P9-CJF-119

Brief Contents

The St. Martin's
Guide to Writing

ELEVENTH EDITION

The St. Martin's Guide to Writing

Rise B. Axelrod
University of California, Riverside

Charles R. Cooper
University of California, San Diego

Bedford/St. Martin's
A Macmillan Education Imprint

Boston • New York

For Bedford/St. Martin's

Vice President, Editorial, Macmillan Higher Education Humanities: Edwin Hill
Editorial Director, English and Music: Karen S. Henry
Senior Publisher for Composition, Business and Technical Writing, Developmental Writing: Leasa Burton
Executive Editor: Molly Parke
Executive Development Manager: Jane Carter
Associate Media Editor: Jonathan Douglas
Senior Project Editor: Peter Jacoby
Media Producer: Melissa Skepo-Masi
Senior Production Supervisors: Dennis J. Conroy and Lisa McDowell
Marketing Manager: Emily Rowin
Copy Editor: Diana Puglisi George
Director of Rights and Permissions: Hilary Newman
Senior Art Director: Anna Palchik
Text Design: Jerilyn Bockorick
Cover Design: Marine Miller
Composition: Cenveo Publisher Services
Printing and Binding: RR Donnelley and Sons

Manufactured in the United States of America.

0 9 8 7 6 5
f e d c b a

For information, write: Bedford/St. Martin's, 75 Arlington Street, Boston, MA 02116 (617-399-4000)

ISBN 978-1-4576-9848-4   (hardcover with Handbook)
ISBN 978-1-319-01603-6   (paperback with Handbook)
ISBN 978-1-319-01606-7   (paperback without Handbook)

Preface

Our goal for *The St. Martin's Guide to Writing* has always been to provide the clear guidance and practical strategies students need to harness their potential as writers, both in college and in the wider world. We also strive to provide both experienced and novice instructors with the time-tested tools they need to coach their students as they develop skills for writing successfully in college and beyond. These goals have guided our development of the core features of the *Guide* as well as the many exciting features that keep the eleventh edition fresh and useful.

Core Features of the *Guide*

The St. Martin's Guide retains its emphasis on active learning by providing practical guides to writing and integrating reading and writing through hands-on activities for critical thinking, reading, analysis, and synthesis.

Practical Guides to Writing

Each chapter in Part One offers practical, flexible guides that help students draft and revise a variety of analytical and persuasive essays. Honed by experience, the acclaimed writing guides offer surefire invention strategies to get students started, sentence strategies to get students writing, and thoughtful peer review and troubleshooting strategies to help students make their writing effective for any rhetorical situation.

Commonsensical and easy to follow, the Guides to Writing teach students how to

- assess the rhetorical situation, focusing on purpose and audience, with special attention to the basic features of each assignment type;
- ask probing analytical questions about what they're reading that can help make students more reflective writers;
- practice finding answers through various kinds of research, including memory search, field research, and traditional source-based research.

Each Guide to Writing begins with a **Starting Points** chart, offering students multiple ways of finding the help they need when they need it. Each also includes a **Peer Review Guide** to help students assess their own writing and the writing of their classmates and a **Troubleshooting Guide** to help students find ways to improve their drafts. All of these guides are organized and color-coded to emphasize the assignment's basic features. In short, the Guides to Writing help students make their writing thoughtful, clear, organized, compelling—and effective for the rhetorical situation.

Purpose-Driven Assignment Chapters

Each chapter in Part One introduces a commonly assigned reason for writing. By working through several assignment types, students learn to identify and use relevant and effective strategies to achieve their purpose with their readers. "Remembering an Event," a memoir assignment, challenges students to reflect on the autobiographical and cultural significance of their experience, for example. "Explaining a Concept," an analysis assignment, asks students to make a new subject interesting and informative for their readers. A cluster of argument chapters—from "Arguing a Position" and "Proposing a Solution" to "Justifying an Evaluation" and "Arguing for Causes or Effects"— requires students to develop an argument that is not only well reasoned and well supported but also responds constructively to readers' likely questions and concerns.

Systematic Integration of Critical Reading and Reflective Writing

Students are asked to read and analyze a range of contemporary selections, attending both to the writer's ideas and to the strategies the writer uses to present those ideas to readers. Each Guide to Reading provides

- an annotated student essay that prompts readers to answer questions about how it is composed;
- a range of compelling professional selections to demonstrate the basic features of writing with that purpose;
- activities following each professional selection that prompt students to read actively by asking them to reflect on the essay and relate it to their own experience and also to read like writers by focusing their attention on the writer's strategies. (Chapter 12 also provides an array of strategies students can use to read critically.)

What's New

Although the eleventh edition of *The St. Martin's Guide to Writing* builds on the success of previous editions, many of the strategies the *Guide* employs have changed in order to connect more effectively with students who are used to visual rhetoric online and are increasingly challenged by demands on their time, attention, and energy.

New Literacy Narrative Chapter

A new introductory chapter, "**Composing Literacy**," offers a quick and engaging way to start off a course. Students first learn about the **rhetorical situation**, a basic literacy concept. They are then invited to read several brief, engaging literacy narratives that demonstrate an array of literacies. Humorist David Sedaris, for example, writes hilariously about the challenges of learning a foreign language. Naturalist Annie Dillard recalls a critical moment when the joy of scientific discovery led her to break free of the need for parental approval. Novelist Amy Tan reflects on the differences between the ways she uses language with family members and the ways she communicates with academic audiences, and cartoonist Lynda Barry looks back on her imaginative interaction with the classifieds. Finally, students are invited to reflect on their own literacy experiences and to compose a literacy narrative.

New Analyzing and Synthesizing Opposing Arguments Project

A newly revised Chapter 5 provides a bridge to help move students from personal and expository to argumentative writing by modeling how to review and critique a variety of positions in preparation for adopting and defending a position of their own. The Guide to Reading shows student Maya Gomez as she works through the stages of analyzing an academic conversation—from summarizing a source to creating an annotated bibliography to reporting on an array of positions to analyzing conflicting positions, all on the same issue. The Guide to Writing provides a host of activities to help students develop their own summary, annotated bibliography, report, or analysis. The argument chapters that follow show students how to apply what they've learned by analyzing a variety of claims and then thoughtfully defending their own.

An Invitation to Reimagine Writing across Genres and Media

Each Guide to Reading in Part One concludes with a Remix activity that invites students to reimagine their writing in a new genre or medium—moving, for example, from remembered event narrative to graphic memoir, from concept analysis to poster presentation, from position argument to Prezi presentation, and more. Considering a change in one aspect of the rhetorical situation forces students to question their earlier composition decisions and deepens their understanding of the rhetorical situation.

Council of Writing Program Administrator's Outcomes Statement

The St. Martin's Guide to Writing, Eleventh Edition, helps students build proficiency in the four categories of learning that writing programs across the country use to assess their students' work: rhetorical knowledge; critical thinking, reading, and writing; writing processes; and knowledge of conventions. The chart below shows in detail how *The St. Martin's Guide* helps students develop these proficiencies. (Note: This chart aligns with the latest WPA Outcomes Statement, ratified in July 2014.)

DESIRED OUTCOMES	RELEVANT FEATURES OF *THE ST. MARTIN'S GUIDE TO WRITING*, ELEVENTH EDITION
Rhetorical Knowledge	
Learn and use key rhetorical concepts through analyzing and composing a variety of texts.	• Chapter 1, "**Composing Literacy**," provides students with a clear, workable definition of the rhetorical situation and asks students to apply that knowledge as they read literacy narratives and compose one of their own.
	• In each of the chapters in Part One, "**Writing Assignments**" (Chapters 2–10), students **read**, **analyze**, and **compose a variety of texts**. A Guide to Reading asks students to analyze texts (including student writing and professional selections), in terms of **purpose**, **audience**, and **genre**. Each Guide to Writing supports students with detailed help for composing in a variety of genres, including memoir, profile, concept analysis, position argument, evaluation, causal argument, and literary analysis.

(continued)

DESIRED OUTCOMES	RELEVANT FEATURES OF *THE ST. MARTIN'S GUIDE TO WRITING*, ELEVENTH EDITION
Rhetorical Knowledge (continued)	

	• Chapter 12, "**A Catalog of Reading Strategies**," provides tools for analyzing texts. • Part Five, "**Composing Strategies for College and Beyond**" (Chapters 26–33), encourages students to consider how genre expectations and discipline requirements affect compositions, particularly in Chapters 26, "**Taking Essay Examinations**"; 27, "**Creating a Portfolio**"; 28, "**Analyzing Visuals**"; 29, "**Writing in Business and Scientific Genres**"; 30, "**Writing for and about Your Community**"; and 32, "**Designing for Page and Screen**."
Gain experience reading and composing in several genres to understand how genre conventions shape and are shaped by readers' and writers' practices and purposes.	• Chapter 1 and the Part One chapters emphasize the connection between **reading and composing**: Each introduces students to the basic features of writing with that purpose; provides a group of engaging reading selections, with apparatus that asks students to think about how the reading demonstrates the basic features; then a Guide to Writing leads them through the process of composing their own text. • A new Chapter 5, "**Analyzing and Synthesizing Opposing Arguments**," invites students to build an essay step-by-step, from **summary** to **annotated bibliography** to **report** and **analysis**. By adapting their writing, students come to understand how academic writers build deep understanding. • A new activity included at the conclusion of each Guide to Reading in Part One invites students to explore how changes to the rhetorical situation affect compositions by asking them to reimagine, or **remix**, their writing in a new genre or medium. • The **readings** in Part One, which represent a range of texts and genres, are annotated and framed with comments and questions that **focus students on key features of the assignment** and help spark ideas for their own compositions. • Chapter 29 covers business and scientific genres.
Develop facility in responding to a variety of situations and contexts, calling for purposeful shifts in voice, tone, level of formality, design, medium, and/or structure.	• In Part One, students practice **responding to a variety of rhetorical situations and contexts**. These chapters also point out what makes a text structurally sound, while the Guides to Writing help students systematically develop their own processes and structures. Sentence strategies in these chapters help composers deal with issues of **voice**, **tone**, and **formality**. • **Remix** boxes in each Part One chapter invite students to consider how changes to the rhetorical situation, especially genre and medium, shape decisions about tone, level of formality, design, medium, and structure. • Chapter 32, "**Designing for Page and Screen**," takes students through the **rhetorical choices** involved in the **design** of any text.
Understand and use a variety of technologies to address a range of audiences.	• One of the book's assumptions is that most students compose in digital spaces for varied audiences and use different media for doing so. This is woven throughout the text. • Online tutorials in the LaunchPad for *The St. Martin's Guide* include **how-tos for using technology**: e.g., digital writing for specific **audiences** and purposes, creating presentations, integrating photos, and appealing to a prospective employer. • Chapter 32, "**Designing for Page and Screen**," helps students understand the needs and requirements involved in the design in print and online. • A dedicated Chapter 33, "**Composing Multimodal Presentations**," offers instruction on how to prepare and deliver a range of presentations, including impromptu and scripted presentations, and those requiring presentation slides.

DESIRED OUTCOMES	RELEVANT FEATURES OF *THE ST. MARTIN'S GUIDE TO WRITING*, ELEVENTH EDITION

Rhetorical Knowledge (continued)

Match the capacities of different environments (e.g., print and electronic) to varying rhetorical situations.	• **Remix** activities in each Part One chapter invite students to consider how a change of medium shapes composition. • Chapter 32, "**Designing for Page and Screen**," provides guidance on how to make effective design choices for electronic documents, from decisions about formatting and font sizes to adding visuals and screen shots. • Advice on composing in a timed writing environment can be found in Chapter 26, "**Taking Essay Examinations**." • See also the section on p. viii: "Understand and use a variety of technologies to address a range of audiences."

Critical Thinking, Reading, and Composing

Use composing and reading for inquiry, learning, thinking, and communicating in various rhetorical contexts.	• Chapter 1, "**Composing Literacy**," asks students to reflect on their own literacy experiences and to extrapolate from the literacy narratives they are reading. • **Analyze and Write activities** in Part One (Chapters 2–10) ask students to **read like a writer**, identifying ideas, techniques, and strategies that they can apply in their own compositions. **Make Connections** activities encourage students to put what they've read in the context of the world they live in. These preliminary reflections come into play in the Guides to Writing, in which students are asked to draw on their thoughts and experiences to write meaningfully. **Thinking Critically** sections, which conclude Chapters 2–10, ask students to consider what they have learned, often in a social/political context. • A new Chapter 5, "**Analyzing and Synthesizing Opposing Arguments**," challenges students to think critically about texts representing a range of positions, to analyze and synthesize information from an array of texts, and to compare and contrast positions on a controversial issue. • Chapter 11, "**A Catalog of Invention and Inquiry Strategies**," and Chapter 12, "**A Catalog of Reading Strategies**," provide strategies students can use to read critically and apply what they've learned.
Read a diverse range of texts, attending especially to relationships between assertion and evidence, to patterns of organization, to interplay between verbal and nonverbal elements, and how these features function for different audiences and situations.	• Chapters 1–10 include a **range of professional selections** and **student essays**. The Guides to Reading and Writing in Chapters 2–10 include advice on **effective strategies for supporting claims, both textual and visual**; the Guides to Writing include **assignment-specific suggestions for organization**, some tailored to specific types of audiences. • The Guides to Writing in the argument chapters (Chapters 6–10) offer advice on **framing** topics to appeal to the audience and recommend techniques and strategies for **responding to alternative views** readers may hold. • The **Remix** activities in each Part One chapter (Chapters 2–10) invite students to consider how a change of audience will affect aspects of the composition. • Part Four, "**Research Strategies**" (Chapters 20–25), especially Chapter 23, "**Using Sources to Support Your Ideas**," emphasizes the importance of **using evidence** effectively to support the students' views.
Locate and evaluate primary and secondary research materials, including journal articles, essays, books, databases, and informal Internet sources.	• Part Four, "**Research Strategies**" (Chapters 20–25), offers extensive coverage of **finding**, **evaluating**, and **using** print and electronic resources with guidance for responsibly using the Internet, e-mail, and online communities for research.

(continued)

DESIRED OUTCOMES	RELEVANT FEATURES OF *THE ST. MARTIN'S GUIDE TO WRITING*, ELEVENTH EDITION

Critical Thinking, Reading, and Composing (continued)

	• Chapter 21, "**Finding Sources and Conducting Field Research**," addresses finding sources using **catalogs** and **databases**, and developing sources through **field research**, and it explains differences between **primary** and **secondary** research. • Chapter 22, "**Evaluating Sources**," emphasizes strategies for **evaluating print** and **digital sources** and distinguishing between **scholarly** and **popular** sources.
Use strategies—such as interpretation, synthesis, response, critique, and design/ redesign—to compose texts that integrate the writer's ideas with those from appropriate sources.	• A new Chapter 5, "**Analyzing and Synthesizing Opposing Arguments**," challenges students to synthesize, analyze, and compare sources from a range of positions on a controversial topic. It provides a bridge to help move students from personal and expository genres to argumentative ones by modeling how to review and critique a variety of informative and persuasive documents in preparation for adopting and defending a position of their own. • Chapters 6–10 ask students to argue for a position, a solution, an evaluation, a preferred cause or effect, and a literary interpretation, and to **anticipate** and **respond to opposing positions** and **readers' objections** to the writer's thesis. • Chapters 6–10 are complemented by Chapter 19, "**Arguing**," which provides strategies for **making assertions**, **offering support**, and **avoiding logical fallacies**. • Chapter 23, "**Using Sources to Support Your Ideas**," offers detailed **strategies** for **integrating research** into an academic research project. Specifically, there is advice on how to integrate and introduce quotations, how to cite paraphrases and summaries so as to distinguish them from the writer's own ideas, and how to avoid plagiarism. Sentence strategies and research coverage in several Part One chapters offer additional support.

Processes

Develop a writing project through multiple drafts.	• In Chapters 2–10, Guides to Writing prompt students to **compose** and **revise**. These chapters include activities for **inventing**, **researching**, **planning**, **composing**, **evaluating**, and **revising** their writing over the course of **multiple drafts**. • The **A Writer at Work** section toward the end of each Part One chapter (Chapters 2–10) demonstrates students' writing processes.
Develop flexible strategies for reading, drafting, reviewing, collaborating, revising, rewriting, rereading, and editing.	• The Guides to Writing in Chapters 2–10 offer extensive, assignment-specific advice on **reading**, **drafting**, **rethinking**, and **revising** at multiple stages. The Ways In activities and Starting Points and Troubleshooting charts encourage students to discover, review, and revise. The activities urge students to start from their strengths, and the charts offer specific, targeted advice for students facing different challenges. • Chapter 11, "**A Catalog of Invention and Inquiry Strategies**," offers numerous helpful suggestions for idea generation. • Chapter 12, "**A Catalog of Reading Strategies**," provides a variety of strategies for reading analytically and critically. • See also the section on p. xi: "Experience the **collaborative** and social aspects of writing processes."

DESIRED OUTCOMES	RELEVANT FEATURES OF *THE ST. MARTIN'S GUIDE TO WRITING*, ELEVENTH EDITION
Processes (continued)	
Use composing processes and tools as a means to discover and reconsider ideas.	• Central to Chapters 2–10 is the idea of using **composing to discover ideas**, especially through the **Ways In activities** in each Guide to Writing. Strategies for **evaluating**, **revising**, and **editing** help students reconsider their ideas over the course of multiple drafts. • **A Writer at Work** sections toward the end of each Part One chapter demonstrate how student writers use writing as a means of discovery and reconsideration. • See also Chapter 11, "**A Catalog of Invention and Inquiry Strategies**," and Chapter 20, "**Planning a Research Project**."
Experience the collaborative and social aspects of writing processes.	• This goal is implicit in several **collaborative activities** in Part One: **Practicing the Genre** activities at the beginning of the chapter; **Make Connections** activities after the readings; and, in the Guides to Writing, **Test Your Choice** activities and **Peer Review Guides** all provide opportunities to work collaboratively. • Chapter 30, "**Writing for and about Your Community**," emphasizes the social nature of writing and real-world applicability in its focus on service learning. • "**Writing Collaboratively**" is the focus of **Chapter 31**, which offers strategies for writing effectively in and managing groups.
Learn to give and act on productive feedback to works in progress.	• The Evaluating the Draft, Peer Review Guide, Improving the Draft, and Troubleshooting Guide sections in the Guides to Writing in each Part One chapter offer students **specific advice on constructively criticizing**—and **praising**—their own work and the work of their classmates, then reflecting and acting upon the comments they've received. • Guidelines in Chapter 31, "**Writing Collaboratively**," offer advice for evaluating another writer's work, from seeking information about the writer's purpose, audience, and genre, to offering support and being sufficiently prepared.
Adapt composing processes for a variety of technologies and modalities.	• As noted in the rhetorical knowledge section on p. viii, one of the book's assumptions is that most students compose in digital spaces for varied audiences and use different media for doing so. This is woven throughout, especially in Chapters 2–10. • **Remix** activities in each Part One chapter (Chapters 2–10) invite students to consider how a change in medium shapes composition. • Chapter 32, "**Designing for Page and Screen**," and Chapter 33, "**Composing Multimodal Presentations**," provide instruction for composing in a variety of modalities. • The **LaunchPad** version of *The St. Martin's Guide to Writing* offers a digital course space and an interactive e-book. It also offers integrated digital tutorials, such as online **how-tos for using technology**: e.g., digital writing, creating presentations, integrating photos, and appealing to a prospective employer.
Reflect on the development of composing practices and how those practices influence their work.	• See the section above: "Use composing processes and tools as a means to discover and reconsider ideas." • In addition, a **Thinking Critically** section concludes each chapter in Part One (Chapters 2–10) and asks students to reflect on what they've learned about the type of writing they've read and written as well as to consider their own composing experiences.

(continued)

DESIRED OUTCOMES	RELEVANT FEATURES OF *THE ST. MARTIN'S GUIDE TO WRITING*, ELEVENTH EDITION

Knowledge of Conventions

Develop knowledge of linguistic structures, including grammar, punctuation, and spelling, through practice in composing and revising.	• Assignment-specific **editing** and **proofreading** advice appears in the Editing and Proofreading sections in each Part One chapter (Chapters 2–10). • The full version of the *Guide* also includes a concise yet remarkably comprehensive handbook that covers syntax, grammar, punctuation, and spelling.
Understand why genre conventions for structure, paragraphing, tone, and mechanics vary.	• Chapters 2–10 emphasize the importance of audience and how expectations differ. For example, several readings emphasize differences in expectations for documenting sources, depending on whether the audience is academic or popular. • **Remix** boxes in each Part One chapter invite students to consider how changes to the rhetorical situation, especially genre and medium, shape decisions about tone, level of formality, design, medium, and structure. • **Assignment-specific issues of structure**, **paragraphing**, **tone**, and **mechanics** are also addressed in the Sentence Strategies and Editing and Proofreading sections of each Guide to Reading in the Part One chapters.
Gain experience negotiating variations in genre conventions.	• Students **read**, **analyze**, and **compose a variety of texts** in Part One, "**Writing Assignments**" (Chapters 2–10). In each of these chapters, a Guide to Reading asks students to analyze texts in terms of **purpose**, **audience**, and the **basic features** of the genre. • Part Four, "**Research Strategies**," allows students to gain experience as they compose an **academic research project**. • The chapters in Part Five, "**Composing Strategies for College and Beyond**," provide students with opportunities to gain experience negotiating genre conventions.
Learn common formats and/or design features for different kinds of texts.	• "**Designing for Page and Screen**" is covered in a dedicated Chapter 32. • Examples of **specific formats for a range of texts** appear on pp. 712–15 (research paper); p. 719 (business letter); p. 721 (e-mail); p. 723 (résumé); p. 725 (job application letter); pp. 727–28 (lab report); pp. 745–48 (table, diagram, graph, chart, map, and other figures); and p. 754 (multimodal presentation).
Explore the concepts of intellectual property (such as fair use and copyright) that motivate documentation conventions.	• Chapter Five, "**Analyzing and Synthesizing Opposing Arguments**," includes coverage of creating an annotated bibliography and invites students to consider the ways in which it is acceptable (and unacceptable) to reuse one's own writing. • Chapter 12, "**A Catalog of Reading Strategies**," covers various strategies useful in working with sources, including annotating, summarizing, and synthesizing. • The book's research coverage (mainly in Chapters 20–25) teaches specific strategies for **integrating** and **citing** source material. A dedicated section on Acknowledging Sources and Avoiding Plagiarism appears on pp. 633–35. Chapter 23, "**Using Sources to Support Your Ideas**," offers detailed coverage of using sources fairly.
Practice applying citation conventions systematically in their own work.	• Several of the activities following reading selections in Chapters 2–9 challenge students to **recognize differences in citation conventions** in popular and academic writing. A number of reading selections include **citations** or **lists of links** to sources. **Research sections** in each Guide to Writing help students with the details of using and documenting sources by providing genre-specific examples of what (and what not) to do. Student essays in Chapters 3–9 offer models for documenting sources in a list of works cited or references.

DESIRED OUTCOMES	RELEVANT FEATURES OF *THE ST. MARTIN'S GUIDE TO WRITING*, ELEVENTH EDITION

Knowledge of Conventions (continued)

- Coverage of applying citation conventions is covered in Part Four, **"Research Strategies."** Chapter 23, **"Using Sources to Support Your Ideas,"** offers detailed advice on how to integrate and introduce quotations, how to cite paraphrases and summaries so as to distinguish them from the writer's own ideas, and how to avoid plagiarism. Chapters 24 and 25 offer instruction and documentation models in **MLA and APA style** in addition to an annotated sample student research paper.
- Chapter 28, **"Analyzing Visuals,"** offers a complete student paper with MLA documentation.

Acknowledgments

We owe an enormous debt to all the rhetoricians and composition specialists whose theory, research, and pedagogy have informed *The St. Martin's Guide to Writing*. We would be adding many pages to an already long book if we were to name everyone to whom we are indebted; suffice it to say that we have been eclectic in our borrowing.

We must also acknowledge immeasurable lessons learned from all the writers, professional and student alike, whose work we analyzed and whose writing we used in this and earlier editions.

Many instructors and students have contributed ideas and criticism over the years. For responding to detailed questionnaires about the tenth edition, we thank Kara Poe Alexander, Baylor University; Berniece Alspach, California Baptist College; Sarah Antinora, California State University, San Bernardino; Leontine Armstrong, California Baptist College; Chris Blankenship, Emporia State University; Mary Brantley, Holmes Community College; Brieanna Casey, Texas Woman's University; Catherine Cucinella, California State University, San Marcos; Cheryl Edelson, Chaminade University; Leona Fisher, Chaffey College; Phyllis Gowdy, Tidewater Community College; Lisa Haag, St. Louis Community College; Lesa Beth Hildebrand, Triton College; Tina Hultgren, Kishwaukee College; Jamie Jones, Texas Woman's University; Mary Jo Keiter, Harrisburg Area Community College; Jason Kolodzyk, University of Wisconsin–Whitewater; Julie Kratt, Cowley College; Courtney Patrick Weber, Texas Woman's University; Kelli Prejean, Marshall University; Dr. Dana Prodoehl, University of Wisconsin–Whitewater; Zina Rodriguez, Moreno Valley College; Matthew Schmeer, Johnson County Community College; Graham (Gray) Scott, Texas Woman's University; Marcia Seabury, University of Hartford; Wes Spratlin, Motlow State Community College; Jenna West, Murray State College; and Marc Wilson, Ivy Tech Community College.

For helping us select new readings, we thank Gretchen Bartels, California Baptist University; Chris Blankenship, Emporia State University; Mary Brantley, Holmes Community College; Wallace Cleaves, University of California, Riverside; Leona Fisher, Chaffey College; Sayanti Ganguly Puckett, Johnson County Community College; Phyllis Gowdy, Tidewater Community College; Laurie Hughes, Richland Community

College; Tina Hultgren, Kishwaukee College; Sarah Hunt, Savannah Technical College; Stephanie Kay, University of California, Riverside; Jason Kolodzyk, University of Wisconsin–Whitewater; Dr. Dana Prodoehl, University of Wisconsin–Whitewater; Matthew Schmeer, Johnson County Community College; Annie Schnarr, Skagit Valley College; Graham (Gray) Scott, Texas Woman's University; Wes Spratlin, Motlow State Community College; David Taylor, St. Louis Community College–Meramec; Karol Walchak, Alpena Community College; Alison Warriner, California State University, East Bay; and Jenna West, Murray State College.

In addition, we'd like to thank reviewers who provided invaluable feedback on a draft of this chapter: Kara Alexander, Baylor University; Gretchen Bartels, California Baptist University; Mary Brantley, Holmes Community College; Sayanti Ganguly Puckett, Johnson County Community College; Julie Kratt, Cowley County Community College; Dana Prodoehl, University of Wisconsin–Whitewater; Matthew Schmeer, Johnson County Community College; Marcia Seabury, University of Hartford; David Taylor, St. Louis Community College–Meramec; Jeana West, Murray State College.

In addition, we gratefully acknowledge the contributions of a number of thoughtful instructors who participated in a focus group that helped us fine-tune the Remix activities that now appear at the end of each Guide to Reading in Part One: Kara Poe Alexander, Baylor University; Daniel Cleary, Lorain County Community College; Sara Fuller, Cuyahoga Community College and Lorain County Community College; Kim Haimes-Korn, Kennesaw State College; Dauvan Mulally, Grand Valley State University; and Amy Rubens, Francis Marion University.

For this new edition of the *Guide*, we are particularly grateful to Alison Warriner, who helped revise several of the Part One chapters; and Gray Scott and Wallace Cleaves, who made recommendations of reading selections, helped draft some of the reading apparatus, and were generally available as a sounding board and a font of good advice, especially in rethinking Chapter 5. Wallace Cleaves we also thank for his astute revisions and updates to the instructor's manual, including writing entirely new content on teaching Chapters 1 and 5 and reading comprehension and summary quizzes (with model summaries as feedback) for all the new reading selections in the text. (The reading comprehension quizzes are auto-graded in the LaunchPad version of *The St. Martin's Guide,* and model summaries are provided as feedback for the summary quizzes. Both are also available in the online instructor's manual.) Danise Hoover, Hunter College, provided expert advice as we updated the research coverage. Finally, we are especially grateful to the student authors for allowing us to use their work in *Sticks and Stones* and the *Guide*.

We want to thank many people at Bedford/St. Martin's, especially Jane Carter, Executive Development Manager and our editor, whose invaluable expertise and indomitable good humor made this book possible; Senior Project Editor Peter Jacoby, who worked miracles keeping all the details straight and keeping the book on schedule; and Associate Media Editor Jonathan Douglas, who singlehandedly managed multiple reviews, while also editing *Sticks and Stones* and overseeing the editorial work on LaunchPad, our customizable course space and interactive e-book for *The St. Martin's Guide to Writing.*

Diana George made many valuable contributions to this revision with her careful copyediting, as did Steve Patterson and Will Rigby with their meticulous proofreading, and Kirsten Kite, with her indexing of the text. Elise Kaiser, Dennis Conroy, and Lisa McDowell kept the whole process running smoothly. Thanks also to the immensely talented design team—book designer Jerilyn Bockorick as well as Bedford/ St. Martin's art director Anna Palchik. Our gratitude also goes to Hilary Newman, Rosemary Spano, Linda Winters, Kathleen Karcher, Julie Tesser, and Martha Friedman for their thoughtful and conscientious work on the permissions program for text and visuals.

We also thank Karen Henry, Editorial Director for English and Music, Leasa Burton, Senior Publisher for Composition, and Molly Parke, Executive Editor for Rhetorics—all of whom offered valued advice at many critical stages in the process. Thanks as well to Edwin Hill, Vice President–Editorial (Humanities), for his adroit leadership of Bedford/St. Martin's, and Marketing Manager Emily Rowin for her tireless efforts on behalf of the *Guide*.

Rise dedicates this book to her husband Steven and their son Jeremiah, who are both distinguished teachers and scholars, and to Sophie and Amalia, two young women whose writing she very much looks forward to reading.

Get the Most Out of Your Course with *The St. Martin's Guide to Writing*

Bedford/St. Martin's offers resources and format choices that help you and your students get even more out of your book and course. To learn more about or to order any of the following products, contact your Bedford/St. Martin's sales representative, e-mail sales support (**sales_support@bfwpub.com**), or visit the Web site at **macmillanhighered.com/theguide/catalog**.

LaunchPad for *The St. Martin's Guide to Writing*: Where Students Learn

LaunchPad provides engaging content and new ways to get the most out of your book. Get an **interactive e-book** combined with **useful, highly relevant materials** in a fully customizable course space; then assign and mix our resources with yours.

- **Autoscored reading quizzes**—a five-question multiple-choice comprehension quiz and a summary quiz with a model summary as feedback—are available for every professional selection in the text.

- **Prebuilt units**—including readings, videos, quizzes, discussion groups, and more—are **easy to adapt and assign** by adding your own materials and mixing them with our high-quality multimedia content and ready-made assessment options, such as **LearningCurve** adaptive quizzing.

- More than forty additional **student essays** from *Sticks and Stones and Other Student Essays*, written using earlier editions of the *Guide*.

- A **Gradebook** that provides a clear window on the performance of your whole class, individual students, and even results of individual assignments.
- A **streamlined interface** helps students focus on what's due, and social commenting tools let them **engage**, make connections, and learn from each other. Use LaunchPad on its own or integrate it with your school's learning management system so that your class is always on the same page.

To get the most out of your book, order LaunchPad for *The St. Martin's Guide to Writing*, Eleventh Edition, packaged with the print book. (LaunchPad for *The St. Martin's Guide to Writing* can also be purchased on its own.) An activation code is required. To order LaunchPad for *The St. Martin's Guide to Writing* with

- *The St. Martin's Guide to Writing*, Eleventh Edition (hardcover), use ISBN 978-1-319-05435-9.
- *The St. Martin's Guide to Writing*, Eleventh Edition (paperback), use ISBN 978-1-319-05433-5.
- *The St. Martin's Guide to Writing*, Short Eleventh Edition, use ISBN 978-1-319-05437-3.

Choose from Alternative Formats of *The St. Martin's Guide to Writing*

Bedford/St. Martin's offers a range of affordable formats, allowing students to choose the one that works best for them. For details, visit **macmillanhighered.com/theguide/catalog**.

- *Hardcover.* To order *The St. Martin's Guide to Writing*, Eleventh Edition, in hardcover, use ISBN 978-1-4576-9848-4.
- *Paperback.* To order *The St. Martin's Guide to Writing*, Eleventh Edition, in paperback, use ISBN 978-1-319-01603-6.
- *Short (without handbook).* To order *The St. Martin's Guide to Writing*, Short Eleventh Edition, in paperback, use ISBN 978-1-319-01606-7.
- *Other popular e-book formats.* For details, visit **macmillanhighered.com/ebooks**.

Select Value Packages

Add value to your text by packaging one of the following resources with *The St. Martin's Guide to Writing*. To learn more about package options for any of the following products, contact your Bedford/St. Martin's sales representative or visit **macmillanhighered.com/theguide/catalog**.

LaunchPad Solo for Readers and Writers allows students to work on whatever they need help with the most. At home or in class, students learn at their own pace, with instruction tailored to each student's unique needs. *LaunchPad Solo for Readers and Writers* features:

- **Prebuilt units that support a learning arc.** Each easy-to-assign unit is comprised of a pretest check; multimedia instruction and assessment; a posttest that assesses what students have learned about critical reading, the writing process, using sources, grammar, style, and mechanics; and help for multilingual writers.

- **A video introduction to many topics.** Introductions offer an overview of the unit's topic, and many include a brief, accessible video to illustrate the concepts at hand.
- **Adaptive quizzing for targeted learning.** Most units include LearningCurve, game-like adaptive quizzing that focuses on the areas in which each student needs the most help.
- **The ability to monitor student progress.** Use our Gradebook to see which students are on track and which need additional help with specific topics.

LaunchPad Solo for Readers and Writers can be **packaged at a significant discount**. To ensure that your students can take full advantage, use the following ISBNs:

- *LaunchPad Solo for Readers and Writers* plus *The St. Martin's Guide to Writing,* Eleventh Edition (hardcover), use ISBN 978-1-319-05562-2.
- *LaunchPad Solo for Readers and Writers* plus *The St. Martin's Guide to Writing,* Eleventh Edition (paperback), use ISBN 978-1-319-05561-5.
- *LaunchPad Solo for Readers and Writers* plus *The St. Martin's Guide to Writing,* Short Eleventh Edition, use ISBN 978-1-319-05563-9.

Visit **macmillanhighered.com/readwrite** for more information.

Writer's Help 2.0 is a powerful online writing resource that helps students find answers, whether they are searching for writing advice on their own or as part of an assignment.

- **Smart search.** Built on research with more than 1,600 student writers, the smart search in *Writer's Help 2.0* provides reliable results even when students use novice terms, such as *flow* and *unstuck*.
- **Trusted content from our best-selling handbooks.** Choose *Writer's Help 2.0 for Hacker Handbooks* or *Writer's Help 2.0 for Lunsford Handbooks* and ensure that students have clear advice and examples for all of their writing questions.
- **Adaptive exercises that engage students.** *Writer's Help 2.0* includes LearningCurve, game-like online quizzing that adapts to what students already know and helps them focus on what they need to learn.

Student access is packaged with *The St. Martin's Guide to Writing* at a significant discount. To ensure that your students have easy access to online writing support, use the following ISBNs:

Writer's Help 2.0 for Hacker Handbooks plus

- *The St. Martin's Guide to Writing,* Eleventh Edition (hardcover): ISBN 978-1-319-05558-5
- *The St. Martin's Guide to Writing,* Eleventh Edition (paperback): ISBN 978-1-319-05559-2
- *The St. Martin's Guide to Writing,* Short Eleventh Edition: ISBN 978-1-319-05560-8

Writer's Help 2.0 for Lunsford Handbooks plus

- *The St. Martin's Guide to Writing*, Eleventh Edition (hardcover): ISBN 978-1-319-05564-6
- *The St. Martin's Guide to Writing*, Eleventh Edition (paperback): ISBN 978-1-319-05565-3
- *The St. Martin's Guide to Writing*, Short Eleventh Edition: ISBN 978-1-319-05566-0

Students who rent a book or buy a used book can purchase access to *Writer's Help 2.0* at **macmillanhighered.com/writershelp2**. **Instructors** may request free access by registering as an instructor at **macmillanhighered.com/writershelp2**. For technical support, visit **macmillanhighered.com/getsupport**.

Sticks and Stones and Other Student Essays, **Ninth Edition**, provides nearly forty essays written by students across the nation using earlier editions of the *Guide*. Each essay is accompanied by a headnote that spotlights some of the ways the writer uses the genre successfully, invites students to notice other achievements, and supplies context where necessary. *Sticks and Stones* is available for free when packaged with new copies of the *Guide*. To order *Sticks and Stones* with

- *The St. Martin's Guide to Writing*, Eleventh Edition (hardcover), use ISBN 978-1-319-05432-8.
- *The St. Martin's Guide to Writing*, Eleventh Edition (paperback), use ISBN 978-1-319-05434-2.
- *The St. Martin's Guide to Writing*, Short Eleventh Edition, use ISBN 978-1-319-05436-6.

Portfolio Keeping, **Third Edition, by Nedra Reynolds and Elizabeth Davis**, provides all the information students need to use the portfolio method successfully in a writing course. *Portfolio Teaching*, a companion guide for instructors, provides the practical information instructors and writing program administrators need to use the portfolio method successfully in a writing course. To order *Portfolio Keeping* packaged with *The St. Martin's Guide to Writing*, Eleventh Edition, or Short Eleventh Edition, contact your sales representative for a package ISBN.

Instructor Resources

macmillanhighered.com/theguide/catalog

You have a lot to do in your course. Bedford/St. Martin's wants to make it easy for you to find the support you need—and to get it quickly.

The **Instructor's Resource Manual** for *The St. Martin's Guide to Writing* is available as a PDF that can be downloaded from the Bedford/St. Martin's online catalog at the URL above; it is also available through LaunchPad. In addition to detailed support for teaching each chapter in *The St. Martin's Guide* (including in-class activities, learning objectives, special challenges, suggestions for teaching, and more), the manual includes teaching and evaluation practices, tips for integrating technology into your teaching, suggested course plans, and a bibliography in composition studies.

Teaching Central offers the entire list of Bedford/St. Martin's print and online professional resources in one place. You'll find landmark reference works, sourcebooks on pedagogical issues, award-winning collections, and practical advice for the classroom—all free for instructors. Visit **macmillanhighered.com/teachingcentral**.

Bedford *Bits* collects creative ideas for teaching a range of composition topics in a frequently updated blog. A community of teachers—leading scholars, authors, and editors such as Andrea Lunsford, Elizabeth Losh, Jack Solomon, and Elizabeth Wardle—discuss assignments, activities, revision, research, grammar and style, multimodal composition, technology, peer review, and much more. Take, use, adapt, and pass the ideas around. Then, come back to the site to comment or share your own suggestion. Visit **community.macmillan.com**.

Contents

3 | Writing Profiles 59

4 | Explaining a Concept 119

5 | Analyzing and Synthesizing Opposing Arguments 170

6   Arguing a Position 229

7 | Proposing a Solution 283

8 | Justifying an Evaluation 335

9 | Arguing for Causes or Effects 385

10 | Analyzing Stories 440

PART 2   Critical Thinking Strategies

PART 3 Writing Strategies

PART 4   Research Strategies

23 | Using Sources to Support Your Ideas 632

24 | Citing and Documenting Sources in MLA Style 644

25 | Citing and Documenting Sources in APA Style 674

PART 5 Composing Strategies for College and Beyond

Handbook

1

Composing Literacy

More people are writing today than ever before, and many are switching comfortably from one genre or medium to another — from tweeting to blogging to creating multimedia Web pages. Learning to be effective as a writer is a continuous process as you find yourself in new writing situations using new technologies and trying to anticipate the concerns of different audiences. "The illiterate of the twenty-first century will not be those who cannot read and write," futurist Alvin Toffler predicted, "but those who cannot learn, unlearn, and relearn."

Understanding the Rhetorical Situation

Central to success in writing across the spectrum of possibilities today is understanding your **rhetorical situation**, any situation in which you produce or receive a text. Ask yourself these questions whenever you encounter a new rhetorical situation:

1. *Who* is the **audience**? How does the audience's prior knowledge, values, and beliefs influence the production and reception of the text?

2. *What* **genre** or type of text is it? How do genre conventions (what we call the text's *basic features*) influence the production and reception of the text?

3. *When*—at what time or for what **occasion**—is the text produced? Is it timely?

4. *Where*—in what social or cultural **context**—will the communication take place? How does the situation influence the production and reception of the text?

5. *How*—in what **medium**—is the text experienced? How does the medium influence the production and reception of the text?

6. *Why* communicate? What is the **purpose** or goal driving the author's choices and affecting the audience's perceptions of the text?

Composing with an awareness of the rhetorical situation means writing not only to express yourself but also to engage your readers and respond to their concerns. You write to influence how your readers think and feel about a subject and, depending on the genre, perhaps also to inspire them to act.

Genres are simply ways of categorizing texts—for example, we can distinguish between fiction and nonfiction; subdivide fiction into romance, mystery, and science fiction genres; or break down mystery even further into hard-boiled detective, police procedural, true crime, and classic whodunit genres. Composing with genre awareness affects your choices—what you write about (topic), the claims you make (thesis), how you support those claims (reasons and evidence), and how you organize it all.

Each genre has a set of conventions, or basic features, readers expect texts in that genre to use. Although individual texts within the same genre vary a great deal—for example, no two *proposals*, even those arguing for the same solution, will be identical—they nonetheless include the same basic features. For example, everyone expects a proposal to identify the problem (usually establishing that it is serious enough to require solving) and to offer a solution (usually arguing that it is preferable to alternative solutions because it is less expensive or easier to implement).

Still, these conventions are not recipes but broad frameworks within which writers are free to be creative. Most writers, in fact, find that frameworks make creativity possible. Depending on the formality of the rhetorical situation and the audience's openness to innovation, writers may also remix features of different genres or media, as you will see in the Genre Remix sections of each Part One chapter.

Like genre, the medium in which you are working also affects many of your design and content choices. For example, written texts can use color, type fonts, charts, diagrams, and still images to heighten the visual impact of the text, delivering information vividly and persuasively. If you are composing Web pages or apps, you have many more options to make your text truly multimedia—for example, by adding hyperlinks, animation, audio, video, and interactivity to your written text.

Reflecting on Your Own Literacy

Learning—especially learning to communicate with new audiences and in new genres—benefits from what we call **reflection** (or metacognition)—thinking critically about *how* as well as *what* you are learning. Extensive research confirms that reflection makes learning easier and faster. In fact, recent studies show that writing even a few sentences about your thoughts and feelings before a high-stress paper or exam can help you reduce stress and boost performance.

Spend a few minutes thinking about your own literacy experiences: *What memories stand out as formative?* You may define *literacy* narrowly as the ability to read and write, as it has been traditionally defined, or you may think of it more broadly as the ability to make meaning in the multiplicity of languages and genres, media and communication practices we are increasingly called upon to use. Here are several questions and examples that may help you remember and reflect on your own literacy experiences:

- *When did you realize that you use language differently for different audiences and purposes?*

  Recently, I was made keenly aware of the different Englishes I do use. I was giving a talk . . . about my writing, my life, and my book, *The Joy Luck Club*. The talk was going along well enough, until I remembered one major difference that made the whole talk sound wrong. My mother was in the room. And it was perhaps the first time she had heard me give a lengthy speech, using the kind of English I have never used with her. I was saying things like, "The intersection of memory upon imagination" and "There is an aspect of my fiction that relates to thus-and-thus"— a speech filled with carefully wrought grammatical phrases, burdened, it suddenly seemed to me, with nominalized forms, past perfect tenses, conditional phrases, all the forms of standard English that I had learned in school and through books, the forms of English I did not use at home with my mother.

  —Novelist Amy Tan, from "Mother Tongue"

- *What do you think are the personal and cultural effects of acquiring new literacies (such as learning another language, using social media, playing sports or video games)?*

  I can remember my father bringing home our first [television] set—this ornate wooden cabinet that was the size of a small refrigerator, with a round cathode-ray picture tube and wooden speaker grilles over elaborate fabric. Like a piece of archaic furniture, even then. Everybody would gather around at a particular time for a broadcast—a baseball game or a variety show or something. . . . We know that something happened then. We know that broadcast television did something—did everything—to us, and that now we aren't the same, though broadcast television, in that sense, is already almost over. I can remember seeing the emergence of broadcast television, but I can't tell what it did to us because I became that which watched broadcast television.

  —Science fiction author William Gibson, from "The Art of Fiction No. 211" The *Paris Reviews* Interviews

■ *When did you discover that you had a talent or enthusiasm for a particular academic subject (such as history, math, literature, or science)?*

Although I usually had to save my tiny allowance for things I wanted, that year for Christmas my parents gave me a microscope kit. . . . All that winter I played with the microscope. I prepared slides from things at hand, as the books suggested. I looked at the transparent membrane inside an onion's skin and saw the cells. I looked at a section of cork and saw the cells, and at scrapings from the inside of my cheek, ditto. I looked at my blood and saw not much; I looked at my urine and saw long iridescent crystals, for the drop had dried.

All this was very well, but I wanted to see the wildlife I had read about. I wanted especially to see the famous amoeba, who had eluded me. He was supposed to live in the hay infusion, but I hadn't found him there. He lived outside in warm ponds and streams, too, but I lived in Pittsburgh, and it had been a cold winter. Finally late that spring I saw an amoeba. . . . In the basement at my microscope table I spread a scummy drop of Frick Park puddle water on a slide, peeked in, and lo, there was the famous amoeba. He was as blobby and grainy as his picture; I would have known him anywhere.

Before I had watched him at all, I ran upstairs. My parents were still at the table, drinking coffee. They, too, could see the famous amoeba. I told them, bursting . . . Mother regarded me warmly. She gave me to understand that she was glad I had found what I had been looking for, but that she and Father were happy to sit with their coffee, and would not be coming down. She did not say, but I understood at once, that they had their pursuits (coffee) and I had mine. She did not say, but I began to understand then, that you do what you do out of your private passion for the thing itself.

—Naturalist and author Annie Dillard, from *An American Childhood*

■ *How did reading stimulate your imagination?*

EACH QUARTER-INCH AD WAS LIKE A CHAPTER IN A BOOK. I'D IMAGINE THE WHOLE STORY: THE FREAKED-OUT PEOPLE, THE FREAKED-OUT ANIMALS, AND ME, ALWAYS COMING TO THE RESCUE AND NEVER ACCEPTING THE REWARD.

NO, KEEP THE FIVE HUNDRED DOLLARS, SIR. ALL I CARE ABOUT IS THAT HENRY IS HOME.

PLEASE, MA'AM, WHAT MY NAME IS DOESN'T MATTER. AND NEITHER DOES THE TEN THOUSAND DOLLARS. ALL THAT MATTERS IS JINGLES.

LIKE MOST WRITERS, I LOVED TO READ WHEN I WAS LITTLE, BUT UNTIL RECENTLY, I NEVER REALLY THOUGHT ABOUT SOME OF THE THINGS I ENJOYED READING MOST. THE CLASSIFIED ADS FASCINATED ME.

CRYPT IN MAUSOLEUM. PRIME LOC. EYE-LEVEL. BEST OFFER. EVENINGS.

SZ. 12 WEDDING DRESS. NEVER WORN. MUST SACRIFICE.

FILL DIRT, VERY CLEAN.

PARTY PIANIST. MY PIANO OR YOURS.

THEY GAVE ME SO MANY WEIRD BLANKS TO FILL IN. LIKE WHO WAS SELLING THEIR CRYPT? I ONLY KNEW THE WORD FROM HORROR MOVIES. ZOMBIES AND VAMPIRES CAME OUT OF THEM. THE AD SAID "EVENINGS." IT SEEMED LIKE SUCH AN OBVIOUS TRICK.

DING! DONG!

WHO IS IT?

UH, I'M HERE ABOUT THE CRYPT?

AAHHHH!!

SAME WITH THE WEDDING DRESS AD. WHO ELSE WAS GOING TO CALL ABOUT IT EXCEPT A MAIDEN? IT SAID "MUST SACRIFICE." WHO ELSE GOT SACRIFICED BUT MAIDENS? THE POLICE WOULD BE BAFFLED BY HOW MAIDENS KEPT DISAPPEARING.

HELLO?

YES?

YOU'VE GOT TO BE KIDDING.

OK.

NOT ANOTHER MAIDEN!

I'M AFRAID SO.

DANG!

—Cartoonist and author Lynda Barry, an excerpt from "Lost and Found"

■ *What was your experience when you were first learning something new (such as another language, an unfamiliar technology, a musical instrument)?*

At the age of forty-one, I am returning to school and have to think of myself as what my French textbook calls "a true debutant." After paying my tuition, I was issued a student ID, which allows me a discounted entry fee at movie theaters, puppet shows, and Festyland, a far-flung amusement park that advertises with billboards picturing a cartoon stegosaurus sitting in a canoe and eating what appears to be a ham sandwich.

I've moved to Paris with hopes of learning the language. My school is an easy ten-minute walk from my apartment, and on the first day of class I arrived early, watching as the returning students greeted one another in the school lobby. Vacations were recounted, and questions were raised concerning mutual friends with names like Kang and Vlatnya. Regardless of their nationalities, everyone spoke in what sounded to me like excellent French. Some accents were better than others, but the students exhibited an ease and confidence I found intimidating. As an added discomfort, they were all young, attractive, and well dressed, causing me to feel not unlike Pa Kettle trapped backstage after a fashion show.

The first day of class was nerve-racking because I knew I'd be expected to perform. That's the way they do it here—it's everybody into the language pool, sink or swim. The teacher marched in, deeply tanned from a recent vacation, and proceeded to rattle off a series of administrative announcements. I've spent quite a few summers in Normandy, and I took a monthlong French class before leaving

New York. I'm not completely in the dark, yet I understood only half of what this woman was saying.

"If you have not *meimslsxp* or *lgpdmurct* by this time, then you should not be in this room. Has everyone *apzkiubjxow*? Everyone? Good, we shall begin." She spread out her lesson plan and sighed, saying, "All right, then, who knows the alphabet?"

It was startling because (a) I hadn't been asked that question in a while and (b) I realized, while laughing, that I myself did *not* know the alphabet. They're the same letters, but in France they're pronounced differently. I know the shape of the alphabet but had no idea what it actually sounded like.

"Ahh." The teacher went to the board and sketched the letter *a*. "Do we have anyone in the room whose first name commences with an *ahh*?"

Two Polish Annas raised their hands, and the teacher instructed them to present themselves by stating their names, nationalities, occupations, and a brief list of things they liked and disliked in this world. The first Anna hailed from an industrial town outside of Warsaw and had front teeth the size of tombstones. She worked as a seamstress, enjoyed quiet times with friends, and hated the mosquito.

"Oh, really," the teacher said. "How very interesting. I thought that everyone loved the mosquito, but here, in front of all the world, you claim to detest him. How is it that we've been blessed with someone as unique and original as you? Tell us, please."

The seamstress did not understand what was being said but knew that this was an occasion for shame. Her rabbity mouth huffed for breath, and she stared down at her lap as though the appropriate comeback were stitched somewhere alongside the zipper of her slacks.

The second Anna learned from the first and claimed to love sunshine and detest lies. It sounded like a translation of one of those Playmate of the Month data sheets, the answers always written in the same loopy handwriting. "Turn-ons: Mom's famous five-alarm chili! Turnoffs: insecurity and guys who come on too strong!!!!"

The two Polish Annas surely had clear notions of what they loved and hated, but like the rest of us, they were limited in terms of vocabulary, and this made them appear less than sophisticated. The teacher forged on, and we learned that Carlos, the Argentine bandonion player, loved wine, music, and, in his words, "making sex with the womens of the world." Next came a beautiful young Yugoslav who identified herself as an optimist, saying that she loved everything that life had to offer.

The teacher licked her lips, revealing a hint of the saucebox we would later come to know. She crouched low for her attack, placed her hands on the young woman's desk, and leaned close, saying, "Oh yeah? And do you love your little war?"

While the optimist struggled to defend herself, I scrambled to think of an answer to what had obviously become a trick question. How often is one asked what he loves in this world? More to the point, how often is one asked and then publicly ridiculed for his answer? I recalled my mother, flushed with wine, pounding the tabletop late one night, saying, "Love? I love a good steak cooked rare. I love my cat, and I love . . ." My sisters and I leaned forward, waiting to hear our names. "Tums," our mother said. "I love Tums."

The teacher killed some time accusing the Yugoslavian girl of masterminding a program of genocide, and I jotted frantic notes in the margins of my pad. While I can honestly say that I love leafing through medical textbooks devoted to severe dermatological conditions, the hobby is beyond the reach of my French vocabulary, and acting it out would only have invited controversy.

When called upon, I delivered an effortless list of things that I detest: blood sausage, intestinal pâtés, brain pudding. I'd learned these words the hard way. Having given it some thought, I then declared my love for IBM typewriters, the French word for *bruise*, and my electric floor waxer. It was a short list, but still I managed to mispronounce *IBM* and assign the wrong gender to both the floor waxer and the typewriter. The teacher's reaction led me to believe that these mistakes were capital crimes in the country of France.

"Were you always this *palicmkrexis*?" she asked. "Even a *fiuscrzsa ticiwelmun* knows that a typewriter is feminine."

I absorbed as much of her abuse as I could understand, thinking—but not saying—that I find it ridiculous to assign a gender to an inanimate object incapable of disrobing and making an occasional fool of itself. Why refer to Lady Crack Pipe or Good Sir Dishrag when these things could never live up to all that their sex implied?

The teacher proceeded to belittle everyone from German Eva, who hated laziness, to Japanese Yukari, who loved paintbrushes and soap. Italian, Thai, Dutch, Korean, and Chinese—we all left class foolishly believing that the worst was over. She'd shaken us up a little, but surely that was just an act designed to weed out the deadweight. We didn't know it then, but the coming months would teach us what it was like to spend time in the presence of a wild animal, something completely unpredictable. Her temperament was not based on a series of good and bad days but, rather, good and bad moments. We soon learned to dodge chalk and protect our heads and stomachs whenever she approached us with a question. She hadn't yet punched anyone, but it seemed wise to protect ourselves against the inevitable.

Though we were forbidden to speak anything but French, the teacher would occasionally use us to practice any of her five fluent languages.

"I hate you," she said to me one afternoon. Her English was flawless. "I really, really hate you." Call me sensitive, but I couldn't help but take it personally.

After being singled out as a lazy *kfdtinvfm*, I took to spending four hours a night on my homework, putting in even more time whenever we were assigned an essay. I suppose I could have gotten by with less, but I was determined to create some sort of identity for myself: David the hard worker, David the cut-up. We'd have one of those "complete this sentence" exercises, and I'd fool with the thing for hours, invariably settling on something like "A quick run around the lake? I'd love to! Just give me a moment while I strap on my wooden leg." The teacher, through word and action, conveyed the message that if this was my idea of an identity, she wanted nothing to do with it.

My fear and discomfort crept beyond the borders of the classroom and accompanied me out onto the wide boulevards. Stopping for a coffee, asking directions, depositing money in my bank account: these things were out of the question, as they involved having to speak. Before beginning school, there'd been no shutting me up, but now I was convinced that everything I said was wrong. When the phone rang, I ignored it. If someone asked me a question, I pretended to be deaf. I knew my fear was getting the best of me when I started wondering why they don't sell cuts of meat in vending machines.

My only comfort was the knowledge that I was not alone. Huddled in the hallways and making the most of our pathetic French, my fellow students and I engaged in the sort of conversation commonly overheard in refugee camps.

"Sometime me cry alone at night."

"That be common for I, also, but be more strong, you. Much work and someday you talk pretty. People start love you soon. Maybe tomorrow, okay."

Unlike the French class I had taken in New York, here there was no sense of competition. When the teacher poked a shy Korean in the eyelid with a freshly sharpened pencil, we took no comfort in the fact that, unlike Hyeyoon Cho, we all knew the irregular past tense of the verb *to defeat*. In all fairness, the teacher hadn't meant to stab the girl, but neither did she spend much time apologizing, saying only, "Well, you should have been *vkkdyo* more *kdeynfulh*."

Over time it became impossible to believe that any of us would ever improve. Fall arrived and it rained every day, meaning we would now be scolded for the water dripping from our coats and umbrellas. It was mid-October when the teacher singled me out, saying, "Every day spent with you is like having a cesarean section."

And it struck me that, for the first time since arriving in France, I could understand every word that someone was saying.

Understanding doesn't mean that you can suddenly speak the language. Far from it. It's a small step, nothing more, yet its rewards are intoxicating and deceptive. The teacher continued her diatribe and I settled back, bathing in the subtle beauty of each new curse and insult.

"You exhaust me with your foolishness and reward my efforts with nothing but pain, do you understand me?"

The world opened up, and it was with great joy that I responded, "I know the thing that you speak exact now. Talk me more, you, plus, please, plus."

—Author and comedian David Sedaris, "Me Talk Pretty One Day"

Composing Your Own Literacy Narrative

This chapter invites you to compose a **literacy narrative**. Your instructor may add specific requirements to this assignment, but in general you are to write about a memorable literacy experience—learning, unlearning, or relearning, as Toffler would say, to communicate with others. Below are some questions and examples to help you choose a subject. But let's begin by considering the assignment's rhetorical situation.

Apply the rhetorical framework: who? what? when? where? how? and why?

Since this is the beginning of a new course, you could view this assignment as an opportunity to introduce yourself to your instructor and classmates by choosing a literacy experience, genre, or medium (assuming your instructor gives you leeway to choose) that would enable you to make a particular impression on your readers. For example, if you want to emphasize the importance of reading graphic novels or playing video games in your literacy development, you might consider composing your literacy narrative as a graphic memoir (like the Lynda Barry selection on pp. 4–6) or video game.

Like the remembered event narrative in Chapter 2, a literacy narrative tells a story about a person or event from your own life. To be effective, it must

- tell a compelling story;
- vividly describe the people and places;
- convey the event or person's significance in your life, how the event or person affected your literacy practices or your understanding of the power and complexity of the ways we try—and sometimes fail—to communicate with one another.

These are the basic features of the genre.

The first part of the Guide to Reading in Chapter 2 (pp. 14–37) provides a more detailed introduction to the basic features of remembered event narratives, and the Guide to Writing in that chapter (pp. 38–54) supports their drafting and revision. Use those sections to help you invent as you draft and revise your literacy narrative.

Devise a topic.

You may already have an idea about what you'd like to write about. But if not, the following ideas may give you a jumping-off point:

- an influential person who played a role—for good or ill—in your literacy education;
- a challenging project that required using a literacy you had not yet mastered;
- an occasion when you had to display literacy in a particular academic discipline;
- a new literacy you had to learn at a workplace;
- an experience learning how to communicate better with classmates, team members, siblings, or people in your community.

Your instructor may ask you to post your thoughts to a class discussion board or compose a fully developed literacy narrative like the example by David Sedaris on pp. 6–9. If your instructor approves, you might also consider using multimedia—for example, creating a Web page with visuals, audio, and video.

© Jahi Chikwendiu/The Washington Post via Getty Images

PART ONE

Writing Activities

2

Remembering an Event

Were you arrested—when you were thirteen? Why would a child remember being chased by an adult stranger as glorious? Have you been haunted by something you did? These are just a few of the exhilarating, disquieting, even terrifying subjects remembered in this chapter. The kind of autobiography you will be reading and writing in this chapter is public, intended to be read by others. Writing for others enables us not only to revisit our past, but also gives us an opportunity to represent ourselves to others. Our own and other people's life stories can help us see ourselves differently. They can give us insight into the cultural influences that helped shape who we are and what we value. They can show us what we have in common with others as well as what makes each of us distinctive.

People write memoirs for various purposes and audiences and publish them as narratives or graphics in a variety of media (print, digital, audiovisual). In college courses, you may be invited to use your own experience as an example or a kind of case study to apply, analyze, or evaluate ideas you are studying. A student in a linguistics course, for example, might analyze a conversation she had with her brother by looking at it through the lens of Deborah Tannen's theory that women tend to view problems as opportunities to share their feelings whereas men typically treat problems as occasions for practical solutions. In the community, writers may reveal personal stories to educate and inspire. For example, a blogger may reveal her own history of domestic violence to help readers understand how some victims become trapped by their own hope and denial. Even in professional and business settings, personal stories can play a role. At a conference, a manager might use the story of his encounter with a disgruntled employee to open a discussion of ways to defuse confrontations in the workplace.

In this chapter, we ask you to write about an event you remember. Choose one that will engage your instructor and classmates, that has significance for you, and that you feel comfortable sharing. From reading and analyzing the selections in the Guide to Reading that follows, you will learn how to make your own story interesting, even exciting, to read. The Guide to Writing (pp. 38–54) will show you ways to use the basic features of the genre to tell your story vividly and dramatically, to entertain readers but also to give them insight into the event's significance—its meaning and importance.

PRACTICING THE GENRE ─────────────────────────────────────

Telling a Story

The success of remembered event writing depends on how well you tell your story. The challenge is to make the story compelling and meaningful for readers, to make readers care about the storyteller and curious to know what happened. To practice creating an intriguing story about an event in your life, get together with two or three other students and follow these guidelines:

Part 1.   Choose an event that you feel comfortable describing and think about what makes it memorable (for example, a conflict with someone else or within yourself, the strong or mixed feelings it evokes, the cultural attitudes it reflects). What will be the turning point, or *climax*, and how will you build up to it? Then take turns telling your stories.

Part 2.   After telling your stories, discuss what you learned:

- **What did you learn about the genre from listening to others' stories?** Tell each other what struck you most on hearing each other's stories. For example, identify something in the story that was engaging (by being suspenseful, edgy, or funny, perhaps) or that helped you identify with the storyteller. What do you think the point or significance of the story is — in other words, what makes the event so memorable?

- **Think of a storytelling strategy someone else used that you could try in your own story.** For example, could you use dialogue to show how someone talks and acts, vivid details to describe how the scene looked and felt, action verbs to make the story exciting, reflection to clarify why the story was significant to you?

Analyzing Remembered Event Essays

As you read the selections in this chapter, you will see how different authors craft stories about an important event in their lives.

- Jean Brandt looks back on getting caught shoplifting (pp. 18–22)
- Annie Dillard recalls the consequences of a childhood prank (pp. 22–24)
- Jenée Desmond-Harris reflects on the death of her idol, rapper Tupac Shakur (pp. 27–29)
- Peter Orner struggles to understand why he swiped something his father valued (pp. 32–34)

Analyzing how these writers tell a dramatic, well-focused story; use vivid, specific description to enliven their writing; and choose details and words that help readers understand why the event was so memorable will help you see how you can employ these same techniques when writing your own autobiographical story.

Determine the writer's purpose and audience.

Many people write about important events in their lives to archive their memories and to learn something about themselves. Choosing events that are important to them personally, writers strive to imbue their stories with meaning and feeling that will resonate with readers. That is, they seek to help readers appreciate what we call the event's autobiographical **significance**—why the event is so memorable for the writer and what it might mean for readers. Often writers use autobiographical stories to reflect on a conflict that remains unresolved or one they still do not fully understand. Autobiographical stories may not only prompt readers to reflect on the writer's complicated and ambivalent emotions, puzzling motivations, and strained relationships. They may also help readers see larger cultural themes in these stories or understand implications the writer may not even have considered.

When reading the selections about remembered events that follow, ask yourself questions like these:

What seems to be the writer's purpose (or multiple, perhaps even conflicting purposes)?

- to understand what happened and why, perhaps to confront unconscious and possibly uncomplimentary motives?
- to relive an intense experience that might resonate with readers and lead them to reflect on similar experiences of their own?
- to win over readers, perhaps to justify or rationalize choices made, actions taken, or words used?
- to use personal experience as an example that readers are likely to understand?
- to reflect on cultural attitudes at the time the event occurred, perhaps in contrast to current ways of thinking?

How does the author want readers to react?

- to understand or empathize with the writer?
- to think anew about a similar experience of their own?
- to see the writer's experience as symptomatic of a broader social phenomenon?
- to assess how well the story applies to other people and situations?

Assess the genre's basic features.

As you read about the remembered events in this chapter, analyze and evaluate how different authors use the basic features of the genre. The examples that follow are taken from the reading selections that appear later in this Guide to Reading.

Basic Features
A Well-Told Story
Vivid Description
Significance

A WELL-TOLD STORY

Read first to see how the story attempts to engage readers:

- by letting readers into the storyteller's (or narrator's) point of view (for example, by using the first-person pronoun *I* to narrate the story);
- by arousing curiosity and suspense;
- by clarifying or resolving the underlying *conflict* through a change or discovery of some kind.

Many of these basic narrative elements can be visualized in the form of a **dramatic arc** (see Figure 2.1), which you can analyze to see how a story creates and resolves dramatic tension.

Exposition/Inciting Incident: Background information and scene setting, introducing the characters and the initial conflict or problem that sets off the action, arousing curiosity and suspense

Rising Action: The developing crisis, possibly leading to other conflicts and complications

Climax: The emotional high point, often a turning point marking a change for good or ill

Falling Action: Resolution of tension and unraveling of conflicts; may include a final surprise

Conclusion/Reflection: Conflicts come to an end but may not be fully resolved, and writer may reflect on the event's meaning and importance—its significance

FIGURE 2.1 Dramatic Arc
The shape of the arc varies from story to story: Not all stories devote the same amount of space to each element, and some may omit an element or include more than one.

*Notice the narrating strategies used to create **action sequences***. Narrating action sequences relies on such strategies as using action verbs (such as *walked*) in different tenses or in conjunction with prepositional phrases or other cues of time or location to depict movement and show the relation among actions in time. In the following example, notice that *I walked* occurred in the past—after *I had found* and before *I was about to drop it*:

Action verbs
> I walked back to the basket where I had found the button and was about to drop it when suddenly, instead, I took a quick glance around, assured myself no one could see, and slipped the button into the pocket of my sweatshirt. (Brandt, par. 3)

In addition to moving the narrative along, action sequences may also contribute to the overall or *dominant impression* and help readers understand the event's significance. In this example, Brandt's actions show her ambivalence or inner conflict. While her actions seem impulsive ("suddenly"), they are also self-conscious, evidenced by her stopping midway to see if anyone is watching.

VIVID DESCRIPTION OF PEOPLE AND PLACES

For more on describing strategies, see Chapter 15.

*Look for the describing strategies of **naming**, **detailing**, and **comparing***. In this example, Annie Dillard uses all three strategies to create a vivid description of a Pittsburgh street on one memorable winter morning:

Naming
Detailing
Comparing
> The cars' tires laid behind them on the snowy street a complex trail of beige chunks like crenellated castle walls. I had stepped on some earlier; they squeaked. (Dillard, par. 5)

Notice the senses the description evokes. In the example above, Dillard relies mainly on visual details to identify color, texture, and shape of the snowy tire tracks. But she also tells us what the chunks of snow sounded like when stepped on.

Think about the impression made by the descriptions, particularly by the comparisons (similes and metaphors). For example, Dillard's comparison of tire tracks to crenellated castle walls suggests a kind of starry-eyed romanticism, an impression that is echoed by her reflections at the end of the story. As you will see, descriptions like this contribute to an overall or *dominant impression* that helps readers grasp the event's significance.

*Finally, notice how **dialogue** is used to portray people and their relationships*. Autobiographers use dialogue to characterize the people involved in the event, showing what they're like by depicting how they talk and interact. Speaker tags identify who is speaking and indicate the speaker's tone or attitude. Here's a brief example that comes at the climax of Dillard's story when the man finally catches the kids he's been chasing:

Speaker tag
> "You stupid kids," he began perfunctorily. (Dillard, par. 18)

Consider why the writer chose to quote, paraphrase, or summarize. **Quoting** can give dialogue immediacy, intensify a confrontation, and shine a spotlight on a relationship. For example, Brandt uses quoting to make an inherently dramatic interaction that much more intense.

"I don't understand. What did you take? Why did you do it? You had plenty of money with you."

"I know but I just did it. I can't explain why. Mom, I'm sorry."

"I'm afraid sorry isn't enough. I'm horribly disappointed in you." (pars. 33–35)

Paraphrasing enables the writer to choose words for their impact or contribution to the dominant impression.

> Next thing I knew, he was talking about calling the police and having me arrested and thrown in jail, as if he had just nabbed a professional thief instead of a terrified kid. (Brandt, par. 7)

Paraphrase cue

The clichés (*thrown in jail* and *nabbed*) mock the security guard, aligning Brandt with her father's criticism of the police at the story's end.

Summarizing gives the gist. Sometimes writers use summary because what was said or how it was said isn't as important as the mere fact that something was said:

> . . . the chewing out was redundant, a mere formality, and beside the point. (Dillard, par. 19)

Summary cue

AUTOBIOGRAPHICAL SIGNIFICANCE

Look for remembered feelings and thoughts from the time the event occurred. Notice in the first example that Brandt announces her thoughts and feelings before describing them, but in the second example she simply shows her feelings by her actions:

> The *thought* of going to jail terrified me. . . . I *felt* alone and scared. (par. 17)

Emotional response

> Long after we got off the phone, . . . I could still distinctly hear the disappointment and hurt in my mother's voice. I cried. (36)

Look also for present perspective reflections about the past. In this example, Desmond-Harris uses rhetorical questions (questions she poses and then answers) to set up her present-day adult perspective on her past.

> Did we take ourselves seriously? Did we feel a real stake in the life of this "hard-core" gangsta rapper, and a real loss in his death? We did, even though we were two mixed-race girls raised by our white moms in a privileged community. . . . (par. 8)

Rhetorical questions

Notice that writers sometimes express both their past and present feelings, possibly to contrast them or to show that they have not changed. Observe the time cues Orner and Desmond-Harris use to distinguish between past and present feelings:

> Now that he is older and far milder, it is hard to believe how scared I used to be of my father. (Orner, par. 8)

Time cues

> I mourned Tupac's death then, and continue to mourn him now, because his music represents the years when I was both forced and privileged to confront what it meant to be black. (Desmond-Harris, par. 9)

Mark word choices in descriptive and narrative passages that contribute to the dominant impression and help to show why the event or person was significant. For example, Brandt shows her feeling of shame vividly in this passage:

> As the officers led me through the mall, I sensed a hundred pairs of eyes staring at me. My face flushed and I broke out in a sweat. (par. 18)

Consider whether the story's **significance** *encompasses mixed or ambivalent feelings and still-unresolved conflicts.* For example, notice the seesawing of feelings Brandt reports:

- Right after shoplifting, Brandt tells us "I thought about how sly [I] had been" and that "I felt proud of [my] accomplishment" (par. 5).

- After she is arrested, she acknowledges mixed feelings: "Being searched, although embarrassing, somehow seemed to be exciting. . . . I was having fun" (19).

- It is only when she has to face her mother that Brandt lets her intense feelings show: "For the first time that night, I was close to tears" (26).

- At the end, however, by transferring the blame from Brandt to the police, her father seems to leave the conflict essentially unresolved and repressed: "Although it would never be forgotten, the incident was not mentioned again" (38).

Readings

Jean Brandt | *Calling Home*

As a first-year college student, Jean Brandt wrote about a memorable event that occurred when she was thirteen: She shoplifted and was caught. As you read about Brandt's experience, you might want to think about these shoplifting factoids (unreliable because they show who is getting caught, but not necessarily who is shoplifting): According to the National Association for Shoplifting Prevention (NASP), shoplifting is pretty equal among genders, socioeconomic classes, and ethnicities, and contrary to expectation, only about 25 percent of shoplifters are kids, including teenagers (shopliftingprevention.org); Christmas season is a peak shoplifting period; some shoplifters report a "high" after getting away with it; shoplifting is seldom premeditated, and is possibly related to peer pressure and what is often called "consumer culture," the ideology that buying things brings intangibles like happiness, status, identity, belonging.

As you read,

To learn about Brandt's process of writing this essay, turn to A Writer at Work on pp. 54–56. How did Brandt discover the central conflict and significance of her story?

- consider which, if any, of this information about shoplifting affects your view of Brandt or your understanding of her story.

- think about Brandt's primary purpose in choosing this event and in presenting it as she does, given that she was writing for her instructor and classmates.

- answer the questions in the margins. Your instructor may ask you to post your answers to a class blog or discussion board or bring your responses to class.

▪▪ Basic Features
A Well-Told Story
Vivid Description
Significance

1   As we all piled into the car, I knew it was going to be a fabulous day. My grandmother was visiting for the holidays; and she and I, along with my older brother and sister, Louis and Susan, were setting off for a day of last-minute Christmas shopping. On the way to the mall, we sang Christmas carols, chattered, and laughed. With Christmas only two days away, we were caught up with holiday spirit. I felt light-headed and full of joy. I loved shopping — especially at Christmas.

2   The shopping center was swarming with frantic last-minute shoppers like ourselves. We went first to the General Store, my favorite. It carried mostly knickknacks and other useless items which nobody needs but buys anyway. I was thirteen years old at the time, and things like buttons and calendars and posters would catch my fancy. This day was no different. The object of my desire was a 75-cent Snoopy button. Snoopy was the latest. If you owned anything with the Peanuts on it, you were "in." But since I was supposed to be shopping for gifts for other people and not myself, I couldn't decide what to do. I went in search of my sister for her opinion. I pushed my way through throngs of people to the back of the store where I found Susan. I asked her if she thought I should buy the button. She said it was cute and if I wanted it to go ahead and buy it.

3   When I got back to the Snoopy section, I took one look at the lines at the cashiers and knew I didn't want to wait thirty minutes to buy an item worth less than one dollar. I walked back to the basket where I had found the button and was about to drop it when suddenly, instead, I took a quick glance around, assured myself no one could see, and slipped the button into the pocket of my sweatshirt.

4   I hesitated for a moment, but once the item was in my pocket, there was no turning back. I had never before stolen anything; but what was done was done. A few seconds later, my sister appeared and asked, "So, did you decide to buy the button?"

5   "No, I guess not." I hoped my voice didn't quaver. As we headed for the entrance, my heart began to race. I just had to get out of that store. Only a few more yards to go and I'd be safe. As we crossed the threshold, I heaved a sigh of relief. I was home free. I thought about how sly I had been and I felt proud of my accomplishment.

6   An unexpected tap on my shoulder startled me. I whirled around to find a middle-aged man, dressed in street clothes, flashing some type of badge and politely asking

How well do these descriptive details help you visualize the scene?

What is your first impression of Brandt?

How do these action verbs (highlighted) and dialogue contribute to the drama?

me to empty my pockets. Where did this man come from? How did he know? I was so sure that no one had seen me! On the verge of panicking, I told myself that all I had to do was give this man his button back, say I was sorry, and go on my way. After all, it was only a 75-cent item.

7   Next thing I knew, he was talking about calling the police and having me arrested and thrown in jail, as if he had just nabbed a professional thief instead of a terrified kid. I couldn't believe what he was saying.

8   "Jean, what's going on?"

9   The sound of my sister's voice eased the pressure a bit. She always managed to get me out of trouble. She would come through this time too.

10   "Excuse me. Are you a relative of this young girl?"

11   "Yes, I'm her sister. What's the problem?"

12   "Well, I just caught her shoplifting and I'm afraid I'll have to call the police."

13   "What did she take?"

14   "This button."

15   "A button? You are having a thirteen-year-old arrested for stealing a button?"

16   "I'm sorry, but she broke the law."

17   The man led us through the store and into an office, where we waited for the police officers to arrive. Susan had found my grandmother and brother, who, still shocked, didn't say a word. The thought of going to jail terrified me, not because of jail itself, but because of the encounter with my parents afterward. Not more than ten minutes later, two officers arrived and placed me under arrest. They said that I was to be taken to the station alone. Then, they handcuffed me and led me out of the store. I felt alone and scared. I had counted on my sister being with me, but now I had to muster up the courage to face this ordeal all by myself.

18   As the officers led me through the mall, I sensed a hundred pairs of eyes staring at me. My face flushed and I broke out in a sweat. Now everyone knew I was a criminal. In their eyes I was a juvenile delinquent, and thank God the cops were getting me off the streets. The worst part was thinking my grandmother might be having the same thoughts. The humiliation at that moment was overwhelming. I felt like Hester Prynne being put on public display for everyone to ridicule.

19   That short walk through the mall seemed to take hours. But once we reached the squad car, time raced by. I was read my rights and questioned. We were at the police

> How does your understanding of Brandt deepen or change through what she reveals about her feelings and thoughts?

station within minutes. Everything happened so fast I didn't have a chance to feel remorse for my crime. Instead, I viewed what was happening to me as if it were a movie. Being searched, although embarrassing, somehow seemed to be exciting. All the movies and television programs I had seen were actually coming to life. This is what it was really like. But why were criminals always portrayed as frightened and regretful? I was having fun. I thought I had nothing to fear—until I was allowed my one phone call. I was trembling as I dialed home. I didn't know what I was going to say to my parents, especially my mother.

20   "Hi, Dad, this is Jean."

21   "We've been waiting for you to call."

22   "Did Susie tell you what happened?"

23   "Yeah, but we haven't told your mother. I think you should tell her what you did and where you are."

24   "You mean she doesn't even know where I am?"

25   "No, I want you to explain it to her."

26   There was a pause as he called my mother to the phone. For the first time that night, I was close to tears. I wished I had never stolen that stupid pin. I wanted to give the phone to one of the officers because I was too ashamed to tell my mother the truth, but I had no choice.

27   "Jean, where are you?"

28   "I'm, umm, in jail."

29   "Why? What for?"

30   "Shoplifting."

31   "Oh no, Jean. Why? Why did you do it?"

32   "I don't know. No reason. I just did it."

33   "I don't understand. What did you take? Why did you do it? You had plenty of money with you."

34   "I know but I just did it. I can't explain why. Mom, I'm sorry."

35   "I'm afraid sorry isn't enough. I'm horribly disappointed in you."

36   Long after we got off the phone, while I sat in an empty jail cell, waiting for my parents to pick me up, I could still distinctly hear the disappointment and hurt in my mother's voice. I cried. The tears weren't for me but for her and the pain I had put her through. I felt like a terrible human being. I would rather have stayed in jail than confront my mom right

How does this dialogue add to the drama?

> What is the effect of interweaving storytelling and describing with remembering thoughts and feelings in this paragraph?

then. I dreaded each passing minute that brought our encounter closer. When the officer came to release me, I hesitated, actually not wanting to leave. We went to the front desk, where I had to sign a form to retrieve my belongings. I saw my parents a few yards away and my heart raced. A large knot formed in my stomach. I fought back the tears.

37   Not a word was spoken as we walked to the car. Slowly, I sank into the back seat anticipating the scolding. Expecting harsh tones, I was relieved to hear almost the opposite from my father.

> What do you learn from Brandt's account of her father's reaction?

38   "I'm not going to punish you and I'll tell you why. Although I think what you did was wrong, I think what the police did was more wrong. There's no excuse for locking a thirteen-year-old behind bars. That doesn't mean I condone what you did, but I think you've been punished enough already."

> How well does this final paragraph help you understand the event's significance?

39   As I looked from my father's eyes to my mother's, I knew this ordeal was over. Although it would never be forgotten, the incident was not mentioned again.

Annie Dillard | From *An American Childhood*

Courtesy of Michele Strub

ANNIE DILLARD, professor emeritus at Wesleyan University, won the Pulitzer Prize for nonfiction writing with her first book, *Pilgrim at Tinker Creek* (1974). Since then, she has written eleven other books in a variety of genres. They include *Teaching a Stone to Talk* (1988), *The Writing Life* (1990), *The Living* (1993), *Mornings Like This* (1996), and *The Maytrees* (2007). Dillard also wrote an autobiography of her early years, *An American Childhood* (1987), from which the following selection (and the excerpt in Chapter 1) comes.

As you read,

• think about how the first two paragraphs in the reading selection prepare readers to understand the story's significance.

• notice how Dillard sets the scene. Why do you think she describes the time and place with so much specificity?

1 Some boys taught me to play football. This was fine sport. You thought up a new strategy for every play and whispered it to the others. You went out for a pass, fooling everyone. Best, you got to throw yourself mightily at someone's running legs. Either you brought him down or you hit the ground flat out on your chin, with your arms empty before you. It was all or nothing. If you hesitated in fear, you would miss and get hurt: you would take a hard fall while the kid got away, or you would get kicked in the face while the kid got away. But if you flung yourself wholeheartedly at the back of his knees — if you gathered and joined body and soul and pointed them diving fearlessly — then you likely wouldn't get hurt, and you'd stop the ball. Your fate, and your team's score, depended on your concentration and courage. Nothing girls did could compare with it.

2 Boys welcomed me at baseball, too, for I had, through enthusiastic practice, what was weirdly known as a boy's arm. In winter, in the snow, there was neither baseball nor football, so the boys and I threw snowballs at passing cars. I got in trouble throwing snowballs, and have seldom been happier since.

3 On one weekday morning after Christmas, six inches of new snow had just fallen. We were standing up to our boot tops in snow on a front yard on trafficked Reynolds Street, waiting for cars. The cars traveled Reynolds Street slowly and evenly; they were targets all but wrapped in red ribbons, cream puffs. We couldn't miss.

4 I was seven; the boys were eight, nine, and ten. The oldest two Fahey boys were there — Mikey and Peter — polite blond boys who lived near me on Lloyd Street, and who already had four brothers and sisters. My parents approved Mikey and Peter Fahey. Chickie McBride was there, a tough kid, and Billy Paul and Mackie Kean too, from across Reynolds, where the boys grew up dark and furious, grew up skinny, knowing, and skilled. We had all drifted from our houses that morning looking for action, and had found it here on Reynolds Street.

5 It was cloudy but cold. The cars' tires laid behind them on the snowy street a complex trail of beige chunks like crenellated castle walls. I had stepped on some earlier; they squeaked. We could not have wished for more traffic. When a car came, we all popped it one.

. . . this time, the only time in all of life, the car pulled over and stopped. Its wide black door opened; a man got out of it, running. He didn't even close the door.

In the intervals between cars we reverted to the natural solitude of children.

6 I started making an iceball — a perfect iceball, from perfectly white snow, perfectly spherical, and squeezed perfectly translucent so no snow remained all the way through. (The Fahey boys and I considered it unfair actually to throw an iceball at somebody, but it had been known to happen.)

7 I had just embarked on the iceball project when we heard tire chains come clanking from afar. A black Buick was moving toward us down the street. We all spread out, banged together some regular snowballs, took aim, and, when the Buick drew nigh, fired.

8 A soft snowball hit the driver's windshield right before the driver's face. It made a smashed star with a hump in the middle.

9 Often, of course, we hit our target, but this time, the only time in all of life, the car pulled over and stopped. Its wide black door opened; a man got out of it, running. He didn't even close the car door.

10 He ran after us, and we ran away from him, up the snowy Reynolds sidewalk. At the corner, I looked back; incredibly, he was still after us. He was in city clothes: a suit and tie, street shoes. Any normal adult would have quit, having sprung us into flight and made his point. This man was gaining on us. He was a thin man, all action. All of a sudden, we were running for our lives.

11 Wordless, we split up. We were on our turf; we could lose ourselves in the neighborhood backyards, everyone for himself. I paused and considered. Everyone had vanished except Mikey Fahey, who was just rounding the corner of a yellow brick house. Poor Mikey, I trailed him. The driver of the Buick sensibly picked the two of us to follow. The man apparently had all day.

12 He chased Mikey and me around the yellow house and up a backyard path we knew by heart: under a low tree, up a bank, through a hedge, down some snowy steps, and across the grocery store's delivery driveway. We smashed through a gap in another hedge, entered a scruffy backyard and ran around its back porch and tight between houses to Edgerton Avenue; we ran across Edgerton to an alley and up our own sliding woodpile to the Halls' front yard; he kept coming. We ran up Lloyd

Street and wound through mazy backyards toward the steep hilltop at Willard and Lang.

13   He chased us silently, block after block. He chased us silently over picket fences, through thorny hedges, between houses, around garbage cans, and across streets. Every time I glanced back, choking for breath, I expected he would have quit. He must have been as breathless as we were. His jacket strained over his body. It was an immense discovery, pounding into my hot head with every sliding, joyous step, that this ordinary adult evidently knew what I thought only children who trained at football knew: that you have to fling yourself at what you're doing, you have to point yourself, forget yourself, aim, dive.

14   Mikey and I had nowhere to go, in our own neighborhood or out of it, but away from this man who was chasing us. He impelled us forward; we compelled him to follow our route. The air was cold; every breath tore my throat. We kept running, block after block; we kept improvising, backyard after backyard, running a frantic course and choosing it simultaneously, failing always to find small places or hard places to slow him down, and discovering always, exhilarated, dismayed, that only bare speed could save us—for he would never give up, this man—and we were losing speed.

15   He chased us through the backyard labyrinths of ten blocks before he caught us by our jackets. He caught us and we all stopped.

16   We three stood staggering, half blinded, coughing, in an obscure hilltop backyard: a man in his twenties, a boy, a girl. He had released our jackets, our pursuer, our captor, our hero: he knew we weren't going anywhere. We all played by the rules. Mikey and I unzipped our jackets. I pulled off my sopping mittens. Our tracks multiplied in the backyard's new snow. We had been breaking new snow all morning. We didn't look at each other. I was cherishing my excitement. The man's lower pants legs were wet; his cuffs were full of snow, and there was a prow of snow beneath them on his shoes and socks. Some trees bordered the little flat backyard, some messy winter trees. There was no one around: a clearing in a grove, and we the only players.

17   It was a long time before he could speak. I had some difficulty at first recalling why we were there. My lips felt swollen; I couldn't see out of the sides of my eyes; I kept coughing.

18   "You stupid kids," he began perfunctorily.

19   We listened perfunctorily indeed, if we listened at all, for the chewing out was redundant, a mere formality, and beside the point. The point was that he had chased us passionately without giving up, and so he had caught us. Now he came down to earth. I wanted the glory to last forever.

20   But how could the glory have lasted forever? We could have run through every backyard in North America until we got to Panama. But when he trapped us at the lip of the Panama Canal, what precisely could he have done to prolong the drama of the chase and cap its glory? I brooded about this for the next few years. He could only have fried Mikey Fahey and me in boiling oil, say, or dismembered us piecemeal, or staked us to anthills. None of which I really wanted, and none of which any adult was likely to do, even in the spirit of fun. He could only chew us out there in the Panamanian jungle, after months or years of exalting pursuit. He could only begin, "You stupid kids," and continue in his ordinary Pittsburgh accent with his normal righteous anger and the usual common sense.

21   If in that snowy backyard the driver of the black Buick had cut off our heads, Mikey's and mine, I would have died happy, for nothing has required so much of me since as being chased all over Pittsburgh in the middle of winter—running terrified, exhausted—by this sainted, skinny, furious redheaded man who wished to have a word with us. I don't know how he found his way back to his car.

[REFLECT]   # Make connections: Acting fearlessly.

At the beginning of the essay, Dillard tells about being taught by the neighborhood boys the joy of playing football, particularly the "all or nothing" of diving "fearlessly" (par. 1). Recall an occasion when you had an opportunity to dive fearlessly into an activity that posed some challenge or risk or required special effort. For example, you may have been challenged, like Dillard, by your teammates at a football game or by a group of volunteers helping during a natural disaster. Or you may have felt pressured by friends to do something that went against your better judgment, was illegal, or was dangerous. Your instructor may ask you to post your thoughts to a class discussion board or to discuss them with other students in class. Use these questions to get started:

- What made you embrace the challenge or resist it? What do you think your choice tells about you at the time of the event?

- Dillard uses the value term *courage* to describe the fearless behavior she learned playing football. What value term would you use to describe your experience? For example, were you being *selfless* or *self-serving; responsible* or *irresponsible;* a *follower, a leader,* or *a self-reliant individual*?

Use the basic features.

[ANALYZE]

A WELL-TOLD STORY: CONSTRUCTING AN ACTION SEQUENCE

Throughout this story, Dillard creates compelling *action sequences* by using a variety of strategies. In this first example, she combines action verbs with prepositional phrases to help readers visualize what it was like to move rapidly from place to place.

> He chased Mikey and me around the yellow house and up a backward path we knew by heart: under a low tree, up a bank, through a hedge, down some snowy steps, and across the grocery store's delivery driveway. We smashed through a gap in a hedge. . . . (par. 12)

Action verb

Prepositional phrases

Here's an example where she uses short phrases, often with similar sounding words and parallel sentence structures, to convey a sense of repeated action:

> He impelled us forward; we compelled him to follow our route. . . . We kept running, block after block; we kept improvising, backyard after backyard. . . . (par. 14)

Similar sounds

Parallel structures

ANALYZE & WRITE

Write a paragraph analyzing one of Dillard's action sequences:

1. Skim paragraphs 11–14, marking similar words and parallel sentence structures, action verbs, and prepositional phrases. (Don't feel you have to mark every instance, but get a sense of how often Dillard uses these strategies.)

2. How well do these narrative strategies work to represent action? How does using the same strategies over and over contribute to the effect?

3. Try writing an action sequence of your own, using parallel sentence structure, prepositional phrases, and/or words that echo one another as Dillard does.

For more about action sequences, see Chapter 14.

VIVID DESCRIPTION: CREATING A DOMINANT IMPRESSION

The describing strategies of naming, detailing, and comparing portray people and places vividly:

> The shopping center was swarming with frantic last-minute shoppers like ourselves. (Brandt, par. 2)

Naming
Detailing
Comparing

Brandt *names* a familiar location for readers. She selects *details* carefully to conjure a specific image of that shopping center before Christmas. Perhaps most evocatively, she uses a metaphor to *compare* the shopping mall to a "swarming" beehive, a comparison that reinforces the image of "frantic" shoppers in a place teeming with hurried, excited people.

Describing strategies, like Brandt's, not only help readers imagine the scene and people at a particular place and time; they also contribute to the *dominant impression*. The description evokes Brandt's youthful excitement, suggests the crowds and chaos that motivated Brandt to pocket the button, and it foreshadows the swarm of intense and conflicted feelings Brandt experiences as the story unfolds.

| ANALYZE & WRITE |

Write a paragraph analyzing Dillard's use of naming, detailing, and comparing to help readers visualize the man who chased her and to create a dominant impression:

For more about describing strategies, see Chapter 15.

1. Skim paragraphs 9–10 and 16–21, highlighting Dillard's use of naming, detailing, and comparing to describe the man.

2. Dillard's description of the man is spare, with only a few carefully chosen details. What kinds of details does Dillard focus on and what do they suggest about the man? Who is he? Where does he come from? Why would he bother to chase the kids?

3. Notice the repetition of the word *normal* in paragraphs 10 and 20. What about the man makes him seem like a "normal adult" and what makes him seem anything but normal? How does Dillard help the reader reconcile these contrasting images to form a dominant impression?

AUTOBIOGRAPHICAL SIGNIFICANCE: SHOWING AND TELLING

Writers use both *showing* and *telling* to convey the autobiographical significance of the event, what it meant at the time and why it continues to be memorable. As you've seen, **showing**, in narrating the story and in describing people and places, not only helps make the writing vivid, but also creates a dominant impression. However, showing alone cannot help readers fully grasp an event's significance. Readers also need **telling**, the writer's explicit comments and reflections. In this example, Brandt uses showing and telling to give readers a clear understanding of how she felt at the time:

Telling
Showing

As the officers led me through the mall, I sensed a hundred pairs of eyes staring at me. My face flushed and I broke out in a sweat. Now everyone knew I was a criminal. . . . The humiliation at that moment was overwhelming. I felt like Hester Prynne being put on public display for everyone to ridicule. (par. 18)

Narrators may use telling to articulate remembered feelings and thoughts from the time the event occurred and to present perspective on the event—what the writer feels and thinks now, looking back on it after time has passed.

To alert readers that they are telling, writers sometimes announce their reflections with words like *felt* and *thought*. But they may also choose words that name or imply a particular emotion or thought (for example, "The humiliation at that moment was overwhelming" [Brandt, 18]).

Similarly, to signal a shift from the past to the present perspective, writers sometimes announce the transition with words such as *then* and *now*. But a more subtle strategy is to use sophisticated word choices that show a deeper, more mature understanding of the experience (for example, when Brandt compares herself to Hester Prynne, from Nathaniel Hawthorne's novel *The Scarlet Letter*, "being put on public display for everyone to ridicule" [par. 18]).

ANALYZE & WRITE

Write a paragraph analyzing Dillard's use of telling to convey the event's significance:

1. Skim paragraphs 11–21, noting where Dillard *tells* readers her thoughts and feelings. (Don't feel you have to mark every instance, but try to get a sense of how much she tells as well as what she tells readers.)

2. Review what you have highlighted to determine which of the passages indicate Dillard's remembered thoughts and feelings from the time the incident occurred and which indicate what she thinks and feels now looking back on the event from her present adult perspective. How can you tell the difference between her past and present perspectives?

Consider possible topics: Remembering unexpected adult actions and reactions.

[RESPOND]

Like Dillard, you could write about a time when an adult did something entirely unexpected during your childhood—an action that seemed dangerous or threatening to you, or something humorous, kind, or generous. Consider unpredictable actions of adults in your immediate or extended family, adults you had come to know outside your family, and strangers. As you consider these possible topics, think about your purpose and audience: What would you want your instructor and classmates to learn from reading about this event?

Jenée Desmond-Harris | *Tupac and My Non-thug Life*

Courtesy of Jenée Desmond-Harris

JENÉE DESMOND-HARRIS is the race, law, and politics reporter at Vox.com. Before that she was White House correspondent and associate editor at *The Root*, an online magazine dedicated to African American news, social justice, and culture. A graduate of Howard University and Harvard Law School, Desmond-Harris has been a contributor to such news outlets as *Time* magazine, CNN, MSNBC, and the *Huffington Post*. The following selection was published in *The Root* in 2011. It chronicles Desmond-Harris's reaction to the murder of gangsta rap icon Tupac Shakur in a Las Vegas drive-by shooting in 1996. Desmond-Harris mentions Tupac's mother, Afeni, as well as the "East Coast–West Coast war"—the rivalry between Tupac and the Notorious B.I.G. (Biggie Smalls), who was suspected of being involved in Tupac's murder.

As you read, consider the photograph that appeared in the article:

• What does the photograph capture about the fifteen-year-old Desmond-Harris?

• What does its inclusion say about Desmond-Harris's perspective on her adolescent self and the event she recollects?

1   I learned about Tupac's death when I got home from cheerleading practice that Friday afternoon in September 1996. I was a sophomore in high school in Mill Valley, Calif. I remember trotting up my apartment building's stairs, physically tired but buzzing with the frenetic energy and possibilities for change that accompany fall and a new school year. I'd been cautiously allowing myself to think during the walk home about a topic that felt frighteningly taboo (at least in my world, where discussion of race was avoided as delicately as obesity or mental illness): what it meant to be biracial and on the school's mostly white cheerleading team instead of the mostly black dance team. I remember acknowledging, to the sound of an 8-count that still pounded in my head as I walked through the door, that I didn't really have a choice: I could memorize a series of stiff and precise motions but couldn't actually dance.

2   My private musings on identity and belonging—not original in the least, but novel to me—were interrupted when my mom heard me slam the front door and drop my bags: *"Your friend died!"* she called out from another room. Confused silence. *"You know, that rapper you and Thea love so much!"*

Mourning a Death in Vegas

3   The news was turned on, with coverage of the deadly Vegas shooting. Phone calls were made. Ultimately my best friend, Thea, and I were left to our own 15-year-old devices to mourn that weekend. Her mother and stepfather were out of town. Their expansive, million-dollar home was perched on a hillside less than an hour from Tupac's former stomping grounds in Oakland and Marin City. Of course, her home was also worlds away from both places.

4   We couldn't "pour out" much alcohol undetected for a libation, so we limited ourselves to doing somber shots of liqueur from a well-stocked cabinet. One each. Tipsy, in a high-ceilinged kitchen surrounded by hardwood floors and Zen flower arrangements, we baked cookies for his mother. We packed them up to ship to Afeni with a handmade card. ("Did we really do that?" I asked Thea this week. I wanted to ensure that this story, which people who know me now find hilarious, hadn't morphed into some sort of personal urban legend over the past 15 years. "Yes," she said. "We put them in a lovely tin.")

5   On a sound system that echoed through speakers perched discreetly throughout the airy house, we played "Life Goes On" on a loop and sobbed. We analyzed lyrics for premonitions of the tragedy. We, of course, cursed Biggie. Who knew that the East Coast–West Coast war had two earnest soldiers in flannel pajamas, lying on a king-size bed decorated with pink toe shoes that dangled from one of its posts? There, we studied our pictures of Tupac and re-created his tattoos on each other's body with a Sharpie. I got "Thug Life" on my stomach. I gave Thea "Exodus 1811" inside a giant cross. Both are flanked by "West Side."

6   A snapshot taken that Monday on our high school's front lawn (seen here) shows the two of us lying side by side, shirts lifted to display the tributes in black marker.

The author (left) with her friend Thea

Despite our best efforts, it's the innocent, bubbly lettering of notes passed in class and of poster boards made for social studies presentations. My hair has recently been straightened with my first (and last) relaxer and a Gold 'N Hot flatiron on too high a setting. Hers is slicked back with the mixture of Herbal Essences and Blue Magic that we formulated in a bathroom laboratory.

7   My rainbow-striped tee and her white wifebeater capture a transition between our skater-inspired Salvation Army shopping phase and the next one, during which we'd wear the same jeans slung from our hip bones, revealing peeks of flat stomach, but transforming ourselves from Alternative Nation to MTV Jams imitators. We would get bubble coats in primary colors that Christmas and start using silver eyeliner, trying—and failing—to look something like Aaliyah.[1]

Mixed Identities: Tupac and Me

8   Did we take ourselves seriously? Did we feel a real stake in the life of this "hard-core" gangsta rapper, and a real loss in his death? We did, even though we were two mixed-race girls raised by our white moms in a privileged community where we could easily rattle off the names of the small handful of other kids in town who also had one black parent: Sienna. Rashea. Brandon. Aaron. Sudan. Akio. Lauren. Alicia. Even though the most subversive thing we did was make prank calls. Even though we hadn't yet met our first boyfriends, and Shock G's proclamations about putting satin on people's panties sent us into absolute giggling fits. And even though we'd been so delicately cared for, nurtured and protected from any of life's hard edges—with special efforts made to shield us from those involving race—that we sometimes felt ready to explode with boredom. Or maybe because of all that.

9   I mourned Tupac's death then, and continue to mourn him now, because his music represents the years when I was both forced and privileged to confront what it meant to be black. That time, like his music, was about exploring the contradictory textures of this identity: The ambience and indulgence of the fun side, as in

"California Love" and "Picture Me Rollin'." But also the burdensome anxiety and outright anger—"Brenda's Got a Baby," "Changes" and "Hit 'Em Up."

10   For Thea and me, his songs were the musical score to our transition to high school, where there emerged a vague, lunchtime geography to race: White kids perched on a sloping green lawn and the benches above it. Below, black kids sat on a wall outside the gym. The bottom of the hill beckoned. Thea, more outgoing, with more admirers among the boys, stepped down boldly, and I followed timidly. Our formal invitations came in the form of unsolicited hall passes to go to Black Student Union meetings during free periods. We were assigned to recite Maya Angelou's "Phenomenal Woman" at the Black History Month assembly.

11   Tupac was the literal sound track when our school's basketball team would come charging onto the court, and our ragtag group of cheerleaders kicked furiously to "Toss It Up" in a humid gymnasium. Those were the games when we might breathlessly join the dance team after our cheer during time-outs if they did the single "African step" we'd mastered for BSU performances.

Everything Black—and Cool

12   . . . Blackness became something cool, something to which we had brand-new access. We flaunted it, buying Kwanzaa candles and insisting on celebrating privately (really, just lighting the candles and excluding our friends) at a sleepover. We memorized "I Get Around"[2] and took turns singing verses to each other as we drove through Marin County suburbs in Thea's green Toyota station wagon. Because he was with us through all of this, we were in love with Tupac and wanted to embody him. On Halloween, Thea donned a bald cap and a do-rag, penciled in her already-full eyebrows and was a dead ringer.

13   Tupac's music, while full of social commentary (and now even on the Vatican's playlist), probably wasn't made to be a treatise on racial identity. Surely it wasn't created to accompany two girls (*little* girls, really) as they embarked on a coming-of-age journey. But it was there for us when we desperately needed it.

---

[1] A hit rhythm-and-blues and hip-hop recording artist. Aaliyah Dana Haughton died in a plane crash at age twenty-two. [Editor's note]

[2] Tupac Shakur's first top-twenty single, released in 1993 on *Strictly 4 My N.I.G.G.A.Z.*, Shakur's second studio album. [Editor's note]

REFLECT

Make connections: Searching for identity.

Remembering high school, Desmond-Harris describes how students chose to group themselves according to what she calls "a vague, lunchtime geography of race: White kids perched on a sloping green lawn and the benches above it. Below, black kids sat on a wall outside the gym" (par. 10).

School, particularly high school, is notorious for students' forming peer groups or cliques of various kinds—by ethnicity, gender, popularity, and so on. Recall the cliques in your own school and think about the roles they played, positive and negative, in the search for identity. Your instructor may ask you to post your thoughts to a class discussion board or blog, or to discuss them with other students in class. Use these questions to get started:

- Did you associate with any particular groups, and if so, why did you choose these groups?
- How did being in a particular group or not being in that group affect your sense of yourself?
- Why do you think it is important for her "coming-of-age journey" that Desmond-Harris felt that the group at the "bottom of the hill beckoned" (par. 10)? The word *beckoned* here can be read in two ways: that she felt the need to be a part of the group or that members of the group invited her to join them. Consider how these possible interpretations affect your understanding of her remembered event.

ANALYZE

Use the basic features.

A WELL-TOLD STORY: FINDING THE ARC OF THE STORY

We have seen that the dramatic arc (Fig. 2.1, p. 15) is often used to organize a remembered event narrative around a central conflict, arousing curiosity and suspense as it builds toward a climax or emotional high point before resolving the conflict or at least bringing it to a conclusion. This is basically the structure Brandt and Dillard use to tell their stories. Writers, however, do not always follow this straightforward pattern. They may emphasize certain elements of the arc and downplay or even skip others.

ANALYZE & WRITE

Write a paragraph analyzing the structure of Desmond-Harris's story.

1. Desmond-Harris could have built up to the surprising news of Tupac's death, using it as the dramatic climax of her story. Why do you think she chose instead to use his death as the "inciting incident" with which to begin her story?

2. How does the opening paragraph shed light on the conflict at the heart of Desmond-Harris's story?

3. What do the girls' actions as they mourn Tupac's death (paragraphs 3–7) as well as their actions later (paragraphs 10–12) suggest about how the inciting incident of Tupac's death led them to deal with the underlying conflict?

VIVID DESCRIPTION OF PEOPLE AND PLACES: USING VISUALS AND BRAND NAMES

Desmond-Harris provides lots of concrete details to enliven her narrative. She also uses a photo and refers to brand names to convey to readers an exact sense of what the girls were like. Notice that she recounts the Sharpie tattooing and then actually shows us a photo of herself and her friend Thea displaying their tattoos. But Desmond-Harris does not let the photo speak for itself; instead, she describes the picture, pointing out features, such as their hairstyles and outfits, that mark the girls' identity. Consider the references to particular styles and brand names (such as "our skater-inspired Salvation Army shopping phase") that tag the various roles they were trying on at that time of their lives (par. 7).

ANALYZE & WRITE

Write a paragraph or two analyzing Desmond-Harris's use of a photograph and brand names to enhance her descriptions:

1. Skim paragraphs 5–7, highlighting the specific details in the photo that Desmond-Harris points out as well as the brand names (usually capitalized) and the modifiers (as in *skater-inspired*) that make them more specific.

2. Look closely at the photograph itself, and consider its purpose.
   - Why do you think Desmond-Harris included it?
   - What does the photograph contribute or show us that the text alone does not convey?

3. Consider the effect that the photo and the brand names have on you as a reader (or might have on readers of about Desmond-Harris's age). How do they help readers envision the girls? What is the dominant impression you get of the young Desmond-Harris from these descriptive details?

For more about analyzing visuals, see Chapter 28.

AUTOBIOGRAPHICAL SIGNIFICANCE: HANDLING COMPLEX EMOTIONS

Remembered events that have lasting significance nearly always involve mixed or ambivalent feelings. Therefore, readers expect and appreciate some degree of complexity. Multiple layers of meaning make autobiographical stories more, not less, interesting. Significance that seems simplistic or predictable makes stories less successful. For example, if Brandt's story had ended with her arrest and left out the conversations with her parents, readers would have less insight into Brandt's still intense and unresolved feelings.

ANALYZE & WRITE

Write a paragraph or two analyzing Desmond-Harris's handling of the complex personal and cultural significance of her remembered event:

1. Skim the last two sections (pars. 8–13), noting passages where Desmond-Harris tells readers her remembered feelings and thoughts at the time and her present perspective as an adult reflecting on the experience. How does Desmond-Harris use her dual perspective—that of the fifteen-year-old experiencing the event and the thirty-year-old writing about it—to help readers understand the event's significance?

2 Look closely at paragraph 8, and consider how Desmond-Harris helps her readers grasp the significance of the event by using sentence strategies like these:

- rhetorical questions (questions writers ask and answer themselves)
- repeated words and phrases
- intentional sentence fragments (incomplete sentences used for special effect)

Note that in academic writing, sentence fragments—even those that are used purposely for rhetorical effect—may be frowned on. One of the instructor's purposes in assigning a writing project is to teach students to use formal academic writing conventions, a process that includes distinguishing between complete sentences and sentence fragments, and knowing how to identify and correct sentence fragments.

[RESPOND]

Consider possible topics: Recognizing a public event as a turning point.

Like Desmond-Harris, you could write about how a public event, like a celebrity death or marriage, an act of heroism or charity, or even the passage of a law helped (or forced) you to confront an aspect of your identity. Consider the complexities of your reaction—the significance the event had for you at the time and the significance the event has for you now. You might make a list of physical traits, as well as beliefs about or aspects of your sense of identity that changed as a result of the event.

Peter Orner | *Writing about What Haunts Us*

YVONNE ZIPP/MLIVE.COM/Landov

PETER ORNER writes in many genres; he has written novels, such as *The Second Coming of Mavala Shikongo* (2006) and *Love and Shame and Love* (2011); short stories, including the collections *Esther Stories* (2001) and *Last Car over the Sagamore Bridge* (2014); screenplays, such as "The Raft" (2014); profiles, including *Underground America* (2008) and *Hope Deferred: Narratives of Zimbabwean Lives* (2010); and autobiographical essays such as "Writing about What Haunts Us."

As you read, think about your first impression of Orner from his admission in the opening sentence about lying:

- What does he risk (or gain) by beginning this way?
- To whom do you think he's been lying?

1 I've been trying to lie about this story for years. As a fiction writer, I feel an almost righteous obligation to the untruth. Fabrication is my livelihood, and so telling something straight, for me, is the mark of failure. Yet in many attempts over the years I've not been able to make out of this tiny—but weirdly soul-defining—episode in my life anything more than a plain recounting of the facts, as best as I can remember them. Dressing them up into fiction, in this case, wrecked what is essentially a long overdue confession.

2 Here's the nonfiction version.

3 I watched my father in the front hall putting on his new, lambskin leather gloves. It was a sort of private ceremony. This was in early November, 1982, in Highland Park, Ill., a town north of Chicago along Lake Michigan. My father had just returned from a business trip to Paris. He'd bought the gloves at a place called Hermès, a mythical wonderland of a store. He pulled one on slowly, then the other, and held them up in the mirror to see how his hands looked in such gloves.

4 A week later, I stole them.

5 I remember the day. I was home from school. Nobody else was around. I opened the left-hand drawer of the front hall table and there they were. I learned for the first time how easy it is to just grab something. I stuffed the gloves in my pants and sprinted upstairs to my room. I hid them in the back of my closet under the wicker basket that held my license plate collection. Then I braced myself, for days. It was a warm November.

6 When we finally left that house—my mother, my brother and me—I took the gloves with me to our new place. I took them with me to college. To Boston, to Cincinnati, to North Carolina, to California. I even took them with me to Namibia for two years. I have them now, on my desk, thirty years later.

7 I've never worn them, not once, although my father and I have the same small hands. I didn't want the gloves. I never wanted the gloves. I only wanted my father not to have them.

8 Now that he is older and far milder, it is hard to believe how scared I used to be of my father. Back then he was so full of anger. Was he unhappy in his marriage? No doubt. He and my mother never had much in common. But his anger—sometimes it was rage—went beyond this not so unusual disappointment. My own totally unscien-

tific, armchair diagnosis is that like other chronically unsatisfied people, the daily business of living caused my father despair. At no time did this manifest itself more powerfully than when he came home from work. A rug askew, a jacket not hung up, a window left open—all could set off a fury. My brother once spilled a pot of ink on the snowy white carpet of my parent's bedroom: Armageddon.

9 His unpredictability is what made his explosions so potent. Sometimes the bomb wouldn't go off, and he'd act like my idea of a normal dad. When he finally noticed those precious gloves were missing, he seemed only confused.

10 "Maybe they're in the glove compartment," my mother said.

11 "Impossible. I never put gloves in the glove compartment. The glove compartment is for maps."

12 "Oh, well," my mother said.

13 He kept searching the front hall table, as if he had somehow overlooked them amid all the cheap imitation leather gloves, mismatched mittens and tasseled Bears hats. I am certain the notion that one of us had taken the gloves never crossed his mind.

14 Haunted by my guilt, a frequent motivation for my fiction in general, I've tried to contort my theft into a story, a made-up story.

15 In my failed attempts, the thief is always trying to give the gloves back. In one abandoned version, the son character (sometimes he's a daughter) mails the gloves back to the father, along with a forged letter, purportedly written by a long-dead friend of the father, a man the father had once betrayed. I liked the idea of a package arriving, out of the blue, from an aggrieved ghost. I'm returning your gloves, Phil. Now at least one of us may be absolved.

I didn't want the gloves. I never wanted the gloves. I only wanted my father not to have them.

16 The problem was that it palmed off responsibility on a third party. And it muddied the story by pulling the thief out of the center of what little action there was.

17 In a simpler but equally bad version, the son character, home for Thanksgiving, slips the gloves back in the top left-hand drawer of the front hall table of the house he grew up in, the house where the father still lives. This attempt was marred not only by cooked-up dialogue but also by a dead end.

18 "Dad! How about we take a walk by the lake?"

19 "It's been years, Son, since we've taken a walk."

20 "Pretty brisk out. Maybe you need your gloves?"

21   The moment arrives: the father slides open the drawer. Voilà! (Note the French.) Cut to the father's face. Describe his bewilderment. I must have checked this drawer a hundred thousand times. Decades drop from the father's eyes, and both father and son face each other as they never faced each other when both were years younger. The son stammers out a confession I could somehow never get right. He tries to explain himself, but can't. Why did he take the gloves? My character could never express it in words and the story kept collapsing.

22   This is where the truth of this always derails the fiction. I can't give the gloves back, in fiction or in this thing we call reality. If I did, I'd have to confront something I've known all along but have never wanted to express, even to myself alone. My father would have given me his gloves. All I had to do was ask. He would have been so pleased that for once we shared a common interest. This happened so few times in our lives. All the years I've been trying to write this, maybe I've always known that this essential fact would stick me in the heart.

23   Our imaginations sometimes fail us for a reason. Not because it is cathartic to tell the truth (I finally told my father last year) but because coming clean may also be a better, if smaller, story. A scared (and angry) kid rips off his father's gloves, carries them around for decades. Sometimes he takes them out and feels them but never puts them on. When I see my father these days, we graze each other's cheeks, a form of kissing in my family. I love my father. I suppose I did even then, in the worst moments of fear.

24   Well-made things eventually deteriorate. The Hermès gloves are no longer baby-soft. All the handless years have dried them up.

25   In 1982, my father wasn't much older than I am at this moment. I think of him now, standing in the front hall. He's holding his hands up in the mirror, pulling on his beautiful gloves, a rare stillness on his face, a kind of hopeful calm. Was this what I wanted to steal?

[REFLECT] Making connections: Explaining yourself to yourself.

In paragraph 21, Orner writes that he cannot "explain himself," even to himself. Occasionally we do or say things for reasons we cannot fully understand or do not want to admit to ourselves. Such memories can haunt us. Think of something you did or said—or failed to do or say—that haunts you. It should be something you don't mind sharing with others because your instructor may ask you to post your thoughts to a class discussion board or blog, or to discuss them with other students in class. Use these questions to get started:

- What was the context in which the event occurred—who was involved, what did you think or feel at the time, what do you think or feel now looking back at it?

- Looking back at the event, how do you see yourself—for example, as having had no choice, as reacting to something someone else did or said, as acting impulsively, or as something else?

- How do you think Orner sees himself?

[ANALYZE] Use the basic features.

A WELL-TOLD STORY: MAKING UP STORIES

Orner tells us that he has tried repeatedly to write about "this tiny—but weirdly soul-defining—episode in [his] life" (par. 1). In his efforts to tell the story, Orner juxtaposes what he calls "the nonfiction version" (2) and two fictional versions.

ANALYZE & WRITE

Write a paragraph analyzing Orner's different versions of this story:

1 Compare the "nonfiction version" (pars. 2–5) with the fictional versions (pars. 15 and 17–21).

2 Which version do you think is most successful? On what criteria do you base your judgment? On what basis does Orner think the made-up stories fail?

3 Notice that Orner bases his fiction on what really happened. Is there any part of his nonfiction version where you think he may have imaginatively invented details to flesh out his story?

VIVID DESCRIPTION OF PEOPLE AND PLACES: PORTRAYING A PERSON

Writers use the describing strategies of naming, detailing, and comparing to describe people. **Naming** identifies people—for example, by the person's name or relationship to the narrator, or both, as Desmond-Harris does when she writes: "my best friend, Thea" (par. 3). **Detailing** means describing how the person looks, acts, gestures, and talks—for example, "a middle-aged man, dressed in street clothes, flashing some type of badge and politely asking me to empty my pockets" (Brandt, par. 6). **Comparing** suggests the narrator's feelings about the person—for example, Dillard calls the man who chased her "sainted" (par. 21). Describing strategies like these help create a dominant impression.

ANALYZE & WRITE

Write a paragraph analyzing the dominant impression you get from the describing strategies Orner uses to portray his father:

1 Highlight the descriptive details that give you a clear picture of what Orner's father looks like and how he acts.

2 What do you learn about Orner's father and Orner's feelings about him from these descriptive details?

3 How does the description in the last paragraph change or deepen the impression you get?

AUTOBIOGRAPHICAL SIGNIFICANCE: USING SYMBOLS

Autobiographers occasionally use *symbols* to enrich the story's significance by adding another level of meaning. The symbol could be an object (such as the Snoopy button for Brandt), a person (such as Tupac for Desmond-Harris), or a place (such as the Panamanian jungle for Dillard). On a literal level, the object, person, or place is simply what it is, nothing more. But on a symbolic level, the object, person, or place takes on additional meaning, often standing for an abstract idea. For example, when Brandt identifies herself with Hester Prynne (the protagonist in the novel *The Scarlet Letter*), she associates herself with a symbol of social injustice and personal heroism, encouraging readers to see her as being mistreated but rising above it. Through this symbol, Brandt reinforces her father's judgment that although she had done something wrong, the police were even "more wrong" (par. 38).

ANALYZE & WRITE

Write a paragraph analyzing how Orner uses symbolism:

1. What do you think the Hermès gloves symbolized for Orner's father? What in the story gives you this impression?
2. What do the Hermès gloves symbolize for Orner himself and for his relationship with his father?

[RESPOND] ## Consider possible topics: Exploring relationships.

Orner focuses on a fairly minor event to explore his complex relationship with his father. Think about whether there is someone in your past with whom you had an intense and perhaps strained relationship. It might be a teacher, coach, relative, or friend. Was there a particular event—a one-time or recurring incident—you could use to show what the person was like and illuminate your relationship? What details do you remember, such as a particular conversation, or the person's typical way of talking, or style of dress, or mannerisms? How do those traits illuminate your relationship or contribute to the dominant impression?

Remembered events are depicted regularly in genres and media besides the college essay. For example, Jean Brandt's story about shoplifting could be remixed as an example in a proposal to curb juvenile delinquincy or as a scene in a coming-of-age movie. (A remix changes all or part of the rhetorical situation—the purpose, audience, context, genre, or medium—to create a new text.) After writing her essay, Brandt decided to remix her story as a graphic memoir for her college newspaper. She thought her chosen genre would appeal to a wide audience of college students, who would be drawn immediately to the graphic form. She also felt that the visuals would allow her to depict her feelings more powerfully and immediately than she could in words.

In the next section of this chapter, we ask you to craft your own remembered event story. After composing it as an essay, consider remixing your story by presenting it (or, a portion of it) in another genre or medium, or using it as part of an essay with a different purpose or audience.

CONSIDER YOUR RHETORICAL SITUATION

Purpose.   The purpose of your story is to express an intense experience dramatically, so readers can appreciate the significance the event had for you and perhaps encourage them to relate the story to their own lives. If you remix your remembered event essay, *which genre or medium would best allow you to depict your story dramatically, portray the people and places vividly, and convey the significance of your story effectively given your audience?*

Audience.   The original audience for your remembered event essay was your instructor and, perhaps, other students in your class. *Who would be the audience if you were to remix your story in another genre or medium? What advantages would that genre or medium have in helping you grab and keep the attention of your audience?*

Genre and medium.   The genre of your remembered event essay was a narrative, and the medium was text, delivered either in print or digitally. If you remix your story, *what genre or medium would best help you achieve your purpose and reach your intended audience?*

The Writing Assignment

Write about an event in your life that will engage readers and that will, at the same time, help them understand the significance of the event. Tell your story dramatically and vividly.

This Guide to Writing will help you depict your own remembered event and apply what you have learned from reading other selections in the same genre. The Starting Points chart will help you find the guidance you need, when you need it.

STARTING POINTS: REMEMBERING AN EVENT

A Well-Told Story

How can I come up with an event to write about?

- Consider possible topics. (pp. 27, 32, 36)
- Choose an event to write about. (p. 40)
- Test Your Topic: Considering Your Purpose and Audience (p. 40–41)

How can I interest my audience and hold its attention?

- Shape your story. (p. 41)
- Test Your Story: Facing an Audience (p. 43)
- Write the opening sentences. (p. 47)

How can I make my story dramatic?

- Assess the genre's basic features: A well-told story. (pp. 15–16)
- A Well-Told Story: Constructing an Action Sequence (p. 25)
- A Well-Told Story: Making Up Stories (p. 34)

How should I organize my story?

- Shape your story. (p. 41)
- Assess the genre's basic features: A well-told story. (pp. 15–16)
- A Well-Told Story: Finding the Arc of the Story (p. 30)
- Clarify the sequence of actions. (pp. 43–44)

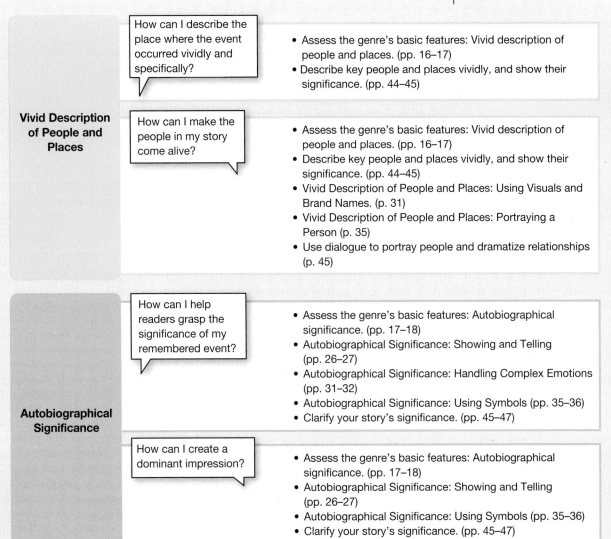

Vivid Description of People and Places

How can I describe the place where the event occurred vividly and specifically?

- Assess the genre's basic features: Vivid description of people and places. (pp. 16–17)
- Describe key people and places vividly, and show their significance. (pp. 44–45)

How can I make the people in my story come alive?

- Assess the genre's basic features: Vivid description of people and places. (pp. 16–17)
- Describe key people and places vividly, and show their significance. (pp. 44–45)
- Vivid Description of People and Places: Using Visuals and Brand Names. (p. 31)
- Vivid Description of People and Places: Portraying a Person (p. 35)
- Use dialogue to portray people and dramatize relationships (p. 45)

Autobiographical Significance

How can I help readers grasp the significance of my remembered event?

- Assess the genre's basic features: Autobiographical significance. (pp. 17–18)
- Autobiographical Significance: Showing and Telling (pp. 26–27)
- Autobiographical Significance: Handling Complex Emotions (pp. 31–32)
- Autobiographical Significance: Using Symbols (pp. 35–36)
- Clarify your story's significance. (pp. 45–47)

How can I create a dominant impression?

- Assess the genre's basic features: Autobiographical significance. (pp. 17–18)
- Autobiographical Significance: Showing and Telling (pp. 26–27)
- Autobiographical Significance: Using Symbols (pp. 35–36)
- Clarify your story's significance. (pp. 45–47)

Writing a Draft: Invention, Research, Planning, and Composing

The activities in this section will help you choose an event to write about and develop it into a story that is well-told, vivid,and meaningful. Do the activities in any order that makes sense to you (and your instructor), and return to them as needed as you revise.

⠒ Choose an event to write about.

To make a compelling story, the event you choose to write about should

- take place over a short period of time (preferably just a few hours);
- center on a conflict (an internal struggle or an external confrontation);
- disclose something significant about your life;
- reveal strong and possibly complex or ambivalent feelings (rather than superficial or sentimental ones).

Make a list of possible events in your life that you would feel comforatble writing about. If you have trouble coming up with promising events to write about, try the following:

- Review the Consider Possible Topics sections on pp. 27, 32, and 36, and reread any notes you made in response to those suggestions.
- Consult Web sites where people post stories about their lives, such as the *Moth, Story Preservation Initiative, Sixties Project,* or *StoryCorps.* Try also typing *memory project, survivor stories,* or a similar word string into the search box of your browser.

If you need more ideas, the following may give you a jumping-off point:

- a difficult situation (for example, when you had to make a tough choice and face the consequences, or when you let someone down or someone you admired let you down)
- an occasion when things did not turn out as expected (for example, when you expected to be criticized but were praised or ignored instead, or when you were convinced you would succeed but failed)
- an incident that changed you or that revealed an aspect of your personality (such as initiative, insecurity, ambition, jealousy, or heroism)
- an incident in which a conflict or a serious misunderstanding with someone made you feel unjustly treated or caused you to mistreat someone else
- an experience that made you reexamine a basic value or belief (such as a time when you were expected to do something that went against your values or had to make a decision about which you were deeply conflicted)
- an encounter with another person that led you to consider seriously someone else's point of view, that changed the way you viewed yourself, or that altered your ideas about how you fit into a group or community
- an event that revealed to you other people's surprising assumptions about you (as a student, friend, colleague, or worker)

| TEST YOUR TOPIC |

Considering Your Purpose and Audience

After you have made a tentative topic choice, ask yourself the following questions:

- Will I be able to reconstruct the story, place, and people in enough detail to help my readers imagine what it was like? (As you probe your memory, you may remember more details, but you may also need to fill in or re-create some details.)

- Do I feel comfortable sharing this experience with my instructor and classmates—revealing what I did, thought, and felt at the time? What concerns or anxieties do I have about the impression they will have of me?
- Will I be able to help my readers understand the personal and social dimensions of the underlying conflict? Will my own understanding of its significance deepen as I write about it?

If you lose confidence in your choice after answering these questions, return to your list and choose another event.

Shape your story.

Once you have selected an event, begin by making a simple sketch of your story. Here is a sample *outline* you can modify to fit your needs. (Remember that each section need not be the same length; the exposition and conclusion/reflection may be very brief—a sentence or two—while the rising action and climax may run for several paragraphs.)

  I. **Exposition/Inciting Incident:** Set the scene and show how the conflict or problem started.
 II. **Rising Action:** Build tension and suspense, showing how the crisis developed or worsened.
III. **Climax:** End the suspense by dramatizing the most critical moment or turning point.
 IV. **Falling Action:** Show how the tension diminished as the conflict moved toward resolution.
  V. **Conclusion/Reflection:** Bring closure to the story and reflect on the event's overall significance.

Then you can use the following "Ways In" suggestions to anticipate your readers' likely questions and flesh out your chronology.

HOW DO I DEVELOP A DRAMATIC ARC?

Ask yourself the following questions:

What is the underlying conflict, the dilemma facing my narrator?
To answer, provide some EXPOSITION, *the background information that will help your readers understand the situation:*

▶ I wanted _____ but didn't want to _____ . So I _____ .

EXAMPLE   The object of my desire was a 75-cent Snoopy button.... I took one look at the lines at the cashiers and knew I didn't want to wait thirty minutes.... (Brandt, pars. 2, 3)

What started it?
To answer, dramatize the INCITING INCIDENT, *the crisis that sets off the conflict or triggered the event.*

WAYS IN

(continued)

Use an action sequence:

▶ I did ⎯⎯⎯⎯. But then ⎯⎯⎯⎯.

EXAMPLE   A black Buick was moving toward us down the street. We all spread out, banged together some regular snowballs, took aim, and, when the Buick drew nigh, fired. (Dillard, par. 7)

Use dialogue:

▶ " ⎯⎯⎯⎯," ⎯⎯⎯⎯ announced excitedly.

EXAMPLE   *"Your friend died!"* she called out from another room. (Desmond-Harris, par. 2)

What will happen?

To answer, intensify the story's RISING ACTION *to arouse curiosity, and build suspense and excitement.*

▶ He ⎯⎯⎯⎯ us. We ⎯⎯⎯⎯.

EXAMPLE   He ran after us, and we ran away from him, up the snowy Reynolds sidewalk. At the corner, I looked back; incredibly, he was still after us. . . . This man was gaining on us. He was a thin man, all action. All of a sudden, we were running for our lives. (Dillard, par. 10)

What did it lead to?

To answer, dramatize the CLIMAX. *It may be the only climax or one of several, as in* Brandt's story.

▶ I thought I had ⎯⎯⎯⎯, but then ⎯⎯⎯⎯.

EXAMPLE   I was home free. I thought about how sly I had been. . . . An unexpected tap on my shoulder startled me. (Brandt, pars. 5–6)

▶ When she told me, " ⎯⎯⎯⎯," I knew I had ⎯⎯⎯⎯.

EXAMPLE   "I'm afraid sorry isn't enough. I'm horribly disappointed in you." Long after we got off the phone, while I sat in an empty jail cell, waiting for my parents to pick me up . . . I cried. (Brandt, pars. 35–36)

How did it turn out?

To answer, summarize the FALLING ACTION, *showing how the conflict subsides and complications unravel.*

▶ Afterwards, I ⎯⎯⎯⎯.

EXAMPLE   When the officer came to release me, I hesitated, actually not wanting to leave. We went to the front desk, where I had to sign a form to retrieve my belongings. (Brandt, par. 36)

Why does my story matter?

To answer, conclude with REFLECTIONS *on the event's significance:*

▶ I realized then that _____ .

EXAMPLE   As I looked from my father's eyes to my mother's, I knew this ordeal was over. Although it would never be forgotten, the incident was not mentioned again. (Brandt, par. 39)

TEST YOUR STORY

Facing an Audience

Get together with two or three other students to try out your story. Your classmates' reactions will help you determine whether you are telling it in an interesting or exciting way.

Storytellers: Take turns telling your stories briefly. Try to pique your listeners' curiosity and build suspense, and watch your audience to see if your story is having the desired reaction.

Listeners: Briefly tell each storyteller what you found most intriguing about the story. For example, consider these questions:

- Were you eager to know how the story would turn out?
- What was the inciting incident? Did it seem sufficient to motivate the climax?
- Was there a clear conflict that seemed important enough to write about?

⠿ Clarify the sequence of actions.

Excerpts from the reading selections in this chapter demonstrate how writers clarify when different actions occur in relation to each other. Try using some of these strategies to help your readers keep track of what happened when.

Manage **tenses** *to show the sequence of actions occurring over time.* You can use the simple past tense (*watched, was, pulled, held*) to depict an action and other tenses (*had . . . returned, continue to mourn*) to show what occurred before or after:

> I watched my father in the front hall putting on his new, lambskin leather gloves. . . . My father had just returned from a business trip to Paris. He'd bought the gloves at a place called Hermès. . . . He pulled one on slowly, then the other, and held them up in the mirror to see how his hands looked in such gloves. (Orner, par. 3)

Past tense
Earlier past (past perfect)

Use **time cues** *(such as* when, now, then, *and* as*) to help readers understand how one action relates to another in the time sequence:*

> As we all piled into the car, I knew. . . . (Brandt, par. 1)

Both actions occur at same time

> When I got back to the Snoopy section, I took one look at the lines . . . and knew I didn't want to wait. . . . (Brandt, par. 3)

One action follows another

Refer to **calendar** *or* **clock time** *to establish when the event took place.*

On one weekday morning after Christmas. . . . (Dillard, par. 3).

For more on transitions of time, see Chapters 13 and 14.

▪▪ Describe key people and places vividly, and show their significance.

The excerpts below show how the writers whose stories appear in this chapter use strategies like naming, detailing comparing, selecting sensory details, and providing an overview of the setting to bring key people and places to life. Try using some of these strategies in your own writing to make people and places vivid.

- *Use* **naming** *and* **detailing** *to help readers visualize people and understand the roles they play in your story.* For example, identify people by name, occupation, or relationship to you; specify how they act, talk, look, and gesture:

   Mikey and Peter—polite blond boys who lived near me on Lloyd Street (Dillard, par. 4)

   My rainbow-striped tee and her white wifebeater capture a transition between our skater-inspired Salvation Army shopping phase and the next one. . . . (Desmond-Harris, par. 7)

- *Add* **comparisons** *to convey what's distinctive about the person and to help create a dominant impression:*

   . . . this sainted, skinny, furious redheaded man (Dillard, par. 21)

   His unpredictability is what made his explosions so potent. Sometimes the bomb wouldn't go off, and he'd act like my idea of a normal dad. (Orner, par. 9)

- *Specify* **sensory details**—*size, shape, color, sounds, textures, smells, tastes*—*of key features of the scene that contribute to the dominant impression you want to create.*

   Tupac was the literal sound track when our school's basketball team would come charging onto the court, and our ragtag group of cheerleaders kicked furiously to "Toss It Up" in a humid gymnasium. (Desmond-Harris, par. 11)

- *Give readers an* **overview** *of the place or take them on a* **tour** *of it.*

   . . . we ran across Edgerton to an alley and up our own sliding woodpile to the Halls' front yard; he kept coming. We ran up Lloyd Street and wound through mazy backyards toward the steep hilltop at Willard and Lang. (Dillard, par. 12)

- *Weave* **active, specific verbs** *and* **vivid descriptive details** *into your action sequences.*

   I whirled around to find a middle-aged man, dressed in street clothes, flashing some type of badge. . . . (Brandt, par. 6)

   I had just embarked on the iceball project when we heard tire chains come clanking from afar. (Dillard, par. 7)

- *Consider scanning, uploading, or attaching a* **photograph** *or* **video** *to help readers picture people and places.* Make sure you introduce it or use a caption to demonstrate its relevance.

   A snapshot taken that Monday on our high school's front lawn (seen here) shows the two of us lying side by side. . . . (Desmond-Harris, par. 6)

Use dialogue to portray people and dramatize relationships.

Dialogue—in the form of quotation, paraphrase, or summary—can give readers a vivid impression of the people and their relationships while also enhancing the drama. The excerpts below may give you ideas of how you might use dialogue in your own story.

- *Insert a* **quotation** *to dramatize a key moment or characterize a relationship:*

   . . . I was too ashamed to tell my mother the truth, but I had no choice.

   " Jean, where are you?"

   "I'm, umm, in jail." (Brandt, pars. 26–28)

   "Maybe they're in the glove compartment," my mother said.

   "Impossible. I never put gloves in the glove compartment. The glove compartment is for maps."

   "Oh, well," my mother said. (Orner, pars. 10–12)

- *Use* **summary** *to emphasize thoughts, feelings, or actions or simply to move the story along.*

   As we crossed the threshold, I heaved a sigh of relief. I was home free. I thought about how sly I had been and I felt proud of my accomplishment.

   An unexpected tap on my shoulder startled me. I whirled around to find a middle-aged man . . . politely asking me to empty my pockets. (Brandt, pars. 5–6)

- *Use* **speaker tags** *to identify each speaker and intersperse remembered thoughts:*

   "Did we really do that?" I asked Thea this week. I wanted to ensure that this story, which people who know me now find hilarious, hadn't morphed into some sort of personal urban legend over the past 15 years. "Yes," she said. "We put them in a lovely tin." (Desmond-Harris, par. 4)

To learn more about quoting, paraphrasing, and summarizing, see Chapter 23.

Clarify your story's significance.

Try using some of these strategies to refine your understanding and presentation of the event's significance. Some of these sentences may make their way into your story; others may simply help you understand your reactions, so you can depict the event's significance more clearly.

WAYS IN

HOW CAN I HELP MY READERS UNDERSTAND THE SIGNIFICANCE OF MY STORY?

Reexamine the **UNDERLYING CONFLICT** *to determine what your story is really about.*

▶ I was confused, torn between _____ and _____ .

EXAMPLE   Did we feel a real stake in the life of this "hard-core" gangsta rapper, and a real loss in his death? We did, even though we were . . . in a privileged community. . . . even though we'd been so delicately cared for, nurtured and protected from any of life's hard edges — with special efforts made to shield us from those involving race — that we sometimes felt ready to explode with boredom. Or maybe because of all that. (Desmond-Harris, par. 8)

Consider whether you now have **INSIGHT** *into your motivation that you did not have at the time or whether you feel just as bewildered today as you did then.*

▶ I still don't understand why I _____ .

EXAMPLE   "I just did it. I can't explain why" (Brandt, par. 34).

▶ How could _____? I now think _____ .

EXAMPLE   What precisely could he have done to prolong the drama of the chase and cap its glory? I brooded about this for the next few years. . . . He could only chew us out there . . . , after months or years of exalting pursuit. (Dillard, par. 20)

Examine any **INCONSISTENCIES** *or* **AMBIVALENCE** *in the language you used to tell the story or describe people and places.* These apparent contradictions may lead you to a deeper understanding of why the event continues to be so fraught for you.

▶ Why did _____?

EXAMPLE   Why did he take the gloves? My character could never express it in words and the story kept collapsing. . . . I can't give the gloves back, in fiction or in this thing we call reality. If I did, I'd have to confront something I've known all along but have never wanted to express, even to myself alone. (Orner, pars. 21–22)

Recall your **REMEMBERED FEELINGS** *and* **THOUGHTS** *from when the event occurred.*

▶ Before / during / after the event, I felt _____ . I showed or expressed these feelings by _____ .

EXAMPLE   I could still distinctly hear the disappointment and hurt in my mother's voice. I cried. . . . I felt like a terrible human being. (Brandt, par. 36)

Explore your **PRESENT PERSPECTIVE**, *what you think and feel now as you look back.*

▶ I realize now that my feelings have not changed. I still _____ .

▶ Looking back at the event, I realize I was probably trying to _____ , though I didn't appreciate that fact at the time.

EXAMPLE   I love my father. I suppose I did even then, in the worst moments of fear. (Orner, par. 23)

Reconsider your PURPOSE *and* AUDIENCE *in light of your developing understanding of the event's significance.* Determine what you want your readers to think and feel after reading your story.

▶ When my readers finish the story, I want them to better appreciate _____ .

▶ The point was that _____ .

EXAMPLE   The point was that he had chased us passionately without giving up, and so he had caught us. Now he came down to earth. I wanted the glory to last forever. (Dillard, par. 19)

Write the opening sentences.

Review what you have already written to see if you have something that would work to launch your story, or try some of these opening strategies:

Begin with a **surprising statement**:

I've been trying to lie about this story for years. (Orner, par. 1)

Set the **scene**—*a specific time and place*—*and* **mood**:

I knew it was going to be a fabulous day . . . [we were] setting off for a day of last-minute Christmas shopping. (Brandt, par. 1)

Reflect on something from your past that provides **context** *for the event*:

I got in trouble throwing snowballs, and have seldom been happier since. (Dillard, par. 2)

But don't agonize over the first sentences because you are likely to discover the best way to begin only after you have written a rough draft.

Draft your story.

By this point, you have done a lot of writing

■ to develop a plan for a well-told story;

■ to come up with vivid details to help your readers imagine what happened;

■ to think of strategies for showing or telling the autobiographical significance of your event;

■ to try out a way to launch your story.

Now stitch that material together to create a draft. The next two parts of this Guide to Writing will help you evaluate and improve your draft.

Evaluating the Draft: Using Peer Review

Your instructor may arrange a peer review session in class or online where you can exchange drafts with your classmates and give each other a thoughtful critical reading, pointing out what works well and suggesting ways to improve the draft. A good critical reading does three things:

1. It lets the writer know how clear, vivid, and meaningful the story seems to readers.

2. It praises what works best.

3. It indicates where the draft could be improved and makes suggestions on how to improve it.

One strategy for evaluating a draft is to use the basic features of remembered event essays as a guide.

A PEER REVIEW GUIDE

A Well-Told Story

How effectively does the writer tell the story?

Summarize: Highlight the inciting incident and the climax of the story.

Praise: Cite a passage where the storytelling is especially effective — for example, a place where the story seems to flow smoothly and maintain the reader's interest, or where narrative action is compelling or exciting.

Critique: Tell the writer where the storytelling could be improved — for example, where the suspense slackens, the story lacks tension or conflict, or the chronology is confusing.

Vivid Description of People and Places

Do the descriptions help you imagine what happened?

Summarize: Choose a passage of description and analyze how and how well it uses the describing strategies of naming, detailing, and comparing.

Praise: Identify a description that is particularly vivid — for example, a graphic sensory description or an apt comparison that makes a person or place come alive.

Critique: Tell the writer where the description could be improved — for example, where objects in the scene are not named or described with enough specific detail (colors, sounds, smells, textures), or where the description is sparse. Note any description that contradicts the dominant impression; it may suggest how the significance can be made more complex and interesting.

Autobiographical Significance	Is it clear why the event was important to the author?

Summarize: Briefly describe the story's dominant impression, and tell the writer why you think the event was significant.

Praise: Give an example where the significance comes across effectively — for example, where remembered feelings are expressed poignantly, where the present perspective seems insightful, or where the description creates a strong dominant impression that clarifies the significance.

Critique: Tell the writer where the significance could be strengthened — for example, if the conflict is too easily resolved, if a moral seems tacked on at the end, or if more interesting meanings could be drawn out of the experience.

Before concluding your peer review, be sure to address any of the writer's concerns that have not been discussed already.

Making Comments Electronically Most word processing software offers features that allow you to insert comments directly into the text of someone else's document. Many readers prefer to make their comments this way because it tends to be faster than writing on hard copy, and space is virtually unlimited; it also eliminates the process of deciphering handwritten comments. Where such features are not available, simply typing comments directly into a document in a contrasting color can provide the same advantages.

Improving the Draft: Revising, Editing, and Proofreading

Start improving your draft by reflecting on what you have written thus far:

- Review comments from your classmates, instructor, or writing center tutor. What are your readers getting at?
- Take another look at your notes and ideas. What else should you consider?
- Review your draft. What else can you do to make your story compelling?

Revise your draft.

If your readers are having difficulty with your draft, try some of the strategies listed in the Troubleshooting Guide below. They can help you fine-tune your presentation of the genre's basic features.

A TROUBLESHOOTING GUIDE

A Well-Told Story

> My readers tell me that the story starts too slowly.

- Shorten the exposition, spread it out more within the story, or move it to a later part of the story.
- Move a bit of dialogue or narrative action up front.
- Start with something surprising but critical to the story.

> My readers find the chronology confusing.

- Add or change time transitions.
- Look for inadvertent tense shifts and fix them.

> My readers feel that the suspense slackens or that the story lacks drama.

- Add remembered feelings and thoughts to heighten anticipation.
- Add an action sequence to build to a climax or high point.
- Cut or shorten background exposition and unnecessary description.
- Build rising action in stages, with multiple high points.

> My readers find the conflict vague or unconnected to the autobiographical significance.

- Think about the conflict's multiple and possibly contradictory meanings.
- Add remembered feelings or thoughts to suggest multiple meanings, and cut those that don't clarify the significance.
- Add your present perspective to make the significance clearer and bring out the implications.
- Add dialogue or narrative action to clarify the conflict.

Vivid Description of People and Places

My readers feel that the people in the story don't come alive.

- Add details about distinctive physical features or mannerisms.
- Add speaker tags to the dialogue to characterize people and relationships.
- Read your dialogue aloud, and revise to make the language more natural and appropriate to the person.

My readers have trouble visualizing the places I describe.

- Name objects in the scene.
- Add sensory details (colors, sounds, smells, textures).
- Use a comparison — metaphor or simile — to evoke a particular mood or attitude.
- Add a visual — a photograph or other memorabilia.

My readers feel that some descriptions weaken the dominant impression.

- Omit unnecessary details.
- Add adjectives, similes, or metaphors to strengthen the dominant impression.
- Rethink the impression you want your writing to convey and the significance it suggests.

Autobiographical Significance

My readers do not identify or sympathize with me.

- Add background details or explain the context.
- Reveal the cultural influences acting on you or emphasize the historical period in which the event occurred.
- Show readers how you have changed or were affected by the experience.

My readers don't understand the significance of the story.

- Use irony or humor to contrast your present perspective with your past behavior, feelings, or attitudes.
- Show that the event ended but that the conflict was not resolved.
- Use dialogue to show how your relationship with people in your story changed.
- Indicate how the event continues to influence your thoughts or actions.

My readers think the significance seems too pat or simplistic.

- Develop contradictions or show ambivalence to enrich the implications.
- Use humor to comment ironically on your past behavior or current contradictory feelings.
- Stress the social or cultural dimensions of the event.
- Revise Hollywood-movie clichés, simple resolutions, or tagged-on morals.

Edit and proofread your draft.

Four problems commonly appear in essays about remembered events: misused words and expressions, dull word choices and flabby sentences, incorrectly punctuated or formatted dialogue, and misused past-perfect verbs. The following guidelines will help you check your essay for these common errors.

Using the Right Word or Expression

The Problem Many familiar sayings and expressions are frequently heard but not often seen in writing, so writers often mistake the expression. Consider the following sentences:

> Chock it up to my upbringing, but having several children play butt naked around my feet certainly curved my appetite for parenthood.

> The deer was still jerking in its death throws, but for all intensive purposes it was dead.

Within those two sentences are five commonly mangled expressions. To the ear, they may sound right, but in each case the author has heard the expression incorrectly and written down the wrong words.

Note: The expressions should be *chalk it up*, *buck naked*, *curbed my appetite*, *death throes*, and *for all intents and purposes*.

The Correction You can find and debug these kinds of errors by following these steps:

1. Highlight or circle common expressions of two or more words in your writing project (especially those you've heard before but haven't seen in writing).

2. Check each expression in a dictionary or in a list of frequently misused words.

3. Consider revising the expression: If you have heard the expression so often that it "sounds right," it may be a cliché. A fresh expression will be more powerful.

Choosing Vivid Language and Cutting Flab

The Problem Early drafts often include vague or overly general word choices and flabby sentences. Cutting words that add little, making verbs active, and replacing weak word choices with stronger ones can greatly increase the power of a remembered event essay.

The Correction The following three steps can help you tighten your language and make it more powerful.

1. Circle empty intensifiers, such as *just, very, certain,* and *really*. Now reread each sentence, omitting the circled word. If the sentence still makes sense without the word, delete it.

2. Circle all forms of the verb *to be* (such as *am, is, are, was,* and *were*). Now reread each sentence that includes a circled word, and ask yourself, "Could I revise the sentence or combine it with another sentence to create an active construction? Examples:

   ▶ The dog was barking. He took off after Jasper, as he raced toward Third Avenue.

   ▶ The rope was tied around the oak in the front yard.

A Note on Grammar and Spelling Checkers

These tools can be helpful, but don't rely on them exclusively to catch errors in your text: Spelling checkers cannot catch misspellings that are themselves words, such as *to* for *too*. Grammar checkers miss some problems, sometimes give faulty advice for fixing problems, and can flag correct items as wrong. Use these tools as a second line of defense after your own (and, ideally, another reader's) proofreading and editing efforts.

3. Review your descriptions, highlighting or underlining adjectives, adverbs, and prepositional phrases. Now reread them, imagining a more specific noun or verb that could convey the same idea in fewer words.

> *A Humvee sped*
> ▶ A large, black truck ~~moved quickly~~ across the parking lot.

Resolving Dialogue Issues

The Problem Remembered event essays often include dialogue, but writers sometimes have trouble using the conventions of dialogue correctly. One common problem occurs with punctuation marks:

- In American English, the opening quotation mark hugs the first word of the quotation. Commas belong inside the closing quotation mark, but end punctuation can go inside or outside the closing quotation mark, depending on whether the end punctuation belongs to the quotation or the end of the sentence.

- Speaker tags reflect what the speaker was thinking, feeling, or doing.

- A new paragraph is typically used to indicate a change in speaker.

The Correction Revise the punctuation, add speaker tags, or start a new paragraph as needed:

> ▶ "⟨"⟩Jean, what's going on ⟨?⟩" ~~/~~ my sister questioned⟨ asked⟩.

> ▶ A few seconds later, my sister appeared and asked, "So, did you decide to buy the button?"⟨¶⟩"No, I guess not."

Using the Past Perfect

The Problem Remembered event essays often mention events that occurred before the main action. To convey this sequence of events, writers use the past-perfect tense rather than the simple past tense:

Past Perfect	Simple Past
had traveled	traveled
had been	was
had begun	began

Failing to use the past perfect when it is needed can make your meaning unclear. (What happened when, exactly?)

The Correction Check places where you recount events to verify that you are using the past perfect to indicate actions that had already been completed at the time of another past action (she *had finished* her work when we saw her).

> *had*
> ▶ I ~~had~~ three people in the car, something my father told me not to do that very morning.

> *had run*
> ▶ Coach Kernow told me I ~~ran~~ faster than ever before.

Note for Multilingual Writers   It is important to remember that the past perfect is formed with *had* followed by a past participle. Past participles usually end in *-ed, -d, -en, -n,* or *-t*—*worked, hoped, eaten, taken, bent*—although some are irregular (such as *begun* or *chosen*).

> ▶ Before Tania went to Moscow last year, she had not really ~~speak~~ Russian.
>   *spoken*

A WRITER AT WORK

Developing Significance in Jean Brandt's Remembered Event Essay

This section compares Jean Brandt's first draft of "Calling Home" to her final revised draft. (See the complete revision on pp. 18–22.)

1   It was two days before Christmas and my older sister and brother, my grandmother, and I were rushing around doing last-minute shopping. After going to a few stores we decided to go to Lakewood Center shopping mall. It was packed with other frantic shoppers like ourselves from one end to the other. The first store we went to (the first and last for me) was the General Store. The General Store is your typical gift shop. They mainly have the cutesy knick-knacks, posters, frames and that sort. The store is decorated to resemble an old-time western general store but the appearance doesn't quite come off.

2   We were all browsing around and I saw a basket of buttons so I went to see what the different ones were. One of the first ones I noticed was a Snoopy button. I'm not sure what it said on it, something funny I'm sure and besides I was in love with anything Snoopy when I was 13. I took it out of the basket and showed it to my sister and she said "Why don't you buy it?" I thought about it but the lines at the cashiers were outrageous and I didn't think it was worth it for a 75 cent item. Instead I figured just take it and I did. I thought I was so sly about it. I casually slipped it into my pocket and assumed I was home free since no one pounced on me.

3   Everyone was ready to leave this shop so we made our way through the crowds to the entrance. My grandmother and sister were ahead of my brother and I. They were

almost to the entrance of May Co. and we were about 5 to 10 yards behind when I felt this tap on my shoulder. I turned around already terror struck, and this man was flashing some kind of badge in my face. It happened so fast I didn't know what was going on. Louie finally noticed I wasn't with him and came back for me. Jack explained I was being arrested for shoplifting and if my parents were here then Louie should go find them. Louie ran to get Susie and told her about it but kept it from Grandma.

4   By the time Sue got back to the General Store I was in the back office and Jack was calling the police. I was a little scared but not really. It was sort of exciting. My sister was telling me to try and cry but I couldn't. About 20 minutes later two cops came and handcuffed me, led me through the mall outside to the police car. I was kind of embarrassed when they took me through the mall in front of all those people. When they got me in the car they began questioning me, while driving me to the police station. Questions just to fill out the report—age, sex, address, color of eyes, etc.

5   Then when they were finished they began talking about Jack and what a nuisance he was. I gathered that Jack had every single person who shoplifted, no matter what their age, arrested. The police were getting really fed up with it because it was a nuisance for them to have to come way out to the mall for something as petty as that. To hear the police talk about my "crime" that way felt good because it was like what I did wasn't really so bad. It made me feel a bit relieved. When we walked into the station I remember the desk sergeant joking with the arresting officers about "well we got another one of Jack's hardened criminals." Again, I felt my crime lacked any seriousness at all.

6   Next they handcuffed me to a table and questioned me further and then I had to phone my mom. That was the worst. I never was so humiliated in my life. Hearing the disappointment in her voice was worse punishment than the cops could ever give me.

Brandt was confident in her choice of a topic. She was sure she could recall enough details to make the story dramatic and was confident it would resonate with readers: "I think many of my readers will be able to identify with my story, even though they won't admit it." Most importantly, Brandt had no doubt that the event was significant:

Being arrested for shoplifting was significant because it changed some of my basic attitudes. Since that night I've never again considered stealing anything. This event would reveal how my attitude toward the law has changed from disrespectful to very respectful.

However, as you compare the following excerpts from her first and last drafts, you will see that Brandt's understanding of the underlying conflict and the event's significance evolved. Initially, she thought the conflict would be about respecting the law. But her first draft doesn't even hint at this conflict and the final draft barely mentions it.

First Draft

. . . I took it out of the basket and showed it to my sister and she said "Why don't you buy it?" I thought about it but the lines at the cashiers were outrageous and I didn't think it was worth it for a 75 cent item. Instead I figured just take it and I did. I thought I was so sly about it. I casually slipped it into my pocket and assumed I was home free since no one pounced on me. (par. 2)

Final Draft

. . . She said it was cute and if I wanted it to go ahead and buy it. . . . I took one look at the lines at the cashiers and knew I didn't want to wait thirty minutes to buy an item worth less than one dollar. . . . I took a quick glance around, assured myself no one could see, and slipped the button into the pocket of my sweatshirt.

I hesitated for a moment, but once the item was in my pocket, there was no turning back. I had never before stolen anything; but what was done was done. . . .

As we headed for the entrance, my heart began to race. I just had to get out of that store. Only a few more yards to go and I'd be safe. As we crossed the threshold, I heaved a sigh of relief. I was home free. I thought about how sly I had been and I felt proud of my accomplishment. (pars. 2–5)

The first draft does not show that Brandt had been conflicted about breaking the law before she stole the button or that she felt guilty afterward. In fact, her only remembered thought or feeling is pride at having pulled it off so neatly: "I thought I was so sly about it" (par. 2). The final draft is not very different, although it does add both a momentary hesitation before and some reflection afterward. But notice her choice of words: she uses clichés ("there was no turning back" and "what was done was done") that neither express guilt nor repentance.

It took some effort and a little help from her instructor for Brandt to realize that she was not really passionate about the conflict she had thought was at the heart of her story and that her strongest, most heartfelt emotions had to do with her mother's disappointment, not with the abstract idea of respecting the law. Pointing out that the first draft ended with a brief but powerful description of Brandt's phone conversation with her mother ("Hearing the disappointment in her voice was worse punishment than the cops could ever give me"), her instructor urged Brandt to try to dramatize the scene by adding dialogue, specific description, and an action sequence.

THINKING CRITICALLY

To think critically means to use all of the knowledge you have acquired from the information in this chapter, your own writing, the writing of other students, and class discussions to reflect deeply on your work for this assignment and the genre (or type) of writing you have produced. The benefit of thinking critically is proven and important: Thinking critically about what you have learned will help you remember it longer, ensuring that you will be able to put it to good use well beyond this writing course.

Reflecting on What You Have Learned

In this chapter, you have learned a great deal about this genre from reading several autobiographical stories and writing one of your own. To consolidate your learning, reflect not only on what you learned but also on how you learned it.

ANALYZE & WRITE

Write a blog post, a letter to your instructor or a classmate, or an e-mail message to a student who will take this course next term, using the writing prompt that seems most productive for you:

- Explain how what you wanted your readers to learn about you from reading your story influenced one of your decisions as a writer, such as how you used the dramatic arc to shape your story around a conflict, how you used dialogue to intensify the drama and convey the significance, or how you integrated your remembered thoughts and feelings into your storytelling.

- Discuss what you learned about yourself as a writer in the process of writing this essay. For example, what part of the process did you find most challenging, or did you try anything new, like getting a critical reading of your draft or outlining your draft in order to revise it? If so, how well did it work?

- If you were to give advice to a fellow student who was about to write a remembered event essay, what would you say?

- Which of the readings (in this chapter or elsewhere) influenced your choice of an event to write about or how you told the story? Explain the influence, citing specific examples comparing the two.

- If you got good advice from a critical reader, explain exactly how the person helped you — perhaps by questioning the conflict in a way that enabled you to develop your story's significance, or by pointing out passages that needed clearer time markers to better orient readers.

Reflecting on the Genre

We've said throughout this chapter that writing about a remembered event leads to self-discovery, but what do we mean by the "self"? Should we think of the self as our "true" essence or as the different roles we play in different situations? If we accept the idea of an essential self, writing about significant events in our lives can help us in the search to discover who we truly are. Given this idea of the self, we might see Jean Brandt, for example, as searching to understand whether she is the kind of person who breaks the law and only cares when she is caught and has to face her parents' disapproval. If, on the other hand, we accept the idea that the various roles we play are ways we construct the self in different situations, then writing about a remembered event allows us to examine a side of our personality and the influences that shaped it. This view of the self assumes that we present different self-images to different people in different situations. Given this idea, we might see Brandt as presenting her sassy teenage side to the police but keeping her vulnerability hidden from them and perhaps also from her family, with some painful loss of intimacy.

ANALYZE & WRITE

Write a page or two explaining how the genre prompts you to think about self-discovery. In your discussion, you might consider one or more of the following:

1. **Consider how writing about your remembered event might be an exercise in self-discovery.** Planning and writing your essay, did you see yourself as discovering your true self or examining how you reacted in a particular situation? Do you think your essay reveals your single, essential, true self, or does it show only an aspect of the person you understand yourself to be?

2. **Write a page or so explaining your ideas about self-discovery and truth in remembered event essays.** Connect your ideas to your own essay and to the readings in this chapter.

3

Writing Profiles

What happens behind the scenes at a mortuary? What happens when kids visit their moms in prison? Is eating twenty corned-beef sandwiches in ten minutes worth $5,000 in prize money? These questions are a few of those explored in the entertaining and thought-provoking profiles in this chapter. Profiles are mini-documentaries, like the podcasts and shows created by the producers of *Radiolab* and *This American Life*. They take us behind the scenes through slice-of-life portraits. As cultural ethnography, profiles range from a day-in-the-life to a longer immersion study of people at work or at play. Intensively researched, they rely primarily on *field research* techniques of observation and interview to provide what is sometimes called *thick description,* because the information is interwoven with the profiler's analysis and interpretation—what we call **perspective**—to capture and convey a full experience.

People compose profiles for various purposes and audiences and publish them in a variety of media (print, digital, audiovisual). For example, a college student studying management might observe and interview a work group's collaborators, and post her profile on the class Web site. A participant in the restoration of a Depression-era mural might construct a multimedia profile of the community effort for the city's Web site to celebrate the project. A security officer might develop a Prezi presentation profiling a number of shoplifters apprehended over the last year to educate sales staff about shoplifting.

In this chapter, we ask you to compose a profile based primarily on your first-hand field research—observational visits and interviews. Whether you choose something you know well or something you want to learn about, you will need to focus on it as if for the first time and choose details that will not only make it come alive for your readers but also show them why your subject is intriguing and important. From reading and analyzing the selections in the Guide to Reading that follows, you will learn how to weave information and insight to construct a rich tapestry that entertains as it informs. The Guide to Writing (pp. 91–112) will show you ways to use the basic features of the genre to depict your subject clearly and compellingly from a perspective that will allow you not only to inform and entertain your readers, but also to convey your subject's cultural, social, or personal significance.

PRACTICING THE GENRE ├──────────────────────────────────

Conducting an Interview

Part 1.   Get together in a small group to practice interviewing, a crucial skill in composing profiles. First, ask for a volunteer from the group to act as the interviewee. It should be someone knowledgeable about a subject that is relatively unfamiliar to the other group members, such as a sport, hobby, type of music, video game, profession, or academic subject. The rest of the group should take a couple of minutes to make a list of questions about the subject. Then have one person serve as the interviewer (or take turns asking questions). Listen to what is being said, and respond with follow-up questions as needed. Take notes not only on what is said (quoting or summarizing) but also on the way it is said. For example, does the interviewee appear to be bored or animated, authoritative or uncertain?

Part 2.   Discuss what you learned about profiles and about conducting an interview:

- **What did you learn about how profiles can make information interesting?** For a profile to be effective, it must depict the subject vividly and be thought provoking. Take turns identifying one thing the interviewee said—for example, an illuminating fact, an amusing anecdote, or a surprising judgment—that would be likely to engage the interest of an audience.

- **What did you learn about conducting an interview?** Compare your thoughts with those of the others in your group on what was easiest and hardest—for example, preparing questions, listening and following up, taking notes, or considering what might be interesting to an audience.

Analyzing Profiles

As you read the selections in this chapter, you will see how different authors create a compelling profile.

- Brian Cable anxiously visits a mortuary and ends up in the embalming room (pp. 65–70).
- Jon Ronson investigates the "sport" of competitive eating (pp. 71–74).
- Amanda Coyne captures Mother's Day in a women's prison (pp. 77–80).
- Gabriel Thompson goes undercover to learn about harvesting lettuce firsthand (pp. 83–86).

Analyzing how these writers organize and present the information they gathered from firsthand observations, interviews, and background research; adopt a role as spectator or participant-observer; and convey a thought-provoking perspective on the subject will help you see how you can employ these same techniques when composing your own observational profile.

Determine the writer's purpose and audience.

Researching a profile gives writers a great deal of information about their subject, enabling them to impart their special perspective or insight into its cultural significance. Profilers seek to enlighten and entertain their audience, creating a fascinating, and occasionally disconcerting, portrait of other people at work or at play. When reading the profiles that follow, ask yourself questions like these:

What seems to be the writer's main purpose?

- to inform readers about some aspect of everyday life that they rarely get to know intimately?
- to give readers a behind-the-scenes look at an intriguing or unusual activity?
- to surprise readers by presenting familiar subjects in unexpected ways?
- to bridge the distance between outsiders' preconceptions and others' experience?

What does the author assume about the audience?

- that readers know nothing or very little about the subject?
- that their expectations will be challenged?
- that their interest will be piqued?
- that they will be intrigued by the writer's ideas or what people do or say?

Assess the genre's basic features.

As you read the profiles in this chapter, analyze and evaluate how profile writers employ the genre's basic features. The examples that follow are drawn from the reading selections that appear later in this Guide to Reading.

> **Basic Features**
> Specific Information
> A Clear, Logical Organization
> Writer's Role
> A Perspective on the Subject

SPECIFIC INFORMATION ABOUT THE SUBJECT

Read first to learn about the subject. Much of the pleasure of reading a profile comes from the way the profile interweaves bits of information and insight into a rich tapestry of lively narrative, arresting quotations, and vivid descriptions.

*Notice the describing strategies of **naming**, **detailing**, and **comparing**.* These strategies help readers visualize places and people and create a dominant impression:

Naming
Detailing
Comparing

For more on describing strategies, see Chapter 15.

> We passed into a bright, fluorescent-lit "display room." Inside were thirty coffins. . . . Like new cars on the showroom floor. . . . (Cable, par. 18)

In this example, using the detail *fluorescent-lit* helps to clarify what Cable means by *bright* and also reinforces the simile comparing the coffins on display to cars in a showroom.

Think about the different kinds *of information, or **topics**, the writer touches on.* In profiling a mortuary, for example, Cable identifies different jobs (funeral director and mortician), explaining the training people undergo and the tasks they perform, and also presents facts about the cost of funerals and ideas about cultural attitudes toward death.

Consider the sources of the information and how the information is presented. Some of the information comes from the writer's firsthand observation, but much of it comes from interviews and background research. To present this information, profile writers rely on three basic strategies—quotation, paraphrase, and summary:

QUOTATION   "We're in *Ripley's Believe It or Not,* along with another funeral home whose owners' names are Baggit and Sackit," Howard told me, without cracking a smile. (Cable, par. 14)

PARAPHRASE   We ask one another where we are from, how long a drive we had. (Coyne, par. 3)

SUMMARY   I came across several articles describing the causes of a farmworker shortage. The stories cited an aging workforce, immigration crackdowns, and long delays at the border that discourage workers with green cards. . . . (Thompson, par. 5)

See Chapters 24 and 25 to learn about the conventions for citing and documenting sources in two popular academic styles.

Profiles in academic contexts—for class and scholarly publication—are expected to cite their sources formally. See, for example, Cable's use of parenthetical citation and a works cited list, But general interest publications seldom include documentation beyond links to other Web pages. Ask your instructor whether you should cite your sources, and if so, what academic style you should follow.

A CLEAR, LOGICAL ORGANIZATION

*Determine whether the profile's basic organizational plan is **narrative**, as a story occurring over time; **spatial**, as a guided tour of a place; or **topical**, as bits of information organized into categories.* Look for cues like these that help orient readers.

Narrative Cues

CALENDAR AND CLOCK TIME	On my first day . . . (Thompson, par. 6)
	It's a ten-minute contest. By minute six, . . . (Ronson, par. 10)
ACTION VERBS	I bend over, noticing that most of the crew has turned to watch. (Thompson, par. 8)
	Joey decided that night to dedicate his life to the pursuit. He became obsessed. . . . (Ronson, par. 14)
TRANSITIONS OF TIME	While the other adults . . . (Coyne, par. 2)
	First, I'm handed . . . Next comes the *gancho* . . . (Thompson, par. 6)

Spatial Cues

PREPOSITIONAL PHRASES	. . . the main lobby, adjacent to the reception room . . . (Cable, par. 6)
	We are standing in front of the double glass doors that lead to the outside world. (Coyne, par. 20)
DIRECTIONS	. . . here in the visiting room . . . (Coyne, par. 1)
	To my left, in the distance . . . To my right . . . (Thompson, par. 2)
LOCATIONS	. . . visiting his mother in prisons in Kentucky, Texas, Connecticut (the Pit of Fire) . . . (Coyne, par. 12)

Topical Cues or Logical Transitions

SEQUENCE	In addition, the burial site . . . (Cable, par. 24)
	Once . . . (Coyne, par. 18)
EMPHASIS	Even, or especially, if that world is a female federal prison camp. (Coyne, par. 4)
CONTRADICTION	But thinking about the next seven weeks doesn't benefit anyone. (Thompson, par. 2)
	On the contrary, his bitterness . . . (Coyne, par. 13)
CAUSE	Because of their difference . . . (Coyne, par. 11)
CONCLUSION	So I am to be very careful and precise . . . (Thompson, par. 12)
SPECULATION	Perhaps such an air of comfort makes it easier for the family to give up their loved one. (Cable, par. 24)

To learn more about cueing the reader, see Chapter 13.

Also notice whether the writer uses a different organizational pattern in particular passages. For example, Cable's profile of a mortuary follows a spatial plan overall: beginning with him across the street from the building, moving first into the reception room, then into a chapel, the display room, and finally the embalming room. But much of the information within this general structure is presented topically: for example, he uses his position in the display room to relate information about caskets—what they are made of, their price range, the cost of funerals and how it has increased over time, and so on.

THE WRITER'S ROLE

Think about the role the writer assumes in relation to the subject:

- As a **spectator**, the writer takes a position, like that of the reader, looking in on the people and their activities. Although profile writers sometimes refer to themselves using the first-person pronoun "I" to place themselves in the scene and tell us what they are thinking, they often maintain the role of a detached observer:

  > I found the funeral director in the main lobby, adjacent to the reception room. Like most people, I had preconceptions about what an undertaker looked like. Mr. Deaver fulfilled my expectations entirely. Tall and thin, he even had beady eyes and a bony face. . . . Indeed, he looked like death on two legs. (Cable, par. 5)

- As a **participant-observer**. the writer participates in the activity being profiled in order to acquire insider knowledge. Participant-observers rely on the first-person pronoun "I" to place themselves in the scene and tell us what they are doing there, as this example from Thompson's investigative profile of his work as a lettuce picker illustrates:

  > I stand up gingerly. It's only my third day in the fields, but already my 30-year-old body is failing me. (par. 2)

A PERSPECTIVE ON THE SUBJECT

*Think about the writer's **perspective** on the subject.* What is the main idea or cultural significance of the profile? To understand the writer's perspective, it might help also to consider the writer's main purpose, the audience to whom the profile was originally addressed, as well as where, when, and how (in what medium) it was published. *Identify any passages where the perspective is communicated to readers* either

- by **telling**—saying explicitly what the writer thinks about the subject:

  > Death may be the great leveler, but one's coffin quickly reestablishes one's status. (Cable, par. 17)

- by **showing**—creating a dominant impression through description and narration:

  > . . . the mothers take deep whiffs from the backs of their children's necks. . . . They hold them tight and take in their own second scent—the scent assuring them that these are still their children and that they still belong to them. (Coyne, par. 2)

Readings

Brian Cable | *The Last Stop*

This profile of a neighborhood mortuary was originally written when Brian Cable was a first-year college student. "Death," as he explains in the opening sentence, "is a subject largely ignored by the living," so it is not surprising that he notices people averting their eyes as they walk past the mortuary on a busy commercial street. Cable, however, walks in and takes readers on a guided tour of the premises. As he presents information he learned from observing how the mortuary works — from the reception room up front to the embalming room in back — and from interviewing the people who work there, Cable invites us to reflect on our own feelings and cultural attitudes toward death.

As you read,

- notice how Cable uses humor to defuse the inherent seriousness of his subject.
- consider the significance of the quotation from Mark Twain with which Cable opens his profile.
- answer the questions in the margin. Your instructor may ask you to post your answers to a class blog or discussion board or to bring them to class.

To learn how Cable conducted his interview with the funeral director and wrote up his notes, turn to A Writer at Work on pp. 113–17. Compare the write-up to pars. 5–22 of the profile, where Cable reports on what he learned from his interview. How did writing up his notes help him draft part of the essay?

Let us endeavor so to live that when we come to die even the undertaker will be sorry.

— Mark Twain, *Pudd'nhead Wilson*

Basic Features
Specific Information
A Clear, Logical Organization
Writer's Role
A Perspective on the Subject

1   Death is a subject largely ignored by the living. We don't discuss it much, not as children (when Grandpa dies, he is said to be "going away"), not as adults, not even as senior citizens. Throughout our lives, death remains intensely private. The death of a loved one can be very painful, partly because of the sense of loss, but also because someone else's mortality reminds us all too vividly of our own.

2   More than a few people avert their eyes as they walk past the dusty-tan building that houses the Goodbody Mortuary. It looks a bit like a church — tall, with gothic arches and stained glass. In the back, it looked somewhat like an apartment complex — low, with many windows stamped out of red brick. (See Fig. 1.)

3   It wasn't at all what I had expected. I thought it would be more like Forest Lawn, serene with lush green lawns and meticulously groomed gardens, a place set apart from the hustle of day-to-day life. Here instead was an odd tan structure set in the middle of a business district.

Cable tells us what he expected. How does the opening — including the title and epigraph (introductory quote) — influence what you expect from his profile?

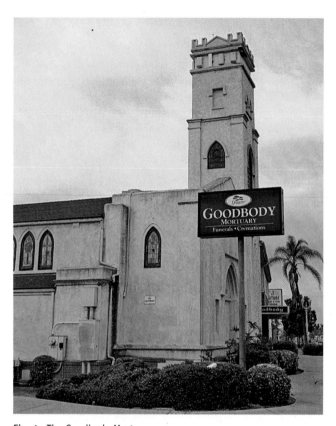

Fig. 1. The Goodbody Mortuary.

What organizational plan for the profile emerges in pars. 4 and 5?

4   I was apprehensive as I climbed the stone steps to the entrance. I feared rejection or, worse, an invitation to come and stay. The door was massive, yet it swung open easily on well-oiled hinges. "Come in," said the sign. "We're always open." Inside was a cool and quiet reception room. Curtains were drawn against the outside glare, cutting the light down to a soft glow.

What does the detailed description of Deaver in pars. 5 and 6 contribute to Cable's profile of the mortuary?

5   I found the funeral director in the main lobby, adjacent to the reception room. Like most people, I had preconceptions about what an undertaker looked like. Mr. Deaver fulfilled my expectations entirely. Tall and thin, he even had beady eyes and a bony face. A low, slanted forehead gave way to a beaked nose. His skin, scrubbed of all color, contrasted sharply with his jet black hair. He was wearing a starched white shirt, gray pants, and black shoes. Indeed, he looked like death on two legs.

6 He proved an amiable sort, however, and was easy to talk to. As funeral director, Mr. Deaver ("Call me Howard") was responsible for a wide range of services. Goodbody Mortuary, upon notification of someone's death, will remove the remains from the hospital or home. They then prepare the body for viewing, whereupon features distorted by illness or accident are restored to their natural condition. The body is embalmed and then placed in a casket selected by the family of the deceased. Services are held in one of three chapels at the mortuary, and afterward the casket is placed in a "visitation room," where family and friends can pay their last respects. Goodbody also makes arrangements for the purchase of a burial site and transports the body there for burial.

7 All this information Howard related in a well-practiced, professional manner. It was obvious he was used to explaining the specifics of his profession. We sat alone in the lobby. His desk was bone clean, no pencils or paper, nothing — just a telephone. He did all his paperwork at home; as it turned out, he and his wife lived right upstairs. The phone rang. As he listened, he bit his lips and squeezed his Adam's apple somewhat nervously.

8 "I think we'll be able to get him in by Friday. No, no, the family wants him cremated."

9 His tone was that of a broker conferring on the Dow Jones. Directly behind him was a sign announcing "Visa and MasterCard Welcome Here." It was tacked to the wall, right next to a crucifix.

10 "Some people have the idea that we are bereavement specialists, that we can handle emotional problems which follow a death: Only a trained therapist can do that. We provide services for the dead, not counseling for the living."

11 Physical comfort was the one thing they did provide for the living. The lobby was modestly but comfortably furnished. There were several couches, in colors ranging from earth brown to pastel blue, and a coffee table in front of each one. On one table lay some magazines and a vase of flowers. Another supported an aquarium. Paintings of pastoral scenes hung on every wall. The lobby looked more or less like that of an old hotel. Nothing seemed to match, but it had a homey, lived-in look.

12 "The last time the Goodbodies decorated was in '99, I believe. It still makes people feel welcome."

13 And so "Goodbody" was not a name made up to attract customers but the owner's family name. The Goodbody family started the business way back in 1915. Today, they do over five hundred services a year.

What role has Cable adopted in writing the profile? When does it become clear?

Why do you think Cable summarizes the information in par. 6 instead of quoting Howard?

What does this observation reveal about Cable's perspective?

Why do you think Cable quotes Howard in par. 10 instead of paraphrasing or summarizing?

What does this observation contribute to the dominant impression?

14   "We're in *Ripley's Believe It or Not*, along with another funeral home whose owners' names are Baggit and Sackit," Howard told me, without cracking a smile.

15   I followed him through an arched doorway into a chapel that smelled musty and old. The only illumination came from sunlight filtered through a stained glass ceiling. Ahead of us lay a casket. I could see that it contained a man dressed in a black suit. Wooden benches ran on either side of an aisle that led to the body. I got no closer. From the red roses across the dead man's chest, it was apparent that services had already been held.

16   "It was a large service," remarked Howard. "Look at that casket—a beautiful work of craftsmanship."

17   I guess it was. Death may be the great leveler, but one's coffin quickly reestablishes one's status.

18   We passed into a bright, fluorescent-lit "display room." Inside were thirty coffins, lids open, patiently awaiting inspection. Like new cars on the showroom floor, they gleamed with high-gloss finishes.

19   "We have models for every price range."

20   Indeed, there was a wide variety. They came in all colors and various materials. Some were little more than cloth-covered cardboard boxes, others were made of wood, and a few were made of steel, copper, or bronze. Howard told me prices started at $500 and averaged about $2,400. He motioned toward the center of the room: "The top of the line."

21   This was a solid bronze casket, its seams electronically welded to resist corrosion. Moisture-proof and air-tight, it could be hermetically sealed off from all outside elements. Its handles were plated with 14-karat gold. The Promethean casket made by the Batesville Casket Company is the choice of celebrities and the very wealthy. The price: a cool $25,000–$30,000 (Russell; see Fig. 2.)

22   A proper funeral remains a measure of respect for the deceased. But it is expensive. In the United States, the amount spent annually on funerals is around $12 billion (Grassley), with the average price about $7,000 ("NFDA Releases")—not counting the burial plot. Among ceremonial expenditures, funerals are second only to weddings. As a result, practices are changing. Howard has been in this business for forty years. He remembers a time when everyone was buried. Nowadays, with

How does Cable make the transition from topic to topic in pars. 15–18?

What does the comparison to a new-car showroom in pars. 18–21 reveal about Cable's perspective?

Where does the information in pars. 22–23 come from? How can you tell?

Fig. 2. "The top of the line." The Promethean casket that Michael Jackson was buried in.

burials costing more than $7,000 a shot (Grassley), people often opt instead for cremation — as Howard put it, "a cheap, quick, and easy means of disposal." In some areas of the country, according to Howard, the cremation rate is now over 60 percent. Observing this trend, one might wonder whether burials are becoming obsolete. Do burials serve an important role in society?

23   For Tim, Goodbody's licensed mortician, the answer is very definitely yes. Burials will remain in common practice, according to the slender embalmer with the disarming smile, because they allow family and friends to view the deceased. Painful as it may be, such an experience brings home the finality of death. "Something deep within us demands a confrontation with death," Tim explained. "A last look assures us that the person we loved is, indeed, gone forever."

24   Apparently, we also need to be assured that the body will be laid to rest in comfort and peace. The average casket, with its innerspring mattress and pleated satin lining, is surprisingly roomy and luxurious. Perhaps such an air of comfort makes it easier for the family to give up their loved one. In addition, the burial site fixes the deceased in the survivors' memory, like a new address. Cremation provides none of these comforts.

25   Tim started out as a clerk in a funeral home but then studied to become a mortician. "It was a profession I could live with," he told me with a sly grin. Mortuary science might be described as a cross between pre-med and cosmetology, with courses in anatomy and embalming as well as in restorative art.

Why do you think Cable uses a rhetorical question here?

Whose perspective does this statement reflect? How do you know?

Is Tim's definition of mortuary science helpful? Why or why not?

Photo credit: REUTERS/Mario Anzuoni/Landov

26   Tim let me see the preparation, or embalming, room, a white-walled chamber about the size of an operating room. Against the wall was a large sink with elbow taps and a draining board. In the center of the room stood a table with equipment for preparing the arterial embalming fluid, which consists primarily of formaldehyde, a preservative, and phenol, a disinfectant. This mixture sanitizes and also gives better color to the skin. Facial features can then be "set" to achieve a restful expression. Missing eyes, ears, and even noses can be replaced.

> Which information in par. 26 comes from observation and which comes from interviewing Tim? How do you know?

27   I asked Tim if his job ever depressed him. He bridled at the question: "No, it doesn't depress me at all. I do what I can for people and take satisfaction in enabling relatives to see their loved ones as they were in life." He said that he felt people were becoming more aware of the public service his profession provides. Grade-school classes now visit funeral homes as often as they do police stations and museums. The mortician is no longer regarded as a minister of death.

28   Before leaving, I wanted to see a body up close. I thought I could be indifferent after all I had seen and heard, but I wasn't sure. Cautiously, I reached out and touched the skin. It felt cold and firm, not unlike clay. As I walked out, I felt glad to have satisfied my curiosity about dead bodies, but all too happy to let someone else handle them.

> How effective is this ending?

Works Cited

Grassley, Chuck. "Opening Statement of Chairman Grassley." U.S. Senate Special Committee on Aging. 21 Sept. 2000. Web. 6 Jan. 2012.

"NFDA Releases Results of Member General Price List Survey." National Funeral Directors Association. NFDA.org, 1 Aug. 2013. Web. 12 Dec. 2014.

Russell, John. "Batesville Casket Is Coy about Starring Role in Jackson Funeral." *Indianapolis Star*. USAToday.com, 9 July 2009. Web. 12 Dec. 2014.

Twain, Mark. *Pudd'nhead Wilson*. New York: Pocket Books, 2004: 45. Print.

Jon Ronson | *The Hunger Games*

JON RONSON has written a number of books, including *The Psychopath Test: A Journey Through the Madness Industry* (2011) and *Out of the Ordinary: True Tales of Everyday Craziness* (2006). Trained in media studies, Ronson regularly contributes profiles and documentaries to the *Guardian* newspaper, the *New York Times Book Review, BBC Radio 4* in the United Kingdom, and *This American Life* in the United States. The film *The Men Who Stare at Goats* (2009) was based on Ronson's 2004 book of the same name, and Ronson himself co-authored the screenplay for the film *Frank* (2014) based on his experience performing with a British band. "The Hunger Games" appeared originally in *GQ* and was anthologized in *Lost at Sea: The Jon Ronson Mysteries* (2012).

As you read,

- notice that Ronson makes three moves in the opening paragraph: beginning with a description, giving a brief anecdote, and then telling us what he thinks.

- how do these moves help interest readers in the subject? Which move works especially well to arouse your interest?

1   Here is a mountain of corned-beef sandwiches, each crammed with meat. Eleven men and one woman—some of the world's top competitive eaters—intently scrutinize the sandwiches as they're wheeled by on a trolley toward the stage. We're at an outdoor shopping mall in Palm Beach Gardens, Florida, the site of the third annual TooJay's World Class Corned Beef Eating Championship. One contestant drove a thousand miles to be here. He got a flat tire and had to double back to Avis in the middle of the night, but he's made it, and he's ready to battle. I'm intrigued and mystified by the dedication of these athletes, as some of them call themselves. Who are they? What motivates them? I notice them glancing at one another in complicated, intense ways.

2   But a sense of fatalistic doom pervades the air. This is because one man is quite simply predestined to win. His name is Joey Chestnut, and he's a charismatic, sweet-natured 28-year-old Californian in surprisingly good shape for someone who bulldozes hideous amounts of food into his stomach on a regular basis. In the past six years, Joey has completely dominated the "sport" of competitive eating as it has expanded from a once-a-year carnival stunt to a worldwide tour. He holds world records for hot dogs, asparagus, funnel cake, jalapeño poppers, gyros, grilled cheese sandwiches, chicken wings, cheesesteaks, shrimp wontons, tacos, and at least a dozen other "disciplines."

3   About 200 people have turned up to watch him try to break his own corned-beef-sandwich record. Fans surround Joey for his autograph. One of them sidles over to me. His name is Sam Barclay. He's such a devotee, he says, that he's actually got himself a job with the International Federation of Competitive Eating (IFOCE), the sport's governing body, as a helper and part-time emcee. And he is in total awe of Joey.

4   The fans are mostly ignoring Joey's challengers. There's the world number two, Pat "Deep Dish" Bertoletti, muscular, wiry, a Mohawk haircut, almost always the bridesmaid, rarely the bride. There's a beautiful woman in her twenties named Maria Edible—a cupcake and a burger tattooed on her arm and the word EDIBLE tattooed inside her mouth. There's a bear of a guy named Bob Shoudt—about the only family man on the circuit. He has three kids and puts any prize money he makes into their college funds. I notice another challenger—a waif of a boy with long dark hair—staring fixedly at Joey from across the crowd.

5   I approach Joey. "Who's that boy?" I whisper.

6   "Matt Stonie," he whispers back. "He's new. He's good. I watched a YouTube video of him in training. You hear his mother in the background encouraging him. When I saw that, I thought, 'Why would she be encouraging him? There must be something wrong with him for her to be encouraging him to eat.'" Joey lowers his voice. "Apparently when he was 15 he was anorexic.". . .

7   Our conversation is interrupted by the emcee, Rich Shea, who is telling the audience how blessed we Americans are to have the freedom to eat as many corned-beef sandwiches as we like under a big blue sky. He introduces the contestants. Each takes his place on the stage. Joey is, of course, last: ". . . the bratwurst and pork rib eating champion of the world, the calzone champion of the world, the Nathan's Famous hot-dog-eating CHAMPION OF THE WORLD! JOEY CHESTNUT!"

8   For two days now, I've been listening to Joey extol the sport as a sensei would a martial art. He has told me, for example, how he has studied the ingestion techniques of snakes: "Their muscles are contracting constantly. You'll see when I'm eating, there's a constant weird up-and-down motion. I'm using my whole rib cage to compact the food." Then there are the years he's spent determining how long to fast before each contest (three days) and which oils best lubricate the digestive system. He's settled on an exact combination of specific brands of olive and fish oils, but he won't divulge more. "I had to figure it out," he said, "so why should I let it be known?"

9   So after all of Joey's talk of science and preparation, I was imagining the corned-beef contest to be somehow more graceful and balletic. But as Shea counts down to zero and the eating begins, what I see instead are twelve people grotesquely cramming huge piles of meat and fat-sodden rye bread into their mouths. The juice drips down their arms, saturating their shirts. Their puffed-out cheeks are beetroot red. They resemble sweaty, meat-smeared squirrels. The sickly smell of fat permeates the hot air. I notice that the fastest eaters are squeezing the sandwiches in their clenched fists before swallowing them. With one hand they're shoveling in the food, with the other they're gulping liters of water or, in the case of Pat Bertoletti, bright red cherry limeade.

Competitive eating is, of course, a manifestation of the American urge to turn absolutely everything, even something as elemental as eating, into a competition.

Coupled with the semi-masticated sandwiches that are spraying from their mouths in globules as they slobber onto themselves and the table, the whole thing looks like an unimaginable crime scene.

10   It's a ten-minute contest. By minute six, most of the field is belching and cramping. But not Joey Chestnut. Pat Bertoletti is doing his level best to keep pace with the champ, and young Matt Stonie seems remarkably adept for someone so slight. But Joey is on another level. He's Usain Bolt, but with sandwiches. He had been telling the truth about the "weird up-and-down motion" in his rib cage. He looks like he's performing a disquieting contemporary dance routine. . . . We are witnessing a new world record! Joey devours twenty corned-beef sandwiches, shattering his previous record by five and a half. Barclay shakes his head in wonder. "It's not pretty," he concedes. "But it *is* beautiful."

11   Joey collects his $5,000 prize money, poses for the cameras, and disappears behind the stage, where I find him looking terrible. . . . "Describe how you're feeling with twenty corned-beef sandwiches inside you," I ask. "I'm used to it," he says. "But . . . pain . . ." He's speaking in fractured sentences, with great difficulty. It seems cruel for me to continue the interview. I congratulate him once again. "Hopefully I'll feel okay," he says, "in four or five hours."

12   Competitive eating is, of course, a manifestation of the American urge to turn absolutely everything, even something as elemental as eating, into a competition. And it is as old as America itself—or maybe it started in the early '70s. The fact is, it's tough to suss out the history of the sport through the thick-as-mustard layer of PR myth that has been slathered onto it by generations of pitchmen. There are tales (possibly true) of pioneers staging contests in the early days of the republic to celebrate bountiful harvests. Nathan's Famous, the Coney Island hot-dog vendor whose annual Fourth of July extravaganza remains the Super Bowl of the sport, claims its event goes back to 1916, when a group of immigrants put on a contest to test their patriotic mettle. This is (almost certainly) untrue. The first Nathan's contest, as best anyone can remember, was actually held on July 4, 1972. . . . And for the next twenty-five years, that's about all competitive eating amounted to—the Nathan's

contest. . . . Until, that is, July 4, 2001—the most extraordinary day in the history of competitive eating. Watching the news footage filmed that day, during the minutes before everything changed forever, I was struck by how lackadaisical things seemed. . . . Until that day, the Nathan's Famous record was twenty-five and one eighth dogs in twelve minutes. Takeru Kobayashi ate fifty. He became an international media sensation, the subject of thousands of gleeful headlines. CNN put him on a list of "Japan's greatest sports heroes." And he remained unbeaten—and virtually synonymous with competitive eating—for six years. But then a new and even greater virtuoso emerged.

13   Joey "Jaws" Chestnut grew up in Vallejo, California. Being the third of four boys, he was always searching for something he could beat his older brothers at. And that thing seemed to be eating very fast. He showed such a talent for it that in 2005, his youngest brother entered him into a lobster competition in Reno. "I'd never eaten lobster before," Joey told me. "I was 21. I didn't know what the heck I was doing. I was scooping guts. But I tied for third. And the two men who beat me didn't look good. One was Bob Shoudt. He seemed in pain. And I felt fine! I was 'Oh, my God, they look like they're dying. And I can eat so much more!' I knew I was made for it after that contest."

14   Joey decided that night to dedicate his life to the pursuit. He became obsessed—"nervous, always nervous"—and his discipline paid off in Coney Island on July 4, 2007, when he scarfed down sixty-six hot dogs before an audience of 40,000. . . . Joey defended his title the next year and every year since. At the 2009 Nathan's contest, he set a new world record with sixty-eight hot dogs. Last year, between his prize money and sponsorships, he raked in $205,000. . . .

15   And now the big one. Coney Island. The Fourth of July. The Nathan's Famous International Hot Dog Eating Championship, with a $10,000 first prize. "The only one," Pat Bertoletti tells me, "the public really cares about."

16   Thousands have gathered on the boardwalk by the beach. Many are chanting "U.S.A.! U.S.A.!" Onto the giant stage marches a procession of stilt walkers, dwarves dressed as Uncle Sam, cheerleaders, bodybuilders, a girl singing "The Star-Spangled Banner." Presiding over the pageantry is the legendary emcee George Shea, wearing a straw boater. ESPN is filming it all for a 3 p.m. broadcast.

Monika Graff/Getty Images

17   The eaters are crowded into a little room backstage where thousands of hot dogs are being mass-cooked. They're like gladiators sharing a dressing room with the lions. . . . Joey and Pat sit next to each other backstage but say nothing. Joey once told me they rarely talk before an event. Sometimes they'll heartily slap each other on the back in the moments before a contest begins, feigning friendliness, when what they're actually trying to do is irritate each other. So it was all the more remarkable when, last night at the hotel, I saw the two men huddled in a corner, speaking quietly. It was a melancholy and surprising conversation. Pat was asking Joey, "When you retire, will you give me the secret?"

18   "You've seen everything I do," Joey replied. I turned to Pat. "Do you sometimes feel like Buzz Aldrin to Joey's Neil Armstrong?"

19   "For sure," he said. Despite the tough-guy mustache and scary Mohawk, there was a real sweetness to Pat. He seemed resigned to the fact that he has hit the ceiling, that he'll always be second best. And he's had enough, he said. He's getting out of this crazy sport.

20   "I don't think I can ever win [hot dogs]," he told Joey and me. "And I've done everything else." "You might quit *everything*?" I asked. "Yeah," said Pat. Then Joey said, "I've thought about getting out, too."

21   "You want out, too?" said Pat, incredulous.

22   "I do," said Joey.

23   "Why?" I asked him.

24   He backpedaled slightly. "It's not that I *want* out," he said, "but I don't want to *linger*."

25   What he meant is that once you're number one, there's nowhere to go. Joey is trapped at number one like Pat is trapped at number two.

26   "My goal is seven [Nathan's titles] in a row," Joey said. "Next year could very well be my last."

27   "Do you also want to quit because you realize it's a bizarre way to live your life?" I asked him.

28   "Probably," Joey said.

29   The truth is, rarely have I done a story about something that's so utterly, existentially pointless and so emblematic of the American tendency to go way too far. . . .

30   Halfway through the contest, something impossible seems to be happening. "Matt Stonie!" George Shea is yelling into the microphone. "Many are calling him the new Joey Chestnut! This is amazing, ladies and gentlemen! Matt Stonie is doing so well he's only four hot dogs behind Joey Chestnut. Nineteen years of age! And yet he's the only one truly putting pressure on Joey Chestnut!" . . . He's gaining on Joey, all those years of pain propelling him on. Twenty-eight hot dogs, twenty-nine hot dogs, thirty hot dogs, thirty-one. . . . But then, suddenly, heartbreakingly, at thirty-four dogs into the contest, Matt hits a wall. ("Died out," he'll later say on Facebook.) The manic pace with which he'd been inhaling hot dogs slows dramatically, and a look of defeat crosses his flushed, sweaty face. . . .

31   The audience—many of whom are wearing Joey Chestnut T-shirts and holding Joey Chestnut signs—is screaming his name as he stands before them, exhausted and utterly spent, basking in their love. A few minutes later, as Joey wades triumphantly into the throng, holding his championship belt aloft, I remember something he told me a few months earlier: "I have to learn to ignore my feelings. Not just the feeling of hunger and the feeling of full, but the feeling of embarrassment, too. I have to remember that this is only weird if I *make* it weird." Soon Joey is swallowed by the crowd, and I lose sight of him. All I can see now is the belt itself, its painted gold glinting in the relentless sun, bobbing along in a surging tide of red, white, and blue.

[REFLECT]

Make connections: Competitive eating as a sport.

Notice that Ronson, who was born and bred in Wales, in the United Kingdom, talks about competitive eating as a typically American "sport" (par. 12). Consider Ronson's take on American values and attitudes toward sports in relation to your own views. Your instructor may ask you to post your thoughts on a class discussion board or to discuss them with other students in class. Use these questions to get started:

- How accurate are Ronson's two assertions: that the sport is "a manifestation of the American urge to turn absolutely everything, even something as elemental as eating, into a competition" (par. 12) and that it is "emblematic of the American tendency to go way too far" (par. 29)?

- How is competitive eating like and unlike other sports that you consider typically American?

- How does Ronson use the genre of the profile to portray competitive eating as a sport? Where in the profile, for example, do you see the kinds of discourse (such as play-by-play narration and up-close-and-personal interview) you associate with sports reporting?

[ANALYZE]

Use the basic features.

SPECIFIC INFORMATION ABOUT THE SUBJECT: DESCRIBING PEOPLE THROUGH NAMING, DETAILING, AND COMPARING

To learn more about these describing strategies, see Chapter 15.

Profiles, like remembered events (Chapter 2), succeed in large part by presenting the people being observed and interviewed. Using the describing strategies of naming, detailing, and comparing, Ronson gives readers a series of graphic images showing us some of the main figures competing with Joey Chestnut, the focus of Ronson's profile.

Write a paragraph analyzing Ronson's use of describing strategies to give readers a vivid impression of a person:

1 Look closely at Ronson's thumbnail portraits of Pat Bertoletti, Maria Edible, Bob Shouldt, and Matt Stonie (par. 4).

2 Choose one portrait that gives you a strong impression, and briefly explain what you think makes that portrait work so well. You might focus, for example, on a specific detail of the person's appearance or a striking comparison (metaphor or simile) that captures something important about the individual's personality.

A CLEAR, LOGICAL ORGANIZATION: USING FLASHBACKS

Profiles organized narratively usually follow a fairly straightforward chronology from past to present. Occasionally, however, they may diverge from this conventional way of storytelling to recount something that occurred in the past, using *flashbacks*. In profiles, flashbacks can be used to interject historical information, a memory, or reflection into the ongoing narrative (as in the following example from Cable's essay). To avoid confusing readers, flashbacks are usually marked by time cues and verb tenses to indicate different points in time:

> Howard has been in this business for forty years. He remembers a time when everyone was buried. (Cable, par. 22)

Ongoing past
Present
Simple past

Write a paragraph analyzing Ronson's use of flashbacks:

1 Skim the profile looking for flashbacks, highlighting the cues Ronson uses to signal time shifts.

2 Consider why Ronson uses flashbacks and how else he could have incorporated the information he presents in this way.

THE WRITER'S ROLE: ACTING AS A SPECTATOR

Like Cable, Ronson assumes the role of a spectator. He places himself in the scene as a sort of eyewitness, using the first-person pronoun "I" to refer to what he was thinking, feeling, seeing, and asking while making observations and conducting interviews.

Here are some typical sentence strategies illustrating the spectator role:

▶ I expected/anticipated/felt/observed _____.

▶ I asked/pondered/wondered _____?

ANALYZE & WRITE

Write a paragraph analyzing Ronson's role:

1. Reread Ronson's profile marking passages where he places himself in the scene. Note whether he uses the first-person pronoun "I" to cue readers or signals in some other way that he is making observations, expressing expectations, or interviewing people.

2. Consider how this profile would be different if Ronson had adopted the role of a participant-observer instead of a spectator. What new insights might he have gotten from participating in an eating contest, for example?

A PERSPECTIVE ON THE SUBJECT: SHOWING AND TELLING

All of the profiles in this chapter use a combination of showing and telling to convey the writer's perspective on or ideas about the subject. Cable shows his anxiety about death, for example, by describing his hesitation to get close to and touch a dead body (pars. 15, 28). He uses comparisons to give readers a dominant impression of the funeral home as all business:

> His tone was that of a broker conferring on the Dow Jones. (par. 9)

> Inside were thirty coffins, lids open, patiently awaiting inspection. Like new cars on the showroom floor. . . . (par. 18)

In addition, Cable tells readers directly about what he observed, for instance, in the opening paragraphs and in his questioning of Tim about whether burials play "an important role in society" (par. 22).

ANALYZE & WRITE

Write a couple of paragraphs analyzing Ronson's use of showing and telling to convey his perspective:

1. Focus first on Ronson's depiction of Joey. Briefly explain the dominant impression you get from the description and dialogue, quoting a few examples to illustrate your explanation.

2. Next, select a couple of examples where Ronson tells readers what he thinks about the sport and about Joey.

3. Finally, consider how the showing and telling work together to create a dominant impression of Joey Chestnut.

[RESPOND]

Consider possible topics: Profiling a sport or a sports figure.

Consider profiling a sport. You could focus on an offbeat sport (curling, extreme skateboarding), follow a team at your high school or college, perhaps focusing on a particular player or coach, or focus on a local children's sports team or karate dojo. If you are interested in health care professions, you might observe and write about a sports injury clinic in your community. To learn about the business side of college sports, consider interviewing the director or business manager of your college athletics association.

Amanda Coyne | *The Long Good-Bye: Mother's Day in Federal Prison*

Courtesy of Amanda Coyne

AMANDA COYNE earned a master of fine arts degree in creative writing at the University of Iowa, where she was the recipient of an Iowa Arts Fellowship. She was the cofounder of and a writer for the *Alaska Dispatch,* an award-winning online news site. Her work has appeared in such publications as *Harper's,* the *New York Times Magazine, Bust, Newsweek,* and the *Guardian.* Coyne coauthored a book about oil and politics in Alaska entitled *Crude Awakening: Money, Mavericks, and Mayhem in Alaska* (2011). She also started a blog about Alaska politics in 2013.

"The Long Good-Bye," her first piece of published writing, originally appeared in *Harper's.* Coyne uses direct observation and interview to study the behavior of a particular community. In this profile, Coyne examines women who have been incarcerated and separated from their children to see how the mothers and children negotiate their difficult relationships.

As you read, consider the following questions:

- What stresses seem to affect the family relationships described in this profile?
- What do you think is the author's attitude toward these stresses? How can you tell what she thinks and feels?

1 You can spot the convict-moms here in the visiting room by the way they hold and touch their children and by the single flower that is perched in front of them—a rose, a tulip, a daffodil. Many of these mothers have untied the bow that attaches the flower to its silver-and-red cellophane wrapper and are using one of the many empty soda cans at hand as a vase. They sit proudly before their flower-in-a-Coke-can, amid Hershey bar wrappers, half-eaten Ding Dongs, and empty paper coffee cups. Occasionally, a mother will pick up her present and bring it to her nose when one of the bearers of the single flower—her child—asks if she likes it. And the mother will respond the way that mothers always have and always will respond when presented with a gift on this day. "Oh, I just love it. It's perfect. I'll put it in the middle of my Bible." Or, "I'll put it on my desk, right next to your school picture." And always: "It's the best one here."

2 But most of what is being smelled today is the children themselves. While the other adults are plunking coins into the vending machines, the mothers take deep whiffs from the backs of their children's necks, or kiss and smell the backs of their knees, or take off their shoes and tickle their feet and then pull them close to their noses. They hold them tight and take in their own second scent—the scent assuring them that these are still their children and that they still belong to them.

3 The visitors are allowed to bring in pockets full of coins, and today that Mother's Day flower, and I know from previous visits to my older sister here at the Federal Prison Camp for women in Pekin, Illinois, that there is always an aberrant urge to gather immediately

around the vending machines. The sandwiches are stale, the coffee weak, the candy bars the ones we always pass up in a convenience store. But after we hand the children over to their mothers, we gravitate toward those machines. Like milling in the kitchen at a party. We all do it, and nobody knows why. Polite conversation ensues around the microwave while the popcorn is popping and the processed-chicken sandwiches are being heated. We ask one another where we are from, how long a drive we had. An occasional whistle through the teeth, a shake of the head. "My, my, long way from home, huh?" "Staying at the Super 8 right up the road. Not a bad place." "Stayed at the Econo Lodge last time. Wasn't a good place at all." Never asking the questions we really want to ask: "What's she in for?" "How much time's she got left?" You never ask in the waiting room of a doctor's office either. Eventually, all of us—fathers, mothers, sisters, brothers, a few boyfriends, and very few husbands—return to the queen of the day, sitting at a fold-out table loaded with snacks, prepared for five or so hours of attempted normal conversation.

4   Most of the inmates are elaborately dressed, many in prison-crafted dresses and sweaters in bright blues and pinks. They wear meticulously applied makeup in corresponding hues, and their hair is replete with loops and curls—hair that only women with the time have the time for. Some of the better seamstresses have crocheted vests and purses to match their outfits. Although the world outside would never accuse these women of making haute-couture fashion statements, the fathers and the sons and the boyfriends and the very few husbands think they look beautiful, and they tell them so repeatedly. And I can imagine the hours spent preparing for this visit—hours of needles and hooks clicking over brightly colored yards of yarn. The hours of discussing, dissecting, and bragging about these visitors—especially the men. Hours spent in the other world behind the door where we're not allowed, sharing lipsticks and mascaras, and unraveling the occasional hair-tangled hot roller, and the brushing out and lifting and teasing . . . and the giggles that abruptly change into tears without warning—things that define any female-only world. Even, or especially, if that world is a female federal prison camp.

5   While my sister Jennifer is with her son in the playroom, an inmate's mother comes over to introduce herself to my younger sister, Charity, my brother, John, and me. She tells us about visiting her daughter in a higher-security prison before she was transferred here. The woman looks old and tired, and her shoulders sag under the weight of her recently acquired bitterness.

6   "Pit of fire," she says, shaking her head. "Like a pit of fire straight from hell. Never seen anything like it. Like something out of an old movie about prisons." Her voice is getting louder and she looks at each of us with pleading eyes. "My *daughter* was there. Don't even get me started on that place. Women die there."

7   John and Charity and I silently exchange glances.

8   "My daughter would come to the visiting room with a black eye and I'd think, 'All she did was sit in the car while her boyfriend ran into the house.' She didn't even touch the stuff. Never even handled it."

9   She continues to stare at us, each in turn. "Ten years. That boyfriend talked and he got three years. She didn't know anything. Had nothing to tell them. They gave her ten years. They called it conspiracy. Conspiracy? Aren't there real criminals out there?" She asks this with hands outstretched, waiting for an answer that none of us can give her.

10   The woman's daughter, the conspirator, is chasing her son through the maze of chairs and tables and through the other children. She's a twenty-four-year-old blonde, whom I'll call Stephanie, with Dorothy Hamill hair and matching dimples. She looks like any girl you might see in any shopping mall in middle America. She catches her chocolate-brown son and tickles him, and they laugh and trip and fall together onto the floor and laugh harder.

11   Had it not been for that wait in the car, this scene would be taking place at home, in a duplex Stephanie would rent while trying to finish her two-year degree in dental hygiene or respiratory therapy at the local community college. The duplex would be spotless, with a blown-up picture of her and her son over the couch and ceramic unicorns and horses occupying the shelves of the entertainment center. She would make sure that her son went to school every day with stylishly floppy pants, scrubbed teeth, and a good breakfast in his belly. Because of their difference in skin color, there would be occasional tension—caused by

the strange looks from strangers, teachers, other mothers, and the bullies on the playground, who would chant after they knocked him down, "Your Momma's white, your Momma's white." But if she were home, their weekends and evenings would be spent together transcending those looks and healing those bruises. Now, however, their time is spent eating visiting-room junk food and his school days are spent fighting the boys in the playground who chant, "Your Momma's in prison, your Momma's in prison."

12   He will be ten when his mother is released, the same age my nephew will be when his mother is let out. But Jennifer, my sister, was able to spend the first five years of Toby's life with him. Stephanie had Ellie after she was incarcerated. They let her hold him for eighteen hours, then sent her back to prison. She has done the "tour," and her son is a well-traveled six-year-old. He has spent weekends visiting his mother in prisons in Kentucky, Texas, Connecticut (the Pit of Fire), and now at last here, the camp — minimum security, Pekin, Illinois.

13   Ellie looks older than his age. But his shoulders do not droop like his grandmother's. On the contrary, his bitterness lifts them and his chin higher than a child's should be, and the childlike, wide-eyed curiosity has been replaced by defiance. You can see his emerging hostility as he and his mother play together. She tells him to pick up the toy that he threw, say, or to put the deck of cards away. His face turns sullen, but she persists. She takes him by the shoulders and looks him in the eye, and he uses one of his hands to swat at her. She grabs the hand and he swats with the other. Eventually, she pulls him toward her and smells the top of his head, and she picks up the cards or the toy herself. After all, it is Mother's Day and she sees him so rarely. But her acquiescence makes him angrier, and he stalks out of the playroom with his shoulders thrown back.

14   Toby, my brother and sister and I assure one another, will not have these resentments. He is better taken care of than most. He is living with relatives in Wisconsin. Good, solid, middle-class, churchgoing relatives. And when he visits us, his aunts and his uncle, we take him out for adventures where we walk down the alley of a city and pretend that we are being chased by

the "bad guys." We buy him fast food, and his uncle, John, keeps him up well past his bedtime enthralling him with stories of the monkeys he met in India. A perfect mix, we try to convince one another. Until we take him to see his mother and on the drive back he asks the question that most confuses him, and no doubt all the other children who spend much of their lives in prison visiting rooms: "Is my Mommy a bad guy?" It is the question that most seriously disorders his five-year-old need to clearly separate right from wrong. And because our own need is perhaps just as great, it is the question that haunts us as well.

15   Now, however, the answer is relatively simple. In a few years, it won't be. In a few years we will have to explain mandatory minimums, and the war on drugs, and the murky conspiracy laws, and the enormous amount of money and time that federal agents pump into imprisoning low-level drug dealers and those who happen to be their friends and their lovers. In a few years he might have the reasoning skills to ask why so many armed robbers and rapists and child-molesters and, indeed, murderers are punished less severely than his mother. When he is older, we will somehow have to explain to him the difference between federal crimes, which don't allow for parole, and state crimes, which do. We will have to explain that his mother was taken from him for five years not because she was a drug dealer but because she made four phone calls for someone she loved.

"Is my Mommy a bad guy?" It is the question that most seriously disorders his five-year-old need to clearly separate right from wrong.

16   But we also know it is vitally important that we explain all this without betraying our bitterness. We understand the danger of abstract anger, of being disillusioned with your country, and, most of all, we do not want him to inherit that legacy. We would still like him to be raised as we were, with the idea that we live in the best country in the world with the best legal system in the world — a legal system carefully designed to be immune to political mood swings and public hysteria; a system that promises to fit the punishment to the crime. We want him to be a good citizen. We want him to have absolute faith that he lives in a fair country, a country that watches over and protects its most vulnerable citizens: its women and children.

17   So for now we simply say, "Toby, your mother isn't bad, she just did a bad thing. Like when you put rocks

in the lawn mower's gas tank. You weren't bad then, you just did a bad thing."

18   Once, after being given this weak explanation, he said, "I wish I could have done something really bad, like my Mommy. So I could go to prison too and be with her."

19   It's now 3:00. Visiting ends at 3:30. The kids are getting cranky, and the adults are both exhausted and wired from too many hours of conversation, too much coffee and candy. The fathers, mothers, sisters, brothers, and the few boyfriends, and the very few husbands are beginning to show signs of gathering the trash. The mothers of the infants are giving their heads one last whiff before tucking them and their paraphernalia into their respective carrying cases. The visitors meander toward the door, leaving the older children with their mothers for one last word. But the mothers never say what they want to say to their children. They say things like, "Do well in school," "Be nice to your sister," "Be good for Aunt Berry, or Grandma." They don't say, "I'm sorry I'm sorry I'm sorry. I love you more than anything else in the world and I think about you every minute and I worry about you with a pain that shoots straight to my heart, a pain so great I think I will just burst when I think of you alone, without me. I'm sorry."

20   We are standing in front of the double glass doors that lead to the outside world. My older sister holds her son, rocking him gently. They are both crying. We give her a look and she puts him down. Charity and I grasp each of his small hands, and the four of us walk through the doors. As we're walking out, my brother sings one of his banana songs to Toby.

21   "Take me out to the—" and Toby yells out, "Banana store!"

22   "Buy me some —"

23   "Bananas!!"

24   "I don't care if I ever come back. For it's root, root, root for the—"

25   "Monkey team!"

26   I turn back and see a line of women standing behind the glass wall. Some of them are crying, but many simply stare with dazed eyes. Stephanie is holding both of her son's hands in hers and speaking urgently to him. He is struggling, and his head is twisting violently back and forth. He frees one of his hands from her grasp, balls up his fist, and punches her in the face. Then he walks with purpose through the glass doors and out the exit. I look back at her. She is still in a crouched position. She stares, unblinking, through those doors. Her hands have left her face and are hanging on either side of her. I look away, but before I do, I see drops of blood drip from her nose, down her chin, and onto the shiny marble floor.

[REFLECT]   # Make connections: Unfair punishment.

Coyne reflects near the end of the essay that she wishes her nephew Toby would "have absolute faith that he lives in a fair country" (par. 16). Yet she expects that, like Stephanie's son, Ellie, Toby will become bitter and angry when he understands that "his mother was taken from him for five years not because she was a drug dealer but because she made four phone calls for someone she loved" (par. 15).

Think about an occasion when you were punished unfairly—for breaking a school rule, perhaps, or neglecting to fulfill an expectation of your parents. Although you willingly admit having done it, you may still feel that the punishment was unjustified. Consider what you did and why you think the punishment was unfair. Your instructor may ask you to post your thoughts on a class discussion board or to discuss them with other students in class. Use these questions to get started:

- Why do you think the punishment was unfair? For example, were the rules or expectations that you broke unclear or unreasonable? Were they applied to everyone or applied selectively or at the whim of those in power?

■ Coyne uses the value term *unfair* to describe what's wrong with the punishment her sister and some of the other women received. Why do you think Coyne believes her sister's punishment is unfair? Why does Stephanie's mother think Stephanie's punishment was unfair? Do you agree or disagree?

Use the basic features.

[ANALYZE]

SPECIFIC INFORMATION ABOUT THE SUBJECT: USING ANECDOTES

Including **anecdotes**—brief narratives about one-time events—can be a powerful way to convey detailed information about a subject. Coyne, for example, exposes the effects of separation on mothers and children through powerful anecdotes portraying what happened between Stephanie and her son, Ellie, during their visit.

ANALYZE & WRITE

Write a few paragraphs analyzing Coyne's use of anecdotes to present information:

1 Reread paragraphs 13 and 26, underlining the words that Coyne uses to present Ellie's actions and putting brackets around the words Coyne uses to present his mother's reactions.

2 What do you learn from these anecdotes about the effects on Stephanie and Ellie of enforced separation?

A CLEAR, LOGICAL ORGANIZATION: NARRATING A DAY IN THE LIFE

Coyne uses narrative as a kind of exoskeleton, a shell within which to hold the information and ideas she wants to present to her readers. The occasion is specific: visiting hours at the Federal Prison on Mother's Day. The opening paragraphs situate the profile in time and space, and the concluding paragraphs—signaled with the time marker "It's now 3:00. Visiting ends at 3:30" (par. 19)—recount what happened at the end of the visit. Within this narrative framework, however, Coyne does not follow a strict chronological order. Some events occur at the same time as other events. For example, paragraphs 1 to 3 present actions that occur at the same time: while mothers are getting reacquainted with their children (pars. 1 and 2), and the family members are using the vending machines and chatting with one another (par. 3).

ANALYZE & WRITE

Write a couple of paragraphs analyzing Coyne's use of narrative organization:

1 Reread the essay, noting in the margin when the events are happening in relation to the events in earlier paragraphs and highlighting any time markers, such as prepositional phrases locating actions in time, clock time, or verb tenses (past, present, future, and so on).

2 Coyne could have organized her essay topically, by presenting a series of insights and impressions from the many visits she has made instead of focusing on one Mother's Day. How does her choice help you understand the situation of the women and their families?

THE WRITER'S ROLE: ACTING AS A PARTICIPANT-OBSERVER

As a participant-observer, Coyne is in a unique situation. Indeed, she was probably only able to gain access to the prison because her sister was an inmate. Having a personal relationship with the subject she is profiling, then, gives Coyne access. It also gives her familiarity, as this is not her first visit to a prison. In addition, it may also give her special insight into both the personal and cultural aspects of the situation she is profiling. Writing about her own family, however, could lead Coyne to blur the distinction between the genres of observational profile and autobiography. This activity invites you to think about these two genres—how they differ yet may intersect or overlap.

ANALYZE & WRITE

Write a paragraph analyzing the genre mixing in "The Long Good-Bye":

1. Reread to find passages in which Coyne refers to her family and reflects on the significance of this Mother's Day visit. One of the distinguishing features of autobiography is that it attempts to shed light on complex, often ambivalent or conflicted feelings and relationships. How does "The Long Good-Bye" explore the writer's relationship with her sister and nephew?

2. Now think about "The Long Good-Bye" as an observational study, a kind of ethnography examining the culture of a community. What do you learn about the community of "convict-moms" (par. 1), as she calls them, and the challenges they face? How does Coyne shift readers' attention from her family to the broader community?

A PERSPECTIVE ON THE SUBJECT: USING CONTRAST

Unlike arguments supporting positions or justifying evaluations, which tell readers directly what the writer thinks and why, profiles often lead readers to draw a particular conclusion on their own, using strategies like comparing and contrasting. For example, Cable quotes the funeral director drawing a distinction between his job and that of a psychologist to clarify what a mortuary does and does not offer clients:

Contrast cue

"We provide services for the dead, not counseling for the living." (par. 10)

Notice that he juxtaposes, or places side by side, the different professions.

Contrasts can also be used to foreground particular aspects of the subject. In this example, Cable uses contrast to call attention to the appearance and location of the mortuary, highlighting the difference between his expectations and the reality he finds:

I thought it would be more like Forest Lawn, serene with lush green lawns and meticulously groomed gardens, a place set apart from the hustle of day-to-day life.

Contrast cue

Here instead was an odd tan structure set in the middle of a business district. (par. 3)

Write a couple of paragraphs analyzing how Coyne uses contrast to convey her perspective:

1. Skim Coyne's profile, highlighting the cues or transitional words and phrases that indicate contrast. Analyze at least one of the contrasts you find. What is being contrasted? How does the contrast help you understand the writer's perspective?

2. Note in the margin which paragraphs focus on Coyne's sister Jennifer and her son Toby and which focus on Stephanie and her son Ellie. Does Coyne juxtapose the two families or use cues to highlight the contrasts — or does she use both strategies? What differences between the two families does Coyne emphasize? Since contrasts tend to be worth pointing out when there are also important similarities, also consider what similarities Coyne wants readers to think about.

3. Consider how Coyne uses contrast — between people, between the world of the prison and the world outside, and between what is and what could have been — to help convey her perspective on the plight of women like her sister and children like her nephew.

To learn more about transitions, see Chapter 13; transitions indicating a contrasting or opposing view are listed on p. 534.

Consider possible topics: Profiling one instance of a recurring event.

[RESPOND]

Like Coyne, you can also profile an activity occurring over a short period of time, in a relatively small space, involving only a few people. Consider, for example, profiling a team practicing, a musical group rehearsing, or researchers working together in a lab. Try to make more than one observational visit to see the group in action, and arrange to talk with people on every visit, perhaps capturing a few digital images you could use to help you understand the group and possibly also to illustrate it.

Gabriel Thompson | *A Gringo in the Lettuce Fields*

Courtesy of Gabriel Thompson

GABRIEL THOMPSON has worked as a community organizer and written extensively about the lives of undocumented immigrants in the United States. His books include *There's No José Here: Following the Hidden Lives of Mexican Immigrants* (2006), *Calling All Radicals: How Grassroots Organizers Can Help Save Our Democracy* (2007), and *Working in the Shadows: A Year of Doing the Jobs (Most) Americans Won't Do* (2010), from which the following selection is taken. The photograph showing lettuce cutters at work (p. 85) is from Thompson's blog, *Working in the Shadows*.

"A Gringo in the Lettuce Fields" falls into the category of immersion journalism, a cultural ethnography that uses undercover participant observation over an extended period of time to get an insider's view of a particular community.

As you read, consider the ethical implications of this kind of profile:

- What does Thompson's outsider status enable him to understand—or prevent him from understanding—about the community?
- How does Thompson avoid—or fail to avoid—stereotyping or exploiting the group being profiled?
- Toward the end, Thompson tells us that one of the workers "guesses" that he "joined the crew . . . to write about it" (par. 17). Not all participant-observers go undercover; why do you think Thompson chose to do so? What concerns would you have if you were the writer or if you were a member of the group being profiled?

1   I wake up staring into the bluest blue I've ever seen. I must have fallen into a deep sleep because I need several seconds to realize that I'm looking at the Arizona sky, that the pillow beneath my head is a large clump of dirt, and that a near-stranger named Manuel is standing over me, smiling. I pull myself to a sitting position. To my left, in the distance, a Border Patrol helicopter is hovering. To my right is Mexico, separated by only a few fields of lettuce. "*Buenos días,*" Manuel says.

2   I stand up gingerly. It's only my third day in the fields, but already my 30-year-old body is failing me. I feel like someone has dropped a log on my back. And then piled that log onto a truck with many other logs, and driven that truck over my thighs. "Let's go," I say, trying to sound energetic as I fall in line behind Manuel, stumbling across rows of lettuce and thinking about "the five-day rule." The five-day rule, according to Manuel, is simple: Survive the first five days and you'll be fine. He's been a farmworker for almost two decades, so he should know. I'm on day three of five—the goal is within sight. Of course, another way to look at my situation is that I'm on day three of what I promised myself would be a two-month immersion in the work life of the people who do a job that most Americans won't do. But thinking about the next seven weeks doesn't benefit anyone. *Day three of five.*

3   "Manuel! Gabriel! Let's go! *¡Vámonos!*" yells Pedro, our foreman. Our short break is over. Two dozen crew members standing near the lettuce machine are already putting on gloves and sharpening knives. Manuel and I hustle toward the machine, grab our own knives from a box of chlorinated water, and set up in neighboring rows, just as the machine starts moving slowly down another endless field.

4   Since the early 1980s, Yuma, Ariz., has been the "winter lettuce capital" of America. Each winter, when the weather turns cold in Salinas, California—the heart of the nation's lettuce industry—temperatures in sunny Yuma are still in the 70s and 80s. At the height of Yuma's growing season, the fields surrounding the city produce virtually all of the iceberg lettuce and 90 percent of the leafy green vegetables consumed in the United States and Canada.

5   America's lettuce industry actually needs people like me. Before applying for fieldwork at the local Dole headquarters, I came across several articles describing the causes of a farmworker shortage. The stories cited an aging workforce, immigration crackdowns, and long delays at the border that discourage workers with green cards who would otherwise commute to the fields from their Mexican homes.[1] Wages have been rising somewhat in response to the demand for laborers (one prominent member of the local growers association tells me average pay is now between $10 and $12 an hour), but it's widely assumed that most U.S. citizens wouldn't do the work at any price. Arizona's own Senator John McCain created a stir in 2006 when he issued a challenge to a group of union members in Washington, D.C. "I'll offer anybody here $50 an hour if you'll go pick lettuce in Yuma this season, and pick for the whole season," he said. Amid jeers, he didn't back down, telling the audience, "You can't do it, my friends."

6   On my first day I discover that even putting on a lettuce cutter's uniform is challenging (no fieldworkers, I learn, "pick" lettuce). First, I'm handed a pair of black

---

[1] A green card is an immigration document that allows noncitizens to work legally in the United States, whether they live here or commute across the border. Undocumented workers (or illegal immigrants, depending on your position) lack green cards. [Editor's note]

Thompson   *A Gringo in the Lettuce Fields*   ▶ **GUIDE TO READING**
GUIDE TO WRITING
A WRITER AT WORK
THINKING CRITICALLY

85

Courtesy of Gabriel Thompson

galoshes to go over my shoes. Next comes the *gancho*, an S-shaped hook that slips over my belt to hold packets of plastic bags. A white glove goes on my right hand, a gray glove, supposedly designed to offer protection from cuts, goes on my left. Over the cloth gloves I pull on a pair of latex gloves. I put on a black hairnet, my baseball cap, and a pair of protective sunglasses. Adding to my belt a long leather sheath, I'm good to go. I feel ridiculous.

7   The crew is already working in the field when Pedro walks me out to them and introduces me to Manuel. Manuel is holding an 18-inch knife in his hand. "Manuel has been cutting for many years, so watch him to see how it's done," Pedro says. Then he walks away. Manuel resumes cutting, following a machine that rolls along just ahead of the crew. Every several seconds Manuel bends down, grabs a head of iceberg lettuce with his left hand, and makes a quick cut with the knife in his right hand, separating the lettuce from its roots. Next, he lifts the lettuce to his stomach and makes a second cut, trimming the trunk. He shakes the lettuce, letting the outer leaves fall to the ground. With the blade still in his hand, he then brings the lettuce toward the gancho at his waist, and with a flick of the wrist the head is bagged and dropped onto one of the machine's extensions. Manuel does this over and over again, explaining each movement. "It's not so hard," he says. Five minutes later, Pedro reappears and tells me to grab a knife. Manuel points to a head of lettuce. "Try this one," he says.

Pedro offers me a suggestion. "Act like the lettuce is a bomb. . . . Imagine you've only got five seconds to get rid of it."

8   I bend over, noticing that most of the crew has turned to watch. I take my knife and make a tentative sawing motion where I assume the trunk to be, though I'm really just guessing. Grabbing the head with my left hand, I straighten up, doing my best to imitate Manuel. Only my lettuce head doesn't move; it's still securely connected to the soil. Pedro steps in. "When you make the first cut, it is like you are stabbing the lettuce." He makes a quick jabbing action. "You want to aim for the center of the lettuce, where the trunk is," he says.

9   Ten minutes later, after a couple of other discouraging moments, I've cut maybe 20 heads of lettuce and am already feeling pretty accomplished. I'm not perfect: If I don't stoop far enough, my stab—instead of landing an inch above the ground—goes right through the head of lettuce, ruining it entirely. The greatest difficulty, though, is in the trimming. I had no idea that a head of lettuce was so humongous. In order to get it into a shape that can be bagged, I trim and trim and trim, but it's taking me upward of a minute to do what Manuel does in several seconds.

10   Pedro offers me a suggestion. "Act like the lettuce is a bomb," he says. "Imagine you've only got five seconds to get rid of it."

11   Surprisingly, that thought seems to work, and I'm able to greatly increase my speed. For a minute or two I feel euphoric. "Look at me!" I want to shout at Pedro; I'm in the zone. But the woman who is packing the lettuce into boxes soon swivels around to face me. "Look, this lettuce is no good." She's right: I've cut the trunk too high, breaking off dozens of good leaves, which will quickly turn brown because they're attached to nothing. With her left hand she holds the bag up, and with her right she smashes it violently, making a loud pop. She turns the bag over and the massacred lettuce falls to the ground. She does the same for the three other bags I've placed on the extension. "It's okay," Manuel tells me. "You shouldn't try to go too fast when you're beginning." Pedro seconds him. "That's right. Make sure the cuts are precise and that you don't rush."

12   So I am to be very careful and precise, while also treating the lettuce like a bomb that must be tossed aside after five seconds.

13   That first week on the job was one thing. By midway into week two, it isn't clear to me what more I can do to keep up with the rest of the crew. I know the techniques by this time and am moving as fast as my body will permit. Yet I need to somehow *double* my current output to hold my own. I'm able to cut only one row at a time while Manuel is cutting two. Our fastest cutter, Julio, meanwhile can handle three. But how someone could cut two rows for an hour—much less an entire day—is beyond me. "Oh, you will get it," Pedro tells me one day. "You will most definitely get it." Maybe he's trying to be hopeful or inspiring, but it comes across as a threat.

14   That feeling aside, what strikes me about our 31-member crew is how quickly they have welcomed me as one of their own. I encountered some suspicion at first, but it didn't last. Simply showing up on the second day seemed to be proof enough that I was there to work. When I faltered in the field and fell behind, hands would come across from adjacent rows to grab a head or two of my lettuce so I could catch up. People whose names I didn't yet know would ask me how I was holding up, reminding me that it would get easier as time went by. If I took a seat alone during a break, someone would call me into their group and offer a homemade taco or two.

15   Two months in, I make the mistake of calling in sick one Thursday. The day before, I put my left hand too low on a head of lettuce. When I punched my blade through the stem, the knife struck my middle finger. Thanks to the gloves, my skin wasn't even broken, but the finger instantly turned purple. I took two painkillers to get through the afternoon, but when I wake the next morning it is still throbbing. With one call to an answering machine that morning, and another the next day, I create my own four-day weekend.

16   The surprise is that when I return on Monday, feeling recuperated, I wind up having the hardest day of my brief career in lettuce. Within hours, my hands feel weaker than ever. By quitting time—some 10 hours after our day started—I feel like I'm going to vomit

from exhaustion. A theory forms in my mind. Early in the season—say, after the first week—a farmworker's body gets thoroughly broken down. Back, legs, and arms grow sore, hands and feet swell up. A tolerance for the pain is developed, though, and two-day weekends provide just enough time for the body to recover from the trauma. My four-day break had been too long; my body actually began to recuperate, and it wanted more time to continue. Instead, it was thrown right back into the mix and rebelled. Only on my second day back did my body recover that middle ground. "I don't think the soreness goes away," I say to Manuel and two other co-workers one day. "You just forget what it's like not to be sore." Manuel, who's 37, considers this. "That's true, that's true," he says. "It always takes a few weeks at the end of the year to get back to normal, to recover."

17   An older co-worker, Mateo, is the one who eventually guesses that I have joined the crew because I want to write about it. "That is good," he says over coffee at his home one Sunday. "Americans should know the hard work that Mexicans do in this country."

18   Mateo is an unusual case. There aren't many other farmworkers who are still in the fields when they reach their 50s. It's simply not possible to do this work for decades and not suffer a permanently hunched back, or crooked fingers, or hands so swollen that they look as if someone has attached a valve to a finger and pumped vigorously. The punishing nature of the work helps explain why farmworkers don't live very long; the National Migrant Resources Program puts their life expectancy at 49 years.

19   "Are you cutting two rows yet?" Mateo asks me. "Yes, more or less," I say. "I thought I'd be better by now." Mateo shakes his head. "It takes a long time to learn how to really cut lettuce. It's not something that you learn after only one season. Three, maybe four seasons—then you start understanding how to really work with lettuce."

[REFLECT]   # Make connections: Switching perspectives.

Thompson temporarily joined a community of lettuce cutters to get an insider's perspective on their work. Think about your own experience as a member of a group that was visited and observed, even for a short period of time. Perhaps an administrator visited one of your classes or a potential coach or recruit observed your team. Consider what it was like being studied by a stranger. Your instructor may ask you to post your thoughts about the experience on a discussion board or to discuss them with other students in class. Use these questions to get started:

- As an insider, how did you and the other group members feel about being the subject of someone else's gaze?

- What were you told about why your group was being visited and what assumptions or concerns did you have about the visitor? Were you concerned about the visitor's motives—for example, wondering if the person was really there to evaluate the group or its members?

- Suppose Thompson wanted to write a piece of immersion journalism about a community (such as a religious group, sports team, fraternity, or sorority) of which you are a member. What elements of Thompson's profile, if any, would cause you to trust or distrust his reporting? What ethical challenges might immersion journalists like Thompson face by going undercover?

Use the basic features.

[ANALYZE]

SPECIFIC INFORMATION ABOUT THE SUBJECT: USING QUOTATION, PARAPHRASE, AND SUMMARY

Profile writers—like all writers—depend on the three basic strategies for presenting source material: quoting, paraphrasing, and summarizing. Each strategy has advantages and disadvantages. It's obvious why Cable chose this quotation: "We're in *Ripley's Believe It or Not*, along with another funeral home whose owners' names are Baggit and Sackit" (par. 14). But making decisions about what to quote and what to paraphrase or summarize is not always that easy.

ANALYZE & WRITE

Write a few paragraphs analyzing Thompson's decisions about how to present information from different sources:

1. Skim the essay to find at least one example of a quotation and one paraphrase or summary of information gleaned from an interview or from background research.

2. Why do you think Thompson chooses to quote certain things and paraphrase or summarize other things? What could be a good rule of thumb for you to apply when deciding whether to quote, paraphrase, or summarize? (Note that when writing for an academic audience, in a paper for a class or in a scholarly publication, all source material — whether it is quoted, paraphrased, or summarized — should be cited.)

To learn more about quotation, paraphrase, and summary, see Chapter 23,

A CLEAR, LOGICAL ORGANIZATION: NARRATING AN EXTENDED PERIOD

Some profile writers do field research, observing and interviewing over an extended period of time. As an immersive journalist, Thompson spent more than two months as a member of one crew. To give readers a sense of the chronology of events, he uses time cues (such as calendar and clock time, transitions like *next*, and prepositional phrases such as *on my first day*). These cues are especially useful because Thompson's narrative does not always follow a straightforward chronology. He also describes the process of cutting lettuce in detail.

For more about time markers, see pp. 62–63 and Chapter 14; for more about process narration, see Chapter 14.

ANALYZE & WRITE

Write a paragraph analyzing Thompson's use of time cues and process narration:

1. Skim the profile, highlighting the time cues. Why do you imagine Thompson decided not to follow a linear chronology? How well does he use time cues to keep readers from becoming confused?

2. Why do you think Thompson devotes so much space (pars. 6–12) to narrating the process of cutting lettuce? What does this detailed narrative offer to readers?

THE WRITER'S ROLE: GOING UNDERCOVER

Like Coyne, Thompson acts as a participant-observer. But unlike Coyne, his role is covert. He does not watch lettuce cutters from the sidelines or announce himself as a journalist but instead works among them for two months. His informal interviews take place during work and on breaks (even at the homes of his coworkers over the weekend). Nevertheless, there is a significant difference between a two-month experiment and a personal account written by a lettuce cutter like Mateo after a lifetime on the job. A profile writer may participate but is always an outsider looking in.

ANALYZE & WRITE

Write a paragraph or two analyzing Thompson's use of the participant-observer role:

1. Skim the text, noting at least one place where Thompson
   - reminds readers of his status as an outsider (for example, when he refers to a coworker as a "near-stranger" [par. 1]);
   - tells readers about something he thinks will be unfamiliar to them (for example, when he explains that people do not "'pick' lettuce" [par. 6]);
   - calls attention to his own incompetence or failings (for example, when he describes his first attempt to cut lettuce [par. 8]).

2. Why do you think Thompson tells us about his errors and reminds us that he is an outsider? What effect are these moves likely to have on his audience?

3. How do the writers whose profiles appear in this chapter use their outsider status to connect with readers?

A PERSPECTIVE ON THE SUBJECT: PROFILING A CONTROVERSIAL ISSUE

Two other profiles in this chapter also touch on a controversial subject about which people have strong opinions. Cable addresses the commercialization of death, and Coyne, the unfairness of the legal system. Although profiles do not usually make an explicit argument the way essays arguing a position do, they convey the writer's perspective on the issue and try to influence readers' thinking about it.

ANALYZE & WRITE

Write a few paragraphs analyzing Thompson's perspective:

1. Skim the profile looking for a passage or two where you get a clear understanding of the issue and what Thompson thinks about it.

2. Consider also what you learn about the issue and Thompson's perspective on it from the title of the profile, "A Gringo in the Lettuce Fields," and the title of the book from which it is excerpted, *Working in the Shadows: A Year of Doing the Jobs (Most) Americans Won't Do.*

3. If Thompson were to make an explicit argument supporting his view of this issue, how do you think his argument would likely differ from this profile? How effectively does Thompson use the genre of the investigative profile to achieve his purpose? How well suited do you think the profile genre is for arguing a position on a controversial issue, as well as informing readers about it?

Consider possible topics: Immersing yourself.

RESPOND

Thompson's experience suggests two possible avenues for research: You could embed yourself in a group, participating alongside group members, and then write about that experience. For example, you might join a club on campus or try an unusual sport. Alternatively, you could observe life in an unfamiliar group, watching how a meeting or event unfolds, interviewing members to learn about their practices, and conducting additional research to learn about the group.

REMIX

Remixing Your Profile

Profiles occur regularly in genres and media besides the college essay. For example, Brian Cable's profile could have been included in a report about greening the mortuary business, or he could have included photos from his visit in a blog post. After writing his essay, Cable decided to remix it as a documentary for a community cable station, so he began by writing a treatment. (A remix takes all or part of a piece in one genre or medium to create a text in another genre or medium.) Cable chose to make a documentary because he thought community members might be interested in an insider's view of a local mortuary, and he knew that video would give interested viewers a strong visual sense of being at the Goodbody Mortuary.

In the next section of this chapter, we ask you to craft your own profile. After composing it as an essay, consider remixing it by presenting it (or a portion of it) in another genre or medium, or using it as part of an essay with a different purpose or audience.

Treatment for *"Come In. We're Always Open.": The Goodbody Mortuary*

Overview
From the cost of a top-of-the-line coffin to the process of embalming and preparing the corpse for viewing, this short (15-minute) documentary will bring viewers behind the scenes at the Goodbody Mortuary, where they will get an insider's view of the death business.

Film Outline

- **Introduction:** A detached observer (or spectator) point of view will convey a "you are there" feeling, as viewers first observe the outside of the funeral home and then walk inside. The mood is wary as will be suggested by the music. The music will fade out as Howard Deaver, the funeral director, greets us.

- **Body:** Deaver will guide us past rose-pink sofas and quasi-religious visitation rooms to his office, with its bone-clean desk, where he will list the services the Goodbody Mortuary provides, from removing the body to preparing the body for viewing, embalming the corpse, placing it in the casket, and moving the casket to a visitation room. Before moving off, the camera will linger on the "Visa and MasterCard Welcome Here" sign on Deaver's desk.

  Deaver will then escort us to the sample room, where a number of casket options are on display. The camera will pan over the array, lingering over the most expensive model—the Promethean—as Deaver describes the costs and luxury features.

  Deaver will lead us downstairs to the preparation area, a white-tiled basement that looks like an operating room, where we will meet Tim, Goodbody's mortician. Tim will tell us about his work, the chemicals used in embalming, and the cosmetic work he does to achieve a resting expression. A body will appear in the background, but we will blur the features of the corpse, so that the privacy of the deceased's family members will be protected.

- **Resolution:** The film will end with an escape to the sunny day outside the gloomy funeral home. An upbeat tune will play and the viewer will get the sense of escape from a dark, confining, slightly oppressive space.

CONSIDER YOUR RHETORICAL SITUATION

Purpose: The purpose of your profile is to inform readers by giving them new insight into your subject or present it from an intriguing slant or angle. If you remix your profile, *which genre or medium would best allow you to convey a compelling portrait of your subject?*

Audience: The original audience for your profile was your instructor and, perhaps, other students in your class. *Who would be the audience if you were to remix your essay in another genre or medium? What advantages would that genre or medium have in helping you grab and keep the attention of your audience?*

Genre and medium: The genre of your assignment was a profile, and the medium was text, delivered either in print or digitally. If you remix your profile, *what genre or medium would best help you achieve your purpose and reach your intended audience?*

The Writing Assignment

Profile an intriguing person, group, place, or activity in your community. Observe your subject closely, and then present what you have learned in a way that both informs and engages readers.

This Guide to Writing is designed to help you compose your own profile and apply what you have learned from reading other profiles. This Starting Points chart will help you find the guidance you need, when you need it.

STARTING POINTS: WRITING A PROFILE

Specific Information about the Subject

How do I come up with an appropriate subject to profile?

- Consider possible topics. (pp. 76–77, 83, 89)
- Choose a subject to profile. (p. 93)
- Test Your Choice: Considering Your Purpose and Audience (pp. 93–94)

How can I gather information on my subject?

- Conduct your field research. (pp. 94–98)
- Chapter 21, Finding Sources and Conducting Field Research

How can I make my subject come to life?

- Assess the genre's basic features: Specific information about the subject. (p. 62)
- Specific Information about the Subject: Describing People through Naming, Detailing, and Comparing (p. 74)
- Specific Information about the Subject: Using Anecdotes (p. 81)
- Specific Information about the Subject: Using Quotation, Paraphrase, and Summary (p. 87)
- Use quotations that provide information and reveal character. (p. 99)
- Consider adding visual or audio elements. (pp. 99–100)
- A Troubleshooting Guide: Specific Information about the Subject (pp. 107–8)

A Clear, Logical Organization

How should I organize my profile?

- Assess the genre's basic features: A clear, logical organization. (pp. 62–64)
- A Clear, Logical Organization: Using Flashbacks (p. 75)
- A Clear, Logical Organization: Narrating a Day in the Life (p. 81)
- A Clear, Logical Organization: Narrating an Extended Period (pp. 87–88)
- Create an outline that will organize your profile effectively for your readers. (p. 100)
- A Troubleshooting Guide: A Clear, Logical Organization (pp. 108–9)

The Writer's Role

What role should I adopt in researching and presenting my subject?

- Assess the genre's basic features: The writer's role. (p. 64)
- The Writer's Role: Acting as a Spectator (pp. 75–76)
- The Writer's Role: Acting as a Participant-Observer (p. 82)
- The Writer's Role: Going Undercover (p. 88)
- Determine your role in the profile. (pp. 100–102)
- A Troubleshooting Guide: The Writer's Role (p. 109)

A Perspective on the Subject

How do I develop and express a clear perspective on the subject?

- Determine the writer's purpose and audience. (p. 61)
- Assess the genre's basic features: A perspective on the subject. (p. 64)
- A Perspective on the Subject: Showing and Telling (p. 76)
- A Perspective on the Subject: Using Contrast (pp. 82–83)
- A Perspective on the Subject: Profiling a Controversial Issue (pp. 88–89)
- Develop your perspective on the subject. (pp. 102–3)
- Clarify the dominant impression. (pp. 103–4)
- A Troubleshooting Guide: A Perspective on the Subject (pp. 109–10)

Writing a Draft: Invention, Research, Planning, and Composing

The activities in this section will help you choose a subject to profile and develop your perspective on the subject. Do the activities in any order that makes sense to you (and your instructor), and return to them as needed as you revise.

Although some of the activities will take only a few minutes each to complete, the essential field research—making detailed observations and conducting interviews—will take a good deal of time to plan and carry out. Your writing in response to many of these activities can be used in a rough draft, which you will be able to improve after receiving feedback from your classmates and instructor.

Choose a subject to profile.

To create an informative and engaging profile, your subject—whether it's a person, a group of people, a place, or an activity—should be

- a subject that sparks your interest or curiosity;
- a subject your readers will find interesting and informative;
- a subject you can gain access to and observe in detail in the time allowed;
- a subject about which (or with whom) you can conduct in-depth interviews.

Note: Whenever you write a profile, consider carefully the ethics involved in such research: You will want to be careful to treat participants fairly and with respect in the way you both approach and depict them. Discuss the ethical implications of your research with your instructor, and think carefully about the goals of your research and the effect it will have on others. You may also need to obtain permission from your school's ethics review board.

Make a list of appropriate subjects. Review the "Consider possible topics" on pp. 76–77, 83, 89 and consult your school's Web site to find intriguing places, activities, or people on campus. The following ideas may suggest additional possibilities to consider:

- A place where people come together because they are of the same age, gender, sexual orientation, or ethnic group (for example, a foreign language–speaking dorm or fraternity or sorority), or a place where people of different ages, genders, sexual orientations, or ethnic groups have formed a community (for example, a Sunday morning pickup basketball game in the park, LGBT club, or barbershop)
- A place where people are trained for a certain kind of work (for example, a police academy, cosmetology program, truck driving school, or boxing ring)
- A group of people working together for a particular purpose (for example, students and their teacher preparing for the academic decathlon, employees working together to produce something, law students and their professor working to help prisoners on death row, or scientists collaborating on a research project)

| TEST YOUR CHOICE |

Considering Your Purpose and Audience
After you have made a tentative choice, ask yourself the following questions:

1 Do I feel curious about the subject?

2 Am I confident that I will be able to make the subject interesting for my readers?

3 Do I believe that I can research this subject sufficiently in the time I have?

Then get together with two or three other students:

Presenters.   Take turns identifying your subjects. Explain your interest in the subject, and speculate about why you think it will interest readers.

Listeners.   Briefly tell each presenter what you already know about his or her subject, if anything, and what might make it interesting to readers.

Conduct your field research.

To learn more about conducting observations and interviews, see Chapter 21.

To write an effective profile, conduct **field research**—*interviews and observations—to collect detailed, firsthand information about your subject.* Many writers begin with observations to get the lay of the land and identify people to interview, but you can start with interviews. You may even be able to make observations and conduct interviews during the same visit. If you are thinking of adopting the role of participant-observer, turn first to "Determine your role in the profile" (pp. 100–102), and consider whether you need to request permission before conducting your research. Before your interview or observation, draft preliminary questions; when you appear for your interview or observation, dress appropriately, and bring equipment for taking notes, recording, or filming. (Be sure to ask permission before recording or filming.) The following activities will help you plan and carry out your field research.

WAYS IN

HOW CAN I MANAGE MY TIME?

Try this **BACKWARD PLANNING** *strategy:*

1. Construct a calendar marking the date the project is due and any other intermediate due dates (such as the date the first draft, thesis, or topic is due).

2. Work backward, adding dates by which key stages or milestones should be reached to make your due dates. For example, mark the following:

   ■ The date by which final revisions to text and images are needed

   ■ The date on which peer review is scheduled

   ■ The date by which the first draft should be completed

   ■ The date by which initial interviews and observations should be conducted (Leave at least a week for this process.)

   ■ The date by which interviews and observations must be scheduled (Leave at least several days for this process.)

A SAMPLE SCHEDULE

Sunday	Monday	Tuesday	Wednesday	Thursday	Friday	Saturday
	1 Arrange interviews & observations	2	3	4	5 Research interview subject, locations	6
7	8 Conduct interviews & observations	9	10	11	12	13
14	15	16 Write-ups completed	17	18	19 First draft due	20 Conduct any extra research
21	22 Call/E-mail with follow-up questions	23 Revise draft	24	25	26 Revised draft due	27
28	29	30	31			

HOW DO I SET UP AND PREPARE FOR INTERVIEWS AND OBSERVATIONS?

WAYS IN

1. *List the people you would like to interview or places you would like to observe.* Include a number of possibilities in case your first choice doesn't work out.

2. *Write out your intentions and goals so you can explain them clearly to others.*

(continued)

3. *Call or e-mail for an appointment with your interview subject, or make arrangements to visit the site.* Explain who you are and what you are doing. Student research projects are often embraced, but be prepared for your request to be rejected.

   Note: Be sure to arrange your interview or site visit as soon as possible. The most common error students report making on this assignment is waiting too long to make that first call. Be aware, too, that the people and places you contact may not respond immediately (or at all); be sure to follow up if you have not gotten an answer to your request within a few days.

4. *Make notes about what you expect to learn before you write interview questions, interview your subject, or visit your site.* Ask yourself questions like these:

Interview

- How would I define or describe the subject?

- What is the subject's purpose or function?

- Who or what is associated with it?

- What about it will interest me and my readers?

- What do I hope to learn about it?

Observation

- How would I define or describe my subject?

- What typically takes place at this location? Who or what will I likely observe?

- What will interest me and my readers?

- What do I expect to learn about my subject?

- How will my presence affect those I am observing?

5. *Write some interview questions in advance, or ask yourself some observation questions to help you determine how best to conduct your site visit.*

Interview

Ask for stories:

▶ Tell me how you got into _____ .

▶ Tell me about something that surprised/pleased/frustrated you.

Let subjects correct misconceptions:

▶ What myths about _____ would you most like to bust?

Ask about the subject's past and future:

▶ How has _____ changed over the years, and where do you think it's going?

Observation

Consider your PERSPECTIVE:

- Should I observe from different vantage points or from the same location?

- Should I visit the location at different times of day or days of the week, or would it be better to visit at the same time every day?

- Should I focus on specific people, or should I identify roles and focus on people as they adopt those roles?

6. *Conduct some preliminary research on your subject or related subjects if possible, and revise your questions or plans accordingly.*

HOW DO I CONDUCT INTERVIEWS?

Take notes:

- Clearly distinguish QUOTATIONS from PARAPHRASES or SUMMARIES by inserting quotation marks where needed.

- Record the interview, if allowed, but also take notes. Politely ask interviewees to speak slowly, repeat themselves, or confirm your quotations if necessary. (Interviewees often fear being misquoted and will usually appreciate your being careful.)

- In addition to writing down what your subject says, use NAMING, DETAILING, and COMPARING to capture the interviewee's tone, gestures, and mannerisms.

- To generate ANECDOTES, ask how the interviewee first got involved with the place or activity; if there was a key event worth noting; what most concerns the interviewee; what has been the biggest influence on his or her experience, for good or ill.

- To elicit PROCESS NARRATIVES, ask how something works; what happens if it breaks; whether it has always been done the same way; how it has changed; how it could be improved.

- To CLASSIFY, COMPARE, or CONTRAST, ask what kind of thing it is; how it's like and unlike others of its kind; how it compares to what it was like in the past.

- To help you with your PERSPECTIVE, ask why the subject is important, how it contributes to the community, or how it could be improved. Ask who would disagree with these perspectives.

- Finally, ask for the interviewee's preferences (e-mail or phone) for handling your follow-up questions, if any.

HOW DO I CONDUCT OBSERVATIONS?

Take notes:

- Note your surroundings, using all of your senses: sight, hearing, smell, taste, touch.

- Describe the place from multiple vantage points, noting furnishings, decor, and so on, and sketch the layout.

- Describe people's appearance, dress, gestures, and actions.

- Make a record of interesting overheard conversation.

- Note your reactions and ideas, especially in relation to your preconceptions. What surprises you?

- If you can get permission, observe how people interact with one another.

Consider your ROLE:

- If you are new to the subject and would like to have a PARTICIPANT-OBSERVER role, ask permission to take part in a small way for a limited time.

- If you are an insider, adopt the position of a SPECTATOR-OBSERVER to help you find a new angle and learn something new. (For example, if you're on the football team, focus on the cheerleaders or the people who maintain the field.)

Collect artifacts, or take videos or photos:

- Collect any brochures or other written material you might be able to use, either to prepare for interviews or to include in your essay.

- Consider taking photographs or videos, if allowed. Try a pan shot scanning the scene from side to side or a tracking shot indicating what you see as you enter or tour the place.

(continued)

Reflect on the interview. Review your notes right after the interview, adding any impressions and marking promising material, such as

- anything that calls into question your or your readers' likely preconceptions;
- details that could paint a vivid portrait of the person;
- quotable phrases that could help you capture the tone or mood of the subject;
- questions you still need answered.

Write up your interview. Write a few paragraphs reporting what you learned from the interview:

- Choose notable quotes and summarize or paraphrase other bits of information.
- Try to add speaker tags to describe the person's tone of voice, gestures, and appearance while speaking.
- Consider whether something important was left unsaid or was misrepresented — and, if so, how that might extend or complicate your understanding of the subject.

Do follow-up interviews or interview another person:

- Follow up to check facts or get clarification, but be careful not to waste your interviewee's time.
- Arrange to talk to another person who has different kinds of information to share.

Reflect on your observations. Take five minutes right after your visit to think about what you observed, and write a few sentences about your impressions of the subject:

- ▶ The most interesting aspect of the subject is _____ because _____ .
- ▶ Although my visit confirmed that _____ , I was surprised to learn that _____ .
- ▶ My dominant impression of the subject is _____ .

Write up your observations:

- Write a few paragraphs reporting what you observed during your visit.
- Include as many sensory details as you can.
- Think of comparisons that might capture what's special or intriguing about the subject.
- Consider the dominant impression you want to make and what impression your word choices actually make. Explore contradictions between your intentions and your words to develop a more nuanced description.

Consider whether you need a follow-up observation:

- Consider a follow-up visit to observe from a new angle.
- Consider a follow-up observation to visit the site at another time.

WAYS IN

HOW SHOULD I PRESENT THE INFORMATION I'VE GLEANED FROM INTERVIEWS AND OBSERVATIONS?

Review the notes from your interviews and observations, selecting the information to include in your draft and how you might present it. Consider including the following:

- **DEFINITIONS** of key terms readers will find unfamiliar;
- **COMPARISONS** or **CONTRASTS** that make information clearer or more memorable;
- **LISTS** or **CATEGORIES** that organize information logically;
- **PROCESSES** that readers will find interesting or surprising.

⠿ Use quotations that provide information and reveal character.

Good profiles quote sources so readers can hear what people have to say in their own voices. The most useful quotations are those that reveal the style and character of the people you interviewed. **Speaker tags** (like *she said*, *he asked*) help readers determine the source of a quotation. You may rely on an all-purpose verb or a more descriptive verb to help readers imagine speakers' attitudes and personal styles:

> "Try this one," he says. (Thompson, par. 7)

> "Take me out to the"—and Toby yells out, "Banana store!" (Coyne, par. 21)

Adding a word or phrase to a speaker tag can reveal something relevant about the speaker's manner or provide context:

> "We're in *Ripley's Believe It or Not,* along with another funeral home whose owners' names are Baggit and Sackit," Howard told me, without cracking a smile. (Cable, par. 14)

> Once, after being given this weak explanation, he said, "I wish I could have done something really bad, like my Mommy. So I could go to prison too and be with her." (Coyne, par. 18)

> "Describe how you're feeling with twenty corned-beef sandwiches inside you," I ask. "I'm used to it," he says. "But . . . pain . . ." He's speaking in fractured sentences, with great difficulty. (Ronson, par. 11)

In addition to being carefully introduced, quotations must be precisely punctuated. Fortunately, there are only two general rules:

1. Enclose all quotations in a pair of quotation marks, one at the beginning and one at the end of the quotation.

2. Separate the quotation from its speaker tag with appropriate punctuation, usually a comma. (Commas and periods usually go inside the closing quotation mark, but question marks go inside or outside, depending on whether the question is the speaker's or the writer's.) If you have more than one sentence (as in the last example above), be careful to punctuate the separate sentences properly.

For more about integrating quotations, see Chapter 23.

⠿ Consider adding visual or audio elements.

Think about whether visual or audio elements—photographs; postcards; menus; or snippets from films, television programs, or songs—would strengthen your profile. If you can recall profiles you've seen in magazines, on Web pages, or on television shows, what visual or audio elements were used to create a strong sense of the subject? Profiles don't require such elements to be effective, but they can be helpful.

Note: Be sure to cite the source of visual or audio elements you didn't create, and get permission from the source if your profile is going to be published on a Web site that is not password protected.

⸬ Create an outline that will organize your profile effectively for your readers.

For more on clustering and outlining, see Chapter 11.

Here are two sample outlines you can modify to fit your needs, depending on whether you prefer a **narrative** plan (to give a tour of a place, for example) or a **topical** plan (to cluster related information). Even if you wish to blend features of both outlines, seeing how each basic plan works can help you combine them. Remember that each section need not be the same length; some sections may require greater detail than others.

Narrative Plan	Topical Plan
I. **Begin by describing the place from the outside.**	I. **Begin with a vivid image of the person in action.**
II. **Present background information.**	II. **Present the first topic** (for example, a trait of the person or of his or her work). Use dialogue, description, narration, process description, evaluation, or interpretation to illustrate this topic. (Presentation of each topic may require several paragraphs.)
III. **Describe what you see as you enter.**	
IV. **Introduce the people and their activities.** (This may require several paragraphs.)	
V. **Tour the place.** Describe what you see as you move from one space to the next. Integrate information wherever you can, and comment about the place or the people as you go. (This may require several paragraphs.)	III. **Present the second topic** (and continue as above until you have presented all topics).
VI. **Conclude with reflections on what you have learned about the place.**	IV. **Conclude with a bit of action or dialogue.**

The tentative plan you choose should reflect the possibilities in your material as well as your purpose and your understanding of your audience. When using a narrative plan, use verb tenses and transitions of space and time to make the succession of events clear; when using a topical plan, use logical transitions to help readers move from topic to topic. As you draft, you will almost certainly discover new ways of organizing parts of your material.

⸬ Determine your role in the profile.

Consider the advantages and disadvantages of the spectator and participant-observer roles, noting the examples and sentence strategies illustrating them. Then choose the role that best allows you to achieve your purpose with your readers.

Writing a Draft

GUIDE TO READING
▶ **GUIDE TO WRITING**
A WRITER AT WORK
THINKING CRITICALLY

101

WHICH ROLE WILL BEST HELP ME CONVEY THE EXPERIENCE OF MY PROFILE SUBJECT?

Choose the SPECTATOR ROLE *to:*

- provide readers with a detailed description or guided tour of the scene.

    ▶ X was dressed in .... with .... and ...., doing ....
       as s/he ....-ed.

    ▶ Inside, you could see .... The room was .... and ....

    EXAMPLE   The door was massive, yet it swung open easily on well-oiled hinges.
    "Come in," said the sign. "We're always open." Inside was a cool and
    quiet reception room. Curtains were drawn against the outside glare,
    cutting the light down to a soft glow. (Cable, par. 4)

- create an aura of objectivity, making it appear as though you're just reporting
  what you see and hear without revealing that you have actually made choices
  about what to include in order to create a DOMINANT IMPRESSION.

    ▶ The shiny new/rusty old tools were laid out neatly/piled helter skelter on the
       workbench, like ....

    EXAMPLE   The juice drips down their arms, saturating their shirts. Their puffed-out
    cheeks are beetroot red. They resemble sweaty, meat-smeared squirrels. . . .
    the whole thing looks like an unimaginable crime scene. (Ronson, par. 9)

Caution: *The* SPECTATOR ROLE *may cause readers to:*

- feel detached, which can lead to a lack of interest in the subject profiled;
- suspect a hidden bias behind the appearance of objectivity, undermining the
  writer's credibility.

Choose the PARTICIPANT-OBSERVER *role to:*

- profile physical activities through the eyes of a novice, so readers can imagine
  doing the activity themselves.

    ▶ I picked up the .... It felt like .... and smelled/tasted/sounded like
       ....

    EXAMPLE   The greatest difficulty, though, is in the trimming. I had no idea that a
    head of lettuce was so humongous. In order to get it into a shape that
    can be bagged, I trim and trim and trim. . . . (Thompson, par. 9)

- reveal how others react to you.

    ▶ X interrupted me as I ....-ed.

    ▶ As I struggled with ...., Y noticed and ....-ed.

    EXAMPLE   People whose names I didn't yet know would ask me how I was holding
    up, reminding me that it would get easier as time went by. (Thompson,
    par. 14)

Caution: The PARTICIPANT-OBSERVER role may cause readers to:

- wonder whether your experience was unique to you, not something they would have experienced;
- think the person, place, group, or activity being profiled seemed secondary in relation to the writer's experience.

⠿ Develop your perspective on the subject.

Try some of these activities to deepen your analysis and enhance your readers' understanding of your subject's cultural significance.

WAYS IN

HOW CAN I DEVELOP A PERSPECTIVE FOR MY PROFILE?

Explore the CULTURAL SIGNIFICANCE *of your subject:*

If you are focusing on a **place** (like a mortuary or prison visiting room), consider what intrigues you about its culture by asking yourself questions like these:

- Who are the insiders at this place and why are they there?
- How does the place affect how insiders talk, act, think, feel?
- What function does the place serve in the wider community?
- What tensions are there between insiders and outsiders or between newcomers and veterans?

▶ X and Y say _____ and _____ because they want to _____ , but they seem to feel _____ because of the way they do _____ .

EXAMPLE   And I can imagine the hours spent preparing for this visit. . . . The hours of discussing, dissecting, and bragging about these visitors — especially the men. . . . and the giggles that abruptly change into tears without warning — things that define any female-only world. Even, or especially, if that world is a female federal prison camp. (Coyne, par. 4)

If you are focusing on an **activity** (like eating competitively or cutting lettuce), ask yourself questions like these:

- Who benefits from it?
- What value does it have for the insider community and for the wider community?
- How has the activity or process changed over time, for good or ill?
- How are outsiders initiated into the activity?

▶ It's important to recognize _____ because _____ .

▶ _____ [date or event] marked a turning point because _____ .

EXAMPLE   July 4, 2001 — the most extraordinary day in the history of competitive eating. Watching the news footage filmed that day, during the minutes before everything changed forever, I was struck by how lackadaisical things seemed. (Ronson, par. 12)

If you are focusing on a **person** or **group of people**, ask yourself questions like these:

- What sense of identity do they have?
- What customs and ways of communicating do they have?
- What are their values and attitudes?
- What are their social hierarchies and what do they think about them?
- How do they see their role in the community?

▶ X values/believes _____ , as you can see from the way s/he _____ .

▶ Members of group X are more likely to _____ than people in the general population because _____ .

EXAMPLES   He said that he felt people were becoming more aware of the public service his profession provides. (Cable, par. 27)

He's settled on an exact combination of specific brands of olive and fish oils, but he won't divulge more. "I had to figure it out," he said, "so why should I let it be known?" (Ronson, par. 8)

Define your PURPOSE *and* AUDIENCE. Write for five minutes exploring what you want your readers to learn about the subject and why. Use sentence strategies like these to help clarify your thinking:

▶ In addition to my teacher and classmates, I envision my ideal readers as _____ .

▶ They probably know _____ about my subject and believe _____ .

▶ They would be most surprised to learn _____ and most interested in _____ .

▶ I can help change their opinions of X by _____ and get them to think about X's social and cultural significance by _____ .

State your main point. Review what you have written, and summarize in a sentence or two the main idea you want readers to take away from your profile. Readers don't expect a profile to have an explicit thesis statement, but the descriptive details and other information need to work together to convey the main idea.

▪▪ Clarify the dominant impression.

The descriptive details, comparisons, and word choices you use and the information you supply should reinforce the dominant impression you are trying to create. For example, the dominant impression of Cable's profile is his—and our—anxiety about death, beginning with his apprehension upon entering the mortuary and ending with his daring to touch a dead body. But, as Cable shows, the dominant impression need not be simplistic. Readers appreciate profiles that reveal the richness and complexity of the subject, as Cable does by describing the Goodbody Mortuary looking "a bit like a church—tall, with gothic arches and stained glass "and" somewhat like an apartment complex" (par. 2). Although he makes fun of the crass commercialism of Howard's side of the business, Cable lets Tim make the joke instead of being the joke: becoming a mortician "'was a profession I could live with,' he told me with a sly grin" (par. 25).

WAYS IN

HOW DO I FINE-TUNE MY DOMINANT IMPRESSION?

Identify your intended DOMINANT IMPRESSION. Write for five minutes sketching out the overall impression you want readers to take away from your profile. What do you want readers to think and feel about your subject?

Reread your notes and write-ups, looking for words and phrases that help convey your overall impression. In Brian Cable's profile, phrases like "His desk was bone clean" (par. 7) help reinforce the sense of death Cable associated with the funeral director. A later sentence—"His tone was that of a broker conferring on the Dow Jones" (par. 9)— complicates his initial assessment and helps create the overall impression of the funeral home and its employees as in the business of death.

If your initial dominant impression seems too simplistic, look for any contradictions or gaps in your notes and write-ups that you can use to develop the subject's complexity. You might start with one of the following sentence strategies and elaborate from there:

▶ Although X clearly seemed ⎯⎯⎯⎯⎯, I couldn't shake the feeling that ⎯⎯⎯⎯⎯ .

▶ Although Y tries to/pretends to ⎯⎯⎯⎯⎯ , overall/primarily he/she/it ⎯⎯⎯⎯⎯ .

Write the opening sentences.

Review your invention writing to see if you have already written something that would work to launch your essay or try some of these opening strategies:

Begin with an **arresting scene:**

> You can spot the convict-moms here in the visiting room by the way they hold and touch their children and by the single flower that is perched in front of them—a rose, a tulip, a daffodil. (Coyne, par. 1)

Offer a **remarkable thought** *or* **occasion** *that triggered your observational visit:*

> Death is a subject largely ignored by the living. (Cable, par. 1)

Start with a **vivid description:**

> Here is a mountain of corned-beef sandwiches, each crammed with meat. (Ronson, par. 1)

Evaluating the Draft
GUIDE TO READING
GUIDE TO WRITING
A WRITER AT WORK
THINKING CRITICALLY
105

But don't agonize over the first sentences because you are likely to discover the best way to begin only as you draft your essay.

Draft your profile.

By this point, you have done a lot of research and writing

- to develop something interesting to say about a subject;
- to devise a plan for presenting that information;
- to identify a role for yourself in the essay;
- to explore your perspective on the subject.

Now stitch that material together to create a draft. The next two parts of this Guide to Writing will help you evaluate and improve your draft.

Evaluating the Draft: Using Peer Review

Your instructor may arrange a peer review session in class or online, where you can exchange drafts with your classmates and give one another a thoughtful critical reading, pointing out what works well and suggesting ways to improve the draft. A good critical reading does three things:

1. It lets the writer know how well the reader understands the cultural significance of the subject.
2. It praises what works best.
3. It indicates where the draft could be improved and makes suggestions on how to improve it.

One strategy for evaluating a draft is to use the basic features of profiles as a guide.

| PEER REVIEW GUIDE |

Specific Information about the Subject

Does the writer portray the subject in enough well-chosen detail to show us why it's interesting?

Summarize: Tell the writer one thing you learned about the subject from reading the essay.

Praise: Point out one passage where the description seems especially vivid, a quotation stands out, or another writing strategy works particularly well to present information.

Critique: Point out one passage where description could be added or where the description could be made more vivid, where a quotation that falls flat should be paraphrased or summarized, or where another writing strategy could be used.

(continued)

A Clear, Logical Organization

Is the profile easy to follow?

Summarize: Identify the kind of organization — narrative, topical, or a blend of the two — that the writer uses.

Praise: Comment on the cues the writer gives that make the profile easy to follow. For example, point to a place where one topic leads logically to the next or where transitions help you follow the tour or narrative. Also, indicate what in the opening paragraphs grabs your attention or why you think the ending works well.

Critique: Point to information that seems out of place or instances where the chronology is confusing. If you think the opening or ending could be improved, suggest an alternative passage in the essay that could work as an opening or an ending.

The Writer's Role

Is the author's role clear, whether it is spectator, participant-observer, or both?

Summarize: Identify the role the writer adopts.

Praise: Point to a passage where the spectator or participant-observer role enables you to identify with the writer, enhancing the essay's immediacy or interest.

Critique: Point out any problems with the role — for example, if the participant-observer role becomes distracting or if the spectator role seems too distant.

A Perspective on the Subject

Does the author have a clear point of view on the subject?

Summarize: State briefly what you believe to be the writer's perspective on the subject and the dominant impression you get from the essay.

Praise: Give an example where you have a strong sense of the writer's perspective through a comment, description, quotation, or bit of information.

Critique: Tell the writer if the essay does not have a clear perspective or convey a dominant impression. To help him or her find one, explain what interests you about the subject and what you think is important. If you see contradictions in the draft that could be developed to make the profile more complex and illuminating, briefly explain.

Before concluding your review, be sure to address any of the writer's concerns that have not already been addressed.

Making Comments Electronically   Most word processing software offers features that allow you to insert comments directly into the text of someone else's document. Many readers prefer to make their comments this way because it tends to be faster than writing on hard copy, and space is virtually unlimited; it also eliminates the process of deciphering handwritten comments. Where such features are not available, simply typing comments directly into a document in a contrasting color can provide the same advantages.

Improving the Draft: Revising, Editing, and Proofreading

Start improving your draft by reflecting on what you have written thus far:

- Review critical reading comments from your classmates, instructor, or writing center tutor. What are your readers getting at?
- Take another look at the notes from your interviews, observations, and earlier writing activities. What else should you consider?
- Review your draft. What else can you do to make your profile fascinating?

Revise your draft.

If your readers are having difficulty with your draft, try some of the strategies listed in the Troubleshooting Guide. It can help you fine-tune your presentation of the genre's basic features.

A TROUBLESHOOTING GUIDE

Specific Information about the Subject

My readers tell me the people do not come alive.

- Describe a physical feature, a mannerism, or an emotional reaction that will help readers imagine or identify with the person.
- Include speaker tags that characterize how people talk.
- Paraphrase long, dry quotations that convey basic information.
- Use short quotations that reveal character or the way someone speaks.
- Make comparisons.
- Use anecdotes or action sequences to show the person in action.

My readers say the place is hard to visualize.

- Name objects in the scene.
- Add sensory detail — sight, sound, smell, taste, touch, temperature.
- Make comparisons.
- Consider adding a visual — a photograph or sketch, for example.

(continued)

Specific Information about the Subject

My readers say there is too much information and it is not clear what is important.

- Prioritize based on the perspective and dominant impression you want to convey, cutting information that does not reinforce the perspective.
- Break up long blocks of informational text with quotations, narration of events, or examples.
- Vary the writing strategies used to present the information: Switch from raw factual reporting to comparisons, examples, or process descriptions.
- Consider which parts of the profile would be more engaging if presented through dialogue or summarized more succinctly.

My readers say visuals could be added or improved.

- Use a photo, a map, a drawing, a cartoon, or any other visual that might make the place or people easier to imagine or the information more understandable.
- Consider adding textual references to any images in your essay or positioning images more effectively.

A Clear, Logical Organization

My readers say the narrative plan drags or rambles.

- Try adding drama through dialogue or action sequences.
- Summarize or paraphrase any dialogue that seems dry or uninteresting.
- Give the narrative shape: Establish a conflict, build tension toward a climax, and resolve it.
- Make sure the narrative develops and has a clear direction.

My readers say my topically arranged essay seems disorganized or out of balance.

- Rearrange topics into new patterns, choosing the structure that makes the most sense for your subject. (Describe a place from outside to inside or from biggest to smallest; describe a process from start to finish or from cause to effect.)
- Add clearer, more explicit transitions or topic sentences.
- Move, remove, or condense information to restore balance.

My readers say the opening fails to engage their attention.

- Consider alternatives: Think of a question, an engaging image, or dialogue you could open with.
- Go back to your notes for other ideas.
- Recall how the writers in this chapter open their profiles: Cable stands on the street in front of the mortuary; Thompson awakens in the lettuce fields, his break over.

Improving the Draft

GUIDE TO READING
▶ **GUIDE TO WRITING**
A WRITER AT WORK
THINKING CRITICALLY

109

A Clear, Logical Organization

> My readers say that transitions are missing or are confusing.

- Look for connections between ideas, and try to use those connections to help readers move from point to point.
- Add appropriate transitional words or phrases.

> My readers say the ending seems weak.

- Consider ending earlier or moving a striking insight to the end. (Often first drafts hit a great ending point and then keep going. Deleting the last few sentences often improves papers.)
- Consider ending by reminding readers of something from the beginning.
- Recall how the writers in this chapter end their profiles: Cable touches the cold flesh of a cadaver; Coyne watches a mother bleed after being punched by her son.

> My readers say the visual features are not effective.

- Consider adding textual references to any images in your essay or positioning images more effectively.
- Think of other design features — drawings, lists, tables, graphs, cartoons, headings — that might make the place and people easier to imagine or the information more understandable.

The Writer's Role

> My readers say the spectator role is too distant.

- Consider placing yourself in the scene as you describe it.
- Add your thoughts and reactions to one of the interviews.

> My readers say my approach to participation is distracting.

- Bring other people forward by adding material about them.
- Reduce the material about yourself.

A Perspective on the Subject

> My readers say the perspective or dominant impression is unclear.

- Try stating your perspective by adding your thoughts or someone else's.
- Make sure the descriptive and narrative details reinforce the dominant impression you want to convey.
- If your perspective is complex, you may need to discuss more directly the contradictions or complications you see in the subject.

(continued)

A Perspective on the Subject

My readers don't find my perspective interesting.

- An "uninteresting" perspective is sometimes an unclear one. Check with your readers to see whether they understood it. If they didn't, follow the tips above.
- Readers sometimes say a perspective is "uninteresting" if it's too simple or obvious. Go back through your notes, looking for contradictions, other perspectives, surprises, or anything else that might help you complicate the perspective you are presenting.

Edit and proofread your draft.

Several errors often occur in profiles, including problems with the punctuation of quotations and the integration of *participial phrases*. The following guidelines will help you check your essay for these common errors.

Checking the Punctuation of Quotations

Because most profiles are based in part on interviews, you have probably quoted one or more people in your essay. When you proofread your writing, check to make sure you have observed the strict conventions for punctuating quotations:

What to Check for

- All quotations should have quotation marks at the beginning and the end.

  ▶ "What exactly is civil litigation? "I asked.

- Commas and periods go *inside* quotation marks.

  ▶ "I'm here to see Anna Post," I replied nervously.

  ▶ Tony explained, "Fraternity boys just wouldn't feel comfortable at the Chez Moi Café."

- Question marks and exclamation points go *inside* closing quotation marks if they are part of the quotation, *outside* if they are not.

  ▶ After a pause, the patient asked, "Where do I sign?"

  ▶ Willie insisted, "You can *too* learn to play Super Mario!"

  ▶ When was the last time someone you just ticketed said to you, "Thank you, Officer, for doing a great job?"

- Use commas with speaker tags (*he said, she asked*) that accompany direct quotations.

  ▶ "This sound system costs only four thousand dollars," Jorge said.

  ▶ I asked, "So where were these clothes from originally?"

Integrating Participial Phrases

The Problem   Consider the following sentence:

▶ Snoring blissfully, <u>Bob</u> reclined in his chair.

You know that "Snoring blissfully" applies to Bob, because in English, modifying phrases or clauses like *snoring blissfully* are understood to apply to the nouns they precede or follow. That's why, when you read

▶ Exhausted after 28 hours of studying, <u>Regina</u> sighed loudly.

you know that Regina studied for twenty-eight hours. So what does the following sentence, taken from a 2003 government press release, mean?

▶ Suspected to have been started by an arsonist, <u>the fire investigation team</u>

. . . continues its search for the person(s) responsible.

—that the fire investigation team was started by an arsonist? That may not be what the author of this sentence meant, but that's what the sentence says. This kind of error—called a *dangling modifier*—can confuse readers (or make them chuckle).

The Correction   When editing or proofreading your writing, look for modifying clauses or phrases. In each case, ask yourself whether the person or thing performing the action in the modifier is named immediately before or after the modifier. If it isn't, you have several options for fixing the error:

Change the subject of the sentence.

▶ Suspected to have been started by an arsonist, <u>the fire</u> burned nearly 60,000 acres before being brought under control.

Change the modifier.

▶ Suspecting that an arsonist started the fire, <u>the fire investigation team</u> . . . continues its search for the person(s) responsible.

Move the modifying phrase or clause.

▶ The fire investigation team continues its investigation into the <u>fire</u>, suspected to have been started by an arsonist.

A Common Problem for Multilingual Writers: Adjective Order

The Problem   In trying to present the subject of your profile vividly and in detail, you have probably included many descriptive adjectives. When you include more than one adjective in front of a noun, you may have difficulty sequencing them. For example, do you write *a large old ceramic pot* or *an old large ceramic pot*?

> **A Note on Grammar and Spelling Checkers**
>
> These tools can be helpful, but don't rely on them exclusively to catch errors in your text: Spelling checkers cannot catch misspellings that are themselves words, such as *to* for *too*. Grammar checkers miss some problems, sometimes give faulty advice for fixing problems, and can flag correct items as wrong. Use these tools as a second line of defense after your own (and, ideally, another reader's) proofreading and editing efforts.

The Correction   The following list shows the order in which adjectives are ordinarily arranged in front of a noun:

1. *Amount* (a/an, the, six)
2. *Evaluation* (good, beautiful, ugly, serious)
3. *Size* (large, small, tremendous)
4. *Shape, length* (round, long, short)
5. *Age* (young, new, old)
6. *Color* (red, black, green)
7. *Origin* (Asian, Brazilian, German)
8. *Material* (wood, cotton, gold)
9. Noun used as an adjective (computer [as in *computer program*], cake [as in *cake pan*])

   1.   3.   6.
Seventeen small green buds appeared on my birch sapling.

       1. 2. 5.   6.   9.
He tossed his daughter a nice new yellow tennis ball.

 1.   4.   7.   8.
The slender German-made gold watch cost a great deal of money.

Brian Cable's Interview Notes and Write-Up

Most profile writers take notes when interviewing people. Later, they may summarize their notes in a short write-up. In this section, you will see some of the interview notes and a write-up that Brian Cable prepared for his mortuary profile, "The Last Stop," on pp. 65–70.

Cable arranged to tour the mortuary and conduct interviews with the funeral director and mortician. Before each interview, he wrote out a few questions at the top of a sheet of paper and then divided it into two columns; he used the left-hand column for descriptive details and personal impressions, and the right-hand column for the information he got directly from the person he interviewed. Following are Cable's notes and write-up for his interview with the funeral director, Howard Deaver.

Cable used three questions to guide his interview with Deaver and then took brief notes during the interview. He did not concern himself too much with notetaking because he planned to spend a half hour directly afterward to complete his notes. He focused his attention on Howard, trying to keep the interview comfortable and conversational and jotting down just enough to jog his memory and catch especially meaningful quotations. A typescript of Cable's interview notes follows.

The Interview Notes

Questions

1. How do families of the deceased view the mortuary business?
2. How is the concept of death approached?
3. How did you get into this business?

Descriptive Details & Personal Impressions	Information
weird-looking	Howard Deaver, funeral director,
tall	Goodbody Mortuary
long fingers	"Call me Howard"
big ears	How things work: Notification, pick up
low, sloping forehead	body at home or hospital, prepare for
like stereotype — skin colorless	viewing, restore distorted features —
	accident or illness, embalm, casket —
	family selects, chapel services (3 in bldg.),
	visitation room — pay respects, family & friends.

Can't answer questions about death —
"Not bereavement specialists. Don't
handle emotional problems. Only a
trained therapist can do that." "We
provide services for dead, not counseling
for the living." (great quote) Concept of
death has changed in last 40 yrs
(how long he's been in the business)

plays with lips
blinks
plays with Adam's apple
desk empty — phone, no
   paper or pen

Phone call (interruption)
"I think we'll be able to get him in
on Friday. No, no, the family wants
him cremated."
Ask about Neptune Society — cremation
Cremation "Cheap, quick, easy means of
disposal."

angry
disdainful of the
   Neptune Society

Recent phenomenon. Neptune Society — erroneous
claim to be only one.

"We've offered them since the beginning. It's only
now it's come into vogue."
Trend now back toward burial.
Cremation still popular in sophisticated areas
60% in Marin Co. and Florida
Ask about paperwork — does it upstairs,
lives there with wife, Nancy.

musty, old stained glass
sunlight filtered

Tour around (happy to show me around)
Chapel — large service just done,
Italian.

man in black suit
roses
wooden benches

"Not a religious institution — a
business."
casket — "beautiful craftsmanship" —
admires, expensive

contrast brightness
fluorescent lights
Plexiglas stands

Display room — caskets, about 30 of them
Loves to talk about caskets "models in every price
range" glossy (like cars in a showroom) cardboard
box, steel, copper, bronze starting at $500, aver-
aging $2,400. Top of line: bronze, electronically
welded, no corrosion

Cable's interview notes include many descriptive details of Deaver as well as of various rooms in the mortuary. Though most entries are short and sketchy, much of the language found its way into the final essay. In describing Deaver, for example, Cable noted that he fits the stereotype of the cadaverous undertaker, a fact that Cable emphasized in his essay.

He put quotation marks around Deaver's actual words, some of them written in complete sentences, others in fragments. We will see how Cable filled these quotes in when he wrote up the interview. In only a few instances did he take down more than he could use. Even though profile writers want good quotes, they should not use quotes to present information that can be more effectively expressed in their own words. In profiles, writers use direct quotation both to provide information and to capture the mood or character of the person speaking.

As you can see, Deaver was not able to answer Cable's questions about the families of the deceased and their attitudes toward death or mortuaries. The gap between these questions and Deaver's responses led Cable to recognize one of his own misperceptions about mortuaries—that they serve the living by helping people adjust to the death of loved ones. This misperception would become an important theme of his essay.

Immediately after the interview, Cable filled in his notes with details while they were still fresh in his mind. Next, he took some time to reflect on what he had learned from his interview with Howard. Here are some of his thoughts:

> I was surprised by how much Howard looked like the undertakers in scary movies. Even though he couldn't answer some of my questions, he was friendly enough. It's obviously a business for him (he loves to talk about caskets and to point out all their features, like a car dealer kicking a tire). Best quote: "We offer services to the dead, not counseling to the living." I have to bring up these issues in my interview with the mortician.

The Interview Write-Up

Writing up an account of the interview a short time afterward helped Cable fill in more details and reflect further on what he had learned. His write-up shows him already beginning to organize the information he had gained from his interview with the funeral director.

I. His physical appearance.

> Tall, skinny, with beady blue eyes embedded in his bony face. I was shocked to see that he looks just like the undertakers in scary movies. His skin is white and colorless, from lack of sunshine. He has a long nose and a low, sloping forehead. He was wearing a clean white shirt. A most unusual man—have you ever seen those Ames Home Loan commercials? But he was friendly, and happy to talk with me. "Would I answer some questions? Sure."

<u>II.   What people want from a mortuary.</u>

A. Well first of all, he couldn't answer my second question, about how families cope with the loss of a loved one. "You'd have to talk to a psychologist about that," he said. He did tell me how the concept of death has changed over the last ten or so years.

B. He has been in the business for forty years(!). One look at him and you'd be convinced he'd been there at least that long. He told me that in the old times, everyone was buried. Embalmed, put in a casket, and paid final homage before being shipped underground forever. Nowadays, many people choose to be cremated instead. Hence comes the success of the Neptune Society and others specializing in cremation. You can have your ashes dumped anywhere. "Not that we don't offer cremation services. We've offered them since the beginning," he added with a look of disdain. It's just that they've become so popular recently because they offer a "quick, easy, and efficient means of disposal." Cheap too — I think it is a reflection of a "no nonsense" society. The Neptune Society has become so successful because it claims to be the only one to offer cremations as an alternative to expensive burial. "We've offered it all along. It's just only now come into vogue."

Sophisticated areas (I felt "progressive" would be more accurate) like Marin County have a cremation rate of over 60 percent. The phone rang. "Excuse me," he said. As he talked on the phone, I noticed how he played with his lips, pursing and squeezing them. He was blinking a lot, too. I meant to ask him how he got into this business, but I forgot. I did find out his name and title: Mr. Howard Deaver, funeral director of Goodbody Mortuary (no kidding, that's the real name). He lives on the premises, upstairs with his wife. I doubt if he ever leaves the place.

<u>III. It's a business!</u>

Some people have the idea that mortuaries offer counseling and peace of mind — a place where everyone is sympathetic and ready to offer advice. "In some mortuaries, this is true. But by and large, this is a business. We offer services to the dead, not counseling to the living." I too had expected to feel an awestruck respect for the dead upon entering the building. I had also expected green lawns, ponds with ducks, fountains, flowers, peacefulness — you know, a "Forest Lawn" type deal. But it was only a tall, Catholic-looking building. "Mortuaries do not sell plots for burial," he was saying. "Cemeteries do that, after we embalm the body and select a casket. We're not a religious institution." He seemed hung up on caskets — though maybe he was just trying to impress upon me the differences between caskets. "Oh, they're very important. A good casket is a sign of respect. Sometimes if the family doesn't have enough money, we rent them a nice one. People pay for what they get just like any other business." I wondered when you had to return the casket you rented.

I wanted to take a look around. He was happy to give me a tour. We visited several chapels and visiting rooms — places where the deceased "lie in state" to be "visited" by family and friends. I saw an old lady in a "fairly decent casket," as Mr. Deaver called

Reflecting on What You Have Learned

GUIDE TO READING
GUIDE TO WRITING
A WRITER AT WORK
▶ **THINKING CRITICALLY**

117

it. Again I was impressed by the simple businesslike nature of it all. Oh yes, the rooms were elaborately decorated, with lots of shrines and stained glass, but these things were for the customers' benefit. "Sometimes we have up to eight or nine corpses here at one time, sometimes none. We have to have enough rooms to accommodate." Simple enough, yet I never realized how much trouble people were after they died. So much money, time, and effort go into their funerals.

As I prepared to leave, he gave me his card. He'd be happy to see me again, or maybe I could talk to someone else. I said I was going to interview the mortician on another day. I shook his hand. His fingers were long and his skin was warm.

Writing up the interview helped Cable probe his subject more deeply. It also helped him express a humorous attitude toward his subject. Cable's interview notes and write-up were quite informal; later, he integrated this material more formally into his full profile of the mortuary.

THINKING CRITICALLY

To think critically means to use all of the knowledge you have acquired from the information in this chapter, your own writing, the writing and responses of other students, and class discussions to reflect deeply on your work for this assignment and the genre (or type) of writing you have produced. The benefit of thinking critically is proven and important: Thinking critically about what you have learned will help you remember it longer, ensuring that you will be able to put it to good use well beyond this writing course.

Reflecting on What You Have Learned

In this chapter, you have learned a great deal about this genre by reading several profiles and writing one of your own. To consolidate your learning, reflect not only on what you learned but on how you learned it.

ANALYZE & WRITE

Write a blog post, a letter to your instructor or a classmate, or an e-mail message to a student who will take this course next term, using the writing prompt that seems most productive for you:

- Explain how your purpose and audience — what you wanted your readers to learn about your subject from reading your profile — influenced *one* of your decisions as a writer, such as what kinds of descriptive detail you included, what method of organization you used, or the role you adopted in writing about your subject.

- Discuss what you learned about yourself as a writer in the process of writing this profile. For example, what part of the process did you find most challenging? Did you try anything new, like getting a critical reading of your draft or outlining your draft in order to revise it? If so, how well did it work?

- If you were to give advice to a fellow student who was about to write a profile, what would you say?

- Which of the readings in this chapter influenced your essay? Explain the influence, citing specific examples from your profile and the reading.

- If you got good advice from a critical reader, explain exactly how the person helped you — perhaps by questioning your perspective in a way that enabled you to refocus your profile's dominant impression, or by pointing out passages that needed more information or clearer chronology to better orient readers.

Reflecting on the Genre

Profiles broaden our view of the world by entertaining and informing us with portraits of people, places, or activities. But even effective profiles sometimes offer a limited view of their subjects. For example, the impulse to entertain readers may lead a profile writer to focus exclusively on the dramatic, colorful, or humorous aspects of a person, place, or activity, ignoring the equally important humdrum, routine, or otherwise less appealing aspects. Imagine a profile that focuses on the dramatic moments in an emergency-room doctor's shift but ignores the routine cases and the slow periods when nothing much is happening. Such a profile would provide a limited and distorted picture. In addition, by focusing on the dramatic or glamorous aspects of a subject, profile writers tend to ignore economic or social consequences and to slight supporting players. Profiling the highly praised chef in a trendy new restaurant, a writer might not ask who the kitchen workers and waitstaff are, how the chef treats them, or how much they are paid.

ANALYZE & WRITE

Write a page or two explaining how the genre prompts you to think about the subject of a profile. In your discussion, you might consider one or more of the following:

1. **Consider whether any of the profiles you have read glamorize or sensationalize their subjects.** Do they ignore less colorful but centrally important people or everyday activities? Is this a problem with your own profile?

2. **Write a page or so explaining what the omissions signify.** What do they suggest about the readers' desires to be entertained and the profile writer's reluctance to present the subject in a more complete way?

4

Explaining a Concept

Is the greatest threat to humanity a natural phenomenon we haven't really considered? Are the complex feelings of love rooted in simple biology? What happens to our judgment when we make too many decisions in one day? These are a few of the questions that are answered in the intriguing concept explanations in this chapter. Much of your reading and writing as a college student involves learning the concepts that are the building blocks of academic subjects. These concepts may include principles (such as *equal justice*), theories (such as *evolution*), ideas (such as *commodification*), conditions (such as *state of flow*), phenomena (such as *inflation*), or processes (such as *socialization*). To communicate effectively and efficiently about a subject—whether you are writing to your instructor, your boss, or your friends; in an essay exam, a blog post, or a presentation; you need to be able to use and explain concepts clearly and compellingly.

People analyze and explain concepts for various purposes and audiences and publish them in a variety of media. For example, a student in a cultural studies course used the concept of cultural framing theory as a lens through which to analyze the politics of sexuality in advertising. She published her essay in a student journal at her school. A parent used Prezi software to explain the concept of surveying in advertising to her child's fifth-grade class. A business consultant created a video to define and demonstrate 3-D imaging and to explain its role to potential buyers of driverless cars.

In this chapter, we ask you to analyze and explain a concept that you think will be unfamiliar to your readers. Whether you tackle a concept you've studied in college or choose one from your work or your favorite pastime, you need to answer your readers' inevitable "So what?" question: Why should they want to understand the concept? Analyzing the selections in the Guide to Reading that follows will help you learn how to make your concept explanation interesting and informative. The Guide to Writing later in the chapter will show you ways to use the basic features of the genre—including how to use visuals and multimedia—to make an unfamiliar concept not only understandable but also compelling to your readers.

PRACTICING THE GENRE ─────────────────────────────────────

Explaining an Academic Concept

Part 1.   First, think of a concept you recently learned in one of your courses. Next, take a few minutes to plan how you will explain it to classmates who may not know anything about the subject. Would it be helpful to

- identify the course and the context in which you learned it?
- give your listeners a dictionary definition?
- tell them what kind of concept it is?
- compare it to something they may already know?
- give them an example?
- explain why the concept is important or useful?

Part 2.   In small groups, take two or three minutes each explaining your concept. Then discuss what you learned:

- **What did you learn about the genre from listening to others' explanations?** To think about purpose and audience in explaining a concept, tell one another whether you felt the "So what?" question was adequately answered: What, if anything, piqued your interest or made you feel that the concept might be worth learning about? What strategies did group members use that you felt were particularly effective?

- **What did you learn about explaining?** Compare your thoughts with others in your group about what was easiest and hardest about explaining a concept—for example, choosing a concept you understood well enough to explain to others; making it interesting, important, or useful to group members; or deciding what would best help your audience understand the concept in the time you had.

Analyzing Concept Explanations

As you read the selections in this chapter, you will see how different authors explain concepts:

- Jonathan Potthast explains the devastating consequences that would follow the eruption of a supervolcano (pp. 124–29).
- Anastasia Toufexis analyzes the biological basis of love (pp. 129–32).
- John Tierney explains the hidden danger of decision fatigue (pp. 135–37).
- Susan Cain examines the benefits of introversion (pp. 141–44).

Analyzing how these writers develop a surprising or interesting focus for their explanation, how they organize the explanation to draw readers in and keep them reading, how they use examples and other writing strategies to make the topic compelling, and how they integrate sources to make their claims convincing will help you see how you can employ these same techniques to make your own concept explanations successful.

Determine the writer's purpose and audience.

How well a writer analyzes and explains a concept can demonstrate how well he or she understands it. That is why this kind of writing is so frequently assigned in college courses. But it is also a popular genre outside of the classroom, where effective writers manage to make the most esoteric topics interesting and important. These authors understand that a concept explanation risks being dry and uninteresting to those not already intrigued by the topic, so they make an effort to zero in on a focus that will excite the curiosity of their readers. When reading the concept explanations that follow, ask yourself questions like these:

What seems to be the writer's main purpose?

- to inform readers about an important idea or theory?
- to show how a concept has promoted original thinking and research in an area of study?
- to better understand the concept by explaining it to others?
- to demonstrate knowledge of the concept and the ability to apply it?

What does the writer assume about the audience?

- that readers will be unfamiliar with the concept and need an introduction that will capture their interest?
- that readers will know something about the concept but want to learn more about it?
- that the primary reader will be an instructor who knows more about the concept than the writer does and who is evaluating the writer's knowledge?

Assess the genre's basic features.

As you read the concept explanations in this chapter, evaluate how effectively different authors employ the genre's basic features. The examples that follow are drawn
from the reading selections that appear later in this Guide to Reading.

A FOCUSED EXPLANATION

Read first to identify the concept. Ask yourself:

- "What is the focus or main point?" This point is the *thesis* of a concept explanation, comparable to what we call autobiographical significance in remembered
  event essays and perspective in profiles. The point answers the "So what?" question: Why are you telling me about this concept? Why is it interesting or
  important?

- "What should I include and what should I leave out?" These decisions are often
  dictated by readers—how much they already know about the topic and how
  interested in the topic they are. For college writing and some other contexts, the
  focus may be dictated by a specific question or prompt. For example, Jonathan
  Potthast's instructor asked students to analyze a concept they had learned about
  in another course, conducting additional research as needed to explain the concept to a reader with little or no background in the subject.

A CLEAR, LOGICAL ORGANIZATION

Consider whether the concept explanation is clearly and logically organized. Notice how
each writer develops a plan that does the following:

- States the thesis or main point early on

  Concept
  Main point

  > Let's put love under a microscope. . . . When rigorous people with Ph.D.s after their
  > names do that, what they see is not some silly senseless thing. No, their probe
  > reveals that love rests firmly on foundations of evolution, biology, and chemistry.
  >
  > (Toufexis, pars. 1–2)

- Divides the information into clearly distinguishable topics and forecasts them in
  the order in which they will be discussed

  Topic
  Forecast

  > Decision fatigue helps explain why ordinarily sensible people get angry at col-
  > leagues and families, splurge on clothes, buy junk food at the supermarket and
  > can't resist the dealer's offer to rustproof their new car. (Tierney, par. 5)

- Guides readers by providing cues or road signs

  Transition

  > Even more astounding, ash in the air after a volcano can temporarily cause
  > dramatic changes to the climate. (Potthast, par. 7)

  > Afterward, all the participants were given one of the classic tests of self-control:
  > holding your hand in ice water for as long as you can. (Tierney, par. 9)

  > If, in nature's design, romantic love is not eternal, neither is it exclusive. (Toufexis,
  > par. 8)

APPROPRIATE EXPLANATORY STRATEGIES

Look for explanatory strategies, such as definition, classification, comparison-contrast, example, illustration, and cause-effect, that help readers understand the topic:

DEFINITION	Each person carries in his or her mind a unique subliminal guide to the ideal partner, a "love map," . . . (Toufexis, par. 17)	Defining characteristic Term being defined
COMPARISON-CONTRAST	Shyness and introversion are not the same thing. Shy people fear negative judgment; introverts simply prefer quiet, minimally stimulating environments. . . . (Cain, par. 9)	Terms being contrasted Cue
	In contrast, . . . (Cain, par. 19)	Cue
EXAMPLE	Despite . . . side effects—nausea, loss of sex drive, seizures—drugs like Zoloft . . . (Cain, par. 3)	Cues Examples
	We find them in recent history, in figures like Charles Darwin, Marcel Proust and Albert Einstein, and, in contemporary times: think of Google's Larry Page, or Harry Potter's creator, J. K. Rowling. (Cain, par. 11)	
ILLUSTRATION (WITH VISUAL)	Like hurricanes, the power of volcanoes is measured using an exponential scale (see the *Volcanic Explosivity Index*, or *VEI*, in Fig. 1). (Potthast, par. 1)	Reference to a visual in the text
CAUSE-EFFECT	To a fatigued judge, denying parole seems like the easier call not only because it preserves the status quo . . . but also because it leaves more options open. . . . (Tierney, par. 11)	Effect Cause For more on writing strategies such as definition and classification, see the chapters in Part 3.

SMOOTH INTEGRATION OF SOURCES

Notice how writers draw on research, as well as their own experiences and observations, to explain the concept. How do writers establish their authority by smoothly integrating information from sources into the explanation? Does the writer quote, paraphrase, or summarize the source material? How does the writer establish the source's expertise and credibility? The examples below demonstrate some strategies:

QUOTE	According to Joel Achenbach, a reporter on science and politics for the *Washington Post*, . . . a super-eruption 2.1 million years ago . . . "[left] a hole in the ground the size of Rhode Island" (1). (Potthast, par. 9)	Signal phrase plus credentials
	In the wake of the . . . eruption, a pyroclastic flow "swept down the mountain, flattening forests, overtaking escaping vehicles and killing several people who stood absolutely no chance of moving out of its path" ("Lahars"). (Potthast, par. 2)	Parenthetical citation
PARAPHRASE	It is the difference between passionate and compassionate love, observes Walsh, a psychobiologist at Boise State University in Idaho. (Toufexis, par. 14)	

SUMMARY   Decision fatigue is the newest discovery involving . . . ego depletion, a term coined by the social psychologist Roy F. Baumeister . . . [who] began studying mental discipline in a series of experiments . . . [that] demonstrated that there is a finite store of mental energy for exerting self-control. (Tierney, par. 6)

How writers treat sources depends on the writing situation. Certain formal situations, such as college assignments or scholarly publications, require writers to cite sources in the text and document them in a bibliography (called a list of **works cited** in many humanities disciplines and a list of **references** in the sciences and social sciences). Students and scholars are expected to cite their sources formally because readers judge their work in part by what the writers have read and how they have used their reading. They may also be interested in locating the sources and reading more about the topic for themselves. (Jonathan Potthast's essay, below, provides an example of academic citation.) For writing in popular sources, like magazine and newspaper articles for example, readers do not expect references or publication information to appear in the article, but they do expect sources to be identified and their expertise established in some way. (The articles by Toufexis, Tierney, and Cain, on pp. 129–32, 135–37, and 141–44, provide examples of informal citation.)

Readings

To learn about how Jonathan Potthast used sources to support his own ideas, turn to A Writer at Work on pp. 167–68: How did he contextualize sources to show their relevance? How did he combine summary and quotation to integrate source material into his essay and avoid simply stringing quotations together?

Jonathan Potthast | *Supervolcanoes: A Catastrophe of Ice and Fire*

ORIGINALLY, Jonathan Potthast wrote this essay analyzing and explaining supervolcanoes for his composition course. Following his instructor's recommendation, Potthast chose a concept he had learned about in another course. He used a number of sources, including articles and books, some of which he accessed through his library's Web site. His instructor required his citation format to be the one used for the humanities, from the Modern Language Association (MLA).

As you read, consider the following questions:

- How does Potthast interest readers in his subject?

- Why do you think he compares supervolcanoes to asteroid impacts and hurricanes?

- Answer the questions in the margin. Your instructor may ask you to post your answers to a class blog or discussion board or to bring them to class.

1   Possibly the most destructive natural disaster, short of a large asteroid impact, would be the eruption of a supervolcano. Supervolcanoes are volcanoes that produce eruptions thousands of times the size of ordinary volcanoes. Like hurricanes, the power of volcanoes is measured using an exponential scale (see the *Volcanic Explosivity Index*, or *VEI*, in fig. 1).

2   A brief synopsis of the effects of regular volcanoes can provide clues as to how destructive the eruption of a supervolcano would be. Volcanic eruptions feature several dangerous physical effects, including pyroclastic flows, pyroclastic surges, lahars, tephra falls, and massive amounts of fine ash particles in the air. Pyroclastic flows, which are dense superheated mixtures of ash, rock, and gas, are the most deadly feature of volcanoes. They are often as hot as 1,400 degrees Fahrenheit and flow at rates of hundreds of miles per hour, making prior evacuation the only possible means of escape.

Fig. 1. Volcanic Explosivity Index (VEI). From "Eruption Styles." *Volcano World*. Dept. of Geosciences, Oregon State U and Oregon Space Grant Consortium, 2014. Web. 22 Dec. 2014.

■■ **Basic Features**
A Focused Explanation
A Clear, Logical Organization
Appropriate Explanatory Strategies
Smooth Integration of Sources

How does Potthast use categories to organize his explanation?

How does the VEI help the reader follow Potthast's explanation?

Driven by gravity, pyroclastic flows destroy everything in their path, and "they pose lethal hazard from incineration, asphyxiation, burial, and impact" ("Pyroclastic"). In the wake of the May 18, 1980, Mt. St. Helens eruption, a pyroclastic flow "swept down the mountain, flattening forests, overtaking escaping vehicles and killing several people who stood absolutely no chance of moving out of its path" ("Lahars").

3   In addition, by rapidly heating phreatic (underground) water, volcanic eruptions can trigger violent steam-driven explosions. The water from these phreatic eruptions can then combine with lava from pyroclastic flows to create devastating mudslides called *lahars*. (Rainwater or melting snow can also combine with lava flows to form lahars.) Lahars flow with enough force to uproot trees, carry away cars, and flatten buildings ("Lahars"). They flow much faster than humans can run, and can kill people instantly. When cooled, they solidify into a sort of concrete. For example, the eruption of Mt. Vesuvius in 79 A.D. produced lahars large enough to bury the entire city of Pompeii in what quickly became solid volcanic rock ("Lahars"). The most dangerous aspect of lahars, however, lies in their ability to form long after a volcanic eruption has apparently ceased, even after evacuated inhabitants have returned to their homes.

4   Pyroclastic surges, another devastating feature of many volcanoes, are composed of gas and particles of volcanic ash which move as quickly as pyroclastic flows but are less dense. P. J. Baxter, a physician specializing in occupational and environmental medicine at Cambridge University and a consultant to the World Health Organization on volcanoes, notes that humans exposed even briefly to pyroclastic surges face serious burns as well as risks of asphyxia (suffocation) and hypoxia (oxygen deprivation to body tissue). The extreme heat of the surges, if not hot enough to kill a person instantly, can kill a person by burning their lungs, throat, and windpipes so severely that those organs swell to the point of preventing any air from getting in.

5   Tephra falls, or showers of pieces of volcanic rock ejected from a volcano, can also be deadly to those nearby. The sheer force of a tephra "rain" can cause roofs to collapse and people without shelter to be battered to death ("Hazards"). While tephra presents an immediate and short-lived danger, however, fine ash particles in the air cause more lasting damage. Heavy ash deposits can destroy vegetation, causing widespread famine and suffering to animals that depend on those plants for food. Inhaling fine volcanic ash can cause silicosis, an irreversible lung disease ("Hazards"). Ash particles also cause damage to moving parts in machinery and vehicles.

6   Aside from the obvious immediate destruction of these physical effects, a volcanic eruption can also have a surprising aftermath. For example, following the 1996 Soufreire Hills volcano, hydrogen sulfide and sulfur dioxide (gases produced in the eruption) combined to form sulfuric acid; this, mixed with the rainwater, destroyed acres of cloud forest (Brosnan). Coral reefs could be destroyed in a similar manner.

7   Even more astounding, ash in the air after a volcano can temporarily cause dramatic changes to the climate. For instance, in the years following the eruption of Tambora in Indonesia on April 5, 1815, fine particles of volcanic ash and aerosols created a fog-like layer in the atmosphere that blocked some of the sun's rays and led to temporary global cooling of about five and a half degrees Fahrenheit ("Mount Tambora"). In Europe and North America, 1816 became known as "the year without a summer"; the New England states, for example, experienced a "killing frost through June, July, and August" ("Mount Tambora"). Although "enough grains, wheat, and potatoes were harvested to prevent a famine," crops such as corn, beans, and squash were destroyed before they could be harvested, hay crops were meager, and "there were reports of people eating raccoons, pigeons, and mackerel" (Foster). Other recent major volcanoes, such as Krakatoa in 1883, have produced similar cooling effects: "On the average, temperature dropped by as much as 1.2°C in the succeeding year. In the years that followed, global climates were very erratic, stabilizing only 4 years after" (Villanueva).

8   Luckily, no supervolcano has erupted in recorded history. Several supervolcanoes exist today, but most are under the ocean, and all are considered dormant or extinct. According to the National Parks Service, a catastrophic eruption would probably provide a good deal—maybe even years—of advance warning, and other geologic events ("strong earthquake swarms and rapid ground deformation") would occur within days or weeks of the eruption (United States).

9   A dormant supervolcano close to home is in Yellowstone National Park. According to Joel Achenbach, a reporter on science and politics for magazines and newspapers such as *National Geographic*, *Slate*, and the *Washington Post*, three super-eruptions have occurred there, with one just 640,000 years ago (a blink of an eye in geologic terms). Even more powerful was a super-eruption 2.1 million years ago that "[left] a hole in the ground the size of Rhode Island" (Achenbach 1). The caldera, or crater, of the Yellowstone supervolcano is about 45 miles across, and over time, has been eroded and covered by glaciers and forests; part of the caldera's rim is invisible, hidden beneath the surface of Lake Butte.

How effectively does Potthast make the transition from the damaging physical features of volcanoes to their unexpected consequences?

How effectively does Potthast weave information together from several sources in this paragraph?

What is the effect on the reader of this transitional paragraph?

10   It was thought that the volcano was extinct, but activity is making scientists rethink that view (Achenbach 2). A huge magma chamber lies deep under the volcano's caldera. When shifted by earthquakes and pressed by hot rock, the land above it rises and falls. An earthquake swarm in the mid-1980s made Yellowstone drop, so that it was about eight inches lower ten years later (Achenbach 2). More recently, "portions of the caldera have surged upward at a rate of nearly three inches a year, much faster than any uplift since close observations began in the 1970's" (Achenbach 3). Such activity indicates a live volcano.

11   Although a catastrophic eruption is far from imminent, one is possible. If a super-eruption were to occur here, the results would be devastating: A Yellowstone eruption, for example, could deposit a 10-foot layer of ash that would destroy vegetation 1,000 miles away. Toxic gases would sweep across much of the nation, making "two-thirds of the U.S. . . . uninhabitable . . . forcing millions to leave their homes" (Bates). Burning plants would generate vast amounts of carbon dioxide that would increase the greenhouse effect and ultimately contribute to global warming, but the immediate effect of a supervolcanic eruption would be dramatic global cooling. While Tambora created a "year without summer," a supervolcanic eruption would "potentially plunge the Earth into years of 'volcanic winter'" (Achenbach 2). According to science writer Charles Choi, a supervolcanic eruption would have an impact comparable to that of a mile-wide asteroid, killing many millions of people and changing the entire global landscape.

Works Cited

Achenbach, Joel. "When Yellowstone Explodes." *National Geographic Magazine*. Aug. 2009: 1–3. *Academic Search Complete*. Web. 5 May 2014.

Bates, Daniel. "Is the World's Largest Super-Volcano Set to Erupt for the First Time in 600,000 Years, Wiping Out Two-Thirds of the U.S.?" *Mail Online*. Associated Newspapers, n.d. Web. 6 May 2014.

Baxter, P. J. "Blast, Burns, Asphyxia and Hypoxia: How Do Pyroclastic Surges Damage Humans?" *Montserrat Volcano Observatory*. Michigan Tech. U, Dept. of Geology, n.d. Web. 6 May 2014.

Brosnan, Deborah M. "Ecological Impacts of the Montserrat Volcano: A Pictorial Account of Its Effects on Land and Sea Life." *Sustainable Ecosystems Institute*. Sustainable Ecosystems Institute, n.d. Web. 5 May 2014.

Choi, Charles Q. "Supervolcano Not to Blame for Humanity's Near-Extinction." *LiveScience*. TechMedia Network, 29 Apr. 2013. Web. 4 May 2014.

What does Potthast achieve in these concluding paragraphs? How does it work for you?

What makes Potthast's sources seem authoritative?

Foster, Lee. "1816—The Year Without Summer." *Climate Corner*. NOAA, Eastern Region
Headquarters, n.d. Web. 6 May 2014.

"Hazards Associated with Soufriere Hills." *Hazards Associated with Soufriere Hills,* n.d.
Web. 6 May 2014.

"Lahars and Pyroclastic Flows." *The Geography Site*. The Geography Site, n.d. Web.
5 May 2014.

"Mount Tambora." *Encyclopaedia Britannica*. Encyclopaedia Britannica, 2015. Web.
6 May 2014.

"Pyroclastic Flow Hazards at Mount St. Helens." *USGS: Volcano Hazards Program — Mount
St. Helens Hazards*. U.S. Geological Survey, 22 Jan. 2013. Web. 6 May 2014.

United States. Natl. Park Service. "Volcano Questions & Answers." *Natl. Parks
Service*. U.S. Dept. of the Interior, 29 Apr. 2014. Web. 4 May 2014.

Villanueva, John Carl. "Mount Krakatoa." *Universe Today*. Universe Today, 18 Sept.
2009. Web. 6 May 2014.

Anastasia Toufexis | *Love: The Right Chemistry*

ANASTASIA TOUFEXIS has been an associate editor of *Time*, senior editor of *Discover*, and editor in chief of *Psychology Today*. She has written on subjects as diverse as medicine, health and fitness, law, the environment, education, science, and national and world news. Toufexis has won a number of awards for her writing, including a Knight-Wallace Fellowship at the University of Michigan and an Ocean Science Journalism Fellowship at Woods Hole Oceanographic Institution. She has also lectured on science writing at Columbia University, the University of North Carolina, and the School of Visual Arts in New York.

As you read, consider the following questions:

- How would you describe the tone Toufexis adopts in this essay, at least in the beginning? How effective do you think this tone was for her original *Time* magazine readers? How appropriate would it be for a college paper?

- Given her purpose and audience, how effective is the visual in helping readers understand her rather technical explanation?

Love is a romantic designation for a most ordinary biological—or, shall we say, chemical?—process. A lot of nonsense is talked and written about it.
                    —Greta Garbo to Melvyn Douglas in *Ninotchka*

1   O.K., let's cut out all this nonsense about romantic love. Let's bring some scientific precision to the party. Let's put love under a microscope.

2   When rigorous people with Ph.D.s after their names do that, what they see is not some silly, senseless thing. No, their probe reveals that love rests firmly on the foundations of evolution, biology and chemistry. What seems on the surface to be irrational, intoxicated behavior is in fact part of nature's master strategy—a vital force that has helped humans survive, thrive and multiply through thousands of years. Says Michael Mills, a psychology professor at Loyola Marymount University in Los Angeles: "Love is our ancestors whispering in our ears."

3   It was on the plains of Africa about 4 million years ago, in the early days of the human species, that the notion of romantic love probably first began to blossom or at least that the first cascades of neurochemicals began flowing from the brain to the bloodstream to produce goofy grins and sweaty palms as men and women gazed deeply into each other's eyes. When mankind graduated from scuttling around on all fours to walking on two legs, this change made the whole person visible to fellow human beings for the first time. Sexual organs were in full display, as were other characteristics, from the color of eyes to the span of shoulders. As never before, each individual had a unique allure.

4   When the sparks flew, new ways of making love enabled sex to become a romantic encounter, not just a reproductive act. Although mounting mates from the rear was, and still is, the method favored among most animals, humans began to enjoy face-to-face couplings; both looks and personal attraction became a much greater part of the equation.

5   Romance served the evolutionary purpose of pulling males and females into long-term partnership, which was essential to child rearing. On open grasslands, one parent would have a hard—and dangerous—time handling a child while foraging for food. "If a woman was carrying the equivalent of a 20-lb.

bowling ball in one arm and a pile of sticks in the other, it was ecologically critical to pair up with a mate to rear the young," explains anthropologist Helen Fisher, author of *Anatomy of Love.*

6   While Western culture holds fast to the idea that true love flames forever (the movie *Bram Stoker's Dracula* has the Count carrying the torch beyond the grave), nature apparently meant passions to sputter out in something like four years. Primitive pairs stayed together just "long enough to rear one child through infancy," says Fisher. Then each would find a new partner and start all over again.

7   What Fisher calls the "four-year itch" shows up unmistakably in today's divorce statistics. In most of the 62 cultures she has studied, divorce rates peak around the fourth year of marriage. Additional youngsters help keep pairs together longer. If, say, a couple have another child three years after the first, as often occurs, then their union can be expected to last about four more years. That makes them ripe for the more familiar phenomenon portrayed in the Marilyn Monroe classic *The Seven-Year Itch.*

8   If, in nature's design, romantic love is not eternal, neither is it exclusive. Less than 5% of mammals form rigorously faithful pairs. From the earliest days, contends Fisher, the human pattern has been "monogamy with clandestine adultery." Occasional flings upped the chances that new combinations of genes would be passed on to the next generation. Men who sought new partners had more children. Contrary to common assumptions, women were just as likely to stray. "As long as prehistoric females were secretive about their extramarital affairs," argues Fisher, "they could garner extra resources, life insurance, better genes and more varied DNA for their biological futures. . . ."

9   Lovers often claim that they feel as if they are being swept away. They're not mistaken; they are literally flooded by chemicals, research suggests. A meeting of eyes, a touch of hands or a whiff of scent sets off a flood that starts in the brain and races along the nerves and through the blood. The results are familiar: flushed skin, sweaty palms, heavy breathing. If love looks suspiciously like stress, the reason is simple: the chemical pathways are identical.

If, in nature's design, romantic love is not eternal, neither is it exclusive.

10   Above all, there is the sheer euphoria of falling in love—a not-so-surprising reaction, considering that many of the substances swamping the newly smitten are chemical cousins of amphetamines. They include dopamine, norepinephrine and especially phenylethylamine (PEA). Cole Porter knew what he was talking about when he wrote, "I get a kick out of you." "Love is a natural high," observes Anthony Walsh, author of *The Science of Love: Understanding Love and Its Effects on Mind and Body.* "PEA gives you that silly smile that you flash at strangers. When we meet someone who is attractive to us, the whistle blows at the PEA factory."

11   But phenylethylamine highs don't last forever, a fact that lends support to arguments that passionate romantic love is short-lived. As with any amphetamine, the body builds up a tolerance to PEA; thus it takes more and more of the substance to produce love's special kick. After two to three years, the body simply can't crank up the needed amount of PEA. And chewing on chocolate doesn't help, despite popular belief. The candy is high in PEA, but it fails to boost the body's supply.

12   Fizzling chemicals spell the end of delirious passion; for many people that marks the end of the liaison as well. It is particularly true for those whom Dr. Michael Liebowitz of the New York State Psychiatric Institute terms "attraction junkies." They crave the intoxication of falling in love so much that they move frantically from affair to affair just as soon as the first rush of infatuation fades.

13   Still, many romances clearly endure beyond the first years. What accounts for that? Another set of chemicals, of course. The continued presence of a partner gradually steps up production in the brain of endorphins. Unlike the fizzy amphetamines, these are soothing substances. Natural pain-killers, they give lovers a sense of security, peace and calm. "That is one reason why it feels so horrible when we're abandoned or a lover dies," notes Fisher. "We don't have our daily hit of narcotics."

14   Researchers see a contrast between the heated infatuation induced by PEA, along with other amphetamine-like chemicals, and the more intimate attachment fostered and prolonged by endorphins. "Early love is when you love the way the other person makes you feel," explains psychiatrist Mark Goulston of the University of California, Los Angeles. "Mature love is when you love the person as he or she is." It is the difference between passionate and compassionate love, observes Walsh, a psychobiologist at Boise State University in Idaho. "It's Bon Jovi vs. Beethoven."

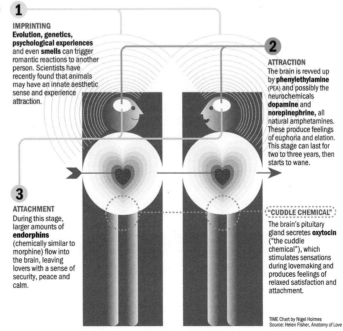

How Do Fools Fall in Love?

1 IMPRINTING
Evolution, genetics, psychological experiences and even **smells** can trigger romantic reactions to another person. Scientists have recently found that animals may have an innate aesthetic sense and experience attraction.

2 ATTRACTION
The brain is revved up by **phenylethylamine** (PEA) and possibly the neurochemicals **dopamine** and **norepinephrine**, all natural amphetamines. These produce feelings of euphoria and elation. This stage can last for two to three years, then starts to wane.

3 ATTACHMENT
During this stage, larger amounts of **endorphins** (chemically similar to morphine) flow into the brain, leaving lovers with a sense of security, peace and calm.

"CUDDLE CHEMICAL"
The brain's pituitary gland secretes **oxytocin** ("the cuddle chemical"), which stimulates sensations during lovemaking and produces feelings of relaxed satisfaction and attachment.

TIME Chart by Nigel Holmes
Source: Helen Fisher, Anatomy of Love

15   Oxytocin is another chemical that has recently been implicated in love. Produced by the brain, it sensitizes nerves and stimulates muscle contraction. In women it helps uterine contractions during childbirth as well as production of breast milk, and seems to inspire mothers to nuzzle their infants. Scientists speculate that oxytocin might encourage similar cuddling between adult women and men. The versatile chemical may also enhance orgasms. In one study of men, oxytocin increased to three to five times its normal level during climax, and it may soar even higher in women.

16   Chemicals may help explain (at least to scientists) the feelings of passion and compassion, but why do people tend to fall in love with one partner rather than a myriad of others? Once again, it's partly a function of evolution and biology. "Men are looking for maximal fertility in a mate," says Loyola Marymount's Mills. "That is in large part why females in the prime childbearing ages of 17 to 28 are so desirable." Men can size up youth and vitality in a glance, and studies indeed show that men fall in love quite rapidly. Women tumble more slowly, to a large degree because their requirements are more complex; they need more time to check the guy out. "Age is not vital," notes Mills, "but the ability to provide security, father children, share resources and hold a high status in society are all key factors."

17   Still, that does not explain why the way Mary walks and laughs makes Bill dizzy with desire while Marcia's gait and giggle leave him cold. "Nature has wired us for one special person," suggests Walsh, romantically. He rejects the idea that a woman or a man can be in love with two people at the same time. Each person carries in his or her mind a unique subliminal guide to the ideal partner, a "love map," to borrow a term coined by sexologist John Money of Johns Hopkins University.

18   Drawn from the people and experiences of childhood, the map is a record of whatever we found enticing and exciting—or disturbing and disgusting. Small feet, curly hair. The way our mothers patted our head or how our fathers told a joke. A fireman's uniform, a doctor's stethoscope. All the information gathered while growing up is imprinted in the brain's circuitry by adolescence. Partners never meet each and every requirement, but a sufficient number of matches can light up the wires and signal, "It's love." Not every partner will be like the last one, since lovers may have different combinations of the characteristics favored by the map.

19   O.K., that's the scientific point of view. Satisfied? Probably not. To most people—with or without Ph.D.s—love will always be more than the sum of its natural parts. It's a commingling of body and soul, reality and imagination, poetry and phenylethylamine. In our deepest hearts, most of us harbor the hope that love will never fully yield up its secrets, that it will always elude our grasp.

[REFLECT]   # Make connections: How love works.

The chemistry of love is easily summarized: Amphetamines fuel romance; endorphins and oxytocin sustain lasting relationships. As Toufexis makes clear, however, these chemical reactions do not explain why people are attracted to each other in the first place. Rather, she claims that an attraction occurs because each of us carries a "unique subliminal guide," or "love map" (par. 17), that leads us unerringly to a partner. Make a short list of the qualities in a partner that would appear on your "love map," and then consider Toufexis's explanation. Your instructor may ask you to post your thoughts on a class discussion board or to discuss them with other students in class. Use these questions to get started:

- What role do factors such as family, friends, community, the media, and advertising play in constructing your love map?

- Why do you think Toufexis ignores the topic of sexual orientation?

- According to Toufexis, men typically look for "maximal fertility," whereas women look for security, resources, status, and a willingness to father children (par. 16). Does this explanation seem convincing to you? Why or why not?

Use the basic features.

[ANALYZE]

A FOCUSED EXPLANATION: EXCLUDING OTHER TOPICS

In writing about a concept as broad as love, Toufexis has to find a way to narrow her focus. Writers choose a focus in part by considering the **rhetorical situation**—the purpose, audience, medium, and genre—in which they are writing. Student Jonathan Potthast is limited by the fact that he is writing in response to his instructor's assignment. As a science writer for *Time* magazine, Toufexis probably also had an assignment—to report on current scientific research. The question is, though, how does she make the science interesting and understandable to her nonscientist readers?

ANALYZE & WRITE

Write a paragraph analyzing how Toufexis focuses her explanation:

1 What is the focus or main point of Toufexis's essay? How do you think she answers readers' potential "So what?" question?

2 How do the title, epigraph, and opening paragraphs help you identify this focus or main point?

3 How do you think Toufexis's purpose, audience, and genre (an article for a popular newsmagazine) affected her focus?

A CLEAR, LOGICAL ORGANIZATION: CUEING THE READER

Experienced writers know that readers often have trouble making their way through new and difficult material. To avoid having them give up in frustration, writers strive to construct a reader-friendly organization: They include a thesis statement that asserts the focus or main point—the answer to the "So what?" question. In addition writers sometimes include a *forecasting statement,* which alerts readers to the main topics to be discussed, and include *transitional words and phrases* to guide readers from topic to topic.

ANALYZE & WRITE

Write a paragraph or two analyzing the strategies Toufexis uses to organize her essay for readers:

1 Skim the essay, and note in the margin where she announces her concept and forecasts the topics she uses to organize her explanation. Then highlight the passage where she discusses each topic. How well does her forecast work to make her essay readable?

2 Study how Toufexis connects the topic of "love maps" (pars. 17–18) to the topics she discussed earlier in the essay. Identify any sentences that connect the two parts of the article, and assess how well they work.

APPROPRIATE EXPLANATORY STRATEGIES: USING VISUALS

Both Potthast and Toufexis use a visual to help explain their concept. In Potthast's case, the visual comes from one of his sources. In contrast, Toufexis's visual was most likely created after her article was written, by the magazine's art editor, Nigel Holmes. Notice also that whereas Potthast, following a convention of academic writing, refers in the text of his essay to the visual he includes, labeling it "Fig. 1" and providing a title and source, Toufexis does not refer to the visual in her text or provide a caption.

ANALYZE & WRITE

Write a paragraph analyzing Toufexis's use of the visual:

1. First, consider it apart from the rest of the article. What can you learn from the visual itself? What makes it easy or hard to read?

2. Then skim Toufexis's essay to mark where she discusses each of the stages in the process described in the flowchart. Considering her original audience, how well does the flowchart work as a map to help readers navigate through the somewhat technical content of her explanation? Would it have been helpful had Toufexis referred to and labeled the visual?

SMOOTH INTEGRATION OF SOURCES: ESTABLISHING CREDIBILITY

To establish their credibility on the subject, writers need to convince readers that the information they are using is authoritative. They can do this in a number of ways, but giving the professional credentials of their sources is a conventional strategy.

ANALYZE & WRITE

Write a paragraph or two analyzing how Toufexis establishes the credentials of her sources:

1. Skim the essay, underlining the name of each source she mentions. Then go back through the essay to highlight each source's credentials. When Toufexis provides credentials, what kinds of information does she include?

2. Consider the effectiveness of Toufexis's strategies for letting readers know the qualifications of her sources. Given her original audience (*Time* magazine readers), how well do you think she establishes her sources' credentials? If she were writing for an academic audience (for example, for your instructor), what would she have to add?

[RESPOND]   # Consider possible topics: Examining other aspects of love.

Like Toufexis, you could write an essay about love or romance, but you could choose a different focus—for example, the history of romantic love (how did the concept of romantic love develop in the West, and when did it become the basis of marriage?), love's cultural characteristics (how is love regarded by different American ethnic groups or in world cultures?), its excesses or extremes (what is sex addiction?), or the phases of falling in and out of love (what is infatuation?). You could also consider writing about other concepts involving personal relationships, such as jealousy, co-dependency, stereotyping, or homophobia.

John Tierney | *Do You Suffer from Decision Fatigue?*

© Fred R. Conrad/The New York Times/Redux

JOHN TIERNEY has been a columnist for the *New York Times* since 1990, where he has worked as a general assignment reporter and a regular columnist, writing for the *New York Times Magazine* and for the Metro section in a column called "The Big City." Currently he writes a column, "Findings," for the Science Times section. He has worked for several other magazines and newspapers, among them the *Atlantic Monthly, Discover, Esquire, Newsweek, Outside,* and the *Wall Street Journal.* In collaboration with novelist Christopher Buckley, Tierney co-wrote the comic novel *God Is My Broker* (2012), a parody of financial and spiritual self-help books. The essay below (originally published in 2011 in the *New York Times Magazine*) was adapted from a book he wrote with Roy F. Baumeister, *Willpower: Rediscovering the Greatest Human Strength* (2011).

As you read,

- Think about the effectiveness of the opening scenario that describes the decisions made by the parole board. What is Tierney's purpose in starting with this anecdote?

- Ponder the relationship you see between decision fatigue and willpower.

1   Three men doing time in Israeli prisons recently appeared before a parole board consisting of a judge, a criminologist and a social worker. The three prisoners had completed at least two-thirds of their sentences, but the parole board granted freedom to only one of them. Guess which one:

> Case 1 (heard at 8:50 a.m.): An Arab Israeli serving a 30-month sentence for fraud.
> Case 2 (heard at 3:10 p.m.): A Jewish Israeli serving a 16-month sentence for assault.
> Case 3 (heard at 4:25 p.m.): An Arab Israeli serving a 30-month sentence for fraud.

2   There was a pattern to the parole board's decisions, but it wasn't related to the men's ethnic backgrounds, crimes or sentences. It was all about timing, as researchers discovered by analyzing more than 1,100 decisions over the course of a year. Judges, who would hear the prisoners' appeals and then get advice from the other members of the board, approved parole in about a third of the cases, but the probability of being paroled fluctuated wildly throughout the day. Prisoners who appeared early in the morning received parole about 70 percent of the time, while those who appeared late in the day were paroled less than 10 percent of the time.

3   The odds favored the prisoner who appeared at 8:50 a.m.—and he did in fact receive parole. But even though the other Arab Israeli prisoner was serving the same sentence for the same crime—fraud—the odds were against him when he appeared (on a different day) at 4:25 in the afternoon. He was denied parole, as was the Jewish Israeli prisoner at 3:10 p.m, whose sentence was shorter than that of the man who was released. They were just asking for parole at the wrong time of day.

4   There was nothing malicious or even unusual about the judges' behavior, which was reported . . . by Jonathan Levav of Stanford and Shai Danziger of Ben-Gurion University.[1] The judges' erratic judgment was due to the occupational hazard of being, as George W. Bush once put it, "the decider." The mental work of ruling on case after case, whatever the individual merits, wore them down. This sort of decision fatigue can make quarterbacks prone to dubious choices late in the game and C.F.O.'s prone to disastrous dalliances late in the evening. It routinely warps the judgment of everyone, executive and nonexecutive, rich and poor—in fact, it can take a special toll on the poor. Yet few people are even aware of it, and researchers are only beginning to understand why it happens and how to counteract it.

5   Decision fatigue helps explain why ordinarily sensible people get angry at colleagues and families, splurge on clothes, buy junk food at the supermarket and can't resist the dealer's offer to rustproof their new car. No matter how rational and high-minded you try to be, you

can't make decision after decision without paying a biological price. It's different from ordinary physical fatigue—you're not consciously aware of being tired—but you're low on mental energy. The more choices you make throughout the day, the harder each one becomes for your brain, and eventually it looks for shortcuts, usually in either of two very different ways. One shortcut is to become reckless: to act impulsively instead of expending the energy to first think through the consequences. (Sure, tweet that photo! What could go wrong?) The other shortcut is the ultimate energy saver: do nothing. Instead of agonizing over decisions, avoid any choice. Ducking a decision often creates bigger problems in the long run, but for the moment, it eases the mental strain. You start to resist any change, any potentially risky move—like releasing a prisoner who might commit a crime. So the fatigued judge on a parole board takes the easy way out, and the prisoner keeps doing time.

6   Decision fatigue is the newest discovery involving a phenomenon called ego depletion, a term coined by the social psychologist Roy F. Baumeister[2] . . . [who] began studying mental discipline in a series of experiments, first at Case Western and then at Florida State University. These experiments demonstrated that there is a finite store of mental energy for exerting self-control. When people fended off the temptation to scarf down M&M's or freshly baked chocolate-chip cookies, they were then less able to resist other temptations. When they forced themselves to remain stoic during a tearjerker movie, afterward they gave up more quickly on lab tasks requiring self-discipline, like working on a geometry puzzle or squeezing a hand-grip exerciser. Willpower turned out to be more than a folk concept or a metaphor. It really was a form of mental energy that could be exhausted. The experiments confirmed the 19th-century notion of willpower being like a muscle that was fatigued with use, a force that could be conserved by avoiding temptation. To study the process of ego depletion, researchers concentrated initially on acts involving self-control—the kind of self-discipline popularly associated with willpower, like resisting a bowl of ice cream. They weren't concerned with routine decision-making, like choosing between chocolate and vanilla, a

When people fended off the temptation to scarf down M&M's or freshly baked chocolate-chip cookies, they were then less able to resist other temptations.

mental process that they assumed was quite distinct and much less strenuous. Intuitively, the chocolate-vanilla choice didn't appear to require willpower.

7   But then a postdoctoral fellow, Jean Twenge, started working at Baumeister's laboratory right after planning her wedding. As Twenge studied the results of the lab's ego-depletion experiments, she remembered how exhausted she felt the evening she and her fiancé went through the ritual of registering for gifts. Did they want plain white china or something with a pattern? Which brand of knives? How many towels? What kind of sheets? Precisely how many threads per square inch?

8   "By the end, you could have talked me into anything," Twenge told her new colleagues. The symptoms sounded familiar to them too, and gave them an idea. A nearby department store was holding a going-out-of-business sale, so researchers from the lab went off to fill their car trunks with simple products—not exactly wedding-quality gifts, but sufficiently appealing to interest college students. When they came to the lab, the students were told they would get to keep one item at the end of the experiment, but first they had to make a series of choices. Would they prefer a pen or a candle? A vanilla-scented candle or an almond-scented one? A candle or a T-shirt? A black T-shirt or a red T-shirt? A control group, meanwhile—let's call them the nondeciders—spent an equally long period contemplating all these same products without having to make any choices. They were asked just to give their opinion of each product and report how often they had used such a product in the last six months.

9   Afterward, all the participants were given one of the classic tests of self-control: holding your hand in ice water for as long as you can. The impulse is to pull your hand out, so self-discipline is needed to keep the hand underwater. The deciders gave up much faster; they lasted 28 seconds, less than half the 67-second average of the nondeciders. Making all those choices had apparently sapped their willpower. . . .

10   Any decision, whether it's what pants to buy or whether to start a war, can be broken down into what psychologists call the Rubicon model of action phases, in honor of the river that separated Italy from the

Roman province of Gaul. When Caesar reached it in 49 BC, on his way home after conquering the Gauls, he knew that a general returning to Rome was forbidden to take his legions across the river with him, lest it be considered an invasion of Rome. Waiting on the Gaul side of the river, he was in the "predecisional phase" as he contemplated the risks and benefits of starting a civil war. Then he stopped calculating and crossed the Rubicon, reaching the "postdecisional phase," which Caesar defined much more felicitously: "The die is cast."

11   The whole process could deplete anyone's willpower, but which phase of the decision-making process was most fatiguing? To find out, Kathleen Vohs, a former colleague of Baumeister's now at the University of Minnesota, performed an experiment [that] showed that crossing the Rubicon is more tiring than anything that happens on either bank—more mentally fatiguing than sitting on the Gaul side contemplating your options or marching on Rome once you've crossed. As a result, someone without Caesar's willpower is liable to stay put. To a fatigued judge, denying parole seems like the easier call not only because it preserves the status quo and eliminates the risk of a parolee going on a crime spree but also because it leaves more options open: the judge retains the option of paroling the prisoner at a future date without sacrificing the option of keeping him securely in prison right now.

12   Once you're mentally depleted, you become reluctant to make trade-offs, which involve a particularly advanced and taxing form of decision making. In the rest of the animal kingdom, there aren't a lot of protracted negotiations between predators and prey. To compromise is a complex human ability and therefore one of the first to decline when willpower is depleted. You become what researchers call a cognitive miser, hoarding your energy. If you're shopping, you're liable to look at only one dimension, like price: just give me the cheapest. Or you indulge yourself by looking at quality: I want the very best (an especially easy strategy if someone else is paying).

13   Decision fatigue leaves you vulnerable to marketers who know how to time their sales, as Jonathan Levav, the Stanford professor, demonstrated in experiments involving . . . new cars. . . . The car buyers . . . had to choose, for instance, among 4 styles of gearshift knobs, 13 kinds of wheel rims, 25 configurations of the engine and gearbox and a palette of 56 colors for the interior. As they started picking features, customers would carefully weigh the choices, but as decision fatigue set in, they would start settling for whatever the default option was. And the more tough choices they encountered early in the process—like going through those 56 colors to choose the precise shade of gray or brown—the quicker people became fatigued and settled for the path of least resistance by taking the default option. By manipulating the order of the car buyers' choices, the researchers found that the customers would end up settling for different kinds of options. . . . Whether the customers paid a little extra for fancy wheel rims or a lot extra for a more powerful engine depended on when the choice was offered and how much willpower was left in the customer. . . .

14   It's simple enough to imagine reforms for the parole board in Israel—like, say, restricting each judge's shift to half a day, preferably in the morning, interspersed with frequent breaks for food and rest. But it's not so obvious what to do with the decision fatigue affecting the rest of society. . . . Today we feel overwhelmed because there are so many choices. . . . Choosing what to have for breakfast, where to go on vacation, whom to hire, how much to spend—these all deplete willpower, and there's no telltale symptom of when that willpower is low. It's not like getting winded or hitting the wall during a marathon. Ego depletion manifests itself not as one feeling but rather as a propensity to experience everything more intensely. When the brain's regulatory powers weaken, frustrations seem more irritating than usual. Impulses to eat, drink, spend and say stupid things feel more powerful (and alcohol causes self-control to decline further). . . . Like the depleted parole judges, [ego-depleted humans] become inclined to take the safer, easier option even when that option hurts someone else.

Links

1. Danziger, Shai, Jonathan Levav, and Liora Avnaim-Pesso. "Extraneous Factors in Judicial Decisions." *Proceedings of the National Academy of Sciences for the United States of America* 108.17 (2011): 6889–92. Print.
2. "Dr. Roy Baumeister," *Faculty Directory, Psychology Dept.* Florida State U, 2013.

[REFLECT]

Make connections: Your own experience with decision fatigue.

Tierney writes about a judge whose fairness is undermined by decision fatigue. Think about your own experience making decisions. Have you ever made a decision that you regretted or avoided making a decision when decisiveness was important? Your instructor may ask you to post your thoughts on a class discussion board or to discuss them with other students in class. Use these questions to get started:

- Think about a decision that you regretted making (or not making). How may decision fatigue have influenced you? What else might have influenced your decision (for example, peer pressure or fear of disappointing a loved one)?

- Tierney points out that it would be easy to reform the schedule of the parole board to take the decision fatigue out of their day, but that "it's not so obvious what to do with the decision fatigue affecting the rest of society" (par. 14). What steps could you take to ease decision fatigue? How would society change if we all had fewer decisions to make? What would we gain, and what would we be giving up?

[ANALYZE]

Use the basic features.

A FOCUSED EXPLANATION: USING AN EXAMPLE

Examples often play a central role in writing about concepts because concepts are general and abstract, and examples help make them specific and concrete. Examples can also be very useful tools for focusing an explanation. Toufexis, for example, uses examples of popular films (*Bram Stoker's Dracula, The Seven-Year Itch*) to illustrate different conceptions of love norms. John Tierney uses Jean Twenge's experience of registering for wedding gifts to illustrate how decision fatigue can erode shoppers' willpower.

⎯⎯| ANALYZE & WRITE |⎯⎯⎯⎯⎯⎯⎯⎯⎯⎯⎯⎯⎯⎯⎯⎯⎯⎯⎯⎯⎯⎯⎯

Write a paragraph analyzing how Tierney uses the example of one judge deciding the fate of three prisoners to illustrate the concept of decision fatigue:

1. Skim paragraphs 1–4. How do they help readers understand the concept of decision fatigue?

2. Now look back at paragraph 4. How does this paragraph answer the "So what?" question readers of concept explanations inevitably ask? In other words, how does it provide a focus for Tierney's explanation of the concept and help readers grasp why the concept is important?

3. Finally, reread paragraph 13, in which Tierney explains how marketers use decision fatigue. Why do you suppose Tierney includes this information in his explanation of the concept?

A CLEAR, LOGICAL ORGANIZATION: CREATING COHESION

Cohesive devices help readers move from paragraph to paragraph and section to section without losing the thread. The most familiar cohesive device is probably the transitional word or phrase (*however, next*), which alerts readers to the relationship among ideas. A less familiar, but equally effective strategy, is to repeat key terms and their synonyms or to use pronouns (*it, they*) to refer to the key term. A third strategy is to provide cohesion by referring back to earlier examples, often bringing a selection full circle by referring to an opening example at the end of the essay.

ANALYZE & WRITE

Write a paragraph or two analyzing how Tierney creates cohesion in "Do You Suffer from Decision Fatigue?":

1. Skim paragraphs 1–4, marking every word (or number) related to time. How does Tierney use time to lend cohesion to his essay? How effectively does this strategy help readers navigate this essay and understand its main point?

2. Select a series of three or four paragraphs and analyze how Tierney knits the paragraphs together. Can you identify any repeated words or concepts, or any pronouns that refer to terms in the preceding paragraph? Does Tierney use transitional words or phrases to link one paragraph to the next?

3. Finally, reread the last paragraph. How does Tierney lend closure to his essay? How effective is his strategy?

APPROPRIATE EXPLANATORY STRATEGIES: USING A VARIETY OF STRATEGIES

Writers typically use a variety of strategies to explain a concept. Potthast, for example, *defines* the concept of *supervolcano*, *classifies* the historic eruptions, *illustrates* their consequences, and explores *causes* and "dangerous physical *effects*" (par. 2) of supervolcanoes. Here are a few examples of sentence patterns Potthast uses to present some of these explanatory strategies:

Definition

> **EXAMPLE**   Supervolcanoes are volcanoes that produce eruptions thousands of times the size of ordinary volcanoes. (par. 1)

▶ X is a member of class Y with _____ , _____ , and _____ [distinguishing traits].

Classification

> **EXAMPLE**   Volcanic eruptions feature several dangerous physical effects, including pyroclastic flows, pyroclastic surges, lahars, tephra falls, and massive amounts of fine ash particles in the air. (par. 2)

▶ X is made up of 3 basic parts: _____ , _____ , _____ .

Cause-Effect Reasoning

EXAMPLE   If a super-eruption were to occur here, the results would be devastating. . . . Toxic gases would sweep across much of the nation, making "two-thirds of the U.S. . . . uninhabitable . . . forcing millions to leave their homes" (Bates). (Potthast, par. 11)

▶ The causes of X are varied, but the most notable are ⎯⎯⎯⎯⎯ and ⎯⎯⎯⎯⎯ .

▶ The effects of X may include ⎯⎯⎯⎯⎯ , ⎯⎯⎯⎯⎯ , and ⎯⎯⎯⎯⎯ .

ANALYZE & WRITE

For more about writing strategies, see Part 3.

Write a paragraph analyzing how Tierney uses definition, classification, cause-effect reasoning, and other strategies (such as example, comparison-contrast, or process analysis) to explain decision fatigue:

1. Skim Tierney's essay looking for and highlighting examples of two or three different types of explanatory strategies.

2. Now select one strategy that you think is particularly effective and explain why you think it works so well. What does the strategy contribute to the explanation of decision fatigue? How does it help answer the "So what?" question?

SMOOTH INTEGRATION OF SOURCES: DECIDING WHEN AND HOW TO CITE SOURCES

Writers of concept explanations nearly always conduct research; incorporate information from sources into their writing using summary, paraphrase, and quotation; and identify their sources so that readers can identify them as experts. But how they acknowledge their sources depends on the conventions of their writing situation. Toufexis, writing for *Time* magazine's general audience, makes clear that her sources are experts by mentioning their credentials in signal phrases:

> Says Michael Mills, a psychology professor at Loyola Marymount University in Los Angeles: "Love is our ancestors whispering in our ears." (par. 2)

But she does not include a formal citation or a list of works cited at the end of the article. Sometimes Potthast uses a signal phrase to make his source's expertise clear; sometimes he merely includes a citation in his text. But in all cases, he includes a full citation in his list of works cited because this is required when writing for an academic audience.

ANALYZE & WRITE

Write a paragraph or two analyzing the kinds of material Tierney incorporates from sources and how he identifies his sources so that his readers know that they can be trusted:

1. Skim the essay, highlighting places where Tierney quotes, paraphrases, or summarizes information from sources. What information does he provide to identify his sources, and how does this information help readers know the source is trustworthy? Try to

determine which information comes from published sources, which from interviews, and which from Tierney's own general knowledge of the topic.

2   Again skim the essay, this time looking for places where Tierney uses an exact quotation from a source. Why do you think he decided to use an exact quotation rather than merely summarizing or paraphrasing the idea?

3   Finally, think about the purpose of citing sources. Why is simply identifying sources with a word or two in the text generally sufficient for nonacademic situations, while academic writing situations require in-text citations and a list of sources? Given your experience reading online, do you think hyperlinks should replace formal citations? Why or why not?

Consider possible topics: Examining how emotions influence behavior.

[RESPOND]

Because behavioral research can help us understand ourselves in new ways, essays that shed light on psychological phenomena can be fascinating to readers. A writer could explore cognitive dissonance, the foot-in-the-door phenomenon, or social loafing, for example. Recent research explores the concept of ego depletion in relation to dieting and depression. Like ego depletion, post-traumatic stress disorder was named only in the last few decades, and scientists are only now discovering new ways to treat it. Consider entering the concept you are seeking to explain into the search field of a database in the social sciences, like *PsycArticles* or *Social Sciences Full Text*, to find an interesting topic you might never have thought of on your own.

Susan Cain | *Shyness: Evolutionary Tactic?*

© Rex Features via AP Images

SUSAN CAIN is the author of the book *Quiet: The Power of Introverts in a World That Can't Stop Talking* (2012). She also writes a popular blog about introversion, and her TED talk has broken viewing records. Her writing has appeared in the *Atlantic*, the *Wall Street Journal*, *Psychology Today*, and many other publications. The selection that appears here was originally published in the *New York Times*. As you read, consider these questions:

• Notice the title of this selection and the title of Cain's book. What do these titles lead you to expect?

• Given that this selection was first published in a newspaper, consider how effective the opening paragraph is as a hook to catch readers' attention.

1   A beautiful woman lowers her eyes demurely beneath a hat. In an earlier era, her gaze might have signaled a mysterious allure. But this is a 2003 advertisement for Zoloft, a selective serotonin reuptake inhibitor (SSRI) approved by the FDA to treat social anxiety disorder. "Is she just shy? Or is it Social Anxiety Disorder?" reads the caption, suggesting that the young woman is not alluring at all. She is sick.

2   But is she?

3   It is possible that the lovely young woman has a life-wrecking form of social anxiety. There are people too afraid of disapproval to venture out for a job interview, a date or even a meal in public. Despite the risk of serious side effects—nausea, loss of sex drive, seizures—drugs like Zoloft can be a godsend for this group.

4   But the ad's insinuation aside, it's also possible the young woman is "just shy," or introverted—traits our society disfavors. One way we manifest this bias is by encouraging perfectly healthy shy people to see themselves as ill.

5   This does us all a grave disservice, because shyness and introversion—or more precisely, the careful, sensitive temperament from which both often spring—are not just normal. They are valuable. And they may be essential to the survival of our species.

6   Theoretically, shyness and social anxiety disorder are easily distinguishable. But a blurry line divides the two. Imagine that the woman in the ad enjoys a steady paycheck, a strong marriage and a small circle of close friends—a good life by most measures—except that she avoids a needed promotion because she's nervous about leading meetings. She often criticizes herself for feeling too shy to speak up.

Shyness and introversion . . . are not just normal. They are valuable. And they may be essential to the survival of our species.

7   What do you think now? Is she ill, or does she simply need public-speaking training?

8   Before 1980, this would have seemed a strange question. Social anxiety disorder did not officially exist until it appeared in that year's Diagnostic and Statistical Manual, the DSM-III, the psychiatrist's bible of mental disorders, under the name "social phobia." It was not widely known until the 1990s, when pharmaceutical companies received FDA approval to treat social anxiety with SSRI's and poured tens of millions of dollars into advertising its existence. The current version of the Diagnostic and Statistical Manual, the DSM-IV, acknowledges that stage fright (and shyness in social situations) is common and not necessarily a sign of illness. But it also says that diagnosis is warranted when anxiety "interferes significantly" with work performance or if the sufferer shows "marked distress" about it. According to this definition, the answer to our question is clear: the young woman in the ad is indeed sick.

9   The DSM inevitably reflects cultural attitudes; it used to identify homosexuality as a disease, too. Though the DSM did not set out to pathologize shyness, it risks doing so, and has twice come close to identifying introversion as a disorder, too. (Shyness and introversion are not the same thing. Shy people fear negative judgment; introverts simply prefer quiet, minimally stimulating environments.)

10   But shyness and introversion share an undervalued status in a world that prizes extroversion. Children's classroom desks are now often arranged in pods, because group participation supposedly leads to better learning; in one school I visited, a sign announcing "Rules for Group Work" included, "You can't ask a teacher for help unless everyone in your group has the same question." Many adults work for organizations that now assign work in teams, in offices without walls, for supervisors who value "people skills" above all. As a society, we prefer action to contemplation, risk-taking to heed-taking, certainty to doubt. Studies show that we rank fast and frequent talkers as more competent, likable and even smarter than slow ones. As the psychologists William Hart and Dolores Albarracin point out, phrases like "get active," "get moving," "do something" and similar calls to action surface repeatedly in recent books.

11   Yet shy and introverted people have been part of our species for a very long time, often in leadership positions. We find them in the Bible ("Who am I, that I should go unto Pharaoh?" asked Moses, whom the Book of Numbers describes as "very meek, above all the men which were upon the face of the earth.") We find them in recent history, in figures like Charles Darwin, Marcel Proust and Albert Einstein, and, in contemporary times: think of Google's Larry Page, or Harry Potter's creator, J. K. Rowling.

12   In the science journalist Winifred Gallagher's words: "The glory of the disposition that stops to consider stimuli rather than rushing to engage with them is its long association with intellectual and artistic achievement. Neither $E = mc^2$ nor *Paradise Lost* was dashed off by a party animal."

13   We even find "introverts" in the animal kingdom, where 15 percent to 20 percent of many species are watchful, slow-to-warm-up types who stick to the

sidelines (sometimes called "sitters") while the other 80 percent are "rovers" who sally forth without paying much attention to their surroundings. Sitters and rovers favor different survival strategies, which could be summed up as the sitter's "Look before you leap" versus the rover's inclination to "Just do it!" Each strategy reaps different rewards.

14   In an illustrative experiment, David Sloan Wilson, a Binghamton evolutionary biologist, dropped metal traps into a pond of pumpkinseed sunfish. The "rover" fish couldn't help but investigate—and were immediately caught. But the "sitter" fish stayed back, making it impossible for Professor Wilson to capture them. Had Professor Wilson's traps posed a real threat, only the sitters would have survived. But had the sitters taken Zoloft and become more like bold rovers, the entire family of pumpkinseed sunfish would have been wiped out. "Anxiety" about the trap saved the fishes' lives.

15   Next, Professor Wilson used fishing nets to catch both types of fish; when he carried them back to his lab, he noted that the rovers quickly acclimated to their new environment and started eating a full five days earlier than their sitter brethren. In this situation, the rovers were the likely survivors. "There is no single best . . . [animal] personality," Professor Wilson concludes in his book, *Evolution for Everyone,* "but rather a diversity of personalities maintained by natural selection."

16   The same might be said of humans, 15 percent to 20 percent of whom are also born with sitter-like temperaments that predispose them to shyness and introversion. (The overall incidence of shyness and introversion is higher—40 percent of the population for shyness, according to the psychology professor Jonathan Cheek, and 50 percent for introversion. Conversely, some born sitters never become shy or introverted at all.)

17   Once you know about sitters and rovers, you see them everywhere, especially among young children. Drop in on your local Mommy and Me music class: there are the sitters, intently watching the action from their mothers' laps, while the rovers march around the room banging their drums and shaking their maracas.

18   Relaxed and exploratory, the rovers have fun, make friends and will take risks, both rewarding and dangerous ones, as they grow. According to Daniel Nettle, a Newcastle University evolutionary psychologist, extroverts are more likely than introverts to be hospitalized as a result of an injury, have affairs (men) and change

relationships (women). One study of bus drivers even found that accidents are more likely to occur when extroverts are at the wheel.

19   In contrast, sitter children are careful and astute, and tend to learn by observing instead of by acting. They notice scary things more than other children do, but they also notice more things in general. Studies dating all the way back to the 1960s by the psychologists Jerome Kagan and Ellen Siegelman found that cautious, solitary children playing matching games spent more time considering all the alternatives than impulsive children did, actually using more eye movements to make decisions. Recent studies by a group of scientists at Stony Brook University and at Chinese universities using functional MRI technology echoed this research, finding that adults with sitter-like temperaments looked longer at pairs of photos with subtle differences and showed more activity in brain regions that make associations between the photos and other stored information in the brain.

20   Once they reach school age, many sitter children use such traits to great effect. Introverts, who tend to digest information thoroughly, stay on task, and work accurately, earn disproportionate numbers of National Merit Scholarship finalist positions and Phi Beta Kappa keys, according to the Center for Applications of Psychological Type, a research arm for the Myers-Briggs personality type indicator—even though their IQ scores are no higher than those of extroverts. Another study, by the psychologists Eric Rolfhus and Philip Ackerman, tested 141 college students' knowledge of 20 different subjects, from art to astronomy to statistics, and found that the introverts knew more than the extroverts about 19 subjects—presumably, the researchers concluded, because the more time people spend socializing, the less time they have for learning.

21   The psychologist Gregory Feist found that many of the most creative people in a range of fields are introverts who are comfortable working in solitary conditions in which they can focus attention inward. Steve Wozniak, the engineer who founded Apple with Steve Jobs, is a prime example: Mr. Wozniak describes his creative process as an exercise in solitude. "Most inventors and engineers I've met are like me," he writes in "iWoz," his autobiography. "They're shy and they live in their heads. They're almost like artists. In fact, the very best of them are artists. And artists work best alone. . . . Not on a committee. Not on a team."

22   Sitters' temperaments also confer more subtle advantages. Anxiety, it seems, can serve an important social purpose; for example, it plays a key role in the development of some children's consciences. When caregivers rebuke them for acting up, they become anxious, and since anxiety is unpleasant, they tend to develop prosocial behaviors. Shy children are often easier to socialize and more conscientious, according to the developmental psychologist Grazyna Kochanska. By six they're less likely than their peers to cheat or break rules, even when they think they can't be caught, according to one study. By seven they're more likely to be described by their parents as having high levels of moral traits such as empathy.

23   When I shared this information with the mother of a "sitter" daughter, her reaction was mixed. "That is all very nice," she said, "but how will it help her in the tough real world?" But sensitivity, if it is not excessive and is properly nurtured, can be a catalyst for empathy and even leadership. Eleanor Roosevelt, for example, was a courageous leader who was very likely a sitter. Painfully shy and serious as a child, she grew up to be a woman who could not look away from other people's suffering—and who urged her husband, the constitutionally buoyant F.D.R., to do the same; the man who had nothing to fear but fear itself relied, paradoxically, on a woman deeply acquainted with it.

24   Another advantage sitters bring to leadership is a willingness to listen to and implement other people's ideas. A groundbreaking study led by the Wharton management professor Adam Grant, to be published this month in *The Academy of Management Journal*, found that introverts outperform extroverts when leading teams of proactive workers—the kinds of employees who take initiative and are disposed to dream up better ways of doing things. Professor Grant notes that business self-help guides often suggest that introverted leaders practice their communication skills and smile more. But, he told me, it may be extrovert leaders who need to change, to listen more and say less.

25   What would the world look like if all our sitters chose to medicate themselves? The day may come when we have pills that "cure" shyness and turn introverts into social butterflies—without the side effects and other drawbacks of today's medications. (A recent study suggests that today's SSRI's not only relieve social anxiety but also induce extroverted behavior.) The day may come—and might be here already—when people are as comfortable changing their psyches as the color of their hair. If we continue to confuse shyness with sickness, we may find ourselves in a world of all rovers and no sitters, of all yang and no yin.

26   As a sitter who enjoys an engaged, productive life, and a professional speaking career, but still experiences the occasional knock-kneed moment, I can understand why caring physicians prescribe available medicine and encourage effective non-pharmaceutical treatments such as cognitive-behavioral therapy.

27   But even non-medical treatments emphasize what is wrong with the people who use them. They don't focus on what is right. Perhaps we need to rethink our approach to social anxiety: to address the pain, but to respect the temperament that underlies it. The act of treating shyness as an illness obscures the value of that temperament. Ridding people of social unease need not involve pathologizing their fundamental nature, but rather urging them to use its gifts.

28   It's time for the young woman in the Zoloft ad to rediscover her allure.

[REFLECT] # Make connections: What's wrong with being quiet?

Cain asserts that "shyness and introversion share an undervalued status in a world that prizes extroversion. . . . As a society, we prefer action to contemplation, risk-taking to heed-taking, certainty to doubt" (par. 10). To explore these categories of introversion and extroversion and to test Cain's assertion about society's valuing one personality type over the other, think of someone you would describe as introverted and someone else who seems to be extroverted. (Include yourself, if you like.) What in particular leads you to classify these individuals as introverts or extroverts? Consider whether personality type has any effect on how other people react to them or whether they are more or less successful in school or in social or work contexts. Your instructor may ask you to post your thoughts on a class discussion board or to discuss them with other students in class. Use these questions to get you started:

- What do you think are the defining characteristics of these two personality types?
- Which, if any, of these characteristics seem to be overvalued or devalued? By whom and in what contexts? Why?
- Cain raises a question about the way psychiatrists and the pharmaceutical industry may be pathologizing shyness or introversion—in other words, "encouraging perfectly healthy shy people to see themselves as ill" (par. 4). What do you think about this issue?

Use the basic features.

[ANALYZE]

A FOCUSED EXPLANATION: PRESENTING ESTABLISHED INFORMATION AND YOUR OWN IDEAS

Writing his essay on decision fatigue, Tierney takes on the job of explaining a concept that is new to his audience. Like many writers of concept explanations, he draws on his research to make an important concept clear and accessible to general readers. Cain, in contrast, explains a concept that many readers think they understand, and she uses her explanation of the concept to make a broader point about the value of introversion.

ANALYZE & WRITE

Write a paragraph or two analyzing how Cain reports information and also presents her own ideas:

1. Reread paragraph 5, in which Cain states her thesis. How does the phrase between dashes in the first sentence ("or more precisely, the careful, sensitive temperament from which both often spring") help unify the different phenomena she describes in this article?

2. Consider the second and third sentences in paragraph 5. How do these sentences help convey Cain's purpose?

3. Skim the rest of the article, looking for places where Cain restates the ideas she conveys in sentences 2 and 3 of paragraph 5. Highlight the words and phrases that restate this theme.

4. Consider how effective Cain's moves are: After reading the article, do you know what shyness is? Are you persuaded that it is underrated? Why or why not?

A CLEAR, LOGICAL ORGANIZATION: CREATING CLOSURE

Toufexis begins her essay by addressing the reader directly: "O.K., let's cut out all this nonsense about romantic love" (par. 1), and she ends by returning to address the reader directly: "O.K., that's the scientific point of view. Satisfied?" (par. 19). By returning to a direct address to the audience, even repeating the word "O.K.," she brings her essay to a satisfying close.

Write a paragraph or two analyzing how Cain creates a sense of closure in her article:

1. Skim paragraphs 1–8 and 25–28 to remind yourself of how Cain begins and ends the reading selection. What image does she start with? What image does she end with? How does she make sense of this image for her readers? What context does she put it in?

2. Notice the pronouns she uses: *she, we, us, they, I*. How does the shift—from talking about the shy, the introverted, the "sitters," in the third person (*she/he/they*) to talking about them in the first person (*I/we*)—change the context in which the Zoloft ad is presented? How does this shift in the pronouns Cain uses add or detract from the sense of closure?

APPROPRIATE EXPLANATORY STRATEGIES: USING COMPARISON-CONTRAST

Writers explaining concepts often use comparison and contrast. Research has shown that seeing how unfamiliar concepts are similar to or different from concepts we already know facilitates the learning of new concepts. Even when both concepts are unfamiliar, comparing foregrounds commonalities, while contrasting makes visible inconsistencies we might not otherwise notice.

Writers employ many strategies to signal comparisons and contrasts, including words that emphasize similarity or difference, and repeating sentence patterns to highlight the differences:

Like emphasizes similarity

The experiments confirmed the 19th-century notion of willpower being like a muscle that was fatigued with use. (Tierney, par. 6)

Repeated sentence pattern emphasizes contrast

"Early love is when you love the way the other person makes you feel." . . . "Mature love is when you love the person as he or she is." It is the difference between passionate and compassionate love. . . . "It's Bon Jovi vs. Beethoven." (Toufexis, par. 14)

To learn more about comparing and contrasting, see Chapter 18.

Write a paragraph or two analyzing Cain's strategies for showing contrast:

1. Find and highlight two or three of the sentence patterns Cain uses for cueing contrast in paragraphs 3–4, 9–10, 13, 18, and 19.

2. Analyze what is being contrasted and how each contrast works.

3. Why do you think Cain uses contrast so often in this essay?

SMOOTH INTEGRATION OF SOURCES: USING EVIDENCE FROM A SOURCE TO SUPPORT A CLAIM

Cain's article first appeared in the *New York Times*. So, like Toufexis and Tierney, whose articles were originally published in popular periodicals, Cain names her sources and mentions their credentials but does not cite them as you must do when writing a paper for a class. While Cain does not cite her sources formally, as academic writing requires, she does integrate her sources effectively by

- making a claim of her own;

- providing appropriate, relevant supporting evidence;

- naming her source author(s) in a signal phrase (name plus an appropriate verb) and mentioning his, her, or their credentials;

- showing how the evidence supports her claim.

Look at how Cain achieves these goals:

> *As a society, we prefer action to contemplation, risk-taking to heed-taking, certainty to doubt.* Studies show that we rank fast and frequent talkers as more competent, likable and even smarter than slow ones. As the psychologists William Hart and Dolores Albarracin point out, phrases like "get active," "get moving," "do something" and similar calls to action surface repeatedly in recent books. (par. 10)

Cain's idea
Supporting evidence
Signal phrase plus credentials
Links Cain's idea and research findings

ANALYZE & WRITE

Write a paragraph analyzing how Cain integrates source material elsewhere in her article:

1 Examine paragraphs 18–19 or 20–21 to see how Cain uses a pattern similar to the one described above.

2 Find and mark the elements: Cain's idea; the name(s) and credentials of the source or sources; what the source found; text linking the source's findings to the original idea or extending the idea in some way.

3 When writers use information from sources, why do you think they often begin by stating their own idea (even if they got the idea from a source)? What do you think would be the effect on readers if the opening sentence of paragraph 18 or 20 began with the source instead of with Cain's topic sentence?

Consider possible topics: Correcting a misunderstood concept.

[RESPOND]

Cain writes in this article about a concept she thinks has been misunderstood or misused. Consider other concepts that you think need clarification. For example, you might consider concepts such as *attention-deficit hyperactivity disorder (ADHD)*, *autism spectrum*, or *transgender*. Alternatively, you might consider contested political concepts such as *liberal, conservative, corporate personhood, American exceptionalism*, or *regime change*.

REMIX

Remixing Your Concept Explanation

Concept explanations regularly appear in genres and media besides the college essay. For example, Jonathan Potthast could have used information from his concept essay to propose that more money be devoted to researching the Yellowstone supervolcano, or he could have presented information from his essay using PowerPoint or Prezi slides. Instead, Potthast decided to remix a portion of his concept explanation on supervolcanoes as a poster that he could display for an information session in the geology department. (A remix takes all or part of a piece in one genre or medium to create a text in another genre or medium). He thought the poster would be an appropriate genre for the information session because it would enable visitors to get information about the destructive power of the Yellowstone supervolcano quickly, as they walked through the exhibits.

In the next section of this chapter, we ask you to craft your own concept explanation. After composing it as an essay, consider remixing it (or a portion of it) in another medium or genre or using it as part of an essay with a different purpose or audience.

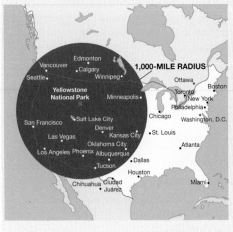

What would happen if the Yellowstone supervolcano erupted?

- A **10-foot layer of ash** would destroy vegetation within 1,000 miles.
- **Toxic gases** would make "two-thirds of the U.S. … uninhabitable … forcing millions to leave their homes" (Bates).
- Burning plants would generate **vast amounts of CO₂**, increasing the greenhouse effect in the long term.
- Volcanic debris high in the atmosphere would "plunge the Earth into a 'volcanic winter'" (Achenbach 2).
- A **"hole … the size of Rhode Island"** (Achenbach 1) would be gouged out of Wyoming, Montana, and Idaho.

CONSIDER YOUR RHETORICAL SITUATION

Purpose: The purpose of your concept explanation is to inform readers about your subject by answering their "So what?" question, showing how your subject is interesting or important. If you remix your concept explanation, *which genre or medium would best allow you to explain the concept so readers would learn something and be engaged by the explanation?*

Audience: The audience for your concept explanation essay was your instructor and other students in your class. *Who would be the audience if you were to remix your essay in another genre or medium? What advantages would that genre or medium have in helping you grab and keep the attention of your audience?*

Genre and medium: The genre of your concept explanation was the essay and the medium was text, delivered either in print or digitally. If you remix your concept explanation, *what genre or medium would best help you achieve your purpose and reach your intended audience?*

The Writing Assignment

Explain an important and interesting concept, one you already know well or are just learning about. Consider what your readers are likely to know and think about the concept, what they are likely to find interesting about the topic, what you might want them to learn about it, and whether you can research it sufficiently in the time you have.

This Guide to Writing is designed to help you compose your own concept explanation and apply what you have learned from analyzing other concept explanations. Use the Starting Points chart to help you find answers to questions you might have about explaining a concept.

STARTING POINTS: EXPLAINING A CONCEPT

A Focused Explanation

How do I come up with a concept to write about?

- Consider Possible Topics (pp. 134, 141, 147)
- Choose a concept to write about. (p. 151)
- Test Your Choice: Considering Your Purpose and Audience (p. 152)

How can I decide on a focus for my concept?

- Assess the genre's basic features: A focused explanation. (p. 122)
- Conduct initial research on the concept. (pp. 152–53)
- Focus your explanation of the concept. (p. 153)
- Test Your Choice: Evaluating Your Focus (p. 154)
- Conduct further research on your focused concept. (p. 154)

How can I make my concept clear and interesting to my readers?

- A Focused Explanation: Excluding Other Topics (p. 133)
- A Focused Explanation: Using an Example (p. 138)
- A Focused Explanation: Presenting Established Information and Your Own Ideas (p. 145)
- Focus your explanation of the concept. (p. 153)
- Test Your Choice: Evaluating Your Focus (p. 154)
- Write the opening sentences. (pp. 159–60)
- A Troubleshooting Guide: A Focused Explanation (pp. 162–63)

A Clear, Logical Organization

How should I organize my explanation so that it's logical and easy to read?

- Assess the genre's basic features: A clear, logical organization. (p. 122)
- A Clear, Logical Organization: Creating Closure (pp. 145–46)
- Draft your working thesis. (p. 154)
- Create an outline that will organize your concept explanation effectively for your readers. (p. 155)
- A Troubleshooting Guide: A Clear, Logical Organization (p. 163)

What kinds of cues should I provide?

- Assess the genre's basic features: A clear, logical organization. (p. 122)
- A Clear, Logical Organization: Cueing the Reader (p. 133)
- A Clear, Logical Organization: Creating Cohesion (p. 139)
- Draft your working thesis. (p. 154)
- Design your writing project. (p. 155)

Appropriate Explanatory Strategies

What's the best way to explain my concept? What writing strategies should I use?

- Assess the genre's basic features: Appropriate explanatory strategies. (p. 123)
- Appropriate Explanatory Strategies: Using Visuals (p. 134)
- Appropriate Explanatory Strategies: Using a Variety of Strategies (pp. 139–40)
- Appropriate Explanatory Strategies: Using Comparison-Contrast (p. 146)
- Consider the explanatory strategies you should use. (pp. 155–56)
- Use summaries, paraphrases, and quotations from sources to support your points. (p. 157)
- Use visuals or multimedia illustrations. (pp. 157–58)
- A Troubleshooting Guide: Appropriate Explanatory Strategies (p. 164)

Smooth Integration of Sources

How should I integrate sources so that they support my argument?

- Assess the genre's basic features: Smooth integration of sources. (pp. 123–24)
- Smooth Integration of Sources: Establishing Credibility (p. 134)
- Use appositives to integrate sources. (p. 158)
- Use descriptive verbs in signal phrases to introduce information from sources. (p. 159)
- A Troubleshooting Guide: Smooth Integration of Sources (p. 165)

Writing a Draft: Invention, Research, Planning, and Composing

The activities in this section will help you choose a concept and develop an explanation that will appeal to your readers, using appropriate explanatory strategies as well as photographs, tables, charts, and other illustrations. Do the activities in any order that makes sense to you (and your instructor), and return to them as needed as you revise.

⠿ Choose a concept to write about.

List possible concepts you might write about. For the best results, your concept should be one that you

- understand well or feel eager to learn more about;
- think is important and will interest your readers;
- can research sufficiently in the allotted time;
- can explain clearly in the length prescribed by your instructor.

Review the Consider Possible Topics activities on pages 134, 141, and 147 and reread notes you made in response to those suggestions. The following list suggests some good concepts:

- **Biology, nursing, and the physical sciences:** morphogenesis, electron transport, phagocytosis, homozygosity, diffusion, mass, energy, gravity, entropy, communicable diseases, epidemiology, toxicology, holistic medicine, pathogen

- **Business and economics:** opportunity cost, elasticity of demand, negative externalities, minimum wage, affirmative action, collective bargaining, robotics, flex time, family leave

- **Environment:** fracking, toxic waste, endangered species, sustainability, climate change

- **Identity and community:** multiculturalism, racism, sexism, social contract, community policing, social Darwinism, identity politics, public space

- **Literature and cultural studies:** irony, semiotics, dystopia, canon, postmodernism, realism, genre, connotation

- **Psychology and sociology:** assimilation/accommodation, social cognition, emotional intelligence, the Stroop effect, trauma, theory of mind, deviance, ethnocentrism, social stratification, acculturation, cultural relativism, patriarchy

- **Management and finance:** risk management, leveraged buyout, deregulation, branding, economy of scale, monopoly capitalism, socially conscious investing

Considering Your Purpose and Audience

To decide whether to proceed with this concept, ask yourself the following questions:

- Can I answer my readers' inevitable "So what?" question and make the concept seem interesting and worth knowing about?
- Am I interested in the concept, and can I focus my explanation?
- Do I know enough about the concept now, or can I research it in the time I have?

⠿ Conduct initial research on the concept.

Start by surveying what you already know about the topic, so you can better determine what gaps you need to fill. The following activities will help you begin putting your ideas into words that you may be able to use as you draft.

WAYS IN

> **WHAT DO I ALREADY KNOW ABOUT THE CONCEPT?**
>
> *To determine what you already know, ask yourself questions like these, using the sentence strategies as jumping-off points to answer them.*
>
> Why is my concept worth writing about?
>
> ▶ My concept is important/useful for the study of .... because .... [list reasons].
>
> What writing strategies can I use to explain the concept?
>
> ▶ My concept can be divided into the following categories: .... , ... , and .... (Classification)
>
> ▶ Examples of my concept include .... , ... , and .... (Examples)
>
> ▶ My concept is a .... [member of a larger category] that is/does/has these defining characteristics: .... , ... , and .... (Definition)

Research your concept in three stages:

1. Gain an overview of the concept.
2. Identify an aspect of the concept to focus on.
3. Conduct enough research to learn about this aspect of the concept.

A reference database, such as the *Gale Virtual Reference Library* or *Web of Science*, can provide you with an overview of your concept as well as the following:

- names of experts on your subject;
- terms, phrases, or synonyms that you might use as search terms later;
- interesting aspects of the concept that you might want to focus on.

You may need to read several articles covering your topic to get the information you need. A search engine can also help you get an overview: Enter the word *overview* or *definition* with the name of your concept, and skim the top ten search results to get a general sense of your topic. You can bookmark useful links or save a copy. Limiting your results to those from *.edu, .gov,* or *.org* domains is more likely to generate reliable results.

To learn more about conducting research, see Chapter 21.

⠿ Focus your explanation of the concept.

What interests you most about your topic? What do you think will most interest your readers? The following activities will help you find a way to focus your explanation.

WAYS IN

WHAT MAKES THE CONCEPT INTERESTING TO ME AND MY READERS?

List two or three aspects of your concept that interest you, and then answer these questions:

- Why does this aspect interest you?

- How is it relevant to your life, family, community, work, or studies?

- What do you already know about this aspect of the concept? What would you like to learn about it?

Analyze your **AUDIENCE** *by brainstorming answers to the following questions:*

- Who are your readers, and in what context will they be reading your explanation?

- What are they likely to know about the concept, about related concepts, or about the subject in general? How can you build on what they already know?

- How would you answer your readers' "So what?" question? Think of at least one aspect of the concept that is relevant to their life, family, community, work, or studies.

- If you suspect your readers are likely to have faulty assumptions, misunderstandings, or outdated ideas about the concept (or about the subject in general), how can you clarify the concept for them?

Consider **WRITING STRATEGIES** *that will help you explain your concept and why it matters.* Write for a few minutes in response to one or more of the following questions:

- What is my concept similar to?

- What parts or features distinguish it from other concepts?

- What are its cultural or historical contexts?

If you find that you don't have enough to write about, return to the previous section to conduct additional research, broaden your concept by adding cultural or historical contexts, or check sources or class readings to look for broader concepts of which your concept is a part.

Evaluating Your Focus

Get together with two or three other students to test the way you've focused your explanation:

Presenters.   Briefly describe your intended audience, identify the aspect of the concept that you will focus on, and explain what you find interesting or relevant about it and what you think your readers will find interesting or relevant. (If your listeners do not find your focus appropriate or interesting, consider returning to your list of possible concepts and repeating the activities above.)

Listeners.   Briefly tell the presenter whether the focus sounds appropriate and interesting for the intended audience. Share what you think readers are likely to know about the concept and what information might be especially interesting to them.

Conduct further research on your focused concept.

To learn more about finding sources, see Chapter 21; evaluating your sources, see Chapter 22; citing sources, see Chapter 24 (MLA style) or Chapter 25 (APA style).

Your instructor may expect you to do in-depth research or may limit the number and type of sources you can use. Readers will want to be sure that your sources are reliable and perhaps read your sources for themselves.

Draft your working thesis.

An essay explaining a concept is made up of three basic parts:

- an opening that will engage readers' interest
- a thesis statement, announcing the concept and its focus, and possibly forecasting the main topics
- information about the concept, organized by topic

You may draft a working thesis statement and other parts of your explanation before deciding on an opening your readers will find engaging. If you prefer to sketch out an opening first, however, turn to the section "Write the opening sentences" (p. 159), and return to this section later.

The **thesis statement** in a concept explanation announces the concept to be explained and identifies the writer's focus on the concept. It may also forecast the topics to be explored. Here's an example of a thesis statement (from "Love: The Right Chemistry") that successfully announces the concept and the writer's focus. It also forecasts the topics the writer will cover:

Concept

Focus

O.K., let's cut out all this nonsense about romantic love. Let's bring some scientific precision to the party. Let's put love under a microscope.
When rigorous people with Ph.D.s after their names do that, what they see is not some silly, senseless thing. No, their probe reveals that love rests firmly on the

Forecast topics

foundations of evolution, biology and chemistry. (Toufexis, pars. 1–2)

To draft your thesis statement, consider using some of your writing from the Ways In activities in the section "Focus your explanation of the concept" (p. 153). You may also want to forecast the topics you will cover.

Writing a Draft   GUIDE TO READING
GUIDE TO WRITING
▶ A WRITER AT WORK
THINKING CRITICALLY   **155**

⠃ Create an outline that will organize your concept explanation effectively for your readers.

Once you have drafted a working thesis, you may want to devise a tentative outline drawing on your invention and research notes. An effective outline for a concept explanation should be divided into separate topics that are conceptually parallel. Toufexis, for example, focuses on the scientific foundations of love, and so she divides the topics she will cover into evolution, biology, and chemistry. Once you have decided on your topics, present them in a logical order (for example, from most familiar to least familiar).

Below is a simple outline for an essay explaining a concept, which you may use as a starting point:

    I. **Introduction:** Attempts to gain readers' interest in the concept, but may not name the concept immediately.

   II. **Thesis:** Identifies the concept in a sentence or two; may include a brief definition, an example, or another strategy to clarify the focus, and may forecast topics that will be addressed later.

  III. **Background:** Social, cultural, historical, or scientific background readers will need to understand the concept.

  IV. **Topic 1:** Any examples, evidence, and explanatory strategies you may use.

   V. **Topic 2:**

  VI. **Topic 3 (etc.):**

 VII. **Conclusion:** Might summarize information, give advice about how to use or apply the information, or speculate about the future of the concept.

Use your outline to guide your drafting, but do not feel tied to it. You may figure out a better way to sequence your topics as you write.

⠃ Design your writing project.

Consider whether you want to use headings to indicate the topics to be discussed; bullets or numbers to highlight lists; and tables, graphics, or other visuals to make your explanation clearer.

To learn more about design, see Chapter 32.

⠃ Consider the explanatory strategies you should use.

To explain your concept, consider which strategies would be most useful. Ask questions like these:

- How would you define it?
- What examples would help your readers understand it?
- How is it similar to or different from other related concepts?
- How does it happen or get done?
- What are its causes or effects?

Keep in mind that your goal is not only to inform your readers but also to engage their interest. The following activities provide sentence strategies you may use to explore the best ways to explain your concept, and they may also help you start drafting your essay.

WAYS IN

WHAT WRITING STRATEGIES CAN I USE TO EXPLAIN MY FOCUSED CONCEPT?

How is the concept DEFINED*? What broader class does it belong to, and how does it differ from other members of its class?*

▸ X is a/an _____ [principle/theory/idea/condition/phenomenon/process] distinguished by _____ [defining characteristics].

What EXAMPLES *or* ANECDOTES *can make the concept less abstract and more understandable?*

▸ Experts/Scientists/The public first became aware of X in [year], when _____ (citation).

▸ Interest in X has been rising/declining because of _____ , _____ , and _____ .

How does this concept COMPARE *or* CONTRAST *with related concepts with which your readers may be more familiar?*

▸ Many people think X means _____ , but it might be more accurate to say it means _____ .

▸ X is similar in some ways to Y. However, unlike Y, X is/has/does _____ , _____ , and _____ .

How can aspects of the concept be CLASSIFIED *to make it easier for readers to understand?*

▸ Professor A says there are several categories/subtypes/versions of X, including _____ , _____ , and _____ (citation).

What PROCESS *must occur? How does this concept happen, or how does one go about doing it?*

▸ To perform X, a person/performer/participant starts by _____ . Then he/she/it does _____ , _____ , and _____ . The process ends when _____ .

What are this concept's CAUSES *or* EFFECTS*?*

▸ X occurs when _____ .

▸ Before X can occur, the following condition[s] must be met: _____ .

▸ Experts disagree over the causes of X. Professor Smith, for example, believes _____ (citation). Professor Jones, in contrast, argues _____ (citation).

Writing a Draft

GUIDE TO READING
▶ **GUIDE TO WRITING**
A WRITER AT WORK
THINKING CRITICALLY

157

Use summaries, paraphrases, and quotations from sources to support your points.

Summaries, paraphrases, and quotations from sources are frequently used to explain concepts or reinforce an explanation. The Ways In activity below can help you decide when to summarize, paraphrase, or quote.

For more about using information from sources to support your own ideas and integrating supporting information into your writing, see Chapter 23.

WAYS IN

WHEN SHOULD I SUMMARIZE, PARAPHRASE, AND QUOTE?

Use **SUMMARY** *to give the gist of a research report or other information.*

▶ Recent research suggests that .... (citation).

Use **PARAPHRASE** *to provide specific details or examples when the language of the source is not especially memorable.*

▶ According to Dr. Smith, the most important element to keep in mind is .... (citation).

Use **QUOTATION** *to capture language that is particularly vivid, clear, or technical; to convey an expert's voice; or to discuss the source's choice of words.*

▶ Professor Y recently noted that "..............." (citation).

Remember that in academic writing projects, you will need to cite the sources of all summaries, paraphrases, and quotations. In most cases, use signal phrases (*Professor Y explained*) so you can provide context for source information and in-text citations (page references in MLA style, year of publication in APA style) so readers can locate the source in your works-cited or references list. A list of works cited or references should be provided at the end of your concept explanation.

Your readers will want you to explain how the ideas from the sources you cite reinforce the points you are making. So comment on sources, making the relationship between your own ideas and the supporting information from sources absolutely clear.

Use visuals or multimedia illustrations.

Concept explanation essays do not require illustrations, but they can be an effective tool. The medium in which your concept explanation appears will determine the types of illustrations you can use. For example, papers can include visual images such as photographs and flowcharts. Web pages can include music, film clips, and animated graphs. Oral presentations can use the Web or presentation slides (such as Power-Point) with still or moving images and sound files embedded in the slides.

When deciding whether to include illustrations, consider the following:

- Can you create your own graphics (for example, using spreadsheet software to create bar graphs or pie charts)?
- Will you need to borrow materials that others have created (for example, downloading materials from the Internet, taking screenshots from Web sites or DVDs, or scanning visuals from books or magazines)? Note: Borrowed material must be cited, including the sources of data you use to create graphs and tables.
- Will your writing be published on a Web site that is not password protected? If so, you may also need to obtain permission from the source.

⠿ Use appositives to integrate sources.

When you write your essay, you'll have to tell readers about the credentials of experts you quote, paraphrase, and summarize. Instead of providing this information in separate sentences, you can use an *appositive* to embed this information smoothly and clearly into another sentence.

An **appositive** is a noun or pronoun that, along with modifiers, gives more information about another noun or pronoun. Here is an example from one of the reading selections earlier in the chapter:

Noun
Appositive

"Love is a natural high," observes Anthony Walsh, author of *The Science of Love: Understanding Love and Its Effects on Mind and Body*. (Toufexis, par. 10)

By placing the credentials right after the expert's name, these sentences provide readers with the information they need, exactly where they need it.

Appositives can also be used for many different purposes, as these examples suggest:

Appositive
Noun

DEFINE A KEY TERM   Each person carries in his or her mind a unique subliminal guide to the ideal partner, a "love map," . . . (Toufexis, par. 17)

IDENTIFY PEOPLE AND THINGS   Decision fatigue is the newest discovery involving a phenomenon called ego depletion, a term coined by the social psychologist Roy F. Baumeister. . . . (Tierney, par. 6)

GIVE EXAMPLES   Despite the risk of serious side effects—nausea, loss of sex drive, seizures—drugs like Zoloft can be a godsend for this group. (Cain, par. 3)

Notice that the last example uses dashes instead of commas to set off the appositive from the rest of the sentence. Although commas are more common, dashes are often used if the writer wants to give the appositive more emphasis or if the appositive itself contains commas.

⸬ Use descriptive verbs in signal phrases to introduce information from sources.

When introducing quotations, paraphrases, or summaries, writers often use a **signal phrase**—the source author's name plus a verb—to alert readers to the fact that they are borrowing someone else's words or ideas. Often the verb is neutral:

> "That is one reason why it feels so horrible when we're abandoned or a lover dies," *notes* Fisher. (Toufexis, par. 13)

> "By the end, you could have talked me into anything," Twenge *told* her new colleagues. (Tierney, par. 8)

Sometimes, however, the verb may be more descriptive—even evaluative:

> "As long as prehistoric females were secretive about their extramarital affairs," *argues* Fisher, "they could garner extra resources, life insurance, better genes and more varied DNA for their biological futures. . . ." (Toufexis, par. 8)

The verb *argues* emphasizes the fact that what is being reported is an interpretation that others may disagree with.

As you refer to sources in your concept explanation, choose carefully among a wide variety of precise verbs to introduce your sources. Here are a number of possibilities: *suggests, reveals, questions, brings into focus, finds, notices, observes, underscores.*

In academic writing, merely mentioning the author's name in a signal phrase is not sufficient. In most cases, you must also include in-text citations that provide the page number from which the borrowed material is taken and include full bibliographic information in a list of works cited or references, so readers can trace the source for themselves.

For more about integrating sources into your sentences and constructing signal phrases, see Chapter 23.

Write the opening sentences.

Review what you have written to see if you have something that would work to launch your concept explanation, or try out some of these opening strategies:

Begin with a **surprising** *or* **provocative quotation** *or* **aspect** *of the concept:*

> O.K., let's cut out all this nonsense about romantic love. Let's bring some scientific precision to the party. Let's put love under a microscope. (Toufexis, par. 1)

Offer an **anecdote** *or* **example** *illustrating the concept:*

> Three men doing time in Israeli prisons recently appeared before a parole board consisting of a judge, a criminologist and a social worker. The three prisoners had completed at least two-thirds of their sentences, but the parole board granted freedom to only one of them. Guess which one:
>
> Case 1 (heard at 8:50 a.m.): An Arab Israeli serving a 30-month sentence for fraud.
>
> Case 2 (heard at 3:10 p.m.): A Jewish Israeli serving a 16-month sentence for assault.
>
> Case 3 (heard at 4:25 p.m.): An Arab Israeli serving a 30-month sentence for fraud. (Tierney, par. 1)

Start with a **concrete example**:

> A beautiful woman lowers her eyes demurely beneath a hat. In an earlier era, her gaze might have signaled a mysterious allure. But this is a 2003 advertisement for Zoloft, a selective serotonin reuptake inhibitor (SSRI) approved by the FDA to treat social anxiety disorder. "Is she just shy? Or is it Social Anxiety Disorder?" reads the caption, suggesting that the young woman is not alluring at all. She is sick.
>
> But is she? (Cain, pars. 1–2)

Make a **comparison** *or* **contrast** *that relates the concept to something readers are likely to know:*

> Possibly the most destructive natural disaster, short of a large asteroid impact, would be the eruption of a supervolcano. Supervolcanoes are volcanoes that produce eruptions thousands of times the size of ordinary volcanoes. Like hurricanes, volcanoes are measured using an exponential scale, called the *Volcanic Explosivity Index*, or *VEI*. (See Fig. 1.) (Potthast, par. 1)

But don't agonize over the first sentences, because you are likely to discover the best way to begin only after you have written a rough draft.

Draft your explanation.

By this point, you have done a lot of research and writing to

- find an interesting focus and develop a working thesis statement;
- try out writing strategies that can help you explain your concept;
- create an outline for presenting that information;
- come up with ways to integrate your sources smoothly;
- try out a way to launch your explanation.

Now stitch that material together to create a draft. The next two parts of this Guide to Writing will help you evaluate and improve your draft.

Evaluating the Draft: Using Peer Review

Your instructor may arrange a peer review session in class or online, where you can exchange drafts with your classmates and give one another a thoughtful critical reading, pointing out what works well and suggesting ways to improve the draft. A good critical reading does three things:

1. It lets the writer know how well the reader understands the concept.
2. It praises what works best.
3. It indicates where the draft could be improved and makes suggestions on how to improve it.

One strategy for evaluating a draft is to use the basic features of concept essays as a guide.

A PEER REVIEW GUIDE

A Focused Explanation

Is the explanation focused?

Summarize: Tell the writer, in one sentence, what you understand the concept to mean and why it is important or useful.

Praise: Identify something in the draft that will especially interest readers.

Critique: Tell the writer about any confusion or uncertainty you have about the concept's meaning, importance, or usefulness. Indicate if the focus could be clearer or more appropriate or if the explanation could have a more interesting focus.

A Clear, Logical Organization

Is the concept explanation clear and easy to follow?

Summarize: Look at the way the essay is organized by making a scratch outline.

Praise: Give an example of where the essay succeeds in being readable—for instance, in its overall organization, forecast of topics, or use of transitions.

Critique: Identify places where readability could be improved—for example, the beginning made more appealing, a topic sentence made clearer, or transitions or headings added.

Appropriate Explanatory Strategies

Are writing strategies used effectively to analyze and explain the concept?

Summarize: Note which explanatory strategies the writer uses, such as definition, comparison, example, cause and effect, classification, or process analysis.

Praise: Point to an explanatory strategy that is especially effective, and highlight research that is particularly helpful in explaining the concept.

Critique: Point to any places where a definition is needed, where more (or better) examples might help, or where another explanatory strategy could be improved or added. Note where a visual (such as a flowchart or graph) would make the explanation clearer.

Smooth Integration of Sources

Are sources incorporated into the essay effectively?

Summarize: Note each source mentioned in the text, and check to make sure it appears in the list of works cited, if there is one. Highlight signal phrases and in-text citations, and identify appositives used to provide experts' credentials.

Praise: Give an example of the effective use of sources—a particularly well-integrated quotation, paraphrase, or summary that supports and illustrates the point. Note any especially descriptive verbs used to introduce information.

Critique: Point out where experts' credentials are needed. Indicate quotations, paraphrases, or summaries that could be more smoothly integrated or more fully interpreted or explained. Suggest verbs in signal phrases that may be more appropriate.

Before concluding your review, be sure to address any of the writer's concerns that have not already been addressed.

Making Comments Electronically   Most word processing software offers features that allow you to insert comments directly into the text of someone else's document. Many readers prefer to make their comments this way because it tends to be faster than writing on hard copy, and space is virtually unlimited; it also eliminates the process of deciphering handwritten comments. Where such features are not available, simply typing comments directly into a document in a contrasting color or different font can provide the same advantages.

Improving the Draft: Revising, Editing, and Proofreading

Start improving your draft by reflecting on what you have written thus far:

- Review critical reading comments from your classmates, instructor, or writing center tutor. What are your readers getting at?
- Take another look at the notes from your earlier research and writing activities. What else should you consider?
- Review your draft. What else can you do to make your explanation effective?

Revise your draft.

If your readers are having difficulty with your draft, or if you think there is room for improvement, try some of the strategies listed in this Troubleshooting Guide. It can help you fine-tune your presentation of the genre's basic features.

A TROUBLESHOOTING GUIDE

A Focused Explanation

My readers think that my topic seems thin, that I don't have enough to write about. (The focus is too narrow.)

- Broaden your concept by adding scientific, cultural, or historical comparisons and contrasts.
- Look up your concept using reference sources to find additional subject terms for larger concepts that include it.
- Conduct a Web search using the name of your concept and *overview* or *definition*. Use the Advanced Search feature to focus on sites with a *.edu, .gov,* or *.org* domain.
- If your concept comes from another course you are taking, check your textbook or lecture notes for broader, related topics.

Improving the Draft

GUIDE TO READING
▶ **GUIDE TO WRITING**
A WRITER AT WORK
THINKING CRITICALLY

163

A Focused Explanation

> My readers don't find my focus interesting.

- Conduct additional research, focusing on finding information likely to be of value and interest to your readers.
- Consider how you can answer your readers' "So what?" question. Show them, perhaps, how they could use the concept; build on their interests or what they already know; or clarify their mistaken, faulty, or outdated assumptions or ideas.
- Consider using humor, anecdotes, or visuals to engage readers' interest.
- Ask yourself whether the focus is interesting to you. If it isn't, choose a different focus. If it is, ask yourself how you can communicate your enthusiasm to your readers—perhaps with anecdotes, examples, or illustrations.

A Clear, Logical Organization

> My readers don't find my organization clear and logical.

- Reread your thesis statement to be sure that it clearly announces the concept and perhaps forecasts the topics.
- Outline your material to be sure that it is divided into separate topics that are presented in a logical order.

> My readers say that the beginning doesn't capture their interest.

- Review your opening paragraphs to be sure that you clearly introduce your concept and your focus.
- Try starting with an anecdote, an interesting quotation, a surprising aspect of the concept, a concrete example, or a similar lead-in.
- Consider stating explicitly what makes the concept worth thinking about and how it relates to your readers' interests.

> My readers feel that the essay doesn't flow smoothly from one part to the next.

- Outline your essay, dividing it into major parts—introduction, main topics, and conclusion. Reread the end of each major part and the beginning of the next to make sure you have provided transitional cues (for example, the strategic repetition of words or phrases, use of synonyms, rhetorical questions). If there are none, add some.
- Consider adding headings to make the topical sections easier to identify.

> My readers feel that the ending falls flat.

- Consider ending by speculating on what the future will bring—how the concept might be redefined, for example.
- Consider relating the ending to the beginning—for example, by recalling an example or a comparison.

(continued)

Appropriate Explanatory Strategies

My readers don't understand my explanation.

- Consider whether you have used the most appropriate writing strategies for your topic—defining, classifying, comparing and contrasting, narrating, illustrating, describing, or explaining cause and effect.
- Recheck your definitions for clarity. Be sure that you have explicitly defined any key terms your readers might not know.
- Add transitional cues (transitional words and phrases, strategic repetition, rhetorical questions, and so on).
- Add headings and bulleted or numbered lists to help readers follow the discussion.

My readers want more information about certain aspects of the concept.

- Expand or clarify definitions by adding examples or using appositives.
- Add examples or comparisons and contrasts to relate the concept to something readers already know.
- Conduct additional research on your topic, and cite it in your essay.

My readers think visuals would help them better understand the concept.

- Check whether your sources use visuals (tables, graphs, drawings, photographs, and the like) that might be appropriate for your explanation. If you are publishing your concept explanation online, consider video clips, audio files, and animated graphics as well.
- Consider drafting your own charts, tables, or graphs, or adding your own photographs or illustrations.

My readers think my summaries are vague, paraphrases are too complicated, or quotations are too long or uninteresting.

- Revise the summaries to emphasize a single key idea.
- Restate the paraphrases more succinctly, omitting irrelevant details. Consider quoting important words.
- Quote only a few memorable words or phrases from a source.

My readers aren't sure how source information supports my explanation of the concept.

- Check to be sure that you have appropriately commented on all cited material, making its relation to your own ideas absolutely clear.
- Expand or clarify accounts of research that your readers find unconvincing on grounds apart from the credibility of the source.

Smooth Integration of Sources

> My readers think that the quotations, summaries, and paraphrases don't flow smoothly with the rest of the essay.

- Reread all passages where you quote sources. Ask yourself whether you provide enough context or clearly establish the author's credentials.
- Use signal phrases to place sources in context. Consider using descriptive verbs in signal phrases to give your readers more information about what your source is saying and why you are referring to it.
- Use appositives to integrate information about your sources smoothly and clearly.

> My readers are concerned that my list of sources is too limited.

- Do additional research to balance your list, taking particular care that you have an adequate number of credible sources.
- If you have difficulty finding sources, ask your instructor or a librarian for help.

> My readers wonder whether my sources are credible.

- Clearly identify all sources, and fully state the credentials of all cited authorities, using appositives where appropriate.
- Eliminate sources that are clearly identified and well integrated but that are not relevant, credible, or otherwise appropriate.

Edit and proofread your draft.

Two kinds of errors occur often in concept explanations: mixed constructions and missing or unnecessary commas around adjective clauses. The following guidelines will help you check your essay for these common errors.

Avoiding Mixed Constructions

What Is a Mixed Construction?   A **mixed construction** in a sentence is a combination of structures that don't work together properly according to the rules of logic or English grammar. Mixed constructions often occur when a writer attributes information to a source, defines a term, or provides an explanation. In particular, watch out for definitions that include *is when* or *is where* and explanations that include *the reason . . . is because,* which are likely to be both illogical and ungrammatical.

The Problem   Sentences are logically or grammatically incoherent.

The Correction   Replace *when* or *where* with a noun that renames the subject or with an adjective that describes the subject.

>   *a disorder in which*
> ▶ Depression is ~~where~~ people feel sad, guilty, or worthless, and lack energy or focus.
>   ^

A Note on Grammar and Spelling Checkers

These tools can be helpful, but don't rely on them exclusively to catch errors in your text: Spelling checkers cannot catch misspellings that are themselves words, such as *to* or *too*. Grammar checkers miss some problems, sometimes give faulty advice for fixing problems, and can flag correct items as wrong. Use these tools as a second line of defense after your own (and, ideally, another reader's) proofreading and editing efforts.

Delete either *the reason . . . is* or *because*.

▶ ~~The reasons~~ ponds become meadows is because plant life collects in the bottom.

Check subjects and predicates to make sure they are logically and grammatically matched, and delete any redundant expressions.

▶ ~~According to Eleanor Smith,~~ she said that the best movie of the year was *Fury Road*.

▶ According to Eleanor Smith, she ~~said that~~ the best movie of the year was *Fury Road*.

Using Punctuation with Adjective Clauses

What Is an Adjective Clause?   An **adjective clause** includes both a subject and a verb, gives information about a noun or a pronoun, and often begins with *who, which,* or *that*:

▶ It is common for schizophrenics to have delusions *that they are being persecuted.*

Because adjective clauses add information about the nouns they follow—defining, illustrating, or explaining—they can be useful in writing that explains a concept.

The Problem   Adjective clauses may or may not need to be set off with a comma or commas. To decide, determine whether the clause is essential to the meaning of the sentence. Essential clauses should *not* be set off with commas; nonessential clauses *must* be set off with commas.

The Correction   Mentally delete the clause. If taking out the clause does not change the basic meaning of the sentence or make it unclear, add a comma or commas.

▶ Postpartum neurosis, which can last for two weeks or longer, can adversely affect a mother's ability to care for her infant.

If the clause follows a proper noun, add a comma or commas.

▶ Nanotechnologists defer to K. Eric Drexler, who speculates imaginatively about the use of nonmachines.

If taking out the clause changes the basic meaning of the sentence or makes it unclear, do *not* add a comma or commas.

▶ Seasonal affective disorders are mood disturbances, that occur in fall/winter.

Jonathan Potthast's Use of Sources

We draw on Jonathan Potthast's essay explaining supervolcanoes to demonstrate a sound strategy for integrating sources into your essay, relying on them fully—as you nearly always must do in explanatory writing—and yet making them your own. Most of the information Potthast uses in this passage comes from one article by Joel Achenbach.

Potthast relies on paraphrase and quotation to present the information he borrowed from Achenbach's article. When you **paraphrase**, you construct your own sentences, using only specific numbers, names, and key terms from the source (like *45 miles, Lake Butte,* and *supervolcano*). In the following comparison, the sections Potthast paraphrases are highlighted in yellow, the quotations he uses are highlighted in gray, and the key words he borrows are underlined:

Jonathan Potthast

A dormant supervolcano close to home is in Yellowstone National Park. According to Joel Achenbach, a reporter on science and politics for the *Washington Post,* three super-eruptions have occurred there, with one just 640,000 years ago (a blink of an eye in geologic terms). Even more powerful was a super-eruption 2.1 million years ago that "[left] a hole in the ground the size of Rhode Island" (Achenbach 1). The caldera, or crater, of the Yellowstone supervolcano is about 45 miles across, and over time, has been eroded and covered by glaciers and forests; part of the caldera's rim is invisible, hidden beneath the surface of Lake Butte (Achenbach 2).

It was thought that the volcano was extinct, but activity is making scientists re-think that view. A huge magma chamber lies deep under the volcano's caldera. When shifted by earthquakes and pressed by hot rock, the land above it rises and falls. An earthquake swarm in the mid-1980s made Yellowstone drop, so that it was about eight inches lower ten years later

Joel Achenbach

The last three super-eruptions have been in Yellowstone itself. The most recent, 640,000 years ago, was a thousand times the size of the Mount St. Helens eruption in 1980, which killed 57 people in Washington. . . . And this wasn't even Yellowstone's most violent moment. An eruption 2.1 million years ago was more than twice as strong, leaving a hole in the ground the size of Rhode Island. . . . For all their violence, the supervolcanoes have left little behind beyond a faintly perceptible sense of absence. The Yellowstone caldera has been eroded, filled in with lava flows and ash from smaller eruptions (the most recent was 70,000 years ago) and smoothed by glaciers. Peaceful forests cover any lingering scars. . . . We're standing atop Lake Butte, . . . But I can't follow the caldera rim visually because much of it is beneath the lake and because of the sheer scale of the thing—roughly 45 miles across. . . . About five to seven miles deep is the top of the magma chamber, a reservoir of partially melted rock roughly 30 miles wide . . .

(Achenbach 2). More recently, "portions of the caldera have surged upward at a rate of nearly three inches a year, much faster than any uplift since close observations began in the 1970's" (Achenbach 3). Such activity indicates a live volcano.

After the 1985 earthquake swarm, Yellowstone fell eight inches over the course of a decade or so. Then it rose again, faster this time. Since 2004, portions of the caldera have surged upward at a rate of nearly three inches a year, much faster than any uplift since close observations began in the 1970s.

Potthast's writing illustrates a careful use of a source (out of many in his paper) in a paragraph in which he wants to impart dense and important information. He quotes when the material is well presented by Achenbach, and he summarizes or paraphrases factual information. For the material he borrows from Achenbach—whether quoted, summarize, or paraphrased—he includes parenthetical citations.

THINKING CRITICALLY

To think critically means to use all of the knowledge you have acquired from the information in this chapter, your own writing, the writing and responses of other students, and class discussions to reflect deeply on your work for this assignment and the genre (or type) of writing you have produced. The benefit of thinking critically is proven and important: Thinking critically about what you have learned will help you remember it longer, ensuring that you will be able to put it to good use well beyond this writing course.

Reflecting on What You Have Learned

In this chapter, you have learned a great deal about this genre from reading several explanations of a concept and writing a concept explanation of your own. To consolidate your learning, reflect not only on what you learned but also on how you learned it.

ANALYZE & WRITE

Write a blog post, a letter to your instructor or a classmate, or an e-mail message to a student who will take this course next term, using the writing prompt that seems most productive for you:

- Explain how your purpose and audience — what you wanted your readers to learn from reading your concept explanation — influenced *one* of your decisions as a writer, such as how you focused the concept, how you organized your explanation, how you used writing strategies to convey information, or how you integrated sources into your essay.

- If you were to give advice to a fellow student who was about to write a concept explanation, what would you say?

- Which of the readings in this chapter influenced your essay? Explain the influence, citing specific examples from your essay and the reading.

- If you got good advice from a critical reader, explain exactly how the person helped you — perhaps by questioning your definitions, your use of visuals, the way you began or ended your essay, or the kinds of sources you used.

- Discuss what you learned about yourself as a writer in the process of writing this essay. For example, what part of the process did you find most challenging? Did you try anything new like getting a critical reading of your draft or outlining your draft in order to revise it?

Reflecting on the Genre

Writers explaining concepts typically present knowledge as established and uncontested. They presume to be unbiased and objective, and they assume that readers will not doubt or challenge the truth or the value of the knowledge they present. This stance encourages readers to feel confident about the validity of the explanation. But should explanatory writing always be accepted at face value? Textbooks and reference materials, in particular, sometimes present a simplified or limited view of knowledge in an academic discipline. Because they must be highly selective, they necessarily leave out certain sources of information and types of knowledge.

ANALYZE & WRITE

Write a page or two considering how concept explanations may distort knowledge. In your discussion, you might consider one or more of the following:

1 **Consider the claim that concept explanations attempt to present their information as uncontested truths.** Identify a reading in this chapter that particularly seems to support this claim, and then think about how it does so. Do the same for a chapter or section in a textbook you are reading for another course.

2 **Write a page or two explaining your initial assumptions about the knowledge or information you presented about the concept in your essay.** When you were doing research on the concept, did you discover that some of the information was being challenged by experts? Or did the body of knowledge seem settled and established? Did you at any point think that your readers might question any of the information you were presenting? How did you decide what information might seem new or even surprising to readers? Did you feel comfortable in your roles as the selector and giver of knowledge?

5

Analyzing and Synthesizing Opposing Arguments

Should people with kidney disease be allowed to buy someone else's extra kidney? Should Americans be required to show a special ID to vote? Should college athletes be paid to play? Should candy-flavored e-cigarettes be banned? Debates on issues like these are rampant in online chat rooms, workplaces, and college classrooms. Whether you want to participate in the debate or simply educate yourself, a good place to start is by researching and analyzing the opposing arguments. This kind of intellectual work is done by individuals at their home computers, by community and business leaders in public forums, by professors in academic journals and at conferences, and by students for class in reports, research projects, and oral presentations.

Unlike other *St. Martin's Guide* chapters, this one does not focus on a single genre but instead presents four interrelated genres on a single controversial topic:

1. **Summary:** A concise recap of one source's main ideas

2. **Annotated Bibliography:** A list of sources with summaries and commentaries exploring how each source could be used

3. **Report:** An informative introduction, explaining the topic's importance and the controversy surrounding it

4. **Analysis of Opposing Arguments:** A perceptive examination of the values underlying two (or more) opposing points of view on the topic

These genres give you the opportunity to practice the fundamental thinking and composing processes of *analysis* and *synthesis* that are required throughout the college curriculum and in most kinds of workplace writing.

Analysis and synthesis are processes that go hand in hand. When you *analyze* what people have said and written about a controversial issue, you take it apart, focusing on important elements—for example, why the topic is significant, what makes it controversial, and what the different points of view on the topic are. When you *synthesize*, you forge connections, showing how different points of view relate to one another, perhaps demonstrating where they agree and disagree or where they fit into a broader framework.

In this chapter, the main purpose of your analysis and synthesis is *explanatory*: to help your audience understand a controversial topic as well as the different points of view and the values on which they are based. In Chapters 6–10, you enter the debate to argue for

- your own point of view on a topic (Chapter 6)

- an alternative solution to a problem (Chapter 7)

- your evaluation of some aspect of the topic (Chapter 8)

- the cause or effect you think is most likely (Chapter 9)

- your interpretation of a work of literature (Chapter 10)

The processes you will engage in for the writing projects in this chapter will be good preparation for writing a thoughtful argument, whether for a college course, for the wider community, or for an employer.

Each of the genres in this chapter—summary, annotated bibliography, report, and comparative analysis—can be used as an end in itself or as a stepping stone in a larger composing process. For example, consider the various purposes and audiences for a summary:

- You can use a summary to help you recall sources you've read and determine what's important, help your audience decide if a text is worth reading, or demonstrate to an instructor that you have read and understood a source.

- You can combine a summary with additional summaries of other sources on a topic, notes about how each of the sources will be used, and bibliographic citations to create an annotated bibliography.

- You can remix the summary, using it, perhaps, in a research report that succinctly describes what various sources have said on a topic, or in an analysis to provide readers with an overview of the topic before delving into what drives a controversy.

Because this chapter covers four genres, the Guides to Reading and Writing in this chapter look different from those in other chapters. Whereas other chapters typically include four reading selections illustrating variations on a single genre, the selections in this chapter illustrate the four different genres. Furthermore, whereas the selections in other chapters are written by different authors, all of the examples in this chapter were composed by the same writer, student Maya Gomez. As you read Gomez's writing, you will see how each genre serves as a part of a multi-stage project. The Guide to Writing later in the chapter offers suggestions for composing each genre independently or as a part of your own multi-stage project.

PRACTICING A GENRE ├──────────────────────────────────────

Analyzing Opposing Arguments

To get a sense of what's involved in analyzing and synthesizing opposing arguments, get together with two or three students to explore how people typically argue about a topic.

Part 1. As a group, choose a controversial issue with which you are all familiar, such as whether there should be a community service requirement for graduation, whether college athletes should be paid, or whether a college education, like kindergarten through twelfth grade, should be free to everyone who qualifies.

Then make a list of several pro and con arguments people use to support their opposing views of the issue you've chosen. For example, a common argument is that student athletes should be paid because colleges gain financially from their hard work and expertise. A con argument against paying student athletes is that colleges already pay them indirectly through expensive coaching programs. (You do not need to have an opinion on this issue yourself; you simply need to recall or guess what others have said or would say.)

Part 2. Discuss what you learned about analyzing and synthesizing opposing arguments:

- Was it easier to think of the pro or the con arguments? How did considering who benefits or whose interests are being served help you think of the opposing arguments?

- Look back at the opposing arguments and try to identify the values driving them. How did you go about identifying an argument's underlying values?

Analyzing Four Genres

As you read the selections in this chapter, you will see how one student, Maya Gomez, moves from summarizing a proposal to solve the shortage of kidneys for transplant, to creating an annotated bibliography of sources on the topic of the kidney shortage, to reporting on the topic, and finally to analyzing the basic values underlying the disagreement between the proponents of two opposing arguments.

- In the summary of "A Moral Market" (p. 178), Gomez recaps the main argument of Eric Posner's proposal.

- In the annotated bibliography "Compensating Kidney Donors" (pp. 179–81), Gomez compiles a list of the sources she consulted, annotating each entry with a summary and a commentary on how she plans to use the source in her report or analysis essay.

- In the report "Possible Solutions to the Kidney Shortage" (pp. 181–86), Gomez introduces the broad topic of kidney transplantation, focusing on the kidney shortage and some of the controversial ideas for encouraging more people to donate their kidneys.

- In the analysis "Satel vs. the National Kidney Foundation: Should Kidney Donors Be Compensated?" (pp. 187–91) Gomez exposes to critical examination the basic values underlying the opposing positions taken by Sally Satel (pp. 225–28) and the National Kidney Foundation (pp. 220–21).

Examining how Maya Gomez summarizes, analyzes, and synthesizes diverse sources—and presents an array of information and different points of view clearly and impartially—will help you see how you can employ the same techniques when composing your own summary, annotated bibliography, report, or comparative analysis on a controversial topic.

Determine the writer's purpose and audience.

The purposes a writer may have will differ, of course, depending on the genre in which he or she is composing and who the intended audience is:

Genre	If the intended audience is . . .	then the purpose is likely to be . . .
Summary	• a reader interested in the topic	• to get a sense of what the source says
	• a writer who has read the source him- or herself	• to identify and record the source's main ideas
	• an instructor who will evaluate the writer's work	• to demonstrate understanding by presenting a clear, concise, and accurate description of the source's main ideas

(continued)

Genre	If the intended audience is . . .	then the purpose is likely to be . . .
Annotated Bibliography	• a writer who is doing research	• to make a record of sources and explore their usefulness
	• other researchers looking for sources for their own project	• to inform others about sources on the topic
	• an instructor who has assigned and will evaluate the bibliography	• to indicate which sources have been consulted and present a clear, accurate summary of the sources' main ideas along with an analysis of how they may be used in a later writing project
Report Explaining a Controversial Topic	• readers who want to learn about the topic	• to inform readers about the topic, explaining its significance and different points of view
	• an instructor who has assigned and will evaluate the report	• to demonstrate understanding by explaining the topic and the different points of view clearly, accurately, and impartially
Analysis of Opposing Arguments	• readers familiar with the topic but not likely to have read the sources	• to identify the crux of the disagreement and clarify the values driving the different points of view
	• an instructor who has assigned and will evaluate the analysis	• to demonstrate understanding by presenting a clear, perceptive, impartial analysis of the values underlying the opposing arguments

Assess the genres' basic features.

As you read the summary, annotated bibliography, report, and analysis in this chapter, consider how the author, Maya Gomez, incorporates the basic features of each genre. You will find that the different genres share some basic features, but may not demonstrate the features in the same way.

AN INFORMATIVE EXPLANATION

To be effective, writing in all four of the genres needs to provide an informative explanation, although each goes about doing so in a slightly different way. A **summary** need only capture the main idea of a source concisely and accurately, answering the question: *What does the source say about the topic?*

An **annotated bibliography** expands on that summary to analyze how useful potential sources might be, given the writer's purpose and audience. An annotated bibliography not only answers the question *What does the source say about the topic?* but also *How might each source be useful to the writer? How might sources be related?* and *What bibliographical information will be needed to cite the source for an academic writing project?*

	Summary	Annotated Bibliography	Report	Comparative Analysis
An Informative Explanation	Analyzes the source's main ideas	Analyzes sources' main ideas and usefulness	Analyzes the topic, its significance, and disagreements	Analyzes the opposing arguments to identify the underlying values at the crux of their disagreement
		Synthesizes sources' relationships	Synthesizes information and points of view	Synthesizes by comparing opposing arguments on the topic
A Clear, Logical Organization	Includes a thesis statement to identify the source's main idea	Includes topic sentences identifying the source's main idea and how it might be used	Includes a thesis statement and topic sentences	
	Includes transitions to signal logical connections			
	May use other types of cues, such as repetition of key terms and synonyms, headings, and a forecast of subtopics			
Smooth Integration of Sources		Includes a formal citation for each source	Includes a formal citation for each source in works-cited list	
	Uses a signal phrase to identify author's credentials, title, and source information	Identifies author and provides credentials in summary of each source	Identifies author of each source, providing credentials in text in a signal phrase or identifying source in a parenthetical citation	
Appropriate Explanatory Strategies	Describes source's main ideas			
	Narrates source's "moves" (for example: whether the source *argues*, *describes*, or *contrasts*)			
			May use a number of writing strategies, such as example, classification, and cause/effect, to help readers understand the topic	
			May present facts or statistics visually	

A **report** analyzes sources further to determine where they stand on the topic. It synthesizes sources to determine where they overlap and diverge, and to categorize information or ideas, so readers readily identify the main issues and conflicts. A report answers the questions *What is the topic? Why is it controversial?* and *What are the main opinions on the topic?*

A **comparative analysis** focuses in on two (or more) sources to identify the positions the different writers hold and probe below the surface to determine what drives their positions apart. It answers the questions *What is the crux of the disagreement? What values, priorities, interests, or fears drive the disagreement on the topic?*

A CLEAR, LOGICAL ORGANIZATION

Similarly, all four genres must be clearly and logically organized. Summaries rely on transitional words and phrases (such as *because* or *therefore*) to make the relationships among sentences clear for readers. Since each summary is only a paragraph long, more cueing devices are unnecessary. The annotations in an annotated bibliography also rely mainly on transitional words and phrases to link sentences, but they may also repeat key terms (or their synonyms) to make clear how sources relate to one another.

To learn more about thesis statements, topic sentences, and headings, see Chapter 13.

Longer writing projects, like reports and analyses, use a full array of strategies. For example, in addition to transitional words and phrases and repetition of key terms and synonyms, Gomez's report includes a thesis statement with a forecast of the subtopics, headings to introduce each subsection, and a topic sentence to state each section's main idea:

Forecast of subtopics

THESIS	This report will survey an array of ideas that have been proposed to encourage people to donate their kidneys, including changing to an opt-out system of organ donation after death, facilitating paired kidney exchanges, reducing financial disincentives, and offering incentives. (par. 3)

Headings keyed to forecast

HEADING	*Change from Opt-In to Opt-Out Organ Donation after Death*
TOPIC SENTENCE	There has been some discussion about changing from an opt-in system that requires a signed pledge to donate organs after death to an opt-out system that presumes consent. (par. 4)

SMOOTH INTEGRATION OF SOURCES

Summaries, annotated bibliographies, reports, and comparative analyses all smoothly integrate sources. A summary is very brief, so it makes sense that it would identify the source in the opening sentence, incorporating the author's name and the title of the selection (and perhaps the author's credentials and publication information) in a signal phrase: "In his article 'A Moral Market,' published by *Slate* in 2014, law professor Eric Posner proposes . . ." (Gomez, p. 178).

Because each entry in an annotated bibliography begins with a formal citation, its summary section need not repeat the title and publication information, although it typically begins with the author's name and credentials: "In this article, law professor Eric Posner proposes . . ." (Gomez, p. 181).

Reports and analyses, both longer writing projects for an academic audience, include a formal citation in a works-cited list and also identify the source of quotations, paraphrases, or summaries as well as visual maternal in in-text citations—a combination of signal phrases and parenthetical citations corresponding to the works-cited list. Consider these examples:

QUOTATION	The key passage of NOTA prohibiting compensation states that "it shall be unlawful for any person to knowingly acquire, receive, or otherwise transfer any human organ for valuable consideration for use in human transplantation" (Sec. 301a). (Report, par. 7; Analysis, par. 2)	Signal phrase Parenthetical citation
PARAPHRASE	As Sigrid Fry-Revere explains in a 2014 CNN op-ed, potential donors like her have been turned down by transplant centers because they cannot afford the estimated $10,000 needed to pay their own expenses. . . . ("Why"). (Report, par. 10)	Paraphrase cue Parenthetical citation
SUMMARY	. . . a number of states have already passed legislation to reduce the burden on living donors ("Financing"). (Report, par. 10)	Parenthetical citation

APPROPRIATE EXPLANATORY STRATEGIES

Both summaries and annotated bibliographies briefly describe the source's main idea. They also narrate the source's moves: Does the source *argue* a position? *State* a claim? *Concede* or *refute* opposing views?

A report or analysis goes further, using a variety of writing strategies. For example, Maya Gomez employs

- *definition* to provide an explanation for a concept:

  "Valuable consideration" is a term used in law to refer to in-kind exchange or monetary value. (Report, par. 7)

- *classification* to group ideas or information into categories:

  . . . an array of ideas . . . have been proposed to encourage people to donate their kidneys, including changing to an opt-out system . . . , facilitating paired kidney exchanges, reducing financial disincentives, and offering incentives. (Report, par. 3)

  Forecast of topics

- *comparison and contrast* to point out similarities and differences:

  Satel's disagreement with the NKF is essentially about morality. Or rather, it is about what she sees as the NKF's moral absolutism in what she assumes is "a morally pluralistic society" (par. 21). (Analysis, par. 7)

  Contrast cue
  Position 1
  Position 2

- *cause-effect* to explain what motivates a writer (in this instance, the NKF) to hold one position rather than another:

  If the act of giving is tainted, for example by self-interest rather than selflessness, then the gift itself becomes unacceptable. (Analysis, par. 5)

  Cause-effect cue

Readings

Maya Gomez   *Summary: "A Moral Market"*

AS A FIRST-YEAR college student, Maya Gomez began a multi-stage project by writing a summary of one of her sources, "A Moral Market" by Eric Posner. Your instructor may ask you to read "A Moral Market" (pp. 302–5) so you can judge how effectively Gomez summarizes the article.

For more about writing a summary, see Chapter 12, pp. 511-12, and Chapter 23, p. 643.

Gomez's instructor gave the class four requirements:

1. summarize the source's main ideas and arguments, leaving out the details,
2. present the source accurately and impartially,
3. keep the summary brief (four to six sentences), and
4. avoid quoting the source (except for occasional key words).

(Other instructors may have different requirements.)

To compose the summary, Gomez used the Ways In activity "How do I write a summary?" (pp. 197–99), in the Guide to Writing later in this chapter.

As you read,

- consider why Gomez begins with information about the source's publication and its author.
- ask yourself whether you get a clear picture of the source's argument from reading the summary.

▪▪ Basic Features

An Informative Explanation

A Clear, Logical Organization

Smooth Integration of Sources

Appropriate Explanatory Strategies

Why do you think Gomez includes a quotation in the summary?

Why does Gomez give a play-by-play description of the source's explanatory strategies?

In his article "A Moral Market," published by *Slate* in 2014, law professor Eric Posner proposes a solution to the kidney shortage. He argues that, unlike the unpopular proposal to sell kidneys, his proposal for an "altruism exchange" would be politically acceptable because it is based on altruism, not the profit motive. He supports this argument by analyzing the public enthusiasm for the Norwood Act, which shows that people do not object to a kidney being exchanged for something of value; rather, they object to the donor profiting from such an exchange. Therefore, Posner proposes that a donor should be rewarded with an organ transplant (for someone other than the donor) or with a monetary donation to the donor's preferred charity.

Maya Gomez | *Annotated Bibliography: Compensating Kidney Donors*

MAYA GOMEZ compiled an annotated bibliography to keep track of the research she was doing for her kidney donor compensation project. Below is a brief excerpt from her bibliography, showing entries for three of her sources. (We include these particular entries because the sources are reprinted in this book, so you can compare Gomez's summaries to the sources themselves.) Note that Gomez titled her bibliography, but did not add an introduction indicating its purpose and scope because she did not intend for it to be read by anyone other than her instructor and herself. (See Chapter 20, p. 608, to see what an introduction to an annotated bibliography might look like.) As she read each source, Gomez used the Ways In activities "How do I write a summary?" (pp. 197–99) and "How do I draft a commentary for an annotated bibliography?" (pp. 199–200).

Notice that each entry in the annotated bibliography has three parts:

1. the MLA style citation (later used in the works-cited lists for the Report and Analysis essays)

2. a *summary* of the source's main ideas and argument

3. a *commentary* reflecting on how the source might be used in a report or analysis

As you read,

- think about how Gomez indicates which part of her annotation is the summary and which is the commentary. Why is distinguishing between these two parts important for an annotated bibliography?

- notice that, following her professor's instructions, Gomez reused the summary of Eric Posner's "A Moral Market" that she had turned in for a grade (see p. 178). Why do you think her professor judged that recycling her work in this context would be acceptable and not be considered self-plagiarism? (If you are not sure whether reusing or remixing your own writing will be acceptable for a particular assigment, be sure to ask your instructor.)

For more about writing an annotated bibliography, see Chapter 20, p. 608.

■■ **Basic Features**
An Informative Explanation
A Clear, Logical Organization
Smooth Integration of Sources
Appropriate Explanatory Strategies

Becker, Gary S., and Julio J. Elías. "Cash for Kidneys: The Case for a Market in Organs." *Wall Street Journal*. Dow Jones, 18 Jan. 2014. Web. 1 May 2015.

Economists Becker and Elías argue for a straightforward but highly controversial proposal to solve the kidney shortage by paying people to donate their extra kidney for transplantation. To demonstrate the dire need for kidneys to transplant, they cite statistics, illustrated by a graph showing the difference between the numbers on the waiting list and the low, flat rate of transplant surgeries. They use their own research to refute the alternative solution that changing from informed to implied consent for

Why do you think citations begin with the last name of the first author?

How well does this thesis statement explain the main idea, or *gist*, of the article?

How helpful is it to identify the authors' explanatory strategies?

Why refer to Becker's credentials?

Why compare this proposal to Posner's? What does this commentary lead you to expect about Gomez's report?

How clear is this analysis of the source's main argument?

How fair and impartial is this annotation?

How important is the date and author in choosing sources?

Compare to Gomez's report and analysis.

deceased donors would reduce the shortage. They also refute objections that payment would not solve the problem, that it is immoral, that it would exploit the poor, and that it would reduce altruistic donations. On the issue of morality (the main criticism made by opponents of compensation), Becker and Elías compare the immorality of paying for kidneys to the immorality of dooming "thousands" on the waiting list to death.

I could use this proposal as an example of a radical or extreme solution, but one offered by Becker, a Nobel Prize–winning economist at the University of Chicago, and Elías, a professor of economics at a university in Argentina. Becker and Elías have the authority to carry off a proposal this bold. Their proposal also stands in sharp contrast to the NKF's opposition to financial compensation and Eric Posner's compromise. I'll certainly use it in my report.

National Kidney Foundation. "Financial Incentives for Organ Donation." *National Kidney Foundation*. National Kidney Foundation, 1 Feb. 2003. Web. 30 Apr. 2015.
This NKF position statement claims that the prohibition against financial incentives in the National Organ Transplant Act (NOTA) should not be removed. It presents a concise summary of the main arguments against payment: paying for body parts devalues human life, paying would be coercive and exploitative, and paying wouldn't be effective in eliminating the shortage and might discourage altruistic donors. After acknowledging that other organizations support pilot studies to see whether payment would help, the NKF asserts its opposition to pilot studies, arguing that, once done, paying for kidneys cannot be undone. The statement concludes by repeating the NKF's commitment to working to solve the problem through improved public relations and professional practices, but not by paying for kidneys.

I think I will use the NKF position statement as the voice of the status quo. Note that it was written in 2003 and hasn't been changed since, even though NOTA has been amended several times to allow paired kidney exchanges and to limit disincentives. I could compare the NKF statement to Becker and Elías's recent proposal, "Cash for Kidneys." Or I could compare it to Satel's op-ed, "When Altruism Isn't Moral." Using Satel's critique of the current altruism-only policy would enable me to contrast the NKF's moral values argument.

Posner, Eric. "A Moral Market." *Slate*. The Slate Group, LLC, 17 Oct. 2014. Web. 1 May 2015.

In this article, law professor Eric Posner proposes a solution to the kidney shortage. He argues that, unlike the unpopular proposal to sell kidneys, his proposal for an "altruism exchange" would be politically acceptable because it is based on altruism, not the profit motive. He supports this argument by analyzing the public enthusiasm for the Norwood Act, which shows that people do not object to a kidney being exchanged for something of value; rather, they object to the donor profiting from such an exchange. Therefore, Posner proposes that a donor should be rewarded with an organ transplant (for someone other than the donor) or with a monetary donation to the donor's preferred charity.

   If I focus my comparative analysis on the morality of altruism, I could use Satel as a critique of Posner. Is Posner's altruism-exchange proposal really different from the NKF-supported altruism-only transplant policy? Satel critiques an altruism-only transplant policy because it forces everyone to follow the same view of morality. (What's the opposite of moral pluralism?)

How do transitions like *unlike*, *because*, and *therefore* help readers?

How does Gomez explore ways of synthesizing her sources?

Maya Gomez | *Report: Possible Solutions to the Kidney Shortage*

FOR THIS REPORT—the third writing project in the sequence—Maya Gomez builds on the research she did on kidney transplantation, exploring the problem of the kidney shortage and solutions that have been tried or proposed. She synthesized information and ideas from sources, categorizing them into three topics. As she composed her report, Gomez relied on her annotated bibliography together with quotations she had included in notes and annotations she had made on copies of her sources.

   As you read,

- consider why Gomez begins her report with an anecdote about the Herrick brothers.

- notice that Gomez includes two graphs and headings. What do you think they contribute to the report?

- answer the questions in the margins. Your instructor may ask you to post to a class blog or discussion board or bring your responses to class.

If your instructor has asked you to compose a report, turn to the Guide to Writing for help choosing a topic, finding sources, synthesizing information from those sources, and composing a report. Use the Starting Points chart (pp. 193–95) to locate the sections you need.

:: Basic Features

An Informative
Explanation

A Clear, Logical
Organization

Smooth Integration of
Sources

Appropriate Explanatory
Strategies

How does knowing this
history help readers
understand the topic?

Why do you think Gomez
explains what Figure 1
shows?

1   The "first successful kidney transplant" took place in 1954 when Ronald Herrick donated one of his kidneys to his identical twin Richard, who was dying of kidney disease (National Kidney Foundation, "Milestones"). Richard and Ronald's successful tandem surgery was an historic event ushering in the era of kidney transplantation. Today, kidney transplantation has become routine. Because of improvements in blood and tissue typing, together with the development of powerful immunosuppressant drugs, it is no longer necessary for an identical twin or even a relative to make the donation. As long as the donor and recipient are compatible, kidneys can be transplanted from strangers as well as relatives, from living as well as deceased donors.

2   Nevertheless, the shortage of kidneys has gotten worse, not better. According to the National Kidney Foundation (NKF), more than 120,000 people with End Stage Renal Disease (ESRD) are on the U.S. transplant waiting list, with "nearly 3,000 new patients" joining the list every month and an estimated 12 patients dying every day waiting for a kidney ("Organ Donation"). As Fig. 1 below shows, the number of people with kidney disease has risen dramatically during recent decades.

3   Even though the number of donated kidneys has doubled, the gap between the number of people on the waiting list and the number of transplantations performed has

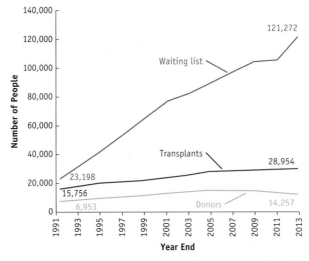

Fig. 1. The Gap Continues to Widen. Data from United States. Dept. of Health and Human Services, Health Resources and Services Administration. *Organ Procurement and Transplantation Network.* HRSA, 1 May 2015. Web. 1 May 2015.

Figure data: hrsa.gov

widened because of the scarcity of available kidneys. Clearly, the number of donated kidneys falls far short of the number needed. This report will survey an array of ideas that have been proposed to encourage people to donate their kidneys, including changing to an opt-out system of organ donation after death, facilitating paired kidney exchanges, reducing financial disincentives, and offering incentives.

How useful is this forecast?

Change from Opt-In to Opt-Out Donation after Death

4   There has been some discussion about changing from an opt-in system that requires a signed pledge to donate organs after death to an opt-out system that presumes consent. But no action has been taken. Currently, two-thirds of the kidneys used for transplant typically come from someone who has recently died. For example, in 2013, a little more than 11,000 of the nearly 17,000 kidney transplants in the U.S. were from deceased donors (National Kidney Foundation, "Organ Donation").

How do the transitions help readers?

5   Those who oppose changing to an opt-out system object either because they don't trust the state not to abuse its power (for example, they fear that the state would order organs to be taken from patients who would not otherwise die), or because they fear medical personnel would make a mistake (for example, that organs would be taken from those who were wrongly considered dead). In contrast, advocates of changing to an opt-out system favor it because they think it would help close the gap between supply and demand. A recent international study "found that countries using opt-out systems had higher total numbers of kidneys donated" than countries with opt-in systems (McIntosh). Nonetheless, economists Becker and Elias argue that the increase in donated kidneys would not be "large enough to eliminate the sizable shortfall in the supply of organs in the U.S." (par. 10). So, although changing to an opt-out system would help, it would not be enough, by itself, to solve the kidney shortage.

How clear are these causal explanations?

Facilitate Paired Kidney Exchanges

6   Unlike the question of whether to change to an opt-out donation system, the question of whether the law should be changed to permit paired kidney exchanges was met with quick action. In 2007, the Charlie W. Norwood Living Organ Donation Act was passed unanimously to amend the 1984 National Organ Transplant Act (NOTA) that established U.S. transplant policy and outlawed any form of compensation for organ donors.

How effective are this subheading and topic sentence?

7   The key passage of NOTA prohibiting compensation states that "it shall be unlawful for any person to knowingly acquire, receive, or otherwise transfer any human organ for valuable consideration for use in human transplantation" (Sec. 301a). "Valuable

consideration" is a term used in law to refer to in-kind exchange or monetary value. A paired kidney exchange essentially trades a biologically incompatible kidney, usually donated by a family member, for a compatible one donated by a stranger. Legalizing paired exchanges enabled relatives to save the life of a loved one even when their kidneys are not compatible. As Fig. 2 shows, most living donor kidneys come from direct donations or paired exchanges from relatives.

8   Advances in computer matching have also made possible long chains of paired kidney exchanges. Unfortunately, however, the total number of living donor transplants, including those from paired kidney exchanges, is relatively low and has been declining in recent years. Research suggests that the decline may be due largely to the financial crisis of 2007 that led to housing foreclosures and high unemployment, making the financial disincentives to donating an even greater hardship for many people (Rodrigue, Schold, and Mandelbrot).

Remove Disincentives

9   Most stakeholders agree that it's a good idea to remove at least some of the disincentives to donation, such as travel expenses to the transplant center. The National Kidney Foundation, one of the most conservative advocacy groups, had been adamantly opposed to financial compensation of any kind since 2002 ("Financial"). But in 2009,

> How clear are these definitions?

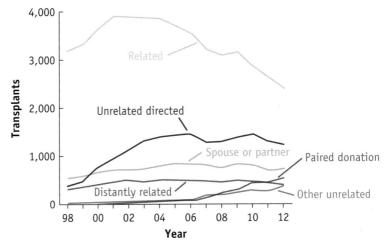

Fig. 2. Kidney transplants from living donors. Data from United States. Dept. of Health and Human Services, Health Resources and Services Administration. *Annual Data Report.* Scientific Registry of Transplant Recipients. HRSA, 2012.

Figure data: hrsa.gov

when the waiting list reached 100,000, the NKF announced that it planned to work with Congress to craft legislation that will address all the barriers to donation ("Organ Shortage"). The NKF's "End the Wait!" campaign supports reimbursing living donors "for all expenses involved in the donation, including lost wages" and also subsidizing donors' "state-of-the-art medical care" and "life insurance coverage" ("Organ Shortage").

10   According to Transplant Living, a service of the nonprofit organization UNOS, a number of states have already passed legislation to reduce the burden on living donors ("Financing"). Congress has also passed two laws: the "Organ Donor Leave Act" (1999), which gives federal employees who donate kidneys paid leave, and the "Organ Donation and Recovery Improvement Act" (2004), which reimburses travel and living expenses for low-income organ donors who qualify for a grant (United States, "Selected"). However, most potential donors do not benefit from these laws.

Offer Incentives

11   The idea that money should be offered, not just to counter the financial costs associated with donating, but also as an incentive to encourage donors, is the most controversial of all the proposals that have been considered. In 2014, the thirtieth anniversary of NOTA, debate heated up on financial incentives. A radical proposal, aptly titled "Cash for Kidneys," was published in the *Wall Street Journal* by two respected economists, Julio Elías and Nobel Laureate Gary Becker, who argue that the only way to "close the gap between the demand and supply of kidneys" is to pay people for their kidneys.

12   For the NKF and other opponents of financial compensation, the Becker and Elías proposal to pay for kidneys recalls the 1983 proposal by Dr. Barry Jacobs to buy kidneys from healthy poor people in Third World countries and sell them to Americans (Sullivan). It was Jacobs' plan that led to NOTA's strict prohibition against compensation in the first place. And, as we have seen, although Congress has been willing to modify NOTA to permit paired kidney exchanges and reimburse some donor expenses, it has staunchly resisted any substantial change to the valuable consideration clause.

13   The main arguments against financial compensation—the immorality of treating body parts as commodities and using poor people's kidneys as spare parts for the rich—have not changed since NOTA was passed (see Gomez). What has changed in the last thirty years, however, is that the kidney shortage has grown to crisis proportions and that desperate people have found ways around the law by means of transplant tourism and the illegal organ trade. But as Sally Satel, herself a kidney transplant recipient,

acknowledges in "The Case for Compensating Kidney Donors": "It is easy to condemn the black market and the patients who patronize it. But you can't fault people for trying to save their own lives" (par. 9).

Works Cited

Becker, Gary S., and Julio J. Elías. "Cash for Kidneys." *Wall Street Journal*. Dow Jones, 18 Jan. 2014. Web. 2 May 2015.

Charlie W. Norwood Living Donation Act. 110th Cong. HR 710. 7 Dec. 2007. *GovTrack*. Civic Impulse, LLC., n.d. Web. 2 May 2015.

"Financing Living Donation." *Transplant Living*. United Network for Organ Sharing, n.d. Web. 1 May 2015.

Gomez, Maya. "Satel vs. the National Kidney Foundation: Should Kidney Donors Be Compensated?" Writing 1101, Huntly College, 2015. Print.

McIntosh, James. "Organ Donation: Is an Opt-In or Opt-Out System Better?" *Medical News Today*. Medi-Lexicon International, Ltd., 24 Sept. 2014. Web. 2 May 2015.

National Kidney Foundation. "Financial Incentives for Organ Donation." *National Kidney Foundation*. National Kidney Foundation, 1 Feb. 2003. Web. 30 Apr. 2015.

---. "Milestones in Organ Transplantation." *National Kidney Foundation*. National Kidney Foundation, n.d. Web. 30 Apr. 2015.

---. "Organ Donation and Transplantation Statistics." *National Kidney Foundation*. National Kidney Foundation, 8 Sept. 2014. Web. 30 Apr. 2015.

---. "Organ Shortage Needs Multi-Faceted Approach." *National Kidney Foundation*. National Kidney Foundation, 29 Jan. 2009. Web. 30 Apr. 2015.

National Organ Transplant Act. 98th Cong. H. Rept. 98-1127. 19 Oct. 1984. *Library of Congress*. USA.gov, n.d. Web. 2 May 2015.

Rodrigue, James R., Jesse D. Schold, and Didier A. Mandelbrot. "The Decline in Living Kidney Donation in the United States: Random Variation or Cause for Concern?" *Transplantation* 96.9 (2013): n. pag. Web. 2 May 2015.

Satel, Sally. "The Case for Compensating Kidney Donors." *Pacific Standard*. The Miller-McCune Center for Research, Media and Public Policy, 12 Mar. 2015. Web. 1 May 2015.

Sullivan, Walter. "Buying of Kidneys of Poor Attacked." *New York Times*. New York Times, 24 Sept. 1983. Web. 1 May 2015.

United States. Dept. of Health and Human Services. "Selected Statutory and Regulatory History of Organ Transplantation." *Legislation and Policy*. Health Resources and Services Administration, n.d. Web. 2 May 2015.

Note the sources' dates, publication venues, and authors. How appropriate do the sources appear to be? Does the selection seem fair and balanced?

Gomez *Analysis: Satel vs. the National Kidney Foundation*

GUIDE TO READING
GUIDE TO WRITING
A WRITER AT WORK
THINKING CRITICALLY

187

Maya Gomez | *Analysis: Satel vs. the National Kidney Foundation: Should Kidney Donors Be Compensated?*

FOR THIS ANALYSIS, Maya Gomez compares two reading selections: the National Kidney Foundation's policy statement "Financial Incentives for Organ Donation" (pp. 220–21) and Sally Satel's op-ed "When Altruism Isn't Moral" (pp. 225–28). From her earlier research, Gomez learned that the National Kidney Foundation (NKF) plays a central role as defender of the status quo, resisting proposals to compensate donors and even opposing a pilot study to see whether financial compensation would encourage donors. To contrast with this position, she selected an article by Sally Satel, an outspoken opponent of the NKF's altruism-only policy.

As you will see, Gomez's comparative analysis builds on her report. Whereas her report gives a brief history of kidney transplantation and introduces the main arguments in the debate, her analysis zeroes in on the pivotal disagreement between the NKF and Satel about moral values—in particular, the virtue of altruism.

Because this was the fourth part of an assignment sequence, Gomez's instructor told the class that remixing their own words and ideas without citation (which could be seen as self-plagiarism) would be acceptable in this context. You will see that Gomez recycles whole sentences from her report, especially in the opening paragraphs. If you write a comparative analysis of your own, you will want to clarify your instructor's expectations regarding the recycling of your own language and ideas from your other projects.

As you read,

- notice how Gomez introduces the two documents and sets up the analysis comparing their underlying values.

- answer the questions in the margins. Your instructor may ask you to post to a class blog or discussion board or bring your responses to class.

If your instructor has asked you to compose an analysis, turn to the Guide to Writing for help choosing a topic, finding sources, analyzing and comparing sources, and composing an analysis. Use the Starting Points chart to locate the sections you need.

■■ Basic Features
An Informative Explanation
A Clear, Logical Organization
Smooth Integration of Sources
Appropriate Explanatory Strategies

1   According to the National Kidney Foundation (NKF), more than 120,000 people are on the U.S. transplant waiting list, with "nearly 3,000 new patients" joining the list every month and an estimated 12 patients dying every day while waiting for a kidney ("Organ Donation"). The NKF, the nation's foremost nonprofit advocacy group for kidney disease patients, bemoans the worsening kidney shortage and "advocates for ways to increase the supply of organs for transplantation" ("Policy"). However, the NKF Web site also claims responsibility for the current U.S. transplant policy that outlaws financial compensation for organ donors—a ban seen by many as the major obstacle to reducing the kidney shortage.

Why do you think Gomez opens with a sentence from her report?

2   In fact, the NKF claims it played a central leadership role not only in drafting the National Organ Transplant Act (NOTA) but also in getting the law passed through its impressive lobbying power ("History"). The key passage of NOTA prohibiting compensation states that "it shall be unlawful for any person to knowingly acquire, receive, or otherwise transfer any human organ for valuable consideration for use in human transplantation" (Sec. 301a). Although the law has been modified to permit kidney exchanges and remove several disincentives to donation (see Gomez), the "valuable consideration" clause has been defended by the NKF. At the same time, it has been criticized by proponents of alternative solutions to the kidney shortage.

Why do you think she refers to her own report?

3   One of the most vocal critics of NOTA's prohibition against compensating donors, and of the NKF's advocacy in particular, is Sally Satel, M.D. A prolific author, Satel has written extensively about transplant policy for distinguished venues such as the *New York Times*, *Washington Post*, and *Wall Street Journal*. She edited the book *When Altruism Isn't Enough: The Case for Compensating Organ Donors*. She is also a lecturer in psychiatry at the Yale University Medical School and a resident scholar at the American Enterprise Institute, a conservative think tank "committed to expanding liberty, increasing individual opportunity and strengthening free enterprise." And she is a kidney transplant recipient. In a 2009 op-ed, Satel gave vent to her disappointment in the NKF, accusing the group of trying "to sabotage any attempt to explore the possibility of rewarding organ donors," and even misrepresenting a study of donor motivation ("National").

Why give so much information about Satel?

4   This essay compares the underlying values driving the arguments in the NKF position statement "Financial Incentives for Organ Donation" and Satel's article "When Altruism Isn't Moral." Their views are diametrically opposed. Whereas the NKF defends the status quo and urges retention of the valuable consideration clause, Satel deplores the "woeful inadequacy of our nation's transplant policy" and proposes "rewards" to "encourage more living and posthumous donation" (pars. 5, 6). The basis of their disagreement is the proper role of altruism. The NKF emphatically endorses the current "altruistic system" (par. 5). Satel, in contrast, argues that current policy is failing precisely because it is an "altruism-only system" (par. 13).

Why wait so long to name the texts being analyzed?

5   Altruism, according to Satel, is "the guiding narrative of the transplant establishment," its underlying ideology or value system (par 5.). The NKF would agree with Satel's description of current policy requiring that "organs should be a 'gift of

life'" and donating should be "an act of selfless generosity" (Satel, par. 5). In using the phrase, "altruistic gift of life," the NKF statement makes explicit the connection between the act of giving and what is being given (par. 2). If the act of giving is tainted, for example by self-interest rather than selflessness, then the gift itself becomes unacceptable. That is why, in the anecdote that Satel uses to begin her article, the transplant surgeons need to be convinced that Matt Thompson, the potential donor, "was donating his kidney for the right reasons" — namely, for purely altruistic reasons (pars. 1-2).

6   Satel's disagreement with the NKF is essentially about morality. Or rather, it is about what she sees as the NKF's moral absolutism in what she assumes is "a morally pluralistic society" (par. 21). The NKF statement represents a worldview in which there are certain moral truths about which it is assumed everyone agrees. Examples of moral certainty in the NKF policy statement include the claims that "payment for organs is wrong" and "inconsistent with our values as a society" (pars. 6, 2).

7   We can see the NKF's and Satel's opposing views of morality played out in their arguments about the commodification of human organs. The NKF statement explains what is wrong with treating the human body as a commodity: "Any attempt to assign a monetary value to the human body, or body parts, either arbitrarily, or through market forces, diminishes human dignity" (par. 2). This argument is based on the belief that the human body is not something to be treated as "property" to be bought and sold (par. 2). Rather, it is sacred, made in God's image.

8   Satel refutes the commodification argument in a number of ways. For example, she points out that commodifying body parts has a long legal tradition from Hammurabi to current personal injury law (par. 19). She also questions the cause-effect reasoning that commodifying body parts is necessarily dehumanizing: "There is little reason to believe — nor tangible evidence to suggest — that these practices depreciate human worth or undermine human dignity in any way" (par. 19). But her main argument is about how we evaluate "the goodness of an act" (par. 18), in other words, our moral reasoning.

9   Satel critiques the NKF's way of assessing moral value by arguing that its moral logic relies on "false choice" reasoning. She summarizes NKF's thinking this way: "Giving a kidney 'for free' is noble but accepting compensation is illegitimate" (par. 11). This distinction between altruistic gift giving and receiving a reward hinges on the idea that

> Why do you think Gomez corrects herself here?

> How effective is this topic sentence?

> What does this paragraph do?

Why do you think Gomez follows Satel's idea with a quotation?

How does Gomez use classification here?

How effective are Gomez's examples?

How effective is this way of concluding the comparative analysis?

inserting a reward into the exchange commercializes it and damages the act's moral purity. Satel quotes Kieran Healy, a professor at Duke University studying economic sociology, to describe the either/or dilemma that framing the debate around altruism creates: "the debate is cast as one in which existing relations of selfless, altruistic exchange are threatened with replacement by market-based, for-profit alternatives" (par. 11).

10   In other words, Satel thinks the NKF sets up a false choice between selflessness and self-interest. In contrast to the NKF, Satel believes that mixed motives probably drive most gift giving. For example, she suggests several self-interested motives that may be involved in giving the "gift of life" — such as offering "an organ as an act of redemption," "a way to elicit praise and social acceptance," or "a way to avoid the shame and guilt of allowing a relative to suffer needlessly and perhaps even die" (par. 13).

11   Purity of motivation plays a key role for the NKF in evaluating "the goodness of an act." But for Satel, what appears to matter most is that the act has the potential to save a human life. For her, it doesn't matter if the donor gains materially, earns enhanced social status, or just gets a "'warm glow'" of self-satisfaction "from performing acts of charity" (par. 16). Instead of "remuneration" crowding out "generosity" (par. 15), as critics of financial compensation like the National Kidney Foundation claim, Satel argues that the opposite is true: the combination of payment with the opportunity to do good could offer a real solution to "increase the pool of transplantable organs" (par. 18).

Works Cited

American Enterprise Institute. "About." *American Enterprise Institute*. American Enterprise Institute, 2015. Web. Apr. 30, 2015.

Gomez, Maya. "Possible Solution to the Kidney Shortage?" Writing 1101, Huntly College, 2015. Print.

National Kidney Foundation. "Financial Incentives for Organ Donation." *National Kidney Foundation*. National Kidney Foundation, 1 Feb. 2003. Web. 30 Apr. 2015.

---. "History." *National Kidney Foundation*. National Kidney Foundation, n.d. Web. 30 Apr. 2015.

---. "Organ Donation and Transplantation Statistics." *National Kidney Foundation*. National Kidney Foundation, 8 Sept 2014. Web. 30 Apr. 2015.

---. "Policy and Legislation." *National Kidney Foundation*. National Kidney Foundation, 8 Sept. 2014. Web. 30 Apr. 2015.

National Organ Transplant Act. (NOTA). Pub. L. 98-507. 98 Stat. 2347. 19 Oct. 1984. Print.

Satel, Sally. "The National Kidney Foundation's Bizarre Logic." American Enterprise Institute, 11 June 2009. Web. 1 May 2015.

---. "When Altruism Isn't Moral." American Enterprise Institute, 30 Jan. 2009. Web. 30 Apr. 2015.

REMIX

Remixing Information from Your Research

In this chapter, you saw how writing in one genre (the summary, for example) could be remixed to become part of a writing project in another genre (the annotated bibliography or report). This writing could also be remixed in another medium: It could be delivered in a PowerPoint or Prezi presentation. Or it could be remixed with a persuasive purpose to become a position argument or a proposal. Maya Gomez decided to remix information she learned while conducting research for her report, presenting that information as a timeline to provide interested readers with a history of kidney transplatation they could understand at a glance.

In the next section of this chapter, we ask you to craft one or more of the genres in this chapter—a summary, annotated bibliography, report, or analysis. Once you have composed a text, consider remixing it in another genre or medium, with another purpose, or for another audience.

© JORGE DAN LOPEZ/ Reuters/Corbis

121,272 patients (like Jonathan, age six) need kidneys, but only 6,953 donors (both live and dead) make kidneys available.

Becker & Elias call for compensating kidney donors.

2014 300 bioethicists, surgeons, and religious leaders call for a pilot study on offering compensation.
The NKF responds, arguing against pilot programs for financial incentives (Delmonico et al.).

2013

The Organ Donation and Recovery Improvement Act passes, allowing reimbursement of travel and living expenses for low-income organ donors (United States, "Selected").

2007 The Charlie W. Norwood Living Organ Donation Act passes, allowing paired kidney exchanges.

2004

© Bettmann/Corbis

The National Organ Transplant Act passes, outlawing compensation for organ donors.

1999 The Organ Donor Leave Act passes, granting federal employees time off to donate a kidney.

1984

Cyclosporine, an immuno-suppressant, is discovered ("Overcoming").

1983 The FDA approves use of the immuno-suppressant cyclosporine in humans ("Overcoming").

1972

© Bettmann/Corbis

The first successful kidney transplant between nonsiblings occurs. Azathioprine, an immunosuppressant, is used, allowing a transplanted kidney to function for 21 months ("Transplant Living").

1968 The Uniform Anatomical Gift Act passes, permitting those over 18 to sign a card allowing organ donation after death ("Embryo project").

1961

Ronald Herrick successfully donates one of his kidneys to his identical twin (National Kidney Foundation, "Milestones").

1960 The first successful kidney transplant occurs between siblings who are not twins ("Overcoming").

1954

CONSIDER YOUR RHETORICAL SITUATION

Purpose: The purpose of your report is to inform readers about a controversial topic, and the purpose of your analysis was to help readers understand opposing views on the topic. *What would your purpose be if you were to remix your report or analysis in another genre or medium? Would you want to persuade readers instead of informing them, for example?*

Audience: The audience for your report or analysis is your instructor and other students in your class. *Who would be the audience if you were to remix your report or analysis in another genre or medium? (For example, you could take a position on the debate and write an op-ed for your school's online newspaper, so members of your school community would be your audience.)*

Genre and medium: In this chapter, you may create a report or analysis essay. Both genres are academic and for each the medium is textual, delivered either in print or online. If you remix your project, *what genre or medium would best help you achieve your purpose and reach your new audience?*

The Writing Assignment

Your instructor may ask you to compose all or part of the following multi-stage project:

1. Summarize one or more sources on a controversial topic.

2. Compile an annotated bibliography on the topic.

3. Synthesize information from the articles you have read to write an informative report introducing the topic to your audience.

4. Analyze two (or more) articles that take conflicting positions on the topic, comparing and contrasting the values underlying the opposing positions.

This Guide to Writing is designed to help you compose your own summaries, annotated bibliography, report, and analysis, applying what you have learned from reading an example of each of these genres. This Starting Points chart will help you find answers to composing questions you might have. Use the chart to find the guidance you need, when you need it.

STARTING POINTS: COMPOSING A SUMMARY, ANNOTATED BIBLIOGRAPHY, REPORT, OR ANALYSIS

An Informative Explanation

How do I find a topic to write about?

- Practicing a Genre: Analyzing Opposing Arguments (p. 172)
- Choose a controversial topic to write about. (pp. 195–96)
- Test Your Choice: Choosing a Topic (pp. 196–97)
- Conduct research to find sources. (p. 197)

How can I summarize my sources?

- Assess the genre's basic features: An informative explanation. (pp. 175–76)
- Summary: "A Moral Market" (Maya Gomez) (p. 178)
- Summarize sources and annotate your working bibliography. (pp. 197–99)

How do I annotate sources for an annotated bibliography?

- Annotated Bibliography: Compensating Kidney Donors (Maya Gomez) (pp. 179–81)
- Summarize sources and annotate your working bibliography. (pp. 197–200)

(continued)

How can I cite my sources properly?

- Chapter 24, Citing and Documenting Sources in MLA Style (pp. 644–73)
- Chapter 25, Citing and Documenting Sources in APA Style (pp. 674–84)

How do I interest my audience?

- Determine the writer's purpose and audience. (pp. 173–74)
- Remix: Remixing Information from Your Report or Analysis (p. 192)
- Test Your Choice: Choosing a Topic (pp. 196–97)
- Analyze your audience. (p. 200)

An Informative Explanation

How can I focus my explanation?

- Brainstorm subtopics for a report. (pp. 200–1)
- Choose opposing argument essays to analyze. (p. 201)
- Synthesize sources for a report or analysis. (pp. 201–2)
- Analyze and compare the opposing argument essays. (pp. 202–3)
- Draft a working thesis for your report or analysis. (p. 204)
- Test Your Choice: Evaluating Your Analysis (p. 204)

How do I organize a report or analysis?

- Assess the genre's basic features: A clear, logical organization. (p. 176)
- Brainstorm subtopics for a report. (pp. 200–1)
- Synthesize sources for a report or analysis. (pp. 201–2)
- Analyze and compare the opposing argument essays. (pp. 202-3)
- Test Your Choice: Evaluating Your Analysis (p. 204)
- Draft a working thesis for your report or analysis. (p. 204)
- Create an outline to organize your report or analysis effectively for your readers. (p. 205)

A Clear, Logical Organization

Writing a Draft

GUIDE TO READING
GUIDE TO WRITING
A WRITER AT WORK
THINKING CRITICALLY

195

Smooth Integration of Sources

How do I integrate sources?

- Assess the genre's basic features: Smooth integration of sources. (pp. 176–77)
- Summarize sources and annotate your working bibliography. (pp. 197–200)
- Develop your report or analysis. (p. 206)

Appropriate Explanatory Strategies

What kinds of explanatory strategies are appropriate in a report and an analysis?

- Assess the genre's basic features: Appropriate explanatory strategies. (p. 177)
- Use visuals or multimedia illustrations to enhance your explanation. (p. 208)
- Draft your report or analysis. (p. 209)

Writing a Draft: Invention, Research, Planning, and Composing

The activities in this section will help you choose a topic and find sources; compose summaries and commentaries for an annotated bibliography; analyze and synthesize your sources; report on the topic; and write an analysis comparing two opposing argument essays. Your writing in response to many of these activities can be used in rough drafts that you will be able to improve after receiving feedback from your classmates and instructor. Do the activities in any order that makes sense to you (and your instructor), and return to them as needed as you revise.

∷ Choose a controversial topic to write about.

When choosing a topic to write about, keep in mind that it must be

- a controversial issue (one that people disagree about);
- a topic about which you can report impartially—you may already be interested in the topic and have a strong opinion about it, but you must be able to represent other views on the topic fairly;

- a topic that you can research in the time you have and on which you are likely to find a range of opinions;

- a topic that is likely to interest you and your readers.

You may already have a controversial topic in mind. (Or perhaps your instructor has already assigned you a topic.) If so, complete the activity Test Your Choice: Choosing a Topic below. If you do not, you could

- search for op-ed articles in newspapers and blogs, using LexisNexis Academic or other databases accessible through your college library;

- survey such Web sites as procon.org or controversialissues.org, or the Room for Debate page on the *New York Times*'s Web site (nytimes.com);

- revisit the topic you discussed in the Practicing a Genre activity (p. 172);

- glance at the reading selections in Chapters 6–9 to see whether any of the readings or topics mentioned there pique your interest. For example, consider using as one of your sources Noam Bramson's opinion essay (pp. 242–44) in the debate about NIMBYism (*NIMBY* stands for "not in my back yard") or Naomi Rose's proposal on the topic of whether marine parks such as SeaWorld should continue to keep orcas in captivity (pp. 296–99).

Here are a few additional controversial topics to get you thinking:

- Voter ID laws: Are they needed to stop voter fraud, or are they a way to suppress voting by poor and ethnic minorities?

- E-cigarettes: Are they safe, or do they perpetuate nicotine addiction?

- School uniforms: Do school uniforms level the socioeconomic playing field or worsen socioeconomic divisions?

TEST YOUR CHOICE

Choosing a Topic

After you have made a provisional choice, ask yourself the following questions:

- What do I already know and think about the topic? Do I find it important and interesting enough to justify spending the time necessary to do the research and writing required?

- What are my readers likely to know about it? Will they have strong opinions, or will I need to show them why they should care about it? Will they be open to learning about different points of view on the topic?

Then get together with two or three other students to take turns trying out your topics with potential readers. Ask group members questions like the following:

- What, if anything, do you already know about the topic? What do you think are the main opposing points of view on it? Do you have an opinion about it?

- What basic values (such as freedom, equality, honesty, justice) seem to be involved in discussions of this topic?

Writing a Draft

GUIDE TO READING
▶ **GUIDE TO WRITING**
A WRITER AT WORK
THINKING CRITICALLY

197

■ What questions about the topic would you like answered? For example, would you like to know how it started or changed over time, who has been involved in discussions of the topic, and what interests they represent?

:: Conduct research to find sources.

Now that you have a tentative topic and a sense of your readers' knowledge of it, along with their questions about it, use the research tips that follow to locate relevant sources:

■ Search a database, such as Academic OneFile (InfoTrac) or Academic Search Complete (EBSCOHost).

■ For topics likely to have been dealt with by a government agency, explore USA.gov, the U.S. government's official Web portal, or conduct an Advanced Google search, limiting results to those with a .gov domain.

■ Follow up on sources cited in the texts and Web sites you have looked at.

For each potential source you find,

1. add a citation to your working bibliography;

2. save a copy of the source or a line for further reference;

3. take notes or draft a summary as you read.

For more about developing key terms and searching for sources, see Chapter 21; for more about evaluating sources, see Chapter 22; for help adding a commentary to a summary in an anno-tated bibliography, complete the Ways In activity "How do I draft a commentary?" (pp. 199–200). For citation models and detailed instruc-tions on creating an entry for a works-cited or refer-ences list, see Chapter 24 (MLA style) or Chapter 25 (APA style).

:: Summarize sources and annotate your working bibliography.

The following activities will be useful if you are writing a summary of a single source or compiling an annotated bibliography of several sources.

The length of the summary will depended on the length of your source, the reason you are writing the summary, and your readers' expectations. Typically, one paragraph is sufficient to summarize a brief source for a stand-alone summary or an annotated bibliography, but consult your instructor if you are not sure.

HOW DO I WRITE A SUMMARY?

WAYS IN

1. *Highlight the* THESIS *and* MAIN SUPPORTING IDEAS (REASONS) *as you read the source. (You may have to reread it several times to distinguish the main points from the details.)*

2. *Compose an* OUTLINE *of the main ideas — using your own words.*

3. *Put the source away and draft the summary from your outline. (This can help you avoid inadvertent plagiarism and retain the order of your source's ideas.)*

   ■ Introduce the source in a SIGNAL PHRASE *(author's name plus a verb that cap-tures the move the author is making, such as* argues, supports, describes, *and so*

(continued)

on). For a summary, include publication information, like the title and date of publication, in the opening sentence.

▶ In his book/article/op-ed _____ [title] (date), X, a professor of _____ at School A, asserts/reports _____ .

EXAMPLE   In his article "A Moral Market," published by *Slate* in 2014, law professor Eric Posner proposes . . . (Gomez, "Summary")

■ In a summary for an annotated bibliography, just include the author's name and credentials; publication information will be included in the bibliographic citation:

▶ In this book/article/op-ed, X, professor of _____ at School A, asserts/reports _____ .

EXAMPLE   In this article, law professor Eric Posner proposes a solution to the kidney shortage. (Gomez, "Annotated Bibliography")

■ State the **THESIS** in your own words.

▶ X argues that the best way to solve the problem is to _____ .

▶ Professor X contradicts Dr. Y, explaining that _____ .

EXAMPLE   Economists Becker and Elías argue for a straightforward but highly controversial proposal to solve the kidney shortage problem by paying people to donate their extra kidney for transplantation. ("Annotated Bibliography")

■ List the main supporting ideas (or reasons) in the same order in which they appear in the source.

▶ X responds to such criticisms as _____ , _____ , and _____ .

▶ X claims that _____ . He also argues that _____ .

EXAMPLE   [Becker and Elías] also refute objections that payment would not solve the problem, that it is immoral, that it would exploit the poor, and that it would reduce altruistic donations. ("Annotated Bibliography")

■ Use **TRANSITIONS** (such as *and, also, but, therefore*) and other cues (such as repeating key terms or using synonyms to refer to key terms) to show readers how the ideas relate to one another.

▶ Although/Whereas/Unlike Dr. A's position, Dr. B's contention is that _____ .

EXAMPLE   [Posner] argues that, unlike the unpopular proposal to sell kidneys, his proposal for an "altruism exchange" would be politically acceptable because it is based on altruism, not the profit motive. ("Summary")

Writing a Draft

GUIDE TO READING
▶ GUIDE TO WRITING
A WRITER AT WORK
THINKING CRITICALLY

199

4. *Check your draft summary against the source to make sure you have*

- captured the author's ideas accurately and succinctly.

- avoided inserting your own ideas or opinions.

- put key terms (such as "altruism exchange" in Gomez's summary of Posner's article) in quotation marks.

- avoided borrowing other words or sentence patterns.

An annotated bibliography for a writing project not only includes a summary of each source, but also a commentary including

- your thoughts on how you might use the source in your report, analysis, or other project;

- your ideas about the relationships among your sources (the beginning of your synthesis); and

- perhaps an evaluation of each source's **credibility** (authority).

Use the following guidelines and sentence strategies as a jumping-off point for drafting the commentary for the sources you include in your annotated bibliography. You can make the sentences you generate your own later, as you revise.

HOW DO I DRAFT A COMMENTARY FOR AN ANNOTATED BIBLIOGRAPHY?

WAYS IN

1. *Explore how you could use the source in your project(s).*

   ▶ I plan to use _____ [title of article/book] to show _____ , _____ , and _____ .

   EXAMPLE I could use [Becker and Elías's] proposal as an example of a radical or extreme solution. . . . (Gomez, "Annotated Bibliography")

   I think I will use the NKF position statement as the voice of the status quo. ("Annotated Bibliography")

2. *Make connections among your sources.*

   ▶ X is like/unlike Y in that _____ .

   EXAMPLE [Becker and Elias's] proposal . . . stands in sharp contrast to the NKF's opposition to financial compensation and Eric Posner's compromise. ("Annotated Bibliography," citation 1, par. 2)

3. *Assess the credibility of your sources.*

   ▶ X is likely to carry authority with most people because _____ .

(continued)

> **EXAMPLE**   . . . Becker, a Nobel Prize–winning economist at the University of Chicago, and Elías, a professor of economics at a university in Argentina. Becker and Elías have the authority to carry off a proposal this bold. ("Annotated Bibliography," citation 1, par. 2)

For citation models and detailed instructions on creating a bibliography citation for your annotated bibliography, see Chapter 24 (MLA style) or Chapter 25 (APA style).

Analyze your audience.

Once you have conducted research and added potential sources to your annotated bibliography, spend a few minutes thinking about your audience. Answering the questions that follow will help you decide on the best approach to take to your report or analysis.

WAYS IN

For more about brainstorming, freewriting, and other idea-generating strategies, see Chapter 11.

WHAT WILL INTEREST READERS OF MY REPORT OR ANALYSIS?

Analyze your **AUDIENCE** *by brainstorming or freewriting answers to the following questions:*

- Who are your readers, and what are they likely to know about the topic? What opinions are they likely to hold? (Reconsider what you learned from the Test Your Choice activity earlier in this Guide to Writing.)
- How would you answer your readers' "So what?" question? Think of at least one aspect of the topic that will clarify its importance for your readers.
- What is your relationship with your readers? What **TONE** is most appropriate for addressing this audience? How do you want your readers to perceive you? (For an academic audience, a rational, dispassionate tone is usually most appropriate.)

Since you are reporting or analyzing a controversial topic, rather than offering your own opinion, be sure to keep your tone impartial.

Brainstorm subtopics for a report.

If you have been asked to write a report, you will need to focus your attention on a few key subtopics that you can address thoroughly. A good way to come up with a list of subtopics to consider is by reviewing what you already know:

- List the milestones in the history of your topic, noting laws, events, and publications that mark important turning points.
- Reread your annotated bibliography and other source notes, highlighting subtopics that are discussed in two or more sources.

Then make a list of the subtopics that seem most relevant. Here's an example from Maya Gomez's report:

Topic: Solving the kidney-shortage problem

Writing a Draft

GUIDE TO READING
▶ **GUIDE TO WRITING**
A WRITER AT WORK
THINKING CRITICALLY

201

Possible Subtopics

- by preventing kidney disease (through education, diet, medication)
- by improving dialysis treatment
- by encouraging everyone to donate their kidneys after death (opt-out instead of the current opt-in system)
- by making kidney exchanges legal
- by removing the obstacles kidney donors face (paid time off)
- by compensating donors (money, health insurance, a kidney for themselves or for a loved one)
- by developing an artificial kidney to replace a non-functioning kidney

Gomez ended up focusing on four of these topics that she knew she had enough information about from her sources to report on in depth.

Choose opposing argument essays to analyze.

If you have been asked to write a comparative analysis, you will need to select texts that

- take different positions on the same controversial topic
- reflect different underlying basic values or worldviews

It may also be helpful to choose opposing arguments that refer explicitly to one other or that at least address the same aspect of the topic from different perspectives.

When compiling your annotated bibliography or writing your report, you may have come across two (or three) essays that looked promising. If you have one promising text but need to find a good opposing one, consider doing additional research on LexisNexis Academic or other databases accessible through your college library using the key words or sources referred to in the essay you've already chosen. Visiting sites like procon.org or the Room for Debate pages on the *New York Times* Web site (nytimes.com) may also be helpful.

Synthesize sources for a report or analysis.

One effective way to make sense of the information you have accumulated is to create a synthesis chart. Once you've devised a list of subtopics, go back to your annotated bibliography and source notes to synthesize the information and ideas you have accumulated.

Gomez selected four possible solutions to the kidney shortage to focus on in her report:

- replace opt-in with opt-out
- allow paired kidney exchanges
- remove disincentives to donation
- offer incentives to donation

She organized the information she found on those subtopics into a synthesis chart. Here is a portion of her chart on one of her subtopics:

Subtopics	Source	My Notes	Location
Offer Incentives	Becker & Elías	Only paying donors will "close the gap between the demand and supply of kidneys"	par. 8
	Delmonico open letter	Like NKF, opposed to pilot studies, $ incentives "would violate global standards and will not work." Favors paying costs for donors. Signed by over 300 national and international doctors, clergy, bioethicists, members of organ procurement organizations.	n. pag., pars. 1-12
	Satel, "Case"	Satel had kidney transplant. "It is easy to condemn the black market and the patients who patronize it. But you can't fault people for trying to save their own lives."	par. 10; quote, par. 9
	Sullivan	1983 proposal by Dr. Barry Jacobs: People in US who need kidneys should be able to buy them from healthy third-world donors. Led to NOTA rules about compensation.	pars. 1-2, pars. 9-10
	US Transplant open letter	Calls on Congress/president for pilot study to find ways to motivate donors, to make more organs available. 300 signers; surgeons, bioethicists, clergy.	open-letter text tab, signer's tab

Notice that Gomez keeps track of where the information in her notes came from, so she can check later to make sure she has represented borrowed ideas fairly and cited her sources accurately.

∷ Analyze and compare the opposing argument essays.

The following activities will help you analyze and compare the opposing argument essays. If you've composed a summary of one or both texts, you've begun your analysis already. You may have highlighted and outlined the essay to identify parts of the argument. Now probe more deeply, exploring the motivating factors—the values, concerns, and priorities—that help explain the fundamental disagreement underlying the opposing points of view. (Most writers will need to reread parts of the opposing argument essays more than once and may need to do some additional research in order to determine the factors motivating each author.) Completing the Comparative Analysis Chart can be very helpful in planning and drafting your analysis.

Writing a Draft

GUIDE TO READING
▶ **GUIDE TO WRITING**
A WRITER AT WORK
THINKING CRITICALLY

203

HOW CAN I ANALYZE AND COMPARE THE OPPOSING ARGUMENTS?

WAYS IN

Reread each essay, noting in the margin where you find indications of the following:

Position: The writer's main idea or **THESIS STATEMENT**, the writer's opinion about the topic

Arguments: How the writer supports the position and responds to alternative points of view

Motivating Factors:

- **Values:** Moral, ethical, or religious principles (for example, justice, equality, "do unto others")

- **Worldviews and ideologies:** Political or religious belief systems (such as libertarianism, progressivism, conservatism, orthodoxy)

- **Ideas and ideals** (for example, democratic ideals, including the right to vote and freedom of speech)

- **Concerns and fears** (for example, personal safety, abuse of power, protecting the environment)

- **Goals and priorities** about what is most important or urgent (for example, whether obedience to authority is more important than independent thinking)

Fill in the Comparative Analysis Chart.

Enter your notes, useful quotations, and the page or paragraph numbers in which you found the borrowed information. Searching the text for evidence of underlying values and other motivating factors will deepen your analysis and help you go beyond summarizing what is said to explaining *why* each author holds her or his opinion. Creating this chart will also help you see points of comparison and contrast between the opposing arguments. (Remember that you may have to leave some sections of the chart blank because you may not find examples of all the features in each essay.)

Chart for Analyzing Opposing Arguments		
TOPIC:		
Source		
Position		
Arguments		
Values		
Worldviews & Ideologies		
Ideas & Ideals		
Concerns & Fears		
Goals & Priorities		

To see Maya Gomez's completed Comparative Analysis Chart, see the "Writer at Work" section (pp. 215–18).

Evaluating Your Analysis

Get together with two or three other students to test the underlying value (or other motivating factor) you think plays an important role in the argument between the texts you're comparing:

Presenters. Briefly tell your listeners what the disagreement is about and what you think is an important motivating factor (such as a value, worldview, or special concern) driving the argument. Provide one or two examples to show where you see the factor you've identified in the opposing texts.

Listeners. Tell the presenter what the examples suggest to you about the motivating factor underlying the disagreement. Share any questions, comments, or insights with the presenter.

⁙ Draft a working thesis for your report or analysis.

The thesis statement announces the purpose and the focus or main idea in both a report and a comparative analysis.

Purpose Focus/Main idea Forecast of subtopics	**REPORT**	This report will survey an array of ideas that have been proposed to encourage people to donate their kidneys, including changing to an opt-out system of organ donation after death, facilitating paired kidney exchanges, reducing financial disincentives, and offering incentives. (Gomez, par. 3)
Purpose Focus/Main idea Forecast of subtopics	**ANALYSIS**	This essay compares the underlying values driving the arguments in the NKF position statement "Financial Incentives for Organ Donation" and Satel's article "When Altruism Isn't Moral." Their views are diametrically opposed. . . . The basis of their disagreement is the proper role of altruism. The NKF emphatically endorses the current "altruistic system" (par. 5). Satel, in contrast, argues that current policy is failing precisely because it is an "altruism-only system" (par. 13). (Gomez, par. 4)

Juxtaposing the thesis statements from Gomez's report and analysis makes clear the different purposes of these two genres. They both focus on the issue of how to encourage more kidney donation. But whereas the report provides an overview, or survey, of different approaches to the problem, the analysis compares two conflicting documents to zero in on the factor (or factors) underlying the disagreement.

∷ Create an outline to organize your report or analysis effectively for your readers.

Once you have drafted a working thesis, you may want to devise a tentative outline, drawing on your invention and research notes. An effective outline for a report typically divides the topic into subtopics. An effective outline for a comparative analysis typically offers a sequenced (or alternating) comparison centered on points of disagreement.

For help organizing a comparison/contrast, see Chapter 18.

Below are simple outlines of Gomez's report and analysis, which you may use as a starting point:

Outline: Gomez's Report

   I. Introduction: Provides a brief history of kidney transplantation and demonstrates the seriousness of the kidney shortage. Thesis statement identifies the topic (proposals to increase the number of kidneys available for transplantation) and forecasts subtopics. (pars. 1–3)

  II. Change from Opt-in to Opt-out System (Subtopic 1). Explains current opt-in system, surveys reasons for and against changing to opt-out, and concludes that this change is not enough to increase the number of kidneys available significantly. (pars. 4–5)

 III. Facilitate Paired Kidney Exchanges (Subtopic 2). Provides history, explains current status, and concludes that paired kidney exchanges will not increase supply significantly. (pars. 6–8)

  IV. Remove Disincentives (Subtopic 3). Explores current efforts and proposed changes. (pars. 9–10)

   V. Offer Incentives (Subtopic 4). Explores history, and positions for and against offering incentives. (pars. 11–13)

  VI. Conclusion: Reiterates the problem, emphasizes significance of problem. (par. 14)

Outline: Gomez's Analysis

   I. Introduction: Demonstrates the seriousness of the kidney shortage and provides background information; introduces the position of the National Kidney Foundation (NKF); introduces Satel, a key critic of the NKF, and her position. (pars. 1–3)

  II. Conflict: Thesis identifies differing attitudes toward altruism as the basis of the conflict underlying Satel's and the NKF's positions on offering incentives to increase the supply of kidneys available for transplantation. (pars. 4–5)

 III. Satel's First Objection: Moral Absolutism. Reviews Satel's argument that the NKF assumes unfairly that altruism is a shared value that trumps all others. (pars. 6–7)

  IV. Satel's Second Objection: Reviews Satel's position that NKF unfairly assumes that all agree that commodification of the human body is wrong. (pars. 8–9)

   V. Satel's Third Objection: Criticizes the NKF's moral logic—claims it commits the false choice fallacy. (pars. 10–11)

  VI. Conclusion: Summarizes basic conflict: NKF emphasizes purity of motive; Satel prioritizes importance of increasing the pool of organs available for donation. (par. 12)

Use your outline to guide your drafting, but do not feel tied to it. You may figure out a better way to organize your ideas as you draft.

⠢ Develop your report or analysis.

Once you have a working thesis statement and outline, review your notes, including the writing you may have done to analyze your audience (p. 200), brainstorm possible subtopics (pp. 200–1), synthesize information and ideas from your sources (pp. 201–2), and complete the comparative analysis chart (p. 203) to determine how you can use the ideas and information you have to support your thesis.

The following Ways In activities provide some sentence strategies to help you analyze opposing arguments and develop supporting paragraphs using writing strategies like classification and comparison or contrast. Use the sentence strategies as a jumping-off point—you can always revise them later—or use language of your own from the start.

WAYS IN →

HOW CAN I PRESENT MY ANALYSIS OF THE OPPOSING ARGUMENTS?

Analyze a quotation. Compose a few sentences explaining why you think a particular quotation (or group of quotations) suggests a **BASIC VALUE** or other **MOTIVATING FACTOR** that plays an important role in the arguments you are analyzing.

▶ Use of the words/phrase " ⎯⎯⎯⎯ " shows that factor A is central to X's way of thinking about ⎯⎯⎯⎯ .

EXAMPLE   Altruism, according to Satel, is "the guiding narrative of the transplant establishment," its underlying ideology or value system. (Gomez, Analysis, par. 5)

SUMMARIZE *or* **PARAPHRASE** *the disagreement.*

▶ X, a member of group A, argues that ⎯⎯⎯⎯ [describe approach] because ⎯⎯⎯⎯ . Y, a member of group B, disagrees, arguing that ⎯⎯⎯⎯ [describe approach] because ⎯⎯⎯⎯ .

EXAMPLE   One of the most vocal critics of NOTA's prohibition against compensating donors . . . is Sally Satel, M.D., . . . a lecturer in psychiatry at the Yale University Medical School and a resident scholar at the American Enterprise Institute, a conservative think tank "committed to expanding liberty, increasing individual opportunity and strengthening free enterprise." And she is a kidney transplant recipient. . . . Whereas the NKF defends the status quo and urges retention of the valuable consideration clause, Satel deplores the "woeful inadequacy of our nation's transplant policy" and proposes "rewards" to "encourage more living and posthumous donation" (par. 5). The basis of their disagreement is the proper role of altruism. The NKF emphatically endorses the current "altruistic system" (par. 5). Satel, in contrast, argues that current policy is failing precisely because it is an "altruism-only system" (par. 13). (Gomez, Analysis, pars. 4–5)

Writing a Draft

GUIDE TO READING
▶ **GUIDE TO WRITING**
A WRITER AT WORK
THINKING CRITICALLY

207

WHAT EXPLANATORY STRATEGIES COULD I USE?

Consider which explanatory strategies would be most useful in reporting on a controversial topic or analyzing conflicting positions on that topic. Ask yourself questions like these:

How can I CLASSIFY aspects of the topic or different points of view?

For more about classification, see Chapter 17; for more about narration, see Chapter 14; for more about comparison and contrast, see Chapter 18; for more about definition, see Chapter 16.

▶ Topic X can be broken down into such categories as _____ , _____ , and _____ .

▶ Some of the reasons Professor X supports _____ include _____ , _____ , and _____ .

EXAMPLE This report will survey an array of ideas that have been proposed to encourage people to donate their kidneys including changing to an opt-out system of organ donation after death, facilitating paired kidney exchanges, reducing financial disincentives, and offering incentives. ("Report," Gomez, par. 3)

How can I use ANECDOTES to tell a story and make the topic less abstract for my readers?

▶ Consider the story of Ms. X, who did _____ in 2015.

▶ For example, in 2015, X and Y stated _____ .

EXAMPLES The "first successful kidney transplant" took place in 1954 when Ronald Herrick donated one of his kidneys to his identical twin Richard, who was dying of kidney disease (National Kidney Foundation, "Milestones"). ("Report," par. 1)

How could I use COMPARISON AND CONTRAST to sharpen similarities and differences among the different points of view?

▶ While/Whereas X believes/argues/claims _____ , Y claims _____ .

▶ X is like Y in these ways: _____ , _____ , _____ .

EXAMPLE Whereas the NKF defends the status quo and urges retention of the valuable consideration clause, Satel deplores the "woeful inadequacy of our nation's transplant policy" and proposes "rewards" to "encourage more living and posthumous donation" (pars. 5, 6). ("Analysis," par. 4)

How do I DEFINE terms or concepts that may be unfamiliar to my readers?

▶ X means _____ .

▶ X, a type of _____ , is characterized by _____ , _____ , and _____ .

EXAMPLE A paired kidney exchange essentially trades a biologically incompatible kidney, usually donated by a family member, for a compatible one donated by a stranger. ("Report," par. 7)

WAYS IN

(continued)

For more about cause and effect, see Chapter 9.

What CAUSES *or* EFFECTS *are important to note?*

▶ The result of .... is ....

▶ Because of .... , we no longer do ....

EXAMPLE   Because of improvements in blood and tissue typing, . . . it is no longer necessary for an identical twin or even a relative to make the donation. ("Report," par. 1)

⸬ Use visuals or multimedia illustrations to enhance your explanation.

Reports explaining a controversial topic may benefit from including visuals, such as timelines, graphs, or tables. Reports published online can include animated graphics and videos. Presentations can use presentation slides (such as PowerPoint or Prezi) with embedded graphics or videos.

When deciding whether to include illustrations, ask yourself questions like the following:

- Can you create your own graphics (for example, by using spreadsheet software to create bar graphs or pie charts)?

- Will you need to borrow materials that others have created (for example, by downloading materials from the Internet, taking screenshots from Web sites, or scanning visuals from books or magazines)? Remember that borrowed material must be cited, including the sources of data you use to create graphs and tables.

- Will your writing be published on a Web site that is available to readers beyond the classroom? If so, you may also need to obtain permission to use borrowed media. (As an alternative, you may want to consider linking to the site, rather than embedding the material in your presentation.)

Write the opening sentences.

Review what you have already written to see if you have something that would help you start your report or analysis, or try out one of these opening strategies:

Cite **statistics** *to impress on readers the importance of the topic:*

According to the National Kidney Foundation (NKF), more than 100,000 people are on the U.S. transplant waiting list, with "nearly 3,000 new patients" joining the list every month and an estimated 12 patients dying every day while waiting for a kidney ("Organ"). (Analysis, par. 1)

Begin with an **anecdote** *to humanize the topic:*

> The "first successful kidney transplant" took place in 1954 when Ronald Herrick donated one of his kidneys to his identical twin Richard, who was dying of kidney disease (National Kidney Foundation, "Milestones"). Richard and Ronald's successful tandem surgery was an historic event ushering in the era of kidney transplantation. (Report, par. 1)

At this point, you simply want an opening sentence to launch your draft. Later, you may discover a better way to capture your readers' attention.

Draft your report or analysis.

By this point, you have done a lot of writing to

- summarize sources accurately and concisely
- comment on how sources relate to one another
- create bibliographic citations for sources
- synthesize an array of information on the topic
- analyze opposing points of view
- find an appropriate focus for your report or analysis
- choose explanatory strategies
- draft a working thesis
- organize your ideas to make them clear, logical, and effective for readers

Now stitch that material together to create a draft. The next two parts of the Guide to Writing will help you evaluate and improve it.

Evaluating the Draft: Using Peer Review

Your instructor may arrange a peer review session in class or online, where you can exchange drafts with your classmates and give one another a thoughtful critical reading. A good critical reading does three things:

1. It lets the writer know how well the reader understands the point of the essay.
2. It praises what works best.
3. It indicates where the draft could be improved and makes suggestions on how to improve it.

One strategy for evaluating a draft is to use the basic features of the genre you are composing as a guide.

A PEER REVIEW GUIDE

An Informative Explanation

Is the report or analysis informative, interesting, and perceptive?

Summarize: Tell the writer what makes the topic important and opposing points of view interesting.

Praise: Give an example of something in the draft that you think will especially interest the intended readers.

Critique: Tell the writer about any confusion or uncertainty you have about the topic's importance. Indicate if the focus of the report or analysis could be clearer, more interesting, or more appropriate for the intended readers.

A Clear, Logical Organization

Does the report or analysis explain the topic and opposing positions clearly, and is it easy to follow?

Summarize: Look at the way the essay is organized by making a scratch outline.

Praise: Give an example of where the essay succeeds in being readable — for instance, in its overall organization, forecast of topics, or use of transitions.

Critique: Identify places where readability could be improved — for example, by adding a forecast, clarifying a topic sentence, or using headings.

Smooth Integration of Sources

Are sources incorporated into the report or analysis effectively?

Summarize: Note each source mentioned in the text, and check to make sure it appears in the list of works cited, if there is one. Highlight signal phrases and other in-text citations.

Praise: Give an example of the effective use of sources — for instance, a particularly well-integrated quotation, paraphrase, or summary that supports and illustrates the point. Note any especially descriptive verbs used to introduce information from sources.

Critique: Point out where adding experts' credentials would make a source more credible. Indicate quotations, paraphrases, or summaries that could be more smoothly integrated or more fully interpreted or explained. Identify verbs in signal phrases that could more clearly signal the writer's moves.

Improving the Draft

GUIDE TO READING
GUIDE TO WRITING
A WRITER AT WORK
THINKING CRITICALLY

211

> Are writing strategies (such as classification, definition, and comparison) used effectively to report on the topic and analyze the underlying values? Is research adequate?

Appropriate Explanatory Strategies

Summarize: Note which explanatory strategies the writer uses, such as classification, definition, comparison, or cause-effect.

Praise: Point to an explanatory strategy that is especially effective, and highlight research that is particularly helpful.

Critique: Point to any places where a definition is needed, where more (or better) examples might help, or where another explanatory strategy could be improved or added. Note where a visual (such as a flowchart or graph) would make the explanation clearer.

Making Comments Electronically Most word processing software offers features that allow you to insert comments directly into the text of someone else's document. Many readers prefer to make their comments this way because it tends to be faster than writing on hard copy and space is virtually unlimited; it also eliminates the process of deciphering handwritten comments. Where such features are not available, simply typing comments directly into a document in a contrasting color can provide the same advantages.

Improving the Draft: Revising, Editing, and Proofreading

Start improving your draft by reflecting on what you have written thus far:

- Review peer review comments from your classmates, as well as feedback from your instructor or a writing center tutor: What basic problems do your readers identify?

- Look back at your invention writing: What else could you add? Is more research needed?

- Review your draft: What can you do to make your report or analysis more informative, interesting, perceptive, or clearly organized?

Revise your draft.

If your readers had difficulty with your draft, or if you think there is room for improvement, try some of the strategies listed in the Troubleshooting Guide that follows. They can help you fine-tune your presentation of each genre's basic features.

A TROUBLESHOOTING GUIDE

An Informative Explanation

My readers are not clear about my topic or the opposing positions I'm exploring.

- State the topic explicitly, perhaps as a question, so the conflicting positions are clear.
- Clarify how your subtopics relate to your topic by forecasting them in your thesis statement.
- Sharpen the contrast between opposing positions by using transitions of contrast (such as *whereas* or *although*).

My readers are not interested or do not appreciate the issue's importance.

- Add information showing the impact of the issue or how it affects people's lives.
- Put the topic in context by providing historical, political, or cultural importance.
- Quote notable authorities to emphasize the issue's importance.
- Cite polls or research studies or use graphics to demonstrate the widespread impact of the issue.

My readers do not understand my analysis.

- Determine whether you are trying to cover too many points.
- Explain in more detail the points that are harder for readers to grasp.
- Consider emphasizing the less obvious points of the disagreement.

My report or analysis seems more like a summary.

- Revisit your sources, brainstorm a list of subtopics some or all of them cover, and create a synthesis chart to help you understand the similarities and differences.
- Consider how the writer's profession or biography could explain why a particular motivating factor (such as a value or priority) has so much persuasive power.
- Think about the social and political situation in which each essay was written and how the writer was trying to appeal to readers.

A Clear, Logical Organization

My readers are confused by my essay or find it difficult to read.

- Outline your report or analysis. If necessary, move, add, or delete sections to strengthen coherence.
- Consider adding a forecasting statement with key terms that are repeated in topic sentences throughout the report or analysis.
- Consider adding headings to highlight subtopics; use key terms from the forecast in your headings.
- Check for appropriate transitions between sentences, paragraphs, and major sections of your report or analysis.
- Consider reorganizing your analysis to alternate between the sources you are comparing.
- Review your opening and closing paragraphs. Be sure you state your thesis explicitly and that your closing paragraph revisits your thesis.

Improving the Draft   GUIDE TO READING
GUIDE TO WRITING
A WRITER AT WORK
THINKING CRITICALLY   213

Smooth Integration of Sources

> Quotations, summaries, and paraphrases don't flow smoothly with the rest of the essay.

- Reread all passages where you quote outside sources. Ask yourself whether you provide enough context for the quotation or establish clearly enough the credentials of the source's author.
- Use signal phrases to put sources in context. Choose descriptive verbs that clearly indicate what the source author is doing (making a claim, asserting a position, reporting on a study, and so forth).
- Add a sentence explaining what the quotation, summary, or paraphrase means or why it is relevant.

> Readers are concerned that my list of sources is too limited or unbalanced.

- Do additional research to balance your list, taking particular care that you have an adequate number of reliable sources from a variety of points of view.
- Ask a librarian or your instructor for help finding sources on your topic.

> My readers wonder whether my sources are credible.

- Clearly identify all sources and state the credentials of cited authorities.
- Eliminate sources that are not relevant, credible, or otherwise appropriate.

Appropriate Explanatory Strategies

> Readers don't understand my report or analysis.

- Consider whether you have used the most appropriate writing strategies (defining, classifying, comparing and contrasting, narrating, illustrating, describing, or explaining causes and effects) for your topic.
- Recheck your definitions for clarity. Be sure that you have explicitly defined any key terms your readers might not know.

> Readers want more information about certain aspects of the topic.

- Expand or clarify definitions by adding examples.
- Add examples or comparisons and contrasts to relate the topic to something readers already know.
- Conduct additional research on your topic, and cite it in your essay.

(continued)

Appropriate Explanatory Strategies

> Readers want visuals to help them understand certain aspects of the topic.

- Check whether your sources use visuals (tables, graphs, drawings, photographs, and the like) that might be appropriate for your report or analysis. (If you are publishing your work online, consider video clips, audio files, and animated graphics as well.)
- Consider drafting your own charts, tables, or graphs, or adding your own photographs or illustrations.

> Summaries lack oomph; paraphrases are too complicated; quotations are too long.

- Revise the summaries to emphasize a single key idea.
- Restate the paraphrases more succinctly, omitting irrelevant details. Consider quoting important words.
- Use ellipses to tighten the quotations to emphasize the memorable words.

A Note on Grammar and Spelling Checkers

These tools can be helpful, but do not rely on them exclusively to catch errors in your text: Spelling checkers cannot catch misspellings that are themselves words, such as *to* for *too*. Grammar checkers miss some problems, sometimes give faulty advice for fixing problems, and can flag correct items as wrong. Use these tools as a second line of defense after your own (and, ideally, another reader's) proofreading and editing efforts.

Edit and proofread your draft.

Our research indicates that particular errors occur often in research reports and analyses of conflicing perspectives on a controversial topic: incorrect comma usage in sentences with interrupting phrases, and vague pronoun reference. The following guidelines will help you check your writing for these common errors.

Using Commas around Interrupting Phrases

What is an *interrupting phrase*? When writers are reporting on a controversial topic or analyzing opposing positions, they need to supply a great deal of information precisely and accurately. They add much of this information in phrases that interrupt the flow of a sentence, as in the following example:

▶ The National Kidney Foundation, one of the most conservative advocacy groups, had been adamantly opposed to financial compensation of any kind since 2002 ("Financial"). (Gomez, "Report," par. 9)

Such interrupting phrases, as they are called, are typically set off with commas.

The Problem   Forgetting to set off an interrupting phrase with commas can make sentences unclear or difficult to read.

How to Correct It   Add a comma on either side of an interrupting phrase.

▶ A radical proposal ∧ aptly titled "Cash for Kidneys ∧" was published in the *Wall Street Journal* by two respected economists ∧ Julio Elías and Nobel Laureate Gary Becker, who argue that the only way to "close the gap between the demand and supply of kidneys" is to pay people for their kidneys. (Gomez, "Report," par. 11)

Analyzing Opposing Arguments

GUIDE TO READING
GUIDE TO WRITING
▶ A WRITER AT WORK
THINKING CRITICALLY

215

Correcting Vague Pronoun Reference

The Problem   **Pronouns** replace and refer to nouns, making writing more efficient and cohesive. If the reference is vague, however, this advantage is lost. A common problem is vague use of *this, that, it,* or *which.*

How to Correct It   Scan your writing for pronouns, taking special note of places where you use *this, that, it,* or *which.* Check to be sure that what *this, that, it, which,* or another pronoun refers to is crystal clear. If it is not, revise your sentence.

- Television evangelists seem to be perpetually raising money, *This habit* which makes some

  viewers question their motives.

- By the late 1960s, plate tectonics emerged as a new area of study. Tectonics was

  based on the notion of the earth's crust as a collection of plates or land masses

  startling new geological theory
  above and below sea level, constantly in motion. This took a while for most people to

  accept, because of its unexpected novelty.

- Inside the Summit Tunnel, the Chinese laborers were using as much as

  500 kegs a day of costly black powder to blast their way through the

  The unexpected expense
  solid rock. It was straining the Central Pacific's budget.

A WRITER AT WORK

Analyzing Opposing Arguments

Below is a two-part illustration of Maya Gomez's work in progress: the notes Gomez made on Satel's article and the Comparative Analysis Chart she filled in. She worked for several hours over a couple of days—rereading both the NKF's position statement and Satel's op-ed and making notes on the texts and in her chart. Notice that the entries in the chart under *Satel* often compare her essay to the NKF's position statement. Note also Gomez's comment in her comparative analysis chart (pp. 217–18), in which she analyzes the commodification argument: "Hard to analyze but core of arg between NKF & Satel. Use to focus: moral values arg is about altruism." If you examine Gomez's comparative analysis essay, you'll see that this is exactly what she did.

Gomez's Annotations on Satel's Op-Ed

11 Arguments from corruption proceed from the belief that donors, and perhaps society at large, will be diminished or corrupted if organs are given in return for something of material value. Giving a kidney "for free" is noble but accepting compensation is illegitimate, a sordid affront to human dignity. Indeed, the debate surrounding incentives for organ donation sometimes resembles a titanic struggle between uplift and greed. "As a rule, the debate is cast as one in which existing relations of selfless, altruistic exchange are threatened with replacement by market-based, for-profit alternatives," observes Kieran Healy, a sociologist at Duke University.

Corruption args: selling kidney diminishes dignity of act. Not selfless but greedy. Contractual, market relationship is sordid, corrupt.

12   Dr. Luc Noel of the World Health Organization subscribes to this false choice. "There are two prevailing concepts of transplantation," he says. "One relies on money and leads to increased inequality, besides putting a price on the integrity of the body and human dignity. The second is based on solidarity and the donor's sole motivation to save a life." The National Kidney Foundation warns against "self-interest on behalf of the donor." . . .

Corruption arg commits false choice fallacy.

13   Paradoxically, our current transplant system makes every donation seem like a "loving, voluntary gift of organ donation." Think about it: there is no other legal option. Some altruistic donations come as close to the technical definition: my experience would be one of those. Yet, our current altruism-only system has a dark side: It imposes coercion of its own by putting friends and family members in a bind. They might not want to donate, but they feel obligated, lest their relative die or deteriorate on dialysis. Sociologists have written about familial dynamics that involve guilt, overt pressure, or subtle threats. Consider the "black-sheep donor," a wayward relative who shows up to offer an organ as an act of redemption, hoping to reposition himself in the family's good graces. Some donate as a way to elicit praise and social acceptance. For others, donation is a sullen fulfillment of familial duty, a way to avoid the shame and guilt of allowing a relative to suffer needlessly and perhaps even die.

Altruism can have a dark side — subtle coercion of the donor

Donation as redemptive act

Donation to win praise

Gomez's Comparative Analysis Chart

Comparative Analysis Chart		
Topic	Should the law be changed to permit financial incentives for kidney donors?	
	National Kidney Foundation, "Financial Incentives for Organ Donation" (2003)	Sally Satel, "When Altruism Isn't Moral" (2009)
Position	Against compensation: "The National Kidney Foundation opposes all efforts to legalize payments" (par. 1)	In favor of compensation: "We need to encourage more living and posthumous donation through rewards, say, tax credits or lifetime health insurance." (par. 6)
Arguments	Moral Values Argument: offering monetary incentives "is inconsistent with our values as a society" (par. 2) Key terms "moral" (5) & "wrong" (6, 7)	Agrees it's a Morality Argument. Satel doesn't say it's always immoral (note title). Satel's view: "these skeptics . . . must not determine binding policy in a morally pluralistic society." (par. 21) Note "right reasons" requirement to donate (2) in Matt Thompson anecdote. How do you measure "the goodness of an act"? (18)
	Commodifies body parts: giving kidneys "a monetary value" is morally wrong because it devalues human life, "diminishes human dignity" (par. 2) This is the main argument for the motivating factor of altruism	Uses "argument from corruption" to refute commodification arg (pars. 11-17): 1. "false choice" reasoning 2. skeptical about whether true human altruism even exists, pure selflessness? (17) 3. the goodness of an act is not diminished b/c someone was paid to perform it" (18) Gives examples (17-18). Hard to analyze but core of arg between NKF & Satel. Use to focus: moral values arg is about altruism.
	Coercion/Exploitation of Poor Argument (par. 3)	Uses "arguments from consequence": Concedes problem but responds "it can be addressed with good policy" (par. 12). Gives examples.
	Effectiveness Argument: "its ability to increase the supply or organs for transplantation is questionable" (par. 4) Response to Pilot Study Proposal: (a) "not be feasible"; (b) "corrosive effect on the ethical, moral, and social fabric of this country"; (c) could not revert to altruistic system (5).	Doesn't claim compensation would solve the shortage: "A donor compensation system operating in parallel with our established mechanism of altruistic procurement is the only way to accommodate us all. Moreover, it represents a promising middle ground" (par. 21)

Values	Values most highly human dignity, therefore opposes commodification.	Values most highly saving lives of kidney patients (like herself)
Ideologies & Worldviews	Moral Certainty	Moral Pluralism (accuses NKF of imposing its morality on everyone else); Satel is member of conservative think tank, favors personal freedom, financial incentives.
Ideas & Ideals	Altruism (selfless giving)	Human life (save more kidney patients)
Concerns & Fears	1. Fears socio-economic fragmentation of society: rich v poor. Claims payments could be viewed as coercion and exploitation. But acknowledges poor get fewer transplants under current system. 2. Fears family dissent over payment.	1. Fears that so many people are dying while waiting for a transplant (fate she was spared) 2. Concerned about exploiting the poor (par. 10), "the dark, corrupt world of organ-trafficking" (21).
Goals & Priorities	To uphold morality	To solve the kidney shortage

THINKING CRITICALLY

To think critically means to use the knowledge you have acquired from the information in this chapter, your own writing, the writing of other students, and class discussions to reflect deeply on your work for this assignment and the genres (or types) of writing you have produced. The benefit of thinking critically is proven and important: Thinking critically about what you have learned will help you remember it longer, ensuring that you will be able to put it to good use well beyond this writing course.

Reflecting on What You Have Learned

In this chapter, you learned a great deal by reading texts in four different genres on the same controversial topic and by composing all or part of a multi-stage project. To consolidate your learning, reflect not only on what you learned but also on how you learned it.

Reflecting on the Genres

GUIDE TO READING
GUIDE TO WRITING
A WRITER AT WORK
▶ **THINKING CRITICALLY**

219

ANALYZE & WRITE

Write a blog post, a letter to your instructor, or an e-mail message to a student who will take this course next term, using the writing prompt below that seems most productive for you:

- Explain how your purpose and audience influenced *one* of your decisions as a writer, such as how much background information you provided, how you categorized the information in your report, or how you organized the comparison in your analysis.

- Discuss what you learned about yourself as a writer in the process of writing one or more of the genres in this chapter. For example, what part of the process did you find most challenging (such as deciding on categories for the report or, for your analysis, understanding the factors motivating the conflict)? Did you try anything new (such as going to the writing center or remixing your writing in a different genre or medium)?

- If you got good advice from a critical reader, explain exactly how the person helped you — perhaps by helping you understand the kinds of evidence you needed to include or by deepening your analysis of the texts you compared.

Reflecting on the Genres

In this chapter, you had an opportunity to compare genres—summary, annotated bibliography, report, and analysis—by reading the student examples in this chapter and by composing one or more of these genres for yourself.

ANALYZE & WRITE

Write a paragraph or two about your own experience of moving from genre to genre on one specific topic. In your discussion, you might do one or more of the following:

1 **Consider how challenging it was to transform your writing from one genre to another.** What decisions did you make as you moved from summary to annotated bibliography to report or analysis? How did your readers' expectations change from genre to genre? What was most challenging about writing a report or writing an analysis? How did writing in multiple genres on the same topic deepen your understanding and enrich your writing?

2 **Think about the tone you used in each genre versus the tone of the selections you included in your report or analysis.** What tone did you aim for and why? How did you craft this tone? Consider how the tone of your academic writing differs from that of your more personal writing and how it differs from that of an op-ed, for example. Why do you think academic writing in general attempts to maintain a fair and impartial tone?

The issue of compensating organ donors is fraught ethically, economically, and geopolitically. Obviously, one needs to have died to donate certain organs, such as the heart, but for organs like the kidney, healthy individuals can live a long life after donating. Therefore, transplanting a kidney from a living person is a realistic option, in addition to harvesting the kidneys from someone who has recently died. But there are not enough people willing to become donors. Demand far exceeds supply.

The following casebook includes three of the selections that Maya Gomez included in her annotated bibliography and that she used to write her report and analysis. The first selection is the strongly worded National Kidney Foundation position paper, "Financial Incentives for Organ Donation" (2003), arguing against liberalizing the 1984 National Organ Transplant Act's restrictions on compensating kidney donors. In the second reading, economists Gary S. Becker and Julio J. Elías propose "Cash for Kidneys: The Case for a Market for Organs," in a 2014 *Washington Post* op-ed. The third piece, "When Altruism Isn't Moral" by kidney transplant recipient Dr. Sally Satel, takes a surprising stance toward the main objection to liberalizing NOTA: the moral argument that claims altruistic gift giving is the only moral solution. (Gomez compared the National Kidney Foundation's position paper with Sally Satel's op-ed to write her analysis.) A fourth selection, "A Moral Market" by law professor Eric Posner, appears in Chapter 7, pp. 302–5. Posner's essay proposes "altruism exchanges" that would compensate kidney donors in a way he argues would be morally acceptable to those that oppose other kinds of compensation.

National Kidney Foundation	*Financial Incentives for Organ Donation*

THE NONPROFIT NATIONAL KIDNEY FOUNDATION (NKF) calls itself "the organization leading the fight against kidney disease" and prides itself on having been "a leader in crafting and passing the National Transplant Act in 1984, which prohibited the sale of organs" (kidney.org). Founded in 1950 as a family support group, the NKF is now led by a board of directors comprised mainly of corporate executives and professors of medicine. It works to promote research and education related to the prevention and treatment of kidney disease. Their position statement "Financial Incentives for Organ Donation," which follows, was adopted in 2003 and is posted on the National Kidney Foundation's Web site.

1   The National Kidney Foundation opposes all efforts to legalize payments for human organs for use in transplantation and urges the federal government to retain the prohibition against the purchase of organs that is codified in Title III of the National Organ Transplant Act of 1984.

2   Offering direct or indirect economic benefits in exchange for organ donation is inconsistent with our values as a society. Any attempt to assign a monetary value to the human body, or body parts, either arbitrarily, or through market forces, diminishes human dignity. By treating the body as property, in the hope of

increasing organ supply, we risk devaluating the very human life we seek to save. Providing any form of compensation for organs may be an affront to the thousands of donor families and living donors who have already made an altruistic gift of life and it could alienate Americans who are prepared to donate life-saving organs out of humanitarian concern. In addition, it disregards families who are unable to donate organs but do consent to tissue donation.

3   Offering money for organs can be viewed as an attempt to coerce economically disadvantaged Americans to participate in organ donation. Furthermore, since the economically disadvantaged have been shown to be less likely to be organ transplant candidates, financial incentives for organ donation could be characterized as exploitation.

4   While payment for organs has real potential to undermine the transplant system in this country, its ability to increase the supply or organs for transplantation is questionable. In a recent survey of families who refused to donate organs of their loved ones who have died, 92% said that payment would not have persuaded them to donate. Public opinion polls and focus groups have disclosed that many Americans are not inclined to be organ donors because they distrust the U. S. health care system, in general, and, in particular, because they are concerned that the health care of potential organ donors might be compromised if their donor status were known. A program of financial incentives for organ donation is not likely to change these perceptions and, indeed, may aggravate mistrust. This is true even with the suggested subterfuge of paying the money to funeral homes. That strategy would most likely simply raise the price of a funeral without benefiting the family at all. Making financial incentives available at the time of death opens the possibility of creating new sources of tension and dissension between family members who are faced with the option of organ donation. Finally, a

The National Kidney Foundation believes that payment for organs is wrong.

program of financial incentives for organ donation could expose transplant recipients to unnecessary risks because living donors and donor families would have an incentive to withhold information concerning the donor's health status so that they can be assured a financial benefit.

5   Proponents of financial incentives for organ donation assert that a demonstration project is necessary to confirm or refute the types of concerns mentioned above. The American Medical Association, the United Network for Organ Sharing and the Ethics Committee of the American Society of Transplant Surgeons have called for pilot studies of financial incentives. Conversely, the National Kidney Foundation maintains that it would not be feasible to design a pilot project that would definitively demonstrate the efficacy of financial incentives for organ donation. Moreover, the implementation of a pilot project would have the same corrosive effect on the ethical, moral and social fabric of this country that a formal change in policy would have. Finally, a demonstration project is objectionable because it will be difficult to revert to an altruistic system once payment is initiated, even if it becomes evident that financial incentives don't have a positive impact on organ donation.

6   The National Kidney Foundation believes that payment for organs is wrong. Such a practice should not be started or tested since its negative message could not be undone if, as research indicates, it will not work. The headline "Local Family Offered Money for Loved One's Organs" should never appear.

7   The National Kidney Foundation remains committed to doing everything that can rightly be done to alleviate the critical organ shortage. However, better understanding by the public, better practices from medical and procurement professionals, better organ preserving-care for post-transplant patients and increased living donation will help, not money. Any attempt to pay families to say yes is wrong.

Gary S. Becker
Julio J. Elías

Cash for Kidneys: The Case for a Market for Organs

GARY S. BECKER, a Nobel Prize–winning professor of economics and sociology at the University of Chicago, collaborated with Julio J. Elías, professor of economics and business at the Universidad del CEMA in Argentina, on this proposal to solve the kidney shortage. As economists who seek real-life solutions to everyday problems, Becker and Elías published "Cash for Kidneys: The Case for a Market for Organs" as an op-ed in the widely read *Wall Street Journal* (2014). It is a briefer, less technical version of their 2007 *Journal of Economic Perspectives* article that stimulated a great deal of debate among economists and bioethicists. Note that the main objection Becker and Elías acknowledge is the moral repugnance many people feel in regard to paying for kidneys (par. 7).

1 In 2012, 95,000 American men, women and children were on the waiting list for new kidneys, the most commonly transplanted organ. Yet only about 16,500 kidney transplant operations were performed that year. Taking into account the number of people who die while waiting for a transplant, this implies an average wait of 4.5 years for a kidney transplant in the U.S.

2 The situation is far worse than it was just a decade ago, when nearly 54,000 people were on the waiting list, with an average wait of 2.9 years. For all the recent attention devoted to the health-care overhaul, the long and growing waiting times for tens of thousands of individuals who badly need organ transplants hasn't been addressed.

3 Finding a way to increase the supply of organs would reduce wait times and deaths, and it would greatly ease the suffering that many sick individuals now endure while they hope for a transplant. The most effective change, we believe, would be to provide compensation to people who give their organs—that is, we recommend establishing a market for organs.

4 Organ transplants are one of the extraordinary developments of modern science. They began in 1954 with a kidney transplant performed at Brigham & Women's Hospital in Boston. But the practice only took off in the 1970s with the development of immunosuppressive drugs that could prevent the rejection of transplanted organs. Since then, the number of kidney and other organ transplants has grown rapidly, but not nearly as rapidly as the growth in the number of people with defective organs who need transplants. The result has been longer and longer delays to receive organs.

5 Many of those waiting for kidneys are on dialysis, and life expectancy while on dialysis isn't long. For example, people age 45 to 49 live, on average, eight additional years if they remain on dialysis, but they live

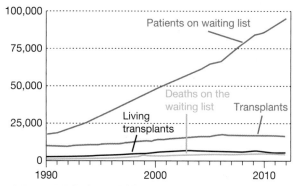

A Long Wait for a Kidney
Since 1990, the number of people on the waiting list for a Kidney transplant has grown sharply, while the number of transplants has increased only slightly.

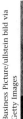

Becker *Cash for Kidneys: The Case for a Market for Organs*
GUIDE TO READING
GUIDE TO WRITING
A WRITER AT WORK
▶ **THINKING CRITICALLY**
223

an additional 23 years if they get a kidney transplant. That is why in 2012, almost 4,500 persons died while waiting for kidney transplants. Although some of those waiting would have died anyway, the great majority died because they were unable to replace their defective kidneys quickly enough.

6   The toll on those waiting for kidneys and on their families is enormous, from both greatly reduced life expectancy and the many hardships of being on dialysis. Most of those on dialysis cannot work, and the annual cost of dialysis averages about $80,000. The total cost over the average 4.5-year waiting period before receiving a kidney transplant is $350,000, which is much larger than the $150,000 cost of the transplant itself.

7   Individuals can live a normal life with only one kidney, so about 34% of all kidneys used in transplants come from live donors. The majority of transplant kidneys come from parents, children, siblings and other relatives of those who need transplants. The rest come from individuals who want to help those in need of transplants.

8   In recent years, kidney exchanges—in which pairs of living would-be donors and recipients who prove incompatible look for another pair or pairs of donors and recipients who would be compatible for transplants, cutting their wait time—have become more widespread. Although these exchanges have grown rapidly in the U.S. since 2005, they still account for only 9% of live donations and just 3% of all kidney donations, including after-death donations. The relatively minor role of exchanges in total donations isn't an accident, because exchanges are really a form of barter, and barter is always an inefficient way to arrange transactions.

9   Exhortations and other efforts to encourage more organ donations have failed to significantly close the large gap between supply and demand. For example, some countries use an implied consent approach, in which organs from cadavers are assumed to be available for transplant unless, before death, individuals indicate that they don't want their organs to be used. (The U.S. continues to use informed consent, requiring people to make an active declaration of their wish to donate.) In our own highly preliminary study of a few countries—Argentina, Austria, Brazil, Chile and Denmark—that have made the shift to implied consent from informed consent or vice versa, we found that the switch didn't lead to consistent changes in the number of transplant surgeries.

10   Other studies have found more positive effects from switching to implied consent, but none of the effects would be large enough to eliminate the sizable shortfall in the supply of organs in the U.S. That shortfall isn't just an American problem. It exists in most other countries as well, even when they use different methods to procure organs and have different cultures and traditions.

11   Paying donors for their organs would finally eliminate the supply-demand gap. In particular, sufficient payment to kidney donors would increase the supply of kidneys by a large percentage, without greatly increasing the total cost of a kidney transplant.

12   We have estimated how much individuals would need to be paid for kidneys to be willing to sell them for transplants. These estimates take account of the slight risk to donors from transplant surgery, the number of weeks of work lost during the surgery and recovery periods, and the small risk of reduction in the quality of life.

13   Our conclusion is that a very large number of both live and cadaveric kidney donations would be available by paying about $15,000 for each kidney. That estimate isn't exact, and the true cost could be as high as $25,000 or as low as $5,000—but even the high estimate wouldn't increase the total cost of kidney transplants by a large percentage. . . .

14   Since the number of kidneys available at a reasonable price would be far more than needed to close the gap between the demand and supply of kidneys, there would no longer be any significant waiting time to get a kidney transplant. The number of people on dialysis would decline dramatically, and deaths due to long waits for a transplant would essentially disappear.

15   Today, finding a compatible kidney isn't easy. There are four basic blood types, and tissue matching is complex and involves the combination of six proteins. Blood and tissue type determine the chance that a kidney will help a recipient in the long run. But the sale of organs would result in a large supply of most kidney types, and with large numbers of kidneys available, transplant surgeries could be arranged to suit the health of recipients (and donors) because surgeons would be confident that compatible kidneys would be available.

16   The system that we're proposing would include payment to individuals who agree that their organs can be used after they die. This is important because transplants for heart and lungs and most liver transplants only use organs from the deceased. Under a new system,

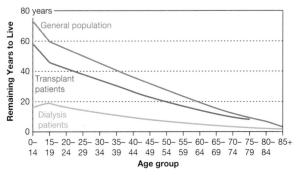

Improving the Prognosis

Across all age ranges, but especially for the young, kidney patients on dialysis tend to have far fewer remaining years to live than those who receive transplants.

individuals would sell their organs "forward" (that is, for future use), with payment going to their heirs after their organs are harvested. Relatives sometimes refuse to have organs used even when a deceased family member has explicitly requested it, and they would be more inclined to honor such wishes if they received substantial compensation for their assent.

17   The idea of paying organ donors has met with strong opposition from some (but not all) transplant surgeons and other doctors, as well as various academics, political leaders and others. Critics have claimed that paying for organs would be ineffective, that payment would be immoral because it involves the sale of body parts and that the main donors would be the desperate poor, who could come to regret their decision. In short, critics believe that monetary payments for organs would be repugnant.

18   But the claim that payments would be ineffective in eliminating the shortage of organs isn't consistent with what we know about the supply of other parts of the body for medical use. For example, the U.S. allows market-determined payments to surrogate moth-ers—and surrogacy takes time, involves great discomfort and is somewhat risky. Yet in the U.S., the average payment to a surrogate mother is only about $20,000.

19   Another illuminating example is the all-volunteer U.S. military. Critics once asserted that it wouldn't be possible to get enough capable volunteers by offering them only reasonable pay, especially in wartime. But the all-volunteer force has worked well in the U.S., even during wars, and the cost of these recruits hasn't been excessive.

20   Whether paying donors is immoral because it involves the sale of organs is a much more subjective matter, but we question this assertion, given the very serious problems with the present system. Any claim about the supposed immorality of organ sales should be weighed against the morality of preventing thousands of deaths each year and improving the quality of life of those waiting for organs. How can paying for organs to increase their supply be more immoral than the injustice of the present system?

21   Under the type of system we propose, safeguards could be created against impulsive behavior or exploitation. For example, to reduce the likelihood of rash donations, a period of three months or longer could be required before someone would be allowed to donate their kidneys or other organs. This would give donors a chance to re-evaluate their decisions, and they could change their minds at any time before the surgery. They could also receive guidance from counselors on the wisdom of these decisions.

22   Though the poor would be more likely to sell their kidneys and other organs, they also suffer more than others from the current scarcity. Today, the rich often don't wait as long as others for organs since some of them go to countries such as India, where they can arrange for transplants in the underground medical sector, and others (such as the late Steve Jobs) manage to jump the queue by having residence in several states or other means. The sale of organs would make them more available to the poor, and Medicaid could help pay for the added cost of transplant surgery.

23   The altruistic giving of organs might decline with an open market, since the incentive to give organs to a relative, friend or anyone else would be weaker when organs are readily available to buy. On the other hand, the altruistic giving of money to those in need of organs could increase to help them pay for the cost of organ transplants.

24   Paying for organs would lead to more transplants—and thereby, perhaps, to a large increase in the overall medical costs of transplantation. But it would save the

Any claim about the supposed immorality of organ sales should be weighed against the morality of preventing thousands of deaths each year. . . .

Satel *When Altruism Isn't Moral*

GUIDE TO READING
GUIDE TO WRITING
A WRITER AT WORK
▶ **THINKING CRITICALLY**

225

cost of dialysis for people waiting for kidney transplants and other costs to individuals waiting for other organs. More important, it would prevent thousands of deaths and improve the quality of life among those who now must wait years before getting the organs they need.

25   Initially, a market in the purchase and sale of organs would seem strange, and many might continue to consider that market "repugnant." Over time, however, the sale of organs would grow to be accepted, just as the voluntary military now has widespread support.

26   Eventually, the advantages of allowing payment for organs would become obvious. At that point, people will wonder why it took so long to adopt such an obvious and sensible solution to the shortage of organs for transplant.

Sally Satel | *When Altruism Isn't Moral*

Courtesy of Sally Satel

SALLY SATEL received a donor kidney in 2006, after living with renal failure for two years. She wrote about her experience in an article published in the *New York Times* and has subsequently written extensively on issues related to organ transplantation, such as the following op-ed, "When Altruism Isn't Moral" (2009). A psychiatrist and resident scholar at the American Enterprise Institute, a conservative nonpartisan think tank that seeks to "expand . . . liberty . . . and strengthen . . . free enterprise," Satel publishes regularly on health care matters. In addition to editing a 2009 collection of essays, *When Altruism Isn't Enough: The Case for Compensating Kidney Donors,* she has authored *The Health Disparity Myth* (2006), *One Nation Under Therapy* (2005), and *BRAINWASHED: The Seductive Appeal of Mindless Neuroscience* (2013).

1   In early 2006, Matt Thompson of San Jose, California, decided to give a kidney to Sonny Davis, a 65-year-old physicist living in nearby Menlo Park. Thompson was moved to donate after reading an impassioned plea from Davis's wife, who had sent 140 letters to friends and relatives asking them to consider helping her husband. One of the recipients happened to be a colleague of Thompson's, who passed it along, thinking Thompson just might heed the call. Sure enough, Thompson, a devout young Christian and former missionary, contacted the transplant program to volunteer.

2   But the transplant program at Kaiser Permanente of Northern California turned him down. Had Davis been a family member or a good friend, he would have been acceptable to the program. Thompson was frustrated and surprised, but he and Davis were determined to do the transplant. According to the *San Jose Mercury News*, they "knew they had to forge a bond that would assure Davis' surgeons that Thompson was donating his kidney for the right reasons." This meant, among other things, that Thompson would not profit financially. So the two developed a relationship and convinced the transplant program that no money was secretly being exchanged. On November 14, 2006, the transplant finally took place.

3   Far more than a human interest tale of a stranger opening his heart to a suffering soul, the story of Sonny Davis and Matt Thompson draws back the curtain on the culture of the organ transplant establishment. It shows that transplant professionals would have allowed a 65-year-old man to languish on dialysis for years or die—a strong probability given his age—while waiting for a kidney, out of fear that he might be remunerating someone for an act that would save his life.

4   There are about 78,000 people in queue for a kidney from a deceased donor. In places like California, the wait can be up to eight years. And unless a friend or

relative gives a kidney to a loved one, he will weaken on dialysis. Four thousand people die each year because they cannot survive the wait. This explains Mrs. Davis's frantic plea to anyone who might volunteer a kidney to her husband.

5   The woeful inadequacy of our nation's transplant policy is due to its reliance on "altruism." According to the guiding narrative of the transplant establishment, organs should be a "gift of life," an act of selfless generosity. It's a beautiful sentiment, no question. In fact, I, myself, am a poster girl for altruism. In 2006, I received a kidney from a (formerly) casual friend who heard secondhand about my need for a transplant. In her act, there was everything for me to gain, and, frankly, not much for her. My glorious donor was moved by empathy and altruism as purely as anyone could ever be.

6   Yet, it is lethally obvious that altruism is not a valid basis for transplant policy. If we keep thinking of organs solely as gifts, there will never be enough of them. We need to encourage more living and posthumous donation through rewards, say, tax credits or lifetime health insurance.

7   But what about the Matt Thompson–Sonny Davis problem: anxiety surrounding the very notion that an organ donor should receive anything of material value for his sacrifice? It is important to understand the nature of this anxiety because it is a formidable obstacle to devising a rational transplant system.

8   Arguments against creating incentives to donate fall into two general categories: arguments from corruption and arguments from consequence. These designations were coined by political philosopher Michael Sandel.

9   Arguments from consequence go like this: there is nothing intrinsically wrong with compensating donors, but it is not possible to design an incentive-based system without exploiting them. The worry is that economic straits could compel reluctant individuals to relinquish a kidney for the sole sake of enrichment.

10   This is indeed a troubling situation. Fortunately, it can be addressed with good policy. For example, a state government could provide compensation such as tax credits, tuition vouchers, a contribution to a tax-free

It is lethally obvious that altruism is not a valid basis for transplant policy.

retirement account, or lifelong health coverage. A non-cash reward won't appeal to those in desperate need of financial help. What they want is quick cash, not delayed in-kind rewards. A months-long waiting period would dampen impulsivity and give more than ample time for donor education and careful medical and psychological screening. Finally, donors would receive quality follow-up care, something the current system does not ensure.

11   Arguments from corruption proceed from the belief that donors, and perhaps society at large, will be diminished or corrupted if organs are given in return for something of material value. Giving a kidney "for free" is noble but accepting compensation is illegitimate, a sordid affront to human dignity. Indeed, the debate surrounding incentives for organ donation sometimes resembles a titanic struggle between uplift and greed. "As a rule, the debate is cast as one in which existing relations of selfless, altruistic exchange are threatened with replacement by market-based, for-profit alternatives," observes Kieran Healy, a sociologist at Duke University.

12   Dr. Luc Noel of the World Health Organization subscribes to this false choice. "There are two prevailing concepts of transplantation," he says. "One relies on money and leads to increased inequality, besides putting a price on the integrity of the body and human dignity. The second is based on solidarity and the donor's sole motivation to save a life." The National Kidney Foundation warns against "self-interest on behalf of the donor." The notion also troubles a primary care physician in Columbus, Ohio: "What sort of organ transplant program do we want," he asks, "one that pressures the financially vulnerable with cash incentives, or one that encourages the show of kindness through a loving, voluntary gift of organ donation?"

13   Paradoxically, our current transplant system makes every donation seem like a "loving, voluntary gift of organ donation." Think about it: there is no other legal option. Some altruistic donations come as close to the technical definition: my experience would be one of those. Yet, our current altruism-only system has a dark side: It imposes coercion of its own by putting friends and family members in a bind. They might not want to donate, but they feel obligated, lest their relative die or

deteriorate on dialysis. Sociologists have written about familial dynamics that involve guilt, overt pressure, or subtle threats. Consider the "black-sheep donor," a wayward relative who shows up to offer an organ as an act of redemption, hoping to reposition himself in the family's good graces. Some donate as a way to elicit praise and social acceptance. For others, donation is a sullen fulfillment of familial duty, a way to avoid the shame and guilt of allowing a relative to suffer needlessly and perhaps even die.

14　As famed anthropologist Marcel Mauss observed in his classic work, *The Gift*, gifts are never free; they demand reciprocity. "The [given] objects are never completely separated from the men who exchange them," he learned from his work with Polynesian natives in the early 1900s. The same applies to organs. The "tyranny of the gift" is an artful term coined by sociologists Renee Fox and Judith Swazey to capture the way in which immense gratitude at receiving a kidney can morph into a sense of constricting obligation. In their 1992 book, *Spare Parts: Organ Replacement in American Society*, the authors write, "The giver, the receiver, and their families, may find themselves locked in a creditor-debtor vise that binds them one to another in a mutually fettering way." Indeed, the virtue of market-like exchanges is that they are emotionally liberating.

15　An unusual take on altruism comes from the National Kidney Foundation, a vocal opponent of incentivizing organ donation. According to Dolph Chianchiano, its senior vice president for health policy and research, the NKF believes that compensating donors will "cheapen the gift." Such an affront to would-be donors will cause them to hold onto their organs. On one level, this seems absurd. Can you imagine a brother telling his ailing sister, "Gee, sis, I would have given you my kidney but now that I hear that someone across town is accepting a tax credit for his donation, well, forget it."

16　But if Chianchiano is correct—that some people will withhold voluntary action if remuneration is available to others—then, paradoxically, a regime of donor compensation would be quite the boon to such "altruists." They would have bragging rights: They were the ones who acted out of generosity, not for material gain, a distinction that not only allows them to retain the "warm glow" that comes from performing acts of charity but also intensifies it. Given the importance of

"social signaling" through gift-giving ("look at me, so generous, so civic-minded!") the opportunity to accentuate the distinction should be most welcome.

17　No wonder scholars ranging from philosophers to evolutionary biologists to psychologists and economists are skeptical about whether true human altruism even exists. It is more realistic to envision a broad middle ground between the poles of selflessness and greed. It is the arena in which most organ donation already plays out. And it is where compensated donation would likely reside, too.

18　Simply look at our daily lives. Financial and humanitarian motives do not reside in discrete realms. Moreover, it is unclear how their commingling is inherently harmful—the goodness of an act is not diminished because someone was paid to perform it. The great teachers who enlighten us and the doctors who heal us inspire no less gratitude because they are paid. A salaried firefighter who risks her life to save a child trapped in a burning building is no less heroic than a volunteer firefighter. Soldiers accept military pay while pursuing a patriotic desire to serve their country. The desire to do well by others while enriching oneself at the same time is as old as humankind. Indeed, the very fact that generosity and remuneration so often intertwine can be leveraged to good ends: to increase the pool of transplantable organs, for instance.

19　The practice of assigning values to body parts has roots in antiquity. The Code of Hammurabi provides an elaborate schedule of compensation for them; for example, it specifies that if an individual should "knock out the teeth of a freed man, he shall pay one-third of a gold mina." Today we routinely assign valuation to the body. Human blood plasma is collected primarily though paid donation. Personal injury lawyers seek damages for bodily harm to their clients. The Veterans Administration puts a price on physical disabilities. We pay for justice in the context of personal injury litigation in the form of legal costs, and for our very lives in the form of medical fees. There is little reason to believe—nor tangible evidence to suggest—that these practices depreciate human worth or undermine human dignity in any way.

20　It is all too easy to romanticize altruism. Sociologist Amitai Etzioni urges the postponement of paying for organs in favor of what he calls a "communitarian" approach "so that members of society will recognize that donating one's organs . . . is the moral (right) thing to do . . . it entails a moral dialogue, in which the public is engaged, leading to a change in what people expect from one another." Thomas A. Shannon, a professor of religion and social ethics, writes, "I would think it a tragedy if . . . we tried to solve the problem of the organ shortage by commodification rather than by the kindness of strangers who meet in the community and recognize and meet the needs of others in generosity."

21   To be sure, these skeptics have a right to their moral commitments, but their views must not determine binding policy in a morally pluralistic society. A donor compensation system operating in parallel with our established mechanism of altruistic procurement is the only way to accommodate us all. Moreover, it represents a promising middle ground between the status quo—a procurement system based on the partial myth of selfless altruism—and the dark, corrupt netherworld of organ trafficking. The current regime permits no room for individuals who would welcome an opportunity to be rewarded for rescuing their fellow human beings; and for those who wait for organs in vain, the only dignity left is that with which they must face death.

Eric Posner | *A Moral Market*

ERIC POSNER is the Kirkland and Ellis Distinguished Service Professor at the University of Chicago Law School. Posner has written many books and hundreds of articles, and he also maintains a blog, www.ericposner.com; a Twitter feed; and a regular column on *Slate.com*, where "A Moral Market" first appeared. Posner first co-wrote an academic study—"Altruism Exchanges and the Kidney Shortage"—with fellow law professors Stephen J. Choi and G. Mitu Gulati. (This article can be found online through a Google search; the *Slate* article appears on pp. 302–5 of Chapter 7.)

6

Arguing a Position

Why should parents think twice before signing up their kids for Little League? Why might it *not* be a good idea for teens to get after-school jobs? Why should you care about online privacy if you haven't done anything wrong? These are some of the compelling issues argued about in this chapter. Because of the in-your-face kind of arguing in blogs and on talk shows, you may associate arguing with quarreling. Although this kind of "argument" lets people vent strong feelings, it seldom leads them to consider other points of view seriously or to think critically about their own reasons or underlying values. A more thoughtful, deliberative kind of argument, one that depends on a critical analysis of an issue, on giving logical reasons rather than raising voices, is more likely to convince others of the validity of your position. Reasoned argument is also more likely to be expected in college courses and in the workplace.

You might compose this thoughful kind of argument for a variety of purposes and audiences and publish them in a variety of media. For example, in a college course on law and society, a student might support the position in a blog post that the race of a murder *victim* is the crucial factor in whether the death penalty is sought. A group of parents might publish an open letter in the local newspaper arguing that the school board should institute the Peacemakers program to help children in the district learn to negotiate conflicts rather than resort to their fists. In the workplace, a consultant may make a presentation, citing statistics and examples, to argue that sustainable business practices are good for business.

In this chapter, we ask you to compose a position argument on a controversial issue. Your argument should try to convince readers to adopt your point of view or at least to consider it seriously. From reading and analyzing the selections in the Guide to Reading that follows, you will learn how writers frame and support a position so readers will take it seriously. The Guide to Writing later in the chapter will support your composing by showing you how to choose and frame an arguable position, marshal compelling evidence to support it, respond to naysayers, and organize it to put your position as compellingly as possible.

PRACTICING THE GENRE ┤──────────────────────────────────

Debating a Position

To get a sense of what's involved in arguing a position, get together with a group of students (preferably four) to discuss an issue you have strong feelings about.

Part 1.   Choose an issue you all know something about, or pick one of the following:

- Should college be paid for by taxes the way K–12 is?
- Should general education requirements be continued (or discontinued) at your college?
- Should drinking alcohol be banned on campuses?
- Should online courses replace large face-to-face lecture courses?

First, decide on your audience and purpose: Is your audience other students, faculty, administrators, or the general public? Is your purpose to persuade audience members to change their minds, confirm their opinions, move them to action, or something else? Then take five minutes to sketch out the arguments for and against your issue. Take turns presenting your arguments to each other.

Part 2.   After your presentations, discuss what you learned:

- **What did you learn about the genre from listening to others' arguments?**
  Were you convinced by the arguments? Would the intended audience have been convinced? That is, was the position presented with the audience's values in mind?
- **What did you learn about the genre from presenting your group's position?**
  Discuss with your group what was easiest and hardest about presenting your position; for example, finding enough evidence that your audience would find convincing, anticipating opposing views, or appealing to the values of your audience.

Analyzing Position Arguments

As you read the selections in this chapter, you will see how different authors argue convincingly for their positions:

- Jessica Statsky argues that organized sports activities can be harmful for children aged six to twelve (pp. 236–41).
- Noam Bramson calls on neighbors to welcome an unpopular group home for people with disabilities (pp. 242–44).
- Amitai Etzioni challenges the idea that after-school work is good for teenagers (pp. 247–50).
- Daniel J. Solove argues that protecting our privacy on the Internet is crucially important even if we feel we have "nothing to hide" (pp. 253–56).

Analyzing how these writers focus and frame their arguments to appeal to the hearts and minds of readers, how they anticipate and respond to opposing views, and how they select and present evidence that will convince readers and undermine objections will also help you see how you can employ these techniques to make your own position argument clear and compelling for your readers.

Determine the writer's purpose and audience.

Although arguing a position helps writers decide where they really stand, typically writers compose arguments to influence their readers. As you read the position arguments that follow, ask yourself questions like these:

What seems to be the writer's main purpose in arguing for a position?

- to change readers' minds by convincing them to look at the issue in a new way?
- to confirm readers' opinions by providing them with authoritative arguments?
- to move readers to take action by stressing the urgency or seriousness of the issue?
- to remind readers what is at stake and establish common ground on which people might be able to agree?

What does the author assume about the audience?

- that readers are already knowledgeable about the issue and likely to be sympathetic to the writer's position?
- that they need to be inspired to care about the issue?
- that they have strong convictions and will likely have serious objections to the writer's position?

Assess the genre's basic features.

As you read position arguments in this chapter, consider how different authors incorporate the basic features of the genre. The examples that follow are taken from the reading selections that appear later in this Guide to Reading.

:: Basic Features
A Focused,
Well-Presented Issue
A Well-Supported Position
An Effective Response
to Opposing Views
A Clear, Logical
Organization

A FOCUSED, WELL-PRESENTED ISSUE

Read first to identify the issue. Look first at the title and the opening paragraphs. For current, hotly debated issues, the title may be enough to identify the issue for readers.

Topic
Position

Why <u>Privacy Matters</u> Even If You Have "Nothing to Hide" (Solove)

Writers may use their opening paragraphs to remind readers about what is at stake or what the position is that they oppose, using a simple sentence pattern like this:

▸ When X happens, most people think _____, but I think _____ because _____.

For example, Solove uses this strategy in the opening paragraph:

> When the government gathers or analyzes personal information, many people say . . . (par. 1)

His "but I think . . . because . . ." response to the common view takes up the bulk of the essay.

To present their positions effectively, writers must focus on a specific aspect of their issue, one they can address fully in the space allowed. An issue like youth employment, for example, is too complex to be tackled fully in a relatively brief essay, so writers must focus on one aspect of the issue, as Amitai Etzioni does (pp. 247–50) when he considers whether working at a fast-food restaurant, like McDonald's or Burger King, is a good idea for high school students.

Notice how the writer establishes the issue's significance. If readers are likely to be unfamiliar with an issue or consider it trivial, a writer will need to establish the issue's significance, as student Jessica Statsky does in her position essay:

> "Organized sports for young people have become an institution in North America," reports sports journalist Steve Silverman, attracting more than 44 million youngsters according to a recent survey by the National Council of Youth Sports ("History"). (par. 1)

To establish the significance of the issue, Statsky quotes a respected authority and also cites statistics.

Also consider how the writer frames the issue. **Framing** an issue is like cropping and resizing a photograph to focus the viewer's eye on one part of the picture (see Figure 6.1). Writers frame an issue to set the stage for their argument and promote their point of view. They may suggest that particular values are at stake or raise in readers' minds certain concerns having to do with the issue. As you read, notice how each writer frames the issue, asking yourself questions like these:

> Who, or what groups of people, does the writer associate with each position, and how

FIGURE 6.1
Framing an Issue
By cropping this photograph of a protest march to focus on the little boy, the photographer softens the message; the broader issue of climate change is framed in terms of saving the planet for this child.

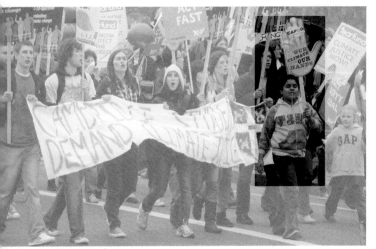

© Patrick Ward/Alamy

does the writer characterize their views? For example, does one side appear thoughtful, moderate, and knowledgeable, and the other side extreme, unreasonable, or self-interested?

What does the writer suggest is really at stake, and for whom? If you were unfamiliar with the issue, what did the writer lead you to think and feel about it? If you were already familiar with it, which of your preconceptions were reinforced and which were challenged by the writer's way of framing the issue?

A WELL-SUPPORTED POSITION

Identify the writer's position, and determine whether the position is appropriately qualified. To argue effectively, writers need to assert an arguable position (an opinion, not a fact that can be proved or disproved or a belief that must be taken on faith). They may also need to *qualify* that position (for example, by using words like *may* and by specifying conditions) to avoid making a claim that is too strong to be defended given the available evidence.

In a position argument, writers typically declare their positions in a thesis statement early on in the essay. Notice, for example, how Jessica Statsky states her thesis:

> When overzealous parents and coaches impose adult standards on children's sports, the result can be activities that are neither satisfying nor beneficial to children.
>
> I am concerned about all organized sports activities for children between the ages of six and twelve. (pars. 1–2)

Qualifying terms

She makes a claim that reasonable people could dispute, and she qualifies her claim by limiting its scope (not all children, just those between six and twelve, for example).

Examine the main reasons and the evidence the writer provides. Make sure that the reasons clearly support the writer's position and that the evidence (facts and statistics, examples and anecdotes, research studies, expert testimony) is credible.

Look for sentence strategies like these that introduce supporting reasons:

▶ What makes issue X problematic / praiseworthy is ....

▶ Because of ...., I support / oppose X.

EXAMPLE   This statistic illustrates another reason I oppose competitive sports for children: because they are so highly selective, very few children get to participate. (Statsky, par. 7)

Credible evidence is both relevant and representative; that is, it must clearly support the reason (which must in turn support the topic sentence and thesis), and it must be typical. The following examples demonstrate some approaches to introducing supporting evidence:

> 24 percent . . . worked . . . five to seven days. . . . There is just no way such amounts of work will not interfere with school work, especially homework. In an informal survey. . . , 58 percent of seniors acknowledged that their jobs interfere with their school work. (Etzioni, par. 13)

Statistics

Reason

Also consider whether the evidence the writer provides appeals to readers' intellect, values, or emotions and avoids logical fallacies. Writers can draw on various types of evidence—from facts and statistics to examples and anecdotes to photographs and flowcharts—to support their positions, but position arguments are most convincing when writers are able to appeal to readers on three levels:

- **Logos:** Appeal to readers' intellect, presenting readers with logical reasoning and reliable evidence.
- **Ethos:** Appeal to readers' perception of the writer's credibility and fairness.
- **Pathos:** Appeal to readers' values and feelings.

Ask yourself how effectively the writers appeals to the reader's intellect, emotions, and sense of fairness:

To learn more about evaluating sources, see Chapters 12 and 22; to learn more about avoiding logical fallacies, see Chapter 19, p. 595.

- Is the argument logical and reasonable (logos)?
- Does the writer appear credible and trustworthy (ethos)?
- Are the values and feelings sincere or manipulative (pathos)?

AN EFFECTIVE RESPONSE TO OPPOSING VIEWS

Notice whether the author anticipates readers' objections and opposing arguments, and whether he or she refutes or concedes those objections and arguments. Writers **refute** (argue against) opposing views when they can show that the opposing view is weak or flawed. A typical refutation states the problem with the opposing view and then explains why the view is problematic, using sentence strategies like these:

▶ One problem with position A is that _____ .

▶ Some claim _____ , but in reality _____ .

Writers often introduce the refutation with a **transition** that indicates contrast, such as *but, although, nevertheless,* or *however*:

Transition
Refutation

The deeper problem with the nothing-to-hide argument is that it myopically views privacy as a form of secrecy. In contrast, understanding privacy as a plurality of related issues demonstrates that the disclosure of bad things is just one among many difficulties caused by government security measure. (Solove, par. 10)

Writers may also **concede** (accept) valid objections, concerns, or reasons. A typical way of conceding is to use sentence strategies like these:

▶ I agree that _____ .

▶ _____ is certainly an important factor.

Here is an example from Jessica Statsky's essay:

Concession

Some children *want* to play competitive sports; they are not being forced to play. These children are eager to learn skills, to enjoy the camaraderie of the team, and earn self-respect by trying hard to benefit their team. I acknowledge that some children may benefit from playing competitive sports. (par. 12)

Conceding a strong opposing view reassures readers that the writer shares their values and builds a bridge of shared concerns.

Frequently, though, writers reach out to readers by making a concession but then go on to point out where they differ. We call this the **concession-refutation move**. Like writers refuting a point, writers making the concession-refutation move often follow their concession with a transition indicating contrast to indicate that an exception or refinement is coming. Here's an example:

> True, you still have to have the gumption to get yourself over to the hamburger stand, but once you don the prescribed uniform, your task is spelled out in minute detail. (Etzioni, par. 7)

Concession
Transition
Refutation

While reading position arguments, assess the effectiveness of the responses by asking yourself questions like these:

- Do they appeal to shared values (pathos) or seem trite or maudlin?

- Do they offer compelling reasons and credible evidence (logos) or simply make unsubstantiated assertions or criticisms?

- Do they draw on authorities whose expertise is established (ethos) or merely refer vaguely to "some" or "many" people with whom they agree? Do the responses to opposing views seem significant and genuine or trivial and insincere?

- Do they misrepresent the opposition (committing a *straw man fallacy*) or attack people personally (committing an *ad hominem fallacy*)?

To learn more about logical fallacies, see Chapter 19, p. 595.

A CLEAR, LOGICAL ORGANIZATION

Look for a thesis statement that asserts the writer's position and a forecast of the reasons the writer will offer as examples. For instance, Amitai Etzioni grabs readers' attention with an alarming sentence—"McDonald's is bad for your kids."—and then goes on to explain just how McDonald's is bad for kids in the next sentence:

> I do not mean the flat patties and the white-flour buns; I refer to the jobs teen-agers undertake, mass-producing these choice items. (par. 1)

In addition to asserting the thesis, writers sometimes preview the reasons in the order they will bring them up later in the essay, as in this example of a *forecasting statement* by Jessica Statsky:

> Highly organized competitive sports . . . are too often played to adult standards, which are developmentally inappropriate for children and can be both physically and psychologically harmful. Furthermore, . . . they are actually counterproductive for developing either future players or fans. Finally, . . . they . . . provide occasions for some parents and coaches to place their own fantasies and needs ahead of children's welfare. (par. 2)

Transition
Reason 1
Reason 2

Reason 3

Notice also where the writer uses *logical transitions* to indicate

- supporting evidence (*because*);

- exceptions (*however*);

- concessions (*admittedly*);
- refutations (*on the other hand*);
- conclusions (*therefore*);
- reasons (*first, finally*).

Transitions may be useful in a forecasting statement, as in the preceding example, or in the *topic sentence* of a paragraph or group of paragraphs, as in the following examples from Solove's position argument:

To learn more about using cues, see Chapter 13.

> One such harm, for example, ... Another potential problem with . . . is. . . . A related problem involves. . . . Yet another problem. . . . (pars. 11–14)

Readings

To learn more about how Jessica Statsky developed her response to readers' likely objections, see A Writer at Work on pp. 278–80. If you could have given Statsky advice in a peer review of her drafts, what objections would you have advised her to respond to, and how do you think she could have responded?

Jessica Statsky | *Children Need to Play, Not Compete*

THIS ESSAY by Jessica Statsky about children's competitive sports was written for a college composition course. When you were a child, you may have had experience playing competitive sports, in or out of school, for example in Peewee Football, Little League Baseball, American Youth Soccer, or some other organization. Or you may have had relatives or friends who were deeply involved in sports.

As you read, consider the following:

- In your experience and observation, was winning unduly emphasized or was more value placed on having a good time, learning to get along with others, developing athletic skills, or something else altogether?

- The questions in the margin: Your instructor may ask you to post your answers to a class blog or discussion board or to bring them to class.

▦ Basic Features

A Focused,
Well-Presented Issue

A Well-Supported Position

An Effective Response
to Opposing Views

A Clear, Logical
Organization

1   "Organized sports for young people have become an institution in North America," reports sports journalist Steve Silverman, attracting more than 44 million youngsters according to a recent survey by the National Council of Youth Sports ("History"). Though many adults regard Little League Baseball and Peewee Football as a basic part of childhood, the games are not always joyous ones. When overzealous parents and coaches impose adult standards on children's sports, the result can be activities that are neither satisfying nor beneficial to children.

2   I am concerned about all organized sports activities for children between the ages of six and twelve. The damage I see results from noncontact as well as contact sports, from sports organized locally as well as those organized nationally. Highly organized competitive sports such as Peewee Football and Little League Baseball are too often played to adult standards, which are developmentally inappropriate for children and can be both physically and psychologically harmful. Furthermore, because they eliminate many children from organized sports before they are ready to compete, they are actually counterproductive for developing either future players or fans. Finally, because they emphasize competition and winning, they unfortunately provide occasions for some parents and coaches to place their own fantasies and needs ahead of children's welfare.

3   One readily understandable danger of overly competitive sports is that they entice children into physical actions that are bad for growing bodies. "There is a growing epidemic of preventable youth sports injuries," according to the STOP Sports Injuries campaign ("Youth Sports"). "Among athletes ages 5 to 14, 28 percent of football players, 25 percent of baseball players, 22 percent of soccer players, 15 percent of basketball players, and 12 percent of softball players were injured while playing their respective sports." Although the official Little League Web site acknowledges that children do risk injury playing baseball, it insists that "severe injuries . . . are infrequent," the risk "far less than the risk of riding a skateboard, a bicycle, or even the school bus" ("What about My Child?"). Nevertheless, Leonard Koppett in *Sports Illusion, Sports Reality* claims that a twelve-year-old trying to throw a curve ball, for example, may put abnormal strain on developing arm and shoulder muscles, sometimes resulting in lifelong injuries (294). Contact sports like football can be even more hazardous. Thomas Tutko, a psychology professor at San Jose State University and coauthor of the book *Winning Is Everything and Other American Myths*, writes:

> I am strongly opposed to young kids playing tackle football. It is not the right stage of development for them to be taught to crash into other kids. Kids under the age of fourteen are not by nature physical. Their main concern is self-preservation. They don't want to meet head on and slam into each other. But tackle football absolutely requires that they try to hit each other as hard as they can. And it is too traumatic for young kids. (qtd. in Tosches A1)

How does Statsky present the issue in a way that prepares readers for her argument?

How does she qualify her position in par. 2?

What reasons does she forecast here, and in which paragraphs does she discuss each reason? Do her reasons appeal primarily to readers' intellect (logos), to their sense of fairness and what's credible (ethos), or to their feelings (pathos)?

How does Statsky try to establish the credibility of her sources in pars. 3–5 (ethos)?

4

As Tutko indicates, even when children are not injured, fear of being hurt detracts from their enjoyment of the sport. The Little League Web site ranks fear of injury as the seventh of seven reasons children quit ("What about My Child?"). One mother of an eight-year-old Peewee Football player explained, "The kids get so scared. They get hit once and they don't want anything to do with football anymore. They'll sit on the bench and pretend their leg hurts..." (qtd. in Tosches A1). Some children are driven to even more desperate measures. For example, in one Peewee Football game, a reporter watched the following scene as a player took himself out of the game:

> "Coach, my tummy hurts. I can't play," he said. The coach told the player to get back onto the field. "There's nothing wrong with your stomach," he said. When the coach turned his head the seven-year-old stuck a finger down his throat and made himself vomit. When the coach turned back, the boy pointed to the ground and told him, "Yes there is, coach. See?" (Tosches A33)

5

Besides physical hazards and anxieties, competitive sports pose psychological dangers for children. Martin Rablovsky, a former sports editor for the *New York Times*, says that in all his years of watching young children play organized sports, he has noticed very few of them smiling. "I've seen children enjoying a spontaneous pre-practice scrimmage become somber and serious when the coach's whistle blows," Rablovsky says. "The spirit of play suddenly disappears, and sport becomes joblike" (qtd. in Coakley 94). The primary goal of a professional athlete — winning — is not appropriate for children. Their goals should be having fun, learning, and being with friends. Although winning does add to the fun, too many adults lose sight of what matters and make winning the most important goal. Several studies have shown that when children are asked whether they would rather be warming the bench on a winning team or playing regularly on a losing team, about 90 percent choose the latter (Smith, Smith, and Smoll 11).

6

Winning and losing may be an inevitable part of adult life, but they should not be part of childhood. Too much competition too early in life can affect a child's development. Children are easily influenced, and when they sense that their competence and worth are based on their ability to live up to their parents' and coaches' high expectations — and on their ability to win — they can become discouraged and depressed. Little League advises parents to "keep winning in perspective" ("Your

Why do you think she uses block quotations instead of integrating these quotes into her own sentences?

How does Statsky try to refute this objection?

Statsky   *Children Need to Play, Not Compete*

GUIDE TO READING
GUIDE TO WRITING
A WRITER AT WORK
THINKING CRITICALLY

239

Role"), noting that the most common reasons children give for quitting, aside from change in interest, are lack of playing time, failure and fear of failure, disapproval by significant others, and psychological stress ("What about My Child?"). According to Dr. Glyn C. Roberts, a professor of kinesiology at the Institute of Child Behavior and Development at the University of Illinois, 80 to 90 percent of children who play competitive sports at a young age drop out by sixteen (Kutner).

7   This statistic illustrates another reason I oppose competitive sports for children: because they are so highly selective, very few children get to participate. Far too soon, a few children are singled out for their athletic promise, while many others, who may be on the verge of developing the necessary strength and ability, are screened out and discouraged from trying out again. Like adults, children fear failure, and so even those with good physical skills may stay away because they lack self-confidence. Consequently, teams lose many promising players who with some encouragement and experience might have become stars. The problem is that many parent-sponsored, out-of-school programs give more importance to having a winning team than to developing children's physical skills and self-esteem.

8   Indeed, it is no secret that too often scorekeeping, league standings, and the drive to win bring out the worst in adults who are more absorbed in living out their own fantasies than in enhancing the quality of the experience for children (Smith, Smith, and Smoll 9). Recent newspaper articles on children's sports contain plenty of horror stories. *Los Angeles Times* reporter Rich Tosches, for example, tells the story of a brawl among seventy-five parents following a Peewee Football game (A33). As a result of the brawl, which began when a parent from one team confronted a player from the other team, the teams are now thinking of hiring security guards for future games. Another example is provided by a *Los Angeles Times* editorial about a Little League manager who intimidated the opposing team by setting fire to one of their team's jerseys on the pitcher's mound before the game began. As the editorial writer commented, the manager showed his young team that "intimidation could substitute for playing well" ("The Bad News").

9   Although not all parents or coaches behave so inappropriately, the seriousness of the problem is illustrated by the fact that Adelphi University in Garden City, New York, offers a sports psychology workshop for Little League coaches, designed to

How effective do you think Statsky's argument in par. 7 is? Why?

In criticizing some parents' behavior in pars. 8–9, Statsky risks alienating her readers. How effective is this part of her argument?

balance their "animal instincts" with "educational theory" in hopes of reducing the "screaming and hollering," in the words of Harold Weisman, manager of sixteen Little Leagues in New York City (Schmitt). In a three-and-one-half-hour Sunday morning workshop, coaches learn how to make practices more fun, treat injuries, deal with irate parents, and be "more sensitive to their young players' fears, emotional frailties, and need for recognition." Little League is to be credited with recognizing the need for such workshops.

How effective is Statsky's use of concession and refutation here?

10   Some parents would no doubt argue that children cannot start too soon preparing to live in a competitive free-market economy. After all, secondary schools and colleges require students to compete for grades, and college admission is extremely competitive. And it is perfectly obvious how important competitive skills are in finding a job. Yet the ability to cooperate is also important for success in life. Before children are psychologically ready for competition, maybe we should emphasize cooperation and individual performance in team sports rather than winning.

11   Many people are ready for such an emphasis. In 1988, one New York Little League official who had attended the Adelphi workshop tried to ban scoring from six- to eight-year-olds' games — but parents wouldn't support him (Schmitt). An innovative children's sports program in New York City, City Sports for Kids, emphasizes fitness, self-esteem, and sportsmanship. In this program's basketball games, every member on a team plays at least two of six eight-minute periods. The basket is seven feet from the floor, rather than ten feet, and a player can score a point just by hitting the rim (Bloch). I believe this kind of local program should replace overly competitive programs like Peewee Football and Little League Baseball. As one coach explains, significant improvements can result from a few simple rule changes, such as including every player in the batting order and giving every player, regardless of age or ability, the opportunity to play at least four innings a game (Frank).

How effectively does Statsky conclude her argument?

12   Some children *want* to play competitive sports; they are not being forced to play. These children are eager to learn skills, to enjoy the camaraderie of the team, and earn self-respect by trying hard to benefit their team. I acknowledge that some children may benefit from playing competitive sports. While some children do benefit from these programs, however, many more would benefit from programs that avoid the excesses and dangers of many competitive sports programs and instead emphasize fitness, cooperation, sportsmanship, and individual performance.

Works Cited

"The Bad News Pyromaniacs?" Editorial. *Los Angeles Times* 16 June 1990: B6. *LexisNexis*. Web. 16 May 2008.

Bloch, Gordon B. "Thrill of Victory Is Secondary to Fun." *New York Times* 2 Apr. 1990, late ed.: C12. *LexisNexis*. Web. 14 May 2008.

Coakley, Jay J. *Sport in Society: Issues and Controversies*. St. Louis: Mosby, 1982. Print.

Frank, L. "Contributions from Parents and Coaches." *CYB Message Board*. AOL, 8 July 1997. Web. 14 May 2008.

Koppett, Leonard. *Sports Illusion, Sports Reality*. Boston: Houghton, 1981. Print.

Kutner, Lawrence. "Athletics, through a Child's Eyes." *New York Times* 23 Mar. 1989, late ed.: C8. *LexisNexis*. Web. 15 May 2008.

Schmitt, Eric. "Psychologists Take Seat on Little League Bench." *New York Times* 14 Mar. 1988, late ed.: B2. *LexisNexis*. Web. 14 May 2008.

Silverman, Steve. "The History of Youth Sports." Livestrong.com. Demand Media, Inc., 26 May 2011. Web. 10 Dec. 2011.

Smith, Nathan, Ronald Smith, and Frank Smoll. *Kidsports: A Survival Guide for Parents*. Reading: Addison, 1983. Print.

Tosches, Rich. "Peewee Football: Is It Time to Blow the Whistle?" *Los Angeles Times* 3 Dec. 1988: A1+. *LexisNexis*. Web. 22 May 2008.

"What about My Child?" *Little League Online*. Little League Baseball, Inc., 1999. Web. 30 May 2008.

"Your Role as a Little League Parent." *Little League Online*. Little League Baseball, Inc., 1999. Web. 30 May 2008.

"Youth Sports Injuries Statistics." *STOPSportsInjuries.org*. American Orthopaedic Society for Sports Medicine, n.d. Web. 10 Dec. 2011.

Are Statsky's sources adequate to support her position, in number and kind? Has she documented them clearly and accurately?

Noam Bramson | *Child, Home, Neighborhood, Community, and Conscience*

John Raiola

NOAM BRAMSON is a native of New Rochelle, a suburb of New York City that is home to about 78,000 residents. After earning a master's degree in public policy from Harvard University, he served on the City Council and is now the mayor, having won re-election with 79 percent of the vote. The argument below originally appeared on his Web site in 2014.

As you read, consider Bramson's intended audience and how he appeals to those readers:

- How does the example of Matthew help build sympathy for Bramson's position? How does it lend credibility to Bramson himself?

- How would you react to Bramson's argument if you and your family lived in New Rochelle? How would you react if you lived near the proposed location of the group home? (The acronym NIMBY stands for "not in my backyard.")

1   Let me tell you a little about Matthew. Next fall, Matthew will enter fourth grade. His favorite food is pizza. He's always happy to jump on his trampoline or go for a swim. He can't wait to return to Disney World. And he loves riding horses.

2   As the school year was wrapping up, Matthew and I, along with his classmates, had lunch together. Their teacher had made the winning bid on "lunch with the mayor" at a Special Education PTA auction. I could not have asked for a warmer, friendlier greeting from the kids, although—let's be honest—the McDonald's happy meals that I brought with me may have accounted for just a bit of the excitement.

3   The students in this small class of five have a range of serious developmental disabilities, including autism ("What Is Autism?"), Down syndrome, and others. All need intensive supervision. Some might require support throughout their lives.

4   Over lunch, we chatted, smiled, joked, took photos. Sometimes a little gentle coaxing was needed to elicit a response or encourage eye contact. A few of the kids communicated more easily with an iPad than through speech. They all presented me with personal artwork and a welcome poster.

5   And then I said good-bye, walked to my car, slumped into the driver's seat, and let out a long breath. These great children and their amazingly dedicated teachers and therapists had overwhelmed me, and that was after just 45 minutes.

6   Every prior experience I've had with children who have developmental disabilities has stirred similar feelings, so I have always been in awe of the parents of kids with profound special needs. The day-to-day challenges are enormous, life-altering, and nearly incomprehensible to those of us whose families face no unusual obstacles. The parents I've known would all say—to a person—that they receive far more from their children than they give. And perhaps a greater depth of humanity is the gift of such relationships, but it is a hard-earned gift.

7   Then consider the emotional strength required to envision and plan for the future—to contemplate the day when many support services will end, when mom and dad can no longer provide care or companionship, and when an uncertain adulthood begins to take shape.

8   That brings me to the real purpose of my writing today. By sheer coincidence, around the same time of my visit to Matthew's class, a controversy was erupting over a proposed group home in a residential area here in New Rochelle.

9   Some background: Group homes (or "community residences") are intended to provide a supportive, neighborhood-based living arrangement to adults with disabilities or other challenges. Unlike institutionalization, they allow the disabled to be part of a community

Bramson *Child, Home, Neighborhood, Community, and Conscience*

▶ GUIDE TO READING
GUIDE TO WRITING
A WRITER AT WORK
THINKING CRITICALLY

243

and to achieve as much independence as their individual circumstances and abilities permit. Typically, a not-for-profit social service agency will purchase a single-family home, make modest renovations as appropriate, and then provide staff and supervision. There are roughly twenty group homes in New Rochelle today, scattered fairly evenly across the city.

10 Group homes are strongly promoted by state law, which pretty much sweeps away the zoning authority that would ordinarily enable municipalities to prevent group homes from being created. In order to block a group home, a municipality must demonstrate that there is already an over-concentration of similar group homes in the proposed area, or the municipality must present a specific alternative location, within the same community, that has the same characteristics as the property that was proposed. (If you want to know more, Google the Padavan Law.)

11 There's lots of variation among group homes, but just about all of them have two things in common: (1) they almost *always* generate serious concern and opposition when they are proposed; and (2) they almost *never* create any serious problems when they are actually up and running.

12 In the case at issue now, an agency called Cardinal McCloskey Community Services is proposing to purchase a property in a pleasant, close-knit, middle-class neighborhood. It will serve as a home for four young men with autism.

13 The neighborhood is opposed—strongly, passionately, and just about universally. At a meeting at City Hall a couple of weeks ago, residents turned out in big numbers to voice their objections in polite, but very forceful terms.

14 With public opinion overwhelmingly against the group home, the City Administration then acted on the neighborhood's request and filed a formal objection with the New York State Office of Mental Health, citing the over-concentration argument noted above. This objection will be adjudicated in the weeks ahead.

15 Now here's where I make an admission that will get me in trouble: *I disagreed with the City's decision to file an objection, and I recommended against submitting it.*

> *Just about all [group homes] . . . generate serious . . . opposition when they are proposed; and . . . almost **never** create any serious problems when they are actually up and running.*

16 Before I get into my reasons, please understand something. I have known many of the residents of this neighborhood for twenty years, and they are *good* people—generous with friends, kind to strangers, trustworthy in their personal relationships, deeply loyal to their community. They are volunteers, church-goers, givers to charity. Some have children or grandchildren with severe disabilities. They are reacting as most neighborhoods react, so I am not singling them out.

17 I simply believe that the objections are wrong. Profoundly wrong. And that the objections should not be validated by the city or its leadership.

18 My thoughts about all this crystallized as I listened to the comments at the meeting. . . .

19 Much was made of the property's location on a cul de sac, presently used by many children as a play area. The group home, speakers argued, would take away a safe haven that is vital to families. That sounds like a fair point, until you start reflecting on it. Why exactly couldn't children just continue playing on the cul de sac?

20 Another speaker asked rhetorically whether the group home operators could "guarantee" that the young men would not pose a safety risk. Again, that seems like a reasonable question, until you think it through. I can't guarantee that my next door neighbor is not a drug dealer, or that the couple moving in across the street aren't spying for the Russians. The question ought to be whether there is any rational basis for fearing such things.

21 There was a suggestion during a prior meeting that these four young men should instead be given a suite of rooms at the hospital—essentially rejecting the entire concept of community-based living for the disabled.

22 One, and only one, speaker contended that the young men with autism presented a threat of sexually predatory behavior. This claim (which lacks any solid evidence) is highly inflammatory, to say the least. I was glad that it wasn't repeated explicitly by others, but I hoped the room would respond with stony silence. Instead, everyone applauded, blurring the line between those who were fair-minded and those who were not.

23 There was more. Speakers said the proposed home was too close to other houses, that the neighborhood would be permanently and irreparably harmed, that

traffic would overwhelm a small street, that property values would collapse.

24   Many took pains to say that they had nothing against the disabled, but surely an alternative site could be found that made more sense for all involved. (If anyone stated the case for why another neighborhood would be happier to welcome a group home, I missed it.)

25   I have no doubt that all the speakers really *believed* what they were saying, and truly felt their positions to be based on logic and reason. But, as I listened, I couldn't shake the feeling that the conclusion—"No!"—had come first, with the arguments following afterwards as a kind of back-engineered rationalization. (In fact, for almost all of us, that's how decision-making tends to work.)

26   It was not about NIMBYism, they said, and so they believed. But of course it was exactly about NIMBYism. It was *only* about NIMBYism.

27   One more factor: even for the most virtuous and self-confident individuals, the dynamic of a group seized by emotion can exert a powerful influence. The crowd ends up being less than the sum of its parts. Often a lot less. I suspect that a few of the neighbors who spoke or applauded will look back in a couple of years and have second thoughts or regrets.

28   But those regrets will pale in comparison to what I felt when the meeting concluded: *shame*. I was ashamed of *myself*, because I simply sat there quietly without saying a word. And I can't imagine a worse display of cowardice.

29   Continued silence would certainly be the politically wise approach. The city's formal objection to the site has no chance whatsoever of succeeding. (In fact, I am told that no such objection has *ever* succeeded in New York, because the threshold established by state law is simply too high.) That means the process will run its course to the inevitable conclusion, the group home will go to the proposed site, and the empty gesture of a city objection will have taken care of the politics. By contrast, this statement of mine will probably anger many people. So why not do the sensible thing and keep my mouth shut?

30   Because there's a cost to all this—to this cycle of too many politicians pretending to fight for people, while really serving only themselves, elevating expediency over conscience, issuing nice-sounding assurances in exchange for applause, until eventually reality overtakes the empty pledges, and then faith in public leadership slips just a little lower into the basement. After two decades in public life, I am neither naive nor pure, but there comes a point when someone has to say *enough* to all that, and I guess this is my moment. Silence is complicity.

31   Our community, which has always been defined by its welcoming spirit, is better than the objections raised at the meeting. *The people who made those objections are better by far than their comments*, and they will eventually come to realize it. Indeed, I have no doubt whatsoever that these four young men will be greeted with courtesy and warmth, even by those who were most concerned about their arrival.

32   How would Catie and I react if a group home was proposed next door to our house? We have asked ourselves this question. Would we raise a host of seemingly fair arguments in opposition? *Pinebrook Boulevard is too heavily trafficked . . . bus service and stores are too far away . . . there's already a group home down the street on Beechmont, and another up the street on Sussex.* Would we band together with our neighbors, reinforcing each others' sense of certainty? Would we have the self-awareness to perceive our own inner, and perhaps less-than-worthy, motivations? It is impossible to know, and I don't pretend to be any more noble than the next person.

33   But I want very much to believe that we would not fight, that we would make the best of it, that we would offer whatever good will we could to our new neighbors, and that we would try to set an example for our own two boys by showing them that every person has worth.

34   At one point or another in our lives, each of us will be expected to step outside our comfort zone or bear some burden for a larger purpose. It can be as simple and broad as the taxes we pay for ADA curb cuts and special ed classes, or as complex and specific as this issue of group home placement. The costs are not always fairly distributed. What we get in return is the chance to live in a decent society.

35   Matthew is nine years old. That means in about a dozen more years, he will age out of the services that support youngsters, and a new chapter of his life will begin. I hope it is a wonderful life, and that when he is older, his neighbors and community will welcome him and take joy in his humanity.

Link

"What Is Autism?" *Autism Speaks.* Autism Speaks, Inc., 2015.

Make connections: Outside the "comfort zone."

Bramson writes that "At one point or another in our lives, each of us will be expected to step outside our comfort zone . . . (par. 34). Think about a time when you were forced "to step outside your comfort zone." For example, you might have moved to a new neighborhood or school or started a new job. Your instructor may ask you to post your thoughts to a class discussion board or blog, or to discuss them with other students in class. Use these questions to get started:

- How did you feel as a newcomer? Did anyone try to make you feel welcome or unwelcome? How did your opinion of group members change as you got to know them (or the rules they followed) better?

- Consider the insights, if any, you gained from stepping outside of your "comfort zone." Did your experience change the way you now respond to others joining a group to which you belong? Did it change the way you respond to the behavior of members of your own group?

Use the basic features.

A FOCUSED, WELL-PRESENTED ISSUE: FRAMING AN ARGUMENT FOR YOUR AUDIENCE

Disagreement over controversial issues often depends on a difference of values and concerns. To argue effectively, writers must anticipate what their readers are likely to think about the issue, and they must frame (or reframe) the issue to influence how their readers think about it. In "Child, Home, Neighborhood, Community, and Conscience," Bramson discusses a meeting at which residents framed the controversy in terms of the danger the group home represents to their neighborhood. In his argument, Bramson reframes the issue, changing it to one of generosity and shared burdens.

ANALYZE & WRITE

Write a few paragraphs analyzing how Bramson reframes the issue of locating group homes in the community:

1. How do the opening and closing paragraphs (pars. 1–7, 35) help Bramson reframe the issue? What role do the paragraphs providing background (pars. 9–12) play in his reframing of the issue?

2. Given his audience and purpose, why do you think Bramson decided that reframing the issue as one of shared burdens would be an effective way to persuade residents to be more accepting of group homes?

A WELL-SUPPORTED POSITION: USING ANECDOTES AND EXAMPLES

Anecdotes (brief stories) and *examples* can be especially effective as evidence because they appeal to readers' values and feelings. Jessica Statsky, for instance, relates an anecdote about a seven-year-old Peewee Football player who made himself vomit to avoid playing. This anecdote delivers the message powerfully, although it runs the risk of being perceived by readers as exaggerated or emotionally manipulative. Writers can also use examples to bring home their claims, making them more concrete, graphic, and convincing, as Statsky does when she tells of "a brawl among seventy-five parents following a Peewee Football game" (par. 8). Because examples are isolated instances, however, they do not necessarily prove the general rule. To get around this, Statsky introduces this example as one of many "horror stories" to suggest that it is not all that unusual, but a fairly typical incident that should be taken seriously as evidence to support her position.

For more on recognizing emotional manipulation, see Chapter 12, p. 520.

ANALYZE & WRITE

Write a paragraph analyzing and evaluating Bramson's use of anecdotes and examples in "Child, Home, Neighborhood, Community, and Consience":

1. Highlight the anecdotes and examples—both real and hypothetical—Bramson uses to support his position.

2. Why do you think, given his original Web site readers, that Bramson thought these anecdotes and examples would be compelling? How effective are they for you?

AN EFFECTIVE RESPONSE: CONCEDING AND REFUTING

Writers of position essays try to anticipate other positions on the issue as well as objections and questions readers might raise, because doing so enhances the writer's credibility (or ethos) and strengthens the argument. They may concede, refute, or combine the two strategies in a concession-refutation move. To review examples of these response strategies and criteria to assess their effectiveness, look back at pp. 234–35 in the Guide to Reading.

ANALYZE & WRITE

Write a paragraph or two analyzing and evaluating how Bramson concedes and refutes anticipated criticism.

1. Skim Bramson's essay, marking where he uses concession, refutation, or both. How did you identify which strategy Bramson is using?

2. Analyze and evaluate Bramson's response: What values does he assume underlie his intended readers' point of view? How does his way of responding bridge the gap between their point of view and his own?

3. How do you think citizens of New Rochelle would respond to Bramson? How would you respond if you were arguing for or against locating a group home in your neighborhood?

A CLEAR, LOGICAL ORGANIZATION: CREATING CLOSURE

A variety of strategies are available to writers to create a sense of closure for readers. They may simply reiterate the main points they've addressed, suggest steps readers can take as a result of what they've learned, or repeat a word or phrase with which the selection opened.

ANALYZE & WRITE

Write a paragraph analyzing how Bramson creates a sense of closure in "Child, Home, Neighborhood, Community, and Consience":

1. Reread paragraphs 1–7 to remind yourself how Bramson begins the essay and paragraph 35 to recall how he concludes it.

2. Now skim the rest of the piece to see how Bramson connects the anecdote about Matthew and his classmates with the broader issue of the location of the group home and the community's response to it.

3. Consider how effective Bramson's conclusion is for persuading readers to accept the group home and to accept, more broadly, the importance of sharing burdens. Were you persuaded? Do you think Bramson's intended readers — the voters of New Rochelle — would have been persuaded? Why or why not?

Consider possible topics: Issues concerning fairness.

[RESPOND]

List some issues that involve what you believe to be unfair distribution of benefits or burdens. For example, should the richest 1 percent of citizens pay a higher rate of taxes than the poorer 99 percent? Should schools in wealthy districts be required to share donations from parents with schools in poorer districts? Should schools create and enforce guidelines to protect individuals from bullying and discrimination? Should taxes be raised so that Medicaid (health insurance for the poor) could be expanded to cover more of the low-income uninsured?

Amitai Etzioni | *Working at McDonald's*

Poklekowski/ullstein bild via Getty Images

AMITAI ETZIONI is a sociologist who has taught at Columbia, Harvard, and George Washington University, where he currently directs the Institute for Communitarian Policy Studies. He has written numerous articles and more than two dozen books, including *The Spirit of Community: The Reinvention of American Society* (1983); *The Limits of Privacy* (2004); *Security First: For a Muscular, Moral Foreign Policy* (2007); and most recently, *The New Normal: Finding a Balance between Individual Rights and the Common Good* (2014). The following reading was originally published on the opinion page of the *Miami Herald* newspaper.

As you read, consider the following:

- What do you imagine Etzioni's teenage son Dari, who helped his father write the essay, contributed?
- What kinds of summer and school-year jobs, if any, have you and your friends held while in high school or college?

1   McDonald's is bad for your kids. I do not mean the flat patties and the white-flour buns; I refer to the jobs teen-agers undertake, mass-producing these choice items.

2   As many as two-thirds of America's high school juniors and seniors now hold down part-time paying jobs, according to studies. Many of these are in fast-food chains, of which McDonald's is the pioneer, trend-setter and symbol.

3   At first, such jobs may seem right out of the Founding Fathers' educational manual for how to bring up self-reliant, work-ethic-driven, productive youngsters. But in fact, these jobs undermine school attendance and involvement, impart few skills that will be useful in later life, and simultaneously skew the values of teen-agers — especially their ideas about the worth of a dollar.

4   It has been a longstanding American tradition that youngsters ought to get paying jobs. In folklore, few pursuits are more deeply revered than the newspaper route and the sidewalk lemonade stand. Here the youngsters are to learn how sweet are the fruits of labor and self-discipline (papers are delivered early in the morning, rain or shine), and the ways of trade (if you price your lemonade too high or too low . . .).

5   Roy Rogers, Baskin Robbins, Kentucky Fried Chicken, et al. may at first seem nothing but a vast extension of the lemonade stand. They provide very large numbers of teen jobs, provide regular employment, pay quite well compared to many other teen jobs and, in the modern equivalent of toiling over a hot stove, test one's stamina.

6   Closer examination, however, finds the McDonald's kind of job highly uneducational in several ways. Far from providing opportunities for entrepreneurship (the lemonade stand) or self-discipline, self-supervision and self-scheduling (the paper route), most teen jobs these days are highly structured — what social scientists call "highly routinized."

7   True, you still have to have the gumption to get yourself over to the hamburger stand, but once you don the prescribed uniform, your task is spelled out in minute detail. The franchise prescribes the shape of the coffee cups; the weight, size, shape and color of the patties; and the texture of the napkins (if any). Fresh coffee is to be made every eight minutes. And so on. There is no room for initiative, creativity, or even elementary rearrangements. These are breeding grounds for robots working for yesterday's assembly lines, not tomorrow's high-tech posts.

8   There are very few studies on the matter. One of the few is a 1984 study by Ivan Charper and Bryan Shore Fraser. The study relies mainly on what teen-agers write in response to questionnaires rather than actual observations of fast-food jobs. The authors argue that the employees develop many skills such as how to operate a food-preparation machine and a cash register. However, little attention is paid to how long it takes to acquire such a skill, or what its significance is.

9   What does it matter if you spend 20 minutes to learn to use a cash register, and then—"operate" it? What "skill" have you acquired? It is a long way from learning to work with a lathe or carpenter tools in the olden days or to program computers in the modern age.

10   A 1980 study by A. V. Harrell and P. W. Wirtz found that, among those students who worked at least 25 hours per week while in school, their unemployment rate four years later was half of that of seniors who did not work. This is an impressive statistic. It must be seen, though, together with the finding that many who begin as part-time employees in fast-food chains drop out of high school and are gobbled up in the world of low-skill jobs.

Far from providing opportunities for entrepreneurship . . . most teen jobs these days are highly structured.

11   Some say that while these jobs are rather unsuited for college-bound, white, middle-class youngsters, they are "ideal" for lower-class, "non-academic," minority youngsters. Indeed, minorities are "over-represented" in these jobs (21 percent of fast-food employees). While it is true that these places provide income, work and even some training to such youngsters, they also tend to perpetuate their disadvantaged status. They provide no career ladders, few marketable skills, and undermine school attendance and involvement.

12   The hours are often long. Among those 14 to 17, a third of fast-food employees (including some school dropouts) labor more than 30 hours per week, according to the Charper-Fraser study. Only 20 percent work 15 hours or less. The rest: between 15 and 30 hours.

13   Often the stores close late, and after closing one must clean up and tally up. In affluent Montgomery County, Md., where child labor would not seem to be a widespread economic necessity, 24 percent of the seniors at one high school in 1985 worked as much as five to seven days a week; 27 percent, three to five. There is just no way such amounts of work will not interfere with school work, especially homework. In an informal survey published in the most recent yearbook of the high school, 58 percent of seniors acknowledged that their jobs interfere with their school work.

14   The Charper-Fraser study sees merit in learning teamwork and working under supervision. The authors have a point here. However, it must be noted that such learning is not automatically educational or wholesome. For example, much of the supervision in fast-food places leans toward teaching one the wrong kinds of compliance: blind obedience, or shared alienation with the "boss."

15   Supervision is often both tight and woefully inappropriate. Today, fast-food chains and other such places of work (record shops, bowling alleys) keep costs down by having teens supervise teens with often no adult on the premises.

16   There is no father or mother figure with which to identify, to emulate, to provide a role model and guidance. The work-culture varies from one place to another: Sometimes it is a tightly run shop (must keep the cash registers ringing); sometimes a rather loose pot party interrupted by customers. However, only rarely is there a master to learn from, or much worth learning. Indeed, far from being places where solid adult work values are being transmitted, these are places where all too often delinquent teen values dominate. Typically, when my son Oren was dishing out ice cream for Baskin Robbins in upper Manhattan, his fellow teen-workers considered him a sucker for not helping himself to the till. Most youngsters felt they were entitled to $50 severance "pay" on their last day on the job.

17   The pay, oddly, is the part of the teen work-world that is most difficult to evaluate. The lemonade stand or paper route money was for your allowance. In the old days, apprentices learning a trade from a master contributed most, if not all, of their income to their parents' household. Today, the teen pay may be low by adult standards, but it is often, especially in the middle class, spent largely or wholly by the teens. That is, the youngsters live free at home ("after all, they are high school kids") and are left with very substantial sums of money.

18   Where this money goes is not quite clear. Some use it to support themselves, especially among the poor. More middle-class kids set some money aside to help pay for college, or save it for a major purchase — often a car. But large amounts seem to flow to pay for an early introduction into the most trite aspects of American consumerism: flimsy punk clothes, trinkets and whatever else is the last fast-moving teen craze.

19   One may say that this is only fair and square; they are being good American consumers and spend their money on what turns them on. At least, a cynic might add, these funds do not go into illicit drugs and booze. On the other hand, an educator might bemoan that these young, yet unformed individuals, so early in life driven to buy objects of no intrinsic educational, cultural or social merit, learn so quickly the dubious merit of keeping up with the Joneses in ever-changing fads, promoted by mass merchandising.

20   Many teens find the instant reward of money, and the youth status symbols it buys, much more alluring than credits in calculus courses, European history or foreign languages. No wonder quite a few would rather skip school—and certainly homework — and instead work longer at a Burger King. Thus, most teen work these days is not providing early lessons in the work ethic; it fosters escape from school and responsibilities,

quick gratification and a short cut to the consumeristic aspects of adult life.

21   Thus, parents should look at teen employment not as automatically educational. It is an activity—like sports—that can be turned into an educational opportunity. But it can also easily be abused. Youngsters must learn to balance the quest for income with the needs to keep growing and pursue other endeavors that do not pay off instantly—above all education.

22   Go back to school.

[REFLECT]   # Make connections: Useful job skills.

Etzioni argues that fast-food jobs do not qualify as meaningful work experience because they do not teach young people the skills and habits they will need for fulfilling careers: "entrepreneurship . . . or self-discipline, self-supervision and self-scheduling" (par. 6).

To judge Etzioni's argument against your own experience and expectations, consider what you have learned or expect people to learn from summer and after-school jobs, either paid or volunteer. Your instructor may ask you to post your thoughts on a class discussion board or to discuss them with other students in class. Use these questions to get started:

- Which, if any, of the skills and habits Etzioni lists as important do you think young people learn at summer or after-school jobs?
- Why do you think these skills and habits are worth learning? If you think other skills and habits are as important or even more important, explain what they are and why you think so.

[ANALYZE]   # Use the basic features.

A FOCUSED, WELL-PRESENTED ISSUE: FRAMING AN ARGUMENT FOR A DIVERSE GROUP OF READERS

When Jessica Statsky wrote "Children Need to Play, Not Compete," she knew she would be addressing her classmates. But writers of position essays do not always have such a homogeneous audience. Often, they have to direct their argument to a diverse group of readers, many of whom do not share their concerns or values. From the first sentence, it is clear that Etzioni's primary audience is the parents of teenagers, but his concluding sentence is a direct address to the teenagers themselves: "Go back to school."

ANALYZE & WRITE

Write a paragraph analyzing and evaluating how Etzioni presents the issue to a diverse group of readers:

1   Reread paragraphs 1–7, highlighting the qualities—values and skills—associated with traditional jobs (the newspaper route and lemonade stand of yesteryear) and with today's McDonald's-type jobs, at least according to Etzioni. How does Etzioni use this comparison to persuade parents to reconsider their assumption that McDonald's-type jobs are good for their kids?

2 Now skim the rest of the essay, looking for places where Etzioni appeals to teenagers themselves. (Notice, for example, how he represents teenagers' experience and values.) How effective do you think Etzioni's appeal would be to teenage readers? How effective do you think it would be for you and your classmates?

A WELL-SUPPORTED POSITION: USING STATISTICS

Numbers can seem impressive—as, for example, when Jessica Statsky refers to the research finding that about 90 percent of children would choose to play regularly on a losing team rather than sit on the bench of a winning team (par. 5). However, without knowing the size of the sample (90 percent of 10 people, 100 people, or 10,000 people?), it is impossible to judge the significance of the statistic. Moreover, without knowing who the researchers are and how their research was funded and conducted, it is also difficult to judge the credibility of the statistic. That's why most critical readers want to know the source of **statistics** to see whether the research is **peer-reviewed**—that is, whether it has been evaluated by other researchers knowledgeable about the subject and able to judge the reliability of the study's findings.

ANALYZE & WRITE

Write a paragraph analyzing and evaluating Etzioni's use of statistics.

1 Reread paragraphs 8–14, and highlight the statistics Etzioni uses. What is each statistic being used to illustrate or prove?

2 Identify what you would need to know about these research studies before you could accept their statistics as credible. Consider also what you would need to know about Etzioni himself before you could decide whether to rely on statistics he calls "impressive" (par. 10). How does your personal experience and observation influence your decision?

AN EFFECTIVE RESPONSE: PRESENTING AND REINTERPRETING EVIDENCE TO UNDERMINE OBJECTIONS

At key points throughout his essay, Etzioni acknowledges readers' likely objections and then responds to them. One strategy Etzioni uses is to cite research that appears to undermine his claim and then offer a new interpretation of that evidence. For example, he cites a study by Harrell and Wirtz (par. 10) that links work as a student with greater likelihood of employment later on. He then reinterprets the data from this study to show that the high likelihood of future employment could be an indication that workers in fast-food restaurants are more likely to drop out of school rather than an indication that workers are learning important employment skills. This strategy of presenting and reinterpreting evidence can be especially effective in academic writing, as Etzioni (a professor of sociology) well knows.

ANALYZE & WRITE

Write a paragraph or two analyzing and evaluating Etzioni's strategy of reinterpreting data elsewhere in his essay:

1. Reread paragraphs 8–9, in which Etzioni responds to the claim that employees in McDonald's-type jobs develop many useful skills.

2. Reread paragraphs 14–16, in which Etzioni discusses the benefits and shortcomings of various kinds of on-the-job supervision.

3. Identify the claim that appears in the research Etzioni cites. How does Etzioni reinterpret it? Do you find his reinterpretation persuasive? Why or why not?

A CLEAR, LOGICAL ORGANIZATION: PROVIDING CUES FOR READERS

Writers of position arguments generally try to make their writing logical and easy to follow. Providing **cues**, or road signs—for example, by forecasting their reasons in a thesis statement early in the argument, using topic sentences to announce each reason as it is supported, and employing transitions (such as *furthermore*, *in addition*, and *finally*) to guide readers from one point to another—can be helpful, especially in newspaper articles, the readers of which do not want to spend a lot of time deciphering arguments.

ANALYZE & WRITE

Write a paragraph analyzing and evaluating the cueing strategies Etzioni uses to help his readers follow his argument:

1. Find and highlight his thesis statement, the cues forecasting his reasons, the transitions he provides, and any other cueing devices Etzioni uses.

2. Identify the paragraphs in which Etzioni develops each of his reasons.

3. How does Etzioni help readers track his reasons, and how effective are his cues?

[RESPOND] ## Consider possible topics: Issues facing students.

Etzioni focuses on a single kind of part-time work, takes a position on how worthwhile it is, and recommends against it. You could write a similar kind of essay. For example, you could take a position for or against students' participating in other kinds of part-time work or recreation during the high school or college academic year or over the summer—for example, playing on a sports team, volunteering, completing an internship, studying a musical instrument or a foreign language, or taking an elective class. If you work to support yourself and pay for college, you could focus on why the job either strengthens or weakens you as a person, given your life and career goals. Writing for other students, you would either recommend the job or activity to them or discourage them from pursuing it, giving reasons and support for your position.

Daniel J. Solove | *Why Privacy Matters Even If You Have "Nothing to Hide"*

DANIEL J. SOLOVE is the John Marshall Harlan Research Professor of Law at the George Washington University Law School. In addition to writing numerous books and articles on issues of privacy and the Internet, Solove is the founder of a company that provides privacy and data security training to corporations and universities. Among his books are *The Future of Reputation: Gossip, Rumor, and Privacy on the Internet* (2007), which won Fordham University's McGannon Award for Social and Ethical Relevance in Communications Policy Research; *Nothing to Hide: The False Tradeoff between Privacy and Security* (2011); and *Privacy Law Fundamentals* (with Paul M. Schwartz, 2013).

An earlier and longer version of this essay in a law review journal included citations that had to be eliminated for publication in the *Chronicle of Higher Education* in 2011, but we have restored them so that you can see how Solove uses a variety of sources to support his position.

As you read, consider the following:

- How do the sources cited in the opening paragraphs contribute to your understanding of why many people think privacy is not something they should be concerned about?

- Do you use Internet privacy settings? How concerned are you about protecting your privacy on social networking and other Web sites?

1   When the government gathers or analyzes personal information, many people say they're not worried. "I've got nothing to hide," they declare. "Only if you're doing something wrong should you worry, and then you don't deserve to keep it private." The nothing-to-hide argument pervades discussions about privacy. The data-security expert Bruce Schneier calls it the "most common retort against privacy advocates." The legal scholar Geoffrey Stone refers to it as an "all-too-common refrain." In its most compelling form, it is an argument that the privacy interest is generally minimal, thus making the contest with security concerns a foreordained victory for security.

2   The nothing-to-hide argument is everywhere. In Britain, for example, the government has installed millions of public-surveillance cameras in cities and towns, which are watched by officials via closed-circuit television. In a campaign slogan for the program, the government declares: "If you've got nothing to hide, you've got nothing to fear" (Rosen 36). Variations of nothing-to-hide arguments frequently appear in blogs, letters to the editor, television news interviews, and other forums. One blogger in the United States, in reference to profiling people for national-security purposes, declares: "I don't mind people wanting to find out things about me, I've got nothing to hide! Which is why I support [the government's] efforts to find terrorists by monitoring our phone calls!" (greatcarrieoakey).

3   On the surface, it seems easy to dismiss the nothing-to-hide argument. Everybody probably has something to hide from somebody. As Aleksandr Solzhenitsyn declared, "Everyone is guilty of something or has something to conceal. All one has to do is look hard enough to find what it is" (192). . . . One can usually think of something that even the most open person would want to hide. As a commenter to my blog post noted, "If you have nothing to hide, then that quite literally means you are willing to let me photograph you naked? And I get full rights to that photograph—so I can show it to your neighbors?" (Andrew) . . .

4   But such responses attack the nothing-to-hide argument only in its most extreme form, which isn't particularly strong. In a less extreme form, the nothing-to-hide argument refers not to all personal information but only to the type of data the government is likely to collect. Retorts to the nothing-to-hide argument about exposing people's naked bodies or their deepest secrets are relevant only if the government is likely to gather this kind of information. In many instances, hardly anyone will see the information, and it won't be disclosed to the public. Thus, some might argue, the privacy interest is minimal, and the security interest in preventing terrorism is much more important. In this less extreme form, the nothing-to-hide argument is a formidable one. However, it stems from certain faulty assumptions about privacy and its value. . . .

5   Most attempts to understand privacy do so by attempting to locate its essence—its core characteristics or the common denominator that links together the various things we classify under the rubric of "privacy." Privacy, however, is too complex a concept to be reduced to a singular essence. It is a plurality of different things that do not share any one element but nevertheless bear a resemblance to one another. For example, privacy can be invaded by the disclosure of your deepest secrets. It might also be invaded if you're watched by a peeping Tom, even if no secrets are ever revealed. With the disclosure of secrets, the harm is that your concealed information is spread to others. With the peeping Tom, the harm is that you're being watched. You'd probably find that creepy regardless of whether the peeper finds out anything sensitive or discloses any information to others. There are many other forms of invasion of privacy, such as blackmail and the improper use of your personal data. Your privacy can also be invaded if the government compiles an extensive dossier about you. Privacy, in other words, involves so many things that it is impossible to reduce them all to one simple idea. And we need not do so. . . .

6   To describe the problems created by the collection and use of personal data, many commentators use a metaphor based on George Orwell's *Nineteen Eighty-Four*. Orwell depicted a harrowing totalitarian society ruled by a government called Big Brother that watches its citizens obsessively and demands strict discipline. The Orwell metaphor, which focuses on the harms of surveillance (such as inhibition and social control), might be apt to describe government monitoring of citizens. But much of the data gathered in computer databases, such as one's race, birth date, gender, address, or marital status, isn't particularly sensitive. Many people don't care about concealing the hotels they stay at, the cars they own, or the kind of beverages they drink. Frequently, though not always, people wouldn't be inhibited or embarrassed if others knew this information.

7   Another metaphor better captures the problems: Franz Kafka's *The Trial*. Kafka's novel centers around a man who is arrested but not informed why. He desperately tries to find out what triggered his arrest and what's in store for him. He finds out that a mysterious court system has a dossier on him and is investigating him, but he's unable to learn much more. *The Trial* depicts a bureaucracy with inscrutable purposes that uses people's information to make important decisions about them, yet denies the people the ability to participate in how their information is used.

8   The problems portrayed by the Kafkaesque metaphor are of a different sort than the problems caused by surveillance. They often do not result in inhibition. Instead they are problems of information processing—the storage, use, or analysis of data—rather than of information collection. They affect the power relationships between people and the institutions of the modern state. They not only frustrate the individual by creating a sense of helplessness and powerlessness, but also affect social structure by altering the kind of relationships people have with the institutions that make important decisions about their lives.

9   Legal and policy solutions focus too much on the problems under the Orwellian metaphor—those of surveillance—and aren't adequately addressing the Kafkaesque problems—those of information processing. The difficulty is that commentators are trying to conceive of the problems caused by databases in terms of surveillance when, in fact, those problems are different. Commentators often attempt to refute the nothing-to-hide argument by pointing to things people want to

The problem with the nothing-to-hide argument is the underlying assumption that privacy is about hiding bad things.

hide. But the problem with the nothing-to-hide argument is the underlying assumption that privacy is about hiding bad things. By accepting this assumption, we concede far too much ground and invite an unproductive discussion about information that people would very likely want to hide. As the computer-security specialist Schneier aptly notes, the nothing-to-hide argument stems from a faulty "premise that privacy is about hiding a wrong." Surveillance, for example, can inhibit such lawful activities as free speech, free association, and other First Amendment rights essential for democracy.

10   The deeper problem with the nothing-to-hide argument is that it myopically views privacy as a form of secrecy. In contrast, understanding privacy as a plurality of related issues demonstrates that the disclosure of bad things is just one among many difficulties caused by government security measures. To return to my discussion of literary metaphors, the problems are not just Orwellian but Kafkaesque. Government information-gathering programs are problematic even if no information that people want to hide is uncovered. In *The Trial*, the problem is not inhibited behavior but rather a suffocating powerlessness and vulnerability created by the court system's use of personal data and its denial to the protagonist of any knowledge of or participation in the process. The harms are bureaucratic ones—indifference, error, abuse, frustration, and lack of transparency and accountability.

11   One such harm, for example, which I call aggregation, emerges from the fusion of small bits of seemingly innocuous data. When combined, the information becomes much more telling. By joining pieces of information we might not take pains to guard, the government can glean information about us that we might indeed wish to conceal. For example, suppose you bought a book about cancer. This purchase isn't very revealing on its own, for it indicates just an interest in the disease. Suppose you bought a wig. The purchase of a wig, by itself, could be for a number of reasons. But combine those two pieces of information, and now the inference can be made that you have cancer and are undergoing chemotherapy. That might be a fact you wouldn't mind sharing, but you'd certainly want to have the choice.

12   Another potential problem with the government's harvest of personal data is one I call exclusion. Exclusion occurs when people are prevented from having knowledge about how information about them is being used, and when they are barred from accessing and correcting errors in that data. Many government national-security measures involve maintaining a huge database of information that individuals cannot access. Indeed, because they involve national security, the very existence of these programs is often kept secret. This kind of information processing, which blocks subjects' knowledge and involvement, is a kind of due-process problem. It is a structural problem, involving the way people are treated by government institutions and creating a power imbalance between people and the government. To what extent should government officials have such a significant power over citizens? This issue isn't about what information people want to hide but about the power and the structure of government.

13   A related problem involves secondary use. Secondary use is the exploitation of data obtained for one purpose for an unrelated purpose without the subject's consent. How long will personal data be stored? How will the information be used? What could it be used for in the future? The potential uses of any piece of personal information are vast. Without limits on or accountability for how that information is used, it is hard for people to assess the dangers of the data's being in the government's control.

14   Yet another problem with government gathering and use of personal data is distortion. Although personal information can reveal quite a lot about people's personalities and activities, it often fails to reflect the whole person. It can paint a distorted picture, especially since records are reductive—they often capture information in a standardized format with many details omitted. For example, suppose government officials learn that a person has bought a number of books on how to manufacture methamphetamine. That information makes them suspect that he's building a meth lab. What is missing from the records is the full story: The person is writing a novel about a character who makes meth. When he bought the books, he didn't consider how suspicious the purchase might appear to government officials, and his records didn't reveal the reason for the purchases. Should he have to worry about government scrutiny of all his purchases and actions? Should he have to be concerned that he'll wind up on a suspicious-persons list? Even if he isn't doing anything wrong, he may want to keep his records away from

government officials who might make faulty inferences from them. He might not want to have to worry about how everything he does will be perceived by officials nervously monitoring for criminal activity. He might not want to have a computer flag him as suspicious because he has an unusual pattern of behavior. . . .

15   Privacy is rarely lost in one fell swoop. It is usually eroded over time, little bits dissolving almost imperceptibly until we finally begin to notice how much is gone. When the government starts monitoring the phone numbers people call, many may shrug their shoulders and say, "Ah, it's just numbers, that's all." Then the government might start monitoring some phone calls. "It's just a few phone calls, nothing more." The government might install more video cameras in public places. "So what? Some more cameras watching in a few more places. No big deal." The increase in cameras might lead to a more elaborate network of video surveillance. Satellite surveillance might be added to help track people's movements. The government might start analyzing people's bank records. "It's just my deposits and some of the bills I pay—no problem." The government may then start combing through credit-card records, then expand to Internet-service providers' records, health records, employment records, and more. Each step may seem incremental, but after a while, the government will be watching and knowing everything about us.

16   "My life's an open book," people might say. "I've got nothing to hide." But now the government has large

> *Privacy is rarely lost in one fell swoop. It is usually eroded over time, little bits dissolving almost imperceptibly until we finally begin to notice how much is gone.*

dossiers of everyone's activities, interests, reading habits, finances, and health. What if the government leaks the information to the public? What if the government mistakenly determines that based on your pattern of activities, you're likely to engage in a criminal act? What if it denies you the right to fly? What if the government thinks your financial transactions look odd—even if you've done nothing wrong—and freezes your accounts? What if the government doesn't protect your information with adequate security, and an identity thief obtains it and uses it to defraud you? Even if you have nothing to hide, the government can cause you a lot of harm. . . .

Works Cited

Andrew. Weblog comment. *Concurring Opinions.* 16 Oct. 2006. Web. 24 May 2012.

greatcarrieoakey. "Reach for the Stars!" *Blogspot.com.* 14 May 2006. Web. 24 May 2012.

Rosen, Jeffrey. *The Naked Crowd: Reclaiming Security and Freedom in an Anxious Age.* New York: Random House, 2004. Print.

Schneier, Bruce. "The Eternal Value of Privacy." *Wired.* 18 May 2006. Web. 24 May 2012.

Solzhenitsyn, Aleksandr. *Cancer Ward.* Trans. Nicholas Bethell and David Burg. New York: Farrar, Straus and Giroux, 1969. Print.

Stone, Geoffrey R. "Freedom and Public Responsibility." *Chicago Tribune* 21 May 2006: 11. Print.

[REFLECT]   # Make connections: Privacy concerns on the Internet.

Whereas Solove's position argument focuses on concerns about government collection and use of personal information, many people today are concerned as well about corporate collection and use of personal information. For example, potential employers review blogs and social media Web sites to gather information about job candidates and to check their résumés. Corporations also use data mining to personalize advertising, sending diaper coupons, for example, to women in their thirties who have recently bought diaper bags or baby monitors online.

Think about the implications of corporate data mining, and reflect on how this could affect your own sense of online privacy. Your instructor may ask you to post your thoughts on a class discussion board or to discuss them with other students in class. Use these questions to get started:

- How, if at all, do you manage the privacy preferences or settings on sites you use? Do you ever de-friend people or click the "do not track" tool when you have the opportunity to do so? Would you untag photos or delete comments on social networking sites like Facebook that you didn't want potential employers to see?

- What are the advantages and disadvantages of corporate data mining? Have targeted advertisements been a boon to you, or are you distressed about a corporation's knowing so much about you?

Use the basic features.

[ANALYZE]

A FOCUSED, WELL-PRESENTED ISSUE: REFRAMING THROUGH CONTRAST

Writers sometimes have to remind their readers why an issue is controversial. Beginning with the title, Solove works to undermine the widely held assumption that the erosion of privacy should not be a concern. He does this primarily by contrasting two different ways of thinking about threats to privacy, which he calls Orwellian and Kafkaesque, based on the novels *Nineteen Eighty-Four,* by George Orwell, and *The Trial,* by Franz Kafka. To present this contrast, Solove uses sentence patterns like these:

▶ Not _____, but _____.

▶ _____ focus on _____, which is characterized by _____, and they don't even notice _____, which is characterized by _____.

Here are a couple of examples from Solove's position argument:

> The problems are not just Orwellian but Kafkaesque. (par. 10)

> Legal and policy solutions focus too much on the problems under the Orwellian metaphor—those of surveillance—and aren't adequately addressing the Kafkaesque problems—those of information processing. (par. 9)

ANALYZE & WRITE

Write a paragraph analyzing and evaluating the effectiveness of Solove's use of contrast to reframe the issue for readers:

1. Reread paragraphs 6–7 to see how Solove explains the two contrasting metaphors.

2. Then skim paragraphs 8–10, highlighting any sentence patterns used to mark the contrast.

3. Has Solove's reframing of the discussion affected your understanding of privacy and your concerns about its loss? Why or why not?

A WELL-SUPPORTED POSITION: USING SOURCES

Writers of position arguments often quote, paraphrase, and summarize sources. Usually, they use sources to support their positions, as Jessica Statsky does in her argument about children's sports. Sometimes, however, they use sources to highlight opposing positions to which they will respond, as Solove does on occasion in this essay.

To learn more about using patterns of opposition to read critically, see Chapter 12, p. 516.

In the following example, Solove signals his opinion through the words he chooses to characterize the source:

> As the computer-security specialist Schneier aptly notes, the nothing-to-hide argument stems from a faulty "premise that privacy is about hiding a wrong." (par. 9)

Elsewhere, readers have to work a little harder to determine how Solove is using the source.

Solove also uses what we might call **hypothetical quotations**—sentences that quote not what someone actually said but what they *might* have said:

Signal phrase

Hypothetical quotation

> Many people say they're not worried. "I've got nothing to hide," they declare. "Only if you're doing something wrong should you worry, and then you don't deserve to keep it private." (par. 1)

> "My life's an open book," people might say. "I've got nothing to hide." (par. 16)

You can tell from a signal phrase like "people might say" or "many people say" that no actual person made the statement, but Solove does not always supply such cues.

| ANALYZE & WRITE |

Write a paragraph analyzing and evaluating Solove's use of quotations:

1. Find and mark the quotations, noting which actually quote someone and which are hypothetical.

2. Identify the quotations—real or hypothetical—that Solove agrees with and those that represent an opposing view.

3. How effective did you find Solove's quoting strategy, given his purpose and audience? (Remember that this article appeared in the *Chronicle of Higher Education*, a weekly newspaper for college faculty and administrators.)

AN EFFECTIVE RESPONSE: REFUTING BY DEMONSTRATING THE EFFECTS

As his title suggests, Solove refutes the claim that privacy does not matter "if you have 'nothing to hide.'" His primary way of refuting the nothing-to-hide argument is to argue that the collection and use of personal information (the cause) has negative effects, which he sometimes calls "problems" and sometimes calls "harms" (par 5).

ANALYZE & WRITE

Write a paragraph or two analyzing and evaluating Solove's use of cause and effect reasoning to refute the claim that privacy only matters if you have something to hide:

1 Reread paragraphs 6–14, noting where Solove discusses potential problems or harms that could result from the collection of personal data.

2 Choose one of these harms, and examine Solove's argument more closely. How does he support this part of the argument — for example, what are his reasons, his evidence, the values and beliefs he uses to appeal to his audience?

3 How effective are Solove's reasons and evidence for you? How effective might they have been for his original audience?

A CLEAR, LOGICAL ORGANIZATION: USING CUEING DEVICES

Solove uses a number of cueing devices to help readers keep track of his argument. Perhaps the most obvious and helpful cues are the topic sentences that begin each paragraph and the logical transitions ("One such harm . . . ," "Another potential problem . . . ," "A related problem . . . ," "Yet another problem . . ." [pars. 11–14]) that signal connections between and within paragraphs. In addition, Solove uses rhetorical questions, such as the series of "What if" questions in the final paragraph.

ANALYZE & WRITE

Write a paragraph or two analyzing and evaluating the effectiveness of Solove's use of cueing devices to help readers follow his argument:

1 Choose a couple of paragraphs that seem to you to use topic sentences and logical transitions effectively. Look closely at the way Solove uses these cueing devices, and determine what makes them so effective.

2 Highlight the rhetorical questions posed in paragraphs 12–14 and 16. Why do you imagine Solove uses so many of them, especially in the final paragraph? Given his purpose and audience, how effective do you think these rhetorical questions were likely to have been? How effective do you find them?

Consider possible topics: Issues concerning privacy.

[RESPOND]

Solove focuses on one concern about the erosion of privacy. You could write a similar type of essay, taking a position on issues such as state laws requiring women to have ultrasounds before terminating a pregnancy; airport security requiring passengers either to go through a full-body scanner or to submit to a "pat-down" before boarding a flight; cell phones making it possible for individuals to be located and tracked without their consent or knowledge; or houses, offices, and even people on the street being depicted on Google Maps without knowledge or consent.

REMIX

Remixing Your Position Argument

Position arguments occur regularly in genres and media besides the college essay. For example, Jessica Statsky's could use information from her argument in a report about injuries in children's sports, or she could have reworked some of the information as an infographic for coaches. Instead, Statsky decided to remix her essay as an article in her local PTA newsletter. (A remix takes all or part of a text in one genre to create a text in another genre or for another purpose or audience.) Since Statsky's position argument warned about the dangers of children's sports, she thought an appropriate target audience would be parents and that the best place to reach them would be through a parenting magazine or newsletter. So after writing her essay, she remixed it as an op-ed for her local PTA newsletter.

In the next section of this chapter, we ask you to craft your own position argument. After composing it as an essay, consider remixing it by presenting it (or a portion of it) in another genre or medium, or using it as part of an essay with a different purpose or audience.

Springfield PTA NEWS

Spring 2015

Connecting Parents, Teachers, and Students across the Valley

Important Dates!

Next PTA Meetings
- March 4
- April 1
- May 6

Parent Teacher Conferences
- March 9, 2-4 p.m. & 6-8 p.m.
- March 10, 3-6 p.m.
- March 11, 2-4 p.m. & 6-8 p.m.

Spring Break
- April 20-24

Could Little League Be Bad for Your Kids?

By Jessica Statsky

You probably knew that your child might face some risk on the playing field, but did you realize that chance of injury could be as high as 28 percent? The STOP Sports Injuries campaign offers these shocking statistics for athletes between 5 and 14. No wonder many children are afraid of being hurt! In fact, the Little League Website ranks fear of injury number 7 on their list of why kids quit.

Chance of Injury to Participants, Ages 5-14

Continued on p. 3

CONSIDER YOUR RHETORICAL SITUATION

Purpose: The purpose of your position argument is to convince readers that an issue is important (or at least open their eyes to it) and maybe persuade them to take action. If you remix your position argument, *which genre or medium would best allow you to make a compelling case for your position?*

Audience: The original audience for your position argument was your instructor and other students in your class. *Which audience would be most affected by your issue or be able to take action on it? What genre or medium would best help you reach that audience?*

Genre and medium: The genre of your position argument was the essay; the medium was textual, delivered either in print or online. If you remix your position argument, *what genre or medium would best help you persuade your target audience?*

The Writing Assignment

Compose a position argument on a controversial issue: Before you take a position, learn more about the issue and the debate surrounding it. Then frame the issue so readers recognize that it merits their attention, consider and respond to views that differ from yours, and develop a well-supported, clearly organized argument that will confirm, challenge, or change your readers' views.

This Guide to Writing will help you compose your own position argument and apply what you have learned from reading other position argument. The Starting Points chart here will help you find answers to many of your questions. Use the chart to find the guidance you need, when you need it.

STARTING POINTS: ARGUING A POSITION

How do I come up with an issue to write about?

- Consider possible topics: Issues concerning fairness. (p. 247)
- Consider possible topics: Issues facing students. (p. 252)
- Consider possible topics: Issues concerning privacy. (p. 259)
- Choose a controversial issue on which to take a position. (pp. 263–64)
- Test Your Choice: Choosing an Issue (p. 264)

A Focused, Well-Presented Issue

How can I effectively frame the issue for my readers?

- Assess the genre's basic features: A focused, well-presented issue. (pp. 232–33)
- A Focused, Well-Presented Issue: Framing an Argument for your Audience (p. 245)
- A Focused, Well-Presented Issue: Framing an Argument for a Diverse Group of Readers (p. 250)
- A Focused, Well-Presented Issue: Reframing through Contrast (p. 257)
- Frame the issue for your readers. (pp. 264–66)
- A Troubleshooting Guide: A Focused, Well-Presented Issue (p. 275)

(continued)

A Well-Supported Position

How do I come up with a plausible position?

- Assess the genre's basic features: A well-supported position. (pp. 233–34)
- Formulate a working thesis stating your position. (p. 266)
- Develop the reasons supporting your position. (p. 267)
- Research your position. (pp. 267–68)
- Use sources to reinforce your credibility. (pp. 268–69)

How do I come up with reasons and evidence supporting my position?

- A Well-Supported Position: Using Anecdotes and Examples (p. 246)
- A Well-Supported Position: Using Statistics (p. 251)
- A Well-Supported Position: Using Sources (p. 258)
- Formulate a working thesis stating your position. (p. 266)
- Develop the reasons supporting your position. (p. 267)
- Research your position. (pp. 267–68)

An Effective Response to Opposing Views

How do I respond to possible objections to my position?

- Assess the genre's basic features: An effective response to opposing views. (pp. 234–35)
- An Effective Response: Conceding and Refuting (p. 246)
- Identify and respond to your readers' likely reasons and objections. (pp. 269–71)
- Write the opening sentences. (p. 272)

How do I respond to possible alternative positions?

- Assess the genre's basic feature: An effective response to opposing views. (pp. 234–35)
- An Effective Response: Conceding and Refuting (p. 246)
- An Effective Response: Presenting and Reinterpreting Evidence to Undermine Objections (pp. 251–52)
- An Effective Response: Refuting by Demonstrating the Effects (pp. 258–59)
- Research your position. (pp. 267–68)
- Identify and respond to your readers' likely reasons and objections. (pp. 269–71)

Writing a Draft

GUIDE TO READING
▶ **GUIDE TO WRITING**
A WRITER AT WORK
THINKING CRITICALLY

263

A Clear, Logical Organization

> How can I help my readers follow my argument?

- Assess the genre's basic features: A clear, logical organization. (pp. 235–36)
- A Clear, Logical Organization: Creating Closure (p. 247)
- A Clear, Logical Organization: Providing Cues for Readers (p. 252)
- A Clear, Logical Organization: Using Cueing Devices (p. 259)
- Create an outline that will organize your argument effectively for your readers. (p. 271)
- A Troubleshooting Guide: A Clear, Logical Organization (p. 276)

Writing a Draft: Invention, Research, Planning, and Composing

The activities in this section will help you choose and research an issue as well as develop and organize an argument for your position. Your writing in response to many of these activities can be used in a rough draft that you will be able to improve after receiving feedback from your classmates and instructor. Do the activities in any order that makes sense to you (and your instructor), and return to them as needed as you revise.

Choose a controversial issue on which to take a position.

When choosing an issue, keep in mind that the issue must be

- controversial—an issue that people disagree about;
- arguable—a matter of opinion on which there is no absolute proof or authority;
- one that you can research, as necessary, in the time you have; and
- one that you care about.

Choosing an issue about which you have special interest or knowledge usually works best. For example, if you are thinking of addressing an issue of national concern, focus on a local or at least a specific aspect of it: For example, instead of addressing censorship in general, write about a local lawmaker's recent effort to propose a law censoring the Internet, a city council attempt to block access to Internet sites at the public library, or your school board's ban on certain textbooks.

You may already have an issue in mind. If you do, skip to Test Your Choice: Choosing an Issue (p. 264). If you do not, the topics that follow, in addition to those following the readings (pp. 247, 252, 259), may suggest an issue you can make your own:

- Should particular courses, community service, or an internship be a graduation requirement at your high school or college?
- Should students attending public colleges be required to pay higher tuition fees if they have been full-time students but have not graduated within four years?

- Should your large lecture or online courses have frequent (weekly or biweekly) exams instead of only a midterm and final?

- Should children raised in this country whose parents entered illegally be given an opportunity to become citizens upon finishing college or serving in the military?

- Should the football conference your school (or another school in the area) participates in be allowed to expand?

- Should you look primarily for a job that is well paid or for a job that is personally fulfilling or socially responsible?

- Should the racial, ethnic, or gender makeup of the police force resemble the makeup of the community it serves?

- Should public employees be allowed to unionize and to bargain collectively for improved working conditions, pay, or pensions?

- Should the state or federal government provide job training for those who are unemployed but able to work?

TEST YOUR CHOICE

Choosing an Issue

First, ask yourself the following questions:

- Does the issue matter to me? If not, could I argue convincingly that it ought to be of concern?

- Do I know enough about the issue to take a position that I can support effectively, or can I learn what I need to know in the time I have?

- Can I frame or reframe the issue in a way that might open readers to my point of view or help them reconsider what's at stake?

Then get together with two or three other students to take turns trying out your issues with potential readers. Ask group members questions like the following:

- What, if anything, do you already know about the issue?

- What about the issue (if anything) seems particularly intriguing or important to you?

- Do you already hold a position on this issue? If so, how strongly do you hold it? Would you be open to considering other points of view? If you don't care about the issue, what might convince you that it matters?

Consider these questions and their responses as you plan and draft your argument.

Frame the issue for your readers.

Once you have made a preliminary choice of an issue, consider how you can frame (or reframe) your issue so that readers who support opposing positions will listen to your argument. Consider how the issue has been debated in the past and what your readers are likely to think. Use the following questions and sentence strategies to help you put your ideas in writing.

Writing a Draft

GUIDE TO READING
▶ **GUIDE TO WRITING**
A WRITER AT WORK
THINKING CRITICALLY

265

WAYS IN

HOW CAN I EXPLORE THE ISSUE?

To explore the ISSUE, ask yourself questions like these and answer them using the sentence strategies as a jumping-off point.

What groups or notable individuals have shaped the debate on this issue? What positions have they taken?

▶ Although many people take Issue X for granted, groups A, B, and C oppose it on the grounds that _____ .

▶ Whereas supporters of Issue X have argued that _____ , opponents such as A, B, and C contend that _____ .

How has the issue, or people's opinions about the issue, changed? What makes the issue important now?

▶ Recent research/new reports have changed some people's minds on this issue. Instead of assuming _____ , many people now think _____ .

▶ The debate over Issue X was initially focused on _____ , but now the main concern seems to be that _____ .

WHAT DO MY READERS THINK?

To determine what your READERS are likely to think, ask yourself questions like these and answer them using the sentence strategies as a jumping-off point.

What values and concerns do my readers and I share regarding the issue?

▶ Concern about Issue X leads many of us to oppose _____ . We worry about the consequences if _____ is implemented.

▶ X is a basic human right that needs to be protected. But what does it mean in everyday practice when _____ ?

What fundamental differences in world-view or experience might keep me and my readers from agreeing?

▶ Those who disagree about Issue X often see it as a choice between _____ and _____ . But we don't have to choose between them.

▶ While others may view it as a matter of _____ , for me what's at stake is _____ .

HOW CAN I FRAME THE ISSUE EFFECTIVELY?

Once you have a good idea of how the issue has been debated and what your readers think, use these sentence strategies to FRAME the issue for your readers.

What is the issue, and why should my readers be concerned about it?

▶ Issue X is of concern to all members of group A because _____ .

EXAMPLE   I'm concerned about the high cost of tuition at state colleges like ours because students have to borrow more money to pay for their education than they will be able to earn once they graduate.

Why are popular approaches or attitudes inappropriate or inadequate?

▶ Although many in the community claim X, I think Y because _____ .

(continued)

> **EXAMPLE**   Some argue that college football players should be paid because of the money the school is earning off players' labor. I disagree. I think the current system should be maintained because without the money earned from football less lucrative sports programs, like fencing and wrestling, would have to be cut.

TEST YOUR CHOICE

Frame Your Issue
Ask two or three other students to consider the way you have framed your issue.

Presenters.   Briefly explain the values and concerns you think are at stake. (The sentence strategies in the Ways In section can help you articulate your position and approach.)

Listeners.   Tell the presenter how you respond to this way of framing the issue and why. You may use the language that follows as a model for structuring your response, or use language of your own.

▶ I'm also/not concerned about Issue X because _____.

▶ I agree/disagree with you about Issue X because _____.

⁞ Formulate a working thesis stating your position.

Try drafting a working thesis statement now. (If you prefer to conduct research or develop your argument before trying to formulate a thesis, skip this activity and return to it when you're ready.) As you develop your argument, rework your assertion to make it a compelling thesis statement by making the language clear and straightforward. You may also need to qualify it with words like *often, sometimes,* or *in part.* Forecast your reasons.

WAYS IN

HOW CAN I DEVISE AN ARGUABLE THESIS?

Begin by describing the **ISSUE,** *possibly indicating where others stand on it or what's at stake, and then stating your* **POSITION.** *These sentence strategies may help you get started:*

▶ At a recent meeting, many people argued _____. Although I sympathize with their point of view, this is ultimately a question of _____, not _____. Therefore, we must do _____.

▶ This issue is dividing our community. Some people argue X, others contend Y, and still others believe Z. However, it is in all of our interests to do _____ because _____.

▶ Conventional wisdom claims that _____. But I take a different view: I believe _____ because _____.

Writing a Draft

GUIDE TO READING
▶ GUIDE TO WRITING
A WRITER AT WORK
THINKING CRITICALLY

267

∷ Develop the reasons supporting your position.

The following activities will help you find plausible reasons and evidence for your position. You can do some focused research later to fill in the details, or skip ahead to conduct research now.

For more idea-generating strategies, see Chapter 11.

> **HOW CAN I COME UP WITH REASONS THAT SUPPORT MY POSITION?**
>
> *Write nonstop for at least five minutes exploring your reasons. Ask yourself questions like these:*
>
> - How can I show readers that my reasons lead logically to my position (**LOGOS**)?
> - How can I convince my readers that I am trustworthy (**ETHOS**)?
> - How can I appeal to their feelings (**PATHOS**)?
>
> At this point, don't worry about the exact language you will use in your final draft. Just write the reasons you hold your position and the evidence (such as anecdotes, examples, statistics, expert testimony) that supports it. Keep your readers and their values in mind—what would they find most convincing and why?
>
> *To brainstorm a list of reasons, try this:*
>
> - Start by writing your position at the top of the page.
> - On the left half of the page, list as many potential reasons as you can think of to support your position. (Don't judge at this point.)
> - On the right half of the page, make notes about the kinds of evidence you would need to provide to convince readers of each reason and to show how each supports your position.

WAYS IN

∷ Research your position.

Do some research to find out how others have argued in support of your position:

- Try entering keywords or phrases related to the issue or your position in the search box of an all-purpose database, such as *Academic OneFile* (InfoTrac) or *Academic Search Complete* (EBSCOHost), to find relevant articles in magazines and journals, or use the database Lexis/Nexis to find articles in newspapers. For example, Jessica Statsky could have tried a combination of keywords, such as *children's sports,* or variations on her terms (*youth sports*) to find relevant articles. A similar search of your library's catalog could also be conducted to locate books and other resources on your topic.

To learn more about searching a database or catalog, consult Chapter 21, pp. 609–13.

- If you think your issue has been dealt with by a government agency, explore the state, local, or tribal sections of USA.gov—the U.S. government's official Web portal—or visit the Library of Congress page on state government information (www.loc.gov/rr/news/stategov/stategov.html) and follow the links.

To learn more about finding government documents, consult Chapter 21, pp. 613–14.

To learn more about documenting sources, consult Chapter 24 or Chapter 25.

Remember to bookmark promising sites and to record the URL and information you will need to cite and document any sources or visuals you use.

Use sources to reinforce your credibility.

How you represent your sources can quickly establish your credibility (ethos)—or the reverse. For example, by briefly describing the author's credentials the first time you *summarize, paraphrase,* or *quote* from a source, you establish the source's authority and demonstrate that you have selected sources appropriately:

Signal phrase and author's credentials

Source summary

In-text citation follows quotation

> Martin Rablovsky, a former sports editor for the *New York Times,* says that in all his years of watching young children play organized sports, he has noticed very few of them smiling. "I've seen children enjoying a spontaneous pre-practice scrimmage become somber and serious when the coach's whistle blows," Rablovsky says . . . (qtd. in Coakley 94).

Quotations can also reinforce the accuracy of your summary or paraphrase and establish your fairness to opposing points of view. In the following sentence, Jessica Statsky demonstrates her fairness by quoting from the Web site of the Little League, a well-known organization, and she establishes her credibility by demonstrating that even those who disagree with her recognize that injuries occur:

Statsky's introduction: Summarizes source

In-text citation follows quotation

> Although the official Little League Web site acknowledges that children do risk injury playing baseball, it insists that "severe injuries . . . are infrequent," the risk "far less than the risk of riding a skateboard, a bicycle, or even the school bus" ("What about My Child?").

In both of these examples from "Children Need to Play, Not Compete" (pars. 5 and 3, respectively), Statsky introduces the source to her readers, explaining the relevance of the source material, including the author's credentials, for readers rather than leaving them to figure out its relevance for themselves.

Whenever you borrow information from sources, be sure to double-check that you are summarizing, paraphrasing, and quoting accurately and fairly. Compare Statsky's sentence with the source passage (that follows). (The portions she uses are highlighted.) Notice that she has inserted ellipsis (. . .) to indicate that she has left out words from her source's second sentence.

Source

> Injuries seem to be inevitable in any rigorous activity, especially if players are new to the sport and unfamiliar with its demands. But because of the safety precautions taken in Little League, severe injuries such as bone fractures are infrequent. Most injuries are sprains and strains, abrasions and cuts and bruises. The risk of serious injury in Little League Baseball is far less than the risk of riding a skateboard, a bicycle, or even the school bus.

Writing a Draft

GUIDE TO READING
GUIDE TO WRITING
A WRITER AT WORK
THINKING CRITICALLY

269

In both of the preceding examples, Statsky uses quotation marks to indicate that she is borrowing the words of a source and provides an in-text citation so that readers can locate the sources in her list of works cited. Doing both is essential to avoiding plagiarism; one or the other is not enough.

For more on integrating language from sources into your own sentences and avoiding plagiarism, see Chapter 23, pp. 633–35.

⁞ Identify and respond to your readers' likely reasons and objections.

The following activity will help you anticipate reasons your readers may use to support their argument or objections they may have. You may want to return to this activity as you do additional research and learn more about the issue and the arguments people make. Return to the section "Research your position" on pp. 267–68 or consult Chapter 21, "Finding Sources and Conducting Field Research."

HOW CAN I FIGURE OUT WHAT MY READERS WILL BE CONCERNED ABOUT?

1. List the **REASONS** you expect your readers to have for their position and the **OBJECTIONS** (including those based on logical fallacies) you expect them to raise to your argument. How do your **VALUES**, **BELIEFS**, and **PRIORITIES** differ from those of your readers?

2. *Analyze your list of likely* **REASONS** *and* **OBJECTIONS**. Which can you refute, and how? Which may you need to concede?

HOW CAN I RESPOND TO READERS' REASONS AND OBJECTIONS?

Now, choose a **REASON** *or* **OBJECTION**, *and try out a response:*

1. Summarize it accurately and fairly. (Do not commit the "straw man" fallacy of knocking down something that no one really takes seriously.)

2. Decide whether you can refute it, need to concede it, or can refute part and concede part.

Try sentence strategies like these to **REFUTE**, **CONCEDE**, *or* **CONCEDE** *and* **REFUTE** *reasons supporting readers' arguments or their objections to your argument:*

To Refute

Reason or Objection Lacks Credible Support

▶ My opponents cite research to support their reason/objection, but the credibility of that research is questionable because _____. In contrast, reliable research by Professor X shows _____.

▶ This reason/objection seems plausible on the surface, but evidence shows _____.

WAYS IN

For more logical fallacies see Chapter 19, p. 595.

(continued)

Readers' Values and Concerns Are Better Served by Your Position

▶ Some insist _____ without realizing that it would take away a basic right/make things even worse.

▶ X and Y think this issue is about _____. But what is really at stake here is _____.

Reasoning Is Flawed

▶ Proponents object to my argument on the grounds that _____. However, they are confusing results with causes. What I am arguing is _____.

▶ Polls show that most people favor _____, but an opinion's popularity does not make it true or right.

▶ While most would agree that _____, it does not necessarily follow that _____.

Times Have Changed

▶ One common complaint is _____. In recent years, however, _____.

To Concede

Accept an Objection Well Taken

▶ To be sure, _____ is true.

▶ Granted, _____ must be taken into consideration.

Qualify on Common Ground

▶ Some people argue that _____. I understand this reservation, and therefore, I think we should _____.

Refocus Your Argument

▶ A common concern about this issue is _____. That's why my argument focuses on [a different aspect of the issue].

To Concede and Refute

And Instead of *Or*

▶ I agree that _____ is important, and so is _____.

Yes, But

▶ I agree that _____ is important, but my opponents also need to consider _____.

On the One Hand . . . On the Other Hand

▶ On the one hand, I accept X's argument that _____, but on the other hand, I still think _____ is ultimately more important because _____.

Note: If a reason or an objection seems so damaging that you cannot refute it convincingly or concede it without undermining your own argument, discuss with your instructor how you could modify your position or whether you should choose a new issue to write about. If you do not know enough about readers' views to anticipate their reasons or likely objections to your argument, do more research.

Create an outline that will organize your argument effectively for your readers.

Whether you have rough notes or a complete draft, making an outline of what you have written can help you organize the essay effectively for your audience. Compare the possible outlines that follow to see how you might organize your essay depending on whether your readers primarily agree or disagree with you.

Readers Primarily Agree with You

Strengthen their convictions by organizing your argument around a series of reasons backed by supporting evidence or by refuting opposing arguments point by point:

I. **Presentation of the issue**

II. **Thesis statement:** A direct statement of your position

III. **Your most plausible reasons and evidence**

IV. **Concession or refutation of opposing reasons or objections to your argument**

V. **Conclusion:** Reaffirmation of your position

Readers Primarily Disagree with You

Begin by emphasizing common ground, and make a concession to show that you have considered the opposing position carefully and with an open mind:

I. **Presentation of the issue:** Reframe the issue in terms of common values

II. **Concession:** Acknowledge the wisdom of an aspect of the opposing position

III. **Thesis statement:** A direct statement of your position, qualified as necessary

IV. **Your most plausible reasons and evidence**

V. **Conclusion:** Reiteration of shared values

Whatever organizational strategy you adopt, do not hesitate to change your outline as necessary while drafting and revising. For instance, you might find it more effective to hold back on presenting your own position until you have discussed unacceptable alternatives. Or you might find a more powerful way to order the reasons for supporting your position. The purpose of an outline is to identify the basic components of your argument and to help you organize them effectively, not to lock you into a particular structure.

For more on outlining, see Chapter 11, pp. 490–94.

⁙ Consider document design.

Think about whether visual or audio elements—photographs, graphics, snippets of interviews with experts—would strengthen your position argument. If you can recall position arguments you've read in newspapers (op-eds and editorials generally argue for positions), on Web pages, and on blogs, what visual or audio elements were used to establish the writer's credibility and to appeal to the reader logically, ethically, or emotionally? Position arguments do not require visual or audio examples to be effective, but these elements can be helpful.

Note: Be sure to cite the source of visual or audio elements you didn't create, and get permission from the source if your essay is going to be published on a Web site that will be accessible outside of your class or college.

Consider also whether your readers might benefit from design features such as headings, bulleted or numbered lists, or other typographic elements that can make your argument easier to follow.

Write the opening sentences.

Review what you have already written to see if you have something that would help you frame or reframe the issue for your readers while also grabbing their attention:

Begin with **statistics** *that would help readers grasp the importance of your topic:*

> "Organized sports for young people have become an institution in North America," reports sports journalist Steve Silverman, attracting more than 44 million youngsters according to a recent survey by the National Council of Youth Sports ("History"). (Statsky, par. 1)

Use a **personal anecdote** *to make the issue tangible or appeal to readers' emotions:*

> Let me tell you a little about Matthew. . . . (Bramson, par. 1)

Start with a **surprising statement** *to capture readers' attention:*

> McDonald's is bad for your kids. (Etzioni, par. 1)

Use a **hypothetical quotation** *to indicate how people typically think about the issue:*

> When the government gathers or analyzes personal information, many people say they're not worried. "I've got nothing to hide," they declare. (Solove, par. 1)

Draft your position argument.

By this point, you have done a lot of writing to

- devise a focused, well-presented issue and take a position on it
- frame your issue so that readers will be open to your argument
- support your position with reasons and evidence your readers will find persuasive
- refute or concede alternative viewpoints on the issue
- organize your ideas to make them clear, logical, and effective for readers

Now stitch that material together to create a draft. The next two parts of this Guide to Writing will help you evaluate and improve that draft.

Evaluating the Draft: Using Peer Review

Your instructor may arrange a peer review session in class or online, where you can exchange drafts with your classmates and give each other a thoughtful critical reading—pointing out what works well and suggesting ways to improve the draft. A good critical reading does three things:

1. It lets the writer know how the reader understands the point of the argument.

2. It praises what works best.

3. It indicates where the draft could be improved and makes suggestions how to improve it.

One strategy for evaluating a draft is to use the basic features of a position argument as a guide.

A PEER REVIEW GUIDE

A Focused, Well-Presented Issue

> How well does the writer present the issue?

Summarize: Tell the writer what you understand the issue to be. If you were already familiar with it and understand it differently, briefly explain.

Praise: Give an example from the essay where the issue and its significance come across effectively.

Critique: Tell the writer where more information about the issue is needed, where more might be done to establish its seriousness, or how the issue could be framed or reframed in a way that would better prepare readers for the argument.

A Well-Supported Position

> How well does the writer argue in support of the position?

Summarize: Underline the thesis statement and the main reasons.

Praise: Give an example in the essay where the argument is especially effective; for example, indicate which reason is especially convincing or which supporting evidence is particularly compelling.

Critique: Tell the writer where the argument could be strengthened; for example, indicate how the thesis statement could be made clearer or more appropriately qualified, how the argument could be developed, or where additional support is needed.

(continued)

An Effective Response to Opposing Views

How effectively has the writer responded to others' reasons and likely objections?

Summarize: Identify where the writer responds to a reason others use to support their argument or an objection they have to the writer's argument.

Praise: Give an example in the essay where a concession seems particularly well done or a refutation is convincing.

Critique: Tell the writer how a concession or refutation could be made more effective, identify a reason or objection the writer should respond to, or note where common ground could be found.

A Clear, Logical Organization

How clearly and logically has the writer organized the argument?

Summarize: Find the sentence(s) in which the writer states the thesis and forecasts supporting reasons, as well as transitions or repeated key words and phrases.

Praise: Give an example of how or where the essay succeeds in being especially easy to read, perhaps in its overall organization, clear presentation of the thesis, clear transitions, or effective opening or closing.

Critique: Tell the writer where the readability could be improved. Can you, for example, suggest better forecasting or clearer transitions? If the overall organization of the essay needs work, make suggestions for rearranging parts or strengthening connections.

Before concluding your peer review, be sure to address any of the writer's concerns that have not been discussed already.

Making Comments Electronically   Most word processing software offers features that allow you to insert comments directly into the text of someone else's document. Many readers prefer to make their comments this way because it tends to be faster than writing on hard copy and space is virtually unlimited; it also eliminates the process of deciphering handwritten comments. Where such features are not available, simply typing comments directly into a document in a contrasting color can provide the same advantages.

Improving the Draft: Revising, Editing, and Proofreading

Start improving your draft by reflecting on what you have written thus far:

- Review critical reading comments from your classmates, instructor, or writing center tutor: What problems are your readers identifying?
- Consider your invention writing: What else should you consider?
- Review your draft: What can you do to support your position more effectively?

Improving the Draft

GUIDE TO READING
GUIDE TO WRITING
A WRITER AT WORK
THINKING CRITICALLY

275

Revise your draft.

If your readers are having difficulty with your draft, or if you think there is room for improvement, try some of the strategies listed in the Troubleshooting Guide that follows. It can help you fine-tune your presentation of the genre's basic features.

A TROUBLESHOOTING GUIDE

A Focused, Well-Presented Issue

My readers don't get the point.

- Quote experts or add information—statistics, examples, anecdotes, and so on—to help readers understand what's at stake.
- Consider adding visuals, such as photos, graphs, tables, or charts to present the issue more clearly.

My readers have a different perspective on the issue than I do.

- Show the limitations of how the issue has traditionally been understood.
- Reframe the issue by showing how it relates to values, concerns, needs, and priorities you share with readers.
- Give concrete examples or anecdotes, facts, and details that could help readers see the issue as you see it.

A Well-Supported Position

My readers do not find my argument clear and/or persuasive.

- Revisit your thesis statement to make sure your position is stated clearly and directly.
- Reconsider your reasons, or explain how they support your position.
- Add supporting evidence—statistics, examples, authorities, and so on.
- Consider adding visuals, graphs, tables, or charts to support your argument.
- Strengthen the logical, ethical, and/or emotional appeals of your argument.
- Try outlining your argument; if your organization is weak or illogical, or if your transitional strategies are not working, try reorganizing the material, adding transitional words and phrases, or repeating key words strategically.

An Effective Response to Opposing Views

My readers question my response to opposing arguments or objections to my argument.

- If your refutation is weak, strengthen it with additional or more compelling reasons and evidence.
- If your concession weakens your argument, qualify your position with words like *sometimes* or *often*.
- Consider adding a refutation to your concession.

(continued)

> My readers are confused by my essay or find it difficult to follow.

A Clear, Logical Organization

- Outline your essay. If necessary, move, add, or delete sections to strengthen coherence.
- Consider adding a forecasting statement with key terms that are repeated in topic sentences throughout the essay.
- Check for appropriate transitions between sentences, paragraphs, and major sections of your essay.
- Review your opening and closing paragraphs. Be sure that your thesis is clearly expressed and that you reaffirm your position in your closing.

Edit and proofread your draft.

Students frequently struggle to maintain a neutral tone when arguing a position they hold dearly. Our research also indicates that incorrect comma usage in sentences with *coordinating conjunctions* and punctuation errors in sentences that use *conjunctive adverbs* are common in position arguments. The following guidelines will help you check your essay for these common errors.

Editing for Tone

To demonstrate that you are treating alternative viewpoints fairly, use words with a positive or neutral connotation (emotional resonance) and avoid name-calling.

▶ Too often . . . the drive to win turns parents ~~into~~ monsters ~~threatening~~ umpires.
                      encourages   *to threaten*

As you edit your position argument, also watch out for language that is puffed up or pompous:

▶ A coach who had attended the Adelphi workshop tried to ~~operationalize~~ what he had *(put into practice)* learned there, but the players' ~~progenitors~~ *(parents)* would not support him.

Using Commas before Coordinating Conjunctions

In essays that argue a position, writers often use coordinating conjunctions (*and, but, for, or, nor, so,* and *yet*) to join related **independent clauses**—groups of words that can stand alone as complete sentences—to create *compound sentences.* Consider this example from Jessica Statsky's essay:

              — independent clause 1 —   coord. conj.   — independent clause 2 —

▶ Winning and losing may be an inevitable part of adult life, but they should not be part of childhood. (par. 6)
                                    comma

Improving the Draft

GUIDE TO READING
GUIDE TO WRITING
▶ A WRITER AT WORK
THINKING CRITICALLY

277

In this sentence, Statsky links two complete ideas of equal importance with the coordinating conjunction *but* to emphasize contrast.

The Problem Two common errors occur in sentences like these:

1. A comma may be left out when two independent clauses are linked by a coordinating conjunction.

2. A comma may be inserted before the coordinating conjunction when one of the sentence parts is not an independent clause.

The Correction Add a comma before coordinating conjunctions that join two independent clauses, as in the following example:

▶ The new immigration laws will bring in more skilled people but their presence will take jobs away from other Americans.

Omit the comma when coordinating conjunctions join phrases that are not independent clauses:

▶ We need people with special talents, and diverse skills to make the United States a stronger nation.

Avoiding Comma Splices When Using Conjunctive Adverbs to Link Independent Clauses

Conjunctive adverbs (such as *consequently, furthermore, however, moreover, therefore,* and *thus*) indicate the logical relationships among ideas. For example, words like *thus* and *therefore* are used to alert readers that a conclusion is coming, and words like *furthermore* and *moreover* are used to alert readers to expect additional ideas on the same topic. When writers take a position, they often use conjunctive adverbs to link independent clauses.

Consider this example:

conj. adv.

├──────── independent clause 1 ────────┤ ├───

▶ Children watching television recognize violence but not its intention ; thus, they

├──── independent clause 2 ────┤   semicolon   comma
become desensitized to violence.

In this sentence, the writer uses the word *thus* to indicate that he is drawing a conclusion.

The Problem A *comma splice* is one error that often occurs when writers use a comma before a conjunctive adverb linking two independent clauses.

The Correction Use a semicolon before and a comma after a conjunctive adverb when it links two independent clauses:

▶ The recent vote on increasing student fees produced a disappointing turnout, moreover, the presence of campaign literature on ballot tables violated voting procedures.

> **A Note on Grammar and Spelling Checkers**
> These tools can be helpful, but do not rely on them exclusively to catch errors in your text: Spelling checkers cannot catch misspellings that are themselves words, such as *to* for *too*. Grammar checkers miss some problems, sometimes give faulty advice for fixing problems, and can flag correct items as wrong. Use these tools as a second line of defense after your own (and, ideally, another reader's) editing and proofreading efforts.

Make sure that both parts of the sentence are independent clauses before inserting a semicolon, a conjunctive adverb, and a comma to link them. If one or both parts cannot stand alone, add a subject, a verb, or both as needed to avoid a *sentence fragment*:

they do not recognize

▶ Children watching television recognize violence; however, not its intention.

Alternatively, you may replace the semicolon, conjunctive adverb, and comma with a coordinating conjunction:

but

▶ Children watching television recognize violence; however, not its intention.

A Common Problem for Multilingual Writers: Subtle Differences in Meaning

Because the distinctions in meaning among some common conjunctive adverbs are subtle, nonnative speakers often have difficulty using them accurately. For example, the difference between *however* and *nevertheless* is small; each is used to introduce a contrasting statement. But *nevertheless* emphasizes the contrast, whereas *however* softens it. Check usage of such terms in an English dictionary rather than a bilingual one. *The American Heritage Dictionary of the English Language* has special usage notes to help distinguish frequently confused words.

A WRITER AT WORK

Jessica Statsky's Response to Opposing Positions

In this section, we look at how Jessica Statsky tried to anticipate opposing positions and respond to them. To understand Statsky's thinking about possible opposing positions, look first at the invention writing she did while analyzing her potential readers.

Three potential groups of readers

Two groups of parents

I think I will write mainly to parents who are considering letting their children get involved in competitive sports and to those whose children are already on teams and who don't know about the possible dangers. Parents who are really into competition and winning probably couldn't be swayed by my arguments anyway. I don't know how to reach coaches (but aren't they also parents?) or league organizers. I'll tell parents some horror stories and present solid evidence from psychologists that competitive sports can really harm children under the age of twelve. I think they'll be impressed with this scientific evidence.

Jessica Statsky's Response to Opposing Positions   GUIDE TO READING
GUIDE TO WRITING
▶ A WRITER AT WORK
THINKING CRITICALLY

279

> I share with parents one important value: the best interests of children. Competition really works against children's best interests. Maybe parents' magazines (don't know of any specific ones) publish essays like mine.

Notice that Statsky lists three potential groups of readers here, but she is already leaning toward making parents her primary audience. Moreover, she divides these parents into two camps: those who are new to organized sports and unaware of the adverse effects of competition, and those who are really into winning. Statsky decides early on against trying to change the minds of parents who place great value on winning. But as you will see in the next excerpt from her invention writing, Statsky gave a lot of thought to the position these parents would likely favor.

Listing Reasons for the Opposing Position

In continuing her invention writing, Statsky listed the following reasons she thought others might have for their position that organized competitive sports teach young children valuable skills:

> --because competition teaches children how to succeed in later life
> --because competition--especially winning--is fun
> --because competition boosts children's self-esteem
> --because competition gives children an incentive to excel

This list appears to pose serious challenges to Statsky's argument, but she benefited by considering the reasons her readers might give for opposing her position before she drafted her essay. By preparing this list, she gained insight into how she had to develop her own argument in light of these predictable arguments, and she could begin thinking about which reasons she might concede and which she had to refute. Her essay ultimately gained authority because she could demonstrate a good understanding of the opposing arguments that might be offered by her primary readers—parents who have not considered the dangers of competition for young children.

Conceding a Plausible Reason

Looking over her list of reasons, Statsky decided that she could accommodate readers by conceding that competitive sports can sometimes be fun for children—at least for those who win. Here are her invention notes:

> It is true that children do sometimes enjoy getting prizes and being recognized as winners in competitions adults set up for them. I remember feeling very excited when our sixth-grade relay team won a race at our school's sports day. And I felt really good when I would occasionally win the candy bar for being the last one standing in classroom spelling contests. But when I think about these events, it's the activity itself I remember as the main fun, not the winning. I think I can concede that winning is exciting to six- to twelve-year-olds, while arguing that it's not as important as adults might think. I hope this will win me some friends among readers who are undecided about my position.

We can see this concession in paragraph 5 of Statsky's revised essay (p. 238), in which she concedes that sports should be fun but quotes an authority who argues that even fun is jeopardized when competition becomes intense.

Refuting an Implausible Reason

Statsky recognized that she had to attempt to refute the other objections in her list. She chose the first reason in her list and tried out the following refutation:

> It irritates me that adults are so eager to make first and second graders go into training for getting and keeping jobs as adults. I don't see why the pressures on adults need to be put on children. Anyway, both my parents tell me that in their jobs, cooperation and teamwork are keys to success. You can't get ahead unless you're effective in working with others. Maybe we should be training children and even high school and college students in the skills necessary for cooperation, rather than competition. Sports and physical activity are important for children, but elementary schools should emphasize achievement rather than competition--race against the clock rather than against each other. Rewards could be given for gains in speed or strength instead of for defeating somebody in a competition.

This brief invention activity led to the argument in paragraph 10 of the revised essay (p. 240), in which Statsky acknowledges the importance of competition for success in school and work, but goes on to argue that cooperation is also important. To support this part of her argument, she gives examples in paragraph 11 of sports programs that emphasize cooperation over competition.

You can see from Statsky's revised essay that her refutation of this opposing argument runs through her entire essay. The invention activities Statsky did advanced her thinking about her readers and purpose; they also brought an early, productive focus to her research on competition in children's sports.

THINKING CRITICALLY

To think critically means to use all of the knowledge you have acquired from the information in this chapter, your own writing, the writing of other students, and class discussions to reflect deeply on your work for this assignment and the genre (or type) of writing you have produced. The benefit of thinking critically is proven and important: Thinking critically about what you have learned will help you remember it longer, ensuring that you will be able to put it to good use well beyond this writing course.

Reflecting on What You Have Learned

In this chapter, you have learned a great deal about arguing for a position from reading several position arguments and from writing one of your own. To consolidate your learning, reflect not only on what you learned but also on how you learned it.

<hr>

ANALYZE & WRITE

Write a blog post to classmates, a letter to your instructor, or an e-mail message to a student who will take this course next term, using the writing prompt that seems most productive for you:

- Explain how your purpose and audience influenced one of your decisions as a writer, such as how you presented the issue, the strategies you used in arguing your position, or the ways in which you attempted to counter possible objections.

- Discuss what you learned about yourself as a writer in the process of writing this essay. For example, what part of the process did you find most challenging? Did you try anything new, like getting a critical reading of your draft or outlining your draft in order to revise it?

- Choose one of the readings in this chapter and explain how it influenced your essay. Be sure to cite specific examples from your essay and the reading.

- If you got good advice from a critical reader, explain exactly how the person helped you—perhaps by questioning the way you addressed your audience or the kinds of evidence you offered in support of your position.

Reflecting on the Genre

While you were writing your position argument, we encouraged you to frame your position in terms of values you share with your readers and to provide logical reasons and evidence in support of your position. However, some critics argue that privileging reasoned argument over other ways of arguing is merely a means to control dissent. Instead of expressing what may be legitimate outrage and inciting public concern through passionate language, dissenters are urged to be dispassionate and reasonable even though they are arguing with people whose views they find repugnant. In the end, trying to present a well-reasoned, well-supported argument may serve to maintain the status quo by silencing the more radical voices within the community. What do you think about this controversy?

<hr>

ANALYZE & WRITE

Write a page or two explaining your ideas about whether the genre's requirement that writers give reasons and support suppresses dissent. Connect your ideas to your own position argument and to the readings in this chapter. In your discussion, you might consider one or more of the following questions:

1. **In your own experience of arguing a position on a controversial issue, did having to give reasons and support discourage you from choosing any particular issue or from expressing strong feelings?** Reflect on the issues you listed as possible subjects for your essay and how you made your choice. Did you reject any issues

because you could not come up with reasons and support for your position? When you made your choice, did you think about whether you could be dispassionate and reasonable about it?

2 **Consider the readings in this chapter and the position arguments you read by other students in the class.** Do you think any of these writers felt limited by the need to give reasons and support for their position? Which of the essays you read, if any, seemed to you to express strong feelings about the issue? Which, if any, seemed dispassionate?

3 **Consider the kind of arguing you typically witness in the media—radio, television, newspapers, magazines, the Internet.** In the media, have giving reasons and support and anticipating readers' objections been replaced with a more contentious, in-your-face style of arguing? Think of media examples of these two different ways of arguing. What do these examples lead you to conclude about the contention that reasoned argument can stifle dissent?

7

Proposing a Solution

Can a student convince his professor that giving infrequent, high-stakes exams is a bad idea? Will a marine biologist's proposal to save orcas by moving them from theme parks to wildlife sanctuaries float? Should we try out a law professor's idea to solve the shortage of kidneys for transplantation? These are some of the problems and solutions addressed by the proposals in this chapter. Proposals like these need, first, to convince their audience that the problem actually exists and is serious and, second, that the proposed solution will not only solve the problem but is the best available option.

284 CHAPTER 7 Proposing a Solution

People make proposals for various purposes and audiences and publish them in a variety of media. For example, students in a health sciences course collaborated on a project to build a Web page that informs the community about a water quality problem, evaluates the feasibility of alternative solutions, and argues for their preferred solution, and a blogger posted a proposal to solve the problem of the rising college loan default rate, arguing that truth in advertising laws should be used to crack down on for-profit colleges that use aggressive recruiting tactics to target low-income students.

In this chapter, we ask you to identify a problem you care about and write a proposal to solve it. By analyzing the selections in the Guide to Reading that follows, you will learn how to make a convincing case for the solution you propose. The Guide to Writing later in the chapter will show you ways to use the basic features of the genre to make your proposal inventive as well as practical.

PRACTICING THE GENRE

Arguing That a Solution Is Feasible

Proposals often succeed or fail on the strength of the argument that the proposed solution is feasible. To practice making a feasibility argument, get together with two or three other students and follow these guidelines:

Part 1. Begin by identifying a problem you face as a student in one of your college courses (this course or a different one). Next, discuss the problem in your group, and choose one of the following solutions (or think of another solution): The instructor should drop one of the assigned books, offer special study sessions, or post study sheets on the readings.

Then discuss the following questions to determine how you could demonstrate to the instructor that your solution is feasible:

- Is it doable? List specific steps that the instructor would need to take.

- Is it worth doing? Identify what implementing the solution would cost the instructor (in terms of time, for example) compared to how much it would benefit the students (in terms of learning, for example).

- Would it work? To prove it would actually help to solve the problem, you could show that it eliminates a cause of the problem or that it has worked elsewhere, for example.

Part 2. As a group, discuss what you learned.

- **What did you learn about demonstrating that your proposed solution is feasible?** Typically, a proposal tries to convince the audience that the solution is doable, worth the time and money, and would actually help solve the problem. Are all three elements of feasibility necessary? If not, which is most important? Why?

- **Think about how the rhetorical situation of your proposal—the purpose, audience, and medium—affects how you need to argue for your solution's feasibility.** For example, how would you change your argument about negative effects of relying on high-stakes exams if you were trying to convince a group of professors at a conference about undergraduate teaching versus an administrator who controls the budget or schedule? Would feasibility be equally important to both groups?

Analyzing Proposals

As you read the selections in this chapter, you will see how different writers argue for a solution:

- Patrick O'Malley argues for more low-stakes quizzes (pp. 290–96).
- Naomi Rose proposes that marine theme parks create orca sanctuaries (pp. 296–99).
- Eric Posner argues for an "altruism exchange" to motivate kidney donors (pp. 302–5).
- Kelly D. Brownell and Thomas R. Frieden propose raising taxes on sugary soft drinks as a way to stem the "obesity epidemic" (pp. 308–12).

Analyzing how these writers define their problems, argue for their solutions, respond to opposing views, and organize their writing will help you see how you can use these techniques to make your own proposals clear and compelling for your readers.

Determine the writer's purpose and audience.

When reading the proposals that follow, ask yourself questions like these:

What seems to be the writer's purpose (or multiple purposes)?

- to convince readers that the problem truly exists and needs immediate action?
- to persuade readers that the writer's proposed solution is better than alternative solutions?
- to rekindle readers' interest in a long-standing problem?

What does the writer assume about the audience?

- that readers will be unaware of the problem?
- that they will recognize the existence of the problem but fail to take it seriously?
- that they will think the problem has already been solved?
- that they will prefer an alternative solution?

Assess the genre's basic features.

As you read the proposals in this chapter, consider how different authors incorporate the basic features of the genre. The examples that follow are taken from the reading selections that appear later in this Guide to Reading.

> **■■ Basic Features**
> A Focused, Well-Defined Problem
> A Well-Argued Solution
> An Effective Response to Objections and Alternative Solutions
> A Clear, Logical Explanation

A FOCUSED, WELL-DEFINED PROBLEM

Read first to see how the writer defines or frames the problem. Framing a problem is a way of preparing readers for the proposed solution by focusing on the aspect of the problem the proposal tries to solve. In "More Testing, More Learning," for example, student Patrick O'Malley frames the problem in terms of the detrimental effects of high-stakes exams on students' learning. If O'Malley were writing to students instead of their teachers, he might have framed the problem in terms of students' poor study habits or procrastination. By framing the problem as he does, he indicates that teachers, rather than students, have the ability to solve the problem and tries to convince readers that it is real and serious.

Determine, how (and how well) the writer frames the problem, for example,

▪ by recounting *anecdotes* or constructing *scenarios* to show how the problem affects people:

EXAMPLE   It's late at night. The final's tomorrow. (O'Malley, par. 1)

▪ by giving *examples* to make the problem less abstract:

EXAMPLE   For example, research by Karpicke and Blunt (2011) published in *Science* found that testing was more effective than other, more traditional methods of studying both for comprehension and for analysis. (O'Malley, par. 4)

▪ by listing the negative *effects* of the problem:

Effect

Transition

Cause

EXAMPLE   The latest data (Rose, 2011) show that orcas are more than three times as likely to die at any age in captivity as they are in the wild. This . . . is probably the result of several factors. . . . Second, they are in artificial and often incompatible social groups. This contributes to chronic stress, which can depress the immune system and leave captive orcas susceptible to infections they would normally fight off in the wild. . . . These factors boil down simply to this: Captivity kills orcas. (Rose, par. 2)

Consider also how the writer uses research studies and statistics to demonstrate the severity of the problem. Look for source material and notice whether the writer emphasizes the credibility of the research by including the expert's name and credentials or by identifying the publication in which the study appeared at the beginning of the sentence in which the study is mentioned:

Emphasizes credibility

▶ Dr. X at University of Y has found that ....

▶ A study published in *Journal X* shows that ....

EXAMPLE   A 2006 study reported in the journal *Psychological Science* concluded that "taking repeated tests . . . leads to better . . . retention" . . . according to the study's coauthors, Henry L. Roediger and Jeffrey Karpicke (ScienceWatch.com, 2008). (O'Malley, par. 4)

Alternatively, the writer may emphasize the data by putting the results of the study up front and identifying the source later in the sentence or in the parenthetical citation, as in the following:

Emphasizes data

▶ .... percent of group X believe/work/struggle ....

EXAMPLE   Very few captive orcas make it to midlife (approximately 30 years for males and 45 for females) and not one out of more than 200 held in captivity has ever come close to old age (60 for males, 80 for females) (*Killer Whale*). (Rose, par. 3)

In contexts where sources are not normally cited (such as newspapers and certain Web sites) or where the information is widely available, the writer may cite statistics without indicating a specific source:

▶ Research findings show that .... (source).

EXAMPLE   More than 100,000 people languish on the waitlist for kidneys, thousands of them dying before they receive a transplant. In 2012, almost 35,000 people joined the waitlist, while only 17,000 received transplants. (Posner, par. 1)

In academic writing the sources of such statistics must be cited.

A WELL-ARGUED SOLUTION

To argue convincingly for a solution to a problem, writers need to *make clear exactly what is being proposed and offer supporting reasons and evidence* showing that the proposed solution

▪ will help solve the problem;

▪ can be implemented;

▪ is worth the expense, time, and effort to do so.

Read first to find the proposed solution, usually declared in a *thesis statement* early in the essay. Typically, the thesis describes the proposed solution briefly and indicates how it would solve the problem, as in this example, which contrasts the problem's disadvantages with the solution's benefits:

So, not only do high-stakes exams *discourage frequent study and undermine students' performance, they also do long-term damage to students' cognitive development.* If professors gave brief exams at frequent intervals, students would be spurred to learn more and worry less. They would study more regularly, perform better on tests, and enhance their cognitive functioning. (O'Malley, par. 2)

Problem and its *disadvantages*

Thesis proposing solution and its benefits

Then check to see how the writer presents the supporting reasons *and* evidence, *and consider how compelling the argument is likely to be, given the writer's purpose and audience.* The following sentence strategies and accompanying examples suggest the kinds of reasons and evidence proposal writers often employ to present their argument, as well as the writing strategies they represent:

▪ The proposed solution would reduce or eliminate a major cause of the problem and would (or could) have beneficial effects:

▶ As research shows, solution X would stop something harmful, change habits, reverse a decline, and would lead to/encourage ....

Cause/effect

EXAMPLE A review conducted by Yale University's Rudd Center for Food Policy and Obesity suggested that . . . a tax on sugared beverages would encourage consumers to switch to more healthful beverages, which would lead to reduced caloric intake and less weight gain. (Brownell and Frieden, par. 3)

▨ A similar solution has worked elsewhere:

Comparison ▶ Solution X has worked for problem Y, so it could work for this problem as well.

EXAMPLE Taxes on tobacco products have been highly effective in reducing consumption, and data indicate that higher prices also reduce soda consumption. (Brownell and Frieden, par. 3)

▨ The necessary steps to put the solution into practice can be taken without excessive cost or inconvenience:

Process analysis ▶ This solution is easy to implement: first do ⎯⎯⎯⎯⎯ and then do ⎯⎯⎯⎯⎯.

EXAMPLE Ideally, a professor would give an in-class test or quiz after each unit. . . . These exams should be given weekly or at least twice monthly. . . . Exams should take no more than 15 or 20 minutes. (O'Malley, par. 3)

▨ Stakeholders could come together behind the proposal ⎯⎯⎯⎯⎯.

▶ X and Y are working together on ⎯⎯⎯⎯⎯.

EXAMPLE Merlin Entertainments is pursuing the establishment of the world's first bottlenose dolphin sanctuary with Whale and Dolphin Conservation ("WDCS," 2009), a nonprofit environmental group. (Rose, par. 6)

AN EFFECTIVE RESPONSE TO OBJECTIONS AND ALTERNATIVE SOLUTIONS

Read to see how the writer responds to readers' likely objections and to the alternative solutions readers may prefer, for example,

▨ by **conceding** (accepting) a valid objection and modifying the argument to accommodate it:

▶ To accommodate critic A's concern, instead of doing ⎯⎯⎯⎯⎯, you could do ⎯⎯⎯⎯⎯.

▨ by **refuting** (arguing against) criticism—for example, by demonstrating that an objection is without merit or arguing that an alternative solution would be more costly or less likely to solve the problem than the proposed solution:

▶ Some object that the proposed solution would cost too much/cause too much disruption. However, when you take into consideration the fact that inaction would cost even more/cause more disruption than implementing solution B, you have to conclude that ⎯⎯⎯⎯⎯.

▶ Although X and Y prefer approach A, solution B would be less expensive/easier to implement because ⎯⎯⎯⎯⎯.

Here are a few examples showing how the proposals in this chapter refute objections or alternative solutions. Notice that proposal writers often introduce the refutation with a transition that indicates contrast, such as *but, although, nevertheless,* or *however*:

EXAMPLES   This system might run afoul of NOTA, but if so, Congress could easily change the law to make it legal, as it has done before. (Posner, par. 12)

Some believe that . . . From the student's perspective, however, . . . (O'Malley, par. 9)

Some argue that . . . , but several considerations support. . . . The first is. . . . The second consideration is. . . . A third consideration is. . . . (Brownell and Frieden, par. 5)

> Contrasts alternative and proposed solutions

▨ by **conceding** and then **refuting** (or the concession-refutation move):

▶ Yes, this solution might result in Problem X , but X can be overcome/avoided by _____ .

EXAMPLE   If weekly exams still seem too time-consuming to some professors, their frequency could be reduced to every other week or their length to 5 or 10 minutes. In courses where multiple-choice exams are appropriate, several questions could be designed to take only a few minutes to answer. (O'Malley, par. 9)

When reading a proposal, consider whether the writer presents others' views fairly and accurately and whether the writer's rebuttal is likely to be convincing to readers. Pay special attention to the writer's tone in responding to other views, noting any place the tone seems sarcastic or dismissive and considering whether such a tone would be effective given the writer's purpose and audience.

To learn more about constructing arguments, see Chapter 19.

A CLEAR, LOGICAL ORGANIZATION

Look for cues or signposts that help readers identify the parts of the proposal. Identify the topic and find the thesis, which in a proposal asserts the solution. Look also for topic sentences, particularly those that announce the parts of the proposal argument. Notice also any transitions and how they function. For example, all of the transitions in the following topic sentences (*another, moreover, still,* and *furthermore*) indicate items in a list. Other transitions you can expect in proposals signal causes or effects (*because, as a result*), exceptions (*but*), concessions (*although*), refutations (*however*), emphasis (*more important*), conclusions (*then, therefore*), and enumerations (*first, second*). Here are the beginnings of several topic sentences from O'Malley's essay:

For more about writing a thesis statement and topic sentences, see Chapter 13.

The main reason professors should give frequent exams is that . . . (par. 4)

Another, closely related argument in favor of multiple exams is that . . . (par. 6)

Moreover, professors object to frequent exams because . . . (par. 10)

Still another solution might be to . . . (par. 12)

Furthermore, professors could . . . (par. 13)

> Transitions

Finally, if headings or visuals (such as flowcharts, graphs, tables, photographs, or cartoons) are included, determine how they contribute. Notice whether visuals are referred to in the text and whether they have titles or captions.

Readings

To learn about how O'Malley responds to professors' likely objections to his proposed solution and argues against their preferred solutions to the problem, look at A Writer at Work on pp. 332–33.

Patrick O'Malley | *More Testing, More Learning*

FRUSTRATED BY what he calls "high-stakes exams," Patrick O'Malley wrote the following proposal while he was a first-year college student. To conduct research into opposing viewpoints, O'Malley interviewed two professors, talked with several students, and read published research on testing. He cited his sources using APA style, as his instructor had requested.

As you read, consider the questions in the margin. Your instructor may ask you to post your answers or bring them to class. Also consider the following:

- Think about your own feelings about high-stakes exams. How well does the opening scenario resonate for you?
- Given O'Malley's audience, how convincing do you think his use of sources is likely to be?

■┇ Basic Features

A Focused, Well-Defined Problem

A Well-Argued Solution

An Effective Response to Objections and Alternative Solutions

A Clear, Logical Organization

What is the function of the opening paragraph?

How does framing the problem this way set up the solution?

1   It's late at night. The final's tomorrow. You got a C on the midterm, so this one will make or break you. Will it be like the midterm? Did you study enough? Did you study the right things? It's too late to drop the course. So what happens if you fail? No time to worry about that now—you've got a ton of notes to go over.

2   Although this last-minute anxiety about midterm and final exams is only too familiar to most college students, many professors may not realize how such major, infrequent, high-stakes exams work against the best interests of students both psychologically and cognitively. They cause unnecessary amounts of stress, placing too much importance on one or two days in the students' entire term, judging ability on a single or dual performance. Reporting on recent research at Cornell University Medical School, Sian Beilock, a psychology professor at the University of Chicago, points out

that "stressing about doing well on an important exam can backfire, leading students to 'choke under pressure' or to score less well than they might otherwise score if the stakes weren't so high." Moreover, Cornell's research using fMRI brain scans shows that "the pressures of a big test can reach beyond the exam itself—stunting the cognitive systems that support the attention and memory skills every day" (Beilock, 2010). So, not only do high-stakes exams discourage frequent study and undermine students' performance, they also do long-term damage to students' cognitive development. If professors gave brief exams at frequent intervals, students would be spurred to learn more and worry less. They would study more regularly, perform better on tests, and enhance their cognitive functioning.

3   Ideally, a professor would give an in-class test or quiz after each unit, chapter, or focus of study, depending on the type of class and course material. A physics class might require a test on concepts after every chapter covered, while a history class could necessitate quizzes covering certain time periods or major events. These exams should be given weekly or at least twice monthly. Whenever possible, they should consist of two or three essay questions rather than many multiple-choice or short-answer questions. To preserve class time for lecture and discussion, exams should take no more than 15 or 20 minutes.

4   The main reason professors should give frequent exams is that when they do and when they provide feedback to students on how well they are doing, students learn more in the course and perform better on major exams, projects, and papers. It makes sense that in a challenging course containing a great deal of material, students will learn more of it and put it to better use if they have to apply or "practice" it frequently on exams, which also helps them find out how much they are learning and what they need to go over again. A 2006 study reported in the journal *Psychological Science* concluded that "taking repeated tests on material leads to better long-term retention than repeated studying," according to the study's coauthors, Henry L. Roediger and Jeffrey Karpicke (ScienceWatch.com, 2008). When asked what the impact of this breakthrough research would be, they responded: "We hope that this research may be picked up in educational circles as a way to improve educational practices, both for students in the classroom and as a study strategy outside of class." The new field of mind, brain, and education research advocates the use of "retrieval testing." For example, research by Karpicke and

How does O'Malley use the key terms introduced here throughout the essay?

What does par. 3 contribute to the argument?

How does O'Malley introduce this reason? What kinds of support does he offer?

How does O'Malley integrate and cite sources in pars. 4 and 5?

Blunt (2011) published in *Science* found that testing was more effective than other, more traditional methods of studying both for comprehension and for analysis. Why retrieval testing works is not known. UCLA psychologist Robert Bjork speculates that it may be effective because "when we use our memories by retrieving things, we change our access" to that information. "What we recall," therefore, "becomes more recallable in the future" (qtd. in Belluck, 2011).

5   Many students already recognize the value of frequent testing, but their reason is that they need the professor's feedback. A Harvard study notes students' "strong preference for frequent evaluation in a course." Harvard students feel they learn least in courses that have "only a midterm and a final exam, with no other personal evaluation." Students believe they learn most in courses with "many opportunities to see how they are doing" (Light, 1990, p. 32). In a review of a number of studies of student learning, Frederiksen (1984) reports that students who take weekly quizzes achieve higher scores on final exams than students who take only a midterm exam and that testing increases retention of material tested.

6   Another, closely related argument in favor of multiple exams is that they encourage students to improve their study habits. Greater frequency in test taking means greater frequency in studying for tests. Students prone to cramming will be required — or at least strongly motivated — to open their textbooks and notebooks more often, making them less likely to resort to long, kamikaze nights of studying for major exams. Since there is so much to be learned in the typical course, it makes sense that frequent, careful study and review are highly beneficial. But students need motivation to study regularly, and nothing works like an exam. If students had frequent exams in all their courses, they would have to schedule study time each week and would gradually develop a habit of frequent study. It might be argued that students are adults who have to learn how to manage their own lives, but learning history or physics is more complicated than learning to drive a car or balance a checkbook. Students need coaching and practice in learning. The right way to learn new material needs to become a habit, and I believe that frequent exams are key to developing good habits of study and learning. The Harvard study concludes that "tying regular evaluation to good course organization enables students to plan their work more than a few days in advance. If quizzes and homework are scheduled on specific days, students plan their work to capitalize on them" (Light, 1990, p. 33).

How does O'Malley support this reason? Why does he include it?

How does O'Malley introduce and respond to this possible objection?

7   By encouraging regular study habits, frequent exams would also decrease anxiety by reducing the procrastination that produces anxiety. Students would benefit psychologically if they were not subjected to the emotional ups and downs caused by major exams, when after being virtually worry-free for weeks they are suddenly ready to check into the psychiatric ward. Researchers at the University of Vermont found a strong relationship among procrastination, anxiety, and achievement. Students who regularly put off studying for exams had continuing high anxiety and lower grades than students who procrastinated less. The researchers found that even "low" procrastinators did not study regularly and recommended that professors give frequent assignments and exams to reduce procrastination and increase achievement (Rothblum, Solomon, & Murakami, 1986, pp. 393–394).

8   Research supports my proposed solution to the problem I have described. Common sense as well as my experience and that of many of my friends support it. Why, then, do so few professors give frequent brief exams?

9   Some believe that such exams take up too much of the limited class time available to cover the material in the course. Most courses meet 150 minutes a week—three times a week for 50 minutes each time. A 20-minute weekly exam might take 30 minutes to administer, and that is one-fifth of each week's class time. From the student's perspective, however, this time is well spent. Better learning and greater confidence about the course seem a good trade-off for another 30 minutes of lecture. Moreover, time lost to lecturing or discussion could easily be made up in students' learning on their own through careful regular study for the weekly exams. If weekly exams still seem too time-consuming to some professors, their frequency could be reduced to every other week or their length to 5 or 10 minutes. In courses where multiple-choice exams are appropriate, several questions could be designed to take only a few minutes to answer.

10   Moreover, professors object to frequent exams because they take too much time to read and grade. In a 20-minute essay exam, a well-prepared student can easily write two pages. A relatively small class of 30 students might then produce 60 pages, no small amount of material to read each week. A large class of 100 or more students would produce an insurmountable pile of material. There are a number of responses to this objection. Again, professors could give exams every other week or make them very short. Instead of reading them closely, they could skim them quickly to see whether students understand an idea or can apply it to an unfamiliar problem; and instead of numerical

How effectively does O'Malley use this source?

What is the purpose of this question?

How does O'Malley argue against possible objections in pars. 9 and 10?

or letter grades, they could give a plus, check, or minus. Exams could be collected and responded to only every third or fourth week. Professors who have readers or teaching assistants could rely on them to grade or check exams. And the Scantron machine is always available for instant grading of multiple-choice exams. Finally, frequent exams could be given *in place of* a midterm exam or out-of-class essay assignment.

How effectively does O'Malley present alternative solutions in pars. 11 and 12?

11   Since frequent exams seem to some professors to create too many problems, however, it is reasonable to consider alternative ways to achieve the same goals. One alternative solution is to implement a program that would improve study skills. While such a program might teach students how to study for exams, it cannot prevent procrastination or reduce "large test anxiety" by a substantial amount. One research team studying anxiety and test performance found that study skills training was not effective in reducing anxiety or improving performance (Dendato & Diener, 1986, p. 134). This team, which also reviewed other research that reached the same conclusion, did find that a combination of "cognitive/relaxation therapy" and study skills training was effective. This possible solution seems complicated, however, not to mention time-consuming and expensive. It seems much easier and more effective to change the cause of the bad habit rather than treat the habit itself. That is, it would make more sense to solve the problem at its root: the method of learning and evaluation.

How do the highlighted words and phrases make the argument easy to follow?

12   Still another solution might be to provide frequent study questions for students to answer. These would no doubt be helpful in focusing students' time studying, but students would probably not actually write out the answers unless they were required to. To get students to complete the questions in a timely way, professors would have to collect and check the answers. In that case, however, they might as well devote the time to grading an exam. Even if it asks the same questions, a scheduled exam is preferable to a set of study questions because it takes far less time to write in class, compared to the time students would devote to responding to questions at home. In-class exams also ensure that each student produces his or her own work.

13   Furthermore, professors could help students prepare for midterm and final exams by providing sets of questions from which the exam questions will be selected or announcing possible exam topics at the beginning of the course. This solution would

O'Malley   *More Testing, More Learning*

GUIDE TO READING
GUIDE TO WRITING
A WRITER AT WORK
THINKING CRITICALLY

295

have the advantage of reducing students' anxiety about learning every fact in the textbook, and it would clarify the course goals, but it would not motivate students to study carefully each new unit, concept, or text chapter in the course. I see this as a way of complementing frequent exams, not as substituting for them.

14   From the evidence and from my talks with professors and students, I see frequent, brief in-class exams as the only way to improve students' study habits and learning, reduce their anxiety and procrastination, and increase their satisfaction with college. These exams are not a panacea, but only more parking spaces and a winning football team would do as much to improve college life. Professors can't do much about parking or football, but they can give more frequent exams. Campus administrators should get behind this effort, and professors should get together to consider giving exams more frequently. It would make a difference.

How effective is this conclusion?

References

Beilock, S. (2010, September 3). Stressing about a high-stakes exam carries consequences beyond the test [Blog post]. Retrieved from http://www.psychologytoday.com /blog/choke/201009/stressing-about-high-stakes-exam-carries-consequences -beyond-the-test

Belluck, P. (2011, January 20). To really learn, quit studying and take a test. *The New York Times*. Retrieved from http://www.nytimes.com/

Dendato, K. M., & Diener, D. (1986). Effectiveness of cognitive/relaxation therapy and study skills training in reducing self-reported anxiety and improving the academic performance of test-anxious students. *The Journal of Counseling Psychology, 33*, 131–135.

Frederiksen, N. (1984). The real test bias: Influences of testing on teaching and learning. *American Psychologist, 39*, 193–202.

Karpicke, J. D., & Blunt, J. R. (2011, January 30). Retrieval practice produces more learning than elaborative studying with concept mapping. *Science Online* doi: 10.1126/science.1199327

Light, R. J. (1990). *Explorations with students and faculty about teaching, learning, and student life*. Cambridge, MA: Harvard University Graduate School of Education and Kennedy School of Government.

Rothblum, E. D., Solomon, L., & Murakami, J. (1986). Affective, cognitive, and behavioral differences between high and low procrastinators. *The Journal of Counseling Psychology, 33*, 387–394.

ScienceWatch.com (2008, February). Henry L. Roediger and Jeff Karpicke talk with ScienceWatch.com and answer a few questions about this month's fast breaking paper in the field of psychiatry/psychology [Interview]. Retrieved from http://sciencewatch.com/dr/fbp/2008/08febfbp/08febfbpRoedigerETAL

Naomi Rose | *Captivity Kills Orcas*

NAOMI ROSE is a scientist specializing in marine mammals at the Animal Welfare Institute in Washington, D.C. Author of numerous articles and book chapters for scientists and the general public, Rose regularly presents university lectures, serves on task forces, and testifies before Congress. She has also worked with the Merlin Entertainments Group to build sanctuaries for bottlenose dolphins. Her proposal here is based on research she conducted and reported in *Killer Controversy: Why Orcas Should No Longer Be Kept in Captivity* (2011) for the Humane Society International. The proposal was originally published by CNN.com in 2013, shortly after the release of the controversial documentary *Blackfish*, which depicts the devastating results—to both the animals and their trainers—of keeping wild orcas in captivity. We have converted Rose's links to in-text citations and have provided a list of the links at the end of the selection.

As you read,

- Think about your own experience with marine parks, zoos, and similar attractions. How did the animals you observed seem to fare in captivity?

- Consider the treatment of animals trained for human entertainment. Given your own experience with animals (as a pet owner, for example), do you think some animals might enjoy performing? Why or why not?

Rose   *Captivity Kills Orcas*
GUIDE TO READING
GUIDE TO WRITING
A WRITER AT WORK
THINKING CRITICALLY
297

1   The film *Blackfish* compellingly describes many of the reasons why keeping orcas in captivity is—and always has been—a bad idea (Magnolia). The main premise of the film is that these large, intelligent, social predators are dangerous to their trainers. But orcas are also directly harmed by being confined in concrete tanks and the science is growing to support this common sense conclusion.

2   The latest data (Rose, 2011) show that orcas are more than three times as likely to die at any age in captivity as they are in the wild. This translates into a shorter life span and is probably the result of several factors. First, orcas in captivity are out of shape; they are the equivalent of couch potatoes, as the largest orca tank in the world is less than one ten-thousandth of one percent (0.0001%) the size of the smallest home range of wild orcas. Second, they are in artificial and often incompatible social groups. This contributes to chronic stress, which can depress the immune system and leave captive orcas susceptible to infections they would normally fight off in the wild. Third, they often break their teeth chewing compulsively on metal gates. These broken teeth, even drilled and cleaned regularly by irrigation, are clear routes for bacteria to enter the bloodstream. These are the obvious factors; there are almost certainly others contributing to the elevated mortality seen in captivity. These factors boil down simply to this: Captivity kills orcas.

3   Yes, they may survive for years entertaining audiences, but eventually the stressors of captivity catch up to them. Very few captive orcas make it to midlife (approximately 30 years for males and 45 for females) and not one out of more than 200 held in captivity has ever come close to old age (60 for males, 80 for females) (*Killer Whale*). Most captive orcas die while they are still very young by wild orca standards.

Tilikum, a bull orca, performing at Sea World in a scene from *Blackfish* (2013).

4   There is a solution to both the trainer safety and orca welfare dilemmas facing marine theme parks around the world, including SeaWorld in the United States. These facilities can work with experts around the world to create sanctuaries where captive orcas can be rehabilitated and retired. These sanctuaries would be sea pens or netted-off bays or coves, in temperate to cold water natural habitat. They would offer the animals respite from performing and the constant exposure to a parade of strangers (an entirely unnatural situation for a species whose social groupings are based on family ties and stability—"strangers" essentially do not exist in orca society). Incompatible animals would not be forced to cohabit the same enclosures and family groups would be preserved. Show business trainers would no longer be necessary. Expert caretakers would continue to train retired whales for veterinary procedures, but would not get in the water and would remain at a safe distance (this is known in zoo parlance as "protected contact"). And the degree to which they interact directly with the whales would be each whale's choice.

5   A fundamental premise of these sanctuaries, however, is that eventually they would empty. Breeding would not be allowed and captive orcas would no longer exist within the next few decades. Many wildlife sanctuaries, for circus, road-side zoo and backyard refugees, exist around the globe for animals such as big cats, elephants and chimpanzees. The business (usually nonprofit) model for these types of facilities is therefore well-established for terrestrial species and can be adapted for orcas. Wildlife sanctuaries are sometimes open to the public, although public interaction with the animals is usually minimized. A visitor's center can offer education, real-time remote viewing of the animals, a gift shop, and in the case of whales and dolphins can even be a base for responsible whale watching if the sanctuary is in a suitable location for that activity. Marine theme parks do not need to lose out financially by phasing out orca shows; this is a transformative proposal, not a punitive one.

Now even staunch SeaWorld supporters are wondering if the time has come to think outside the (concrete) box.

6   Creating a whale or dolphin sanctuary is not entirely theoretical. Merlin Entertainments is pursuing the establishment of the world's first bottlenose dolphin sanctuary with Whale and Dolphin Conservation ("WDCS," 2009), a nonprofit environmental group. Whale and Dolphin Conservation put together a team to determine the feasibility of such a concept and the company has now identified potential sites and is studying the infrastructure that will be needed to support a group of retired dolphins.

7   Before the tragic death of SeaWorld trainer Dawn Brancheau in 2010 ("SeaWorld"), the ethical arguments against keeping orcas in captivity came largely from the animal welfare/animal rights community, with the marine theme parks basically ignoring or dismissing their opponents as a vocal and out-of-touch minority. Now even staunch SeaWorld supporters are wondering if the time has come to think outside the (concrete) box.

8   Furthermore, the marine mammal science community, which has long maintained a neutral stance on the question of whether orcas are a suitable species for captive display, has finally recognized the need to engage. An informal panel discussion on captive orcas is scheduled at the 20th Biennial Conference on the Biology of Marine Mammals in December, the first time this topic will be openly addressed by the world's largest marine mammal science society.

9   The first orca was put on public display in 1964. The debate on whether that was a good idea—for people or the whales—began the next day but didn't really heat up until the 1970s. It raged mostly on the fringe for the next 25 years. It picked up steam in the mid-1990s, with the release of the film *Free Willy* and the rehabilitation of its orca star Keiko. And now, thanks in part to *Blackfish*, it is mainstream and consensus is building that orcas don't belong in captivity. The marine theme parks can shift with the paradigm or be left behind—it is up to them.

Links

"Killer Whale (*Orcinus orca*)." *Office of Protected Resources.* NOAA Fisheries, 25 June 2014. Web. 8 Dec. 2014.

Magnolia Pictures and Magnet Releasing. "Blackfish— Official Trailer." blackfishfilm.com. *YouTube.* 3 June 2013. Web. 8 Dec. 2014.

Rose, Naomi A. *Killer Controversy: Why Orcas Should No Longer Be Kept in Captivity. Humane Society International and The Humane Society of the United States*. Humane Society International, 2011. Web. 8 Dec. 2014.

"SeaWorld Trainer Killed by Killer Whale." *CNN.com.* Cable News Network, 25 Feb. 2010. Web. 8 Dec. 2014.

"WDCS to Work with Merlin Entertainments on Better Future for Captive Dolphins." *Whale and Dolphin Conservation.* WDCS, 17 Mar. 2009. Web. 8 Dec. 2014.

Make connections: Thinking about corporate and consumer responsibility.

[**REFLECT**]

Rose argues that for-profit marine parks should eliminate orca shows and send their captive orcas to nonprofit sanctuaries. Think about the responsibilities corporations like SeaWorld owe to the animals they use to make a profit. Your instructor may ask you to post your thoughts to a class discussion board or blog, or to discuss them with other students in class. Use these questions to get started:

- What aspects of the problem seem most important: that businesses are profiting, that orcas and dolphins are highly intelligent mammals, that they are being taken out of their habitats and put into captivity, that the mammals are being trained to do tricks for our entertainment, or something else?

- Thinking about animals more generally, should business ventures such as zoos, scuba diving tours, fishing boats, race tracks, and circuses—or movies that feature animals—contribute in some way to ensure the well-being of the animals from which they profit?

- Reflect also on the consumer's responsibilities in supporting businesses that profit from animals. The documentary *Blackfish* and Rose's CNN.com proposal are addressed to the general public. What role, if any, do you think consumers should play?

Use the basic features.

[**ANALYZE**]

A FOCUSED, WELL-DEFINED PROBLEM: CONVINCING THE AUDIENCE

If the audience doesn't care about the problem, or if people aren't convinced it exists, any solution may seem too expensive or hard to implement. For this reason, proposal writers must frame the problem so that their audience will want a solution.

In his proposal, Patrick O'Malley begins by addressing his fellow students: "You got a C on the midterm . . ." (par. 1). But he knows that students are not his primary audience because the most they can do is help him pressure the real decision makers—their instructors. To convince professors that the problem is important, O'Malley uses a couple of strategies:

- He addresses the intended audience:

  "many professors may not realize" (par. 2)

- He grabs the intended audience's attention and enlists readers' sympathy, using the opening scenario and rhetorical questions to remind professors what it was like to be a student:

  "It's late at night. . . . Did you study enough? Did you study the right things?" (par. 1)

- He gains the audience's respect by demonstrating that he is not just whining about a personal problem. He cites sources and establishes their reliability by identifying the researchers' credentials and where the research was presented, and by showing that it is current:

  "Reporting on recent research at Cornell University Medical School, Sian Beilock, a psychology professor at the University of Chicago. . . ." (par. 2)

ANALYZE & WRITE

Write a paragraph analyzing the strategies Rose uses to frame the problem, establish its seriousness, and persuade her audience:

1. Based on what you can infer about the audience of *CNN.com*, who do you think Rose hopes to influence by publishing her proposal on that Web site? For example, does she appear to be addressing SeaWorld executives who could take action on her proposal, advertisers who could put pressure on decision makers, the general public who could boycott the theme park? What signs, if any, help you identify Rose's intended audience and her purpose in addressing them?

2. Reread paragraphs 1–3. What strategies does Rose employ to convince the members of her audience that the problem is serious and they should care about it? Does Rose employ strategies like those O'Malley uses? If so, where? If not, what alternative strategies does Rose employ?

3. Considering Rose's purpose and audience, how effective do you think her opening paragraphs were and what else might she have done to persuade her readers to take the problem seriously?

A WELL-ARGUED SOLUTION: DEMONSTRATING FEASIBILITY

To persuade readers that more testing would help students, O'Malley makes clear in his thesis statement exactly what he wants faculty to do and why:

Proposal
Results

If professors gave brief exams at frequent intervals, students would be spurred to learn more and worry less. They would study more regularly, perform better on tests, and enhance their cognitive functioning. (par. 4)

He then cites scientific studies and news reports about scientific studies to persuade readers that the results he promises are realistic.

ANALYZE & WRITE

Write a paragraph analyzing Rose's strategy to demonstrate that her proposal is feasible:

1 Reread paragraph 4, highlighting the sentences in which Rose spells out her proposal. What does she propose, and what does she claim the result would be if her proposal were implemented?

2 Now skim paragraphs 5–8. What writing strategies (such as cause-effect reasoning, comparison and contrast, process analysis, statistics, examples) does Rose use to support her claim?

3 Evaluate the effectiveness of the evidence Rose supplies. What other kinds of evidence would have made Rose's proposal more convincing for you?

AN EFFECTIVE RESPONSE TO OBJECTIONS AND ALTERNATIVE SOLUTIONS: ANTICIPATING NEGATIVE SIDE EFFECTS

Effective proposals respond to readers' potential objections. O'Malley, for example, suggests ways faculty can reduce the negative side effects of offering more low-stakes quizzes by making exams shorter and simplifying grading systems (pars. 9–10).

ANALYZE & WRITE

Write a paragraph evaluating how Rose responds to objections to marine sanctuaries:

1 Skim paragraphs 5–8. What are some of the objections that Rose implies owners of facilities like SeaWorld would make?

2 How effective are Rose's suggestions for mitigating the negative effects that retiring captive orcas to sanctuaries would have on marine parks? Why do you think she claims that "this is a transformative proposal, not a punitive one" (par. 5)? Why do you think she feels the needs to reassure her audience that her proposal is "not a punitive one"? Who would care if it was?

3 Now skim paragraphs 7–9. If you're not familiar with the film Rose mentions, watch the *Blackfish* trailer. What sort of resistance does Rose seem to be anticipating from her audience? How effective is her response?

A CLEAR, LOGICAL ORGANIZATION: CREATING UNITY

It's important, especially in complicated proposals, to provide cues to help the audience move from paragraph to paragraph without losing sight of the main point. O'Malley, for example, provides a forecast of what his essay will cover by repeating key terms or their synonyms from his thesis statement in each of his topic sentences:

> If professors gave brief exams at frequent intervals, students would be spurred to learn more and worry less. They would study more regularly, perform better on tests, and enhance their cognitive functioning. (par. 2)

Thesis statement

> The main reason professors should give frequent exams is that when they do and when they provide feedback to students on how well they are doing, students learn more in the course and perform better on major exams. . . . (par. 4)

Topic sentence

O'Malley also uses transitions—"The main reason" (par. 4), "Another, closely related argument reason" (par. 6)—to remind readers how each paragraph relates to the thesis and to the paragraphs that precede and follow it. Writers may also use the conclusion to unify their writing by coming full circle: revisiting an idea, example, or comparison at the end of the essay that they had introduced at the beginning.

ANALYZE & WRITE

Write a paragraph analyzing and evaluating how Rose cues readers and creates unity:

1 Reread the first and last paragraphs of Rose's essay. What idea does Rose mention in both paragraphs? How does paragraph 9 close a circle started in paragraph 1?

2 Now skim paragraphs 2–8, highlighting Rose's topic sentences and any transitional words or phrases she uses.

3 What else might Rose have done to unify her proposal and make it easier to follow?

[RESPOND]

Consider possible topics: Representing the voiceless.

In her proposal to free captive orcas, Rose speaks for creatures that cannot speak for themselves—at least, not in English. You could propose a solution to a problem faced by those who cannot effectively advocate for themselves, perhaps because they belong to another species, do not speak the language of power, lack access to the technologies they would need to be heard, or lack the credibility or status necessary to get a fair hearing. For example, consider writing a proposal that would reduce the number of abandoned pets on campus or in the community. Or propose ways to help elderly and infirm people in your community who need transportation or elementary-school kids who need after-school programs.

Eric Posner | *A Moral Market*

Lloyd DeGrane

ERIC POSNER is the Kirkland and Ellis Distinguished Service Professor at the University of Chicago Law School. A prolific author, Posner has over a dozen books and more than a hundred legal articles and book chapters to his credit. As a public intellectual, he also maintains a blog (www.ericposner.com) and an active Twitter feed, as well as a regular column on *Slate.com*, where "A Moral Market" first appeared. Like Naomi Rose, Posner first composed a well-researched academic study on "altruism exchanges" before writing a shorter, more accessible version of the proposal he later published online for a general audience. (Posner's legal article "Altruism Exchanges and the Kidney Shortage," written in collaboration with law professors Stephen J. Choi and G. Mitu Gulati, is available online at chicagounbound.uchicago.edu.) We have converted Posner's links to in-text citations and provided a list of links at the end of the selection. You also may have noticed that Chapter 5 of this book includes student writing on "A Moral Market" as well as other sources on the question of whether to compensate kidney donors. Your instructor may invite you to read Chapter 5 or you may choose to do so on your own. The activities following this selection, however, do not require familiarity with the material in Chapter 5.

As you read,

- What might lead you to consider donating one of your kidneys, assuming you could do so without damaging your own health?

- It is currently against the law, as Posner points out, to buy and sell kidneys. Why do you imagine people object to a cash market for organs for transplantation?

1   Sunday is the thirtieth anniversary of the National Organ Transplant Act, but no one wants to celebrate. U.S. policy on organ transplants—especially as applied to kidneys—is a mess. More than 100,000 people languish on the waitlist for kidneys, thousands of them dying before they receive a transplant. In 2012, almost 35,000 people joined the waitlist, while only 17,000 received transplants.

2   Every year the waitlist lengthens. NOTA virtually guaranteed this shortage by shutting down an incipient market in kidneys. Some economists have argued that the best way to encourage people to donate kidneys is to allow people to sell them. Since almost everyone has one unneeded kidney, and most people could use some money, a market would form. The estimated price—perhaps in the range of $100,000 per kidney—would be less than the cost of dialysis (more than $70,000 per patient per year [Costs]), even taking into account transplant surgery, and so the donor fee would be paid by insurers, including Medicare and Medicaid.

3   The law reflected a popular, inchoate repugnance at the idea of kidney-selling. Ethicists have tried to supply a philosophical argument. They argue that, if a market for kidneys existed, poor people would be taken advantage of; moreover, we should not treat body parts as "commodities." Neither of these arguments is persuasive. A regulated market that required informed consent would eliminate the worst forms of exploitation and could ensure (as under current law) that kidneys were equally available to rich and poor. If poor people really can't be trusted to make good decisions on their own behalf, then a simple solution is to ban poor people from selling their kidneys while allowing everyone else to do so. Nor is it clear why it's more objectionable to sell a kidney than, say, one's hair, blood plasma, egg

> *More than 100,000 people languish on the waitlist for kidneys, thousands of them dying before they receive a transplant.*

cells, or sperm (sale of which is legal in most places within the United States).

4   But political opposition to selling kidneys will not go away, and so the question is how to increase the supply of kidneys without creating a market. Most proposals, including a recent open letter (Open Letter) by transplant experts and bioethicists to top government officials, try to thread the needle by giving donors implicit or in-kind compensation, such as travel expenses to the hospital, a tax credit, or priority on the waitlist if they ever need a kidney themselves. The proposals amount to attempts to evade moral objections by allowing limited, implicit compensation rather than a price in dollars.

5   But it is possible to be more imaginative. It may help to sort out the source of moral objections to a market in kidneys. One possible view is that people should not *exchange* their body parts for other things of value. Another is that people shouldn't *profit* on the sale of their body parts. These ideas are different. To see why, imagine that Martha wants to donate her kidney to her daughter (this is legal, of course), but the daughter's body would reject her mother's kidney because the mother's and daughter's antigens are not matched (Transplant Rejection), or similar enough. Meanwhile, an unrelated person named Frank wants to donate his kidney to his son, but also cannot do so because of immunological incompatibility. But it happens that Martha matches with Frank's son and Frank matches with Martha's daughter. Could Martha donate her kidney to Frank's son in exchange for Frank donating his kidney to Martha's daughter? Under NOTA, the answer was (or was believed to be) no: An exchange of any kind was illegal. In a subsequent law, called the Charlie W. Norwood Living Organ Donation Act, Congress clarified that this type of exchange, called a "paired donation," is

lawful. But only a few hundred transplants per year are arranged through paired donations because it is hard to find and arrange matches between strangers.

6   So while the Norwood Act did not solve the problem of undersupply of kidneys, it did reveal a key feature of public morality—that people don't object to exchanges of kidneys. That means the feature of markets they must object to is not exchange but profit. A donor like Martha may give her kidney to a stranger like Frank, who wants it for his son, as long as what she gets in return is not money that she spends on herself, but something different—a benefit for another person, her daughter.

7   But if that's true, we can do better than paired donations, as I argue in a paper (Posner) written with law professors Stephen Choi and Mitu Gulati. Suppose that Martha needs a kidney for her daughter but Frank's son does not need a kidney. Martha proposes to Frank that if Frank donates his kidney to her daughter, Martha (or, actually, Martha's insurer, which, remember, wants to avoid the high cost of dialysis) will make a $100,000 contribution to Frank's favorite charity—say, Doctors Without Borders, which could use the money to combat Ebola in Liberia. Frank, of course, might say no; but there are likely other people who might be willing to take Martha up on the deal.

8   If you're skeptical, you should be aware that every year a few hundred people donate their kidneys to strangers in return for nothing at all. There must certainly be additional people who would stop short of donating a kidney to help merely a single stranger but would be willing to do so to help hundreds or thousands of desperate people—who need medical care, disaster relief, or basic infrastructure like irrigation systems. There are also probably thousands of people who can't help a friend or loved one who needs a kidney because of the lack of a match but who would be willing to donate their own kidney to a pool of organs if it would secure the matched kidney of someone else. And friends and relatives who can't donate a kidney would surely donate money if doing so enabled them to secure a kidney for a friend or loved one. Frank might donate his kidney to Martha's daughter for another reason. Suppose Frank's son does not yet have end-stage renal disease but he does suffer from a medical condition that will probably lead to kidney shutdown decades from now. Frank worries that by the time his son needs a kidney, Frank will be too old to participate in a paired donation. So Frank agrees to donate a kidney to Martha's

daughter today in return for the right to have his son receive a kidney from someone else when the son needs it.

9   How would this work? Imagine that charities set up "altruism exchanges" that accept donations of various types—kidneys, money, whatever. The charities then do two things. First, they distribute kidneys and other resources to those who need them. Second, they give to donors "credits" that the donors can take back to the charity in the future. The credits can then be used to obtain kidneys for loved ones, cash distributions to causes that they care about, and other resources as long as they are allocated to people other than the donors themselves.

10   The charities would vastly strengthen people's incentives to donate a kidney. If you donate your kidney at age 20, you would be given a credit, which you could then use—immediately or later in life—to obtain a charitable benefit for someone you care about or a cause that matters to you. It could be a kidney for your own child, or it could be housing, food, and water for victims of natural disasters. It could be for malaria control in Africa or girls' education in Pakistan. The charity would also make it much easier to arrange kidney matches. Martha would no longer need to find someone who matched with her daughter. Instead, Martha would donate her kidney to a stranger via the altruism exchange, and then could use her credit when the first match for her daughter came along, which could be immediately or years later.

11   The system would increase the supply of kidneys by giving donors the power to help more than a single stranger. Everyone would get to be a major philanthropist, and the more people who participated, the larger the benefits. At the same time, the profit motive would be avoided. All exchanges must be altruistically motivated. The system would not necessarily help everyone. People who don't have generous friends and relatives may still find themselves on the wait list for transplants. But those people would still be better off than under the current system because the larger supply of kidneys—donated by people who exchanged their kidneys for other types of charitable benefits financed by people who donated money—would shorten the waitlist considerably.

12   This system might run afoul of NOTA, but if so, Congress could easily change the law to make it legal, as it has done before. Congress would simply need to provide that anyone may donate a kidney and receive in exchange the right to allocate future charitable benefits

through a government-approved charity. The dollar value of those benefits could be based on the avoided costs of dialysis. Donors would be forbidden to receive cash or goods. So people couldn't donate kidneys to raise money to buy a Tesla Model D. They could donate kidneys only to help others.

Links

An Open Letter to President Barack Obama, Secretary of Health and Human Services Sylvia Mathews Burwell, Attorney General Eric Holder, and Leaders of Congress. W. Kramer, 2014. Web. 20 Feb. 2015.

"Costs of End-Stage Renal Disease." *U.S. Renal Data System Annual Data Report 2014.* Vol. 2: 326–32. U.S. RDS Coordinating Center, 2014. Web. 20 Feb. 2015.

"Transplant Rejection." *Medline Plus.* U.S. National Library of Medicine and National Institutes of Health, 2013. Web. 20 Feb. 2015.

Posner, Eric, Stephen J. Choi, and G. Mitu Gulati. "Altruism Exchanges and the Kidney Shortage." *Chicago Unbound: Coase-Sandor Working Paper Series in Law and Economics.* Coase-Sandor Institute for Law and Economics, University of Chicago Law School, 2013. Web. 20 Feb. 2015.

Make connections: Compromising on a solution.

`[ REFLECT ]`

Because he is determined to find a pragmatic solution—one that will garner widespread public support—Posner seems willing to forge a compromise. That is, although he appears to support the idea of a market in kidneys, he understands that "political opposition to selling kidneys will not go away, and so the question is how to increase the supply of kidneys without creating a market" (par. 4). Think about some conditions under which compromising is the right thing to do. Your instructor may ask you to post your thoughts to a class discussion board or blog, or to discuss them with other students in class. Use these questions to get started:

- What makes this problem so important? How does Posner try to inspire his audience to join with him in the search for a solution?

- How does Posner present his solution as a compromise? What is being compromised by those who support a kidney market and by those who oppose it?

- How does Posner try to convince his readers that this solution would not require them to compromise their moral values? How convincing do you think his argument is likely to be?

Use the basic features.

`[ ANALYZE ]`

A FOCUSED, WELL-DEFINED PROBLEM: FRAMING THE PROBLEM

Every proposal begins with a problem. What writers say about the problem and how much space they devote to it depends on what they assume their audience already knows and thinks about it. Savvy proposal writers try to present even familiar problems in a way that reminds readers of the problem's seriousness and prepares them for the writer's preferred solution. They often *frame* the problem by focusing attention on *values* they share with their audience. For example, knowing that professors care about learning, Patrick O'Malley says he wants his audience of professors to "realize" that their current exam policy impairs learning and has a detrimental effect on "students' cognitive development" (par. 2).

Write a paragraph analyzing how Posner frames the problem:

1. Given his *Slate.com* audience, why do you think Posner opens his proposal by pointing out that it is the anniversary of the National Organ Transplant Act (NOTA)?

2. Skim paragraphs 1–3. What kinds of information does Posner include here, and how does this information help him frame the problem around shared values?

3. Consider how, in these paragraphs, Posner introduces the debate between economists and ethicists over what to do about the lack of organs for transplantation. How does setting up these opposing views help Posner frame the problem in a way that prepares his audience for the solution he proposes?

A WELL-ARGUED SOLUTION: MAKING A PERSUASIVE ARGUMENT

To be persuasive, a proposal must demonstrate to the audience that the proposed solution would work—that it would solve or at least lessen the problem—and that it could be implemented without too much effort, time, and cost. Proposals attempting to solve a highly controversial problem, like whether to pay people to donate their kidneys, must also meet a feasibility test. That is, the solution has to be seen as realistic. If your solution (or something like it) has never been implemented, then you might use sentence strategies like these to describe one or more hypothetical **scenarios** to show the audience the result of implementing your solution:

Cues indicating
hypotheticals

▶ Suppose X does _____ .

▶ If solution X were implemented, then _____ would result.

EXAMPLE   Ideally, a professor would give an in-class test. . . . A physics class might require a test on concepts . . . while a history class could necessitate. . . . Exams should be given weekly. . . . (O'Malley, par. 3)

If students had frequent exams in all their courses, they would have to schedule study time each week and would gradually develop a habit of frequent study. (O'Malley, par. 6)

Note that sometimes these hypotheticals use an "if-then" construction, as in the last example above. Scenarios work like examples by giving the audience a graphic image of what could happen. But, like an example or anecdote, a scenario will not be effective unless the audience sees it as a credible, realistic possibility.

Write a paragraph or two analyzing Posner's argument for his proposed solution:

1. Skim paragraphs 9–11. How does Posner try to convince his audience that his proposed solution can be implemented and that it would indeed help solve the problem?

2. Now reread paragraphs 5–8 and 10. Notice the Martha-and-Frank scenarios and the sentence strategies Posner uses. How effective do you think these scenarios are likely to be in convincing Posner's *Slate* audience that his solution is workable?

AN EFFECTIVE RESPONSE TO OBJECTIONS AND ALTERNATIVE SOLUTIONS: FINDING A WAY TO BRIDGE DIFFERENCES

In addition to arguing for the proposed solution, proposal writers also need to show that their solution is preferable to alternatives their readers might favor. Patrick O'Malley, for example, identifies several alternative solutions his intended audience (instructors) might bring up, including implementing programs to improve students' study skills, giving students study questions, and handing out possible exam topics to help students prepare. He concedes the benefits of some of these solutions, but he also points out their shortcomings, showing how his solution is better.

ANALYZE & WRITE

Write a paragraph or two analyzing how Posner attempts to show that his solution is the best option:

1. Skim paragraphs 2–5, in which Posner reviews three alternative solutions and the objections raised to each of them:

   ■ the economists' proposed solution (pars. 2–3);

   ■ the solution offered by "transplant experts and bioethicists" (par. 4);

   ■ the "paired donation" solution (par. 5).

   What, if anything, do the objections to all three proposed solutions have in common?

2. Choose one of these alternative solutions to examine closely, identifying the solution being proposed and the objections that have been raised to it.

3. Think about Posner's strategy to "sort out the source of moral objections to a market in kidneys" (par. 5) before proposing his own solution. How does Posner's "altruism exchange" (par. 9) emerge from his analysis of objections to the other solutions? How effective do you think his solution would be in avoiding the same objections?

A CLEAR, LOGICAL ORGANIZATION: CREATING COHERENCE

Writers use a variety of strategies to make a proposal clear and easy to follow. One common strategy is to use a rhetorical question (a question to which no answer is expected) to make a transition from one topic to the next. For example, O'Malley uses a rhetorical question at the end of paragraph 8—"Why, then, do so few professors give frequent brief exams?"—as a transition to the section dealing with likely objections. The two paragraphs following the rhetorical question begin with an answer:

"Some believe that such exams . . ." (par. 9)

"Moreover, professors object to frequent exams because . . ." (par 10)

Another strategy is to use transitions. O'Malley, for example, uses transitions such as *moreover* (par. 10), *still another* (12), and *furthermore* (13) in the opening sentence of a paragraph to connect it to the preceding one. Notice the different functions transitions have:

See Chapter 13, pp. 533–36, for more about transitions.

To add an idea	*moreover, also, in addition*
To indicate an opposing idea	*but, however, neither*
To cue a cause-effect relationship	*so, since, because*

ANALYZE & WRITE

Write a paragraph analyzing Posner's use of rhetorical questions and transitions:

1 Reread paragraphs 6 and 9, and highlight the rhetorical question in each. How do these rhetorical questions function as transitions?

2 Now skim the essay, highlighting some of the transitional words or phrases you find. How many appear at the beginning of a paragraph to link it to the preceding paragraph? What role does each play? For example, does the transition indicate that another related idea is coming or that the writer is going to offer an opposing idea?

[RESPOND]

Consider possible topics: Moving the masses.

Although Posner proposes a change to law, ultimately he hopes to change the way large numbers of people behave. Think about problems that cannot be solved unless many people change what they are doing. Many such problems can be referred to collectively as the "tragedy of the commons": resources that no one owns—like air, water, and public spaces—are neglected, damaged, or recklessly depleted. For example, consider a proposal that would encourage dorm residents to change sloppy behavior in common areas, that would encourage those drinking communal coffee to help clean up or make the next pot, or that would discourage residents from dropping garbage in public parks or playgrounds. The challenge to solving such problems is, of course, that you're unlikely to change public behavior just by making a good argument. Like Posner, you may have to propose a policy change or come up with an incentive, a process that often starts with figuring out why people aren't already doing what you want them to do.

Kelly D. Brownell
Thomas R. Frieden

Ounces of Prevention—The Public Policy Case for Taxes on Sugared Beverages

Courtesy of Kelly Brownell

KELLY D. BROWNELL is a professor of psychology and neuroscience at Duke. An international expert who has published numerous books and articles, including *Food Fight: The Inside Story of the Food Industry, America's Obesity Crisis, and What We Can Do About It* (2003), Brownell received the 2012 American Psychological Association Award for Outstanding Lifetime Contributions to Psychology. He was also featured in the Academy Award–nominated film *Super Size Me.*

Brownell and Frieden   *Ounces of Prevention*

GUIDE TO READING
GUIDE TO WRITING
A WRITER AT WORK
THINKING CRITICALLY

309

THOMAS R. FRIEDEN, a physician specializing in public health, is the director of the U.S. Centers for Disease Control and Prevention (CDC) and served for several years as the health commissioner for the City of New York.

Brownell and Frieden's proposal "Ounces of Prevention—The Public Policy Case for Taxes on Sugared Beverages" was originally published in 2009 in the highly respected *New England Journal of Medicine*, which calls itself "the most widely read, cited, and influential general medical periodical in the world." In fact, research published there is often referred to widely throughout the media.

As you read, consider the effect that Brownell and Frieden's use of graphs and formal citation of sources has on their credibility:

- How do the graphs help establish the seriousness of the problem? How do they also help demonstrate the feasibility of the solution the authors propose?

- How do the citations help persuade you to accept the authors' solution? What effect might they have had on their original readers? (Note that the authors use neither of the two citation styles covered in Part 4 of this text. Instead, they use one common to medical journals and publications of the U.S. National Library of Medicine.)

Sugar, rum, and tobacco are commodities which are nowhere necessaries of life, which are become objects of almost universal consumption, and which are therefore extremely proper subjects of taxation.

— Adam Smith, *The Wealth of Nations*, 1776

1   The obesity epidemic has inspired calls for public health measures to prevent diet-related diseases. One controversial idea is now the subject of public debate: food taxes. Forty states already have small taxes on sugared beverages and snack foods, but in the past year, Maine and New York have proposed large taxes on sugared beverages, and similar discussions have begun in other states. The size of the taxes, their potential for generating revenue and reducing consumption, and vigorous opposition by the beverage industry have resulted in substantial controversy. Because excess consumption of unhealthful foods underlies many leading causes of death, food taxes at local, state, and national levels are likely to remain part of political and public health discourse.

2   Sugar-sweetened beverages (soda sweetened with sugar, corn syrup, or other caloric sweeteners and other carbonated and uncarbonated drinks, such as sports and energy drinks) may be the single largest driver of the obesity epidemic. A recent meta-analysis found that the intake of sugared beverages is associated with increased body weight, poor nutrition, and displacement of more healthful beverages; increasing consumption increases risk for obesity and diabetes; the strongest effects are seen in studies with the best methods (e.g., longitudinal and interventional vs. correlational studies);* and interventional studies show that reduced intake of soft drinks improves health.[1] Studies that do not support a relationship between consumption of sugared beverages and health outcomes tend to be conducted by authors supported by the beverage industry.[2] Sugared beverages are marketed extensively to children and adolescents, and in the mid-1990s, children's intake of sugared beverages surpassed that of milk. In the past decade, per capita intake of calories

---

*In a *longitudinal* study, researchers observe changes taking place over a long period of time; in an *interventional* study, investigators give research subjects a measured amount of whatever is being studied and note its effects; and in a *correlational* study, researchers examine statistics to see if two or more variables have a mathematically significant similarity. [Editor's note]

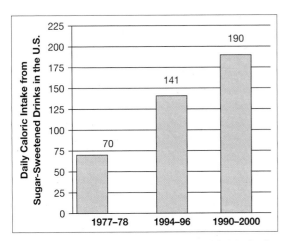

Daily Caloric Intake from Sugar-Sweetened Drinks in the United States.
Data are from Nielsen and Popkin.[3]

from sugar-sweetened beverages has increased by nearly 30 percent (see bar graph Daily Caloric Intake from Sugar-Sweetened Drinks in the United States);[3] beverages now account for 10 to 15 percent of the calories consumed by children and adolescents. For each extra can or glass of sugared beverage consumed per day, the likelihood of a child's becoming obese increases by 60 percent.[4]

3   Taxes on tobacco products have been highly effective in reducing consumption, and data indicate that higher prices also reduce soda consumption. A review conducted by Yale University's Rudd Center for Food Policy and Obesity suggested that for every 10 percent increase in price, consumption decreases by 7.8 percent. An industry trade publication reported even larger reductions: as prices of carbonated soft drinks increased by 6.8 percent, sales dropped by 7.8 percent, and as Coca-Cola prices increased by 12 percent, sales dropped by 14.6 percent.[5] Such studies—and the economic principles that support their findings—suggest that a tax on sugared beverages would encourage consumers to switch to more healthful beverages, which would lead to reduced caloric intake and less weight gain.

4   The increasing affordability of soda—and the decreasing affordability of fresh fruits and vegetables (see line graph)—probably contributes to the rise in obesity in the United States. In 2008, a group of child and health care advocates in New York proposed a one-penny-per-ounce excise tax on sugared beverages, which would be expected to reduce consumption by 13 percent—about two servings per week per person. Even if one quarter of the calories consumed from sugared beverages are replaced by other food, the decrease in consumption would lead to an estimated reduction of 8,000 calories per person per year—slightly more than 2 pounds each year for the average person. Such a reduction in calorie consumption would be expected to substantially reduce the risk of obesity and diabetes

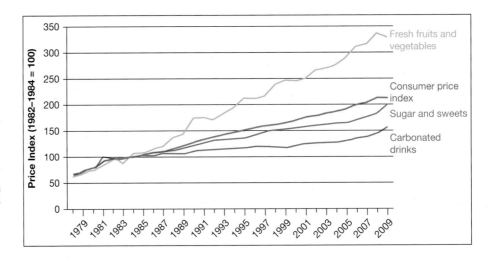

Relative Price Changes for Fresh Fruits and Vegetables, Sugar and Sweets, and Carbonated Drinks, 1978–2009.
Data are from the U.S. Bureau of Labor Statistics and represent the U.S. city averages for all urban consumers in January of each year.

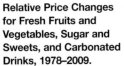

and may also reduce the risk of heart disease and other conditions.

5   Some argue that government should not interfere in the market and that products and prices will change as consumers demand more healthful food, but several considerations support government action. The first is externality—costs to parties not directly involved in a transaction. The contribution of unhealthful diets to health care costs is already high and is increasing—an estimated $79 billion is spent annually for overweight and obesity alone—and approximately half of these costs are paid by Medicare and Medicaid, at taxpayers' expense. Diet-related diseases also cost society in terms of decreased work productivity, increased absenteeism, poorer school performance, and reduced fitness on the part of military recruits, among other negative effects. The second consideration is information asymmetry between the parties to a transaction. In the case of sugared beverages, marketers commonly make health claims (e.g., that such beverages provide energy or vitamins) and use techniques that exploit the cognitive vulnerabilities of young children, who often cannot distinguish a television program from an advertisement. A third consideration is revenue generation, which can further increase the societal benefits of a tax on soft drinks. A penny-per-ounce excise tax would raise an estimated $1.2 billion in New York State alone. In times of economic hardship, taxes that both generate this much revenue and promote health are better options than revenue initiatives that may have adverse effects.

6   Objections have certainly been raised: that such a tax would be regressive, that food taxes are not comparable to tobacco or alcohol taxes because people must eat to survive, that it is unfair to single out one type of food for taxation, and that the tax will not solve the obesity problem. But the poor are disproportionately affected by diet-related diseases and would derive the greatest benefit from reduced consumption; sugared beverages are not necessary for survival; Americans consume about 250 to 300 more calories daily today than they did several decades ago, and nearly half this increase is accounted for by consumption of sugared beverages; and though no single intervention will solve the obesity problem, that is hardly a reason to take no action.

7   The full impact of public policies becomes apparent only after they take effect. We can estimate changes in sugared-drink consumption that would be prompted by a tax, but accompanying changes in the consumption of other foods or beverages are more difficult to predict. One question is whether the proportions of calories consumed in liquid and solid foods would change. And shifts among beverages would have different effects depending on whether consumers substituted water, milk, diet drinks, or equivalent generic brands of sugared drinks.

8   Effects will also vary depending on whether the tax is designed to reduce consumption, generate revenue, or both; the size of the tax; whether the revenue is earmarked for programs related to nutrition and health; and where in the production and distribution chain the tax is applied. Given the heavy consumption of sugared beverages, even small taxes will generate substantial revenue, but only heftier taxes will significantly reduce consumption. Sales taxes are the most common form of food tax, but because they are levied as a percentage of the retail price, they encourage the purchase of less-expensive brands or larger containers. Excise taxes structured as a fixed cost per ounce provide an incentive to buy less and hence would be much more effective in reducing consumption and improving health. In addition, manufacturers generally pass the cost of an excise tax along to their customers, including it in the price consumers see when they are making their selection, whereas sales taxes are seen only at the cash register.

9   Although a tax on sugared beverages would have health benefits regardless of how the revenue was used, the popularity of such a proposal increases greatly if revenues are used for programs to prevent childhood obesity, such as media campaigns, facilities and programs for physical activity, and healthier food in schools. Poll results show that support of a tax on sugared beverages ranges from 37 to 72 percent; a poll of New York residents found that 52 percent supported a "soda tax," but the number rose to 72 percent when respondents were told that the revenue would be used for obesity prevention. Perhaps the most defensible approach is to use revenue to subsidize the purchase of healthful foods. The public would then see a relationship between tax and benefit, and

any regressive effects would be counteracted by the reduced costs of healthful food.

10   A penny-per-ounce excise tax could reduce consumption of sugared beverages by more than 10 percent. It is difficult to imagine producing behavior change of this magnitude through education alone, even if government devoted massive resources to the task. In contrast, a sales tax on sugared drinks would generate considerable revenue, and as with the tax on tobacco, it could become a key tool in efforts to improve health.

References

1. Vartanian LR, Schwartz MB, Brownell KD. Effects of soft drink consumption on nutrition and health: a systematic review and meta-analysis. Am J Public Health 2007;97:667–675.

2. Forshee RA, Anderson PA, Storey ML. Sugar-sweetened beverages and body mass index in children and adolescents: a meta-analysis. Am J Clin Nutr 2008;87:1662–71.

3. Nielsen SJ, Popkin BM. Changes in beverage intake between 1977 and 2001. Am J Prev Med 2004; 27:205–210.

4. Ludwig DS, Peterson KE, Gortmaker SL. Relation between consumption of sugar-sweetened drinks and childhood obesity: a prospective, observational analysis. Lancet 2001;357: 505–508.

5. Elasticity: big price increases cause Coke volume to plummet. Beverage Digest. November 21, 2008:3–4.

[REFLECT]   # Make connections: Government problem solving.

Brownell and Frieden explicitly argue in favor of the federal and/or state government taking action to address public health problems such as those related to obesity and smoking. Imposing taxes is one thing government can do. Another action is to require that foods be labeled with accurate nutritional information.

Write a few paragraphs considering the right and responsibility of government to solve public health problems. Your instructor may ask you to post your thoughts on a class discussion board or to discuss them with other students in class. Use these questions to get started:

- Consider what actions government *could* take to address public health problems and whether government *should* take such actions.

- Think about how you would respond to Brownell and Frieden's argument that "though no single intervention will solve the obesity problem, that is hardly a reason to take no action" (par. 6).

[ANALYZE]   # Use the basic features.

A FOCUSED, WELL-DEFINED PROBLEM: CITING RESEARCH STUDIES

Brownell and Frieden identify the problem for which they are proposing a solution in broad terms as the "obesity epidemic" (par. 1). However, they frame the issue by focusing on "sugar-sweetened beverages" (par. 2). To support a causal connection between consuming sugar-sweetened beverages and obesity, they cite research studies.

ANALYZE & WRITE

Write a paragraph or two analyzing more closely how Brownell and Frieden use research to establish a causal connection between sweetened drinks and obesity:

1. Skim paragraph 3 to identify the findings Brownell and Frieden summarize there. Note that these are the findings of a "meta-analysis," which compares different studies researching the same question.

2. Consider how effectively, if at all, these findings support Brownell and Frieden's argument about a cause-effect relationship between consuming sugar-sweetened beverages and obesity.

3. Think about what kinds of studies were done and consider how Brownell and Frieden rate these different kinds of studies. Why might it be helpful for Brownell and Frieden's readers from the *New England Journal of Medicine* to know the kinds of studies that have been used and which ones employ "the best methods" and get "the strongest effects"?

A WELL-ARGUED SOLUTION: USING COMPARISON-CONTRAST AND CLASSIFICATION

Like O'Malley, Brownell and Frieden use their title to announce the solution they are proposing: the imposition of a tax on certain beverages. They use writing strategies such as comparison-contrast and classification to support their claims. Even the epigraph quoting Adam Smith, the father of free market economics, is a kind of comparison in that it implicitly associates a figure linked to conservative politics with their proposal, which would generally be considered liberal.

ANALYZE & WRITE

Write a few paragraphs analyzing and evaluating how Brownell and Frieden use comparison and contrast as well as classification strategies to support their proposal:

1. Reread paragraphs 3–4. How do Brownell and Frieden use comparison and contrast there to argue for a tax on sweetened beverages?

2. Reread paragraphs 8–9. How do they use classification there?

3. Consider the strengths and weaknesses of using these two strategies to support their proposed solution. How are these two writing strategies effective ways of supporting their proposal? What other strategies might work better?

AN EFFECTIVE RESPONSE TO OBJECTIONS AND ALTERNATIVE SOLUTIONS: HANDLING OBJECTIONS

Proposal writers usually try to anticipate readers' objections and questions and concede or refute them. How writers handle objections and questions affects their credibility with readers, who usually expect writers to be respectful of other points of view and to take criticism seriously while still arguing assertively for their solution. Brownell and Frieden anticipate and respond to five objections they would expect their readers to raise.

To learn more about using
graphics, see Chapter 32,
pp. 744–50.

ANALYZE & WRITE

Write a couple of paragraphs analyzing and evaluating how Brownell and Frieden respond
to objections:

1 Reread paragraph 5. First, summarize the objection and their argument refuting it. Then
evaluate their response: How effective is their refutation likely to be with their readers?

2 Reread paragraph 6, in which the authors respond to a number of objections. What
cues do they provide to help you follow their argument?

3 Given their purpose and audience, why do you think Brownell and Frieden focus so
much attention on the first objection and group the other objections together in a
single paragraph?

4 How would you describe the tone of Brownell and Frieden's refutation? How is their
credibility with readers likely to be affected by the way they respond to objections?

A CLEAR, LOGICAL ORGANIZATION: USING GRAPHS

Brownell and Frieden include two graphs in their proposal—a bar graph and a line
graph. Bar graphs and line graphs can be used to display numerical and statistical
information at different points in time and also to compare groups or data sets by using different color bars or lines.

ANALYZE & WRITE

Write a paragraph analyzing and evaluating how well Brownell and Frieden integrate these
graphs:

1 Highlight the sentences in paragraphs 2 and 4 in which Brownell and Frieden introduce
each graph. How else do they integrate the graphs into their argument?

2 Consider the sections in which these graphs appear. How might the graphs help
demarcate sections and move readers from one section to the next?

3 Look closely at the graphs themselves to see how the information is presented. What
do the graphs contribute? Given Brownell and Frieden's purpose and audience, why
do you think they chose to include these graphs?

[RESPOND]   # Consider possible topics: Improving a group to which you belong.

Consider making a proposal to improve the operation of an organization, a business,
or a club to which you belong. For example, you might propose that your college
keep administrative offices open in the evenings or on weekends to accommodate
working students, or that a child-care center be opened for students who are parents
of young children. For a business, you might propose a system to handle customer
complaints or a fairer way for employees to arrange their schedules. If you belong
to a club that has a problem with the collection of dues, you might propose a new
collection system or suggest alternative ways of raising money.

Proposals occur regularly in genres and media besides the college essay. For example, proposals to obtain grant funding generally appear as reports, with sections for an executive summary, background, project narrative, timeline, and budget. They may be delivered electronically with links in a table of contents, so readers can click to read each section.

Patrick O'Malley thought his target audience (professors) would be more likely to replace a few high-stakes exams with a greater number of lower-stakes quizzes and tests if he remixed his essay as a presentation that laid out the evidence clearly. (A remix takes all or part of a piece in one genre to create a text in another genre or for another purpose or audience.) He planned to deliver it face to face at a faculty meeting and then post his presentation slides online.

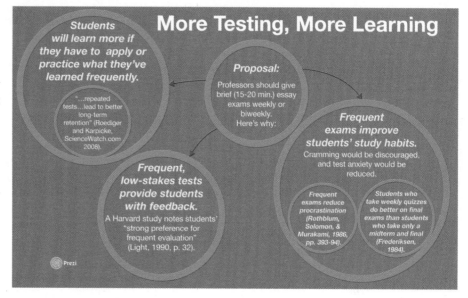

In the next section of this chapter, we ask you to craft your own proposal. After composing it as an essay, consider remixing it by presenting it (or a portion of it) in another genre or medium, or using it as part of text with a different purpose or audience.

CONSIDER YOUR RHETORICAL SITUATION

Purpose: The purpose of your propsal is to convince your readers that a serious problem exists and persuade them that your solution is feasible. If you remix your proposal, *which genre or medium would best allow you to make a compelling case for your proposed solution?*

Audience: The audience for your proposal is your instructor and other students in your class. *What audience will be most affected by the problem you identify or will be able to take action on your proposal?*

Genre and medium: The genre of your proposal was the essay; the medium was textual, delivered either in print or online. If your remix you proposal, *what genre or medium would best help you convince your target audience?*

The Writing Assignment

Write an essay proposing a solution to a problem. Choose a problem faced by a community or group to which you belong, and address your proposal to one or more members of the group or to outsiders who might help solve the problem.

This Guide to Writing is designed to help you compose your own proposal and apply what you have learned from reading other essays in the same genre. This Starting Points chart will help you find answers to questions you might have about composing a proposal. Use the chart to find the guidance you need, when you need it.

STARTING POINTS: PROPOSING A SOLUTION

A Focused, Well-Defined Problem

How do I come up with a problem to write about?

- Assess the genre's basic features: A focused, well-defined problem. (pp. 285–87)
- Consider possible topics: Representing the voiceless. (p. 302)
- Consider possible topics: Moving the masses. (p. 308)
- Consider possible topics: Improving a group to which you belong. (p. 314)
- Choose a problem for which you can propose a solution. (p. 318)

How can I best define the problem for my readers?

- A Focused, Well-Defined Problem: Convincing the Audience (pp. 299–300)
- A Focused, Well-Defined Problem: Framing the Problem (pp. 305–6)
- A Focused, Well-Defined Problem: Citing Research Studies (pp. pp. 312–13)
- Frame the problem for your readers. (pp. 319–20)
- Test Your Choice: Defining the Problem (p. 321)
- Assess how the problem has been framed, and reframe it for your readers. (pp. 321–22)
- A Troubleshooting Guide: A Focused, Well-Defined Problem (p. 329)

A Well-Argued Solution

How do I come up with a plausible solution?

- Assess the genre's basic features: A well-argued solution. (pp. 287–88)
- A Well-Argued Solution: Demonstrating Feasibility (pp. 300–301)
- A Well-Argued Solution: Making a Persuasive Argument (p. 306)
- A Well-Argued Solution: Using Comparison-Contrast and Classification (p. 313)
- Develop a possible solution. (pp. 322–23)
- Research your proposal. (p. 324)

How do I construct an argument supporting my solution?

- Assess the genre's basic features: A well-argued solution. (pp. 287–88)
- A Well-Argued Solution: Demonstrating Feasibility (pp. 300–301)
- Explain your solution. (p. 323)
- Research your proposal. (p. 324)
- A Troubleshooting Guide: A Well-Argued Solution (p. 329)

An Effective Response to Objections and Alternative Solutions

How do I respond to possible objections and alternative solutions?

- Assess the genre's basic features: An effective response to objections and alternative solutions. (pp. 288–89)
- An Effective Response to Objections and Alternative Solutions: Anticipating Negative Side Effects (p. 301)
- An Effective Response to Objections and Alternative Solutions: Finding a Way to Bridge Differences (p. 307)
- An Effective Response to Objections and Alternative Solutions: Handling Objections (p. 313)
- Develop a response to objections or alternative solutions. (pp. 324–25)

A Clear, Logical Organization

How can I help my readers follow my argument?

- Assess the genre's basic features: A clear, logical organization. (pp. 289–90)
- A Clear, Logical Organization: Creating Unity (pp. 301–2)
- A Clear, Logical Organization: Creating Coherence (pp. 307–8)
- A Clear, Logical Organization: Using Graphs (p. 314)
- Create an outline that will organize your proposal effectively for your readers. (p. 325)
- A Troubleshooting Guide: A Clear, Logical Organization (p. 330)

Writing a Draft: Invention, Research, Planning, and Composing

The activities in this section will help you choose and research a problem as well as develop and organize an argument for your proposed solution. Your writing in response to many of these activities can be used in a rough draft that you will be able to improve after receiving feedback from your classmates and instructor. Do the activities in any order that makes sense to you (and your instructor), and return to them as needed as you revise.

▪▪ Choose a problem for which you can propose a solution.

When choosing a problem, keep in mind that it must be

- important to you and of concern to your readers;
- solvable, at least in part;
- one that you can research sufficiently in the time you have.

Choosing a problem affecting a group to which you belong (for example, as a classmate, teammate, participant in an online game site, or garage band member) or a place at which you have worked (a coffee shop, community pool, or radio station) gives you an advantage: You can write as an expert. You know the history of the problem, you know who to interview, and perhaps you have already thought about possible solutions. Moreover, you know who to address and how to persuade that audience to take action on your proposed solution.

If you already have a problem and possible solution(s) in mind, skip to Frame the Problem for Your Readers on the facing page. If you need to find a problem, consider the possible topics following the readings and the suggestions here.

	Problems	**Possible Solutions**
School	Can't get into required courses	Make them large lecture courses.
		Make them online or hybrid courses.
		Give priority to majors.
Community	No safe place for children to play	Use school yards for after-school sports.
		Get high school students or senior citizens to tutor kids.
		Make pocket parks for neighborhood play.
		Offer programs for kids at branch libraries.
Work	Inadequate training for new staff	Make a training video or Web site.
		Assign experienced workers to mentor trainees (for bonus pay).

Writing a Draft

GUIDE TO READING
▶ **GUIDE TO WRITING**
A WRITER AT WORK
THINKING CRITICALLY

319

:: Frame the problem for your readers.

Once you have made a preliminary choice of a problem, consider what you know about it, what research will help you explore what others think about it, and how you can interest your readers in solving it. Then determine how you can frame or reframe it in a way that appeals to readers' values and concerns. Use the questions and sentence strategies that follow as a jumping-off point; you can make them your own as you revise later.

To learn more about conducting surveys and interviews, consult Chapter 24. For advice on listing, cubing, and freewriting, see Chapter 11.

WAYS IN

WHAT IS THE PROBLEM?

What do I already know about the problem?

BRAINSTORM *a list:* Spend 10 minutes listing everything you know about the problem. Write quickly, leaving judgment aside for the moment. After the 10 minutes are up, you can review your list and highlight or star the most promising information.

Use **CUBING**: Probe the problem from a variety of perspectives:

- Describe the problem.
- Compare the problem to other, similar problems, or contrast it with other, related problems.
- Connect the problem to other problems in your experience.
- Analyze the problem to identify its parts, its causes, or its effects.
- Apply the problem to a real-life situation.

FREEWRITE (write without stopping) for 5 or 10 minutes about the problem. Don't stop to reflect or consider; if you hit a roadblock, just keep coming back to the problem. At the end of the specified time, review your writing and highlight or underline promising ideas.

WHY SHOULD READERS CARE?

How can I convince readers the problem is real and deserves attention?

Give an **EXAMPLE** *to make the problem specific:*

- ▶ Recently, ... has been in the news/in movies/a political issue because of [name event].

EXAMPLE   The film *Blackfish* compellingly describes many of the reasons why keeping orcas in captivity is—and always has been—a bad idea. (Rose, par. 1)
Sunday is the thirtieth anniversary of the National Organ Transplant Act, but no one wants to celebrate. U.S. policy on organ transplants—especially as applied to kidneys—is a mess. (Posner, par. 1)

Use a **SCENARIO** *or* **ANECDOTE** *to dramatize the problem:*

EXAMPLE   It's late at night. The final's tomorrow. You got a C on the midterm, so this one will make or break you. (O'Malley, par. 1)

Cite **STATISTICS** *to show the severity of the problem:*

- ▶ It has recently been reported that .... percent of group A are [specify problem].

(continued)

What do others think about the problem?

Conduct **SURVEYS**:

- Talk to a variety of students at your school (your friends and others).
- Discuss the problem with neighbors or survey shoppers at a local mall.
- Discuss the problem with coworkers or people who work at similar jobs.

Conduct **INTERVIEWS**:

- Interview faculty experts.
- Discuss the issue with businesspeople in the community.
- Interview local officials (members of the city council, the fire chief, the local labor union representative).

What do most of my potential readers already think about the problem?

▶ Many complain about .... but do nothing because solving it seems too hard/too costly.

▶ Some think .... is someone else's responsibility/not that big of a problem.

▶ Others see .... as a matter of fairness/human decency.

Who suffers from the problem?

▶ Studies have shown that .... mostly affects groups A, B, and C.

EXAMPLE These . . . predators are dangerous to their trainers. But orcas are also directly harmed by being confined in concrete tanks. . . . (Rose, par. 1)

EXAMPLE More than 100,000 people languish on the waitlist for kidneys, thousands of them dying before they receive a transplant. In 2012, almost 35,000 people joined the waitlist, while only 17,000 received transplants.

Every year the waitlist lengthens. NOTA virtually guaranteed this shortage by shutting down an incipient market in kidneys. (Posner, pars. 1–2)

Describe the problem's **NEGATIVE CONSEQUENCES**:

▶ According to Professor X, group A is suffering as a result of .... [insert quote from expert].

EXAMPLE Sian Beilock, a psychology professor at the University of Chicago, points out that "stressing about doing well on an important exam can backfire, leading students to 'choke under pressure' or to score less well than they might otherwise score if the stakes weren't so high." (O'Malley, par. 2)

Why should readers care about solving the problem?

▶ We're all in this together. .... is not a win-lose proposition. If group A loses, we all lose.

▶ If we don't try to solve ...., no one else will.

▶ Doing nothing will only make .... worse.

▶ We have a moral responsibility to do something about ....

Writing a Draft

GUIDE TO READING
GUIDE TO WRITING
A WRITER AT WORK
THINKING CRITICALLY

321

TEST YOUR CHOICE

Defining the Problem

Ask two or three other students to help you develop your plan to frame the problem.

Presenters.   Briefly explain how you are thinking of framing or reframing the problem for your audience. Use the following language as a model for presenting your problem, or use language of your own.

▶ I plan to define the problem not as _____ but as _____ /in terms of _____ because I think my readers will share my concerns/values/priorities.

Listeners.   Tell the presenter what response this way of framing the problem elicits from you and why. You may also explain how you think other readers might respond. Use the following language as a model for structuring your response, or use your own words.

▶ I'm also/not concerned about X because of _____ , _____ , and _____ .

▶ I agree/disagree that _____ because _____ .

⠿ Assess how the problem has been framed, and reframe it for your readers.

Once you have a good idea of what you and your readers think about the problem, consider how others have framed the problem and how you might be able to reframe it for your readers.

HOW HAS THE PROBLEM BEEN FRAMED?	HOW CAN I REFRAME THE PROBLEM?
Sink or Swim Argument	**Teaching Should Not Be Punitive Argument**
EXAMPLE Providing tutoring for students who are failing a course is wrong because students should do what they need to do to pass the course or face the consequences. That's the way the system is supposed to work.	EXAMPLE Providing tutoring for students who are failing a course assumes the purpose of education is learning, not testing for its own sake or punishing those who have not done well.
Don't Reward Failure Argument	**Encourage Success Argument**
EXAMPLE Providing tutoring for students who are failing a course is like a welfare system that makes underprepared students dependent and second-class citizens.	EXAMPLE Providing tutoring for students who are failing a course encourages students to work hard and value doing well in school.

WAYS IN

(continued)

Reverse Discrimination Argument

EXAMPLE   Providing tutoring for students who are failing a course is unfair to the other students who don't need assistance.

Win-Lose Argument

EXAMPLE   Providing tutoring for students who are failing a course ignores the fact that grades should fall on a bell curve — that is, an equal proportion of students should get an *F* as get an *A*.

Level Playing Ground Argument

EXAMPLE   Providing tutoring for students who are failing a course is a way to make up for inadequacies in previous schooling.

Win-Win Argument

EXAMPLE   Providing tutoring for students who are failing a course assumes that it would be a good thing if every student earned an *A*. Providing tutoring enhances learning.

⁛ Develop a possible solution.

The following activities will help you devise a solution and develop an argument to support it. If you have already found a solution, you may want to skip this activity and go directly to the Explain Your Solution section (p. 323).

WAYS IN

HOW CAN I SOLVE THIS PROBLEM?

One way to generate ideas is to write steadily for at least five minutes, exploring some of the possible ways of solving the problem. Consider using the following approaches as a jumping-off point:

- Adapt a solution that has been tried or proposed for a similar problem.

    EXAMPLE   Rose's proposal for an orca sanctuary is based on a similar proposal for a dolphin sanctuary that is being developed by Merlin Entertainments.

- Focus on eliminating a cause or minimizing an effect of the problem.

    EXAMPLE   O'Malley's solution to stressful high-stakes exams is to eliminate the cause of the stress by inducing instructors to give more frequent low-stakes exams.

- See the problem as part of a larger system, and explore solutions to the system.

    EXAMPLE   Posner's solution to the problem of organ waiting lists is to reform the system for compensating donors.

- Focus on solving a small part of the problem.

EXAMPLE   Brownell and Frieden's solution to obesity is to reduce the consumption of sugared beverages through taxation.

- Look at the problem from different points of view.

  EXAMPLE   Consider what students, teachers, parents, or administrators might think could be done to help solve the problem.

- Think of a specific example of the problem, and consider how you could solve it.

  EXAMPLE   O'Malley could have focused on solving the problem of high-stakes exams in his biology course.

For more idea-generating strategies, see Chapter 11.

Explain your solution.

You may not yet know for certain whether you will be able to construct a convincing argument to support your solution, but you should choose a solution that you feel motivated to pursue. Use the questions and sentence strategies that follow to help you put your ideas in writing. You will likely want to revise what you come up with later, but the questions and sentence strategies below may provide a convenient jumping-off point.

WAYS IN

HOW CAN I EXPLAIN HOW MY SOLUTION WOULD HELP SOLVE THE PROBLEM?

It would eliminate a cause of the problem.

- ▶ Research shows it would reduce ....

It has worked elsewhere.

- ▶ It works in ...., ..., and ...., as studies evaluating it show.

It would change people's behavior.

- ▶ .... would discourage/encourage people to ....

HOW CAN I EXPLAIN THAT MY SOLUTION IS FEASIBLE?

It could be implemented.

Describe the major stages or steps necessary to carry out your solution.

We can afford it.

Explain what it would cost to put the solution into practice.

It would not take too much time.

Create a rough schedule or timeline to show how long it would take to make the necessary arrangements.

⚌ Research your proposal.

You may have already begun researching the problem and familiarizing yourself with alternative solutions that have been offered, or you may have ideas about what you need to research. If you are proposing a solution to a problem about which others have written, use the following research strategies to help you find out what solutions others have proposed or tried. You may also use these strategies to find out how others have defined the problem and demonstrated its seriousness.

For more about searching for information, consult Chapter 21. For more about avoiding plagiarism, see Chapter 23. For more about documenting sources, consult Chapter 24 (MLA style) or Chapter 25 (APA style).

- Enter keywords or phrases related to your solution (or problem) into the search box of an all-purpose database, such as *Academic OneFile* (InfoTrac) or *Academic Search Complete* (EBSCOHost), to find relevant articles in magazines and journals; in the database Lexis/Nexis to find articles in newspapers; or in library catalogs to find books and other resources. (Database names may change, and what is available will differ from school to school. Some libraries may even combine all three into one search link on the library's home page. Ask a librarian if you need help.) Patrick O'Malley could have tried a combination of keywords, such as *learning* and *test anxiety,* or variations on his terms (*frequent testing, improve retention*) to find relevant articles.

- Bookmark or keep a record of the URLs of promising sites, and download or copy information you could use in your essay. When available, download PDF files rather than HTML files, because these are likely to include visuals, such as graphs and charts. If you copy and paste relevant information into your notes, be careful to distinguish all material from sources from your own ideas.

- Remember to record source information and to cite and document any sources you use, including visuals and interviews.

⚌ Develop a response to objections or alternative solutions.

The topics you considered when developing an argument for your solution may be the same topics you need to consider when developing a response to likely criticisms of your proposal—answering possible objections to your solution or alternative solutions readers may prefer. The following sentence strategies may help you start drafting an effective response.

WAYS IN

HOW CAN I DRAFT A REFUTATION OR CONCESSION?

To draft a REFUTATION, *try beginning with sentence strategies like these:*

- ▶ Some people think we can't afford to do X, but it would only cost $........ to put my solution in place compared to $ .... , the cost of doing nothing/implementing an alternative solution.

- ▶ Although it might take X months/years to implement this solution, it would actually take longer to implement solution A.

▶ There are critics who think that only a few people would benefit from solving this problem, but _____ would benefit because _____ .

▶ Some may suggest that I favor this solution because I would benefit personally; however, the fact is we would all benefit because _____ .

▶ Some may claim that this solution has been tried and hasn't worked. But research shows that [explain how proposed solution has worked] *or* my solution differs from past experiments in these important ways: _____ , _____ , and _____ .

To draft a CONCESSION, *try beginning with sentence strategies like these:*

▶ I agree with those who claim X/object on X grounds; therefore, instead of _____ , I think we should pursue _____ .

▶ If _____ seems too time-consuming/expensive, let's try _____ .

▶ Where _____ is a concern, I think _____ [name alternative] should be followed.

▶ Although _____ is the best way to deal with a problem like this, under _____ [describe special circumstances], I agree that _____ should be done.

⠿ Create an outline that will organize your proposal effectively for your readers.

For more on outlining, see Chapter 11, pp. 490–94.

Whether you have rough notes or a complete draft, making an outline of what you have written can help you organize your essay effectively for your audience. Compare the possible outlines below to see how you might organize the essay depending on whether your readers agree that a serious problem exists and are open to your solution—or not.

If you are writing primarily for readers who *acknowledge that the problem exists and are open to your solution:*

   I. **Introduce the problem,** concluding with a thesis statement asserting your solution.

  II. **Demonstrate the problem's seriousness:** Frame the problem in a way that prepares readers for the solution.

 III. **Describe the proposed solution:** Show what could be done to implement it.

 IV. **Refute objections.**

  V. **Conclude:** Urge action on your solution.

If you are writing primarily for readers who *do not recognize the problem or are likely to prefer alternative solutions:*

   I. **Reframe the problem:** Identify common ground, and acknowledge alternative ways readers might see the problem.

  II. **Concede strengths, but emphasize the weaknesses of alternative solution(s) that readers might prefer.**

 III. **Describe the proposed solution:** Give reasons and provide evidence to demonstrate that it is preferable to the alternative(s).

 IV. **Refute objections.**

  V. **Conclude:** Reiterate shared values.

Whatever organizational strategy you adopt, do not hesitate to change your outline as necessary while drafting and revising. For instance, you might find it more effective to hold back on presenting your solution until you have discussed unacceptable alternatives. The purpose of an outline is to identify the basic components of your proposal and to help you organize it effectively, not to lock you into a particular structure.

Write the opening sentences.

Review what you have written to see if you have something that would work to launch your proposal, or try out one or two of these opening strategies:

Begin with an **engaging scenario:**

> It's late at night. The final's tomorrow. You got a C on the midterm, so this one will make or break you. Will it be like the midterm? Did you study enough? Did you study the right things? It's too late to drop the course. So what happens if you fail? No time to worry about that now—you've got a ton of notes to go over. (O'Malley, par. 1)

Cite a **recent event** *or* **film** *demonstrating the seriousness of the problem:*

> The film *Blackfish* compellingly describes many of the reasons why keeping orcas in captivity is—and always has been—a bad idea (Magnolia). (Rose, par. 1)

Use **statistics** *to demonstrate the seriousness of the problem:*

> Sunday is the thirtieth anniversary of the National Organ Transplant Act, but no one wants to celebrate. U.S. policy on organ transplants—especially as applied to kidneys—is a mess. More than 100,000 people languish on the waitlist for kidneys, thousands of them dying before they receive a transplant. (Posner, par. 1)

Offer a **quotation** *that highlights support for your solution:*

> Sugar, rum, and tobacco are commodities which are nowhere necessaries of life, which are become objects of almost universal consumption, and which are therefore extremely proper subjects of taxation.
> —Adam Smith, *The Wealth of Nations*, 1776 (Brownwell and Frieden, par. 1)

But don't agonize over the first sentences, because you are likely to discover the best way to begin only after you have written a rough draft.

Draft your proposal.

By this point, you have done a lot of research and writing to

- focus and define a problem, and develop a solution to it;
- support your solution with reasons and evidence your readers will find persuasive;
- refute or concede objections and alternative solutions;
- organize your ideas to make them clear, logical, and effective for readers.

Now stitch that material together to create a draft. The next two parts of this Guide to Writing will help you evaluate and improve that draft.

Evaluating the Draft

GUIDE TO READING
GUIDE TO WRITING
A WRITER AT WORK
THINKING CRITICALLY

327

Evaluating the Draft: Using Peer Review

Your instructor may arrange a peer review session in class or online, where you can exchange drafts with your classmates and give each other a thoughtful critical reading, pointing out what works well and suggesting ways to improve the draft. A good critical reading does three things:

1. It lets the writer know how well the reader understands the point of the draft.

2. It praises what works best.

3. It indicates where the draft could be improved and makes suggestions on how to improve it.

One strategy for evaluating a draft is to use the basic features of a proposal as a guide.

A PEER REVIEW GUIDE

A Focused, Well-Defined Problem

> How well does the writer establish that the problem exists and is serious?

Summarize: Tell the writer what you understand the problem to be.

Praise: Give an example where the problem and its significance come across effectively such as where an example dramatizes the problem or statistics establish its significance.

Critique: Tell the writer where readers might need more information about the problem's causes and consequences, or where more might be done to establish its seriousness.

A Well-Argued Solution

> Has the writer argued effectively for the solution?

Summarize: Tell the writer what you understand the proposed solution to be.

Praise: Give an example in the essay where support for the solution is presented especially effectively—for example, note particularly strong reasons, writing strategies that engage readers, or design or visual elements that make the solution clear and accessible.

Critique: Tell the writer where the argument for the solution could be strengthened—for example, where steps for implementation could be laid out more clearly, where the practicality of the solution could be established more convincingly, or where additional support for reasons should be added.

(continued)

An Effective Response to Objections and Alternative Solutions

Has the writer responded effectively to objections or alternative solutions?

Summarize: Tell the writer what you understand to be the objections or alternative solutions that he or she is responding to.

Praise: Give an example in the essay where the writer concedes or refutes a likely objection to the argument effectively, and where reasons showing the limitations of alternative solutions are most effectively presented.

Critique: Tell the writer where concessions and refutations could be more convincing, where possible objections or reservations should be taken into account or alternative solutions should be discussed, where reasons for not accepting other solutions need to be strengthened, or where common ground should be sought with advocates of other positions.

A Clear, Logical Organization

Is the proposal clearly and logically organized?

Summarize: Underline the sentence(s) in which the writer establishes the problem and proposes a solution. Also identify the places where the writer forecasts the argument, supplies topic sentences, and uses transitions or repeats key words and phrases.

Praise: Give an example of how the essay succeeds in being readable—for example, in its overall organization, its use of forecasting statements or key terms introduced in its thesis and strategically repeated elsewhere, its use of topic sentences or transitions, or an especially effective opening or closing.

Critique: Tell the writer where the readability could be improved. For example, point to places where using key terms would help or where a topic sentence could be made clearer, where the use of transitions could be improved or added, or indicate whether the beginning or ending could be more effective.

Before concluding your peer review, be sure to address any of the writer's concerns that have not been discussed already.

Making Comments Electronically   Most word processing software offers features that allow you to insert comments directly into the text of someone else's document. Many readers prefer to make their comments this way because it tends to be faster than writing on hard copy and space is virtually unlimited; it also eliminates the process of deciphering handwritten comments. Where such features are not available, simply typing comments directly into a document in a contrasting color can provide the same advantages.

Improving the Draft

GUIDE TO READING
GUIDE TO WRITING
A WRITER AT WORK
THINKING CRITICALLY

329

Improving the Draft: Revising, Editing, and Proofreading

Start improving your draft by reflecting on what you have written thus far:

- Review the Test Your Choice responses and critical reading comments from your classmates, instructor, or writing center tutor: What are your readers getting at?
- Take another look at the notes from your earlier research and writing activities: What else should you consider?
- Review your draft: What else can you do to make your proposal more effective?

Revise your draft.

If your readers are having difficulty with your draft, or if you think there is room for improvement, try some of the strategies listed in the Troubleshooting Guide that follows. It can help you fine-tune your presentation of the genre's basic features.

A TROUBLESHOOTING GUIDE

A Focused, Well-Defined Problem	**My readers aren't convinced that my problem is serious or even exists.** • Change the way you present the problem to address readers' concerns more directly. • Add information—statistics, examples, description, and so on—that members of your audience are likely to find persuasive or that they can relate to. • Consider adding visuals, such as graphs, tables, or charts, if these would help clarify the problem for your audience.
A Well-Argued Solution	**My readers aren't convinced that my solution is a good one.** • Try to make your solution more convincing by discussing similar solutions used successfully elsewhere or by demonstrating more clearly how it will solve the problem. • Add evidence (such as facts, statistics, and examples) to support your reasons. • Review the steps needed to enact your solution; if necessary, lay them out more clearly.

(continued)

An Effective Response to Objections and Alternative Solutions

My readers have raised objections to my solution.

- Cite research studies, statistics, or examples to refute readers' objections.
- Concede valid points or modify your solution to accommodate the criticism.
- If you can neither refute nor accommodate objections, rethink your solution.

My readers have proposed alternative solutions that I don't discuss.

- If possible, establish shared values with those who propose alternative solutions, but show why their solutions will not work as well as yours.
- If you cannot demonstrate that your solution is preferable, consider arguing that both solutions deserve serious consideration.

A Clear, Logical Organization

My readers are confused by my proposal or find it hard to follow.

- Try outlining your proposal to be sure that the overall organization is strong; if it is not, try moving, adding, or deleting sections to strengthen coherence.
- Consider adding a forecasting statement and using key terms in your thesis and repeating them when you discuss your main points.
- Check to see that you use topic sentences to introduce your main points and that you provide appropriate transitions.

Edit and proofread your draft.

Several errors occur often in essays that propose solutions: ambiguous use of *this* and *that,* and sentences that lack an agent. The following guidelines will help you check your essay for these common errors.

Avoiding Ambiguous Use of *This* and *That*

The Problem   Because you must frequently refer to the problem and the solution in a proposal, you will often use pronouns to avoid the monotony or wordiness of repeatedly referring to them by name. Using *this* and *that* vaguely to refer to other words or ideas, however, can confuse readers.

The Correction   Add a specific noun after *this* or *that.* For example, in his essay in this chapter, Patrick O'Malley writes:

> Furthermore, professors could help students prepare for midterm and final exams by providing sets of questions from which the exam questions will be selected. . . . *This solution* would have the advantage of reducing students' anxiety about learning every fact in the textbook. . . . (par. 13)

Improving the Draft

GUIDE TO READING
GUIDE TO WRITING
A WRITER AT WORK
THINKING CRITICALLY

331

O'Malley avoids an ambiguous *this* in the second sentence by adding the noun *solution*. (He might just as well have used *preparation* or *action* or *approach*.) Here's another example:

> increase
> ▶ Students would not resist a reasonable fee increase of $40 a year if that would pay
> for needed dormitory remodeling.

Revising Sentences That Lack an Agent

The Problem A writer proposing a solution to a problem usually needs to indicate who should take action to solve it. Those who are in a position to take action are called "agents." Look, for example, at this sentence from Patrick O'Malley's proposal:

> To get students to complete the questions in a timely way, professors would have to collect and check the answers. (par. 12)

In this sentence, *professors* are the agents. They have the authority to assign and collect study questions, and they would need to take this action in order for this solution to be successfully implemented.

Had O'Malley instead written "the answers would have to be collected and checked," the sentence would lack an agent. Failing to name an agent would have made his argument less convincing, because it would have left unclear one of the key parts of any proposal: who is going to take action.

The Correction When you revise your work, ask yourself *who* or *what* performed the action in any given sentence. If there's no clear answer, rewrite the sentence to give it an agent. Watch in particular for forms of the verb *to be* (the ball *was* dropped, exams should *be* given, etc.), which often signal agentless sentences.

> *Your staff should plan a survey*
> ▶ A~~survey could be planned~~ to find out more about students' problems in scheduling the courses they need.

> *The registrar should extend*
> ▶ ~~Extending~~ the deadline to mid-quarter ~~would make sense.~~

Note: Sometimes, however, agentless sentences are appropriate, as when the agent is clear from the context, unknown, or less important than the person or thing acted upon.

A Note on Grammar and Spelling Checkers

These tools can be helpful, but do not rely on them exclusively to catch errors in your text: Spelling checkers cannot catch misspellings that are themselves words, such as *to* for *too*. Grammar checkers miss some problems, sometimes give faulty advice for fixing problems, and can flag correct items as wrong. Use these tools as a second line of defense after your own (and, ideally, another reader's) proofreading and editing efforts.

Patrick O'Malley's Revision Process

This section focuses on student writer Patrick O'Malley's successful efforts to strengthen his argument for the solution he proposes in his essay, "More Testing, More Learning." Compare the following three paragraphs from his draft with paragraphs 4–7 of his final essay on pp. 291–93. As you read, take notes on the differences you observe.

The predominant reason students perform better with multiple exams is that they improve their study habits. Greater regularity in test taking means greater regularity in studying for tests. Students prone to cramming will be forced to open their textbooks more often, keeping them away from long, "kamikaze" nights of studying. Regularity prepares them for the "real world" where you rarely take on large tasks at long intervals. Several tests also improve study habits by reducing procrastination. An article about procrastination from the *Journal of Counseling Psychology* reports that "students view exams as difficult, important, and anxiety provoking." These symptoms of anxiety leading to procrastination could be solved if individual test importance was lessened, reducing the stress associated with the perceived burden.

With multiple exams, this anxiety decrease will free students to perform better. Several, less important tests may appear as less of an obstacle, allowing the students to worry less, leaving them free to concentrate on their work without any emotional hindrances. It is proven that "the performance of test-anxious subjects varies inversely with evaluation stress." It would also be to the psychological benefit of students if they were not subjected to the emotional ups and downs of large exams where they are virtually worry-free one moment and ready to check into the psychiatric ward the next.

Lastly, with multiple exams, students can learn how to perform better on future tests in the class. Regular testing allows them to "practice" the information they learned, thereby improving future test scores. In just two exams, they are not able to learn the instructor's personal examination style, and are not given the chance to adapt their study habits to it. The *American Psychologist* concludes: "It is possible to influence teaching and learning by changing the type of tests."

One difference you may have noted between O'Malley's draft and revised paragraphs is the sequence of reasons he offers.

Draft	Revision
1. Improve study habits	1. Learn more
2. Decrease anxiety and improve performance	2. Perform better on tests
3. Perform better on future tests	3. Improve study habits
	4. Decrease anxiety

O'Malley made learning more his first reason after a classmate commented that professors (the target audience) would probably be more convinced by students' learning than by their improving their study habits or decreasing their anxiety. Here are some other improvements you may have noticed:

Reflecting on What You Have Learned

GUIDE TO READING
GUIDE TO WRITING
A WRITER AT WORK
▶ **THINKING CRITICALLY**

333

- **O'Malley's revised paragraphs are better focused.** For example, in the first draft paragraph, O'Malley switches from study habits to procrastination to anxiety. The revised paragraph (par. 6), by contrast, focuses on study habits. Also, reduced anxiety as a result of less procrastination is discussed in a single paragraph in the revision (par. 7), whereas in the draft it is mixed in with intellectual benefits in the first two paragraphs.
- **O'Malley's language is more precise.** For example, he changes "predominant reason" to "main reason" and "future tests" to "major exams, projects, and papers."
- **O'Malley's supporting evidence is more relevant.** For example, in the first draft paragraph, O'Malley includes a quotation that adds nothing, whereas in the revised paragraph (par. 6) the quotation he uses from the Harvard report provides convincing support for his claims and offers an effective conclusion to the paragraph.

Can you find other examples of better focus, more precise language, or relevant support? Did you notice any other improvements?

THINKING CRITICALLY

To think critically means to use all of the knowledge you have acquired from the information in this chapter, your own writing, the writing of other students, and class discussions to reflect deeply on your work for this assignment and the genre (or type) of writing you have produced. The benefit of thinking critically is proven and important: Thinking critically about what you have learned will help you remember it longer, ensuring that you will be able to put it to good use well beyond this writing course.

Reflecting on What You Have Learned

In this chapter, you have learned a great deal about this genre from reading several proposals and writing one of your own. To consolidate your learning, reflect not only on what you learned but also on how you learned it.

ANALYZE & WRITE

Write a blog post, a letter to your instructor, or an e-mail message to a student who will take this course next term, using the writing prompt below that seems most productive for you:

- Explain how your purpose and audience influenced *one* of your decisions as a writer, such as how you defined the problem, the strategies you used in presenting your solution, or the ways in which you attempted to counter possible objections.

- Discuss what you learned about yourself as a writer in the process of writing this particular essay. For example, what part of the process did you find most challenging? Did you try anything new, like getting a critical reading of your draft or outlining your draft in order to revise it?

- If you were to give advice to a friend who was about to write an essay proposing a solution to a problem, what would you say?

- Which of the readings in this chapter influenced your essay? Explain the influence, citing specific examples from your essay and the reading.

- If you got good advice from a critical reader, explain exactly how the person helped you—perhaps by questioning the way you addressed your audience or the kinds of evidence you offered in support of your proposed solution.

Reflecting on the Genre

No matter how well researched and well argued, many proposals are simply never carried out. In choosing among competing proposals, decision makers—who usually hold the power of the purse strings and necessarily represent a fairly conservative position—often go for the one that is cheapest, most expedient, and least disruptive. They may also choose small, incremental changes over more fundamental, radical solutions. While sometimes the most pragmatic choice, such immediately feasible solutions may merely patch over a problem, failing to solve it structurally. They may even inadvertently maintain the status quo. Worse, they can cause people to give up all attempts to resolve a problem after superficial treatments fail.

ANALYZE & WRITE

Write a page or two explaining how the genre pushes writers to select problems that are easy to solve or that reinforce the status quo. In your discussion, you might consider one or more of the following:

1. **Consider how proposals, because they invite us to select problems that are solvable, might inadvertently push us to focus on minor problems that are only a small part of a major problem.** Do any of the proposals you have read or written reveal this misdirection? If so, what do you think is the major problem in each case? Is the minor problem worth solving as a first step toward solving the major problem, or is it perhaps an unfortunate diversion?

2. **Reflect on arguments that we should not try to solve fundamental social problems by "throwing money at them."** Do you think this objection is a legitimate criticism of most proposals to solve social problems, or is it a justification for allowing the rich and powerful to maintain the status quo? What else, besides money, is required to solve serious social problems? Where are these other resources to come from?

3. **Write a page or two explaining your ideas about the frustrations of effecting real change.** Connect your ideas to your own essay and to the readings in this chapter.

8

Justifying an Evaluation

D oes *Scott Pilgrim vs. the World* deserve its status as a cult film? Is binge-watching the HBO series *Game of Thrones* worthwhile? Does the popular *U.S. News* "Best Colleges" guide use a reliable system for ranking schools? These are some of the questions the evaluations in this chapter answer.

People make evaluations for various purposes and audiences and publish them in a variety of media. For example, students in a history course were asked to write and post to the class blog a review of a scholarly book that included a summary of the book's main assertions and an assessment of how well the author supports those claims with factual evidence and authoritative sources. A business executive used Prezi slides to present her evaluation of how the company could benefit from investing in 3-D printer technology. A motorcycle enthusiast reviewed his tour of the Harley Davidson factory in York, Pennsylvania, and published it in a newsletter for motorcyle hobbyists.

In this chapter, we ask you to choose a subject for evaluation that you can examine closely. By analyzing the selections in the Guide to Reading that follows, you will learn how to use appropriate *criteria* to support your judgment. The Guide to Writing later in the chapter will show you ways to use the basic features of the genre to make your evaluation interesting and persuasive.

PRACTICING THE GENRE

Choosing Appropriate Criteria

The success of evaluation depends on whether readers agree that the criteria being applied are sound and based on widely accepted standards of judgment. To practice developing an evaluative argument based on appropriate criteria, get together with two or three other students and follow the guidelines below.

Part 1.   First, choose a film everyone in the group has seen. Then take turns giving a quick review of the film:

1. Identify the type of film you think it was (for example, romantic comedy, science fiction, action, and so on).

2. Say one thing you expect from films of this type.

3. Say whether this particular film surpassed, met, or fell short of your expectations for this type of film and why.

For example, do you usually expect a film like this to have a surprising or predictable story; to present believable characters in realistic situations; to be all about special effects or exciting action sequences; to be funny, scary, or thought-provoking?

Part 2.   As a group, discuss what you learned:

- **What did you learn about criteria, or standards, appropriate for evaluating the film you chose?** To think about criteria in evaluating a film, discuss the similarities and differences between what you expected and what others expected for the film. Our expectations represent the criteria we think are important when evaluating a subject. What is a *must have* (your main criterion) for judging a comedy? An action film? Were you surprised by how your partners categorized the film or any of the criteria they applied? Why?

- **Think about how the context for your review — the purpose, audience, and medium — affects the criteria you use.** If you were going to post your evaluation on Facebook, be graded on your review, or submit it to an audience review Web site such as Flixster, would you use the same criteria you used in your group? What would you assume about your audience: Why do you think audience members would be likely or unlikely to share your criteria? How could you justify the criteria you think are most important?

Analyzing Evaluations

As you read the selections in this chapter, you will see how different writers argue for an evaluation:

- William Akana argues that *Scott Pilgrim vs. the World* is "a hell of a ride" (pp. 341–46).
- Emily Nussbaum tries to persuade readers that *Game of Thrones* is an engrossing series well worth watching, despite its gruesome violence (pp. 346–49).
- Malcolm Gladwell argues that the *U.S. News* college rankings uses a flawed ranking system (pp. 352–55).
- Sherry Turkle tries to convince readers that texting is no substitute for face-to-face relationships (pp. 358–60).

Analyzing how these writers present their subject, assert and justify their judgment, respond to alternative viewpoints, and organize their writing will help you see how you can use these techniques to make your own evaluations clear and compelling for your readers.

Determine the writer's purpose and audience.

Although writing a review usually helps writers better understand the criteria they use when making evaluations, most writers also hope to influence people as well. As you read the evaluations that follow, ask yourself questions like these:

What seems to be the writer's main purpose?

- to influence readers' judgments and possibly their actions?
- to inspire readers to think critically about which criteria are appropriate for judging subjects of this kind?
- to get readers to look at the subject in a new way?

What does the writer assume about the audience?

- that readers will accept the writer's judgment?
- that they will use the review to make their own independent, informed judgment?
- that they already made up their minds and want to see what others think?
- that they will have serious objections to the writer's argument?

Assess the genre's basic features.

As you read the evaluations in this chapter, consider how different authors make their evaluations helpful and convincing. The examples that follow are taken from the reading selections that appear later in this Guide to Reading.

> ■■ **Basic Features**
> A Well-Presented Subject
> A Well-Supported Judgment
> An Effective Response to Objections and Alternative Judgments
> A Clear, Logical Organization

A WELL-PRESENTED SUBJECT

Read first to identify the subject of the review, which is often named in the title (for example, "*Scott Pilgrim vs. the World:* A Hell of a Ride") and described briefly in the opening paragraphs. Look also to see how the writer classifies the subject in terms of its genre. Here's an example from the first reading selection in the chapter, by student William Akana:

subgenres
genre

> From start to finish, *Scott Pilgrim vs. the World* delivers intense action in a hilarious slacker movie that also somehow reimagines romantic comedy. (par. 1)

Even if readers don't recognize the title, Akana makes clear that the film he is reviewing combines elements of three different kinds of movies (or subgenres), so readers can determine whether he is using appropriate criteria, as you will see in the next section.

Knowing the genre is also important because readers need different kinds of information for different genres. For example, most readers of film reviews want to know what the story is about but do not want to know how it turns out. Film reviewers, therefore, try not to give too much plot detail, as you can see in this concise plot summary from Akana's essay:

> Pilgrim's life takes a dramatic turn when he falls in love with Ramona Flowers (Mary Elizabeth Winstead), who is, quite literally, the girl of his dreams. However, he soon discovers that Ramona's former lovers have formed a league of evil exes to destroy him, and he is forced to fight to the death to prove his love. (par. 2)

A WELL-SUPPORTED JUDGMENT

Identify the judgment the writer asserts, and determine whether the reviewer thinks the subject is good or bad, better or worse than other things in the same genre. Typically, writers announce their judgment in a *thesis statement* early in the evaluation. Below are a couple of sentence strategies typically used for thesis statements in evaluations, followed by examples from reviews in this chapter:

▶ What makes X a success/a failure is _____ and _____ .

▶ X can be appreciated/criticized for _____ , _____ , and _____ , but ultimately it is a success/failure because of _____ .

Genre
Subject
Judgment
Reasons

EXAMPLES   Although the film is especially targeted for old-school gamers, anime fans, and comic book fanatics, *Scott Pilgrim vs. the World can be appreciated and enjoyed* by all audiences because of its inventive special effects, clever dialogue, and artistic cinematography and editing. (Akana, par. 2)

Game of Thrones is the latest entry in television's most esteemed category: the sophisticated cable drama about a patriarchal subculture. . . . These worlds are picturesque, elegantly filmed, and ruled by rigid etiquette—lit up, for viewers, by the thrill of seeing brutality enforced (or, in the case of *Downton Abbey*, a really nice house kept in the family). And yet the undergirding strength of each series is its insight into what it means to be excluded from power: to be a woman, or a bastard, or a "half man." (Nussbaum, par. 3)

Examine the thesis to see whether the writer asserts an overall judgment *and also note the features of the subject that are being praised or criticized and the* reasons *supporting the judgment. Finally, consider whether the reasons are based on criteria you would expect to be used for evaluating something of this kind.* For example, one of William Akana's reasons is that the film uses "special effects" that are "inventive." To support this reason, he devotes two paragraphs to detailing some of the film's special effects. He also gives examples of "video-game-like gimmicks" such as "gamertags," describing them and also providing a screen shot to show what they look like (par. 3).

Consider the types of evidence provided, such as examples and visuals, and whether the writer cites sources by quoting, paraphrasing, *or* summarizing *source material.* Also notice whether the writer uses a *signal phrase* to identify the source and establish its credibility.

> A businessman laments that he no longer has colleagues at work. He doesn't stop by to talk; he doesn't call. He says that he doesn't want to interrupt them. He says they're "too busy on their e-mail." But then he pauses and corrects himself. "I'm not telling the truth. I'm the one who doesn't want to be interrupted. I think I should. But I'd rather just do things on my BlackBerry." (Turkle, par. 2)

How writers treat sources depends on the rhetorical situation. Certain formal situations, such as college assignments or scholarly publications, require writers to cite sources in the text and document them in a bibliography (called a list of *works cited* in many humanities disciplines or a list of *references* in the sciences and social sciences), as we can see in Akana's essay. In writing for a general audience—blogs and newspaper articles, for example—readers do not expect references to appear in the article, but they do expect sources to be named and their credentials to be identified in a signal phrase.

Notice also whether the reviewer uses comparison and contrast. Malcolm Gladwell, for example, sets up his evaluation of the ranking system used by *U.S. News & World Report*'s annual "Best Colleges" guide by comparing it to the system used by *Car and Driver* magazine. Similarly, Emily Nussbaum compares and contrasts *Game of Thrones* with other programs to support her judgment:

> Like *Mad Men*, *Game of Thrones* is elementally concerned with the way that meaningful consent dissolves when female bodies are treated as currency. (par. 8)

> Artistically, *Game of Thrones* is in a different class from *House of Lies*, *Californication*, and *Entourage*. (par. 10)

AN EFFECTIVE RESPONSE TO OBJECTIONS AND ALTERNATIVE JUDGMENTS

Notice how the writer responds to objections to the argument or to alternative judgments readers might prefer. Writers may **concede** (accept) or **refute** (argue against) alternatives, providing a transition or other cues to alert readers.

Side notes: For advice on when to indent quotations rather than use quotation marks, see Chapter 23, pp. 639–41. · Signal phrase · Paraphrase · Quotation · For more on citing sources, see Chapters 23, 24, and 25. · Comparison cue · Contrast cue

The basic structure of a concession is:

Transition indicating concession

▶ Of course, ... is an important factor.

▶ Granted, ... must be taken into consideration.

CONCESSION   Neil Genzlinger called it "vileness for voyeurism's sake," directed at "Dungeons & Dragons types."
    It's true that "Game of Thrones" is unusually lurid, even within the arms race of pay cable. . . . (Nussbaum. pars. 2-3)

The basic structure of a refutation is:

Transition indicating refutation

▶ Although .... , I think ....

▶ X says .... , but I think .... because ....

REFUTATION   Some reviewers have criticized the film because they think that in the end it fails as a romantic comedy. . . . But I agree with *New York Times* reviewer A. O. Scott, who argues that "the movie comes home to the well-known territory of the coming-of-age story, with an account of lessons learned and conflicts resolved." (Akana, par. 9)

A CLEAR, LOGICAL ORGANIZATION

Read to see if the reviewer provides cues *to help readers follow the logic of the argument.* Notice, for example, if the reasons are *forecast* in the thesis or elsewhere in the opening and, if so, where they are brought up again later in the essay. Here are examples from William Akana's film review:

Thesis with topics forecast

Scott Pilgrim vs. the World can be appreciated and enjoyed by all audiences *because* of its inventive special effects, clever dialogue, and artistic cinematography and editing. (par. 2)

Topic sentences with reasons forecast

Scott Pilgrim vs. the World shines bright with superb special effects that serve to reinforce the ideas, themes, and style of the film. (par. 3)

Another strong point of *Scott Pilgrim vs. the World* is its clever and humorous dialogue. (par. 6)

The best attribute by far is the film's creative cinematography and editing. (par. 7)

Also notice how the writer uses logical transitions — such as *because* to introduce reasons and *another* to indicate the next reason in a list.

Finally, where visuals — *such as film stills, cartoons, screen shots, and diagrams* — *are included, determine how they are integrated into the text.* Akana, for example, uses the conventional phrase "see fig. 1" in parentheses following his written description and includes a descriptive caption with the visual. In contrast, writers publishing in newspapers and magazines may simply intersperse screen shots following their descriptions to illustrate their points.

To see how Akana integrated visuals into his essay, see pp. 341–45.

Readings

William Akana | # Scott Pilgrim vs. the World: *A Hell of a Ride*

THIS EVALUATION ESSAY was written by student William Akana for his composition course. The assignment prompt asked students to choose a film and write a review that includes a close analysis of the cinematic techniques used in at least one important scene. Akana's instructor illustrated various cinematic techniques, such as camera angles and movements, and demonstrated how to take screen shots, explaining that students can use visuals for a class project without asking permission, but to publish them they would have to get permission, as we did. As you read, consider these questions as well as those in the margin:

To learn how Akana developed his thesis and responses to objections, turn to A Writer at Work on pp. 382–83.

- How well do the screen shots illustrate Akana's analysis and support his evaluation?

- How would you describe Akana's tone in this essay? How is his tone affected by the fact that he uses the first person pronoun "I" to refer to himself only in the opening and closing paragraphs?

1   As I leaned back in the movie theater seat, accompanied by my friends on a typical Saturday night, I knew I was in for something special. I was reassured; not only had my friends and I reached a unanimous vote to watch *Scott Pilgrim vs. the World*, but two of my friends had already seen the film and were eager to see it again. As soon as the film began, with its presentation of the classic Universal Studios introduction in old-timer eight-bit music and pixilated format, I knew I was in for one hell of a ride. From start to finish, *Scott Pilgrim vs. the World* delivers intense action in a hilarious slacker movie that also somehow reimagines romantic comedy.

▪▪ Basic Features

A Well-Presented Subject

A Well-Supported Judgment

An Effective Response to Objections and Alternative Judgments

A Clear, Logical Organization

How appropriate is this narrative and informality for a film review? For a college paper?

2   *Scott Pilgrim vs. the World,* released in 2010 by Universal Studios, came into production as a comic book adaptation film under the direction of Edgar Wright (best known for the zombie movie masterpiece *Shaun of the Dead*). Scott Pilgrim (Michael Cera) is a twenty-two-year-old Canadian who plays bass for his indie band, Sex Bob-omb, located in Toronto, Canada. Pilgrim's life takes a dramatic turn when he falls in love with Ramona Flowers (Mary Elizabeth Winstead), who is, quite literally, the girl of his dreams. However, he soon discovers that Ramona's former lovers have formed a league of evil exes to destroy him, and he is forced to fight to the death to prove his love. Although the film is especially targeted for old-school gamers, anime fans, and comic book fanatics, *Scott Pilgrim vs. the World* can be appreciated and enjoyed by all audiences because of its inventive special effects, clever dialogue, and artistic cinematography and editing.

3   *Scott Pilgrim vs. the World* shines bright with superb special effects that serve to reinforce the ideas, themes, and style of the film. Special effects are plentiful throughout the entire film, ranging from superimposed annotations echoing classic gaming features to artful backgrounds and action sequences modeled on colorful comic book pages. For example, each of the main characters is described for the first time with "gamertags," short-timed boxes of information that include name, age, and rating (see fig. 1).

> **Why do you think Akana gives readers this information?**

> **How well does this thesis statement forecast Akana's argument? Skim the essay, noting where he discusses each of these reasons.**

Fig. 1. Screen shot showing gamertags

4   *Scott Pilgrim vs. the World* contains numerous amounts of other fun video-game-like gimmicks that were made possible through special effects. One humorous scene presents a pee bar that depletes as Pilgrim relieves himself. Another scene presents a bass battle between Pilgrim and one of the evil exes in the format of PlayStation's popular Guitar Hero (see fig. 2). It goes without saying that anyone who has ever dabbled in video games will greatly appreciate the gaming-culture inside jokes. As the reviewer for the Web site *Cinema Sight* wrote, this film is intended for "the video game generation" ("Review").

5   Comic book references are also installed using special effects. In almost every battle between Pilgrim and his enemies, comic-book-like backgrounds, added through CGI, enhance the eye-popping fight sequences as characters fly into the air to deliver devastating punches accompanied with traditional onomatopoeic "POWs" and "KAPOWs" (see fig. 3). However, comic book annotations are not reserved merely for fight scenes. Annotations range from even the simplest "RIIIINGs" of a telephone to trails of shouting "AAAAHs" of Pilgrim as he is thrown into the air in battle. To make the film even more visually appealing, *Scott Pilgrim vs. the World* portrays flashbacks using white and black comic strips similar to the original Scott Pilgrim comic books. Special effects play a truly vital part in enlivening the style of the film.

> How well do these details and the illustration he chose support Akana's claim that the special effects are "inventive" and "superb"?

Fig. 2. Guitar face-off

Image credit: © Universal/Everett Collection

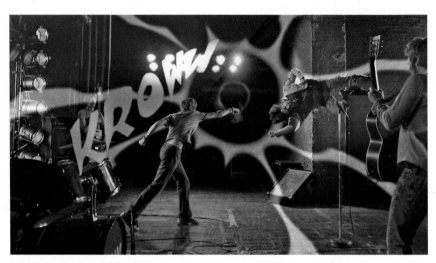

Fig. 3. Comic-book-style annotations

6   Another strong point of *Scott Pilgrim vs. the World* is its clever and humorous dialogue. One memorable scene in the film involves Knives Chau (Ellen Wong) and Scott Pilgrim in an awkward situation where Knives states sheepishly: "I've never even kissed a guy." In a supposedly intimate gesture of affection, Pilgrim moves closer only to pause shortly before saying "Hey . . . me neither." Additionally, *Scott Pilgrim vs. the World* is rich in cultural satire that pokes fun at adolescent and young adult behaviors. One scene contains Pilgrim telling Ramona Flowers: "I feel like I'm on drugs when I'm with you, not that I do drugs, unless you do—in which case, I do drugs all the time." Dialogue like this gives the film a raw yet rich sense of humor that is one of the many inventive risks of the film that pay off.

7   The best attribute by far is the film's creative cinematography and editing, which can be illustrated in the ultimate fight scene of the movie. Pilgrim finally confronts his former band members, who are playing in an underground lair for Ramona's seventh evil ex, Gideon (Jason Schwartzman). As Pilgrim admits his faults and proceeds to apologize to the band for former wrongs, the shot assumes a point of view from Pilgrim's perspective looking up to the band on stage. Shortly before Pilgrim is finished, Gideon, sitting on his throne atop a miniature pyramid, interrupts him. The shot quickly cuts to a close-up of Gideon's eyes, emphasizing his anger at Pilgrim. From this point, soft focusing is utilized to blur the background as a tracking shot follows Pilgrim in a medium close-up as he marches to the base of the pyramid. Then, reverse shots are used between high- and low-angled frames to illustrate Pilgrim's challenge to Gideon for a final duel.

How do the highlighted transitions help readers follow Akana's analysis?

Fig. 4. Threshold of a new beginning?

8   Gideon, in response to the challenge, asks Pilgrim if he is fighting for Ramona, which leads to a climactic epiphany for Pilgrim as he realizes his true motive, admitting in a tight close-up: "No. I want to fight you for me." As Pilgrim finishes this confession, a deep narrating voice announces that "Scott Pilgrim has earned the power of self-respect," and in turn, he is awarded a magical sword with which he can defeat Gideon. Subsequently, the camera pans from left to right in a subjective shot to illustrate Gideon's goons closing in on Pilgrim. Pilgrim, in a series of fast-paced jump cuts, quickly dispatches the bad guys before charging up the pyramid. After an extended battle, deep focusing is used with a long shot to establish that the hierarchy has changed between hero and villain: Pilgrim is seen standing atop the pyramid, looking down at the kneeling Gideon before Pilgrim kicks him to smithereens.

9   This brilliantly executed scene illustrates the artful cinematography of *Scott Pilgrim vs. the World*. More importantly, it delivers the film's thematic message, which undercuts the cliché "love conquers all" and instead focuses on the fresh concept that, in the grand scheme of things, the only person you are fighting for is yourself. Some reviewers have criticized the film because they think that in the end it fails as a romantic comedy. For example, *Miami Herald* film reviewer Rene Rodriguez argues that the film ultimately fails because of the lack of "chemistry" or "emotional involvement" in the romance between Pilgrim and Ramona. But I agree with *New York Times* reviewer A. O. Scott, who argues that "the movie comes home to the well-known territory of the coming-of-age story, with an account of

For what purposes does Akana use these sources? How effective is his response to an opposing view?

lessons learned and conflicts resolved." Fighting Ramona's exes forces Pilgrim to wake up out of his slacker stupor. Before he can begin a grown-up relationship with Ramona, he has to come to terms with his own failures, especially in relation to his own exes. The film ends, as director Edgar Wright explained in an interview, on the threshold of a new beginning: "Scott and Ramona might not make it past the end credits, or it might be the start of a beautiful relationship" (Cozzalio).

Works Cited

Cozzalio, Dennis. "Scott Pilgrim's Dreamscape and the Glories of the Wright Stuff II: An Interview with Director Edgar Wright." *Sergio Leone and the Infield Fly Rule*. SergioLeoneIFR.blogspot.com, 15 Jan. 2011. Web. 30 Mar. 2011.

Rodriguez, Rene. Rev. of *Scott Pilgrim vs. the World. Miami Herald*. Miami.com, 11 Aug. 2010. Web. 28 Mar. 2011.

Scott, A. O. "This Girl Has a Lot of Baggage, and He Must Shoulder the Load." *New York Times*. New York Times, 12 Aug. 2010. Web. 29 Mar. 2011.

Rev. of *Scott Pilgrim vs. The World. Cinema Sight*. CinemaSight.com, 13 Sept. 2010. Web. 30 Mar. 2011.

Emily Nussbaum | *The Aristocrats: The Graphic Arts of* Game of Thrones

Courtesy Emily Nussbaum

EMILY NUSSBAUM has written for numerous publications including the *New York Times, Slate*, and *New York* magazine, for which she worked as culture editor. Currently, she is the television critic for the *New Yorker*, in which this review originally appeared. Her initial fascination with analyzing and critiquing television programs sprang from an obsession with *Buffy the Vampire Slayer*. Her reviews and commentary have become influential particularly in discussions about the effects of technology and social media on television as a medium and on our viewing habits. As you read,

- notice that Nussbaum begins with a little narrative about her job as a television reviewer. How does this story prepare you for what follows?

- consider how effectively Nussbaum establishes her credibility as a reviewer. What in her evaluation helps demonstrate her expertise?

1   For critics, sorting through television pilots is an act of triage. Last year, when *Game of Thrones* landed on my desk, I skimmed two episodes and made a quick call: we'd have to let this one go. The HBO series, based on the best-selling fantasy books by George R. R. Martin, looked as if it were another guts-and-corsets melodrama, like *The Borgias*. In the première, a ten-year-old boy was shoved out of a tower window. The episode climaxed with what might be described as an Orientalist gang rape/wedding dance. I figured I might catch up later, if the buzz was good.

2   It was the right decision, even if I made it for the wrong reason. *Game of Thrones* is an ideal show to binge-watch on DVD: with its cliffhangers and Grand Guignol[1] dazzle, it rewards a bloody, committed immersion in its foreign world—and by this I mean not only the medieval-ish landscape of Westeros (the show's mythical realm) but the genre from which it derives. Fantasy—like television itself, really—has long been burdened with audience condescension: the assumption that it's trash, or juvenile, something intrinsically icky and low. Several reviews of *Game of Thrones* have taken this stance, including two notable writeups in the *Times*: Ginia Bellafante sniffed that the show was "boy fiction" and Neil Genzlinger called it "vileness for voyeurism's sake," directed at "Dungeons & Dragons[2] types."

3   It's true that *Game of Thrones* is unusually lurid, even within the arms race of pay cable: the show is so graphic that it was parodied on *Saturday Night Live*, with a "behind-the-scenes" skit in which a horny thirteen-year-old boy acted as a consultant. To watch it, you must steel yourself for baby-stabbing, as well as rat torture and murder by molten gold. But, once I began sliding in disks in a stupor, it became clear that, despite the show's Maltese vistas and asymmetrical midriff tops, this was not really an exotic property. To the contrary, *Game of Thrones* is the latest entry in television's most esteemed category: the sophisticated cable drama about a patriarchal subculture. This phenomenon launched with *The Sopranos*, but it now includes shows such as *Deadwood*, *Mad Men*, *Downton Abbey*, and *Big Love*. Each of these acclaimed series is a sprawling, multi-character exploration of a closed, often violent hierarchical system. These worlds are picturesque, elegantly filmed, and ruled by rigid etiquette—lit up, for viewers, by the thrill of seeing brutality enforced (or, in the case of *Downton Abbey*, a really nice house kept in the family). And yet the undergirding strength of each series is its insight into what it means to be excluded from power: to be a woman, or a bastard, or a "half man."

4   The first season of *Game of Thrones* built up skillfully, sketching in ten episodes a conflict among the kingdoms of Westeros, each its own philosophical ecosystem. There were the Northern Starks, led by the gruffly ethical Ned Stark and his dignified wife, Catelyn, and their gruffly ethical and dignified children. There were the Southern Lannisters, a crowd of high-cheekboned beauties (and one lusty dwarf, played by the lust-worthy Peter Dinklage), who form a family constellation so twisted, charismatic, and cruel that it rivals *Flowers in the Attic*[3] for blond dysfunction. Across the sea, there were the Dothraki, a Hun-like race of horseman warriors, whose brutal ruler, Drogo, took the delicate, unspellable Daenerys as a bride. A teen girl traded like currency by her brother, Daenerys was initiated into marriage through rape; in

> *The show is so graphic that it was parodied on* Saturday Night Live, *with a "behind-the-scenes" skit in which a horny thirteen-year-old boy acted as a consultant.*

---

[1] An over-the-top style of entertainment designed to shock and thrill viewers, originally of the kind produced at the Grand Guignol Theater in Paris. [Editor's note]

[2] A role-play war game in a fantasy setting. [Editor's note]

[3] A popular novel by V. C. Andrews in which a newly widowed (and indebted) mother moves her children into the attic of her estranged parents' home, while she tries to win back their affections so she will inherit their fortune. This novel has formed the basis of a number of movies and made-for-TV movies since it was published in 1979. [Editor's note]

time, she began to embrace both that marriage and her desert queenhood. (Although the cast is mostly white, the dusky-race aesthetics of the Dothraki sequences are head-clutchingly problematic.) By the finale, she was standing naked in the desert—widowed, traumatized, but triumphant, with three baby dragons crawling over her like vines. (This quick summary doesn't capture the complexity of the series' ensemble, which rivals a Bosch painting: there's also the whispery eunuch Spider; a scheming brothel owner named Littlefinger; and a ketchup-haired sorceress who gives birth to shadow babies.)

5   In the season's penultimate episode, the show made a radical move: it killed off the protagonist. On a public stage, Ned Stark was beheaded, on the orders of the teen-age sadist King Joffrey, a sequence edited with unusual beauty and terror—birds fluttering in the air, a hushed soundtrack, and a truly poignant shot from Ned's point of view, as he looked out toward his two daughters. This primal act suggested the limits of ethical behavior in a brutalized universe, and also dramatized the show's vision of what aristocracy means: a succession of domestic traumas, as each new regent dispatches threats to his bloodline. (Or, as Joffrey's mother, Cersei, puts it, kinghood means "lying on a bed of weeds, ripping them out one by one, before they strangle you in your sleep.") It demonstrated, too, a willingness to risk alienating its audience. . . .

6   Still, the most compelling plots remain those of the subalterns, who are forced to wield power from below. These characters range from heroic figures like the tomboy Arya Stark to villains like Littlefinger, but even the worst turn out to have psychic wounds that complicate their actions. If the show has a hero, it's Tyrion (Dinklage), who is capable of cruelty but also possesses insight and empathy, concealed beneath a carapace of Wildean wit. So far, his strategic gifts have proved more effective than the torture-with-rats approach. Power is "a trick, a shadow on the wall," the eunuch tells Tyrion. "And a very small man can cast a very large shadow."

7   Then, of course, there are the whores. From the start, the show has featured copious helpings of pay-cable nudity, much of it in scenes that don't strictly require a woman to display her impressive butt dimples as the backdrop for a monologue about kings. (The most common fan idiom for these sequences is "sexposition," but I've also seen them referred to as "data humps.") These scenes are at once a turn-on and a turn-off. At times, I found myself marveling at the way that HBO has solved the riddle of its own economic existence, merging *Hookers at the Point*[4] with quasi-Shakespearean narrative. In the most egregious instance so far, Littlefinger tutored two prostitutes in how to moan in fake lesbianism for their customers, even as they moaned in fake lesbianism for us.

8   Viewed in another light, however, these sex scenes aren't always so gratuitous. Like *Mad Men*, *Game of Thrones* is elementally concerned with the way that meaningful consent dissolves when female bodies are treated as currency. War means raping the enemy's women; princesses go for a higher price, because their wombs are the coin of the realm, cementing strategic alliances. It helps that the narrative is equally fascinated by the ways in which women secure authority, and even pleasure, within these strictures, and that in the second season its bench of female characters has got even deeper—among them, a seafaring warrior princess, a butch knight, and Tyrion's prostitute girlfriend.

9   *Game of Thrones* is not coy about the way the engine of misogyny can grind the fingers of those who try to work it in their favor. An episode two weeks ago featured a sickening sequence in which King Joffrey ordered one prostitute—a character the audience had grown to care about—to rape another. The scenario . . . seemed designed not to turn viewers on but to confront them with the logical endgame of this pornographic system. . . . But while the scene may have been righteous in theory, in practice it was jarring, and slightly incoherent, particularly since it included the creamy nudity we've come to expect as visual dessert.

10   As with *True Blood*, the show's most graphic elements—the cruel ones, the fantasy ones, and the

---

[4] A 2002 HBO documentary about prostitutes working the Hunts Point neighborhood in New York's South Bronx. [Editor's note]

cruel-fantasy ones—speak to female as well as male viewers. (One of the nuttiest quotes I've ever read came from Alan Ball, *True Blood*'s showrunner,[5] who said that a focus group had revealed that men watched his series for the sex and women for the romance. Please.) But there is something troubling about this sea of C.G.I.[6]-perfect flesh, shaved and scentless and not especially medieval. It's unsettling to recall that these are not merely pretty women; they are unknown actresses who must strip, front and back, then mimic graphic sex and sexual torture, a skill increasingly key to attaining employment on cable dramas. During the filming of the second season, an Irish actress walked off the set when her scene shifted to what she termed "soft porn." Of course, not everyone strips: there are no truly explicit scenes of gay male sex, fewer lingering shots of male bodies, and the leading actresses stay mostly buttoned up. Artistically, *Game of Thrones* is in a different class from *House of Lies*, *Californication*, and *Entourage*. But it's still part of another colorful patriarchal subculture, the one called Los Angeles.

Make connections: Binge-watching.

[REFLECT]

Binge-watching is a marathon viewing of multiple episodes of the same television show in a single sitting. According to Nussbaum, "*Game of Thrones* is an ideal show to binge-watch" (par. 2). Her reason is that "with its cliffhangers and Grand Guignol dazzle, it rewards a bloody, committed immersion in its foreign world." But what Nussbaum seems to think makes *Game of Thrones* so good for sustained viewing is not primarily the horror or titillation it provides, but its immersive power to draw viewers into a complex imaginary world (par. 3). Think of your own experience. What, if anything, have you binge-watched or been tempted to binge-watch? What would make a program worth bingeing on? Your instructor may ask you to post your thoughts to a class discussion board or blog, or to discuss them with other students in class. Use these questions to get started:

- Is being immersed in an imagined world a—or even *the*—main attraction of binge-watching for you, or does something else matter more? If you think something else does matter more, what is it and why is it so important?

- Nussbaum suggests that the kinds of imagined worlds viewers gravitate toward (at least at the time she was writing) portray "a closed, often violent hierarchical system" that shows "what it means to be excluded from power" (par. 3). Why do you imagine viewers might be enticed by this theme?

Use the basic features.

[ANALYZE]

A WELL-PRESENTED SUBJECT: PROVIDING INFORMATION

Reviews usually begin by providing basic information about the subject. For example, William Akana's title identifies his subject by name, "*Scott Pilgrim vs. the World*: A Hell of a Ride." The second paragraph also provides the kinds of information

---

[5] The producer responsible for day-to-day management of a television program. [Editor's note]
[6] Computer-generated imagery. [Editor's note]

readers expect to learn from film reviews, such as the name of the director (and his or her well-known films), the main actors and their roles, the setting, and a brief summary of the plot.

> *Scott Pilgrim vs. the World*, released in 2010 by Universal Studios, came into produc-
> tion as a comic book adaptation film under the direction of Edgar Wright (best
> known for the zombie movie masterpiece *Shaun of the Dead*). Scott Pilgrim (Michael
> Cera) is a twenty-two-year-old . . . in Toronto, Canada. Pilgrim's life takes a dramatic
> turn when he falls in love with Ramona Flowers (Mary Elizabeth Winstead) . . . and
> he is forced to fight to the death to prove his love. (Akana, par. 2)

Because Akana knows that his audience, particularly his instructor, might not have heard of *Scott Pilgrim vs. the World* (a cult classic but not a box office hit), he opens the review with a brief anecdote. Recounting a personal experience in a review is an unusual move, but it allows Akana to take the same position vis-à-vis his readers that his friends had taken with him—sharing a favorite film with a friend—and as a consequence may contribute to his credibility with his audience.

ANALYZE & WRITE

Write a paragraph analyzing how Nussbaum identifies her subject:

1. Compare Nussbaum's way of presenting the subject with Akana's. For example, how does she use the series' name and what kinds of information does she give her audience about it?

2. Why do you think Nussbaum, like Akana, begins with an anecdote? Notice that Akana uses the first-person pronoun "I" only in the opening paragraph where he presents the anecdote. Skim Nussbaum's review, noting where she uses "I." Why do you think she uses the first person in those passages?

A WELL-SUPPORTED JUDGMENT: BASING A JUDGMENT ON CRITERIA

Reviewers assert an overall judgment of the subject in a thesis statement that usually appears early in the review. Akana, for example, concludes his opening paragraph with this thesis statement:

Evaluation
Genre

> From start to finish, *Scott Pilgrim vs. the World* delivers intense action in a
> hilarious slacker movie that also somehow reimagines romantic comedy.

Notice that Akana praises the film here, making his overall judgment clear. (Of course, an evaluation doesn't have to be all positive or all negative; reviews are often mixed.) He also uses specific evaluative language: He doesn't claim simply that *Scott Pilgrim* is good. Instead, he points out what is good about the film based on the three genres it draws upon (action, slacker, and romantic comedy) and the criteria usually used for evaluating those film genres. And he supports his judgment with evaluative analysis, explaining what is noteworthy about the climactic fight scene:

> This brilliantly executed scene illustrates the artful cinematography of *Scott
> Pilgrim vs. the World*. More importantly, it delivers the film's thematic message,

which undercuts the cliché "love conquers all" and instead focuses on the fresh concept that, in the grand scheme of things, the only person you are fighting for is yourself. (par. 9)

ANALYZE & WRITE

Write a paragraph or two analyzing how Nussbaum presents and supports her judgment of *Game of Thrones*:

1. Skim the essay to find the thesis statement in which Nussbaum asserts her overall judgment, and highlight the evaluative language she uses.

2. What genre or combination of genres does Nussbaum use to categorize *Game of Thrones*? Consider whether Nussbaum's evaluative language is typical of the criteria usually used when evaluating the genre (or genres) she identifies.

3. Now reread paragraph 4, 5, or 6 and analyze Nussbaum's use of examples to support her judgment. How does she present an example or examples and use evaluative language?

AN EFFECTIVE RESPONSE TO OBJECTIONS AND ALTERNATIVE JUDGMENTS: CONCEDING AND REFUTING ALTERNATIVE JUDGMENTS

Reviewers often acknowledge an alternative judgment and then either refute or concede it. To do so, they may use a sentence strategy like one of these:

▶ Programs in this genre have been dismissed as ⸺ . But this misses the point because ⸺ .

▶ Some reviewers criticize the film because it ⸺ . However, I think ⸺ because ⸺ .

> **EXAMPLE** Some reviewers have criticized the film because they think that in the end it fails as a romantic comedy. . . . But I agree with *New York Times* reviewer A. O. Scott, who argues that "the movie comes home to the well-known territory of the coming-of-age story, with an account of lessons learned and conflicts resolved." (Akana, par. 9)

ANALYZE & WRITE

Write a paragraph or two considering the role of the initial negative evaluations of *Game of Thrones*:

1. Reread paragraphs 2–3, noting the negative evaluations and Nussbaum's response. Does she refute, concede, or make the refutation-concession move?

2. Now look at paragraphs 7–10, where Nussbaum returns to the criticism of sex in *Game of Thrones*. How does she respond to the criticism this time? What point is she making about "the logical endgame of this pornographic system" (par. 9)?

3. What's implied by the phrase "graphic arts" in the subtitle: "The Graphic Arts of *Game of Thrones*"?

A CLEAR, LOGICAL ORGANIZATION: CUEING READERS

Nussbaum's evaluation is complicated. She interweaves plot summary with analysis to support her claims about the merits (and demerits) of *Game of Thrones,* and she compares the series with other cable series, both good and bad. To keep her readers on track, she must use a variety of cueing strategies.

ANALYZE & WRITE

Write a paragraph analyzing how Nussbaum helps her audience follow her evaluation:

1. Skim the essay, noting Nussbaum's main topics and marking any key terms that she uses to orient readers.

2. Mark any transitions, considering how each transition helps readers follow the logical movement from topic to topic.

3. Consider how effective Nussbaum's strategies are. How difficult did you find it to follow the logic of the review? What would you suggest Nussbaum do, if anything, to make her evaluation easier to follow?

[RESPOND] ## Consider possible topics: Offering a mixed judgment.

Some of the most effective and interesting evaluations are neither wholly positive or negative. Instead, they point out both strengths and weaknesses while developing a clear overall judgment. Try to think of a subject about which you have mixed feelings—such as a sports team, video game, film, musical performance, or course you've taken. What is your overall judgment? What would you praise about your subject and what would you criticize? What are the criteria you think should be used in evaluating examples of this genre?

Malcolm Gladwell | *What College Rankings Really Tell Us*

Photo by Theo Wargo/WireImage for Bragman Nyman Cafarelli/Getty Images

MALCOLM GLADWELL is a staff writer for the *New Yorker* magazine and has written a number of best-selling books, including *Outliers: The Story of Success* (2008) and *Blink: The Power of Thinking without Thinking* (2005). He received the American Sociological Association Award for Excellence in the Reporting of Social Issues and was named one of the hundred most influential people by *Time* magazine. As he explains on his Web site (gladwell.com), giving public readings, particularly to academic audiences, has helped him "re-shape and sharpen [his] arguments."

"What College Rankings Really Tell Us" (2011) evaluates the popular *U.S. News* annual "Best Colleges" guide. You may be familiar with this guide and may have even consulted it when selecting a college. Excerpted from a longer *New Yorker* article, Gladwell's evaluation focuses on the *U.S. News* ranking system. As you read Gladwell's review, consider these questions:

- Note the numbered list of "variables" the *U.S. News* uses to rank colleges. For whom do you suppose *U.S. News*'s criteria are important? Why?

- If they are important for you, why? If they are not important for you, why not? What criteria for choosing a college are important for you?

1   *Car and Driver* conducted a comparison test of three sports cars, the Lotus Evora, the Chevrolet Corvette Grand Sport, and the Porsche Cayman S. . . . Yet when you inspect the magazine's tabulations it is hard to figure out why *Car and Driver* was so sure that the Cayman is better than the Corvette and the Evora. The trouble starts with the fact that the ranking methodology *Car and Driver* used was essentially the same one it uses for all the vehicles it tests—from S.U.V.s to economy sedans. It's not set up for sports cars. Exterior styling, for example, counts for four per cent of the total score. Has anyone buying a sports car ever placed so little value on how it looks? Similarly, the categories of "fun to drive" and "chassis"—which cover the subjective experience of driving the car—count for only eighty-five points out of the total of two hundred and thirty-five. That may make sense for S.U.V. buyers. But, for people interested in Porsches and Corvettes and Lotuses, the subjective experience of driving is surely what matters most. In other words, in trying to come up with a ranking that is heterogeneous—a methodology that is broad enough to cover all vehicles—*Car and Driver* ended up with a system that is absurdly ill-suited to some vehicles. . . .

2   A heterogeneous ranking system works if it focuses just on, say, how much fun a car is to drive, or how good-looking it is, or how beautifully it handles. The magazine's ambition to create a comprehensive ranking system—one that considered cars along twenty-one variables, each weighted according to a secret sauce cooked up by the editors—would also be fine, as long as the cars being compared were truly similar. It's only when one car is thirteen thousand dollars more than another that juggling twenty-one variables starts to break down, because you're faced with the impossible task of deciding how much a difference of that degree ought to matter. A ranking can be heterogeneous, in other words, as long as it doesn't try to be too comprehensive. And it can be comprehensive as long as it doesn't try to measure things that are heterogeneous. But it's an act of real audacity when a ranking system tries to be comprehensive and heterogeneous—which is the first thing to keep in mind in any consideration of *U.S. News & World Report*'s annual "Best Colleges" guide.

3   The *U.S. News* rankings . . . relies on seven weighted variables:

1. Undergraduate academic reputation, 22.5 per cent
2. Graduation and freshman retention rates, 20 per cent
3. Faculty resources, 20 per cent
4. Student selectivity, 15 per cent
5. Financial resources, 10 per cent
6. Graduation rate performance, 7.5 per cent
7. Alumni giving, 5 per cent

From these variables, *U.S. News* generates a score for each institution on a scale of 1 to 100. . . . This ranking system looks a great deal like the *Car and Driver* methodology. It is heterogeneous. It doesn't just compare U.C. Irvine, the University of Washington, the University of Texas–Austin, the University of Wisconsin–Madison, Penn State, and the University of Illinois, Urbana–Champaign—all public institutions of roughly the same size. It aims to compare Penn State—a very large, public, land-grant university with a low tuition and an economically diverse student body, set in a rural valley in central Pennsylvania and famous for its football team—with Yeshiva University, a small, expensive, private Jewish university whose undergraduate program is set on two campuses in Manhattan (one in midtown, for the women, and one far uptown, for the men) and is definitely not famous for its football team.

4   The system is also comprehensive. It doesn't simply compare schools along one dimension—the test scores of incoming freshmen, say, or academic reputation. An algorithm takes a slate of statistics on each college and transforms them into a single score: it tells us that Penn State is a better school than Yeshiva by one point. It is easy to see why the *U.S. News* rankings are so popular. A single score allows us to judge between entities (like Yeshiva and Penn State) that otherwise would be impossible to compare. . . .

5   A comprehensive, heterogeneous ranking system was a stretch for *Car and Driver*—and all it did was rank inanimate objects operated by a single person. The Penn State campus at University Park is a complex institution with dozens of schools and departments, four thousand faculty members, and forty-five thousand students. How on earth does anyone propose to assign a number to something like that?

6   The first difficulty with rankings is that it can be surprisingly hard to measure the variable you want to rank—even in cases where that variable seems perfectly objective. . . . There's no direct way to measure the quality of an institution—how well a college manages to inform, inspire, and challenge its students. So the *U.S. News* algorithm relies instead on proxies for quality—and the proxies for educational quality turn out to be flimsy at best.

7   Take the category of "faculty resources," which counts for twenty per cent of an institution's score (number 3 on the chart above). "Research shows that the more satisfied students are about their contact with professors," the College Guide's explanation of the category begins, "the more they will learn and the more likely it is they will graduate." That's true. According to educational researchers, arguably the most important variable in a successful college education is a vague but crucial concept called student "engagement"—that is, the extent to which students immerse themselves in the intellectual and social life of their college—and a major component of engagement is the quality of a student's contacts with faculty. . . . So what proxies does *U.S. News* use to measure this elusive dimension of engagement? The explanation goes on:

> We use six factors from the 2009–10 academic year to assess a school's commitment to instruction. Class size has two components, the proportion of classes with fewer than 20 students (30 percent of the faculty resources score) and the proportion with 50 or more students (10 percent of the score). Faculty salary (35 percent) is the average faculty pay, plus benefits, during the 2008–09 and 2009–10 academic years, adjusted for regional differences in the cost of living. . . . We also weigh the proportion of profes-

sors with the highest degree in their fields (15 percent), the student-faculty ratio (5 percent), and the proportion of faculty who are full time (5 percent).

8   This is a puzzling list. Do professors who get paid more money really take their teaching roles more seriously? And why does it matter whether a professor has the highest degree in his or her field? Salaries and degree attainment are known to be predictors of research productivity. But studies show that being oriented toward research has very little to do with being good at teaching. Almost none of the *U.S. News* variables, in fact, seem to be particularly effective proxies for engagement. As the educational researchers Patrick Terenzini and Ernest Pascarella concluded after analyzing twenty-six hundred reports on the effects of college on students:

> After taking into account the characteristics, abilities, and backgrounds students bring with them to college, we found that how much students grow or change has only inconsistent and, perhaps in a practical sense, trivial relationships with such traditional measures of institutional "quality" as educational expenditures per student, student/faculty ratios, faculty salaries, percentage of faculty with the highest degree in their field, faculty research productivity, size of the library, [or] admissions selectivity. . . .

9   There's something missing from that list of variables, of course: it doesn't include price. That is one of the most distinctive features of the *U.S. News* methodology. Both its college rankings and its law-school rankings reward schools for devoting lots of financial resources to educating their students, but not for being affordable. Why? [Director of Data Research Robert] Morse admitted that there was no formal reason for that position. It was just a feeling. "We're not saying that we're measuring educational outcomes," he explained. "We're not saying we're social scientists, or we're subjecting our rankings to some peer-review process. We're just saying we've made this judgment. We're saying we've interviewed a lot of experts, we've developed these academic indicators, and we think these measures measure quality schools."

> *The first difficulty with rankings is that it can be surprisingly hard to measure the variable you want to rank.*

Gladwell   *What College Rankings Really Tell Us*

GUIDE TO READING
GUIDE TO WRITING
A WRITER AT WORK
THINKING CRITICALLY

355

10   As answers go, that's up there with the parental "Because I said so." But Morse is simply being honest. If we don't understand what the right proxies for college quality are, let alone how to represent those proxies in a comprehensive, heterogeneous grading system, then our rankings are inherently arbitrary. . . . *U.S. News* thinks that schools that spend a lot of money on their students are nicer than those that don't, and that this niceness ought to be factored into the equation of desirability. Plenty of Americans agree: the campus of Vanderbilt University or Williams College is filled with students whose families are largely indifferent to the price their school charges but keenly interested in the flower beds and the spacious suites and the architecturally distinguished lecture halls those high prices make possible. Of course, given that the rising cost of college has become a significant social problem in the United States in recent years, you can make a strong case that a school ought to be rewarded for being affordable. . . .

11   The *U.S. News* rankings turn out to be full of these kinds of implicit ideological choices. One common statistic used to evaluate colleges, for example, is called "graduation rate performance," which compares a school's actual graduation rate with its predicted graduation rate given the socioeconomic status and the test scores of its incoming freshman class. It is a measure of the school's efficacy: it quantifies the impact of a school's culture and teachers and institutional support mechanisms. Tulane, given the qualifications of the students that it admits, ought to have a graduation rate of eighty-seven per cent; its actual 2009 graduation rate was seventy-three per cent. That shortfall suggests that something is amiss at Tulane. Another common statistic for measuring college quality is "student selectivity." This reflects variables such as how many of a college's freshmen were in the top ten per cent of their high-school class, how high their S.A.T. scores were, and what percentage of applicants a college admits. Selectivity quantifies how accomplished students are when they first arrive on campus.

12   Each of these statistics matters, but for very different reasons. As a society, we probably care more about efficacy: America's future depends on colleges that make sure the students they admit leave with an education and a degree. If you are a bright high-school senior and you're thinking about your own future, though, you may well care more about selectivity, because that relates to the prestige of your degree. . . .

13   There is no right answer to how much weight a ranking system should give to these two competing values. It's a matter of which educational model you value more—and here, once again, *U.S. News* makes its position clear. It gives twice as much weight to selectivity as it does to efficacy. . . .

14   Rankings are not benign. They enshrine very particular ideologies, and, at a time when American higher education is facing a crisis of accessibility and affordability, we have adopted a defacto standard of college quality that is uninterested in both of those factors. And why? Because a group of magazine analysts in an office building in Washington, D.C., decided twenty years ago to value selectivity over efficacy.

Make connections: Ideology underlying judgments.   [REFLECT]

Gladwell asserts that "implicit ideological choices" underlie ranking systems (par. 11). The word *ideology* refers to the values and beliefs that influence people's thinking. An important sign of underlying ideology is the fact that the *U.S. News* rankings leave out how much it costs to go to each college. This omission is significant, especially at a time when there is "a crisis of accessibility and affordability" (par. 14).

To think about the role of ideology in your own choice of a college, reflect on your personal experience as well as your observations of others choosing a college. Your instructor may ask you to post your thoughts on a class discussion board or to discuss them with other students in class. Use these questions to get started:

- What colleges did you consider, and what criteria (cost, location, standing in the *U.S. News* college ranking, and so on) did you use?

- Choose one or two of your criteria, and consider what values and beliefs were behind your choice. For example, was it important to you to attend a college with a winning football team, with a particular religious orientation, with opportunities for undergraduates to do scientific research?

- How would comparing the criteria you used with the criteria your classmates used help you better understand the ideology—values and beliefs—behind your choices?

[ANALYZE]   # Use the basic features.

A WELL-PRESENTED SUBJECT: INTRODUCING A COMPLICATED SUBJECT

Every year, *U.S. News* publishes a special edition that ranks colleges and universities across the nation. In his essay, Gladwell does not simply evaluate one year's ratings; he evaluates the ranking system itself. But he begins by focusing on the ranking system of another magazine, *Car and Driver*.

⎡ ANALYZE & WRITE ⎤────────────────────────────────

Write a paragraph analyzing and evaluating how Gladwell introduces *U.S. News*'s ranking system:

1 Reread paragraph 1. Why do you think Gladwell begins his evaluation of *U.S. News*'s college ranking system by discussing the system used by another magazine to rank cars? How does Gladwell's evaluation of *Car and Driver*'s ranking system prepare readers for his evaluation of *U.S. News*'s ranking system?

2 Now reread paragraph 2. What cues does Gladwell provide to help readers follow his transition from the ranking system of *Car and Driver* to that of *U.S. News*?

3 What does Gladwell mean when he describes *U.S. News*'s ranking system as striving to be both comprehensive and heterogeneous?

A WELL-SUPPORTED JUDGMENT: DEFINING CRITERIA

In paragraph 3, Gladwell lists the "seven weighted variables" *U.S. News* uses to represent a school's quality. Then, in paragraph 6, he states his main reason for criticizing any system for ranking colleges: "There's no direct way to measure the quality of an institution. . . . So the *U.S. News* algorithm"—its formula or set of rules—"relies instead on proxies for quality—and the proxies for educational quality turn out to be flimsy at best."

⎡ ANALYZE & WRITE ⎤────────────────────────────────

Write a paragraph or two analyzing and evaluating how Gladwell supports his argument:

1 Reread paragraphs 7 and 8, in which Gladwell focuses on one criterion — "faculty resources" — from the list of variables *U.S. News* uses to measure a school's quality. Why does *U.S. News* focus on faculty resources, and what do the editors of the magazine use to measure this quality?

[2] Now consider Gladwell's claim that faculty resources are an inappropriate criterion for evaluating student engagement. What reasons and evidence does Gladwell supply? Given your own experience as a student, how convincing is this part of his argument?

[3] What single criterion would you consider most important in evaluating a school's quality? How would you measure that criterion?

AN EFFECTIVE RESPONSE TO OBJECTIONS AND ALTERNATIVE JUDGMENTS: SINGLING OUT A COMMENT FOR RESPONSE

Because it is a negative evaluation, one could say that Gladwell's entire essay is an implied refutation of those who think well of the *U.S. News* college rankings. However, Gladwell also responds specifically to comments made by Robert Morse, the director of data research for *U.S. News* & *World Report*.

ANALYZE & WRITE

Write a paragraph analyzing Morse's response to Gladwell and Gladwell's response to Morse:

[1] Reread paragraph 9. How would you describe Morse's response to Gladwell's criticism: Which of Gladwell's points does Morse concede or refute? Is Morse's response effective? Why or why not?

[2] Now reread paragraphs 10–12. How does Gladwell respond to Morse? How does he concede or refute Morse's response? How would you describe the tone of Gladwell's response? Is he fair, mean, sarcastic, something else?

[3] Given Gladwell's purpose and audience, how do you imagine readers would react to Morse's response to criticism as well as to Gladwell's handling of Morse's response? How did you respond?

A CLEAR, LOGICAL ORGANIZATION: USING COMPARISON AND CONTRAST

Lengthy evaluations can be difficult to follow, but writers have a number of strategies at their disposal to help guide readers. They may use transitional words and phrases or numbered lists, as Gladwell does. But they may also use more subtle strategies to help create cohesion. Gladwell, for example, uses comparison and contrast and strategic repetition to help readers follow his analysis.

ANALYZE & WRITE

Write a paragraph analyzing how Gladwell uses these two strategies:

[1] Skim paragraphs 1–3, 5, and 10, noting where Gladwell mentions *Car and Driver* or compares *Car and Driver*'s ranking system with the ranking system used by *U.S. News*, and highlight Gladwell's repeated use of the word *heterogeneous* to describe these ranking systems. Consider the comparison Gladwell is making between *Car and Driver*'s and *U.S. News*'s ranking systems. How does this comparison help him structure his article logically?

2 Skim paragraphs 3, 8, and 11–14, underlining the words *selectivity* and *efficacy*. How does Gladwell use the contrast between selectivity and efficacy? How does this contrast help him guide readers and make his point?

3 Finally, evaluate Gladwell's use of these strategies. How effective are they in helping you follow Gladwell's logic? What, if anything, would you suggest Gladwell do to make his analysis easier to follow?

RESPOND   ## Consider possible topics: Evaluating a text.

List several texts you would consider evaluating, such as an essay from one of the chapters in this book; a children's book that you read when you were young or that you now read to your own children; a magazine for people interested in a particular topic, like computers or cars; or a scholarly article you read for a research paper. If you choose an argument from Chapters 6–9, you could evaluate its logic, its use of emotional appeals, or its credibility. You need not limit yourself to texts written on paper. You might also evaluate a Web site or blog, a radio or television program or advertisement, or even a work of art (such as a story from Chapter 10). Choose one possibility from your list, and then come up with two or three criteria for evaluation.

Sherry Turkle | *The Flight from Conversation*

Pat Greenhouse/The Boston Globe/Getty Images

SHERRY TURKLE is the Abby Rockefeller Mauzé Professor of the Social Studies of Science and Technology at the Massachusetts Institute of Technology and the founder and director of the MIT Initiative on Technology and Self. In addition to being a professor, Turkle is also a licensed clinical psychologist. Her recent books include *Alone Together: Why We Expect More from Technology and Less from Each Other* (2011) and *Reclaiming Conversation: The Power of Talk in a Digital Age* (2015). In addition to book chapters and articles for scholarly publications, Turkle addresses popular audiences in such venues as TED.com, *Scientific American*, *Wired*, and the *New York Times* where this selection was originally published.

As you read, consider these questions:

• Turkle describes our lives today as "plugged-in." In what ways is your life plugged-in? Are there any ways in which your life is "unplugged"?

• What are the benefits and losses of being plugged-in? What advantages or disadvantages do you think older people or people in different social groups might see?

1   We live in a technological universe in which we are always communicating. And yet we have sacrificed conversation for mere connection. At home, families sit together, texting and reading e-mail. At work executives text during board meetings. We text (and shop and go on Facebook) during classes and when we're on dates. My students tell me about an important new skill: it involves maintaining eye contact with someone while you text someone else; it's hard, but it can be done. Over the past 15 years, I've studied technologies of mobile connection and talked to hundreds of people of all ages and circumstances about their plugged-in lives. I've learned that the little devices most of us carry around are so powerful that they change not only what we do, but also who we are.

2   We've become accustomed to a new way of being "alone together." Technology-enabled, we are able to be with one another, and also elsewhere, connected to wherever we want to be. We want to customize our lives. We want to move in and out of where we are because the thing we value most is control over where we focus our attention. . . . To some this seems like a good idea, but we can end up hiding from one another, even as we are constantly connected to one another. A businessman laments that he no longer has colleagues at work. He doesn't stop by to talk; he doesn't call. He says that he doesn't want to interrupt them. He says they're "too busy on their e-mail." But then he pauses and corrects himself. "I'm not telling the truth. I'm the one who doesn't want to be interrupted. I think I should. But I'd rather just do things on my BlackBerry." A 16-year-old boy who relies on texting for almost everything says almost wistfully, "Someday, someday, but certainly not now, I'd like to learn how to have a conversation." In today's workplace, young people who have grown up fearing conversation show up on the job wearing earphones. Walking through a college library or the campus of a high-tech start-up, one sees the same thing: we are together, but each of us is in our own bubble, furiously connected to keyboards and tiny touch screens. A senior partner at a Boston law firm describes a scene in his office. Young associates lay out their suite of technologies: laptops, iPods and multiple phones. And then they put their earphones on. "Big ones. Like pilots. They turn their desks into cockpits." With the young lawyers in their cockpits, the office is quiet, a quiet that does not ask to be broken.

3   In the silence of connection, people are comforted by being in touch with a lot of people—carefully kept at bay. We can't get enough of one another if we can use technology to keep one another at distances we can control: not too close, not too far, just right. I think of it as a Goldilocks effect. Texting and e-mail and posting let us present the self we want to be. This means we can edit. And if we wish to, we can delete. Or retouch: the voice, the flesh, the face, the body. Not too much, not too little—just right. Human relationships are rich; they're messy and demanding. We have learned the habit of cleaning them up with technology. And the move from conversation to connection is part of this. But it's a process in which we shortchange ourselves.

4   Worse, it seems that over time we stop caring; we forget that there is a difference. We are tempted to think that our little "sips" of online connection add up to a big gulp of real conversation. But they don't. E-mail, Twitter, Facebook, all of these have their places—in politics, commerce, romance and friendship. But no matter how valuable, they do not substitute for conversation. Connecting in sips may work for gathering discrete bits of information or for saying, "I am thinking about you." Or even for saying, "I love you." But connecting in sips doesn't work as well when it comes to understanding and knowing one another. In conversation we tend to one another. (The word itself is kinetic; it's derived from words that mean to move, together.) We can attend to tone and nuance. In conversation, we are called upon to see things from another's point of view.

5   Face-to-face conversation unfolds slowly. It teaches patience. When we communicate on our digital devices, we learn different habits. As we ramp up the volume and velocity of online connections, we start to expect faster answers. To get these, we ask one another simpler questions; we dumb down our communications, even on the most important matters. It is as though we have all put ourselves on cable news. Shakespeare might have said, "We are consum'd with that which we were nourish'd by." And we use conversation with others to learn to converse with ourselves. So our flight from conversation can mean diminished chances to learn skills of self-reflection. These days, social media continually asks us what's "on our mind," but we have little motivation to say something truly self-reflective. Self-reflection in conversation requires trust. It's hard to do anything with 3,000 Facebook friends except connect.

6   As we get used to being shortchanged on conversation and to getting by with less, we seem almost willing to dispense with people altogether. Serious people muse about the future of computer programs as psychiatrists. A high school sophomore confides to me that he wishes he could talk to an artificial intelligence program instead of his dad about dating; he says the A.I. would have so much more in its database. Indeed, many people tell me they hope that as Siri, the digital assistant on Apple's iPhone, becomes more advanced, "she" will be more and more like a best friend—one who will listen when others won't.

7   During the years I have spent researching people and their relationships with technology, I have often heard the sentiment "No one is listening to me." I believe this feeling helps explain why it is so appealing to have a Facebook page or a Twitter feed—each provides so many automatic listeners. And it helps explain why—against all reason—so many of us are willing to talk to machines that seem to care about us. Researchers around the world are busy inventing sociable robots, designed to be companions to the elderly, to children, to all of us.

8   One of the most haunting experiences during my research came when I brought one of these robots, designed in the shape of a baby seal, to an elder-care facility, and an older woman began to talk to it about the loss of her child. The robot seemed to be looking into her eyes. It seemed to be following the conversation. The woman was comforted. And so many people found this amazing. Like the sophomore who wants advice about dating from artificial intelligence and those who look forward to computer psychiatry, this enthusiasm speaks to how much we have confused conversation with connection and collectively seem to have embraced a new kind of delusion that accepts the simulation of compassion as sufficient unto the day. And why would we want to talk about love and loss with a machine that has no experience of the arc of human life? Have we so lost confidence that we will be there for one another?

9   We expect more from technology and less from one another and seem increasingly drawn to technologies that provide the illusion of companionship without the demands of relationship. Always-on/always-on-you devices provide three powerful fantasies: that we will always be heard; that we can put our attention wherever we want it to be; and that we never have to be alone. Indeed our new devices have turned being alone into a problem that can be solved.

10   When people are alone, even for a few moments, they fidget and reach for a device. Here connection works like a symptom, not a cure, and our constant, reflexive impulse to connect shapes a new way of being. Think of it as "I share, therefore I am." We use technology to define ourselves by sharing our thoughts and feelings as we're having them. We used to think, "I have a feeling; I want to make a call." Now our impulse is, "I want to have a feeling; I need to send a text." So, in order to feel more, and to feel more like ourselves, we connect. But in our rush to connect, we flee from solitude, our ability to be separate and gather ourselves. Lacking the capacity for solitude, we turn to other people but don't experience them as they are. It is as though we use them, need them as spare parts to support our increasingly fragile selves. We think constant connection will make us feel less lonely. The opposite is true. If we are unable to be alone, we are far more likely to be lonely. If we don't teach our children to be alone, they will know only how to be lonely.

11   I am a partisan for conversation. To make room for it, I see some first, deliberate steps. At home, we can create sacred spaces: the kitchen, the dining room. We can make our cars "device-free zones." We can demonstrate the value of conversation to our children. And we can do the same thing at work. There we are so busy communicating that we often don't have time to talk to one another about what really matters. Employees asked for casual Fridays; perhaps managers should introduce conversational Thursdays. Most of all, we need to remember—in between texts and e-mails and Facebook posts—to listen to one another, even to the boring bits, because it is often in unedited moments, moments in which we hesitate and stutter and go silent, that we reveal ourselves to one another.

> *We . . . seem increasingly drawn to technologies that provide the illusion of companionship without the demands of relationship.*

Make connections: Evaluating social media.

Turkle is writing a cultural critique, which is a specialized form of evaluation focusing on contemporary culture. Her essay addresses the way technologically mediated communication has affected how we relate to one another and how we think of ourselves.

Reflect on your own observations and experiences with social media, virtual communities, and other ways of being plugged in. Your instructor may ask you to post your thoughts on a class discussion board or to discuss them with other students in class. Use these questions to get started:

- What kinds of social media, if any, do you and your friends use? What do you primarily use social media for?
- User-generated news sites like *Demotix*, *CNN iReport*, and *Newsvine* have been criticized as unauthoritative and possibly biased or incomplete compared to more traditional newspapers and television news outlets. Such sites have also been praised for democratizing news and for empowering active instead of passive information consumers. What is your view of the value of user-generated news and other social media for information and news? Where, if anywhere, do you go for information and news about current events and why?
- Given the concerns she expresses in "The Flight from Conversation," how do you think Turkle would respond to the debate about social media's impact on the news?

Use the basic features.

A WELL-PRESENTED SUBJECT: IDENTIFYING THE SUBJECT

To identify a film or television series, reviewers simply rely on the subject's name, usually announced in the review's title and opening paragraph and then repeated throughout the review, as you have seen in "*Scott Pilgrim vs. The World:* A Hell of a Ride" (pp. 341–46) and "*The Aristocrats:* The Graphic Arts of *Game of Thrones*" (pp. 346–49). For other subjects, a key term may perform the same function as a film title. For example, Gladwell uses the key term *ranking* in his title and throughout "What College Rankings Really Tell Us" (pp. 352–55).

ANALYZE & WRITE

Write a paragraph analyzing how Turkle presents her subject:

1. Skim the article, highlighting the term *conversation* in the essay's title and elsewhere in the evaluation.

2. Now skim paragraphs 4 and 5. How does Turkle modify *conversation* to clarify what she means by this term?

3. Analyze the way Turkle defines *conversation* in contrast with "mere connection." How well does this contrast, along with the examples Turkle offers, help readers to understand her subject? How well do Turkle's examples fit your own experience and observation?

A WELL-SUPPORTED JUDGMENT: PROVIDING SUPPORTING EVIDENCE

The support a reviewer uses depends on what is being evaluated. Film reviews typically give examples to illustrate and support their argument. Akana, for instance, narrates plot elements: "Gideon, in response to the challenge, asks Pilgrim if he is fighting for Ramona, which leads to a climactic epiphany for Pilgrim as he realizes his true motive" (par. 8); he describes important scenes and illustrates them with screen shots: "Another scene presents a bass battle between Pilgrim and one of the evil exes in the format of PlayStation's popular Guitar Hero (see fig. 2)" (par. 4); and he quotes authorities from other reviews and interviews: "The film ends, as director Edgar Wright explained in an interview. . . ." (par. 9). In addition to these strategies, evaluations can draw on a broad array of support, including comparison and contrast, analysis of causes and effects, and anecdotal evidence.

ANALYZE & WRITE

Write a paragraph or two analyzing how Turkle supports her argument:

1. Examine how Turkle uses comparison and contrast to discuss the differences between conversation and connection in paragraphs 3–5, for example. How are they different? What characteristics or qualities, if anything, do they share? How does Turkle use comparison and contrast to support her judgment about the lost art of conversation?

2. Skim the essay, noting where Turkle describes the effects of the shift from conversation to online connection. Are all the effects negative or are some of them positive? Which effects seem most important to Turkle? Why? How does she use cause-effect to support her argument?

AN EFFECTIVE RESPONSE TO OBJECTIONS AND ALTERNATIVE JUDGMENTS: APPEALING TO SHARED VALUES

Values, of course, play a defining role in evaluation. What people value determines the criteria they apply when making evaluative judgments as well as how they respond to their audience's objections and alternative judgments. To convince their audience that their judgment is sound, writers of evaluations usually appeal to values shared with most, if not all, of their readers. For example, Gladwell tries to convince his audience to accept his judgment of the *U.S. News* college ranking system because it does not share with most Americans the values of "accessibility and affordability" (par. 14). Similarly, in conceding the validity of criticism of *Game of Thrones*'s pornographic and sadistic sexuality, Nussbaum shows her audience that she shares their values.

ANALYZE & WRITE

Write a paragraph analyzing and evaluating how Turkle appeals to values she likely shares with her audience:

1. Skim the essay, noting where Turkle refers to values. How does she let her readers know whether the values she's referring to are ones that are commonly shared?

Turkle   *The Flight from Conversation*

GUIDE TO READING
GUIDE TO WRITING
A WRITER AT WORK
THINKING CRITICALLY

363

2 How would you describe Turkle's tone? For example, does she come across as concerned, condescending, respectful, rigid, nostalgic, or something else? Illustrate with a quotation. How would her tone likely have affected her original *New York Times* audience? How did it affect you?

A CLEAR, LOGICAL ORGANIZATION: CREATING COHERENCE

Repeating key terms can be a powerful tool for creating coherence—especially when the terms are introduced early to forecast the main topics and repeated in topic sentences. Another powerful tool is the use of transitions (such as *although, nevertheless, since, therefore,* and *of course*), sometimes in combination with a demonstrative pronoun (*this, that, these, those*) and a key term or summary to remind readers of the preceding paragraph's main point before introducing the new paragraph's topic:

> There's something missing from that list of variables, of course: it doesn't include price. (Gladwell, par. 9)

Demonstrative pronoun

Key term(s)

> Viewed in another light, however, these sex scenes aren't always so gratuitous. (Nussbaum, par. 8)

Transition

ANALYZE & WRITE

Write a paragraph analyzing and evaluating how Turkle creates coherence:

1 Track one key term through Turkle's essay. How does the repetition of this term (or variations on it) help the reader follow Turkle's evaluation argument?

2 Notice that paragraph 6 introduces a new topic. What is the topic and how does it relate to what went before? What strategy does Turkle use to make the transition from paragraph 5 to paragraph 6? Is it effective? Why or why not?

Consider possible topics: Evaluating a technology-related subject.

RESPOND

List several technology-related subjects you could evaluate. For example, you could review a wearable technology product (like the Apple Watch or Google Glass), an app, or a new smartphone or tablet. Alternatively, you could evaluate a controversial issue related to technology such as Net neutrality (the proposal by communications companies to offer tiered service, so companies like Netflix could stream at a faster rate than average consumers), the use of body cameras by the police, or the collection of cell phone records by the National Security Agency (NSA).

REMIX

Remixing Your Evaluation

Evaluations occur regularly in genres and media besides the college essay. For example, newspapers regularly publish reviews of the latest films and books, and Web sites galore review the latest movies and digital gadgets. William Akana could have remixed his evaluation as a proposal to persuade his college entertainment committee to screen *Scott Pilgrim* on campus, or he could have posted his review to his Facebook page. (A remix takes all or part of a piece in one genre or medium to create a new text in another genre or medium.) Instead, Akana revised his evaluation for publication in his college newspaper.

In the next section of this chapter, we ask you to craft your own evaluation. After composing it as an essay, consider remixing it by presenting it (or a portion of it) in another genre or medium, or using it as part of an essay with a different purpose or audience.

HOME   ABOUT ▾   MULTIMEDIA ▾   NEWS ▾   LIFESTYLE & CULTURE ▾

LEVEL UP!
CUTE -3
HEART-3
KARATE-4
WILL-4

06
MAY 2015

***SCOTT PILGRIM VS. THE WORLD:* A MUST-SEE CULT MOVIE CLASSIC!   Free! At the Student Center, 11 p.m.**

WILL AKHANA

Whether you're a slacker, old-school gamer, animé/ comic book fan, or just someone who likes a good rom-com with inventive special effects, clever dialogue, and artistic cinematography and editing, *Scott Pilgrim vs. the World* is a film you shouldn't miss.
Directed by Edgar Wright (best known for the zombie movie masterpiece *Shaun of the Dead*), *Scott Pilgrim* stars Michael Cera (of *Arrested Development* and *Juno* fame) as the twenty-two-year-old Pilgrim, whose life takes a dramatic turn when he falls in love with Ramona Flowers (Mary Elizabeth Winstead), quite literally, the girl of his dreams. ...*more*

Image credit: © Universal/Everett Collection

CONSIDER YOUR RHETORICAL SITUATION

Purpose: The purpose of your evaluation is to persuade your readers to accept your judgment. If you remix your evaluation, *which genre or medium would best allow you to make a compelling case for or against the subject of your evaluation?*

Audience: The audience for your evaluation was your instructor and other students in your class. If you remix your evaluation, *what audience would be most interested in your subject and in your evaluation of it? What genre or medium would best help you reach that audience?*

Genre and medium: The genre of your evaluation was the essay, and the medium of your evaluation was textual, delivered either in print or online. If you remix your evaluation, *what medium would best help you reach and persuade your target audience?*

GUIDE TO WRITING

The Writing Assignment

Write an essay evaluating a specific subject. Examine your subject closely, and make a judgment about it. Give reasons for your judgment that are based on widely recognized criteria or standards for evaluating a subject like yours. Support your reasons with examples and other details primarily from your subject.

This Guide to Writing is designed to help you compose your own evaluation and apply what you have learned from reading other essays in the same genre. This Starting Points chart will help you find answers to questions you might have about composing an essay evaluating a subject. Use the chart to find the guidance you need, when you need it.

STARTING POINTS: JUSTIFYING AN EVALUATION

A Well-Presented Subject	How do I come up with a subject to write about?	• Consider possible topics: Offering a mixed judgment. (p. 352) • Consider possible topics: Evaluating a text. (p. 358) • Consider possible topics: Evaluating a technology-related subject. (p. 363) • Choose a subject to evaluate. (p. 367) • Test Your Choice: Choosing a Subject (pp. 367–68) • Assess your subject and consider how to present it to your readers. (pp. 368–69)
	How can I present my subject clearly and convincingly?	• Determine the writer's purpose and audience. (p. 337) • Assess the genre's basic features: A well-presented subject. (p. 338) • A Well-Presented Subject: Providing Information (pp. 349–50) • A Well-Presented Subject: Introducing a Complicated Subject (p. 356) • A Well-Presented Subject: Identifying the Subject (p. 361) • Assess your subject and consider how to present it to your readers. (pp. 368–69)
A Well-Supported Judgment	How do I come up with a thesis statement?	• Assess the genre's basic features: A well-supported judgment. (pp. 338–39) • Formulate a working thesis stating your overall judgment. (pp. 369–70)

(continued)

A Well-Supported Judgment

How do I construct an argument supporting my judgment?

- Assess the genre's basic features: A well-supported judgment. (pp. 338–39)
- A Well-Supported Judgment: Basing a Judgment on Criteria (pp. 350–51)
- A Well-Supported Judgment: Defining Criteria (pp. 356–57)
- A Well-Supported Judgment: Providing Supporting Evidence (p. 362)
- Develop the reasons and evidence supporting your judgment. (pp. 370–71)
- Research your evaluation. (p. 371)

An Effective Response to Objections and Alternative Judgments

How do I respond to possible objections and alternative judgments?

- Assess the genre's basic features: An effective response to objections and alternative judgments. (pp. 339–40)
- An Effective Response to Objections and Alternative Judgments: Conceding and Refuting Alternative Judgments (p. 351)
- An Effective Response to Objections and Alternative Judgments: Singling Out a Comment for Response (p. 357)
- An Effective Response to Objections and Alternative Judgments: Appealing to Shared Values (pp. 362–63)
- Respond to a likely objection or alternative judgment. (pp. 371–73)

A Clear, Logical Organization

How can I help my readers follow my argument?

- Assess the genre's basic features: A clear, logical organization. (pp. 340–41)
- A Clear, Logical Organization: Cueing Readers (p. 352)
- A Clear, Logical Organization: Using Comparison and Contrast (pp. 357–58)
- A Clear, Logical Organization: Creating Coherence (p. 363)
- Organize your draft to appeal to your readers. (p. 373)

Writing a Draft: Invention, Research, Planning, and Composing

The activities in this section will help you choose and research a subject as well as develop and organize an evaluative argument. Do the activities in any order that makes sense to you (and your instructor), and return to them as needed as you revise. Your writing in response to many of these activities can be used in a rough draft that you will be able to improve after receiving feedback from your classmates and instructor.

⠶ Choose a subject to evaluate.

When choosing a subject for evaluation, keep in mind that it must be

- one that has strengths or weaknesses you could write about;
- one that you can view and review (for example, a location you can visit; a printed text; or a Web site or digital recording from which you can capture stills or video clips to use as examples in a multimedia presentation);
- one typically evaluated according to criteria or standards of judgment that you understand and share with your readers.

You may already have a subject in mind. If you do, skip to Test Your Choice below. If you do not, the following topics, in addition to those following the readings (pp. 352, 358, and 363), may suggest one you can write about effectively.

Subjects Related to School

- Evaluate some aspect of your high school or college—for example, a particular program or major you are considering; a residence hall, library, or lab; the sports facilities or teams; a campus research institute or center; or campus work-study or student support services.
- Evaluate an article, an essay, a textbook, or another book assigned in a course; a campus newspaper blog, editorial, or opinion piece; or a campus performance, exhibit, or film series.

Subjects Related to Your Community

- Evaluate how well one of the following meets the needs of residents of your town or city: public library, health clinic, neighborhood watch or block parent program, meals-on-wheels program, theater, or symphony.
- Evaluate a law or a proposed law, such as the Dream Act, the Stop Online Piracy Act, the Defense of Marriage Act, the balanced budget amendment, or the equal rights amendment to the Constitution.

Subjects Related to Work

- Evaluate a job you have had or currently have, or evaluate someone else you have observed closely, such as a coworker or supervisor.
- Evaluate a local job-training program, either one in which you have participated or one that will allow you to observe and interview trainees.

⌐ TEST YOUR CHOICE ⌐

Choosing a Subject

After you have made a provisional choice, ask yourself the following questions:

- Do I know enough about the subject, or can I learn enough in the time I have?
- Do I already have a judgment (either tentative or certain) about this subject?
- Do I know what criteria or standards my readers are likely to use for judging something of this kind? Would I use the same criteria?

(continued)

To try out your choice of a subject and ideas about criteria, get together with two or three other students:

Presenters.   Take turns describing your subject.

Listeners.   Briefly tell the presenter what criteria or standards of judgment you would use to evaluate a subject of this kind.

As you plan and draft your evaluation, you may need to reconsider your choice of subject (for example, if you discover your criteria for evaluating are different from those your readers would use). If you have serious doubts about your choice, discuss them with your instructor before starting over with a new subject.

⸬ Assess your subject and consider how to present it to your readers.

Once you have made a preliminary choice of a subject, consider how you can frame or reframe it so that readers will be open to your evaluation. To do this, consider first how you regard the subject and what your readers are likely to think. Use the following questions and sentence strategies as a jumping-off point. You can make the sentences you generate your own later, as you revise.

WAYS IN

WHAT DO I THINK?

List those qualities of your **SUBJECT** that you like and dislike, or list its strengths and weaknesses or advantages and disadvantages.

▶ What makes X good/bad is _____, _____, and _____.

▶ Although X is stellar in _____ [ways], it falls short in _____ [other ways].

What **GENRE** or kind of subject is it?

▶ X is a _____ [name genre or category of subject, such as romantic comedy or horror movie].

▶ X is an innovative example of _____ [name category in which the subject belongs] that combines elements of _____ and _____.

▶ X is rather unconventional for a _____ [name category in which your subject belongs].

WHAT DO MY READERS THINK?

Who are your **READERS**, and why will they be reading your review? Is the subject new or familiar to them?

▶ My readers are _____ and are probably reading my review to learn about the subject/to decide whether to see it, play it, or buy it.

▶ My readers will probably be familiar with the subject. They may be curious to know what I think because _____.

How might **DEMOGRAPHIC FACTORS** such as the readers' age, gender, cultural background, or work experience affect their judgment of the subject?

▶ Older/Younger readers are less/more likely to _____.

Writing a Draft

GUIDE TO READING
▶ **GUIDE TO WRITING**
A WRITER AT WORK
THINKING CRITICALLY

369

What **CRITERIA** or standards of judgment do you usually use to evaluate things of this kind?

- ▶ I expect X to be .... or ....
- ▶ I dislike it when X is ....

How does your subject **COMPARE** to other examples of the genre?

- ▶ Compared to Y, X has the best/worst .... [name trait].
- ▶ X is like Y in that both are/do/make .... , but X is more/less ....
- ▶ Whereas Y can be faulted/praised for .... , X ....

- ▶ People who work in .... or who are familiar with .... may be more/less critical, or apply different standards to a subject like this one.

What **CRITERIA** or standards of judgment do you expect your readers to use when evaluating subjects of this kind? What other **EXAMPLES** of the genre would they be familiar with?

- ▶ I expect readers to share my criteria.
- ▶ If they like/dislike Y, they are sure to like/dislike X.
- ▶ Judging X on the basis of .... is likely to surprise readers because they probably are more familiar with .... and ....

▪▪ Formulate a working thesis stating your overall judgment.

You may already have a good idea about how you want to assert your thesis: stating whether your subject is good or bad, or better or worse than something else in the same genre or category. Remember that evaluations can be mixed—you can concede shortcomings in a generally favorable review or concede admirable qualities in a mostly negative assessment. If you feel comfortable drafting a working thesis statement now, do so. You may use the following sentence strategies as a jumping-off point—you can always revise them later—or use language of your own. (Alternatively, if you prefer to develop your argument before trying to formulate a thesis, skip this activity now and return to it later.)

As you develop your argument, you may want to rework your thesis to make it more compelling by sharpening the language and perhaps also by forecasting your reasons. You may also need to qualify your judgment with words like *generally, may,* or *in part.*

WAYS IN

HOW CAN I ASSERT A TENTATIVE OVERALL JUDGMENT?

A good strategy is to begin by NAMING the subject and IDENTIFYING the kind of subject it is, and then using VALUE TERMS to state your judgment of the subject's strengths and weaknesses:

▶ X is a brilliant embodiment of _____ [genre/category], especially notable for its superb _____ and thorough _____ .

▶ Because I admire _____ [another artist's other work], I expected X to be _____ . But I was disappointed/surprised by _____ .

▶ X has many good qualities including _____ and _____ ; however, the pluses do not outweigh its one major drawback, namely that _____ .

▪▪ Develop the reasons and evidence supporting your judgment.

For more idea-generating strategies, see Chapter 11.

The following activities will help you find reasons and evidence to support your evaluation. Begin by writing down what you already know. You can do some focused research later to fill in the details.

WAYS IN

HOW CAN I COME UP WITH REASONS AND EVIDENCE TO SUPPORT MY JUDGMENT?

List the good and bad qualities of the subject. Begin by reviewing the CRITERIA and the VALUE TERMS you have already used to describe the good and bad qualities of the subject. These are the potential REASONS for your judgment. Try restating them using this basic sentence strategy, which is also illustrated by an example from student William Akana's film review:

▶ X is _____ [your overall judgment] *because* _____ , _____ , and _____ .

Example:

> *Scott Pilgrim vs. the World* can be appreciated and enjoyed by all audiences *because* of its inventive special effects, clever dialogue, and artistic cinematography and editing. (par. 2)

Write steadily for at least five minutes, developing your reasons. Ask yourself questions like these:

▶ Why are the characteristics I'm pointing out for praise or criticism so important in judging my subject?

Example:

> Akana singles out special effects, dialogue, cinematography and editing because of the particular kind of film *Scott Pilgrim vs. the World* is—"a hilarious slacker movie that also somehow reimagines romantic comedy" (par. 1).

Writing a Draft

GUIDE TO READING
GUIDE TO WRITING
A WRITER AT WORK
THINKING CRITICALLY

371

▶ How can I prove to readers that the value terms I'm using to evaluate these characteristics are fair and accurate?

Example:

Akana analyzes the film's special effects and gives readers specific examples, including screen shots, to demonstrate that they are indeed "inventive."

Make notes of the **EVIDENCE** you will use to support your judgment. Evidence you might use to support each reason may include the following:

- Examples
- Quotations from authorities
- Textual evidence (quotations, paraphrases, or summaries)
- Images
- Statistics
- Comparisons or contrasts

You may already have some evidence you could use. If you lack evidence for any of your reasons, make a *Research To Do* note for later.

Research your evaluation.

Consult your *Research To Do* notes to determine what you need to find out. If you are evaluating a subject that others have written about, try searching for articles or books on your topic. Enter keywords or phrases related to the subject, genre, or category into the search box of

- an all-purpose database—such as *Academic OneFile* (InfoTrac) or *Academic Search Complete* (EBSCOHost)—to find relevant articles in magazines and journals;
- the database *Lexis/Nexis* to find newspaper reviews;
- a search engine like *Google* or *Yahoo!* (Akana used *Movie Review Query Engine* [mrqe.com] and *Rotten Tomatoes* to find film reviews of *Scott Pilgrim vs. the World*);
- your library's catalog to locate books on your topic.

Turn to databases and search engines for information on more recent items, like films and popular novels; use books, databases, and search engines to find information on classic topics. (Books are more likely to provide in-depth information, but articles in print or online are more likely to be current.)

To learn more about searching a database or catalog, see Chapter 21.

Respond to a likely objection or alternative judgment.

Start by identifying an objection or an alternative judgment you expect some readers to raise. To come up with likely objections or alternative judgments, you might try the following:

- *Brainstorm* a list on your own or with fellow students.
- *Freewrite* for ten minutes on this topic.

For more on idea-generating strategies, see Chapter 11; for more on conducting research, see Chapter 21.

- Conduct research to learn what others have said about your subject.
- Conduct interviews with experts.
- Distribute a survey to a group of people similar to your intended readers.

Then figure out whether to concede or refute a likely objection or alternative judgment. You may be able simply to acknowledge an objection or alternative judgment. But if the criticism is serious, consider conceding the point and qualifying your judgment. You might also try to refute an objection or alternative judgment by arguing that the standards you are using are appropriate and important. Use the following strategies for generating ideas and sentences as a jumping-off point, and revise them later to make them your own.

WAYS IN

HOW CAN I RESPOND EFFECTIVELY TO MY READERS?

1. Start by listing OBJECTIONS you expect readers to have as well as their preferred ALTERNATIVE JUDGMENTS. In the Ways In activity on p. 368, you considered your readers and the criteria they are likely to favor. If their criteria differ from yours, you may need to explain or defend your criteria.

2. Analyze your list of objections and alternative judgments to determine which are likely to be most powerful for your readers.

3. Draft REFUTATIONS and CONCESSION statements:

To Refute

▶ Reviewer A claims that .... But I agree with Reviewer B who argues that
....

▶ Some people claim that subject X is .... because of .... , ... , and
.... Although one can see why they might make this argument, the evidence does not back it up because ....

▶ In contrast to popular opinion, a recent study of .... showed that ....

To Concede

▶ Indeed, the more hard-core enthusiasts, like A, B, and C, may carp that .... is not sufficiently ....

▶ The one justifiable criticism that could be made against X is ....

▶ As some critics have pointed out, X follows the tried-and-true formula of ....

To Concede and Refute

Frequently, writers concede a point only to come back with a refutation. To make the CONCESSION-REFUTATION MOVE, follow concessions like those above with sentences that begin with a TRANSITION like *but, however, yet,* or *nevertheless,* and then explain why you believe that your interpretation or position is more powerful or compelling.

> ► As some critics have pointed out, X follows the tried-and-true formula of .... Still, the director/writer/artist is using the formula effectively to ....

Research Note: You may want to return to this activity after conducting further research. (For example, when he researched published reviews of *Scott Pilgrim,* student William Akana found objections to his argument as well as alternative judgments he could quote and refute.)

For more on the concession-refutation move, see Chapter 6, p. 235.

▓ Organize your draft to appeal to your readers.

Whether you have rough notes or a complete draft, making an *outline* of what you have written can help you organize the essay effectively for your audience. An evaluative essay contains as many as four basic parts:

1. Presentation of the subject
2. Judgment of the subject
3. Presentation of reasons and support
4. Consideration of readers' objections and alternative judgments

These parts can be organized in various ways; two options follow:

If you are writing primarily for readers who disagree with your judgment, you could start by showing them what you think they have overlooked or misjudged about the subject. Then you could anticipate and refute their likely objections before presenting your own reasons.	If you expect some readers to disagree with your judgment even though they share your standards, you could begin by restating these standards and then demonstrate how the subject fails to meet them. Then you could present your reasons and support before responding to alternative judgments.

I. **Presentation of the subject:** Reframe subject in terms that support your judgment	I. **Presentation of the issue:** Reassert shared criteria
II. **Thesis statement:** State your judgment directly	II. **Thesis statement:** State judgment that subject fails to meet shared criteria
III. **Refutation of alternative judgments**	III. **First reason and support showing how subject falls short**
IV. **First reason and support with refutation of objection**	IV. **Second reason and support**
V. **Second reason and support**	V. **Third reason and support (and so on)**
VI. **Third reason and support (and so on)**	VI. **Refutation of alternative judgment**
VII. **Conclusion:** Reiterate why your judgment is preferable to the alternatives	VII. **Conclusion:** Reassert judgment based on shared criteria

For more on outlining,
see Chapter 11.

Never be a slave to an outline: As you draft, you may see ways to improve your original plan, and you should be ready to shift parts around or drop or add parts as needed. If you use the outlining function of your word processing program, changing your outline will be simple, and you may be able to write the essay simply by expanding that outline.

Consider document design.

Because evaluations depend heavily on excerpts from the subject, they frequently include quotations, paraphrases, or summaries of the subject. When the subject of evaluation is in a visual medium (as with films, television shows, works of art, and Web sites), writers may use movie stills, photographs, or screen shots as evidence to support their claims. Consider how William Akana used film stills from *Scott Pilgrim vs. the World* as evidence to support his claim that this film "can be appreciated and enjoyed by all audiences because of its inventive special effects" (par. 2).

Uses a film still to support his claim that the film offers inventive special effects (film still shows "gamertags")

Connects text discussion to the illustration with a figure callout

Scott Pilgrim vs the World shines bright with superb special effects that serve to reinforce the ideas, themes, and style of the film. Special effects are plentiful throughout the entire film, ranging from superimposed annotations echoing classic gaming features to artful backgrounds and action sequences modeled on colorful comic book pages. For example, each of the main characters is described for the first time with "gamertags," short-timed boxes of information that include name, age, and rating (see fig. 1).

Uses a caption to highlight what the illustration shows

Fig. 1. Screen shot showing gamertags

Image credit: © Universal/Everett Collection

Writing a Draft

GUIDE TO READING
GUIDE TO WRITING
A WRITER AT WORK
THINKING CRITICALLY

375

Write the opening sentences.

Review what you have already written to see if you have something that would work to launch your concept explanation, or try out some of these opening strategies:

Offer an **anecdote** *or* **example***:*

> As I leaned back in the movie theater seat, accompanied by my friends on a typical Saturday night, I knew I was in for something special. I was reassured; not only had my friends and I reached a unanimous vote to watch *Scott Pilgrim vs. the World*, but two of my friends had already seen the film and were eager to see it again. (Akana, par. 1)

> For critics, sorting through television pilots is an act of triage. Last year, when *Game of Thrones* landed on my desk, I skimmed two episodes and made a quick call: we'd have to let this one go. (Nussbaum, par. 1)

Begin with a **comparison** *your readers are likely to be familiar with:*

> *Car and Driver* conducted a comparison of three sports cars, the Lotus Evora, the Chevrolet Corvette Grand Sport, and the Porsche Cayman S. . . . (Gladwell, par. 1)

Offer a **surprising or provocative statement***:*

> We live in a technological universe in which we are always communicating. And yet we have sacrificed conversation for mere connection. (Turkle, par. 1)

But don't agonize over the first sentences, because you are likely to discover the best way to begin only after you have written a rough draft.

Draft your evaluation.

By this point, you have done a lot of writing to

- devise a well-presented subject and made a judgment about it;
- support your judgment with reasons and evidence that your readers will find persuasive;
- refute or concede objections and alternative judgments;
- organize your ideas to make them clear, logical, and effective for readers.

Now stitch that material together to create a draft. The next two parts of this Guide to Writing will help you evaluate and improve that draft.

Evaluating the Draft: Using Peer Review

Your instructor may arrange a peer review session in class or online where you can exchange drafts with your classmates to give each other a thoughtful critical reading, pointing out what works well and suggesting ways to improve the draft. A good critical reading does three things:

1. It lets the writer know how well the reader understands the point of the essay.

2. It praises what works best.

3. It indicates where the draft could be improved and makes suggestions on how to improve it.

One strategy for evaluating a draft is to use the basic features of evaluative essays as a guide.

A PEER REVIEW GUIDE

A Well-Presented Subject

> Has the writer presented the subject effectively?

Summarize: Tell the writer what you understand the subject of the evaluation to be, and identify the kind of subject it is.

Praise: Point to a place where the subject is presented effectively — for example, where it is described vividly and accurately, where it is named, or where it is clearly placed in a recognizable genre or category.

Critique: Tell the writer where readers might need more information about the subject, and whether any information about it seems inaccurate or possibly only partly true. Suggest how the writer could clarify the kind of subject it is, either by naming the category or by giving examples of familiar subjects of the same type.

A Well-Supported Judgment

> Has the writer supported the judgment effectively?

Summarize: Tell the writer what you understand the overall judgment to be, and list the criteria on which it is based.

Praise: Identify a passage in the essay where support for the judgment is presented effectively — for example, note particularly strong supporting reasons, appeals to criteria readers are likely to share, or especially compelling evidence.

Critique: Let the writer know if you cannot find a thesis statement or think the thesis is vague or overstated. Tell the writer where the evaluation could be improved — for example, suggest another reason that could be added; propose a way to justify one of the criteria on which the evaluation is based; or recommend a source or an example that could be used to bolster support for the judgment.

An Effective Response to Objections and Alternative Judgments

Has the writer responded effectively to objections and alternative judgments?

Summarize: Choose an objection or alternative judgment about the subject, and explain it in your own words.

Praise: Identify a passage in the essay where the writer responds effectively to an objection or alternative judgment. An effective response may include making a concession — for example, agreeing that a subject the writer is primarily criticizing has some good points, or agreeing that the subject has weaknesses as well as strengths.

Critique: Tell the writer where a response is needed or could be made more effective — for example, suggest a likely objection or alternative judgment that should be taken into account, help the writer understand the criteria behind an alternative judgment, or offer an example that could be used to refute an objection.

A Clear, Logical Organization

Is the evaluation clearly and logically organized?

Summarize: Briefly describe the strategies used to make the essay clear and easy to follow.

Praise: Give an example of where the essay succeeds in being readable — in its overall organization, in its clear presentation of the thesis, in its effective opening or closing, or by other means.

Critique: Tell the writer where the readability could be improved. Can you, for example, suggest a better beginning or a more effective ending? If the overall organization of the essay needs work, make suggestions for rearranging parts or strengthening connections.

Before concluding your peer review, be sure to address any of the writer's concerns that have not been discussed already.

Making Comments Electronically   Most word processing software offers features that allow you to insert comments directly into the text of someone else's document. Many readers prefer to make their comments this way because it tends to be faster than writing on hard copy and space is virtually unlimited; it also eliminates the process of deciphering handwritten comments. Where such features are not available, simply typing comments directly into a document in a contrasting color can provide the same advantages.

Improving the Draft: Revising, Editing, and Proofreading

Start improving your draft by reflecting on what you have written thus far:

- Review critical reading comments from your classmates, instructor, or writing center tutor: What are your readers getting at?
- Consider whether you can add any of the notes from your earlier writings: What else should you consider?
- Review your draft: What can you do to present your position more compellingly?

Revise your draft.

If your readers are having difficulty with your draft, or if you think there is room for improvement, try some of the strategies listed in the Troubleshooting Guide that follows. It can help you fine-tune your presentation of the genre's basic features:

A TROUBLESHOOTING GUIDE

A Well-Presented Subject

> My readers find my subject vague or do not think it has been identified clearly.

- Identify the subject, name the author or director, and give the title.
- Describe the subject — summarize what it is about, cite statistics that establish its importance, or give examples to make it concrete.
- Consider adding visuals — photographs, tables, or charts — to help clarify the subject.

> My readers aren't sure what kind of subject it is.

- Classify the subject by naming the genre or category it fits into.
- Refer to reviews or reviewers of subjects of this kind.
- Compare your subject to other, better-known subjects of the same kind.

A Well-Supported Judgment

> My readers don't find my thesis or overall judgment clear.

- State your thesis early in the essay.
- Clarify the language in your thesis statement to indicate your overall judgment.
- Consider whether your judgment is arguable (not simply a matter of taste). If you cannot provide reasons and support for it, then your judgment probably isn't arguable; ask your instructor about modifying your judgment or writing about a different subject.

A Well-Supported Judgment

> My readers aren't convinced that my evaluation is reasonable and/or persuasive.

- Clarify the criteria on which you base your judgment, and justify them by citing authorities or reviews of similar subjects, making comparisons, or explaining why your criteria are appropriate and perhaps preferable to criteria readers may be more familiar with.
- Add support for your reasons by, for example, quoting respected experts or research studies; providing facts or statistics; giving specific examples; or quoting, summarizing, or paraphrasing the subject of your evaluation.

> My readers don't understand my evaluation.

- Review the way you present your evaluation to make sure that you have explained it clearly and that you state your supporting reasons clearly.
- Outline your argument to be sure that it is clearly organized; if it is not, try rearranging parts or strengthening connections.
- Make sure that you have cut out any irrelevant content, and revise to strengthen the connections among your ideas.

An Effective Response to Objections and Alternative Judgments

> My readers raise objections I haven't considered or find fault with my response to alternative judgments.

- If readers raise only a minor concern, you may be able to ignore or dismiss it. (Not every objection requires a response.)
- If readers raise a serious objection, one that undermines your argument, try to refute it by showing that it's not based on widely held or appropriate criteria or that it's based on a misunderstanding of your argument or the subject.
- If readers raise a serious objection that you can't refute, acknowledge it but try to demonstrate that it doesn't invalidate your judgment.

> My readers have proposed alternative judgments or have found fault with how I handle alternatives.

- Address the alternative judgments directly by conceding good or bad qualities of the subject that others focus on, but emphasize that you disagree about the overall value of the subject.
- Point out where you and your readers agree on criteria but disagree on how well the subject meets the criteria.
- Where you disagree with readers on criteria, try to justify the standards you are applying by citing authorities or establishing your own authority.

(continued)

My readers find my essay confusing or hard to follow.

A Clear, Logical Organization

- Outline your essay to review its structure, and move, add, or delete sections as necessary to strengthen coherence.
- Consider adding a forecasting statement early in your essay.
- Repeat your key terms or use synonyms of key terms to keep readers oriented.
- Check to see that you introduce your reasons clearly in topic sentences.
- Check to be sure that you provide appropriate transitions between sentences, paragraphs, and sections of your essay, especially at points where your readers have trouble following your argument.
- Review your opening and closing paragraphs to be sure that your overall judgment is clear and appropriately qualified.

Edit and proofread your draft.

Our research indicates that particular errors occur often in essays that justify an evaluation: incomplete and illogical comparisons, and short, choppy sentences. The following guidelines will help you check your essay for these common errors.

Making Complete, Logical, and Grammatically Correct Comparisons

The Problem   In essays that justify an evaluation, writers often engage in comparison—showing, for example, that one film is stronger than another, a new recording is inferior to an earlier one, or one restaurant is better than another. When comparisons are expressed incompletely, illogically, or incorrectly, however, the point of the comparison can be dulled or lost completely.

The Correction   Reread your comparisons, checking for completeness, logic, and correctness.

A comparison is complete if two terms are introduced, and the relationship between them is clearly expressed:

> ▶ *Jazz* is as good, *as* if not better than, Morrison's other novels.

> ▶ I liked the Lispector story because it's so different, *from anything else I've ever read.*

A comparison is logical if the terms compared are parallel (and therefore comparable):

> ▶ Will Smith's Muhammad Ali is more serious than any *other* role he's played.

> ▶ Ohio State's offense played much better than ~~Michigan.~~ *Michigan's did.*

Note that *different from* is correct; *different than,* though commonly used, is incorrect:

Improving the Draft

GUIDE TO READING
GUIDE TO WRITING
A WRITER AT WORK
THINKING CRITICALLY

381

▶ Carrying herself with a confident and brisk stride, Katherine Parker seems

from
different ~~than~~ the other women in the office.
        ^

▶ Films like *Drive*, which glorify violence for its own sake, are different ~~than~~
    from
films like *Apocalypse Now*, which use violence to make a moral point.

Combining Sentences

The Problem   When writers justify an evaluation, they generally present their sub-ject in some detail—defining it, describing it, placing it in some context. Inexperi-enced writers often present such details one after another, in short, choppy sentences. These sentences can be difficult or irritating to read, and they provide the reader with no help in determining how the different details relate to one another.

The Correction   Combine sentences to make your writing more readable and to clarify the relationships among ideas. Two common strategies for sentence combin-ing involve converting full sentences into **appositive phrases** (a noun phrase that renames the noun or pronoun that immediately precedes it) or **verbal phrases** (phrases using words derived from verbs that function as adjectives, adverbs, or nouns). Consider the following example:

▶ In paragraph 5, the details provide a different impression,/^ ~~It is~~ a comic or

                                                            based on
perhaps even pathetic impression,/^ ~~The impression comes from~~ the boy's
                                                                    ^

attempts to dress up like a real westerner.

From three separate sentences, this writer smoothly combines details about the "different impression" into a single sentence, using an appositive phrase ("a comic or perhaps even pathetic impression") and a verbal phrase ("based on the boy's attempts to dress up like a real westerner").

Here are two additional examples of the first strategy (conversion into an apposi-tive phrase):

▶ "Something Pacific" was created by Nam June Paik,/^ ~~He is~~ a Korean artist who is considered a founder of video art.

                        ^ *"Talkin' John Birch Paranoid Blues"* ^ "
▶ One of Dylan's songs ridiculed the John Birch Society. ~~This song was called~~
~~"Talkin' John Birch Paranoid Blues."~~

Finally, here are two additional examples of the second strategy (conversion into a verbal phrase):

                                                        carrying
▶ Spider-Man's lifesaving webbing sprung from his wristbands,/^ ~~They carried~~
                                                                ^
Mary Jane Watson and him out of peril.

        enticing
▶ The coffee bar flanks the bookshelves,/^ ~~It entices~~ readers to relax with a book.
                                        ^

William Akana's Thesis and Response to Objections

In this section, we look at how William Akana anticipated his readers' objections. Using the Ways In activity on pp. 368–69, Akana determined that readers would be interested in his review to "learn about whether the movie is worth going to see," although he realized that his instructor would read the review to assess how effectively he used the basic features of evaluative essays and whether he included an insightful analysis of the cinematic techniques used in at least one important scene.

After writing for a few minutes on the first part of the Test Your Choice activity on pp. 367–68, Akana got together with three other students in the class to test out his idea for a subject and his criteria for evaluation. One of his group's members told him that she had gone to see the movie on a date and had found the film lacking as a romantic comedy. Akana realized that this was an objection that he could respond to.

A few days later, Akana received some helpful advice from a student who read his draft. Using the Peer Review Guide in this chapter (pp. 376–77), the student noted that she could not find a clear statement of his judgment in the draft. She told him that the evidence he provided made it pretty clear that he liked the movie but that she couldn't find where he stated his judgment directly. So he went back to the Ways In activity on drafting a tentative overall judgment (pp. 369–70), and used one of the sentence strategies to help him draft a thesis:

> *Scott Pilgrim vs. the World* is a brilliant embodiment of the slacker film, especially notable for its superb special effects and clever dialogue.

When he finished his first draft, he revisited his thesis to polish it and to add another reason discussed in his supporting paragraphs. He also realized that he needed to acknowledge the target audience but wanted to make sure readers who were *not* video game or anime enthusiasts knew they would also enjoy the movie. Here's the final version of his thesis:

> Although the film is especially targeted for old-school gamers, anime fans, and comic book fanatics, *Scott Pilgrim vs. the World* can be appreciated and enjoyed by all audiences because of its inventive special effects, clever dialogue, and artistic cinematography and editing.

Another student reader noted that Akana's draft provided lots of strong evidence, especially the analysis of film stills, but she found his response to an objection weak and unconvincing. This assessment hit home because Akana had inserted his classmate's criticism—that the movie failed as a romantic comedy—without really thinking about it. To strengthen his response to the criticism, Akana conducted research and found an expert reviewer who agreed with his classmate. He found a review by Rene Rodriguez in the *Miami Herald* that offered a reason why the romance was not convincing, and then he brainstormed his own response—that the romance is really secondary to Pilgrim's personal development. Akana then did more research and found a review that he could use to support this claim. His paragraph (par. 9), which originally focused solely on Rodriguez's criticism of the romance theme, developed into one in which Akana argued what he really believed—that the romance is pretty much beside the point.

THINKING CRITICALLY

To think critically means to use all of the knowledge you have acquired from the information in this chapter, your own writing, the writing of other students, and class discussions to reflect deeply on your work for this assignment and the genre (or type) of writing you have produced. The benefit of thinking critically is proven and important: Thinking critically about what you have learned will help you remember it longer, ensuring that you will be able to put it to good use well beyond this writing course.

Reflecting on What You Have Learned

In this chapter, you have learned a great deal about this genre from reading several essays that justify an evaluation and from writing an evaluation of your own. To consolidate your learning, reflect not only on what you learned but also on how you learned it.

ANALYZE & WRITE

Write a blog post, a letter to your instructor, or an e-mail message to a student who will take this course next term, using the writing prompt that seems most productive for you:

- Explain how your purpose and audience influenced *one* of your decisions as a writer, such as how you presented the subject, the strategies you used in justifying your evaluation, or the ways in which you attempted to counter possible objections.

- Discuss what you learned about yourself as a writer in the process of writing this particular essay. For example, what part of the process did you find most challenging? Did you try anything new, like getting a critical reading of your draft or outlining your draft in order to revise it?

- If you were to give advice to a friend who was about to write an essay justifying an evaluation, what would you say?

- Which of the readings in this chapter influenced your essay? Explain the influence, citing specific examples from your essay and from the reading.

- If you got good advice from a critical reader, explain exactly how the person helped you — perhaps by questioning the way you addressed your audience or the kinds of support you offered in support of your position.

Reflecting on the Genre

Good evaluative writing provides readers with reasons and support for the writer's judgment. However, the writer's personal experiences, cultural background, and political ideology are also reflected in evaluations. Even the most fair-minded evaluators write from the perspective of their ethnicity, religion, gender, age, social class, sexual orientation, academic discipline, and so on. Writers seldom make their assumptions explicit, however. Consequently, while the reasons presented within an evaluation may make it seem fair and objective, the writer's judgment may result from hidden assumptions that even the writer has not examined critically.

| ANALYZE & WRITE |

Write a page or two explaining how the genre disguises the writer's assumptions. In your discussion, you might do one or more of the following:

1 **Identify one of the hidden assumptions of a writer in this chapter.** Think of a personal or cultural factor that may have influenced the writer's judgment of the subject. For example, how do you imagine that Akana's gender may have influenced his judgment of the film *Scott Pilgrim vs. the World*?

2 **Reflect on your own experience of writing an evaluation essay.** How do you think factors such as gender, age, social class, ethnicity, religion, geographical region, or political perspective may have influenced your own evaluation? Recall the subjects that you listed as possibilities for your essay and how you chose one to evaluate. Also recall how you arrived at your overall judgment and how you decided which reasons to use and which not to use in your essay.

3 **Write a page or two explaining your ideas about how hidden assumptions play a role in evaluation essays.** Connect your ideas to the readings in this chapter and to your own essay.

9

Arguing for Causes or Effects

Why is social media *really* so popular? Why do we watch horror movies, even though they make our skin crawl? Is "multitasking" the answer to our busy lives? Why are people moved more by the plight of an individual than by the plight of a crowd? The quest for answers to our questions inspires scientific inquiry, which can fully and satisfactorily explain the causes and effects of many things. But for questions like those addressed by the readings in this chapter, the causes and effects are uncertain and may never be known conclusively. For such subjects, it is helpful to think of analyzing causes or effects as a special kind of *argument* that considers evidence to determine whether one cause is likely to play an important — perhaps surprising — role in bringing about the effect or whether surprising effects might be the result of a particular cause.

People make causal arguments for various purposes and audiences and publish them in a variety of media. For example, a college student in an ecology course might write a research paper analyzing why coral reefs are dying off, a serious problem that could alter coastal communities around the world. The captain of a neighborhood watch committee might write to the op-ed page of his community's online newspaper arguing that ignoring vandalism can lead to more serious deterioration of a neighborhood (the "broken-window effect"). A teacher might write an article on why boys are falling behind in educational achievement and the consequences to society of such a fact.

In this chapter, we ask you to choose a subject that does not have a single, definitive cause or effect that everyone accepts as fact, and then to *argue* that one (or more than one) cause or effect is the most plausible culprit, providing *reasons* and *evidence* to support your claim. By analyzing the reading selections that follow, you will learn how to develop your own causal analysis. The Guide to Writing later in the chapter will show you ways to use the basic features of the genre to compose an original, thought-provoking causal argument of your own.

PRACTICING THE GENRE ├─────────────────────────────────

Arguing That a Cause Is Plausible

To think about how you could make a convincing causal argument, get together with two or three other students and follow these guidelines:

Part 1.   The detrimental health effects of smoking are well known, and smoking by everyone, including teens, has been declining for at least twenty years. However, some high school students still choose to smoke cigarettes.

First, choose your audience and purpose:

- Are you addressing other college students, faculty, administrators, the general public, or teens themselves?

- Is your goal to change opinions or behavior, or to inspire the creation of useful school policies?

Then brainstorm a list of causes that could explain why some high school students choose to smoke. Finally, pick your most plausible cause and discuss these questions:

- What evidence would you need to support an argument for your preferred cause?

- Where could you find the supporting evidence you need?

Part 2.   As a group, discuss what you learned from this activity:

- **How did your group initially come up with possible causes?** For example, did you recall your own experiences and observations? Did you consider different categories of causes, such as cultural, biological, psychological, or social?

- **What did you assume about your audience?** Did you think audience members would already be interested in your argument or perhaps that they would resent being the focus of this kind of inquiry? What kinds of supporting evidence did you think your audience would find persuasive?

Analyzing Causal Arguments

As you read the selections in this chapter, you will see how different authors make a provocative causal argument:

- Clayton Pangelinan argues that the popularity of social media is driven, not only by our need to connect, but also by our curiosity and our narcissism (pp. 391–95).
- Stephen King offers causes for why we crave horror movies—beyond the simple shiver effect (pp. 396–98).
- Claudia Wallis argues that multitasking is not the wonderful way to achieve more productivity that many people think it is (pp. 401–7).
- Shankar Vedantam tries to explain why people are often generous toward individuals or small groups but do not help large groups (pp. 409–13).

Analyzing how these writers present their subjects to their readers, persuade readers that their cause-effect reasoning is plausible, respond to alternative viewpoints, and organize their writing will help you see how you can employ similar strategies to make your own causal argument clear and compelling for your readers.

Determine the writer's purpose and audience.

In analyzing possible causes or effects, writers exercise their imagination along with their logical thinking skills, but they also want to influence the way their readers think. As you read the causal arguments that follow, ask yourself questions like these:

What seems to be the writer's main purpose in arguing for a cause or effect?

- to engage readers in thinking about the subject in creative new ways?
- to convince readers to contemplate causes or effects that have not been considered or taken seriously before?
- to persuade readers that surprising causes or effects are likely to play a significant role?

What does the author assume about the audience?

- that readers know little about the subject and need to be inspired to care?
- that they know little about the subject but are likely to be curious about it?
- that they know a lot about the subject and are likely to have their own ideas about causes or effect?
- that they know a lot about the subject but are open to new ideas?

Assess the genre's basic features.

As you analyze the causal arguments in this chapter, consider how different authors incorporate the basic features of the genre. The examples that follow are taken from the reading selections that appear later in this Guide to Reading.

Basic Features
A Well-Presented Subject
A Well-Supported Causal Analysis
An Effective Response to Objections and Alternative Causes or Effects
A Clear, Logical Organization

A WELL-PRESENTED SUBJECT

Look first at the title and opening paragraphs to see what the subject is and whether it is clearly and vividly established. Frequently, the title of a causal argument will identify the focus:

> #socialnetworking: Why It's *Really* So Popular (Pangelinan, title)
> Why We Crave Horror Movies (King, title)

To establish the subject, a writer may cite statistics or provide graphic illustrations:

> As Figure 1 below shows, the rise in popularity [of social media] cuts across all age groups. The most dramatic growth has been among young adults. . . . A 2015 survey reported that 71% of all teens use Facebook, along with sites like Instagram and Snapchat (Lenhart). Facebook has tended to outpace other networking outlets for adults as well, with 71% of online adults reporting they use Facebook ("Social Networking Fact Sheet"). (Pangelinan, par. 1)

A common approach to arousing the reader's curiosity is to begin with a compelling anecdote:

> It's 9:30 p.m., and Stephen and Georgina Cox know exactly where their children are. Well, their bodies, at least. Piers, 14, is holed up in his bedroom—eyes fixed on his computer screen. . . . His twin sister Bronte is planted in the living room, having commandeered her dad's iMac—as usual. (Wallis, par. 1)

> The *Insiko 1907* was a tramp tanker that roamed the Pacific Ocean. . . . The ship was about eight hundred miles south of Hawaii's Big Island, and adrift. Its crew could not call on anyone for help, and no one who could help knew of the *Insiko*'s existence, let alone its problems. (Vendantam, par. 1)

Another common strategy for stimulating the audience to read on is to pose *why* questions:

> The fact *that* social networking is popular is well established. The question is *why* is it so popular? (Pangelinan, par. 2)

> When we [see] a horror movie, we are daring the nightmare. Why? Some of the reasons are simple and obvious. . . . (King, par. 2)

> Why did so many people come forward to save Hokget? . . . Why did they feel a single abandoned dog on a stateless ship was *their* problem? (Vedantam, par. 11)

> Why can we so easily walk down the street while engrossed in a deep conversation? Why can we chop onions while watching *Jeopardy*? (Wallis, par. 16)

A WELL-SUPPORTED CAUSAL ANALYSIS

Find where the writer identifies and discusses each possible cause or effect, and note which one(s) the writer favors as being the most plausible (the most likely to have played a significant role) *as well as the most interesting* (possibly because the cause or effect has been overlooked or underappreciated).

EXAMPLE   When we [see] a horror movie, we are daring the nightmare. Why? Some
of the reasons are simple and obvious. . . . To show that we can, that we
are not afraid. . . .
. . . to re-establish our feelings of essential normality. . . .
. . . to have fun.
Ah, but this is where the ground starts to slope away, isn't it? . . . (King,
pars. 2–5)

Then assess the persuasiveness of the supporting evidence:

Although such habits may prepare kids for today's frenzied workplace, many
cognitive scientists are positively alarmed by the trend. "Kids that are instant
messaging while doing homework, playing games online and watching TV, I predict,
aren't going to do well in the long run," says Jordan Grafman, chief of the cognitive
neuroscience section of the National Institute of Neurological Disorders and Stroke
(NINDS). . . . (Wallis, par. 13).

Quotation
from expert

The evidence for what I am going to call the telescope effect comes from a series of
fascinating experiments. . . . (Vedantam, par. 14)

Research
studies

Also check that the cause-effect argument makes sense—in particular, that the
cause (or causes) could actually bring about the effect (or effects). Note whether either
of these logical fallacies or errors of causal reasoning have been made:

- **Mistaking chronology for causation:** Assuming that because one thing preceded another, the former caused the latter. (This fallacy is often called by its
Latin name, *post hoc, ergo propter hoc*, which means "after this, therefore because
of this.")

- **Mistaking correlation for causation:** Assuming that because two things seem
to be related or complementary that one thing caused the other. (This fallacy is
sometimes called "with this, therefore because of this.")

For more about logical
fallacies, see Chapter 19,
p. 595.

AN EFFECTIVE RESPONSE TO OBJECTIONS AND ALTERNATIVE CAUSES OR EFFECTS

*Notice where the author anticipates and responds to objections and alternative causes or
effects.* Often writers mention the well-known, predictable causes or effects first, but
quickly put them aside to make room for a more detailed consideration of the writer's
preferred cause or effect. Here are a couple of sentence strategies that you might look
for, followed by examples of these strategies in context:

▶ Most people assume X; however, _____ .

▶ X and Y and are the usual suspects, but let's look at a totally new possibility: _____ .

EXAMPLES   Saving the dog . . . was an act of pure altruism, and a marker of the
remarkable capacity human beings have to empathize with the plight
of others.

Acknowledges positive
aspects of rescue

There are a series of disturbing questions, however. . . . (Vedantam,
pars. 6–7)

Prepares reader for
alternative perspective

Concedes but puts aside alternative explanations	**EXAMPLES**	Some of the reasons are simple and obvious. To show that we can, that we are not afraid, that we can ride this roller coaster. . . . We also go to re-establish our feelings of essential normality. . . . And we go to have fun. Ah, but this is where the ground starts to slope away, isn't it? Because this is a very peculiar sort of fun, indeed. The fun comes from seeing others menaced—sometimes killed. (King, pars. 2–5)
Offers surprising, new explanation		

States alternative explanation

Refutes alternative

There are many explanations for the discrepancy between our response to Hokget and our response to genocide. Some argue that Americans care little about foreign lives—but then what should we make about their willingness to spend thousands of dollars to rescue a dog, a foreign dog on a stateless ship in international waters? Well, perhaps Americans care more about pets than people? But that does not stand up to scrutiny either. . . . I believe our inability to wrap our minds around large numbers is responsible for our apathy toward mass suffering. (Vedantam, pars. 8–9)

A CLEAR, LOGICAL ORGANIZATION

Read to see if the writer provides cues to help readers follow the logic of the causal argument. Essays arguing for causes or effects tend to be rather complicated because the writer has to establish that the subject exists, present a variety of causes or effects, and argue for those that are more likely to play an important role. So cues to help readers follow the argument are needed. Notice whether the writer asserts the preferred cause or effect in a thesis statement:

Cause
Effect

I believe our inability to wrap our minds around large numbers is responsible for our apathy toward mass suffering. (Vedantam, par. 9)

Some thesis statements may also include a forecasting statement. Typically, a forecasting statement in a causal argument identifies the main causes, effects, key supporting topics, or examples in the order they will be explored in the essay.

The fact *that* social networking is popular is well established. The question is *why* is it so popular? The most basic answer is that social networking is popular because it's available. . . . A better answer, though, is that social media offer people a way to satisfy their desire to connect with others and maybe also be "world-famous for fifteen minutes" (to quote Andy Warhol). (Pangelinan, par. 2)

Writers may cue readers by repeating key terms from the forecasting statement. They may also repeat sentence patterns from the forecasting statement in the essay's *topic sentences* to emphasize that another cause or effect, response to objections, or supporting example is coming.

Repeats sentence structure	**FORECASTING STATEMENT**	Why? Some of the reasons are simple and obvious. To show that we can, that we are not afraid, that we can ride this roller coaster. (King, par. 2)
	TOPIC SENTENCE	We also go to re-establish our feelings of essential normality. (3)
	TOPIC SENTENCE	And we go to have fun. (4)

By repeating the same subject (*we*) and an active verb (*can, are, go*), King helps readers identify each new cause.

Writers may also use parallel grammatical structures to help readers recognize a series of supporting examples:

> Consider the story of Emmalene Pruden, a YouTube sensation who began posting her video blogs on YouTube. . . . Consider also the story of Lisa Sargese, who "started blogging as a way to tell the truth about her life. . . ." (Pangelinan, pars. 3–4)

Each of these examples provides support for the claim that "our wiring impels us not only to share, but also to hear" (par. 2). Other cues writers may provide to guide readers include the following:

- a thesis statement and possibly a forecast of the main cause or causes

- topic sentences announcing each new cause or example

- clear transitional words and phrases

- visuals (such as charts, graphs, and tables) that present information in an easy-to-read format

- headings that break selections up into sections by topic or cause

Readings

Clayton Pangelinan | *#socialnetworking: Why It's Really So Popular*

ORIGINALLY WRITTEN for Clayton Pangelinan's first-year college composition course, this essay analyzes what may be some surprising reasons for social networking's popularity. Before reading, reflect on your own attitudes about social media:

- Why do you think social networking is so popular? What are your own reasons for using social media (or for avoiding them)?

- Does the author address any of the causes you speculated about or that have motivated you?

  Your instructor may ask you to post to a class blog or discussion board or bring to class your responses to these questions as well as those in the margin of Pangelinan's essay.

To learn how Pangelinan generated ideas for his essay, turn to A Writer at Work on pp. 436–37.

▪▪ Basic Features
A Well-Presented Subject
A Well-Supported Causal Analysis
An Effective Response to Objections and Alternative Causes or Effects
A Clear, Logical Organization

What is the effect on you of this opening paragraph?

How effective are the data Pangelinan provides to establish the fact that social networking has increased significantly?

1 Complain about problems in a *tweet* over Twitter; add a *friend*, virtually *poke* each other, and *like* friends' postings and ramblings on Facebook; send images and videos to each other using Snapchat; capture a *selfie* with Instagram, edit it, add hashtags, and share it for your friends to see and comment on: Social networking is only a click away with apps like Vine and YouTube, Twitter, Facebook, Snapchat, Instagram, and Whatsapp on smartphones and tablets everywhere. Over the last decade or so, there has been a remarkable increase in the popularity of social networking. As Figure 1 below shows, the rise in popularity cuts across all age groups. The most dramatic growth has been among young adults. The percentage of 18 to 29-year-olds using social media rose from 9% to 49% in just 18 months, from February 2005 to August 2006. Like young adults, teenagers have flocked to social media. A 2015 survey reported that 71% of all teens use Facebook, along with sites like Instagram and Snapchat (Lenhart). Facebook has tended to outpace other networking outlets for adults as well, with 71% of online adults reporting they use Facebook ("Social Networking Fact Sheet"). Preferences among social networking sites have changed over the years, but the bottom line is that social networking continues to be enormously popular.

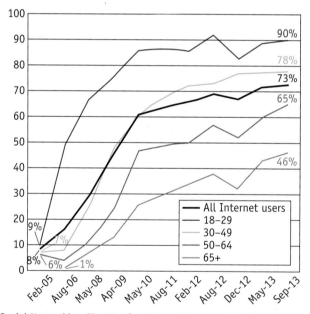

Fig. 1. Social Networking Site Use for Internet Users by Age Group, 2005-2013. Figure from "Social Networking Fact Sheet." *Internet Project Library Survey, 18 July-30 Sept., 2013.* Pew Research Center, Sept. 2013. Web. 14 Oct. 2015.

Pangelinan   *#socialnetworking: Why It's Really So Popular*

GUIDE TO READING
GUIDE TO WRITING
A WRITER AT WORK
THINKING CRITICALLY

393

2   The fact *that* social networking is popular is well established. The question is *why is it so popular?* The most basic answer is that social networking is popular because it's available. Without the technological advances that transformed the static read-only Web into the dynamic, interactive virtual community known as Web 2.0, none of the social networking we all engage in today would have been possible. A better answer, though, is that social media offer people a way to satisfy their desire to connect with others and maybe also be "world-famous for fifteen minutes" (as Andy Warhol supposedly remarked). When people were asked what their motivations were for using social networking sites like Facebook and Twitter, two-thirds of those surveyed reported that they go online primarily to connect with friends and family and meet new people (Fig. 2). As social animals, people have an inherent need for human connection. Professor Matthew Lieberman, in his recent book *Social: Why Our Brains Are Wired to Connect*, reports experiments using fMRIs to prove that the need to connect is hard-wired. According to Lieberman, our wiring impels us not only to share, but also to hear. Communication naturally flows both ways: Not only are we

Fig. 2. Motivations for using social networking sites. Figure from Smith, Aaron. "Why Americans Use Social Media." *Pew Research Center*. Pew Research Center, 15 Nov. 2011. Web. 14 Oct. 2015.

How is the rhetorical question and its answer a response to objections?

How do these two answers help structure Pangelinan's essay?

Why does Pangelinan include this chart?

How does this source support Pangelinan's argument?

"driven by deep motivations to stay connected with friends and family" but we are also "naturally curious about what is going on in the minds of other people" (ix).

How does Pangelinan make a connection between this paragraph and the one before?

3   Social media outlets offer a way to satisfy both impulses. Consider the story of Emmalene Pruden, a YouTube sensation who began posting her video blogs on YouTube after moving and feeling "cut off from her friends" (Niedzviecki 37). Emmalene is one example of how social media allow individuals to feel connected to a larger community: "If nothing else," as Niedzviecki claims, "peeping your problem, suspicion, or outrage is guaranteed to make you feel less alone" (142). But Emmalene's popularity also suggests that — as Hal Niedzviecki, author of *The Peep Diaries: How We're Learning to Love Watching Ourselves and Our Neighbors*, puts it — "it is these quotidian revelations that make her enticing to her viewers" (39). Viewers may feel less lonely knowing that their own everyday struggles and daily trivialities are no different than Emmalene's.

How does repeating this phrase cue readers?

4   Consider also the story of Lisa Sargese, who "started blogging as a way to tell the truth about her life as a morbidly obese, single woman determined to return to mobility and health via stomach-shrinking surgery" (Niedzviecki 51-52). She chronicled the effects of her surgery, growing her readership as she lost weight. Like Emmalene and her YouTube videos, Lisa was able to produce something that made her audience adore her: the sympathy effect. Readers also found hope by watching her overcome her problems. Niedzviecki makes a powerful statement that applies to both Emmalene and Lisa, as well as to their fans, when he concludes:

> We're alone all the time. We're alone on the bus, we're alone walking down the street, we're alone at the office and in the classroom, alone waiting in line at Disney World. We're tired of being alone, which is why increasingly we are barely hesitating to do whatever we feel we need to do to push out of solitude. (212-213)

5   This statement rings true throughout the social networking world but especially on Facebook, where users often post whatever is on their minds, however intimate. From the status of their relationships to pornographic home videos, social networkers can find it in a Facebook post. What motivates the extreme sharers?

How effective is a rhetorical question here?

How effective is this transition to a new topic?

6   One answer might be a desire for celebrity. Consider the story of a woman who calls herself Padme. For her, social networking has turned into an obsession apparently motivated by her need for fame: "In our case you get to 1.6 million readers it's really hard to just walk away from that" (quoted in Niedzviecki 26). Padme appears to be a typical suburban housewife and mother, except that she is also a fantastically popular writer of a sexually explicit Star Wars–themed blog, *Journey to the Darkside*. Padme's popularity appears to come not only

from her sexual confessions (and visuals), but also from her story of living a double life, as both a mother and as a Star Wars sex slave. In addition to recording her rather ordinary day-to-day activities as a stay-at-home mom, she also writes "about her need to be dominated by the man she calls Master Anakin, the man she's been . . . 'married to for 4 years, living with for 12 years, and best friends with for 18 years'" (Niedzviecki, 23).

7   Writing in the American Psychological Association journal *Psychology of Popular Media Culture,* Dara Greenwood reviews research showing that "a craving for positive feedback and validation may be a common thread that links a desire for fame with social media use" (223). More specifically, she points to the correlation between the desire to be seen and valued and the need to feel connected, "to feel meaningfully embedded in social networks," as Greenwood puts it (223). While Padme carries her blogging to extremes that Emmalene and Lisa don't reach, what Greenwood writes applies to all three. The underlying cause of this need for visibility may be narcissism, fairly obvious in all three cases but especially so in Padme's as demonstrated by the "increased tendency to engage in exhibitionist postings on social media sites" (224).

8   Of course, most of us participate in social networks without getting as carried away as Emmalene, Lisa, or Padme. In fact, if you understood the first paragraph in this essay, then chances are you sign in, sign up, tune in, and engage in many of these forms of social media. So ask yourself: What are your reasons for joining in? To connect? To tune in to what others are up to? To show off? Whatever your reasons, you can be sure you are not alone.

How does this source support Pangelinan's argument?

How is Pangelinan's conclusion a response to objections? How effective is his conclusion?

Works Cited

Greenwood, Dara N. "Fame, Facebook, and Twitter: How Attitudes about Fame Predict the Frequency and Nature of Social Media Use." *Psychology of Popular Media Culture* 2 (2013): 222-36. Web. 16 Oct. 2015.

Lenhart, Amanda. "Teens, Social Media & Technology Overview 2015." *Pew Research Center.* Pew Research Center. 9 Apr. 2015. Web. 14 Oct. 2015.

Lieberman, Matthew. *Social: Why Our Brains Are Wired to Connect.* New York: Crown, 2013. Print.

Niedzviecki, Hal. *The Peep Diaries: How We're Learning to Love Watching Ourselves and Our Neighbors.* San Francisco: City Lights, 2009. Print.

Smith, Aaron. "Why Americans Use Social Media." *Pew Research Center.* Pew Research Center, 15 Nov. 2011. Web. 15 Oct. 2015.

"Social Networking Fact Sheet." *Internet Project Library Survey, 18 July-30 Sept., 2013.* Pew Research Center, Sept. 2013. Web. 15 Oct. 2015.

Stephen King | *Why We Crave Horror Movies*

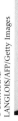
© BERTRAND LANGLOIS/AFP/Getty Images

STEPHEN KING is America's best-known writer of horror fiction. In 2015, he won the prestigious Edgar Award for best novel, for *Mr. Mercedes* (2014), in which a serial killer taunts the retired cop who never solved the crime. He has also won many other awards, including a Lifetime Achievement Award from the Horror Writers Association and the National Book Foundation Medal for Distinguished Contribution to American Letters, both in 2003. A prolific writer in many genres and media, King has recently published *Finders Keepers* (2015), *Revival* (2014), and *A Good Marriage* (2014), novels; *The Wind through the Keyhole* (2012), the latest in his Dark Tower graphic novel series; *Road Rage* (2012), a comic book series co-written with his son Joe Hill; *11/22/63* (2012), a time-travel novel about the assassination of President John F. Kennedy; and *Stephen King Goes to the Movies* (2009), a short story collection. Many films and television movies have been based on King's work, including the classics *The Shawshank Redemption* (1994) and *Stand by Me* (1986). King offers this wise advice to beginning writers in *On Writing* (2000): "You have to read a lot and write a lot. There's no way around these two things . . . no shortcut."

In this classic essay, King analyzes why some of us love horror movies. As you read, consider the following:

- What's your feeling about horror films, roller coasters, or other scary rides? For you personally, what makes them attractive or something to avoid?

- What reasons can you think of for why we like horror movies?

1   I think that we're all mentally ill; those of us outside the asylums only hide it a little better — and maybe not all that much better, after all. We've all known people who talk to themselves, people who sometimes squinch their faces into horrible grimaces when they believe no one is watching, people who have some hysterical fear—of snakes, the dark, the tight place, the long drop . . . and, of course, those final worms and grubs that are waiting so patiently underground.

2   When we [see] a horror movie, we are daring the nightmare. Why? Some of the reasons are simple and obvious. To show that we can, that we are not afraid, that we can ride this roller coaster. Which is not to say that a really good horror movie may not surprise a scream out of us at some point, the way we may scream when the roller coaster twists through a complete 360 or plows through a lake at the bottom of the drop. And horror movies, like roller coasters, have always been the special province of the young; by the time one turns 40 or 50, one's appetite for double twists or 360-degree loops may be considerably depleted.

3   We also go to re-establish our feelings of essential normality; the horror movie is innately conservative, even reactionary. Freda Jackson as the horrible melting woman in *Die, Monster, Die!* confirms for us that no matter how far we may be removed from the beauty of a Robert Redford or a Diana Ross, we are still light-years from true ugliness.

4   And we go to have fun.

5   Ah, but this is where the ground starts to slope away, isn't it? Because this is a very peculiar sort of fun, indeed. The fun comes from seeing others menaced—sometimes killed. One critic has suggested that if pro football has become the voyeur's version of combat, then the horror film has become the modern version of the public lynching.

can you face the ULTIMATE in DIABOLISM
.....can you stand PURE TERROR?

STARRING
BORIS KARLOFF
NICK ADAMS
SUSAN FARMER

It COULD happen!
It MAY happen!
It MIGHT happen!
to YOU!

IN AMERICAN INTERNATIONAL'S
Die MonsteR Die! in COLORSCOPE

Directed by DANIEL HALLER · PAT GREEN · JAMES H. NICHOLSON & SAMUEL Z. ARKOFF · JERRY SOHL

Courtesy Everett Collection

6   It is true that the mythic, "fairy tale" horror film intends to take away the shades of gray. . . . It urges us to put away our more civilized and adult penchant for analysis and to become children again, seeing things in pure blacks and whites. It may be that horror movies provide psychic relief on this level because this invitation to lapse into simplicity, irrationality, and even outright madness is extended so rarely. We are told we may allow our emotions a free rein . . . or no rein at all.

7   If we are all insane, then sanity becomes a matter of degree. If your insanity leads you to carve up women like Jack the Ripper or the Cleveland Torso Murderer, we clap you away in the funny farm (but neither of

those two amateur-night surgeons was ever caught, heh-heh-heh); if, on the other hand, your insanity leads you only to talk to yourself when you're under stress or to pick your nose on your morning bus, then you are left alone to go about your business . . . though it is doubtful that you will ever be invited to the best parties.

8   The potential lyncher is in almost all of us (excluding saints, past and present; but then, most saints have been crazy in their own ways), and every now and then, he has to be let loose to scream and roll around in the grass. Our emotions and our fears form their own body, and we recognize that it demands its own exercise to maintain proper muscle tone. Certain of these emotional muscles are accepted—even exalted—in civilized society; they are, of course, the emotions that tend to maintain the status quo of civilization itself. Love, friendship, loyalty, kindness—these are all the emotions that we applaud, emotions that have been immortalized in the couplets of Hallmark cards and in the verses (I don't dare call it poetry) of Leonard Nimoy.

9   When we exhibit these emotions, society showers us with positive reinforcement; we learn this even before we get out of diapers. When, as children, we hug our rotten little puke of a sister and give her a kiss, all the aunts and uncles smile and twit and cry, "Isn't he the sweetest little thing?" Such coveted treats as chocolate-covered graham crackers often follow. But if we deliberately slam the rotten little puke of a sister's fingers in the door, sanctions follow—angry remonstrance from parents, aunts, and uncles; instead of a chocolate-covered graham cracker, a spanking.

10   But anticivilization emotions don't go away, and they demand periodic exercise. We have such "sick" jokes as "What's the difference between a truckload of bowling balls and a truckload of dead babies?" ("You can't unload a truckload of bowling balls with a pitchfork" . . . a joke, by the way, that I heard originally from a ten-year-old.) Such a joke may surprise a laugh or a grin out of us even as we recoil, a possibility that confirms the thesis: If we share a brotherhood of man, then we also share an insanity of man. None of which is intended as a defense of either the sick joke or insanity but merely as an explanation of why the best horror films, like the best fairy tales, manage to be

reactionary, anarchistic, and revolutionary all at the same time.

11   The mythic horror movie, like the sick joke, has a dirty job to do. It deliberately appeals to all that is worst in us. It is morbidity unchained, our most base instincts let free, our nastiest fantasies realized . . . and it all happens, fittingly enough, in the dark. For those reasons, good liberals often shy away from horror films. For myself, I like to see the most aggressive of them—*Dawn of the Dead*, for instance—as lifting a trap door in the civilized forebrain and throwing a basket of raw meat to the hungry alligators swimming around in that subterranean river beneath.

12   Why bother? Because it keeps them from getting out, man. It keeps them down there and me up here. It was Lennon and McCartney who said that all you need is love, and I would agree with that.

13   As long as you keep the gators fed.

[REFLECT]   # Make connections: Media violence.

"The potential lyncher is in almost all of us," says Stephen King, ". . . and every now and then, he has to be let loose to scream and roll around in the grass" (par. 8). King seems to say that horror films perform a social function by allowing us to exercise (or possibly exorcise) our least civilized emotions. In fact, King even argued against a proposed ban on the sale of violent video games to people under the age of eighteen.

To analyze King's ideas about violence in the media, reflect on your own observation and personal experience with film, video games, or other media that may be considered violent. Your instructor may ask you to post your thoughts on a class discussion board or to discuss them with other students in class. Use these questions to get you started:

- King asserts that we all have what he calls "anticivilization emotions" (par. 10). What does King give as an example of these emotions? What have you seen, heard, or felt that suggests you or others harbor such emotions?

- The argument against violence in the media is basically that images of violence— or in the case of video games, performing virtual acts of violence—arouse anticivilization feelings and perhaps even inspire people (especially young people) to commit acts of real violence. King seems to agree that there is a cause-effect relationship, but what does he think is the cause and the effect? What do you think?

- If you think media violence inspires real violence, do you support censorship of movies, television programs, books, or Internet sites that portray violence? If so, should this material be censored just for children or for all viewers? If you oppose outright censorship, do you support movie rating systems or the television V-chip, which gives parents some control over what their children watch? Explain your responses.

Use the basic features.

[ANALYZE]

A WELL-PRESENTED SUBJECT: REFRAMING THE SUBJECT FOR READERS

Writers try to present their subjects in an intriguing way that makes readers wonder about it. To do so, they typically frame or reframe their subjects, emphasizing new ways of looking at and understanding them. How does King make room for his less predictable causes and convince readers to go along for the ride?

ANALYZE & WRITE

Write a couple of paragraphs analyzing and evaluating how King reframes his subject:

1   The title suggests that the subject of this essay is horror movies, but the key term in the title is the word "crave." Look up the verb *crave* and the related noun *craving* to see what they mean. Also highlight some of the other words and phrases King associates with the appeal of horror movies, such as "mentally ill" and "hysterical fear" (par. 1). How do the words you highlighted relate to the word *crave*?

2   Given these key terms, how would you describe the way King reframes the subject for readers? How do these key terms enable him to plant the seed of his main idea at the very beginning of the essay?

A WELL-SUPPORTED CAUSAL ANALYSIS: USING EXAMPLES AND COMPARISONS

In writing about horror movies, you might expect King to provide a lot of examples of the genre or to go into detail about one or two particularly memorable films. But, interestingly, King names only two films, neither of which is that memorable. By limiting the number and only referring to them briefly, King leaves a lot of space for readers to fill with their own favorite horror movies.

ANALYZE & WRITE

Write a couple of paragraphs analyzing and evaluating the examples and comparisons King uses to support his argument and the films that come to mind for you:

1   In addition to horror movies, King gives several other examples. Find one or two of them, and consider how well they confirm his thesis that we all harbor anticivilization emotions.

2   King also compares horror movies to various other things, such as roller coasters (par. 2). Skim the essay, highlighting the comparisons King makes. Then, consider how they help support his causal argument.

3   Taken together, how effective are the examples and comparisons as support for King's analysis? What examples did you think of as you read? How would the reading have been different had King supplied more examples of horror films?

AN EFFECTIVE RESPONSE: PUTTING ASIDE OBVIOUS CAUSES OR EFFECTS

People analyzing causes sometimes consider an array of possibilities before focusing on one or two serious probabilities. They may concede that these other causes or effects play some role, or they may simply dismiss them as trivial or irrelevant. "Some of the reasons," King explicitly declares, "are simple and obvious" (par. 2).

ANALYZE & WRITE

Write a couple of paragraphs analyzing and evaluating how well King uses concession and refutation:

1. Look closely at the causes King considers in the opening paragraphs to determine how he actually responds to them. For example, how does he support the assertion that some of them are "simple and obvious"? What other arguments, if any, does he use to refute them?

2. Given his purpose and audience, why do you think King chooses to begin by presenting reasons he thinks are simple and obvious?

A CLEAR, LOGICAL ORGANIZATION: USING CAUSE-EFFECT SENTENCE STRATEGIES

Writers of essays arguing for causes or effects sometimes rely on certain sentence strategies to present cause-effect relationships:

▶ When _____ happens, _____ is the result.

▶ If X does/says/acts like _____, then Y will do/say/act like _____.

EXAMPLE   When we exhibit these emotions, society showers us with positive reinforcement; we learn this even before we get out of diapers. When, as children, we hug our rotten little puke of a sister and give her a kiss, all the aunts and uncles smile and twit and cry, "Isn't he the sweetest little thing?" Such coveted treats as chocolate-covered graham crackers often follow. But if we deliberately slam the rotten little puke of a sister's fingers in the door, sanctions follow —angry remonstrance from parents, aunts, and uncles; instead of a chocolate-covered graham cracker, a spanking. (par. 9)

Both of these sentence strategies establish a chronological relationship—one thing happens and then another thing happens. They also establish a cause-effect relationship. (Chronology and causality, of course, do not always go together. See p. 389.)

ANALYZE & WRITE

Write a paragraph or two analyzing and evaluating how King uses these patterns elsewhere in this reading selection:

1 Skim the essay to find and mark the sentences that use these strategies. How do you know whether they each present a cause-effect relationship as well as a chronological sequence?

2 Why do you think King repeats these sentence strategies so often in this essay? Is this repetition an effective or ineffective strategy?

Consider possible topics: Popular culture.

RESPOND

Following King, you could consider writing about some aspect of popular culture. Consider, for example, why particular social networking sites, apps or video games, or genres of fiction or film are so popular with college students or other demographic groups. Why do ads appealing to sex work so well to sell cars and other consumer products? Why are negative political ads so effective?

Claudia Wallis | *The Multitasking Generation*

Courtesy Claudia Wallis

CLAUDIA WALLIS has been an associate dean for strategic communication at the Mailman School of Public Health at Columbia University and a writer and editor for *Time* magazine. She is currently a freelance writer, journalist, editor, and communications strategist specializing in medicine, education, family, and social issues. She has won citations from the Newspaper Guild of New York, the National Mental Health Association, and the Susan G. Komen Breast Cancer Foundation, among other organizations. Her most recent work is on autism.

"The Multitasking Generation" was published in 2006, so some of the references may seem dated. (For example, texting has moved from Instant Messenger to our mobile phones.) Nevertheless, the effects Wallis describes are still relevant.

As you read, consider the following:

• Do you generally multitask or "uni-task" (focus on one thing at a time)?

• When and where do you use technology? Can you easily resist the temptation to multitask in situations where multitasking is inappropriate (for example, texting while driving or surfing the Web in class)?

1   It's 9:30 p.m., and Stephen and Georgina Cox know exactly where their children are. Well, their bodies, at least. Piers, 14, is holed up in his bedroom—eyes fixed on his computer screen—where he has been logged onto a MySpace chat room and AOL Instant Messenger (IM) for the past three hours. His twin sister Bronte is planted in the living room, having commandeered her dad's iMac—as usual. She, too, is busily IMing, while chatting on her cell phone and chipping away at homework.

2   By all standard space-time calculations, the four members of the family occupy the same three-bedroom home in Van Nuys, Calif., but psychologically each exists in his or her own little universe. Georgina, 51, who works for a display-cabinet maker, is tidying up the living room as Bronte works, not that her daughter notices. Stephen, 49, who juggles jobs as a squash coach, fitness trainer, event planner and head of a cancer charity he founded, has wolfed down his dinner alone in the kitchen, having missed supper with the kids. He, too, typically spends the evening on his cell phone and returning e-mails—when he can nudge Bronte off the computer. "One gets obsessed with one's gadgets," he concedes.

3   Zooming in on Piers' screen gives a pretty good indication of what's on his hyperkinetic mind. O.K., there's a Google Images window open, where he's chasing down pictures of Keira Knightley. Good ones get added to a snazzy Windows Media Player slide show that serves as his personal e-shrine to the actress. Several IM windows are also open, revealing such penetrating conversations as this one with a MySpace pal:

MySpacer: suuuuuup!!! (Translation: What's up?)
Piers: wat up dude
MySpacer: nmu (Not much. You?)
Piers: same

4   Naturally, iTunes is open, and Piers is blasting a mix of Queen, AC/DC, classic rock and hip-hop. Somewhere on the screen there's a Word file, in which Piers is writing an essay for English class. "I usually finish my homework at school," he explains to a visitor, "but if not, I pop a book open on my lap in my room, and while the computer is loading, I'll do a problem or write a sentence. Then, while mail is loading, I do more. I get it done a little bit at a time."

5   Bronte has the same strategy. "You just multitask," she explains. "My parents always tell me I can't do homework while listening to music, but they don't understand that it helps me concentrate." The twins also multitask when hanging with friends, which has its own etiquette. "When I talk to my best friend Eloy," says Piers, "he'll have one earpiece [of his iPod] in and one out." Says Bronte: "If a friend thinks she's not getting my full attention, I just make it very clear that she is, even though I'm also listening to music."

6   The Coxes are one of 32 families in the Los Angeles area participating in an intensive, four-year study of modern family life, led by anthropologist Elinor Ochs, director of UCLA's Center on Everyday Lives of Families. While the impact of multitasking gadgets was not her original focus, Ochs found it to be one of the most dramatic areas of change since she conducted a similar study 20 years ago. "I'm not certain how the children can monitor all those things at the same time, but I think it is pretty consequential for the structure of the family relationship," says Ochs, whose work on language, interaction and culture earned her a MacArthur "genius" grant.

7   One of the things Ochs' team of observers looks at is what happens at the end of the workday when parents and kids reunite—and what doesn't happen, as in the case of the Coxes. "We saw that when the working parent comes through the door, the other spouse and the kids are so absorbed by what they're doing that they don't give the arriving parent the time of day," says Ochs. The returning parent, generally the father, was greeted only about a third of the time, usually with a perfunctory "Hi." "About half the time the kids ignored him or didn't stop what they were doing, multitasking and monitoring their various electronic gadgets," she says. "We also saw how difficult it was for parents to penetrate the child's universe. We have so many videotapes of parents actually backing away, retreating from kids who are absorbed by whatever they're doing."

8   Human beings have always had a capacity to attend to several things at once. Mothers have done it since the hunter-gatherer era—picking berries while suckling an infant, stirring the pot with one eye on the toddler. Nor is electronic multitasking entirely new: we've been driving while listening to car radios since they became popular in the 1930s. But there is no doubt that the phenomenon has reached a kind of warp speed in the era of Web-enabled computers, when it has become routine to conduct six IM conversations, watch *American*

Idol on TV and Google the names of last season's finalists all at once.

9   That level of multiprocessing and interpersonal connectivity is now so commonplace that it's easy to forget how quickly it came about. Fifteen years ago, most home computers weren't even linked to the Internet. In 1990 the majority of adolescents responding to a survey done by Donald Roberts, a professor of communication at Stanford, said the one medium they couldn't live without was a radio/CD player. How quaint. In a 2004 follow-up, the computer won hands down.

10   Today 82% of kids are online by the seventh grade, according to the Pew Internet and American Life Project. And what they love about the computer, of course, is that it offers the radio/CD thing and so much more—games, movies, e-mail, IM, Google, MySpace. The big finding of a 2005 survey of Americans ages 8 to 18 by the Kaiser Family Foundation, co-authored by Roberts, is not that kids were spending a larger chunk of time using electronic media—that was holding steady at 6.5 hours a day (could it possibly get any bigger?)—but that they were packing more media exposure into that time: 8.5 hours' worth, thanks to "media multitasking"—listening to iTunes, watching a DVD and IMing friends all at the same time. Increasingly, the media-hungry members of Generation M, as Kaiser dubbed them, don't just sit down to watch a TV show with their friends or family. From a quarter to a third of them, according to the survey, say they simultaneously absorb some other medium "most of the time" while watching TV, listening to music, using the computer or even while reading.

11   Parents have watched this phenomenon unfold with a mixture of awe and concern. The Coxes, for instance, are bowled over by their children's technical prowess. Piers repairs the family computers and DVD player. Bronte uses digital technology to compose elaborate photo collages and create a documentary of her father's ongoing treatment for cancer. And, says Georgina, "they both make these fancy PowerPoint presentations about what they want for Christmas." But both parents worry about the ways that kids' compulsive screen time is affecting their schoolwork and squeezing out family life. "We rarely have dinner together anymore," frets Stephen. "Everyone is in their own little world, and we don't get out together to have a social life."

12   Every generation of adults sees new technology—and the social changes it stirs—as a threat to the rightful order of things: Plato warned (correctly) that reading would be the downfall of oral tradition and memory. And every generation of teenagers embraces the freedoms and possibilities wrought by technology in ways that shock the elders: just think about what the automobile did for dating.

13   As for multitasking devices, social scientists and educators are just beginning to assess their impact, but the researchers already have some strong opinions. The mental habit of dividing one's attention into many small slices has significant implications for the way young people learn, reason, socialize, do creative work and understand the world. Although such habits may prepare kids for today's frenzied workplace, many cognitive scientists are positively alarmed by the trend. "Kids that are instant messaging while doing homework, playing games online and watching TV, I predict, aren't going to do well in the long run," says Jordan Grafman, chief of the cognitive neuroscience section at the National Institute of Neurological Disorders and Stroke (NINDS). Decades of research (not to mention common sense) indicate that the quality of one's output and depth of thought deteriorate as one attends to ever more tasks. Some are concerned about the disappearance of mental downtime to relax and reflect. Roberts notes Stanford students "can't go the few minutes between their 10 o'clock and 11 o'clock classes without talking on their cell phones. It seems to me that there's almost a discomfort with not being stimulated—a kind of 'I can't stand the silence.'"

14   Gen M's multitasking habits have social and psychological implications as well. If you're IMing four friends while watching *That '70s Show*, it's not the same as sitting on the couch with your buddies or your sisters and watching the show together. Or sharing a family meal across a table. Thousands of years of evolution created human physical communication—facial expressions, body language—that puts broadband to shame in its ability to convey meaning and create bonds. What happens, wonders UCLA's Ochs, as we replace side-by-side and

> *Every generation of adults sees new technology — and the social changes it stirs — as a threat to the rightful order of things . . .*

eye-to-eye human connections with quick, disembodied e-exchanges? Those are critical issues not just for social scientists but for parents and teachers trying to understand—and do right by—Generation M.

Your Brain When It Multitasks

15 Although many aspects of the networked life remain scientifically uncharted, there's substantial literature on how the brain handles multitasking. And basically, it doesn't. It may seem that a teenage girl is writing an instant message, burning a CD and telling her mother that she's doing homework—all at the same time— but what's really going on is a rapid toggling among tasks rather than simultaneous processing. "You're doing more than one thing, but you're ordering them and deciding which one to do at any one time," explains neuroscientist Grafman.

16 Then why can we so easily walk down the street while engrossed in a deep conversation? Why can we chop onions while watching *Jeopardy*? "We, along with quite a few others, have been focused on exactly this question," says Hal Pashler, psychology professor at the University of California at San Diego. It turns out that very automatic actions or what researchers call "highly practiced skills," like walking or chopping an onion, can be easily done while thinking about other things, although the decision to add an extra onion to a recipe or change the direction in which you're walking is another matter. "It seems that action planning—figuring out what I want to say in response to a person's question or which way I want to steer the car—is usually, perhaps invariably, performed sequentially" or one task at a time, says Pashler. On the other hand, producing the actions you've decided on—moving your hand on the steering wheel, speaking the words you've formulated—can be performed "in parallel with planning some other action." Similarly, many aspects of perception—looking, listening, touching—can be performed in parallel with action planning and with movement.

17 The switching of attention from one task to another, the toggling action, occurs in a region right behind the forehead called Brodmann's Area 10 in the brain's anterior prefrontal cortex, according to a functional magnetic resonance imaging (fMRI) study by Grafman's team. Brodmann's Area 10 is part of the frontal lobes, which "are important for maintaining long-term goals and achieving them," Grafman explains. "The most anterior part allows you to leave something when it's incomplete and return to the same place and continue from there." This gives us a "form of multitasking," he says, though it's actually sequential processing. Because the prefrontal cortex is one of the last regions of the brain to mature and one of the first to decline with aging, young children do not multitask well, and neither do most adults over 60. New fMRI studies at Toronto's Rotman Research Institute suggest that as we get older, we have more trouble "turning down background thoughts when turning to a new task," says Rotman senior scientist and assistant director Cheryl Grady. "Younger adults are better at tuning out stuff when they want to," says Grady. "I'm in my 50s, and I know that I can't work and listen to music with lyrics; it was easier when I was younger."

18 But the ability to multiprocess has its limits, even among young adults. When people try to perform two or more related tasks either at the same time or alternating rapidly between them, errors go way up, and it takes far longer—often double the time or more—to get the jobs done than if they were done sequentially, says David E. Meyer, director of the Brain, Cognition and Action Laboratory at the University of Michigan: "The toll in terms of slowdown is extremely large—amazingly so." Meyer frequently tests Gen M students in his lab, and he sees no exception for them, despite their "mystique" as master multitaskers. "The bottom line is that you can't simultaneously be thinking about your tax return and reading an essay, just as you can't talk to yourself about two things at once," he says. "If a teenager is trying to have a conversation on an e-mail chat line while doing algebra, she'll suffer a decrease in efficiency, compared to if she just thought about algebra until she was done. People may think otherwise, but it's a myth. With such complicated tasks [you] will never, ever be able to overcome the inherent limitations in the brain for processing information during multitasking. It just can't be, any more than the best of all humans will ever be able to run a one-minute mile."

The bottom line is that you can't simultaneously be thinking about your tax return and reading an essay . . .

19   Other research shows the relationship between stimulation and performance forms a bell curve: a little stimulation—whether it's coffee or a blaring soundtrack—can boost performance, but too much is stressful and causes a fall-off. In addition, the brain needs rest and recovery time to consolidate thoughts and memories. Teenagers who fill every quiet moment with a phone call or some kind of e-stimulation may not be getting that needed reprieve. Habitual multitasking may condition their brain to an overexcited state, making it difficult to focus even when they want to. "People lose the skill and the will to maintain concentration, and they get mental antsyness," says Meyer.

Is This Any Way To Learn?

20   Longtime professors at universities around the U.S. have noticed that Gen M kids arrive on campus with a different set of cognitive skills and habits than past generations. In lecture halls with wireless Internet access—now more than 40% of college classrooms, according to the Campus Computing Project—the compulsion to multitask can get out of hand. "People are going to lectures by some of the greatest minds, and they are doing their mail," says Sherry Turkle, professor of the social studies of science and technology at M.I.T. In her class, says Turkle, "I tell them this is not a place for e-mail, it's not a place to do online searches and not a place to set up IRC [Internet relay chat] channels in which to comment on the class. It's not going to help if there are parallel discussions about how boring it is. You've got to get people to participate in the world as it is."

21   Such concerns have, in fact, led a number of schools, including the M.B.A. programs at UCLA and the University of Virginia, to look into blocking Internet access during lectures. "I tell my students not to treat me like TV," says University of Wisconsin professor Aaron Brower, who has been teaching social work for 20 years. "They have to think of me like a real person talking. I want to have them thinking about things we're talking about."

22   On the positive side, Gen M students tend to be extraordinarily good at finding and manipulating information. And presumably because modern childhood tilts toward visual rather than print media, they are especially skilled at analyzing visual data and images, ob-

serves Claudia Koonz, professor of history at Duke University. A growing number of college professors are using film, audio clips and PowerPoint presentations to play to their students' strengths and capture their evanescent attention. It's a powerful way to teach history, says Koonz. "I love bringing media into the classroom, to be able to go to the website for Edward R. Murrow and hear his voice as he walked with the liberators of Buchenwald." Another adjustment to teaching Generation M: professors are assigning fewer full-length books and more excerpts and articles. (Koonz, however, was stunned when a student matter-of-factly informed her, "We don't read whole books anymore," after Koonz had assigned a 350-page volume. "And this is Duke!" she says.)

23   Many students make brilliant use of media in their work, embedding audio files and video clips in their presentations, but the habit of grazing among many data streams leaves telltale signs in their writing, according to some educators. "The breadth of their knowledge and their ability to find answers has just burgeoned," says Roberts of his students at Stanford, "but my impression is that their ability to write clear, focused and extended narratives has eroded somewhat." Says Koonz: "What I find is paragraphs that make sense internally, but don't necessarily follow a line of argument."

24   Koonz and Turkle believe that today's students are less tolerant of ambiguity than the students they taught in the past. "They demand clarity," says Koonz. They want identifiable good guys and bad guys, which she finds problematic in teaching complex topics like Hutu-Tutsi history in Rwanda. She also thinks there are political implications: "Their belief in the simple answer, put together in a visual way, is, I think, dangerous." Koonz thinks this aversion to complexity is directly related to multitasking: "It's as if they have too many windows open on their hard drive. In order to have a taste for sifting through different layers of truth, you have to stay with a topic and pursue it deeply, rather than go across the surface with your toolbar." She tries to encourage her students to find a quiet spot on campus to just think, cell phone off, laptop packed away.

Got 2 Go. Txt Me L8er

25 But turning down the noise isn't easy. By the time many kids get to college, their devices have become extensions

of themselves, indispensable social accessories. "The minute the bell rings at most big public high schools, the first thing most kids do is reach into their bag and pick up their cell phone," observes Denise Clark Pope, lecturer at the Stanford School of Education, "never mind that the person [they're contacting] could be right down the hall."

26   Parents are mystified by this obsession with e-communication—particularly among younger adolescents who often can't wait to share the most mundane details of life. Dominique Jones, 12, of Los Angeles, likes to IM her friends before school to find out what they plan to wear. "You'll get IMs back that say things like 'Oh, my God, I'm wearing the same shoes!' After school we talk about what happened that day, what outfits we want to wear the next day."

> *By the time many kids get to college, their devices have become extensions of themselves, indispensable social accessories.*

27   Turkle, author of the recently reissued *The Second Self: Computers and the Human Spirit*, has an explanation for this breathless exchange of inanities. "There's an extraordinary fit between the medium and the moment, a heady, giddy fit in terms of social needs." The online environment, she points out, "is less risky if you are lonely and afraid of intimacy, which is almost a definition of adolescence. Things get too hot, you log off, while in real time and space, you have consequences." Teen venues like MySpace, Xanga and Facebook—and the ways kids can personalize their IM personas—meet another teen need: the desire to experiment with identity. By changing their picture, their "away" message, their icon or list of favorite bands, kids can cycle through different personalities. "Online life is like an identity workshop," says Turkle, "and that's the job of adolescents—to experiment with identity."

28   All that is probably healthy, provided that parents set limits on where their kids can venture online, teach them to exercise caution and regulate how much time they can spend with electronics in general. The problem is that most parents don't. According to the Kaiser survey, only 23% of seventh- to 12th-graders say their family has rules about computer activity; just 17% say they have restrictions on video-game time.

29   In the absence of rules, it's all too easy for kids to wander into unwholesome neighborhoods on the Net and get caught up in the compulsive behavior that psychiatrist Edward Hallowell dubs "screen-sucking" in his new book, *CrazyBusy*. Patricia Wallace, a techno-psychologist who directs the Johns Hopkins Center for Talented Youth program, believes part of the allure of e-mail—for adults as well as teens—is similar to that of a slot machine. "You have intermittent, variable reinforcement," she explains. "You are not sure you are going to get a reward every time or how often you will, so you keep pulling that handle. Why else do people get up in the middle of the night to check their e-mail?"

Getting Them To Log Off

30   Many educators and psychologists say parents need to actively ensure that their teenagers break free of compulsive engagement with screens and spend time in the physical company of human beings—a growing challenge not just because technology offers such a handy alternative but because so many kids lead highly scheduled lives that leave little time for old-fashioned socializing and family meals. Indeed, many teenagers and college students say overcommitted schedules drive much of their multitasking.

31   Just as important is for parents and educators to teach kids, preferably by example, that it's valuable, even essential, to occasionally slow down, unplug and take time to think about something for a while. David Levy, a professor at the University of Washington Information School, has found, to his surprise, that his most technophilic undergraduates—those majoring in "informatics"—are genuinely concerned about getting lost in the multitasking blur. In an informal poll of 60 students last semester, he says, the majority expressed concerns about how plugged-in they were and "the way it takes them away from other activities, including exercise, meals and sleep." Levy's students talked about difficulties concentrating and their efforts to break away, get into the outdoors and inside their head. "Although it wasn't a scientific survey," he says, "it was the first evidence I had

that people in this age group are reflecting on these questions."

32   For all the handwringing about Generation M, technology is not really the problem. "The problem," says Hallowell, "is what you are not doing if the electronic moment grows too large"—too large for the teenager and too large for those parents who are equally tethered to their gadgets. In that case, says Hallowell, "you are not having family dinner, you are not having conversations, you are not debating whether to go out with a boy who wants to have sex on the first date, you are not going on a family ski trip or taking time just to veg. It's not so much that the video game is going to rot your brain, it's what you are not doing that's going to rot your life."

33   Generation M has a lot to teach parents and teachers about what new technology can do. But it's up to grownups to show them what it can't do, and that there's life beyond the screen.

Make connections: Multitasking's effect on your daily life. ⌈REFLECT⌉

Wallis quotes experts to show that multitasking can have a number of negative effects, such as making one "less tolerant of ambiguity" and the ability to sustain attention. Think about whether your experience with multitasking confirms or contradicts these experts. Your instructor may ask you to post your thoughts on a class discussion board or to discuss them with other students in class. Use these questions to get started:

- What do you see as the advantages and disadvantages of multitasking? Have you experienced any of the negative effects Wallis writes about?

- Do you think multitasking is more appropriate when engaged in certain kinds of tasks? If so, what criteria would you consider appropriate for multitasking?

- Under what circumstances, if any, do you practice "uni-tasking"? Why might certain kinds of tasks or situations be better for uni-tasking than for multitasking?

Use the basic features. ⌈ANALYZE⌉

A WELL-PRESENTED SUBJECT: USING EXAMPLES TO REFRAME THE SUBJECT

Because she is criticizing something she knows most of her readers accept as natural or at least unavoidable, Wallis needs to reframe her subject. That is, she needs to reintroduce the phenomenon in a way that leads readers to see that multitasking has serious disadvantages. To do this, she starts the essay with an extended example of the Cox family—Georgina, Stephen, and their twins, Piers and Bronte—describing a typical evening for the four members of the family.

ANALYZE & WRITE

Write a paragraph analyzing how Wallis uses examples to reframe her subject:

1 Reread paragraphs 1–5. As you read, list the forms of multitasking each family member engages in.

2 Now skim paragraphs 6–14. How does Wallis move from the multitasking habits of the Cox family in particular to those of families in general? How does she shape the conversation as one about how members of what she calls "Generation M" multitask?

A WELL-SUPPORTED CAUSAL ANALYSIS: USING A VARIETY OF SOURCES

Causal arguments require writers to provide evidence in favor of the preferred cause. Pangelinan, for example, cites the research of a psychologist as well as the "expert testimony" of a number of social media celebrities to make his case.

ANALYZE & WRITE

Write a paragraph or two analyzing and evaluating Wallis's use of evidence to support her claims about the effects of multitasking on "Gen M":

1 Skim the selection, identifying the types of evidence Wallis relies on (for example, anecdotes, facts and statistics, expert testimony, and results from research studies). How convincing do you find the evidence she provides? What other evidence could she provide to convince you that multitasking is bad for Gen M?

2 Wallis seems to limit her findings to Gen M. Do you think her research could be extended to other generations, such as the parents of generation M? Why or why not?

AN EFFECTIVE RESPONSE: PRESENTING, CONCEDING, AND REFUTING OPPOSING VIEWS

Presenters of causal arguments often must respond to objections that their preferred cause is not sufficiently serious to warrant a change in attitude or behavior. Wallis, for example, concedes that "human beings have always had a capacity to attend to several things at once" (par. 8). She spends the rest of the essay explaining why multitasking in a digital environment is different, especially for members of Generation M.

ANALYZE & WRITE

Write a paragraph of two analyzing how Wallis responds to the objection that people have always multitasked:

1 Skim paragraphs 9–14. How does Wallis use changes in technology to respond to this objection?

2 Now reread the section "Your Brain When It Multitasks" (pars. 15–19). How does Wallis use evidence from cognitive neuroscience to support her claim that digital technology has changed the way people multitask?

3 In paragraph 12, Wallis responds to another objection, that "every generation of adults sees new technology . . . as a threat to the rightful order of things. . . ." Do you think Wallis successfully responds to this second objection? Why or why not?

A CLEAR, LOGICAL ORGANIZATION: USING HEADINGS AND OTHER STRATEGIES

Writers use headings to signal a change in topic. Since they allow readers to see at a glance how an argument is structured, headings are particularly helpful in long, complicated selections. Writers may also use other strategies to guide readers. For example, they may introduce a section with a topic sentence that identifies the focus of the section. They may also link the new topic to the previous topic by repeating key terms or synonyms or by using transitional words and phrases to clarify the relationship between sections (for example, by indicating that the upcoming section will refute a view presented previously or that it will extend the discussion in a slightly different direction).

ANALYZE & WRITE

Write a paragraph analyzing Wallis's use of headings and other strategies for cueing the reader:

1. Look at each heading. Consider both the way each heading is written and its placement in the essay. What purpose do the headings serve?

2. Now skim the paragraphs before and after each heading. What other cues does Wallis provide readers with to help them make the transition from section to section? Does the logical progression of her ideas make sense? Why or why not?

Consider possible topics: Self-destructive behavior.

[RESPOND]

Wallis is writing about the effects of multitasking with digital technology. You could consider writing about the causes of teen multitasking: If multitasking is so bad for teens, why do they find it so hard to resist? Similarly, you could consider the surprising or less well known reasons for other kinds of bad or self-destructive behavior. For example, what might motivate members of a fraternity to record offensive chants or songs and post them online when the repercussions for such behavior (such as having the chapter's license revoked) are so dire?

Shankar Vedantam | *The Telescope Effect*

© Julio Vitullo-Martin

SHANKAR VEDANTAM is a correspondent for National Public Radio reporting on the psychology of human behavior. He also writes a column called "The Hidden Brain" for *Slate,* and for ten years he was a reporter for the *Washington Post.* He has been honored with fellowships and awards by Harvard University, the World Health Organization, the Society of Professional Journalists, and the American Public Health Association. In addition to his many articles, Vedantam writes plays and fiction, including his short story collection, *The Ghosts of Kashmir* (2005). "The Telescope Effect" is excerpted from his book *The Hidden Brain: How Our Unconscious*

Minds Elect Presidents, Control Markets, Wage Wars, and Save Our Lives (2010). The photograph of the rescued dog, Hokget, which appears in the reading selection, is from the *Honolulu Star-Bulletin*. As you read, consider the following questions:

- How does Vedantam engage readers' interest in the opening paragraphs?
- How do you think including a photograph of the dog affects readers' perspectives?
- What do you think is the most thought-provoking question Vedantam raises in this selection?

1   The *Insiko 1907* was a tramp tanker that roamed the Pacific Ocean. Its twelve-man Taiwanese crew hunted the seas for fishing fleets in need of fuel; the *Insiko* had a cargo of tens of thousands of gallons of diesel. It was supposed to be an Indonesian ship, except that it was not registered in Indonesia because its owner, who lived in China, did not bother with taxes. In terms of international law, the *Insiko 1907* was stateless, a two-hundred-sixty-foot microscopic speck on the largest ocean on earth. On March 13, 2002, a fire broke out in the *Insiko*'s engine room. . . . The ship was about eight hundred miles south of Hawaii's Big Island, and adrift. Its crew could not call on anyone for help, and no one who could help knew of the *Insiko*'s existence, let alone its problems.[1]

2   Drawn by wind and currents, the *Insiko* eventually got within two hundred twenty miles of Hawaii, where it was spotted by a cruise ship called the *Norwegian Star* on April 2. The cruise ship diverted course, rescued the Taiwanese crew, and radioed the United States Coast Guard. But as the *Norwegian Star* pulled away from the *Insiko* and steamed toward Hawaii, a few passengers on the cruise ship heard the sound of barking. The captain's puppy had been left behind on the tanker.

3   It is not entirely clear why the cruise ship did not rescue the Jack Russell mixed terrier, or why the Taiwanese crew did not insist on it. . . . Whatever the reason, the burned-out tanker and its lonely inhabitant were abandoned on the terrible immensity of the Pacific. The *Norwegian Star* made a stop at Maui. A passenger who heard the barking dog called the Hawaiian Humane Society in Honolulu. . . . The Humane Society alerted fishing boats about the lost tanker. Media reports began appearing about the terrier, whose name was Hokget.

4   Something about a lost puppy on an abandoned ship on the Pacific gripped people's imaginations. Money poured into the Humane Society to fund a rescue. One

check was for five thousand dollars. . . . "It was just about a dog," [Hawaiian Humane Society president Pamela] Burns told me. . . . "This was an opportunity for people to feel good about rescuing a dog. People poured out their support. A handful of people were incensed. These people said, 'You should be giving money to the homeless.'" But Burns felt the great thing about America was that people were free to give money to whatever cause they cared about, and people cared about Hokget. . . .

5   On April 26, nearly one and a half months after the puppy's ordeal began, the *American Quest* found the *Insiko* and boarded the tanker. The forty-pound female pup was still alive, and hiding in a pile of tires. It was a hot day, so Brian Murray, the *American Quest*'s salvage supervisor, went in and simply grabbed the terrier by the scruff of her neck. The puppy was terrified and shook for two hours. Her rescuers fed her, bathed her, and applied lotion to her nose, which was sunburned.

6   The story of Hokget's rescue is comical, but it is also touching. Human beings from around the world came together to save a dog. The vast majority of people who sent money to the Humane Society knew they would never personally see Hokget, never have their hands licked in gratitude. Saving the dog, as Pamela Burns suggested to me, was an act of pure altruism, and a marker of the remarkable capacity human beings have to empathize with the plight of others.

7   There are a series of disturbing questions, however. Eight years before Hokget was rescued, the same world that showed extraordinary compassion in the rescue of a dog sat on its hands as a million human beings were killed in Rwanda. . . . The twentieth century reveals a shockingly long list of similar horrors that have been ignored by the world as they unfolded. . . . Why have successive generations of Americans—a people with extraordinary powers of compassion—done so little to halt suffering on such a large scale? . . .

Vedantam *The Telescope Effect*

GUIDE TO READING
GUIDE TO WRITING
A WRITER AT WORK
THINKING CRITICALLY

411

Hokget, the rescued dog, with Dr. Becky Rhoades, the veterinarian with the Kauai (Hawaii) Humane Society who examined her

© Craig T. Kojima, Honolulu Star-Advertiser

8   There are many explanations for the discrepancy between our response to Hokget and our response to genocide. Some argue that Americans care little about foreign lives—but then what should we make about their willingness to spend thousands of dollars to rescue a dog, a foreign dog on a stateless ship in international waters? Well, perhaps Americans care more about pets than people? But that does not stand up to scrutiny, either. Hokget's rescue was remarkable, but there are countless stories about similar acts of compassion and generosity that people show toward their fellow human beings every day. No, there is something about genocide, about mass death in particular, that seems to trigger inaction.

9   I believe our inability to wrap our minds around large numbers is responsible for our apathy toward mass suffering. We are unconsciously biased in our moral judgment, in much the same way we are biased when we think about risk. Just as we are blasé about heart disease and lackadaisical about suicide, but terrified about psychopaths and terrorists, so also we make systematic errors in thinking about moral questions—especially those involving large numbers of people.

10   The philosopher Peter Singer once devised a dilemma that highlights a central contradiction in our moral reasoning. If you see a child drowning in a pond, and you know you can save the child without any risk to your own life—but you would ruin a fine pair of shoes worth two hundred dollars if you jumped into the water—would you save the child or save your shoes?[2] Most people react incredulously to the question; obviously, a child's life is worth more than a pair of shoes. If this is the case, Singer asked, why do large numbers of people hesitate to write a check for two hundred dollars to a reputable charity that could save the life of a child halfway around the world—when there are millions of such children who need our help? Even when people are absolutely certain their money will not be wasted and will be used to save a child's life, fewer people are willing to write the check than to leap into the pond.

11   Our moral responsibilities feel different in these situations even though Singer is absolutely right in arguing they are equivalent challenges; one feels immediate and visceral, the other distant and abstract. We feel personally responsible for one child, whereas the other is one of millions who need help. Our responsibility feels diffused when it comes to children in distant places—there are many people who could write that check. But distance and diffusion of responsibility do not explain why we step forward in some cases—why did so many people come forward to save Hokget? Why did they write checks for a dog they would never meet? Why did they feel a single abandoned dog on a stateless ship was *their* problem?

12   I want to offer a disturbing idea. The reason human beings seem to care so little about mass suffering and death is precisely *because* the suffering is happening on a mass scale. The brain is simply not very good at grasping the implications of mass suffering. Americans would be far more likely to step forward if only a few

people were suffering, or a single person were in pain. Hokget did not draw our sympathies because we care more about dogs than people; she drew our sympathies because she was a *single* dog lost on the biggest ocean in the world. If the hidden brain biases our perceptions about risk toward exotic threats, it shapes our compassion into a telescope. We are best able to respond when we are focused on a single victim. We don't feel twenty times sadder when we hear that twenty people have died in a disaster than when we hear that one person has died, even though the magnitude of the tragedy *is* twenty times larger. . . . We can certainly reach such a conclusion abstractly, in our conscious minds, but we cannot *feel it viscerally,* because that is the domain of the hidden brain, and the hidden brain is simply not calibrated to deal with the difference between a single death and a million deaths.

13   But the paradox does not end there. Even if ten deaths do not make us feel ten times as sad as a single death, shouldn't we feel five times as sad, or even at least twice as sad? There is disturbing evidence that shows that in many situations, not only do we not care twice as much about ten deaths as we do about one, but we may actually care *less.* I strongly suspect that if the *Insiko* had been carrying a hundred dogs, many people would have cared less about their fate than they did about Hokget. A hundred dogs do not have a single face, a single name, a single life story around which we can wrap our imaginations—and our compassion. . . .

14   The evidence for what I am going to call the telescope effect comes from a series of fascinating experiments.[3] At the University of Oregon, the psychologist Paul Slovic asked . . . groups of volunteers to imagine they were running a philanthropic foundation. Would they rather spend ten million dollars to save 10,000 lives from a disease that caused 15,000 deaths a year, or save 20,000 lives from a disease that killed 290,000 people a year? Overwhelmingly, volunteers preferred to spend money saving the ten thousand lives rather than the twenty thousand lives. Rather than tailor their investments to saving the largest number of lives, people sought to save the largest *proportion* of lives among the different groups of victims. An investment directed

We respond to mass suffering in much the same way we respond to most things in our lives. We fall back on rules of thumb, on feelings, on intuitions.

toward disease A could save two-thirds of the victims, whereas an investment directed at disease B could save "only" seven percent of the victims.

15   We respond to mass suffering in much the same way we respond to most things in our lives. We fall back on rules of thumb, on feelings, on intuitions. People who choose to spend money saving ten thousand lives rather than twenty thousand lives are not bad people. Rather, like those who spend thousands of dollars rescuing a single dog rather than directing the same amount of money to save a dozen dogs, they are merely allowing their hidden brain to guide them.

16   I have often wondered why the hidden brain displays a telescope effect when it comes to compassion. Evolutionary psychology tends to be an armchair sport, so please take my explanation for the paradox as one of several possible answers. The telescope effect may have arisen because evolution has built a powerful bias into us to preferentially love our kith and kin. It is absurd that we spend two hundred dollars on a birthday party for our son or our daughter when we could send the same money to a charity and save the life of a child halfway around the world. How can one child's birthday party mean more to us than another child's life? When we put it in those terms, we sound like terrible human beings. The paradox, as with the rescue of Hokget, is that our impulse springs from love, not callousness. Evolution has built a fierce loyalty toward our children into the deepest strands of our psyche. Without the unthinking telescope effect in the unconscious mind, parents would not devote the immense time and effort it takes to raise children; generations of our ancestors would not have braved danger and cold, predators and hunger, to protect their young. The fact that you and I exist testifies to the utility of having a telescope in the brain that caused our ancestors to care intensely about the good of the few rather than the good of the many.

17   This telescope is activated when we hear a single cry for help—the child drowning in the pond, the puppy abandoned on an ocean. When we think of human suffering on a mass scale, our telescope does not work, because it has not been designed to work in such situations.

18   What makes evolutionary sense rarely makes moral sense. (One paradox of evolution is that ruthless natural selection has produced a species that recoils at the ruthlessness of natural selection.) Humans are the first and only species that is even aware of large-scale suffering taking place in distant lands; the moral telescope in our brain has not had a chance to evolve and catch up with our technological advances. When we are told about a faraway genocide, we can apply only our conscious mind to the challenge. We can reason, but we cannot feel the visceral compassion that is automatically triggered by the child who is drowning right before us. Our conscious minds can tell us that it is absurd to spend a boatload of money to save one life when the same money could be used to save ten—just as it can tell us it is absurd to be more worried about homicide than suicide. But in moral decision-making, as in many other domains of life where we are unaware of how unconscious biases influence us, it is the hidden brain that usually carries the day.

Editor's Notes

1. Chris Lee and George Butler, "Complex Response to Tankship *Insiko 1907*," *Proceedings of the Marine Safety Council,* Vol. 60, No. 1 (January–March 2003), pp. 49–51.
2. Peter Singer has mentioned the story about the drowning child in a number of publications, including his 2009 book, *The Life You Can Save,* Random House, Inc.
3. Paul Slovic, "'If I Look at the Mass I Will Never Act': Psychic Numbing and Genocide," *Judgment and Decision Making,* Vol. 2, No. 2 (April 2007), pp. 79–95.

Make connections: Thinking about — and feeling — others' suffering.

[REFLECT]

Moral dilemma experiments—scenarios that challenge our ability to decide what is the right thing to do—can be useful in helping us analyze our moral intuitions. Consider one of the moral dilemmas that follow, and then think about how scenarios like these help you think through a moral decision:

- Vedantam's scenario: Would you have sent money to support the lost dog Hokget's rescue?

- Singer's dilemma: Would you be more likely to ruin expensive shoes to save a drowning child than to send the same amount of money to save an anonymous child halfway around the world?

- Slovic's dilemma: Would you rather spend $10 million to save 10,000 lives from a disease that caused 15,000 deaths a year or save 20,000 lives from a disease that killed 290,000 people a year?

- Sinking Lifeboat dilemma: Your cruise ship has sunk and you are in a dangerously overcrowded lifeboat. One person is gravely ill and not likely to survive the journey. Could you throw the sick person overboard in order to increase the chances of survival of the rest of the people in the lifeboat?

- Runaway Trolley dilemma: A runaway trolley is heading toward a group of people who can't be warned in time. Throwing a switch would shift the train from the track headed toward the group of people to another track on which one person is standing. Only you can divert the trolley by throwing the switch. What would you do?

Your instructor may ask you to post your thoughts on a class discussion board or to discuss them with other students in class. Use these questions to get started:

- What would you do if you were in the situation described in the dilemma? Briefly explain your choice. If you and your classmates are considering the same dilemma, discuss your various responses to it.

- How did you decide what was the right thing to do? For example, how did your feeling of closeness or identification with the potential victims or beneficiaries of your action influence you? How did the magnitude or the consequences of your action or inaction affect your choice?

- What is the value of participating in a thought experiment like this?

[ANALYZE]   # Use the basic features.

A WELL-PRESENTED SUBJECT: USING AN ANECDOTE TO DRAMATIZE THE SUBJECT

In "The Telescope Effect," Vedantam begins his causal analysis with an *anecdote,* a story about an actual event. Vedantam could have summarized the anecdote about Hokget in a sentence or two:

> A dog was stranded on a ship adrift in the ocean, and after an outpouring of concern, the dog was ultimately rescued.

Instead, he gives readers a brief but dramatic *narrative* about how Hokget got stranded (in pars. 1–3) and rescued (par. 5).

| ANALYZE & WRITE |

Write a paragraph or two analyzing how Vedantam uses anecdote and examples to support his causal analysis:

1. Reread paragraphs 1–3 and 5, highlighting the details that help dramatize Hokget's story. What feelings do these narrative details evoke in you as a reader? Given his purpose, why do you think Vedantam would want to arouse readers' feelings at the beginning of his analysis?

2. Reread paragraph 7, contrasting the detail Vedantam provides in telling Hokget's story with the concise way in which he presents the example of the genocide in Rwanda. Why do you think Vedantam says so much about Hokget's story but so little about the Rwandan genocide?

A WELL-SUPPORTED CAUSAL ANALYSIS: USING A SOURCE

Although Vedantam is writing for a general audience, he follows the academic convention of explicitly acknowledging his sources. In fact, Vedantam states at the beginning of paragraph 14 that psychologist Paul Slovic's research provides the main "evidence" supporting his favored cause and cites Slovic's research in the notes.

| ANALYZE & WRITE |

Write a paragraph or two analyzing how Vedantam uses Slovic's research:

1. Reread paragraph 14. How does Vedantam use Slovic's research to support his causal analysis?

2. Reread paragraphs 12 and 15–18. What could Vedantam have added, if anything, to clarify the connection between Slovic's research and Vedantam's ideas about "the hidden brain" and "the telescope effect"?

AN EFFECTIVE RESPONSE: USING COUNTEREXAMPLES

A common strategy writers use to refute alternative causes or effects is to give counterexamples. A counterexample contradicts the causal explanation and shows that the analysis is flawed or at least incomplete. We can see this strategy at work in Vedantam's response to the cause proposed by Pamela Burns, the president of the Hawaiian Humane Society:

> Saving the dog, as Pamela Burns suggested to me, was an act of pure altruism, and a marker of the remarkable capacity human beings have to empathize with the plight of others.
>
>   There are a series of disturbing questions, <u>however</u>. Eight years before Hokget was rescued, the same world that showed extraordinary compassion in the rescue of a dog sat on its hands as a million human beings were killed in Rwanda. (pars. 6–7)

Paraphrase of Burns's cause

Transition cueing refutation

Counterexample

| ANALYZE & WRITE |

Write a paragraph or two analyzing and assessing how Vedantam refutes philosopher Peter Singer's causal analysis:

1. Reread paragraphs 10 and 11. What example and counterexample does Singer use? How does Vedantam explain what Singer's thought experiment demonstrates?

2. Now examine paragraph 11, noting where Vedantam appears to accept Singer's causal analysis and also where he cues readers that he is about to question it. How does Vedantam use the counterexample of Hokget to refute Singer's explanation?

3. How effective is Vedantam's response? Does Singer's thought experiment raise interesting moral issues outside the context of Hogket?

A CLEAR, LOGICAL ORGANIZATION: USING RHETORICAL QUESTIONS

Writers sometimes use **rhetorical questions**—questions posed to make a point rather than to elicit an answer—to guide readers through a causal argument. In this selection, Vedantam presents several important rhetorical questions, such as these:

Why have successive generations of Americans . . . done so little to halt suffering on such a large scale? (par. 7)

Why did so many people come forward to save Hokget? . . . Why did they feel a single abandoned dog on a stateless ship was *their* problem? (par. 11)

ANALYZE & WRITE

Write a paragraph or two analyzing how Vedantam uses rhetorical questions to help readers follow the logic of his causal argument:

1 Reread paragraphs 7–13, in which Vedantam poses rhetorical questions. What is the "discrepancy" (par. 8) or "paradox" (par. 13) that Vedantam is trying to explain? How do these rhetorical questions convey to readers this central problem?

2 Skim the rest of the selection, highlighting the other rhetorical questions Vedantam includes. Which are Vedantam's own questions, and which are questions paraphrased from sources? How do these additional rhetorical questions help guide readers' understanding of the subject?

[RESPOND] ## Consider possible topics: Current events.

Following Vedantam, you could consider the causes of a current event. For example, think about why people voted a certain way in a recent election, or why a particular news story or YouTube video went viral. Also think about the causes of something ongoing, such as why the risk of auto accidents is higher among teenage drivers than among older motorists, or why the rate of teen pregnancy is the lowest it has been in twenty years.

Causal arguments appear frequently in genres and media besides the printed college essay. The proposal genre, for example, may include a causal analysis as a first step in framing a plan to solve a problem. Interactive graphics may depict a causal analysis to show users what the effects might be if one or more causal factors were changed. After writing his essay, Clayton Pangelinan decided to use his causal analysis of what motivates users to engage with social media as a jumping-off point for a proposal for developing training to help high school students avoid inappropriate sharing that could harm them later. (The first page is included here.)

In the next section of this chapter, we ask you to craft your own causal argument. After composing it as an essay, consider remixing it by presenting it (or a portion of it) in another genre or medium, with another purpose, or for another audience.

CONSIDER YOUR RHETORICAL SITUATION

Purpose: The purpose of your causal argument is to persuade your audience to accept your preferred cause or effect as the most likely. If you remix your argument, *which genre or medium would best help you persuade your audience to accept your causal analysis?*

Audience: The audience for your causal argument was your instructor and other students in your class. *Who would be the audience if you were to remix your causal argument as another genre or in another medium?*

Genre and medium: The genre of your causal analysis was the essay; the medium was textual, delivered either in print or online. If you remix your ideas, *what genre and medium would best help you achieve your purpose and reach your intended audience?*

Project Proposal Submitted to the Principal, Mitchell High School
Project Title: Social Media Responsibility Assembly
Project Leader: Clayton Pangelinan
Start Date: Oct. 12, 2015   **Completion Date:** Oct. 29, 2015

Objectives
My research shows that the desire to connect with others or to receive attention from a large number of people fuels much of the appeal of social media such as Facebook, Instagram, Twitter, etc. Unfortunately, it can be easy to overshare personal information on these social networks. By presenting a school-wide Social Media Responsibility Assembly highlighting entertaining but informative examples of oversharing, students at Mitchell High School will become aware of the risks of oversharing and gain the knowledge necessary to make wise choices about their virtual content.

Action Plan and Calendar
Oct. 12-19: Research and plan assembly, create PowerPoint
Oct. 20: Rehearse assembly, distribute surveys to classroom instructors
Oct. 21: Hold assembly in school auditorium & distribute survey
Oct. 22-29: Analyze survey responses and present findings to school board

Budget Estimate
Labor costs (@$10/hr):	$250
Develop & photocopy survey: 4 hrs	
Plan assembly and draft PowerPoint presentation: 5 hrs	
Revise presentation in response to comments: 5 hrs	
Rehearse assembly and set up equipment: 2 hrs	
Collect surveys, tabulate responses, & write-up findings: 9 hrs	
Printing expenses:	$50
Total	$300

Evidence of Success
Before and after the assembly, students will fill out questionnaires gauging their knowledge of the scope of social networking and the limits of privacy settings. The project will have succeeded if students are more knowledgeable or say that they will now be more wary of what they choose to share on social media.

GUIDE TO WRITING

The Writing Assignment

Write an essay about an important or intriguing subject, and speculate about why it might have occurred or what its effects might be. Make sure that it is an appropriate subject for a speculative causal analysis and not simply a report of widely accepted causes or effects. Be sure to demonstrate that the subject exists and to argue for the plausibility of certain causes or effects, while anticipating your readers' likely objections to your argument as well as their preferred alternative.

This Guide to Writing is designed to help you compose your own causal analysis and apply what you have learned from reading other selections in the same genre. The Starting Points chart (below) will help you find answers to questions you might have about composing an essay arguing for causes or effects. Use the chart to find the guidance you need, when you need it.

STARTING POINTS: ARGUING FOR CAUSES OR EFFECTS

How do I come up with a subject to write about?

- Consider possible topics: Popular culture. (p. 401)
- Consider possible topics: Self-destructive behavior. (p. 409)
- Consider possible topics: Current events. (p. 416)
- Choose a subject to analyze. (pp. 420–21)
- Test Your Choice: Choosing a Topic (p. 421)

A Well-Presented Subject

How can I present my subject clearly and effectively?

- Determine the writer's purpose and audience. (p. 387)
- Assess the genre's basic features: A well-presented subject. (p. 388)
- A Well-Presented Subject: Reframing the Subject for Readers (p. 399)
- A Well-Presented Subject: Using Examples to Reframe the Subject (p. 407)
- A Well-Presented Subject: Using Anecdote to Dramatize the Subject (p. 414)
- Present the subject to your readers. (p. 422)
- A Troubleshooting Guide: A Well-Presented Subject (p. 433)

A Well-Supported Causal Analysis

How do I come up with a list of possible causes to explore?

- Analyze possible causes or effects. (p. 423)
- Conduct research. (p. 424)

The Writing Assignment

GUIDE TO READING
GUIDE TO WRITING
A WRITER AT WORK
THINKING CRITICALLY

419

A Well-Supported Causal Analysis

How can I convince my readers that the causes I identify are plausible?

- Assess the genre's basic features: A well-supported causal analysis. (pp. 388–89)
- A Well-Supported Causal Analysis: Using Examples and Comparisons (p. 399)
- A Well-Supported Causal Analysis: Using a Variety of Sources (p. 408)
- A Well-Supported Causal Analysis: Using a Source (pp. 414–15)
- Analyze possible causes or effects. (p. 423)
- Conduct research. (p. 424)
- Cite a variety of sources to support your causal analysis. (p. 425)
- Formulate a working thesis stating your preferred cause(s) or effect(s). (pp. 425–26)

An Effective Response to Objections and Alternative Causes or Effects

How do I deal with my readers' likely objections or alternative causes?

- Assess the genre's basic features: An effective response to objections and alternative causes or effects. (pp. 389–90)
- An Effective Response: Putting Aside Obvious Causes or Effects (p. 400)
- An Effective Response: Presenting, Conceding, and Refuting Opposing Views (p. 408)
- An Effective Response: Using Counterexamples (p. 415)
- Draft a response to objections readers are likely to raise. (pp. 426–27)
- Draft a response to the causes your readers are likely to favor. (427–28)
- A Troubleshooting Guide: An Effective Response (p. 433)

A Clear, Logical Organization

How can I help my readers follow my argument?

- Assess the genre's basic features: A clear, logical organization. (pp. 390–91)
- A Clear, Logical Organization: Using Cause-Effect Sentence Strategies (p. 400)
- A Clear, Logical Organization: Using Headings and Other Strategies (p. 409)
- A Clear, Logical Organization: Using Rhetorical Questions (pp. 415–16)
- Create an outline that will organize your causal analysis effectively for your readers. (p. 429)
- A Troubleshooting Guide: A Clear, Logical Organization (p. 434)

Writing a Draft: Invention, Research, Planning, and Composing

The activities in this section will help you choose and research a subject as well as develop and organize your causal analysis. Your writing in response to many of these activities can be used in a rough draft that you will be able to improve after receiving feedback from your classmates and instructor. Do the activities in any order that makes sense to you (and your instructor), and return to them as needed as you revise.

▪▪ Choose a subject to analyze.

When choosing a subject for a causal analysis, keep in mind that it must be

- one that you can show exists (such as with examples or statistics);
- one that has no definitive, proven causes or effects;
- one that you can research, as necessary, in the time you have;
- one that will puzzle—or at least interest—you and your readers.

You may already have a subject in mind and a clear idea of the causes or effects you want to discuss. If so, go to Test Your Choice (p. 421). If you do not, the subjects that follow, in addition to those following the readings (pp. 401, 409, and 416), may suggest a cause you can analyze effectively:

Subjects Related to School

- Why do some parents choose to homeschool their children, send their children to private instead of public schools, or oppose or advocate for publishing teacher evaluations? Or what are the results of such choices?
- What are the most or the least popular majors among undergraduates at your college? Why do you think these fields are so popular or unpopular?
- What were the underlying causes or effects of a recent surprising or controversial event at your college, such as the closing of the tutoring center or the firing of a coach or popular teacher?

Subjects Related to Your Community

- Why has hooking up replaced dating, or living together replaced getting married, for many young people? Or what are the results of such social changes?
- What are the causes or effects of more or less political activity nowadays—for example, voting; working for candidates; blogging; or joining Occupy, Tea Party, or other movements?
- Why are people embracing or abandoning social media, getting or removing tattoos or body piercings, or becoming vegetarians or giving up vegetarianism?

Subjects Related to Work

- Why is collaborating with others or being able to communicate clearly in writing especially valuable in the workplace today?

- Why is the attitude that one should "work to live" more prevalent among young people than the attitude that one should "live to work"? How might such a change affect society for good or ill?

- Why do employees choose to join or not join a union, or why have so many state legislatures passed so-called right-to-work laws? What surprising effects might these decisions have had?

Writers often find it helpful to consider several possibilities before choosing a subject. Making a chart listing subjects that interest you and their possible causes or effects can help you decide which subject is most promising.

Subject	Possible Causes
Example: What causes bullies?	Putting down others makes them feel powerful.
	They are mean.
	They are performing for their friends.
	They are sociopaths without empathy for others.
Example: Why do students often procrastinate in writing papers or studying for exams?	They have better things to do.
	They are lazy.
	They are actually using time efficiently.

TEST YOUR CHOICE

Choosing a Topic

After you have made a provisional choice, ask yourself the following questions:

- Do I know enough about the subject, or can I learn enough in the time I have?

- Do I know what causes or effects readers would be likely to think of, and do I have any ideas about what causes or effects might surprise and interest them?

To try out your subject and learn what other people think caused it, get together with two or three other students:

Presenters. Take turns describing your subject.

Listeners. Briefly tell each presenter what you think is a likely cause and why you think so.

Research Note

As you begin exploring the subject and its possible causes or effects, you may discover that you need to conduct research before you can go further. If so, skip ahead to the Conduct Research section (p. 424), and return to the activities here later on in the writing process. Alternatively, you may be able simply to make a *Research To Do* list for later.

⠿ Present the subject to your readers.

Once you have made a preliminary choice of a subject and have some idea about its possible causes or effects, consider how you can present the subject in a way that will interest your readers. To do this, consider what you think about the subject and what your readers are likely to think. Use the questions and sentence strategies that follow to help you put your ideas in writing.

WAYS IN →

WHAT DO I THINK?

Why do I find this subject intriguing?

▶ I think X is important because _____.

▶ X is changing the way we think/do _____.

▶ X has widespread effects, such as _____.

▶ I know what the obvious causes/effects of X are, but I'm curious about the underlying cultural/psychological/ideological causes/effects because _____.

Which possible causes/effects will surprise readers or help them think about the subject in a constructive new way?

▶ I think X will enable readers to understand that _____.

▶ Thinking about X will challenge readers to _____.

How do your subject and its causes/effects compare or contrast with other, more familiar subjects?

▶ X is like Y in that they are both caused by _____.

▶ Whereas Y is _____, X is _____.

WHAT DO MY READERS THINK?

What will readers know about the subject?

▶ My readers will probably be familiar with X because _____.

▶ X is likely to be new to my readers, so I will need to show that it is widespread and serious by providing evidence such as _____.

▶ My readers are likely to be curious about X because _____.

How might readers' age, gender, work, or cultural background affect their thinking?

▶ Readers who are/have trait A may assume that X is caused by individuals who should have _____.

▶ Readers who are/have trait B are likely to think the causes/effects are part of a larger system that involves _____.

▶ Readers who have experienced C may think of X in terms of _____.

What causes or effects are readers likely to know about?

▶ My readers will have heard of X from _____ [name source].

▶ Readers' experience of D will lead them to assume that X was caused by _____.

Writing a Draft

GUIDE TO READING
▶ GUIDE TO WRITING
A WRITER AT WORK
THINKING CRITICALLY

423

⸬ Analyze possible causes or effects.

The following activity will help you analyze an array of possible causes or effects and decide which ones you could use in your essay. Remember that causal analysis essays often speculate about several possible causes or effects but usually also argue for an especially interesting or plausible cause or effect.

HOW CAN I ANALYZE POSSIBLE CAUSES OR EFFECTS?

WAYS IN

1. List the possible causes or effects you've identified so far—ones that your readers are likely to think of, that your classmates suggested, that you found doing research, and that you thought of yourself.

2. Write a few sentences about each cause or effect, answering questions like these:

   ▶ Why do my readers think _____ could have caused X?

   ▶ Why do I think _____ could have caused X?

   ▶ Is _____ necessary to bring about X; that is, could X not happen without X? Is X sufficient — enough in itself — to cause _____?

   ▶ If X is one of several contributing factors, what role does it play? For example, is it a minor or a major cause, an obvious or a hidden cause, a triggering cause (the one that got the cause-effect process started) or a continuing cause (the one that keeps it going)?

   ▶ What kinds of evidence could I use to argue in favor of or against X? (If you don't already have supporting evidence, make a *Research To Do* note indicating what kind of evidence you need and where you might possibly find it.)

3. Classify the causes or effects you plan to discuss in your essay into three categories: plausible cause(s)/effect(s) you want to argue for, causes/effects your readers may favor that you can CONCEDE but put aside as obvious or minor, and causes/effects you should REFUTE because your readers are likely to think they are important.

Plausible cause(s)/ effect(s) to argue for	Readers' causes/effects to concede/put aside	Readers' causes/effects to refute

Turn to A Writer at Work on pp. 436–37 to see how Clayton Pangelinan used this activity to analyze his list of possible causes.

Remember that the only category you must include in your essay is the first: one or more causes or effects you will argue played a major, and perhaps surprising, role.

:: Conduct research.

If you are analyzing a cause that others have written about, try searching for articles or books on your topic. Enter keywords or phrases related to your cause/effect or subject into the search box of

To learn more about searching a database, consult Chapter 21, pp. 609–16.

- an all-purpose database, such as *Academic OneFile* (InfoTrac) or *Academic Search Complete* (EBSCOHost), to find relevant articles in magazines and journals;
- a database like *Lexis/Nexis* to find articles in newspapers;
- a search engine like *Google* to find relevant Web sites, blogs, podcasts, and discussion lists;
- your library's catalog, to find books and other resources on your topic.

To locate numerical or statistical evidence that you could use or to draw graphs or tables, try the following sites:

- USA.gov, the U.S. government's official Web portal, to find information about the federal government
- Library of Congress page on State Government Information, loc.gov/rr/news/stategov /stategov.html; follow the links for information on state and local government
- U.S. Census Bureau, census.gov, especially the Quick Facts and Fact Finder pages, and the Statistical Abstracts for various years (to compare years), for demographic information
- The Centers for Disease Control and Prevention, cdc.gov, especially the FastStats pages, for statistics about diseases and illnesses

To learn more about finding government documents, consult Chapter 21, pp. 613–14.

- National Center for Education Statistics, nces.ed.gov, for reports, such as *America's Youth: Transitions to Adulthood*
- Pew Research Center, pewresearch.org, for research data and public opinion polling data
- Gallup, gallup.com, or Rasmussen Reports, rasmussenreports.com, for public opinion polling data

Bookmark or keep a record of the URLs of promising sites. If you find useful information, you may want to download or copy it to use in your essay. When they are available, download PDF files rather than HTML files, because the PDFs are more likely to include visuals, such as graphs and charts. If you copy and paste relevant information from sources into your notes, be careful to distinguish all source material from your own ideas and to record source information, so you can cite and document any sources you use, including graphics.

Another option is to conduct field research and to use personal experience. Field research, such as interviews, surveys, and direct observation, can offer statistical data and information about public opinion. Your own experience may also provide anecdotal evidence that might interest readers.

Writing a Draft

GUIDE TO READING
► **GUIDE TO WRITING**
A WRITER AT WORK
THINKING CRITICALLY

425

Cite a variety of sources to support your causal analysis.

Writers of causal analyses often rely on evidence from experts to support some causes or effects and refute others. For college assignments, the instructor may require that certain kinds of sources be used and may even specify a minimum number of sources. But for most writing situations, you have to decide whether your sources are appropriate and sufficient. Using too few sources or sources that are too narrow in scope can undercut the effectiveness of your analysis. Consequently, it can be important to offer information from a number of sources and from sources that reflect a variety of areas of expertise.

Look, for example, at the sources Wallis uses to support her causal analysis in "The Multitasking Generation" (pp. 401–407). Because her essay was originally published in a popular magazine, she does not include a works cited list or parenthetical citations, but she does identify each of her sources by giving their credentials and academic affiliations: professors from a range of distinguished universities (such as MIT, Duke, and the University of Michigan) and different disciplines (such as history, psychology, and neuroscience). She uses as support for her analysis the specific findings of a number of academic research projects. The number and variety of expert sources adds to the credibility of Wallis's analysis.

Similarly, student Clayton Pangelinan uses a number of sources to support his causal analysis in "#socialnetworking: Why It's *Really* So Popular" (pp. 391–95). Because he is writing for a class, Pangelinan includes both in-text citations and a list of works cited. Like Wallis, he uses *signal phrases* (the author's name and an appropriate verb, plus the author's background where context is needed). He also cites independent sources his readers are likely to find credible, such as the Pew Research Center and an academic article. The number of sources, their authority, and their variety lend credibility to Pangelinan's own speculations.

As you determine how many and what kinds of sources to cite in your essay, ask yourself questions like these:

- Are my sources **appropriate**—will my audience accept them as authoritative?
- Are my sources **sufficient**—do I have enough sources and do they reflect a variety of areas of expertise?
- Do I paraphrase or summarize my sources accurately, without borrowing too much of the source's language or sentence structures?
- Do I use signal phrases to provide the credentials of my sources?

Formulate a working thesis stating your preferred cause(s) or effect(s).

Once you have identified one or more interesting and plausible causes or effects that could be the focus of your analysis, try drafting a working thesis. (Some writers may want to skip this activity now and return to it after they have developed their analysis and completed some research.)

WAYS IN

> **HOW CAN I ASSERT MY THESIS?**
>
> To get an idea about how you might formulate your thesis, take a look at the thesis statements from the reading selections you've studied in this chapter.
>
> > The fact *that* social networking is popular is well established. The question is *why* is it so popular? . . . A better answer . . . is that social media offer people a way to satisfy their desire to connect with others and maybe also be "world-famous for fifteen minutes" (as Andy Warhol supposedly remarked). (Pangelinan, par. 2)
>
> > The mythic horror movie, like the sick joke, has a dirty job to do. It deliberately appeals to all that is worst in us. It is morbidity unchained, our most base instincts let free, our nastiest fantasies realized . . . and it all happens, fittingly enough, in the dark. (King, par. 11)
>
> > The mental habit of dividing one's attention into many small slices has significant implications for the way young people learn, reason, socialize, do creative work and understand the world. (Wallis, par. 13)
>
> > I want to offer a disturbing idea. The reason human beings seem to care so little about mass suffering and death is precisely *because* the suffering is happening on a mass scale. The brain is simply not very good at grasping the implications of mass suffering. (Vedantam, par. 12)
>
> Now draft your own thesis statement, using the examples from the readings or the sentence strategies that follow as a jumping-off point. You can put your ideas into your own words now or when you revise:
>
> ▶ The reasons for X may surprise you, such as _____, _____, and _____ .
>
> ▶ The effects of X may be alarming, but they are clear: _____ .
>
> ▶ X plays a disturbing role in our lives/our families/our communities/our workplaces: It does/is/provides _____ .
>
> ▶ For many years, Group A has believed that _____ . Now there is research supporting this claim, but not for the reasons you may think. It's not _____ that has been causing this phenomenon but _____ .

⁞⁞ Draft a response to objections readers are likely to raise.

The following activity will help you respond to possible objections your readers might raise. Start by analyzing the reasons your readers object to your cause or effect, and then consider ways you might respond to their objections.

Writing a Draft

GUIDE TO READING
GUIDE TO WRITING
A WRITER AT WORK
THINKING CRITICALLY

427

WAYS IN

HOW CAN I RESPOND EFFECTIVELY TO MY READERS' OBJECTIONS?

1. For each of your preferred causes or effects, consider the questions your readers might raise. Some possibilities include the following:

   ▶ Even if you can prove that X and Y increased/decreased at the same time, how do you know X actually caused Y?

   ▶ Even if you can prove that Y occurred after X, how do you know X actually caused Y?

   ▶ Could X and Y both have been caused by something else altogether?

   ▶ X seems to have been an effect of Y but was it really a major effect or just one of many insignificant results?

2. Use the following sentence strategies or language of your own to respond to one of these objections:

   ▶ The objection that Y may result from things other than X may be true. But there is strong evidence showing that X played a central role by _____.

   ▶ Researchers studying _____ have shown a causal connection between X and Y. They claim that _____ [quote/paraphrase/summarize information from source] (cite source).

   ▶ A large number of people have been polled on this question, and it appears that X was an important factor in their decision to _____.

Research Note

You may need to conduct research to find evidence to support your refutation. If so, revisit the sections Conduct Research (p. 424) and Cite a Variety of Sources to Support Your Causal Analysis (p. 425).

Draft a response to the causes or effects your readers are likely to favor.

In the preceding activity, you analyzed and drafted a response to the objections your readers are likely to raise. The next activity will help you respond to your readers' preferred causes or effects.

WAYS IN

- **Choose an alternative cause or effect, and summarize it.** Be sure to summarize it accurately and fairly. Do not commit the straw man fallacy of knocking down something that no one really takes seriously.

- **Decide whether you can REFUTE the alternative cause or effect or whether you need to CONCEDE it.** Refute the alternative cause or effect if you can show that it lacks credible support or if the underlying reasoning is flawed. Concede it by pointing out that the cause or effect is obvious and setting it aside or by showing that it plays a less important role than the cause or effect you are championing. Try the following sentence strategies, or use language of your own.

To *Refute*

Lacks Credible Support

- ▶ Just because Y caused _____ does not mean that it caused _____ [a similar subject]. Here's why: _____ .

- ▶ The scenario/anecdote others sometimes use to explain why X caused/occurred certainly helps dramatize _____ , but it doesn't really explain why X happened.

- ▶ If X is the result of Y, then one would expect _____ to happen, too, but it hasn't/the opposite has happened.

Reasoning Is Flawed

Mistakes correlation for causation.

- ▶ Some argue that Y caused X because X and Y occurred/began rising sharply at the same time. But, in fact, this is merely a coincidence/both were caused by something else altogether.

Mistakes chronology for causation.

- ▶ Just because Y occurred before/after X doesn't prove that X caused/resulted from Y.

- ▶ Proponents of _____ have not provided convincing evidence to show how Y could have caused X.

To *Concede*

Set Aside a Well-Known Cause

- ▶ An obvious explanation is _____ . But if we dig deeper, we find that _____ .

- ▶ Typical explanations include _____ and _____ , but let's consider a totally different possibility: _____ .

Show That an Alternative Cause Is Minor

- ▶ _____ is one of the answers but may not play as central a role as most people think it does.

- ▶ _____ may have kept the process going, but X was the trigger: Without it, Y would never have gotten started.

- ▶ _____ may have been a factor at the outset, getting the process started, but what keeps it going is X.

Writing a Draft

GUIDE TO READING
GUIDE TO WRITING
A WRITER AT WORK
THINKING CRITICALLY

429

∷ Create an outline that will organize your causal argument effectively for your readers.

Whether you have rough notes or a complete draft, making an outline of what you have written can help you organize the essay effectively for your audience. A causal argument may contain as many as four basic parts:

1. A presentation of the subject
2. Plausible causes/effects, logically sequenced
3. Convincing support for each cause or effect
4. A consideration of readers' questions, objections, and alternative causes or effects

Compare the possible outlines that follow to see how you might organize your essay depending on whether your readers primarily agree with you—or not.

If your readers are *not* likely to favor any alternatives, you may want to anticipate and respond to their possible objections to your causes or effects.

I. **Presentation of the subject:** Demonstrate that the subject exists and that its causes/effects are uncertain

II. **Thesis and forecasting statement:** Announce the causes/effects you will offer

III. **First cause/effect with supporting evidence and refutation of objection**

IV. **Second cause/effect with supporting evidence and refutation of objection (and so on)**

V. **Conclusion:** Reassertion of judgment

If you expect readers *are* likely to favor alternatives, you may want to concede or refute them before offering your own cause or effect.

I. **Presentation of the subject:** Demonstrate that the subject exists and that its causes/effects are uncertain

II. **Thesis statement:** Acknowledge alternative causes/effects readers are likely to know about

III. **Concession of first alternative cause/effect to set it aside**

IV. **Refutation of second alternative cause/effect with supporting evidence**

V. **Writer's preferred cause/effect with supporting evidence**

VI. **Refutation of objection(s)**

VII. **Conclusion:** Reassertion of judgment based on shared criteria

---

Whatever organizational strategy you adopt, do not hesitate to change your outline as necessary while drafting and revising. For instance, you might find it more effective to begin with your own preferred cause or effect and to hold back on presenting unacceptable alternatives until you've made the case you think is most plausible and interesting. The purpose of an outline is to identify the basic components of your analysis and to help you organize them effectively, not to lock you into a particular structure.

For more on outlining, see Chapter 11.

Write the opening sentences.

Review what you have already written to see if you have something that would help you present the subject of your causal argument effectively for your audience:

*Demonstrate the **relevance** of your topic by putting it in context for your reader:*

> Complain about problems in a *tweet* over Twitter; add a *friend*, virtually *poke* each other, and *like* friends' postings and ramblings on Facebook; send images and videos to each other using Snapchat; capture a *selfie* with Instagram, edit it, add hashtags, and share it for your friends to see and comment on: Social networking is only a click away . . . (Pangelinan, par. 1)

*Begin with a **surprising assertion** that would help grab your readers' attention:*

> I think that we're all mentally ill; those of us outside the asylums only hide it a little better—and maybe not all that much better, after all. (King, par. 1)

*Begin with a **scenario** or an **anecdote**:*

> It's 9:30 p.m., and Stephen and Georgina Cox know exactly where their children are. Well, their bodies, at least. (Wallis, par. 1)

> The *Insiko 1907* was a tramp tanker that roamed the Pacific Ocean. Its twelve-man Taiwanese crew hunted the seas for fishing fleets in need of fuel; the *Insiko* had a cargo of tens of thousands of gallons of diesel. (Vedantam, par. 1)

Draft your causal argument.

By this point, you have done a lot of writing to:

- devise a well-presented subject and analyze its causes or effects;
- support your preferred causes or effects with evidence your readers will find persuasive;
- refute or concede objections and alternative causes or effects;
- organize your ideas to make them clear, logical, and effective for readers.

Now stitch that material together to create a draft. The next two parts of this Guide to Writing will help you evaluate and improve that draft.

Evaluating the Draft: Using Peer Review

Your instructor may arrange a peer review session in class or online, where you can exchange drafts with your classmates and give each other a thoughtful critical reading, pointing out what works well and suggesting ways to improve the draft. A good critical reading does three things:

1. It lets the writer know how well the reader understands the causal analysis.
2. It praises what works best.
3. It indicates where the draft could be improved and makes suggestions for how to improve it.

One strategy for evaluating a draft is to use the basic features of the causal analysis as a guide.

Evaluating the Draft

GUIDE TO READING
GUIDE TO WRITING
A WRITER AT WORK
THINKING CRITICALLY

431

A PEER REVIEW GUIDE

A Well-Presented Subject

How effectively does the writer present the subject?

Summarize: Tell the writer what you understand the subject to be and why he or she thinks it is important and worth analyzing.

Praise: Give an example of something in the draft that you think will especially interest the intended readers and help them understand the subject.

Critique: Tell the writer if you have any confusion or uncertainty about the subject. What further explanation, examples, or statistics do you need to understand it better? If you can think of a more interesting way to present the subject, share your ideas with the writer.

A Well-Supported Causal Analysis

How plausible are the proposed causes or effects, and how well does the writer support the causal analysis?

Summary: Identify the possible causes or effects the writer argues are the most plausible and interesting.

Praise: Tell the writer which cause or effect seems most convincing. Point to any support (such as a particular example, a statistic, a research study, or a graph) that you think is especially strong.

Critique: Tell the writer if any of the causes or effects seem too obvious or minor, and if you think an important cause or effect has been left out. Where the support seems lacking or unconvincing, explain what is missing or seems wrong. If the reasoning seems flawed, what makes you think so?

An Effective Response to Objections and Alternative Causes or Effects

How effectively does the writer respond to readers' objections and alternative causes or effects?

Summary: Identify the objections or alternative causes or effects to which the writer responds.

Praise: Point out any response you think is especially effective, and tell the writer what makes you think so. For example, indicate where the support is especially credible and convincing.

Critique: Point to any objections or alternative causes or effects that the writer could have responded to more effectively, and suggest how the response could be improved. Also indicate if the writer has overlooked any serious objections.

(continued)

A Clear, Logical Organization

How clear and logical is the causal analysis?

Summary: Underline the thesis statement and topic sentences.

Praise: Give an example of where the essay succeeds in being especially clear and easy to follow — for example, in its overall organization, its use of key terms and transitions, or its use of visuals.

Critique: Point to any passages where the writing could be clearer, where topic sentences or transitions could be added, or where key terms could be repeated to make the essay easier to follow. Try suggesting a better beginning or a more effective ending.

Before concluding your peer review, be sure to address any of the writer's concerns that have not been discussed already.

Making Comments Electronically   Most word processing software offers features that allow you to insert comments directly into the text of someone else's document. Many readers prefer to make their comments this way because it tends to be faster than writing on hard copy and space is virtually unlimited; it also eliminates the process of deciphering handwritten comments. Where such features are not available, simply typing comments directly into a document in a contrasting color can provide the same advantages.

Improving the Draft: Revising, Editing, and Proofreading

Start improving your draft by reflecting on what you have written thus far:

- Review critical reading comments from your classmates, instructor, or writing center tutor: What are your readers getting at?
- Consider your invention writing: What else should you consider?
- Review your draft: What can you do to present your causal analysis more compellingly?

Revise your draft.

If your readers are having difficulty with your draft, or if you think there is room for improvement, try some of the strategies listed in the Troubleshooting Guide that follows. It can help you fine-tune your presentation of the genre's basic features.

Improving the Draft

GUIDE TO READING
▶ GUIDE TO WRITING
A WRITER AT WORK
THINKING CRITICALLY

433

A TROUBLESHOOTING GUIDE

A Well-Presented Subject

> My readers don't understand the subject or see why it is important.

- Reconsider what your readers already know, and provide additional background if necessary.
- Try providing examples or an anecdote to interest readers in the subject.
- Quote authorities and explain research findings, including statistics, to demonstrate the subject's importance — that it is widespread and significant.
- Use visuals — graphs, tables, photographs, or screen shots — to make the subject more vivid.
- Review your research to see if you can add anything to help clarify the subject for your readers, or do some additional research.
- Pose the subject directly or indirectly as a *why* question, and then answer it.

A Well-Supported Causal Analysis

> My readers don't understand which of the causes or effects I am arguing are the most plausible.

- Be explicit about which causes or effects are the ones you think are most plausible, and why you think so.
- Use a thesis and forecasting statement followed by topic sentences with key terms to announce your main causes or effects.

> My readers do not find my causal argument convincing.

- Whenever possible, explain how the cause-effect relationship works, backing up your explanation with appropriate support.
- Cite more credible experts, being sure to give their credentials.
- Cite research studies and statistics rather than limiting yourself to examples and anecdotes.
- Review your sources to make sure they are varied, or do additional focused research to fill in where your analysis is weak.
- Make sure your sources are cited properly.

An Effective Response to Objections and Alternative Causes or Effects

> My readers do not think my responses are effective.

- Respond directly to criticism of your reasoning by showing that you are not mistaking correlation or chronology for causation.
- Demonstrate that you understand the complexity of the cause-effect relationship you are analyzing, for example, by indicating how your cause relates to other contributing causes.
- If your readers think you have overlooked an objection, consider it seriously and do further research to respond to it if necessary.

(continued)

A Clear, Logical Organization

My readers think my analysis is not clear or logical.

- If readers have difficulty finding the thesis statement or topic sentences, consider revising them.
- Add a forecasting statement early in the essay to help guide readers.
- Review your use of transitions, and consider adding transitions to make the logical relationships among sentences and paragraphs clear to readers.
- Refer to visuals explicitly (for example, by adding the direction, "see fig. 1"), and include a caption tying each visual to the text discussion.
- Outline your essay to review its structure, and move, add, or delete sections as necessary to strengthen coherence.

Edit and proofread your draft.

Two kinds of errors occur often in causal analysis essays: mechanical errors in using numbers, and use of the wordy and illogical construction *the reason is because*. The following guidelines will help you check your essay for these common errors.

Checking Your Use of Numbers

A Note on Grammar and Spelling Checkers

These tools can be helpful, but do not rely on them exclusively to catch errors in your text: Spelling checkers cannot catch misspellings that are themselves words, such as *to* for *too*. Grammar checkers miss some problems, sometimes give faulty advice for fixing problems, and can flag correct items as wrong. Use these tools as a second line of defense after your own (and, ideally, another reader's) proofreading and editing efforts.

Whether they are indicating the scope of a phenomenon or citing the increase or decrease of a trend, writers who are speculating about causes or effects often cite dates, percentages, fractions, and other numbers. Academic writing prescribes conventional ways of writing such numbers. Look, for example, at these sentences from an essay about increasing reports of sexual harassment in the workplace:

> According to a 1994 survey conducted by the Society for Human Resource Management, the percentage of human resource professionals who have reported that their departments handled at least one sexual harassment complaint rose from 35 percent in 1991 to 65 percent in 1994. The jury awarded Weeks $7.1 million in punitive damages, twice what she sought in her lawsuit.

The writer follows the convention of spelling out numbers (*one*) that can be written as one or two words and using a combination of numerals and words for a large number (*$7.1 million*). (She could also have used numerals for the large number: *$7,100,000*.) She uses numerals for dates and percentages.

The Problem Ignoring the rules for writing dates, percentages, fractions, and other numbers in academic writing can confuse your readers or make them question your attention to detail.

Improving the Draft

GUIDE TO READING
GUIDE TO WRITING
A WRITER AT WORK
THINKING CRITICALLY

435

The Correction

- Spell out numbers and fractions of one or two words.

  ▶ According to the World Health Organization, as many as ~~1~~ *one* person in every ~~50~~ *fifty* may be infected with HIV.

  ▶ Approximately ~~2/3~~ *two-thirds* of the smoke from a cigarette is released into the air.

- Use numbers when fractions and numbers are more than two words.

  ▶ That year the Japanese automobile industry produced only ~~four thousand eight hundred thirty-seven~~ *4,837* vehicles, mostly trucks and motorbikes.

  ▶ This study shows that Americans spend an average of ~~five and one-third~~ *5⅓* hours a day watching television.

- Write percentages and dates with figures.

  ▶ Comparing 1980 to 1960, we can see that time spent viewing television increased ~~twenty-eight~~ *28* percent.

- Spell out numbers that begin a sentence.

  ▶ ~~30~~ *Thirty* percent of commercial real estate in Washington, D.C., is owned by foreigners.

Checking for *Reason Is Because* Constructions

When you analyze causes, you need to offer reasons and support for your claims. Consequently, essays that analyze causes often contain sentences constructed around a *reason is because* pattern, as in the following example:

> The *reason* we lost the war *is because* troop morale was down.

The Problem   Since *because* means "for the reason that," such sentences say essentially that "the reason is the reason."

The Correction   Rewrite the sentence so that it uses either *the reason . . . is* or *because,* but not both:

> The *reason* we lost the war *is* that troop morale was down.

> We lost the war *because* troop morale was down.

  ▶ Her research suggests that one reason women attend women's colleges is ~~because~~ *that* they want to avoid certain social pressures.

  ▶ ~~A reason~~ *Older* ~~older~~ Americans watch so much television is because they tend to be sedentary.

Clayton Pangelinan's Analysis of Possible Causes

Using the "Ways In" activity "How can I analyze possible causes or effects?" on p. 423, Clayton Pangelinan sorted through the notes he had made doing preliminary research for his essay "#socialnetworking: Why It's *Really* So Popular" (pp. 391–95). He began with the vague idea of examining the popularity of social networking, which he could establish easily with information he found from the Pew Research Center—a solid source. The Pew Research Center also offered reasons for the popularity of social media based on polling; its research suggested that staying in touch with friends and family and connecting with people with shared interests were the main reasons people use social media. But Pangelinan thought these reasons seemed too obvious and wanted to delve more deeply.

Following is the list of possible causes and a few sentences he wrote analyzing each cause. Notice that in a few cases he refers to research he has already found.

Possible Causes	Analysis of Causes
1. We have the technology for it now.	The Pew Research Center shows how social networking increased hugely in all age groups in 2005–6. We had to have Web 2.0 to create interactive use; without the technology, it simply couldn't have existed. So I will establish that the increase exists with a useful chart from Pew, and then I'll examine why social media is the form interactive behavior has taken.
2. People can connect with the lives and activities of friends and family.	The phone increased our connections, and e-mail did too, but not until people joined social media did they have a chance to be in touch daily—sometimes hourly—with everyone they cared about all at once. This is an obvious cause. You can share what you want with friends, acquaintances, and followers, and learn about their lives, too. It's interactive rather than read-only. (Research To Do note: Find Matthew Lieberman's article recommended by my professor about why our brains are "wired to connect.")
3. People can shape how their lives look and how other people see them.	When people post to social media, they can revise what they write to create the impression they want. However, some people post really spontaneously, so I don't know whether this is a valid cause. Interview friends? This would be a more hidden cause.
4. People can reach more than one person at a time.	You have a larger audience when you post to social media. It's not like writing a letter or making a phone call—you can reach countless people all at once. This is a continuing cause. Appeals to people who want attention? Narcissists?

Clayton Pangelinan's Analysis of Possible Causes

GUIDE TO READING
GUIDE TO WRITING
▶ A WRITER AT WORK
THINKING CRITICALLY

437

5. People can satisfy a desire for celebrity.

Could use Andy Warhol's 15 minutes of fame. Find examples of people who are clearly posting so they will get attention (Padme). Other examples?

6. It is a way to keep current in the world.

Can be a way to be "up" on current events without having to read newspapers, magazines, and books—too time-consuming? Twitter, for example, provides snippets of news that keep you up to date on what's happening right now. You can choose your own topics—politics, movies, animal rights, climate change, cartoons—it's all out there—and get different perspectives on the same sites. Some sites attract only one kind of perspective, though, and that might be a drawback—but keeping current is still a cause.

Pangelinan decided he couldn't use all of these causes because of the time and space limits for his essay, so he decided to concentrate on humans' need for connection, their curiosity about other people's lives, and the desire to be the center of attention. He began with cause 1 because it was obvious that the technology had to have reached a certain point to allow social networking. He merged causes 2 and 3 because they were related and he knew these causes were valid from his own experience; he was sure he could find good examples to support them. He then developed cause 4 into a significant portion of his essay, folding in cause 5 because you can't get fame without an audience. *Narcissism* is a strong word that would generate strong opinions, and he thought some people might find it surprising. Finally, he dropped cause 6 altogether because he could write a whole essay just on that cause, and he found causes 2 through 5 more interesting.

To think critically means to use all of the knowledge you have acquired from the information in this chapter, your own writing, the writing of other students, and class discussions to reflect deeply on your work for this assignment and the genre (or type) of writing you have produced. The benefit of thinking critically is proven and important: Thinking critically about what you have learned will help you remember it longer, ensuring that you will be able to put it to good use well beyond this writing course.

Reflecting on What You Have Learned

In this chapter, you have learned a great deal about the genre from reading several causal arguments and from writing one of your own. To consolidate your learning, reflect not only on what you learned but also on how you learned it.

ANALYZE & WRITE

Write a blog post, a letter to your instructor, or an e-mail message to a student who will take this course next term, using the writing prompt that seems most productive for you:

- Explain how your purpose and audience influenced *one* of your decisions as a writer, such as how you explained the subject, how you supported your preferred causes or effects, or how you responded to readers' likely objections.

- Discuss what you learned about yourself as a writer in the process of writing this argument or from remixing it in another genre or medium. For example, what part of the process did you find most challenging? Did you try anything new, like getting a critical reading of your draft or re-envisioning your essay as a proposal or a presentation?

- If you were to give advice to a friend who was about to write a causal argument, what would you say?

- Which of the readings in this chapter influenced your essay? Explain the influence, citing specific examples from your essay and the reading.

- If you got good advice from a critical reader, explain exactly how the person helped you — perhaps by questioning your use of support, your choice of medium, your use of visuals, the way you began or ended your essay, or the kinds of sources you used.

Reflecting on the Genre

Causal arguments are always shaped by the writer's expertise and special interests. For example, Stephen King—a horror writer—has a personal investment in establishing the horror movie as a legitimate literary and cinematic form; not surprisingly, then, he emphasizes the psychological benefits of horror movies. Shankar Vedantam, a science journalist, is clearly sympathetic to the work of the evolutionary psychologists and philosophers he quotes to support his claim that human beings are unable to respond viscerally (from the gut) to information about mass suffering.

Reflecting on the Genre

GUIDE TO READING
GUIDE TO WRITING
A WRITER AT WORK
▶ THINKING CRITICALLY

439

ANALYZE & WRITE

Write a page or two explaining how causal arguments disguise the writer's assumptions. In your discussion, you might do one or more of the following:

1. **Consider how the readings and your own argument are exercises in exerting authority.** We have said that because causal arguments deal with possibilities instead of certainties, writers must be somewhat tentative about their speculations. However, if a causal argument is to be convincing, it cannot be too timid. Writers who have studied a subject carefully may feel that they are justified in exerting their authority. Compare two or more of the essays by Pangelinan, King, Wallis, and Vedantam. Which seems most assertive? What accounts for your response? What seems to you assertive or unassertive about your own essay? Was it your knowledge or your **ideology** (your way of looking at the world), or both, that gave you (or withheld from you) the confidence to be authoritative?

2. **Consider how easy it is to accept a causal argument.** If not alert, readers may begin to think that the argument a selection offers is the only possible one. Are any of the selections in this chapter so seductive that you find yourself accepting their causal arguments without question? Explain briefly.

3. **Write a page or two explaining your ideas about authority and ideology in essays analyzing causes or effects.** Connect your ideas to your own essay and to the readings in this chapter.

10

Analyzing Stories

Stories have a special place in most cultures. They can lead us to look at others with sensitivity and, for a brief time, to see the world through another person's eyes. They can also lead us to see ourselves differently, to gain insight into our innermost feelings and thoughts. Although writing about stories is an important academic kind of discourse, many people who are not in school enjoy discussing stories and writing about how a story resonates in their lives. That is why book clubs, reading groups, and online discussion forums are so popular. Good stories tend to be enigmatic in that they usually do not reveal themselves fully on first reading. So it can be enjoyable and enlightening to analyze stories and discuss them with other readers. Even very short stories can elicit fascinating analyses. For example, Ernest Hemingway wrote this six-word story, which he reportedly claimed was his best work:

For sale: baby shoes, never worn.

Analyzing a Story Collaboratively

Sharing the experience of reading stories with others exposes us to different ways of interpreting and responding to them — expanding our openness to new perspectives, deepening our insight, and enhancing our pleasure. To benefit from this kind of discussion with
others, work together with one or two other students to analyze the ultrabrief Hemingway
story above. Here are some guidelines to follow:

Part 1.   Discuss the story, using these questions to get started:

- It looks like an ad, but who would try to sell baby shoes, and why? What is the likely
  relationship between the person trying to sell the shoes and the baby for whom the
  shoes were originally bought?

- Who could be a potential buyer for the shoes?

- Where and when was the ad written? (In a country where there are land mines? In a
  time of severe economic depression?)

- Why is the story so short? What could the brevity say about emotion? What could
  the fact that the story is written in the form of an advertisement suggest about
  commercialism?

Part 2.   After you have discussed the story for half of the time allotted for this activity,
reflect on the process of analyzing the story in your group:

- Before you began, what were your expectations of how the group would work
  together? For example, did you think your group should or would agree on one "right
  answer" to the questions, or did you expect significant disagreement? What actually
  happened once you began to discuss the story?

- How did the discussion affect your attitude about the story or about the process of
  analyzing stories? What, if anything, did you learn?

Your instructor may ask you to write about what you learned and to present your conclusions to the rest of the class.

In this chapter, we ask you to write an analysis of a story. Analyzing the selections in the Guide to Reading that follows will help you learn the basic features and strategies writers typically use when writing about stories. The readings, as well as the questions and discussion surrounding them, will help you consider strategies you might want to try out when writing your own analysis.

Analyzing Essays That Analyze Stories

As you read the essays in this chapter, you will see how two students have analyzed the short story "The Use of Force" by William Carlos Williams (pp. 482–84).

- Iris Lee interprets the story through the lens of the doctor's Hippocratic Oath to "do no harm" (pp. 446–49).
- Isabella Wright interprets the story as a breaking away from convention (pp. 450–52).

Examining how these writers present an arguable thesis about the story, support this thesis, and guide readers through their argument will help you write an insightful literary analysis of your own. The example passages in the sections that follow are drawn from these two essays.

Determine the writer's purpose and audience.

When reading the short story analysis essays that appear in this chapter, ask yourself the following questions:

What seems to be the writer's main purpose?

- to illuminate the story?
- to change or expand the way readers understand the story?
- to impress readers with the writer's insight and close reading?

What does the writer assume about the audience?   The short story analyses from this chapter were written by students in a college course in which the entire class had read the same story. These writers assumed that their primary reader, the instructor, not only had read the story but also knew a fair amount about its context and the conversation surrounding it — enough, at least, to be able to judge whether the essayist had read the story with sufficient care and thought. In cases such as these, plot summaries and recitals of well-known facts about the short story and its author are not necessary.

Assess the genre's basic features.

As you read the essays that analyze stories in this chapter, you will see how different writers incorporate the basic features of the genre. The following discussions of these features include examples from the essays as well as sentence strategies you can experiment with later, as you write your own analysis of a story.

> **▪▪ Basic Features**
> A Clear, Arguable Thesis
> A Well-Supported Argument
> A Clear, Logical Organization

A CLEAR, ARGUABLE THESIS

Read first to find the thesis statement, *which is often one or two sentences long but that may run to several paragraphs.* A good thesis statement in an essay analyzing a story

- asserts the main idea or claim;

- is arguable, not a simple statement of fact (for example, "'The Use of Force' tells the story of a doctor's visit to a sick little girl") or an obvious conclusion (for example, "The doctor grows frustrated by the little girl's behavior");

- is appropriately qualified, not overgeneralized or exaggerated (for example, "The behavior of the doctor at the center of 'The Use of Force' shows that no medical professional can be trusted");

- is clearly stated, not vague or ambiguous.

Often, the thesis is part of an introduction that is at least a paragraph in length. In most cases, this introduction identifies the story being analyzed by giving the title and author, and it may also provide some historical, biographical, or cultural context. In effective writing, the thesis and other sentences in the opening paragraph (or paragraphs) introduce *key terms* for ideas that are echoed and further developed later in the essay. In this way, the introductory sentences and thesis *forecast* how the argument will be developed.

Inexperienced writers are sometimes afraid to ruin the surprise by forecasting their argument at the beginning of their essays. But explicit forecasting is a convention of literary analysis, similar in purpose to the abstract that precedes many articles in academic journals.

Take a look at Iris Lee's lead-up to the thesis in her essay on "The Use of Force." In it, she introduces key terms that are *repeated* (exactly, closely, or through synonyms) and underscored in her thesis:

> The Hippocratic Oath binds doctors to practice ethically and, above all, to "do no harm." The doctor narrating William Carlos Williams's short story "The Use of Force" comes dangerously close to breaking that oath, yet ironically is able to justify his actions by invoking his professional image and the pretense of preserving his patient's well-being. As an account of a professional doing harm under the pretense of healing, the story uncovers how a doctor can take advantage of the intimate nature of his work and his professional status to overstep common forms of conduct, to the extent that his actions actually hurt rather than help a patient. In this way, the doctor-narrator actually performs a valuable service by warning readers, indirectly through his story, that blindly trusting members of his profession can have negative consequences. (par. 1)

Key terms

Thesis

Sometimes, the thesis of a literary analysis contradicts or complicates a surface reading of a work. Look for sentence strategies like this one:

▶ A common/superficial reading of X [title or author] is that _____ [surface reading], but in fact _____ [insert your own interpretation].

In Isabella Wright's essay on "The Use of Force," the surface reading actually appears in the sentences leading up to the thesis. A transitional sentence and a transitional word introduce the contradiction/complication that constitutes the thesis:

Surface reading

Transitional sentence
Transitional word

Contradiction/
complication

> By any reasonable standards, the story of a doctor prying a little girl's mouth open as she screams in pain and fear should leave readers feeling nothing but horror and disgust at the doctor's actions. William Carlos Williams's story "The Use of Force" is surprising in that it does not completely condemn the doctor for doing just that. *Instead,* through his actions and words (uttered or thought), readers are able to see the freeing, transformative power of breaking with social conventions. (par. 1)

A WELL-SUPPORTED ARGUMENT

Consider how the writer provides support for the argument. Because essays analyzing stories usually present new ideas that are not obvious and that readers may disagree with, writers need to make an argument that includes

- *reasons*—the supporting ideas or points that develop the essay's thesis or main claim;

- *evidence* or *examples* from the story;

- *explanations* or *analyses* showing how the examples support the argument.

In addition, writers may provide other kinds of support—for example, *quotations from experts* or historical, biographical, or cultural evidence. But *textual evidence* from the work of literature is the primary support readers expect in literary analysis essays.

Evidence from the text often takes the form of *quotation* of words, phrases, sentences, and, occasionally, even paragraphs. Quoting is the most important method of providing support for essays that analyze short stories, but effective writers do not expect a quotation to do the work by itself. Instead, they analyze the language of the story to show how particular words' **connotations** (cultural and emotional associations), their *figurative* use in *images* and *metaphors,* or their **symbolism** (ideas or qualities they suggest) enrich the story's meanings.

When reading a literary analysis, look for sentence strategies like this one:

▶ _____ [type of evidence from the text], such as "_____" and "_____" [quotations] demonstrates/shows _____ [analysis].

Now look at the extended example from paragraph 4 of Iris Lee's essay. In this excerpt, Lee supports an assertion about the author's use of "militaristic diction" by quoting from several parts of the story:

Description of evidence

Supporting
quotations

Analysis

> Examples of militaristic diction include calling his struggle with the girl a "battle" (502), the tongue depressor a "wooden blade" (503), his bodily effort an "assault" (503). She too is a party in this war, moving from fighting "on the defensive" to surging forward in an attack (503). Such metaphors of fighting and warfare, especially those associated with the doctor and his actions, figuratively convey that his character crosses a crucial boundary. They present the argument that, despite his

honorable pretentions, his actions—at least during the height of his conflict with the girl—align more with violence than with healing. The doctor's thoughts even turn more obviously (and more consciously) violent at times, such as when, in a bout of frustration, he wants "to kill" the girl's father, (502) or when he says, "I could have torn the child apart in my own fury and enjoyed it" (503). Although these statements are arguably exaggerated, they, like the metaphors of war, imply a tendency to do harm that goes directly against the narrator's duty as a doctor. While the story's opening introduces him as a person whose occupation is reason to overcome the parents' distrust, by the end of the story he leaves his readers thoroughly horrified by his forceful handling of the little girl. *By investigating the calculated artifice and military metaphors, we might conclude that the narrator is conscious both of his deceptive rhetoric and of the harm it allows him to inflict upon his patient.*

Writer's conclusions

In addition to quoting, evidence can also take the form of *summary* or *paraphrase*. Writers can use this type of evidence to set up an extended close textual analysis like that shown above. Or they might use summary or paraphrase in brief snippets of analysis, as in sentence strategies like the following:

▶ When X says/does _____ [summary/paraphrase] readers can readily see _____ [analysis].

For more on quotation, summary, and paraphrase, see Chapter 23.

For example, to support her thesis, Isabella Wright summarizes the doctor's conflict with the girl instead of describing it in detail. The summary is introduced by repeating key terms from the thesis statement:

The doctor also breaks with social conventions by willingly engaging in a physical struggle with the little girl. (par. 5)

Analysis

Summary

A CLEAR, LOGICAL ORGANIZATION

To make the argument in a literary analysis easy to follow, writers usually include some or all of the following:

- *Topic sentences* introducing paragraphs or groups of paragraphs (often using key terms from the thesis statement)

- Key terms—words or phrases—introduced in the thesis or other introductory text as a way of forecasting the development of the argument (see the previous section); these key terms are repeated strategically throughout the essay

- Clear *transitional words* and *phrases* (such as "although," "in addition," and "at the story's beginning")

Writers tend to place topic sentences at or near the beginning of a paragraph because these sentences help readers make sense of the details, examples, and explanations that follow. Often, topic sentences repeat key terms from the thesis or other introductory text. Look, for example, at the first topic sentence of Iris Lee's essay, which repeats key terms from the introduction in paragraph 1.

Key terms

In the way the story and its characters introduce us to the narrator, we see how people automatically grant a doctor status and privilege based on his profession alone, creating an odd sort of intimacy that is uncommon in ordinary social relations. (par. 2)

The paragraph then gives examples of the extreme politeness the young patient's parents show to the doctor, and in describing and analyzing the scene, Lee repeats the words "privilege" and "intimacy."

Topic sentences can also serve as transitions from one paragraph to the next. In reading literary analyses, look for sentence strategies like the following:

▶ In comparison with/in contrast to/in addition to/because of subject A [discussed in the previous paragraph], subject B [discussed in this paragraph] does _____.

In her analysis of "The Use of Force," Isabella Wright uses this strategy:

Subject A
Subject B

EXAMPLE   *In contrast to* the little girl's parents, the doctor breaks social conventions in his interactions with the family and in doing so highlights the absurdity of these rules. (par. 3)

Notice that Wright repeats the phrase "social conventions," which she introduces in her thesis.

Readings

The following essays by students Iris Lee and Isabella Wright analyze the short story "The Use of Force," by William Carlos Williams (pp. 482–84). As you will see, both Lee and Wright attempt to answer questions that many readers have asked of this story: What is the purpose—aside from vividly describing his anger and frustration—of portraying a doctor's use of force on an uncooperative patient? What larger points are being made? Lee and Wright arrive at different answers to these questions. By reading their essays, you will learn a great deal about how writers argue for their own analysis of a story.

For guidelines on formatting a writing project and acknowledging sources in MLA style, see Chapter 24.

Iris Lee | *Performing a Doctor's Duty*

WRITTEN FOR A FIRST-YEAR COMPOSITION COURSE, this essay by Iris Lee emphasizes the "doctor's duty." As you read, consider the following:

• What, from Lee's perspective, is the doctor's duty, as indicated in the title?

• What evidence from the story does Lee use to support her main idea?

Also consider the questions in the margin. Your instructor may ask you to post your answers to a class blog or discussion board or to bring them to class.

1   The Hippocratic Oath binds doctors to practice ethically and, above all, to "do no harm." The doctor narrating William Carlos Williams's short story "The Use of Force" comes dangerously close to breaking that oath, yet ironically is able to justify his actions by invoking his professional image and the pretense of preserving his patient's well-being. As an account of a professional doing harm under the pretense of healing, the story uncovers how a doctor can take advantage of the intimate nature of his work and his professional status to overstep common forms of conduct, to the extent that his actions actually hurt rather than help a patient. In this way, the doctor-narrator actually performs a valuable service by warning readers, indirectly through his story, that blindly trusting members of his profession can have negative consequences.

2   In the way the story and its characters introduce us to the narrator, we see how people automatically grant a doctor status and privilege based on his profession alone, creating an odd sort of intimacy that is uncommon in ordinary social relations. At the story's beginning, the narrator identifies the family he visits as "new patients" (482), and he establishes that they are virtual strangers to him — "all [he] had was the name, Olson" (482). After the mother confirms that he is the doctor, however, she immediately invites him into the most intimate part of her home, the kitchen, where her husband and sick daughter are waiting (482). Later, the mother reassures the child that the doctor is a "nice man" and "won't hurt you," though she can base those assertions only on what little she knows of him: his occupation (483). At the same time, the narrator senses that the family is "very nervous, eyeing me up and down distrustfully" (482). The parents' eagerness in offering their home and hospitality, coupled with the betrayal of their nervousness, hints at the dubious nature of the intimacy between a doctor and his patient. Although the doctor's profession gives him privilege to overstep certain boundaries, the basis of real trust is lacking, thus casting the doctor-patient relationship as something strange and artificial.

3   The narrator communicates to readers that he perceives both sides of the interaction and also admits to intentionally using the weight of his professional status against the family's natural distrust of outsiders. The young girl, who is not yet "adult" enough to follow social conventions (484), might be read as representing the family's instinct for self-protection. In the face of the child's resistance, the narrator "smiled in [his] best professional manner" (483), trying to invoke the special form of trust that

█▪ Basic Features
A Clear, Arguable Thesis
A Well-Supported Argument
A Clear, Logical Organization

How do the highlighted transitions help the reader? Is this merely plot summary or does it serve an analytical purpose?

Highlight the topic sentences of paragraphs 3–5. How well do they work?

doctors typically assume. The phrase "professional manner" shows that the narrator acknowledges he is using the power of his occupation, while also admitting that his reassuring smile is only part of his professional performance. As the doctor's struggle to examine the little girl's throat becomes more heated, he repeatedly brings up his expert concern to justify his rough actions. He tells readers, "I had to do it . . . for her own protection" (483). Later, he reminds readers (and himself) that "I have seen at least two children lying dead in bed of neglect in such cases, and [feel] that I must get a diagnosis now or never" (483). He also notes that "others must be protected" against the sick child before him (484). The narrator repeatedly brings up his duty as a doctor and the privilege that comes with it to defend his use of force. Yet at other points, he admits to having "grown furious" (483), to being unable to "hold [himself] down" (483), and to have "got beyond reason" (483). In acknowledging the loss of his capacity for reason and self-control, he essentially admits that his "professional manner" and attempts to be gentle in getting the girl to follow his commands are empty artifice (483). When these attempts fail, emotion alone drives his actions. In effect, he uses the medical art as a pretense to justify otherwise unacceptable interventions.

4   Beyond admitting his personal motivations in his treatment of the girl, the narrator sketches a more disturbing and potentially incriminating image of himself in his use of militaristic diction, for it aligns his character more with harming than healing — the perfect contradiction of a doctor. Examples of militaristic diction include calling his struggle with the girl a "battle" (483), the tongue depressor a "wooden blade" (483), his bodily effort an "assault" (484). She too is a party in this war, moving from fighting "on the defensive" to surging forward in an attack (484). Such metaphors of fighting and warfare, especially those associated with the doctor and his actions, figuratively convey that his character crosses a crucial boundary. They present the argument that, despite his honorable pretentions, his actions — at least during the height of his conflict with the girl — align more with violence than with healing. The doctor's thoughts even turn more obviously (and more consciously) violent at times, such as when, in a bout of frustration, he wants "to kill" the girl's father (483), or when he says, "I could have torn the child apart in my own fury and enjoyed it" (483–84). Although these statements are arguably exaggerated or hyperbolic, they, like the metaphors of war, imply a tendency to do harm that goes directly against the narrator's duty as a doctor. While the story's opening introduces him as a person whose occupation is

How clear is Lee's analysis here? How does she support it?

How well do the quoted words illustrate Lee's analysis?

enough to overcome the parents' distrust, by the end of the story he leaves his readers thoroughly horrified by his forceful handling of the little girl. By investigating the calculated artifice and military metaphors, we might conclude that the narrater is conscious both of his deceptive rhetoric and of the harm it allows him to inflict upon his patient.

5   Curiously, the narrator readily pleads guilty on both counts, which leads one to wonder why any person would willingly paint such a damning picture of himself—one that would surely destroy his livelihood. I would argue that the doctor of this story does not take ownership of his despicable actions but uses them to blame the parents and more generally to warn against blindly trusting those in positions of authority. Looking back to the story's opening, we note that the narrator presents himself generically. He does not name or describe himself or provide any information beyond the fact that he is a doctor. The lack of specification renders him the "every doctor" and expands the possible reference points for the pronoun "I" as it is used in this story. That is to say, although the story is told in the first person, attaching the actions and events to the singular narrator, that narrator turns himself into a placeholder for every doctor by leaving out all identifying features. I would argue, furthermore, that speaking in the first person, as he must to make his story credible, the narrator offers a cautionary tale about a doctor who exploits the privileges of his profession. The warning implied in the story of a doctor's exploitation of professional privilege is for patients to protect themselves. Thus, through his cautionary tale, the doctor-as-narrator does the opposite of the doctor-as-actor in the story: he performs a doctor's duty to his readers of preventing harm.

6   For readers who distinguish between the different layers of Williams's first-person narrator, the story is ultimately both a damning and a flattering depiction of the doctor figure. The doctor-as-actor in the story becomes a despicable specimen of professionalism corrupted, someone capable of brutality and rhetorical manipulation. Above him stands another—the doctor-as-narrator—who counteracts these crimes through his art. The way he tells the story conveys a powerful story and serious message.

> Why do you think Lee poses an implied question ("wonder why")? How do her answers ("I would argue") make her analysis deeper?

> Why do you think Lee provides so many transitions (highlighted in purple) here?

> What are the strengths of this ending? How could it be improved?

Work Cited

Williams, William Carlos. "The Use of Force." *The St. Martin's Guide to Writing*. Ed. Rise B. Axelrod and Charles R. Cooper. 11th ed. Boston: Bedford/St. Martin's, 2016. 482–84. Print.

To learn about how Isabella Wright used the activities in the Analyze the Story section (pp. 457–60), turn to A Writer at Work on pp. 472–74.

Isabella Wright | *"For Heaven's Sake!"*

USING THE WAYS IN ACTIVITIES in the Guide to Writing section Analyze the Story (pp. 457–60), Isabella Wright explored and wrote about how the doctor's thoughts and actions in "The Use of Force" might be justified. We have not annotated or highlighted this essay, but you may want to do so as you read and as you respond to the Analyze & Write questions in the sections that follow. As you read, notice how Wright's analysis differs from Lee's. Consider which essay you find more convincing and why.

1   By any reasonable standards, the story of a doctor prying a little girl's mouth open as she screams in pain and fear should leave readers feeling nothing but horror and disgust at the doctor's actions. William Carlos Williams's story "The Use of Force" is surprising in that it does not completely condemn the doctor for doing just that. Instead, through his actions and words (utterred or thought), readers are able to see the freeing, transformative power of breaking with social conventions. Thus, they are also encouraged to rethink what is acceptable and unacceptable in polite society.

2   Social conventions and proper conduct are prominent themes in Williams's story, in which the mother and father of the sick little girl are fixated on acting and speaking within the boundaries of politeness. The parents demonstrate this tendency most obviously in how they go out of their way to be respectful to the doctor. Upon his arrival at their home, the mother preemptively says that "[he] must excuse [them]" for bringing him into the kitchen, where they are keeping the child warm (482). There, the father makes an effort to "get up" to greet the doctor (482). The parents' efforts continue and take on even greater urgency when the child is uncooperative with the doctor as he tries to examine her throat. When she succeeds in knocking his glasses to the floor, her parents "almost [turn] themselves inside out in embarrassment and apology" (483). At certain moments, keeping up appearances seems to become disproportionately important, overshadowing their concern for their daughter's well-being. The mother's ultimate argument, meant to be stronger even than her threat to take the girl to the hospital, is to shame her daughter over her discourteous behavior. "Aren't you ashamed to act like that in front of the doctor?" she asks (483). The ending of her statement is key because it raises the question, would the daughter's misbehavior be shameful if no one outside of the family witnessed it? In other words, to what extent should concerns over appearances determine rightful and wrongful conduct?

3   In contrast to the little girl's parents, the doctor breaks social conventions in his interactions with the family and in doing so highlights the absurdity of these rules. From the beginning we see him as someone who pushes aside polite but pointless practices; for example, he "motion[s] for [the father] not to bother" standing for a greeting when it would have disturbed the child on his lap (482). The doctor's disregard for social conventions applies most to his tendency to give voice to thoughts rather than to keep them to himself for fear of sounding rude or causing discomfort. When the mother scolds her daughter for knocking the glasses off the "nice man" (483), the doctor's reaction borders on outright rudeness: "For heaven's sake, I broke in. Don't call me a nice man to her. I'm here to look at her throat on the chance that she might have diphtheria and possibly die of it" (483).

4   But is the doctor *really* giving voice to such reactions? The absence of quotation marks in the story leaves it uncertain which lines are and are not spoken aloud, creating a thought-provoking ambiguity. For example, does the doctor actually respond with "Oh yeah?" to the mother's threat to take the girl to the hospital, or does he care enough to keep such an irreverent reaction to himself (483)? In any case, readers are presented with the possibility of imagining that all the doctor's thoughts — no matter how offensive, belittling, or inappropriate — are expressed aloud. In fact, the very existence of the text and our reading of it give these thoughts expression, turning a stylistic choice into the ultimate statement on how social considerations limit our actions and expressions.

5   The doctor also breaks with social conventions by willingly engaging in a physical struggle with the little girl. This conflict might be interpreted as a process of reverse socialization or reverse civilization, a transformation that, surprisingly, the story presents as a potentially positive change. While the doctor stoops to the primitive tactics of the little girl, he does not view her in a negative light. To the contrary, from the beginning, he — and, through him, readers — sees the little girl as "unusually attractive" and "strong," with "magnificent blonde hair" (482). This description of her seems almost angelic. Through the doctor's conflict with her, his admiration grows. He comes to respect, even "love," the girl for her raw spirit that allows her to "[rise] to magnificent heights" in her struggle against him (483). Such worshipful language — note the repetition of the word "magnificent," for example — leads readers to understand the girl and her strength as something closer to glory and divinity than to savagery. The doctor's entering a similar state might thus be read as his reeducation

into a finer, truer self. Indeed, it is at these points in the story when he uses the most sophisticated language and the most involved metaphors. Thus, the story demonstrates, through the doctor's transformation, that the casting off of social conventions might lead not to a reduced state of humanity but to a purer, more admirable state of being.

6   In a story where politeness is made to seem absurd, the doctor's tactless words and his inappropriate use of force actually have the potential to be improvements on his character. By tossing aside social conventions, he brings himself closer to the glorious heights of the little girl, who, from the story's beginning, is magnificent and strong in her stubbornness. In the characters of the mother and father, readers come to understand also that politeness can stand in the way of accomplishing a task or communicating a clear meaning, and thus the doctor's actions are in the service of honesty and efficiency. Thus framed, the story leads readers to a point where they cannot fully condemn the doctor's outwardly abhorrent actions and instead must reconsider their own metric of what is and is not socially appropriate.

Work Cited

Williams, William Carlos. "The Use of Force." *The St. Martin's Guide to Writing.* Ed. Rise B. Axelrod and Charles R. Cooper. 11th ed. Boston: Bedford/St. Martin's, 2016. 482–84. Print.

[ANALYZE]   # Use the basic features.

A CLEAR, ARGUABLE THESIS: GETTING BENEATH THE SURFACE

Earlier, we discussed how the thesis of a literary analysis can contradict or complicate a surface reading of a work. After asserting her thesis about how "The Use of Force" helps readers see the "freeing, transformative power of breaking with social conventions," Wright supports her thesis with examples from the text and with her own analysis. Often, she returns to a key term from her thesis: "social conventions."

| ANALYZE & WRITE |──────────────────────────────

Write a paragraph or two about how well Wright gets below the surface in her reading of "The Use of Force."

1. Reread the thesis statement, and highlight the term "social conventions" whenever it appears later in the essay, paying attention to what Wright says about it in each instance.

2 Do you think Wright's thesis accurately forecasts the argument she develops in the rest of her essay? If not, what changes to the thesis might you suggest?

3 In her discussion of how the doctor breaks with social conventions, do you think Wright makes an adequate case for the "freeing, transformative power" of his thoughts and actions? Why or why not?

A WELL-SUPPORTED ARGUMENT: PAIRING TEXTUAL EVIDENCE WITH ANALYSIS

As we have noted, an essay about a short story relies primarily on textual evidence— gleaned from a close reading of the story—to support the argument. We have also discussed how simply quoting, summarizing, or paraphrasing passages from the text is not enough; instead, effective writing about a literary work must use such evidence in support of an analysis: the writer's original, thoughtful examination of the text. Earlier, we looked at Lee's analysis of militaristic diction in "The Use of Force," an analysis that drew on quotations from the story. Now let's turn to Wright's essay.

ANALYZE & WRITE

Write a paragraph or two about how well Wright uses textual evidence and analysis:

1 Focus on quotations, highlighting the one in the title as well as those in paragraphs 2–5. Consider how — and how well — these quotations support Wright's argument.

2 What improvements might you suggest to the choice of quotations? For example, in paragraph 5, Wright refers to the "most involved metaphors" of the story but does not quote any of them. Which metaphors, if any, might she have quoted? Or is summarizing these parts of the story sufficient to support her analysis?

3 What improvements might you suggest to Wright's analysis of textual evidence? For example, in paragraph 2, Wright discusses how the parents of the sick child go out of their way to be polite and respectful to the doctor. However, read paragraph 3 of the story (p. 482), and consider in what ways this part of the story might complicate Wright's analysis of the parents' behavior.

A CLEAR, LOGICAL ORGANIZATION: COORDINATING KEY WORDS AND TOPIC SENTENCES

As we have seen, writers try to help readers follow their argument by making their plan or organization clear to readers. For example, topic sentences that repeat key terms from the thesis statement help readers connect individual paragraphs to the larger argument the writer is making.

ANALYZE & WRITE

Write a paragraph or two about Wright's use of key words in topic sentences:

1 Underline the topic sentences of paragraphs 2, 3, and 5, and circle any key terms that are repeated in these sentences.

2 Pay special attention to the key terms, noting the way they are used in each topic sentence and built upon in the paragraph. Assess how well each topic sentence helps you follow the argument as it is developed in these paragraphs.

REMIX

Remixing Your
Literary
Analysis

Literary analyses may appear in genres and media besides the printed college essay. A literary analysis, for example, may be excerpted as an example in a writing project in another genre or it may be included as a whole as a review for a newspaper or magazine published in print or online. After turning in her literary analysis, Iris Lee decided to remix it as a review for her college newspaper, so more students at her school would be prompted to read the powerful short story "The Use of Force."

HOME   ABOUT ▾   MULTIMEDIA ▾   NEWS ▾   LIFESTYLE & CULTURE ▾

14
Apr 2015

***The Use of Force:* William Carlos Williams' Classic Parable of Blind Trust Is a Must-Read**

IRIS LEE

Though William Carlos Williams' short story *The Use of Force* was first published in 1938, the captivating and disturbing tale of medical malpractice still resonates with readers today. How far will a family go in trusting the care of their sick young daughter to a strange doctor, just because of the credibility his profession seems to afford him?

This story offers an important and somber warning, reminding us to be alert and to question the intentions of the authority figures around us. *...more*

In the next section of this chapter, we ask you to craft your own literary analysis. After composing it as an essay, consider remixing it by presenting it (or a portion of it) in another genre or medium, with another purpose, or for another audience.

CONSIDER YOUR RHETORICAL SITUATION

Purpose: The purpose of your literary analysis is to persuade your audience to accept your interpretation of the story. If you remix your essay, *which genre or medium would best allow you to persuade your readers to accept your take?*

Audience: The audience for your literary analysis was your instructor and, perhaps, other students in your class. If you remix your analysis, *what audience would be most interested in your subject and in your analysis of it?*

Genre and medium: The genre of your literary analysis was the essay; the medium was textual, delivered either in print or online. If you remix your literary analysis, *what genre and medium would best help you reach and persuade your target audience?*

The Writing Assignment

Write an essay analyzing one or more aspects of a story. Aim to convince readers that your analysis is interesting and contributes to the conversation about the story. Back up your ideas with supporting quotations and examples from the story.

This Guide to Writing is designed to help you write your own analysis of a story and apply what you have learned from reading other students' essays. This Starting Points chart will help you find answers to questions you might have about analyzing a story. Use the chart to find the guidance you need, when you need it.

STARTING POINTS: ANALYZING STORIES

How can I find a good story to write about?

- Find a story to write about. (p. 456)
- Analyze the story. (pp. 457–60)

A Clear, Arguable Thesis

How do I decide on a main idea and develop a thesis?

- Determine the writer's purpose and audience. (p. 442)
- Assess the genre's basic features: A clear, arguable thesis. (pp. 443–44)
- A Clear, Arguable Thesis: Getting Beneath the Surface (p. 452)
- Analyze the story. (pp. 457–60)
- Formulate a working thesis. (pp. 461–62)
- A Troubleshooting Guide: A Clear, Arguable Thesis (p. 468)

A Well-Supported Argument

How do I support my ideas?

- Assess the genre's basic features: A well-supported argument. (pp. 444–45)
- A Well-Supported Argument: Pairing Textual Evidence with Analysis (p. 453)
- Analyze the story. (pp. 457–60)
- Formulate a working thesis. (pp. 461–62)
- Provide support for your argument. (pp. 463–64)
- To build on your support, consider doing outside research. (p. 464)
- A Troubleshooting Guide: A Well-Supported Argument (p. 469)

(continued)

A Clear, Logical Organization

How should I organize my argument so that my audience can follow it easily?

- Assess the genre's basic features: A clear, logical organization. (pp. 445–46)
- A Clear, Logical Organization: Coordinating Key Words and Topic Sentences (p. 453)
- Create an outline that will organize your argument effectively. (pp. 464–65)
- Write the opening sentences. (p. 465)
- Draft your analysis. (p. 466)
- A Troubleshooting Guide: A Clear, Logical Organization (p. 469)

Writing a Draft: Invention, Research, Planning, and Composing

The activities in this section will help you find a story to write about, analyze it thoughtfully, and develop and organize an essay that argues for the position you are taking on the story. Your writing in response to many of these activities can be used in a rough draft that you will be able to improve after receiving feedback from your classmates and instructor. Do the activities in any order that makes sense to you (and your instructor), and return to them as needed as you revise.

Find a story to write about.

Your instructor may have given you a list of stories to choose from or assigned a particular story for the class to write about. If so, go on to the next section, Analyze the Story (pp. 457–60). If you need to find a story on your own, look for one that meets your instructor's approval and does one or more of the following:

- Deals with a culturally, politically, or historically significant theme
- Surprises or puzzles you with apparent contradictions
- Leads you to wonder what is left out of the story—the backstory or *context*
- Raises questions about characters' motivations, relationships, or development
- Uses conventional story motifs, setting, or other features in unconventional ways
- Resonates emotionally, perhaps giving you insight into human frailty or moral ambiguity

To find a story on your own, browse any literature anthology or short story collection in a library or bookstore, or try one of the following online sites:

- *American Literature* short story library (americanliterature.com)
- *Classic Short Stories* (classicshorts.com)
- *Classic Reader:* Short Stories (classicreader.com/browse/6)
- *Short Story Archive* (shortstoryarchive.com)

⠸ Analyze the story.

Use the following suggestions as a way into the story. Try out more than one to discover how different aspects of the story work together and to generate ideas for a thoughtful analysis. To read the story closely and critically, *annotate* it as you work through the suggestions, highlighting key passages and noting your ideas and questions.

For more on annotating, see Chapter 12.

WHAT ELEMENTS COULD I ANALYZE, AND WHY?	WHAT APPROACH MIGHT I TAKE?	WHAT SHOULD I ASK MYSELF?
Character You want to know ■ why a character acts in a particular way ■ how gender or ethnicity affects relationships ■ whether a character changes or grows ■ whether we should approve of a character's actions or accept his or her justifications	Psychological	■ Does the character change/learn anything in the course of the story? ■ How does the character relate to other characters? For instance, how does he or she deal with intimacy, commitment, and responsibility? ■ Does the character seem depressed, manic, abusive, fearful, egotistical, or paranoid? ■ Does any other character seem to represent the character's double or opposite?
	Ethical or moral	■ What are the character's virtues and/or vices? ■ What influences your judgment of the character? Something in the story (such as what the narrator or another character says)? Something you bring to the story (your views of right and wrong, based on your family upbringing or religious teachings)? Something else? ■ Do any of the other characters have different moral values that could be compared or contrasted to the character's values?
	Social or cultural	■ How does the character fit into and appear to be defined by society in terms of race, ethnicity, socioeconomic class, sexual orientation, age, or gender?

WAYS IN

(continued)

		▪ Who in the story exercises power over whom? What causes the difference in power? What are the effects of this difference? Does the balance of power change during the story?
Setting You want to know ▪ how much time and place matter ▪ what the description of the setting symbolizes ▪ how the setting affects characters	In relation to the mood, characters, or actions	▪ How does the setting affect the mood? For example, does it create feelings of suspense or foreboding? ▪ Are there any cause-effect connections between the setting and what characters are doing, thinking, or feeling?
	Historical or cultural	▪ How does the historical period or cultural context in which the story is set affect what happens and does not happen? ▪ How might the story's meaning be different if the historical time or cultural situation were changed?
	Metaphoric or symbolic	▪ Assuming that the setting is a projection of the thoughts and feelings of the narrator, what does the setting tell you about the narrator's state of mind? ▪ Assuming that the setting symbolizes the social relations among characters in the story, what does the setting tell you about these relationships? ▪ Assuming that the setting stands for something outside the characters' control (such as nature, God, or some aspect of society), what does the setting tell you about the pressures and rules under which the characters function?
Plot Structure You want to know ▪ what the ending means ▪ whether there is a turning point in the story	As realistic (resembling real-life experience)	▪ After marking where each new stage of the story begins, how can the sequence of scenes or events be understood? In what ways do subplots mirror, undercut, or comment on the main plot?

Writing a Draft

GUIDE TO READING
GUIDE TO WRITING
A WRITER AT WORK
THINKING CRITICALLY

459

▪ how a subplot relates to the main plot	As surrealistic (having symbolic rather than literal meaning)	▪ Thinking of the story as a series of images (more like a collage or a dream than a realistic portrayal of actual events), what meanings do you find in the arrangement of these images?
Point of View You want to know ▪ whether the narrator can be believed ▪ whose values and interests are represented ▪ how readers' sympathies are manipulated	In terms of what the narrator actually sees	▪ Is the narrator a character in the story or an all-knowing, disembodied voice who knows what every character thinks, feels, and does? ▪ What important insights or ideas does the narrator have? ▪ How do factors such as the narrator's gender, age, and ethnicity influence what he or she notices as important? ▪ Are there things that the narrator is not able to see or that he or she distorts—for example, certain truths about himself or herself, about other characters, or about what happens in the story?
	In terms of how the narrator represents what he or she sees	▪ How would you characterize the narrator's tone at various points in the story? For example, is the tone satirical, celebratory, angry, bitter, or optimistic? ▪ What about the narrator (or about the situation) might account for each tone you identify? ▪ What special agenda or motive might have led the narrator to this particular way of describing characters and scenes or telling the story?
Literary Motif or Theme You want to know ▪ whether the story is about a break with social conventions, the initiation into adulthood, or some other common literary motif	In terms of a traditional story motif (or an ironic reversal of the tradition)	▪ Could you analyze the text as . . . an initiation (or coming-of-age or rite-of-passage) story? . . . a quest (for love, truth, fame, fortune, or salvation of oneself or the community)? . . . a story about a character's disillusionment or fall from innocence?

(continued)

■ what the story says about war, poverty, love, alienation, or some other general theme ■ how the story illuminates a historical or current issue	In terms of a common literary theme	. . . a story about family or surrogate families? . . . a story about storytelling (or some other art) or becoming a writer or an artist? ■ Might you focus on the theme of . . . the American dream? . . . the social construction of femininity or masculinity? . . . race relations in America? . . . alienation? . . . the urban or suburban experience?

In addition to generating ideas by taking one of the approaches listed above, you can consider the details and use those to generate an approach. Or you can list ideas you had while reading the story and use those to locate supporting details. The Ways In box that follows can help you generate ideas using these two approaches.

WAYS IN

HOW CAN I GENERATE IDEAS BY MOVING FROM SPECIFIC DETAILS TO GENERAL IDEAS?

1. Select two or three quotations, and write several sentences answering this question: What idea or ideas does each quotation suggest, and what in the quotation makes you think so?

2. Write a paragraph analyzing one or more patterns you found in the story. Here are a few patterns to help you get started:

   • Imagery (for example, the militaristic images in "The Use of Force" that Lee analyzes)

   • Characters as contrasts (for example, differences between the parents and the doctor in "The Use of Force" that Wright discusses)

   • Events that echo or reverse one another (for example, the doctor's fury echoes the young girl's)

HOW CAN I GENERATE IDEAS BY MOVING FROM GENERAL IDEAS TO SPECIFIC DETAILS?

1. List ideas you thought of as you analyzed the story, without worrying about how these ideas relate to one another or whether they are contradictory. For example, here are two of Isabella Wright's ideas about the doctor in "The Use of Force" (see A Writer at Work, pp. 472–74).

   He has no time for the social conventions upheld by the parents.

   His break with social conventions feels freeing—maybe even transformative.

2. Review the story to find quotations or other details you could use to illustrate your ideas.

3. Write for a few minutes about your most interesting ideas and how they connect. For example, in exploring her ideas about "The Use of Force," Wright connected ideas about breaking social conventions to develop her main claim about the transformative power of disobeying the rules of social behavior.

Writing a Draft

GUIDE TO READING
▶ **GUIDE TO WRITING**
A WRITER AT WORK
THINKING CRITICALLY

461

TEST YOUR CHOICE

Choosing a Topic

Get together with two or three other students who have read your story, and offer responses to one another's ideas.

Presenters. Take turns telling one another your two or three most promising ideas, giving an example from the story to support each idea.

Listeners. Briefly respond to each presenter's ideas, identifying what you find interesting in them, what you agree or disagree with, and how the ideas could be extended or complicated productively.

∷ Formulate a working thesis.

Remember that an arguable thesis is not a simple statement of fact or an obvious conclusion. To get a sense of how you might formulate an arguable thesis, take a look at the thesis statements from the student essays you've studied in this chapter.

> As an account of a professional doing harm under the pretense of healing, the story uncovers how a doctor can take advantage of the intimate nature of his work and his professional status to overstep common forms of conduct, to the extent that his actions actually hurt rather than help a patient. In this way, the doctor-narrator actually performs a valuable service by warning readers, indirectly through his story, that blindly trusting members of his profession can have negative consequences. (Lee, par. 1)

> Through [the doctor's] actions and words (uttered or thought), readers are able to see the freeing, transformative power of breaking with social conventions. Thus, they are also encouraged to rethink what is acceptable and unacceptable in polite society. (Wright, par. 1)

You may have already decided on the main claim you want to make in your short story analysis; if so, try drafting a working thesis statement now. The Ways In activities that follow may help. (Alternatively, if you prefer to develop your analysis before trying to formulate a thesis, skip this activity and return to it when you're ready.)

HOW CAN I FORMULATE AN ARGUABLE THESIS?

Write for ten minutes about your most promising ideas. After writing, read what you have written and see if you can find one main idea or claim that can serve as the thesis for your essay. Focus your exploratory writing on questions like these:

- How can readers understand a character's internal conflict or apparent change?
- How is the story's theme reflected in the way the story is told, the way the setting is described, how characters relate to one another, or some other aspect of the story?

WAYS IN

(continued)

- How does the language used to describe the setting or the characters' actions illuminate such things as the main character's internal conflict, the relationship between characters, or the theme? (For example, the doctor-patient struggle described in "The Use of Force" forms the basis of Iris Lee's argument that the story warns readers against blindly trusting doctors.)

- What does the trajectory of the story (the plot structure) say about the characters or the culture? (For example, Isabella Wright's analysis of the increasing tension between repression and expression, social conventions and human willfulness, underlies her argument about the value of breaking with these conventions.)

Reread the story with one of the following questions (or a question of your own) in mind, underlining passages or taking notes as you read:

- How do my ideas about the story form links in a chain leading to some general conclusion? For example, Wright links two ideas: (1) pressure to adhere to social conventions and (2) reasons for breaking with these conventions. She is *not* simply retelling the story; she is stating her ideas about what happens in the story.

- How can I present my ideas as a response to a question — either a question my instructor asked or one I composed myself? For example, in their essays, Lee and Wright responded to the first question we pose in the Analyze & Write section for "The Use of Force" (p. 484).

- What, if anything, does the story say about what may be universally true about people and society versus what may result from specific historical, economic, or cultural conditions? About what is usually considered normal versus what is considered abnormal? About how some groups exert power while others may be oppressed or subversive?

Now reread your notes. Do they suggest one MAIN IDEA or CLAIM that can serve as the thesis for your essay?

Use the sentence strategies that follow as a jumping-off point; put your thesis into your own words when you revise, or use your own words and sentence patterns now:

▶ Many readers of X point to .... [state feature(s) of the story], but an important aspect of the story that is often overlooked is ....

▶ A common/superficial reading of X [name story or character] is that .... [common conclusion], but in fact .... [your own conclusion].

▶ Through the actions of X [name character], we are led to this surprising conclusion: ....

▶ Through the events unfolded in X [name story], readers are led to this disturbing conclusion: ....

Writing a Draft

GUIDE TO READING
▶ **GUIDE TO WRITING**
A WRITER AT WORK
THINKING CRITICALLY

463

⫶ Provide support for your argument.

Look back on the ideas that you have generated so far, and ask yourself these questions:

- How can I present my ideas as reasons supporting my central claim, the essay's thesis? For example, Isabella Wright shaped the ideas she generated moving from general ideas to specific details (pp. 472–73) into reasons supporting her thesis about the value of breaking with social conventions.

- Have I remembered to include my own analysis in the support instead of just retelling the story through quotation, paraphrase, or summary? (If you are unsure, work through the Ways In activities that follow.)

HOW CAN I INTEGRATE EVIDENCE FROM THE STORY?

WAYS IN

As noted earlier, to provide support for a short story analysis, writers may QUOTE, PARAPHRASE, or SUMMARIZE parts of the story. However, this evidence should be offered in the service of a thoughtful examination of the story and go beyond a simple repetition of description, dialogue, and so on. To effectively integrate material from a story, try these strategies:

- **Use short quotations frequently to support your** ANALYSIS. Brief quotations are not in themselves superior to sentence-length and longer quotations, but they allow you to stay focused on your own argument while bringing in key information or vivid details from the story. Look at these examples from the student essays in this chapter:

  > To the contrary, from the beginning, he—and, through him, readers—sees the little girl as "unusually attractive" and "strong," with "magnificent blonde hair" (482). This description of her seems almost angelic. (Wright, par. 5)

  > Later, the mother reassures the child that the doctor is a "nice man" and "won't hurt you," though she can base those assertions only on what little she knows of him: his occupation (483). (Lee, par. 2)

- **Comment directly on what you have** QUOTED, PARAPHRASED, **or** SUMMARIZED **so that readers will understand the relevance of this material to your** ANALYSIS. These comments should connect the quotation, paraphrase, or summary to the idea you are trying to support. One good strategy is to refer to quotations or paraphrases with *this, these,* or *they* statements, which are highlighted in the following examples:

  > After quoting the doctor's violent thoughts about the girl, Lee comments, "Although these statements are arguably exaggerated or hyperbolic, they, like the metaphors of war, imply a tendency to do harm that goes directly against the narrator's duty as a doctor" (Lee, par. 4).

  > After summarizing the doctor's struggle with the girl, Wright notes, "This conflict might be interpreted as a process of reverse socialization or reverse civilization, a transformation that, surprisingly, the story presents as a potentially positive change" (Wright, par. 5).

(continued)

Another good strategy is to repeat key nouns from quotations, paraphrases, or summaries in your analysis. These nouns are highlighted in the following examples:

> After quoting part of the story that refers to the doctor smiling in his "best professional manner," Lee explains that, in using the "phrase 'professional manner,'" the narrator admits his actions are not sincere but a calculated "professional performance" (Lee, par. 3).

> After quoting and paraphrasing information about the parents' politeness to the doctor, Wright observes, "In a story where politeness is made to seem absurd, the doctor's tactless words and his inappropriate use of force actually have the potential to be improvements on his character" (Wright, par. 6).

To build on your support, consider doing outside research.

Many analyses of short stories rely on a close reading of the text alone; the writer's analysis is the only tool brought to bear on the work. Some approaches to analysis, however, also consider biographical information on the author, his or her other works, or various critical responses to the short story in question. If your instructor has asked you to include such information, or if you are curious about some aspect of the text that you do not understand—or that you suspect your readers will not understand—you might want to conduct some research and include your findings in your essay. Here are a few suggestions for getting started:

- Do a *Google* search, using keywords relevant to your analysis. For example, if you want more information about the context of "The Use of Force," you could try key words such as *diphtheria epidemic*.

- To see what others have said about an author's work, conduct a search using a specialized periodical database, such as the *MLA International Bibliography*, which specializes in academic writing about languages and literature. You should have access to periodical databases through your school's library. If you are not sure how to use them, see Chapter 21. Ask a reference librarian for help if you encounter problems.

As you work, bookmark or keep a record of promising sites. If you download or copy information you could use in your essay, remember to record source information.

Create an outline that will organize your argument effectively.

Whether you have rough notes or a complete draft, making an outline of what you have written can help you organize the essay effectively for your audience. One way to outline a literary analysis is to lay out your argument as a series of *because* sentences. For example, here's how Iris Lee might have outlined her argument:

Writing a Draft

GUIDE TO READING
GUIDE TO WRITING
A WRITER AT WORK
THINKING CRITICALLY

465

I. The story performs a valuable service because, through the doctor's actions, readers see that it's unwise to trust members of his profession blindly.

    A. Although he displays his "best professional manner," the doctor does so only because he knows it will encourage the family's deference to him despite his rude and rough behavior.

    B. The doctor shows his untrustworthiness because he seems more interested in harming the girl than healing her.

II. Readers who see the doctor purely as a bad person are wrong because the author presents two sides of him.

    A. The doctor-as-actor deserves our scorn because he is capable of brutality under the guise of professionalism.

    B. The doctor-as-narrator deserves our thanks because he depicts the crimes of the doctor-as-actor, warning readers about the dangers of placing too much trust in medical professionals.

Once you have a working outline, you should not hesitate to change it as necessary while drafting and revising. For instance, you might find you left out an important idea that is needed to make the chain of reasoning complete. Remember that the purpose of an outline is to help you organize your ideas logically, not to lock you into a particular structure.

Write the opening sentences.

The section "Formulate a working thesis" (pp. 461–62) and the Ways In activities there suggest several ways to present an arguable thesis. In writing your introduction, avoid creating a "funnel paragraph," which begins with a broad generalization and then becomes more and more focused and narrow, culminating in what is usually the essay's thesis. The problem with this kind of paragraph structure is that broad generalizations are not very interesting and add nothing to the essay. Look, for example, at the italicized sentences in this modified version of Isabella Wright's opening paragraph:

> *As all of us know, being the subject of a medical examination, especially if you are a child, is rarely fun. Patients can be nervous and uncooperative, and in the worst cases, doctors can act like real jerks.* William Carlos Williams's story "The Use of Force" is surprising in that it does not completely condemn the doctor for doing just that.

It is best to get rid of sentences like these and simply begin by presenting your ideas about the story.

Draft your analysis.

By this point, you have done a lot of writing to

- come up with ideas for your short story analysis;
- draft an arguable thesis;
- provide support for your argument;
- organize your ideas to present them logically to readers.

Now stitch that material together to create a draft. As you write, ask yourself questions like the following:

- Early in my essay, should I name the story and also identify the author?
- How much do I need to tell my readers about what happens in the story? Should I assume, as both Iris Lee and Isabella Wright do, that my readers have read the story?
- Should I consider placing the story in the context of the author's other writing or in its historical context?
- How can I revise my topic sentences to use the key terms introduced in my thesis? What synonyms could I use to avoid repeating my key terms too often?
- How can I use logical transitions to help readers see how one point connects to the next? For example, could I use transitions that announce contrasts, such as *but, although,* and *yet*?
- Should I consider ending with a new idea that grows out of my argument? Could I, for example, expand on the cultural or historical implications of my reading of the story?

Evaluating the Draft: Using Peer Review

Your instructor may arrange a peer review session in class or online, where you can exchange drafts with your classmates and give each other a thoughtful critical reading, pointing out what works well and suggesting ways to improve the draft. A good critical reading of a literary analysis does three things:

1. It lets the writer know how well the point of his or her analysis comes across to readers.
2. It praises what works best.
3. It indicates where the draft could be improved and makes suggestions on how to improve it.

One strategy for evaluating a draft is to use the basic features of a literary analysis as a guide.

Evaluating the Draft

GUIDE TO READING
GUIDE TO WRITING
A WRITER AT WORK
THINKING CRITICALLY

467

A PEER REVIEW GUIDE

A Clear, Arguable Thesis

How well does the writer present the thesis?

Summarize: Tell the writer what you understand the essay's thesis to be and what its key terms are.

Praise: Tell the writer what seems most interesting to you about his or her main claim about the story, whether you agree with it or not.

Critique: If you cannot find the thesis statement or cannot identify the key terms, let the writer know. Evaluate the thesis statement on the basis of whether

- it makes an interesting and arguable assertion (rather than making a statement of fact or an obvious point)
- it is clear and precise (neither ambiguous nor vague)
- it is appropriately qualified (neither overgeneralized nor exaggerated)

A Well-Supported Argument

How well does the writer develop and support the argument?

Summarize: Underline the thesis statement and the major support for it. (Often, the major support appears in the topic sentences of paragraphs.)

Praise: Give an example in the essay where support for a reason is presented especially effectively — for instance, note where brief quotations (words and short phrases), a longer quotation, or summaries of particular events are introduced and explained in a way that clearly illustrates a particular point that is being argued.

Critique: Tell the writer where the connection between a reason and its support seems vague, where too much plot is being relayed with no apparent point, or where a quotation is left to speak for itself without explanation. Let the writer know if any part of the argument seems to be undeveloped or does not support the thesis.

A Clear, Logical Organization

Has the writer clearly and logically organized the argument?

Summarize: Underline the sentence(s) in which the writer forecasts supporting reasons, and circle transitions or repeated key words and phrases.

Praise: Give an example of something that makes the essay especially easy to read — where, for example, the key terms introduced in the thesis recur throughout the essay in topic sentences and elsewhere, or where transitions are used logically.

Critique: Tell the writer where readability could be improved. For example, point to places where key terms could be added or where a topic sentence could be made clearer, indicate where the use of transitions might be improved, or note where transitions are lacking and could be added.

Before concluding your peer review, be sure to address any of the writer's concerns that have not been discussed already.

Making Comments Electronically   Most word processing software offers features that allow you to insert comments directly into the text of someone else's document. Many readers prefer to make their comments this way because it tends to be faster than writing on hard copy and space is virtually unlimited; it also eliminates the process of deciphering handwritten comments. Where such features are not available, simply typing comments directly into a document in a contrasting color can provide the same advantages.

Improving the Draft: Revising, Editing, and Proofreading

Start improving your draft by reflecting on what you have written thus far:

- Review critical reading comments from your classmates, instructor, or writing center tutor: What are your readers getting at?
- Consider your invention writing: What else should you consider?
- Review your draft: What can you do to present your argument more compellingly?

Revise your draft.

If your readers are having difficulty with your draft, or if you think there is room for improvement, try some of the strategies listed in the Troubleshooting Guide that follows. It can help you fine-tune your presentation of the genre's basic features.

A TROUBLESHOOTING GUIDE

A Clear, Arguable Thesis

My thesis is unclear or overgeneralized.

- Add more explanation.
- Refer to the story specifically.
- Add qualifying words like *some* or *usually*.

My thesis is not arguable or interesting.

- Respond to a question or class discussion.
- Summarize an alternative argument.
- Try additional suggestions for analysis from the Ways In boxes on pp. 457–60.

Improving the Draft

GUIDE TO READING
GUIDE TO WRITING
A WRITER AT WORK
THINKING CRITICALLY

469

A Well-Supported Argument

My argument seems superficial or thin.

- Develop your ideas by connecting them.
- Link your ideas to make a chain of reasoning.
- Connect to a literary motif or theme.
- Add textual evidence by quoting, paraphrasing, or summarizing important passages.
- Focus on the writer's choice of words, explaining how particular word choices support your ideas.
- Consider using other kinds of support, such as information about the story's historical or cultural context.

The connection between a reason and its support seems vague.

- Explain why the support illustrates the point you are making.
- Explain what the quoted words imply — their connotative (cultural or emotional) associations as well as their denotative (literal or dictionary) meanings.
- Introduce quotations, and follow them with some analysis or explanation.
- Explain more fully and clearly how your reasons relate logically to one another as well as to your thesis.
- Fill in the gaps.
- Use contradictions or gaps to extend or complicate your argument.

A Clear, Logical Organization

My essay is hard to follow.

- Repeat key terms from the thesis and other introductory text.
- Provide explicit topic sentences.
- Add logical transitions.

Edit and proofread your draft.

Our research has identified several errors that occur often in essays that analyze short stories, including problems with parallelism and the use of ellipsis marks. The following guidelines will help you check your essay for these common errors.

Using Parallel Structure

The Problem   When you present items as a pair or in a series (for example, *I gave him x and y;* or *I gave him x, y, and z*), you must present the items in the series in the same grammatical form—all nouns, all prepositional phrases, all adverb clauses, and so on. Mixing and matching leads to lack of clarity and lessens the impact of your prose. Take as an example one of Iris Lee's first-draft sentences:

The doctor's actions actually hurt rather than providing any benefit to the patient.

A Note on Grammar and Spelling Checkers

These tools can be helpful, but do not rely on them exclusively to catch errors in your text: Spelling checkers cannot catch misspellings that are themselves words, such as *to* for *too*. Grammar checkers miss some problems, sometimes give faulty advice for fixing problems, and can flag correct items as wrong. Use these tools as a second line of defense after your own (and, ideally, another reader's) proofreading and editing efforts.

"Hurt" is a one-word verb; "providing any benefit to," which should be a parallel item, combines an *-ing* verb, an adjective, an object, and a preposition. The resulting sentence is unnecessarily complicated and clumsy.

The Correction   Lee eventually edited the sentence as follows:

> ▶ The doctor's actions actually hurt rather than ~~providing any benefit~~ *help* to a patient.

The parallelism of *hurt* and *help* puts the verbs in the same form and emphasizes the contrast between these two actions in a way that the first-draft wording did not. For more examples, see the following sentences:

> ▶ This image comes more from ~~his reading~~ *what he's read* than from anything he's observed.

> ▶ To Kafka, loneliness, ~~being isolated~~ *isolation*, and regrets are the price of freedom.

> ▶ Sarah really cares about her brother and to ~~maintain~~ *values* their relationship. She lets us know that she was injured by her mother's abuse but avoids saying what she felt after the incident, how others reacted to the incident, and ~~that~~ *what* physical pain she endured.

Using Ellipsis Marks Correctly

You will often quote sources when you analyze a story, and you must be careful to use **ellipsis marks** (or **ellipses**)—three spaced periods—to indicate places where you delete material from a quotation. Look, for example, at how Iris Lee, in an early draft of her essay, used ellipsis marks in quoting from "The Use of Force."

Passage from Story	**Quotation with Ellipsis Marks**
When finally I got the wooden spatula behind the last teeth and just the point of it into the mouth cavity, she opened up for an instant but before I could see anything she came down again and gripping the wooden blade between her molars she reduced it to splinters before I could get it out again. (Williams, par. 29)	In describing his attempts to get the wooden spatula into the girl's mouth, the narrator says "she opened up for an instant but . . . came down again and gripping the wooden blade between her molars reduced it to splinters . . ."

The Problem   Failing to use ellipsis marks to indicate the omission of material misrepresents the quote, which is a serious breach of convention. Using ellipsis marks incorrectly makes your readers doubt your knowledge of conventions.

Improving the Draft

GUIDE TO READING
▶ **GUIDE TO WRITING**
A WRITER AT WORK
THINKING CRITICALLY

471

The Correction   If you are using MLA style, follow these rules about using ellipsis marks:

- When you delete words from the *middle of a quoted sentence,* add ellipsis marks, and leave a single space before and after each ellipsis point.
- When you delete words from the *end of a quoted sentence* and a grammatically complete sentence remains, add a period after the last word and then three ellipsis marks.
- Leave a single space after the period and each of the first two ellipsis marks. Do not leave a space between the last mark and the closing quotation mark.
- When you delete material from the middle of a passage of *two or more sentences,* use ellipsis marks where the text is omitted and a period after the preceding text if it is a grammatically complete sentence.
- When you delete words from the *beginning of a quoted sentence,* use ellipsis marks only if the remainder of the sentence begins with a capitalized word and is a grammatically complete sentence.
- Single words and brief phrases can be quoted without ellipsis marks.

Examples of sentences edited to show correct usage follow:

For more on using ellipsis marks to indicate a deletion from a quotation, see Chapter 23.

▶ The narrator describes his patient as "She did not move and seemed, inwardly,

quiet; an unusually attractive little thing, and as strong as a heifer in appearance.

But her face was flushed, she was breathing rapidly, and I realized that she had a

high fever. She had magnificent blonde hair, in profusion."

▶ According to the narrator, the little girl's mother was "a big startled-looking

woman, very clean and apologetic, who merely said, Is this the doctor? and let me in."

Isabella Wright's Invention Work

In this section, you will see some of the work that Isabella Wright did in developing her essay analyzing the story "The Use of Force." Using the Guide to Writing in this book, Wright chose the suggestions for interpreting character to guide her analysis of the story. As you will see,

- she annotated a portion of the story focusing on the doctor's first attempts to examine the young patient's throat;
- she wrote to explore her annotations on the passages;
- she listed ideas for formulating her tentative thesis statement.

You will be able to infer from her invention work how her ideas came to form the thesis she developed for her final essay.

Annotating

Wright annotated paragraphs 12–22 of "The Use of Force" as she reread them with the suggestions for analyzing character in mind. The annotated passages are reproduced here. Notice the diversity of her annotations:

- In the text itself, she underlined key words and circled words to be defined.
- In the margin, she defined words, made comments, and posed questions. She also expressed her tentative insights, reactions, and judgments.

smile really sincere? 12   Well, I said, suppose we take a look at the throat first. I <u>smiled</u> in my best professional manner and asking for the child's first name I said, come on, Mathilda, open your mouth and let's take a look at your throat.

13   Nothing doing.

14   Aw, come on, I coaxed, just open your mouth wide and let me take a look. <u>Look, I said opening both hands wide, I haven't anything in my hands. Just open up and let me see.</u>

he's trying to come across as unthreatening

mother's politeness continues 15   Such a <u>nice man</u>, put in the mother. Look how kind he is to you. Come on, do what he tells you to. He won't hurt you.

16   At that I ground my teeth in <u>disgust</u>. If only they wouldn't use the word "hurt" I might be able to get somewhere. But I did not allow myself to be hurried or disturbed but speaking quietly and slowly I approached the child again.

not willing to promise he won't hurt girl

unlike parents, child showing her true self 17   As I moved my chair a little nearer suddenly with one catlike movement both her hands clawed instinctively for my eyes and she almost reached them too. In fact she knocked my glasses flying

Isabella Wright's Invention Work

GUIDE TO READING
GUIDE TO WRITING
▶ A WRITER AT WORK
THINKING CRITICALLY

473

and they fell, though unbroken, several feet away from me on the kitchen floor.

18   Both the mother and father almost turned themselves inside out in embarrassment and apology. You bad girl, said the mother, taking her and shaking her by one arm. Look what you've done. The nice man . . .

parents very embarrassed— concerned with social conventions

19   For heaven's sake, I broke in. Don't call me a nice man to her. I'm here to look at her throat on the chance that she might have (diphtheria) and possibly die of it. But that's nothing to her. Look here, I said to the child, we're going to look at your throat. You're old enough to understand what I'm saying. Will you open it now by yourself or shall we have to open it for you?

possibly deadly infection

he's losing his patience

Rude. Is he really saying this? No quotation marks

20   Not a move. Even her expression hadn't changed. Her breaths however were coming faster and faster. Then the battle began. I had to do it. I had to have a throat culture for her own protection. But first I told the parents that it was entirely up to them. I explained the danger but said that I would not insist on a throat examination so long as they would take the responsibility.

battle of the wills as much as a physical battle?

"her own protection"— he's trying to justify his actions

21   If you don't do what the doctor says you'll have to go to the hospital, the mother admonished her severely.

22   Oh yeah? I had to smile to myself. After all, I had already fallen in love with the savage brat, the parents were contemptible to me. In the ensuing struggle they grew more and more (abject,) crushed, exhausted while she surely rose to magnificent heights of insane fury of effort bred of her terror of me.

hopeless

Now here's a sincere smile!

struggle has transformed him— and his view of her?

As you can see, annotating this section of the story with the suggestions for analyzing character in mind led Wright to notice how much the doctor's direct, and sometimes rude, manner is butting up against the parents' politeness and embarrassment over their child's behavior.

Examining Patterns in the Story

Following the instructions for generating ideas by moving from details to general ideas (p. 460), Wright explored a pattern of contrast she saw between the doctor and the parents in the story. Here is what she wrote:

From the start of this scene, it feels like the whole experience between the doctor and the family is going to go from bad to worse. The doctor's smile feels forced, almost as if he's warning the little girl that she's in for an unpleasant time. The parents' attempts to smooth things over do nothing but irritate him, and he's actually angered by being referred to as a "nice man." It's as if he has no time for the social conventions so important to the parents; these rules mean nothing to him, much less to the girl. In some ways, the doctor and the girl seem more alike than the doctor and the parents because he and the girl are showing their true selves. For that reason, maybe he even respects her more than he does the parents. The longer the two of them struggle, the more he seems to admire her. From the parents' and the girl's point of view, the experience is pretty clearly a bad one, but perhaps there's something freeing about it from the doctor's perspective.

As Wright wrote about the contrasts between the characters, she became increasingly confident that she not only had an interesting idea but also had one she could find support for in the story.

Listing Ideas

Wright tried out the activity on listing ideas from the Ways In feature on p. 460. In doing so, she drew on both her annotations and on the exploratory writing she did about the doctor and the family (above):

> The doctor comes across in a bad light: He's rude and impatient and able to justify the use of force against the girl.
> He has no time for the social conventions upheld by the parents.
> He's more annoyed than flattered by the mother's compliments and attempts to smooth things over.
> In this way, maybe he is more like the little girl than the parents.
> They both seem to be showing their true selves.
> In the end, it's hard to condemn the doctor.
> His break with social conventions feels freeing—maybe even transformative.

From these ideas about the doctor's behavior and how his views about social conventions differ from those of the parents, Wright was able to devise the thesis statement she eventually used in her essay.

To think critically means to use all of the knowledge you have acquired from the information in this chapter, your own writing, the writing of other students, and class discussions to reflect deeply on your work for this assignment and the genre (or type) of writing you have produced. The benefit of thinking critically is proven and important: Thinking critically about what you have learned will help you remember it longer, ensuring that you will be able to put it to good use well beyond this writing course.

Reflecting on What You Have Learned

In this chapter, you have learned a great deal about arguing for your analysis of a short story by reading two essays in this genre and by writing one of your own. To consolidate your learning, reflect not only on what you learned but also on how you learned it.

ANALYZE & WRITE

Write a blog post to classmates, a letter to your instructor, or an e-mail message to a student who will take this course next term, using the writing prompt that seems most productive for you:

- Explain how your purpose and audience influenced *one* of your decisions as a writer, such as how you chose the suggestions for analysis you used, the key words you used in presenting your thesis, or the quotations you chose to support your argument.

- Discuss what you learned about yourself as a writer in the process of writing this essay. For example, what part of the process did you find most challenging? Did you try anything new, like getting a critical reading of your draft or summarizing an alternative argument to improve your thesis? If so, would you do it again?

- Choose one of the readings in this chapter, and explain how it influenced your essay. Be sure to cite specific examples from your essay and the reading.

- If you got good advice from a critical reader, explain exactly how the person helped you—perhaps by questioning the way you stated your thesis or how you explained one of your reasons.

Reflecting on the Genre

Some genres, like position papers, have a broad general audience, composed of people whose knowledge of current controversial issues varies widely. Other genres, like essays analyzing stories, are highly specialized, read and written by a comparatively small group of people who share certain kinds of knowledge and interests.

Students in English courses learn certain ways of reading and writing about stories, and they also discover what kinds of analyses are likely to interest their readers—people engaged in an ongoing conversation about stories and other works of literature. They need to know some of the specialized vocabulary used in writing about literature, such as *point of view,* as well as the critical approaches to analyzing stories they find useful. English instructors determine which approaches their students need to become familiar with, and they introduce these subjects in lectures and class discussions. They choose stories to read and assign essays to write that will give students opportunities to use these approaches.

ANALYZE & WRITE

Write a page or two about your experience analyzing literature in this course and, if relevant, in other English classes. Connect your ideas to your experience with writing a short story analysis and to the readings in this chapter. In your discussion, you might consider one or more of the following questions:

1 **List some of the subjects you and your classmates discussed in class and wrote about.** Where did these subjects come from — class discussion, this chapter, your instructor's questions or lectures, other English classes?

2 **Consider whether any subjects were deemed by your instructor or other students to be uninteresting or not appropriate for analyzing stories.** Why were these subjects rejected? Do you agree with their exclusion?

3 **Did you become part of the conversation about the literature you studied?** If so, what made you feel most connected to the stories (or other works) you read and the discussions about them? If not, can you name anything in particular that made you feel left out?

AN ANTHOLOGY OF SHORT STORIES

In this section, you will find four short stories: "The Story of an Hour," by Kate Chopin; "Araby," by James Joyce; "The Use of Force," by William Carlos Williams; and "Girl" by Jamaica Kincaid. Each is followed by questions to help you get started analyzing the story. Your instructor may ask you to choose one of these stories for your essay analyzing a story.

Kate Chopin | *The Story of an Hour*

The Granger Collection, New York

KATE CHOPIN (1851–1904) was born in St. Louis and lived in Louisiana until her husband died in 1882, leaving her with six children. Encouraged by friends, Chopin wrote her first novel, *At Fault* (1890), when she was nearly forty years old. She wrote many short stories for such popular magazines as *Century, Harper's,* and *Vogue,* in which "The Story of an Hour" first appeared in 1894. She published two collections of stories and a second novel, her best-known work, *The Awakening* (1899).

1 Knowing that Mrs. Mallard was afflicted with a heart trouble, great care was taken to break to her as gently as possible the news of her husband's death.

2 It was her sister Josephine who told her, in broken sentences; veiled hints that revealed in half concealing. Her husband's friend Richards was there, too, near her. It was he who had been in the newspaper office when intelligence of the railroad disaster was received, with Brently Mallard's name leading the list of "killed." He had only taken the time to assure himself of its truth by a second telegram, and had hastened to forestall any less careful, less tender friend in bearing the sad message.

3 She did not hear the story as many women have heard the same, with a paralyzed inability to accept its significance. She wept at once, with sudden, wild abandonment, in her sister's arms. When the storm of grief had spent itself she went away to her room alone. She would have no one follow her.

4 There stood, facing the open window, a comfortable, roomy armchair. Into this she sank, pressed down by a physical exhaustion that haunted her body and seemed to reach into her soul.

5 She could see in the open square before her house the tops of trees that were all aquiver with the new spring life. The delicious breath of rain was in the air. In the street below a peddler was crying his wares. The notes of a distant song which some one was singing reached her faintly, and countless sparrows were twittering in the eaves.

6 There were patches of blue sky showing here and there through the clouds that had met and piled one above the other in the west facing her window.

7 She sat with her head thrown back upon the cushion of the chair, quite motionless, except when a sob came up into her throat and shook her, as a child who has cried itself to sleep continues to sob in its dreams.

8 She was young, with a fair, calm face, whose lines bespoke repression and even a certain strength. But now there was a dull stare in her eyes, whose gaze was fixed away off yonder on one of those patches of blue sky. It was not a glance of reflection, but rather indicated a suspension of intelligent thought.

9 There was something coming to her and she was waiting for it, fearfully. What was it? She did not know; it was too subtle and elusive to name. But she felt it, creeping out of the sky, reaching toward her through the sounds, the scents, the color that filled the air.

10 Now her bosom rose and fell tumultuously. She was beginning to recognize this thing that was approaching to possess her, and she was striving to beat it back with her will—as powerless as her two white slender hands would have been.

11 When she abandoned herself a little whispered word escaped her slightly parted lips. She said it over and over under her breath: "free, free, free!" The vacant stare and the look of terror that had followed it went from her eyes. They stayed keen and bright. Her pulses beat fast, and the coursing blood warmed and relaxed every inch of her body.

12 She did not stop to ask if it were or were not a monstrous joy that held her. A clear and exalted perception enabled her to dismiss the suggestion as trivial.

13 She knew that she would weep again when she saw the kind, tender hands folded in death; the face that had never looked save with love upon her, fixed and gray and dead. But she saw beyond that bitter moment a long procession of years to come that would belong to her absolutely. And she opened and spread her arms out to them in welcome.

14 There would be no one to live for during those coming years; she would live for herself. There would be no powerful will bending hers in that blind persistence with which men and women believe they have a right to impose a private will upon a fellow-creature. A kind intention or a cruel intention made the act seem no less a crime as she looked upon it in that brief moment of illumination.

15 And yet she had loved him—sometimes. Often she had not. What did it matter! What could love, the unsolved mystery, count for in face of this possession of self-assertion which she suddenly recognized as the strongest impulse of her being!

16 "Free! Body and soul free!" she kept whispering.

17 Josephine was kneeling before the closed door with her lips to the keyhole, imploring for admission. "Louise, open the door! I beg; open the door—you will make yourself ill. What are you doing, Louise? For heaven's sake open the door."

18 "Go away. I am not making myself ill." No; she was drinking in a very elixir of life through that open window.

19 Her fancy was running riot along those days ahead of her. Spring days, and summer days, and all sorts of days that would be her own. She breathed a quick prayer that life might be long. It was only yesterday she had thought with a shudder that life might be long.

20   She arose at length and opened the door to her sister's importunities. There was a feverish triumph in her eyes, and she carried herself unwittingly like a goddess of Victory. She clasped her sister's waist, and together they descended the stairs. Richards stood waiting for them at the bottom.

21   Some one was opening the front door with a latchkey. It was Brently Mallard who entered, a little travel-stained, composedly carrying his gripsack and umbrella. He had been far from the scene of accident, and did not even know there had been one. He stood amazed at Josephine's piercing cry; at Richards' quick motion to screen him from the view of his wife.

22   But Richards was too late.

23   When the doctors came they said she had died of heart disease—of joy that kills.

ANALYZE & WRITE

Use the following questions to begin analyzing "The Story of an Hour":

1 **Irony** refers to a gap or discrepancy between what is said and what is true, or between a result that is expected and what actually happens. In literature, readers often perceive irony that characters are unable to see. What is the central irony of "The Story of an Hour"? To get started, take a look at how the story is framed in the opening and closing paragraphs. What gap or discrepancy do you notice? Do the characters share your insight?

2 What do you learn from the setting and, in particular, the language Chopin uses to describe what Mrs. Mallard experiences when, beginning in paragraph 4, she sits in her armchair, looking out the window?

3 This story was originally published at the end of the nineteenth century. With this context in mind, what do you think Chopin is saying about marriage, gender, power, and sexuality in American society? To get started, you could look at how Richards tries to "screen [Mr. Mallard] from the view of his wife" (par. 21).

James Joyce | *Araby*

The Granger Collection, New York

JAMES JOYCE (1882–1941), a native of Dublin, Ireland, is considered one of the most influential writers of the early twentieth century. "Araby," one of his most often anthologized stories, first appeared in the collection *Dubliners* in 1914. Like his novel *Portrait of the Artist as a Young Man*, published two years later, it relies on scenes from Joyce's own boyhood.

1   North Richmond Street, being blind,[1] was a quiet street except at the hour when the Christian Brothers' School set the boys free. An uninhabited house of two storeys stood at the blind end, detached from its neighbours in a square ground. The other houses of the street, conscious of decent lives within them, gazed at one another with brown imperturbable faces.

2   The former tenant of our house, a priest, had died in the back drawing-room. Air, musty from having been long enclosed, hung in all the rooms, and the waste

---

[1]A dead end. The young Joyce in fact lived for a time on North Richmond Street in Dublin. [Editor's note]

room behind the kitchen was littered with old useless papers. Among these I found a few paper-covered books, the pages of which were curled and damp: *The Abbot*, by Walter Scott, *The Devout Communicant* and *The Memoirs of Vidocq*.[2] I liked the last best because its leaves were yellow. The wild garden behind the house contained a central apple-tree and a few straggling bushes under one of which I found the late tenant's rusty bicycle-pump. He had been a very charitable priest; in his will he had left all his money to institutions and the furniture of his house to his sister.

3   When the short days of winter came dusk fell before we had well eaten our dinners. When we met in the street the houses had grown sombre. The space of sky above us was the colour of ever-changing violet and towards it the lamps of the street lifted their feeble lanterns. The cold air stung us and we played till our bodies glowed. Our shouts echoed in the silent street. The career of our play brought us through the dark muddy lanes behind the houses where we ran the gauntlet of the rough tribes from the cottages, to the back doors of the dark dripping gardens where odours arose from the ashpits, to the dark odorous stables where a coachman smoothed and combed the horse or shook music from the buckled harness. When we returned to the street light from the kitchen windows had filled the areas. If my uncle was seen turning the corner we hid in the shadow until we had seen him safely housed. Or if Mangan's sister came out on the doorstep to call her brother in to his tea we watched her from our shadow peer up and down the street. We waited to see whether she would remain or go in and, if she remained, we left our shadow and walked up to Mangan's steps resignedly. She was waiting for us, her figure defined by the light from the half-opened door. Her brother always teased her before he obeyed and I stood by the railings looking at her. Her dress swung as she moved her body and the soft rope of her hair tossed from side to side.

4   Every morning I lay on the floor in the front parlour watching her door. The blind was pulled down to within an inch of the sash so that I could not be seen. When she came out on the doorstep my heart leaped. I ran to the hall, seized my books and followed her. I kept her brown figure always in my eye and, when we came near the point at which our ways diverged, I quickened my pace and passed her. This happened morning after morning. I had never spoken to her, except for a few casual words, and yet her name was like a summons to all my foolish blood.

5   Her image accompanied me even in places the most hostile to romance. On Saturday evenings when my aunt went marketing I had to go to carry some of the parcels. We walked through the flaring streets, jostled by drunken men and bargaining women, amid the curses of labourers, the shrill litanies of shop-boys who stood on guard by the barrels of pigs' cheeks, the nasal chanting of street-singers, who sang a *come-all-you* about O'Donovan Rossa,[3] or a ballad about the troubles in our native land. These noises converged in a single sensation of life for me: I imagined that I bore my chalice safely through a throng of foes. Her name sprang to my lips at moments in strange prayers and praises which I myself did not understand. My eyes were often full of tears (I could not tell why) and at times a flood from my heart seemed to pour itself out into my bosom. I thought little of the future. I did not know whether I would ever speak to her or not or, if I spoke to her, how I could tell her of my confused adoration. But my body was like a harp and her words and gestures were like fingers running upon the wires.

6   One evening I went into the back drawing-room in which the priest had died. It was a dark rainy evening and there was no sound in the house. Through one of the broken panes I heard the rain impinge upon the earth, the fine incessant needles of water playing in the sodden beds. Some distant lamp or lighted window gleamed below me. I was thankful that I could see so little. All my senses seemed to desire to veil themselves and, feeling that I was about to slip from them, I pressed the palms of my hands together until they trembled, murmuring: *"O love! O love!"* many times.

---

[2]*The Abbot* is a historical romance set in the court of Mary, Queen of Scots, a Catholic, who was beheaded for plotting to assassinate her Protestant cousin, Queen Elizabeth I. *The Devout Communicant* is a collection of religious meditations. *The Memoirs of Vidocq* is a collection of sexually suggestive stories about a French criminal turned detective. [Editor's note]

[3]A contemporary leader of an underground organization opposed to British rule of Ireland. [Editor's note]

7   At last she spoke to me. When she addressed the first words to me I was so confused that I did not know what to answer. She asked me was I going to Araby. I forgot whether I answered yes or no. It would be a splendid bazaar, she said she would love to go.[4]

8   "And why can't you?" I asked.

9   While she spoke she turned a silver bracelet round and round her wrist. She could not go, she said, because there would be a retreat that week in her convent. Her brother and two other boys were fighting for their caps and I was alone at the railings. She held one of the spikes, bowing her head towards me. The light from the lamp opposite our door caught the white curve of her neck, lit up her hair that rested there and, falling, lit up the hand upon the railing. It fell over one side of her dress and caught the white border of a petticoat, just visible as she stood at ease.

10   "It's well for you," she said.

11   "If I go," I said, "I will bring you something."

12   What innumerable follies laid waste my waking and sleeping thoughts after that evening! I wished to annihilate the tedious intervening days. I chafed against the work of school. At night in my bedroom and by day in the classroom her image came between me and the page I strove to read. The syllables of the word *Araby* were called to me through the silence in which my soul luxuriated and cast an Eastern enchantment over me. I asked for leave to go to the bazaar on Saturday night. My aunt was surprised and hoped it was not some Freemason affair.[5] I answered few questions in class. I watched my master's face pass from amiability to sternness; he hoped I was not beginning to idle. I could not call my wandering thoughts together. I had hardly any patience with the serious work of life which, now that it stood between me and my desire, seemed to me child's play, ugly monotonous child's play.

13   On Saturday morning I reminded my uncle that I wished to go to the bazaar in the evening. He was fussing at the hallstand, looking for the hatbrush, and answered me curtly:

14   "Yes, boy, I know."

15   As he was in the hall I could not go into the front parlour and lie at the window. I left the house in bad humour and walked slowly towards the school. The air was pitilessly raw and already my heart misgave me.

16   When I came home to dinner my uncle had not yet been home. Still it was early. I sat staring at the clock for some time and, when its ticking began to irritate me, I left the room. I mounted the staircase and gained the upper part of the house. The high cold empty gloomy rooms liberated me and I went from room to room singing. From the front window I saw my companions playing below in the street. Their cries reached me weakened and indistinct and, leaning my forehead against the cool glass, I looked over at the dark house where she lived. I may have stood there for an hour, seeing nothing but the brown-clad figure cast by my imagination, touched discreetly by the lamplight at the curved neck, at the hand upon the railings and at the border below the dress.

17   When I came downstairs again I found Mrs. Mercer sitting at the fire. She was an old garrulous woman, a pawnbroker's widow, who collected used stamps for some pious purpose. I had to endure the gossip of the tea-table. The meal was prolonged beyond an hour and still my uncle did not come. Mrs. Mercer stood up to go: she was sorry she couldn't wait any longer, but it was after eight o'clock and she did not like to be out late, as the night air was bad for her. When she had gone I began to walk up and down the room, clenching my fists. My aunt said:

18   "I'm afraid you may put off your bazaar for this night of Our Lord."

19   At nine o'clock I heard my uncle's latchkey in the halldoor. I heard him talking to himself and heard the hallstand rocking when it had received the weight of his overcoat. I could interpret these signs. When he was midway through his dinner I asked him to give me the money to go to the bazaar. He had forgotten.

20   "The people are in bed and after their first sleep now," he said.

21   I did not smile. My aunt said to him energetically:

22   "Can't you give him the money and let him go? You've kept him late enough as it is."

---

[4] Traveling bazaars featured cafés, shopping stalls, and entertainment. Araby was the name of an English bazaar that visited Dublin when Joyce was a boy. [Editor's note]

[5] The Freemasons is a secretive fraternal order that has a long history and that has traditionally been opposed by the Catholic Church. [Editor's note]

23   My uncle said he was very sorry he had forgotten. He said he believed in the old saying: "All work and no play makes Jack a dull boy." He asked me where I was going and, when I had told him a second time he asked me did I know *The Arab's Farewell to His Steed*. When I left the kitchen he was about to recite the opening lines of the piece to my aunt.

24   I held a florin tightly in my hand as I strode down Buckingham Street towards the station. The sight of the streets thronged with buyers and glaring with gas recalled to me the purpose of my journey. I took my seat in a third-class carriage of a deserted train. After an intolerable delay the train moved out of the station slowly. It crept onward among ruinous houses and over the twinkling river. At Westland Row Station a crowd of people pressed to the carriage doors; but the porters moved them back, saying that it was a special train for the bazaar. I remained alone in the bare carriage. In a few minutes the train drew up beside an improvised wooden platform. I passed out on to the road and saw by the lighted dial of a clock that it was ten minutes to ten. In front of me was a large building which displayed the magical name.

25   I could not find any sixpenny entrance and, fearing that the bazaar would be closed, I passed in quickly through a turnstile, handing a shilling to a weary-looking man. I found myself in a big hall girdled at half its height by a gallery. Nearly all the stalls were closed and the greater part of the hall was in darkness. I recognised a silence like that which pervades a church after a service. I walked into the centre of the bazaar timidly. A few people were gathered about the stalls which were still open. Before a curtain, over which the words *Café Chantant*[6] were written in coloured lamps, two men were counting money on a salver. I listened to the fall of the coins.

26   Remembering with difficulty why I had come I went over to one of the stalls and examined porcelain vases and flowered tea-sets. At the door of the stall a young lady was talking and laughing with two young gentlemen. I remarked their English accents and listened vaguely to their conversation.

27   "O, I never said such a thing!"

28   "O, but you did!"

29   "O, but I didn't!"

30   "Didn't she say that?"

31   "Yes. I heard her."

32   "O, there's a . . . fib!"

33   Observing me the young lady came over and asked me did I wish to buy anything. The tone of her voice was not encouraging; she seemed to have spoken to me out of a sense of duty. I looked humbly at the great jars that stood like eastern guards at either side of the dark entrance to the stall and murmured:

34   "No, thank you."

35   The young lady changed the position of one of the vases and went back to the two young men. They began to talk of the same subject. Once or twice the young lady glanced at me over her shoulder.

36   I lingered before her stall, though I knew my stay was useless, to make my interest in her wares seem the more real. Then I turned away slowly and walked down the middle of the bazaar. I allowed the two pennies to fall against the sixpence in my pocket. I heard a voice call from one end of the gallery that the light was out. The upper part of the hall was now completely dark.

37   Gazing up into the darkness I saw myself as a creature driven and derided by vanity; and my eyes burned with anguish and anger.

ANALYZE & WRITE

Use the following questions to begin analyzing "Araby":

1. "Araby" can be read as a coming-of-age story about an adolescent boy's first crush. If you read it on this level, what changes would you say the boy goes through? What, if anything, does he learn? To get started, take a look at paragraph 4.

2. The boy describes himself as carrying the "image" of Mangan's sister like a "chalice," "even in places the most hostile to romance," such as the crowded, raucous streets of

---

6 Literally, *singing café* (French), a music hall. [Editor's note]

early twentieth-century Dublin, Ireland (par. 5). How does the boy's experience on Saturday evening shopping trips with his aunt compare to his experience at Araby (par. 25)? What makes the experiences so different?

3 This story is saturated with the culture of Dublin, Ireland, particularly its Catholicism and its attitudes about gender and sexuality. How are these or other important cultural influences expressed in the story? To get started, take a look at paragraph 2.

William Carlos Williams | *The Use of Force*

Library of Congress, Prints & Photographs Division, LC-USZ62109601

WILLIAM CARLOS WILLIAMS (1883–1963) is one of the most important poets of the twentieth century, best known for his long poem *Paterson* (1946–1958). He also wrote essays, plays, novels, and short stories. "The Use of Force" was initially published in *The Doctor Stories* (1933), a collection loosely based on Williams's experiences as a pediatrician.

1   They were new patients to me, all I had was the name, Olson. Please come down as soon as you can, my daughter is very sick.

2   When I arrived I was met by the mother, a big startled-looking woman, very clean and apologetic, who merely said, Is this the doctor? and let me in. In the back, she added. You must excuse us, doctor, we have her in the kitchen where it is warm. It is very damp here sometimes.

3   The child was fully dressed and sitting on her father's lap near the kitchen table. He tried to get up, but I motioned for him not to bother, took off my overcoat and started to look things over. I could see that they were all very nervous, eyeing me up and down distrustfully. As often, in such cases, they weren't telling me more than they had to, it was up to me to tell them; that's why they were spending three dollars on me.

4   The child was fairly eating me up with her cold, steady eyes, and no expression to her face whatever. She did not move and seemed, inwardly, quiet; an unusually attractive little thing, and as strong as a heifer in appearance. But her face was flushed, she was breathing rapidly, and I realized that she had a high fever. She had magnificent blonde hair, in profusion. One of those picture children often reproduced in advertising leaflets and the photogravure sections of the Sunday papers.

5   She's had a fever for three days, began the father, and we don't know what it comes from. My wife has given her things, you know, like people do, but it don't do no good. And there's been a lot of sickness around. So we tho't you better look her over and tell us what is the matter.

6   As doctors often do I took a trial shot at it as a point of departure. Has she had a sore throat?

7   Both parents answered me together, No . . . No, she says her throat don't hurt her.

8   Does your throat hurt you? added the mother to the child. But the little girl's expression didn't change nor did she move her eyes from my face.

9   Have you looked?

10   I tried, said the mother, but I couldn't see.

11   As it happens we had been having a number of cases of diphtheria in the school to which this child went during that month and we were all, quite apparently, thinking of that, though no one had as yet spoken of the thing.

12   Well, I said, suppose we take a look at the throat first. I smiled in my best professional manner and asking for the child's first name I said, come on, Mathilda, open your mouth and let's take a look at your throat.

13   Nothing doing.

14   Aw, come on, I coaxed, just open your mouth wide and let me take a look. Look, I said opening both hands wide, I haven't anything in my hands. Just open up and let me see.

15   Such a nice man, put in the mother. Look how kind he is to you. Come on, do what he tells you to. He won't hurt you.

16   At that I ground my teeth in disgust. If only they wouldn't use the word "hurt" I might be able to get somewhere. But I did not allow myself to be hurried or disturbed but speaking quietly and slowly I approached the child again.

17   As I moved my chair a little nearer suddenly with one catlike movement both her hands clawed instinctively for my eyes and she almost reached them too. In fact she knocked my glasses flying and they fell, though unbroken, several feet away from me on the kitchen floor.

18   Both the mother and father almost turned themselves inside out in embarrassment and apology. You bad girl, said the mother, taking her and shaking her by one arm. Look what you've done. The nice man . . .

19   For heaven's sake, I broke in. Don't call me a nice man to her. I'm here to look at her throat on the chance that she might have diphtheria and possibly die of it. But that's nothing to her. Look here, I said to the child, we're going to look at your throat. You're old enough to understand what I'm saying. Will you open it now by yourself or shall we have to open it for you?

20   Not a move. Even her expression hadn't changed. Her breaths however were coming faster and faster. Then the battle began. I had to do it. I had to have a throat culture for her own protection. But first I told the parents that it was entirely up to them. I explained the danger but said that I would not insist on a throat examination so long as they would take the responsibility.

21   If you don't do what the doctor says you'll have to go to the hospital, the mother admonished her severely.

22   Oh yeah? I had to smile to myself. After all, I had already fallen in love with the savage brat, the parents were contemptible to me. In the ensuing struggle they grew more and more abject, crushed, exhausted while she surely rose to magnificent heights of insane fury of effort bred of her terror of me.

23   The father tried his best, and he was a big man, but the fact that she was his daughter, his shame at her behavior and his dread of hurting her made him release her just at the critical times when I had almost achieved success, till I wanted to kill him. But his dread also that she might have diphtheria made him tell me to go on, go on though he himself was almost fainting, while the mother moved back and forth behind us raising and lowering her hands in an agony of apprehension.

24   Put her in front of you on your lap, I ordered, and hold both her wrists.

25   But as soon as he did the child let out a scream. Don't, you're hurting me. Let go of my hands. Let them go I tell you. Then she shrieked terrifyingly, hysterically. Stop it! Stop it! You're killing me!

26   Do you think she can stand it, doctor! said the mother.

27   You get out, said the husband to his wife. Do you want her to die of diphtheria?

28   Come on now, hold her, I said.

29   Then I grasped the child's head with my left hand and tried to get the wooden tongue depressor between her teeth. She fought, with clenched teeth, desperately! But now I also had grown furious—at a child. I tried to hold myself down but I couldn't. I know how to expose a throat for inspection. And I did my best. When finally I got the wooden spatula behind the last teeth and just the point of it into the mouth cavity, she opened up for an instant but before I could see anything she came down again and gripping the wooden blade between her molars she reduced it to splinters before I could get it out again.

30   Aren't you ashamed, the mother yelled at her. Aren't you ashamed to act like that in front of the doctor?

31   Get me a smooth-handled spoon of some sort, I told the mother. We're going through with this. The child's mouth was already bleeding. Her tongue was cut and she was screaming in wild hysterical shrieks. Perhaps I should have desisted and come back in an hour or more. No doubt it would have been better. But I have seen at least two children lying dead in bed of neglect in such cases, and feeling that I must get a diagnosis now or never I went at it again. But the worst of it was that I too had got beyond reason. I could have torn

the child apart in my own fury and enjoyed it. It was a pleasure to attack her. My face was burning with it.

32   The damned little brat must be protected against her own idiocy, one says to oneself at such times. Others must be protected against her. It is a social necessity. And all these things are true. But a blind fury, a feeling of adult shame, bred of a longing for muscular release are the operatives. One goes on to the end.

33   In a final unreasoning assault I overpowered the child's neck and jaws. I forced the heavy silver spoon back of her teeth and down her throat till she gagged. And there it was—both tonsils covered with membrane. She had fought valiantly to keep me from knowing her secret. She had been hiding that sore throat for three days at least and lying to her parents in order to escape just such an outcome as this.

34   Now truly she was furious. She had been on the defensive before but now she attacked. Tried to get off her father's lap and fly at me while tears of defeat blinded her eyes.

ANALYZE & WRITE

Use the following questions to begin analyzing "The Use of Force":

1 This story is told from the doctor's point of view. How does he justify his use of force? What are the pros and cons he weighs in using it? To get started, look in particular at paragraph 34.

2 How do the sexual overtones of the story — for example, in the doctor's describing the girl as "an unusually attractive little thing" (par. 4) and admitting "I had already fallen in love with the savage brat" (par. 22) — affect your understanding and judgment of the doctor's and the girl's behavior?

3 Because this story came out of the era of the Great Depression, you might expect it to say something about the impoverished material conditions in which people lived at the time and how these hardships affected them. Are these expectations borne out? What seems to be the economic status of the family and the doctor, and how does class affect what happens in the story? To get started, take a look at paragraphs 2 and 3.

Jamaica Kincaid | *Girl*

© ZUMA Press/Newscom

JAMAICA KINCAID was born Elaine Potter Richardson in 1949 in St. Johns, Antigua, in the West Indies. As Kincaid's mother had more children, the once-close relationship between mother and daughter became strained, and Kincaid began to feel increasingly restricted by life in Antigua under British rule. At seventeen, she left Antigua to work as an au pair in New York, where she attended night classes and began working as a freelance writer. At the start of her writing career, she changed her name to Jamaica Kincaid to shed the "weights" (as she put it) of her past life. Kincaid's stories have appeared in such prestigious venues as *Rolling Stone,* the *Paris Review,* and the *New Yorker,* where she became a staff writer in 1978. "Girl" was published first in the *New Yorker* and later in Kincaid's first book, *At the Bottom of the River* (1984), an anthology of short stories that won the Morton Dauwen Zabel Award. Her next book, *Annie John* (1985), also a collection of stories, centered on a girl growing up in the West Indies. In addition to two novels—*Lucy* (1990) and *The Autobiography of My Mother* (1996)—Kincaid has published two books of nonfiction: *My Brother* (1997), the story of her brother Devon Drew's short life, and *A Small Place* (2000), an examination of her native Antigua. Kincaid now makes her home in Vermont, where her husband is a composer and professor of music at Bennington College.

As you read "Girl," listen to the rhythms of the language, and consider how the almost poetic litany of instructions reflects and shapes the relationship between mother and daughter.

Wash the white clothes on Monday and put them on the stone heap; wash the color clothes on Tuesday and put them on the clothesline to dry; don't walk barehead in the hot sun; cook pumpkin fritters in very hot sweet oil; soak your little cloths right after you take them off; when buying cotton to make yourself a nice blouse, be sure that it doesn't have gum on it, because that way it won't hold up well after a wash; soak salt fish overnight before you cook it; is it true that you sing benna[1] in Sunday school?; always eat your food in such a way that it won't turn someone else's stomach; on Sundays try to walk like a lady and not like the slut you are so bent on becoming; don't sing benna in Sunday school; you mustn't speak to wharf-rat boys, not even to give directions; don't eat fruits on the street—flies will follow you; *but I don't sing benna on Sundays at all and never in Sunday school;* this is how to sew on a button; this is how to make a button-hole for the button you have just sewed on; this is how to hem a dress when you see the hem coming down and so to prevent yourself from looking like the slut I know you are so bent on becoming; this is how you iron your father's khaki shirt so that it doesn't have a crease; this is how you iron your father's khaki pants so that they don't have a crease; this is how you grow okra—far from the house, because okra tree harbors red ants; when you are growing dasheen,[2] make sure it gets plenty of water or else it makes your throat itch when you are eating it; this is how you sweep a corner; this is how you sweep a whole house; this is how you sweep a yard; this is how you smile to someone you don't like too much; this is how you smile to someone you don't like at all; this is how you smile to someone you like completely; this is how you set a table for tea; this is how you set a table for dinner; this is how you set a table for dinner with an important guest; this is how you set a table for lunch; this is how you set a table for breakfast; this is how to behave in the presence of men who don't know you very well, and this way they won't recognize immediately the slut I have warned you against becoming; be sure to wash every day, even if it is with your own spit; don't squat down to play marbles—you are not a boy, you know; don't pick people's flowers—you might catch something; don't throw stones at blackbirds, because it might not be a blackbird at all; this is how to make a bread pudding; this is how to make doukona;[3] this is how to make pepper pot;[4] this is how to make a good medicine for a cold; this is how to make a good medicine to throw away a child before it even becomes a child; this is how to catch a fish; this is how to throw back a fish you don't like, and that way something bad won't fall on you; this is how to bully a man; this is how a man bullies you; this is how to love a man; and if this doesn't work there are other ways, and if they don't work don't feel too bad about giving up; this is how to spit up in the air if you feel like it, and this is how to move quick so that it doesn't fall on you; this is how to make ends meet; always squeeze bread to make sure it's fresh; *but what if the baker won't let me feel the bread?;* you mean to say that after all you are really going to be the kind of woman who the baker won't let near the bread?

---

[1] Calypso, popular Afro-Caribbean music from the West Indies. [Editor's note]
[2] Taro, a starchy root vegetable with edible leaves that is a staple crop of the Caribbean. [Editor's note]
[3] Spicy pudding made from plantains. [Editor's note]
[4] A West Indian stew that is typically made for special occasions. [Editor's note]

ANALYZE & WRITE

Use the following questions to begin analyzing "Girl":

1 This story is told almost exclusively from the mother's point of view; with the exception of two italicized interjections from the daughter ("but I don't sing benna on Sundays at all and never in Sunday school"; "but what if the baker won't let me feel the bread?"), the words are entirely the mother's. How does the language the mother uses, and the instructions she gives, shape your understanding of the mother's character? How would you describe her relationship with her daughter based on her litany of advice?

2 If irony is the discrepancy between the truth and what is said or the gap between what is expected and what actually happens, is "Girl" ironic? Why or why not?

3 Kincaid grew up in St. John's, Antigua, in the 1950s and 1960s, and while the setting is not specified, "Girl" seems to have been set in a similar place and time. What can you infer about the society in which "Girl" is set from the advice the mother gives and the language she uses? How might the story's first readers (subscribers to the *New Yorker* magazine in 1978) have reacted and why? How might your reaction differ from that of the story's initial audience?

PART 2

Critical Thinking Strategies

11

A Catalog of Invention and Inquiry Strategies

Writers are like scientists: They ask questions, systematically inquiring about how things work, what they are, where they occur, and how more information can be learned about them. Writers are also like artists in that they use what they know and learn to create something new and imaginative.

The invention and inquiry strategies described in this chapter are not mysterious or magical. They represent ways writers, engineers, scientists, composers—in fact, all of us—solve problems. Once you have mastered these strategies, you can use them to tackle many of the writing situations you will encounter in college, on the job, and in the community.

The strategies for invention and inquiry in this chapter are arranged alphabetically within two categories:

Mapping: A brief visual representation of your thinking or planning

Writing: The composition of phrases or sentences to discover information and ideas and to make connections among them

These invention and inquiry strategies will help you explore and research a topic fully before you begin drafting, and then help you creatively solve problems as you draft and revise.

Mapping

Mapping strategies, like clustering, listing, and outlining, involve making a visual record of invention and inquiry. In making maps, writers usually use key words and phrases to record material they want to remember, questions they need to answer, and new sources of information they want to check. The maps show the ideas, details, and facts as well as possible ways to connect and focus them. Mapping can be especially useful for working collaboratively, preparing presentations, and creating multimedia illustrations for written texts you will submit either on paper or electronically.

Create a cluster diagram to reveal relationships among ideas.

Software-based diagramming tools
Software vendors have created a variety of electronic tools to help people better visualize complex projects. These flowcharts, webs, and outlines can make it easier for you to see how to proceed at any stage of your project.

Clustering is a strategy for revealing possible relationships among facts and ideas. Clustering works as follows:

1. In a word or phrase, write your topic in the center of a piece of paper. Circle it.

2. Also in words or phrases, write down the main parts or ideas of your topic. Circle these, and connect them with lines to the topic in the center.

3. Next, write down facts, details, and examples related to these main parts or ideas. Connect them with lines to the relevant main parts or ideas.

Clustering can be useful in the early stages of composing to narrow a topic, find subtopics, and organize information. You may try out and discard several clusters before finding one that is promising. Many writers also use clustering to plan brief sections of a writing project as they are drafting or revising. (A model of clustering is shown in Figure 11.1.)

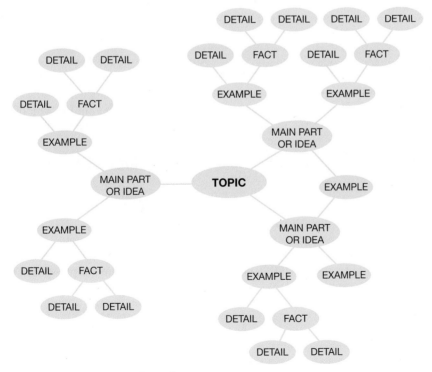

FIGURE 11.1   A Model of Clustering

Make a list to generate a plan quickly.

Listing is a familiar activity. You probably make shopping or to-do lists every day. But listing can also be a great help in planning a writing project. It enables you to recall what you already know about a topic and suggests what else you may need to find out. Listing is especially useful to those who have little time for planning—for example, reporters facing deadlines and college students taking essay exams—because it lets you order your ideas quickly. It can also serve as a first step in discovering possible writing topics.

Here is how listing works best for invention work:

1. Give your list a title that indicates your main idea or topic.
2. Write as fast as you can, relying on short phrases.
3. Include anything that seems at all useful. Try not to be judgmental at this point.
4. After you have finished or even as you write, reflect on and organize the list:
   - Put an asterisk next to the most promising items.
   - Number or reorder key items in order of importance.
   - Put items in related groups.
   - Cross out or delete items that do not seem promising.
   - Add new items.

Create an outline to invent and organize.

Like listing and clustering, **outlining** is both a means of inventing what you want to say and a way of organizing your ideas and information. As you outline, you nearly always see new possibilities in your subject, discovering new ways of dividing or grouping information and seeing where you need additional information to develop your ideas. Because outlining lets you see strengths and weaknesses at a glance, it can also help you read and revise with a critical eye.

There are two main forms of outlining: informal outlining and formal topic or sentence outlining. Among the several types of informal outlining, *scratch outlines* are perhaps the most adaptable to a variety of situations.

A **scratch outline** is little more than a list of the essay's main points. You have no doubt made scratch outlines many times—to plan essay exams, to revise your own writing, and to analyze a difficult reading passage. Here are sample scratch outlines for two different kinds of essays. The first is an outline of Annie Dillard's essay in Chapter 2 (pp. 22–24), and the second shows one way to organize a position paper (Chapter 6):

Scratch Outline: Essay about a Remembered Event

¶1. explains what she learned from playing football

¶2. identifies other sports she learned from boys in the neighborhood

¶3. sets the scene by describing the time and place of the event

¶4. describes the boys who were playing with her

¶5. describes what typically happened: a car would come down the street, they would throw snowballs, and then they would wait for another car

¶6. describes the iceball-making project she had begun while waiting

¶7. describes the Buick's approach and how they followed the routine

Scratch Outline: Essay Arguing a Position

Presentation of the issue

Concession of some aspect of an opposing position

Thesis statement

First reason with support

Second reason with support

(etc.)

Conclusion

Remember that the items in a scratch outline do not necessarily coincide with paragraphs. Sometimes two or more items may be developed in the same paragraph or one item may be covered in two or more paragraphs.

Chunking, a type of scratch outline commonly used by professional writers in business and industry and especially well suited to collaborative and multimodal composing, consists of a set of headings describing the major points to be covered in the final document. What makes chunking distinctive is that the blocks of text—or "chunks"—under each heading are intended to be roughly the same length and scope. These headings can be discussed and passed around among several writers and editors before writing begins, and different chunks may be written by different authors, simply by typing notes into the space under each heading.

The list of headings is subject to change during the writing, and new headings may be added or old ones subdivided or discarded as part of the drafting and revising processes.

The advantage of chunking in your own writing is that it breaks the large task of drafting into smaller tasks in a simple, evenly balanced way; once the headings are determined, the writing becomes a matter of filling in the specifics that go in each chunk. Organization tends to improve as you get a sense of the weight of different parts of the document while filling in the blanks. Places where the writing project needs more information or where there is a problem with pacing tend to stand out because of the chunking structure, and the headings can be either taken out of the finished project or left in as devices to help guide readers. If they are left in, they should be edited into parallel grammatical form like the items in a formal topic or sentence outline, as discussed below.

For more on parallelism, see Chapter 10, pp. 469–70, and Chapter 13, p. 536.

Topic outlines and **sentence outlines** are considered more formal than scratch outlines because they follow a conventional format of numbered and lettered headings and subheadings:

Period follows numbers and letters

First word of each item is capitalized

```
I.  Main topic
    A. Subtopic of I
    B.
        1. Subtopic of I.B
        2.
            a. Subtopic of I.B.2
            b.
                (1) Subtopic of I.B.2.b
                (2)
    C.
        1. Subtopic of I.C
        2.
```

The difference between a topic and sentence outline is obvious: Topic outlines simply name the topics and subtopics, whereas sentence outlines use complete or abbreviated sentences. To illustrate, here are two partial formal outlines of an essay arguing a position, Jessica Statsky's "Children Need to Play, Not Compete," from Chapter 6 (pp. 236–41).

Formal Topic Outline

I. Organized sports harmful to children
   A. Harmful physically
      1. Curve ball (Koppett)
      2. Tackle football (Tutko)
   B. Harmful psychologically
      1. Fear of being hurt
         a. Little League Online
         b. Mother
         c. Reporter
      2. Competition
         a. Rablovsky
         b. Studies

Formal Sentence Outline

I. Highly organized competitive sports such as Peewee Football and Little League Baseball can be physically and psychologically harmful to children, as well as counterproductive for developing future players.
   A. Physically harmful because sports entice children into physical actions that are bad for growing bodies.
      1. Koppett claims throwing a curve ball may put abnormal strain on developing arm and shoulder muscles.
      2. Tutko argues that tackle football is too traumatic for young kids.
   B. Psychologically harmful to children for a number of reasons.
      1. Fear of being hurt detracts from their enjoyment of the sport.
         a. Little League Online ranks fear of injury seventh among top reasons children quit.
         b. One mother says, "Kids get so scared. . . . They'll sit on the bench and pretend their leg hurts."
         c. A reporter tells about a child who made himself vomit to get out of playing Peewee Football.
      2. Too much competition poses psychological dangers for children.
         a. Rablovsky reports: "The spirit of play suddenly disappears, and sport becomes joblike."
         b. Studies show that children prefer playing on a losing team to "warming the bench on a winning team."

Every level of a formal outline except the top level (identified by the roman numeral *I*) must include at least two items. Items at the same level of indentation in a topic outline should be grammatically parallel—all beginning with the same part of speech. For example, *I.A* and *I.B* are parallel when they both begin with an adverb

(*Physically harmful* and *Psychologically harmful*) or with an adjective (*Harmful physically* and *Harmful psychologically*); they would not be parallel if one began with an adverb (*Physically harmful*) and the other with an adjective (*Harmful psychologically*).

Writing

Writing strategies—including cubing, dialoguing, dramatizing, freewriting, keeping a journal, looping, and questioning—invite you to produce complete sentences, so they provide considerable generative power. Because they are complete statements, they take you further than listing or clustering, enabling you to explore ideas and define relationships, bring ideas together or show how they differ, identify causes and effects, and develop a logical chain of thought.

Use cubing to explore a topic from six perspectives.

Cubing allows you to explore a writing topic from six different perspectives (the number of sides in a cube):

> **Describing:** What does your subject look like? What size is it? What is its color? Its shape? Its texture? Name its parts.

> **Comparing:** What is your subject similar to? Different from?

> **Associating:** What does your subject make you think of? What connections does it have to anything else in your experience?

> **Analyzing:** What are the origins of your subject? What are the functions or significance of its parts? How are its parts related?

> **Applying:** What can you do with your subject? What uses does it have?

> **Arguing:** What arguments can you make for your subject? Against it?

> These guidelines can help you use cubing productively:

1. **Select a topic, subject, or part of a subject.** This can be a person, a scene, an event, an object, a problem, an idea, or an issue. Hold it in focus.

2. **Limit your writing to three to five minutes for each perspective.** The whole activity should take no more than half an hour.

3. **Keep going until you have written about your subject from all six perspectives.** Remember that cubing offers the special advantage of enabling you to generate multiple perspectives quickly.

4. **As you write from each perspective, begin with what you know about your subject.** However, do not limit yourself to your present knowledge. Indicate what else you would like to know about your subject, and suggest where you might find that information.

5. **Reread what you have written.** Look for bright spots, surprises. Recall the part that was easiest for you to write. Recall the part where you felt a special momentum and pleasure in writing. Look for an angle or an unexpected insight. These special parts may suggest a focus or topic within a larger subject, or they may provide specific details to include in a draft.

Construct a dialogue to explore an experience or alternative view.

A *dialogue* is a conversation between two or more people. You can use **dialoguing** to search for topics, find a focus, explore ideas, or consider opposing viewpoints. When you write a dialogue as an invention strategy, you need to make up all parts of the conversation (unless, of course, you are writing collaboratively). Following these steps can help:

1. **Write a conversation between two speakers.** Label the participants *Speaker A* and *Speaker B,* or make up names for them.

2. **Write brief responses to keep the conversation moving fast.** Do not spend much time planning or rehearsing responses. Write what first occurs to you, just as in a real conversation, in which people take quick turns to prevent any awkward silences.

3. **If you get stuck, you might have one of the speakers ask the other a question.**

Dialogues can be especially useful in writing based on personal experience and persuasive essays because they help you remember conversations and anticipate objections.

Use dramatizing to analyze behavior.

Dramatizing is an invention activity developed by the philosopher Kenneth Burke as a way of thinking about how people interact and as a way of analyzing stories and films. Thinking about human behavior in dramatic terms can be very productive for writers. Drama has action, actors, setting, motives, and methods. A five-pointed star can help you remember these five points of dramatizing (see Figure 11.2).

Action   *Action* answers the question "what?" An action is anything that happens, has happened, will happen, or could happen. Action includes events that are physical (running a marathon), mental (thinking about a book you have read), and emotional (falling in love).

Actor   The *actor* answer the question "who?" The actor is either responsible for or affected by the action. The actor may be anything that causes an action. For example, if the action is a rise in the price of gasoline, the actor could be increased demand or short supply. Dramatizing may also include a number of actors working together or at odds.

Setting   *Setting* answers the questions "when?" and "where?" We usually think of setting as the place and time of an event, but it may also be the historical background of an event or the childhood of a person.

METHOD

MOTIVE   ACTION

SETTING   ACTOR

FIGURE 11.2 Dramatizing

Motive   *Motive* answers the question "why?" The motive is the purpose or reason for an action—the actor's intention. Actions may have multiple, even conflicting, motives.

Method   *Method* answers the question "how?" The method explains how an action occurs, including the techniques an actor uses. It refers to whatever makes things happen.

This list answers the questions reporters typically ask. But dramatizing goes further: It enables us to consider relations among these five elements. You can also use this invention strategy to analyze the readers you want to inform or convince.

Freewrite to generate ideas freely and creatively.

Freewriting is a technique that requires you to stop judging what you write and simply let your mind wander in order to generate ideas freely and creatively. To freewrite, set a certain amount of time, say ten to fifteen minutes, and then simply write, generating as much text as you can in the allotted time. While freewriting, try not to stop; if you cannot think of anything to say, simply write "don't know what to say" over and over until an idea comes to you. If you find it difficult to avoid editing yourself, try turning down the brightness on your monitor or lowering the screen on your laptop until you can no longer see what it says.

A variation on freewriting is **focused freewriting**. In focused freewriting, you begin from a specific topic, returning to the beginning topic whenever you find yourself getting off track.

Use looping to explore aspects of a topic.

Looping is especially useful for the first stages of exploring a topic. Like focused freewriting, **looping** involves writing quickly to explore some aspect of a topic. But it differs in that the focus is on looping back to your original starting point or to a new starting point to explore another aspect. Beginning with almost any starting point, looping enables you to find a center of interest and eventually a thesis for your essay. The steps are simple:

1. **Write down your area of interest.** You may know only that you have to write about another person or a movie or a cultural trend that has caught your attention. Or you may want to search for a topic in a broad historical period or for one related to a major political event. Although you may wander from this topic as you write, you will want to keep coming back to it. Your purpose is to find a focus for writing.

2. **Write nonstop for ten minutes.** Start with the first thing that comes to mind. Write rapidly, without looking back to reread or to correct anything. *Do not stop writing. Keep your pencil moving or keystrokes clacking.* Continuous writing is the key to looping. If you get stuck for a moment, rewrite the

last sentence. Follow diversions and digressions, but keep returning to your topic.

3. **After ten minutes, pause to reread what you have written.** Decide what is most important—a single insight, a pattern of ideas, an emerging theme, a visual detail, anything at all that stands out. Some writers call this a "center of gravity" or a "hot spot." To complete the first loop, restate this center in a single sentence.

4. **Beginning with this sentence, write nonstop for another ten minutes.** Summarize in one sentence again to complete the second loop. Keep looping until one of your summary sentences produces a focus or thesis. You may need only two or three loops; you may need more.

Take notes in a journal.

Professional writers often use **journals** to keep notes. Starting one is easy. Buy a special notebook, or open a new file on your computer, and start writing. Here are some possibilities:

- Keep a list of new words and concepts you learn in your courses. You could also write about the progress and direction of your learning in particular courses—the experience of being in the course, your feelings about what is happening, and what you are learning.

- Respond to your reading, both assigned and personal. As you read, write about your personal associations, reflections, reactions, and evaluations. Summarize or copy memorable or especially important passages, and comment on them. (Copying and commenting have been practiced by students and writers for centuries in special journals called *commonplace books*.)

- Write to prepare for particular class meetings. Write about the main ideas you have learned from assigned readings and about the relationship of these new ideas to other ideas in the course. After class, write to summarize what you have learned. List questions you have about the ideas or information discussed in class. Journal writing of this kind involves reflecting, evaluating, interpreting, synthesizing, summarizing, and questioning.

- Write for ten or fifteen minutes every day about whatever is on your mind. Focus these meditations on your new experiences as you try to understand, interpret, and reflect on them or write sketches of people who catch your attention, recording observations and overheard conversation.

- Organize your time. Write about your goals and priorities, or list specific things to accomplish and what you plan to do.

- Keep a log over several days or weeks about a particular event unfolding in the news—a sensational trial, an environmental disaster, a political campaign, a campus controversy, or the fortunes of a sports team.

Ask questions to explore a subject systematically.

Asking questions about a subject is a way to learn about it and decide what to write. When you first encounter a subject, however, your questions may be scattered. Also, you are not likely to think right away of all the important questions you ought to ask. The advantage of having a basic list of questions for invention, like the ones for cubing and for dramatizing discussed earlier in this chapter, is that it provides a systematic approach to exploring a subject.

The questions that follow are based on the work of linguist Kenneth Pike. Here are the steps in using questions for invention:

1. **In a sentence or two, identify your subject.** A subject could be any event, person, problem, project, idea, or issue—in other words, anything you might write about.

2. **Start by writing a response to the first question in the lists below, and move right through the lists.** Try to answer each question at least briefly with a word or a phrase. Some questions may invite several sentences or even a page or more of writing. You may draw a blank on a few questions. Skip them. Later, when you have more experience with questions for invention, you can start anywhere in the list.

3. **Write your responses quickly, without much planning.** Follow digressions or associations. Do not screen anything out. Be playful.

What Is Your Subject?

- What is your subject's name? What other names does it have or has it had?
- What aspects of the subject do these different names emphasize?
- Imagine a photograph or movie of your subject. What would it look like?
- What would you put into a time capsule to stand for your subject?
- What are its causes and effects?
- How would it look from different vantage points or perspectives?
- What experiences have you had with the subject? What have you learned?

What Parts or Features Does Your Subject Have, and How Are They Related?

- Name the parts or features of your subject.
- Describe each one, using the questions in the preceding subject list.
- How is each part or feature related to the others?

How Is Your Subject Similar to and Different from Other Subjects?

- What is your subject similar to? In what ways?
- What is your subject different from? In what ways?
- What seems to you most unlike your subject? In what ways? Now, just for fun, note how they are alike.

How Much Can Your Subject Change and Still Remain the Same?

- How has your subject changed from what it once was?

- How is it changing now—moment to moment, day to day, year to year?

- How does each change alter your way of thinking about your subject?

- What are some different forms your subject takes?

- What does it become when it is no longer itself?

Where Does Your Subject Fit in the World?

- When and where did your subject originate?

- What would happen if at some future time your subject ceased to exist?

- When and where do you usually experience your subject?

- What is your subject a part of, and what are the other parts?

- What do other people think of your subject?

12

A Catalog of
Reading Strategies

This chapter presents strategies for reading critically that you can apply to the selections in this book as well as to your other college reading.

- **Annotating:** Recording your reactions to, interpretations of, and questions about a text as you read it

- **Taking inventory:** Listing and grouping your annotations and other notes to find meaningful patterns

- **Outlining:** Listing the text's main ideas to reveal how it is organized

- **Paraphrasing:** Restating what you have read to clarify or refer to it

- **Summarizing:** Distilling the main ideas or gist of a text

- **Synthesizing:** Integrating into your own writing ideas and information gleaned from different sources

- **Contextualizing:** Placing a text in its historical and cultural context

- **Exploring the significance of figurative language:** Examining how metaphors, similes, and symbols are used in a text to convey meaning and evoke feelings

- **Looking for patterns of opposition:** Inferring the values and assumptions embodied in the language of a text

- **Reflecting on challenges to your beliefs and values:** Examining the bases of your personal responses to a text

- **Evaluating the logic of an argument:** Determining whether an argument is well reasoned and adequately supported

- **Recognizing emotional manipulation:** Identifying texts that unfairly and inappropriately use emotional appeals based on false or exaggerated claims

- **Judging the writer's credibility:** Considering whether writers represent different points of view fairly and know what they are writing about

For more about annotating, see Chapter 5; for more about outlining, see Chapter 11; for more about paraphrasing, see Chapter 23; for more about summarizing and synthesizing, see Chapters 5 and 23; for more about logical fallacies, see Chapter 19.

Annotating

Annotations are the marks—underlines, highlights, and comments—you make directly on the page as you read. Annotating can be used to record immediate reactions and questions, outline and summarize main points, and evaluate and relate the reading to other ideas, readings, and points of view. Annotating can be done on paper with a pencil, pen, or highlighter, or on-screen by using your software's highlighting and commenting functions (or simply by typing annotations into the text using a different color or font).

Your annotations can take many forms, such as the following:

- Inserting comments, questions, or definitions in the margins
- Underlining or circling words, phrases, or sentences
- Connecting ideas with lines or arrows
- Numbering related points
- Bracketing sections of the text
- Noting anything that strikes you as interesting, important, or questionable

Most readers annotate in layers, adding further annotations on second and third readings. Annotations can be light or heavy, depending on your purpose and the difficulty of the material. Your purpose for reading also determines how you use your annotations.

The following selection, excerpted from Martin Luther King Jr.'s "Letter from Birmingham Jail," illustrates some of the ways you can annotate as you read. Add your own annotations, if you like.

Martin Luther King Jr. | *An Annotated Sample from "Letter from Birmingham Jail"*

MARTIN LUTHER KING JR. (1929–1968) first came to national notice in 1955, when he led a successful boycott against the policy of restricting African American passengers to rear seats on city buses in Montgomery, Alabama, where he was minister of a Baptist church. He subsequently formed the Southern Christian Leadership Conference, which brought people of all races from all over the country to the South to fight nonviolently for racial integration. In 1963, King led demonstrations in Birmingham, Alabama, that were met with violence; a bomb was detonated in a black church, killing four young girls. King was arrested for his role in organizing the protests, and while in prison, he wrote his "Letter from Birmingham Jail" to justify his strategy of civil disobedience, which he called "nonviolent direct action."

King begins his letter by discussing his disappointment with the lack of support he has received from white moderates, such as the group of clergy who published criticism of his organization in the local newspaper.

As you read, try to infer what the clergy's specific criticisms might have been, and notice the tone King uses. Would you characterize the writing as apologetic, conciliatory, accusatory, or something else?

¶1. White moderates block progress.

I must confess that over the past few years I have been gravely 1 disappointed with the <u>white moderate</u>. I have almost reached the regrettable conclusion that the Negro's [great stumbling block in his stride toward freedom] is not the White Citizen's Counciler or the Ku Klux Klanner, but the white moderate, who is more devoted to "<u>order</u>" than to <u>justice</u>; who prefers a <u>negative peace</u> which is the <u>absence of tension</u> to a <u>positive peace</u> which is the presence of justice; who constantly says: "I agree with you in the <u>goal</u> you seek, but I cannot agree with your <u>methods</u> of direct action"; who

Contrasts: order vs. justice, negative vs. positive peace, ends vs. means

(treating others like children)

(paternalistically) believes he can set the timetable for another man's freedom; who lives by a mythical concept of time and who constantly advises the Negro to wait for a "more convenient season." <u>Shallow understanding</u> from people of good will is more frustrating than <u>absolute misunderstanding</u> from people of ill will. [Lukewarm acceptance is much more bewildering than outright rejection.]

more contrasts

I had hoped that the white moderate would understand that 2 <u>law and order exist for the purpose of establishing justice</u> and that when they fail in this purpose they become the [dangerously structured dams that block the flow of social progress.] I had hoped that the white moderate would understand that the <u>present tension in the South</u> is a <u>necessary phase of the transition</u> from an [obnoxious <u>negative peace</u>,] in which the Negro passively accepted his unjust plight, to a [substantive and <u>positive peace</u>,] in which all men will respect the dignity and worth of human personality. Actually, we <u>who engage in nonviolent direct action are not the creators of tension</u>. We merely bring to the surface the <u>hidden tension</u> that is already alive. We bring it out in the open, where it can be seen

¶2. What the moderates don't understand

metaphor: law and order = dams (faulty?)

repeats contrast (negative/positive)

Tension already exists: We help dispel it. (True?)

and dealt with. [Like a boil that can never be cured so long as it is covered up but must be opened with all its ugliness to the natural medicines of air and light, injustice must be exposed, with all the tension its exposure creates, to the light of human conscience and the air of national opinion before it can be cured.]

simile: hidden tension is "like a boil"

In your statement you assert that our actions, even though peaceful, must be condemned because they precipitate violence. But is this a logical assertion? [Isn't this like condemning a robbed man because his possession of money precipitated the evil act of robbery? Isn't this like condemning Socrates because his unswerving commitment to truth and his philosophical inquiries precipitated the act by the misguided populace in which they made him drink hemlock? Isn't this like condemning Jesus because his unique God-consciousness and never-ceasing devotion to God's will precipitated the evil act of crucifixion?] We must come to see that, as the federal courts have consistently affirmed, it is wrong to urge an individual to cease his efforts to gain his basic constitutional rights because the question may precipitate violence. [Society must protect the robbed and punish the robber.]

3

¶3. Questions clergymen's logic: condemning his actions = condemning robbery victim, Socrates, Jesus.

repetition ("Isn't this like . . .")

(Yes!)

I had also hoped that the white moderate would reject the myth concerning time in relation to the struggle for freedom. I have just received a letter from a white brother in Texas. He writes: "All Christians know that the colored people will receive equal rights eventually, but it is possible that you are in too great a religious hurry. It has taken Christianity almost two thousand years to accomplish what it has. The teachings of Christ take time to come to earth." Such an attitude stems from a tragic misconception of time, from the strangely irrational notion that there is something in the very flow of time that will inevitably cure all ills. Actually, time itself is neutral; it can be used either destructively or constructively. More and more I feel that the people of ill will have used time much more effectively than have the people of good will. We will have to repent in this generation not merely for the [hateful words and actions of the bad people] but for the [appalling silence of the good people.] Human progress never rolls in on [wheels of

4

example of a white moderate's view

¶4. Time must be used to do right.

Silence/passivity is as bad as hateful words and actions.

*metaphor
(mechanical?)*

inevitability;| it comes through the tireless efforts of men willing to be co-workers with God, and without this hard work, time itself becomes an ally of the forces of social (stagnation.) |We must use time creatively, in the knowledge that the time is always ripe to do right.| Now is the time to make real the promise of democracy and transform our pending |national elegy| into a creative |psalm of brotherhood.| Now is the time to lift our national policy from the |quicksand of racial injustice| to the |solid rock of human dignity.|

stop developing

metaphors (song, natural world)

King accused of being an extremist.

You speak of our activity in Birmingham as extreme. At first I was rather disappointed that fellow clergymen would see my non-violent efforts as those of an extremist. I began thinking about the fact that I stand in the middle of two opposing forces in the Negro community. One is a |force of complacency,| made up in part of Negroes who, as a result of long years of oppression, are so drained of self-respect and a sense of "somebodiness" that they have adjusted to segregation; and in part of a few middle-class Negroes, who because of a degree of academic and economic security and because in some ways they profit by segregation, have become insensitive to the problems of the masses. The other |force is one of bitterness and hatred,| and it comes perilously close to advocating violence. It is expressed in the various black nationalist |groups that are springing up| across the nation, the largest and best-known being Elijah Muhammad's Muslim movement. Nourished by the Negro's frustration over the continued existence of racial discrimination, this movement is made up of people who have lost faith in America, who have absolutely repudiated Christianity, and who have concluded that the white man is an incorrigible "devil."

5

¶5. Puts self in middle of two extremes: complacency and bitterness.

Malcolm X?

I have tried to stand between these two forces, saying that we need emulate neither the "do-nothingism" of the complacent nor the hatred and despair of the black nationalist. For there is the more excellent way of love and nonviolent protest. I am grateful to God that, through the influence of the Negro church, the way of nonviolence became an integral part of our struggle.

6

¶6. Offers better choice: nonviolent protest.

(How did nonviolence become part of King's movement?)

If this philosophy had not emerged, by now many streets of the South would, I am convinced, be flowing with blood. And I am further convinced that if our white brothers dismiss as "rabble-

7

¶7. Says movement prevents racial violence. (Threat?)

(comfort)

rousers" and "outside agitators" those of us who employ nonviolent direct action, and if they refuse to support our nonviolent efforts, millions of Negroes will, out of frustration and despair, seek solace and security in black-nationalist ideologies—a development that would inevitably lead to a frightening racial nightmare.

[Oppressed people cannot remain oppressed forever.] The 8 yearning for freedom eventually manifests itself, and that is what has happened to the American Negro. Something within has reminded him of his birthright of freedom, and something without has reminded him that it can be gained. Consciously or unconsciously, he has been caught up by the Zeitgeist, and with *(spirit of the times)* his black brothers of Africa and his brown and yellow brothers of Asia, South America and the Caribbean, the United States Negro is moving with a sense of great urgency toward the [promised land of racial justice.] If one recognizes this [vital urge that has engulfed the Negro community,] one should readily understand why public demonstrations are taking place. The Negro has many [pent-up resentments] and latent frustrations, and he must release them. So let him march; let him make prayer pilgrimages to the city hall; let him go on freedom rides—and try to understand why he must do

Not a threat, but a fact — ?

so. If his repressed emotions are not released in nonviolent ways, they will seek expression through violence; this is not a threat but a fact of history. So I have not said to my people: "Get rid of your discontent." Rather, I have tried to say that this normal and healthy

¶8. Discontent is normal, healthy, and historically inevitable, but it must be channeled.

discontent can be [channeled into the creative outlet of nonviolent direct action.] And now this approach is being termed extremist.

But though I was initially disappointed at being categorized as 9 an extremist, as I continued to think about the matter I gradually gained a measure of satisfaction from the label. Was not Jesus an extremist for love: "Love your enemies, bless them that curse you, do good to them that hate you, and pray for them which despitefully use you, and persecute you." Was not Amos an extremist for justice: "Let justice roll down like waters and righteousness like an ever-flowing stream." Was not Paul an extremist for the Christian gospel: "I bear in my body the marks of the Lord Jesus." Was not Martin Luther an extremist: "Here I stand; I cannot do otherwise,

¶9. Redefines "extremism," embraces "extremist" label.

(Hebrew prophet)

(Christian apostle)
(founder of Protestantism)

(English preacher)

so help me God." And John Bunyan: "I will stay in jail to the end of my days before I make a butchery of my conscience." And Abraham Lincoln: "This nation cannot survive half slave and half free." And Thomas Jefferson: "We hold these truths to be self-evident, that all men are created equal. . . ." [So the question is not whether we will be extremists, but what kind of extremists we will be.] Will we be extremists for hate or for love? Will we be extremists for the preservation of injustice or for the extension of justice? In that dramatic scene on Calvary's hill three men were crucified. We must never forget that all three were crucified for the same crime—the crime of extremism. Two were extremists for immorality, and thus fell below their environment. The other, Jesus Christ, was an extremist for love, truth and goodness, and thereby rose above his environment. Perhaps the South, the [nation and the world are in dire need of creative extremists.]

Compares self to great "extremists"— including Jesus

I had hoped that the white moderate would see this need. 10 Perhaps I was too optimistic; perhaps I expected too much. I suppose I should have realized that few members of the oppressor race can understand the deep groans and passionate yearnings of the oppressed race, and still fewer have the vision to see that [injustice must be rooted out] by strong, persistent and determined action. I am thankful, however, that some of our white brothers in the South have grasped the meaning of this social revolution and committed themselves to it. They are still all too few in quantity, but they are big in quality. Some—such as Ralph McGill, Lillian Smith, Harry Golden, James McBride Dabbs, Ann Braden and Sarah Patton Boyle—have written about our struggle in eloquent and prophetic terms. Others have marched with us down nameless streets of the South. They have languished in filthy, roach-infested jails, suffering the abuse and brutality of policemen who view them as "dirty nigger-lovers." Unlike so many of their moderate brothers and sisters, they have recognized the urgency of the moment and sensed the need for [powerful "action" antidotes] to combat the [disease of segregation.]

Disappointed in the white moderate

¶10. Praises whites who have supported movement.

(Who are they?)

(been left unaided)

Metaphor: segregation is a disease.

1. Select a reading from chapters 2–9 or from another text, and mark the text using annotations like these:
   - Circle words to be defined in the margin.
   - Underline key words and phrases.
   - Bracket important sentences and passages.
   - Use lines or arrows to connect ideas or words.
2. Write marginal comments like these:
   - Number and summarize each paragraph.
   - Define unfamiliar words.
   - Note responses and questions.
   - Identify interesting writing strategies.
   - Point out patterns.
3. Layer additional markings in the text and comments in the margins as you reread for different purposes.

Taking Inventory

Taking inventory helps you analyze your annotations for different purposes. When you take inventory, you make various kinds of lists to explore patterns of meaning you find in the text. For instance, in reading the annotated passage by Martin Luther King Jr., you might have noticed that certain similes and metaphors are used or that many famous people are named. By listing the names (Socrates, Jesus, Luther, Lincoln, and so on) and then grouping them into categories (people who died for their beliefs, leaders, teachers, and religious figures), you could better understand why the writer refers to these particular people. Taking inventory of your annotations can be helpful if you plan to write about a text you are reading.

1. Examine the annotations you made in the activity above for patterns or repetitions, such as recurring images, stylistic features, repeated words and phrases, repeated examples or illustrations, and reliance on particular writing strategies.
2. List the items that make up a pattern.
3. Decide what the pattern might reveal about the reading.

Outlining

Outlining is an especially helpful reading strategy for understanding the content and structure of a reading. **Outlining**, which identifies the text's main ideas, may be part of the annotating process, or it may be done separately. Writing an outline in the margins of the text as you read and annotate makes it easier to find information later. Writing an outline on a separate piece of paper or online gives you more space to work with, and therefore such an outline usually includes more detail.

The key to outlining is distinguishing between the main ideas and the supporting material, such as examples, quotations, comparisons, and reasons. The main ideas form the backbone that holds the various parts of the text together. Outlining the main ideas helps you uncover this structure.

For more about the conventions of formal outlines, see Chapter 11.

Making an outline, however, is not simple. The reader must exercise judgment in deciding which are the most important ideas. The words used in an outline reflect the reader's interpretation and emphasis. Readers also must decide when to use the writer's words, their own words, or a combination of the two.

You may make either a formal, multileveled outline or an informal scratch outline. You might choose to make a formal outline of a reading about which you are writing an in-depth analysis or evaluation and a scratch outline to help you identify the main idea in each paragraph of a reading assignment. For example, here is a formal outline a student wrote for an essay evaluating the logic of the King excerpt.

Formal Outline of "Letter from Birmingham Jail"

I. "[T]he Negro's great stumbling block in his stride toward freedom is . . . the white moderate . . ." (par. 1).

    A. White moderates are more devoted to "order" than to justice; however,

        1. law and order exist only to establish justice (par. 2).

        2. law and order *without* justice actually threaten social order ("dangerously structured dams" metaphor, par. 2).

    B. White moderates prefer "negative peace" (absence of tension) to "positive peace" (justice); however,

        1. tension already exists; it is not created by movement (par. 2).

        2. tension is a necessary phase in progress to a just society (par. 2).

        3. tension must be allowed outlet if society is to be healthy ("boil" simile, par. 2).

    C. White moderates disagree with methods of movement; however,

        1. nonviolent direct action can't be condemned for violent response to it (analogies: robbed man; Socrates; Jesus, par. 3).

        2. federal courts affirm that those who seek constitutional rights can't be held responsible for violent response (par. 3).

    D. White moderates paternalistically counsel patience, saying time will bring change; however,

       1. time is "neutral"—we are obligated to use it *actively* to achieve justice (par. 4).

       2. the time for action is now (par. 4).

II. Contrary to white moderates' claims, the movement is not "extremist" in the usual sense (par. 5 ff.).

   A. It stands between extremes in black community: passivity, seen in the oppressed and the self-interested middle-class; and violent radicalism, seen in Elijah Muhammad's followers (pars. 5–6).

   B. In its advocacy of love and nonviolent protest, the movement has forestalled bloodshed and kept more blacks from joining radicals (pars. 5–7).

   C. The movement helps blacks channel urge for freedom that's part of historical trend and the prevailing *Zeitgeist* (par. 8).

III. The movement can be defined as extremist if the term is redefined: "Creative extremism" is extremism in the service of love, truth, and goodness (examples of Amos, Paul, Luther, Bunyan, Lincoln, Jefferson, Jesus, par. 9).

IV. Some whites—"few in quantity, but . . . big in quality"—have recognized the truth of the arguments above and, unlike the white moderates, have committed themselves to the movement (par. 10).

The annotations include a summary of each paragraph's topic. Here is a scratch outline that lists the topics:

For more about making a scratch outline, see Chapter 11.

Scratch Outline of "Letter from Birmingham Jail"

¶1. White moderates block progress

¶2. What the moderates don't understand

¶3. Questions clergymen's logic

¶4. Time must be used to do right

¶5. Puts self in middle of two extremes: complacency and bitterness

¶6. Offers better choice: nonviolent protest

¶7. Says movement prevents racial violence

¶8. Discontent normal, healthy, and historically inevitable, but it must be channeled

¶9. Redefines "extremism," embraces "extremist" label

¶10. Praises whites who have supported movement

ANALYZE & WRITE

1   Reread each paragraph of the selection you have been working with in the previous activities in this chapter. Identify the topic and the comments made about the topic. Do not include examples, specific details, quotations, or other explanatory and supporting material.

2   List the author's main ideas in the margin, on a separate piece of paper, or in a new document.

Paraphrasing

To learn more about paraphrasing, see Chapter 23.

Paraphrasing is restating a text you have read by using mostly your own words. It can help you clarify the meaning of an obscure or ambiguous passage. It is one of the three ways of integrating other people's ideas and information into your own writing, along with **quoting** (reproducing exactly the language of the source text) and **summarizing** (distilling the main ideas or gist of the source text). You might choose to paraphrase rather than quote when the source's language is not especially arresting or memorable. You might paraphrase short passages but summarize longer ones.

Following are two passages. The first is from paragraph 2 of the excerpt from King's "Letter." The second passage is a paraphrase of the first:

Original

> I had hoped that the white moderate would understand that law and order exist for the purpose of establishing justice and that when they fail in this purpose they become the dangerously structured dams that block the flow of social progress. I had hoped that the white moderate would understand that the present tension in the South is a necessary phase of the transition from an obnoxious negative peace, in which the Negro passively accepted his unjust plight, to a substantive and positive peace, in which all men will respect the dignity and worth of human personality.

Paraphrase

> King writes that he had hoped for more understanding from white moderates—specifically that they would recognize that law and order are not ends in themselves but means to the greater end of establishing justice. When law and order do not serve this greater end, they stand in the way of progress. King expected the white moderate to recognize that the current tense situation in the South is part of a transition process that is necessary for progress. The current situation is bad because although there is peace, it is an "obnoxious" and "negative" kind of peace based on blacks passively accepting the injustice of the status quo. A better kind of peace—one that is "substantive," real and not imaginary, as well as "positive"—requires that all people, regardless of race, be valued.

When you compare the paraphrase to the original, you can see that the paraphrase contains all the important information and ideas of the original. Notice also that the paraphrase is somewhat longer than the original, refers to the writer by name, and encloses King's original words in quotation marks. The paraphrase tries to be *neutral*, to avoid inserting the reader's opinions or distorting the original writer's ideas.

1. Select an important passage from the selection you have been working with. (The passage need be only two or three sentences.) Then reread the passage, looking up unfamiliar words in a college dictionary.

2. Translate the passage into your own words and sentences, putting quotation marks around any words or phrases you quote from the original.

3. Revise to ensure coherence.

Summarizing

Summarizing is important because it not only helps you understand and remember what is most significant in a reading, but also creates a condensed version of the reading's ideas and information that you can refer to later or insert into your own writing. Along with quoting and paraphrasing, summarizing enables you to integrate other writers' ideas into your own writing.

To learn more about summarizing, see Chapter 5.

A **summary** is a relatively brief restatement, primarily in the reader's own words, of the reading's main ideas. Summaries vary in length, depending on the reader's purpose. Some summaries are very brief—a sentence or even a subordinate clause. For example, if you were referring to the excerpt from "Letter from Birmingham Jail" and simply needed to indicate how it relates to your other sources, your summary might look something like this: "There have always been advocates of extremism in politics. Martin Luther King Jr., in 'Letter from Birmingham Jail,' for instance, defends nonviolent civil disobedience as an extreme but necessary means of bringing about racial justice." If, however, you were surveying the important texts of the civil rights movement, you might write a longer, more detailed summary that not only identifies the reading's main ideas but also shows how the ideas relate to one another.

Many writers find it useful to outline the reading as a preliminary to writing a summary. A paragraph-by-paragraph scratch outline (like the one on p. 509) lists the reading's main ideas in the sequence in which they appear in the original. But summarizing requires more than merely stringing together the entries in an outline; it must fill in the logical connections between the author's ideas. Notice how, in the summary, the reader repeats selected words and phrases and refers to the author by name, indicating, with verbs like *expresses*, *acknowledges*, and *explains*, the writer's purpose and strategy at each point in the argument.

Summary

King expresses his disappointment with white moderates who, by opposing his program of nonviolent direct action, have become a barrier to progress toward racial justice. He acknowledges that his program has raised tension in the South, but he explains that tension is necessary to bring about change. Furthermore, he argues that tension already exists, but because it has been unexpressed, it is unhealthy and potentially dangerous.

> He defends his actions against the clergy's criticisms, particularly their argument that he is in too much of a hurry. Responding to charges of extremism, King claims that he has actually prevented racial violence by channeling the natural frustrations of oppressed blacks into nonviolent protest. He asserts that extremism is precisely what is needed now — but it must be creative, rather than destructive, extremism. He concludes by again expressing disappointment with white moderates for not joining his effort as some other whites have.

A summary presents only ideas. Although it may use certain key terms from the source, it does not otherwise attempt to reflect the source's language, imagery, or tone; and it avoids even a hint of agreement or disagreement with the ideas it summarizes. Of course, a writer might summarize ideas in a source like "Letter from Birmingham Jail" to show readers that he or she has read it carefully and then proceed to use the summary to praise, question, or challenge King's argument. In doing so, the writer might quote specific language that reveals word choice, imagery, or tone.

ANALYZE & WRITE

---

1. Make a scratch outline of the reading you have been working with, or use the outline you created in the activity on page 509.

2. Write a paragraph or more that presents the author's main ideas in your own words and sentences, omitting supporting details and examples. Use the outline as a guide, but reread parts of the original text as necessary.

3. To make the summary coherent, fill in connections between the ideas you present.

Synthesizing

For more on synthesizing information and ideas from sources, see Chapters 5 and 23.

Synthesizing involves presenting ideas and information gleaned from different sources. It can help you see how different sources relate to one another. For example, one reading may provide information that fills out the information in another reading, or a reading could present arguments that challenge arguments in another reading.

When you synthesize material from different sources, you construct a conversation among your sources, a conversation in which you also participate. Synthesizing contributes most when writers use sources not only to support their ideas but to challenge and extend them as well.

In the following example, the reader uses a variety of sources related to the King passage (pp. 502–506) and brings them together around a central idea. Notice how quotation, paraphrase, and summary are all used.

Synthesis

When King defends his campaign of nonviolent direct action against the clergymen's criticism that "our actions, even though peaceful, must be condemned because they precipitate violence" (King excerpt, par. 3), he is using what Vinit Haksar calls Mohandas Gandhi's "safety-valve argument" ("Civil Disobedience and Non-Cooperation" 117). According to Haksar, Gandhi gave a "non-threatening warning of worse things to come" if his demands were not met. King similarly makes clear that advocates of actions more extreme than those he advocates are waiting in the wings: "The other force is one of bitterness and hatred, and it comes perilously close to advocating violence" (King excerpt, par. 5). King identifies this force with Elijah Muhammad, and although he does not name him, King's contemporary readers would have known that he was referring also to his disciple Malcolm X, who, according to Herbert J. Storing, "urged that Negroes take seriously the idea of revolution" ("The Case against Civil Disobedience" 90). In fact, Malcolm X accused King of being a modern-day Uncle Tom, trying "to keep us under control, to keep us passive and peaceful and nonviolent" (*Malcolm X Speaks* 12).

ANALYZE & WRITE

1. Find and read two or three sources on the topic of the selection you have been working with, annotating the passages that give you ideas about the topic.

2. Look for patterns among your sources, possibly supporting or challenging your ideas or those of other sources.

3. Write a paragraph or more synthesizing your sources, using quotation, summary, and paraphrase to present what they say on the topic.

Contextualizing

All texts reflect historical and cultural assumptions, values, and attitudes that may differ from your own. To read thoughtfully, you need to become aware of these differences. **Contextualizing** is a critical reading strategy that enables you to make inferences about a reading's historical and cultural context and to examine the differences between its context and your own.

The excerpt from King's "Letter from Birmingham Jail" is a good example of a text that benefits from being read contextually. If you knew little about the history of slavery and segregation in the United States, it would be difficult to understand the passion expressed in this passage. To understand the historical and cultural context in which King wrote his "Letter from Birmingham Jail," you could do some library or Internet research. Comparing the situation at the time to situations with which you are familiar would help you understand some of your own attitudes toward King and the civil rights movement.

Here is what one reader wrote to contextualize King's writing:

I have seen documentaries showing civil rights demonstrators being attacked by dogs, doused by fire hoses, beaten and dragged by helmeted police. Such images give me a sense of the violence, fear, and hatred that King was responding to. The creative tension King refers to comes across in his writing. He uses his anger and frustration to inspire his critics. He also threatens them, although he denies it. I saw a film on Malcolm X, so I could see that King was giving white people a choice between his own nonviolent way and Malcolm's more confrontational way.

Things have certainly changed since the 1960s. For one: Barack Obama was elected president for two terms! When I read King's "Letter" today, I feel like I'm reading history. But then again, there have been a number of reports recently—often caught as cell-phone videos—of police brutality (like the death of Walter Scott, an unarmed black man who was shot in the back eight times by a cop in North Charleston, South Carolina). Some people have also suggested that in recent elections, there have been efforts to deprive African Americans and other minorities of the right to vote in some areas of the country.

ANALYZE & WRITE

1 Describe the historical and cultural situation as it is represented in the reading you have been working with and in other sources with which you are familiar. Your knowledge may come from other reading, television or film, school, or elsewhere. (If you know nothing about the historical and cultural context, you could do some library or Internet research.)

2 Compare the historical and cultural situation in which the text was written with your own historical and cultural situation. Consider how your understanding and judgment of the reading are affected by your own context.

Exploring the Significance of Figurative Language

Figurative language—*metaphor, simile,* and *symbolism*—enhances literal meaning by implying abstract ideas through vivid images and by evoking feelings and associations.

Metaphor implicitly compares two different things by identifying them with each other. For instance, when King calls the white moderate "the Negro's great stumbling block in his stride toward freedom" (par. 1), he does not mean that the white moderate literally trips the Negro who is attempting to walk toward freedom. The sentence makes sense only if understood figuratively: The white moderate trips up the Negro by frustrating every effort to achieve justice.

Simile, a more explicit form of comparison, uses the word *like* or *as* to signal the relationship of two seemingly unrelated things. King uses simile when he says that injustice is "like a boil that can never be cured so long as it is covered up" (par. 2). This simile makes several points of comparison between injustice and a boil. It suggests that injustice is a disease of society as a boil is a disease of the skin and that injustice, like a boil, must be exposed or it will fester and infect the entire body.

Symbolism compares two things by making one stand for the other. King uses the white moderate as a symbol for supposed liberals and would-be supporters of civil rights who are actually frustrating the cause.

How these figures of speech are used in a text reveals something of the writer's feelings about the subject. Exploring possible meanings in a text's figurative language involves (1) annotating and then listing the metaphors, similes, and symbols you find in a reading; (2) grouping and labeling the figures of speech that appear to express related feelings or attitudes; and (3) writing to explore the meaning of the patterns you have found. The following example shows the process of exploring figures of speech in the King excerpt.

Listing Figures of Speech

"stumbling block in his stride toward freedom" (par. 1)

"law and order . . . become the dangerously structured dams" (2)

"the flow of social progress" (2)

"Like a boil that can never be cured" (2)

"the light of human conscience and the air of national opinion" (2)

"the quicksand of racial injustice" (4)

Grouping and Labeling Figures of Speech

Sickness: "like a boil" (2); "the disease of segregation" (10)

Underground: "hidden tension" (2); "injustice must be exposed" (2); "injustice must be rooted out" (10)

Blockage: "dams," "block the flow" (2); "Human progress never rolls in on wheels of inevitability" (4); "pent-up resentments" (8); "repressed emotions" (8)

Writing to Explore Meaning

The patterns labeled underground and blockage suggest a feeling of frustration. Inertia is a problem; movement forward toward progress or upward toward the promised land is stalled. The strong need to break through the resistance may represent King's feelings about both his attempt to lead purposeful, effective demonstrations and his effort to write a convincing argument.

The simile of injustice being "like a boil" links the two patterns of underground and sickness, suggesting that something bad, a disease, is inside the people or the society. The cure is to expose or to root out the blocked hatred and injustice as well as to release the tension or emotion that has long been repressed. This implies that repression itself is the evil, not simply what is repressed. Therefore, writing and speaking out through political action may have curative power for individuals and society alike.

ANALYZE & WRITE

1. Annotate all the figures of speech you find in the reading you have been working with (or another selection) — metaphors, similes, and symbols — and then list them.

2. Group the figures of speech that appear to express related feelings and attitudes, and label each group.

3. Write one or two paragraphs exploring the meaning of these patterns. What do they tell you about the text?

Looking for Patterns of Opposition

All texts carry within themselves voices of opposition. These voices may echo the views and values of readers the writer anticipates or predecessors to whom the writer is responding in some way; they may even reflect the writer's own conflicting values. Careful readers look closely for such a dialogue of opposing voices within the text.

When we think of oppositions, we ordinarily think of polarities: *yes* and *no*, *up* and *down*, *black* and *white*, *new* and *old*. Some oppositions, however, may be more subtle. The excerpt from King's "Letter from Birmingham Jail" is rich in such oppositions: *moderate* versus *extremist*, *order* versus *justice*, *direct action* versus *passive acceptance*, *expression* versus *repression*. These oppositions are not accidental; they form a significant pattern that gives a reader important information about the essay.

A careful reading will show that King always values one of the two terms in an opposition over the other. In the passage, for example, *extremist* is valued over *moderate* (par. 9). This preference for extremism is surprising. The reader should ask why, when white extremists like members of the Ku Klux Klan have committed so many outrages against African Americans, King would prefer extremism. If King is trying to convince his readers to accept his point of view, why would he represent himself as an extremist? Moreover, why would a clergyman advocate extremism instead of moderation?

Studying the **patterns of opposition** in the text enables you to answer these questions. You will see that King sets up this opposition to force his readers to examine their own values and realize that they are in fact misplaced. Instead of working toward justice, he says, those who support law and order maintain the unjust status quo. By getting his readers to think of white moderates as blocking rather than facilitating peaceful change, King brings readers to align themselves with him and perhaps even embrace his strategy of nonviolent resistance.

Looking for patterns of opposition involves annotating words or phrases in the reading that indicate oppositions, listing the opposing terms in pairs, deciding which term in each pair is preferred by the writer, and reflecting on the meaning of the patterns. Here is a partial list of oppositions from the King excerpt, with the preferred terms marked by an asterisk:

Listing Patterns of Opposition

moderate	*extremist
order	*justice
negative peace	*positive peace
absence of justice	*presence of justice
goals	*methods
*direct action	passive acceptance
*exposed tension	hidden tension

ANALYZE & WRITE

1 Annotate the selection you have been working with (or another selection) for words or phrases indicating oppositions.

2 List the pairs of oppositions. (You may have to paraphrase or even supply the opposite word or phrase if it is not stated directly in the text.)

3 For each pair of oppositions, put an asterisk next to the term that the writer seems to value or prefer over the other.

4 Study the patterns of opposition. How do they contribute to your understanding of the essay? What do they tell you about what the author wants you to believe?

Reflecting on Challenges to Your Beliefs and Values

To read thoughtfully, you need to scrutinize your own assumptions and attitudes as well as those expressed in the text you are reading. If you are like most readers, however, you will find that your assumptions and attitudes are so ingrained that you are not always fully aware of them. A good strategy for getting at these underlying beliefs and values is to identify and reflect on the ways the text challenges you and how it makes you feel—disturbed, threatened, ashamed, combative, pleased, exuberant, or some other way.

For example, here is what one student wrote about the King passage:

Reflections

In paragraph 1, Dr. King criticizes people who are "more devoted to 'order' than to justice." This criticism upsets me because today I think I would choose order over justice. When I reflect on my feelings and try to figure out where they come from, I realize that what I feel most is fear. I am terrified by the violence in society today. I'm afraid of sociopaths who don't respect the rule of law, much less the value of human life.

> I know Dr. King was writing in a time when the law itself was unjust, when order was apparently used to keep people from protesting and changing the law. But things are different now. Today, justice seems to serve criminals more than it serves law-abiding citizens. That's why I'm for order over justice.

ANALYZE & WRITE

1. Identify challenges by marking the text you have been working with (or another text) where you feel your beliefs and values are being opposed, criticized, or unfairly characterized.

2. Write a few paragraphs reflecting on why you feel challenged. Do not defend your feelings; instead, search your memory to discover where they come from.

Evaluating the Logic of an Argument

For more on argument, including logical fallacies, see Chapter 19.

An *argument* includes a thesis backed by reasons and support. The **thesis** asserts a position on a controversial issue or a solution to a problem that the writer wants readers to accept. The **reasons** tell readers why they should accept the thesis, and the **support** (such as examples, statistics, authorities, and textual evidence) gives readers grounds for accepting it. For an argument to be considered logically acceptable, it must meet the three conditions of what we call the ABC test:

The ABC Test

A. The reasons and support must be *appropriate* to the thesis.
B. The reasons and support must be *believable*.
C. The reasons and support must be *consistent* with one another as well as *complete*.

Test for appropriateness.

To evaluate the logic of an argument, first decide whether the argument's reasons and support are appropriate. To test for appropriateness, ask these questions:

- How does each reason or piece of support relate to the thesis?

- Is the connection between reasons and support and the thesis clear and compelling?

Readers most often question the appropriateness of reasons and support when the writer argues by analogy or by invoking authority. For example, in paragraph 2, King argues that when law and order fail to establish justice, "they become the dangerously structured dams that block the flow of social progress." The analogy asserts the following logical relationship: Law and order are to progress toward justice what a dam is to water. If you do not accept this analogy, the argument fails the test of appropriateness.

For more about analogy, see Chapter 18. For more about invoking authorities, see Chapter 19.

King uses both analogy and authority in paragraph 3: "Isn't this like condemning Socrates because his unswerving commitment to truth and his philosophical inquiries precipitated the act by the misguided populace in which they made him drink hemlock?" Not only must you judge the appropriateness of the analogy comparing the Greeks' condemnation of Socrates to the white moderates' condemnation of King, but you must also judge whether it is appropriate to accept Socrates as an authority. Since Socrates is generally respected for his teachings on justice, his words and actions are likely to be considered appropriate to King's situation in Birmingham.

Test for believability.

Believability is a measure of your willingness to accept as true the reasons and support the writer gives in defense of a thesis. To test for believability, ask:

- On what basis am I being asked to believe this reason or support is true?
- If it cannot be proved true or false, how much weight does it carry?

In judging facts, examples and anecdotes, statistics, and authorities, consider the following points:

Facts are statements that can be proved objectively to be true. The believability of facts depends on the following:

- their a*ccuracy* (they should not distort or misrepresent reality)
- their *completeness* (they should not omit important details)
- the *trustworthiness* of their sources (sources should be qualified and unbiased)

King, for instance, asserts as fact that the African American will not wait much longer for racial justice (par. 8). His critics might question the factuality of this assertion by asking: Is it true of all African Americans? How does King know what African Americans will and will not do?

Examples and anecdotes are particular instances that may or may not make you believe a general statement. The believability of examples depends on the following:

- their *representativeness* (whether they are truly typical and thus generalizable)
- their *specificity* (whether particular details make them seem true to life)

Even if a vivid example or gripping anecdote does not convince readers, it usually strengthens argumentative writing by clarifying the meaning and dramatizing the point. In paragraph 5 of the King excerpt, for example, King supports his generalization that some African American extremists are motivated by bitterness and hatred by citing the specific example of Elijah Muhammad's Black Muslim movement. Conversely, in paragraph 9, he refers to Jesus, Paul, Luther, and others as examples of extremists motivated by love and Christianity. These examples support his assertion that extremism is not in itself wrong and that any judgment of extremism must be based on its motivation and cause.

Statistics are numerical data. The believability of statistics depends on the following:

- the *comparability* of the data (the price of apples in 1985 cannot be compared with the price of apples in 2015 unless the figures are adjusted to account for inflation)
- the *precision* of the methods employed to gather and analyze data (representative samples should be used and variables accounted for)
- the *trustworthiness* of the sources

Authorities are people to whom the writer attributes expertise on a given subject. Not only must such authorities be appropriate, as mentioned earlier, but they must be credible as well—that is, the reader must accept them as experts on the topic at hand. King cites authorities repeatedly throughout his essay. He refers to religious leaders (Jesus and Luther) as well as to American political leaders (Lincoln and Jefferson). These figures are likely to have a high degree of credibility among King's readers.

Test for consistency and completeness.

In looking for consistency, you should be concerned that all the parts of the argument work together and that they are sufficient to convince readers to accept the thesis or at least take it seriously. To test for consistency and completeness, ask:

- Are any of the reasons and support contradictory?
- Do the reasons and support provide sufficient grounds for accepting the thesis?
- Does the writer fail to acknowledge, concede, or refute any opposing arguments or important objections?

A thoughtful reader might regard as contradictory King's characterizing himself first as a moderate and later as an extremist opposed to the forces of violence. (King attempts to reconcile this apparent contradiction by explicitly redefining extremism in par. 9.) Similarly, the fact that King fails to examine and refute every legal recourse available to his cause might allow a critical reader to question the sufficiency of his argument.

For more on responding to objections and alternatives, see Chapter 19.

ANALYZE & WRITE

Use the ABC test on the selection you have been working with (or another selection):

A *Test for appropriateness* by checking that the reasons and support are clearly and directly related to the thesis.

B *Test for believability* by deciding whether you can accept the reasons and support as likely to be true.

C *Test for consistency and completeness* by deciding whether the argument has any contradictions and whether any important objections or opposing views have been ignored.

Recognizing Emotional Manipulation

Writers often try to arouse emotions in readers to excite their interest, make them care, or move them to take action. There is nothing wrong with appealing to readers' emotions. What is wrong is manipulating readers with false or exaggerated appeals. Therefore, you should be suspicious of writing that is overly sentimental, that cites alarming statistics and frightening anecdotes, that demonizes others and identifies itself with revered authorities, or that uses potent symbols (for example, the American flag) or emotionally loaded words (such as *racist*).

King, for example, uses the emotionally loaded word *paternalistically* to refer to the white moderate's belief that "he can set the timetable for another man's freedom" (par. 1). In the same paragraph, King uses symbolism to get an emotional reaction from readers when he compares the white moderate to the "Ku Klux Klanner." To get readers to accept his ideas, he also relies on authorities whose names evoke the greatest respect, such as Jesus and Lincoln. But some readers might object that comparing his own crusade to that of Jesus is pretentious and manipulative. A critical reader might also consider King's discussion of African American extremists in paragraph 7 to be a veiled threat designed to frighten readers into agreement.

ANALYZE & WRITE

1. Annotate places in the text you have been working with (or another text) where you sense emotional appeals are being used.

2. Assess whether any of the emotional appeals are unfairly manipulative.

Judging the Writer's Credibility

Writers try to persuade readers by presenting an image of themselves in their writing that will gain their readers' confidence. This image must be created indirectly, through the arguments, language, and system of values and beliefs expressed or implied in the writing. Writers establish credibility in their writing in three ways:

- By showing their knowledge of the subject
- By building *common ground* with readers
- By responding fairly to objections and opposing arguments

Test for knowledge.

Writers demonstrate their knowledge through the facts and statistics they marshal, the sources they rely on for information, and the scope and depth of their understanding. You may not be sufficiently expert on the subject yourself to know whether the facts are accurate, the sources are reliable, and the understanding is sufficient. You may need to do some research to see what others say about the subject. You can also check credentials—the writer's educational and professional qualifications, the respectability of the publication in which the selection first appeared, and reviews of the writer's work—to determine whether the writer is a respected authority in the field. For example, King brings with him the authority that comes from being a member of the clergy and a respected leader of the Southern Christian Leadership Conference.

For more about evaluating sources, see Chapter 22.

Test for common ground.

One way writers can establish **common ground** with their readers is by basing their reasoning on shared values, beliefs, and attitudes. They use language that includes their readers (*we*) and qualify their assertions to keep them from being too extreme. Above all, they acknowledge differences of opinion. You want to notice such appeals.

King creates common ground with readers by using the inclusive pronoun *we*, suggesting shared concerns between himself and his audience. Notice, however, his use of masculine pronouns and other references ("the Negro . . . he," "our brothers"). Although King addressed his letter to male clergy, he intended it to be published in the local newspaper, where it would be read by an audience of both men and women. By using language that excludes women—a common practice at the time the selection was written—King may have missed the opportunity to build common ground with more than half of his readers.

Test for fairness.

Writers reveal their character by how they handle opposing arguments and objections to their argument. As a critical reader, pay particular attention to how writers treat possible differences of opinion. Be suspicious of those who ignore differences and pretend that everyone agrees with their viewpoints. When objections or opposing views are represented, consider whether they have been distorted in any way; if they are refuted, be sure they are challenged fairly—with sound reasoning and solid support.

One way to gauge the author's credibility is to identify the tone of the argument, for it conveys the writer's attitude toward the subject and toward the reader. Is the text angry? sarcastic? evenhanded? shrill? condescending? bullying? Do you feel as if the writer is treating the subject—and you, as a reader—with fairness? King's tone might be characterized in different passages as patient (he doesn't lose his temper), respectful (he refers to white moderates as "people of good will"), or pompous (comparing himself to Jesus and Socrates).

ANALYZE & WRITE

---

1. Using the selection you have been working with (or another selection), annotate for the writer's knowledge of the subject, how well common ground is established, and whether the writer deals fairly with objections and opposing arguments.

2. Decide what in the essay you find credible and what you question.

PART 3

Writing
Strategies

13

Cueing the Reader

Readers need guidance. To guide readers through a piece of writing, a writer can provide five basic kinds of **cues**, or signals:

1. Thesis and forecasting statements, to orient readers to ideas and organization
2. Paragraphing, to group related ideas and details
3. Cohesive devices, to connect ideas to one another and bring about clarity
4. Transitions, to signal relationships or shifts in meaning
5. Headings and subheadings, to group related paragraphs and help readers locate specific information quickly

This chapter illustrates how each of these cueing strategies works.

Orienting Statements

To help readers find their way, especially in difficult and lengthy texts, you can provide two kinds of **orienting statements**: a *thesis statement*, which declares the main point, and a *forecasting statement*, which previews subordinate points, showing the order in which they will be discussed in the essay.

Use thesis statements to announce the main idea.

To help readers understand what is being said about a subject, writers often provide a thesis statement early in the essay. The **thesis statement**, which can comprise one or more sentences, operates as a cue by letting readers know which is the most important general idea among the writer's many ideas and observations. In "Love: The Right Chemistry" in Chapter 4, Anastasia Toufexis expresses her thesis in the second paragraph:

> O.K., let's cut out all this nonsense about romantic love. Let's bring some scientific precision to the party. Let's put love under a microscope.

When rigorous people with Ph.D.s after their names do that, what they see is not some silly, senseless thing. No, their probe reveals that love rests firmly on the foundations of evolution, biology and chemistry.

Readers naturally look for something that will tell them the point of an essay, a focus for the many diverse details and ideas they encounter as they read. They expect to find some information early on that will give them a context for reading the essay, particularly if they are reading about a new or difficult subject. Therefore, a thesis statement, like Toufexis's, placed at the beginning of an essay enables readers to anticipate the content of the essay and helps them understand the relationships among its various ideas and details.

Occasionally, however, particularly in fairly short, informal pieces, a writer may save a direct statement of the thesis until the conclusion. Ending with the thesis brings together the various strands of information or supporting details introduced over the course of the essay and makes clear the essay's main idea.

Some essays, particularly autobiographical essays, offer no direct thesis statement. Although this can make the point of the essay more difficult to determine, it can be appropriate when the essay is more expressive and personal than it is informative. In all cases, careful writers keep readers' needs and expectations in mind when deciding how—and whether—to state the thesis.

EXERCISE 13.1

In the essay by Jessica Statsky in Chapter 6, underline the thesis statement, the last sentence in paragraph 1. Notice the key terms: "overzealous parents and coaches," "impose adult standards," "children's sports," "activities . . . neither satisfying nor beneficial." Then skim the essay, stopping to read the sentence at the beginning of each paragraph. Also read the last paragraph.

Consider whether the idea in every paragraph's first sentence is anticipated by the thesis's key terms. Consider also the connection between the ideas in the last paragraph and the thesis's key terms. What can you conclude about how a thesis might assert the point of an essay, anticipate the ideas that follow, and help readers relate the ideas to one another?

Use forecasting statements to preview topics.

Some thesis statements include a **forecast**, which overviews the way a thesis will be developed, as in the following example:

> In the three years from 1348 through 1350 the pandemic of plague known as the Black Death, or, as the Germans called it, the Great Dying, killed at least a fourth of the population of Europe. It was undoubtedly the worst disaster that has ever befallen mankind. Today we can have no real conception of the terror under which people lived in the shadow of the plague. For more than two centuries plague has not been a serious threat to mankind in the large, although it is still a grisly presence in parts of the Far East and Africa. Scholars continue to study the Great Dying, however, as a historical example of human behavior under the stress of universal catastrophe. In these days when the threat of plague has been replaced by the threat of mass human extermination

by even more rapid means, there has been a sharp renewal of interest in the history of the fourteenth-century calamity. With new perspective, students are investigating its manifold effects: demographic, economic, psychological, moral and religious.

—WILLIAM LANGER, "The Black Death"

As a reader would expect, Langer divides his essay into explanations of the research into these five effects, addressing them in the order in which they appear in the forecasting statement.

EXERCISE 13.2

Turn to Patrick O'Malley's essay in Chapter 7, and underline the forecasting statement in paragraph 2. Then skim the essay. Notice whether O'Malley takes up every point he mentions in the forecasting statement and whether he sticks to the order he promises readers. How well does his forecasting statement help you follow his essay? What suggestions for improvement, if any, would you offer him?

Paragraphing

Paragraph cues as obvious as indentation keep readers on track. You can also arrange material in a paragraph to help readers see what is important or significant. For example, you can begin with a topic sentence, help readers see the relationship between the previous paragraph and the present one with an explicit transition, and place the most important information toward the end.

Paragraph indents signal related ideas.

One paragraph cue—the indentation that signals the beginning of a new paragraph—is a relatively modern printing convention. Old manuscripts show that paragraph divisions were not always marked. To make reading easier, scribes and printers began to use the symbol ¶ to mark paragraph breaks, and later, indenting became common practice. Indenting has been abandoned by most online and business writers, who now distinguish one paragraph from another by leaving a line of space between paragraphs.

Paragraphing helps readers by signaling when a sequence of related ideas begins and ends. Paragraphing also helps readers judge what is most important in what they are reading. Writers typically emphasize important information by placing it at the two points in the paragraph where readers are most attentive—the beginning and the end.

You can give special emphasis to information by placing it in its own paragraph.

EXERCISE 13.3

Turn again to Patrick O'Malley's essay in Chapter 7, and read paragraphs 4–7 with the following questions in mind: Does all the material in each paragraph seem to be related? Do you feel a sense of closure at the end of each paragraph? Does the last sentence offer the most important or significant or weighty information in the paragraph?

Topic sentences announce the paragraph's focus.

A **topic sentence** lets readers know the focus of a paragraph in simple and direct terms. It is a cueing strategy for the paragraph, much as a thesis or forecasting statement is for the whole essay. Because paragraphing usually signals a shift in focus, readers expect some kind of reorientation in the opening sentence. They need to know whether the new paragraph will introduce another aspect of the topic or develop one already introduced.

Announcing the Topic   Some topic sentences simply announce the topic. Here are some examples taken from Barry Lopez's book *Arctic Dreams:*

> A polar bear walks in a way all its own.

> What is so consistently striking about the way Eskimos used parts of an animal is the breadth of their understanding about what would work.

> The Mediterranean view of the Arctic, down to the time of the Elizabethan mariners, was shaped by two somewhat contradictory thoughts.

The following paragraph shows how one of Lopez's topic sentences (highlighted) is developed:

> What is so consistently striking about the way Eskimos used parts of an animal is the breadth of their understanding about what would work. Knowing that muskox horn is more flexible than caribou antler, they preferred it for making the side prongs of a fish spear. For a waterproof bag in which to carry sinews for clothing repair, they chose salmon skin. They selected the strong, translucent intestine of a bearded seal to make a window for a snowhouse — it would fold up for easy traveling and it would not frost over in cold weather. To make small snares for sea ducks, they needed a springy material that would not rot in salt water — baleen fibers. The down feather of a common eider, tethered at the end of a stick in the snow at an angle, would reveal the exhalation of a quietly surfacing seal. Polar bear bone was used anywhere a stout, sharp point was required, because it is the hardest bone.
>
> —Barry Lopez, *Arctic Dreams*

EXERCISE 13.4

Turn to Jessica Statsky's essay in Chapter 6. Underline the topic sentence (the first sentence) in paragraphs 3 and 5. Consider how these sentences help you anticipate the paragraph's topic and method of development.

Making a Transition   Not all topic sentences simply point to what will follow. Some also refer to earlier sentences. Such sentences work both as topic sentences, stating the main point of the paragraph, and as *transitions,* linking that paragraph to the previous one. Here are a few topic sentences from "Quilts and Women's Culture," by Elaine Hedges, with transitions highlighted:

Transitions tie each topic sentence to a previous statement.

Within its broad traditionalism and anonymity, however, variations and distinctions developed.

Regionally, too, distinctions were introduced into quilt making through the interesting process of renaming.

Finally, out of such regional and other variations come individual, signed achievements.

Quilts, then, were an outlet for creative energy, a source and emblem of sisterhood and solidarity, and a graphic response to historical and political change.

Sometimes the first sentence of a paragraph serves as a transition, and a subsequent sentence states the topic, as in the following example:

Transition sentences

What a convenience, what a relief it will be, they say, never to worry about how to dress for a job interview, a romantic tryst, or a funeral!

Convenient, perhaps, but not exactly a relief. Such a utopia would give most of us the same kind of chill we feel when a stadium full of Communist-bloc athletes in identical sports outfits, shouting slogans in unison, appears on TV. Most people do not want to be told what to wear any more than they want to be told what to say. In Belfast recently four hundred Irish Republican prisoners "refused to wear any clothes at all, draping themselves day and night in blankets," rather than put on prison uniforms. Even the offer of civilian-style dress did not satisfy them; they insisted on wearing their own clothes brought from home, or nothing. Fashion is free speech, and one of the privileges, if not always one of the pleasures, of a free world.

—ALISON LURIE, *The Language of Clothes*

Occasionally, whole paragraphs serve as transitions, linking one sequence of paragraphs with those that follow, as in the following:

Transition paragraph summarizes contrasts and sets up an analysis of the similarities.

Yet it was not all contrast, after all. Different as they were—in background, in personality, in underlying aspiration—these two great soldiers had much in common. Under everything else, they were marvelous fighters. Furthermore, their fighting qualities were really very much alike.

—BRUCE CATTON, "Grant and Lee: A Study in Contrasts"

EXERCISE 13.5

Turn to Jessica Statsky's essay in Chapter 6 and read paragraphs 3–7. As you read, underline the part of the first sentence in paragraphs 4, 5, and 7 that refers to the previous paragraph, creating a transition from one to the next. Notice the different ways Statsky creates these transitions. Consider whether they are all equally effective.

Positioning the Topic Sentence   Although topic sentences may occur anywhere in a paragraph, stating the topic in the first sentence has the advantage of giving readers a sense of how the paragraph is likely to be developed. The beginning of the paragraph is therefore the most common position.

A topic sentence that does not open a paragraph is most likely to appear at the end. When a topic sentence concludes a paragraph, it usually summarizes or generalizes preceding information:

> Even black Americans sometimes need to be reminded about the deceptiveness of television. Blacks retain their fascination with black characters on TV: Many of us buy *Jet* magazine primarily to read its weekly television feature, which lists every black character (major or minor) to be seen on the screen that week. Yet our fixation with the presence of black characters on TV has blinded us to an important fact that *Cosby,* which began in 1984, and its offshoots over the years demonstrate convincingly: There is very little connection between the social status of black Americans and the fabricated images of black people that Americans consume each day. The representation of blacks on TV is a very poor index to our social advancement or political progress.
>
> —Henry Louis Gates Jr., "TV's Black World Turns—but Stays Unreal"

Topic is not stated until the last sentence.

When a topic sentence is used in a narrative, it often appears as the last sentence as a way to evaluate or reflect on events:

> A cold sun was sliding down a gray fall sky. Some older boys had been playing tackle football in the field we took charge of every weekend. In a few years, they'd be called to Southeast Asia, some of them. Their locations would be tracked with pushpins in red, white, and blue on maps on nearly every kitchen wall. But that afternoon, they were quick as young deer. They leapt and dodged, dove from each other and collided in midair. Bulletlike passes flew to connect them. Or the ball spiraled in a high arc across the frosty sky one to another. In short, they were mindlessly agile in a way that captured as audience every little kid within running distance of the yellow goalposts.
>
> —Mary Karr, *Cherry*

Topic sentence reflects on narrated events described earlier in paragraph.

It is possible for a single topic sentence to introduce two or more paragraphs. Subsequent paragraphs in such a sequence have no separate topic sentences of their own:

> Anthropologists Daniel Maltz and Ruth Borker point out that boys and girls socialize differently. Little girls tend to play in small groups or, even more common, in pairs. Their social life usually centers around a best friend, and friendships are made, maintained, and broken by talk—especially "secrets." If a little girl tells her friend's secret to another little girl, she may find herself with a new best friend. The secrets themselves may or may not be important, but the fact of telling them is all-important. It's hard for newcomers to get into these tight groups, but anyone who is admitted is treated as an equal. Girls like to play cooperatively; if they can't cooperate, the group breaks up.
>
> Little boys tend to play in larger groups, often outdoors, and they spend more time doing things than talking. It's easy for boys to get into the group, but not everyone is accepted as an equal. Once in the group, boys must jockey for their status in it. One of the most important ways they do this is through talk: verbal display such as telling stories and jokes, challenging and sidetracking the verbal

Topic sentence states topic of this paragraph and next.

displays of other boys, and withstanding other boys' challenges in order to maintain their own story — and status. Their talk is often competitive talk about who is best at what.

—Deborah Tannen, *That's Not What I Meant!*

EXERCISE 13.6

Consider the variety and effectiveness of the topic sentences in your most recent writing project. Begin by underlining the topic sentence in each paragraph after the first one. The topic sentence may not be the first sentence in a paragraph, though it will often be.

Then double-underline the part of the topic sentence that provides an explicit transition from one paragraph to the next. You may find a transition that is separate from the topic sentence. You may not always find a topic sentence.

Reflect on your topic sentences, and evaluate how well they serve to orient your readers to the sequence of topics or ideas in your essay.

Cohesive Devices

Cohesive devices guide readers, helping them follow your train of thought by connecting key words and phrases throughout a passage. Among such devices are pronoun reference, word repetition, synonyms, sentence structure repetition, and collocation.

Pronouns connect phrases or sentences.

One common cohesive device is *pronoun reference*. As noun substitutes, pronouns refer to nouns that either precede or follow them and thus serve to connect phrases or sentences. The nouns that come before pronouns are called **antecedents**.

> In New York from dawn to dusk to dawn, day after day, you can hear the steady rumble of tires against the concrete span of the George Washington Bridge. The bridge is never completely still. It trembles with traffic. It moves in the wind. Its great veins of steel swell when hot and contract when cold; its span often is ten feet closer to the Hudson River in summer than in winter.
>
> —Gay Talese, "New York"

Pronouns form a chain of connection with antecedent.

This example has only one pronoun-antecedent chain, and the antecedent comes first, so all the pronouns refer back to it. When there are multiple pronoun-antecedent chains with references forward as well as back, writers have to make sure that readers will not mistake one pronoun's antecedent for another's.

Word repetition aids cohesion.

To avoid confusion, writers often use *word repetition*. The device of repeating words and phrases is especially helpful if a pronoun might confuse readers:

Some odd optical property of our highly polarized and unequal society makes the poor almost invisible to their economic superiors. The poor can see the affluent easily enough—on television, for example, or on the covers of magazines. But the affluent rarely see the poor or, if they do catch sight of them in some public space, rarely know what they're seeing, since—thanks to consignment stores and, yes, Wal-Mart—the poor are usually able to disguise themselves as members of the more comfortable classes.

—Barbara Ehrenreich, *Nickel and Dimed*

Repeated words

In the next example, several overlapping chains of word repetition prevent confusion and help the reader follow the ideas:

Natural selection is the central concept of Darwinian theory—the fittest survive and spread their favored traits through populations. Natural selection is defined by Spencer's phrase "survival of the fittest," but what does this famous bit of jargon really mean? Who are the fittest? And how is "fitness" defined? We often read that fitness involves no more than "differential reproductive success"—the production of more surviving offspring than other competing members of the population. Whoa! cries Bethell, as many others have before him. This formulation defines fitness in terms of survival only. The crucial phrase of natural selection means no more than "the survival of those who survive"—a vacuous tautology. (A tautology is a phrase—like "my father is a man"—containing no information in the predicate ["a man"] not inherent in the subject ["my father"]. Tautologies are fine as definitions, but not as testable scientific statements—there can be nothing to test in a statement true by definition.)

— Stephen Jay Gould, *Ever Since Darwin*

Repeated words with some variation of form

Synonyms connect ideas.

In addition to word repetition, you can use **synonyms**, words with identical or very similar meanings, to connect important ideas. In the following example, the author develops a careful chain of synonyms and word repetitions:

Over time, small bits of knowledge about a region accumulate among local residents in the form of stories. These are remembered in the community; even what is unusual does not become lost and therefore irrelevant. These narratives comprise for a native an intricate, long-term view of a particular landscape. . . . Outside the region this complex but easily shared "reality" is hard to get across without reducing it to generalities, to misleading or imprecise abstraction.

—Barry Lopez, *Arctic Dreams*

Synonym sequences:

region, particular landscape

local residents, native

stories, narratives

are remembered, does not become lost

intricate, . . . view, complex . . . "reality"

The result is a coherent paragraph that constantly reinforces the author's point.

Repetition of sentence structure emphasizes connections.

Writers occasionally use *sentence structure repetition* to emphasize the connections among their ideas, as in this example:

But the life forms are as much part of the structure of the Earth as any inanimate portion

Repeats the if/then
sentence structure

is. It is all an inseparable part of a whole. If any animal is isolated totally from other forms of life, then death by starvation will surely follow. If isolated from water, death by dehydration will follow even faster. If isolated from air, whether free or dissolved in water, death by asphyxiation will follow still faster. If isolated from the Sun, animals will survive for a time, but plants would die, and if all plants died, all animals would starve.

— Isaac Asimov, "The Case against Man"

Collocation creates networks of meaning.

Collocation—the positioning of words together in expected ways around a particular topic—occurs quite naturally to writers and usually forms recognizable networks of meaning for readers. For example, in a paragraph on a high school graduation, a reader might expect to encounter such words as *valedictorian, diploma, commencement, honors, cap and gown,* and *senior class.* The paragraph that follows uses five collocation chains:

Collocation chains:

housewife, cooking, neighbor, home

clocks, calculated, progression, precise

obstinacy, vagaries, problem

sun, clear days, cloudy ones, sundial, cast its light, angle, seasons, sun, weather

cooking, fire, matches, hot coals smoldering, ashes, go out, bed-warming pan

The seventeenth-century housewife not only had to make do without thermometers, she also had to make do without clocks, which were scarce and dear throughout the sixteen hundreds. She calculated cooking times by the progression of the sun; her cooking must have been more precise on clear days than on cloudy ones. Marks were sometimes painted on the floor, providing her with a rough sundial, but she still had to make allowance for the obstinacy of the sun in refusing to cast its light at the same angle as the seasons changed; but she was used to allowing for the vagaries of sun and weather. She also had a problem starting her fire in the morning; there were no matches. If she had allowed the hot coals smoldering under the ashes to go out, she had to borrow some from a neighbor, carrying them home with care, perhaps in a bed-warming pan.

—Waverly Root and Richard de Rouchement, *Eating in America*

EXERCISE 13.7

Now that you know more about pronoun reference, word repetition, synonyms, sentence structure repetition, and collocation, turn to Brian Cable's essay in Chapter 3 and identify the cohesive devices you find in paragraphs 1–5. Underline each cohesive device you can find; there will be many. You might also want to connect with lines the various pronoun, related-word, and synonym chains you find. You could also try listing the separate collocation chains. Consider how these cohesive devices help you read and make sense of the passage.

EXERCISE 13.8

Choose one of your recent writing projects, and select any three contiguous paragraphs. Underline every cohesive device you can find; there will be many. Try to connect with lines the various pronoun, related-word, and synonym chains you find. Also try listing the separate collocation chains.

You will be surprised and pleased at how extensively you rely on cohesive ties. Indeed, you could not produce readable text without cohesive ties. Consider these questions relevant to your development as a writer: Are all of your pronoun references clear? Are you straining for synonyms when repeated words would do? Do you ever repeat sentence structures to emphasize connections? Do you trust yourself to put collocation to work?

Transitions

A **transition** serves as a bridge to connect one paragraph, sentence, clause, or word with another. It also identifies the kind of connection by indicating to readers how the item preceding the transition relates to the one that follows it. Transitions help readers anticipate how the next paragraph or sentence will affect the meaning of what they have just read. There are three basic groups of transitions, based on the relationships they indicate: logical, temporal, and spatial.

Transitions emphasize logical relationships.

Transitions help readers follow the *logical relationships* within an argument. How such transitions work is illustrated in this tightly and passionately reasoned paragraph by James Baldwin:

> The black man insists, by whatever means he finds at his disposal, that the white man cease to regard him as an exotic rarity and recognize him as a human being. This is a very charged and difficult moment, for there is a great deal of will power involved in the white man's naïveté. Most people are not naturally malicious, and the white man prefers to keep the black man at a certain human remove because it is easier for him thus to preserve his simplicity and to avoid being called to account for crimes committed by his forefathers, or his neighbors. He is inescapably aware, nevertheless, that he is in a better position in the world than black men are, nor can he quite put to death the suspicion that he is hated by black men therefore. He does not wish to be hated, neither does he wish to change places, and at this point in his uneasiness he can scarcely avoid having recourse to those legends which white men have created about black men, the most unusual effect of which is that the white man finds himself enmeshed, so to speak, in his own language which describes hell, as well as the attributes which lead one to hell, as being black as night.
>
> —JAMES BALDWIN, "Stranger in the Village"

Transitions reinforce the logic of the argument.

Transitions Showing Logical Relationships

- *To introduce another item in a series:* first . . . , second; in the second place; for one thing . . . , for another; next; then; furthermore; moreover; in addition; finally; last; also; similarly; besides; and; as well as

- *To introduce an illustration or other specification:* in particular; specifically; for instance; for example; that is; namely

- *To introduce a result or a cause:* consequently; as a result; hence; accordingly; thus; so; therefore; then; because; since; for

- *To introduce a restatement:* that is; in other words; in simpler terms; to put it differently

- *To introduce a conclusion or summary:* in conclusion; finally; all in all; evidently; clearly; actually; to sum up; altogether; of course

- *To introduce an opposing point:* but; however; yet; nevertheless; on the contrary; on the other hand; in contrast; still; neither; nor

- *To introduce a concession to an opposing view:* certainly; naturally; of course; it is true; to be sure; granted

- *To resume the original line of reasoning after a concession:* nonetheless; all the same; even though; still; nevertheless

Transitions can indicate a sequence in time.

In addition to showing logical connections, transitions may indicate **temporal relationships**—a sequence or progression in time—as this example illustrates:

Transitions to relationships of time

That night, we drank tea and then vodka with lemon peel steeped in it. The four of us talked in Russian and English about mutual friends and American railroads and the Rolling Stones. Seryozha loves the Stones, and his face grew wistful as we spoke about their recent album, *Some Girls*. He played a tape of "Let It Bleed" over and over, until we could translate some difficult phrases for him; after that, he came out with the phrases at intervals during the evening, in a pretty decent imitation of Jagger's Cockney snarl. He was an adroit and oddly formal host, inconspicuously filling our teacups and politely urging us to eat bread and cheese and chocolate. While he talked to us, he teased Anya, calling her "Piglet," and she shook back her bangs and glowered at him. It was clear that theirs was a fiery relationship. After a while, we talked about ourselves. Anya told us about painting and printmaking and about how hard it was to buy supplies in Moscow. There had been something angry in her dark face since the beginning of the evening; I thought at first that it meant she didn't like Americans; but now I realized that it was a constant, barely suppressed rage at her own situation.

—Andrea Lee, *Russian Journal*

Transitions Showing Temporal Relationships

- *To indicate frequency:* frequently; hourly; often; occasionally; now and then; day after day; every so often; again and again

- *To indicate duration:* during; briefly; for a long time; minute by minute; while

- *To indicate a particular time:* now; then; at that time; in those days; last Sunday; next Christmas; in 2003; at the beginning of August; at six o'clock; first thing in the morning; two months ago; when

- **To indicate the beginning:** at first; in the beginning; since; before then
- **To indicate the middle:** in the meantime; meanwhile; as it was happening; at that moment; at the same time; simultaneously; next; then
- **To indicate the end and beyond:** eventually; finally; at last; in the end; subsequently; later; afterward

Transitions can indicate relationships in space.

Transitions showing **spatial relationships** orient readers to the objects in a scene, as illustrated in these paragraphs:

> On Georgia 155, I crossed Troublesome Creek, then went through groves of pecan trees aligned one with the next like fenceposts. The pastures grew a green almost blue, and syrupy water the color of a dusty sunset filled the ponds. Around the farmhouses, from wires strung high above the ground, swayed gourds hollowed out for purple martins.
>
> The land rose again on the other side of the Chattahoochee River, and Highway 34 went to the ridgetops where long views over the hills opened in all directions. Here was the tail of the Appalachian backbone, its gradual descent to the Gulf. Near the Alabama stateline stood a couple of LAST CHANCE! bars.
>
> —WILLIAM LEAST HEAT MOON, *Blue Highways*

Transitions to show relationships in space

Transitions Showing Spatial Relationships

- **To indicate closeness:** close to; near; next to; alongside; adjacent to; facing
- **To indicate distance:** in the distance; far; beyond; away; there
- **To indicate direction:** up/down; sideways; along; across; to the right/left; in front of/behind; above/below; inside/outside; toward/away from

---

| EXERCISE 13.9 |

Turn to William Akana's essay in Chapter 8. Relying on the lists of transitions just given, underline the transitions in paragraphs 4–6. Consider how the transitions connect the ideas from sentence to sentence. Suggest any further transitions that could be added to make the relationships even clearer.

| EXERCISE 13.10 |

Select a recent writing project of your own. Choose at least three paragraphs, and underline the logical, temporal, and spatial transitions. Depending on the kind of writing you were doing, you may find few, if any, transitions in one category or another. For example, an essay speculating about causes may not include any spatial transitions; writing about a remembered event might not contain transitions showing logical relationships.

Consider how your transitions relate the ideas from sentence to sentence. Compare your transitions with those in the lists in this text. Do you find that you are making full use of the repertoire? Do you find gaps between any of your sentences that a well-chosen transition would close?

Headings and Subheadings

Headings and **subheadings** — brief phrases set off from the text in various ways — can provide visible cues to readers about the content and organization of a text. Headings can be distinguished from the text in numerous ways, including the selective use of capital letters, bold or italic type, or different sizes of type. To be most helpful to readers, headings should be phrased similarly and follow a predictable system.

Headings indicate sections and levels.

In this chapter, the headings in the section Paragraphing, beginning on p. 526, provide a good example of a system of headings that can readily be outlined:

Paragraphing
Paragraph indents signal related ideas.
Topic sentences announce the paragraph's focus.
Announcing the Topic

Making a Transition

Positioning the Topic Sentence

To learn more about distinguishing headings from surrounding text and about setting up systems of headings, see Chapter 32.

Notice that in this example, the heading system has three levels. The first-level heading sits on its own line and is set in a large, red font; this heading stands out most visibly among the others. (It is one of five such headings in this chapter.) The second-level heading also sits on its own line but is set in a smaller font (and uses black type). The first of these second-level headings has no subheadings beneath it, while the second has three. These third-level headings, in black, do not sit on their own lines but run into the paragraph they introduce, as you can see if you turn back to pp. 527–28.

All of these headings follow a parallel grammatical structure: "-ing" nouns at the first level; complete sentences at the second level; and "-ing" nouns at the third level.

Headings are not common in all genres.

Headings may not be necessary in short essays: thesis statements, forecasting statements, well-positioned topic sentences, and transition sentences may be all the cues the reader needs. Headings are rare in some genres, such as essays about remembered events (Chapter 2) and essays profiling people and places (Chapter 3). Headings appear more frequently in such genres as concept explanations, finding-common-ground essays, position papers, public policy proposals, evaluations, and causal analyses (Chapters 4–9). Headings are required in résumés and lab reports (Chapter 29).

At least two headings are needed at each level.

Before dividing their essays into sections with headings and subheadings, writers need to make sure their discussion is detailed enough to support at least two headings at each level. The frequency and placement of headings depend entirely on the content and how it is divided and organized. Keep in mind that headings do not reduce the need for other cues to keep readers on track.

EXERCISE 13.11

Turn to Maya Gomez's report "Possible Solutions to the Kidney Shortage" in Chapter 5 (pp. 181–86) and survey that essay's system of headings. If you have not read the essay, read or skim it now. Consider how the headings help readers anticipate what is coming and how the argument is organized. Decide whether the headings substitute for or complement other cues for keeping readers on track. Consider whether the headings are grammatically parallel.

EXERCISE 13.12

Select one of your writing projects that might benefit from headings. Develop a system of headings, and insert them where appropriate. Be prepared to justify your headings in light of the discussion about headings in this section.

14

Narrating

Narrating is a basic strategy for representing action and events. It can be used to report on events, present information, illustrate abstract ideas, support arguments, explain procedures, and entertain with stories. This chapter begins by describing and illustrating five basic narrating strategies, it includes two types of process narrative—explanatory and instructional—and it concludes with some sentence strategies you might use to get started drafting a narrative.

Narrating Strategies

Strategies such as calendar and clock time, temporal transitions, verb tense, action sequences, and dialogue give narrative its dynamic quality, the sense of events unfolding in time. They also help readers track the order in which the events occurred and understand how they relate to one another.

Use calendar and clock time to create a sequence of events.

One of the simplest ways of constructing a clear time sequence is to place events on a timeline, with years or precise dates and times clearly marked. Look, for example, at the excerpted portion of a timeline in Figure 14.1, which presents a series of events in the history of U.S. savings bonds. A timeline is not itself a narrative, but it shares with narrative two basic elements:

1. Events are presented in chronological order.
2. Each event is "time-stamped," so that readers can clearly understand when events occurred in relation to one another.

Look now at a brief but fully developed narrative reconstructing the discovery of the bacterial cause of stomach ulcers. This narrative was written by Martin J. Blaser for *Scientific American,* a journal read primarily by nonspecialists interested in science. As you read, notice the same narrating strategies you saw in the timeline in Figure 14.1: sequencing events in chronological order and specifying when each event occurred:

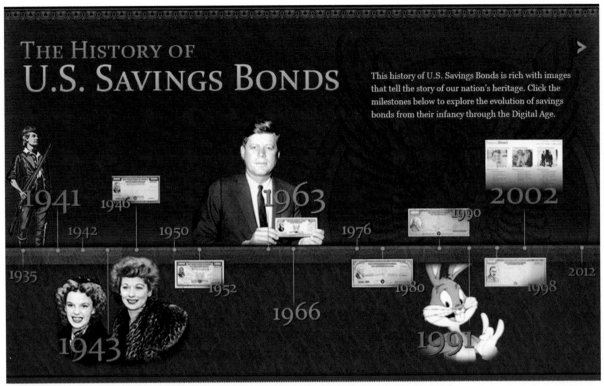

FIGURE 14.1 Chronology of events in the history of U.S. Savings Bonds (U.S. Department of the Treasury)

In 1979 J. Robin Warren, a pathologist at the Royal Perth Hospital in Australia, made a puzzling observation. As he examined tissue specimens from patients who had undergone stomach biopsies, he noticed that several samples had large numbers of curved and spiral-shaped bacteria. Ordinarily, stomach acid would destroy such organisms before they could settle in the stomach. But those Warren saw lay underneath the organ's thick mucus layer—a lining that coats the stomach's tissues and protects them from acid. Warren also noted that the bacteria were present only in tissue samples that were inflamed. Wondering whether the microbes might somehow be related to the irritation, he looked to the literature for clues and learned that German pathologists had witnessed similar organisms a century earlier. Because they could not grow the bacteria in culture, though, their findings had been ignored and then forgotten.

Warren, aided by an enthusiastic young trainee named Barry J. Marshall, also had difficulty growing the unknown bacteria in culture. He began his efforts in 1981. By April 1982 the two men had attempted to culture samples from 30-odd patients—all without success. Then the Easter holidays arrived. The hospital laboratory staff accidentally held some of the culture plates for five days instead of

Blaser cites specific years, months, days, and a holiday to convey the passage of time and indicate when each event occurred.

the usual two. On the fifth day, colonies emerged. The workers christened them *Campylobacter pyloridis* because they resembled pathogenic bacteria of the *Campylobacter* genus found in the intestinal tract. Early in 1983 Warren and Marshall published their first report, and within months scientists around the world had isolated the bacteria.

—Martin J. Blaser, "The Bacteria behind Ulcers"

In addition to calendar time (years, months, days), writers sometimes also refer to clock time (hours, minutes, seconds). Here is a brief narrative from an essay profiling the emergency room at Bellevue Hospital in New York City:

> 9:05 p.m. An ambulance backs into the receiving bay, its red and yellow lights flashing in and out of the lobby. A split second later, the glass doors burst open as a nurse and an attendant roll a mobile stretcher into the lobby. When the nurse screams, "Emergency!" the lobby explodes with activity as the way is cleared to the trauma room. Doctors appear from nowhere and transfer the bloodied body of a black man to the treatment table. Within seconds his clothes are stripped away.
>
> — George Simpson, "The War Room at Bellevue"

The references to clock time establish the sequence and contribute to dramatic intensity.

EXERCISE 14.1

Skim Gabriel Thompson's "A Gringo in the Lettuce Fields" in Chapter 3, and underline the references to calendar and clock time. How do you think these time markers function in the narrative? What do they tell you about the impression Thompson wants to create about that period of his life?

Use temporal transitions to establish an action sequence.

For a more extensive list of transitions showing temporal relationships, see Chapter 13.

Whereas writers tend to use calendar and clock time sparingly, they regularly use **temporal transitions** such as *when, at that moment, before,* and *while* to establish a clear sequence of actions in narrating onetime or recurring events.

Onetime Events   To see how temporal transitions work, let us look at the concluding paragraphs of a remembered-event essay in which Russell Baker recounts what happened after his final flight test, his last chance to become a pilot. The "he" Baker refers to is the flight check pilot, T. L. (nicknamed "Total Loss") Smith:

Baker uses temporal transitions to show what he and Smith were doing after the flight test.

> Back at the flight line, when I'd cut the ignition, he climbed out and tramped back toward the ready room while I waited to sign the plane in. When I got there he was standing at a distance talking to my regular instructor. His talk was being illustrated with hand movements, as pilots' conversations always were, hands executing little loops and rolls in the air. After he did the falling-leaf motion with his hands, he pointed a finger at my instructor's chest, said something I couldn't hear, and trudged off. My instructor, who had flown only with the pre-hangover Baker, was slack-jawed when he approached me.

"Smith just said you gave him the best check flight he's ever had in his life," he said. "What the hell did you do to him up there?"

"I guess I just suddenly learned to fly," I said.

— Russell Baker, "Smooth and Easy"

Look closely at the two transitions in the first sentence. The word *when* presents actions in chronological order (first Baker stopped the plane, and then Smith got out). *While* performs a different function, showing that the next two actions occurred at the same time (Baker waited to sign in as the check pilot returned to the ready room). There is nothing complicated or unusual about this set of actions, but it would be hard to represent them in writing without temporal transitions.

Recurring Events   Temporal transitions also enable writers to narrate recurring events. In the following narrative by Monica Sone about her daily life in an internment camp for Japanese Americans during World War II, we can see how transitions (highlighted) help the writer represent actions she routinely performed:

> First I typed on pink, green, blue and white work sheets the hours put in by the 10,000 evacuees, then sorted and alphabetized these sheets, and stacked them away in shoe boxes. My job was excruciatingly dull, but under no circumstances did I want to leave it. The Administration Building was the only place which had modern plumbing and running hot and cold water; in the first few months and every morning, after I had typed for a decent hour, I slipped into the rest room and took a complete sponge bath with scalding hot water. During the remainder of the day, I slipped back into the rest room at inconspicuous intervals, took off my head scarf and wrestled with my scorched hair. I stood upside down over the basin of hot water, soaking my hair, combing, stretching and pulling at it.
>
> — Monica Sone, "Camp Harmony"

With the time marker *first,* Sone starts describing her typical work routine. In the third sentence, she tells of her surreptitious actions *in the first few months and every morning.*

EXERCISE 14.2

Turn to Anastasia Toufexis's "Love: The Right Chemistry" in Chapter 4. Read paragraph 3, underlining the temporal transitions Toufexis uses to present the sequence of evolutionary changes that may have contributed to the development of romantic love. How important are these transitions in helping you follow her narrative?

Use verb tense to place actions in time.

In addition to time markers like calendar time and temporal transitions, writers use *verb tense* to represent action in writing and to help readers understand when each action occurred in relation to other actions.

Onetime Events   Writers typically use the past tense to represent onetime events that began and ended in the past. Here is a brief passage from a remembered-person essay by Amy Wu. In addition to the temporal transitions *once* and *when* in the opening sentence, which let readers know that this particular event occurred many years earlier, the writer also uses simple past-tense verbs (highlighted):

Wu uses the simple past tense to indicate that actions occurred in a linear sequence.

> Once, when I was 5 or 6, I interrupted my mother during a dinner with her friends and told her that I disliked the meal. My mother's eyes transformed from serene pools of blackness into stormy balls of fire. "Quiet!" she hissed, "do you not know that silent waters run deep?"
>
> — AMY WU, "A Different Kind of Mother"

In the next example, by Chang-Rae Lee, we see how verb tense can be used to show more complicated relationships between past actions that occurred at different times in the past:

Lee uses both the simple past (*amassed, needed, moved*) and past perfect (*had hoped*) tenses.

> When Uncle Chul amassed the war chest he needed to open the wholesale business he had hoped for, he moved away from New York.
>
> — CHANG-RAE LEE, "Uncle Chul Gets Rich"

You do not have to know that *amassed* is simple past tense and *had hoped* is past perfect tense to know that the uncle's hopes came before the money was amassed. In fact, most readers of English can understand complicated combinations of tenses without knowing their names.

Let us look at another verb tense combination used frequently in narrative: the simple past and the past progressive:

Malcolm *X* uses the simple past (*overheard, was*) and past progressive (*was leaving, was appearing*) tenses.

> When Dinah Washington was leaving with some friends, I overheard someone say she was on her way to the Savoy Ballroom where Lionel Hampton was appearing that night — she was then Hamp's vocalist.
>
> — MALCOLM X, *The Autobiography of Malcolm X*

This combination of tenses plus the temporal transition *when* shows that the two actions occurred at the same time in the past. The first action ("Dinah Washington was leaving") continued during the period that the second action ("I overheard") occurred.

Occasionally, writers use the present instead of the past tense to narrate onetime events. Process narratives and profiles typically use the present tense to give the story a sense of "you are there" immediacy:

Edge uses present-tense verbs to give readers a sense that they are in the room with him.

> Slowly, the dank barroom fills with grease-smeared mechanics from the truck stop up the road and farmers straight from the fields, the soles of their brogans thick with dirt clods. A few weary souls make their way over from the nearby sawmill. I sit alone at the bar, one empty bottle of Bud in front of me, a second in my hand. I drain the beer, order a third, and stare down at the pink juice spreading outward from a crumpled foil pouch and onto the bar.
>
> *I'm not leaving until I eat this thing*, I tell myself.
>
> — JOHN T. EDGE, "I'm Not Leaving Until I Eat This Thing"

Recurring Events   Verb tense, usually combined with temporal transitions, can also help writers narrate events that occurred routinely:

Many times, walking home from work, I would see some unknowing soul venture across that intersection against the light and then freeze in horror when he saw the cars ripping out of the tunnel toward him. . . . Suddenly, the human reflex would take over, and the pedestrian would jackknife first one way, then another, arms flaying the empty air, and often the car would literally skim the man, brushing by him so close it would touch his coat or his tie. . . . On one occasion, feeling sorry for the person who had brushed against the speeding car, I hurried across the intersection after him to cheer him up a little. Catching up with him down by 32nd I said, "That was good legwork, sir. Excellent moves for a big man!" but the man looked at me with an empty expression in his eyes, and then moved away mechanically and trancelike, heading for the nearest bar.

— WILLIE MORRIS, *North toward Home*

> Morris uses the helping verb *would* along with temporal transitions to show recurring actions.

Notice also that Morris shifts to the simple past tense when he moves from recurring actions to an action that occurred only once. He signals this shift with the temporal transition *on one occasion.*

| EXERCISE 14.3 |

Turn to Jean Brandt's essay, "Calling Home," in Chapter 2. Read paragraph 3 and underline the verbs, beginning with *got*, *took*, *knew*, and *didn't want* in the first sentence. Brandt uses verb tense to reconstruct her actions and reflect on their effectiveness. Notice also how verb tense helps you follow the sequence of actions Brandt took.

Use action sequences for vivid narration.

The narrating strategy we call **action sequences** uses active verbs and modifying phrases and clauses to present action vividly. Action sequences are especially suited to representing intense, fast-moving events like chase scenes and sports. The following example by George Plimpton shows how well action sequences work to show what happened during a practice scrimmage. Plimpton participated in the Detroit Lions football training camp while writing a book profiling professional football. This is what he experienced:

> Since in the two preceding plays the concentration of the play had been elsewhere, I had felt alone with the flanker. Now, the whole heave of the play was toward me, flooding the zone not only with confused motion but noise—the quick stomp of feet, the creak of football gear, the strained grunts of effort, the faint *ah-ah-ah* of piston-stroke regularity, and the stiff calls of instruction, like exhalations. "Inside, inside! Take him inside!" someone shouted, tearing by me, his cleats thumping in the grass. A call—a parrot squawk— may have erupted from me. My feet splayed in hopeless confusion as Barr came directly toward me, feinting in one direction, and then stopping suddenly, drawing me toward him for the possibility of a buttonhook pass, and as I leaned almost off balance toward him, he turned and came on again, downfield, moving past me at high speed, leaving me poised on one leg, reaching for him, trying to grab at him despite the illegality, anything to

> Though Plimpton uses active verbs, he describes most of the action through modifying phrases and clauses.

keep him from getting by. But he was gone, and by the time I had turned to set out after him, he had ten yards on me, drawing away fast with his sprinter's run, his legs pinwheeling, the row of cleats flicking up a faint wake of dust behind.

—GEORGE PLIMPTON, *Paper Lion*

By piling up action sequences, Plimpton reconstructs for readers the texture and excitement of his experience on the football field. He uses the two most common kinds of modifiers that writers employ to present action sequences:

Participial phrases: *tearing by me, stopping suddenly, moving past me at high speed*

Absolute phrases: *his cleats thumping in the grass, his legs pinwheeling, the row of cleats flicking up a faint wake of dust behind*

Combined with vivid *sensory description* (*the creak of football gear, the strained grunts of effort, the faint* ah-ah-ah *of piston-stroke regularity*), these action sequences re-create the sights and sounds of people in motion.

EXERCISE 14.4

Turn to paragraph 2 of Amanda Coyne's profile essay "The Long Good-Bye: Mother's Day in Federal Prison" in Chapter 3. Underline any action sequences you find in this brief paragraph. Then reflect on how they help the reader envision the scene in the prison's visiting room.

EXERCISE 14.5

Record several brief—two- or three-minute—televised segments of a fast-moving sports competition, such as a soccer or basketball game. Then review the recording, and choose one segment to narrate using action sequences to describe in detail what you see.

If you cannot record a televised game, narrate a live-action event (for example, people playing touch football, a dog catching a Frisbee, or a skateboarder or inline skater practicing a trick). As you watch the action, take detailed notes of what you see. Then, based on your notes, write a few sentences using action sequences to describe what you witnessed firsthand.

Use dialogue to dramatize events.

Dialogue is most often used in narratives that dramatize events. It reconstructs choice bits of conversation, rather than trying to present an accurate and complete record. In addition to showing people interacting, dialogue can give readers insight into character and relationships. Dialogue may be *quoted* to make it resemble the give-and-take of actual conversation, or it may be *summarized* to give readers the gist of what was said.

The following example from Gary Soto's *Living up the Street* shows how a narrative can combine quoted and summarized dialogue. In this passage, Soto recalls his first experience as a migrant worker in California's San Joaquin Valley:

"Are you tired?" she asked.

"No, but I got a sliver from the frame," I told her. I showed her the web of skin between my thumb and index finger. She wrinkled her forehead but said it was nothing.

"How many trays did you do?"

I looked straight ahead, not answering at first. I recounted in my mind the whole morning of bend, cut, pour again and again, before answering a feeble "thirty-seven." No elaboration, no detail. Without looking at me she told me how she had done field work in Texas and Michigan as a child. But I had a difficult time listening to her stories. I played with my grape knife, stabbing it into the ground, but stopped when Mother reminded me that I had better not lose it. I left the knife sticking up like a small, leafless plant. She then talked about school, the junior high I would be going to that fall, and then about Rick and Debra, how sorry they would be that they hadn't come out to pick grapes because they'd have no new clothes for the school year. She stopped talking when she peeked at her watch, a bandless one she kept in her pocket. She got up with an "Ay, Dios," and told me that we'd work until three, leaving me cutting figures in the sand with my knife and dreading the return to work.

— Gary Soto, "One Last Time"

Soto uses signal phrases with the first two quotations but not with the third, where it is clear who is speaking.

The fourth quotation, "thirty-seven," is preceded by a narrative that tells what Soto did and thought before speaking and is followed by a summary of further conversation.

Quoted dialogue is easy to recognize, of course, because of the quotation marks. Summarized dialogue can be harder to identify. In this case, however, Soto embeds *signal phrases* (*she told me* and *she then talked*) in his narrative. Summarizing leaves out information the writer decides readers do not need. In this passage about a remembered event, Soto has chosen to focus on his own feelings and thoughts rather than his mother's.

For more on deciding when to quote, see Chapter 2 and Chapter 26.

EXERCISE 14.6

Read the essay "A Gringo in the Lettuce Fields" in Chapter 3, and consider Gabriel Thompson's use of both direct quotation and summaries for reporting speech. When does Thompson choose to quote directly, and why might he have made this decision?

EXERCISE 14.7

If you wrote a remembered-event essay in Chapter 2 or used narration in some other essay, reread your essay, looking for one example of each of the following narrating strategies: calendar and clock time, temporal transitions, past-tense verbs in onetime events, action sequences, and dialogue. Do not worry if you cannot find examples of all of the strategies. Pick one strategy you did use, and comment on what it contributes to your narrative.

Narrating a Process

Process narratives explain how something was done or instruct readers on how it could or should be done. Whether the purpose is explanatory or instructional, process narratives must clearly convey each necessary action and the exact order in which the actions occur.

Use process narratives to explain.

Explanatory process narratives often relate particular experiences or elucidate processes followed by machines or organizations. Consider this excerpt from a remembered-event essay by Mary Mebane. She uses process narrative to let readers know what happened the first time she worked on an assembly line putting tobacco leaves on the conveyor belt:

Temporal transitions and simple past-tense verbs place the actions in time.

> The job seemed easy enough as I picked up bundle after bundle of tobacco and put it on the belt, careful to turn the knot end toward me so that it would be placed right to go under the cutting machine. Gradually, as we worked up our tobacco, I had to bend more, for as we emptied the hogshead we had to stoop over to pick up the tobacco, then straighten up and put it on the belt just right. Then I discovered the hard part of the job: the belt kept moving at the same speed all the time and if the leaves were not placed on the belt at the same tempo there would be a big gap where your bundle should have been. So that meant that when you got down lower, you had to bend down, get the tobacco, straighten up fast, make sure it was placed knot end toward you, place it on the belt, and bend down again. Soon you were bending down, up; down, up; down, up. All along the line, heads were bobbing—down, up; down, up—until you finished the barrel. Then you could rest until the men brought you another one.
>
> —MARY MEBANE, "Summer Job"

Here, actions sequences (*bend down, get the tobacco, straighten up fast*) become a series of staccato movements (*down, up; down, up; down, up*) that emphasize the speed and machinelike actions Mebane had to take to keep up with the conveyor belt.

The next example shows how a laser printer functions:

Because the objects performing the action change from sentence to sentence, the writers must construct a clearly marked chain, introducing the object's name in one sentence and repeating the name or using a synonym in the next.

> To create a page, the computer sends signals to the printer, which shines a laser at a mirror system that scans across a charged drum. Whenever the beam strikes the drum, it removes the charge. The drum then rotates through a toner chamber filled with thermoplastic particles. The toner particles stick to the negatively charged areas of the drum in the pattern of characters, lines, or other elements the computer has transmitted and the laser beam mapped.
>
> Once the drum is coated with toner in the appropriate locations, a piece of paper is pulled across a so-called transfer corona wire, which imparts a positive electrical charge. The paper then passes across the toner-coated drum. The positive charge on the paper attracts the toner in the same position it occupied on the drum. The final phase of the process involves fusing the toner to the paper with a set of high-temperature rollers.
>
> —RICHARD GOLUB AND ERIC BRUS, *Almanac of Science and Technology*

Like Mebane's process narrative, this one sequences the actions chronologically from beginning ("the computer sends signals to the printer") to end ("fusing the toner to the paper"). Temporal transitions (*then, once, then, final*) and present-tense verbs (*sends, shines, scans, strikes*) convey the passage of time and place the actions clearly in this chronological sequence.

In Chapter 3, read paragraph 6 of Brian Cable's profile of a local mortuary, "The Last Stop." Here Cable narrates the process that the company follows once it has been notified of a client's death. As you read, look for and mark the narrating strategies discussed in this chapter that Cable uses. Then reflect on how well you think the narrative presents the actions and their sequence.

Use process narratives to instruct.

Unlike explanatory process narratives, **instructional process narratives** must include all of the information a reader needs to perform the procedure presented. Depending on the reader's experience, the writer might need to define technical terms, list tools that should be used, give background information, and account for alternatives or possible problems.

For guidelines on designing documents, see Chapter 32.

Figure 14.3 presents a detailed instructional process narrative from the *Home Repair Handbook,* which gives readers directions for replacing a broken plug. The first graphic includes four steps that are clearly numbered, illustrated, and narrated. Each step presents several actions to be taken, and its graphic shows what the plug should look like when these actions have been completed. We can identify the actions by looking at the verbs. Step 1 in "Replacing plugs with terminal screws," for example, instructs readers to take four separate actions, each signaled by the verb (italicized here): "*Unscrew* and *remove* the new plug's insulating barrier. Using a utility knife, *split* the end of the cord to *separate* the wires; *push* the cord through the plug body." These are active verbs, and the sentences are in the form of clear and efficient commands. The anonymous authors do not assume that readers know very much, as they label every element of each drawing, including the screws. They also instruct readers precisely what to do. For example, in Step 4, they tell readers to "form loops on wires and wrap them clockwise three-quarters of the way around the screws."

Unscrew and remove the new plug's insulating barrier. Using a utility knife, split the end of the cord to separate the wires; push the cord through the plug body.

Make two loops with the wires, pass the loose ends of the wires through the loops, and pull to form an Underwriter's knot (to prevent strain on connections).

Strip 1/2 to 3/4 inch of insulation off the wire ends, being careful not to nick the wires *(page 159).* Unscrew the terminal screws to allow space for the wires.

Form loops on wires and wrap them clockwise three-quarters of the way around screws. Tighten the screws, trim excess wire, and reattach the barrier to the body.

FIGURE 14.3 Replacing plugs with terminal screws

Write a one- to two-page instructional process narrative that tells readers how to make a peanut butter and jelly sandwich or perform some other equally simple procedure, such as hemming a pair of pants, potting a plant, or changing a tire. Address your narrative to readers who have never done the procedure before.

Sentence Strategies for Narration

When writing about a remembered event, writers often struggle to convey the event's significance. If you are writing about a remembered event, why not try out some of these sentence strategies to help you capture your experience in words, first for yourself and then for your readers? You will probably want to rework these sentences to make them your own, but they may give you a jumping-off point for articulating your thoughts.

To Think about Your Main Point

▶ When readers finish my story, they will better appreciate how society and culture/an individual person/the human condition _____ .

To Sketch Out the Backstory (Exposition) Readers Need to Understand What Happened and Why It Mattered

▶ In [year], while I was _____ing in [location], _____ .

▶ John knew all about _____ because he was a/an _____ologist, an expert on _____ .

▶ In past years, I had previously _____ .

To Explore the Significance of Your Story's Conflict

▶ During this event, I found myself locked in conflict with _____ . [Elaborate.]

▶ Although I struggled with X [a factor outside myself], I also was _____ . [Elaborate.]

▶ I kept wondering, should I _____ or should I _____ ? [Elaborate.]

To Explore How You Felt at the Time

▶ As the event started [or during or right after the event], I felt _____ and _____ . I hoped others would think of me as _____ .

▶ I showed or expressed these feelings by _____ .

To Explore Your Present Perspective

▶ My feelings since the event have/have not changed: _____. [Elaborate.]

▶ At the time, I had been going through _____, which may have affected my experience by _____.

▶ Looking back at the event now, I realize I was probably trying to _____, though I didn't appreciate that fact at the time.

To Alert Readers to What You Were Thinking or Feeling

▶ I felt _____.

▶ The thought of _____ made me feel _____.

▶ The terror/exhilaration/excitement was _____.

To Make Clear Who Is Speaking and to Convey Their Attitude or Position

▶ She asked, "_____?"

▶ "_____," he complained.

▶ She snapped, "_____."

15

Describing

Vivid *description* creates an intense, distinctive image, one that seems to bring words to life. Good description can also be evocative, calling up memories or suggesting feelings associated with the subject being described. Writers use description to give readers an impression of people and places, to illustrate abstract ideas, to make information memorable, and to support an argument. This chapter presents the three basic descriptive techniques of *naming, detailing,* and *comparing;* it surveys the words writers typically use to evoke vivid sense impressions; it examines how writers use description to create a dominant impression; and it provides some sentence strategies you might use to get started drafting a description.

Naming

For more on naming, see Chapter 2

Naming calls readers' attention to observable features of the subject being described. To describe a room, for example, you might name objects you see as you look around, such as a bed, pillows, blankets, a dresser, clothes, books, and a laptop. These objects suggest what kind of room it is and begin to give readers an impression of what it is like to be in this particular room.

Look closely at the following passage describing a weasel that the writer, Annie Dillard, encountered in the woods:

> He was ten inches long, thin as a curve, a muscled ribbon, brown as fruitwood, soft-furred, alert. His face was fierce, small and pointed as a lizard's; he would have made a good arrowhead. There was just a dot of chin, maybe two brown hairs' worth, and then the pure white fur began that spread down his underside. He had two black eyes I didn't see, any more than you see a window.
>
> — ANNIE DILLARD, *Teaching a Stone to Talk*

With these names, readers can begin to put together a mental image of the animal Dillard is describing. She uses simple, everyday nouns, like *chin,* to identify the weasel's features, not technical words like *maxilla* or *mandible.* The piling up of simple, concrete nouns helps readers imagine what the weasel looked like to Dillard.

Although writers most commonly name what they see, sight is not the only sense that contributes to vivid descriptions:

> When the sun fell across the great white pile of the new Telephone Company building, you could smell the stucco burning as you passed; then some liquid sweetness that came to me from deep in the rings of the freshly cut lumber stacked in the yards, and the fresh plaster and paint on the brand-new storefronts. Rawness, sunshiny rawness down the end streets of the city, as I thought of them then — the hot ash-laden stink of the refuse dumps in my nostrils and the only sound at noon the resonant metal plunk of a tin can I kicked ahead of me as I went my way.
>
> — ALFRED KAZIN, *A Walker in the City*

Names smells, sounds, tastes, and tactile qualities

EXERCISE 15.1

Go to a place where you can sit for a while and observe the scene. It might be a landscape or a cityscape, indoors or outdoors, crowded or solitary. For five minutes, list everything in the scene that you can name using nouns. (A simple way to test if a word is a noun is to see if you can put the word *the, a,* or *an* in front of it.) Remember, you can name objects you see (*dog, hydrant*) as well as impressions such as smells or sounds you experience at the place (*stench, hiss*).

Then write a paragraph or two that describes the scene for someone who is not there with you. Write for readers who have never been to this particular place to let them know what to expect when they get there.

EXERCISE 15.2

Turn to Annie Dillard's "An American Childhood" in Chapter 2. Read paragraphs 12 and 13, and underline the names that Dillard uses to describe the circuitous route she runs while the stranger is chasing her. Begin underlining with the words *house, path, tree,* and *bank* in the opening sentence. How do you think the amount of naming Dillard does contributes to the description's vividness, measured by your ability to imagine the chase scene?

Detailing

Naming identifies the notable features of the subject being described; **detailing** makes the features more specific or particularized. Naming answers the questions What is it? and What are its parts or features? Detailing answers questions like these:

For more on detailing, see Chapter 2.

- What size is it?
- How many are there?
- What is it made of?
- Where is it located?
- What is its condition?

- How is it used?
- Where does it come from?
- What is its effect?
- What is its value?

To add details to names, add modifiers—adjectives and adverbs, phrases and clauses. **Modifiers** make nouns more specific by supplying additional information. Notice how many modifying details Dillard provides in her description of the weasel:

> He was ten inches long, thin as a curve, a muscled ribbon, brown as fruitwood, soft-furred, alert. His face was fierce, small and pointed as a lizard's; he would have made a good arrowhead. There was just a dot of chin, maybe two brown hairs' worth, and then the pure white fur began that spread down his underside. He had two black eyes I didn't see, any more than you see a window.
>
> — Annie Dillard, *Teaching a Stone to Talk*

In addition to providing details that show readers what this specific weasel looked like, Dillard also conveys her thoughts and feelings during the encounter. For example, when she writes that the weasel's "face was fierce," she is making a judgment. She uses details like this to make readers see the weasel as a wild animal, not a soft and cuddly pet.

In describing people, writers often combine physical details with details characterizing aspects of the individual's personality. These characterizations or evaluations let readers know something about the writer's thoughts about the person, as the following examples illustrate:

Physical description
Evaluative details

> My father, a fat, funny man with beautiful eyes and a subversive wit . . .
>
> — Alice Walker, "Beauty: When the Other Dancer Is the Self"

> I was afraid of her higharched bony nose, her eyebrows lifted in half-circles above her hooded, brilliant eyes, and of the Kentucky R's in her speech, and the long steps she took in her hightop shoes. I did nothing but fear her bearing-down authority.
>
> — Eudora Welty, "Miss Duling"

Sometimes physical details alone can be enough to symbolize a person's character or the writer's feelings toward that person, as in the following passage:

Physical details
suggesting a powerful,
threatening character

> Rick was not a friendly looking man. He wore only swim trunks, and his short, powerful legs rose up to meet a bulging torso. His big belly was solid. His shoulders, as if to offset his front-heaviness, were thrown back, creating a deep crease of excess muscle from his sides around the small of his back, a crease like a huge frown. His arms were crossed, two medieval maces placed carefully on their racks, ready to be swung at any moment. His round cheeks and chin were darkened by traces of black whiskers. His hair was sparse. Huge, black, mirrored sunglasses replaced his eyes. Below his prominent nose was a thin, sinister mustache. I couldn't believe this menacing-looking man was the legendary jovial Rick.
>
> — Brad Benioff, "Rick"

EXERCISE 15.3

Return to the description you wrote in Exercise 15.1. Put brackets around the details you used to help describe the scene. Add any other details you think of now—details that indicate size, quantity, makeup, location, condition, use, source, effect, value, or any other quality that would make the description more specific and particularized for readers. Then reread your description. What do you think the detailing contributes to the description you wrote?

EXERCISE 15.4

Look again at paragraphs 12 and 13 of Annie Dillard's "An American Childhood" in Chapter 2. In Exercise 15.2, you underlined the names Dillard used. Now put brackets around the details. You might begin, for example, with the modifiers *yellow* and *backyard*. How do you think detailing contributes to Dillard's description? How do these details help you imagine Dillard's experience of the chase?

EXERCISE 15.5

Turn to paragraphs 10 and 13 of Amanda Coyne's "The Long Good-Bye: Mother's Day in Federal Prison" in Chapter 3. Read and put brackets around the words that detail the description of Stephanie and her son, Ellie. If you have not read the entire essay, read it now, and consider how Coyne uses these contrasting descriptions of the inmate and her son to emphasize her main point in the essay.

Comparing

In addition to naming and detailing, writers sometimes use *comparing* to make their description more vivid for readers. Look again at Annie Dillard's description of a weasel, paying attention this time to the comparisons:

> He was ten inches long, thin as a curve, a muscled ribbon, brown as fruitwood, soft-furred, alert. His face was fierce, small and pointed as a lizard's; he would have made a good arrowhead. There was just a dot of chin, maybe two brown hairs' worth, and then the pure white fur began that spread down his underside. He had two black eyes I didn't see, any more than you see a window.
>
> — ANNIE DILLARD, *Teaching a Stone to Talk*

Similes
Metaphors

Dillard uses simile and metaphor, both of which point out similarities in things that are essentially dissimilar. A **simile** expresses the similarity directly by using the words *like* or *as* to announce the comparison. A **metaphor**, by contrast, is an implicit comparison in which one thing is described as though it were the other.

Similes and metaphors can enhance the vividness of a description by giving readers additional information to help them picture the subject. For example, Dillard uses the word *thin* to detail the weasel's body shape. But *thin* is a relative term, leading readers to wonder, how thin? Dillard gives readers two images for comparison, a curve and a ribbon, to help them construct a fuller mental image of the weasel.

Comparing can also convey to readers what the writer feels about the subject. The following comparison from Brad Benioff's description of Coach Rick suggests the writer's feelings: "His arms were crossed, two medieval maces placed carefully on their racks, ready to be swung at any moment." Sometimes the similes or metaphors writers use are suggestive but hard to pin down. What do you think Dillard means, for example, by comparing the weasel's eyes to a window: "He had two black eyes I didn't see, any more than you see a window"?

EXERCISE 15.6

Return to the description you wrote in Exercise 15.1 and may have added to in Exercise 15.3. Reread it, and mark any comparing you did. Try to add one or two similes or metaphors to your description. How do you think your use of comparing may help readers imagine the subject or get a sense of what you feel about it?

Using Sensory Description

When writers use **sensory description** to describe animals, people, or scenes, they usually rely on the sense of sight more than the other senses. In general, our vocabulary for reporting what we see is larger and more varied than our vocabulary for reporting other sense impressions. Nevertheless, writers can detail the qualities and attributes of nonvisual sensations—the loudness or tinniness or rumble of an engine, for instance. They can also use comparing to help readers imagine what something sounds, feels, smells, or tastes like.

Describe what you saw.

When people describe what they see, they identify the objects in their field of vision. Here are two brief examples of visual description:

> On Christmas Eve I saw that my mother had outdone herself in creating a strange menu. She was pulling black veins out of the backs of fleshy prawns. The kitchen was littered with appalling mounds of raw food: A slimy rock cod with bulging eyes that pleaded not to be thrown into a pan of hot oil. Tofu, which looked like stacked wedges of rubbery white sponges. A bowl soaking dried fungus back to life. A plate of squid, their backs crisscrossed with knife markings so they resembled bicycle tires.
>
> — AMY TAN, "Fish Cheeks"

She was thirty-four. She wore a white skirt and yellow sweater and a thin gold necklace, which she held in her fingers, as if holding her own reins, while waiting for children to answer. Her hair was black with a hint of Irish red. It was cut short to the tops of her ears, and swept back like a pair of folded wings. She had a delicate cleft chin, and she was short—the children's chairs would have fit her. . . . Her hands kept very busy. They sliced the air and made karate chops to mark off boundaries. They extended straight out like a traffic cop's, halting illegal maneuvers yet to be perpetrated. When they rested momentarily on her hips, her hands looked as if they were in holsters.

— TRACY KIDDER, *Among Schoolchildren*

EXERCISE 15.7

Write a few sentences describing a teacher, friend, or family member. Do not rely on memory for this exercise; describe someone who is before you as you write so that you can describe in detail what you see. Later, when you are alone, reread what you have written, and make any changes you think will help make this visual description more vivid for your readers.

Describe what you heard.

In reporting auditory impressions, writers seldom name sounds without also specifying what the sounds come from: the murmur of a voice, the rustle of the wind, the squeak of a hinge, the sputter of an engine. *Onomatopoeia* is the term for names of sounds that echo the sounds themselves: *squeak, murmur, hiss, boom, plink, tinkle, twang, jangle, rasp, chirr*. Sometimes writers make up words like *sweesh* and *cara-wong* to imitate sounds they wish to describe. Qualitative words like *powerful* and *rich* as well as relative terms like *loud* and *low* often specify sounds further. For detailing sounds, writers sometimes use the technique called *synesthesia*, applying words commonly used to describe one sense to another, such as describing sounds as *sharp* and *soft;* they sometimes also use simile or metaphor to compare one sound to another.

To write about the sounds along Manhattan's Canal Street, Ian Frazier uses many of these describing and naming techniques:

> The traffic on Canal Street never stops. It is a high-energy current jumping constantly between the poles of Brooklyn and New Jersey. It hates to have its flow pinched in the density of Manhattan, hates to stop at intersections. Along Canal Street, it moans and screams. Worn brake shoes of semitrucks go "Ooohhhh nooohhhh" at stoplights, and the sound echoes in the canyons of warehouses and Chinatown tenements. People lean on their horns from one end of Canal Street to the other. They'll honk nonstop for ten minutes at a time, until the horns get tired and out of breath. They'll try different combinations: shave-and-a-hair-cut, long-long-long, short-short-short-long. Some people have musical car horns; a person purchasing a musical car horn seems to be limited to a choice of four tunes— "La Cucaracha," "Theme from *The Godfather*," "Dixie," and "Hava Nagila."

> — IAN FRAZIER, "Canal Street"

Metaphor
Onomatopoeia

Auditory details

EXERCISE 15.8

Find a noisy spot — a restaurant, a football game, a nursery school, a laundry room — where you can perch for about half an hour. Listen attentively to the sounds of the place, and make notes about what you hear. Then write a paragraph or two describing the place through its sounds.

Describe what you smelled.

The English language has a meager stock of words to express the olfactory sense. In addition to the word *smell*, fewer than a dozen commonly used nouns name this sensation: *odor, scent, vapor, fume, aroma, fragrance, perfume, bouquet, stench,* and *stink.* Although there are other, rarer words like *fetor* and *effluvium,* few writers use them, probably for fear that their readers will not know them. Few verbs describe receiving or sending odors — *smell, sniff, waft* — but a fair number of detailing adjectives are available: *redolent, pungent, aromatic, perfumed, stinking, musty, rancid, putrid, rank, fetid, malodorous, foul, acrid, sweet,* and *cloying.*

Here is an example of how Amanda Coyne, in her essay in Chapter 3, uses smell in a description:

> Occasionally, a mother will pick up her present and bring it to her nose when one of the bearers of the single flower — her child — asks if she likes it. . . . But most of what is being smelled today is the children themselves. While the other adults are plunking coins into the vending machines, the mothers take deep whiffs from the backs of their children's necks, or kiss and smell the backs of their knees, or take off their shoes and tickle their feet and then pull them close to their noses. They hold them tight and take in their own second scent — the scent assuring them that these are still their children and that they still belong to them.
>
> — AMANDA COYNE, "The Long Good-Bye: Mother's Day in Federal Prison"

In addition to using *smell* as a verb, Coyne describes the repeated action of bringing the object being smelled to the nose, an act that not only signifies the process of smelling but also underscores its intimacy. To further emphasize intimacy, Coyne connects smelling with other intimate acts of kissing, tickling, pulling close, and holding tight.

Because she is not describing her own experience of smell, Coyne does not try to find words to evoke the effect the odor has on her. In the next passage, however, Frank Conroy uses comparing in addition to naming and detailing to describe how the smell of flowers affected him:

> The perfume of the flowers rushed into my brain. A lush aroma, thick with sweetness, thick as blood, and spiced with the clear acid of tropical greenery.
>
> — FRANK CONROY, *Stop-Time*

Naming the objects from which smells come can also be very suggestive:

> The odor of these houses was different, full of fragrances, sweet and nauseating. On 105th Street the smells were of fried lard, of beans and car fumes, of factory smoke and home-made brew out of backyard stills. There were chicken smells and goat smells in grassless yards filled with engine parts and wire and wood planks, cracked and sprinkled with rusty nails. These were the familiar aromas: the funky earth, animal and mechanical smells which were absent from the homes my mother cleaned.
>
> — Luis J. Rodriguez, *Always Running: Gang Days in L.A.*

EXERCISE 15.9

Turn to Jon Ronson's "The Hunger Games" in Chapter 3, and read paragraph 9. Underline the words describing the sense of smell. How do you think this bit of sensory description helps readers imagine the scene?

EXERCISE 15.10

Choose a place with noticeable, distinctive smells where you can stay for ten or fifteen minutes. You may choose an eating place (a cafeteria, a doughnut shop), a place where something is being manufactured (a sawmill, a bakery), or some other place that has strong, identifiable odors (a fishing dock, a garden, a locker room). While you are there, take notes on what you smell, and then write a paragraph or two describing the place primarily through its smells.

Describe tactile sensations.

Relatively few nouns and verbs name tactile sensations besides words like *touch, feel, tickle, brush, scratch, sting, itch,* and *tingle*. Probably as a consequence, writers describing the sense of touch tend not to name the sensation directly or even to report the act of feeling. Nevertheless, a large stock of words describes temperature (*hot, warm, mild, tepid, cold, arctic*), moisture content (*wet, dry, sticky, oily, greasy, moist, crisp*), texture (*gritty, silky, smooth, crinkled, coarse, soft, leathery*), and weight (*heavy, light, ponderous, buoyant, feathery*). Read the following passages with an eye for descriptions of touch:

> A small slab of roughly finished concrete offered a place to stand opposite a square of tar from which a splintered tee protruded.
>
> — William Rintoul, "Breaking One Hundred"

> The earth was moldy, a dense clay. No sun had fallen here for over two centuries. I climbed over the brick retaining wall and crawled toward the sound of the kitten. As I neared, as it sensed my presence was too large to be its mother, it went silent and scrabbled away from the reach of my hand. I brushed fur, though, and that slight warmth filled me with what must have been a mad calm because when the creature squeezed into a bearing wall of piled stones, I inched forward on my stomach.
>
> — Louise Erdrich, "Beneath the House"

Here is an example of a writer recalling a childish fantasy of aggression toward her younger sister. Notice the tactile description she uses:

> She was baby-soft. I thought that I could put my thumb on her nose and push it bonelessly in, indent her face. I could poke dimples into her cheeks. I could work her face around like dough.
>
> — Maxine Hong Kingston, "The Quiet Girl"

EXERCISE 15.11

Do something with your hands, and then write a sentence or two describing the experience of touch. For example, you might pet a dog, dig a hole and put a plant into the earth, make a pizza, sculpt with clay, bathe a baby, or scrub a floor. As you write, notice the words you consider using to describe temperature, moisture content, texture, weight, or any other tactile quality.

EXERCISE 15.12

Turn to Brian Cable's "The Last Stop" in Chapter 3, and read the last paragraph. Underline the language that describes the sense of touch. What does this detail add to your understanding of the scene, and why might Cable have chosen to save it for the last paragraph of his profile?

Describe flavors.

Other than *taste, savor,* and *flavor,* few words name gustatory sensations directly. Certain words do distinguish among types of tastes — *sweet (saccharine, sugary, cloying); sour (acidic, tart); bitter (acrid, biting); salty (briny, brackish)* — and several other words describe specific tastes (*piquant, spicy, pungent, peppery, savory*).

In the following passage, M. F. K. Fisher describes the surprisingly "delicious" taste of tar:

> Tar with some dust in it was perhaps even more delicious than dirty chips from the iceman's wagon, largely because if we worked up enough body heat and had the right amount of spit we could keep it melted so that it acted almost like chewing gum, which was forbidden to us as vulgar and bad for the teeth and in general to be shunned. Tar was better than anything ever put out by Wrigley and Beechnut, anyway. It had a high, bright taste. It tasted the way it smelled, but better.
>
> — M. F. K. Fisher, "Prejudice, Hate, and the First World War"

Words not typically associated with taste

Fisher tries to evoke the sense of taste by comparing tar that acted like chewing gum to actual Wrigley and Beechnut chewing gum. More surprisingly, she compares the taste of tar to its smell.

Ernest Hemingway, in a more conventional passage, tries to describe taste primarily by naming the foods he consumed and giving details that indicate the intensity and quality of the tastes:

As I ate the oysters with their strong taste of the sea and their faint metallic taste that the cold wine washed away, leaving only the sea taste and the succulent texture, and as I drank their cold liquid from each shell and washed it down with the crisp taste of the wine, I lost the empty feeling and began to be happy and to make plans.

— ERNEST HEMINGWAY, *A Moveable Feast*

Combines taste and touch (the feel of the food in the mouth)

Writers often use words like *juicy, chewy,* and *chunky* to evoke both the taste and the feel of food in the mouth.

EXERCISE 15.13

In the manner of Hemingway, take notes as you eat a particular food or an entire meal. Then write a few sentences describing the tastes you experienced.

Creating a Dominant Impression

The most effective description creates a **dominant impression**, a mood or an atmosphere that reinforces the writer's purpose. Naming, detailing, comparing, and sensory language — all the choices about what to include and what to call things — come together to create this effect, as the following passage by Mary McCarthy illustrates. Notice that McCarthy directly states the idea she is trying to convey in the last sentence of the paragraph:

Whenever we children came to stay at my grandmother's house, we were put to sleep in the sewing room, a bleak, shabby, utilitarian rectangle, more office than bedroom, more attic than office, that played to the hierarchy of chambers the role of a poor relation. It was a room seldom entered by the other members of the family, seldom swept by the maid, a room without pride; the old sewing machine, some cast-off chairs, a shadeless lamp, rolls of wrapping paper, piles of pins, and remnants of material united with the iron folding cots put out for our use and the bare floor boards to give an impression of intense and ruthless temporality. Thin, white spreads, of the kind used in hospitals and charity institutions, and naked blinds at the windows reminded us of our orphaned condition and of the ephemeral character of our visit; there was nothing here to encourage us to consider this our home.

— MARY MCCARTHY, *Memories of a Catholic Girlhood*

Like McCarthy and her brothers, the things in the room were unwanted, discarded, orphaned. Even the room itself is described in terms applicable to the children: Like them, it "played to the hierarchy of chambers the role of a poor relation."

Sometimes writers comment directly in a description, as McCarthy does. Often, however, writers want description to speak for itself, as in the following example:

Hanging from the ceiling there was a heavy glass chandelier on which the dust was so thick that it was like fur. And covering most of one wall there was a huge hideous piece of junk, something between a sideboard and a hall-stand, with lots of carving and little drawers and strips of looking-glass, and there was a once-gaudy carpet ringed by the slop-pails of years, and two gilt chairs with burst seats, and one of those old-fashioned armchairs which you slide off when you try to sit on them. The room had been turned into a bedroom by thrusting four squalid beds in among the wreckage.

— GEORGE ORWELL, *The Road to Wigan Pier*

EXERCISE 15.14

Turn to "The Long Good-Bye: Mother's Day in Federal Prison" by Amanda Coyne in Chapter 3 and read paragraph 3. What seems to you to be the dominant impression of this description? What do you think contributes most to this impression?

Sentence Strategies for Description

Effective descriptions not only create a distinctive image but also contribute to the overall impression the writer wants to convey. To create this overall impression, writers must determine not only what is most relevant, important, or interesting about what they are describing but also what role the description is playing. The sentence strategies that follow may provide you with a jumping-off point for writing descriptions that are both powerful and effective. To make these sentences your own, though, you may need to rework them as you revise.

To Describe as a Participant

▶ As I tried to _____ like the _____ , I was surprised to find that _____ .

▶ I picked up X. It felt like _____ , and it looked/smelled/tasted/sounded like _____ .

▶ Above/around/before me, activity A happened. I tried to _____ , and found it _____ . "_____," X said, watching.

▶ Although X clearly seemed _____ , I couldn't shake the feeling that/ignore/stop thinking about _____ .

▶ After hours/minutes/days of doing X, I felt like _____ .

To Describe as a Spectator

▶ On the other side of _____ , a/an _____ appeared/came into view/did something.

▶ X talked as he _____ . "_____," he said.

▶ Gazing at/down/along/with/on _____ , X remarked that _____ .

▶ X is impressive/strange/easy to miss, with its/his/her _____, _____, and _____ .

▶ _____ makes X angry. She/he says it's because _____ : " _____ ."

▶ Although X tries to/pretends to/has made progress toward _____ , overall/for the most part/primarily he/she/it is _____ .

To Reflect on Your Observations

▶ The most interesting aspect of X is _____ , because _____ .

▶ Although my visit confirmed that _____ , I was surprised to learn that _____ .

▶ My dominant impression of X is _____ .

16

Defining

Defining is an essential strategy for all writing. Autobiographers, for example, must occasionally define objects, conditions, events, and activities for readers likely to be unfamiliar with particular terms, as in the following example:

Term to be defined
Definition

My father's hands are grotesque. He suffers from psoriasis, a chronic skin disease that covers his massive, thick hands with scaly, reddish patches that periodically flake off, sending tiny pieces of dead skin sailing to the ground.

— JAN GRAY, "Father"

When writers share information or explain how to do something, they must often define important terms for readers who are unfamiliar with the subject, as in this example:

Shifting baselines are the chronic, slow, hard-to-notice changes in things, from the disappearance of birds and frogs in the countryside to the increased drive time from L.A. to San Diego.

— RANDY OLSON, "Shifting Baselines: Slow-Motion Disaster below the Waves"

To convince readers of a position or an evaluation or to move them to act on a proposal, a writer must often define concepts important to an argument:

You would come across news of a study showing that the percentage of Wisconsin food-stamp families in "extreme poverty" — defined as less than 50 percent of the federal poverty line — has tripled in the last decade to more than 30 percent.

— BARBARA EHRENREICH, *Nickel and Dimed*

Some writing is primarily concerned with the definition of a little-understood or problematic concept or thing. Usually, however, a long piece of writing, like a term paper, textbook, or research report, will include many kinds of brief and extended definitions, all of them integrated with other writing strategies.

This chapter illustrates various types of sentence definitions, the most common in writing. When writers use sentence definitions, they rely on various sentence patterns to provide concise definitions. The chapter also provides illustrations of multi-sentence extended definitions, including definition by word history, or etymology, and by stipulation. It concludes with some sentence strategies you might use to get started drafting a definition.

Sentence Definitions

Coming to a new field of study, institution, or activity for the first time, a participant is often baffled by the many unfamiliar concepts and terms. In college, introductory courses in all the academic disciplines often seem like courses in definitions of new terms. In the same way, newcomers to a sport like sailing or rock climbing often need to learn a great deal of specialized terminology. Writers of textbooks and manuals that cover such topics rely on brief **sentence definitions** to explain terms and concepts. The most obvious strategies simply announce a definition:

> A karyotype is a graphic representation of a set of chromosomes.   Term to be defined

> Then, within the first week, the cells begin to differentiate — to specialize in   Definition
> structure and function.

> Posthypnotic suggestions (suggestions to be carried out after the hypnosis session has ended) have helped alleviate headaches, asthma, warts, and stress-related skin disorders.

Other, less direct strategies for integrating definitions are signaled by *subordinate clauses*:

> During the oral stage, which lasts throughout the first 18 months, the infant's sensual pleasures focus on sucking, biting, and chewing.

> Hemophilia is called the bleeder's disease because the affected person's blood does not clot.

Another common defining strategy is to use an *appositive*—a brief, inserted word or phrase that presents either the definition or the word to be defined:

> Taxonomy, the science of classifying groups (taxa) of organisms in formal groups, is hierarchical.

> The actual exchange of gases takes place in small air sacs, the alveoli, which are clustered in branches like grapes around the ends of the smallest bronchioles.

EXERCISE 16.1

Look up any three of the following words or phrases in a dictionary. Define each one in a sentence. Try to use a different sentence pattern for each of your definitions.

bull market	ecumenism	samba
carcinogen	edema	seasonal affective disorder
caricature	harangue	sonnet
clinometer	hyperhidrosis	testosterone
ectomorph	mnemonic	zero-based budgeting

EXERCISE 16.2

Turn to the essay in Chapter 8 entitled "What College Rankings Really Tell Us" by Malcolm Gladwell and analyze the sentence definition in paragraph 2. Notice the strategy Gladwell relies on. Keeping in mind that Gladwell's purpose is to persuade readers to accept his criticism of the *U.S. News* staff's college rankings, how helpful do you find this sentence definition?

Extended Definitions

At times a writer may need to go further than a brief sentence definition and provide readers with a fuller, **extended definition**, as in the following example:

Compares TV addiction with drug and alcohol addiction

People often refer to being "hooked on TV." Does this, too, fall into the light-hearted category of cookie eating and other pleasures that people pursue with unusual intensity, or is there a kind of televison viewing that falls into the more serious category of destructive addiction? . . .

Let us consider television viewing in the light of the conditions that define serious addictions.

Not unlike drugs or alcohol, the television experience allows the participant to blot out the real world and enter into a pleasurable and passive mental state. The worries and anxieties of reality are as effectively deferred by becoming absorbed in a television program as by going on a "trip" induced by drugs or alcohol. And just as alcoholics are only inchoately aware of their addiction, feeling that they control their drinking more than they really do ("I can cut it out any time I want—I just like to have three or four drinks before dinner"), people similarly overestimate their control over television watching. Even as they put off other activities to spend hour after hour watching television, they feel they could easily resume living in a different, less passive style. But somehow or other while the television set is present in their homes, the click doesn't sound. With television pleasures available, those other experiences seem less attractive, more difficult somehow. . . .

The self-confessed television addict often feels he "ought" to do other things—but the fact that he doesn't read and doesn't plant his garden or sew or crochet or play games or have conversations means that those activities are no longer as desirable as television viewing. In a way a heavy viewer's life is as imbalanced by his television "habit" as a drug addict's or an alcoholic's. He is living in a holding pattern, as it were, passing up the activities that lead to growth or development or a sense of accomplishment. This is one reason people talk about their television viewing so ruefully, so apologetically. They are aware that it is an unproductive experience, that almost any other endeavor is more worthwhile by any human measure.

Finally, it is the adverse effect of television viewing on the lives of so many people that defines it as a serious addiction. The television habit distorts the sense of time. It renders other experiences vague and curiously unreal while taking on a greater reality for itself. It weakens relationships by reducing and sometimes eliminating normal opportunities for talking, for communicating.

And yet television does not satisfy, else why would the viewer continue to watch hour after hour, day after day? "The measure of health," writes Lawrence Kubie, "is flexibility . . . and especially the freedom to cease when sated." But the television viewer can never be sated with his television experiences—they do not provide the true nourishment that satiation requires—and thus he finds that he cannot stop watching.

— MARIE WINN, "TV Addiction"

In this example, Marie Winn offers an extended definition of television addiction that begins with a comparison. *Comparison or contrast* is often the most effective way to present an unfamiliar term or concept to readers. The key is to know your readers well enough to find a term nearly all of them will know to compare to the unfamiliar term.

Extended definitions may also include *negative definitions*—explanations of what the thing being defined is *not:*

It's important to be clear about the reverse definition, as well: what dinosaurs are not. Dinosaurs are not lizards, and vice versa. Lizards are scaly reptiles of an ancient bloodline. The oldest lizards antedate the earliest dinosaurs by a full thirty million years. A few large lizards, such as the man-eating Komodo dragon, have been called "relics of the dinosaur age," but this phrase is historically incorrect. No lizard ever evolved the birdlike characteristics peculiar to each and every dinosaur. A big lizard never resembled a small dinosaur except for a few inconsequential details of the teeth. Lizards never walked with the erect, long-striding gait that distinguishes the dinosaur like ground birds today or the birdlike dinosaurs of the Mesozoic.

Defines by saying what dinosaurs are not

— ROBERT T. BAKKER, *The Dinosaur Heresies*

EXERCISE 16.3

Choose one term that names some concept or feature of central importance in an activity or a subject you know well. For example, if you are studying biology, you have probably encountered terms like *morphogenesis* and *ecosystem*. Choose a word with a well-established definition. Write an extended definition of several sentences for this important term. Write for readers your own age who will be encountering the term for the first time when they read your definition.

EXERCISE 16.4

In his essay in Chapter 4, "Do You Suffer from Decision Fatigue?," John Tierney presents an extended definition. After reading his essay, how would you define *decision fatigue*? Reread the essay to see which strategies he uses to define the term.

Historical Definitions

Occasionally, a writer will provide a **historical definition**, tracing the evolution of a term from its first use to its adoption into other languages to its shifting meanings over the centuries. Such a strategy can be a rich addition to an essay, bringing surprising depth and resonance to the definition of a concept. In this example on the future uses of cyberspace and its potential impact on the economy, Philip Elmer-DeWitt provides a historical definition of the term *cyberspace*:

> It started, as the big ideas in technology often do, with a science-fiction writer. William Gibson, a young expatriate American living in Canada, was wandering past the video arcades on Vancouver's Granville Street in the early 1980s when something about the way the players were hunched over their glowing screens struck him as odd. "I could see in the physical intensity of their postures how *rapt* the kids were," he says. "It was like a feedback loop, with photons coming off the screens into the kids' eyes, neurons moving through their bodies and electrons moving through the video game. These kids clearly *believed* in the space the games projected."
>
> That image haunted Gibson. He didn't know much about video games or computers—he wrote his breakthrough novel *Neuromancer* (1984) on an ancient manual typewriter—but he knew people who did. And as near as he could tell, everybody who worked much with the machines eventually came to accept, almost as an article of faith, the reality of that imaginary realm. "They develop a belief that there's some kind of *actual space* behind the screen," he says. "Some place that you can't see but you know is there."
>
> Gibson called that place "cyberspace," and used it as the setting for his early novels and short stories. In his fiction, cyberspace is a computer-generated landscape that characters enter by "jacking in"—sometimes by plugging electrodes directly into sockets implanted in the brain. What they see when they get there is a three-dimensional representation of all the information stored in "every computer in the human system"—great warehouses and skyscrapers of data. He describes it in a key passage in *Neuromancer* as a place of "unthinkable complexity," with "lines of light ranged in the nonspace of the mind, clusters and constellations of data. Like city lights, receding. . . ."
>
> In the years since, there have been other names given to that shadowy space where our computer data reside: the Net, the Web, the Cloud, the Matrix, the Metaverse, the Datasphere, the Electronic Frontier, the information superhighway. But Gibson's coinage may prove the most enduring. By 1989 it had been borrowed by the online community to describe not some science-fiction fantasy but today's increasingly interconnected computer systems—especially the millions of computers jacked into the Internet.
>
> — Philip Elmer-DeWitt, "Welcome to Cyberspace"

The historical definition serves Elmer-DeWitt's larger purpose in writing this essay: to help readers acquire a deeper understanding of the new technologies that continue to profoundly affect the ways in which we live our lives.

You can consult a historical, or etymological, dictionary, such as the *Oxford English Dictionary, A Dictionary of American English,* or *A Dictionary of Americanisms,* to trace changes in the use of a word over long periods of time or to survey different theories of a word's or phrase's origins. Online you can search the *Phrase Finder,* search the *Urban Dictionary,* or just Google the word or phrase plus definition. Look up the historical definition of any one of the following words — or a word or phrase you're curious about — in one or more sources, and write several sentences on its roots and development.

bedrock	eye-opener	lobbying	rubberneck
bogus	filibuster	lynching	sashay
bushwhack	gerrymander	pep	23 skidoo
dugout	head over heels	podunk	two-bit

Stipulative Definitions

To stipulate means to seek or assert agreement on something. In a **stipulative definition**, the writer declares a certain meaning, generally not one found in the dictionary.

In the excerpt from her autobiography *An American Childhood* that appears in Chapter 2, Annie Dillard offers a stipulative definition of *football* as she understood it as a nine-year-old:

> Some boys taught me to play football. This was fine sport. You thought up a new strategy for every play and whispered it to the others. You went out for a pass, fooling everyone. Best, you got to throw yourself mightily at someone's running legs. Either you brought him down or you hit the ground flat out on your chin, with your arms empty before you. It was all or nothing. If you hesitated in fear, you would miss and get hurt: you would take a hard fall while the kid got away, or you would get kicked in the face while the kid got away. But if you flung yourself wholeheartedly at the back of his knees—if you gathered and joined body and soul and pointed them diving fearlessly— then you likely wouldn't get hurt, and you'd stop the ball. Your fate, and your team's score, depended on your concentration and courage. Nothing girls did could compare with it.
>
> — ANNIE DILLARD, *An American Childhood*

There are recognizable elements of grown-up football in Dillard's definition. Her focus is less on rules and strategy, however, than on the "concentration and courage" required to make a successful tackle and, of course, on the sheer thrill of doing so.

In the next example, the writer stipulates a definition of the term *environmentalism* to support an argument:

> A sane environmentalism, the only kind of environmentalism that will win universal public support, begins by unashamedly declaring that nature is here to serve man. A sane environmentalism is entirely anthropocentric: it enjoins man to preserve nature, but on the grounds of self-preservation.

A sane environmentalism does not sentimentalize the earth. It does not ask people to sacrifice in the name of other creatures. After all, it is hard enough to ask people to sacrifice in the name of other humans. (Think of the chronic public resistance to foreign aid and welfare.) Ask hardworking voters to sacrifice in the name of the snail darter, and, if they are feeling polite, they will give you a shrug.

— CHARLES KRAUTHAMMER, "Saving Nature, but Only for Man"

EXERCISE 16.6

Write several sentences of a stipulative definition for one of the following:

1. Define in your own way game shows, police dramas, horror movies, or some other form of entertainment. Try for a stipulative definition of what your subject is generally like. In effect, you will be saying to your readers—other students in your class who are familiar with these entertainments—"Let's define it this way for now."

2. Define in your own way some hard-to-define concept, such as "loyalty," "love," "bravery," "shyness," or "masculinity."

3. Think of a new development or phenomenon in contemporary romance, music, television, leisure, fashion, or eating habits, or in your line of work. Invent a name for it, and write a stipulative definition for it.

Sentence Strategies for Definition

Writers frequently include definitions in essays that explain concepts. Essay exams also may require students to define terms. If you need to integrate a definition into an essay or exam, one or more of the following sentence strategies may provide a jumping-off point. Remember to rework the definition to make it your own as you revise.

▶ X is a/an phenomenon/event/process in which _____ [list defining characteristics].

▶ Many people think the term X means _____ , but it might be more accurate to say it means _____ .

▶ What makes X a good example of _____ is _____ , _____ , and _____ .

▶ X should be considered a/an _____ [name genre or category of subject, such as romantic comedy or horror movie] because _____ .

▶ X is an innovative _____ [name genre or category to which your subject belongs] because it not only includes _____ [name standard features] but also offers _____ [name additional features].

▶ X is rather unconventional for a/an _____ [name genre or category to which your subject belongs] because _____ .

▶ X is a brilliant embodiment of [name genre or category to which your subject belongs], especially notable for its superb _____ and thorough _____ .

17

Classifying

Classifying is an essential writing strategy for thinking about and organizing ideas, information, and experience. The process of **classifying** involves either grouping or dividing. Writers group related items (such as *apples, oranges, bananas, strawberries, cantaloupes,* and *cherries*) and label the general class of items they grouped together (*fruit*). Or they begin classifying with a general class (such as *fruit*) and then divide it into subclasses of particular types (*apples, oranges,* etc.).

This chapter shows how you can organize and illustrate a classification you have read about or constructed yourself, and it concludes with some sentence strategies you might use when classifying information.

Organizing Classification

Classifying in writing serves primarily as a means of **organization**—of creating a framework for the presentation of information, whether in a few paragraphs of an essay or in an entire book. This section surveys several examples of classifying, ranging from a simple two-level classification to a complex multilevel system.

The simplest classification divides a general topic into two subtopics. Here is an example by Edward J. Loughram from a proposal to keep at-risk teenagers out of jail and help them lead productive lives. Before he can present his proposed solution, Loughram has to get readers to see that juvenile offenders are not all the same. He does this by explaining that although statistics show that the number of juvenile offenders is rising, they do not take into account the fact that there are two distinct groups of young people getting into trouble. He classifies juvenile offenders into these two categories to argue that the problem of delinquency can be solved, at least in part, by interrupting the criminal paths of the second group:

> Two primary factors explain the growing numbers of juvenile offenders. First, there is indeed a rise in serious crime among young people, fueled by the steady stream of drugs and weapons into their hands. These dangerous offenders are committed—legitimately—to juvenile-correction agencies for long-term custody or treatment.
>
> But a second, larger group is also contributing to the increase. It consists of 11-, 12-, and 13-year-old first-time offenders who have failed at home, failed in

school, and fallen through the cracks of state and community social-service agencies. These are not serious offenders, or even typical delinquents. But they are coming into the correctional system because we have ignored the warning signs among them.

— EDWARD J. LOUGHRAM, "Prevention of Delinquency"

From Loughram's essay, we see how a writer can use a simple two-category classification to advance an argument. The concept analysis by John Tierney in Chapter 4 also offers a two-category classification to analyze the effects of decision fatigue. The following figure below offers a *tree diagram* of his analysis:

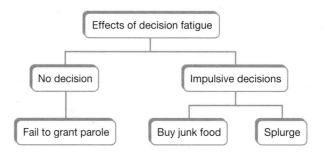

What the tree diagram shows at a glance is that in a classification system, some categories, such as "do nothing" and "act impulsively," are on the same level, or *coordinate;* others (in this case "effects of decision fatigue") are on a higher level, or *superordinate;* and some ("fail to grant parole," "buy junk food," "splurge") are on a lower level, or *subordinate*. The highest level represents the most general category, and lower levels identify increasingly specific types. Tierney takes his classification to the most specific level by offering examples of individuals who suffered from decision fatigue. For example, he begins with a lengthy example of a judge who failed to grant parole because of decision fatigue, and he quotes Jean Twenge on her impulsive decisions while creating a gift registry for her wedding.

EXERCISE 17.1

Turn to Anastasia Toufexis's concept explanation in Chapter 4, "Love: The Right Chemistry," and make a tree diagram of the classification she offers of romantic love. What do you think is Toufexis's basis for classification? Does each item seem to be placed in an appropriate category and at the proper level?

EXERCISE 17.2

Review the essays you have written so far for this class or for another class, looking for an essay in which you used classifying. What was the purpose of your essay and your basis for classifying? Construct a tree diagram of your classification to see whether each item can be placed in an appropriate category and on the proper level.

Illustrating Classification

We used tree diagrams as an *illustration* of the categories and levels of Tierney's classification of reasons. Similarly, writers sometimes integrate graphics to make their classification easy for readers to see at a glance.

Here is an example in which Sharon Begley and Martha Brant explain the abuse of performance-enhancing drugs by Olympic athletes, classifying the drugs into five categories:

> If doping is, as [the head of IOC's Medical Commission Prince Alexandre] de Merode noticed, suddenly "an important problem," it is partly because the newest doping agents pose the risk of serious health problems, and even death. But the larger reason is that it is ridiculously easy to dope and not get caught. Doping and detection are like an arms race. First, trainers discover a performance-enhancing drug. Then, sports officials develop a test for it. Trainers retaliate by inventing a way to elude the detectors. So far, doping has stayed a lap ahead. "Undetectable drugs are 90 percent of estimated doping cases," says Hein Verbruggen, head of international cycling.
>
> Czech tennis pro Petr Korda tested positive for the steroid nandrolone after the Wimbledon quarterfinals last May, for instance. (Protesting that he did not know how the chemicals got into his system, he avoided the one-year suspension the International Tennis Association is supposed to impose.) But American pro Jim Courier charged that steroids are far from the worst abuse in tennis. "EPO is the problem," Courier told *Newsweek*. "I have pretty strong suspicions that guys are using it on the tour. I see guys who are out there week in and week out without taking rests. EPO can help you when it's the fifth set and you've been playing for four-and-a-half hours." Although the endurance-building effects of EPO last for about two weeks, its use can't be detected in urine at all or in blood for more than a day or so after the athlete stops taking it.
>
> EPO is only one weapon in a pharmaceutical arsenal of performance-enhancing substances flowing through sports. Stimulants like amphetamines, ephedrine and caffeine were the first substances to land on the IOC's list of banned agents, and they're still popular. They provide a quick pop of energy, and so are a favorite of sprinters, cyclists and swimmers. They are an ingredient of many asthma medications. Exercise-induced asthma has inexplicably stricken many Olympians, including 60 percent of the U.S. team in 1994, and medical use of stimulant inhalants is allowed. Are stimulants detectable? Sure, if your trainer's IQ matches his hat size. They clear the urine in hours, so all an athlete has to do is not take them too close to her event. If you've been using too soon before your race, there are always "masking agents." Probenecid, for one, inhibits substances from reaching the urine. And urine tests are all the IOC requires: blood tests, which can detect more substances, are deemed too invasive.
>
> Anabolic steroids, almost all of them derivatives of the hormone testosterone, are the mothers of all doping agents. They build muscles. By most estimates, an athlete can improve strength at least 5 percent by taking steroids either orally or through injection during high-intensity training. Drug-detection machines, such as the high-resolution mass spectrometer used at the Atlanta Games in 1996,

Five types of performance-enhancing drugs

Drug	What Does It Do?	Masking/Detection	Risks
Human growth hormone (hGH)	Stimulates the intracellular breakdown of body fat, allowing more to be used for energy.	This is a natural hormone, so added amounts don't show up in blood or urine tests.	Muscle and bone disfigurement — jutting forehead, elongated jaw. Also: heart and metabolic problems.
Erythropoietin (EPO)	Increases the number of red blood cells without having to "dope" using one's own blood.	It's extremely difficult to detect because the extra blood cells are the athlete's own.	Extra cells can make blood the consistency of yogurt. This can lead to a clot, heart attack, or stroke.
Testosterone	Used to build muscles. It lets the body recover quickly from strenuous exercise.	Rules allow up to five times the natural body level, giving athletes latitude.	Unnatural levels can cause heart disease, liver cancer, and impotence.
Steroids/ androstenedione	Anabolic steroids are incarnations of testosterone; androstenedione is a precursor molecule.	Water-based steroids (most common) are undetectable in urine after several weeks.	Synthetic testosterone carries the same risks as naturally occurring testosterone.
Stimulants	The first category that the IOC tested for. They delay the symptoms of fatigue.	Stimulants such as amphetamines can be detected; diuretics can dilute them in urine.	Fatigue is the body saying "stop" — overriding that message can be dangerous.

Chart illustrates organizational plan

can be tuned to detect any synthetic steroid; the Atlanta lab tested for 100 different types. But the Dr. Feelgoods of sport can tinker with the molecular structure of common steroids, so they slip through. "There are 72 banned steroids," says one American coach who says he developed drug regimes for athletes in Atlanta, "but the testosterone molecule is changeable in millions of ways. All you have to do is make a steroid not on the list." Or, simply by going cold turkey a few weeks before competition, an athlete can get the muscle-bulking effects without getting caught. If that seems too chancy, athletes can use a diuretic. These drugs, which are also banned, dilute the urine. That makes illicit substances virtually undetectable.

More and more athletes are turning to the source of all steroids: testosterone itself. Natural levels vary, so sports federations and the IOC try to detect doping indirectly. They measure the relative amounts of testosterone and another natural steroid called epitestosterone. In most people, testosterone levels are no more than twice epi levels. But to allow for individual variation, the IOC set the prohibited level at anything over 6 to 1. That means an athlete can dope himself up to, say, five times his normal testosterone levels, and get away with it. How much of an edge would that provide? A male athlete with a typical testosterone/epitestosterone ratio of 1.3 to 1 could boost that to 6 to 1, stay within the IOC limit and improve his performance at least 10 percent. Women, with a natural ratio of 2.5 to 1, could do even better, since they have less testosterone to begin with and so are more sensitive to added amounts. Testosterone can give women beards, deep voices and tough skin. It can make men's breasts swell and testicles shrivel.

The doping agents of choice today are substances that cannot be detected in urine: EPO and human growth hormone. Even though the performance-enhancing effects of hGH are unproved, many athletes believe it boosts energy. (Athletes dubbed the Atlanta Olympics "The Growth Hormone Games.") hGH can also cause grotesque skeletal deformations by stimulating abnormal bone growth. EPO, by increasing the production of red blood cells up to tenfold, can turn blood the consistency of yogurt, making it too thick to flow freely. The misuse of EPO has apparently killed at least 18 Dutch and Belgian cyclists since 1987.

— SHARON BEGLEY AND MARTHA BRANT, "The Real Scandal"

For more information on designing documents with graphics, see Chapter 32.

Maintaining Clarity and Coherence

The next example illustrates how writers can help readers follow a classification system by maintaining *clarity* and *coherence*—even when the subject is new and difficult. The passage comes from a book on physics by Gary Zukav. He uses classifying to explain the concept of mass. Simply defined, mass in physics is a measure of the matter in an object:

> There are two kinds of mass, which means that there are two ways of talking about it. The first is gravitational mass. The gravitational mass of an object, roughly speaking, is the weight of the object as measured on a balance scale. Something that weighs three times more than another object has three times more mass. Gravitational mass is the measure of how much force the gravity of the earth exerts on an object. Newton's laws describe the effects of this force, which vary with the distance of the mass from the earth. . . .
>
> The second type of mass is inertial mass. Inertial mass is the measure of the resistance of an object to acceleration (or deceleration, which is negative acceleration). For example, it takes three times more force to move three railroad cars from a standstill to twenty miles per hour (positive acceleration) than it takes to move one railroad car from a standstill to twenty miles per hour. . . . Similarly, once they are moving, it takes three times more force to stop three cars than it takes to stop the single car. This is because the inertial mass of the three railroad cars is three times more than the inertial mass of the single railroad car.
>
> — GARY ZUKAV, *The Dancing Wu Li Masters: An Overview of the New Physics*

Cues alerting readers to classification scheme

From this passage, we can see some of the cues writers use to make a classification clear and coherent. Zukav begins by *forecasting* the classification he will develop (*There are two kinds of mass*). He then introduces each category in its own paragraph, announced with a *transition* (*first* and *second*) and presented in the same sentence pattern (*The first is . . .* and *The second type of mass is . . .*). Careful *cueing* like this can help make a classification clear to readers.

General strategies for coherence are discussed in Chapter 13.

EXERCISE 17.3

Look back at Anastasia Toufexis's essay "Love: The Right Chemistry" (Chapter 4), which you used to make a tree diagram in Exercise 17.1, or at the example by Begley and Brant earlier in this chapter to examine the strategies these authors use to make their classifications clear and coherent. Notice how each category is introduced and how transitions are used to help readers keep track of the categories. What conclusions can you draw about how writers maintain clarity and coherence from your analysis?

EXERCISE 17.4

Look back at the classification you examined in Exercise 17.2 to see how well you were able to maintain clarity and coherence in your classification. What changes would you make, if any, to improve clarity and coherence?

Sentence Strategies for Classification

Many genres invite the use of classification, including concept explanations, proposals, evaluations, and speculations about causes. If classifying ideas, information, or experience will help your readers understand a concept or accept a proposal or an evaluation, use these sentence strategies to begin putting your ideas into words. You will probably want to rework these sentences to make them your own, but they may give you a jumping-off point for articulating your thoughts.

Use Rhetorical Questions to Establish the Categories

▶ How does X develop, and how does it continue in _____ [name stage or period]? Researchers A and B provide answers to these questions.

Use Comparison or Contrast to Establish the Categories

▶ X is similar to/different from Y in these ways: _____, _____, and _____.

Use Causes and Effects as Categories

▶ Recent research on X demonstrates that when _____ [state cause], it often _____ [state effect].

Use Reasons as Categories

▶ What makes X problematic/praiseworthy is _____, _____, and _____.

▶ I'm also/not concerned about X because _____, _____, and _____ [state reasons].

List the Categories

▶ X can be divided into 4 categories: _____, _____, _____, and _____.

▶ Experts like Professor A say there are _____ categories/types/subtypes/versions of X ranging from _____ to _____ (citation).

▶ Experts disagree over the causes of X. Some, like Dr. A, believe _____ (citation). Others, like Dr. B, contend that _____ (citation).

Use Cues to Forecast Categories

▶ Researcher A identified three basic types/categories of X. The first type/category is _____. It does/is/has _____ [name distinguishing characteristics]. The second/next type/category is _____. It does/is/has _____ [name distinguishing characteristics]. The final/third type/category is _____. It does/is/has _____ [name distinguishing characteristics].

18

Comparing and Contrasting

Most of us compare things all the time: You might compare two people you know well, two motorcycles you are considering buying for a cross-country tour, three Stephen King novels, four tomato plants being grown under different laboratory conditions, or two theories about the relationship between inflation and wages. But as soon as you begin to compare two things, you usually begin to contrast them as well, for rarely are two things alike in all respects. The contrasts, or differences, between the two motorcycles are likely to be more enlightening than the similarities, many of which may be so obvious as to need no analysis. **Comparison**, then, brings similar things together for examination, to see how they are alike. **Contrast** is a form of comparison that emphasizes differences. According to research on learning, we acquire new concepts most readily if we can see how they are similar to or different from concepts we already know.

Chances are that you will confront many test questions and essay assignments asking you to compare and contrast—two poems, three presidents, four procedures. This strategy is popular in all academic disciplines, for it is one of the best ways to challenge students intellectually. This chapter shows how you can organize a comparison/contrast, and it concludes with some sentence strategies you might use when comparing or contrasting.

Organizing Comparisons and Contrasts

There are two ways to organize comparison and contrast in writing: You can present the items being compared in chunks or in sequence. In **chunking**, each object of the comparison is presented separately; in **sequencing**, the items are compared point by point. For example, a chunked comparison of two motorcycles would first detail all pertinent features of the Harley-Davidson SuperLow 1200T, and then consider all features of the Kawazuki Z1000 ABS, whereas a sequenced comparison would analyze the Harley and the Kawazuki feature by feature. In a chunked comparison, the discussion is organized around the items being compared. In a sequenced comparison, it is organized around characteristics of the items being compared.

In the following example of chunked comparison, Jane Tompkins contrasts popular nineteenth-century sentimental novels with the Western novels that provided a reaction against them:

> The female, domestic, "sentimental" religion of the best-selling women writers— Harriet Beecher Stowe, Susan Warner, Maria Cummins, and dozens of others—whose novels spoke to the deepest beliefs and highest ideals of middle-class America, is the real antagonist of the Western.
>
> You can see this simply by comparing the main features of the Western with the sentimental novel. In these books . . . a woman is always the main character, usually a young orphan girl, with several other main characters being women too. Most of the action takes place in private spaces, at home, indoors, in kitchens, parlors, and upstairs chambers. And most of it concerns the interior struggles of the heroine to live up to an ideal of Christian virtue—usually involving uncomplaining submission to difficult and painful circumstances, learning to quell rebellious instincts, and dedicating her life to the service of God through serving others. In these struggles, women give one another a great deal of emotional and material support, and they have close relationships verging on what today we would identify as homosocial and homoerotic. There's a great deal of Bible reading, praying, hymn singing, and drinking of tea. Emotions other than anger are expressed very freely and openly. Often there are long, drawn-out death scenes in which a saintly woman dies a natural death at home. . . .
>
> The elements of the typical Western plot arrange themselves in stark opposition to this pattern, not just vaguely and generally but point for point. First of all, in Westerns (which are generally written by men), the main character is always a full-grown adult male, and almost all of the other characters are men. The action takes place either outdoors—on the prairie, on the main street—or in public places—the saloon, the sheriff's office, the barber shop, the livery stable. The action concerns physical struggles between the hero and a rival or rivals, and culminates in a fight to the death with guns. In the course of these struggles the hero frequently forms a bond with another man—sometimes his rival, more often a comrade—a bond that is more important than any relation he has with a woman and is frequently tinged with homoeroticism. There is very little free expression of the emotions. The hero is a man of few words who expresses himself through physical action—usually fighting. And when death occurs it is never at home in bed but always sudden death, usually murder.
> — JANE TOMPKINS, *West of Everything: The Inner Life of Westerns*

Presents each point of contrast for the two subjects in the same order (chunking)

Signals shift from one subject to the other with a transition sentence at the start of the third paragraph

Schematically, a chunked comparison looks simple enough. As the preceding example shows, it is easy to block off such a discussion in a text and then provide a clean *transition* between the various parts. And yet it can in fact be more complicated for a writer to plan than a sequenced comparison. Sequenced comparison may be closer to the way people perceive and think about similarities or differences in things. For example, you may have realized all at once that two navy jackets are different, but you would identify the specific differences—buttons, tailoring, fabric—one at a time. A sequenced comparison would point to the differences in just this way, one at a time, whereas a chunked comparison would present all the features of one jacket and then do the same for the second. A writer using the chunked strategy, then, must organize all the points of comparison before starting to write and then be sure that the points of comparison are presented in the same order in the discussion of each item being compared. With sequencing, however, the writer can take up each point of comparison as it comes to mind.

In the next example, from a natural history of the earth, David Attenborough uses sequencing to contrast bird wings and airplane wings:

> Bird wings have a much more complex job to do than the wings of an aeroplane, for in addition to supporting the bird they must act as its engine, rowing it through the air. Even so the wing outline of a bird conforms to the same aerodynamic principles as those eventually discovered by man when designing his aeroplanes, and if you know how different kinds of aircraft perform, you can predict the flight capabilities of similarly shaped birds.
>
> Short stubby wings enable a tanager and other forest-living birds to swerve and dodge at speed through the undergrowth just as they helped the fighter planes of the Second World War to make tight turns and aerobatic manoeuvres in a dog-fight. More modern fighters achieve greater speeds by sweeping back their wings while in flight, just as peregrines do when they go into a 130 kph dive, stooping to a kill. Championship gliders have long thin wings so that, having gained height in a thermal up-current, they can soar gently down for hours and an albatross, the largest of flying birds, with a similar wing shape and a span of 3 metres, can patrol the ocean for hours in the same way without a single wing beat. Vultures and hawks circle at very slow speeds supported by a thermal and they have the broad rectangular wings that very slow flying aircraft have. Man has not been able to adapt wings to provide hovering flight. He has only achieved that with the whirling horizontal blades of a helicopter or the downward-pointing engines of a vertical landing jet. Hummingbirds have paralleled even this. They tilt their bodies so that they are almost upright and then beat their wings as fast as 80 times a second producing a similar down-draught of air. So the hummingbird can hover and even fly backwards.
>
> — DAVID ATTENBOROUGH, *Life on Earth*

Uses a limited, focused basis for the comparison: shape

Attenborough finds a valid—and fascinating—basis for comparison between birds and airplanes and develops it in a way that both informs and entertains his readers. A successful comparison always has these qualities: a valid basis for comparison, a limited focus, and information that will catch a reader's attention.

EXERCISE 18.1

Identify the specific items contrasted in Tompkins's passage comparing sentimental novels and Westerns. Number in sequence each contrast, and underline both parts of the contrast. To get started, in the paragraph about sentimental novels, underline "a woman is always the main character, usually a young orphan girl," and number it "1" in the margin. In the paragraph about Westerns, underline "the main character is always a full-grown adult male," and number this "1" also to complete your identification of both parts of the comparison. Then look for contrast 2, underline and number the contrasted items, and so on.

Look over your work and consider the pattern of these contrasts. What, if anything, made them easy to identify? Was any contrast left incomplete? In general, how successful and informative do you find this set of contrasts?

EXERCISE 18.2

Identify the specific items compared in Attenborough's passage comparing bird wings and aircraft wings. Underline both items, and number the pair in the margin. To get started, underline "tanager" and "fighter planes" in the first sentence of the second paragraph. In the margin, number this pair "1." Then identify pair 2 and so on.

Consider the pattern and ordering of the comparisons you have identified. What, if anything, made the pairs of items easy to identify? Some comparisons begin by naming a bird, some by identifying a category of aircraft. Did this lack of predictability present problems for you? Do you see any possible justification for the writer's having given up the predictability of always beginning each comparison with either a bird or an aircraft? In general, how successful and informative did you find this comparison?

EXERCISE 18.3

Write a page or so comparing or contrasting any one of the following subjects. Be careful to limit the basis for your comparison, and underline the sentence that states that basis. Use chunking or sequencing to organize the comparison.

Two ways of achieving the same goal (for example, traveling by bus or subway, or using flattery or persuasion to get what you want)

A good and bad job interview or date

Your relationship with two friends or relatives

Two or more forms of music, dance, film, or social networking sites

Two methods of doing some task at home or on the job

EXERCISE 18.4

Read paragraph 14 from "Love: The Right Chemistry" in Chapter 4 and paragraph 3 from "The Aristocrats: The Graphic Arts of *Game of Thrones*" in Chapter 4. How is each comparison organized? (It may or may not be neatly chunked or sequenced.) Why do you think the writer organizes the comparison in that way?

Using Analogy to Compare

An **analogy** is a special form of comparison in which one part of the comparison is used simply to explain the other, as in the following example:

> In like manner, geologists will sometimes use the calendar year as a unit to represent the time scale, and in such terms the Precambrian runs from New Year's Day until well after Halloween. Dinosaurs appear in the middle of December and are gone the

Uses two analogies — the twelve-month calendar and the distance along two widespread arms — to explain the duration of geologic time day after Christmas. The last ice sheet melts on December 31st at one minute before midnight, and the Roman Empire lasts five seconds. With your arms spread wide . . . to represent all time on earth, look at one hand with its line of life. The Cambrian begins in the wrist, and the Permian Extinction is at the outer end of the palm. All of the Cenozoic is in a fingerprint, and in a single stroke with a medium-grained nail file you could eradicate human history. Geologists live with the geologic scale. Individually, they may or may not be alarmed by the rate of exploitation of the things they discover, but, like the environmentalists, they use these repetitive analogies to place the human record in perspective—to see the Age of Reflection, the last few thousand years, as a small bright sparkle at the end of time.

— John McPhee, *Basin and Range*

Analogies are not limited to abstract, scientific concepts. Writers often use analogies to make nontechnical descriptions and explanations more vivid or to make an imaginative point of comparison that serves a larger argument. Consider the following example:

But now that government has largely withdrawn its "handouts" [to the welfare poor], now that the overwhelming majority of the poor are out there toiling in Wal-Mart or Wendy's—well, what are we to think of them? Disapproval and condescension no longer apply, so what outlook makes sense?

> The "working poor," as they are approvingly termed, are in fact the major philanthropists of our society. They neglect their own children so that the children of others will be cared for; they live in substandard housing so that other homes will be shiny and perfect; they endure privation so that inflation will be low and stock prices high. To be a member of the working poor is to be an anonymous donor, a nameless benefactor, to everyone else. As Gail, one of my restaurant coworkers put it, "you give and you give."

— Barbara Ehrenreich, *Nickel and Dimed*

Suggests that the working poor in the United States are among society's "major philanthropists"

Analogies are tricky. They can be useful, but they are rarely consistently accurate at all major points of comparison. For example, in the preceding analogy, the working poor can be seen as philanthropists in the sense that they have "made a great sacrifice" but not in the sense that they are selflessly sharing their wealth. Analogies can powerfully bring home a point, but skilled writers use them with caution.

Nevertheless, you will run across analogies regularly; indeed, it would be hard to find a book without at least one. For abstract information and in certain writing situations, analogy is often the writing strategy of choice.

| EXERCISE 18.5 |

Write a one-paragraph analogy that explains a principle or process to a reader who is unfamiliar with it. Choose a principle or process that you know well. You might select a basic principle from the natural or social sciences, like dark matter or ethnocentrism; a bodily movement, like running; a physiological process, like digestion; or a process from your job, like assembling a product. Look for something very familiar to compare it with that will help the reader understand the principle or process without a technical explanation.

Sentence Strategies for Comparison and Contrast

Writers frequently use comparison and contrast in writing of almost all genres to present ideas and information. You, too, are likely to use comparison and contrast in your writing, so these sentence strategies may provide a jumping-off point for articulating your thoughts. Remember to make them your own as you revise.

▶ X is similar to/different from Y in these ways: _____ , _____ , and _____ .

▶ Many people think that X means _____ , but it might be more accurate to say it means _____ .

▶ X is similar in some ways to Y: _____ [list areas of similarity]. However, unlike Y, it _____ [list areas of difference].

▶ X, a kind of grown-up/children's/bigger/smaller/local/international version of _____ , is/does/has _____ .

▶ X and Y are frequently confused, but they are not the same; X has/is/does _____ , whereas Y has/is/does _____ .

▶ Most people assume _____ ; however, _____ .

▶ X and Y are the usual suspects, but let's look at a totally new possibility: _____ .

▶ People focus on X, which is characterized by _____ , and they don't even notice Y, which is characterized by _____ .

▶ Whereas supporters of X have argued that _____ , opponents such as Y contend that _____ .

▶ Although some argue X, I think Y because _____ .

▶ On this issue, Professor A and Doctor B say _____ . Although I understand and to some degree sympathize with their point of view, this is ultimately a question of _____ . What's at stake is not _____ but _____ . Therefore, we must _____ .

▶ This issue is dividing our community. Some people argue X. Others contend Y. And still others believe Z. It is in all of our interests to A, however, because _____ .

▶ Conventional wisdom is that _____ . But I take a different view: _____ .

▶ One common complaint is _____ . In recent years, however, _____ .

19

Arguing

This chapter presents the basic strategies for making *arguments* in writing. In it, we focus on asserting a thesis, backing it up with reasons and support, and anticipating readers' questions and objections. It concludes with some sentence strategies you might use when composing an argument.

Asserting a Thesis

Central to any argument is the **thesis**. In a sentence or two, a thesis asserts or states the main point of any argument you want to make. It can be assertive only if you make it clear and direct. The thesis statement usually appears at the beginning of an argument essay.

Chapters 6–10 contain essays that argue for each of these kinds of assertions, along with guidelines for constructing an argument to support such an assertion.

There are five kinds of argument essays in Part One of this book. Each of these essays requires a special kind of assertion and reasoning:

- *Assertion of opinion:* What is your position on a controversial issue? (Chapter 6, "Arguing a Position")

    When overzealous parents and coaches impose adult standards on children's sports, the result can be activities that are neither satisfying nor beneficial to children.
    — Jessica Statsky, "Children Need to Play, Not Compete"

- *Assertion of policy:* What is your understanding of a problem, and what do you think should be done to solve it? (Chapter 7, "Proposing a Solution")

    Although this last-minute anxiety about midterm and final exams is only too familiar to most college students, many professors may not realize how such major, infrequent, high-stakes exams work against the best interests of students both psychologically and cognitively. . . . If professors gave brief exams at frequent intervals, students would be spurred to learn more and worry less.
    — Patrick O'Malley, "More Testing, More Learning"

- *Assertion of evaluation:* What is your judgment of a subject? (Chapter 8, "Justifying an Evaluation")

    Although the film is especially targeted for old school gamers, anime fans, and comic book fanatics, *Scott Pilgrim vs. the World* can be appreciated and enjoyed by all audiences because of its inventive special effects, clever dialogue, and artistic cinematography and editing.

—WILLIAM AKANA, "*Scott Pilgrim vs. the World*: A Hell of a Ride"

- ■ *Assertion of cause:* What do you think made a subject the way it is? (Chapter 9, "Arguing for Causes or Effects")

  The fact *that* social networking is popular is well established. The question is *why* is it so popular? The most basic answer is that social networking is popular because it's available. . . . A better answer, though, is that social media offer people a way to satisfy their desire to connect with others and maybe also be "world-famous for fifteen minutes" (as Andy Warhol supposedly remarked).

  —CLAYTON PANGELINAN, "#socialnetworking: Why It's *Really* So Popular"

- ■ *Assertion of story analysis:* What does a story mean, or what is significant about it? (Chapter 10, "Analyzing Stories")

  As an account of a professional doing harm under the pretense of healing, the story uncovers how a doctor can take advantage of the intimate nature of his work and his professional status to overstep common forms of conduct, to the extent that his actions actually hurt rather than help a patient. In this way, the doctor-narrator actually performs a valuable service by warning readers, indirectly through his story, that blindly trusting members of his profession can have negative consequences.

  —IRIS LEE, "Performing a Doctor's Duty"

As these different thesis statements indicate, the kind of thesis you assert depends on the occasion for which you are writing and the question you are trying to answer for your readers. Whatever the writing situation, to be effective, every thesis must satisfy the same three standards: It must be *arguable, clear,* and *appropriately qualified.*

Make arguable assertions.

Reasoned argument is called for when informed people disagree over an issue or remain divided over how best to solve a problem, as is so often the case in social and political life. Hence, the thesis statements in reasoned arguments make **arguable assertions**—possibilities or probabilities, not certainties.

Therefore, a statement of fact could not be an arguable thesis statement because facts are easy to verify—whether by checking an authoritative reference book, asking an authority, or observing the fact with your own eyes. For example, these statements assert facts:

Jem has a Ph.D. in history.

I am less than five feet tall.

Eucalyptus trees were originally imported into California from Australia.

Each of these assertions can be easily verified. To find out Jem's academic degree, you can ask him, among other things. To determine a person's height, you can use a tape measure. To discover where California got its eucalyptus trees, you can search the library or Internet. There is no point in arguing such statements (though you might question the authority of a particular source or the accuracy of someone's measurement). If a writer asserts something as fact and attempts to support the assertion with *authorities* or *statistics,* the resulting essay is not an argument but a *report.*

Like facts, expressions of personal feelings are not arguable assertions. Whereas facts are unarguable because they can be definitively proved true or false, feelings are unarguable because they are purely subjective.

You can declare, for example, that you detest eight o'clock classes, but you cannot offer an argument to support this assertion. All you can do is explain why you feel as you do. If, however, you were to restate the assertion as "Eight o'clock classes are counterproductive," you could then construct an argument that does not depend solely on your subjective feelings, memories, or preferences. Your argument could be based on *reasons* and *support* that apply to others as well as to yourself. For example, you might argue that students' ability to learn is at an especially low ebb immediately after breakfast and provide scientific support for this assertion—in addition, perhaps, to personal experience and reports of interviews with your friends.

Use clear and precise wording.

The way a thesis is worded is as important as its arguability. The wording of a thesis, especially its key terms, must be *clear* and *precise.*

Consider the following assertion: "Democracy is a way of life." The meaning of this claim is uncertain, partly because the word *democracy* is abstract and partly because the phrase *way of life* is inexact. Abstract ideas like democracy, freedom, and patriotism are by their very nature hard to grasp, and they become even less clear with overuse. Too often, such words take on *connotations* that may obscure the meaning you want to emphasize. *Way of life* is fuzzy: What does it mean? Does it refer to daily life, to a general philosophy or attitude toward life, or to something else?

Thus, a thesis is vague if its meaning is unclear; it is ambiguous if it has more than one possible meaning. For example, the statement "My English instructor is mad" can be understood in two ways: The teacher is either angry or insane. Obviously, these are two very different assertions. You would not want readers to think you mean one when you actually mean the other.

Whenever you write an argument, you should pay special attention to the way you phrase your thesis and take care to avoid vague and ambiguous language.

Qualify the thesis appropriately.

In addition to being arguable and clear, the thesis of an argument must make **appropriate qualifications** that suit your writing situation. If you are confident that your case is so strong that readers will accept your argument without question, state your thesis emphatically and unconditionally. If, however, you expect readers to challenge your assumptions or conclusions, you must qualify your statement. Qualifying a thesis makes it more likely that readers will take it seriously. Expressions like *probably, very likely, apparently,* and *it seems* all serve to qualify a thesis.

EXERCISE 19.1

Write an assertion of opinion that states your position on one of the following controversial issues:

- Should English be the official language of the United States and the only language used in local, state, and federal governments' oral and written communications?

- Should teenagers be required to get their parents' permission to obtain birth control information and contraceptives?

- Should high schools or colleges require students to perform community service as a condition for graduation?

- Should parents be able to demand access to the social media accounts of their children under eighteen?

Constructing a persuasive argument on any of these issues would obviously require careful deliberation and research. For this exercise, however, all you need to do is construct an arguable, clear, and appropriately qualified thesis.

EXERCISE 19.2

Find the thesis in the student essays in one of the argument chapters (Chapters 6–10). Then decide whether the thesis is arguable, clear, and appropriately qualified.

EXERCISE 19.3

If you have written or are currently working on one of the argument assignments in Chapters 6–10, consider whether your thesis is arguable, clear, and appropriately qualified. If you believe it does not meet these requirements, revise it accordingly.

Giving Reasons and Support

Whether you are arguing a position, proposing a solution, justifying an evaluation, or speculating about causes, you need to give reasons and support for your thesis.

Think of **reasons** as the main points supporting your thesis. Often they answer the question *Why do you think so?* For example, if you assert among friends that you value a certain movie highly, one of your friends might ask, "Why do you like it so much?" And you might answer, "*Because* it has challenging ideas, unusual camera work, and memorable acting." Similarly, you might oppose restrictions on students' use of offensive language at your college *because* such restrictions would make students reluctant to enter into frank debates, *because* offensive speech is hard to define, and *because* restrictions violate the free-speech clause of the First Amendment. These *because* phrases are your reasons. You may have one or many reasons, depending on your subject and your writing situation.

For your argument to succeed with your readers, you must not only give reasons but also support your reasons. The main kinds of **support** writers use are examples, statistics, authorities, anecdotes, and textual evidence. Following is a discussion and illustration of each kind of support, along with standards for judging its reliability.

Use representative examples for support.

Examples may be used as support in all types of arguments. For examples to be believable and convincing, they must be representative (typical of all the relevant examples you might have chosen), consistent with the experience of your readers (familiar to them and not extreme), and adequate in number (numerous enough to be convincing and yet not likely to overwhelm readers).

The following illustration comes from a book on illiteracy in America by Jonathan Kozol, a prominent educator and writer:

Uses examples to support argument that human costs of illiteracy are high

> Illiterates cannot read the menu in a restaurant.
>
> They cannot read the cost of items on the menu in the window of the restaurant before they enter.
>
> Illiterates cannot read the letters that their children bring home from their teachers. They cannot study school department circulars that tell them of the courses that their children must be taking if they hope to pass the SAT exams. They cannot help with homework. They cannot write a letter to the teacher. They are afraid to visit in the classroom. They do not want to humiliate their child or themselves.
>
> Illiterates cannot read instructions on a bottle of prescription medicine. They cannot find out when a medicine is past the year of safe consumption; nor can they read of allergenic risks, warnings to diabetics, or the potential sedative effect of certain kinds of nonprescription pills. They cannot observe preventive health care admonitions. They cannot read about "the seven warning signs of cancer" or the indications of blood-sugar fluctuations or the risks of eating certain foods that aggravate the likelihood of cardiac arrest.
>
> — JONATHAN KOZOL, *Illiterate America*

Kozol collected these examples in his many interviews with people who could neither read nor write. Though all of his readers are literate and have presumably never experienced the frustrations of adult illiteracy, Kozol assumes they will accept that the experiences are a familiar part of lives of adults who cannot read. Most readers will believe the experiences to be neither atypical nor extreme.

EXERCISE 19.4

Identify the examples in paragraphs 9 and 11 in Jessica Statsky's essay "Children Need to Play, Not Compete" and paragraphs 16–18 in Amitai Etzioni's essay "Working at McDonald's" (both in Chapter 6). If you have not read the essays, pause to skim them so that you can evaluate these examples within the context of the entire essay. How well do the examples meet the standards of representativeness, consistency with experience of readers, and adequacy in number? You will not have all the information you need to evaluate the examples—you rarely do unless you are an expert on the subject—but make a judgment based on the information available to you in the headnotes and the essays.

Use up-to-date, relevant, and accurate statistics.

In many kinds of arguments about economic, educational, or social issues, *statistics* may be essential. When you use statistics in your own arguments, you will want to ensure that they are up-to-date, relevant, and accurate. In addition, take care to select statistics from reliable sources and to cite them from the sources in which they originally appeared if at all possible. For example, you would want to get medical statistics directly from a reputable and authoritative professional periodical like the *New England Journal of Medicine* rather than secondhand from a supermarket tabloid or an unaffiliated Web site, neither of which can be relied on for accuracy. If you are uncertain about the most authoritative sources, ask a reference librarian or a professor who knows your topic.

The following selection, written by a Harvard University professor, comes from an argument speculating about the decline of civic life in the United States. Civic life includes all of the clubs, organizations, and communal activities in which people choose to participate:

> The culprit is television.
>
> First, the timing fits. The long civic generation was the last cohort of Americans to grow up without television, for television flashed into American society like lightning in the 1950s. In 1950 barely 10 percent of American homes had television sets, but by 1959, 90 percent did. . . . The reverberations from this lightning bolt continued for decades, as viewing hours grew by 17–20 percent during the 1960s and by an additional 7–8 percent during the 1970s. In the early years, TV watching was concentrated among the less educated sectors of the population, but during the 1970s the viewing time of the more educated sectors of the population began to converge upward. Television viewing increases with age, particularly upon retirement, but each generation since the introduction of television has begun its life cycle at a higher starting point. By 1995 viewing per TV household was more than 50 percent higher than it had been in the 1950s.
>
> Most studies estimate that the average American now watches roughly four hours per day (excluding periods in which television is merely playing in the background). Even a more conservative estimate of three hours means that television absorbs 40 percent of the average American's free time, an increase of about one-third since 1965. Moreover, multiple sets have proliferated: By the late 1980s three-quarters of all U.S. homes had more than one set, and these numbers too are rising steadily, allowing ever more private viewing. . . . This massive change in the way Americans spend their days and nights occurred precisely during the years of generational civic disengagement.
>
> — ROBERT D. PUTNAM, "The Strange Disappearance of Civic America"

Uses statistics to support claim that Americans devote less time to civic life because they are watching more television

Chapter 21, provides help finding statistical data in the library.

These statistics come primarily from the U.S. Bureau of the Census, a nationwide count of the number of Americans and a survey, in part, of their buying habits, levels of education, and leisure activities. The Census reports are widely considered to be accurate and trustworthy. They qualify as original sources of statistics.

EXERCISE 19.5

In Chapter 6, underline the statistics in paragraphs 5 and 6 of Jessica Statsky's essay "Children Need to Play, Not Compete." If you have not read the essay, pause to skim it so that you can evaluate the writer's use of statistics within the context of the whole essay. How well do the statistics meet the standards of up-to-dateness, relevance, accuracy, and reliance on the original source? Does the writer indicate where the statistics come from? What do the statistics contribute to the argument?

Cite reputable authorities on relevant topics.

To support an argument, writers often cite experts on the subject. *Quoting, paraphrasing,* or even just referring to a respected **authority** can add to a writer's *credibility*. Authorities must be selected as carefully as are facts and statistics, however. One qualification for authorities is suggested by the way we refer to them: They must be authoritative—that is, trustworthy and reputable. They must also be specially qualified to contribute to the subject you are writing about. For example, a well-known expert on the American presidency might be a perfect choice to support an argument about the achievements of a past president but a poor choice to support an argument on whether adolescents who commit serious crimes should be tried as adults. Finally, qualified authorities must have training at respected institutions or have unique real-world experiences, and they must have a record of research and publications recognized by other authorities.

The following example comes from a *New York Times* article about some parents' and experts' heightened concern over boys' behavior. The author believes that the concern is exaggerated and potentially dangerous. In the full argument, she is particularly concerned about the number of boys who are being given Ritalin, a popular drug for treating attention-deficit hyperactivity disorder (ADHD):

> Today, the world is no longer safe for boys. A boy being a shade too boyish risks finding himself under the scrutiny of parents, teachers, guidance counselors, child therapists—all of them on watch for the early glimmerings of a medical syndrome, a bona fide behavioral disorder. Does the boy disregard authority, make snide comments in class, push other kids around and play hooky? Maybe he has a conduct disorder. Is he fidgety, impulsive, disruptive, easily bored? Perhaps he is suffering from attention-deficit hyperactivity disorder, or ADHD, the disease of the hour and the most frequently diagnosed behavioral disorder of childhood. Does he prefer computer games and goofing off to homework? He might have dyslexia or another learning disorder.

"There is now an attempt to pathologize what was once considered the normal range of behavior of boys," said Melvin Konner of the departments of anthropology and psychiatry at Emory University in Atlanta. "Today, Tom Sawyer and Huckleberry Finn surely would have been diagnosed with both conduct disorder and ADHD." And both, perhaps, would have been put on Ritalin, the drug of choice for treating attention-deficit disorder.

— Natalie Angier, "Intolerance of Boyish Behavior"

Establishes Konner's professional qualifications by naming the university where he teaches and his areas of study

In this example, Angier relies on **informal citation** within her essay to introduce Melvin Konner, the authority she quotes, along with a reference to his professional qualifications. Such informal citation is common in newspapers, magazines, and some books intended for general audiences. In other scholarly books and articles, and in other academic contexts, writers use **formal citation**, providing a list of works cited at the end of their own writing.

For examples of two formal citation styles often used in college essays, see Chapters 24 and 25.

EXERCISE 19.6

Analyze how authorities are used in paragraphs 4 and 6 of Patrick O'Malley's essay "More Testing, More Learning" in Chapter 7. Begin by underlining the authorities' contributions to these paragraphs, whether through quotation, summary, or paraphrase. On the basis of the evidence you have available, decide to what extent each source is authoritative on the subject: qualified to contribute to the subject, trained appropriately, and recognized widely. How does O'Malley establish each authority's credentials? Then decide what each authority contributes to the argument as a whole. (If you have not read the essay, take time to read or skim it.)

Use vivid, relevant anecdotes.

Anecdotes are brief stories about events or experiences. If they are relevant to the argument, well told, and true to life, they can provide convincing support. To be relevant, an anecdote must strike readers as more than an entertaining diversion; it must seem to make an irreplaceable contribution to an argument. A well-told story is easy to follow, and the people and scenes are described memorably, even vividly. A true-to-life anecdote seems believable, even if the experience is foreign to readers' experiences.

The following anecdote appeared in an argument taking a position on gun control. The writer, an essayist, poet, and environmentalist who is also a rancher in South Dakota, always carries a pistol and believes that other people should have the right to do so:

One day, while driving to the highway mailbox, I saw a vehicle parked about halfway to the house. Several men were standing in the ditch, relieving themselves. I have no objection to emergency urination; we always need moisture. But I noticed they'd also dumped several dozen beer cans, which can blow into pastures and slash a cow's legs or stomach.

Tells an engaging anecdote and explains its relevance

As I drove slowly closer, the men zipped their trousers ostentatiously while walking toward me, and one of them demanded what the hell I wanted.

"This is private land. I'd like you to pick up the beer cans."

"What beer cans?" said the belligerent one, putting both hands on the car door and leaning in my window. His face was inches from mine, and the beer fumes were strong. The others laughed. One tried the passenger door, locked; another put his foot on the hood and rocked the car. They circled, lightly thumping the roof, discussing my good fortune in meeting them and the benefits they were likely to bestow upon me. I felt small and trapped; they knew it.

"The ones you just threw out," I said politely.

"I don't see no beer cans. Why don't you get out here and show them to me, honey?" said the belligerent one, reaching for the handle inside my door.

"Right over there," I said, still being polite, "—there and over there." I pointed with the pistol, which had been under my thigh. Within one minute the cans and the men were back in the car and headed down the road.

I believe this incident illustrates several important principles. The men were trespassing and knew it; their judgment may have been impaired by alcohol. Their response to the polite request of a woman alone was to use their size and numbers to inspire fear. The pistol was a response in the same language. Politeness didn't work; I couldn't intimidate them. Out of the car, I'd have been more vulnerable. The pistol just changed the balance of power.

— LINDA M. HASSELSTROM, "Why One Peaceful Woman Carries a Pistol"

Most readers would readily agree that this anecdote is well told: It has many concrete, memorable details; there is action, suspense, climax, resolution, and even dialogue. It is about a believable, possible experience. Finally, the anecdote is clearly relevant to the author's argument about gun control.

See Chapter 14, "Narrating," and Chapter 2, "Remembering an Event," for more information about narrating anecdotes.

EXERCISE 19.7

Evaluate the way an anecdote is used in paragraph 16 of Amitai Etzioni's essay "Working at McDonald's" in Chapter 6. Consider whether the story is well told and true to life. Decide whether it seems to be relevant to the whole argument. Does the writer make the relevance clear? Does the anecdote support Etzioni's argument?

Use relevant textual evidence.

See Chapter 5 for more about summarizing; see Chapter 12 for more about paraphrasing; see Chapter 23 for more about quoting, paraphrasing, and summarizing and integrating material from sources into your own writing.

When you argue claims of value (Chapter 8) and offer an analysis (Chapter 10), **textual evidence** will be very important. In your college courses, if you are asked to evaluate a controversial article, you must quote, paraphrase, or summarize passages so that readers can understand why you think the author's argument is or is not credible. If you are analyzing a novel, you must include numerous excerpts to show just how you arrived at your conclusion.

For textual evidence to be considered effective support for an argument, it must be carefully selected to be relevant. You must help readers see the connection between each piece of evidence and the reason it supports. Textual evidence must also be highly selective—that is, chosen from among all the available evidence to provide the support needed without overwhelming the reader or weakening the argument with marginally relevant evidence. Textual evidence usually has more impact if it is balanced between quotation and paraphrase, and quotations must be smoothly *integrated* into the sentences of the argument.

The following example comes from a student essay in which the writer argues that the main character (referred to as "the boy") in the short story "Araby" by James Joyce is so self-absorbed that he learns nothing about himself or other people:

You can read "Araby" in Chapter 10.

> The story opens and closes with images of blindness—a framing device that shows the boy does not change but ends up with the same lack of understanding that he began with. The street is "blind" with an "uninhabited house . . . at the blind end" (par. 1). As he spies on Mangan's sister, from his own house, the boy intentionally limits what he is able to see by lowering the "blind" until it is only an inch from the window sash (par. 4). At the bazaar in the closing scene, the "light was out," and the upper part of the hall was "completely dark" (par. 36). The boy is left "gazing up into the darkness," seeing nothing but an inner torment that burns his eyes (par. 37).
>
> The boy's blindness appears to be caused by his obsession with Mangan's sister. When he tries to read at night, for example, the girl's "image [comes] between [him] and the page," in effect blinding him (par. 12). In fact, he seems blind to everything except this "image" of the "brown-clad figure cast by [his] imagination" (par. 16). The girl's "brown-clad figure" is also associated with the houses on "blind" North Richmond Street, with their "brown imperturbable faces" (par. 1). The houses stare back at the boy, unaffected by his presence and gaze.
>
> — SALLY CRANE, "Gazing into the Darkness"

Cites textual evidence from "Araby" to convince readers to take her argument seriously

Notice how the writer quotes selected words and phrases about blindness to support her reasoning that the boy learns nothing because he is blinded. There are twelve smoothly integrated quotations in these two paragraphs, along with a number of paraphrases, all of them relevant. The writer does not assume that the evidence speaks for itself; she comments and interprets throughout.

EXERCISE 19.8

Analyze the use of evidence in paragraphs 2 and 3 of Iris Lee's essay "Performing a Doctor's Duty" in Chapter 10. If you have not read this essay, read it now. Identify the quotes and paraphrases Lee uses, and then try to identify the phrases or sentences that comment on or explain this evidence. Consider whether Lee's evidence in these two paragraphs seems relevant to her thesis and reasons, appropriately selective, well balanced between quotes and paraphrases, integrated smoothly into the sentences she creates, and explained helpfully.

Responding to Objections and Alternatives

For more about conceding and refuting, see Chapters 6–9.

Asserting a thesis and backing it with reasons and support are essential to a successful argument. Thoughtful writers go further, however, by anticipating and responding to their readers' objections or their alternative position or solutions to a problem.

To respond to objections and alternatives, writers rely on three basic strategies: acknowledging, conceding, and refuting. Writers show they are aware of readers' objections and questions (*acknowledge*), modify their position to accept readers' concerns they think are legitimate (*concede*), or explicitly argue that readers' objections may be invalid or that their concerns may be irrelevant (*refute*). Writers may use one or more of these three strategies in the same essay. Readers find arguments more convincing when writers have anticipated their concerns in these ways.

Acknowledge readers' concerns.

When you **acknowledge** readers' questions or objections, you show that you are aware of their point of view and take it seriously even if you do not agree with it, as in the following example:

> The homeless, it seems, can be roughly divided into two groups: those who have had marginality and homelessness forced upon them and want nothing more than to escape them, and a smaller number who have at least in part chosen marginality, and now accept, or, in a few cases, embrace it.
>
> _Acknowledges three doubts his readers may have_
>
> I understand how dangerous it can be to introduce the idea of choice into a discussion of homelessness. It can all too easily be used for all the wrong reasons by all the wrong people to justify indifference or brutality toward the homeless, or to argue that they are getting only what they deserve.
>
> And I understand, too, how complicated the notion can become: Many of the veterans on the street, or battered women, or abused and runaway children, have chosen this life only as the lesser of evils, and because, in this society, there is often no place else to go.
>
> And finally, I understand how much that happens on the street can combine to create an apparent acceptance of homelessness that is nothing more than the absolute absence of hope.
>
> Nonetheless we must learn to accept that there may indeed be people on the street who have seen so much of our world, or have seen it so clearly, that to live in it becomes impossible.
>
> — PETER MARIN, "Go Ask Alice"

You might think that acknowledging readers' objections in this way—addressing readers directly, listing their possible objections, and discussing each one—would weaken your argument. It might even seem reckless to suggest objections that not all readers would think of. On the contrary, however, most readers respond positively to this strategy because it makes you seem thoughtful and reasonable. By researching your subject and your readers, you will be able to use this strategy confidently in your own argumentative essays. And you will learn to look for it in arguments you read and use it to make judgments about the writer's credibility.

EXERCISE 19.9

Jessica Statsky acknowledges readers' concerns in paragraphs 10 and 12 of her essay "Children Need to Play, Not Compete" in Chapter 6. How, specifically, does Statsky attempt to acknowledge her readers' concerns? What do you find most and least successful in her acknowledgment? How does the acknowledgment affect your judgment of her credibility?

Concede readers' concerns.

To argue effectively, you must often take special care to acknowledge readers' objections; questions; and alternative positions, causes, or solutions. Occasionally, however, you may have to go even further. Instead of merely acknowledging your readers' concerns, you may decide to accept some of them and incorporate them into your own argument. This strategy, called **concession**, can be very disarming to readers, for it recognizes that opposing views have merit. The following example comes from an essay enthusiastically endorsing e-mail:

> To be sure, egalitarianism has its limits. The ease and economy of sending email, especially to multiple recipients, makes us all vulnerable to any bore, loony, or commercial or political salesman who can get our email address. It's still a lot less intrusive than the telephone, since you can read and answer or ignore email at your own convenience. . . .
>
> Another supposed disadvantage of email is that it discourages face-to-face communication. At Microsoft, where people routinely send email back and forth all day to the person in the next office, this is certainly true. Some people believe this tendency has more to do with the underdeveloped social skills of computer geeks than with Microsoft's role in developing the technology email relies on. I wouldn't presume to comment on that. Whether you think email replacing live conversation is a good or bad thing depends, I guess, on how much of a misanthrope you are. I like it.
>
> — MICHAEL KINSLEY, "Email Culture"

Accommodates readers' likely reservations by conceding that e-mail poses certain problems

Notice that Kinsley's accommodation or concession is not grudging. He readily concedes that e-mail brings users a lot of unwanted messages and may discourage conversation in the workplace.

EXERCISE 19.10

How does Patrick O'Malley respond to readers' objections and alternatives in paragraphs 9 and 10 of his essay "More Testing, More Learning" in Chapter 7, which argues for more frequent exams? What seems successful or unsuccessful in his argument? How do his efforts to acknowledge readers' concerns or make concessions affect his argument and his credibility?

Refute readers' objections.

Your readers' possible objections and views cannot always be conceded. Sometimes they must be refuted. When you **refute readers' objections**, you assert that they are wrong and argue against them. Refutation does not have to be delivered arrogantly or dismissively, however. Because differences are inevitable, reasoned argument provides a peaceful and constructive way for informed, well-intentioned people who disagree strongly to air their differences.

In the following example, social sciences professor Todd Gitlin refutes one argument for giving college students the opportunity to purchase lecture notes prepared by someone else:

Concedes a possible objection

Now, it may well be argued that universities are already shortchanging their students by stuffing them into huge lecture halls where, unlike at rock concerts or basketball games, the lecturer can't even be seen on a giant screen in real time. If they're already shortchanged with impersonal instruction, what's the harm in offering canned lecture notes?

The amphitheater lecture is indeed, for all but the most engaging professors, a lesser form of instruction, and scarcely to be idealized. Still, Education by Download misses one of the keys to learning. Education is a meeting of minds, a process through which the student educes, draws from within, a response to what the teacher teaches.

Refutes the objection

The very act of taking notes—not reading someone else's notes, no matter how stellar—is a way of engaging the material, wrestling with it, struggling to comprehend or take issue, but in any case entering into the work. The point is to decide, while you are listening, what matters in the presentation. And while I don't believe that most of life consists of showing up, education does begin with that— with immersing yourself in the activity at hand, listening, thinking, judging, offering active responses. A download is a poor substitute.

— TODD GITLIN, "Disappearing Ink"

As this selection illustrates, writers cannot simply dismiss readers' possible concerns with a wave of their hand. Gitlin states a potential objection fully and fairly but then goes on to refute it by claiming that students need to take their own lecture notes to engage and comprehend the material that is being presented to them.

Effective refutation requires a restrained tone and careful argument. Although you may not accept this particular refutation, you can agree that it is well reasoned and supported. You need not feel attacked personally because the writer disagrees with you.

EXERCISE 19.11

Evaluate Kelly D. Brownell and Thomas R. Frieden's use of refutation in paragraphs 5 and 6 of "Ounces of Prevention — The Public Policy Case for Taxes on Sugared Beverages" (Chapter 7). How do Brownell and Frieden signal or announce the refutation? How do they support the refutation? What is the tone of the refutation, and how effective do you think the tone would be in convincing readers to take the writers' argument seriously?

Logical Fallacies

Fallacies are errors or flaws in reasoning. Although essentially unsound, fallacious arguments seem superficially plausible and often have great persuasive power. Fallacies are not necessarily deliberate efforts to deceive readers. Writers may introduce a fallacy accidentally by not examining their own reasons or underlying assumptions, by failing to establish solid support, or by using unclear or ambiguous words. Here is a summary of the most common logical fallacies (listed alphabetically):

- ■ *Begging the question:* Arguing that a claim is true by repeating the claim in different words (also called *circular reasoning*). (More and more often, writers are using *begging the question* to mean *raising the question*, but this is incorrect. Asking questions is a legitimate strategy in reasoned argument.)

- ■ *Confusing chronology with causality:* Assuming that because one thing preceded another, the former caused the latter (also called *post hoc, ergo propter hoc*—Latin for "after this, therefore because of this")

- ■ *Either-or reasoning:* Assuming that there are only two sides to a question and representing yours as the only correct one

- ■ *Equivocating:* Misleading or hedging with ambiguous word choices

- ■ *False analogy:* Assuming that because one thing resembles another, conclusions drawn from one also apply to the other

- ■ *Hasty generalization:* Offering only weak or limited evidence to support a conclusion

- ■ *Overreliance on authority:* Assuming that something is true simply because an expert says so and ignoring evidence to the contrary

- ■ *Oversimplifying:* Giving easy answers to complicated questions, often by appealing to emotions rather than logic

- ■ *Personal attack:* Demeaning the proponents of a claim instead of refuting their argument (also called *ad hominem*—Latin for "against the man"—*attack*)

- ■ *Red herring:* Attempting to misdirect the discussion by raising an essentially unrelated point

- ■ *Slanting:* Selecting or emphasizing the evidence that supports your claim and suppressing or playing down other evidence

- ■ *Slippery slope:* Pretending that one thing inevitably leads to another

- ■ *Sob story:* Manipulating readers' emotions to lead them to draw unjustified conclusions

- ■ *Straw man:* Directing the argument against a claim that nobody actually makes or that everyone agrees is very weak

Sentence Strategies for Argument

Writers frequently argue to persuade others, whether they are arguing for an intepretation of a story in a literature class or for an interpretation of sales data to a supervisor. You, too, are likely to assert and support positions, respond to alternatives, and concede or refute objections. Sentence strategies like these may provide a jumping-off point for articulating your thoughts. Of course, you will probably want to rework the sentences they inspire.

To Assert a Position

▶ When issue/event X happens, most people think _____, but I think _____ because _____.

▶ People focus on X, which is characterized by _____, and they don't even notice Y, which is characterized by _____.

▶ Although many people take X for granted, Groups A, B, and C oppose it on the grounds that _____.

▶ Whereas supporters of X have argued that _____, opponents such as A, B, and C contend that _____.

▶ Though others may view it as a matter of _____, for me, the issue hinges on _____.

▶ According to A, what's at stake in this issue is _____. For me, however, what is most important is _____.

▶ On this issue, A and B say _____. Although I understand and to some degree sympathize with their point of view, this is ultimately a question of _____. What's at stake is not _____ but _____. Therefore, we must _____.

▶ This issue is dividing our community. Some people argue _____. Others contend _____. And still others believe _____. It is in all of our interests to _____, however, because _____.

▶ Conventional wisdom is that _____. But I take a different view: _____.

▶ X has many good qualities, including _____ and _____; however, the pluses do not outweigh its one major drawback, namely that _____.

▶ X is a brilliant embodiment of _____ [name genre or category], especially notable for its superb _____ and thorough _____.

▶ Because I admire A's other work, I expected X to be _____. But I was disappointed/surprised by it because _____.

▶ Many complain about problem X but do nothing because solving it seems too hard/too costly. I think we need to tackle problem X because _____.

To Support a Position

▶ What makes X problematic/praiseworthy is _____.

▶ Because _____, I support/oppose X.

▶ Studies such as _____ have shown that X mostly affects groups A, B, and C because _____.

- Studies by Professors A and B at University C show that X has worked in cases such as _____ , _____ , and _____ .

- The reasons for X may surprise you, such as _____ , _____ , and _____ .

- The cause(s) of X may be surprising/alarming/disturbing/amazing, but they are clear: _____ [state cause(s) and provide evidence].

- X plays a surprising/alarming/disturbing/amazing role in our lives/our families/our communities/our workplaces: It does/is/provides _____ [describe role].

- For many years, group A has believed that _____ . Now there is research supporting this claim, but not for the reasons you may think. It's not _____ that has been causing this phenomenon but _____ .

- Researchers studying X have shown a causal connection between _____ [my causes] and _____ [my subject]. They claim _____ [quote/paraphrase/summarize information from source] (cite source).

- A large number of people have been polled on this question, and it appears that X was an important factor in their decision to _____ .

- Reliable research by Professor A shows _____ .

To Refute an Opposing Position

- One problem with position Y is that _____ .

- Some claim position Y, but in reality _____ .

- My opponents cite research to support position Y, but the credibility of that research is questionable because _____ .

- This argument seems plausible because it is consistent with our preconceptions. Nevertheless, evidence shows _____ .

- Activists insist _____ . Still, in spite of their good intentions, doing _____ would take away a basic right/make things even worse.

- A and B think this issue is about _____ . But what is really at stake here is _____ .

- Proponents object to my argument on the grounds that _____ . However, they are confusing results with causes. What I am arguing is X.

- Polls show that most people favor Y, but an opinion's popularity does not make it true or right.

- Though most would agree that Y is true, it does not necessarily follow that _____ .

- One common complaint is _____ . In recent years, however, _____ .

- Some people think we can't afford to implement solution X but it would only cost $ _____ to put my solution in place compared to $ _____ , the cost of doing nothing/implementing an alternative solution.

▶ Although it might take _____ months/years to implement my solution, it would actually take longer to implement solution Y.

▶ Some may suggest that I favor this solution because I would benefit personally; however, the fact is we would all benefit because _____ .

▶ Some may claim that this solution has been tried and hasn't worked. But research shows that my solution differs from past experiments in several important ways: _____ , _____ , and _____ [list differences].

▶ X, reviewer for newspaper A, claims that _____ . But I agree with Y, reviewer for newspaper B, who argues that _____ .

▶ Some people think Y occurs because of _____ , _____ , and _____ . Although it is easy to see why they might make this argument, the evidence does not back it up: _____ [explanation].

▶ Reviewers have remarked that X is a pale imitation of Y. I disagree. Whereas Y is _____ , X is _____ .

▶ X has generated criticism for its supposed _____ . But X is not _____ . Instead, it is _____ .

▶ A recent study of X showed that _____ .

To Concede an Objection

▶ I agree that _____ .

▶ _____ is certainly an important factor.

▶ To be sure, _____ is true.

▶ Granted, _____ must be taken into consideration.

▶ Some people argue that _____ . I understand this reservation, and therefore, I think we should _____ .

▶ A common concern about this issue is _____ . That's why my argument focuses on _____ [name a different aspect] of the issue.

▶ I agree with those who claim X/object on X grounds; therefore, instead of implementing option A, I think we should pursue option B.

▶ If _____ seems too time-consuming/expensive, let's try _____ .

▶ Where _____ is a concern, I think X should be considered because _____ .

▶ The one justifiable criticism that could be made against X is _____ .

▶ As some critics have pointed out, X does follow the tried-and-true formula of _____ .

To Concede and Refute an Objection

▶ Indeed, hard-core enthusiasts like A, B, and C, may carp that X is not sufficiently _____ [list shortcomings]. However, _____ .

▶ _____ may be true for Y but not for X.

▶ Although _____ , I think _____ .

▶ A and B insist that _____ . Nevertheless, in spite of their good intentions, _____ .

▶ I agree that _____ is important, but so is _____ .

▶ I agree that _____ is important, but my opponents need to consider _____ .

▶ On the one hand, I accept A's argument that _____ , but on the other hand, I still think X is ultimately more important because _____ .

▶ As some critics have pointed out, X does follow the tried-and-true formula of _____ . Still, the director/writer/artist is using the formula effectively to _____ .

▶ The objection that X can be caused by things other than cause Y may be true. But there is strong evidence showing that cause Y played a central role in making X happen by _____ .

▶ Those who disagree about X often see it as a choice between _____ and _____ . But both are important. We don't have to choose between them because _____ .

PART 4

Research Strategies

20

Planning a Research Project

To research a topic effectively at the college level requires a plan. A clear sense of your rhetorical situation, as well as the practical needs of your research task (such as the due date and the level of detail required), will help you create one. Figure 20.1 lists common elements that you will need to consider not only as you plan your research project, but also as you continue to find and evaluate sources and draft your project.

Define your research task and set a schedule.

Analyze your rhetorical situation.

- Determine your purpose.
- Analyze your audience to understand the interest and background your readers bring to the project, and analyze your attitude to determine how you want your readers to think of you.
- Determine the genre, or type, of research project you are creating, such as a proposal or laboratory report, and the expectations for research, writing, and design associated with this genre.
- Determine the medium you will use to present your research project and the medium's advantages and disadvantages for achieving your purpose and reaching your audience.

Understand the assignment.

- Check your syllabus or consult your instructor about the requirements of the assignment (such as the number and types of resources required, the length of the project, and so forth).
- Determine the final due date, and assign interim due dates to keep your project on track.

Establish a research log.

- Create a list of keywords.
- Create a working bibliography (list of sources), and annotate entries.
- Take notes on your sources.

Choose a topic, get an overview, and narrow your topic.

Choose a topic that answers an interesting question relevant to the assignment and of interest to you and your readers.

- Consult with your instructor.
- Review textbooks and other course materials.
- Explore newspapers, magazines, and Internet sites.

Get an overview, and narrow your topic (if necessary).

- Consult subject guides or a librarian to determine the availability of sources on your topic.
- Get necessary background by consulting encyclopedias and other general reference sources.
- Start a working bibliography to keep track of the sources you are beginning to explore.
- Draft questions to guide your research.

FIGURE 20.1   Overview of a Research Project

Search for in-depth information on your topic.

Conduct a search for sources, using carefully selected search terms.

- Check the library's resources (such as the catalog, databases, or home page) for books, articles, and multimedia.
- If acceptable to your instructor, search the Internet for relevant Web sites, blogs, groups.

- Keep a list of search terms in your research log, and annotate your working bibliography to keep track of sources.
- Add relevant sources to your working bibliography, and annotate each entry to record the genre (or type) of source, the source's main points, and how you would use the source.
- Refine your research questions, and draft a thesis.

REFINE YOUR SEARCH.

Ask yourself questions like these about the sources you have found:

- Is this what I expected to find?
- Am I finding enough information?
- Am I finding too much?
- Do I need to modify my keywords?

- Do I need to recheck background sources?
- Do I need to revise my research questions?
- Do I need to modify my thesis statement?

Continue searching for relevant and reliable sources in response to your answers.

Evaluate your sources.

Determine the relevance of potential sources.

- Does the source explain terms or concepts or provide background?
- Does the source provide evidence to support my claims?
- Does the source offer alternative viewpoints or lend authority?

Determine the reliability of potential sources.

- Who wrote it?
- How recently was it published?
- Who published it and what is the reputation of the publisher?
- Is the source scholarly or popular (or something else)?
- Is the source printed or online?
- What does the source say?

Continue to evaluate and refine your search strategy based on your research results.

Use your research to support your ideas.

Use evidence from sources to support your ideas.

- Synthesize ideas from multiple sources.
- Support your ideas with summaries, paraphrases, and quotations as appropriate.
- Include your own analysis to demonstrate how source information supports your ideas.

Avoid plagiarism.

- Paraphrase carefully to avoid plagiarism.
- Carefully integrate source material into your text.
- Cite sources using an appropriate citation style.

Analyzing Your Rhetorical Situation and Setting a Schedule

Making your research project manageable begins with defining the scope and goals of your research project. Begin by analyzing your *rhetorical situation:*

- What is your *purpose?* Is it to explain a concept, report on or argue for a position, or analyze the causes of an event or a behavior?

To learn more about primary and secondary research, see Chapter 21.

- Who is your *audience* and what will your readers' interests, attitudes, and expectations for the project be? How many and what kinds of resources does your audience expect you to consult? (For college research projects, your audience will likely be your instructor.)

- What *genre* (or *type*) is the research project, and how will that affect the kinds of sources you use? An observational report in the social sciences may demand mainly *primary research,* whereas an argument essay for a history course may require a variety of *secondary* and primary sources.

- What medium will you use to present your research project? A research project presented in print will allow you to incorporate visuals and use parenthetical citations and a works cited or references list to acknowledge your sources; a project presented using PowerPoint or Prezi slides may allow you to incorporate video and sound but require you to name your sources during the presentation.

Also be sure you consider the following practical issues before you begin your research project:

- How long should the research project be?

- When is it due?

- Are any interim assignments required (such as an outline or an annotated bibliography)?

If you're not sure of the answers to these questions, ask your instructor to clarify the assignment or define any confusing terms so that you can work most efficiently.

Finally, set a schedule. Be sure to take into consideration the projects you have due for other classes as well as other responsibilities (to work or family, for example) or activities. A sample schedule is shown in Figure 20.2.

Some library Web sites may offer an online scheduler to help you with this process. Look for a link on your library's Web site, or try out an assignment calculator, such as one of those listed on the "Guides" page of the Web site for the University of Missouri Libraries: library.missouri.edu/guides/assigncalc/.

Choosing a Topic and Getting an Overview

Often students will be assigned a topic for a research project. If you are free to choose your own topic, consult course materials, such as textbooks and handouts, to get ideas, and consult your instructor to make sure your topic is appropriate. Sometimes conducting an Internet search may give you an idea for a topic.

Once you've chosen an appropriate topic, an overview can help you determine the kinds of issues you should consider.

Wikipedia offers a wealth of information, and it is often the first stop for students who are accustomed to consulting the Internet first for information. Be aware, though, that *Wikipedia* is user generated rather than traditionally published, and for this reason, the quality of information found there can be inconsistent. Many instructors do not consider *Wikipedia* a reliable source, so you should ask your teacher for advice on consulting it at this stage.

Sunday	Monday	Tuesday	Wednesday	Thursday	Friday	Saturday
	1 *Analyze writing situation & choose topic*	**2**	**3** *Check resources available and get an overview*	**4**	**5** *Draft research questions & narrow topic further (?)*	**6**
7	**8** *Set up a working bibliog.*	**9** *List search terms and start searching for sources*	**10** *Topic and working bib with 3 sources due!*	**11** *Evaluate the sources I've found so far*	**12**	**13** *Draft a thesis statement*
14 *Write a first draft*	**15** *Peer review—in class*	**16** *More research? Revise research questions and search terms?*	**17** *Don't forget to evaluate new sources!*	**18** *Start revising!*	**19**	**20**
21	**22** *Draft the works-cited list*	**23**	**24** *Revise the 2nd draft*	**25**	**26**	**27**
28 *Edit, spell-check, and proofread*	**29** *Final project due in class today!*	**30**	**31**			

FIGURE 20.2   Sample Schedule for a 3- to 5-Page Research Project

Your library will likely subscribe to databases, such as Gale Virtual Reference Library or Oxford Reference Online, that you can search to find information from general encyclopedias and dictionaries as well as specialized, or subject-specific encyclopedias and dictionaries.

General dictionaries, like Britannica Online, provide basic information about many topics. **Specialized encyclopedias** provide a comprehensive introduction to your topic, including the key terms you will need to find relevant material in catalogs and databases, and they present subtopics, enabling you to see many possibilities for focusing your research.

Frequently, libraries prepare **research guides**—lists of reliable sources on popular topics. A guide can offer very useful suggested resources for research, so check your library to find out if such a guide is available. You may also find resources that provide good overviews of topics, such as *CQ Researcher.* A reference librarian can help point you in the right direction.

Focusing Your Topic and Drafting Research Questions

After you have gotten a sense of the kinds of sources available on your topic, you may be ready to narrow it. Focus on a topic that you can explore thoroughly in the number of pages assigned and the length of time available. Finding your own take on a subject can help you narrow it as well. The invention strategies in Chapter 11 can help you focus in on one aspect of your topic.

You may also want to write questions about your topic and then focus in on one or two that can be answered through research. These will become the research questions that will guide your search for information. You may need to add or revise these questions as you conduct your search. The answers you devise can form the basis for your thesis statement.

Establishing a Research Log

One of the best ways to keep track of your research is to keep all your notes in one place, in a **research log.** Your log may be digital (a folder on your computer with files for notes, lists of keywords, and your working bibliography) or analog (a notebook with pockets for copies of sources works well).

Listing Keywords

Finding useful sources depends on determining the right **keywords**—words or phrases that describe your topic—to use while searching catalogs, databases, and the Internet. Start your list of keywords by noting the main words from your research question or thesis statement. Look for useful terms in your search results, and use these to expand your list. Then add synonyms (or words with a similar meaning) to expand your list. Keep in mind that different databases use different terms, and terms that work well for one subject might not be successful in another. For example, databases covering education and psychology might index sources on some of the same subjects, but they might not use the same keywords.

For example, student Cristina Dinh might have started with a term like *home schooling.* She might have added *home education* or *home study.* After reading an article in an encyclopedia about her subject, she might have added *student-paced education* or *autonomous learning* to expand her scope. After consulting the thesaurus in ERIC, a database focusing on education, she might have added *parents as teachers;* after consulting the thesaurus in the database PSYCArticles, she might have added *nontraditional education.*

Creating a Working Bibliography

A **working bibliography** is an ongoing record of the sources you discover as you research your subject. In your final project, you will probably not end up citing all the sources you list in your working bibliography, but recording the information you will need to cite a source—*as you identify it*—will save you time later. (Just be sure to double-check that your entries are accurate!) Your working bibliography should include the following for each source:

- **Author(s) name(s)**
- **Title and subtitle**
- **Publication information:** A book's edition number (for example, *revised edition, 3rd ed.*), the name and location of the book's publisher, and the page numbers of the section(s) you consulted; a periodical's name, volume and issue number or date, and the article's page numbers
- **Access information:** The call number of a book; the name of the database through which you accessed the source; the URL of the article (if available without a subscription), the URL of the source's home page, or the **DOI** (digital object identifier—a permanent identifying code that won't change over time or from database to database); the date you last accessed the source (for a Web page or Web site)
- **Medium of publication:** *Print* for printed books and articles, *Web* for online books and articles accessed through a database or found online, *DVD* for a film you watched at home, *MP3* for a music file, and so on

You can store your working bibliography in a computer file, in specialized bibliography software, or even on note cards. Each method has its advantages:

- A **computer file** allows you to move citations into order and incorporate the bibliography into your research project easily using standard software (such as Word or Excel).
- A **citation manager** (such as RefWorks, Zotero, EndNote, or the Bedford Bibliographer) designed for creating bibliographies helps you create the citation in the specific citation style (such as MLA or APA) required by your discipline. These software programs are not perfect, however; you still need to double-check your citations against the models in the style manual you are using or in Chapter 24 or 25 of this text.
- A **notebook** allows you to keep everything—working bibliography, annotations, notes, copies of chapters or articles—all in one place.

Chapters 24 and 25 present two common documentation styles—one created by the Modern Language Association (MLA) and widely used in the humanities, and the other advocated by the American Psychological Association (APA) and used in the social sciences. Other disciplines have their own preferred styles of documentation. Confirm with your instructor which documentation style is required for your assignment so that you can follow that style for all the sources you put into your working bibliography.

Annotating Your Working Bibliography

An **annotated bibliography** provides an overview of sources that you have considered for your research project. Researchers frequently create annotated bibliographies to keep a record of sources and their thoughts about them. Researchers

For more about annotating a bibliography, see Chapter 5.

sometimes also publish annotated bibliographies to provide others with a useful tool for beginning a research project of their own.

What an annotated bibliography includes depends on the researcher's rhetorical situation. But most entries answer these questions:

- What kind of source is this?
- What is the main point of the source?
- How might I use the source?
- How might my sources be related?
- What information will I need to cite the source?

Some also include an introduction that explains the purpose and scope of the annotated bibliography and may describe how and why the researcher selected the sources. The annotated bibliography in Chapter 5 by Maya Gomez, written for her composition instructor, might include an introduction like this:

> My annotated bibliography is intended to provide me with the sources I need to write a report on compensating organ donors. It includes sources that provide background on evolving government policy and that offer arguments for and against compensating donors. These sources represent a number of perspectives, including economic, political, moral, and personal; they have been written by well-respected scholars (for example, the Nobel Prize-winning economist Gary S. Becker) and organizations (the National Kidney Foundation).

Taking Notes on Your Sources

For more on synthesizing, see Chapters 12 and 23.

The summaries that you include in a working bibliography or the annotations that you make on a printed or digital copy of a source are useful reminders, but you should also make notes that analyze the text, that synthesize what you are learning with ideas you have gleaned elsewhere or with your own ideas, and that evaluate the quality of the source.

You will mine your notes for language to use in your draft, so be careful to

- summarize accurately, using your own words and sentence structures;
- paraphrase without borrowing the language or sentence structure of the source;
- quote accurately and place all language from the source in quotation marks.

For more on annotating, sources, see Chapter 12; for more on avoiding plagiarism, see Chapter 23.

You can take notes on a photocopy of a printed text or use comments or highlighting to annotate a digital text. Whenever possible, download, print, photocopy, or scan useful sources, so that you can read and make notes at your leisure and so that you can double-check your summaries, paraphrases, and quotations of sources against the original. These strategies, along with those discussed in Chapter 23. "Using Sources to Support Your Ideas," will keep you from plagiarizing inadvertently.

21

Finding Sources and Conducting Field Research

Students are surrounded by a wealth of information—in print, online, in videos and podcasts, even face to face! Much of this information is excellent, but some is of dubious quality. This can make finding the information you need to support your ideas exciting, but it also means you will have to develop a research strategy and sift possible sources carefully. What you are writing about, who will read your writing project, and the type of writing you are doing (a story for your college newspaper, a proposal for your employer, or a research project for your U.S. history course) will help you decide which types of sources are most appropriate. Does your writing project require you to depend mainly on **secondary sources**—like books and articles that analyze and summarize a subject—or develop **primary sources**, such as interviews with experts, surveys, or observational studies you conduct yourself and laboratory reports, historical documents, diaries, letters, or works of literature written by others? Whatever sources you decide will best help you support your claims, this chapter will help you find or develop the resources you need.

To learn how to devise a research strategy, see Chapter 20; to learn how to evaluate sources, see Chapter 22.

Searching Library Catalogs and Databases

For most college research projects, finding appropriate sources starts with your library's home page, where you can

- find (and sometimes access) books, reference sources (such as general and subject-specific encyclopedias and dictionaries), reports, documents, multimedia resources (such as films and audio recordings), and much more;
- use your library's database to find (and sometimes access) articles in newspapers, magazines, and scholarly journals, as well as in reference sources;
- find **research guides**, lists of reliable sources on topics frequently studied by students.

Many libraries now offer unified search, which allows patrons to search for books and articles in magazines, newspapers, and scholarly journals simultaneously, from the home page. If you aren't sure whether you will need to search for books and articles using separate catalogs and databases, consult a librarian.

Your library's home page is also the place to find information about the brick-and-mortar library—its floor plan, its hours of operation, and the journals it has available in print. You might even be able to find links to what you need in other libraries or get online help from a librarian.

Use appropriate search terms.

Just as with a search engine like *Google,* you can search a library catalog or database by typing your search terms—an author's name, the title of a work, a subject term or keyword, even a call number—into the search box. To search successfully, put yourself in the position of the people writing about your topic to figure out what words they might have used. If your topic is "ecology," for example, you may find information under the keywords *ecosystem, environment, pollution,* and *endangered species,* as well as a number of other related keywords, depending on the focus of your research and your area of study.

Broaden or narrow your results.

When conducting a search, you may get too few hits and have to broaden your topic. To broaden your search, try the following:

Replace a specific term with a more general term	Replace *sister* or *brother* with *sibling*
Substitute a synonym for one of your keywords	Replace *home study* with *home schooling* or *student-paced education*
Combine terms with *or* to get results with either or both terms	Search *home study or home schooling* to get results that include both *home study* and *home schooling*
Add a wildcard character, usually an asterisk (*) or question mark (?) (Check the search tips to find out which wildcard character is in use.)	Search *home school** or *home school?* to retrieve results for *home school, home schooling,* and *home schooled*

Most often, you'll get too many hits and need to narrow your search. To narrow a search, try the following:

Add a specific term	Search not just *home schooling* but *home schooling statistics*
Combine search terms into phrases or word strings	Search *home schooling and California* or *"home schooling California"*

In many cases, using phrases or word strings will limit your results to items that include *all* the words you have specified. You may need to insert quotation marks around the terms or insert the word *and* between them to create a search phrase or word string. Check the search tips for the database, catalog, or search engine you are using.

Find books (and other sources).

Books housed in academic library collections offer two distinct advantages to the student researcher:

1. They provide in-depth coverage of topics.
2. They are likely to be published by reputable presses that strive for accuracy and reliability.

You can generally search for books and other library resources, like reference works and multimedia resources, by author's name, title, keyword, or subject heading, and narrow your search by using advanced search options.

Though you can search by keywords, most college libraries use special *subject headings* devised by the Library of Congress (the national library of the United States) to catalog books. Finding and using the subject headings most relevant to your search will make your research more productive. You can locate the subject headings your library uses by pulling up the record of a relevant book you have already found and looking for the list of words under the heading "Subject" or "Subject headings" (Figure 21.1). Including these terms in your search may help you find additional relevant resources. Ask a librarian for help if you cannot identify the headings.

FIGURE 21.1 A Book's Catalog Record

An item's record provides a lot more information than just the author, title, and call number. You can also find the subject headings by which it was cataloged and perhaps also the item's status (whether it has been checked out) and its location. Some libraries may allow you to place a hold on a book or find similar items. Some libraries, such as the one whose catalog is depicted here, even allow you to capture the book's record with your smartphone or have the information texted or e-mailed to you.

Some libraries also allow you to search by call number, which makes it easy to find other items on the same or a similar topic. (You might think of a call-number search as the electronic equivalent of looking at books shelved nearby.) For example, typing LC40 (the first part of the call number from the library record shown in Figure 21.1) into the search box calls up the records of other items on the subject of home schooling:

Title	Call number
Well-Trained Mind: A Guide to Classical Education at Home	**LC40**.B39 2004
Love in a Time of Homeschooling: A Mother and Daughter's Uncommon Year	**LC40**.B76 2010
Homeschool: An American History	**LC40**.G34 2008
Family Matters: Why Homeschooling Makes Sense	**LC40**.G88 1992
Home Schooling: Parents as Educators	**LC40**.H65 1995
How Children Learn at Home	**LC40**.T48 2007

If your search for books in your college library turns up little that is useful to you, do not give up. You may be able to request an item from another library via your library's interlibrary loan service. Inquire at your library for services available to you that can connect you to resources in other libraries.

Many libraries also house **archives and special collections** comprising manuscripts, rare books, and specialized materials or resources of local or worldwide interest. Whereas some libraries may list these items in their online catalog, others may provide links to these special collections in a different location on their Web sites; still others may provide access only through a catalog in the archives or special-collections room. Ask a librarian whether such materials may be useful to you.

Find articles in periodicals.

Much of the information you will use to write your research project will come from articles in **periodicals**, publications such as newspapers, magazines, or scholarly journals that are published at regular intervals. To locate relevant articles on your topic, start your search with one of your library's databases. Why not just start with a *Google* search? There are two very good reasons:

1. *Google* will pull up articles from any publication it indexes, from personal Web sites to scholarly journals. Results rise to the top of the list based on a number of factors but not necessarily the reliability of the source. A *Google* search will turn up helpful sources, but you will need to spend a good deal of time sifting through the numerous hits you get to find sources that are both relevant and reliable. (*Google Scholar* may help you locate more reliable sources than those you might find through a typical *Google* search.)

2. Sources you find through *Google* may ask you to pay for access to articles, or they may require a subscription. Your library may already subscribe to these sources on your behalf. Also, adding databases to your search strategy will diversify your search and provide you with access to resources not available through a search engine such as *Google*.

Most college libraries subscribe at least to **general databases** and **subject-specific databases** as well as databases that index newspapers. General databases (such as *Academic OneFile, Academic Search Premier* or *Elite* or *Complete*,[1] and *ProQuest Central*) index articles from both scholarly journals and popular magazines. Subject-specific databases (such as *ERIC—Education Resources Information Center, MLA International Bibliography, PsycINFO,* and *General Science Full Text*) index articles only in their discipline. Newspaper databases (such as *Alt-Press Watch, LexisNexis Academic, National Newspaper Index,* and *ProQuest Newspapers*) index newspaper articles. For college-level research projects, you may use all three types of databases to find appropriate articles. (Note that many libraries also offer ways to search multiple databases at once.) For the research project on home schooling that appears in Chapter 24, "Citing and Documenting Sources in MLA Style," Cristina Dinh might have consulted both a general database and a subject-specific database like *ERIC.*

If your database search returns too many unhelpful results, use the search strategies for choosing keywords and narrowing results discussed earlier in this chapter (p. 610) or use the database's advanced search options to refine your search. Many databases allow users to restrict results to articles published in academic journals, for example, or to articles that were published only after a certain date (see Figure 21.2, p. 610). Use the Help option or ask a librarian for assistance.

Increasingly, databases provide access to full-text articles, either in HTML or PDF format. When you have the option, choose the PDF format, as this will provide you with photographs, graphs, and charts in context, and you will be able to include the page numbers in your citation. If you find a citation to an article that is not accessible through a database, however, do not ignore it. Check with a librarian to find out how you can get a copy of the article.

Find government documents and statistical information.

Federal, state, and local governments make many of their documents available directly through the Web. For example, you can access statistical data about the United States through the U.S. Census Bureau's Web site (census.gov), and you can learn a great deal about other countries through the Web sites of the U.S. State Department (travel .state.gov) and the CIA (cia.gov/library/publications/the-world-factbook).

The Library of Congress provides a useful portal for finding government documents (federal, state, local, and international) through its Web site (loc.gov), and the U.S. Government Printing Office provides free electronic access to documents produced by the federal government through its FDsys Web page (gpo.gov/fdsys).

---

[1] The names of databases change over time and vary from library to library, so ask your instructor or a reference librarian if you need help.

Database

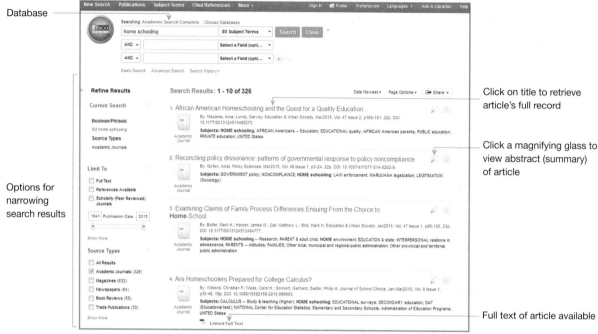

Options for narrowing search results

Click on title to retrieve article's full record

Click a magnifying glass to view abstract (summary) of article

Full text of article available

FIGURE 21.2   Database Search Results
Database search results may allow you to access an article directly or provide the information you need to locate (and cite) it, including the title, the author(s), and the article's publication information. The database may also provide options for narrowing a search by publication date, source type (academic journal versus newspaper, for example), and so on.

To learn more about the domains of Web sites, see Chapter 22.

Some libraries have collections of government publications and provide access to government documents through databases or catalogs. Your library may also offer statistical resources and data sets. See if your library has a guide to these resources, or ask a librarian for advice. You can also find government documents online using an advanced *Google* search (google.com/advanced_search) and specifying *.gov* as the type of site, or *domain,* you want to search (see Figure 21.3).

Find Web sites and interactive sources.

By now, you are likely quite familiar with searching the Web. This section introduces you to some tools and strategies to use it more efficiently. But first, a few cautions:

- ***Your research project will be only as credible as the sources you use.*** Because search engines index Web sources without evaluating them, not all the results a search engine like *Google* generates will be reliable and relevant to your purposes.

- **Web sources may not be stable.** A Web site that existed last week may no longer be available today, or its content may have changed. Be sure to record the information you need to cite a source when you first find it.

- **Web sources must be documented.** No matter what your source—a library book, a scholarly article, or a Web site or Web page—you will need to cite and document your source in your list of works cited or references. If you are publishing your report online, check also to determine whether you will need permission to reproduce an image or any other elements.

Google Scholar and Google Book Search

Although you may use search engines like *Google* with great rapidity and out of habit, as a college researcher you are likely to find it worthwhile to familiarize yourself with other parts of the *Google* search site. Of particular interest to the academic writer are *Google Scholar* and *Google Book Search*. *Google Scholar* retrieves articles from a number of scholarly databases and a wide range of general-interest and scholarly books. *Google Book Search* searches both popular and scholarly books. Both *Google Scholar* and *Google Book Search* offer overviews and, in some cases, the full text of a source.

Note: Whatever search engine you use, always click on the link called Help, Hints, or Tips on the search tool's home page to find out more about the commands and advanced-search techniques it offers. Most search engines allow searches using the techniques discussed earlier in the chapter (p. 610). Many also provide advanced searching options that allow you to limit results to those created between specific dates, in specific languages, and so on.

Other Useful Search Options

No matter how precisely you search the Web with a standard search engine, you may not hit on the best available resources. Starting your search from a subject guide, such as those provided by the *Internet Public Library* (ipl.org/div/special) or the librarians at your school can direct you to relevant and reliable sources of online information.

Interactive Sources

Interactive sources, including blogs, wikis, RSS feeds, social networking sites (like *Facebook* and *Twitter*), and discussion lists, can also be useful sources of

FIGURE 21.3 An Advanced Google search
Use *Google*'s advanced search (google.com /advanced_search) to locate information within specific sites or domains (such as *.edu* or *.gov*) or to narrow results to sites that include or exclude specific words, appear only in English or another language, and so on.

For guidelines on how to cite Web sources, see Chapter 24, "Citing and Documenting Sources in MLA Style," or Chapter 25, "Citing and Documenting Sources in APA Style"; for more on evaluating sources, especially Web sources, see Chapter 22.

information, especially if your research project focuses on a current event or late-breaking news.

- **Blogs** are Web sites that are updated regularly, often many times a day. They are usually organized chronologically, with the newest posts at the top, and may contain links or news stories, but generally focus on the opinions of the blog host and visitors. Blogs by experts in the field are likely to be more informative than blogs by amateurs or fans.

- **Wikis**—of which *Wikipedia* is the best known example—offer content contributed and modified collaboratively by a community of users. Wikis can be very useful for gleaning background information, but because (in most cases) anyone can write or revise wiki entries, many instructors will not accept them as reliable sources for college-level research projects. Use wikis cautiously.

- **RSS (Really Simple Syndication) feeds** aggregate frequently updated sites, such as news sites and blogs, into links in a single Web page or e-mail. Most search engines provide this service, as do sites such as *NewzCrawler* (newzcrawler.com) and *FeedDemon* (feeddemon.com). RSS feeds can be useful if you are researching news stories or political campaigns.

- **Social networking sites**, like *Facebook* and *Twitter*, allow users to create groups or pages on topics of interest or to follow the thoughts and activities of newsmakers.

- **Discussion lists** are electronic mailing lists that allow members to post comments and get feedback from others interested in the same topic. The most reliable discussion lists are moderated and attract experts on the topic. Many online communities provide some kind of indexing or search mechanism so that you can look for "threads" (conversations) related to your topic.

Although you need to evaluate the information you find in all sources carefully, you must be especially careful with information from social networking sites and discussion lists. However, such sources can provide up-to-the-minute information. Also be aware that whereas most online communities welcome guests and newcomers, others may perceive your questions as intrusive or naive. It may be useful to "lurk" (that is, just to read posts) before making a contribution.

Conducting Field Research

In universities, government agencies, and the business world, field research can be as important as library research. In some majors, like education or sociology, as well as in service-learning courses, primary research projects are common. Even in the writing projects covered in Chapters 2–9, observations, interviews, and surveys may be useful or even necessary. As you consider how you might use field research in your writing projects, ask your instructor whether your institution requires you to obtain approval, and check Chapter 24, "Citing and Documenting Sources in MLA Style," or 25, "Citing and Documenting Sources in APA Style," for information about citing interviews you conduct yourself.

Conduct observational studies.

Observational studies, such as you would conduct when profiling a place (see Chapter 3), are common in college. To conduct an observational study effectively, follow these guidelines:

Planning an Observational Study

To ensure that your observational visits are productive, plan them carefully:

- **Arrange access if necessary.** Visits to a private location (such as a school or business) require special permission, so be sure to arrange your visit in advance. When making your request, state your intentions and goals for your study directly and fully. You may be surprised at how receptive people can be to a college student on assignment. But have a fallback plan in case your request is refused or the business or institution places constraints on you that hamper your research.

- **Develop a hypothesis.** In advance, write down a tentative assumption about what you expect to learn from your study—your **hypothesis**. This will guide your observations and notes, and you can adjust your expectations in response to what you observe if necessary. Consider, too, how your presence will affect those whom you are observing, so you can minimize your impact or take the effect of your presence into consideration.

- **Consider how best to conduct the observation.** Decide where to place yourself to make your observations most effective. Should you move around to observe from multiple vantage points, or will a single perspective be more productive?

Making Observations

Strategies for conducting your observation include the following:

- **Description:** *Describe* in detail the setting and the people you are observing. Note the physical arrangement and functions of the space, and the number, activities, and appearance of the people. Record as many details as possible, draw diagrams or sketches if helpful, and take photographs or videos if allowed (and if those you are observing do not object).

  For more about narration, description, and classification, see Chapters 14, 15, and 17.

- **Narration:** *Narrate* the activities going on around you. Try initially to be an innocent observer: Pretend that you have never seen anything like this activity or place before, and explain what you are seeing step by step, even if what you are writing seems obvious. Include interactions among people, and capture snippets of conversations (in quotation marks) if possible.

- **Analysis and classification:** Break the scene down into its component parts, identify common threads, and organize the details into categories.

Take careful notes during your visit if you can do so unobtrusively or immediately afterwards if you can't. You can use a notebook and pencil, a laptop or tablet, or even a smartphone to record your notes. Choose whatever is least disruptive to those around you. You may need to use abbreviations and symbols to capture your observations on-site, but be sure to convert such shorthand into words and phrases as soon as possible after the visit so that you don't forget its significance.

Writing Your Observational Study

For more about mapping, clustering, or outlining strategies, see Chapter 11.

Immediately after your visit, fill in any gaps in your notes, and review your notes to look for meaningful patterns. You might find *mapping strategies,* such as *clustering* or *outlining,* useful for discovering patterns in your notes. Take some time to reflect on what you saw. Asking yourself questions like these might help:

- How did what I observed fit my own or my readers' likely preconceptions of the place or activity? Did my observations upset any of my preconceptions? What, if anything, seemed contradictory or out of place?

- What interested me most about the activity or place? What are my readers likely to find interesting about it?

- What did I learn?

Your purpose in writing about your visit is to share your insights into the meaning and significance of your observations. Assume that your readers have never been to the place, and provide enough detail for it to come alive for them. Decide on the perspective you want to convey, and choose the details necessary to convey your insights.

PRACTICING THE GENRE ——————————————————————————————————

Collaborating on an Observational Study

Arrange to meet with a small group (three or four students) for an observational visit somewhere on campus, such as the student center, gym, or cafeteria. Have each group member focus on a specific task, such as recording what people are wearing, doing, or saying, or capturing what the place looks, sounds, and smells like. After twenty to thirty minutes, report to one another on your observations. Discuss any difficulties that arise.

Conduct interviews.

A successful interview involves careful planning before the interview, but it also requires keen listening skills and the ability to ask appropriate follow-up questions while conducting the interview. Courtesy and consideration for your subject are crucial at all stages of the process.

Planning the Interview

Planning an interview involves the following:

- **Choosing an interview subject.** For a profile of an individual, your interview will be with one person; for a profile of an organization, you might interview several people, all with different roles or points of view. Prepare a list of interview candidates, as busy people might turn you down.

- **Arranging the interview.** Give your prospective subject(s) a brief description of your project, and show some sincere enthusiasm for it. Keep in mind that the person you want to interview will be donating valuable time to you, so call ahead to arrange the interview, allow your subject to specify the amount of time she or he can spare, and come prepared.

Preparing for the Interview

In preparation for the interview, consider your objectives:

- Do you want details or a general orientation (the "big picture") from this interview?
- Do you want this interview to lead you to interviews with other key people?
- Do you want mainly facts or opinions?
- Do you need to clarify something you have observed or read? If so, what?

Making an observational visit and doing some background reading beforehand can be helpful. Find out as much as you can about the organization or company (size, location, purpose, etc.), as well as the key people.

Good questions are key to a successful interview. You will likely want to ask a few **closed questions** (questions that request specific information) and a number of **open questions** (questions that give the respondent range and flexibility and encourage him or her to share anecdotes, personal revelations, and expressions of attitudes):

Open Questions	Closed Questions
▶ What do you think about _____ ?	▶ How do you do _____ ?
▶ Describe your reaction when _____ happened.	▶ What does _____ mean?
▶ Tell me about a time you were _____ .	▶ How was _____ developed?

The best questions encourage the subject to talk freely but stick to the point. You may need to ask a follow-up question to refocus the discussion or to clarify a point, so be prepared. If you are unsure about a subject's answer, follow up by rephrasing the answer, prefacing it by saying something like "Let me see if I have this right" or "Am I correct in saying that you feel _____ ?" Avoid *forced-choice questions* ("Which do you think is the better approach: _____ or _____ ?") and *leading questions* ("How well do you think _____ is doing?").

During the Interview

Another key to good interviewing is flexibility. Ask the questions you have prepared, but also be ready to shift gears to take full advantage of what your subject can offer.

- **Take notes.** Take notes during the interview, even if you are recording your discussion. You might find it useful to divide several pages of a notebook into two columns or to set up a word processing file in two columns. Use the left-hand

For an example of a student's interview notes, see the "Writer at Work" section in Chapter 3 (pp. 113–17).

column to note details about the scene and your subject or about your impressions overall; in the right-hand column, write several questions and record the answers. Remember that how something is said is as important as what is said. Look for material that will give texture to your writing—gesture, verbal inflection, facial expression, body language, physical appearance (dress, hair) or anything that makes the person an individual.

- **Listen carefully.** Avoid interrupting your subject or talking about yourself; rather, listen carefully and guide the discussion by asking follow-up questions and probing politely for more information.

- **Be considerate.** Do not stay longer than the time you were allotted unless your subject agrees to continue the discussion, and show your appreciation for the time you have been given by thanking your subject and offering her or him a copy of your finished project.

Following the Interview

After the interview, do the following:

- **Reflect on the interview.** As soon as you finish the interview, find a quiet place to reflect on it and to review and amplify your notes. Asking yourself questions like these might help: What did I learn? What seemed contradictory or surprising about the interview? How did what was said fit my own or my readers' likely expectations about the person, activity, or place? How can I summarize my impressions?

  Also make a list of any questions that arise. You may want to follow up with your subject for more information, but limit yourself to one e-mail or phone call to avoid becoming a bother.

- **Thank your subject.** Send your interview subject a thank-you note within twenty-four hours of the interview. Try to reference something specific from the interview, something surprising or thought-provoking. And send your subject a copy of your finished project with a note of appreciation.

PRACTICING THE GENRE

Interviewing a Classmate

Practice interviewing a classmate:

- Spend five to ten minutes writing questions and thinking about what you'd like to learn.

- Spend ten minutes asking the questions you prepared, but also ask one or more follow-up questions in response to something your classmate has told you.

- Following the interview, spend a few minutes thinking about what you learned about your classmate and about conducting an interview. What might you do differently when conducting a formal interview?

Conduct surveys.

Surveys let you gauge the opinions and knowledge of large numbers of people. You might conduct a survey to gauge opinion in a political science course or to assess familiarity with a television show for a media studies course. You might also conduct a survey to assess the seriousness of a problem for a service-learning class or in response to an assignment to propose a solution to a problem (Chapter 7). This section briefly outlines procedures you can follow to carry out an informal survey, and it highlights areas where caution is needed. Colleges and universities have restrictions about the use and distribution of questionnaires, so check your institution's policy or obtain permission before beginning the survey.

Designing Your Survey

Use the following tips to design an effective survey:

- **Conduct background research.** You may need to conduct background research on your topic. For example, to create a survey on scheduling appointments at the student health center, you may first need to contact the health center to determine its scheduling practices, and you may want to interview health center personnel.

- **Focus your study.** Before starting out, decide what you expect to learn (your *hypothesis*). Make sure your focus is limited—focus on one or two important issues—so you can craft a brief questionnaire that respondents can complete quickly and easily and so that you can organize and report on your results more easily.

- **Write questions.** Plan to use a number of *closed questions* (questions that request specific information), such as *two-way questions, multiple-choice questions, ranking scale questions,* and *checklist questions* (see Figure 21.4, p. 622). You will also likely want to include a few *open questions* (questions that give respondents the opportunity to write their answers in their own words). Closed questions are easier to tally, but open questions are likely to provide you with deeper insight and a fuller sense of respondents' opinions. Whatever questions you develop, be sure that you provide all the answer options your respondents are likely to want, and make sure your questions are clear and unambiguous.

- **Identify the population you are trying to reach.** Even for an informal study, you should try to get a reasonably representative group. For example, to study satisfaction with appointment scheduling at the student health center, you would need to include a representative sample of all the students at the school—not only those who have visited the health center. Determine the demographic makeup of your school, and arrange to reach out to a representative sample.

- **Design the questionnaire.** Begin your questionnaire with a brief, clear introduction stating the purpose of your survey and explaining how you intend to use the results. Give advice on answering the questions, estimate the amount of time

This is a survey about scheduling appointments at the student health center. Your participation will help determine how long students have to wait to use the clinic's services and how these services might be more conveniently scheduled. The survey should take only 3 to 4 minutes to complete. All responses are confidential.

Two-way question ——— 1. Have you ever made an appointment at the clinic?
❏ Yes   ❏ No

Filter ——— If you answered "No" to question 1, skip to question 5.

2. How frequently have you had to wait more than 10 minutes at the clinic for a scheduled appointment?

Multiple-choice questions ——— ❏ Always   ❏ Usually   ❏ Occasionally   ❏ Never

3. Have you ever had to wait more than 30 minutes at the clinic for a scheduled appointment?
❏ Yes   ❏ No   ❏ Uncertain

4. Based on your experience with the clinic, how would you rate its system for scheduling appointments?

❏ 1 (poor)   ❏ 2 (adequate)   ❏ 3 (good)   ❏ 4 (excellent)

5. Given your present work and class schedule, which times during the day (Monday through Friday) would be the most and least convenient for you to schedule appointments at the clinic? (Rank your choices from 1 for most convenient time to 4 for least convenient time.)

Ranking questions ———

	1 (most convenient)	2 (more convenient)	3 (less convenient)	4 (least convenient)
morning (7 a.m.–noon)	❏	❏	❏	❏
afternoon (noon–5 p.m.)	❏	❏	❏	❏
dinnertime (5–7 p.m.)	❏	❏	❏	❏
evening (7–10 p.m.)	❏	❏	❏	❏

6. If you have had an appointment at the student health center within the last six months, please evaluate your experience.

7. If you have had an appointment at the student health center within the last six months, please indicate what you believe would most improve scheduling of appointments at the clinic.

Open questions ———

8. If you have *never* had an appointment at the student health center, please indicate why you have not made use of this service.

Thank you for your participation.

FIGURE 21.4   Sample Questionnaire: Scheduling at the Student Health Center

needed to complete the questionnaire, and—unless you are administering the survey in person—indicate the date by which completed surveys must be returned. Organize your questions by topic, from least to most complicated, or in any order that seems logical, and format your questionnaire so that it is easy to read and complete.

- **Test the questionnaire.** Ask at least three readers to complete your questionnaire before you distribute it. Time them as they respond, or ask them to keep track of how long they take to complete it. Discuss with them any confusion or problems they experience. Review their responses with them to be certain that each question is eliciting the information you want it to elicit. From what you learn, revise your questions and adjust the format of the questionnaire.

Administering the Survey

The more respondents you have, the better, but constraints of time and expense will almost certainly limit the number. As few as twenty-five could be adequate for an informal study, but to get twenty-five responses, you may need to solicit fifty or more participants.

You can conduct the survey in person or over the telephone; use an online service such as *SurveyMonkey* (surveymonkey.com) or *Zoomerang* (zoomerang.com); e-mail the questionnaires; or conduct the survey using a social media site such as *Facebook*. You may also distribute surveys to groups of people in class or around campus and wait to collect their responses.

Each method has its advantages and disadvantages. For example, face-to-face surveys allow you to get more in-depth responses, but participants may be unwilling to answer personal questions face to face. Though fewer than half the surveys you solicit using survey software are likely to be completed (your invitations may wind up in a spam folder), online software will tabulate responses automatically.

Writing the Report

When writing your report, include a summary of the results, as well as an interpretation of what the results mean.

- **Summarize the results.** Once you have the completed questionnaires, tally the results from the closed questions. (If you conducted the survey online, this will have already been done for you.) You can give the results from the closed questions as percentages, either within the text of your report or in one or more tables or graphs. Next, read all respondents' answers to each open question to determine the variety of responses they gave, and classify the answers. You might classify them as positive, negative, or neutral or try grouping them into more specific categories. Finally, identify quotations that express a range of responses succinctly and engagingly to use in your report.

- **Interpret the results.** Once you have tallied the responses and read answers to open questions, think about what the results mean. Does the information you gathered support your hypothesis? If so, how? If the results do not support your hypothesis, where did you go wrong? Was there a problem with the way you worded your questions or with the sample of the population you contacted? Or was your hypothesis in need of adjustment?

For more about writing a laboratory report, see Chapter 29.

- **Write the report.** Research reports in the social sciences use a standard format, with headings introducing the following categories of information:

  - **Abstract:** A brief summary of the report, usually including one sentence summarizing each section

  - **Introduction:** Includes context for the study (other similar studies, if any, and their results), the question or questions the researcher wanted to answer and why this question (or these questions) is important, and the limits of what the researcher expected the survey to reveal

  - **Methods:** Includes the questionnaire, identifies the number and type of participants, and describes the methods used for administering the questionnaire and recording data

  - **Results:** Includes the data from the survey, with limited commentary or interpretation

  - **Discussion:** Includes the researcher's interpretation of results, an explanation of how the data support the hypothesis (or not), and the conclusions the researcher has drawn from the research

22

Evaluating Sources

As soon as you start your search for sources, you should begin evaluating what you find not only to decide whether they are *relevant* to your research project but also to determine how *credible,* or reliable, they are.

Choosing Relevant Sources

Sources are **relevant** when they help you achieve your aims with your readers. Relevant sources may

- explain terms or concepts;
- provide background information;
- provide evidence in support of your claims;
- provide alternative viewpoints or interpretations;
- lend authority to your point of view.

A search for sources may reveal more books and articles than any researcher could ever actually consult. A search on the term *home schooling* in one database, for example, got 1,172 hits. Obviously, a glance at all the hits to determine which are most relevant would take far too much time. To speed up the process, resources such as library catalogs, databases, and search engines provide tools to narrow the results. For example, in one popular all-purpose database, you can limit results by publication date, language, and publication or source type (such as articles from newspapers or scholarly journals), among other options. (Check the Help screen to learn how to use these tools.) In this database, limiting the *home schooling* results to articles published in scholarly journals in English over the last ten years reduced the number of hits to fifty-six, a far more reasonable number to review. (Remember that if you have too few results or your results are not targeted correctly, you can expand your search by changing your search terms or removing limits selectively.)

Once you've reduced your search results to a manageable number, click on the remaining titles to look closely at each record. The analysis of an article's detailed record in Figure 22.1 shows what to look for.

For more on focusing search results and selecting search terms, see Chapter 21.

Publication: What do you know about the periodical? Is it well respected?

Date: Is the article recent enough for your area of study, or is it a classic? (Some older, "classic" sources may offer authoritative perspectives, but for current controversies or recent developments, use recent sources.)

Title: Does the article address your topic?

Length: Does the length suggest the topic is treated in depth?

Subject terms: Are any of your keywords listed? Should any of these terms be added to your keywords list?

Abstract: Does the article address your topic? What angle does it take?

Authors: Are they experts in the field? Do they have relevant background?

FIGURE 22.1   Analyzing the Detailed Record of an Article from a Periodicals Database
Analyze the detailed record of an article to determine whether the article itself is worth reading by asking yourself the following questions: Does the title suggest that the article addresses your topic? Are the authors experts in the field? Was the article published in a periodical that is likely to be reliable, was it published recently, and is it lengthy enough to indicate that the topic is treated in depth? Does the abstract (or summary) suggest that the article addresses your topic? If so, what angle does it take?

After you have identified a reasonable number of relevant sources, examine the sources themselves:

- Read the preface, introduction, or conclusion of books, or the first or last few paragraphs of articles, to determine which aspect of the topic is addressed or which approach to the topic is taken. To obtain a clear picture of a topic, researchers need to consider sources that address different aspects of the topic or take different approaches.

- Look at the headings or references in articles, or the table of contents and index in books, to see how much of the content relates specifically to your topic.

- Consider the way the source is written: Sources written for general readers may be accessible but may not analyze the subject in depth. Extremely specialized works may be too technical. Poorly written sources may be unreliable. (See Choosing Reliable Sources, below, for more on scholarly versus popular sources and for a discussion of why researchers should avoid sources that are poorly written or riddled with errors.)

If close scrutiny leaves you with too few sources—or too many sources from too few perspectives—conduct a search using additional or alternative keywords, or explore links to related articles, look at the references in a particularly useful article, or look for other sources by an author whose work you find useful.

Choosing Reliable Sources

Choosing relevant sources is crucial to assembling a useful working bibliography. Determining which of those relevant sources is also likely to be *reliable* is even more important. To determine reliability, ask yourself the questions below.

Who wrote it?

Consider, first, whether the author is an *expert* in the field. The fact that someone has a PhD in astrophysics is no indication that he or she will be an expert in military history, for example, so be careful that the area of expertise is directly relevant to the topic.

To determine the author's area of expertise, look for the author's professional affiliation (where he or she works or teaches). This may be indicated at the bottom of the first page of an article (often labeled "Author Affiliations") or in an "About the Author" section in a book or on a Web site. Frequently, Googling the author will also reveal the author's affiliation, but double-check to make sure the affiliation is current and that you have located the right person. You may also consult a biographical reference source available through a reference database at your library. Looking to see what other works the author has published, and with whom, can also help you ascertain his or her areas of expertise.

Contributors to blogs, wikis, and online discussion forums may or may not be experts in the field. Determine whether the site screens contributors, and double-check any information taken from sites for which you cannot determine the credentials of contributors.

Also consider the author's *perspective*. Most writing is not neutral or objective and does not claim to be. Knowledge of the author's perspective enables you to assess *bias* and determine whether the author's perspective affects the presentation of his or her argument. To determine the author's perspective, look for the main point and ask yourself questions like these:

- What evidence does the author provide to support this point? Is it from authoritative sources? Is it persuasive?

For more details on these argumentative strategies, see Chapter 19.

- Does the author make concessions to or refute opposing arguments?

- Does the author avoid fallacies, confrontational phrasing, and loaded words?

How recently was it published?

For more help locating
publication information, see
the documentation maps in
Chapter 24.

In general, especially when you are writing about science or technology, current events, or emerging trends, you should consult the most up-to-date sources available on your subject. The date of publication for articles you locate will be indicated in your search results. For a print book, look for the copyright date on the copyright page (usually on the back of the title page); for an e-book, look for the copyright date at the beginning or end of the electronic file. If your source is a Web site, consider when it, and the content within it, was last updated (often indicated at the bottom of the Web page or home page).

You may also need older, "classic" sources that establish the principles, theories, and data on which later work is based; classics may also provide a useful perspective for evaluating other works. To determine which sources are classics, note the ones that are cited most often in encyclopedia articles, lists of works cited or references, and recent works on the subject. You may also want to consult your instructor or a librarian to help you determine which works are classics in your field.

Is the source scholarly, popular, or for a trade group?

Scholarly sources (whether books or articles) are written by and for experts in a field of study, frequently professors or academic researchers. They can be challenging to read and understand because they use the language of the field, which may be unfamiliar to those outside the discipline, but they are considered reliable because the contents are written by specialists and peer-reviewed (reviewed by specialists) before publication. Scholarly sources also tend to delve deeply into a subject, often a narrowly defined subject. Scholarly sources may be published by a university press, a scholarly organization, or a commercial publisher (such as Kluwer Academic or Blackwell). Though scholarly sources may provide an overview of the subject, they generally focus on a specific issue or argument and generally contain a great deal of original research.

In contrast, **popular sources** are written to entertain and educate the general public. For the most part, they are written by journalists who have conducted research and interviewed experts. They may include original research, especially on current events or emerging trends. Mainly, though, they report on and summarize original research and are written for interested, nonspecialist readers.

Of course, popular sources range widely along the reliability spectrum. Highly respected newspapers and magazines, such as the *New York Times*, the *Guardian*, the *Economist*, and *Harper's Magazine*, publish original research on news and culture. These newspapers and magazines check facts carefully and are often considered appropriate sources for research projects in entry-level courses (although you should check with your instructor to find out her or his expectations). Magazines that focus on celebrity gossip, such as *People* and *Us Weekly*, are unlikely to be considered appropriate sources for a college-level research project.

Trade publications—periodicals that report on news and technical advances in a specific industry—are written for those employed in the industry and include such titles as *Advertising Age, World Cement,* and *American Machinist.* Some trade publications may be appropriate for college research projects, especially in the sciences, but keep in mind that these publications are intended for a specialist audience and may focus on marketing products to professionals in the field. Table 22.1 summarizes some of the important differences between scholarly journals, popular magazines, and trade publications.

Who published it?

Determining who published or sponsored a source you are considering can help you gauge its reliability and ascertain the publication's slant (or point of view). Look to see

TABLE 22.1 Scholarly Journals versus Popular Magazines and Trade Publications

Scholarly Journals	Popular Magazines	Trade Publications
Journals are usually published 4 to 6 times per year.	Magazines are usually published weekly or monthly.	Trade publications may be published daily, weekly, monthly, or quarterly, depending on the industry covered.
Articles are usually written by scholars (with *PhD* or academic affiliations after their names).	Authors of articles are journalists but may quote experts.	Articles may be written by professionals or by journalists with quotes from experts.
Many articles have more than one author.	Most articles have a single author.	Authors of articles may or may not be named.
In print journals, the title page often appears on the cover, and the covers frequently lack artwork.	Photographs, usually in color, appear on the covers of most print magazines and their Web sites.	Photographs, usually in color, appear on the covers of most print trade publications and on their Web sites.
Articles may include charts, tables, figures, and quotations from other scholarly sources.	Articles frequently include color pictures and sidebars.	Articles frequently include color pictures and sidebars.
An abstract (summary) of the article may appear on the first page.	A headline or engaging description may precede the article.	Headlines often include names or terms familiar only to industry insiders.
Most articles are fairly long—5 to 20 pages.	Most articles are fairly short—1 to 5 pages.	Most articles are fairly short—1 to 5 pages.
Articles cite sources and provide a bibliography (works-cited or reference list).	Articles rarely include a list of works cited or references but may mention or quote experts.	Articles rarely include a list of works cited or references but may mention or quote experts.

whether the source was published by a commercial publisher (such as St. Martin's or Random House); a university press (such as the University of Nebraska Press); a corporation, an organization, or an interest group (such as the RAND Corporation, the World Wildlife Fund, or the National Restaurant Association); a government agency (such as the Internal Revenue Service or the U.S. Census Bureau); or the author on his or her own. Determining the publisher or sponsor is particularly important for material published on the Web.

If your source is a Web page, look at the URL (uniform resource locator) to find its top-level domain, which is indicated by a suffix. Some of the most useful ones are listed here:

.gov	U.S. federal government and some state or local government institutions
.org	nonprofit organizations
.edu	educational institutions
.com	businesses and commercial enterprises
.net	usually businesses or organizations associated with online networks
.mil	the U.S. military

For the most part, *.gov* and *.edu* are the most likely to offer reliable sources of information for a college research project. However, sources with any of these domains may vary in reliability. For example, a file with a *.com* suffix may offer a highly reliable history of a corporation and be an appropriate source for someone writing a history of corporate America, whereas a file with a *.edu* suffix may have been posted by a student or by a faculty member outside his or her area of expertise.

It is essential to look at Web sites carefully. Determine who sponsors the site: Is it a business, a professional group, a private organization, an educational institution, a government agency, or an individual? Look for a link, usually at the top or the bottom of the home page, called something like "Who We Are" or "About Us." If you cannot determine who sponsors a site, carefully double-check any information you find there.

Consider, too, checking how often the Web site has been linked to and the types of links provided by the Web site. That a site has been linked to repeatedly does not guarantee reliability, but that information may be helpful in conjunction with other recommendations in this chapter. To determine the number of times a Web page has been linked to, type *link:* plus the URL into a *Google* search box. To check the links provided, click on them and apply the criteria in this chapter.

If the source was published by a commercial publisher, check out the publisher's Web site, and ask yourself questions like these:

- Does the publisher offer works from a single perspective or from multiple perspectives?
- Do the works it publishes cover a wide variety of topics or focus on a particular array?
- Does the publisher's Web site host links to a particular type of site?

The Web sites of book publishers may offer a link to a catalog. If so, look at the works the catalog lists. Does the publisher seem to focus on a particular topic or take a particular point of view? Does the publisher generally offer popular, academic, or professional works?

If your source is a periodical (a magazine, newspaper, newsletter, or scholarly journal), consider whether it focuses on a particular topic or offers a single point of view. In addition to looking at the article you are considering and back issues of the periodical, visit the publisher's Web site, which may help you determine topic and point of view.

How is the source written?

Most works that are published professionally (including popular newspapers and magazines, as well as scholarly journals and trade magazines) will have been edited carefully. These sources will generally avoid errors of grammar, punctuation, and spelling, and have been fact-checked carefully. Web sites sponsored by professional organizations, too, will generally avoid these kinds of errors. Personal Web sites, however, are unlikely to have been professionally edited and fact-checked. If a Web site is riddled with errors, be very careful to double-check any information you take from that site.

What does the source say?

Finally, and perhaps most importantly, consider the source itself. Answering the following questions can help you determine whether the source is worth consideration:

- What is the intended audience of the source? Does the source address an audience of experts or a general audience?

- What is the purpose of the source? Does it review a number of different positions, or does it argue for a position of its own? If it makes its own argument, analyze the argument closely.

To learn more about analyzing an argument, see Chapter 19.

- What is the tone of the source? Is the tone reasonable? Does the source respond to alternative viewpoints, and are those responses logical and reasonable?

- What evidence is offered to support the argument? Is the evidence relevant and reliable? What kinds of citations or links does the source supply?

23

Using Sources to Support Your Ideas

Writing a college research project requires you to

- analyze sources to understand the arguments those sources are making, the information they are using to support their claims, and the ways those arguments and the supporting evidence they use relate to your topic;

- synthesize information from sources to support, extend, and challenge your own ideas;

- integrate information from sources with your own ideas to contribute something new to the "conversation" on your topic.

Synthesizing Sources

Synthesizing means making connections among information and ideas from texts and from your own experience. Once you have analyzed a number of sources on your topic, consider questions like the following to help you synthesize ideas and information:

- Do any of the sources you read use similar approaches or come to similar conclusions? What common themes do they explore? Do any of them use the same evidence (facts, statistics, research studies, examples) to support their claims?

- What differentiates their various positions? Where do the writers disagree, and why? Does one writer seem to be responding to or challenging one or more of the others?

- Do you agree with some sources and disagree with others? What makes one source more convincing than the others? Do any of the sources you have read offer support for your claims? Do any of them challenge your conclusions? If so, can you *refute* the challenge or do you need to *concede* a point?

Sentence strategies like the following can help you clarify where you differ from or agree with the sources you have read:

▶ A study by X supports my position by demonstrating that _____ .

▶ X and Y think this issue is about _____ . But what is really at stake here is _____ .

▶ X claims that _____ . But I agree with Y, who argues that _____ .

▶ On this issue, X and Y say _____ . Although I understand and to some degree sympathize with their point of view, I agree with Z that this is ultimately a question of _____ .

The report by Maya Gomez (pp. 181–86) and the synthesis chart she created (p. 202) show how ideas and information from sources can be synthesized.

To learn more about synthesis, see Chapters 5 and 12.

Acknowledging Sources and Avoiding Plagiarism

In your college writing, you will be expected to use and acknowledge **secondary sources**—books, articles, published or recorded interviews, Web sites, lectures, and other print and nonprint materials—in addition to your own ideas, insights, and field research. The following information will help you decide what does and does not need to be acknowledged and will enable you to avoid *plagiarizing* inadvertently.

What does and does not need to be acknowledged?

For the most part, any ideas, information, or language you borrow from a source—whether the source is in print or online—must be acknowledged by including an in-text citation and an entry in your list of works cited (MLA style) or references (APA style). The only types of information that do not require acknowledgment are common knowledge (for example, John F. Kennedy was assassinated in Dallas), facts widely available in many sources (U.S. presidents used to be inaugurated on March 4 rather than January 20), well-known quotations ("To be or not to be / That is the question"), and material you created or gathered yourself, such as photographs that you took or data from surveys that you conducted.

For more on citing sources in MLA and APA style, see Chapters 24 and 25.

Remember that you need to acknowledge the source of any visual (photograph, table, chart, graph, diagram, drawing, map, screen shot) that you did not create yourself as well as the source of any information that you used to create your own visual. (You should also request permission from the source of a visual if your essay is going to be posted online without password protection.) When in doubt about whether you need to acknowledge a source, do so.

The documentation guidelines in the next two chapters present two styles for citing sources: MLA and APA. Whichever style you use, the most important thing is that your readers be able to tell where words or ideas that are not your own begin and end. You can accomplish this most readily by placing parenthetical source citations correctly and by separating your words from those of the source with **signal phrases** such as "According to Smith," "Peters claims," and "As Olmos asserts." (When you cite a source for the first time in a signal phrase, use the author's full name; after that, use just the last name.)

Avoid plagiarism by acknowledging sources and quoting, paraphrasing, and summarizing carefully.

When you use material from another source, you need to acknowledge the source, usually by citing the author and page or publication date in your text and including a list of works cited or references at the end of your essay. Failure to acknowledge sources—even by accident—constitutes plagiarism, a serious transgression. By citing sources correctly, you give appropriate credit to the originator of the words and ideas you are using, offer your readers the information they need to consult those sources directly, and build your own credibility.

Writers—students and professionals alike—occasionally fail to acknowledge sources properly. Students sometimes mistakenly assume that plagiarizing occurs only when another writer's exact words are used without acknowledgment. In fact, plagiarism can also apply to paraphrases as well as to such diverse forms of expression as musical compositions, visual images, ideas, and statistics. Therefore, keep in mind that you must indicate the source of any borrowed information, idea, language, or visual or audio material you use in your essay, whether you have *paraphrased, summarized,* or *quoted* directly from the source or have reproduced it or referred to it in some other way.

Remember especially the need to document electronic sources fully and accurately. Perhaps because it is so easy to access and distribute text and visuals online and to copy material from one electronic document and paste it into another, some students do not realize, or may forget, that information, ideas, and images from electronic sources require acknowledgment just as those from print sources do. At the same time, the improper (unacknowledged) use of online sources is often very easy for readers to detect.

Some people plagiarize simply because they do not know the conventions for using and acknowledging sources. Others plagiarize because they keep sloppy notes and thus fail to distinguish between their own and their sources' ideas. If you keep a working bibliography and careful notes, you will not make this serious mistake. If you are unfamiliar with the conventions for documentation, this and the next two chapters will clarify how you can incorporate sources into your writing and properly acknowledge your use of those sources.

Another reason some people plagiarize is that they feel intimidated by the writing task or the deadline. If you experience this anxiety about your work, speak to your instructor. Do not run the risk of failing a course or being expelled from your college because of plagiarism.

If you are confused about what is and what is not plagiarism, be sure to ask your instructor, or consult your school's plagiarism policy.

Using Information from Sources to Support Your Claims

When writing a research project, remember that the goal is to use the ideas and information you find in sources *to support your own ideas*. Make sure that each of your supporting paragraphs does three things:

1. States a claim that supports your thesis

2. Provides evidence that supports your claim

3. Explains to readers how the evidence supports your claim

Consider this paragraph from Patrick O'Malley's proposal in Chapter 7, "More Testing, More Learning" (pp. 290–96):

> The main reason professors should give frequent exams is that when they do and when they provide feedback to students on how well they are doing, students learn more in the course and perform better on major exams, projects, and papers. It makes sense that in a challenging course containing a great deal of material, students will learn more of it and put it to better use if they have to apply or "practice" it frequently on exams, which also helps them find out how much they are learning and what they need to go over again. A 2006 study reported in the journal *Psychological Science* concluded that "taking repeated tests on material leads to better long-term retention than repeated studying," according to the study's coauthors, Henry L. Roediger and Jeffrey Karpicke (ScienceWatch.com, 2008). When asked what the impact of this breakthrough research would be, they responded: "We hope that this research may be picked up in educational circles as a way to improve educational practices, both for students in the classroom and as a study strategy outside of class." The new field of mind, brain, and education research advocates the use of "retrieval testing." For example, research by Karpicke and Blunt (2011) published in *Science* found that testing was more effective than other, more traditional methods of studying both for comprehension and for analysis. Why retrieval testing works is not known. UCLA psychologist Robert Bjork speculates that it may be effective because "when we use our memories by retrieving things, we change our access" to that information. "What we recall," therefore, "becomes more recallable in the future" (qtd. in Belluck, 2011).

States claim

Explains how evidence supports claim

Provides evidence

O'Malley connects this body paragraph to his thesis by beginning with the transition *The main reason* and by repeating the phrase *perform better* from his forecasting statement. He synthesizes information from a variety of sources, and doesn't merely stitch quotations and summary together; rather, he explains how the evidence supports his claim by stating that it "makes sense" that students "apply or 'practice'" what they learn on frequent exams, for example.

Decide whether to quote, paraphrase, or summarize.

As illustrated in O'Malley's paragraph (p. 635), writers integrate supporting evidence by quoting, paraphrasing, or summarizing information or ideas from sources. This section provides guidelines for deciding when to use each of these three methods and how to quote, paraphrase, and summarize effectively. Note that all examples in this section follow MLA style for in-text citations, which is explained in detail in Chapter 24.

As a rule, quote only in these situations:

- When the wording of the source is particularly memorable or vivid or expresses a technical point you can't rephrase clearly
- When the words of reliable and respected authorities would lend support to your position
- When you wish to cite an author whose opinions challenge or vary greatly from those of other experts
- When you are going to discuss the source's choice of words

Paraphrase passages whose details you wish to use but whose language is not particularly striking. Summarize any long passages whose main points you wish to record as support for a point you are making.

Copy quotations exactly, or use italics, ellipses, and brackets to indicate changes.

Quotations should duplicate the source exactly, even if they contain spelling errors. Add the notation *sic* (Latin for "thus") in brackets immediately after any such error to indicate that it is not your error but your source's. As long as you signal them appropriately, you may make changes to

- emphasize particular words;
- omit irrelevant information;
- insert information necessary for clarity;
- make the quotation conform grammatically to your sentence.

Using Italics for Emphasis   You may italicize any words in the quotation that you want to emphasize; add a semicolon and the words *emphasis added* (in regular type, not italicized or underlined) to the parenthetical citation:

> In her 2001 exposé of the struggles of the working class, Ehrenreich writes, "The wages Winn-Dixie is offering--*$6 and a couple of dimes to start with*--are not enough, I decide, to compensate for this indignity" (14; emphasis added).

Using Ellipsis Marks for Omissions You may decide to omit words from a quotation because they are not relevant to the point you are making. When you omit words from within a quotation, use **ellipses**—three spaced periods (. . .)—in place of the missing words. When the omission occurs within a sentence, include a space before the first ellipsis mark and after the last mark:

> Hermione Roddice is described in Lawrence's *Women in Love* as a "woman of the new school, full of intellectuality and . . . nerve-worn with consciousness" (17).

When the omission falls at the end of a sentence, place a period *directly after* the final word of the sentence, followed by a space and three spaced ellipsis marks:

> But Grimaldi's commentary contends that for Aristotle rhetoric, like dialectic, had "no limited and unique subject matter upon which it must be exercised. . . . Instead, rhetoric as an art transcends all specific disciplines and may be brought into play in them" (6).

A period plus ellipses can indicate the omission not just of the rest of a sentence but also of whole sentences, paragraphs, or even pages.

When a parenthetical reference follows the ellipses at the end of a sentence, place the three spaced periods after the quotation, and place the sentence period after the final parenthesis:

> But Grimaldi's commentary contends that for Aristotle rhetoric, like dialectic, had "no limited and unique subject matter upon which it must be exercised. . . . Instead, rhetoric as an art transcends all specific disciplines . . ." (6).

When you quote only single words or phrases, you do not need to use ellipses because it will be obvious that you have left out some of the original:

> More specifically, Wharton's imagery of suffusing brightness transforms Undine before her glass into "some fabled creature whose home was in a beam of light" (21).

For the same reason, you need not use ellipses if you omit the beginning of a quoted sentence unless the rest of the sentence begins with a capitalized word and appears to be a complete sentence.

Using Brackets for Insertions or Changes Use brackets around an insertion or a change needed to make a quotation conform grammatically to your sentence, such as a change in the form of a verb or pronoun or in the capitalization of the first word of the quotation. In this example from an essay on James Joyce's short story "Araby," the writer adapts Joyce's phrases "we played till our bodies glowed" and "shook music from the buckled harness" to fit the grammar of her sentences:

> In the dark, cold streets during the "short days of winter," the boys must generate their own heat by "play[ing] till [their] bodies glowed." Music is "[shaken] from the buckled harness" as if it were unnatural, and the singers in the market chant nasally of "the troubles in our native land" (30).

You may also use brackets to add or substitute explanatory material in a quotation:

> Guterson notes that among Native Americans in Florida, "education was in the home; learning by doing was reinforced by the myths and legends which repeated the basic value system of their [the Seminoles'] way of life" (159).

Some changes that make a quotation conform grammatically to another sentence may be made without any signal to readers:

- A period at the end of a quotation may be changed to a comma if you are using the quotation within your own sentence.
- Double quotation marks enclosing a quotation may be changed to single quotation marks when the quotation is enclosed within a longer quotation.

Adjusting the Punctuation within Quotations   Although punctuation within a quotation should reproduce the original, some adaptations may be necessary. Use single quotation marks for quotations within the quotation:

Original from David Guterson's *Family Matters* (pp. 16–17)	**Quoted Version**
E. D. Hirsch also recognizes the connection between family and learning, suggesting in his discussion of family background and academic achievement "that the significant part of our children's education has been going on outside rather than inside the schools."	Guterson claims that E. D. Hirsch "also recognizes the connection between family and learning, suggesting in his discussion of family background and academic achievement 'that the significant part of our children's education has been going on outside rather than inside the schools' " (16-17).

If the quotation ends with a question mark or an exclamation point, retain the original punctuation:

> "Did you think I loved you?" Edith later asks Dombey (566).

If a quotation ending with a question mark or an exclamation point concludes your sentence, retain the question mark or exclamation point, and put the parenthetical reference and sentence period outside the quotation marks:

> Edith later asks Dombey, "Did you think I loved you?" (566).

Avoiding Grammatical Tangles   When you incorporate quotations into your writing, and especially when you omit words from quotations, you run the risk of creating ungrammatical sentences. Avoid these three common errors:

- Verb incompatibility
- Ungrammatical omissions
- Sentence fragments

Verb incompatibility occurs when the verb form in the introductory statement is grammatically incompatible with the verb form in the quotation. When your quotation has a verb form that does not fit in with your text, it is usually possible to use just part of the quotation, thus avoiding verb incompatibility:

▶ The narrator suggests his bitter disappointment when "~~I saw myself~~ *he describes seeing himself "* as a creature

driven and derided by vanity" (35).

As this sentence illustrates, use the present tense when you refer to events in a literary work.

Ungrammatical omissions may occur when you delete text from a quotation. To avoid this problem, try adapting the quotation (with brackets) so that its parts fit together grammatically, or use only one part of the quotation:

▶ From the moment of the boy's arrival in Araby, the bazaar is presented as a

commercial enterprise: "I could not find any sixpenny entrance and . . .

hand[ed]
~~hand~~ing a shilling to a weary-looking man" (34).

▶ From the moment of the boy's arrival in Araby, the bazaar is presented as a

He "
commercial enterprise: "~~I~~ could not find any sixpenny entrance ~~and~~ "

so he had to pay a shilling to get in
~~. . . handing a shilling to a weary-looking man~~" (34).

Sentence fragments sometimes result when writers forget to include a verb in the sentence introducing a quotation, especially when the quotation itself is a complete sentence. Make sure you introduce a quotation with a complete sentence:

leads
▶ The girl's interest in the bazaar ~~leading~~ the narrator to make what amounts to a sacred

oath: "If I go . . . I will bring you something" (32).

Use in-text or block quotations.

Depending on its length, you may incorporate a quotation into your text by enclosing it in quotation marks or by setting it off from your text in a block without quotation marks. In either case, be sure to integrate the quotation into your essay using the strategies described here:

In-Text Quotations   Incorporate brief quotations (no more than four typed lines of prose or three lines of poetry) into your text. You may place a quotation virtually anywhere in your sentence:

At the Beginning

"To live a life is not to cross a field," Sutherland, quoting Pasternak, writes at the beginning of her narrative (11).

In the Middle

Woolf begins and ends by speaking of the need of the woman writer to have "money and a room of her own" (4)--an idea that certainly spoke to Plath's condition.

At the End

In *The Second Sex*, Simone de Beauvoir describes such an experience as one in which the girl "becomes an object, and she sees herself as object" (378).

Divided by Your Own Words

"Science usually prefers the literal to the nonliteral term," Kinneavy writes, "--that is, figures of speech are often out of place in science" (177).

When you quote poetry within your text, use a slash (/) with spaces before and after to signal the end of each line of verse:

Alluding to St. Augustine's distinction between the City of God and the Earthly City, Lowell writes that "much against my will / I left the City of God where [faith] belongs" (4-5).

Block Quotations In MLA style, use the block form for prose quotations of five or more typed lines and for poetry quotations of four or more lines. Indent the quotation an inch from the left margin, as shown in the following example:

In "A Literary Legacy from Dunbar to Baraka," Margaret Walker says of Paul Lawrence Dunbar's dialect poems:

> He realized that the white world in the United States tolerated his literary genius only because of his "jingles in a broken tongue," and they found the old "darky" tales and speech amusing and within the vein of folklore into which they wished to classify all Negro life. This troubled Dunbar because he realized that white America was denigrating him as a writer and as a man. (70)

In APA style, use block form for quotations of forty words or more. Indent the block quotation half an inch.

In a block quotation, double-space between lines just as you do in your text. *Do not* enclose the passage within quotation marks. Use a colon to introduce a block quotation unless the context calls for another punctuation mark or none at all. When quoting a single paragraph or part of one in MLA style, do not indent the first line of the quotation more than the rest. In quoting two or more paragraphs, indent the first line of each paragraph an extra quarter inch. If you are using APA style, indent the first line of subsequent paragraphs in the block quotation an additional half inch from the indention of the block quotation.

Note that in MLA style the parenthetical page reference follows the period in block quotations.

Use punctuation to integrate quotations into your writing.

Statements that introduce in-text quotations take a range of punctuation marks and lead-in words. Here are some examples of ways writers typically introduce quotations:

Introducing a Quotation Using a Colon   A colon usually follows an independent clause placed before the quotation:

> As George Williams notes, protection of white privilege is critical to patterns of discrimination: "Whenever a number of persons within a society have enjoyed for a considerable period of time certain opportunities for getting wealth, for exercising power and authority, and for successfully claiming prestige and social deference, there is a strong tendency for these people to feel that these benefits are theirs 'by right'" (727).

Introducing a Quotation Using a Comma   A comma usually follows an introduction that incorporates the quotation in its sentence structure:

> Similarly, Duncan Turner asserts, "As matters now stand, it is unwise to talk about communication without some understanding of Burke" (259).

Introducing a Quotation Using *That*   No punctuation is generally needed with *that*, and no capital letter is used to begin the quotation:

> Noting this failure, Alice Miller asserts that "the reason for her despair was not her suffering but the impossibility of communicating her suffering to another person" (255).

Paraphrase sources carefully.

In a **paraphrase**, the writer restates in his or her own words all the relevant information from a passage, without any additional comments or any suggestion of agreement or disagreement with the source's ideas. A paraphrase is useful for recording details of the passage when the source's wording is not important. Because all the details of the passage are included, a paraphrase is often about the same length as the original passage. It is better to paraphrase than to quote ordinary material in which the author's way of expressing things is not worth special attention.

Here is a passage from a book on home schooling and an example of an acceptable paraphrase of it:

Original Source

Bruner and the discovery theorists have also illuminated conditions that apparently pave the way for learning. It is significant that these conditions are unique to each learner, so unique, in fact, that in many cases classrooms can't provide them. Bruner also contends that the more one discovers information in a great variety of circumstances, the more likely one is to develop the inner categories required to organize that information. Yet life at school, which is for the most part generic and predictable, daily keeps many children from the great variety of circumstances they need to learn well.

—David Guterson, *Family Matters: Why Homeschooling Makes Sense*, p. 172

Acceptable Paraphrase

According to Guterson, the "discovery theorists," particularly Bruner, have found that there seem to be certain conditions that help learning take place. Because individuals require different conditions, many children are not able to learn in the classroom. According to Bruner, when people can explore information in many different situations, they learn to classify and order what they discover. The general routine of the school day, however, does not provide children with the diverse activities and situations that would allow them to learn these skills (172).

The highlighting shows that some words in the paraphrase were taken from the source. Indeed, it would be nearly impossible for paraphrasers to avoid using any key terms from the source, and it would be counterproductive to try to do so, because the original and the paraphrase necessarily share the same information and concepts. Notice, though, that of the total of eighty-five words in the paraphrase, the paraphraser uses only a name (*Bruner*) and a few other key nouns and verbs for which it would be awkward to substitute other words or phrases. If the paraphraser had wanted to use other, more distinctive language from the source—for example, the description of life at school as "generic and predictable"—these adjectives would need to be enclosed in quotation marks. In fact, the paraphraser puts quotation marks around only one of the terms from the source: "discovery theorists"—a technical term likely to be unfamiliar to readers.

Paraphrasers must, however, avoid borrowing too many words and repeating the sentence structures from a source. Here is an unacceptable paraphrase of the first sentence in the Guterson passage:

Unacceptable Paraphrase: Too Many Borrowed Words and Phrases

Repeated phrase

Repeated words

Apparently, some conditions, which have been illuminated by Bruner and other discovery theorists, pave the way for people to learn.

Here, the paraphrase borrows almost all of its key language from the source sentence, including the entire phrase *pave the way for*. Even if you cite the source, this heavy borrowing would be considered plagiarism.

Here is another unacceptable paraphrase of the same sentence:

Unacceptable Paraphrase: Sentence Structure Repeated Too Closely

Bruner and other *researchers* have also *identified circumstances* that *seem to ease the path* to learning.

Repeated words

Synonyms

Repeated sentence structure

If you compare the source's first sentence and this paraphrase of it, you will see that the paraphraser has borrowed the phrases and clauses of the source and arranged them in an almost identical sequence, simply substituting synonyms for most of the key terms. This paraphrase would also be considered plagiarism.

Write summaries that present the source's main ideas in a balanced and readable way.

Unlike a paraphrase, a **summary** presents only the main ideas of a source, leaving out examples and details.

For more about how to summarize, see Chapter 5.

Here is one student's summary of five pages from Guterson's book *Family Matters*. You can see at a glance how drastically summaries can condense information, in this case from five pages to five sentences. Depending on the summarizer's purpose, the five pages could be summarized in one sentence, the five sentences here, or two or three dozen sentences.

> In looking at different theories of learning that discuss individual-based programs (such as home schooling) versus the public school system, Guterson describes the disagreements among "cognitivist" theorists. One group, the "discovery theorists," believes that individual children learn by creating their own ways of sorting the information they take in from their experiences. Schools should help students develop better ways of organizing new material, not just present them with material that is already categorized, as traditional schools do. "Assimilationist theorists," by contrast, believe that children learn by linking what they don't know to information they already know. These theorists claim that traditional schools help students learn when they present information in ways that allow children to fit the new material into categories they have already developed (171-75).

Summaries like this one are more than a dry list of main ideas from a source. They are instead a coherent, readable new text composed of the source's main ideas. Summaries provide balanced coverage of a source, following the same sequence of ideas and avoiding any hint of agreement or disagreement with them.

24

Citing and Documenting Sources in MLA Style

When using the MLA system of documentation, include both an in-text citation and a list of works cited. **In-text citations** tell your readers where the ideas or words you have borrowed come from, and the entries in the **works-cited list** allow readers to locate your sources so that they can read more about your topic.

In most cases, include the author's last name and the page number on which the borrowed material appears in the text of your research project. You can incorporate this information in two ways:

SIGNAL PHRASE By naming the author in the text of your research project with a signal phrase (*Simon described*) and including the page reference (in parentheses) at the end of the borrowed passage:

author's last name   *appropriate verb*

> Simon, a well-known figure in New York literary society, described the impression Dr. James made on her as a child in the Bronx: He was a "not-too-skeletal Ichabod Crane" (68).

page number

PARENTHETICAL CITATION By including the author's name and the page number together in parentheses at the end of the borrowed passage:

author's last name + page number

> Dr. James is described as a "not-too-skeletal Ichabod Crane" (Simon 68).

WORKS-CITED ENTRY Simon, Kate. "Birthing." *Bronx Primitive: Portraits in a Childhood.* New York: Viking, 1982. 68-77. Print.

In most cases, you will want to use a *signal phrase* because doing so lets you put your source in context. The signal-phrase-plus-page-reference combination also allows you to make crystal clear where the source information begins and ends. Use a parenthetical citation alone when you have already identified the author or when citing the source of an uncontroversial fact.

The in-text citation should include as much information as is needed to lead readers to the source in your list of works cited and allow them to find the passage you are citing in that source. In most cases, that means the author's last name and the page number on which the borrowed material appears. In some cases, you may need to include other information in your in-text citation (such as a brief version of the title if the author is unnamed or if you cite more than one work by this author). In a few cases, you may not be able to include a page reference, as, for example, when you cite a Web site. In such cases, you may include other identifying information, such as a paragraph number or section heading.

The most common types of in-text citations follow. For other, less common citation types, consult the *MLA Handbook for Writers of Research Papers,* Seventh Edition. Most libraries will own a copy. If the handbook does not provide a model citation, use the information here to create a citation that will lead your readers to the source. (Citation managers like *EndNote* and *RefWorks* will format your citations in MLA style, but check them carefully, as the software sometimes makes errors.)

Citing Sources in the Text
Directory to In-Text-Citation Models

One author   When citing most works with a single author, include the author's name (usually the last name is enough*) and the page number on which the cited material appears.

author's last name + appropriate verb   *page number*

SIGNAL PHRASE   Simon describes Dr. James as a "not-too-skeletal Ichabod Crane" (68).

author's last name + page number

PARENTHETICAL CITATION   Dr. James is described as a "not-too-skeletal Ichabod Crane" (Simon 68).

---

* But see entries for "Two or more works by the same author," "Two or more authors with the same last name," and "Work without page numbers or a one-page work" on pp. 646, 647, and 648.

author's name

BLOCK QUOTATION   In Kate Simon's story "Birthing," the description of Dr. James captures both his physical appearance and his role in the community:

> He looked so much like a story character—the gentled Scrooge of a St. Nicholas Magazine Christmas issue, a not-too-skeletal Ichabod Crane. . . . Dr. James was, even when I knew him as a child, quite an old man, retired from a prestigious and lucrative practice in Boston. . . . His was a prosperous intellectual family, the famous New England Jameses that produced William and Henry, but to the older Bronx doctors, *the* James was the magnificent old driven scarecrow. (68)

page number

(A works-cited entry for "Birthing" appears on page 644.)

More than one author   To cite a source by two or three authors, include all the authors' last names. To cite a source with four or more authors, model your in-text citation on the entry in your works-cited list: Use either all the authors' names or just the first author's name followed by *et al.* ("and others" in Latin, not italicized).

SIGNAL PHRASE   Dyal, Corning, and Willows (1975) identify several types of students, including the "Authority-Rebel" (4).

PARENTHETICAL CITATION   The Authority-Rebel "tends to see himself as superior to other students in the class" (Dyal, Corning, and Willows 4).

The drug AZT has been shown to reduce the risk of transmission from HIV-positive mothers to their infants by as much as two-thirds (Van de Perre et al. 4-5).

Unknown author   If the author's name is unknown, use a shortened version of the title, beginning with the word by which the title is alphabetized in the works-cited list.

An international pollution treaty still to be ratified would prohibit ships from dumping plastic at sea ("Plastic Is Found" 68).

The full title of the work is "Plastic Is Found in the Sargasso Sea; Pieces of Apparent Refuse Cover Wide Atlantic Region."

Two or more works by the same author   If you cite more than one work by the same author, include a shortened version of the title.

When old paint becomes transparent, it sometimes shows the artist's original plans: "a tree will show through a woman's dress" (Hellman, *Pentimento* 1).

Two or more authors with the same last name   When citing works by authors with the same last name, include each author's first name in the signal phrase or first initial in the parenthetical citation.

> Chaplin's *Modern Times* uses montage to make an editorial statement (E. Roberts 246).

Corporation, organization, or government agency as author   In a signal phrase, use the full name of the corporation, organization, or government agency. In a parenthetical citation, use the full name if it is brief or a shortened version if it is long.

SIGNAL PHRASE   The Washington State Board for Community and Technical Colleges will raise tuition to offset budget deficits from Initiative 601 (4).

PARENTHETICAL CITATION   A tuition increase has been proposed for community and technical colleges to offset budget deficits from Initiative 601 (WA State Board 4).

Literary work (novel, play, poem)   Provide information that will help readers find the passage you are citing no matter what edition of the novel, play, or poem they are using. In a signal phrase, spell out titles; in a parenthetical citation, abbreviate famous works. For a novel or other prose work, provide the part or chapter number as well as the page numbers from the edition you used.

NOVEL OR OTHER PROSE WORK   In *Hard Times,* Tom reveals his utter narcissism by blaming Louisa for his own failure: "'You have regularly given me up. You never cared for me'" (Dickens 262; bk. 3, ch. 9).

For a play in verse, use act, scene, and line numbers instead of page numbers.

PLAY (IN VERSE)   At the beginning, Regan's fawning rhetoric hides her true attitude toward Lear: "I profess / myself an enemy to all other joys . . . / And find that I am alone felicitate / In your dear highness' love" (*Lr.* 1.1.74-75, 77-78).

For a poem, indicate the line numbers and stanzas or sections (if they are numbered) instead of page numbers.

POEM   In "Song of Myself," Whitman finds poetic details in busy urban settings, as when he describes "the blab of the pave, tires of carts . . . the driver with his interrogating thumb" (8.153-54).

If the source gives only line numbers, use the term *lines* in your first citation and use only the numbers in subsequent citations.

> In "Before you thought of spring," Dickinson at first identifies the spirit of spring with a bird, possibly a robin--"A fellow in the skies / Inspiriting habiliments / Of indigo and brown" (lines 4, 7-8)--but by the end of the poem, she has linked it with poetry and perhaps even the poet herself, as the bird, like Dickinson "shouts for joy to nobody / But his seraphic self!" (15-16).

Work in an anthology   Use the name of the author of the work, not the editor of the anthology, in your in-text citation.

SIGNAL PHRASE
> In "Six Days: Some Rememberings," Grace Paley recalls that when she was in jail for protesting the Vietnam War, her pen and paper were taken away and she felt "a terrible pain in the area of my heart--a nausea" (191).

PARENTHETICAL CITATION
> Writers may have a visceral reaction--"a nausea" (Paley 191)-- to being deprived of access to writing implements.

Religious work   In your first citation, include the element that begins your entry in the works-cited list, such as the edition name of the religious work you are citing (see p. 653), and include the book or section name (using standard abbreviations in parenthetical citations) and any chapter or verse numbers.

> She ignored the admonition "Pride goes before destruction, and a haughty spirit before a fall" (*New Oxford Annotated Bible,* Prov. 16.18).

Multivolume work (one volume, more than one volume)   If you cite only one volume of a multivolume work, treat the in-text citation as you would any other work, but include the volume number in the works-cited entry (see p. 654).

ONE VOLUME
> Forster argued that modernist writers valued experimentation and gradually sought to blur the line between poetry and prose (150).

When you use two or more volumes of a multivolume work, include the volume number and the page number(s) in your in-text citation.

MORE THAN ONE VOLUME
> Modernist writers valued experimentation and gradually sought to blur the line between poetry and prose (Forster 3: 150).

Indirect citation (quotation from a secondary source)   If possible, locate the original source and cite that. If not possible, name the original source but also include the secondary source in which you found the material you are citing, plus the abbreviation *qtd. in.* Include the secondary source in your list of works cited.

> E. M. Forster says, "the collapse of all civilization, so realistic for us, sounded in Matthew Arnold's ears like a distant and harmonious cataract" (qtd. in Trilling 11).

Entire work   Include the reference in the text without any page numbers or parentheses.

> In *The Structure of Scientific Revolutions,* Thomas Kuhn discusses how scientists change their thinking.

Work without page numbers or a one-page work (with/without other section numbers)
If a work (such as a Web page) has no page numbers or is only one page long, omit the page number. If it uses screen numbers or paragraph numbers, insert a comma after the author's name, an identifying term (such as *screen*) or abbreviation (*par.* or *pars.*), and the number.

WITHOUT PAGE OR OTHER NUMBERS	The average speed on Montana's interstate highways, for example, has risen by only 2 miles per hour since the repeal of the federal speed limit, with most drivers topping out at 75 (Schmid).
WITH OTHER SECTION NUMBERS	Whitman considered African American speech "a source of a native grand opera" (Ellison, par. 13).

Two or more works cited in the same parentheses   If you cite two or more sources for a piece of information, include them in alphabetical order in the same parentheses, separated by semicolons.

> A few studies have considered differences between oral and written discourse production (Gould; Scardamalia, Bereiter, and Goelman).

Creating a List of Works Cited

Directory to Works-Cited-List Models

Format your list of works cited.

In your MLA-style research paper, every source you cite must have a corresponding entry in the list of works cited, and every entry in your list of works cited must correspond to at least one citation in your research project.

Follow these rules when formatting your list of works cited in MLA style:

- On a new page, type "Works Cited" (centered), and double-space the whole works-cited list.

- Alphabetize entries by the first word in the citation (usually the first author's last name, or the title if the author is unknown, ignoring *A, An,* or *The*).

- Use a "hanging indent" for all entries: Do not indent the first line, but indent second and subsequent lines of the entry by half an inch (or five spaces).

- Shorten publishers' names: Abbreviate compound or hyphenated names to the first name only (*Bedford/St. Martin's* becomes *Bedford,* for example); omit words like *Company* or *Books*; and for university presses, shorten the words *University* and *Press* to *U* and *P.*

Cite all sources, regardless of medium.

Nowadays, many print sources are also available in an electronic format, either online or through a database your school's library subscribes to. For most online versions of a source, follow the form of the corresponding print version. For example, if you are citing an article from an online periodical, put the article title in quotation marks and italicize the name of the periodical. If the source has also been published in print (as with most e-books and many magazines and newspapers that appear online), include the print publication information if it is available. Also include information specific to the version of the source you used.

For sources accessed through a database, include the following:

- Title of the database (in italics)
- Medium of publication (*Web*)
- Date you last accessed the source

For other online sources, include the following:

- Title of the Web site (in italics)
- Version or edition used (if any)
- Publisher or sponsor of the site; if not available, use *n.p.*
- Date of publication or last update; if not available, use *n.d.*
- Medium of publication (*Web*)
- Date you last accessed the source

Content on the Web frequently changes or disappears, and because the same information that traditionally published books and periodicals provide is not always included for Web sources, giving your reader a complete citation is not always possible. Always keep your goal in mind: to provide enough information so that your reader can track down the source. If you cannot find all of the information listed here, include what you can.

Author Listings

One author   List the author last name first (followed by a comma), and insert a period at the end of the name.

> Isaacson, Walter.

Two or three authors   List the first author last name first (followed by a comma). List the other authors in the usual first-name/last-name order. Insert the word *and* before the last author's name, and follow it with a period.

> Saba, Laura, and Julie Gattis.

> Wilmut, Ian, Keith Campbell, and Colin Tudge.

Four or more authors   List the first author last name first (followed by a comma). Then either list all the authors' names (in the usual first-name/last-name order, with a comma between authors, the word *and* before the last name, and a period after it) *or* insert *et al.* (which means *and others* in Latin) in regular type (not italics). Whichever you decide to do, be sure to use the same format in your in-text citation.

> Hunt, Lynn, Thomas R. Martin, Barbara H. Rosenwein, R. Po-chia Hsia,
>   and Bonnie G. Smith.

> Hunt, Lynn, et al.

Unknown author   Begin the entry with the title.

> *Primary Colors: A Novel of Politics.*

> "Out of Sight."

Corporation, organization, or government agency as author   Use the name of the corporation, organization, or government agency as the author.

> RAND Corporation.

> United States. Natl. Commission on Terrorist Attacks.

Two or more works by the same author   Replace the author's name in subsequent entries with three hyphens, and alphabetize the works by the first important word in the title:

> Eugenides, Jeffrey. *The Marriage Plot.*

> ---. *Middlesex.*

> ---. "Walkabout."

Books (Print, Electronic, Database)

Basic format

PRINT

Author, last name first — *Title (and subtitle, if any), italicized* — *Publication info* — *Medium*

Eugenides, Jeffrey. *The Marriage Plot.* New York: Farrar, 2011. Print.

City of publication — *Publisher (abbreviated)* — *Year of publication*

E-BOOK

Print publication info — *Medium*

Eugenides, Jeffrey. *The Marriage Plot.* New York: Farrar, 2011. Kindle e-book file.

DATABASE

Print publication info — *Database name, italicized*

Whitman, Walt. *Leaves of Grass.* Philadelphia: McKay, 1900. *Bartleby.com.*
Web. 28 Nov. 2011.

Medium   Access date

Figure 24.1 (p. 653) shows you where to find the source information you will need to create a works-cited entry for a book.

Anthology or edited collection   If you are referring to the anthology as a whole, put the editor's name first.

> Masri, Heather, ed. *Science Fiction: Stories and Contexts.* Boston: Bedford, 2009. Print.

Work in an anthology or edited collection   If you're referring to a selection in an anthology, begin the entry with the name of the selection's author.

> Hopkinson, Nalo. "Something to Hitch Meat To." *Science Fiction: Stories and Contexts.* Ed. Heather Masri. Boston: Bedford, 2009. 838-50. Print.

If you cite more than one selection from an anthology or collection, you may create an entry for the collection as a whole (see the model above) and then cross-reference individual selections to that entry.

Selection author — *Selection title* — *Anthology editor*

Hopkinson, Nalo. "Something to Hitch Meat To." Masri 838-50. Print.

Selection pages in anthology

Introduction, preface, foreword, or afterword

> Murfin, Ross C. Introduction. *Heart of Darkness.* By Joseph Conrad. 3rd ed. Boston: Bedford, 2011. 3-16. Print.

Translation

> Tolstoy, Leo. *War and Peace.* Trans. Richard Pevear and Larissa Volokhonsky. New York: Vintage, 2009. Print.

Graphic narrative   If the graphic narrative was a collaboration between a writer and an illustrator, begin your entry with the name of the person on whose work your research project focuses. If the author also created the illustrations, then follow the basic model for a book with one author (p. 652).

> Pekar, Harvey, and Joyce Brabner. *Our Cancer Year*. Illus. Frank Stack. New York: Four Walls Eight Windows, 1994. Print.

Religious work   Include an entry in the list of works cited only if you cite a specific edition of a sacred text.

> *The Qu'ran: English Translation and Parallel Arabic Text*. Trans. M. A. S. Abdel Haleem. New York: Oxford UP, 2010. Print.

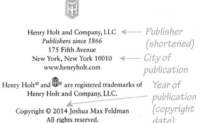

FIGURE 24.1   Documentation Map for a Book

Look for the author, title, publisher, and city of publication on the title page (at the front of the book) and the year of publication (or copyright date) on the copyright page (usually on the back of the title page in print books). The title page and copyright page may appear in a different location or look a little different in an e-book or a book accessed through a database, but the information provided should be the same.

Multivolume work   If you use only one volume from a multivolume work, indicate the volume number after the title. If you use more than one volume, indicate the total number of volumes after the title.

One volume cited

Sandburg, Carl. *Abraham Lincoln*. Vol. 2. New York: Scribner's, 1939. Print. 6 vols.

More than one volume cited

Sandburg, Carl. *Abraham Lincoln*. 6 vols. New York: Scribner's, 1939. Print.

Later edition of a book   Include the edition name (such as *Revised*) or number following the title.

Rottenberg, Annette T., and Donna Haisty Winchell. *The Structure of Argument*. 6th ed. Boston: Bedford, 2009. Print.

Republished book   Provide the original year of publication after the title of the book, followed by publication information for the edition you are using.

Original publication date

Alcott, Louisa May. *An Old-Fashioned Girl*. 1870. New York: Puffin, 1995. Print.

Republication information

Title within a title   When a title that is normally italicized appears within a book title, do not italicize it. If the title within the title would normally be enclosed in quotation marks, include the quotation marks and also set the title in italics.

Hertenstein, Mike. *The Double Vision of* Star Trek: *Half-Humans, Evil Twins, and Science Fiction*. Chicago: Cornerstone, 1998. Print.

Miller, Edwin Haviland. *Walt Whitman's "Song of Myself": A Mosaic of Interpretation*. Iowa City: U of Iowa P, 1989. Print.

Book in a series   Include the series title and number (if any) after the medium of publication. If the word *Series* is part of the name, include the abbreviation *Ser.* before the series number. (This information will appear on the title page or on the page facing the title page.) Abbreviate any commonly abbreviated words in the series title.

Zigova, Tanya, et al. *Neural Stem Cells: Methods and Protocols*. Totowa: Humana, 2002. Print. Methods in Molecular Biology 198.

Dictionary entry or article in another reference book   If no author is listed, begin with the entry's title. (But check for initials following the entry or article and a list of authors in the front of the book.) If the reference work is familiar, omit the publication information.

PRINT   "Homeopathy." *Webster's New World College Dictionary*. 4th ed. 1999. Print.

PRINT   Trenear-Harvey, Glenmore S. "Farm Hall." *Historical Dictionary of Atomic Espionage.*
Lanham: Scarecrow, 2011. Print.

Web site (italics)   *Site sponsor*   *Medium*

ONLINE   "Homeopathy." *Merriam-Webster.com.* Merriam-Webster, Inc., 2011. Web.
29 Nov. 2011.

Access date

DATABASE   Powell, Jason L. "Power Elite." *Blackwell Encyclopedia of Sociology*. Ed. George
Ritzer. Wiley-Blackwell, 2007. *Blackwell Reference Online.* Web. 29 Nov. 2011.

Database (italics)   *Medium*   *Access date*

Government document   If no author is named, begin with the government and agency
that issued the document. If the author is named, include that information either before
or after the document's title (introduced with the word *By*). In the United States, the
publication information for most print government documents is *Washington: GPO. (GPO*
stands for *Government Printing Office.*) But most government documents are now published
online.

Issuing government   *Issuing department*

PRINT   United States. Dept. of Health and Human Services. *Trends in Underage*
Drinking in the United States, 1991-2007. By Gabriella Newes-Adeyi et al.
Washington: GPO, 2009. Print.   *Authors*

Issuing agency

ONLINE   United States. Centers for Disease Control. "Youth Risk Behavior Surveillance—
United States, 2009." *Morbidity and Mortality Weekly Report.*
Centers for Disease Control. Dept. of Health and Human Services,

Web site (italics)   *Site sponsor*

4 June 2010. Web. 30 Nov. 2011.

Publication date   Medium   Access date

Published proceedings of a conference   If the name of the conference is part of the
title of the publication, it need not be repeated. If it isn't part of the title, insert the
name of the conference following the title. Use the format for a work in an anthology
(p. 652) to cite an individual presentation.

Conference name included in title

Duffett, John, ed. *Against the Crime of Silence: Proceedings of the International War Crimes*
Tribunal. Nov. 1967, Stockholm. New York: Clarion-Simon, 1970. Print.

Pamphlet or brochure

U.S. Foundation for Boating Safety and Clean Water. *Hypothermia and Cold Water Survival.*
Alexandria: U.S. Foundation for Boating, 2001. Print.

Doctoral dissertation　Cite a published dissertation as you would a book, but add pertinent dissertation information before the publication data. Enclose the title of an unpublished dissertation in quotation marks.

Title in italics

PUBLISHED　　　Jones, Anna Maria. *Problem Novels/Perverse Readers: Late-Victorian Fiction and the Perilous Pleasures of Identification*. Diss. U of Notre Dame, 2001. Ann Arbor: UMI, 2001. Print.

Dissertation information

Title in quotation marks

UNPUBLISHED　　Bullock, Barbara. "Basic Needs Fulfillment among Less Developed Countries: Social Progress over Two Decades of Growth." Diss. Vanderbilt U, 1986. Print.

Dissertation information

Articles (Print, Online, Database)

Articles appear in periodicals—works that are issued at regular intervals such as scholarly journals, newspapers, and magazines. Most periodicals today are available both in print and in electronic form (online or through an electronic database); some are available only in electronic format. If you are using the online version of an article, use the models provided here. If no model matches your source exactly, choose the closest print match, and add the site sponsor, the medium, and the date you last accessed the site, along with any other information your reader will need to track down the source.

For help distinguishing between scholarly journals and magazines, see Chapter 22.

From a scholarly journal　Scholarly journals are typically identified using their volume and issue numbers, separated by a period. If a journal does not use volume numbers, provide the issue number only. Online journals may not include page numbers; if paragraph or other section numbers are provided, use them instead. Otherwise, insert *n. pag.* (for *no page numbers*). If an article in a printed journal is not on a continuous sequence of pages, give the first page number followed by a plus sign. (See entry for a print version of a newspaper for an example.)

Figure 24.2 shows where to find the source information you will need to create a works-cited entry for three of the journal articles cited here.

Author, last name first　　　　　　　　　　　*Article in quotation marks*

PRINT　　　Haas, Heather A. "The Wisdom of Wizards--and Muggles and Squibs: Proverb Use in the World of Harry Potter." *Journal of American Folklore* 124.492 (2011): 29-54. Print.

Date of publication (year)　*Page numbers*　　*Medium*

Garas-York, Keli. "Overlapping Student Environments: An Examination of the Homeschool Connection and Its Impact on Achievement." *Journal of College Admission* 42.4 (2010): 430-49. Print.

Article from Printed Journal

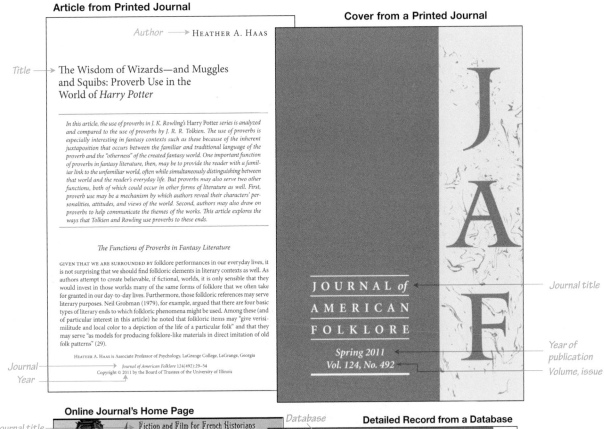

Author → HEATHER A. HAAS

Title → The Wisdom of Wizards—and Muggles and Squibs: Proverb Use in the World of *Harry Potter*

In this article, the use of proverbs in J. K. Rowling's Harry Potter series is analyzed and compared to the use of proverbs by J. R. R. Tolkien. The use of proverbs is especially interesting in fantasy contexts such as these because of the inherent juxtaposition that occurs between the familiar and traditional language of the proverb and the "otherness" of the created fantasy world. One important function of proverbs in fantasy literature, then, may be to provide the reader with a familiar link to the unfamiliar world, often while simultaneously distinguishing between that world and the reader's everyday life. But proverbs may also serve two other functions, both of which could occur in other forms of literature as well. First, proverb use may be a mechanism by which authors reveal their characters' personalities, attitudes, and views of the world. Second, authors may also draw on proverbs to help communicate the themes of the works. This article explores the ways that Tolkien and Rowling use proverbs to these ends.

The Functions of Proverbs in Fantasy Literature

GIVEN THAT WE ARE SURROUNDED BY FOLKLORE performances in our everyday lives, it is not surprising that we should find folkloric elements in literary contexts as well. As authors attempt to create believable, if fictional, worlds, it is only sensible that they would invest in those worlds many of the same forms of folklore that we often take for granted in our day-to-day lives. Furthermore, those folkloric references may serve literary purposes. Neil Grobman (1979), for example, argued that there are four basic types of literary ends to which folkloric phenomena might be used. Among these (and of particular interest in this article) he noted that folkloric items may "give verisimilitude and local color to a depiction of the life of a particular folk" and that they may serve "as models for producing folklore-like materials in direct imitation of old folk patterns" (29).

HEATHER A. HAAS is Associate Professor of Psychology, LaGrange College, LaGrange, Georgia

Journal / *Year* → *Journal of American Folklore* 124(492):29–54
Copyright © 2011 by the Board of Trustees of the University of Illinois

Cover from a Printed Journal

Journal title
JOURNAL *of* AMERICAN FOLKLORE

Year of publication
Spring 2011

Volume, issue
Vol. 124, No. 492

Online Journal's Home Page

Journal title — Fiction and Film for French Historians A Cultural Bulletin

HOME   WHAT IS FFFH?   ISSUE INDEX   AUTHOR INDEX   TITLE INDEX   PREVIOUS ISSUES   BACK TO FRANCE

Volume, issue, year → Volume 5, Issue 6, April 2015
Table of Contents

Author

The Buzz
Waterloo (1970): A Critical Review, by Charles Esdaile

Article title →

Maybe Missed
"When Vice Meets Crime": Jean-Claude Brisville's Le Souper, by Philip Dwyer

Database

Detailed Record from a Database

Article title
The Wisdom of Wizards—and Muggles and Squibs: Proverb Use in the World of Harry Potter.

Authors: HAAS, HEATHER A.

Source: *Journal of American Folklore*, Spring2011, Vol. 124 Issue 492, p29-54, 26p

Publication information: journal, year, volume, issue, page numbers

Document Type: Literary Criticism

Subject Terms: *OTHER (Philosophy) in literature* *PROVERBS in literature* *FANTASY fiction*

Reviews & Products: HARRY Potter book series

People: ROWLING, J. K., 1965– TOLKIEN, J. R. R. (John Ronald Reuel), 1892-1973

Abstract: In this article, the use of proverbs in J. K. Rowling's Harry Potter series is analyzed and compared to the use of proverbs by J. R. R. Tolkien. The use of proverbs is especially interesting in fantasy contexts such as these because of the inherent juxtaposition that occurs between the familiar and traditional language of the proverb and the "otherness" of the created fantasy world. One important function of proverbs in fantasy literature, then, may be to provide the reader with a familiar link to the unfamiliar world, often while simultaneously distinguishing between that world and the reader's everyday life. But proverbs may also serve two other functions, both of which could occur in other forms of literature as well. First, proverb use may be a mechanism by which authors reveal their characters' personalities, attitudes, and views of the world. Second, authors may also draw on proverbs to help communicate the themes of the works. This article explores the ways that Tolkien and Rowling use proverbs to these ends. [ABSTRACT FROM AUTHOR]

Copyright of Journal of American Folklore is the property of University of Illinois Press and its content may not be copied or emailed to multiple sites or posted to a listserv without the copyright holder's express written permission. However, users may print, download, or email articles for individual use. This abstract may be abridged. No warranty is given about the accuracy of the copy. Users should refer to the original published version of the material for the full abstract. (Copyright applies to all Abstracts.)

Author Affiliations: ¹Associate Professor of Psychology, LaGrange College, LaGrange, Georgia.

ISSN: 0021-8715

Accession Number: 63144966

FIGURE 24.2   Documentation Map for a Journal Article   For a print journal, look for the title of the journal on the front cover or in the table of contents. The author and article title will also be listed there; they will, of course, appear on the first page of the article (shown here) as well. The information you will need to cite an article you access through a database will appear in the list of results, the detailed record of the article, and the PDF (or HTML) version of the article itself. For an article published in an electronic journal, look for the information you need to create the works-cited entry on the journal's home page or on the page on which the article appears.

ONLINE   Markel, J. D. "Religious Allegory and Cultural Discomfort in Mike Leigh's
Happy-Go-Lucky: And Why *Larry Crowne* Is One of the Best Films of 2011."
Bright Lights 74 (2011): n. pag. Web. 29 Nov. 2011.

Issue number only   *No page*   *Medium*   *Access date*
numbers

Saho, Bala S. K. "The Appropriation of Islam in a Gambian Village: Life and
Times of Shaykh Mass Kay, 1827-1936. *African Studies Quarterly* 12.4
(2011): n pag. Web. 12 Dec. 2011.

DATABASE   Haas, Heather A. "The Wisdom of Wizards--and Muggles and Squibs: Proverb
Use in the World of *Harry Potter*." *Journal of American Folklore* 124.492
(2011): 29-54. *Academic Search Complete*. Web. 29 Nov. 2011.

Database (italics)

Garas-York, Keli. "Overlapping Student Environments: An Examination of the
Homeschool Connection and Its Impact on Achievement." *Journal of
College Admission* 42.4 (2010): 430-49. *Academic Search Complete*.
Web. 13 Dec. 2011.

From a newspaper   Newspapers are identified by date, not volume and issue
numbers, with the names of months longer than four letters abbreviated. If the article
is from a special edition of the newspaper (*early ed., natl ed.*), include the edition name
after the date. If articles are not on a continuous series of pages, give only the first
page number followed by a plus sign. For unpaginated articles accessed through a
database, use *n. pag.* Notice that the online version of the article was posted before
the print edition was published. The version in the database was from a later edition
of the printed publication.

PRINT   Weisman, Jonathan, and Jennifer Steinhauer. "Patriot Act Faces Revisions Backed
by Both Parties." *New York Times* 1 May 2015: A1+. Print.

Noncontinuous pages

ONLINE   Weisman, Jonathan, and Jennifer Steinhauer. "Patriot Act Faces Revisions Backed
by Both Parties." *New York Times*. New York Times, 30 Apr. 2015. Web.
1 May 2015.   *Web site (italics)*   *Site sponsor*   *Publication date*   *Medium*

Access date

DATABASE   Weisman, Jonathan, and Jennifer Steinhauer. "Patriot Act Faces Revisions
Backed by Both Parties." *New York Times* 1 May 2015, late ed.: A1+.
LexisNexis Academic. Web. 1 May 2015.   *Edition*   *Noncontinuous*
name   *pages*
Database
(italics)

From a magazine   Magazines (like newspapers) are identified by date, with the names
of months longer than four letters abbreviated. For magazines published weekly or

biweekly, include the day, month, and year; for magazines published monthly or bimonthly, include the month and year. If the article is unsigned, alphabetize by the first important word in the title (ignoring *A, An,* and *The*).

Publication date (weekly)

PRINT   Stillman, Sarah. "Where Are the Children?" *New Yorker* 27 Apr. 2015: 40-41. Print.

Publication date (monthly)

Bennet, James. "To Stay or to Go." *Atlantic* Apr. 2015: 8. Print.

Web site (italics)   *Site sponsor*

ONLINE   Bennet, James. "To Stay or to Go." *The Atlantic.com.* Atlantic Monthly Group, Apr. 2015. Web. 2 May 2015.

Medium   *Access date*

DATABASE   Stillman, Sarah. "Where Are the Children?" *New Yorker* 27 Apr. 2015: 40-41. *Academic Search Complete.* Web. 2 May 2015.

Database (italics)   *Medium*   *Access date*

Editorial or letter to the editor

"Stay Classy." Editorial. *New Republic* 1 Dec. 2011: 1. Print.

Wegeiser, Art. "How Does He Know?" Letter. *Pittsburgh Post-Gazette* 30 Nov. 2011: B6. Print.

Review   If the review does not include an author's name, start the entry with the title of the review. If the review is untitled, begin with *Rev. of* and alphabetize under the title of the work being reviewed. For a review in an online newspaper or magazine, add the site sponsor and access date and change the medium to *Web*. For a review accessed through a database, add the database title (in italics) and access date and change the medium to *Web*.

DeParle, Jason. "Immigration Nation." Rev. of *Exodus: How Migration Is Changing Our World*, by Paul Collier. *Atlantic* Nov. 2013: 44-46. Print.

Multimedia Sources (Live, Print, Electronic, Database)

Lecture or public address

Title of lecture   *Conference title*

Stephenson, Brittany. "Wading Out of Web Stew: Reader-Centric Course Design." Conf. on College Composition and Communication. Marriott Waterside, Tampa. 20 Mar. 2015. Lecture.

Location   *Date of lecture*

Medium

Letter   If the letter has been published, treat it like a work in an anthology (p. 652), but add the recipient, the date, and any identifying number after the author's name. If the letter is unpublished, change the medium to *MS* ("manuscript") if written by hand or *TS* ("typescript") if typed.

Sender   Recipient   Date   Medium

DuHamel, Grace. Letter to the author. 22 Mar. 2008. TS.

Map or chart (print, online)

PRINT   *Map of Afghanistan and Surrounding Territory*. Map. Burlington: GiziMap, 2001. Print.

ONLINE   "North America, 1797." Map. *Perry-Castañeda Library Map Collection*. U of Texas at Austin, 1909. Web. 1 Dec. 2011.

Cartoon or comic strip   Provide the title (if given) in quotation marks directly following the artist's name.

PRINT   Wheeler, Shannon. Cartoon. *New Yorker* 11 May 2015: 50. Print.

ONLINE   Hunt, Tarol. "Goblins." Comic strip. *Goblinscomic.com*. Tarol Hunt, 29 Sept. 2011. Web. 30 Nov. 2011.

Advertisement

PRINT   Hospital for Special Surgery. Advertisement. *New York Times* 13 Apr. 2009: A7. Print.

BROADCAST   Norweigian Cruise Line. Advertisement. *WNET.org*. PBS, 29 Apr. 2012. Television.

ONLINE   Volkswagen Passat. Advertisement. *Slate*. Slate Group, 1 Dec. 2011. Web. 1 Dec. 2011.

Work of art   Include the year the work was created, the medium (*Oil on canvas*), and the museum or collection and its location. If the work was accessed online, include the Web site name and your date of access and change the medium to *Web*.

Medium

MUSEUM   Palmer Payne, Elsie. *Sheep Dipping Time*. c. 1930s. Oil on canvas. Nevada Museum of Art, Reno.

Location

PRINT   Chihuly, Dale. *Carmine and White Flower Set*. 1987. Glass. Tacoma Art Museum, Tacoma. New York: Abrams, 2011. 109. Print.

Print publication information

WEB SITE   Sekaer, Peter. *A Sign Business Shop, New York*. 1935. Intl. Center of Photography, New York. *Intl. Center of Photography*. Web. 5 Dec. 2011.

Web site

Medium   Access date

Musical composition

> Beethoven, Ludwig van. Violin Concerto in D Major, Op. 61. 1809. New York: Kalmus, n.d. Print.

> Gershwin, George. *Porgy and Bess*. 1935. New York: Alfred, 1999. Print.

Performance

> *The Agony and the Ecstasy of Steve Jobs*. Writ. and perf. Mike Daisey. Dir. Jean-Michele Gregory. Public Theater, New York. 25 Nov. 2011. Performance.

Television or radio program   Include the network, local station, and broadcast date. Treat a show you streamed as you would a Web page, but include information about key contributors (host or performers, for example) as you would for a broadcast television or radio program. If you downloaded the program as a podcast, include the information as for a broadcast program, but change the medium to match the type of file you accessed (*MP3, JPEG file*).

	Episode *Program* *Key contributors*
BROADCAST	"Being Mortal." *Frontline*. Writ., Atul Gawande and Tom Jennings. Dir. Tom Jennings and Nisha Pahuja. PBS. WNET, New York, 22 Nov. 2011. Television. *Network Local Location Broadcast date* *station*
	Medium
STREAMED	"Being Mortal." *Frontline*. Writ., Atul Gawande and Tom Jennings. Dir. Tom Jennings and Nisha Pahuja. *WNET.org*. PBS, 10 Feb. 2015. Web. 2 May 2015. *Web site Sponsor Post date Medium Access date*
DOWNLOADED	"Patient Zero." *Radio Lab*. Host. Jad Abumrad and Robert Krulwich. Natl. Public Radio. WNYC, New York, 14 Nov. 2011. MP3. *Medium*

Podcast   Treat a podcast you listened to or watched online as you would an online television or radio program (see *Streamed* entry above). Treat a podcast you downloaded as you would a television or radio program you downloaded (see *Downloaded* entry above).

Film

THEATER	*Space Station*. Prod. and dir. Toni Myers. Narr. Tom Cruise. IMAX, 2002. Film.
DVD	*Casablanca*. Dir. Michael Curtiz. Perf. Humphrey Bogart, Ingrid Bergman, and Paul Henreid. 1942. Warner Home Video, 2003. DVD.
STREAMED	*The Social Network*. Dir. David Fincher. Writ. Aaron Sorkin. Perf. Jesse Eisenberg, Justin Timberlake, and Andrew Garfield. Columbia Pictures, 2010. iTunes. Web. 2 May 2015.

Online video

Film School. "Sunny Day." *YouTube*. YouTube, 12 June 2010. Web. 2 May 2015.

Music recording

Beethoven, Ludwig van. Violin Concerto in D Major, Op. 61. Perf. David Oistrakh. U.S.S.R. State Orchestra. Cond. Alexander Gauk. Allegro, 1980. CD.

Maroon 5. "Moves Like Jagger." *Hands All Over*. A&M/Octone Records, 2011. MP3.

Interview   If a personal interview takes place through e-mail, change "Personal interview" to "E-mail interview."

PRINT   Ashrawi, Hanan. "Tanks vs. Olive Branches." Interview by Rose Marie Berger. *Sojourners* Feb. 2005: 22-26. Print.

BROADCAST   Dobbs, Bill. "Occupy Wall Street." Interview by Brooke Gladstone. *On the Media*. Natl. Public Radio. WNYC, New York, 7 Oct. 2011. Web. 1 Dec. 2011.

PERSONAL   Ellis, Trey. Personal interview. 3 Sept. 2015.

Other Electronic Sources

For help evaluating online sources, see Chapter 22.

Online sources have proliferated in the last ten years. With that proliferation has come access to more information than ever before. But not all of that information is of equal value. Before including a source found on *Google* in your research project, be sure that it is appropriate for a college-level writing project, and evaluate its reliability carefully.

If you are using the online version of a source for which there is no model shown here, choose the model that best matches your source, change the medium as appropriate, add the date you last accessed the source, and add any other information that readers will need to find the source themselves.

Web page or other document on a Web site

Author/editor, last name first   *Document title (in quotation marks)*

McGann, Jerome J., ed. "Introduction to the Final Installment of the Rossetti Archive."

Title of site (italicized)

The Complete Writings and Pictures of Dante Gabriel Rossetti: A Hypermedia Archive.

Sponsor   *Publication date/last update*

Inst. for Advanced Technology in the Humanities, U Virginia, 2008. Web.

Access date

16 Oct. 2012.

Figure 24.3 shows where to find the source information you will need to create a works-cited entry for the Web page cited here.

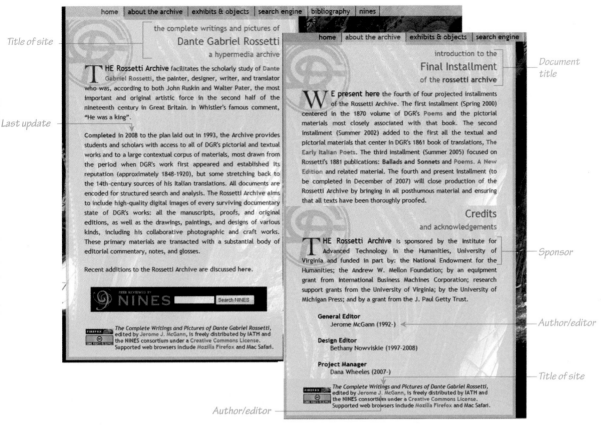

FIGURE 24.3 Documentation Map for a Web Page
Look for the author or editor and title of the Web page on the Web page itself. The title of the Web site may appear on the Web page, on the site's home page, or both. The sponsor may be listed at the bottom of the Web page, on the home page, or somewhere else. (Look for an "About Us," "Who We Are," or "Contact Us" page.) If no publication or copyright date or "last update" appears on the Web page, the home page, or elsewhere on the site, insert *n.d.* in its place.

Entire Web site If the author's name is not given, begin the citation with the title. For an untitled personal site, put a description such as *Home page* where the Web site's title would normally appear (but with no quotation marks or italics). If no site sponsor or publisher is named, insert *n.p.* (for *no publisher*).

Gardner, James Alan. *A Seminar on Writing Prose*. N.p., 2001. Web. 1 Dec. 2011.

The Complete Writings and Pictures of Dante Gabriel Rossetti: A Hypermedia Archive. Ed. Jerome J. McGann. Inst. for Advanced Technology in the Humanities, U Virginia, 2008. Web. 16 Oct. 2012.

Chesson, Frederick W. Home page. N.p., 1 Apr. 2003. Web. 26 Apr. 2015.

Online scholarly project   Treat an online scholarly project as you would a Web site, but include the name of the editor, if given.

> *The Darwin Correspondence Project.* Ed. Janet Browne. Amer. Council of Learned Socs. and
>   U Cambridge, 2015. Web. 2 May 2015.

Book or a short work in an online scholarly project   Treat a book or a short work in an online scholarly project as you would a Web page or another document on a Web site, but set the title in italics if the work is a book and in quotation marks if it is an article, essay, poem, or other short work, and include the print publication information (if any) following the title.

> Heims, Marjorie. "The Strange Case of Sarah Jones." *The Free Expression Policy Project.*
>   FEPP, 2 Nov. 2011. Web. 1 Dec. 2011.

Original publication information

> Corelli, Marie. *The Treasure of Heaven.* London: Constable, 1906. *Victorian Women Writers*
>   *Project.* Ed. Percy Willett. Indiana U, 10 July 1999. Web. 10 Sept. 2008.

Blog   Cite an entire blog as you would an entire Web site (see p. 663). If the author of the blog or blog post uses a pseudonym, begin with the pseudonym and put the blogger's real name in brackets.

	Blog title	*Sponsor*

ENTIRE BLOG   *Talking Points Memo.* Ed. Josh Marshall. TPM Media, 1 Dec. 2011. Web. 1 Dec. 2011.

Pseudonym   *Real name*

Negative Camber [Todd McCandless]. *Formula1blog.* F1b., 2011. Web.
    1 Dec. 2011.

Post author   *Post title*

BLOG POST   Marshall, Josh. "Coke and Grass at Amish Raid." *Talking Points Memo.* TPM
    Media, 1 Dec. 2011. Web. 1 Dec. 2011.

Wiki article   Since wikis are written and edited collectively, start your entry with the title of the article you are citing. But check with your instructor before using information from a wiki in your research project; because content is written and edited collectively, it is difficult to assess its reliability and impossible to determine the expertise of the contributers.

> "John Lydon." *Wikipedia.* Wikipedia Foundation, 27 Apr. 2015. Web. 2 May 2015.

Discussion group or newsgroup posting   Use the subject line of the posting (in quotation marks) as the title, and include the name of the discussion or newsgroup.

Post author   *Subject line*   *Group name*   *Site sponsor*

Martin, Francesca Alys. "Wait--Did Somebody Say 'Buffy'?" *Cultstud-L.* U of S FL,
    8 Mar. 2000. Web. 8 Mar. 2008.

Post date

E-mail message

Sender   *Subject line*   *Recipient*   *Date sent*

Olson, Kate. "Update on State Legislative Grants." Message to the author. 5 Nov. 2015.

E-mail.

Medium

Student Research Project in MLA Style

On the following pages is a student research project speculating about the causes of a trend—the increase in home schooling. The author, Cristina Dinh, cites statistics, quotes authorities, and paraphrases and summarizes background information to support her argument. She uses MLA documentation style.

Double-spaced

Double-spaced

Title centered; no underlining, quotes, or italics

Paragraphs indented one-half inch

Author named in text; no parenthetical page reference because source not paginated

Abbreviated title used in parenthetical citation because works cited lists two sources by government author (named in text); no punctuation between title and page number

Author named in text; parenthetical page reference falls at end of sentence

1/2"
Dinh 1   1"

1"

1"

Cristina Dinh

Professor Cooper

English 100

15 May 2015

Educating Kids at Home

Every morning, Mary Jane, who is nine, doesn't have to worry about gulping down her cereal so she can be on time for school. School for Mary Jane is literally right at her doorstep.

In this era of serious concern about the quality of public education, increasing numbers of parents across the United States are choosing to educate their children at home. These parents believe they can do a better job teaching their children than their local schools can. *Home schooling*, as this practice is known, has become a national trend over the past thirty years, and according to education specialist Brian D. Ray, the home-schooled population is growing at a rate between 5% and 12% per year. A 2008 report by the U.S. Department of Education's Institute of Education Sciences estimated that, nationwide, the number of home-schooled children rose from 850,000 in 1999 to approximately 1.5 million in 2007 (*1.5 million* 1). Some home-schooling advocates believe that even these numbers may be low because not all states require formal notification when parents decide to teach their children at home.

What is home schooling, and who are the parents choosing to be home-schoolers? David Guterson, a pioneer in the home-schooling movement, defines home schooling as "the attempt to gain an education outside of institutions" (5). Home-schooled children spend the majority of the conventional school day learning in or near their homes rather than in traditional schools; parents or guardians are the prime educators. Former teacher and home-schooler Rebecca Rupp notes that home-schooling parents vary considerably in what they teach and how they teach, ranging from those who follow a highly traditional curriculum within a structure that parallels the typical classroom to those who

1"

Dinh 2

essentially allow their children to pursue whatever interests them at
their own pace (3). Home-schoolers commonly combine formal instruction
with life skills instruction, learning fractions, for example, in terms
of monetary units or cooking measurements (Saba and Gattis 89).   Work by two authors cited
According to the U.S. Department of Education's 2008 report, while home-
schoolers are also a diverse group politically and philosophically--
libertarians, conservatives, Christian fundamentalists--most say they
home school for one of three reasons: they are concerned about the
quality of academic instruction, the general school environment, or the
lack of religious or moral instruction (*1.5 million* 2).

    The first group generally believes that children need individual
attention and the opportunity to learn at their own pace to learn well. This
group says that one teacher in a classroom of twenty to thirty children
(the size of typical public-school classes) cannot give this kind of attention.
These parents believe they can give their children greater enrichment and
more specialized instruction than public schools can provide. At home,
parents can work one-on-one with each child and be flexible about time,
allowing their children to pursue their interests at earlier ages. Many of
these parents, like home-schooler Peter Bergson, believe that

> home schooling provides more of an opportunity to continue the   Quotation of more than four lines typed as a block and indented 1 inch
> natural learning process that's in evidence in all children.
> [In school,] you change the learning process from self-directed   Brackets indicate alteration of quotation
> to other-directed, from the child asking questions to the
> teacher asking questions. You shut down areas of potential
> interest. (qtd. in Kohn 22)   Parenthetical citation of secondary source falls after period when quotation indented as a block

This trend can be traced back to the 1960s, when many people
began criticizing traditional schools. Various types of "alternative" schools
were created, and some parents began teaching their children at home
(Friedlander 150). Parents like this mention several reasons for their
disappointment with public schools and for their decision to home school.
A lack of funding, for example, leaves children without new textbooks.

Dinh 3

In a 2002 survey, 31% of teachers said that their students are using textbooks that are more than ten years old, and 29% said that they do not have enough textbooks for all of their students (National Education Association). Many schools also cannot afford to buy laboratory equipment and other teaching materials. At my own high school, the chemistry teacher told me that most of the lab equipment we used came from a research firm he worked for. In a 2006 Gallup poll, lack of proper financial support ranked first on the list of the problems in public schools (Rose and Gallup 45).

Parents also cite overcrowding as a reason for taking their kids out of school. The more students in a classroom, the less learning that goes on, as Cafi Cohen discovered before choosing to home school; after spending several days observing what went on in her child's classroom, she found that administrative duties, including disciplining, took up to 80% of a teacher's time, with only 20% of the day devoted to learning (6). Moreover, faced with a large group of children, a teacher ends up gearing lessons to the students in the middle level, so children at both ends miss out. Gifted children and those with learning disabilities particularly suffer in this situation. At home, parents of these children say they can tailor the material and the pace for each child. Studies show that home-schooling methods seem to work well in preparing children academically. Lawrence Rudner, director of the ERIC Clearinghouse on Assessment and Evaluation at the University of Maryland and a researcher on home schooling, found that testing of home-schooled students showed them to be between one and three years ahead of public school students their age (xi). Home-schooled children have also made particularly strong showings in academic competitions; since the late 1990s, 10% of National Spelling Bee participants have been home schooled, as have two National Spelling Bee and two National Geographic Bee winners (Lyman). More and more selective colleges are admitting, and even recruiting, home-schooled applicants (Basham, Merrifield, and Hepburn 15).

[margin note: Corporate author's name cited]

[margin note: Work by three authors cited]

Dinh 4

Parents in the second group--those concerned with the general school environment--claim that their children are more well-rounded than those in school. Because they don't have to sit in classrooms all day, home-schooled kids can pursue their own projects, often combining crafts or technical skills with academic subjects. Home-schoolers participate in outside activities, such as 4-H competitions, field trips with peers in home-school support groups, science fairs, musical and dramatic productions, church activities, and Boy Scouts or Girl Scouts (Saba and Gattis 59-62). In fact, they may even be able to participate to some extent in actual school activities. A 1999 survey conducted by the U.S. Department of Education's Institute of Education Sciences found that 28% of public schools allowed home-schooled students to participate in extracurricular activities alongside enrolled students, and 20% allowed home-schooled students to attend some classes (*Homeschooling* 12).

Many home-schooling parents believe that these activities provide the social opportunities kids need without exposing their children to the peer pressure they would have to deal with as regular school students. For example, many kids think that drinking and using drugs are cool. When I was in high school, my friends would tell me a few drinks wouldn't hurt or affect driving. If I had listened to them, perhaps I wouldn't be alive today. Four of my friends were killed under the influence of alcohol. Between 1992 and 2008, the number of high school seniors surveyed who had used any illicit drug in the last year climbed from 27.1% to 36.6% (Johnston et al. 59). ← Work by four or more authors cited

Another reason many parents decide to home school their kids is that they are concerned for their children's safety. Samuel L. Blumenfeld notes that "physical risk" is an important reason many parents remove their children from public schools as "[m]ore and more children are assaulted, robbed, and murdered in school" and a "culture of violence, abetted by rap music, drug trafficking, . . . and racial tension, has engulfed teenagers" (4). Beginning in the mid-1990s, a string of school shootings--including the 1999 massacres in Littleton, Colorado, and Conyers, Georgia, and the 2001 massacre in Santee, California--has led to increasing fears that young people are simply not safe at school.

While all of the reasons mentioned so far are important, perhaps the single most significant cause of the growing home-schooling trend is Christian fundamentalist dissatisfaction with "godless" public schools. Sociologist Mitchell L. Stevens, author of one of the first comprehensive studies of home schooling, cites a mailing sent out by Basic Christian Education, a company that markets home-schooling materials, titled "What Really Happens in Public Schools." This publication sums up the fears of fundamentalist home-schoolers about public schools: that they encourage high levels of teenage sexual activity and pregnancies "out of wedlock"; expose children to "violence, crime, lack of discipline, and, of course, drugs of every kind"; present positive portrayals of communism and socialism and negative portrayals of capitalism; and undermine children's Christian beliefs by promoting "New Age philosophies, Yoga, Transcendental Meditation, witchcraft demonstrations, and Eastern religions" (51).

As early as 1988, Luanne Shackelford and Susan White, two Christian home-schooling mothers, were claiming that because schools expose children to "[p]eer pressure, perverts, secular textbooks, values clarification, TV, pornography, rock music, bad movies . . . [h]ome schooling seems to be the best plan to achieve our goal [to raise good Christians]" (160). As another mother more recently put it:

> I don't like the way schools are going. . . . What's wrong with Christianity all of a sudden? You know? This country was founded on Christian, on religious principles. [People] came over here for religious freedom, and now all of a sudden all religious references seem to be stricken out of the public school, and I don't like that at all. (qtd. in Stevens 67)

Although many nonfundamentalist home-schoolers make some of these same criticisms, those who cite the lack of "Christian values" in

Brackets used to indicate changes in capitalization and addition to quotation for clarification

Ellipsis marks used to indicate words left out of quotations

Quotation cited in a secondary source

Dinh 6

public schools have particular concerns of their own. For example, home-schooling leader Raymond Moore talks of parents who are "'sick and tired of the teaching of evolution in the schools as a cut-and-dried fact,' along with other evidence of so-called secular humanism" (Kohn 21), such as textbooks that contain material contradicting Christian beliefs. Moreover, parents worry that schools undermine their children's moral values. In particular, some Christian fundamentalist parents object to sex education in schools, saying that it encourages children to become sexually active early, challenging values taught at home. They see the family as the core and believe that the best place to instill family values is within the family. These Christian home-schooling parents want to provide their children not only with academic knowledge but also with a moral grounding consistent with their religious beliefs.

Still other home-schooling parents object to a perceived government-mandated value system that they believe attempts to override the values, not necessarily religious in nature, of individual families. For these parents, home schooling is a way of resisting what they see as unwarranted intrusion by the federal government into personal concerns (*Alliance*).

Armed with their convictions, parents such as those who belong to the Christian Home School Legal Defense Association have fought in court and lobbied for legislation that allows them the option of home schooling. In the 1970s, most states had compulsory attendance laws that made it difficult, if not illegal, to keep school-age children home from school. Today, home schooling is permitted in every state, with strict regulation required by only a few (Home School). As a result, Mary Jane is one of hundreds of thousands of American children who can start their school day without leaving the house.

Single quotation marks indicate a quotation within a quotation

Citation placed close to quotation, before comma but after closing quotation mark

Internet source cited by shortened form of title; author's name and page numbers unavailable

Shortened form of corporate author's name cited

Works-cited entries begin on a new page; entries are in alphabetical order.

Title centered

Double-spaced

Entries begin flush with left margin; subsequent lines indent half an inch.

Periods separate author, title, publication information, medium, and date of access.

1/2"

Dinh 7

1"

1"

Works Cited

Alliance for the Separation of School and State. "Is There a Problem?" *Alliance for the Separation of School and State*. Alliance for the Separation of School and State, 29 Jan. 2008. Web. 5 May 2015.

Basham, Patrick, John Merrifield, and Claudia R. Hepburn. *Home Schooling: From the Extreme to the Mainstream*. 2nd ed. Vancouver: Fraser Inst., 2007. Studies in Education Policy. *Fraser Inst*. Web. 5 May 2015.

Blumenfeld, Samuel L. *Homeschooling: A Parents Guide to Teaching Children*. Bridgewater: Replica, 1999. Print.

Cohen, Cafi. *And What about College? How Home-Schooling Leads to Admissions to the Best Colleges and Universities*, 2nd ed. Cambridge: Holt, 2000. Print.

Friedlander, Tom. "A Decade of Home Schooling." *The Home School Reader*. Ed. Mark Hegener and Helen Hegener. Tonasket: Home Educ., 1988. 147-56. Print.

Guterson, David. *Family Matters: Why Homeschooling Makes Sense*. San Diego: Harcourt, 1992. Print.

Home School Legal Defense Association. "State Action Map." HSLDA, 2009. Web. 9 May 2015.

Johnston, Lloyd D., et al. *Monitoring the Future: National Results on Adolescent Drug Use, Overview of Key Findings, 2008*. Bethesda: Natl. Inst. on Drug Abuse, 2009. Web. 9 May 2015.

Kohn, Alfie. "Home Schooling." *Atlantic Monthly* Apr. 1988: 20-25. Print.

Lyman, Isabel. "Generation Two." *American Enterprise* Oct./Nov. 2002: 48-49. *InfoTrac OneFile*. Web. 5 May 2015.

National Education Association. *2002 Instructional Materials Survey*. Assn. of Amer. Pubs., Sept. 2002. Web. 7 May 2015.

Ray, Brian D. "Research Facts on Home Schooling." *National Home Education Research Institute*. NHERI, 2008. Web. 7 May 2015.

Dinh 8

Rose, Lowell C., and Alec M. Gallup. "The 38th Annual Phi Delta Kappa/Gallup
    Poll of the Public's Attitudes toward the Public Schools." *Phi Delta*
    Kappan 88.1 (2006): 41–56. *Phi Delta Kappa International*. Web.
    7 May 2015.

Rudner, Lawrence. Foreword. *The McGraw-Hill Home-Schooling Companion*.
    By Laura Saba and Julie Gattis. New York: McGraw, 2002. xi-xiii. Print.

Rupp, Rebecca. *The Complete Home Learning Source Book*. New York: Three
    Rivers, 1998. Print.

Saba, Laura, and Julie Gattis. *The McGraw-Hill Home-Schooling Companion*.
    New York: McGraw, 2002. Print.

Shackelford, Luanne, and Susan White. *A Survivor's Guide to Home*
    Schooling. Westchester: Crossway, 1988. Print.

Stevens, Mitchell L. *Kingdom of Children: Culture and Controversy in the*
    Homeschooling Movement. Princeton: Princeton UP, 2001. Print.

United States. Dept. of Education. Inst. of Education Sciences.
    Homeschooling in the United States: 2003. Washington: GPO, 2006.
    Natl. Center for Educ. Statistics. Web. 7 May 2015.

- - -. *1.5 Million Homeschooled Students in the United States in 2007*.
    Washington: GPO, 2008. *Natl. Center for Educ. Statistics*. Web.
    5 May 2015.

Untitled section labeled

For multiple sources by the same author, replace author's name with three hyphens followed by a period. (The name of this government source has three separate components.)

25

Citing and Documenting Sources in APA Style

When using the APA system of documentation, include both an in-text citation and a list of references at the end of the research project. **In-text citations** tell your readers where the ideas or words you have borrowed come from, and the entries in the **list of references** allow readers to locate your sources so that they can read more about your topic.

The most common types of in-text citations follow. For other, less common citation types, consult the *Publication Manual of the American Psychological Association,* Sixth Edition. Most libraries will own a copy.

Citing Sources in the Text

Directory to In-Text-Citation Models

When citing ideas, information, or words borrowed from a source, include the author's last name and the date of publication in the text of your research project. In most cases, you will want to use a *signal phrase* to introduce the works you are citing, since doing so gives you the opportunity to put the work and its author in context. A signal phrase includes the author's last name, the date of publication, and a verb that describes the author's attitude or stance:

Smith (2015) complained that . . .

Jones (2015) defended her position by . . .

Use a parenthetical citation—*(Jones, 2015)*—when you have already introduced the author or the work or when citing the source of an uncontroversial fact. When quoting from a source, also include the page number: *Smith (2015) complained that he "never got a break" (p. 123).* When you are paraphrasing or summarizing, you may omit the page reference, although including it is not wrong.

One author

SIGNAL PHRASE	Upton Sinclair (2005), a crusading journalist, wrote that workers sometimes "fell into the vats; and when they were fished out, there was never enough of them left to be worth exhibiting" (p. 134).
PARENTHETICAL CITATION	*The Jungle*, a naturalistic novel inspired by the French writer Zola, described in lurid detail the working conditions of the time, including what became of unlucky workers who fell into the vats while making sausage (Sinclair, 2005, p. 134).
	author's last name + date + page
REFERENCE-LIST ENTRY	Sinclair, U. (2005). *The jungle*. New York, NY: Oxford University Press. (Original work published 1906)

More than one author In a signal phrase, use the word *and* between the authors' names; in a parenthetical citation, use an ampersand (&). When citing a work by three to seven authors, list all the authors in your first reference; in subsequent references, just list the first and use *et al.* (Latin for *and others*).

SIGNAL PHRASE	As Jamison and Tyree (2001) have found, racial bias does not diminish merely through exposure to individuals of other races.
PARENTHETICAL CITATION	Racial bias does not diminish through exposure (Jamison & Tyree, 2001).
FIRST CITATION	Rosenzweig, Breedlove, and Watson (2005) wrote that biological psychology is an interdisciplinary field that includes scientists from "quite different backgrounds" (p. 3).
LATER CITATIONS	Biological psychology is "the field that relates behavior to bodily processes, especially the workings of the brain" (Rosenzweig et al., 2005, p. 3).

For works with more than seven authors, list the first six, an ellipsis (. . .), and the last author.

Unknown author To cite a work when the author is unknown, the APA suggests using a shortened version of the title.

> An international pollution treaty still to be ratified would prohibit all plastic garbage from being dumped at sea ("Plastic Is Found," 1972).

The full title of the article is "Plastic Is Found in the Sargasso Sea; Pieces of Apparent Refuse Cover Wide Atlantic Region."

Two or more works by the same author in the same year   When your list of references includes two works by the same author, the year of publication is usually enough to distinguish them. Occasionally, though, you may have two works by the same author in the same year. If this happens, alphabetize the works by title in your list of references, and add a lowercase letter after the date (2005a, 2005b).

> Middle-class unemployed are better off than their lower-class counterparts, because they "are likely to have some assets to invest in their job search" (Ehrenreich, 2005b, p. 16).

Two or more authors with the same last name   Include the author's initials.

> F. Johnson (2010) conducted an intriguing study on teen smoking.

Corporation, organization, or government agency as author   Spell out the name of the organization the first time you use it, but abbreviate it in subsequent citations if readers will know what the abbreviation refers to.

> (National Institutes of Health, 2015)

> (NIH, 2015)

Indirect citation (quotation from a secondary source)   To quote material taken not from the original source but from a secondary source that quotes the original, give the secondary source in the reference list, and in your essay acknowledge the original source and cite the secondary source.

> E. M. Forster said "the collapse of all civilization, so realistic for us, sounded in Matthew Arnold's ears like a distant and harmonious cataract" (as cited in Trilling, 1955, p. 11).

Two or more works cited in the same parentheses   List sources in alphabetical order, separated by semicolons.

> (Johnson, 2014; NIH, 2015)

Creating a List of References
Directory to Reference-List Models

Author Listings
One author   677
More than one author   678
Unknown author   678
Corporation, organization, or government
   agency as author   678
Two or more works by the same
   author   678

Books (Print, Electronic)
Basic format for a book   678
Author and editor   679
Edited collection   679
Work in an anthology or edited
   collection   679
Translation   679

Author Listings

When the list of references includes several works by the same author, the APA provides the following rules for arranging these entries in the list:

- Same-name single-author entries precede multiple-author entries:

Zettelmeyer, F. (2000).

Zettelmeyer, F., Morton, F. S., & Silva-Risso, J. (2006).

- Entries with the same first author and a different second author are alphabetized under the first author according to the second author's last name:

Dhar, R., & Nowlis, S. M. (2004).

Dhar, R., & Simonson, I. (2003).

- Entries by the same authors are arranged by year of publication, in chronological order:

Golder, P. N., & Tellis, G. J. (2003).

Golder, P. N., & Tellis, G. J. (2004).

- Entries by the same authors with the same publication year should be arranged alphabetically by title (according to the first word after *A, An,* or *The*), and lower-case letters (*a, b, c,* and so on) should be appended to the year in parentheses:

Aaron, P. (1990a). Basic . . .

Aaron, P. (1990b). Elements . . .

One author

Schneier, B. (2015). *Data and Goliath: The hidden battles to collect your data and control your world.* New York, NY: Norton.

More than one author

Robinson, K., & Aronica, L. (2015). *Creative schools: The grassroots revolution that's transforming education*. New York, NY: Viking.

Hunt, L., Po-Chia Hsia, R., Martin, T. R., Rosenwein, B. H., Rosenwein, H., & Smith, B. G. (2001). *The making of the West: Peoples and cultures*. Boston, MA: Bedford.

If there are more than seven authors, list only the first six, insert an ellipsis (. . .), and add the last author's name.

Unknown author   Begin the entry with the title.

Communities blowing whistle on street basketball. (2003, June 2). *USA Today*, p. 20A.

If an author is designated as "Anonymous," include the word *Anonymous* in place of the author, and alphabetize it as "Anonymous" in the reference list.

Anonymous. (2006). *Primary colors*. New York, NY: Random House.

Corporation, organization, or government agency as author

American Medical Association. (2004). *Family medical guide*. Hoboken, NJ: Wiley.

Two or more works by the same author

When you cite two or more works by the same author, arrange them in chronological (time) order.

Pinker, S. (2005). So how does the mind work? *Mind and Language, 20*(1): 1-24. doi:10.1111/j.0268-1064.2005.00274.x

Pinker, S. (2011). *The better angels of our nature: Why violence has declined*. New York, NY: Viking.

When you cite two works by the same author in the same year, alphabetize entries by title and then add a lowercase letter following each year.

Pinker, S. (2005a). *Hotheads*. New York, NY: Pocket Penguins.

Pinker, S. (2005b). So how does the mind work? *Mind and Language, 20*(1), 1-24. doi: 10.1111/j.0268-1064.2005.00274.x

Books (Print, Electronic)

When citing a book, capitalize only the first word of the title and subtitle and any proper nouns (*Dallas, Darwin*). Book titles are italicized.

Basic format for a book

Author	Year		Title

PRINT   Pinker, S. (2011). *The better angels of our nature: Why violence has declined.* New York, NY: Viking.

City, State (abbr)   Publisher

| E-BOOK | Pinker, S. (2011). *The better angels of our nature: Why violence has declined.* New York, NY: Viking. [Nook version.] |

E-publication information

| DATABASE | Darwin, C. (2001). *The origin of species*. Retrieved from http://bartleby.com (Original work published 1909-14)   *Database information* |

If an e-book has been assigned a **digital object identifier** (or *doi*)—a combination of numbers and letters assigned by the publisher to identify the work—add that information at the end of the citation.

Author and editor

Arnold, M. (1994). *Culture and anarchy* (S. Lipman, Ed.). New Haven, CT: Yale University Press. (Original work published 1869)

Edited collection

Waldman, D., & Walker, J. (Eds.). (1999). *Feminism and documentary*. Minneapolis: University of Minnesota Press.

Work in an anthology or edited collection

Fairbairn-Dunlop, P. (1993). Women and agriculture in western Samoa. In J. H. Momsen & V. Kinnaird (Eds.), *Different places, different voices* (pp. 211-226). London, England: Routledge.

Translation

Tolstoy, L. (2002). *War and peace* (C. Garnett, Trans.). New York, NY: Modern Library. (Original work published 1869)

Dictionary entry or article in another reference book

Rowland, R. P. (2001). Myasthenia gravis. In *Encyclopedia Americana* (Vol. 19, p. 683). Danbury, CT: Grolier.

Introduction, preface, foreword, or afterword

Graff, G., & Phelan, J. (2004). Preface. In M. Twain, *Adventures of Huckleberry Finn* (pp. iii-vii). Boston, MA: Bedford.

Later edition of a book

Axelrod, R., & Cooper, C. (2016). *The St. Martin's guide to writing* (11th ed.). Boston, MA: Bedford.

Government document

U.S. Department of Health and Human Services. (2009). *Trends in underage drinking in the United States, 1991-2007*. Washington, DC: Government Printing Office.

Note: When the author and publisher are the same, use the word *Author* (not italicized) as the name of the publisher.

Unpublished doctoral dissertation

Bullock, B. (1986). *Basic needs fulfillment among less developed countries: Social progress over two decades of growth* (Unpublished doctoral dissertation). Vanderbilt University, Nashville, TN.

Articles (Print, Electronic)

For articles, capitalize only the first word of the title, proper nouns (*Barclay, Berlin*), and the first word following a colon (if any). Omit quotation marks around the titles of articles, but capitalize all the important words of journal, newspaper, and magazine titles, and set them in italics. If you are accessing an article through a database, follow the model for a comparable source.

From a scholarly journal

Author   *Year*   *Article title*

PRINT   Kardefelt-Winther, D. (2015). A critical account of DSM-5 criteria for Internet
            gaming disorder. *Addiction Research and Theory, 23*(2), 93-98.
                                  Journal title   *Volume (issue) Pages*

            Goodboy, A. K., & Martin, M. M. (2015). The personality profile of a cyberbully:
            Examining the dark triad. *Computers in Human Behavior, 49,* 1-4.
                                                              Volume only Pages

Include the digital object identifier (or *doi*) when available. When a doi has not been assigned, include the journal's URL.

ELECTRONIC Goodboy, A. K., & Martin, M. M. (2015). The personality profile of a cyberbully:
            Examining the dark triad. *Computers in Human Behavior, 49,* 1-4.
            doi: 10.1016/j.chb.2015.02.052
                              DOI

            Houston, R. G., & Toma, F. (2003). Home schooling: An alternative
            school choice. *Southern Economic Journal, 69*(4), 920-936. Retrieved from
            http://www.southerneconomic.org/
                              URL

From a newspaper

            Year Month Day

PRINT   Peterson, A. (2003, May 20). Finding a cure for old age. *The Wall Street
            Journal,* pp. D1, D5.

ELECTRONIC Zimmer, C. (2015, May 6). Under the sea, a missing link in the evolution of
            complex cells. *The New York Times.* Retrieved from http://www.nytimes.com/

From a magazine   If a magazine is published weekly or biweekly (every other week), include the full date following the author's name. If it is published monthly or bimonthly, include just the year and month (or months).

Weekly or biweekly

PRINT   Gladwell, M. (9 September 2013). Man and superman. *The New Yorker, 89*(27), 76-80.

Monthly or bimonthly

Freeland, C. (2015, May). Globalization bites back. *Atlantic, 315*(4), 82-86.

ELECTRONIC   Freeland, C. (2015, May). Globalization bites back. *Atlantic*. Retrieved from http://theatlantic.com/

Editorial or letter to the editor

Kosinski, T. (2012, May 15). Who cares what she thinks? [Letter to the editor]. *The Chicago Sun-Times*. Retrieved from http:// www.suntimes.com/opinions/letters/12522890-474/who-cares-what-she-thinks.html

Review

"Review of" + item type + title of item reviewed

Nussbaum, E. (2015, January 26). House of chords [Review of the television series *Empire* and *Mozart in the Jungle*.] *The New Yorker, 90*(45), 70–72.

If the review is untitled, use the bracketed information as the title, retaining the brackets.

Multimedia Sources (Print or Electronic)

Television program

Label

O'Connell, C. (Writer and director). (2015, Jan. 6). Ripley: Believe it or not. [Television series episode]. In H. Hampton and S. Fitzmeyer (Creators), *American Experience*. Boston, MA: WGBH.

Film, video, or DVD

Label

Nolan, C. (Writer and director). (2010). *Inception* [Motion picture]. Los Angeles, CA: Warner Bros.

Sound recording

PODCAST   Dubner, S. (2012, May 17). Retirement kills [Audio podcast]. *Freakonomics Radio*. Retrieved from http://www.freakonomics.com/

Label

RECORDING   Maroon 5. (2010). Moves like Jagger. On *Hands all over* [CD]. New York, NY: A&M/Octone Records.

Interview   Do not list personal interviews in your reference list. Instead, cite the interviewee in your text (last name and initials), and in parentheses give the notation *personal communication* (in regular type, not italicized) followed by a comma and the date of the interview. For published interviews, use the appropriate format for an article.

For more information on finding sources, see Chapter 22.

Other Electronic Sources

A rule of thumb for citing electronic sources not covered in one of the preceding sections is to include enough information to allow readers to access and retrieve the source. For most online sources, provide as much of the following as you can:

- Name of author
- Date of publication or most recent update (in parentheses; if unavailable, use the abbreviation *n.d.*)
- Title of document (such as a Web page)
- Title of Web site
- Any special retrieval information, such as a URL; include the date you last accessed the source only when the content is likely to change or be updated (as on a wiki, for example)

Web site   The APA does not require an entry in the list of references for entire Web sites. Instead, give the name of the site in your text with its Web address in parentheses.

Web page or document on a Web site

American Cancer Society. (2011, Oct. 10). *Child and teen tobacco use*. Retrieved from http://www.cancer.org/Cancer/CancerCauses/TobaccoCancer/ ChildandTeenTobaccoUse/child-and-teen-tobacco-use-what-to-do

Heins, M. (2014, September 4). Untangling the Steven Salaita case. In *The Free Expression Policy Project*. Retrieved from http://www.fepproject.org/commentaries/Salaita.html/

Discussion list and newsgroup postings   Include online postings in your list of references only if you can provide data that would allow others to retrieve the source.

Paikeday, T. (2005, October 10). "Esquivalience" is out [Electronic mailing list message]. *Label*
Retrieved from http://listserv.linguistlist.org/cgi-bin/wa?A1=ind0510b&L=ads-1#1

Ditmire, S. (2005, February 10). NJ tea party [Newsgroup message]. Retrieved from *Label*
http://groups.google.com/group/TeaParty

Blog post

Mestel, R. (2012, May 17). Fructose makes rats dumber [Blog post]. Retrieved from *Label*
http://www.latimes.com/health/boostershots/la-fructose-makes-rats-stupid-brain-
20120517,0,2305241.story?track=rss

Wiki entry   Start with the article title and include the post date (or *n.d.*, if there is no date), since wikis may be updated frequently, as well as the retrieval date.

Sleep. (2011, November 26). Retrieved May 21, 2011, from Wiki of Science: http://wikiofscience.wikidot.com/science:sleep

E-mail message   Personal correspondence, including e-mail, should not be included in your reference list. Instead, cite the person's name in your text, and in parentheses give the notation *personal communication* (in regular type, not italicized) and the date.

Computer software   If an individual has proprietary rights to the software, cite that person's name as you would for a print text. Otherwise, cite as you would for an anonymous print text.

Label

How Computers Work [Software]. (1998). Available from Que: http://www.howcomputers work.net/

A Sample Reference List

To see the complete text of this student research project in APA style, see Patrick O'Malley's proposal, "More Testing, More Learning" in Chapter 7, pp. 290–96.

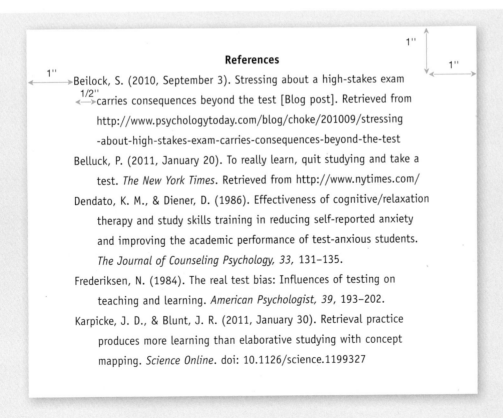

References

Beilock, S. (2010, September 3). Stressing about a high-stakes exam carries consequences beyond the test [Blog post]. Retrieved from http://www.psychologytoday.com/blog/choke/201009/stressing -about-high-stakes-exam-carries-consequences-beyond-the-test

Belluck, P. (2011, January 20). To really learn, quit studying and take a test. *The New York Times*. Retrieved from http://www.nytimes.com/

Dendato, K. M., & Diener, D. (1986). Effectiveness of cognitive/relaxation therapy and study skills training in reducing self-reported anxiety and improving the academic performance of test-anxious students. *The Journal of Counseling Psychology, 33,* 131–135.

Frederiksen, N. (1984). The real test bias: Influences of testing on teaching and learning. *American Psychologist, 39,* 193–202.

Karpicke, J. D., & Blunt, J. R. (2011, January 30). Retrieval practice produces more learning than elaborative studying with concept mapping. *Science Online*. doi: 10.1126/science.1199327

Light, R. J. (1990). *Explorations with students and faculty about teaching, learning, and student life*. Cambridge, MA: Harvard University Graduate School of Education and Kennedy School of Government.

Rothblum, E. D., Solomon, L., & Murakami, J. (1986). Affective, cognitive, and behavioral differences between high and low procrastinators. *The Journal of Counseling Psychology, 33,* 387–394.

ScienceWatch.com (2008, February). Henry L. Roediger and Jeff Karpicke talk with ScienceWatch.com and answer a few questions about this month's fast breaking paper in the field of psychiatry/psychology [Interview]. Retrieved from http://sciencewatch.com/dr/fbp/2008/08febfbp/08febfbpRoedigerETAL

Nicolas Ayer/EyeEm/Getty Images

PART 5

Composing Strategies for College and Beyond

26

Taking Essay Examinations

Many instructors believe that essay exams are the best way to find out what you have learned and, more important, help you consolidate and reinforce your learning. Essay exams demonstrate that you can sort through the large body of information covered in a course, identify what is significant, and explain your decision. They show whether you understand basic concepts and can use those concepts to interpret specific materials, make connections, draw comparisons and find contrasts, and synthesize information in support of an original assertion. They may even ask you to justify your own evaluations and argue for your opinions with convincing reasons and supporting evidence. All instructors want students to think critically and analytically about a subject; many feel that essay exams provide the best demonstration that you can do so.

As a college student, then, you will face a variety of essay exams, from short-answer identifications to take-home exams. The writing activities and strategies discussed in Parts One and Three of this book—particularly narrating, describing, defining, classifying, comparing and contrasting, and arguing—as well as the critical thinking strategies in Part Two will help you do well on these exams. This chapter provides specific guidelines for you to follow in preparing for and taking essay exams, and analyzes a group of typical exam questions and answers to help you determine which strategies will be most useful.

Preparing for an Exam

The best way to ensure that you will do well on essay exams is to keep up with readings and assignments from the very start of the course: Do the reading, go to lectures, take careful notes, participate in discussion sessions, and organize study groups with classmates to explore and review course material throughout the term. Trying to cram weeks of information into a single night of study will never allow you to do your best.

As you study, avoid simply memorizing information aimlessly. Instead, clarify the important issues of the course and use these issues to focus your understanding of specific facts and particular readings. Try to see relations among topics; concentrate on the central concerns of each study unit, and see what connections you can discover; and place all you have learned into a meaningful context.

As an exam approaches, find out what you can about the form it will take. No question is more irritating to instructors than "Do we need to know this for the exam?" but it is generally legitimate to ask whether the questions will require short or long answers, how many questions there will be, whether you may choose which questions to answer, and what kinds of thinking and writing will be required of you. Some instructors may hand out study guides for exams or even lists of potential questions.

If yours does not, make up questions you think the instructor might ask and then plan answers to them with classmates. Returning to your notes and to assigned readings with specific questions in mind can help enormously in your process of understanding. The important thing to remember is that an essay exam tests more than your memory of specific information; it requires you to use this information to demonstrate a comprehensive grasp of the material covered in the course.

Taking the Exam

Doing well on an essay exam begins with a plan of attack. Once you analyze the questions to determine what is wanted, apportion your time.

Read the exam carefully.

Before you answer a question, read the entire exam so that you can apportion your time realistically. Pay particular attention to how many points you may earn in different parts of the test; notice any directions that suggest how long an answer should be or how much space it should take up. As you are doing so, you may wish to make tentative choices of the questions you will answer and decide on the order in which you will answer them. If you have ideas about how you would organize any of your answers, you might also jot down scratch outlines. But before you start to complete any answers, write down the actual clock time you expect to be working on each question or set of questions. Careful time management is crucial to your success on essay exams; devoting some time to each question is always better than using up your time on only a few.

Before beginning to write your first answer, analyze the question carefully so that you can focus your attention on the information that will be pertinent to your answer. Consider this question from a sociology final:

> Drawing from lectures and discussions on the contradictory aspects of American values, the "bureaucratic personality," and the behaviors associated with social mobility, discuss the problems of attaining economic success in a relatively "open," complex, post-industrial society such as the United States.

Though the question looks confusing at first, once you sort it out, you will find that it contains the key terms for the answer's thesis, as well as the main points of development. Look first at the words that give you directions: *draw from* and *discuss*. The term *discuss* invites you to list and explain the problems of attaining economic success. The categories of these problems are already identified in the opening phrases: "contradictory . . . values," "bureaucratic personality," and "behaviors associated with social mobility." Therefore, you would begin with a thesis that includes the key words in the final clause ("attaining economic success in a relatively open, complex, post-industrial society") and then take up each category of problem—and perhaps other problems you can think of—in separate paragraphs.

Review typical essay exam questions.

The next section presents questions in nine common categories (on the left) with an explanation of how students should respond to each question (on the right). All the examples are drawn from short quizzes, midterms, and final exams for a variety of first- and second-year courses. These questions demonstrate the range of writing you may be expected to do on exams. Pay particular attention to how the directions and key words in each case help you define the writing task.

Notice that each question indicates the amount of time students should devote to their answer. In reality, students are often expected to determine how much time to spend, depending on the number of points allocated to the question—for example, students should spend half the exam period answering a question that could earn half the exam's points. In general, instructors expect students to need the entire exam period to write an effective essay exam. If you find that you have finished the exam in half the time, review your answers: You probably have not included all the information your instructor was looking for.

Define or Identify   Questions that require you to write a few sentences defining or identifying material from readings or lectures may ask for a brief overview of a large topic, or a more detailed definition or identification of a more narrowly defined topic. In composing a *definition* or identification, always ask yourself why this item is important enough to be on the exam.

See Chapter 16 for more about defining.

Question 26.1 (15/100 points; 15 minutes)

What are the three stages of African literature?

This question asks for a brief overview of a large topic. Answering this question would involve naming the periods in historical order and then describing each period in a sentence or two.

Question 26.2 (20/100 points; 20 minutes)

Define and state some important facts concerning each of the following:
a. demographics
b. Instrumental model
c. RCA
d. telephone booth of the air
e. penny press

With no more than three or four minutes for each part, students answering Question 26.2 would offer a concise definition for each item (probably in a sentence) and add facts relevant to the main topics in the course.

Recall Details of a Specific Source   Sometimes instructors will ask for a straightforward *summary* or *paraphrase* of a specific source (often, assigned reading). To answer such questions, the student must recount details directly from the source without interpretation or evaluation. In the following example from a sociology exam, students were allowed about fifteen minutes to complete the answer on one lined page provided with the exam.

Question 26.3 (10/100 points; 15 minutes)

For more about paraphrasing and summarizing, see Chapter 5, Chapter 12, and Chapter 23.

In his article "Is There a Culture of Poverty?" Oscar Lewis addresses a popular question in the social sciences: What is the "culture of poverty"? How is it able to come into being, according to Lewis? That is, under what conditions does it exist? When does he say a person is no longer a part of the culture of poverty? What does Lewis say is the future of the culture of poverty?

The phrasing in Question 26.3 invites a fairly clear-cut structure: Each of the five questions can be turned into an assertion and supported with examples from Lewis's article. For example, the first two questions could become assertions like these: "Lewis defines the culture of poverty as _____," and "According to Lewis, the culture of poverty comes into being through _____." The important thing in this case is to summarize accurately what the writer said and not waste time evaluating or criticizing his ideas.

Explain the Importance or Significance   Another kind of essay exam question asks students to explain the importance of something covered in the course. Such questions require specific examples as the basis for a more general discussion of what has been studied. This type of question is often used when instructors want students to interpret a text or visual work by concentrating on a particular aspect of it.

Question 26.4 (10/100 points; 15 minutes)

In the last scene of *Paths of Glory,* the owner of a café brings a young German woman onto a small stage in his café to sing for the French troops, while Colonel Dax looks on from outside the café. Briefly explain the significance of this scene in relation to the movie as a whole.

In answering this question, a student's first task would be to reconsider the whole movie, looking for ways in which this one brief scene illuminates or explains larger issues or themes. Then, in a paragraph or two, the student would summarize these themes and point out how each element of the scene fits into the overall context.

Question 26.5 (10/100 points; 20 minutes)

Chukovsky gives many examples of cute expressions and statements uttered by small children. Give an example of two of the kinds of statements that he finds interesting. Then state their implications for understanding the nature of language in particular and communication more generally.

For Question 26.5 (on a communications exam), students would start by choosing examples of children's utterances from Chukovsky's book. These examples would then provide the basis for demonstrating the student's grasp of the larger subject. Questions like these require students to decide for themselves the significance of the information and to organize the answer so that the general ideas are clearly developed.

Apply Concepts   Very often, courses in the humanities and the social sciences emphasize significant themes, ideologies, or concepts. A common type of essay exam question asks students to apply the concepts to works studied in the course.

See Chapter 4 for more on explaining a concept.

Question 26.6 (45/130 points; 40 minutes)

Several works studied in this course depict scapegoat figures. Select two written works and two films, and discuss how their authors or directors present and analyze the social conflicts that lead to the creation of scapegoats.

The answer to Question 26.6 would provide an introductory paragraph defining the concept "scapegoat" and referring to the works to be discussed. Then the student would devote a paragraph or two to the works, pointing out specific examples to illustrate the concept. A concluding paragraph would probably attempt to bring the concept into clearer focus.

Comment on a Quotation   On essay exams, an instructor will often ask students to comment on a quotation they are seeing for the first time. Usually, such quotations will express some surprising or controversial opinion that complements or challenges basic principles or ideas in the course. Sometimes the writer being quoted is identified, sometimes not. In fact, it is not unusual for instructors to write the quotation themselves.

Question 26.7 (75/100 points; 90 minutes)

"Some historians believe that economic hardship and oppression breed social revolt, but the experience of the United States and Mexico between 1900 and 1920 suggests that people may rebel also during times of prosperity."

Question 26.7, from a midterm exam in a history course, asks students to "comment," but the three questions make clear that a successful answer would require an *argument*: a clear *thesis* stating a position on the views

Comment on this statement. Why did large numbers of Americans and Mexicans wish to change conditions in their countries during the years from 1900 to 1920? How successful were their efforts? Who benefited from the changes that took place?

expressed in the quotation, specific *reasons* for that thesis, and *support* for the thesis from readings and lectures. In general, such questions do not have a "correct" answer: Whether students agree or disagree with the quotation is not as important as whether they can argue their case reasonably and convincingly, demonstrating a firm grasp of the subject matter.

See Chapter 19 for more about these components of an argument.

Compare and Contrast   Instructors are particularly fond of essay exam questions that require a *comparison and contrast* of two or three principles, ideas, works, activities, or phenomena. To answer this kind of question, you need to explore fully the relations between the things to be compared, analyze each one separately, and then search out specific points of likeness or difference. Students must thus show a thorough knowledge of the things being compared, as well as a clear understanding of the basic issues on which comparisons and contrasts can be made. Whether the point of comparison is stated in the question or left for you to define for yourself, your answer needs to be limited to the aspects of similarity or difference that are most relevant to the general concepts or themes covered in the course.

See Chapter 18 for more about comparing and contrasting.

Question 26.8 (50/100 points; 1 hour)

Compare and analyze the views of colonialism presented in Memmi's *Colonizer and the Colonized* and Pontecorvo's *Battle of Algiers*. What are the significant differences between these two views?

Often, as in Question 26.8, the basis of comparison will be limited to a particular focus; here, for example, students are asked to compare two works in terms of their views of colonialism.

Question 26.9 (50/100 points; 1 hour)

What was the role of the United States in Cuban affairs from 1898 until 1959? How did its role there compare with its role in the rest of Spanish America during the same period?

Sometimes instructors will simply identify what is to be compared, as in Question 26.8. In this question from a Latin American history exam, students are left the task of choosing the basis of the comparison.

Synthesize Information from Various Sources   In a course with several assigned readings, an instructor may ask students to pull together, or *synthesize,* information from several or even all the readings.

For more about synthesizing, see Chapter 5, Chapter 12, and Chapter 23.

Question 26.10 (25/100 points; 30 minutes)

On the basis of the articles read on El Salvador, Nicaragua, Peru, Chile, Argentina, and Mexico, what would you say are the major problems confronting Latin America today? Discuss the major types of problems with references to particular countries as examples.

Question 26.10, from the final in a Latin American studies course, asks students to decide which major problems to discuss, which countries to include in each discussion, and how to use material from many readings to develop their answers, all in half an hour. To compose a coherent essay, a student will need a carefully developed *forecasting statement*.

For more about forecasting statements, see Chapter 13.

See Chapter 9 for more about analyzing causes.

Analyze Causes In humanities and social science courses, much of what students study concerns the causes of trends, actions, and events. Hence, it is not surprising to find questions about causes on essay exams. In such cases, the instructor expects students to *analyze* causes of various phenomena discussed in readings and lectures.

Question 26.11 (25/100 points; 30 minutes)

Given that we occupy several positions in the course of our lives and given that each position has a specific role attached to it, what kinds of problems or dilemmas arise from those multiple roles, and how are they handled?

Question 26.11 comes from a midterm exam in sociology. The question requires students to develop a list of causes in the answer. The causes would be organized under a thesis statement, and each cause would be argued and supported by referring to lectures or readings.

See Chapter 8 for more about evaluation.

Criticize or Evaluate Occasionally, instructors will include essay exam questions that invite students to *evaluate* a concept or a work. They want more than opinion: They expect a reasoned, documented evaluation based on appropriate standards of judgment. Such questions test students' ability to recall and synthesize pertinent information and to understand and apply criteria taught in the course.

Question 26.12 (10/85 points; 20 minutes)

Eisenstein and Mukerji both argue that movable print was important to the rise of Protestantism. Cole extends this argument to say that print set off a chain of events that was important to the history of the United States. Summarize this argument, and evaluate any part of it if you choose.

Question 26.12 appeared on a communications course midterm that asked students to answer "in two paragraphs." The question asks students to summarize and evaluate an argument that appears in several course readings. The students would probably use the writing strategies of comparison and contrast to analyze and evaluate the authors' views.

Write your answer.

Your strategy for writing depends on the length of your answer. For short identifications and definitions, start with a general identifying statement and then move on to describe specific applications or explanations. Two complete sentences will almost always suffice.

For longer answers, begin with a clear and explicit thesis statement. Use key terms from the question in your thesis, and use the same key terms throughout your essay. If the question does not supply any key terms, provide your own. Outlining your answer will enable you to forecast your points in your opening sentences. Use transitions such as *first, second, moreover, however,* and *thus* to signal clear relations among paragraphs.

See Chapter 13 for more about forecasting and transitions.

As you write, you will certainly think of new ideas or facts to include. If you find that you want to add a sentence or two to sections you have already completed, write them in the margin or at the top of the page, with a neat arrow pointing to where they fit in your answer. Strike out words or even sentences you want to change by drawing through them neatly with a single line. If you run out of time when you are writing an answer, jot down the remaining ideas, just to show that you know the material and with more time could have continued your answer.

Model Answers

Here we analyze several successful answers and give you an opportunity to analyze one for yourself. These analyses, along with the information we have provided elsewhere in this chapter, should greatly improve your chances of writing successful exam answers.

Short Answers   A literature midterm opened with ten items to identify, each worth 3 points. Students had about two minutes for each item. Here are three of Brenda Gossett's answers, each one earning her the full 3 points:

> Rauffenstein: He was the German general who was in charge of the castle where Boeldieu, Maréchal, and Rosenthal were finally sent in *The Grand Illusion*. He, along with Boeldieu, represented the aristocracy, which was slowly fading out at that time.

> Iges Peninsula: This peninsula is created by the Meuse River in France. It is there that the Camp of Hell was created in *The Debacle*. The Camp of Hell is where the French army was interned after the Germans defeated them in the Franco-Prussian War.

> Pache: He was the "religious peasant" in the novel *The Debacle*. It was he who inevitably became a scapegoat when he was murdered by Loubet, La poulle, and Chouteau because he wouldn't share his bread with them.

The instructor said only "identify the following" but clearly wanted students both to identify the item and to indicate its significance to the work in which it appeared. Gossett does both and gets full credit. She mentions particular works, characters, and events. Although she is rushed, she answers in complete sentences. She does not misspell any words or leave out any commas or periods. Her answers are complete and correct.

Paragraph-Length Answers The following question is from a weekly literature quiz. With only a few minutes to respond, students were instructed to "answer in a few sentences." Here is the question and Camille Prestera's answer:

> In *Things Fall Apart,* how did Okonkwo's relationship with his father affect his attitude toward his son? (20/100 points)
>
> Okonkwo despised his father, who was lazy, cowardly, and in debt. Okonkwo tried to be everything his father wasn't. He was hardworking, wealthy, and a great warrior and wrestler. Okonkwo treated his son harshly because he was afraid he saw the same weakness in Nwoye that he despised in his father. The result of this harsh treatment was that Nwoye left home.

Prestera begins by describing Okonkwo and his father, contrasting the two sharply. Then she explains Okonkwo's relationship with his son Nwoye. Her answer is coherent and straightforward.

Long Answers Many final exams include at least one question requiring an essay-length answer. John Pixley had an hour to plan and write this essay for a final exam in a literature course in response to the following question applying a concept:

> Many American writers have portrayed their characters or their poetic speaker as being engaged in a quest. The quest may be explicit or implicit, it may be external or psychological, and it may end in failure or success. Analyze the quest motif in the work of four of the following writers: Edwards, Franklin, Hawthorne, Thoreau, Douglass, Whitman, Dickinson, James, Twain.

Key term, *quest*, mentioned in introduction and thesis

1   Americans pride themselves on being ambitious and on being able to strive for goals and to tap their potential. Some say that this is what the "American Dream" is all about. It is important for one to do and be all that one is capable of. This entails a quest or search for identity, experience, and happiness. Hence, the idea of the quest is a vital one in the United States, and it can be seen as a theme throughout American literature.

First writer identified immediately

2   In eighteenth-century colonial America, Jonathan Edwards dealt with this theme in his autobiographical and personal writings. Unlike his fiery and hard-nosed sermons, these autobiographical writings present a sensitive, vulnerable man trying to find himself and his proper, satisfying place in the world. He is concerned with his spiritual growth, in being free to find and explore religious experience and happiness. For example, in *Personal Narrative*, he very carefully traces the stages of religious beliefs. He tells about periods of abandoned ecstasy, doubts, and rational revelations. He also notes that his best insights and growth came at times when he was alone in the wilderness, in nature. Edwards's efforts to find himself in relation to the world can also be seen in his "Observations of the Natural World," in which he relates various meticulously observed and described natural phenomena to religious precepts and occurrences. Here, he is trying to give the world and life, of which he is a part, some sense of meaning and purpose.

Edwards's work and the details of his quest presented

3   Although he was a contemporary of Edwards, Benjamin Franklin, who was very involved in the founding of the United States as a nation, had a different conception of the quest. He sees the quest as being one of practical accomplishment, success, and wealth. In his *Autobiography*, he stresses that happiness involves working hard to accomplish things, getting along with others, and establishing a good reputation. Unlike Edwards's, his quest is external and bound up with society. He is concerned with his morals and behavior, but as seen in part 2 of the *Autobiography*, he deals with them in an objective, pragmatic, even statistical way, rather than in sensitive pondering. It is also evident in this work that Franklin, unlike Edwards, believes so much in himself and his quest that he is able to laugh at himself. His concern with society can be seen in *Poor Richard's Almanac*, in which he gives practical advice on how to find success and happiness in the world, how to "be healthy, wealthy, and wise."

4   Still another version of the quest can be seen in the mid-nineteenth-century poetry of Walt Whitman. The quest that he portrays blends elements of those of Edwards and Franklin. In "Song of Myself," which is clearly autobiographical, the speaker emphasizes the importance of finding, knowing, and enjoying oneself as part of nature and the human community. He says that one should come to realize that one is lovable, just as are all other people and all of nature and life. This is a quest for sensitivity and awareness, as Edwards advocates, and for great self-confidence, as Franklin advocates. Along with Edwards, Whitman sees that peaceful isolation in nature is important; but he also sees the importance of interacting with people, as Franklin does. Being optimistic and feeling good--in both the literal and the figurative sense--are the objects of this quest. Unfortunately, personal disappointment and national crisis (i.e., the Civil War) shattered Whitman's sense of confidence, and he lost the impetus of this quest in his own life.

5   This theme of the quest can be seen in prose fiction as well as in poetry and autobiography. One interesting example is "The Beast in the Jungle," a short story written by Henry James around 1903. It is interesting in that not only does the principal character, John Marcher, fail in his lifelong quest, but his failure comes about in a most subtle and frustrating way. Marcher believes that something momentous is going to happen in his future. He talks about his belief to only one person, a woman named May. May decides to befriend him for life and watch with him for the momentous occurrence to come about, for "the beast in the jungle" to "pounce." As time passes, May seems to know what this occurrence is and eventually even says that it has happened; but John is still in the dark. It is only long after May's death that the beast pounces on him in his recognition that the "beast" was his failure to truly love May, the one woman of his life, even though she gave him all the encouragement that she possibly, decently could. Marcher never defined the terms of his quest until it was too late. By just waiting and watching, he failed to find feeling and passion. This tragic realization, as someone like Whitman would view it, brings about John Marcher's ruin.

Side annotations:

Second writer identified in transition sentence; key term (*quest*) repeated

Contrast with Edwards added for coherence

Another key term from question, *external*, used

Franklin's particular kind of quest described

Third writer identified in transition sentence; key term repeated

Coherence sustained by comparison of Whitman to Edwards and Franklin

Whitman's quest defined

Transition: Key term repeated; fourth writer identified

Quest of James character described

Key term repeated in conclusion

6   As seen in these few examples, the theme of the quest is a significant one in American literature. Also obvious is the fact that there are a variety of approaches to, methods used in, and outcomes of the quest. This is an appropriate theme for American literature, seeing how much Americans cherish the right of "the pursuit of happiness."

Pixley's answer is strong for two reasons: He has the information he needs, and he has organized it carefully and presented it coherently.

EXERCISE 26.1

The following essay was written by Dan Hepler. He answered the same essay exam question as his classmate John Pixley. Analyze Hepler's essay to discover whether it meets the criteria of a good essay exam answer. Review the criteria mentioned earlier in this chapter (in the section Write Your Answer, pp. 693–96) and in the annotated commentary of John Pixley's answer. Try to identify the features of Hepler's essay that contribute to or work against its success.

Dan Hepler's Answer

The quest motif is certainly important in American literature. By considering Franklin, Thoreau, Douglass, and Twain, we can see that the quest may be explicit or implicit, external or psychological, a failure or a success. Tracing the quest motif through these four authors seems to show a developing concern in American literature with transcending materialism to address deeper issues. It also reveals a drift toward ambiguity and pessimism.   1

Benjamin Franklin's quest, as revealed by his *Autobiography*, is for material comfort and outward success. His quest may be considered an explicit one because he announces clearly what he is trying to do: perfect a systematic approach for living long and happily. The whole *Autobiography* is a road map intended for other people to use as a guide; Franklin apparently meant rather literally for people to imitate his methods. He wrote with the assumption that his success was reproducible. He is possibly the most optimistic author in American literature because he enjoys life, knows exactly *why* he enjoys life, and believes that anyone else willing to follow his formula may enjoy life as well.   2

By Franklin's standards, his quest is clearly a success. But his *Autobiography* portrays only an external, not a psychological, success. This is not to suggest that Franklin was a psychological failure. Indeed, we have every reason to believe the contrary. But the fact remains that Franklin *wrote* only about external success; he never indicated how he really felt emotionally. Possibly it was part of Franklin's overriding optimism to assume that material comfort leads naturally to emotional fulfillment.   3

Henry David Thoreau presents a more multifaceted quest. His *Walden* is, on the simplest level, the chronicle of Thoreau's physical journey out of town and into the woods. But the moving itself is not the focus of *Walden*. It is really more of a metaphor for some kind of spiritual quest going on within Thoreau's mind. Most of the action in *Walden* is mental, as Thoreau contemplates and philosophizes, always using the lake, the woods, and his own daily actions as symbols of higher, more eternal truths. This spiritual quest is a success in   4 that Thoreau is able to appreciate the beauty of nature and to see through much of the sham and false assumptions of town life and blind materialism.

Thoreau does not leave us with nearly as explicit a "blueprint" for success as Franklin does. Even Franklin's plan is limited to people of high intelligence, personal discipline, and sound character; Franklin sometimes seems to forget that many human beings are in fact weak and evil and so would stand little chance of success similar to his own. But at least Franklin's quest could be duplicated by another Franklin. Thoreau's quest is more problematic, for even as great a mystic and naturalist as Thoreau himself could not remain in the woods indefinitely. This points toward the idea that the real quest is all internal and psychological; Thoreau seems to have gone to the woods to develop a spiritual strength that he could keep and take elsewhere on subsequent dealings with the "real world."

The quest of Frederick Douglass was explicit in that he needed physically to get north and escape slavery, but it was also implicit because he sought to discover and redefine himself through his quest, as Thoreau did. Douglass's motives were more sharply focused than either Franklin's or Thoreau's; his very humanness was at stake, as well as his physical well-being and possibly even his life. But Douglass also makes it clear that the most horrible part of slavery was the mental anguish of having no hope of freedom. His learning to read, and his maintenance of this skill, seems to have been as important as the maintenance of his material comforts, of which he had very few. In a sense, Douglass's quest is the most psychological and abstract so far because it is for the very essence of freedom and humanity, both of which were mostly taken for granted by Franklin and Thoreau. Also, Douglass's quest is the most pessimistic of the three; Douglass concludes that physical violence is the only way out, as he finds with the Covey incident.

Finally, Mark Twain's *Huckleberry Finn* is an example of the full range of meaning that the quest motif may assume. Geographically, Huck's quest is very large. But again, there is a quest defined implicitly as well as one defined explicitly, as Huck (without consciously realizing it) searches for morality, truth, and freedom. Twain's use of the quest is ambiguous, even more so than the previous writers', because while he suggests success superficially (i.e., the "happily ever after" scene in the last chapter), he really hints at some sort of ultimate hopelessness inherent in society. Not even Douglass questions the good or evil of American society as deeply as Twain does; for Douglass, everything will be fine when slavery is abolished; but for Twain, the only solution is to "light out for the territories" altogether--and when Twain wrote, he knew that the territories were no more.

Twain's implicit sense of spiritual failure stands in marked contrast to Franklin's buoyant confidence in material success. The guiding image of the quest, however, is central to American values and, consequently, a theme that these writers and others have adapted to suit their own vision.

Analyze the following essay exam questions to decide what kind of writing task they present. What is being asked of the student as a participant in the course and as a writer? Given the time constraints of the exam, what plan would you propose for writing the answer? Following each question is the number of points it is worth and the amount of time allotted to answer it.

1. Cortazar is a producer of fantastic literature. Discuss first what fantastic literature is. Then choose any four stories by Cortazar as examples, and discuss the fantastic elements in these stories. Refer to the structure, techniques, and narrative styles that he uses in these four stories. If you like, you may refer to more than four, of course. (Points: 30 of 100. Time: 40 of 150 minutes.)

2. During the course of the twentieth century, the United States experienced three significant periods of social reform—the progressive era, the age of the Great Depression, and the decade of the 1960s. What were the sources of reform in each period? What were the most significant reform achievements of each period as well as the largest failings? (Points: 35 of 100. Time: 75 of 180 minutes.)

3. Since literature is both an artistic and an ideological product, writers comment on their material context through their writing.

   a. What is Rulfo's perspective of his Mexican reality, and how is it portrayed through his stories?

   b. What particular themes does he deal with, especially in these stories: "The Burning Plain," "Luvina," "They Gave Us the Land," "Paso del Norte," and "Tell Them Not to Kill Me!"?

   c. What literary techniques and structures does he use to convey his perspective? Refer to a specific story as an example.

   (Points: 30 of 100. Time: 20 of 50 minutes.)

4. Why is there a special reason to be concerned about the influence of television watching on kids? In your answer, include a statement of the following:

   a. Your own understanding of the *general communication principles* involved for any television watcher.

   b. What is special about television and kids.

   c. How advertisers and producers use this information. (You should draw from the relevant readings as well as lectures.)

   (Points: 20 of 90. Time: 25 of 90 minutes.)

5. Analyze the autobiographical tradition in American literature, focusing on differences and similarities among authors and, if appropriate, changes over time. Discuss four authors in all. In addition to the conscious autobiographers—Edwards, Franklin, Thoreau, and Douglass—you may choose one or two figures from among the following fictional or poetic quasi-autobiographers: Hawthorne, Whitman, Dickinson, and Twain. (Points: 50 of 120. Time: 60 of 180 minutes.)

6. How does the system of (media) sponsorship work, and what, if any, ideological control do sponsors exert? Be specific and illustrative. (Points: 33 of 100. Time: 60 of 180 minutes.)

7   Several of the works studied in this course analyze the tension between myth and reality. Select two written works and two films, and analyze how their authors or directors present the conflict between myth and reality and how they resolve it, if they resolve it. (Points: 45 of 130. Time: 60 of 180 minutes.)

8   *Man's Hope* is a novel about the Spanish Civil War written while the war was still going on. *La Guerre Est Finie* is a film about Spanish revolutionaries depicting their activities nearly thirty years after the civil war. Discuss how the temporal relationship of each of these works to the civil war is reflected in the character of the works themselves and in the differences between them. (Points: 58 of 100. Time: 30 of 50 minutes.)

9   Write an essay on one of these topics: The role of the narrator in *Tom Jones* and *Pride and Prejudice* or the characters of Uncle Toby and Miss Bates. (Points: 33 of 100. Time: 60 of 180 minutes.)

27

Creating a Portfolio

A **portfolio** displays your work. Portfolios for college composition courses usually include a selection of your writing for the course and an essay reflecting on your writing and on what you learned in the course. The contents of a portfolio will, of course, vary from writer to writer and from instructor to instructor. This chapter provides some advice for assembling a writing portfolio using the resources in *The St. Martin's Guide to Writing*.

Purposes of a Writing Portfolio

Portfolios are generally used to display an individual's accomplishments. Artists present portfolios of their best work to gallery owners. Designers and architects present portfolios of their most successful work to potential clients. Writing students may be asked to submit a portfolio of their work for evaluation. No matter what the occasion, a portfolio presents a rich opportunity to show what you can do.

Creating a portfolio for a composition course enables you to present your best, most representative, or most extensively revised writing. Your instructor will assign the final grade, but how you select the materials included in your portfolio and describe them in your introductory essay may have some influence on your instructor's judgment. Most important, selecting your work and composing an introductory reflective essay give you an opportunity to review, reinforce, and therefore better remember and apply what you have learned. Reviewing your work can increase your satisfaction with the course, give you insights into your intellectual development, and help you recognize your strengths and weaknesses.

Assembling a Portfolio for Your Composition Course

Some instructors give students free rein in deciding what to include in their portfolio, but most specify what the portfolio should include. Instructors usually ask students to select a certain number of essays, and they may specify that certain types of essays be included, such as one based on personal experience or observation and another based on research, along with other materials like in-class writing or responses to readings. Many instructors also ask students to include materials that reflect their writing process (such as invention work, drafts, and critical responses). In addition to a selection of course materials, instructors usually require a reflective essay or letter that introduces the portfolio and evaluates the writer's own work.

Instructors who require portfolios often do not assign grades to individual drafts or revisions but wait until the end of the term to grade the entire portfolio. In such cases, instructors may ask students to submit a midterm portfolio for an in-progress course evaluation. A midterm portfolio usually includes plans for revising one or more of the essays included.

There are many ways to assemble portfolios, and you will need to determine exactly what your instructor expects your portfolio to include. Here are some of the variables to consider:

- How many essays should be included in the portfolio?
- May essays be revised further for the portfolio?
- What other material should be included (such as invention or research notes, exercises, notes from collaborative activities, analyses of readings, or downloaded Web pages)?
- May material from other courses, workplace projects, or service-learning projects be included?

For more about service learning, see Chapter 31.

- Should the portfolio be introduced by a reflective essay or letter? If so, how long should it be? Are there any special requirements for it?
- How should the portfolio be organized?

The following sections review specific resources in the *Guide* that can help you compose your portfolio.

Select your work.

Even if your instructor specifies what to include in your portfolio, you have some important decisions to make. Here are some suggestions to help you:

- If you are asked to select only your best essays, begin by rereading them to see how well each one develops the basic features of its genre. Also review any feedback you received from your instructor, classmates, writing center tutors, or other readers.
- If you are asked to make further revisions to one or more of your essays, reread the essay, using the Peer Review Guide for that genre, or get a response to it from your instructor, a classmate, or a writing center tutor. It may also help to review any responses you received on earlier drafts as well as the Troubleshooting Guide for that genre to see what else you could do to improve the essay. Be sure to edit and proofread your essays carefully.
- If you are asked to select an essay based on personal experience, you might choose the remembered event essay you wrote for Chapter 2. If you are asked for essays based on firsthand observation and analysis, look at what you wrote for the profile (Chapter 3), the concept explanation (Chapter 4), the comparative

analysis (Chapter 5), or the short story analysis (Chapter 10). If you are asked to include argument essays, review the writing you did for Chapters 6–9.

- If you are asked to select essays incorporating research, look at the essays you wrote for Chapters 4–9.

- If you are asked to select essays with a range of different purposes and audiences, you might begin by reviewing the Determining the Writer's Purpose and Audience sections of the Part One chapters you used. Then reread your invention notes defining the particular purpose and audience for each essay you wrote.

- If you are asked to include examples of your writing process work, look for your most thoughtful invention work; a first draft from the Drafting section in any of the Guides to Writing in Chapters 2–10; one or more revisions showing significant rethinking or reorganization; your critical reading response to another student's draft showing perceptive criticism and helpful suggestions; or a draft you edited heavily.

- If you are asked to include a complete process for one essay, you should choose process materials that show the quality as well as quantity of work you have done. Look for examples of thoughtful invention and substantive revision you can point out in your reflective essay.

- If you are asked to select essays that show the progress you have made in the course, you may want to choose essays that underwent radical change during the term.

Reflect on your work and what you have learned.

Many instructors require a written statement in the form of an essay or letter introducing the portfolio. Some ask for a simple description of the work presented in your portfolio; others prefer an evaluation of your work; still others may want you to connect your learning in this course to other courses and to work you hope to do in the future. Keeping the following considerations in mind will help you write a thoughtful, well-organized statement to your instructor about what you have learned:

- ***Introduce and describe your work.*** Because you will need to refer to several works or parts of a work, name each item in your portfolio in a consistent way. In describing an essay, give its title, genre (using the title of the chapter in *The St. Martin's Guide*), purpose, audience, and topic.

If you need help writing an evaluation, review Chapter 8.

- ***Justify your choices.*** When you justify what you see as your "best" work, you think critically about the standards you are using to evaluate good writing in each genre. The *Guide* sets forth clear criteria for each kind of writing in the Use the Basic Features and Peer Review Guide sections in Chapters 2–10. Review these sections as you judge the success of your essay, and refer to them as you explain your analysis.

- ***Illustrate your growth as a writer with specific examples.*** You may have selected work to show how you have grown as a writer, but you should not assume your readers will read the portfolio as you do without some guidance. You need to show them where they can find evidence that supports your analysis by citing relevant examples from the work included in your portfolio. Summarize or quote your examples, and be sure to tell readers what you think the examples illustrate. Also refer to them in a way that will help readers locate them with ease—perhaps by page and paragraph number (see the next section for some suggestions for organizing your portfolio).

- ■ *Use the* **Guide** *to help you reflect on your learning.* Your instructor may ask you to consider what you learned in writing and revising a particular essay as well as what you learned about the process of writing that essay. In either case, it will help you to anchor your reflections in the specific work you have done using this book. Consider what you have learned analyzing and discussing the readings, drafting and researching, participating in groups, getting and giving critical comments, and revising and editing. Look again at the Thinking Critically sections in Chapters 2–10. There you will find questions that will help you reflect on how you solved problems when revising an essay and how your writing can be situated and understood in a larger social context. You may well be able to use your responses to these questions in your portfolio's reflective essay.

Organize your portfolio.

Some instructors prescribe the portfolio's design and organization, while others allow students to be creative. Follow your instructor's specific guidelines. If your instructor doesn't supply guidelines, here are some possibilities for organizing your portfolio:

- ■ *Include a table of contents.* Portfolios need a table of contents so that readers can see at a glance what is included and where it is located. Be sure to identify all of the parts and specify the page on which each part begins. For online portfolios, link each item in your table of contents to your work.

- ■ *Label each item.* If your instructor does not specify how you should label your work, you need to develop a clear system on your own. You may need to explain your system briefly in a note on the table of contents or in your introductory reflective essay, where you refer to particular items in your portfolio. For example, you could use the *Guide* chapter number to identify each essay assignment. To indicate process materials, consider using the chapter number and title and the relevant heading from that chapter's Guide to Writing section (such as Chapter 2, Writing a Draft). To identify different drafts, you could write on the top left margin of every page the chapter number, essay title, and draft number. For drafts that received a critical reading, you might want to add the notation "Read by *S*." You should also date all of your work.

- ■ *Sequence the material.* If your instructor does not indicate how you should order the work included in your portfolio, you will have to decide yourself. If your instructor asks you to present two or more examples of your best work, you may want to begin with the essay you consider your very best. If your instructor asks you to show the progress you have made in the course, you could begin with your weakest essay and either show how you improved it or present later essays that were stronger. If your instructor asks you to demonstrate growth, you might organize your work by the particular areas that improved. For example, you could show that you learned to rework your writing substantially by presenting multiple drafts. Or to show that you learned to edit effectively or to avoid certain sentence errors, you could give examples of a particular error you made one or two times early on but avoided in later drafts.

28

Analyzing Visuals

We live in a highly visual world. Every day we are deluged with a seemingly endless stream of images, all of them competing for our attention, and all of them loaded with information and ideas. Forms of communication that traditionally used only the written word (letters, books, term papers) or the spoken word (telephone conversations, lectures) are today increasingly enhanced with visual components (calls on FaceTime or Skype, presentation slides in Prezi or PowerPoint) for greater impact. And most of us would agree that visuals do, indeed, have an impact: A picture, as the saying goes, is worth a thousand words.

In part because of their potentially powerful effect on us, visuals should be approached the way we approach written texts: analytically and critically. Whether their purpose is to sell us an idea or a car, to spur us to action, or inspire us to dream, visuals invite analysis both of their key components and their *rhetorical context*. As we "read" a visual, therefore, we should ask ourselves a series of questions: Who created it? Where was it published? What *audience* is it addressing? What is it trying to get this audience to think and feel about the subject? How does it attempt to achieve this *purpose*?

Let's look, for example, at Figure 28.1, a public service announcement (PSA) from the World Wildlife Fund (WWF).

The central image in this PSA is a photo of an attractive, smiling young couple. Most of us will immediately recognize the dress, posture, and facial expressions of the young man and woman as those of a newly married couple; the photo-mounting corners make the image seem like a real wedding album photo, as opposed to an ad agency's creation (which would be easier to ignore). After noting these things, however, we are immediately struck by what is wrong with the picture: a hurricane rages in the background, blowing hair, clothing, and the bride's veil forcefully to one side showering the bride's pure white dress with spots (of rain? mud?) and threatening to rip the bridal bouquet from her hand.

So what do we make of the disruption of the convention (the traditional wedding photo) on which the PSA image is based? In trying to decide, most of us will look next to the text below the image: "Ignoring global warming won't make it go away." The disjunction between the couple's blissful expression and the storm raging around them turns out to be the point of the PSA: Like the young couple in the picture, the PSA implies, we are all blithely ignoring the impending disaster that global warming represents. The reputable, nonprofit WWF's logo and URL, which constitute its "signature," are meant to be an assurance that this threat is real, and not just an idea a profit-seeking ad agency dreamt up to manipulate us.

People continue to argue about how urgent the problem of climate change is and what, if anything, we need to do about it. The WWF suggests that, like the clueless young couple, too many of us have adopted a "head-in-the-sand" attitude about the problem. Lest the implied criticism be construed as an outright insult and alienate viewers, the implied connection to the couple also flatters us by implying that we are attractive, hopeful, and well intentioned. Global warming, in the WWF's view, threatens the bright future we all like to imagine we have ahead of us.

Not everyone will be convinced by this PSA to support the work of the WWF, and some viewers may feel manipulated by the visual image. They may disagree that the problem is as dire as the depiction implicitly claims it is. They may feel that our resources and energy would be better directed toward other problems facing the world. Nevertheless, most people would agree that with a single cleverly constructed image, a single line of text, and a logo, the PSA delivers its message clearly and forcefully.

FIGURE 28.1
"Wedding," from the WWF's "Beautiful Day U.S." Series

Criteria for Analyzing Visuals

The primary purpose of this chapter is to help you analyze visuals and write about them. In your college courses, some of you will be asked to write entire papers in which you analyze one or more visuals (a painting or a photo, for example). Some of you will write papers in which you include analysis of one or more visual texts within the context of a larger written essay (say, by analyzing the brochures and ads authorized by a political candidate, in an argument about her campaign).

Of course, learning to analyze visuals effectively can also help you gain a more complete understanding of any document that *uses* visuals but that is not entirely or predominantly composed of them. Why did Jenée Desmond-Harris, for example, choose to include a particular photo of her friend Thea in her remembered-event essay "Tupac and My Non-Thug Life" (see Chapter 2)? Does it reinforce the written description, add to it, or contradict it in some way? If there is a caption under the photo, how does it affect the way we read it? Jonathan Potthast includes a graphic of the volcanic explosivity index in his concept explanation "Supervolcanoes: A Catastrophe of Ice and Fire" (see Chapter 4), but he doesn't include a chart of the serious effects of volcanic eruptions. Why? How well does the graphic help Potthast explain supervolcanoes? Understanding what visuals can do for a text can also help you effectively integrate images, charts, graphs, and other visuals into your own essays, whatever your topic.

The chart "Criteria for Analyzing Visuals" outlines key criteria for analyzing visuals and provides questions for you to ask about documents that include them.

CRITERIA FOR ANALYZING VISUALS

KEY COMPONENTS

Composition

- Of what elements is the visual composed?

- What is the focal point—that is, the place your eyes are drawn to?

- From what perspective do you view the focal point? Are you looking straight ahead at it, down at it, or up at it? If the visual is a photograph, what angle was the image shot from—straight ahead, looking down or up?

- What colors are used? Are there obvious special effects employed? Is there a frame, or are there any additional graphical elements? If so, what do these elements contribute to your "reading" of the visual?

People/Other Main Figures

- If people are depicted, how would you describe their age, gender, subculture, ethnicity, profession, level of attractiveness, and socioeconomic class? How do these factors relate to other elements of the image?

- Who is looking at whom? Do the people represented seem conscious of the viewer's gaze?

- What do the facial expressions and body language tell you about power relationships (equal, subordinate, in charge) and attitudes (self-confident, vulnerable, anxious, subservient, angry, aggressive, sad)?

Scene

- If a recognizable scene is depicted, what is its setting? What is in the background and the foreground?

- What has happened just before the image was "shot"? What will happen in the next scene?

- What, if anything, is happening just outside of the visual frame?

Words

- If text is combined with the visual, what role does the text play? Is it a slogan? A famous quote? Lyrics from a well-known song?

- If the text helps you interpret the visual's overall meaning, what interpretive clues does it provide?

- What is the tone of the text? Humorous? Elegiac? Ironic?

A Sample Analysis

In a composition class, students were asked to do a short written analysis of a photograph. In looking for ideas, Paul Taylor came across the Library of Congress's *Documenting America,* an exhibit of photographs taken 1935–45. Gordon Parks's photographs struck Paul as particularly interesting, especially those of Ella Watson, a poorly paid office cleaner employed by the federal government. (See Figure 28.2, p. 708)

Tone

- What tone, or mood, does the visual convey? Is it lighthearted, somber, frightening, shocking, joyful? What elements in the visual (color, composition, words, people, setting) convey this tone?

CONTEXT(S)

Rhetorical Context

- **What is the visual's main purpose?** Are we being asked to buy a product? Form an opinion or judgment about something? Support a political party's candidate? Take some other kind of action?

- **Who is its target audience?** Children? Men? Women? Some sub- or super-set of these groups (e.g., African American men, "tweens," seniors)?

- **Who is the author? Who sponsored its publication?** What background/associations do the author and the sponsoring publication have? What other works have they produced?

- **Where was it published, and in what form?** Online? On television? In print? In a commercial publication (a sales brochure, billboard, ad) or an informational one (newspaper, magazine)?

- **If the visual is embedded within a document that is primarily written text, how do the written text and the visual relate to each other?** Do they convey the same message, or are they at odds in any way? What does the image contribute to the written text? Is it essential or just eye candy?

- ***Social Context.* What is the immediate social and cultural context within which the visual is operating?** If we are being asked to support a certain candidate, for example, how does the visual reinforce or counter what we already know about this candidate? What other social/cultural knowledge does the visual assume its audience already has?

- ***Historical Context.* What historical knowledge does it assume the audience already possesses?** Does the visual refer to other historical images, figures, events, or stories that the audience would recognize? How do these historical references relate to the visual's audience and purpose?

- ***Intertextuality.* How does the visual connect, relate to, or contrast with any other significant texts, visual or otherwise, that you are aware of?** How do such considerations inform your ideas about this particular visual?

FIGURE 28.2 *Ella Watson,* Gordon Parks (1942)
Library of Congress,

FIGURE 28.3 *American Gothic,* Grant Wood (1930)
Superstock/Art © Figge Art Museum, successors to the estate of Nan Wood Graham/ VAGA, New York, NY.

After studying the photos, Paul read about Parks's first session with Watson:

My first photograph of [Watson] was unsubtle. I overdid it and posed her, Grant Wood style, before the American flag, a broom in one hand, a mop in the other, staring straight into the camera.[1]

Paul didn't understand Parks's reference to Grant Wood in his description of the photo, so he did an Internet search and discovered that Parks was referring to a classic painting by Wood called *American Gothic* (Figure 28.3). Reading further about the connection, he discovered that Parks's photo of Watson is itself commonly titled *American Gothic* and discussed as a parody of Grant Wood's painting.

---

[1]Gordon Parks, *A Choice of Weapons* (New York: Harper & Row, 1966), 230–31. Print.

FIGURE 28.4 *Emerging Man,* Gordon Parks (1952)
Courtesy of and copyright The Gordon Parks Foundation

After learning about the connection with *American Gothic,* Paul read more about the context of Parks's photos:

> Gordon Parks was born in Kansas in 1912. . . . During the Depression a variety of jobs . . . took him to various parts of the northern United States. He took up photography during his travels. . . . In 1942, an opportunity to work for the Farm Security Administration brought the photographer to the nation's capital; Parks later recalled that "discrimination and bigotry were worse there than any place I had yet seen."[2]

Intrigued by what he had learned so far, Paul decided to delve into Parks's later career. A 2006 obituary of Parks in the *New York Times* reproduced his 1952 photo *Emerging Man* (see Figure 28.4), which Paul decided to analyze for his assignment. First he did additional research on the photo. Then he made notes on his responses to the photo using the "Criteria for Analyzing Visuals" earlier in the chapter.

---

[2]Martin H. Bush, "A Conversation with Gordon Parks," in *The Photographs of Gordon Parks* (Wichita, KS: Wichita State University, 1983), 36. Print.

PAUL TAYLOR'S ANALYSIS OF *EMERGING MAN*

KEY COMPONENTS OF THE VISUAL

Composition

- **Of what elements is the visual composed?**
  It's a black-and-white photo showing the top three-quarters of a man's face and his hands (mostly fingers). He appears to be emerging out of the ground -- out of a sewer? There's what looks like asphalt in the foreground, and buildings (out of focus) in the far background.

- **What is the focal point — that is, the place your eyes are drawn to?** The focal point is the face of the man staring directly into the camera's lens. There's a shaft of light angled (slightly from the right?) onto the lower-middle part of his face. His eyes appear to glisten slightly. The rest of his face, his hands, and the foreground are in shadow.

- **From what perspective do you view the focal point?** We appear to be looking at him at eye level -- weird, since eye level for him is just a few inches from the ground. Was the photographer lying down? The shot is also a close-up -- a foot or two from the man's face. Why so close?

- **What colors are used? Are there obvious special effects employed? Is there a frame, or are there any additional graphical elements?** There's no visible frame or any graphic elements. The image is in stark black and white, and there's a "graininess" to it: we can see the texture of the man's skin and the asphalt on the street.

People/Other Main Figures

- **If people are depicted, how would you describe their age, gender, subculture, ethnicity, profession, level of attractiveness, and socioeconomic class?** The man is African American and probably middle-aged (or at least not obviously very young or very old). We can't see his clothing or any other marker of class, profession, etc. The fact that he seems to be emerging from a sewer implies that he's not hugely rich or prominent, of course -- a "man of the people"?

- **Who is looking at whom? Do the people represented seem conscious of the viewer's gaze?** The man seems to be looking directly into the camera and at the viewer (who's in the position of the photographer). I guess, yes, he seems to look straight at the viewer -- perhaps in a challenging or questioning way.

- **What do the facial expressions and body language tell you about power relationships (equal, subordinate, in charge) and attitudes (self-confident, vulnerable, anxious, subservient, angry, aggressive, sad)?** We can only see his face from the nose up, and his fingertips. It looks like one eyebrow is slightly raised, which might mean he's questioning or skeptical. The expression in his eyes is definitely serious. The position of his fingers implies that he's clutching the rim of the manhole -- that, and the title, indicate that he's pulling himself up out of the hole. But since we see only the fingers, not the whole hand, does his hold seem tenuous -- he's "holding on by his fingertips"? Not sure.

Scene

- **If a recognizable scene is depicted, what is its setting? What is in the background and the foreground?** It looks like an urban setting (asphalt, manhole cover, buildings, and lights in the blurry distant background). Descriptions of the photo note that Parks shot the image in Harlem. Hazy buildings and objects are in the distance. Only the man's face and fingertips are in focus. The sky behind him is light gray, though -- is it dawn?

- **What has happened just before the image was "shot"? What will happen in the next scene?** He appears to be coming up and out of the hole in the ground (the sewer).

- **What, if anything, is happening just outside of the visual frame?** It's not clear. There's no activity in the background at all. It's deserted, except for him.

Words

- **If text is combined with the visual, what role does the text play?** There's no text on or near the image. There is the title, though--*Emerging Man*.

- **Does the text help you interpret the visual's overall meaning?** The title is a literal description, but it might also refer to the civil rights movement --the gradual racial and economic integration--of African Americans into American society.

- **What is the tone of the text?** Hard to say. I guess, assuming wordplay is involved, it's sort of witty (merging traffic?).

Tone

- **What tone, or mood, does the visual convey? What elements in the visual (color, composition, words, people, setting) convey this tone?** The tone is serious, even perhaps a bit spooky. The use of black and white and heavy shadows lends a somewhat ominous feel, though the ray of light on the man's face, the lightness of the sky, and the lights in the background counterbalance this to an extent. The man's expression is somber, though not obviously angry or grief-stricken.

CONTEXT(S)

Rhetorical Context

- **What is the visual's main purpose?** Given Parks's interest in politics and social justice, it seems fair to assume that the image of the man emerging from underground--from the darkness into the light?--is a reference to social progress (civil rights movement) and suggests rebirth of a sort. The use of black and white, while certainly not unusual in photographs of the era, emphasizes the division between black and white that is in part the photo's subject.

- **Who is its target audience?** Because it appeared first in *Life*, the target audience was mainstream-- a broad cross-section of the magazine-reading U.S. population at mid-twentieth century.

- **Who is the author? Who sponsored its publication?** During this era, Gordon Parks was best known as a photographer whose works documented and commented on social conditions. The fact that this photo was originally published in *Life* (a mainstream periodical read by white Americans throughout the country) is probably significant.

- **If the visual is embedded within a document that is primarily written text, how do the written text and the visual relate to each other?** The photo accompanied an article about Ellison's *Invisible Man,* a novel about a man who goes underground to escape racism and conflicts within the early civil rights movement. Now the man is reentering mainstream society?

- *Social Context.* **What is the immediate social and cultural context within which the visual is operating?** The civil rights movement was gaining ground in post–World War II society.

- *Historical Context.* **What historical knowledge does it assume the audience already possesses?** For a viewer in 1952, the image would call to mind the current and past situation of African Americans. Uncertainty about what the future would hold (Would the emergence be successful? What kind of man would eventually emerge?) would be a big part of the viewer's response. Viewers today obviously feel less suspense about what would happen in the immediate (post-1952) future. The "vintage" feel of the photo's style and even the man's hair, along with the use of black and white, probably have a "distancing" effect on the viewer today. At the same time, the subject continues to be relevant--most viewers will likely think about the progress we've made in race relations and where we're currently headed.

- *Intertextuality.* **How does the visual connect, relate to, or contrast with any other significant texts, visual or otherwise, that you are aware of?** *Invisible Man,* which I've already discussed, was a best-seller and won the National Book Award in 1953.

After writing and reviewing these notes and doing some further research to fill in gaps in his knowledge about Parks, Ellison, and the civil rights movement, Paul drafted his analysis. He submitted this draft to his peer group for comments, and then revised. His final draft follows.

Taylor 1

Paul Taylor

Professor Stevens

Writing Seminar I

4 October 2015

The Rising

Gordon Parks's 1952 photograph *Emerging Man* (Fig. 1) is as historically significant a reflection of the civil rights movement as are the speeches of Martin Luther King and Malcolm X, the music of Mahalia Jackson, and the books of Ralph Ellison and James Baldwin. Through striking use of black and white--a reflection of the racial divisions plaguing American cities and towns throughout much of the nineteenth and twentieth centuries--and a symbolically potent central subject--an African American man we see literally "emerging" from a city manhole--Parks's photo evokes the centuries of racial and economic marginalization of African Americans, at the same time as it projects a spirit of determination and optimism regarding the civil rights movement's eventual success.

In choosing the starkest of urban settings and giving the image a gritty feel, Parks alerts the viewer to the gravity of his subject and gives

Fig. 1. Gordon Parks, *Emerging Man* (1952)

Taylor 2

Fig. 2. Gordon Parks, *Ella Watson* (1942)

it a sense of immediacy. As with the documentary photographs Parks took of office cleaner Ella Watson for the Farm Security Administration in the 1940s--see Fig. 2 for one example--the carefully chosen setting and the spareness of the treatment ensure the viewer's focus on the artist's social statement (*Documenting*). Whereas the photos of Watson document a particular woman and the actual conditions of her life and work, *Emerging Man* strips away any particulars, including the man's name, with the result that the photo enters the symbolic or even mythic realm.

The composition of *Emerging Man* makes it impossible for us to focus on anything other than the unnamed subject rising from the manhole--we are, for instance, unable to consider what the weather might be, though we might surmise from the relatively light tone of the sky and the emptiness of the street that it is dawn. Similarly, we are not given any specifics of the setting, which is simply urban and, apart from the central figure, unpopulated. Reducing the elements to their outlines in this way keeps the viewer focused on the grand central theme of the piece: the role of race in mid-twentieth-century America and the future of race relations.

The fact that the man is looking directly at the camera, in a way that's challenging but not hostile, speaks to the racial optimism of the period among many African Americans and whites alike. President Truman's creation of the President's Committee on Civil Rights in 1946 and his 1948 Executive Order for the integration of all armed services were significant steps toward the emergence of the full-blown civil rights movement, providing hope that African Americans would be able, for perhaps the first time in American history, to look directly into the eyes of their white counterparts and fearlessly emphasize their shared humanity (Leuchtenburg). The "emerging man" seems to be daring us to try to stop his rise from the manhole, his hands gripping its sides, his eyes focused intently on the viewer.

According to several sources, Parks planned and executed the photograph as a photographic counterpart to Ralph Ellison's 1952 *Invisible Man,* a breakthrough novel about race and society that was both a best-seller and a critical success. *Invisible Man* is narrated in the first person by an unnamed African American man who traces his experiences from boyhood. The climax of the novel shows the narrator hunted by policemen controlling a Harlem race riot; escaping down a manhole, the narrator is trapped at first but eventually decides to live permanently underground, hidden from society ("Ralph Ellison"). The correspondences between the photo and the book are apparent. In fact, according to the catalog accompanying an exhibit of Parks's photos selected by the photographer himself before his death in 2006, Ellison actually collaborated on the staging of the photo (*Bare Witness* 17).

More than just a photographic counterpart, however, it seems that Parks's *Emerging Man* can be read as a sequel to *Invisible Man,* with the emphasis radically shifted from resignation to optimism. The man who had decided to live underground now decides to emerge, and does so with determination. In this compelling photograph, Parks--himself an "emerging man," considering he was the first African American photographer to be hired full-time by *Life* magazine--created a photograph that celebrated the changing racial landscape in American society.

Works Cited

Bare Witness: Photographs by Gordon Parks. Ed. Maren Stange. Milan: Skira, 2007. Print.

"Documenting America: Photographers on Assignment." *America from the Great Depression to World War II: Black-and-White Photographs from the FSA-OWI, 1935-1945*. Prints and Photographs Div., Lib. of Cong., n.d. Web. 27 Sept. 2015.

Leuchtenburg, William E. "The Conversion of Harry Truman." *American Heritage* 42.7 (1991): 55-68. *America: History & Life*. Web. 29 Sept. 2015.

Parks, Gordon. *Ella Watson*. Aug. 1942. *America from the Great Depression to World War II: Black-and-White Photographs from the FSA-OWI, 1935-1945*. Prints and Photographs Div., Lib. of Cong., n.d. Web. 27 Sept. 2015.

---. *Emerging Man*. 1952. *PhotoMuse*. George Eastman House and ICP, n.d. Web. 26 Sept. 2015.

"Ralph Ellison: *Invisible Man*." *Literature and Its Times: Profiles of 300 Notable Literary Works and the Historical Events That Influenced Them*. Ed. Joyce Moss and George Wilson. Vol. 4. Gale Research, 1997. *Literature Resource Center*. Web. 30 Sept. 2015.

Dorothea Lange's *First-Graders at the Weill Public School* shows children of Japanese descent reciting the Pledge of Allegiance in San Francisco, California, in 1942. Following the steps below, write an essay suggesting what the image means.

Library of Congress

First-Graders at the Weill Public School, Dorothea Lange (1942)

1. Do some research on Lange's work. (Like Paul Taylor, you might start at the Library of Congress's online exhibit *Documenting America,* which features Lange, along with Gordon Parks and other photographers.)

2. Analyze the image using the Criteria for Analyzing Visuals on pp. 706–707.

3. From this preliminary analysis, develop a tentative thesis that says what the image means and how it communicates that meaning.

4. With this thesis in mind, plan your essay, using your analysis of the image to illustrate your thesis. Be aware that as you draft your essay, your thesis will develop and may even change substantially.

Analyze one of the ads that follow by using the Criteria for Analyzing Visuals on pp. 706–707. Be sure to consider the role that writing plays in the ad's overall meaning. Write an essay with a thesis that discusses the ad's central meaning and significance.

Mini-Cooper Magazine Ad

Billboard Ad for Jell-O (Text under percentage reads: "Smiley Tweets" and "Frowny Tweets.")

Coca-Cola TV Ad

Find an ad or public service announcement that you find compelling in its use of visuals. Analyze the ad by using the Criteria for Analyzing Visuals on pp. 706–707. Be sure to consider the role that writing plays in the ad's overall meaning. Write an essay with a thesis that discusses the ad's central meaning and significance.

29

Writing in Business and Scientific Genres

Genres are simply categories or types of texts. Movies, for example, may be categorized into genres such as action adventure, romantic comedy, or film noir. Audiences for each of these genres of film have likely seen romantic comedies or noir films in the past, so they bring certain expectations based on that experience to the next romantic comedy or film noir they see. The same is true for genres that you are likely to read or create: Many of your decisions—from what to write about (subject choice) to the organizational structure, length, formatting, and design—are affected by the audience's genre expectations. While writers usually try to satisfy readers' expectations, genre conventions also provide opportunities for creativity. Depending on the *rhetorical situation* and the audience's openness to innovation, writers may play with genre conventions. But anticipating when your audience will respond to a genre surprise with delight rather than rejection is crucial.

Each of the genres you will encounter in this chapter—from business documents such as résumés and business letters to laboratory reports—are highly conventional genres in which surprises are unlikely to be met with delight. Readers of each of these genres expect writers to get directly to the point in clear, unadorned prose and to follow the format prescribed for the genre. As you examine the documents in this chapter, analyze the way language and design (*typography, color, white space,* and *visuals*) are used to inform and guide readers. What language choices and design features make the documents easy to read? What choices and features make finding specific information within the documents easy? What choices and features make the documents easy to use?

For more about design, see Chapter 32.

Business Letters

The **business letter** (such as the one shown in Figure 29.1) is the document most often used for correspondence between representatives of one organization and another, though e-mail messages are increasingly being used in place of business letters.

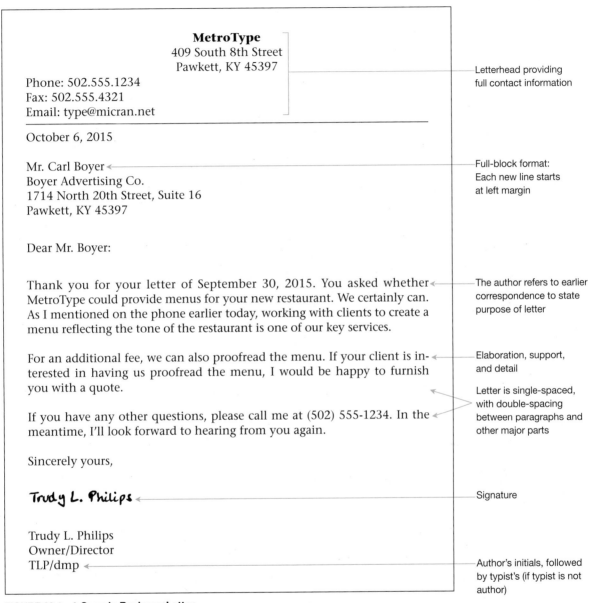

FIGURE 29.1   A Sample Business Letter

Business letters are written to obtain information about a company's products, to register or respond to a complaint, to introduce other documents (such as a proposal) that accompany the letter, or to apply for a job.

Whether a letter is delivered electronically or in print, the expectations are the same: The writer should state the purpose of the letter in the first few lines, provide supporting information in the paragraphs that follow, and maintain a courteous and professional tone throughout. Include enough information to identify clearly any documents you refer to in the letter.

The design conventions of business letters are long established:

- **Return address** (included in your company's letterhead or typed at the top of the page), plus any additional contact information for your company

- **Date:** The date, with the name of the month spelled out, follows the return address.

- **Inside address:** Include the name, title, and street address of the recipient, with words like *Street* or *Avenue* spelled out.

- **Salutation:** The convention is to address recipients of business letters as *Dear,* even if you've never met the person before. Use the recipient's title (abbreviated), such as *Gen., Rev., Mr.,* or *Ms.,* and address your letter to a specific person, even if you have to telephone the company to find out the name to use.

- **Body:** Most business letters are written in block style, with the paragraphs flush with the left margin. But look at other business letters from your organization to make sure that this is the preferred style.

- **Closing and signature:** Business letters, even if sent by e-mail, typically conclude with a formal closing, such as *Yours truly* or *Sincerely,* but your relationship with the recipient may influence your choice here. Four lines below the closing, type your full name, and sign the letter above it.

- **Additional information:** If you include items with the letter, such as a proposal or brochure, indicate this with the abbreviation *Enc.* below your name. If other people, such as your boss, will receive a copy of the letter, insert the abbreviation *cc:* followed by the initials of the recipient's name. If you are typing the letter for someone else, include the author's initials (in capital letters), a slash, and the typist's initials (in lowercase letters).

E-mail

Many students and instructors rely on **e-mail** to exchange information about assignments and schedules as well as to follow up on class discussions (see Figure 29.2). Like other business correspondence, e-mail messages are usually concise, direct, and limited to a single subject. Although most business letters sent by e-mail should be fairly formal, other e-mail messages may be polite but informal. Because of the deluge of e-mails, e-mail messages should always include a clear, accurate subject line.

If you are part of a large or complex organization, you may want to repeat your name and add such information as your job title, division, and telephone extension in a "signature" at the end of the document.

E-mail is a broader medium of communication than the business letter. Nevertheless, in anything other than quick e-mails to friends, you should maintain a professional tone.

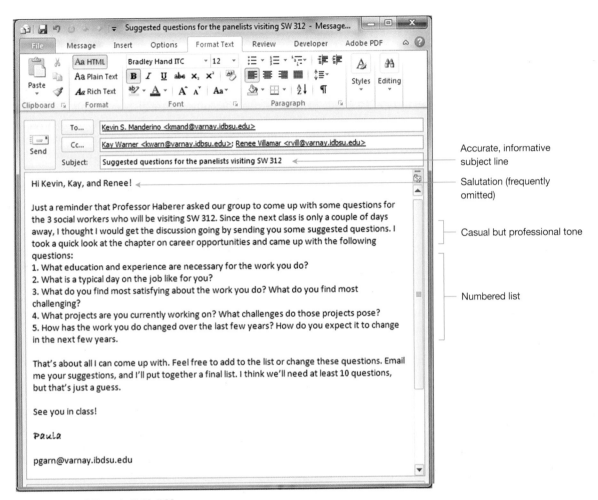

FIGURE 29.2 A Sample E-Mail Message

Avoid sarcasm and humor, which may not come across as you intend, and be sure to proofread and spell-check your message before sending it. Also, because e-mail messages are accessible to many people besides the intended recipient, always be careful about what you write in an e-mail message.

Though e-mail messages themselves are among the simplest forms of electronic documents, software programs allow you to attach files, insert hypertext links, and insert pictures and graphics into your e-mail documents. If you have promised to insert an attachment to an e-mail message, always pause before sending to make sure the promised attachment is included.

Résumés

A **résumé** is used to acquaint a prospective employer with your work experience, education, and accomplishments. All résumés contain such basic information as your name, address, phone number, and e-mail address.

The résumé is a good example of why the context in which a document is read is so important. An employer may receive dozens of résumés for one position. Your résumé may not be read closely in a first screening. Consequently, your résumé should highlight your important qualifications visually so that the reader can quickly find the pertinent information by scanning the page.

The format of résumés varies among disciplines and professions. Some professions require traditional formatting, while others allow for some flexibility in design. Be sure to research your field and potential employers to see if a particular résumé format is preferred; consider consulting recently published reference books that show examples of good résumés. Also consider whether posting your résumé on a Web site such as *Monster.com* might be advisable. Always tailor your résumé to the job for which you are applying.

Résumés may also vary in terms of what is emphasized—educational or work experience, for example. If you have little work experience, focus your résumé on your grade-point average, the courses you have taken, the projects and internships (if any) you have completed, and the applicable skills and abilities you have acquired in college. (For an example of such a résumé, see Figure 29.3.) If you have extensive, relevant, and continuous work experience, consider a reverse-chronological résumé, listing the jobs you have held (beginning with the most recent job) and describing the duties, responsibilities, and accomplishments associated with each one. If you have shifted directions during your adult life, consider organizing your résumé in a way that emphasizes the strengths and skills you have acquired and used in different settings—for instance, your experience speaking in front of groups, handling money, or working with specific software programs.

Do not include such personal information as your height, weight, and age. Mention personal interests or hobbies only if they are relevant to the position. Finally, proofread your résumé carefully; it must be error-free. Your résumé is the first impression you make on a potential employer. Do everything you can to make a good first impression.

Job-Application Letters

A **job-application letter** (sometimes called a **cover letter**) is sent with a résumé when you apply for a job. The primary purpose of the job-application letter is to persuade your reader that you are a qualified candidate for employment and to introduce your résumé. For college students and recent graduates, most job-application letters (such as the one shown in Figure 29.4, p. 725) consist of four paragraphs:

1. **Paragraph 1:** Identify the position you are applying for and how you became aware of its availability. If you are not applying for a particular position, the first paragraph should express your desire to work for the particular organization.

Kim Hua
Current Address: MS 1789, Union College, Union, PA 55342
Permanent Address: 702 Good Street, Borah, ID 83702
Phone: (412) 555-1234 E-mail: khua@mailer.union.edu
                                                        — Contact information

EDUCATION
Union College   Bachelor of Arts,   Anticipated May 2016
Union, PA   Child Development   GPA: 3.7

Relevant Courses: Lifespan Human Development, Infancy and Early
Childhood, Parent-Child Relations, Fundamentals of Nutrition, Education
of the Preschool Child

Relevant Projects: Coordinator, collaborative research project analyzing
educational goals for local Head Start program. Lead writer, report on
parent-child relations, delivered to the Borah, Idaho, School Board.

CHILD DEVELOPMENT WORK EXPERIENCE
- *Summer 2015, Union College Child-Care Center, Union College, Union, PA* ← Work experience begins
  with most current
  employment
  Child Care Provider: Provided educational experiences and daily care for
  three 2-year-olds and four 3-year-olds. Prepared daily activity agendas.

- *Summer 2014, St. Alphonsus Day Care Center, St. Alphonsus Hospital,*
  Union, PA
  Child Care Provider: Provided educational experiences and daily care
  for a group of nine children ages six through ten.

- *Fall 2013, Governor's Commission for the Prevention of Child Abuse, Union, PA*
  Intern: Located online resources relevant to the prevention of child
  abuse. Recommended which resources to include in the Web site of   — Relevant volunteer work
  the Governor's Commission.

OTHER WORK EXPERIENCE
2014 to present, Union Falls Bed & Breakfast, Union, PA
Payroll Manager: Maintain daily payroll records for all employees, ← Other experience
compile daily and weekly reports of payroll costs for the manager, and   showing dependability
ensure compliance with all applicable state and federal laws governing   and responsibility
payroll matters.

PROFESSIONAL AFFILIATIONS
Past President, Union College Child and Family Studies Club; Student
Member, American Society of Child Care Professionals; Member,
National Child Care Providers

FIGURE 29.3   A Sample Résumé

2. **Paragraph 2:** Briefly describe your education, focusing on specific achievements, projects, and relevant coursework.

3. **Paragraph 3:** Briefly describe your work experience, focusing on relevant responsibilities and accomplishments.

Note that paragraphs 2 and 3 should not merely restate what is in your résumé; rather, they should help persuade your reader that you are qualified for the job.

4. **Paragraph 4:** Express your willingness to provide additional information and to be interviewed at the employer's convenience.

When writing a printed job-application, follow the format for a business letter (see pp. 718–20).

Web Pages

Although Web pages offer the potential for expanded use of color and visuals (including animation and video), the general principles of design used for paper documents can be applied to them. Again, you will want to evaluate the context in which the document will be read. For example, consider how big your readers' screens are and how good the resolution is likely to be. Keep in mind that sans serif fonts (like Arial and Verdana) are easier to read than serif fonts (like Times New Roman).

For more about designing for screens, see Chapter 32.

Web pages and other electronic texts differ from print texts in large part because of the links they can include to additional text or graphics, to other Web pages, or to video, animation, or sound files. As an author, you must consider that because of these links, readers may navigate your text in a nonlinear fashion, starting almost anywhere they like and branching off whenever a link piques their curiosity. To help readers find their way around, Web authors often provide a navigation scheme, usually in the form of site maps or "index" pages.

HTML (hypertext markup language) is the standard language used for creating Web pages. Software programs called **HTML editors** provide novices with an easy way to create Web pages, and most word processing programs allow a document to be converted into HTML and saved as a Web page.

As you design a Web page, beware of letting unnecessary graphics and multimedia elements distract from your message. Yes, you *can* add a textured background to the screen that will make it look like marble or cloth, but will that background make reading the text easier? Will a sound file improve communication of your main points, or are you adding sound simply because you can? Consider the following guidelines when designing a Web page:

- *Make sure your text is easy to read.* Many Web pages are difficult to read because of textured and brightly colored backgrounds. Keep the background of a Web page light in tone so that your text can be read with ease. Because color type can also be difficult to read, avoid vibrant colors for long blocks of text. Bear in mind that most readers are used to reading dark (typically black) text on a light (typically white) background.

308 Fairmont Street ←————— Modified block format:
Warren, CA 07812   Address, date, and signature
June 6, 2016   block begins five spaces to
                                 the right of center

Ms. Ronda Green
Software Engineer
Santa Clara Technology
P.O. Box 679
Santa Clara, CA 09145

Dear Ms. Green:

I am responding to your June 5 posting on Monster.com (reference ←————— Purpose of the letter
#91921) announcing that Santa Clara Technology is accepting résumés
for an entry-level engineer position in the Quality Assurance Department.
I think that my experience as an intern in quality assurance and my
educational background qualify me for this position.

As my résumé states, I graduated this past May from the University of Southern ←————— Education paragraph
California (USC) with a bachelor of science degree in Interdisciplinary Studies.
The Interdisciplinary Studies program at USC allows students to develop a
degree plan spanning at least two disciplines. My degree plan included
courses in computer science, marketing, and technical communication. In
addition to university courses, I have completed courses in team dynamics,
project management, and C, C++, and C# programming offered by the
training department at PrintCom, a manufacturer of high-end laser printers.

Throughout last summer, I worked as an intern in the quality-assurance ←————— Work-experience paragraph
department of PrintCom. I assisted quality-assurance engineers in testing
printer drivers, installers, and utilities. In addition, I maintained a database
containing the results of these tests and summarized the results in weekly
reports. This experience gave me valuable knowledge of the principles of
quality assurance and of the techniques used in testing software.

I would appreciate the opportunity to discuss further the education, skills, ←————— Concluding paragraph
and abilities I could bring to Santa Clara Technology. You can reach me any
workday after 3 p.m. (PDT) at (907) 555-1234 or by e-mail at sstur17@axl.com.

Sincerely yours,

Shelley Sturman

Shelley Sturman

Enclosure: résumé

FIGURE 29.4 A Sample Job-Application Letter

- ***Chunk information carefully, and keep your Web pages short.*** Because many people have difficulty reading long documents on a computer screen, be sure to chunk your information into concise paragraphs. Also, readers often find it difficult to read a Web page that requires extensive scrolling down the screen. Break up long text blocks into separate Web pages that require no more than one or two screens of scrolling. Use hypertext links to connect the text blocks and to help readers navigate across the pages.

- ***Include date posted or updated.*** To help readers who will want to know whether your Web site has been updated recently and who may need to cite your Web site in the list of works cited or references, always include the date you post or update your Web page.

- ***Include an "About the Author" page.*** Provide relevant information about yourself. If you are interested in hearing from readers, you may want to include your e-mail address, but avoid providing a link. Instead, write out your email address—johnsmithatgmaildotcom—to avoid getting robot-generated messages.

- ***Use links effectively.*** Make sure that all of your links work correctly and that all the pages of your Web site include a link back to your home page, so that readers can access it easily. You can make your text easier to read by judiciously limiting the number of links you embed in it. In addition to embedded text links, consider including a list of important links on a separate page for readers' convenience.

For more about design, see Chapter 32.

- ***Use the elements of document design.*** Most principles of good print document design apply to Web page design as well.

Lab Reports

A **lab report** is written to summarize the results of an experiment or test and to provide a road map for others who wish to repeat the experiment; it generally consists of the following five sections:

1. **Introduction:** Provides background information: the hypothesis of the experiment, the question to be answered, how the question arose
2. **Methods:** Describes how the research was conducted or the experiment performed
3. **Results:** Describes what happened as a result of your research or experiment
4. **Discussion:** Explains your results
5. **References:** Cites the sources used in conducting the research, performing the experiment, or writing the report

The content, style, and format of a lab report may vary from discipline to discipline or from course to course. Before writing a lab report, be certain that you understand your instructor's requirements, and look at sample lab reports in your field. The sample in Figure 29.5 shows excerpts from a lab report written by two students in a soils science course. It uses the documentation format advocated by the Council of Science Editors (CSE).

Bulk Density and Total Pore Space

Joe Aquino and Sheila Norris

Soils 101, Lab Section 1

October 6, 2016

Title, authors, and course number (centered) on title page

Introduction

Soil is an arrangement of solids and voids. The voids, called pore spaces, are important for root growth, water movement, water storage, and gas exchange between the soil and atmosphere. A medium-textured soil good for plant growth will have a pore-space content of about 0.50 (half solids, half pore space). The total pore space is the space between sand, silt, and clay particles (micropore space) plus the space between soil aggregates (macropore space).[1]

Background information that the reader will need to understand the experiment

Methods

To determine the bulk density[2] and total pore space of two soil samples, we hammered cans into the wall of a soil pit (Hagerstown silt loam). We collected samples from the Ap horizon and a Bt horizon. We then placed a block of wood over the cans so that the hammer did not smash them. After hammering the cans into the soil, we dug the cans, now full of soil, out of the horizons; we trimmed off any excess soil. The samples were dried in an oven at 105°C for two days and weighed. We then determined the volume of the cans by measuring the height and radius, as follows:

volume = 1/4 r^2h

We used the formulas noted in the Introduction to determine bulk density and porosity of the samples. Particle density was assumed to be 2.65 g/cm^3. The textural class of each horizon was determined by feel; that is, we squeezed and kneaded each sample and assigned it to a particular textural class.

Detailed explanation of the methods used

FIGURE 29.5   A Sample Lab Report

Presents the results of the experiment, with a table showing quantitative data

Results

We found both soils to have relatively light bulk densities and large porosities, but the Bt horizon had greater porosity than the Ap. Furthermore, we determined that the Ap horizon was a silt loam, whereas the Bt was a clay (see Table 1).

Table 1

Textural class, bulk density, and porosity of two Hagerstown soil horizons

Textural Class	Ap Silt Loam	Bt Clay
Bulk density (g/cm^3)	1.20	1.08
Porosity	0.55	0.59

Explains what was significant about the results of the research

Discussion

Both soils had bulk densities and porosities in the range we would have expected from the discussions in the lab manual and textbook. The Ap horizon is a medium-textured soil and is considered a good topsoil for plant growth, so a porosity around 0.5 is consistent with those facts. The Bt horizon is a fine-textured horizon (containing a large amount of clay), and the bulk density is in the predicted range.

The references are in the format recommended by the Council of Science Editors (CSE). They begin on a new page.

References

1. Brady NC, Weil RR. The nature and properties of soils. 11th ed. New York: Prentice-Hall; 1996. 291 p.
2. Blake GR, Hartge KH. Bulk density. In: Klute A, editor. Methods of soil analysis. Part 1. 2nd ed. Agronomy 1986; 9:363-376.

30

Writing for and about Your Community

Service learning combines classroom education with life experience. In service-learning programs, students are most often placed in off-campus positions with government bureaus such as local parks and recreation departments or nonprofit organizations that offer community support services such as tutoring or computer skills. In these positions, students have an opportunity to apply what they are studying in class. Here are a few examples:

- Nursing students teach expectant mothers about prenatal and infant care.
- Chemistry students tour local elementary schools demonstrating science "magic."
- Botany students teach fourth graders about plants native to their region.
- Zoology students help researchers gather samples for a study of local amphibian populations.
- Political science students work with the local government to increase voter turnout.
- English-speaking students tutor grade school children who are having trouble learning to read and write English.

Though you will probably find much to write about in your community service experience, you may also find writing to a wider audience to be part of your service.

Writing *about* Your Service Experience

Service learning may put you in a position to write for a nonacademic audience. For example, you might write an editorial for your campus or local newspaper in which you argue for increased support for your service organization or project. You might craft a letter to local government officials or even representatives to the state or national legislature suggesting a solution to a specific problem.

For many of the writing assignments in Part One, you might also draw on your service experience for source material. Here are some ideas for using the writing activities discussed in Part One of this textbook:

Chapter 2: Remembering an Event

- Write about your first day of service. What happened? How did you feel? What did you learn? How did it differ from what you expected to learn?

- Write about a particularly difficult day. Why was it difficult? How did you handle the situation? What would you do differently? What did you learn from the experience?

Chapter 3: Writing Profiles

- Write about the place where you are doing your service. What does it look like? How does it make you feel? How does the location reflect or affect what goes on there? What does go on there?

- Write about one of the people you have met doing your service. What is he or she like? How is he or she typical (or atypical) of other people in the same position? What makes this person special or different?

Chapter 4: Explaining a Concept

- Write about a concept with which you were unfamiliar before you did your service. What does the concept mean? How is it important in the context of your service experience? How does what you learned about this concept make you think differently now?

- Write about a concept that you knew but now understand differently because of your service. How has your understanding of the concept changed? What caused that change? How might you explain that change to someone who does not share your experience?

Chapter 5: Analyzing and Synthesizing Opposing Arguments

- Write about a debate that is relevant to the type of service you are doing, and analyze each position in the debate. (Note that there may be more than two.) Who are the major proponents of each position? What are the main reasons and evidence given to support each position? What are factors motivating the adherents of each position?

Chapter 6: Arguing a Position

- Write an argument in support of the service organization you are working with. Why should people support it? How can they support it? Why is it a worthwhile endeavor?

- Write an argument about the value of service learning. What have you gained from this experience? Who should participate? What are the advantages of service learning to individuals and the community?

Chapter 7: Proposing a Solution

- Write about a process or procedure within or affecting the organization you are working with that you think needs to be improved. Why does it need to be improved? How might it be improved?

- Write about a policy, law, or practice that you think should be eliminated or revised because it negatively affects the organization you are working with. What would be the benefit of eliminating or revising it? What steps would need to be taken in order to change the policy, law, or practice?

Chapter 8: Justifying an Evaluation

- Write about how effectively the organization you are working with satisfies its objectives. How do you measure its effectiveness?
- Write about your school's service-learning program. In what ways is it most successful? In what ways could it be improved?

Chapter 9: Arguing for Causes or Effects

- Write about the causes for a problem or situation that you have encountered through your service-learning experience. What brought the problem about? What circumstances perpetuate it?
- Write about why service-learning programs have become common. What function do they serve that traditional education models do not? What demands do they meet?

Find a topic.

One of the many advantages of service learning is that it can present numerous topics that might be fruitfully explored through your writing. To generate a substantial list of ideas, you need only ask yourself some simple questions:

- Who is most affected by the situation, and how are these people affected?
- How long has this situation existed?
- What forces shape the situation? Can anything be done to alter them?
- How have other organizations handled this issue? How might the situation be improved?
- What common perceptions do people hold about this situation? What are my own perceptions?
- If perceptions are inaccurate, how might they be changed?

Gather sources.

A service-learning environment can provide field research sources that would otherwise be difficult to tap. The most significant of these potential sources is the people who run the organization in which you are doing your service. If you have focused your writing on the kinds of issues that are relevant to your service, these people can provide expertise. Many of the people you work with will have years of experience and specialized training and probably will have researched the subject themselves. Take advantage of your opportunity to tap their knowledge. When approached courteously, people are often more than willing to share what they know.

For suggestions on making observations, conducting interviews, and creating questionnaires, see Chapter 21.

Depending on the situation, your service site might also be a good place to circulate a questionnaire or conduct a survey to help you gather information about your subject. Of course, your own observations and experiences as you perform your service will be valuable as well. You might consider keeping a daily journal in which you record these experiences and observations. When you are ready to begin writing, you will have already done some early invention work.

The service organization itself might also be a good source of information. Such organizations often collect and produce literature that is relevant to their mission. Your organization might even maintain its own small library of resource materials. Frequently, such organizations are also part of a network of similar groups that share their expertise through newsletters, trade journals, Web sites, or online discussion groups. Explore these unique resources.

Keep in mind the ethical considerations that are involved. Many service-learning environments, such as those that involve counseling, tutoring, or teaching, can give you access to information that should be kept confidential, especially if you are working with minors. Be sure that you are open about your information gathering and that everyone whom you might use as a source knows your intentions. Any questionnaires should state what you intend to do with the information gathered. Any information gained from interviews should be properly attributed, but obtain your subjects' explicit permission before using their names. Err on the side of caution and consideration, and ask your instructor for guidance if you have any questions about how to treat sensitive material.

Writing *for* Your Service Organization

Some service-learning situations will put you in a position not just to write *about* your service experience but also to write *for* your service experience. You might be asked to create flyers, brochures, press releases, or Web pages for a community organization. You might help craft presentations or reports. Though these may not be academic writing activities, the strategies presented in this text still apply. You might be asked, for example, to write a brochure that explains the purpose and function of the organization. In effect, you would be writing an explanation, and you would need to keep in mind the basic features of this genre outlined in Chapter 4.

In such writing situations, it is important to consider your rhetorical situation: What is your purpose? Who is your audience? How do you want readers to think of you or the organization you represent? In what medium will you be communicating? While in class you might be asked to select a topic and write an essay in which you argue for a position (Chapter 6) or a solution (Chapter 7), in your service experience you might be asked to create a presentation that explains the importance of a no-kill animal shelter to potential donors or a brochure that urges commuters to carpool to reduce pollution and ease traffic congestion. Identifying your rhetorical situation will help you communicate your goals more effectively.

Writing in organizations is frequently a collaborative process. Everyone involved in the process is expected to do his or her part. When your written document will be used to represent your organization in any way, respect the expertise of the staff, especially when their assessment of the audience differs from your own. In some situations, your service writing may be heavily edited—or not used at all. Make sure your instructor and service-learning program administrators are aware of any instances in which you and members of the organization are having difficulty reaching a consensus.

For suggestions on how to make such collaboration run smoothly and successfully, see Chapter 31.

Finally, remember that nonacademic writing often requires greater attention to presentation than most kinds of academic writing. One-inch margins and double-spaced text are simply not enough when you are trying to create eye-catching documents such as brochures and press releases. Document design can not only make a piece of writing more visually attractive and thereby stimulate readers' interest but also help readers with different needs identify which parts of the document are most relevant. Therefore, carefully consider the layout and configuration of your document, and take advantage of the flexibility that even a simple word processing program can give you.

For more about design, see Chapter 32.

31

Writing Collaboratively

Writers often seek advice and feedback from friends, colleagues, or mentors on individual writing projects. For instance, they may consult a librarian for advice on research, try out an argument on a coworker or fellow student, or ask a trusted friend to check for grammar errors. On some occasions, writers also work in small groups to research, plan, and compose joint writing projects.

Working with others is often referred to as *collaboration*. Collaborating with others on individual projects and especially on joint writing projects can be challenging but also rewarding. The following advice will help you anticipate the difficulties so that you can get the most out of the collaboration.

Working with Others on Your Individual Writing Projects

This book assumes that you will collaborate with others, at least with your instructor and classmates, to write your essays. Class discussion of the readings will help you understand more about the genres you will be writing, and responses to your invention work and to drafts of your essays will give you ideas for writing more effectively.

Collaboration is also built directly into the activities in the writing assignment chapters. In every assignment chapter, four activities ask you to collaborate with other students in a purposeful way. Chapter 6, "Arguing a Position," for example, has these activities:

> *Practicing the Genre: Debating a Position.* This activity asks you to get together with a small group of your classmates to develop reasons for and against a position. Afterward, your group is encouraged to discuss the process, reflecting on what parts presented the biggest challenges, and why.

> *Make connections.* This activity, following each of the professional readings, invites you to examine some of the important ideas and underlying assumptions of the reading. In small-group discussion, face to face or online, you can explore your responses and develop your understanding.

Test Your Choice. As you choose an issue and decide how best to frame it for your audience, you can get feedback to determine whether your choice will be effective with readers.

Peer Review Guide. Once you have a draft of your essay, anyone using the Peer Review Guide can give you a comprehensive evaluation of your work, and you can do likewise for others. Because the Chapter 6 Peer Review Guide reflects the particular requirements of an essay arguing a position, anyone using it to evaluate your draft will be able to give you focused, relevant advice.

In these four activities, you collaborate with others to develop your individual writing by discovering what you may know about a project before you get very far into it, assessing your progress after a period of initial work, and evaluating your first attempts to draft a complete essay. There are many other occasions for fruitful collaboration in the assignment chapters. For instance, in Chapter 6 you might work with other students to complete the Analyze & Write activities that follow the readings. You and another student might exchange revisions of your essays to help each other with final editing and proofreading. Or you might meet or exchange e-mail messages with two or three other students to work on the Reflecting on the Genre section that concludes the chapter. Working collaboratively on these activities may not only make them easier or more enjoyable but also make them more productive, through the exchange of many more ideas than you might have come up with on your own.

Following are guidelines for successful collaboration on individual writing projects:

- Whenever you read someone else's writing, have the writer inform you about his or her purpose and readers. Collaboration is always more effective when writers focus on helping other writers achieve their purposes for their particular readers. If a writer is explaining a concept to readers who know nothing about it, as might be the case in Chapter 4, "Explaining a Concept," your comments are likely to be unhelpful if you assume the essay is addressed to someone who shares your understanding of the concept.

- Know the genre the writer is working in. If a writer is proposing a solution to a problem and you are evaluating the writing as though it were an essay arguing a position, your advice is likely to be off the mark.

- When you evaluate another writer's work, be sure you know the stage of its development. Is it a set of tentative notes for a first draft? A partial draft? A complete draft? A revision? If it is a draft, you want to focus on helping the writer develop and organize ideas; if it is a revision, you might focus exclusively on cueing and coherence or editing and proofreading.

- When you evaluate someone's writing, be helpful and supportive but also frank and specific. You do a writing partner no favor if you shrink from criticizing and giving advice. If your criticism seems grounded in the purpose, audience, and genre, it will probably not seem arbitrary or personal to your partner.

- Bring as much writing as possible to a scheduled meeting with other writers. The further along your writing is, the more you can learn from the collaboration.

- Try to be receptive to criticism. Later, you can decide whether to change your essay, and how.

Collaborating on Joint Writing Projects

In addition to collaborating with others on your individual writing projects, you may have the opportunity to collaborate to produce a single essay. For instance, in Chapter 6, "Arguing a Position," you could collaborate to construct a persuasive argument for a position you share with two or three other students. In Chapter 4, "Explaining a Concept," you could work with a few other students to research and explain a concept, perhaps using graphics or hands-on activities to help others grasp the concept and its implications. In Chapter 7, "Proposing a Solution," you have an opportunity to practice researching and writing proposals, by far the most common type of joint writing project in college, the workplace, and the community.

When people collaborate on joint projects, they often share responsibility for the final product but divide up tasks for the preparation of the final draft. For example, each team member might take on responsibilities related to his or her areas of expertise. Someone who knows the problem firsthand might work on developing ways to explain the problem to those who have not experienced it directly. People who have experience making forecasts and planning budgets might be assigned to research and draft those aspects of the proposal. Or you might divide the work in sections, with one person conducting the research, another doing the initial drafting, a third taking responsibility for revising.

Everyone in the group might suggest ways of improving the draft, and individuals might be assigned parts to strengthen and clarify. When a final draft seems near, one person might be assigned the job of improving cueing and coherence, another might be in charge of editing and proofreading, and a third might work on document design. Because the team shares responsibility for the final document, most teams collectively review the final draft so that errors do not slip through the cracks.

Consider the following workplace writing example. A pharmaceuticals company decided to invest time and money in finding a solution to a problem the company saw as damaging to its business as well as to the community. The company assigned a team of seven division managers and a technical writer, gave them a budget to pay for outside consultants, and asked them to present a written proposal to the state legislature and local school board in six months' time. The pharmaceuticals team divided the project into a series of research and writing tasks like those outlined in the Guide to Writing in Chapter 7. The team members scheduled due dates for each task and progress reports to identify problems as they arose. They assigned responsibility for each task and identified which tasks might need consultation with outside experts.

Writing collaboratively on a joint project certainly has benefits. Collaboration not only draws on the expertise and energy of different people but also creates an outcome that is greater than the sum of its parts. One difficulty of collaborative writing projects, however, is that learning how to work effectively with others takes time and effort. Writers working on a joint project need to spend a lot of time communicating with one another, anticipate conflicts and resolve them constructively, be realistic in scheduling and complete their assigned tasks responsibly, be flexible in their writing processes, and be open to different points of view.

To help group members work together constructively on joint writing projects, here are some ground rules you will want to discuss and implement:

- Begin by establishing clear and easy means of communicating with one another. Will you e-mail, text, or call? Exchange e-mail addresses, but also exchange phone numbers as a backup.

- Think about the technology that will enable you to work together most easily. For example, you may decide that creating documents on a sharing site like *Google Drive* will make it easiest for all members of the group to access the documents. Or you may decide to e-mail versions to group members as work progresses to make sure all group members can work independently until it is time to share.

- Expect to spend a lot of time planning the project together and discussing who will do what and when. Discuss how the group should divide responsibilities. Remember, however, to remain flexible and keep lines of communication open to deal with problems as they arise.

- Set a schedule of regular meetings, and agree on how to run the meetings. For example, should someone lead each discussion? Should the role of discussion leader fall to one person or rotate among group members? Should each meeting have an agenda? If so, how and when should it be set?

- Make sure each team member has a say in major decisions, such as choosing a topic and devising a thesis statement. This isn't always easy: Some team members might be inclined to agree with whatever the team seems to want, even if they privately have concerns. However, you can get frank input from every person on the team if you periodically collect comments or votes anonymously.

- Treat each other with respect and consideration, but do not be surprised by disagreements and personality conflicts. Arguing can stimulate thinking—inspiring creativity as well as encouraging each person to explain ideas clearly and systematically—but arguing can also encourage aggressiveness in some people and withdrawal in others. If there is a problem in the way the group interacts, address it immediately, perhaps by calling a special meeting to work out a solution. Try to avoid placing blame. Consider, for example, whether taking turns would ensure that everyone contributes to the discussion and no one dominates. Urge everyone to refrain from characterizing other people and instead to speak only about what they themselves think and feel by making "I" rather than "you" statements.

- Keep track of everyone's progress. Consider creating a chart so that all members can see at a glance what they need to do and when. Schedule regular progress reports so that any problems can be identified immediately.

- If the group will make a presentation of the final proposal, plan it carefully, giving each person a role. Rehearse the presentation as a group to make sure it satisfies the time limit and other requirements of the assignment.

For more on multimodal presentations, see Chapter 33.

32

Designing for Page and Screen

The way a document is designed—the arrangement of text, visuals, and white space on a page or screen—has a major impact on the readability of a document and may influence the reader's attitude toward it. This chapter introduces basic components of design, offers guidelines for designing effective projects, and discusses some common formats for documents you may be asked to create in your college courses or in the workplace. You may also want to look at Chapters 24 and 25, which include research projects annotated to point out the formatting requirements in MLA and APA style.

The Impact of Design

We can probably all agree that effectively written documents are easy to navigate, and their meanings are accessible to the intended audience. Good design also makes readability easier and the intended meaning clearer and more vivid.

The ways in which design affects the way we read documents can be illustrated fairly simply. Consider this familiar phrase, rendered in four different ways:

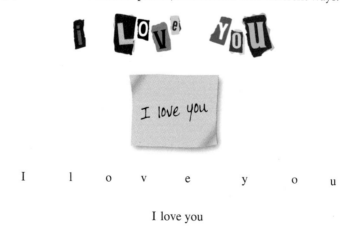

I   l   o   v   e   y   o   u

I love you

The words in each rendering are the same, but the different uses of fonts, colors, and white space encourage us to read them very differently. The first message is vaguely unsettling (is that a ransom note? a message from a stalker?); the second seems conventionally sweet; the third carries no emotional or context clues, but the spacing makes it irritatingly difficult to read; and the fourth offers no tone or context clues at all (though this in itself might strike us as odd, given the meaning of the words). Thus, design does far more than add visual interest: It actually directs how we read and, to a certain extent, determines the meaning we derive.

The freedom you have in terms of using design elements and visuals in the college projects you compose will vary quite a bit, depending on your instructors' preferences and the nature of the projects. As you write, however, you should always remain aware of the impact design can have on your reader. And any time you read a document—whether it is a textbook, a blog, or even an ad on the side of a bus—you should stop to think about how that document was designed and how that design affects your reading of it.

Considering Purpose, Audience, Context, and Medium

Purpose, audience, context, and medium of delivery are the key components to consider in designing any document. For instance, if you are writing an essay for a college course, you can expect that your instructor and your classmates will read it carefully. Your design decisions should therefore make sustained reading as easy as possible; fonts that are too small to read easily or print that is too light to see clearly will make the reader's job unnecessarily difficult. Additionally, instructors usually ask students to submit hard-copy work that is double-spaced with one-inch margins to give the reviewers room to write comments on the page.[*]

In most college courses, guidelines on design have traditionally followed a "less is more" rule—written assignments were generally expected to be printed on white, 8.5- by 11-inch paper, and the use of colors, extravagant fonts, sheerly decorative visuals, and the like, was in most cases discouraged. However, in many college classrooms, what constitutes an acceptable course "paper" or project is in transition; many instructors now allow or in some cases require the creation of multimodal projects—blogs, collages, timelines, videos, presentations with Prezi or PowerPoint slides, even playlists—in place of traditional papers.

Developments like these, driven largely by advances in technology, have obviously required some adjustments to traditional notions of acceptable design for college writing. "Less is more" still applies, however, in principle. Good design gives priority to clarity:

---

[*] It is important to note that MLA, APA, and other style systems have specific rules regarding such things as spacing, margins, and heading formats. Be sure to ask your instructor whether you will be expected to adhere closely to these rules; if so, your choices regarding document design will be limited. For more on MLA and APA style, see Chapters 24 and 25.

Whatever the project, you should use design not for its own sake but to make your points as clearly, effectively, and efficiently as possible.

Of course, the same principle of clarity applies to most *non*academic documents you will write. In writing for nonacademic audiences, however, you cannot expect all readers to read your writing equally closely. Some readers may skim through your blog entries looking for interesting points; others might scan a report or memo for information important specifically to them. Design elements such as *headings, bullets,* and *chunking* will help these readers find the information of most interest to them.

Frequently, too, your document design decisions will be determined by the kind of document you are preparing. Business letters and e-mails, for example, traditionally follow specific formats. Because your readers will bring certain expectations to these kinds of documents, altering an established format can cause confusion and should therefore be considered carefully.

For more about business writing, see Chapter 29.

To analyze the context in which a composition will be "consumed," ask yourself the following questions:

- ***Where will my document be read?*** Will the document be read on paper in a well-lighted, quiet room, or in another context—perhaps on a laptop in a noisy, dimly lit coffee shop or on a presentation slide in a meeting?

- ***Do my readers have specific expectations for this kind of document?*** Am I composing a presentation, proposal, letter, or report that requires certain design conventions? Does my instructor expect me to follow MLA style, APA style, or another system?

- ***How will the information be used?*** Is my audience expecting to learn or to be entertained? Do I expect my readers to skim the document for tidbits or information or to read it carefully?

Elements of Design

Readable *fonts;* informative *headings; bulleted* or *numbered lists;* and appropriate use of *color, white space,* and *visuals* like photographs, charts, and diagrams all help readers learn from your compositions.

Choose readable fonts.

Typography is a design term for the letters and symbols that make up the print on a page or a screen. You are already using important aspects of typography when you use capital letters, italics, boldface, or different sizes of type to signal a new sentence, identify the title of a book, or distinguish a heading from body text.

Word processing programs enable you to use dozens of different **fonts**, or typefaces; bold and italic versions of these fonts; and a range of font sizes. Fortunately, you can rely on some simple design principles to make good typographic choices for your compositions.

Perhaps the most important advice for working with typography is to choose fonts that are easy to read. Some fonts are meant for decorative or otherwise very minimal use, and are hard to read in extended passages. Font style, font size, and combinations of style and size are features that can add to or detract from readability.

Considering Font Style   For most academic and business writing, you will probably want to choose a traditional font that is easy to read, such as Arial or Times New Roman. Texts that will be read on paper may be easier to read if composed in a serif font like Georgia, Times Roman, or Calisto. (A serif is the little line projecting from the ends of letters.) Texts that will be read on screen may be easier to read if composed in sans serif fonts like Arial, Tahoma, and Verdana.

Sentences and paragraphs printed in fonts that imitate calligraphy (typically called *script fonts*) or those that mimic Handwriting are not only difficult to read but also too informal for most academic and business purposes.

Considering Font Size   To ensure that your documents can be read easily, you also need to choose an appropriate font size (traditionally measured in units called **points**). For most types of academic writing, a 12-point font is standard for the main (body) text. For Web pages, however, you should consider using a slightly larger font to compensate for the difficulty of reading from a computer monitor. For presentation slides, you should use an even larger font size (such as 32-point, and typically no smaller than 18-point) to ensure that the text can be read from a distance.

Combining Font Styles and Sizes   Although technology now makes hundreds of font styles and sizes available to writers, you should avoid confusing readers with too many different fonts in one composition. Limit the number of fonts to one or two that complement each other well. A common practice, for instance, is to choose one font for all titles and headings (such as Arial, 14-pt, boldface for printed text) and another for the body text (such as Times New Roman, 12-pt for printed texts). (For texts delivered and read online, you might reverse the fonts, using Arial in 12-pt. type for the body text and Times New Roman, 14-pt, boldface for headings.)

Use headings to organize your writing.

Titles and headings are often distinguished from body text by boldface, italics, or font size. Headings are helpful in calling attention to certain parts or sections of a piece of writing and in offering readers visual cues to its overall organization. Always check with your instructor about the conventions for using (or not using) these elements in the particular discipline you are studying.

Distinguishing between Headings and Subheadings   Typically, headings for major sections (level-one headings) must have more visual impact than those subdividing these sections (level-two headings), which should be more prominent than headings within the subdivisions (level-three headings). The typography should reflect this hierarchy of headings. Here is one possible system for distinguishing among three levels of headings:

LEVEL-ONE HEADING
Level-Two Heading
Level-Three Heading

Notice that the level-one and level-two headings are given the greatest prominence by the use of boldface and that they are distinguished from one another by the use of all capital letters for the major heading versus capital and lowercase letters for the subheading. The third-level heading, italicized but not boldfaced, is less prominent than the other two headings but can still be readily distinguished from body text. Whatever system you use to distinguish headings and subheadings, be sure to apply it consistently throughout your document.

For more on selecting appropriate headings and subheadings, see Chapter 13.

Positioning Headings Consistently   In addition to keeping track of the font size and style of headings, you need to position headings in the same way throughout a piece of writing. You will want to consider the spacing above and below headings and determine whether the headings should be aligned with the left margin, indented a fixed amount of space, or centered. In this book, headings like the one that begins this paragraph—**Positioning Headings Consistently**—are aligned with the left margin and followed by a fixed amount of space.

Using Type Size to Differentiate Headings from Text   In documents that do not need to observe MLA or APA style, which have specific rules about formatting, you may wish to use font size to help make headings visually distinct from the body of the text. If you do so, avoid making the headings too large. To accompany 12-point body text, for instance, a 14-point heading will do. The default settings for heading and body text styles on most word processing and desktop publishing programs are effective, and you may want to use them to autoformat your heading and text styles.

Use lists to highlight steps or key points.

Lists are often an effective way to present information in a logical and visually coherent way. Use a **numbered list** (1, 2, 3) to present the steps in a process or to list items that readers will need to refer to easily (for instance, see the sample e-mail message in Chapter 29). Use a **bulleted list** (marking each new item with a "bullet"—a dash, circle, or box) to highlight key points when the order of the items is not significant. Written instructions, such as recipes, are typically formatted using numbered lists, whereas a list of supplies, for example, is more often presented in the form of a bulleted list.

Use colors with care.

Color printers, photocopiers, and online technology facilitate the use of color, but color does not necessarily make text easier to read. In most academic print documents, the only color you should use is black. Though color is typically used more freely in academic writing produced in other media (for example, Web pages or multimodal presentations), it should still be used in moderation and always with the aim

FIGURE 32.1   Document with Too Little Color Contrast

of increasing your readers' understanding of what you have to say. Always consider, too, whether your readers might be color-blind and whether they will have access to a full-color version of the document.

Although the slideshow design in Figure 32.1 is visually interesting and the heading is readable, the bulleted text is very hard to read because there is too little contrast between the text color and the background color.

In Figure 32.2, it is clear that the person who created the pie chart carefully chose the colors to represent the different data. What the person did not consider, however, is how the colors would look when printed out on a black-and-white printer. It is nearly impossible to associate the labels with the slices of the pie and thus to read the

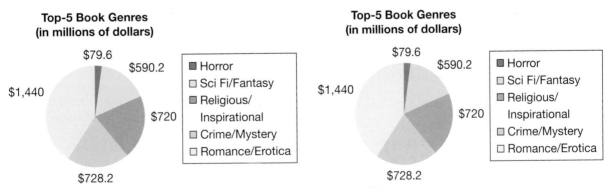

FIGURE 32.2 A Pie Chart That Requires a Color Printer to Be Understandable

chart. If your work is likely to be photocopied, consider using patterns to distinguish pie slices or lines and bars in graphs, or use a line to connect labels.

Also consider the meanings associated with different colors. For example, in the United States and other Western cultures, white is typically associated with goodness and purity; in China, however, white represents grief and mourning. Although your use of color in a report, blog, or multimodal presentation might not carry such deep meaning, bear in mind that most people have emotional or psychological responses to colors and color combinations.

Use white space to make text readable.

Another basic element of document design, **white space**, is the open, or blank, space surrounding the text. White space is usually used between a heading and the paragraph that follows the heading. You also use white space when you set the margins on the page, and even when you double-space between lines of text and indent paragraphs. In all of these cases, the space makes your document easier to read. When used generously, white space facilitates reading by keeping the pages of a document uncluttered and by helping the eye find and follow the text.

Chunking **Chunking**, the breaking up of text into smaller units, also facilitates reading. **Paragraphing** is a form of chunking that divides text into units of closely related information. In most academic essays and reports, text is double-spaced, and paragraphs are distinguished by indenting the first line one-half inch.

In single-spaced text or text that will be read on-screen, you may want to make reading easier by adding extra space between paragraphs rather than indenting the first lines of paragraphs. This format, referred to as **block style**, is often used in business letters, e-mails, and other electronic documents. When creating electronic documents, especially Web pages, you might consider chunking your material into separate "pages" or screens, with links connecting the chunks.

Margins Adequate margins are an important component of readability, especially in printed documents. If the margins are too small, your page will seem cluttered. For academic essays, use one-inch margins on all sides unless your instructor (or the style manual you are following) advises differently.

Adding Visuals

Tables, graphs, charts, diagrams, photographs, maps, and screen shots add visual interest and are often more effective in conveying information than prose alone. Choose the type of visual that will best suit your purpose (see Figure 32.3). In academic writing, be certain, too, that each visual has a valid role to play in your work; if the visual is merely a decoration, leave it out or replace it with a visual that is more appropriate.

Use a/an . . .	to . . .	
table	display detailed numerical or textual data	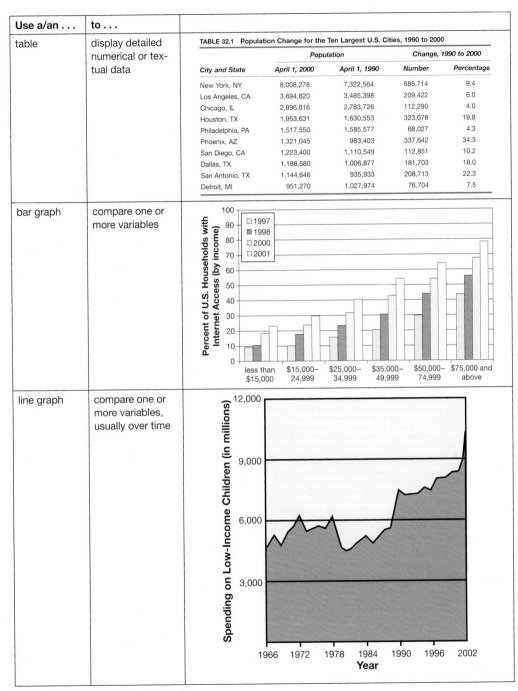
bar graph	compare one or more variables	
line graph	compare one or more variables, usually over time	

TABLE 32.1   Population Change for the Ten Largest U.S. Cities, 1990 to 2000

	Population		Change, 1990 to 2000	
City and State	April 1, 2000	April 1, 1990	Number	Percentage
New York, NY	8,008,278	7,322,564	685,714	9.4
Los Angeles, CA	3,694,820	3,485,398	209,422	6.0
Chicago, IL	2,896,016	2,783,726	112,290	4.0
Houston, TX	1,953,631	1,630,553	323,078	19.8
Philadelphia, PA	1,517,550	1,585,577	68,027	4.3
Phoenix, AZ	1,321,045	983,403	337,642	34.3
San Diego, CA	1,223,400	1,110,549	112,851	10.2
Dallas, TX	1,188,580	1,006,877	181,703	18.0
San Antonio, TX	1,144,646	935,933	208,713	22.3
Detroit, MI	951,270	1,027,974	76,704	7.5

(continued)

Figure 32.3   When to Use a Visual

Use a/an . . .	to . . .	
pie chart	show the parts that make up a whole (usually adding up to 100%)	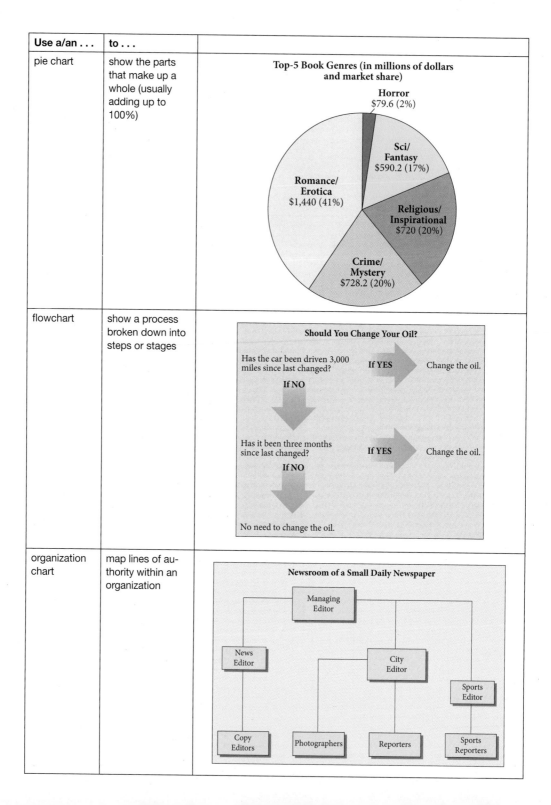 **Top-5 Book Genres (in millions of dollars and market share)**
flowchart	show a process broken down into steps or stages	
organization chart	map lines of authority within an organization	

Top-5 Book Genres (in millions of dollars and market share)

Horror $79.6 (2%)

Sci/ Fantasy $590.2 (17%)

Romance/ Erotica $1,440 (41%)

Religious/ Inspirational $720 (20%)

Crime/ Mystery $728.2 (20%)

Should You Change Your Oil?

Has the car been driven 3,000 miles since last changed?   If YES   Change the oil.

If NO

Has it been three months since last changed?   If YES   Change the oil.

If NO

No need to change the oil.

Newsroom of a Small Daily Newspaper

Managing Editor

News Editor

City Editor

Sports Editor

Copy Editors

Photographers

Reporters

Sports Reporters

Use a/an . . .	to . . .	
diagram	depict an item or its properties, often using symbols	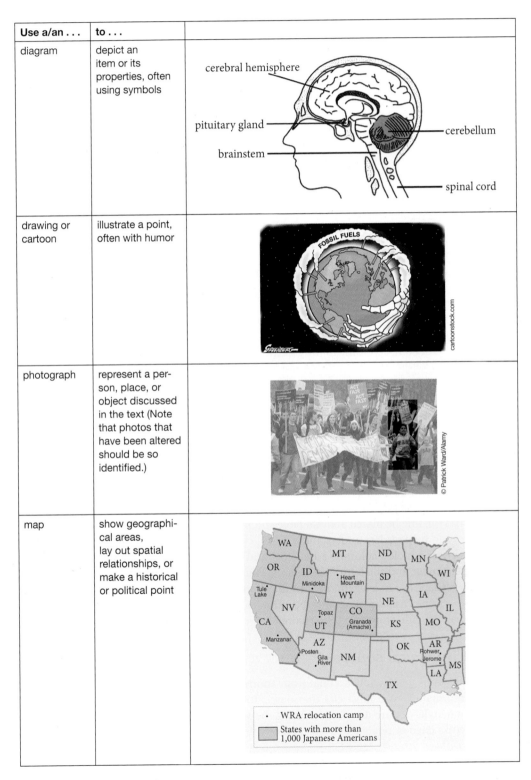
drawing or cartoon	illustrate a point, often with humor	
photograph	represent a person, place, or object discussed in the text (Note that photos that have been altered should be so identified.)	
map	show geographical areas, lay out spatial relationships, or make a historical or political point	

(continued)

Use a/an . . .	to . . .	
screen shot	duplicate a computer screen or window	www.whitehouse.gov

You can create visuals on a computer, using the drawing tools of a word processing program, the charting tools of a spreadsheet program, or software specifically designed for creating visuals. You can also download visuals from the Internet or photocopy or scan visuals from print materials. If your composition is going to be posted on the Web on a site that is not password-protected and a visual you want to use is from a source that is copyrighted, you may need to request written permission from the copyright holder (such as the photographer, publisher, or site sponsor). For any visual that you borrow from or create based on data from a source, be sure to cite the source in the caption, your bibliography, or both, according to the guidelines of the documentation system you are using.

For more about citing visual sources, see Chapters 24 and 25.

Number, title, and label visuals.

Number your visuals in sequential order, and give each one a title. Refer to tables as *Table 1, Table 2,* and so on, and to other types of visuals as *Figure 1, Figure 2,* and so on. (In a long work with chapters or sections, also include the chapter or section number [*Figure 32.1*], as is done here.) In MLA style, use the abbreviation *Fig.*

Make sure each visual has a title that reflects its subject (for example, income levels) and its purpose (to compare changes in those income levels over time): *Figure 1. Percentage of U.S. Households in Three Income Ranges, 2000–2012.* MLA style requires that the title be placed above a table and below a figure.

To help readers understand a visual, clearly label all of its parts. For instance, give each of a table's columns a heading, and label each section of a pie chart with the percentage and the item it represents. You may place the label on the chart itself if it is readable, or in a legend next to the chart.

Some visuals may require a caption to provide a fuller description or explanation than the title alone can. (See Figure 32.2, p. 743, for example.)

Cite visual sources.

Finally, if you borrow a visual from another source or create a visual from borrowed information, you must cite the source, following the guidelines for the documentation style you are using. In addition, be sure to document the source in your list of works cited or references at the end of your document.

Integrate the visual into the text.

Visuals should facilitate, not disrupt, the reading of the body text. To achieve this goal, you need to introduce and discuss the visual in your text first and then insert the visual in an appropriate location.

For models demonstrating how to integrate and label visuals in college writing projects, see the student papers in Chapters 3–5, 8–9, and 28.

Introducing the Visual   Ideally, you should introduce each visual by referring to it in your text immediately *before* the visual appears. An effective textual reference answers the following questions:

- What is the number of the visual?
- Where is it located?
- What kind of information does it contain?
- What important point does it make or support?

Here is an example of a paragraph from page 712 that effectively refers to a visual; it is taken from "The Rising," the student paper by Paul Taylor that appears in Chapter 28:

> The Rising
>
> Gordon Parks's 1952 photograph *Emerging Man* (Fig. 1) is as historically significant a reflection of the civil rights movement as are the speeches of Martin Luther King and Malcolm X, the music of Mahalia Jackson, and the books of Ralph Ellison and James Baldwin. Through striking use of black and white--a reflection of the racial divisions plaguing American cities and towns throughout much of the nineteenth and twentieth centuries--and a symbolically potent central subject--an African American man we see literally "emerging" from a city manhole--Parks's photo evokes the centuries of racial and economic marginalization of African Americans, at the same time as it projects a spirit of determination and optimism regarding the civil rights movement's eventual success.

Placing the Visual in an Appropriate Location   MLA style requires that you place a visual in the body of your text as soon after the discussion as possible (as Paul Taylor does), particularly when the reader will need to consult the visual. (Note that Taylor discusses the figures in the text and places them as close after he first mentions them as he can. The photograph *Emerging Man* appears at the bottom of the page on which the paragraph above appears. He also includes them in his list of works cited [p. 715], with a descriptive title and source information.)

Use common sense when creating visuals on a computer.

If you use a computer program to create visuals, keep this advice in mind:

- *Make the decisions that your computer cannot make for you.* A computer can automatically turn spreadsheet data into a pie chart or bar graph, but only you can decide which visual—or what use of color, if any—is most appropriate for your purpose.

- *Avoid "chart junk."* Many computer programs provide an array of special effects that can be used to alter visuals, including three-dimensional renderings, textured backgrounds, and shadowed text. Such special effects often detract from the intended message of the visual by calling attention to themselves instead. Use them sparingly, and only when they emphasize key information.

- *Use clip art sparingly, if at all, in academic writing.* Clip art consists of icons, symbols, and other simple, typically abstract, copyright-free drawings. Because clip art simplifies ideas, it is of limited use in conveying the complex information contained in most academic writing. While clip art may be acceptable in some nonacademic contexts, always consider your audience before including it.

33

Composing Multimodal Presentations

At some point in your academic career, you will probably be asked to give a presentation. In fact, you may give many presentations before you graduate, and you almost certainly will give presentations on the job. This chapter contains practical suggestions for preparing and giving effective presentations, with or without a multimedia component.

Preparing

Many people are terrified at the thought of public speaking, particularly people who have little experience with it. Even experienced public speakers can become jittery before giving a presentation. The key to defeating nervousness and anxiety is to research and prepare. If you have researched your subject thoroughly and have planned your presentation in detail, then you should be able to relax. If you find that you are still anxious, take a few slow, deep breaths before starting your presentation. It is also helpful not to think of your presentation as a performance. Remember that you are communicating a message. Think of your presentation as simply talking to an audience.

Understand the kind of presentation you have been asked to give.

The list that follows identifies the four basic types of presentations:

- **_Impromptu presentation._** An impromptu presentation is given without preparation. In a history class, for example, your instructor may call on you to explain briefly a concept you are studying, such as "manifest destiny." As best you can, you would recall what you have read and summarize the information. Although impromptu presentations are given without preparation, they do require knowledge of the subject matter.

- **_Extemporaneous presentation._** In an extemporaneous presentation, you prepare beforehand and speak from notes or an outline. For example, in a management class, you might prepare a report on a business that you recently visited. In most academic and business situations, extemporaneous talks are preferred because they are informal yet well organized. Extemporaneous presentation often includes outlining your major points using presentation software, such as PowerPoint or Prezi.

- ***Scripted presentation.*** Reading from a script is one way to ensure that you say exactly what you want to say—and that you take no more than the time you have been allotted. Because you read to your audience, a scripted presentation can be stiff and boring unless it is carefully planned and rehearsed. To be sure the audience can easily follow the presentation by just hearing it, sentences should be kept short, and explicit transition words and phrases should be used. In fact, more transitions and cues are needed in presentations than in documents that are read (see Use Cues to Orient Listeners, on the facing page). A simple guideline to remember is that if your writing is difficult for you to read aloud, it will be difficult to listen to as well.

- ***Memorized presentation.*** This type of presentation is written and committed to memory beforehand. For instance, at a sales meeting, you might evaluate a new product in relation to its competition. However, most people prefer scripted talks because of the difficulty of memorizing a lengthy presentation.

Assess your audience and purpose.

To give effective presentations, you need to assess your audience and your purpose. Even for an impromptu presentation, you should take a few moments to think about why and to whom you are speaking. To assess your audience, ask the same questions you would ask about readers: Why are the members of my audience here? What do they already know about my subject? How do they feel about my topic? What objections might they have to my argument? What kind of media will help me convey my points most effectively? What kind of media (including presentation slides, like PowerPoint or Prezi) will they expect?

Define your purpose by completing the following statement:

▶ In this presentation, I want to ....

For instance, you may want to speculate on the causes of companies' hiring part-time instead of full-time workers, or you may want to argue your position on the ethics of this new hiring policy.

Determine how much information you can present in the allotted time.

Your presentation should be exactly as long as the time allotted. Using substantially less time will make your presentation seem incomplete or superficial; using substantially more time may alienate your audience. Plan your presentation to allocate sufficient time for an introduction, concluding remarks, and follow-up questions (if a question-and-answer session is to be part of the presentation). If you are giving a scripted presentation, each double-spaced page of text will probably take two minutes to deliver. Time yourself to be sure.

Use cues to orient listeners.

Listening is one of the most difficult ways to comprehend information, in part because listeners cannot look back at previous information or scan forward, as readers can. To help your audience follow your presentation, use the same cues you would use to orient readers—but use them more frequently and overtly. Here are four basic cues that are especially helpful for listeners:

- ■ *Thesis and forecasting statements.* Begin your presentation with thesis and forecasting statements that announce to audience members what you intend to communicate (your thesis) and the order in which you will present your material (your forecast). For instance, if you will present an argument about deregulation of Internet service providers, you can begin by asserting your position and previewing the reasons you will offer to support your position.

- ■ *Transitions.* Provide transitions when you move from one point to the next to help your audience follow the twists and turns of your presentation. For example, when you have finished discussing your first reason, state explicitly that you are now turning to your second reason.

- ■ *Summaries.* End your presentation with a summary of the main points you have made. Also look for opportunities to use summaries throughout the presentation, particularly when you have spent a long time discussing something complicated. A brief summary that indicates the point you are making and its relation to your overall thesis can help listeners understand how the parts of your argument fit together to support your thesis.

- ■ *Visuals.* Visual presentation of these cues will reinforce them. An outline of your presentation, including your thesis and main topics (in a bulleted or numbered list), can all be included on a presentation slide.

For further discussion and illustration of orienting cues, see Chapter 13.

Prepare effective and appropriate multimedia aids.

For planned presentations, you can use a variety of media to help both you and your audience. As mentioned previously, presentation software, such as PowerPoint or Prezi, allows you to list the major points of your presentation, helping your listeners understand and remember what you say. Presentation slides also allow you to incorporate images, like photos or graphics, video, and sound files, all of which can be used to illustrate your points and provide supporting evidence.

But there are other ways to incorporate visuals. Writing on a board or flip chart has several advantages: low cost, high visibility, and simplicity for composing or altering on the spot. To present a long passage or detailed graphic, photocopied handouts are preferable, although they can be distracting.

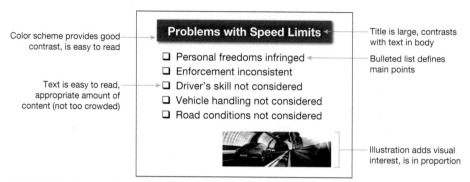

Color scheme provides good contrast, is easy to read

Text is easy to read, appropriate amount of content (not too crowded)

Title is large, contrasts with text in body

Bulleted list defines main points

Illustration adds visual interest, is in proportion

Problems with Speed Limits

❑ Personal freedoms infringed
❑ Enforcement inconsistent
❑ Driver's skill not considered
❑ Vehicle handling not considered
❑ Road conditions not considered

FIGURE 33.1   Sample PowerPoint Slide
The Advertising Archives

Simple presentation slides, such as the one in Figure 33.1, can be created and displayed with relative ease. Presentation software has the advantage of allowing the use of animation, video, and audio. Just be sure that the bells and whistles don't drown you out.

If you use presentation software, think of it as integral to your presentation, not just decorative. The text you include should be concise, easy to read, and uncluttered. You may use it to list the main points of your presentation, to signal transitions from one topic to another, to provide multimedia examples, or to summarize information you have presented.

As you prepare multimedia aids of any kind, keep in mind that everyone in your audience, including people seated in the back of the room, must be able to see or hear them easily. Use a large, easy-to-read font, allow generous amounts of space around text, and maintain sharp contrast; also, control any sound files so volume is consistent and clearly audible, but not deafening.

For more on designing for page and screen see Chapter 32.

Verify that you will have the correct equipment and supplies.

Well before your presentation is scheduled to begin, verify that the presentation room contains all of the equipment and supplies you will need. For example, if you plan to use a projector, make sure it is in the room, placed correctly, and working well. Anticipating your needs as well as potential problems (for example, by bringing a backup copy of any files you need) will make your presentation go smoothly and help reduce your anxiety.

Rehearse your presentation.

Rehearsing will help you become more familiar with your material, fit the material into the allotted time, and feel more confident about speaking in public. If possible, rehearse in the same room in which you will give the presentation, using the same equipment. Be sure to practice with any multimedia aids, so you can time your presentation realistically. Also try to rehearse before an audience of colleagues or friends who can give you feedback. Rehearsing a script or memorized presentation will enable you to plan your delivery. For a scripted talk, mark cues selectively on your printed text to remind yourself when to pause or emphasize a word or phrase.

Delivering Your Presentation

Before your presentation, try to relax: Take a few deep breaths, drink some water, or step outside for some fresh air. If someone is to introduce you, give that person information about yourself and your presentation. Otherwise, begin by introducing yourself and your title or topic. These guidelines will help you make a professional impression:

- As you speak, try to make eye contact with the people in the room.
- If you are behind a lectern, avoid slouching, leaning on it, or gripping it tightly throughout the presentation.
- If you are using presentation slides, be careful not to block the audience's view of them. After introducing a new slide, resume making eye contact with audience members; talk to the audience, not the screen.
- Try to avoid distracting vocal mannerisms, such as repeatedly saying "uh," "like," or "you know," or fidgeting with your hair or clothes.
- Speak loudly enough that all members of the audience can hear you, and speak clearly and distinctly. Nervousness may cause you to speak too rapidly, so watch your pace.
- Do not speak in a monotone. Instead, let the pitch of your voice rise and fall naturally, especially when giving a scripted presentation, and use your hands naturally, gesturing as you would in a conversation.
- Dress appropriately for your audience and the formality of the situation in which you are speaking. The focus should be on your message, not on how you are dressed.

End the presentation by thanking your audience for giving you the opportunity to speak. If appropriate, offer to answer any questions in a question-and-answer session following the presentation, in a private conversation, or in a follow-up correspondence.

Handbook

Contents

How to Use This Handbook

You may use the Handbook on your own when you edit your essays, or your instructor may refer you to specific sections to correct errors in your writing. If using the Handbook on your own, check the Handbook Contents on the previous page, or look in the index for the kind of error you are concerned about.

Your instructor may use the Handbook's letter-and-number system to lead you directly to information about a specific topic—for example, if your instructor noted "P1-b" in the margin of your essay, it would mean you had omitted a necessary comma following an introductory word, phrase, or clause. The Handbook Contents connects codes to page numbers (in this case, H-51) in the Handbook. As an alternative, you can find P1-b by looking through the tabs at the tops of the pages. Each tab indicates the section code for that page and an abbreviation or symbol for the topic covered. If your instructor indicates errors with correction symbols such as *frag* or *ww,* you can find the section where the error is covered by checking the list of correction symbols in the back of this book.

When you locate the section that will help you correct an error or make a sentence more concise or graceful, you will find a brief explanation and examples of correct usage, along with one or more hand-corrected sentences that demonstrate how to edit a sentence. Terms are defined in the margin. If your instructor has assigned this book with LaunchPad (an online course space and e-book), use your activation code to practice these skills in LearningCurve, an adaptive, game-like quizzing program that quickly learns what you already know and helps you practice what you don't yet understand. LearningCurve activities appear in the Handbook and other relevant sections of the e-book.

While developing this Handbook, ten college writing instructors and four professional editors worked together to identify the twenty-five most common errors* in more than five hundred student essays written in first-year composition courses. These errors are listed below in order of descending frequency. The codes in bold following each error indicate the section number in this Handbook where you can find help with understanding and correcting each error in your own writing.

Top 25 Errors in Student Papers

1. Wordiness **W1-a–W1-c**

2. Misused word **W2-a, W2-e**

3. Incorrect or ambiguous pronoun reference **G1**

4. Verb tense errors **G5-a, G5-b**

5. Missing comma between independent clauses **P1-a**

6. Problems with hyphens between compound adjectives **M1-a**

7. Missing comma after introductory elements **P1-b**

8. Capitalization of proper or common nouns **M2-a**

9. Unnecessary comma between compound elements **P2-a**

---

* Spelling errors were not included.

10. Incorrect spacing **M3**

11. Missing words **E1-a–E1-d**

12. Missing comma with nonrestrictive word groups **P1-c**

13. Comma splice or fused sentence **S1, S2**

14. Problems in using quotation marks with other punctuation **P6-b**

15. Missing or unnecessary hyphens in compound nouns **M1-b**

16. Missing comma with transitional and parenthetical expressions, absolute phrases, and contrasted elements **P1-d**

17. Problems of pronoun-antecedent agreement **G2**

18. Incorrect preposition **W2-b, T3**

19. Misuse of *who, which,* or *that* **G3**

20. Unnecessarily complex sentence structure **W1-b**

21. Spelling out or using figures for numbers incorrectly **M4**

22. Problems with apostrophes in possessive nouns **P7-a**

23. Sentence fragment **S3**

24. Missing comma in items in a series **P1-e**

25. Unnecessary comma with restrictive word groups **P2-b**

This list of the top twenty-five errors can be categorized into the following five major patterns of errors. You may find it useful to keep these patterns in mind as you edit your work.

1. Missing or unnecessary commas **(P1-a–P1-d, P2-a–P2-g)**

2. Errors in word choice **(W1-a–W1-d, W2-a–W2-d)**

3. Errors in pronoun reference, agreement, or use **(G1, G2, G3)**

4. Verb tense errors **(G5-a, G5-b)**

5. Errors in recognizing and punctuating sentences — comma splices, fused sentences, fragments **(S1, S2, S3)**

Keeping a Record of Your Own Errors

In addition to checking your work for the errors college students usually make, you will find it useful to keep a record of the errors that *you* usually make. You can then work toward avoiding them.

To use the Record of Errors form on the next page, note the name and section number of each error you make in the left-hand column. (See the Handbook Contents on p. H-1 or the list of correction symbols at the back of the book for the names of errors.) For example, if in your first essay your instructor or another student marks a vague use of the pronoun *this* at the beginning of two of your sentences, locate the section that provides help in correcting this error (G1), and enter the error name in the left column along with the section number. Then under *Essay 1* and next to the name of the error, enter the number *2* to indicate how many times you made this error. As you edit subsequent essays, you can easily review this section in the Handbook to make sure you have avoided this pronoun problem.

By your second or third essay, you should begin to see patterns in the errors you make and to understand how to recognize and correct them.

RECORD OF ERRORS

Name of Error and Section Number in the Handbook	Frequency						
	Essay 1	Essay 2	Essay 3	Essay 4	Essay 5	Essay 6	Essay 7

S   Sentence Boundaries

S1   Comma Splices

In a comma splice, two **independent clauses** are improperly joined by a comma.

COMMA SPLICE

┌— independent clause —┐ ┌——— independent clause ———┐
I know what to do, I just don't know how to do it.
                 comma

> **independent clause** A word group with a subject and a predicate that can stand alone as a separate sentence.

Because a comma splice can be edited in many ways, first consider how the ideas in the two independent clauses relate. For example, are they equally important, or does one depend on or explain the other? Then select the strategy from the following that will best clarify this relationship for a reader.

Add a **subordinating conjunction** to one clause, rewording as necessary.

> *After*
> ▶ I started to exercise, my health began to improve.
>   ^

> *Though*
> ▶ I know what to do, I just don't know how to do it.
>   ^

> **subordinating conjunction** A word or phrase (such as *although* or *because*) that introduces a dependent clause and relates it to an independent clause.

By beginning a clause with a subordinating conjunction, you indicate that the clause is subordinate to—and dependent on—the main clause. Usually, the **dependent clause** explains or qualifies the **independent clause**. Select the subordinating conjunction carefully so that it tells the reader how the ideas in the clauses relate to each other.

> **dependent clause** A word group that has a subject and a predicate but cannot stand by itself as a sentence; it must be connected to an independent clause.

Separate the independent clauses with a comma and a **coordinating conjunction**.

> ▶ On *Muppets: The Green Album*, a wide variety of musicians and bands covered songs
>
>   *and*
>   made famous by the beloved puppets, the result inspired cross-generational nostalgia
>   ^
>
>   and extra buzz for 2011's new Muppets movie.

> ▶ In 2015, the average fuel consumption by a Japanese car was 40 mpg, the average
>   *but*
>   ^
>   American car was still getting only 22 mpg.

> **coordinating conjunction** A word that joins comparable and equally important sentence elements: *for, and, or, but, nor, yet,* or *so.*

The coordinating conjunction tells the reader that the ideas in the two clauses are closely related and equally important.

Separate the independent clauses with a semicolon.

▶ The tattoo needle looked like an extension of his arm; the needle was his

brush, and the human body, his canvas.

▶ Nate was very lucky; he lived to see his hundredth birthday.

The semicolon tells the reader that the ideas in the two clauses are closely connected, but it *implies* the connection rather than stating it. Occasionally, a colon may be used to introduce a second independent clause. See P4-a.

Separate the independent clauses with a semicolon or a period, and add a conjunctive adverb or transitional phrase.

conjunctive adverb A word or phrase (such as *finally, however,* or *therefore*) that tells how the ideas in two sentences or independent clauses are connected.

▶ He doesn't need the map right now; *instead,* he is following the direction Kiem pointed

out to him and checking it with the compass.

▶ He doesn't need the map right now. *Instead,* he is following the direction Kiem pointed

out to him and checking it with the compass.

The period shows a stronger break. Conjunctive adverbs are used more frequently in formal than in informal writing.

Turn the independent clauses into separate sentences.

▶ At high noon we were off, paddling down the Potomac River. *We* we were two

to a canoe, leaving space in the middle for our gear.

The period at the end of the first independent clause tells the reader that one complete sentence is ending and another is beginning.

Turn one independent clause into a phrase that modifies the other.

▶ At high noon we were off, paddling down the Potomac River, ~~we were~~ two to a

canoe with space in the middle for our gear.

modifying phrase A word group that serves as an adjective or adverb.

Eliminating the subject and verb in the second clause turns it into a **modifying phrase**, reducing the number of words and closely connecting the ideas.

S2 Fused Sentences

A fused or run-on sentence consists of two **independent clauses** run together with no punctuation.

FUSED
SENTENCE

┌── independent clause ──┐┌────────── independent clause ──────────┐
Her mood was good I took the opportunity to ask if she had a few minutes
to answer some questions.

> **independent clause** A word group with a subject and a predicate that can stand alone as a separate sentence.

Because a fused sentence can be edited in many ways, first consider how the ideas in the two independent clauses are related, and then select the most appropriate strategy from among the following.

Make one of the clauses subordinate to the other by adding a subordinating conjunction and rewording as necessary.

> **subordinating conjunction** A word or phrase (such as *although* or *because*) that introduces a dependent clause and relates it to an independent clause.

>   so   that
> ▶ Her mood was good I took the opportunity to ask if she had a few minutes to answer
>
> some questions.

>   *Although childhood*
> ▶ Childhood is often remembered as delightful, kids can be extremely cruel to one another.

By beginning a clause with a subordinating conjunction, you indicate that the clause is subordinate to—and dependent on—the main clause. Usually, the **dependent clause** explains or qualifies the independent clause. Choose the subordinating conjunction carefully so that it tells the reader how the dependent clause relates to the independent clause. For example, the writer might emphasize the causal relationship between two clauses by using the word *because.*

> **dependent clause** A word group that has a subject and a predicate but cannot stand by itself as a sentence; it must be connected to an independent clause.

>   *Because her*
> ▶ Her mood was good I took the opportunity to ask if she had a few minutes
>
> to answer some questions.

Add a comma and a coordinating conjunction to separate the independent clauses.

> **coordinating conjunction** A word that joins comparable and equally important sentence elements: *for, and, or, but, nor, yet,* or *so.*

>   , and
> ▶ The beast was upon me I could feel his paws pressing down on my chest.

The coordinating conjunction tells the reader that the ideas in the two clauses are equally important.

Separate the independent clauses with a semicolon.

▶ I looked around at the different displays ; most were large plasma screens, many

of which were connected to the central unit.

The semicolon tells the reader that the ideas in the two clauses are closely connected, but it *implies* the connection rather than stating it. Occasionally, a colon may be used to introduce a second independent clause. See P4-a.

Separate the independent clauses with a semicolon or a period, and add a conjunctive adverb or a transitional phrase such as *for example* or *in other words*.

▶ Most students do not do their homework during the day they do it in the evening.
_{; instead,}

▶ Most students do not do their homework during the day they do it in the evening.
_{. Instead,}

The period indicates a stronger break.

Turn the independent clauses into separate sentences.

▶ He was only eight . his life hadn't even started.
_{His}

▶ I couldn't believe it . I had fallen into the campus fountain.

The period at the end of the first independent clause tells the reader that one complete sentence is ending and another is beginning.

Turn one independent clause into a phrase that modifies the other.

▶ I almost dropped my phone ; ~~I could feel~~ my hand slipping as I tried to text and use

the self-checkout lane at the same time.

Eliminating the subject and verb in the second clause turns it into a **modifying phrase**, reducing the number of words and closely linking the ideas.

S3 Sentence Fragments

A fragment is either an incomplete sentence, lacking a complete **subject** or **predicate**, or a **dependent clause** punctuated incorrectly as a sentence.

FRAGMENT   Tonight it's my turn. *A ride-along with Sergeant Rob Nether of the Green Valley Police Department.*

---

conjunctive adverb A word or phrase (such as *finally*, *however*, or *therefore*) that tells how the ideas in two sentences or independent clauses are connected.

modifying phrase A word group that serves as an adjective or adverb.

subject The part of a clause that identifies who or what is being discussed.

predicate The part of a clause that includes a complete verb and describes the action or state of the subject.

dependent clause A word group that has a subject and a predicate but cannot stand by itself as a sentence; it must be connected to an independent clause.

Because a fragment can often be edited in several ways, begin by considering what the fragment lacks and how its ideas relate to those in the sentences before and after it. Then use one of the following strategies to change the fragment into a complete sentence.

Connect the fragment to a complete sentence.

To edit the fragment in the opening example, the writer might connect it to the preceding sentence.

▶ Tonight it's my turn. *for a* A ride-along with Sergeant Rob Nether of the Green Valley

 Police Department.

▶ A unique design has the distinct advantage of becoming associated with its

 role. *for* For example, the highly successful Coke bottle shape, which is now

 associated with soft drinks.

Eliminate the subordinating word(s) that make a clause dependent.

▶ The world that I was born into demanded continuous work. *Nobody* ~~Where nobody~~ got

 ahead, and everyone came home tired.

Add or complete the verb or subject to change a fragment into a complete sentence.

▶ The crowd in the lounge is basically young. Teenagers and twenty-somethings. *gather there*

▶ Children are brought up in different ways. Some. *grow up* around violence.

Exception: Use fragments intentionally for emphasis or special effect.

▶ The bare utility of the clock echoes the simplicity of the office. No sign of a large hardwood desk, a pillowy leather chair, or even a wall of imposing law books.

Use intentional fragments cautiously. Especially in academic writing, readers may perceive them as errors, regardless of your intentions. In the preceding example, the same impact might also be achieved by using a colon or dash.

▶ The bare utility of the clock echoes the simplicity of the office. *:* No sign of a large

 hardwood desk, a pillowy leather chair, or even a wall of imposing law books.

G Grammatical Sentences

G1 Pronoun Reference

pronoun A word that replaces a specific noun (such as *it, his, them, yours, myself,* or *which*), points out a specific noun (such as *this, these,* or *that*), or refers to an unspecified person or object (such as *everybody* or *each*).

antecedent The word or words that a pronoun replaces and to which it refers.

Make sure that each **pronoun** clearly refers to one specific **antecedent**.

▸ ──── antecedent ────   pronoun
The elderly and children are victims when no one bothers to check on *them*.

Eliminate vague uses of *they, it,* or *you*.

▸ Lani explained that everything is completely supported by individual

                   The organization receives
contributions. ~~They receive~~ no tax support.

▸ Often, a guest such as Neil DeGrasse Tyson or Al Franken appears

                 having the same guest return
more than once. Although it may seem repetitious, it is not when the

guest discusses different topics each time.

▸ Parents argue that beginning the program in the sixth grade is too early.

 They say that   *encourages*
By exposing teens to sex education early, ~~you encourage~~ them to go out and

have sex.

Add a noun, change the pronoun to a noun, or eliminate vague uses of *this, that,* or *which*.

▸ Researchers have found that men interrupt women more than women

           finding
interrupt men. This may explain why women sometimes find it difficult to start

and sustain conversations with men.

▸   *getting good grades*
I was an *A* student, and I thought that should have been enough for any teacher.

▸ The brevity of the first story prevents the reader from dwelling on the plot

                     Because these
and caring about the outcome. ~~These~~ faults are not present in "The Soft

                      is
Voice of the Serpent," ~~which~~ makes it much more fulfilling to read.

Add a missing antecedent, or eliminate a pronoun with no clear antecedent.

▸ In addition to the cars your tenants actually drive, five or six vehicles are

your tenants
always on and around the property. As a result, not only do they park some of
                                                                    ^

them in front of their neighbors' homes, but their questionable visitors park up

and down the street as well.

Adding an antecedent (specifying *your tenants* instead of *they*) and eliminating a
pronoun (reducing *park some of them* to *park*) simplify and clarify the sentence.

**Identify a specific antecedent if a pronoun refers vaguely to a clause or a whole
sentence.**

▸ After the long ride, we reached the place for our expedition at Pine Heaven

the trip
Forest in western Virginia. At my age, it seemed to take forever.
                                       ^

Clarify an ambiguous reference to two possible antecedents.

if
▸ Students may now sue their schools if they are underperforming.
                                    ^

underperforming
▸ Students may now sue their schools⊙ if they are underperforming.
                                   ^

Specify an implied reference.

In this   ⌃the singer
▸ This song tells about being carefree and going through life without any worries.
   ^   ^

Years later, though, he starts to remember his past, and things do not seem so

problem-free anymore.

In this example, adding *the singer* specifies an antecedent for *he*.

Note: Sometimes the implied noun may be present in another form, such as a possessive (*Mary's* for *Mary*) or as part of another word (*child* in *childhood*).

▸ Radaker's arguments irritated everyone at the lecture because he failed to

his arguments
support them with examples or evidence.
           ^

G2 Pronoun Agreement

pronoun A word that replaces a specific noun (such as *it, his, them, yours, myself,* or *which*), points out a specific noun (such as *this, these,* or *that*), or refers to an unspecified person or object (such as *everybody* or *each*).

antecedent The word or words that a pronoun replaces and to which it refers.

number The form of a word that shows whether it refers to one thing (singular: *parent*) or more than one (plural: *parents*).

person The form of a word that shows whether it refers to *I* or *we* (first person), to *you* (second person), or to *he, she, it,* or *they* (third person).

gender The form of a word that shows whether it refers to a male (*he*) or a female (*she*).

Make sure that a **pronoun** and its **antecedent** agree in **number**, in **person**, and in **gender**. In the following examples, the arrows connect the pronouns to their antecedents.

▶ The *scientists* did not know what *they* were creating.

▶ *I* thought about Punita's offer while watching the movie. *My* curiosity won.

▶ After we went back to the lab, *Punita* started concentrating on *her* work.

The form of the antecedent and the form of the pronoun must correspond so that a reader is not troubled by inconsistencies or confused about how many, who, or which gender you mean.

G2-a   Use pronouns and antecedents that agree in number.

If the antecedent of a pronoun is singular, the pronoun must be singular so that both agree in number. Likewise, if the antecedent is plural, the pronoun must be plural.

▶ The *shelter* gets most of *its* cats and dogs from *owners* who cannot keep *their* pets.

When the pronoun and its antecedent do not agree, change one so that both are singular or plural, or rewrite the sentence to eliminate the inconsistency. (See also E2-b.)

Change either the pronoun or its antecedent so that both are singular or plural.

▶ The patient is fully aware of the decision that ~~they are~~ making.
   he or she is

▶ ~~The patient is~~ fully aware of the decisions that they are making.
   Patients are

Note: As an alternative, you may be able to eliminate the pronoun.

▶ The patient is fully aware of the decision that ~~they are making~~.
   each

Revise the sentence to eliminate the inconsistency.

▶ Roommates get agitated at always being told to clean, and the roommate
   doing the telling gets tired of hearing ~~their own voice complain~~.
   complaining

indefinite pronoun A pronoun that does not refer to a particular person or object. Examples: **Singular**—*anybody, anyone, each, everyone, everything, somebody, something, neither, none,* or *nobody;* **Plural**—*few, many,* and *several;* **Singular or plural**—*all, most,* and *some.*

Use a singular pronoun to refer to a singular indefinite pronoun, or reword the sentence.

▶ Whether student, teacher, faculty member, graduate, or parent, each wants
   their school to be the one that remains open.
   his or her

▸ *All students~ teachers~ faculty members~ graduates~ and parents want*
Whether student, teacher, faculty member, graduate, or parent, each wants
  ^

their school to be the one that remains open.

▸ This event would be a good chance for ~~everyone~~ *students* to come out, socialize, and
  ^

enjoy themselves.

Consider the level of formality of your writing. Friends in a casual conversation may not mind if an indefinite pronoun and its antecedent do not agree, but such errors are not acceptable in formal writing.

Use a singular pronoun if the antecedent is a collective noun.

▸ The Santa Barbara School District has a serious problem on ~~their~~ *its* agenda.
  ^

collective noun A noun (such as *class* or *family*) that refers to a group as a unit and is usually considered singular.

Exception: A collective noun may sometimes be considered plural if it refers to the group members as individuals: The *couple* decided it was time to consolidate *their* bank accounts. (See also G6-b.)

G2-b **Use masculine, feminine, or gender-free forms to match a pronoun with its antecedent.**

Match a masculine pronoun with a masculine antecedent and a feminine pronoun with a feminine antecedent so that the pronoun and its antecedent agree in gender.

▸ I first met *Mark* the day *he* was hired.

If an antecedent might be either masculine or feminine, avoid using a pronoun that stereotypes by gender. (See also W3-c.)

Match a plural antecedent with a plural pronoun to include both sexes.

▸ Many people believe that ~~a boy or girl is~~ *children are* better off with a family that is able to
  ^

provide for all of their needs than with a poverty-stricken parent.

Use a phrase that includes both masculine and feminine singular pronouns (such as *his or her*) to refer to both sexes.

▸ Many people believe that a child is better off with a family that is able to

his or her
provide for all of ~~their~~ needs than with a poverty-stricken family.
  ^

Note: If repeating a phrase such as *his or her* seems cumbersome or repetitious, try using plural forms or eliminating the pronouns altogether, as the following strategy suggests.

Eliminate unneeded or awkward pairs of masculine and feminine pronouns.

▶ This solution, of course, assumes that the bus ~~driver~~ *drivers* will be where ~~he/she is~~ *they are*

supposed to be; boredom sometimes inspires a ~~driver~~ *drivers* to make up new

and exciting variations on ~~his or her~~ *their* designated routes.

Note: Avoid using *he/she* in all but the most informal writing situations.

G3 Relative Pronouns

relative pronoun A pronoun that introduces an adjective clause.

Use personal **relative pronouns** to refer to people: *who, whom, whoever, whomever,* and *whose.*

▶ This reaction is unlike the response of the boys, *who* had trouble focusing on a

subject.

Use nonpersonal relative pronouns to refer to things—*which, whichever, whatever,* and *whose.* **Note:** *Whose* can be used as a nonpersonal relative pronoun as well as a personal one.

▶ These interruptions, 75 percent of *which* come solely from males, disrupt

conversations.

Use *that* for general references to things and groups.

▶ Sensory modalities are governed by the side of the brain *that* is not damaged.

(See also G6-e.)

nonrestrictive clause A clause, set off by commas, that provides extra or nonessential information and could be eliminated without changing the meaning of the noun or pronoun it modifies.

restrictive clause A clause, not set off by commas, that provides information essential to defining or identifying the noun or pronoun it modifies.

G3-a Select *who* for references to people, *which* for **nonrestrictive** references to things, and *that* for **restrictive** references to groups and things.

▶ My attention focused on a little dark-haired boy *who* was crying.

▶ The tournament, *which* we had worked for all year, was the most prestigious event

of the season.

▶ Save Our Sharks tried to promote a bill *that* would forbid the killing of certain sharks.

Change *that* to *who* to refer to a person.

▶ Illness phobics have countless examinations despite the reassurance of each

    who
  physician ~~that~~ examines them.
        ^

Note: Rewriting a sentence to simplify its structure sometimes eliminates a problem with pronouns.

  His
▶ ~~It was his~~ parents that made him run for student council, play the piano, and
  ^

  go out for sports.

(See also G3-b for information on *who* and *whom*.)

Change *that* to *which* when a nonrestrictive clause supplies extra, nondefining information.

Introduce a nonrestrictive clause with *which,* not *that.*

                                which
▶ Caroline had the prettiest jet-black hair, ~~that~~ went down to the middle of her back.
                                    ^

See P1-c on using commas with nonrestrictive word groups.

Change *which* to *that* when a restrictive clause supplies essential information defining a thing or a group.

                                          that
▶ From the moment we are born, we come into a society ~~which~~ assimilates us into
                                          ^

  its culture.

Introduce a restrictive clause with *that,* not *which.*

                                     that
▶ In addition to the equipment and technology ~~which~~ fill the trauma room,
                                    ^

  a team of experts assembles before the patient arrives.

See P2-b on unnecessary commas with restrictive word groups.

G3-b   Use *who* as a subject and *whom* as an **object.**

Two strategies can help you figure out whether to use *who* or *whom.*

1. Arrange the phrase's or clause's words in subject-verb-object order or **preposition-object** order. In this standard order, a subject (*who*) is followed by a verb, but an object (*whom*) follows a subject and verb or a preposition.

object The part of a clause that receives the action of the verb, or the part of a phrase that follows a preposition.

preposition A word (such as *between, in,* or *of*) that indicates the relation between a word in a sentence and its object.

2. Look for the subject of the clause. If the verb in the clause has another subject, use *whom;* if the verb in the clause has no other subject, use *who.* If it is the object of a preposition, use *whom.*

SUBJECT

We remember [*who* tips well] and [*who* doesn't].

I will always admire Mr. Stewart.

OBJECT OF VERB

Mr. Stewart is someone [*whom* I will always admire].

OBJECT OF PREPOSITION

The university employs a large number of international teaching assistants [for *whom* English is a second language].

Change *who* to *whom* when the pronoun is an object within another clause that has a subject and a verb.

whom

▶ He has the ability to attract guests who people want to hear.
                                        ^

Change *who* to *whom* when the pronoun is the object of a preposition.

to whom

▶ He also met his wife, who he was married to for fifty-two years.
                       ^

Change *whom* to *who* when the pronoun is the subject of a clause and is followed by a verb.

who

▶ The libraries are staffed by professionals whom have instituted methods to keep
                                             ^

students informed of new materials.

G4   Pronoun Case

A pronoun can take different forms or cases, depending on its role in a sentence.

subject complement
A word or word group that follows a linking verb and describes or restates the subject.

■ Subject or **subject complement**: *I, we, you, he, she, it, they* (subjective form)

▶ "*You*'d better be careful," *she* said.

▶ It is *we* you owe the money to.

preposition A word (such as *between, in,* or *of*) that indicates the relation between a word in a sentence and its object.

■ Object of a verb or a **preposition**: *me, us, you, him, her, it, them* (objective form)

▶ This realization spurred *me* to hasten the search.

▶ Her dog, Peter the Great, went with *her* on the excavation in southern Siberia.

- Possession or ownership: *mine, ours, yours, his, hers, theirs, my, our, your, her, its, their* (possessive form)

  ▶ I trusted *his* driving.

  ▶ I finished putting *my* gear on and rolled over backward into the ocean.

See R2-a for more on pronouns.

Replace a reflexive pronoun that does not refer to another noun or pronoun in the clause.

> **reflexive pronoun** A pronoun such as *myself* or *ourselves* that refers to a noun or a personal pronoun in the same clause.

  ▶ Kyle and ~~myself~~ *I* went upstairs to see how she was doing.

A reflexive pronoun does not belong in this sentence because *myself* does not refer to a preceding *I*.

Change a pronoun to the subjective form if it is part of a compound subject.

> **compound subject** Two or more words acting as a subject, linked by *and*.

  ▶ Even though Annie and ~~me~~ *I* went through the motions, we did not understand the customs of our host.

Change a pronoun to the objective form if it is an object (or part of a compound object) of a preposition or a verb.

> **compound object** Two or more words acting as an object, linked by *and*.

  ▶ There was an invisible wall between ~~she~~ *her* and ~~I~~ *me*.

Change a pronoun to the possessive form when it modifies a gerund.

> **gerund** A verb form that is used as a noun and ends in *-ing: arguing, throwing.*

  ▶ One of the main reasons for ~~me~~ *my* wanting to stay home with my children until they enter grade school is that otherwise I would miss so much.

Change the form of a pronoun to fit the implied or understood wording of a comparison using *than* or *as*.

  ▶ I was still faster than ~~her~~ *she*.

Test whether a pronoun form fits by filling in the implied wording.

INCORRECT PRONOUN   I was still faster than *her* [was fast].

CORRECT PRONOUN   I was still faster than *she* [was fast].

Use *we* to precede a subject, or *us* to precede an object.

We is the subjective form, and *us* is the objective form. Select the form that matches the role of the noun in the sentence.

▶ Whenever ~~us~~ ^we^ neighborhood kids would go out to play, I would always be goalie.

Test your choice of pronoun by reading the sentence with the noun left out.

INCORRECT PRONOUN	Whenever *us* would go out to play, I would always be goalie.
CORRECT PRONOUN	Whenever *we* would go out to play, I would always be goalie.

G5 Verbs

tense The form of a verb that shows the time of the action or state of being.

mood The form of a verb that shows the writer's attitude toward a statement.

voice The form of a verb that either emphasizes the performer of an action (active) or deemphasizes it (passive).

Use standard verb forms in the appropriate **tense**, **mood**, and **voice**.

G5-a Select the appropriate verb tense to place events in past, present, and future time.

When selecting the correct verb tense for a sentence, pay special attention to conventional usage or to the relationships among different verbs within the context of your essay. See R2-a for a review of the basic verb tenses.

FOR MULTILINGUAL WRITERS

See T2 for advice on how to use the correct tense in conditional clauses, two-word verbs, and helping (auxiliary) verbs and whether to use a gerund or an infinitive form after a verb.

Change verbs from the past tense to the present when discussing events in a literary work or film, general truths, ongoing principles, and facts.

Readers expect the use of the present tense in a literary analysis, as if the action in a work were always ongoing.

▶ In "The Monkey Garden," the girl ~~knew~~ ^knows^ it ~~was~~ ^is^ time to grow up but still
~~wanted~~ ^wants^ to play with the other kids in her make-believe world.

▶ In the show *The Good Wife*, Alicia (Julianna Margulies) ~~was~~ ^is^ an attorney
who ~~returned~~ ^returns^ to work after her husband is imprisoned.

Readers also expect general truths, facts, and ongoing principles to be stated in the present tense. (See also E2-a.)

GENERAL TRUTH	The family *is* the foundation for a child's education.
ONGOING PRINCIPLE	Attaining self-sufficiency *is* one of the most important priorities of our energy policy.
FACT	The earth *is tilted* at an angle of 23 degrees.

Note: Some style guides make different recommendations about verb tense, depending on the field and its conventions. The style guide of the American Psychological Association (APA), for example, recommends using the past tense for past studies but using the present tense for research implications and conclusions.

APA STYLE	Davidson *stated* that father absence *is* more than twice as common now as in our parents' generation.

Change the verb from the past tense to the past perfect (using *had*) to show that one past action took place before another.

> ► The student's roommate also claimed that she ^*had* called the dorm office two days

before the suicide attempt.

The past action identified by the verb *had called* occurred before the past action identified by the verb *claimed*.

┌─────────────────────────┐
│ **FOR MULTILINGUAL WRITERS** │
└─────────────────────────┘

Certain verbs—ones that indicate existence, states of mind, and the senses of sight, smell, touch, and so on—are rarely used in the **progressive tense**. Such verbs include *appear, be, belong, contain, feel, forget, have, hear, know, mean, prefer, remember, see, smell, taste, think, understand,* and *want*.

> ► I am ^*belong*ing to the campus group for foreign students.

progressive tense A tense that shows ongoing action, consisting of a form of *be* plus the *-ing* form of the main verb: I *am waiting*.

G5-b Use the correct verb endings and verb forms.

The five basic forms of regular verbs (such as *talk*) follow the same pattern, adding *-s*, *-ed*, and *-ing*, as shown here. The forms of irregular verbs (such as *speak*) do not consistently follow this pattern in forming the past and the past participle (see R2-a).

- Infinitive or base: *talk* or *speak*

  > ► Every day I *talk* on the phone and *speak* to my friends.

- Third-person singular present (*-s* form): *talks* or *speaks*

▶ He *talks* softly, and she *speaks* slowly.

▪ Past: *talked* or *spoke*

▶ I *talked* to my parents last week, and I *spoke* to Jed on Tuesday.

▪ Present participle (*-ing* form): *talking* or *speaking*

▶ She is *talking* on the phone now, and he is *speaking* to a friend.

▪ Past participle (*-ed* form): *talked* or *spoken*

▶ I have *talked* to her many times, but she has not *spoken* to him yet.

Add an *-s* or *-es* ending to a verb when the subject is in the third-person singular (*he, she, it,* or a singular noun).

▶ The national drug control policy ~~treat~~ *treats* drug abuse as a law enforcement problem.

▶ This group ~~account~~ *accounts* for more than 10 percent of the total U.S. population.

FOR MULTILINGUAL WRITERS

Choosing the correct verb form is sometimes complicated by English expressions. For example, *used to* followed by the base form of the verb does not mean the same as *get used to* followed by a gerund.

▶ In the United States, most people *used to live* in rural areas. [This situation existed in the past but has changed.]

▶ My daughter *is getting used to going* to school every day. [She is getting in the habit of attending school.]

For more on choosing correct word forms, see W2.

Delete an *-s* or *-es* ending from a verb when the subject is in the first person (*I, we*), second person (*you*), or third-person plural (*they*).

▶ Because I think you'll really like it, I ~~suggests~~ *suggest* that you go see the movie *Boyhood*.

Add a *-d* or an *-ed* ending to a regular verb to form the past tense or the past participle.

▶ This movie was filmed in New Orleans because it resembles the city where the story is ~~suppose~~ *supposed* to take place.

▶ As we walked through the library, she ~~explain~~ *explained* the meaning of the yellow signs.

Check to be sure you have used the correct form of an irregular verb.

If you are uncertain about a verb form, refer to the list of irregular verbs in R2-a, or check your dictionary.

▶ The hostess greeted us and ~~lead~~ ^led^ us to our seats.

▶ We could tell our food had just ~~came~~ ^come^ off the grill because it still sizzled.

Note: Some verbs with different meanings are confusing because they have similar forms. For example, the verb *lie* (*lie, lay, lain, lying*) means "recline," but the verb *lay* (*lay, laid, laid, laying*) means "put or place." Consult the Glossary of Frequently Misused Words on pp. H-111–14 or a dictionary to make sure that you are using the correct form of the word you intend.

▶ I thought everyone was going to see my car ~~laying~~ ^lying^ on its side.

G5-c Choose the correct form of a verb to show the **indicative**, **imperative**, or **subjunctive mood**.

INDICATIVE There *is* Homer, the father, who *serves* as sole provider for the family.

Where *are* the Simpsons today?

IMPERATIVE *Take* me to the mall.

SUBJUNCTIVE If it *were* to rain on the day of the picnic, we would simply bring everything indoors.

> **indicative mood** The verb form ordinarily used for statements and questions.
>
> **imperative mood** The verb form used for commands or directions.
>
> **subjunctive mood** The verb form used for wishes, suggestions, and conditions that are hypothetical, impossible, or unlikely.

The subjunctive is often used in clauses with *if* or *that*. Always use the **base form** of the verb for the present subjunctive. (See G5-b.) For the past tense of the verb *be*, the subjunctive form is *were*, not *was*.

> **base form** The uninflected form of a verb: I *eat*; to *play*.

▶ Even if this claim ~~was~~ ^were^ true, it would raise a very controversial issue.

G5-d Use verbs primarily in the active voice.

The **active voice** calls attention to the actor performing an action. By contrast, the **passive voice** emphasizes the recipient of the action or the action itself over the actor.

ACTIVE The monkey *lived* in the garden.

PASSIVE The story *is told* by a girl as she reflects on her own childhood.

> **active voice** The verb form that shows the subject in action.
>
> **passive voice** The verb form that shows something happening to the subject.

Change passive verbs to active in most writing situations.

Straightforward and direct, the active voice creates graceful, clear writing that emphasizes actors.

> *girl tells the story*
> ▶ The ~~story is told by the girl~~ as she reflects on her own childhood.
>   ^

> *The*   *attract physicians.*
> ▶ ~~Physicians are attracted by the~~ monetary rewards of high-tech research.
>   ^   ^

Eliminate awkward, unnecessary passive verbs.

>   *∧ seeking others with similar interests.*
> ▶ The guests cluster like grapes ~~as similar interests are sought.~~
>   ^

Note: The passive voice is sometimes useful if you want to shift information to the end of a sentence. It is also frequently used in impersonal writing that focuses on an action rather than an actor, as in a scientific research report.

> ▶ When the generator *is turned on,* water *is forced* down the tunnel, and the animals swim against the current. Their metabolism *is measured.* They have participated in this experiment before, and the results from that run and this new one *will be compared.*

G6   Subject-Verb Agreement

subject The part of a clause that identifies who or what is being discussed.

verb A word or phrase that expresses action or being and, along with a subject, is a basic component of a sentence.

person The form of a word that shows whether it refers to *I* or *we* (first person), to *you* (second person), or to *he, she, it,* or *they* (third person).

number The form of a word that shows whether it refers to one thing (singular) or more than one (plural): *parent, parents; child, children.*

Use **subjects** and **verbs** that agree in **person** and **number**. Agreement problems often occur when a sentence has a complicated subject or verb, especially when the subject and verb are separated by other words.

>   ┌─ subject ─┐   ┌verb┐
>   *are*
> ▶ The large amounts of money that are associated with sports is not the problem.
>   ∧∧

The plural subject, *amounts,* requires a plural verb, *are.* (See also R2-a to check the correct forms of *be* and other irregular verbs.)

G6-a   Make sure the subject and verb agree even if they are separated by other words.

>   ┌─ subject ─┐   ┌──verb──┐
> ▶ The *relationship* between artists and politicians *has become* a controversial issue.

First identify the subject and the verb; then change one to agree with the other.

>   *is*
> ▶ The pattern of echoes from these sound waves are converted by computer into a
>   ^
>   visual image.

> ▶ The ~~pattern of echoes from these sound waves are~~ converted by computer into a
>   visual image.

G6-b   Use a singular verb with a subject that is a **collective noun**.

▶ The *association distributes* information on showing bison, selling bison, and

marketing bison meat.

collective noun / singular verb

Change the verb to a singular form if the subject is a collective noun.

fights

▶ If a military team ~~fight~~ without spirit and will, it will probably lose.

Note: A collective noun is generally considered singular because it treats a group as a single unit. If it refers to the members of the group as individuals, however, it may be considered plural.

SINGULAR (GROUP AS A UNIT)   The *staff is* amiable.

PLURAL (INDIVIDUAL MEMBERS)   The *staff exchange* greetings and small talk as *they begin* putting on *their* surgical garb.

G6-c   Use a verb that agrees with a subject placed after it.

In most sentences, the subject precedes the verb, but some sentences are inverted. For example, sentences beginning with *there is* and *there are* put the subject after the verb.

verb / subject

▶ There are no busy lines and brushstrokes in the paintings.

verb / subject

▶ There is interaction between central and peripheral visual fields.

In inverted sentences, change the verb so that it agrees with the subject that follows it, or rewrite the sentence to put the subject (which still must agree with the verb) first.

were

▶ The next morning, there ~~was~~ Mike and Cindy, acting as if nothing had happened.

were

▶ The next morning, ~~there was~~ Mike and Cindy, acting as if nothing had happened.

G6-d   Use a plural verb with a **compound subject**.

subject / verb

▶ She and her husband have a partnership with her in-laws.

Two subjects joined by *and* require a plural verb.

accumulate

▶ Dust and dirt ~~accumulates~~, bathrooms get mildewy, and kitchens get greasy.

---

collective noun A noun (such as *class* or *family*) that refers to a group as a unit and is usually considered singular.

compound subject Two or more words acting as a subject, linked by *and*.

Note: If two subjects are joined by *or* or *nor*, the verb should agree with the subject that is closer to it.

▸ Most nights, my daughter or my sons *start* dinner.

antecedent The word or words that a pronoun replaces and to which it refers.

G6-e Use a verb that agrees with the **antecedent** of the pronouns *who,* *which,* or *that.*

▸ Its staff consists of nineteen people who drive to work in any kind of weather to make sure the station comes through for its listeners.

To check agreement, identify the antecedent of the pronoun.

▸ Within the ordered chaos of the trauma room are diagnostic tools, surgical

devices, and X-ray equipment, which is *are* required for Sharp to be designated a

trauma center.

▸ Some students choose topics that enable them to establish dominance over classmates

in the group, while others tell personally moving stories that encourages *encourage*

partners to show their feelings.

Note: With the phrase *one of the* followed by a plural noun, use a verb that agrees with that noun.

▸ One of the *features* that *make* the player different is that it doubles as a streaming device.

indefinite pronoun
A pronoun that does not refer to a particular person or object. Examples: **Singular**—*anybody, anyone, each, everyone, everything, somebody, something, neither, none,* or *nobody;* **Plural**—*few, many,* and *several;* **Singular or plural**—*all, most,* and *some.*

G6-f Use a singular verb with an **indefinite pronoun.**

▸ Everything on the playground is child friendly.

In formal writing, an indefinite pronoun usually refers to a single person or object and agrees with a singular verb.

▸ There are two alternatives to this solution, and neither seem *seems* feasible.

If an indefinite pronoun such as *all, none,* or *some* refers to a plural noun, use a plural form of the verb. If it refers to a singular noun, use a singular form.

▸ *Some manage* to find jobs that fit their schedule, the surf schedule.

▸ *Most are* respectable people.

G6-g Use a verb that agrees with the subject rather than a **subject complement.**

subject [and verb] ——— subject complement ———

▶ The shark's favorite diet is elephant seals and sea lions.

subject complement
A word or word group that follows a linking verb and describes or restates the subject.

When either the subject or the subject complement names a group or category, the choice between a singular or plural verb can be confusing. Make sure that the verb agrees with the actual subject.

are
▶ Big blocks of color in a simple flat shape is his artistic trademark.
^

He favors big
▶ Big blocks of color in a simple flat shape is his artistic trademark.
^

G7 Adjectives and Adverbs

Distinguish **adjectives** from **adverbs** so that you select the correct forms of these **modifiers**. (See also R2-a.)

ADJECTIVES	Because *angry* drivers are *dangerous* drivers, it is *imperative* that the county implement *a* solution.
ADVERB	Installing traffic lights would *quickly* alleviate three important aspects of the problem.

adjective A word that modifies a noun or a pronoun, adding information about it.

adverb A word that modifies a verb, an adjective, or another adverb.

G7-a Select an adverb, not an adjective, to modify an adjective, another adverb, or a verb.

modifier A word, phrase, or clause functioning as an adjective or adverb that adds information about another word.

Often ending in -*ly,* adverbs tell how, when, where, why, and how often.

▶ Despite a *very* busy work schedule, Caesar finds time in the afternoon to

come *directly* to the high school and work as a volunteer track coach.

Change an adjective that modifies another adjective, an adverb, or a verb to an adverb form.

loudly
▶ The man yelled at me so loud that I began to cry.
^

Adjective forms that are common in informal, spoken conversation should be changed to adverb forms in more formal writing.

SPOKEN	The day was going *slow,* and I repeatedly caught my lure on the riverbed or a tree limb.
WRITTEN	The day was going *slowly,* and I repeatedly caught my lure on the riverbed or a tree limb.

G7-b   Select an adjective, not an adverb, to modify a noun or pronoun.

▶ I am enamored of the *cool* motor, the *massive* boulder in the middle of the lake, and the sound of the *splashing* wake against the side of the two-seater.

Change an adverb that modifies a noun or a pronoun to an adjective.

> *traditional*

▶ Working within a ~~traditionally~~ chronological plot, Joyce develops the

protagonist's emotional conflict.

An adjective generally appears immediately before or after the word it modifies. When an adjective acts as a **subject complement**, however, it is separated from the word it modifies by a **linking verb**.

▶ My grandfather is *amazing*.

subject complement
A word or word group that follows a linking verb and describes or restates the subject.

linking verb *Be, seem, appear, become, taste,* or another verb that connects a subject with a subject complement that describes or modifies it: The chips *taste* salty.

Note: Some verbs (such as *looked*) act as linking verbs only in certain contexts. When one of these verbs connects a subject and its complement, use an adjective form: She looked *ill*. However, when the verb expresses an action and is modified by the word that follows it, use an adverb: She looked *quickly*.

┌─────────────────────────┐
│ **FOR MULTILINGUAL WRITERS** │
└─────────────────────────┘

Multilingual writers sometimes have trouble choosing between past and present participles (*looked, looking*) used as adjectives. See T6 for help in selecting the correct form.

G7-c   Select the correct forms of adjectives and adverbs to show comparisons.

Add -*er* or -*est* to short words (one or two syllables), and use *more, most, less,* and *least* with longer words and all -*ly* adverbs.

▶ The southern peninsula's *smallest* kingdom was invaded continually by its two *more powerful* neighbors.

Use -*er, more,* or *less* (the comparative form) to compare two things.

▶ I had always been a little bit *faster* than she was.

Use -*est, most,* or *least* (the superlative form) to compare three or more things.

▶ The team's undefeated status soon gained it the respect of even its *most bitter* rivals.

Change the forms of adjectives and adverbs to show comparison precisely.

> *less*

▶ She has clearly been the ~~least~~ favored candidate in the sense that she is not as well known or as experienced as her opponent.

E Effective Sentences

E1 Missing Words

To write effective prose, you need to supply all words necessary for clarity, completeness, and logic. Proofread your essays carefully, even out loud, to catch any omitted words.

FOR MULTILINGUAL WRITERS

If English is not your native language, you may have trouble with omitted words. See also T4.

E1-a Supply **prepositions, conjunctions**, infinitive parts, articles, and verb parts when needed for clarity.

In many instances, when you forget to include these small words, the reader may be puzzled or have to pause to figure out what you mean.

Insert missing prepositions.

> *in*
> ▶ The car began to skid the other direction.
>   ^

> *from*
> ▶ He graduated high school at the top of his class.
>   ^

> *at*
> ▶ A child his age shouldn't be playing outside that time of night.
>   ^

preposition A word (such as *between, in,* or *of*) that indicates the relation between a word in a sentence and its object.

conjunction A word that relates sentence parts by coordinating, subordinating, or pairing elements, such as *and, because,* or *either . . . or.*

FOR MULTILINGUAL WRITERS

If you are not a native speaker of American English, prepositions may be challenging because native speakers of English use prepositions in ways that do not translate directly. The best way to understand when prepositions are needed is to read widely and study the work of other writers. See also T3.

Insert missing conjunctions.

> *and*
> ▶ Most families and patients will accept the pain, inconvenience, financial and
>   ^
>
> emotional strain as long as the patient can achieve a certain quality of life.

> The heads of these golf clubs can be made of metal, wood, *or* graphite and often
>
> have special inserts in the part of the club that hits the ball.

A conjunction is generally needed to connect the final item in a series, such as *financial and emotional strain* in the first example and *graphite* in the second.

infinitive A verb form consisting of the word *to* plus the base form of the verb: *to run*.

Restore the *to* omitted from an infinitive if needed for clarity.

> They decided *to* start the following Monday morning.

> I noticed how he used his uncanny talent for acting *to* make a dreary subject
>
> come alive.

article An adjective that precedes a noun and identifies a definite reference to something specific (*the*) or an indefinite reference to something less specific (*a* or *an*).

Insert missing articles.

> This incident ruined the party, but it was only *the* beginning of the trouble.

> But such *a* condition could be resolved by other means.

FOR MULTILINGUAL WRITERS

Nonnative speakers of English may be unsure when and when not to use the articles *a, an,* and *the.* For more advice on the use of articles, see T1.

Insert other missing words that help clarify or complete a sentence.

> Malaria was once a widespread disease *it may* and become so again.

> In these scenes, women are often *shown* with long, luxurious hair.

> Finally, and I'm embarrassed to admit, *it* I pushed Bella.

E1-b **Insert the word *that* if needed to prevent confusion or misreading.**

CONFUSING   I would like to point out golf is not just a game for rich old men in ugly pants.

CLEARER   I would like to point out *that* golf is not just a game for rich old men in ugly pants.

Without *that,* the reader may think at first that the writer is pointing out *golf* and have to double back to understand the sentence. In the revised sentence, *that* tells the reader exactly where the **dependent clause** begins.

dependent clause A word group that has a subject and a predicate but cannot stand by itself as a sentence; it must be connected to an independent clause.

▶ Dryer says, *that* as people grow older, they may find themselves waking up early,

usually at dawn.

▶ One problem parents will notice is *that* the child leaves out certain words.

Note: If the meaning of a sentence is clear without *that,* it may be left out.

E1-c Add words to a comparison to make it logical, clear, and complete.

Because a comparison connects two or more things for the reader, you should name both things and state the comparison fully. In addition, the items compared should be of the same kind. For example, compare a person with another person, not with an activity or a situation. This sentence compares two stores:

▶ The old student center has a *general store* that carries *as many books or supplies as*

the *Saver Center.*

(See also E7-c.)

Reword a comparison to specify comparable items of the same kind.

▶ Five-foot-five-inch Maria finds climbing to be more challenging *for her than it is for* than her six-

foot-five-inch companions, who can reach the handholds more easily.

The original version of this sentence says that climbing is more challenging than companions (illogically comparing an activity to people). The edited sentence says that climbing is more challenging for Maria than it is for her companions (logically comparing one person to other people).

Reword a comparison to identify clearly and completely all items being compared.

▶ Danziger's article is definitely more entertaining. *than Solomon's article.*

In some comparative sentences, formal academic English requires the coordinated use of *as.*

▶ Millie is *as* graceful *as,* if not more graceful than, Margot.

▶ Students opting for field experience credits would learn as much, *as*⌃ or more, than⌃

students who take only classes.

compound structure
A sentence element, such as a subject or a verb, that consists of two or more items linked by *and* or another conjunction.

E1-d Supply all words needed to clarify the parts of a **compound structure.**

Although words may be left out of compound structures to avoid unnecessary repetition, omitted words must fit grammatically in each part of the compound.

▶ Women tend to express feelings *in the form of* requests, whereas men tend to

express them *in* [*the form of*] commands.

When the same structure would not fit in each part, you need to supply the missing words—even if they are simply different forms of the same word.

▶ Water buffalo meat has been gaining popularity in America and *is*⌃ being sold to

the public.

▶ Observable behaviors that relate to classroom assault can be dealt with prior, *to*⌃

during, and after an attack.

E2 **Shifts**

Follow the same pattern throughout a sentence or passage to avoid a shift in tense, person, number, mood, voice, or type of discourse.

tense The form of a verb that shows the time of the action or state of being.

E2-a Use one verb **tense** consistently in a passage unless a tense change is needed to show a time change.

▶ The nurse tried to comfort me by telling jokes and explaining that the needle

wouldn't hurt. With a slight push, the long, sharp needle *pierced*⌃ pierces my skin

found
and ⌃finds its way to the vein.

If you tend to mix verb tenses as you draft, perform a special edit of your entire essay concentrating on this one issue.

Change the tense of any verbs that do not follow the established tense in a passage unless they show logical time changes.

▶ I noticed much activity around the base. Sailors and chiefs *were*~~are~~ walking all over

the place. At 8:00 a.m., all traffic, foot and vehicle, halted. Toward the piers,

rose   *ended*   *were*
the flag ~~is rising~~ up its pole. After the national anthem ~~ends~~, salutes ~~are~~

went   *had been*
completed, and people ~~go~~ on with what they ~~are~~ doing.

Change verbs to the present tense to discuss events in literature, general truths, facts, and other ongoing principles.

▶ In 2003, the Supreme Court ruled that antisodomy laws are unconstitutional

go
because such laws ~~went~~ against "our tradition [that] the state is not

omnipresent in our homes."

dies   *realizes*   *is*
▶ In the story, when the boy ~~died~~, Kathy ~~realized~~ that it ~~was~~ also time for her

returns
childhood to die, and so she ~~returned~~ to her South African home as an adult.

Discussing such events may require tense shifts in a sentence or text. (See also G5-a.)

PRESENT TENSE   Each cell *has* forty-six chromosomes that *carry* the genetic traits the
WITH LOGICAL   individual *will have* when he or she *is* born.
SHIFT TO FUTURE

E2-b **Change the nouns and pronouns in a passage to a consistent person and number.**

them and their pets.
▶ Lynn informs all the members about helpful programs for ~~you and your pet.~~

you
▶ Lynn informs ~~all the members~~ about helpful programs for you and your pet.

In casual conversation, people often shift between singular and plural or between the third person and the second. In writing, however, such shifts may be confusing.

Note: Also consider how your choice of person suits the tone or approach of your essay. The first or second person, for example, will usually strike a reader as less formal than the third person.

person The form of a word that shows whether it refers to *I* or *we* (first person), to *you* (second person), or to *he, she, it,* or *they* (third person).

number The form of a word that shows whether it refers to one thing (singular: *parent*) or more than one (plural: *parents*).

mood The form of a verb that shows the writer's attitude toward a statement.

voice The form of a verb that either emphasizes the performer of an action (active) or deemphasizes it (passive).

E2-c Establish a consistent **mood** and **voice** in a passage.

▶ Each time I entered his house, I ~~could~~ always ^*knew*^ know when he was home.

The original sentence shifts from the indicative mood (*I entered*), used for statements and questions, to the subjunctive mood (*I could know*), used to indicate hypothetical, impossible, or unlikely conditions.

▶ I stepped out of the car with my training permit, a necessary document ~~for the~~ ^*to take the test.*^

~~test to be taken.~~

Although mood and voice may need to change to fit the context of a sentence, unneeded shifts may seem inconsistent. (See also G5-c on mood, G5-d on voice, and T2-a on conditional clauses.)

Change the verbs in a conditional clause or passage to a consistent mood.

▶ If the mother should change her mind and keep the child, the couple ^*would*^ ~~will~~ be

reimbursed for their expenses.

▶ If the mother ~~should change~~ ^*changes*^ her mind and ~~keep~~ ^*keeps*^ the child, the couple will be

reimbursed for their expenses.

Make the verbs in a passage consistent, preferably using the active voice.

▶ I will judge the song according to the following criteria: the depth with which

the lyrics treat each issue, and the clarity with which ~~each idea is presented in~~ ^*the music presents each idea.*^

~~the music.~~

(See also G5-d.)

E2-d Use either direct or indirect quotation without mixing the two.

Writers use direct quotation to present statements or questions in a speaker's or another writer's own words; they use indirect quotation to present the person's words without quoting directly.

▶ "Do whatever ~~they wanted to her,~~ ^*you want to me,*^" she cried, "but don't harm Reza."

▶ Do whatever ^*They could do*^ they wanted to her, she cried, but ^*they shouldn't*^ don't harm Reza.

To avoid shifts between direct and indirect quotation, make sure that your pronouns are consistent in **person** (see G2) and your verbs are consistent in mood (see G5-c).

E3   Noun Agreement

In most instances, use nouns that agree in **number** when they refer to the same topic, person, or object.

▶ The treatment consists of *injections* of minimal *doses* of the *allergens*, given at regular *intervals*.

Sometimes, however, the context calls for both singular and plural nouns.

▶ *Students* who want to make the most of *their* college years should pursue *a major course of study* while choosing *electives* or *a few minor courses of study* from the liberal arts.

> **person** The form of a word that shows whether it refers to *I* or *we* (first person), to *you* (second person), or to *he, she, it,* or *they* (third person).
>
> **number** The form of a word that shows whether it refers to one thing (singular: *parent*) or more than one (plural: *parents*).

E3-a   Select corresponding singular or plural forms for related references to a noun.

When several nouns are used to develop a topic, they may describe and expand the characteristics of a key noun, act as synonyms for one another, or develop related points in the discussion. A sentence or passage that includes such nouns will generally be clearer and more effective if the nouns agree in number.

▶ Many people tend to "take their jobs to bed" with them and lie awake

thinking about what needs to be done the next day. They also worry about a *promotions*̭

layoffs̭ *or shifts*
~~promotion, layoffs, or a shift~~ in responsibilities.

E3-b   Decide whether a noun should be singular or plural.

A noun may need to agree with another word in the sentence or may need to be singular or plural to fit the context or idiomatic usage. Be sure to consider the meaning of the sentence as a whole.

▶ *Minnows* are basically inedible because *they* have very little meat on *their bodies*.

In this sentence, the writer consistently uses plural forms (*they, their,* and *bodies*) to refer to the minnows but also uses *meat,* which takes a singular form in this context.

Note: Nouns such as *kind* are singular, although they have plural forms (*kinds*). Use *this* and *that* instead of *these* and *those* to modify the singular forms of *kind* and similar words. Expressions with *kind of* or *sort of* are usually singular.

▶ To comprehend *this* ~~these~~ type of articles~~,~~ *article*, it helps to have a strong background in statistics.

▶ RAs are allowed to choose what kind of ~~programs~~ *program* they want to have.

Change a noun to singular or plural to agree with a preceding indefinite adjective.

indefinite adjective A word that modifies a noun or another adjective and indicates an unspecific quantity, such as *each, few, many,* or *some.*

▶ Under some ~~circumstance~~, *circumstances* parents aren't there to supervise their kids.

Consider changing a noun to singular or plural to reflect its context.

Sometimes it is customary to treat an abstract quality (such as *justice* or *power*) as a singular noun. In other cases, a noun should be singular or plural to fit with the grammar or logic of the rest of the sentence.

▶ As soon as immigrants get to the United States, they realize that to get a ~~better~~ *better jobs*

job and better living conditions, they need to learn English.

Some common idiomatic expressions mix singular and plural forms.

IDIOMATIC WORDING   The penalties set for offenders might be enough to help them see *the error of their ways* and eventually reform their social habits.

E4 Modifiers

modifier A word, phrase, or clause functioning as an adjective or adverb that adds information about another word.

A **modifier**'s position in a sentence generally tells the reader what word the modifier qualifies.

E4-a Place a word, phrase, or clause next to or close to the word that it modifies.

▶ My *frozen* smile faltered as my chin quivered.

▶ The flurry *of fins, masks, weights, and wet suits* continued.

▶ Beyond the chairs loomed the object *that I feared most*—

a beautiful, black Steinway grand piano *that gleamed under the bright stage lights.*

If a modifier is too far away from the word it modifies, a reader may assume that it modifies another word closer to it. As a result, a *misplaced modifier* can create confusion, ambiguity, or even unintended humor.

Move a modifier closer to the word it modifies.

▶ The ~~attempted~~ number of *attempted* suicides this semester was four.

▶ The women have to do all the hard work, *needed to maintain the family* especially in subsistence cultures, ~~needed to maintain the family.~~

▶ He and the other people start to look *as hard as they can* for any sign of a boat, an island, or an oil platform ~~as hard as they can.~~

Rewrite to clarify the sentence.

▶ *In organizing meetings open to all neighbors* Community ~~leaders~~ *community* should ~~organize meetings open to all neighbors~~ *select* at convenient times and locations.

▶ We were friends until I ~~became~~ *turned eighteen and* became too popular and obnoxious for anyone to stand ~~when I turned eighteen.~~

E4-b Place a modifier so that it qualifies the meaning of a particular word in the sentence instead of dangling.

A phrase that does not modify a specific word is called a *dangling modifier*. A dangling modifier usually occurs at the beginning of a sentence and is likely to be a **participial phrase** or a **prepositional phrase**.

▶ Rather than receiving several painful shots in the mouth before a cavity is filled, *a patient may find that* hypnosis can work just as effectively.

▶ After surveying the floor on which I live, *I concluded that* the residents of my dorm don't care much for floor programs.

Place a word or phrase being modified immediately after the modifying phrase.

▶ By far the best song on the album, *"Rolling in the Deep" has a* the vocal performance and musical arrangement of ~~"Rolling in the Deep"~~ *that* create a perfect harmony.

participial phrase A group of words that begins with a present participle (*dancing, freezing*) or a past participle (*danced, frozen*) and modifies a noun or a pronoun: We boarded the bus, *expecting to leave immediately.*

prepositional phrase A group of words that begins with a preposition and indicates the relation between a word in a sentence and the object following the preposition: Her sunglasses slid *under the seat.*

dependent clause A word group that has a subject and a predicate but cannot stand by itself as a sentence; it must be connected to an independent clause.

subject The part of a clause that identifies who or what is being discussed.

predicate The part of a clause that includes a complete verb and describes the action or state of the subject.

Change the modifying phrase into a dependent clause.

Unlike a phrase, a clause includes both a **subject** and a **predicate**. By changing a phrase to a clause, you can correct a dangling modifier by supplying the information or connection that is missing. Be sure to rewrite so that both the subject and the predicate are clearly stated and the clause fits the rest of the sentence.

▶ *If the school board decides to close*
By closing Dos Pueblos, the remaining high schools ~~would~~ *will* have larger student bodies and increased budgets.

▶ *I concluded*
After ~~concluding~~ my monologue on the hazards of partying, she smiled broadly and said, "OK, Mom, I'll be more careful next time."

limiting modifier A modifier such as *almost, just,* or *only* that should directly precede the word or word group it limits.

E4-c Place a **limiting modifier** just before the word it modifies.

A limiting modifier can create confusion or ambiguity when it is misplaced because it could modify several words in the same sentence.

▶ Landfills in Illinois are going to be filled to capacity by 2020, and some
even
experts ~~even~~ say sooner.

When *even* precedes *say* in the example above, the sentence suggests that the experts are "even saying," not that the date will be even sooner.

infinitive A verb form consisting of the word *to* plus the base form of the verb: *to run*.

E4-d Keep the two parts of an **infinitive** together.

When other words follow the *to*, they "split" the infinitive, separating *to* from the base form of the verb. These other words can usually be moved elsewhere in the sentence. Be especially alert to limiting modifiers that split infinitives. (See also E4-c.)

▶ *always*
His stomach seemed to ~~always~~ hang over his pants.

Note: Occasionally, moving intervening words creates a sentence more awkward than the version with the split infinitive. In such cases, leaving the split infinitive may be the better choice.

E5 **Mixed Constructions**

The beginning and ending of a sentence must match, and its parts should fit together. If a sentence changes course in the middle or its parts are mixed up, a reader will have to guess at the pattern or connection you intend.

E5-a Begin and end a sentence with the same structural pattern.

A sentence is mixed if it combines several grammatical patterns. You usually need to rewrite a mixed construction so that its parts fit together.

> *If we save*   *we will have*
> ▶ The more oil ~~that we save now~~ means ~~much~~ more in the future.
>   ^   ^   ^

Choose one of the grammatical patterns in a mixed sentence, and use it consistently throughout the sentence.

>   *place where*
> ▶ School is another ~~resource for~~ children who don't have anyone to talk to can
>   ^
>
>   get educated about the problem of teen pregnancy.

> ▶ School is another resource for children who don't have anyone to talk to can
>   ^
>   *provide information*
>   ~~get educated~~ about the problem of teen pregnancy.
>   ^

Rewrite a mixed sentence if neither part supplies a workable pattern for the whole.

>   *The*
> ▶ ~~This is something~~ the shelter prides itself on ~~and is~~ always looking for new
>   ^
>
>   volunteers and ideas, ~~for the shelter.~~

>   *next detailed*
> ▶ The ~~next part of the essay~~ was ~~where~~ the results of the study ~~were detailed~~
>   ^
>   *concluded with*
>   and ~~finally included~~ a commentary section, ~~concluding the article.~~
>   ^

E5-b Match the subject and the predicate in a sentence so that they are compatible.

You can solve the problem of a logically mismatched subject and predicate—called *faulty predication*—by rewriting either the subject or the predicate so that the two fit together.

>   *Students attending schools*   *those at*
> ▶ Schools ~~that prohibited~~ corporal punishment behaved as well as schools ~~that~~
>   ^   ^
>
>   permitted it.

To test a sentence for faulty predication, ask yourself whether the subject can do what the predicate says: For example, do schools behave? If not, revise the sentence.

Revise the subject so that it can perform the action described in the predicate.

>   *the staff*
> ▶ Bean's service is top notch, and is striving continually to meet student needs.
>   ^   ^

Revise the predicate so that it fits logically with the subject.

▶ Ironically, the main character's memory of Mangan's sister on the porch step

always includes
~~cannot recall the image without~~ the lamplight.
⌃

E5-c **Order words logically so that the meaning of the sentence will be clear.**

Entering traffic
▶ ~~Traffic entering~~ will be dispersed into a perimeter pattern of flow.
⌃

E5-d **Eliminate the phrase *is where, is when,* or *the reason is because,* and then rewrite the sentence so that it is clear and logical.**

Often you can replace an *is where* or *is when* phrase with a noun specifying a category or type.

part makes   *seem*
▶ This ~~is where~~ the irony ~~seems to be~~ most evident.
        ⌃   ⌃

a stance taken by someone who
▶ An absolutist position is ~~when someone~~ strongly opposes any restrictions on speech.
                            ⌃

To eliminate *the reason is because,* rewrite the sentence, or use either *the reason is that* or *because* instead.

In addition ⌃
▶ ~~Another reason~~ radio stations should not play songs with sexually explicit lyrics
   ⌃

is because children like to sing along.

▶ Another reason radio stations should not play songs with sexually explicit lyrics

that
is ~~because~~ children like to sing along.
   ⌃

E6 **Integrated Quotations, Questions, and Thoughts**

When you use sources or write dialogue, merge your quotations, questions, and thoughts smoothly into your text so that the reader can tell who is speaking, thinking, or providing information.

▶ The expense of being a teenager has caused many young people to join the workforce just because "they were offered a job" (Natriello 60).

▶ "Hello," I replied, using one of the few words I knew in her language.

▶ I told myself, *Don't move.*

Use introductory phrases to link ideas and provide necessary background and context. Refer to the source or the speaker in the sentence. (See also P6.)

E6-a   Integrate **direct quotations** into sentences responsibly and correctly.

> **direct quotation** A speaker's or writer's exact words, which are enclosed in quotation marks.

Writers often introduce quotations by mentioning the name of the person being quoted. Although *says* and *states* are acceptable, consider using more precise verbs and phrases that establish logical connections and provide variety. Examples include *agrees, asserts, charges, claims, confirms, discusses, emphasizes,* and *suggests.*

▶ As American Motors President M. Paul Tippitt asserts, "The cardinal rule of the new ballgame is change" (Sobel 259).

Readers expect quotations and text to fit gracefully so that the writer's ideas and the material from supporting sources are both distinct and coherent. (See also E2-d.)

Cite a source smoothly, guiding readers from text to quotation.

Identifying the author of your source in the main part of your sentence often supplies the context and transition a reader needs.

▶ Most people are not even aware of the extent to which television plays a role

As Mitroff and Bennis point out^

in their lives. "Television defines our problems and shapes our actions; in

*(xi)*₀

short, [it is] how we define our world" (Mitroff and Bennis xi).

Mitroff and Bennis assert that most

▶ Most ~~people are not even aware of the extent to which~~ television ~~plays a role~~

~~television~~ *(xi)*₀

~~in their lives.~~ "Television defines our problems and shapes our actions; in

~~short, how we define our world" (Mitroff and Bennis xi).~~

> For more on integrating source information in an academic essay, see Chapter 23; for more on citing and documenting sources, see Chapters 24 (MLA) and 25 (APA).

Carefully select the text that introduces or integrates the quotation, as well as the exact words you are quoting.

▶ The average American child is exposed to "violence from every medium

and

~~. . . in addition listens to~~ music that advocates drug use" (Hollis 624).

E6-b   Integrate a question so that its source is clear.

> **indirect quotation** A restatement of a speaker's or writer's ideas without quoting directly or using quotation marks.

Enclose a direct quotation in quotation marks, identifying the speaker and using his or her exact words. Do not use quotation marks for an **indirect quotation** or a question that you address to the reader.

DIRECT QUOTATION	"Can you get my fins?" he asked.
INDIRECT QUOTATION	Without much hesitation, I explained my mission to her and asked whether she would help me out.
QUESTION ADDRESSED TO READER	Should sex education be a required class in public schools?

Begin a new paragraph to show each change of speaker.

▶ "The refrigeration system is frozen solid. Come back later/ ." *he said*. *once* Once again

turning his back to me. ~~I asked~~

I asked.
    "When would it be best for me to come back?"

E6-c Integrate thoughts so that they are clearly identified and consistently punctuated.

If you supply the exact words that you or someone else thinks, follow the guidelines for direct quotations. Quotation marks (or sometimes italics, for emphasis) are optional, but be consistent throughout an essay.

▶ Go north eighty miles, she reminded herself.

▶ *Wife and kids?* I thought.

▶ "Wife and kids?" I thought.

E7 Parallelism

Use parallel form to present items as a pair or in a series.

PAIR	Imagine that you and your daughter are *walking* in the mall or *eating* in a popular restaurant.
SERIES	By implementing this proposal, administrators could enhance the reputation of the university with quality *publications, plays, concerts,* and *sports teams.*
SERIES OF PHRASES	An interruption has the potential *to disrupt turns at talk, to disorganize the topic of conversation,* and *to violate the current speaker's right to talk.*

The grammatical similarity of the items in the pair or series strongly signals to the reader that they are equally important, similar in meaning, and related in the same way to the rest of the sentence.

E7-a **Each item in a series must follow the same grammatical pattern as the other items.**

Items in a series are usually linked by *and* or *or*. Each item should be parallel to the others, presented as a **noun**, an **infinitive**, a **gerund**, or another grammatical form.

▶ The children must deal with an overprotective parent, sibling rivalry, and living *life* in a single-parent home.

▶ Drivers destined for Coronado can choose to turn left, right, or proceeding *turn* *proceed* straight into the city.

> **noun** A word that names a specific or general thing, person, place, concept, characteristic, or other idea.
>
> **infinitive** A verb form consisting of the word *to* plus the base form of the verb: *to run.*
>
> **gerund** A verb form that is used as a noun and ends in *-ing: arguing, throwing.*

E7-b **Both items in a pair must follow the same grammatical pattern.**

Items in a pair are usually linked by *and* or *or*.

▶ While Maddox is growing up, he is told of things he should do and things not to do. *he should*

E7-c **In a comparison using *than* or *as,* the items must use the same grammatical form.**

▶ They feel that using force is more comprehensible to the children than abstract *threatening* consequences.

In this example, "using force" was not parallel with "abstract consequences," so the latter has been changed to "threatening abstract consequences."

E7-d **Use parallel form for items joined by correlative conjunctions.**

▶ At that time, the person is surprised not only about where he is but also *about* ~~unable to account~~ for what has happened.

> **correlative conjunctions** Word pairs that link sentence elements; the first word anticipates the second: *both . . . and, either . . . or, neither . . . nor, not only . . . but also.*

Also position the conjunctions so that each introduces a comparable point.

E8 Coordination and Subordination

Use coordination and subordination to indicate the relationships among sentence elements.

E8-a   Use coordination to join sentence elements that are equally important.

▶ The sheriff's department lacks both the *officers* and the *equipment* to patrol every road in the county.

▶ The evil queen's magic mirror declares that this Disney girl, with her *skin as white as snow*, *lips as red as blood*, and *hair as black as ebony*, is "the fairest one of all."

Writers use coordination to bring together in one sentence two or more elements of equal importance to the meaning. These elements can be words, phrases, or clauses, including **independent clauses** within the same sentence.

> **independent clause** A word group with a subject and a predicate that can stand alone as a separate sentence.

▶ ┌─────── independent clause 1 ───────┐ ┌─── independent clause 2 ───┐
The sport of windsurfing dates back only to 1969, but it has already achieved full status as an Olympic event.

▶ ┌─────── independent clause 1 ───────┐
Children like to sing along with songs their parents listen to. Consequently, radio
┌─────── independent clause 2 ───────┐
stations should not play songs with language that demeans women.

E8-b   Use subordination to indicate that one sentence element is more important than other elements.

▶ *After Dave finished his mutinous speech,* the corners of Dan's mouth slowly formed a nearly expressionless grin.

▶ Political liberals, *who trace their American roots to the Declaration of Independence,* insist that the federal government should attempt to reduce inequalities of income and wealth.

> **phrase** A group of words that does *not* contain both a subject and a verb and is always part of an independent clause.
>
> **dependent clause** A word group that has a subject and a predicate but cannot stand by itself as a sentence; it must be connected to an independent clause.

Writers frequently subordinate information within a single sentence. The most important information appears in an independent clause, and the less important or subordinate information appears in words, **phrases**, or **dependent clauses** attached to the independent clause or integrated into it.

W Word Choice

Effective language is concise and appropriate for the context.

W1 Concise Sentences

Sentences with redundant phrasing, wordy expressions, and unnecessary intensifiers are tiresome to read and may be difficult to understand. Concentrate on choosing words well, simplifying sentence stucture, and avoiding words that are unnecessary or evasive.

> *This*   *occur because*   *have had no*
> ▸ ~~In many cases,~~ this situation may ~~be due to the fact that~~ these women ~~were~~
>
> ~~not given~~ the opportunity to work.

Note: Even though you may need to add detail or examples to clarify your ideas, cutting out useless words will make your writing more focused.

W1-a Eliminate redundancies and repetition.

Redundant phrasing adds unnecessary words to a sentence. Repetitive wording says the same thing twice.

Eliminate or rewrite redundant expressions.

The phrase *blue in color* is redundant because it repeats obvious information. Expressions such as *past memories, advance planning,* and *mix together* include modifiers that repeat information already provided in the word modified. Expressions such as *the fact is true* and *in my opinion, I believe* are redundant because they contain obvious implications.

> *modernized.*
> ▸ Many machines in the drilling area need to be updated ~~to better and more~~
>
> ~~modern equipment.~~

> ▸ All these recommendations are interconnected~~, to one another.~~

> *California colleges*
> ▸ ~~The colleges in the state of California~~ rely too much on the annual income of a
>
> student's parents and not enough on the parents' true financial situation.

Delete extra words from a redundant or repetitive sentence.

> *convenient*
> ▸ In addition, there is a customer service center~~, for the convenience of the~~
>
> ~~customers.~~

▶ Student volunteers will no longer be ~~overworked, overburdened, and~~ *exhausted*

~~overexhausted~~ from working ~~continuously at the jobs~~ without any breaks

because of the shortage ~~of labor~~. *labor*

W1-b   Eliminate words that do not add to a sentence's meaning.

Rewrite a wordy sentence to reduce the number of clauses and phrases.

Concentrate on turning clauses into phrases or replacing phrases, especially strings of **prepositional phrases**, with individual words. Sometimes you can even consolidate a series of sentences into one.

prepositional phrase
A group of words that begins with a preposition and indicates the relation between a word in a sentence and the object following the preposition: Her sunglasses slid *under the seat.*

▶ ~~One of the best examples of~~ an athlete ~~being completely~~ *Michael Phelps is an excellent example* *overexposed*

~~overexposed is that of Michael Phelps.~~

▶ ~~There are many other possible alternative solutions to teen pregnancy. One~~ *No single alternative will solve the problem of teen pregnancy, and all the possible*

~~solution is not going to work alone to solve the problem. But there are~~ *solutions have disadvantages.*

~~disadvantages that come along with them.~~

Eliminate wordy expressions.

Extra, empty words can creep into a sentence in many ways.

▶ Demanding Eldridge's resignation ~~at this point in time~~ will not solve the problem. *now*

▶ However, in most neighborhoods, the same ~~group of~~ people who write the

newsletters ~~are the ones who~~ organize and participate in the activities. *also*

Here are examples of common wordy phrases and more concise alternatives.

Wordy Phrases	More Concise Alternatives
due to the fact that	
in view of the fact that	
the reason for	
for the reason that	for, because, why, since
this is why	
in light of the fact that	
on the grounds that	

despite the fact that regardless of the fact that	although, though
as regards in reference to concerning the matter of where . . . is concerned	concerning, about, regarding
it is necessary that there is a need for it is important that	should, must
has the ability to is able to is in a position to	can
in order to for the purpose of	to
at this point in time	now
on the subject of	on, about
as a matter of fact	actually
be aware of the fact that	know [that]
to the effect that	that
the way in which	how
in the event that	if, when

Rewrite a wordy sentence to simplify its structure.

Often you can express your ideas more directly and forcefully by editing to eliminate *there is* or *there are* from the beginning of a sentence, or by changing from the passive to the active **voice**. (See also G5–d.)

>   *Five*   *are always*
▶ ~~There are always~~ five or six spots open at the ends of the rows.

>   *A*   *initiates*
▶ ~~The topic is initiated by~~ a member who has nothing to gain by the discussion of
>
> the topic.

voice The form of the verb that either emphasizes the performer of an action (active) or deemphasizes it (passive).

Note: Whenever possible, replace *am, are, is, was,* and other forms of *be* with a stronger verb that clearly defines an action.

W1-c Eliminate unnecessary intensifiers or hedges.

Delete unnecessary intensifiers.

Although intensifiers such as *very, really, clearly, quite,* and *of course* can strengthen statements, eliminating them or substituting more forceful words is often more effective.

> ▸ The plot of this movie is ~~really~~ great.
> *thrilling*

Some intensifiers are unnecessary because the words they modify are already as strong as possible, such as *unique.*

> *unique*
> ▸ The arrangement of the plain blocks ~~is so unique that it~~ makes the sculpture
>
> seem textured.

Eliminate unnecessary hedges.

Writers use hedges such as *apparently, seem, perhaps, possibly, to a certain extent, tend,* and *somewhat* to avoid making claims that they cannot substantiate. Hedges add subtlety to prose and acknowledge the possibility of important exceptions. Too many hedges, however, make writing too tentative.

> *Realistic*   *often*
> ▸ ~~In most cases, realistic~~ characteristics ~~tend to~~ undermine comedy's primary
>
> function of making us laugh at exaggerated character traits.

W1-d Eliminate unnecessary prepositions.

preposition A word (such as *between, in,* or *of*) that indicates the relation between a word in a sentence and its object.

If the word following a preposition is the object of a verb, the preposition may be unnecessary.

> ▸ Nothing happened, and my doctor ordered ~~for~~ them to stop inducing labor.

Another alternative is to change the verb.

> *seek*
> ▸ Consequently, student volunteers will not be inclined to leave and ~~look for~~
>
> smaller hospitals with less intense shifts.

FOR MULTILINGUAL WRITERS

Prepositions also combine with verbs to form two- or three-word (or phrasal) verbs whose meaning cannot be understood literally (*handed in, longed for*). When a preposition is part of a two- or three-word verb, it is called a *particle.* See T2-b.

W2 Exact Words

Effective writers choose words carefully, paying attention to meaning, form, idiomatic phrasing, and freshness.

W2-a Replace incorrect words with intended words.

Check a dictionary when you are uncertain of meaning. Watch for incorrect words and for words similar in meaning or sound. (See also the Glossary of Frequently Misused Words.)

▶ Louis kicked him into a river ~~invested~~ *infested* with crocodiles.

▶ How do we stop offshore oil drilling and yet offer an alternative to ~~appease~~ *alleviate* the energy crisis?

W2-b Use correct prepositions.

Short as they generally are, prepositions define crucial relationships for the reader.

▶ A building's beauty must be determined *by* the harmony *of* its design.

If prepositions are a problem in your writing, note how other writers use them.

▶ Unlike many of the other pieces of art ~~about~~ *on* campus, the statues seemed to fit well.

FOR MULTILINGUAL WRITERS

If you find prepositions difficult, pay special attention to them as you read. For a review of the meanings of some common prepositions, see T3.

W2-c Use standard idioms.

Read and listen carefully to get a sense of standard idioms, especially the ones that consist of small words, such as prepositions, and verb forms.

▶ The most serious problems of many developing countries stem ~~to~~ *from* lack of educational and economic opportunities.

idiom An expression whose meaning cannot be determined from its parts but must be learned (*call off* for "cancel").

FOR MULTILINGUAL WRITERS

Idiomatic two- and three-word verbs (*put down, set up*) and combinations of verbs or adjectives and prepositions (*look for, afraid of*) can be especially troublesome for writers whose first language is not English. See T2-b.

---

cliché An overused expression that has lost its original freshness, such as *hard as a rock*.

W2-d Eliminate **clichés** or overused expressions.

Readers prefer lively, original expressions to worn phrases.

▶ The audience is on pins and needles, wondering whose plan will falter first.
erupts in gasps and nervous giggles

W2-e Select the correct form of the word that you intend.

If you are learning to use an unfamiliar word or are struggling to find a word whose meaning fits, you may use the wrong form. A good dictionary can help you determine which form of a word fits your context.

▶ The phrase "you know" is an introductory to someone's opinion.
introduces

figures of speech Images such as similes and metaphors that suggest a comparison between objects that are generally unlike each other.

simile A direct comparison that uses *like* or *as*.

metaphor An indirect comparison that refers to or describes one thing as if it were the other.

mixed metaphor An inconsistent metaphor, one that mixes several images rather than completing one.

W2-f Use appropriate **figures of speech.**

Figures of speech, such as **similes** and **metaphors**, can express comparisons, make a complex idea easier to understand, or bring a scene or character to life for your readers.

SIMILE To Sam, high school was like a nursing home.

METAPHOR Tupac was the Beethoven of his age.

Make sure that any figure of speech that you use is clear, appropriate, and consistent.

INACCURATE METAPHOR The children would jump from car to car *as if they were mushrooms*. [Mushrooms cannot jump.]

Also avoid **mixed metaphors**, as in the following example, in which the soul is compared to both a criminal defendant and a plant.

MIXED METAPHOR Karma is an inorganic process of development in which the soul not only *pays the price* for its misdeeds but also *bears the fruit* of the *seeds sown* in former lives.

W3 Appropriate Words

Choose words carefully to give your writing the appropriate level of formality, without slang, bias, or pretentious language. The following sentences illustrate how appropriate words can convey a sense of environment.

▶ At 6:50 p.m., the hospital's paging system comes alive.

▶ Lying on the stretcher, the unidentified victim can only groan and move his left leg.

W3-a Use the level of formality expected in your writing situation.

Many problems with inappropriate language occur when writers use informal language in a more formal writing situation.

INFORMAL   Treating old people badly gets everyone upset because that's your family, and no one wants to get judged for putting their mom in a home.

MORE FORMAL   Mistreatment of the elderly is an unusually sensitive problem because it involves such value-laden ideas as *home* and *family*.

Taking your essay assignment into account, reword as necessary to avoid shifts in the level of formality.

▸ What makes an excellent church, auditorium, or theater makes a ~~lousy~~ *poor* library.

W3-b Limit the use of **slang** in formal writing situations.

Although slang may be appropriate in dialogue used to define a character or a situation in a narrative, it should not be used in formal academic writing. Replace inappropriate slang expressions with more formal words.

▸ The ~~guy~~ *investor* is ~~for real~~ *completely serious*.

▸ The cast of the movie was ~~awesome~~ *impressive*.

slang Informal language that tends to change rapidly.

W3-c Use nonsexist language.

Avoid using gender-based pronouns (such as *he* or *his*) to refer to people who might be either men or women. (See also G2-b.)

Revise a sentence that uses masculine pronouns to represent people in general.

Use plural forms, eliminate the pronouns, or use both masculine and feminine pronouns.

▸ *Students'* A ~~student's~~ eligibility for alternative loans is based on whether or not ~~his~~ *their*

they are school decides ~~he is~~ entitled to financial aid.

▸ Abstract expressionism is art that is based on the artist's spontaneous feelings

or she *a* at the moment when he is creating ~~his~~ work.

Substitute more inclusive words to represent people in general.

▶ Oligarchies have existed throughout the *human history.* ~~history of man.~~

Rewrite language that implies or reinforces stereotypes or discrimination.

▶ Oligarchies were left to ~~barbaric~~ *the tribes* tribesmen and herders ~~who were beyond the~~ *outside the empire.*

~~reach of civilization.~~

▶ A doctor who did not keep up with his *or her* colleagues would be forced to update

his procedures.

pretentious language
Fancy or wordy language used primarily to impress.

W3-d Replace **pretentious language** with simpler, more direct wording.

Use words that best express your idea, and balance or replace distractingly unusual words with simpler, more familiar choices.

▶ Perhaps ~~apprehension toward instigating~~ *fear of* these changes stems from financial

concern.

▶ Expanded oil exploration may seem relatively innocuous, but this proposal is a

deplorable suggestion to all but the most *deceptive,~destructive groups.* ~~pernicious, specious entities.~~

P Punctuation

P1 Commas

Use a comma to set off and separate sentence elements.

P1-a Add a comma between **independent clauses** joined by a **coordinating conjunction.**

When independent clauses are joined by a coordinating conjunction, a comma is required to tell the reader that another independent clause follows the first one.

> ⎡———— independent clause ————⎤   ⎡———— independent clause ————⎤
> ▶ Perhaps my father had the same dream‸and perhaps my grandfather did as well.
>   ‸,

If the independent clauses are brief and unambiguous, a comma is not required, though it is never wrong to include it.

> ▶ The rescue attempt fails and the climber must let go.

independent clause
A word group with a subject and a predicate that can stand alone as a separate sentence.

coordinating conjunction
A word that joins comparable and equally important sentence elements: *for, and, or, but, nor, yet,* or *so.*

P1-b Place a comma after an introductory word, phrase, or clause.

Sentences often begin with words, phrases, or clauses that precede the independent clause and modify an element within it. The comma following each introductory element lets the reader know where the modifying word or phrase ends and the main clause begins.

> ▶ *Naturally,* this result didn't help him any.

> ▶ *With a jerk,* I lofted the lure in a desperate attempt to catch a fish and please my dad.

> ▶ *When we entered the honeymoon suite,* the room smelled of burnt plastic and was the color of Pepto-Bismol.

If an introductory phrase or clause is brief—four words or fewer—the comma may be omitted unless it is needed to prevent misreading.

> ▶ Without hesitation I dived into the lake.

P1-c Use commas to set off a nonrestrictive word group.

To test whether a word group is *nonrestrictive* (supplemental, nondefining, and thus nonessential) or *restrictive* (defining and thus essential), read the sentence with and without the word group. If the sentence is essentially unchanged in meaning without it, the word group is nonrestrictive. Use commas to set it off.

NONRESTRICTIVE The oldest fishermen, *grizzly sea salts wrapped in an aura of experience,* led the way.

Conversely, if omitting the word group changes the meaning of the sentence, it is restrictive. In this case, do not use commas.

RESTRICTIVE   Body-mapping technologies can give video games a sense of realism *that was not previously available*.

Use a comma to set off a nonrestrictive word group at the end of a sentence.

▶ We all stood, anxious and prepared for what he was about to say.

Use a pair of commas to set off a nonrestrictive word group in the middle of a sentence.

▶ The most common moods are happiness, when the music is in a major key, or

sadness, when the music is in a minor key.

(See also P2-b.)

P1-d **Use commas to set off a transitional, parenthetical, or contrasting expression or an absolute phrase.**

Transitional expressions help the reader follow a writer's movement from point to point. *Parenthetical comments* interrupt a sentence with a brief aside. *Contrasting expressions* are introduced by *not, no,* or *nothing. Absolute phrases* modify the whole clause and often include a past or present **participle** as well as modifiers. By using commas to set off such expressions, you signal that they are additions, supplementing or commenting on the information in the rest of the sentence.

participle A verb form showing present tense (*dancing, freezing*) or past tense (*danced, frozen*) that can also act as an adjective.

TRANSITIONAL   *Besides,* it is summer.

PARENTHETICAL   These are all indications, *I think,* of Jan's drive for power and control.

CONTRASTING   Nick is the perfect example of a young, hungry manager trying to climb to the top, *not bothered by the feelings of others.*

ABSOLUTE   "Did I ever tell you about the time I danced with the Rockettes at Radio City Music Hall?" she asked, *her eyes focusing dreamily into the distance.*

P1-e **Use commas to separate three or more items in a series, placing the final comma before the conjunction.**

The commas in a series separate the items for the reader.

▶ He always tells me about the loyalty, honor, and pride he feels as a Marine.

▶ Our communities would get relief from the fear and despair that come from having

unremitting violence, addiction, and open-air drug markets in their midst.

Note: Newspapers, magazines, and British publications often omit the comma before the conjunction. In your academic writing, however, include it for clarity.

P1-f Use a comma before a trailing nonrestrictive **participial phrase**.

Participial phrases are generally **nonrestrictive word groups**. When they follow the **independent clause** in a sentence, they should be set off with commas. See P1-c.

PARTICIPIAL   The plane taxied as he turned on his phone, *expecting to find*
PHRASE   *a mushy text* from his girlfriend.

The comma before the phrase signals the end of the main clause and sets off the important modifying phrase.

▶ Every so often, a pelican agilely arcs high over the water, twisting downward gracefully

to catch an unsuspecting mackerel.

Note: If the participial phrase is restrictive, providing essential information, do not use a comma. See P1-c and P2-b.

P1-g Place a comma between a complete **direct quotation** and the text identifying the speaker.

The comma, along with the quotation marks, helps the reader determine where the quotation begins and ends. (See also P6.)

▶ "It will be okay," Coach reassured me, as he motioned for the emergency

medical technicians to bring a board.

P1-h Add a comma (or pair of commas in the middle of a sentence) to set off expressions commonly included in dialogue.

Use commas to set off from the main part of the sentence the name of a person **directly addressed** by a speaker, words such as *yes* and *no*, and mild **interjections**. Also use a comma to set off questions added to the end of sentences.

▶ "Well, son, what are you doing?"

▶ "No, sir."

---

participial phrase A group of words that begins with a present participle (*dancing, freezing*) or a past participle (*danced, frozen*) and modifies a noun or a pronoun.

nonrestrictive word group A group of words, set off by commas, that provides nonessential information and could be eliminated without changing the meaning of the noun or pronoun it modifies.

independent clause A word group with a subject and a predicate that can stand alone as a separate sentence.

direct quotation A speaker's or writer's exact words, which are enclosed in quotation marks.

direct address Words that are spoken directly to someone else who is named.

interjection An exclamatory word that indicates strong feeling or attempts to command attention: *Shhh! Oh! Ouch!*

▸ "Boy, did we underestimate her."

▸ "That's not very efficient, is it?"

▸ "Besides, it'll be good for me."

coordinate adjectives Two or more adjectives that modify a noun equally and independently: the *large, red* hat.

P1-i   Use a comma between **coordinate adjectives**.

If you can change the order of a series of adjectives or add *and* between them without changing the meaning, they are coordinate and should be separated with a comma.

▸ There are reasons for her *erratic, irrational* behavior.

The comma signals that the adjectives are equal, related in the same way to the word modified.

cumulative adjectives Two or more adjectives that do not modify a noun equally. Instead, one or two of the adjectives closest to the noun form a noun phrase that the remaining adjectives modify: *colorful hot-air* balloons.

If the adjectives closest to the noun cannot be logically rearranged or linked by *and,* they are **cumulative adjectives** and should not be separated by commas.

▸ I pictured myself as a *professional race car* driver.

P1-j   Add commas where needed to set off dates, numbers, and addresses.

When you include a full date (month, day, and year), use a pair of commas to set off the year.

▸ In the May 11, 2015, issue of the *New Yorker,* Emily Nussbaum describes "Inside Amy

   Schumer" as a "destablizing mixture of daffy and caustic" (68).

If you present a date in reverse order (day, month, and year) or if the date is partial, do not add commas.

In large numbers (except four-digit years), separate groups of three digits (thousands, millions, and so forth) with commas.

▸ As of 2015, there were about 905,000 speakers of Russian in the United States.

When you write out an address, add commas between the street address, the city, and the state.

▸ Mrs. Wilson relocated to Bowie, Maryland, after years of telecommuting from

   Delaware.

P2 Unnecessary Commas

Because commas are warranted in so many instances, it is easy to use them unnecessarily or incorrectly.

P2-a Omit the comma when items in a pair are joined by a **coordinating conjunction.**

Many word pairs can be joined by *and* or another coordinating conjunction, including **compound predicates**, **compound objects**, and **compound subjects**. None of these pairs should be interrupted by a comma.

▶ I grabbed my lunchbox,/and headed out to the tree.
  ┌─────── compound predicate ───────┐

▶ As for me, I wore a pink short set with ruffles,/and a pair of sneakers.
  ┌──────── compound object ────────┐

▶ My father,/and brother wore big hiking boots.
  ┌ compound subject ┐

Note: This rule does not apply when the items in a pair are both independent clauses.

P2-b Omit any comma that sets off a restrictive word group.

A *restrictive word group* distinguishes the noun it modifies from similar nouns or precisely defines its distinguishing characteristics. See P1-c for a review of nonrestrictive word groups that need commas.

  If a comma incorrectly sets off a restrictive word group, it undermines the meaning, suggesting to the reader that essential information is not important.

▶ Although divorce is obviously a cause of the psychological problems,/a child

  will face, the parents need to support their child through the anxiety and turmoil.

P2-c Omit any commas that unnecessarily separate a **subject** and **verb** or a verb and its **object.**

A comma that separates two of a sentence's core elements—**subject**, **verb**, and **object**—confuses matters by suggesting that some other material has been added.

▶ *Bilateral,*/means that both the left and the right sides of the brain are involved
  ┌ subject ┐┌ verb ┐

  in processing a stimulus.

▶ Many singers try without success to incorporate in their works,/music from different
  ┌──── verb ────┐   ┌ object ┐

  cultures.

---

coordinating conjunction
A word that joins comparable and equally important sentence elements: *for, and, or, but, nor, yet,* or *so.*

compound predicate
Two or more verbs or verb phrases linked by *and.*

compound object Two or more words acting as an object and linked by *and.*

compound subject Two or more words acting as a subject and linked by *and.*

subject The part of a clause that identifies who or what is being discussed.

verb A word or phrase that expresses action or being and, along with a subject, is a basic component of a sentence.

object The part of a clause that receives the action of the verb, or the part of a phrase that follows a preposition: At the checkpoint, we unloaded *the canoes.*

adverbial clause A clause that nearly always modifies a verb, indicating time, place, condition, reason, cause, purpose, result, or another logical relationship.

P2-d Omit a comma that separates the main part of the sentence from a trailing **adverbial clause**.

When an adverbial clause appears at the end of a sentence, a comma is ordinarily not needed.

▶ I found the tables turned, when he interviewed me about the reasons for my tattoo.

cumulative adjectives Two or more adjectives that do not modify a noun equally. Instead, one or two of the adjectives closest to the noun form a noun phrase that the remaining adjectives modify: *colorful hot-air* balloons.

P2-e Leave out commas that separate **cumulative adjectives**.

▶ Wearing a pair of jeans, ⎡— coordinate adjectives —⎤ *cutoff, bleached,* and *torn,* with an embroidered blouse and ⎡cumulative adjectives⎤ *soft leather* sandals, she looked older and more foreign than Julie.

Leather modifies *sandals,* and *soft* modifies *leather sandals* as a unit. Thus the meaning is cumulative, and a comma would interrupt the connection between the adjectives and the noun. (See P1-i to review the use of commas with coordinate adjectives.)

P2-f Omit any comma that appears before or after a series of items.

Although commas should be used to separate the items in a list, they should not be used before the first item or after the final one.

▶ Race, sex, religion, financial situation, or any other circumstance beyond the control of the applicant, should not be considered.

(See also P1-e.)

P2-g Omit or correct any other unnecessary or incorrect commas.

Check your essays carefully to correct typical comma problems.

Omit commas that follow **coordinating conjunctions**.

coordinating conjunction A word that joins comparable and equally important sentence elements: *for, and, or, but, nor, yet,* or *so.*

▶ But, since sharks are not yet classified as endangered species, the members of

Congress were not very sympathetic, and the bill was not passed.

Omit commas that follow coordinating conjunctions joining two independent clauses.

▶ The ominous vision of the piano wavered before my eyes and, before I knew it,

I was at the base of the steps to the stage, steps that led to potential public

humiliation.

▶ I had finally felt the music deep in my soul, and, when I sang, I had a great

feeling of relief knowing that everything was going to be all right.

Omit commas following subordinating conjunctions such as *who, that, although,* or *since*.

Watch for words such as *who, which, that, whom, whose, where, when, although, because, since, though,* and other subordinating conjunctions.

▶ The drinking age should be raised because, drunk driving has become the leading

cause of death among young people between the ages of fifteen and twenty-five.

> **subordinating conjunction**
> A word or phrase (such as *although* or *because*) that introduces a dependent clause and relates it to an independent clause.

Omit commas preceding *that* when it introduces an indirect quotation.

Unlike a direct quotation, an indirect quotation is not set off by a comma or quotation marks.

▶ After looking at my tests, the doctor said, that I had calcification.

> **indirect quotation**
> A restatement of a speaker's or writer's ideas without quoting directly or using quotation marks.

Omit commas immediately following a preposition.

▶ Despite, multiple recruitment and retention problems, the number of public

school teachers remained about the same between 2000 and 2014.

> **preposition** A word (such as *between, in,* or *of*) that indicates the relation between a word in a sentence and its object: The water splashed *into* the canoe.

Omit commas setting off a prepositional phrase in the middle or at the end of a sentence.

When a prepositional phrase appears in the middle or at the end of a sentence, it is usually not set off by commas.

▶ The children's trauma team gathers in the Resuscitation Room, at the same time

that John Doe is being treated.

> **prepositional phrase**
> A group of words that begins with a preposition and indicates the relation between a word in a sentence and the object following the preposition: Her sunglasses slid *under the seat.*

Rewrite a sentence that is full of phrases and commas to simplify both the sentence structure and the punctuation.

By   *the researchers could monitor*
▶ ~~The researchers could monitor~~, by looking through a porthole window, how

Noah spent
much time ~~was spent, by Noah,~~ in the dome.

P3   Semicolons

Use semicolons to join closely related independent clauses and to make long sentences with commas easier to read.

independent clause
A word group with a subject and a predicate that can stand alone as a separate sentence.

P3-a Use a semicolon to join **independent clauses** if the second clause restates or sets up a contrast to the first.

Although two independent clauses could be separated by a period, the semicolon tells the reader that they are closely related, emphasizing the restatement or sharpening the contrast.

▶ Davie was not an angel; he was always getting into trouble with the teachers.

Note: When the independent clauses are linked by *and, but,* or another coordinating conjunction, use a comma rather than a semicolon (see P1-a) unless the independent clauses include internal punctuation (see P3-c).

P3-b Use semicolons to separate items in a series when they include internal commas.

Because the reader expects items in a series to be separated by commas, other commas within items can be confusing. The solution is to leave the internal commas as they are but to use a stronger mark, the semicolon, to signal the divisions between items.

▶ Appliances that use freon include air conditioners, small models as well as

central systems; refrigerators; and freezers, both home and industrial types.

P3-c Use a semicolon to join a series of independent clauses when they include other punctuation.

When independent clauses include elements set off by internal punctuation, use semicolons between them if other punctuation may confuse a reader or make the sentence parts difficult to identify.

▶ He was the guide; and he was driving us in this old Ford sedan, just the two of

us and him; and I had noticed early on that the car didn't have a gas cap.

conjunctive adverb A word or phrase (such as *finally, however,* or *therefore*) that tells how the ideas in two sentences or independent clauses are connected.

transitional expression
A word or group of words that expresses the relationship between one sentence and the next.

P3-d Use a semicolon to join two independent clauses when the second clause contains a **conjunctive adverb** or a **transitional expression**.

Because a semicolon shows a strong relationship between independent clauses, writers often use it to reinforce the connection expressed by the adverb or transition.

▶ Ninety-five percent of Americans recognize the components of a healthy diet;

however, they fail to apply their nutritional IQ when selecting foods.

P3-e Omit a semicolon used incorrectly to replace a comma or another punctuation mark.

Take care not to use semicolons in place of other punctuation.

Replace a semicolon with a comma to link an independent clause to a phrase or to set off an appositive.

> ▶ The threat of a potentially devastating malpractice suit promotes the practice of
>
> defensive medicine; doctors ordering excessive and expensive tests to confirm a
>
> diagnosis.

appositive A word or word group that identifies or gives more information about a noun or pronoun that precedes it.

Replace a semicolon with a comma to join two independent clauses linked by a coordinating conjunction.

> ▶ The ashtrays would need to be relocated to that area; and it could then become
>
> an outdoor smoking lounge.

(See also P1-a.)

coordinating conjunction A word that joins comparable and equally important sentence elements: *for, and, or, but, nor, yet,* or *so.*

Replace a semicolon with a colon to introduce a list.

> ▶ Our county ditches fill up with old items that are hard to get rid of; old
>
> refrigerators, mattresses, couches, and chairs, just to name a few.

Note: For introducing an in-text list as in this example, a dash (see P5-b) is a less formal and more dramatic alternative to the colon (see P4-a).

P4 Colons

Besides introducing specific sentence elements, colons conventionally appear in works cited or bibliography entries, introduce subtitles, express ratios and times, and follow the salutations in formal letters.

P4-a Use a colon to introduce a list, an appositive, a quotation, a question, or a statement.

Usually, a colon follows an independent clause that makes a general statement; after the colon, the rest of the sentence often supplies specifics—a definition, a quotation or question, or a list.

Use the colon selectively to alert readers to closely connected ideas, a significant point, a crucial definition, or a dramatic revelation.

independent clause
A word group with a subject and a predicate that can stand alone as a separate sentence.

Note: Because a colon follows but does not interrupt an **independent clause**, do not use a colon after words such as *is, are, consists of, including, such as, for instance,* and *for example* to introduce a list (see P4-b).

Consider using a colon to introduce a list.
You can use a colon to introduce a list if the list is preceded by an independent clause. Be careful not to interrupt the clause in the middle (see P4-b).

▶ Most young law school graduates become trial lawyers in one of three ways/: by

going to work for a government prosecutor's office, by working for a private law

firm, or by opening private offices of their own.

appositive A word or word group that identifies or gives more information about a noun or pronoun that precedes it.

Consider using a colon to emphasize an appositive.
Although you can always use commas to set off an appositive, try using a colon occasionally when you need special emphasis.

▶ The oldest fishermen are followed by the younger generation of middle-aged

fathers, excited by the chance to show their sons what their fathers once taught

them. Last to arrive are the novices/: the thrill seekers.

Consider using a colon to introduce a formal quotation, a question, a statement, or another independent clause.

▶ We learn that the narrator is a troublemaker in paragraph twelve/: "I got thrown

out of the center for playing pool when I should've been sewing."

▶ I ran around the office in constant fear of his questions/: What do you have

planned for the day? How many demonstrations are scheduled for this week?

How many contacts have you made?

▶ Both authors are clearly of the same opinion/: Recycling scrap tires is no longer

an option.

▶ I guess the saying is true/: Absence does make the heart grow fonder.

Do not capitalize the word following a colon if it introduces an incomplete sentence. However, when the word group following a colon is a complete sentence, you can either capitalize the first word or not, depending on your preference. Whichever choice you prefer, be consistent. When you introduce a quotation with a colon, always capitalize the word that begins the quotation. (See also M2-c.)

P4-b Correct unnecessary or incorrect colons.

Omit a colon that interrupts an independent clause, especially after words such as *is, are, include, composed of, consists of, including, such as, for instance,* and *for example*.

▶ The tenets include; courtesy, integrity, perseverance, self-control, indomitable

spirit, and modesty.

Replace an inappropriate colon with the correct punctuation mark.

▶ As I was touring the different areas of the shop, I ran into one of the owners;,

"Hi, Kim," she said with a smile on her face.

P5 Dashes

A dash breaks the rhythm or interrupts the meaning of a sentence, setting off information with greater emphasis than another punctuation mark could supply. Writers often use dashes to substitute for other punctuation in quick notes and letters to friends. In many kinds of published writing, dashes are used sparingly—but often to good effect.

P5-a Type, space, and position a dash correctly.

Type a dash (—) as two hyphens (--) in a row with no spaces before or after. (Your word processing program likely provides the option of converting two hyphens into a dash.) Use one dash before a word or words set off at the end of the sentence. Use two dashes—one at the beginning and one at the end—if the word or words are in the middle of the sentence.

▶ The rigid structure and asymmetrical arrangements of the sculpture blend well with three different surroundings —the trees, the library building, and the parking lots.

Use a pair of dashes, not just one, to mark the beginning and end of a word group that needs emphasis.

▶ I could tell that the people in the room work in uncomfortable conditions —

they all wear white lab coats, caps, and gloves—but they joke or laugh while

building the guns.

P5-b **Consider using a dash to set off material from the rest of the sentence.**

Because the dash marks a strong break, it alerts the reader to the importance of the material that follows it.

Use a dash or a pair of dashes to emphasize a definition, a dramatic statement, a personal comment, or an explanation.

▶ Binge eating—larger than normal consumption of high-calorie foods—starts with

emotional distress and depression.

▶ But unlike the boys, the girls often turn to something other than violence—

motherhood.

Consider inserting a dash or a pair of dashes to emphasize a list.
If the list appears in the middle of the sentence, use one dash at the beginning and another at the end to signal exactly where the list begins and ends.

▶ Another problem is that certain toy figures—The Hulk, Spider-Man, and the

X-Men, to name just a few—are characters from movies that portray violence.

P5-c **Rewrite a sentence that uses the dash inappropriately or excessively.**

Use dashes purposefully; avoid relying on them instead of using other punctuation marks or developing clear sentences and transitions.

▶ Finally the TV people were finished with their interviewing —*and* now they wanted

to do a shot of the entrance to the restaurant.

> " "

If you are not sure whether you have used a dash or a pair of dashes appropriately, try removing the material that is set off. If the sentence does not make logical and grammatical sense, one or both of the dashes are misused or misplaced.

▶ That's a tall order — and a reason to start ~~/~~ amassing some serious capital soon.

P6 Quotation Marks

Use double quotation marks, always in pairs, to indicate direct quotations and to mark some types of titles.

P6-a Set off direct quotations with quotation marks.

A direct quotation is set off by a pair of quotation marks and by an initial capital letter. **Indirect quotations**, however, do not use quotation marks or capital letters.

direct quotation A speaker's or writer's exact words, which are enclosed in quotation marks.

DIRECT QUOTATION	Ms. Goldman told her colleagues: "It's time to face the real issues!"
INDIRECT QUOTATION	Ms. Goldman told her colleagues that it was time to face the real issues.

indirect quotation A restatement of a speaker's or writer's ideas without quoting directly or using quotation marks.

When a phrase such as *she said* interrupts the quotation, do not capitalize the first word after the phrase unless the word actually begins a new quoted sentence. (See also M2-c.)

▶ "The only way to get rid of a temptation," says Lord Henry in Oscar Wilde's *The Picture*

is

of Dorian Gray, "~~I~~s to yield to it" (29; ch. 2).

Note: In a research paper, indent a long quotation as a block, double-spaced, and omit quotation marks.

For more on using block quotations in MLA and APA style, see Chapter 23.

P6-b Follow convention in using punctuation at the end of a quotation, after a signal phrase or speaker tag (*she said*), and with other punctuation.

Place a comma or a period inside the closing quotation mark.

▶ Fishman also discusses utterances such as "umm," "oh," and "yeah."

▶ Grandpa then said, "I guess you haven't heard what happened."

In a research paper following either MLA style or APA style, the closing quotation mark should follow the last quoted word, but the period at the end of the sentence should follow the parentheses enclosing the citation.

▶ Senator Gabriel Ambrosio added that "an override would send a terrible

   message, particularly to the young people (Schwaneberg 60)."

Note: Place a colon or semicolon outside the closing quotation mark.

▶ The doctor who tells the story says that the girl is "furious"; she shrieks

   "terrifyingly, hysterically" as he approaches her.

Follow an introductory phrase with either a comma or the word *that*.

▶ I looked down and said, "I was trying on your dress blues."

When you introduce a formal quotation with an independent clause, you can instead follow the introduction with a colon. (See P4-a.)

Place a question mark or an exclamation point inside the closing quotation mark if it is part of the quotation, or outside if it is part of your own sentence.

PART OF QUOTATION   My father replied, "What have I ever done to you?"

PART OF SENTENCE   How is it possible that he could have kept repeating to our class,

   "You are too dumb to learn anything?"

You do not need to add a period if a question mark or an exclamation point concludes a quotation at the end of the sentence.

▶ Miriam produces a highlighter from her bookbag with an enthusiastic "Voilà!"

Supply a closing quotation mark at the end of a paragraph to show that a new quotation begins in the next paragraph.

▶ "Come on, James," Toby said. "Let's climb over the fence." "I don't think it's a

   good idea!" I replied.

Omit the closing quotation mark if a quotation continues in the next paragraph.

▶ "I enjoy waiting on these people because they also ask about my life, instead

of treating me like a servant."

"However, some customers can be rude and very impatient."

P6-c Enclose titles of short works in quotation marks.

Short works include articles, chapters, essays, short stories, short poems, episodes in a television program, and songs. Place the quotation marks around the exact title of the work mentioned. Titles of longer works, such as books, magazines, and newspapers, are italicized; see M5-a.

"The Use of Force,"
▶ The short story ~~The Use of Force,~~ by William Carlos Williams, is an account of a

doctor's unpleasant experience with his patient.

Note: Do not enclose the title of your own essay in quotation marks.

P6-d Use single quotation marks inside double quotation marks to show a quotation within a quotation.

▶ Flanagan and McMenamin say, "Housing values across the United States have

acted more like a fluctuating stock market than the ʻ"sure"ʼ investment they

once were."

P6-e Omit or correct quotation marks used excessively or incorrectly.

Omit unneeded quotation marks used for emphasis, irony, or distance.
Avoid using quotation marks just to emphasize certain words, to show irony, or to distance yourself from **slang**, **clichés**, or trite expressions.

▶ Environmental groups can wage war in the hallways of Washington and

Sacramento and drive oil companies away from our "sacred shores."

slang Informal language that tends to change rapidly.

cliché An overused expression that has lost its original freshness, such as *hard as a rock.*

indirect quotation
A restatement of a speaker's
or writer's ideas without
quoting directly or using
quotation marks.

indirect quotation
A restatement of a speaker's
or writer's ideas without
quoting directly or using
quotation marks.

possessive form The form
that shows that a thing
belongs to someone or to
something.

Omit quotation marks from indirect quotations.

▶ He said that ⁗when he was eighteen years old and living in Liberty, Texas, a vision

inspired him to move to Houston.⁗

P7 Apostrophes

Use an apostrophe to mark the **possessive form** of nouns and some pronouns, the omission of letters or figures, and in some cases, the plural of letters or figures.

P7-a   Use an apostrophe to show the possessive form of a noun.

The form of a possessive noun depends on whether it is singular (one item) or plural (two or more items).

Add -'s to a singular noun to show possession.

  a student's parents   the rabbit's eye   Ward's essay

Be sure to include the apostrophe and to place it before the -*s* so that the reader does not mistakenly think that the noun is plural.

  apartment's
▶ The apartments design is spare to the point of dullness.

Indicate shared or joint possession by adding -'s to the final noun in a list; indicate individual possession by adding -'s to each noun.

  ▶ father and mother's room (joint or shared possession)

  ▶ father's and mother's patterns of conversation (individual possession)

Indicate possession by adding -'s to the last word in a compound.

  ▶ mother-in-law's

Even if a singular noun ends in *s,* add an apostrophe and -*s.*

  ▶ Louis's life

  ▶ Williams's narrator

  ▶ Cisneros's story

If the second *s* makes the word hard to pronounce, it is acceptable to add only an apostrophe.

  ▶ Sophocles' plays

To make plural nouns possessive, add -'s if the noun does not already end in *s,* and add only an apostrophe if it does.

▶ The guard was horrified by the children's behavior in the museum.

▶ Males tend to interrupt *females'* ~~females~~ conversations.

Note: Form the plural of a family name by adding *-s* without an apostrophe (the Harrisons); add the apostrophe only to show possession (the Harrisons' house).

P7-b   Add an apostrophe to show where letters or figures are omitted from a contraction.

▶ *Let's* "~~Lets~~ go back inside and see if you can do it my way now."

▶ Many people had cosmetic surgery in the *'90s.* ~~90s.~~

P7-c   Check your style guide to determine whether to include an apostrophe to form the plural of a number, a letter, or an abbreviation.

Some style guides encourage writers to form the plural of a number, a letter, or an abbreviation by adding *-'s*.

▶ The participants were shown a series of *3's* 3s that configured into a large 5.

However, the *MLA Handbook* (the most commonly used style guide in courses in English literature and composition) does not. So check with your instructor to be sure what is appropriate.

P7-d   Add *-'s* to form the possessive of an **indefinite pronoun** but not a personal pronoun.

INDEFINITE PRONOUN   Everyone knows that good service can make or break *one's* ~~ones~~ dining experience.

The possessive forms of **personal pronouns**, however, do not have apostrophes: *my, mine, your, yours, her, hers, his, its, our, ours, their, theirs*.

PERSONAL PRONOUN   That company does not use animals to develop *its* it's products.

P7-e   Omit unnecessary or incorrect apostrophes.

Watch for an apostrophe incorrectly added to a plural noun ending in *s* when the noun is not a possessive.

▶ Autistic *patients* patient's can be high, middle, or low functioning.

indefinite pronoun A pronoun that does not refer to a particular person or object, such as *all, anybody, anywhere, each, enough, every, everyone, everything, one, somebody, something, either, more, most, neither, none*, and *nobody*.

personal pronoun A pronoun that refers to a specific person or object and changes form depending on its function in a sentence, such as *I, me, my, we, us,* and *our.*

P8   Parentheses

Parentheses are useful for enclosing material—a word, a phrase, or even a complete sentence—that interrupts a sentence.

P8-a   Add parentheses to enclose additions to a sentence.

Parentheses are useful for enclosing citations of research sources (following the format required by your style guide); for enclosing an **acronym** or abbreviation at first mention; for adding dates, definitions, illustrations, or other elaborations; and for numbering or lettering a list (always using a pair of marks).

acronym A word formed from the first letters of the phrase that it abbreviates, such as *BART* for *Bay Area Rapid Transit*.

▶ Americans are not applying their knowledge, and as a result, their children are

not benefiting (*American Dietetic Association* 582).

▶ People for the Ethical Treatment of Animals (PETA) is a radical animal liberation group.

▶ The bill called (S-2232) was introduced to protect people who smoke off the job

against employment discrimination.

▶ Signals would (1) prevent life-threatening collisions, (2) provide more efficient and

speedy movement of traffic, and (3) decrease frustration and loss of driver judgment.

Note: Use commas to separate the items in a numbered list. If the items include internal commas, use semicolons. (See P3-b.)

P8-b   Correct the punctuation used with parentheses, and omit unnecessary parentheses.

When you add information in parentheses, the sentence should remain logical and complete, and the punctuation should be the same. Delete any comma *before* a parenthesis mark.

▶ As I stood at the salad bar, a young lady asked if the kitchen had any cream

cheese, (normally served only at breakfast,).

Parentheses are unnecessary if they enclose information that could simply be integrated into the sentence.

▶ He didn't exhibit the uncontrollable temper and the high-velocity swearing

(typical of many high school coaches).

P9 Brackets

Use brackets to insert editorial notes into a quotation and to enclose parenthetical material within text that is already in parentheses. In a quotation, the brackets tell the reader that the added material is yours, not the original author's. (See also P10.)

For more about brackets, see Chapter 23.

▶ " 'The gang is your family,' he [Hagan] explains."

If the original quotation includes a mistake, add [sic], the Latin word for "so," in brackets to tell the reader that the error occurs in the source. Often you can reword your sentence to omit the error.

Replace inappropriate brackets with parentheses.

▶ The American Medical Society has linked "virtual" violence (violence in the

media) to real-life acts of violence (Hollis 623).

P10 Ellipsis Marks

Use ellipsis marks to indicate a deliberate omission within a quotation or to mark a dramatic pause in a sentence. Type ellipsis marks as three spaced periods (. . .), with a space before the first period and following the last period.

▶ Aries also noticed this reaction in her research: "The mixed group setting seems to benefit men more than women . . . allowing men more variation in the ways they participate in discussions" (32).

If you omit the end of a quoted sentence or if you omit a sentence or more from the middle of a quoted passage, add a sentence period and a space before the first ellipsis mark.

Do not use opening or closing ellipsis marks if the quotation is clearly only part of a sentence.

▶ According to the environmental group Earthgreen, U.S. oil reserves "... will be

economically depleted by 2018 at the current consumption rate ..."

For more about ellipsis marks, see Chapter 10 and Chapter 23.

(Miller 476).

P11 Slashes

Use a slash to separate quoted lines of poetry and to separate word pairs that present options or opposites.

▶ In "A Poison Tree," William Blake gives the same advice: "I was angry with my friend: / I told my wrath, my wrath did end."

Note: When you use a slash to show the lines in poetry, leave a space before and after the mark. If you quote four lines or more, omit the quotation marks and slashes and present the poetry line for line as a block quotation.

P12   Periods

declarative sentence
A sentence that makes a statement rather than asking a question or exclaiming.

indirect question A statement that tells what a question asked without directly asking the question.

Use a period to mark the end of a **declarative sentence**, an **indirect question**, or an abbreviation.

▶ Another significant use for clinical hypnosis would be to replace anesthesia.

▶ She asked her professor why he was not as tough on her as he was on the male

  students?.

▶ Mrs. Drabin was probably one of the smartest people I knew.

Note: Some abbreviations do not include periods (see M6); always check your dictionary to be sure. In addition, many specialized professional and academic fields have their own systems for handling abbreviations.

P13   Question Marks

Add a question mark after a direct question.

▶ Did they even read my information sheet/?

  Avoid using question marks to express irony or sarcasm. Use them sparingly to question the accuracy of a preceding word or figure.

P14   Exclamation Points

Use an exclamation point to show strong emotion or emphasis.

▶ He fell on one knee and exclaimed, "Marry me, my beautiful princess!"

  Use exclamation points sparingly. Replace inappropriate or excessive exclamation points with periods.

▶ If parents know which disciplinary methods to use, they can effectively protect

  their children!.

M Mechanics

M1 Hyphens

Hyphens are used to form select **compound words** and to break words at the end of a line.

M1-a Use a hyphen to join **compound adjectives** that *precede* nouns.

Before Noun	After Noun
after-school activities	activities after school
well-known athlete	athlete who is well known

When a compound adjective precedes a noun, the hyphen clarifies that the compound functions as a unit.

▶ People usually think of locusts as hideous‚looking creatures that everyone dislikes

and wants to squash.

▶ I was a nineteen year old second semester sophomore.

▶ People are becoming increasingly health‑conscious.

When two different prefixes or initial words go with the same second word, use a hyphen and a space at the end of the first prefix or word.

▶ An army of green- and blue-hooded medical personnel crowded the small trauma room.

Note: Some compound adjectives are nearly always hyphenated, before or after a noun, including those beginning with *all-* or *self-*. Check a dictionary if you are not sure whether a hyphen is needed.

▶ The use of ethanol will be a self perpetuating trend.

A compound with an *-ly* **adverb** preceding an **adjective** or a **participle** is always left as two words.

▶ brilliantly clever scheme

▶ rapidly growing business

compound word A word formed from two or more words that function together as a unit.

compound adjective An adjective formed from two or more words that function as a unit.

adverb A word that modifies a verb, an adjective, or another adverb.

adjective A word that modifies a noun or a pronoun, adding information about it.

participle A verb form showing present tense (*dancing, freezing*) or past tense (*danced, frozen*) that can also act as an adjective.

M1-b Present a compound noun as one word, as separate words, or as a hyphenated compound.

Close up the parts of a compound noun spelled as one word.

▶ Another road in our county now looks like an appliance grave yard.

Omit hyphens in a compound noun spelled as separate words.

▶ First, make the community aware of the problem by writing a letter-to-the-editor.

Hyphenate fractions, compound numbers (up to ninety-nine), and other nouns that are hyphenated in your dictionary.

▶ Almost two thirds of couples married before age eighteen end up divorced,

twice the number of couples married at twenty one or older.

Note: If using compound words that have more than one acceptable spelling (*workforce* and *work force,* for example), choose one spelling and use it consistently. If you are unsure about whether to use a hyphen, check your dictionary, or follow the common usage of professional publications in that field.

M1-c Spell words formed with most prefixes as one word with no hyphen.

antismoking	coauthor	multicultural	nonviolent
postwar	repossess	submarine	unskilled

▶ This possibility is so rare as to be non-existent.

Insert a hyphen in a compound noun beginning with *ex-, great-,* or *self-* (unless it is followed by a suffix, as in *selfhood*) or ending in *-elect* or *-in-law.*

ex-husband   self-esteem   secretary-elect

▶ Self sufficiency is not the only motivation.

proper noun The capitalized name of a specific person, group, place, or thing.

Use a hyphen in a word that includes a prefix and a **proper noun**.

un-American   anti-American   pro-American

M1-d Use a hyphen when necessary to avoid ambiguity.

Sometimes a hyphen is necessary to prevent a reader from confusing a word with a prefix (*re-cover, re-creation*) with another word (*recover, recreation*) or from stumbling over a word in which two or three of the same letters fall together (*anti-inflammatory, troll-like*).

▶ The police officers asked for the *recreation* facility's log to help them *re-create* the circumstances surrounding the crime.

M1-e Insert a hyphen between syllables to divide a word at the end of a line.

If you must divide a word, look for a logical division, such as between syllables, between parts of a compound word, or between the root and a prefix or suffix. If you are uncertain about where to divide a word, check your dictionary.

go-ing	height-en	mus-cu-la-ture	back-stage
dis-sat-is-fied	com-mit-ment	hon-or-able	phi-los-o-phy

Although many published works divide words, writing is easier to read without numerous broken words.

M2 Capitalization

Capitalize proper nouns, the first word in a sentence or a quotation that is a sentence, and the main words in a title.

M2-a Capitalize proper nouns.

Capitalize specific names of people, groups, places, streets, events, historical periods, monuments, holidays, days, months, and directions that refer to specific geographic areas.

World War II	the Great Depression	Lincoln Memorial
Independence Day	Passover	Ramadan
Monday	January	Colorado College
the Northeast	Native Americans	Magnolia Avenue

▶ It is difficult for ᴀamericans to comprehend the true meaning of freedom.

Capitalize adjectives derived from proper nouns.

Mexican   Dickensian

▶ The ɴnapoleonic code influenced Louisiana law.

When a reference is general, use a **common noun** (uncapitalized) rather than a proper one (capitalized). Do not capitalize general names of institutions, seasons, compass directions, or words that you simply want to emphasize.

common noun The general name of a person, place, or thing.

summer vacation	last winter	university requirements
church service	southern exposure	western life

▶ I work in a ₗLaw ᴏOffice that specializes in settling accident cases.

Note: Common nouns such as *street* and *river* are capitalized only when they are part of a proper noun: *Main Street, the Mississippi River.*

M2-b Capitalize the word that begins a sentence.

▶ ~~t~~The garden was their world.

If a complete sentence appears within parentheses and is not part of a larger sentence, capitalize the first word.

See P4-a for information on capitalizing **independent clauses** following colons.

independent clause
A word group with a subject and a predicate that can stand alone as a separate sentence.

M2-c Capitalize the first word in a quotation unless it is integrated into your own wording or continues an interrupted quotation.

▶ Lucy Danziger says, "Forget about the glass ceiling" (81).

▶ Lucy Danziger argues that we should "forget about the glass ceiling."

▶ Marilyn describes the adult bison as having an "ugly, shaggy, brown coat."

Writers often incorporate short quotations and quotations introduced by *that* into their sentences; neither needs an initial capital letter. When a phrase such as *she said* interrupts a quotation, capitalize the first word in the quotation but not the first word after the phrase unless it begins a new sentence. (See also P6-a.)

▶ Toby said, "~~t~~Trust me — we won't get caught."

▶ "~~r~~Renting," she insists, "deprives you of big tax breaks."

Note: If you quote from a poem, capitalize words exactly as the poet does.

article An adjective that precedes a noun and identifies a definite reference to something specific (*the*) or an indefinite reference to something less specific (*a* or *an*).

coordinating conjunction A word that joins comparable and equally important sentence elements: *for, and, or, but, nor, yet,* or *so.*

preposition A word (such as *between, in,* or *of*) that indicates the relation between a word in a sentence and its object.

M2-d Capitalize titles and subtitles of longer works, such as books, magazines, and newspapers.

Capitalize the first and last words in a title and subtitle plus all other words except for **articles**, **coordinating conjunctions**, and **prepositions**.

War and Peace   *The Grand Canyon Suite*

Tragedy: Vision and Form   "On First Looking into Chapman's Homer"

(See also P6-c and M5-a.)

▶ In her article "The Gun ~~In~~ In ~~The~~ The Closet," Straight tells of booming Riverside,

California, a city east of Los Angeles.

M2-e Capitalize a title that precedes a person's name.

Capitalize titles only when they precede a name, not when they follow a name or appear without a name.

Professor John Ganim   Aunt Alice

John Ganim, my professor   Alice Jordan, my favorite aunt

▶ At the state level, Reverend Green is ~~P~~president of the State Congress of Christian

Education and ~~M~~moderator of the Old Landmark Association.

Note: References to the President (of the United States) and other major public figures are sometimes capitalized in all contexts.

M2-f Avoid overusing capitalization for emphasis.

Although in some writing situations a word that appears entirely in capital letters can create a desired effect, you should limit this use of capital letters to rare occasions.

▶ The powerful SMACK of the ball on the rival's thigh brings an abrupt, anticlimactic end to the rising tension.

In most cases, follow the conventions for capitalizing described in this section.

▶ The principles are called the ~~TENETS OF TAE KWON DO.~~ *tenets of Tae Kwon Do.*

M3 Spacing

Allow standard spacing between words and punctuation marks. Most style guides recommend leaving one space after a sentence and supply specific directions about spacing source citations.

M3-a Supply any missing space before or after a punctuation mark.

Although spell-checkers can help identify some misspelled words, they do not indicate spacing errors unless the error links two words or splits a word. Always proofread carefully for spacing errors around punctuation marks.

▶ My curiosity got the best of me, so I flipped through the pages to see what would happen.

▶ "I found to my horror, " Nadine later wept, "that I was too late!"

▶ "I would die without bread!" Roberto declared. "In my village, they made fresh bread every morning."

▶ Pet adoption fees include the cost of spaying or neutering all dogs and cats four

months old or older(if needed).

M3-b **Close up any unnecessary space between words and punctuation marks.**

▶ Karl did not know why this war was considered justifiable ͡ .

▶ The larger florist shops require previous experience ͡ , but the smaller ͡ , portable

wagons require only a general knowledge of flowers.

▶ Do you remember the song " ͡ The Wayward Wind" ͡ ?

M4 Numbers

Conventions for the treatment of numbers vary widely. In the humanities, writers tend to spell out numbers (*one out of ten*), but in the sciences and social sciences, writers are far more likely to use numerals (*1 out of 10*).

M4-a **Spell out select types of numbers in most nonscientific college writing.**

Spell out whole numbers *one* through *ninety-nine*.

▶ A hefty $7,000 per week is paid to Wells Fargo Security for ₄4 guards who patrol the *four*

grounds ₄24 hours a day. *twenty-four*

▶ Only ₁15 years ago, it was difficult to find any public figures who were openly gay. *fifteen*

Note: Depending on the type of writing that you do and the conventions of your field, you may decide to spell out only numerals up to ten. Choose a rule and follow it consistently.

If two numbers occur in succession, use a combination of spelled-out words and numerals for clarity.

eight 45-cent stamps   ten 3-year-olds

Spell out a number that begins a sentence, or rewrite so that the number is no longer the first word.

▶ ₄41,000 women die from breast cancer each year. *Forty-one thousand*

▶ ₄41,000 women die from breast cancer each~~year~~. *Each year,*

Spell out very large round numbers, or use a combination of numerals and words.

3.5 million dollars *or* $3.5 million   nearly 14 million

five thousand   a billion

M4-b   **Use numerals for numbers over a hundred, in fractions and percentages, with abbreviations and symbols, in dates and addresses, and for page numbers and sections of books.**

289 cards	1/2	18.5	99%
73 percent	5 a.m.	10:30 p.m.	3 cm
185 lb	$200	May 6, 2012	175 Fifth Avenue
page 44	part 5	chapter 2	volume 8

▶ A woman with the same skills as her coworkers may earn an additional eight to ^8^

twenty percent just by being well groomed. ^20^

Note: Depending on the style guide you are using, either the word *percent* or the % symbol will be required. Whichever you choose, use it consistently throughout a paper.

M5   Italics

M5-a   **Italicize titles of long or self-contained works.**

Titles of books, newspapers, magazines, scholarly journals, pamphlets, long poems, movies, television and radio programs, long musical compositions, plays, comic strips, and works of art are italicized.

the *Georgia Review*	*Beowulf*	*Citizen Kane*
the *Washington Post*	*60 Minutes*	*Pride and Prejudice*

▶ I found that the article in the *Journal of the American Medical Association* had more information and stronger scientific proof than the article in *American Health*.

Note: The Bible and its divisions are not italicized.

▶ "The Hunger Games" film was based on the novel by Suzanne Collins.   *The Hunger Games*

Titles of short works or works contained in other works are not italicized but are placed in quotation marks. (See also P6-c.)

▶ The original "Star Trek" episode "The Trouble with Tribbles" was hugely popular.   *Star Trek*

M5-b Italicize words used as words and letters and numbers used as themselves.

the word *committed*   three *7*s   a *q* or a *g*

▶ *Rank order* is a term that Aries uses to explain the way that some individuals take the role as the leader and the others fall in behind.

M5-c Italicize names of planes, ships, and other vehicles; foreign words not commonly used in English; and, on occasion, words that need special emphasis.

Lindbergh's *Spirit of St. Louis*   Amtrak's *Silver Star*

Resist the temptation to emphasize words by putting them in bold type. In most writing situations, italics provides enough emphasis.

▶ On every table is a vase adorned with a red carnation, symbolizing *amore*.

▶ This situation could exist because it is just that, *reverse* socialization.

M5-d Italicize when appropriate, but not in place of or in addition to other conventional uses of punctuation and mechanics.

Eliminate any unusual uses of italics.

UNUSUAL   Former NFL commissioner Paul Tagliabue said, *"I do not believe playing [football] in Arizona is in the best interests of the NFL."*

APPROPRIATE   Former NFL commissioner Paul Tagliabue said, "I do not believe playing [football] in Arizona is in the best interests of the NFL."

M6 Abbreviations

Although abbreviations are more common in technical and business writing than in academic writing, you may sometimes want to use them to avoid repetition. Use the full word in your first reference, followed by the abbreviation in parentheses. Then use the abbreviation in subsequent references.

▶ She was a member of the San Diego Humane Society (SDHS).

Abbreviations composed of all capital letters are generally written without periods or spaces between letters. When capital letters are separated by periods, do not include a space after the period, except for the initials of a person's name, which should be spaced.

USA   CNN   UPI   B.A.   Ph.D.   T. S. Eliot

M6-a Use abbreviations that your readers will recognize for names of agencies, organizations, countries, and common technical terms.

FBI   IRS   CBS   NATO   NOW   DNA   GNP   CPM

▶ NOW is an independently run nonprofit organization.

Note: Do not abbreviate geographic names in formal writing unless the areas are commonly known by their abbreviations (*Washington, D.C.*).

M6-b Use a.m., p.m., no., $, BC, and AD only with specific numerals or dates.

7:15 a.m.   10:30 p.m.
$172.18 or $38   No. 18 or no. 18 [item or issue number of a source]
72 BC [before Christ]   72 BCE [before the Common Era]
AD 378 [anno Domini]   378 CE [Common Era]

Note: AD is placed before the date, not after it.

M6-c Use commonly accepted abbreviations for titles, degrees, and Latin terms.

Use an accepted abbreviation for titles and degrees.

Rev. Jesse Jackson   Mr. Roger Smith   Ring Lardner Jr.
Diana Lee, M.D.   Dr. Diana Lee   James Boyer, D.V.M.

Avoid duplication by using a title before a person's name or a degree after the name but not both.

▶ According to Dr. Ira Chasnoff, M. D., cocaine produces a dramatic fluctuation in blood pressure.

Reserve Latin terms, such as those listed here, primarily for source citations or comments in parentheses rather than in the text of your essay.

c. (*or* ca.)   "circa" or about (used with dates)
cf.   compare
e.g.   for example
et al.   and others (used with people)
etc.   and so forth
i.e.   that is

M6-d Use abbreviations when appropriate, but do not use them to replace words in most writing.

In formal writing, avoid abbreviating units of measurement or technical terms (unless your essay is technical), names of time periods, titles of courses or names of departments, names of states or countries (unless the abbreviation is the more common form), names of companies, and parts of books.

▶ The Pets for People program gives older people the companionship they need,
especially
~esp. if they live alone.

Street
▶ I called the closest site on Hancock~St. to ask for a tour.

September
▶ The walkout followed an incident on ~Sept. 27.

M7 Spelling

Spell-checkers can be helpful, but they will not catch all errors. To be sure that your spelling is correct, you must proofread your final draft yourself. The following suggestions for catching and correcting your spelling errors will help:

- Proofread your writing carefully to catch transposed letters (*becuase* for *because*), omitted letters (*becaus*), and other careless errors (*then* for *than*). When you proofread for spelling, read the text backward, beginning with the last word. This strategy keeps you from reading for content and lets you focus on each word.

- Check a good dictionary for any words you are uncertain about. When you are writing and doubt the spelling of a word, put a question mark by the word but wait to check it until you have finished drafting.

- Keep a list of words you often misspell so that you can try to pinpoint your personal patterns. Although misspellings nearly always follow a pattern, you are not likely to misspell every word of a particular type, or you may spell the same word two different ways in the same essay.

prefix A word part, such as *pre-*, *anti-*, or *bi-*, that is attached to the beginning of a word to form another word: *preconceived, unbelievable.*

suffix A word part, such as *-ly*, *-ment*, or *-ed*, that is added to the end of a word to change the word's form (*bright, brightly*) or tense (*call, called*) or to form another word (*govern, government*).

M7-a Study the spelling rules for adding **prefixes** and **suffixes** to words.

Although English has a large number of words with unusual spellings, many follow the patterns that spelling rules describe.

Add a prefix to a root without doubling or dropping letters.

<u>dis</u>trust	<u>mis</u>behave	<u>un</u>able
<u>dis</u>satisfy	<u>mis</u>spell	<u>un</u>natural

Add a suffix beginning with a vowel (such as -*ing*) in accord with the form of the root word.

Double the final consonant if the word has a single syllable that ends in a single consonant preceded by a single vowel.

beg<u>ging</u>	hid<u>den</u>	fit<u>ting</u>

Do the same if the word has a final stressed syllable that ends in a single consonant preceded by a single vowel.

beginning   occurrence

The final consonant does not double if the word ends in two consonants or two vowels.

acting   parted   seeming   stooped

In some cases, the stress shifts to the first syllable when a suffix is added. When it does, do not double the final consonant.

prefér: preférring,   preférred

     préference,   préferable

Add a suffix that begins with *y* or a vowel by dropping a final silent *e*.

achieving   icy   location

grievance   lovable   continual

Keep the final silent *e* to retain a soft *c* or *g* sound, to prevent mispronunciation, or to prevent confusion with other words.

changeable   courageous   noticeable

eyeing   mileage   canoeist

dyeing   singeing

Add a suffix that begins with a consonant by keeping a final silent *e*.

achievement   discouragement   sincerely

Exceptions: acknowledgment, argument, awful, judgment, truly, wholly

Form the plural of a singular noun in accord with its form.

If a singular noun ends in a consonant followed by *y*, change *y* to *i* and add *-es*.

► baby, babies ► cry, cries

Note: Simply add *-s* to names: her cousin *Mary,* both *Marys.*

If a singular noun ends in a vowel followed by *y*, add *-s*.

► trolley, trolleys ► day, days

If a singular noun ends in a consonant and *o*, add *-es*.

► potato, potatoes ► echo, echoes ► veto, vetoes

Exceptions: autos, dynamos, pianos, sopranos

If a singular noun ends in a vowel and *o*, add *-s*.

► video, videos ► rodeo, rodeos ► radio, radios

If a singular noun ends in *s, ss, sh, ch, x,* or *z,* add *-es.*

▶ Jones, Joneses   ▶ hiss, hisses   ▶ bush, bushes

▶ match, matches   ▶ suffix, suffixes   ▶ buzz, buzzes

Note: The plural of *thesis* is *theses.*

Check the dictionary for the plural of a word that originates in another language.

criterion, criteria   datum, data

medium, mediums *or* media

hors d'oeuvre, hors d'oeuvres *or* hors d'oeuvre

M7-b   **Study the spelling rules (and the exceptions) that apply to words you routinely misspell.**

Add *i* before *e* except after *c.*

Most people remember this rule because of the jingle "Write *i* before *e* / Except after *c* / Or when sounded like *ay* / As in *neighbor* and *weigh.*" *Exceptions:* either, foreign, forfeit, height, leisure, neither, seize, weird

Spell most words ending in the sound "seed" as *-cede.*

precede   recede   secede   intercede

Exceptions: proceed, succeed, supersede

FOR MULTILINGUAL WRITERS

If you have learned Canadian or British English, you may have noticed some differences in the way that words are spelled in U.S. English.

U.S. English	**Canadian or British English**
color	colour
realize	realise (*or* realize in Canadian English)
center	centre
defense	defence

M7-c   **Watch for words that are often spelled incorrectly because they sound like other words.**

In English, many words are not spelled as they sound. The endings of some words may be dropped in speech but need to be included in writing. For example, speakers often pronounce *and* as *an'* or drop the *-ed* ending on verbs. Other common words sound the same but have entirely different meanings. Watch carefully for words such as the following:

already ("by now": He is *already* in class.)

all ready ("fully prepared": I'm *all ready* for the test.)

an (article: Everyone read *an* essay last night.)

and (conjunction: The class discussed the problem *and* the solution.)

its (possessive pronoun: The car lost *its* shine.)

it's ("it is": *It's* too cold to go for a walk.)

maybe ("perhaps": *Maybe* we should have tacos for dinner.)

may be (verb showing possibility: They *may be* arriving tonight.)

than (conjunction showing comparison: The house was taller *than* the tree.)

then (adverb showing time sequence: First she knocked and *then* she opened the door.)

their (possessive pronoun: They decided to sell *their* old car.)

there (adverb showing location: The car dealer is located *there* on the corner.)

they're ("they are": *They're* going to pick up the new car tonight.)

your (possessive pronoun: I can see *your* apartment.)

you're ("you are": Call me when *you're* home.)

For distinctions between other words, such as *affect/effect, principal/principle,* and *to/too,* see the Glossary of Frequently Misused Words.

Watch for and correct misspelled words that sound the same as other words.

▶ I started packing my gear, still ~~vary~~ *very* excited about the trip.

▶ The campfire had ~~burn~~ *burned* down to a sizzle.

▶ I just ~~new~~ *knew* it was a bear, and I was going to be its dinner.

▶ As students pay ~~there~~ *their* fees, part of this money goes toward purchasing new

books and materials.

M7-d Watch for words that are often misspelled.

Check your essays for the following words, which are often spelled incorrectly. Look up any other questionable words in a dictionary, and keep a personal list of words that you tend to misspell.

absence	choose	friend	preferred
accidentally	chose	government	prejudice
accommodate	coming	harass	preparation
accomplish	commitment	height	privilege
achievement	committed	heroes	probably
acknowledge	competitive	immediately	proceed
acquaintance	conscience	incredible	professor
acquire	conscious	indefinitely	quiet
against	convenient	interesting	quite
aggravate	criticize	irrelevant	receive
all right	definitely	knowledge	recommend
a lot	dependent	loose	reference
although	desperate	lose	referred
analyze	develops	maintenance	roommate
apparently	disappear	maneuver	schedule
appearance	eighth	mischievous	separate
appropriate	eligible	necessary	similar
argument	embarrass	noticeable	studying
arrangement	emphasize	occasion	succeed
attendance	environment	occur	success
basically	especially	occurred	successful
before	every day	occurrences	therefore
beginning	exaggerated	particularly	thorough
believe	exercise	performance	truly
benefited	exercising	phenomena	unnecessarily
business	experience	phenomenon	until
businesses	explanation	physically	usually
calendar	finally	playwright	whether
cannot	foreign	practically	without
categories	forty	precede	woman
changeable	fourth	preference	women

T   Troublespots for Multilingual Writers

This section provides advice about problems of grammar and standard usage that are particularly challenging for writers whose first language is not English.

T1   Articles

The rules for using articles (*a, an,* and *the*) are complicated. Your choice depends on whether the article appears before a **count, noncount,** or **proper noun**. An *article* is used before a common noun to indicate whether the noun refers to something specific (*the* moon) or whether it refers to something that is one among many or has not yet been specified (*a* planet, *an* asteroid). In addition, for some nouns, the absence of an article indicates that the reference is not specific.

count noun A noun that names people and things that can be counted: one *teacher,* two *teachers;* one *movie,* several *movies.*

noncount noun A noun that names things or ideas that are not or cannot be counted: thunder, money, happiness.

proper noun The capitalized name of a specific person, group, place, or thing.

T1-a   Select the correct article to use with a count noun.

- Use *a* or *an* with nonspecific singular count nouns.
- Use no article with nonspecific plural count nouns.
- Use *the* with specific singular and plural count nouns.

Note: The article *a* is used before a consonant and *an* before a vowel; exceptions include words beginning with a long *u* sound, such as *unit*.

Use *a* or *an* before a singular count noun when it refers to one thing among many or something that has not been specifically identified.

▸ We, as ^*a* society, have to educate our youth about avoiding teen pregnancy.

▸ *A darkroom*
  ^Darkroom is a room with no light where photographs are developed.

Use *the* before a singular or plural count noun when it refers to one or more specific things.

After you have used *a* or *an* with a count noun, subsequent references to the noun become specific and are marked by *the*.

▸ When I walked into the office, *a* woman in her midforties was waiting to be called. As I sat down, I looked at *the* woman.

Exceptions include a second reference to one among many.

▸ I was guided to *a* classroom. It was *a* bright room, filled with warm rays of Hawaiian sunlight.

In most situations, use *the* with a count noun modified by a superlative adjective.

the most frightening moment   the smallest person

Nouns such as *sun* generally refer to unique things. Nouns such as *house* and *yard* often refer to things that people own. In most situations, both types of nouns can be preceded by the definite article *the*.

▶ Don't look directly at *the sun*. [Only one sun could be meant.]

▶ I spent Saturday cleaning *the house*. [The reader will infer that the writer is referring to his or her own house.]

You can also introduce count nouns referring to specific entities with possessive nouns or pronouns (*Maya's* friends) or demonstrative pronouns (*these* friends). Indefinite count and noncount nouns can also be introduced by words that indicate amount (*few* friends, *some* sand).

COUNT NOUN   She starred in a reality show with *her* eight children.

NONCOUNT NOUN   Her family wanted *some* happiness.

Delete any article before a nonspecific plural count noun.

▶ ~~The~~ people like Dee cannot forget their heritage.
People

T1-b Select the correct article to use with a noncount noun.

The many kinds of noncount nouns include the following:

Natural phenomena: *thunder, steam, electricity*

Natural elements: *gold, air, sunlight*

Manufacturing materials: *steel, wood, cement*

Fibers: *wool, cotton, rayon*

General categories made up of a variety of specific items: *money, music, furniture*

Abstract ideas: *happiness, loyalty, adolescence, wealth*

Liquids: *milk, gasoline, water*

Some nouns naming foodstuffs are always noncount (*pork, rice, broccoli*); others are noncount when they refer to food as it is eaten (*We ate barbecued chicken and fruit*) but count when they refer to individual items or varieties (*We bought a plump chicken and various fruits*).

Delete any article before a general noncount noun.

▶ What is needed is a reasonable and measured legislation.

▶ The destruction caused by the war drew artists away from the reality, which is

painful and cruel, and toward the abstract art that avoids a sense of despair.

Use *the* before a noncount noun when it refers to something specific or when it is specified by a **prepositional phrase** or an **adjective clause**.

- ▶ *The* coffee is probably cold by now.

- ▶ *The* water on the boat has to be rationed.

- ▶ *The* water that we have left has to be rationed.

You can also introduce noncount nouns referring to specific things with possessive nouns or pronouns (*her* money) or demonstrative pronouns (*that* money). Indefinite noncount nouns can also be introduced by words that indicate amount (*some* money).

T1-c Select the correct article to use with a **proper noun.**

Most plural proper nouns require *the: the* United States, *the* Philippines, *the* Black Hills, *the* Clintons, *the* Los Angeles Dodgers. Exceptions include business names (Hillshire Farms, Miller Auto Sales).

Delete any article before most singular proper nouns.

In general, singular proper nouns are not preceded by an article: Dr. Livingston, New York City, Hawaii, Disneyland, Mount St. Helens, Wrigley Field.

- ▶ ~~The~~ Campus Security is a powerful deterrent against parties, because if you are written up twice, you can lose your housing contract.

The is used before proper noun phrases that include *of* (*the* Rock of Gibraltar, *the* Gang of Four). *The* is also required before proper nouns that name the following things:

1. Bodies of water, except when the generic part of the name precedes the specific name: *the* Atlantic Ocean, *the* Red River, but Lake Erie
2. Geographic regions: *the* West Coast, *the* Sahara, *the* Grand Canyon
3. Vehicles for transportation: *the Concorde*
4. Named buildings and bridges: *the* Empire State Building, *the* Golden Gate Bridge
5. National or international churches: *the* Russian Orthodox Church
6. Governing bodies preceded by a proper adjective: *the* British Parliament
7. Titles of religious and political leaders: *the* Dalai Lama
8. Religious and historical documents: *the* Bible, *the* Magna Carta
9. Historical periods and events: *the* Gilded Age, *the* Civil War

prepositional phrase
A group of words that begins with a preposition and indicates the relation between a word in a sentence and the object following the preposition: Her sunglasses slid *under the seat.*

adjective clause A clause that modifies a noun or pronoun and is generally introduced by a relative pronoun (such as *that* or *which*).

proper noun The capitalized name of a specific person, group, place, or thing.

T2 Verbs

Section R2-a reviews the basic English verb forms and includes a list of common irregular verbs. As you edit your writing, pay particular attention to conditional clauses, two-word verbs, helping (auxiliary) verbs, and gerund or infinitive forms after verbs.

independent (main) clause
A word group with a subject and a predicate that can stand alone as a separate sentence.

T2-a Select verb tenses carefully in **main clauses** and conditional clauses.

Conditional clauses beginning with *if* or *unless* generally indicate that one thing causes another (a factual relationship); predict future outcomes or possibilities; or speculate about the past, present, or future, or impossible events or circumstances.

┌─────── conditional clause ───────┐ ┌─────── main clause ───────┐
If we *use* media outlets responsibly, they *can give* us information and entertainment.

┌─────── conditional clause ───────┐ ┌─────── main clause ───────┐
If we *use* the media carelessly, it *will control* our families and our society.

Change both verbs to the same tense to express general or specific truths or actions that happen together habitually.

> ▶ When we moved to America, my family ~~has~~ *had* good communication.

Change the verb in the main clause to the future and the verb in the conditional clause to the present to express future possibilities or predictions.

> ▶ If you ask about the servers in any of her restaurants, the manager ~~could~~ *can* tell you
>
> about their quirks.

base form The uninflected form of a verb: I *eat*; to *play*.

To speculate about events or conditions that are unreal, improbable, or contrary to fact, change the verb in the main clause to *would, could,* or *might* plus the **base form**, and change the verb in the *if* conditional clause to the past tense.
  Use *were* rather than *was* in an *if* clause.

> ▶ Some people believe that if the Health Department ~~gives~~ *were to give* out clean needles, the
>
> number of people using drugs would increase.

participle A verb form showing present tense (*dancing, freezing*) or past tense (*danced, frozen*) that can also act as an adjective.

To speculate about past actions that did not in fact occur, change the verb in the main clause to *would have, might have, could have,* or *should have* plus the past **participle**, and change the verb in the *if* clause to the past perfect.

> ▶ If the lab ~~added~~ *had* added more hours during finals week, students would not have had
>
> to wait to use a computer.

Note: Do not add *would have* to the *if* clause.

T2-b Learn the meanings of idiomatic two- and three-word verbs used in English.

Idiomatic two- or three-word (or phrasal) verbs usually combine a verb with a word that appears to be a preposition or an adverb (called a *particle*). The combined meaning cannot be understood literally, and similar expressions often have very different meanings.

> *hand in* means "submit"
>
> *hand out* means "distribute"
>
> *look into* means "investigate"
>
> *look out for* means "watch carefully"
>
> *run away* means "leave without warning"
>
> *run into* means "meet by chance"
>
> *walk out on* means "abandon"
>
> *want out* means "desire to be free of responsibility"

Native speakers of English will notice misuses of these idiomatic verbs even though they use the verbs without thinking about their literal meanings. When you are unsure of the meaning or usage of such verbs, consult a dictionary or ask a native speaker.

T2-c Use the correct verb forms after helping verbs.

After the helping (auxiliary) verbs *do, does,* and *did,* always use the **base form** of the main verb. After the helping verbs *have, has,* and *had,* always use the past participle form of the main verb. (See R2-a and G5.)

>   *cooperate*
> ▶ They do not cooperated with the police.

>   *done*
> ▶ They have doing these things for a long time.

base form The uninflected form of a verb: I *eat;* to *play.*

A **modal** such as *will* sometimes precedes *have, has,* or *had.*

> ▶ By Friday I *will have finished* this project.

Following the helping verbs *be, am, is, are, was, were,* and *been* (forms of *be*), use the present participle to show ongoing action (progressive tense).

>   *giving*
> ▶ The President is given a speech on all major networks.

modals The helping verbs *can, could, may, might, must, shall, should, will,* and *would,* which must be used in conjunction with another (main) verb: I *may go* to the bank.

Use one of the modal verbs with *be.* Use *have, has,* or *had* with *been.*

> ▶ Terence *could be making* some calls while I am out.

> ▶ I *have been working* hard.

passive voice The verb form that shows something happening to the subject.

After the helping verbs *am, is, are, was,* and *were* (forms of *be*), use the past participle to form the **passive voice**.

> *canceled*
> ▶ Regular programming is ~~cancel~~ for tonight.
>   ^

To form the passive, *be, being,* and *been* need another helping verb in addition to the past participle.

> ▶ Tonya will be challenged in graduate school this fall.

After a modal, use the base form.

> ▶ The Senate *might* vote on this bill next week.

gerund A verb form that is used as a noun and ends with *-ing: arguing, throwing.*

infinitive A verb form consisting of the word *to* plus the base form of the verb: *to run.*

T2-d   Follow verbs with **gerunds** or **infinitives**.

1. Some verbs can be followed by either a gerund or an infinitive with no change in meaning:

begin	continue	like	prefer
can't stand	hate	love	start

> ▶ The roof *began leaking.*

> ▶ The roof *began to leak.*

2. Some verbs change their meaning, depending on whether a gerund or an infinitive follows:

forget	remember	stop	try

> ▶ Salam *remembered going* to the park on Saturday. [Salam recalled a weekend visit to the park.]

> ▶ Salam *remembered to go* to the park on Saturday. [Salam remembered that he had to go to the park on Saturday.]

3. Some verbs can be followed by a gerund but not an infinitive:

admit	deny	keep	recall
appreciate	discuss	miss	resist
avoid	dislike	postpone	risk
can't help	enjoy	practice	suggest
consider	finish	put off	tolerate
delay	imagine	quit	

> *seeing*
> ▶ I recall ~~to see~~ Michel there.
>   ^

Not or *never* can separate the verb and the gerund.

▶ We discussed *not* having a party this year.

4. Some verbs can be followed by an infinitive but not a gerund:

agree   expect   need   refuse

ask   fail   offer   venture

beg   have   plan   wait

choose   hope   pretend   want

claim   manage   promise   wish

decide   mean

to eat
▶ Children often only pretend ~~eating~~ food they dislike.

In a sentence with a verb followed by an infinitive, the meaning changes depending on the placement of a negative word such as *not* or *never*.

▶ I *never* promised to eat liver. [I did not make the promise.]

▶ I promised *never* to eat candy. [I promised not to do it.]

5. Some verbs must be followed by a noun or pronoun and an infinitive:

advise   encourage   order   teach

allow   force   persuade   tell

cause   instruct   remind   urge

command   invite   require   warn

convince   need

▶ Magda taught *her parrot to say* a few words.

Use an infinitive, not *that,* following a verb such as *want* or *need.*

to stay
▶ José wants ~~that his new car stays~~ in good condition.

6. The verbs *let, make* ("force"), and *have* ("cause") must be followed by a noun or pronoun and the base form of the verb (not the infinitive):

▶ He *let me borrow* the car.

▶ The drill sergeant *makes the recruits stand* at attention.

▶ I *had the children draw* in their notebooks.

T3 Prepositions

preposition A word (such as *between*, *in*, or *of*) that indicates the relation between a word in a sentence and its object.

Use the **prepositions** *in, on,* and *at* to indicate location and time.

Location

- *In* usually means within a geographic place or enclosed area (*in* Mexico, *in* a small town, *in* the park, *in* my bedroom, *in* a car).

- *On* means *on top of* (*on* the shelf, *on* a hill, *on* a bicycle); it is also used with modes of mass transportation (*on* a train, *on* the subway), streets (*on* Broadway), pages (*on* page 5), floors of buildings (*on* the tenth floor), and tracts of private land (*on* a farm, *on* the lawn).

- *At* refers to specific addresses and named locations (*at* 1153 Grand Street, *at* Nana's house, *at* Macy's), to general locations (*at* work, *at* home, *at* the beach), and to locations that involve a specific activity (*at* the mall, *at* the gym, *at* a party, *at* a restaurant).

Time

- *In* is used with months (*in* May), years (*in* 1999), and seasons (*in* the fall), as well as with *morning, afternoon,* and *evening* (*in* the morning).

- *On* is used with days of the week (*on* Wednesday) and dates (*on* June 2, 2006).

- *At* is used with specific times (*at* 7:30, *at* noon, *at* midnight) and with *night* (*at* night).

Change any incorrect prepositions so that *in*, *on*, and *at* convey location and time correctly.

▶ People are driving at 55 or 60 miles per hour in the highway.
on
^

Change any incorrect prepositions to idiomatic usage.

▶ Is life worse in the refugee camps or in Vietnam? You would find answers from
in
^

his article.

▶ Williams gives readers insight to the doctor's insecurity.
into
^

T4 Omitted or Repeated Words

subject The part of a clause that identifies who or what is being discussed.

verb A word or phrase that expresses action or being and, along with a subject, is a basic component of a sentence.

In English, every sentence, with rare exceptions, should have both a **subject** and a **verb**.

⌐ subject ⌐⌐ verb ⌐
▶ My brother has been very successful in his job.

If your native language allows you to omit either subject or verb, check your drafts carefully to be sure that you include both in your writing. Supply both a subject and a verb in each sentence, but do not repeat the subject or other words that duplicate grammatical functions.

Add a missing subject.

▶ On the contrary, *the compliments* increase his irritability.

Add a missing verb.

▶ Mr. Yang *is* a man who owns a butcher shop.

Supply a missing expletive (*there* or *it*) if the subject follows the verb.

▶ *There are* Are many ways to help the unemployed get jobs.

Delete a repeated subject.

▶ The elderly woman ~~she~~ must have an eye infection.

Delete other words that repeat grammatical functions.

▶ People say that the cost of insurance has never ~~goes~~ down anymore.

▶ Only a few people ~~that are~~ rich.

T5 Adjective Order

Adjectives generally appear in the following order in English sentences.

1. Article, pronoun, or other determiner: *a, an, the, that, his, their, Janine's*
2. Evaluation or judgment: *beautiful, ugly, elegant, magnificent, impressive*
3. Size or dimension: *short, tall, long, large, small, big, little*
4. Shape: *round, rectangular, square, baggy, circular, octagonal*
5. Age: *new, young, old, aged, antique*
6. Color: *pink, turquoise, gray, orange*
7. History or origin (country and religion): *Asian, Norwegian, Thai, American, Protestant, Mongolian, Buddhist, Muslim, Catholic, Jewish*
8. Material: *copper, cotton, plastic, oak, linen*
9. Noun used as a descriptive adjective: *kitchen* (sink), *bedroom* (lamp)

When you use several adjectives to modify a noun, arrange them in the order expected in English.

   1   2   4   6   1   3   5

▶ *a beautiful, round, turquoise* stone   ▶ *her skinny, young* cousin

T6 Participles

participle A verb form showing present tense (*dancing, freezing*) or past tense (*danced, frozen*) that can also act as an adjective.

Use the present form of the **participle** (*-ing*) if it describes someone or something *causing* or *producing* a mental state. Use the past form (*-ed*) if it describes someone or something *experiencing* the mental state. Problem participles include the following pairs:

annoying/annoyed	exhausting/exhausted
boring/bored	pleasing/pleased
confusing/confused	surprising/surprised
disappointing/disappointed	terrifying/terrified
exciting/excited	tiring/tired

▶ The class was *confused* by the *confusing* directions.

▶ The teacher was *surprised* by the *surprising* number of questions.

Change a participle to its present form (*-ing*) if it describes someone or something causing or producing a situation.

▶ Parents must not accept the ~~frightened~~ *frightening* behavior that their children learn in gangs.

Change a participle to its past form (*-ed*) if it describes someone or something experiencing a situation.

▶ I was not ~~pleasing~~ *pleased* with the information about religion in this article.

R   Review of Sentence Structure

As you write, your primary concern will be with the ideas you want to convey to your audience, not parts of speech or sentence structure. Still, writing clear and correct sentences is an important part of communicating effectively with your audience. This and the other sections in the Handbook will help you achieve that goal.*

R1   Basic Sentence Structure

This review of basic sentence structure will look first at the elements that make up simple sentences and then at how simple sentences produce compound and complex sentences.

R1-a   Words, Phrases, and Clauses

The basic building blocks of sentences are, of course, words, which can be combined into discrete groupings or *phrases.*

Words and phrases are further combined to create *clauses,* groups of at least two words that both name a topic and make some point about that topic; every clause can be divided into a subject and a predicate. The *subject* identifies the topic or theme of the sentence—what is being discussed—while the *predicate* says something about the subject and is the focus of information in the clause.

R1-b   Sentence Units

A *simple sentence* includes a single independent clause made up of a subject and a predicate. The subject and the predicate may each be a single word or a group of words. In addition to its verb, the predicate may include **objects**, **complements**, and **adverbial modifiers**.

> ┌─── subject ───┐ ┌──────────── predicate ─────────────┐
> ▶ Native Americans introduced baked beans to the New England settlers.

Simple sentences, then, are composed of some combination of these basic units:

Subject (S)   The simplest subject can be a single noun or pronoun, but a subject may also consist of a noun phrase (including adjectives and other sentence elements) or even a noun clause. Subjects may also be *compound* when two or more nouns or

object The part of a clause that receives the action of the verb, or the part of a phrase that follows a preposition.

complement A word or word group that describes or restates a subject or an object.

adverbial modifier A word or word group that modifies a verb, an adjective, or another adverb.

---

* This brief review is based on an extraordinary book: *A Grammar of Contemporary English* (New York: Harcourt, 1972). If you need more information than is provided here, consult a stand-alone handbook, such as Diana Hacker and Nancy Sommers's *The Bedford Handbook* or Andrea Lunsford's *The St. Martin's Handbook.*

pronouns are linked by a conjunction. (See R2 for definitions and examples of these various elements.)

Verb (V)   These can be classified as *transitive*, when they occur with an object, or *intransitive*, when they occur without an object. Intransitive verbs that occur with complements are often called *linking verbs*. Like subjects, verbs may be compound.

Objects (DO, IO)   These include *direct objects* (DO) and *indirect objects* (IO), which, like subjects, can be nouns, noun phrases, noun clauses, or pronouns. Objects usually follow the subject and verb.

Complements (SC, OC)   These are either subject complements or object complements: *Subject complements* (SC) refer to the subject, *object complements* (OC) to an object. Like subjects and objects, complements can be nouns or pronouns, noun phrases, or noun clauses (sometimes referred to as *predicate nominatives*). Complements can also be adjectives or adjective phrases (sometimes called *predicate adjectives*). Like objects, complements usually follow the subject and verb. They also follow any objects.

Adverbial (A)   These are modifiers that refer to the verb in the sentence. They can be adverbs, adverb phrases, or adverb clauses.

Of these seven units, two—subject and verb—are required in every sentence.

R1-c   Types of Simple Sentences

The basic sentence elements listed in R1-b can be put together in various ways to produce seven general types of simple sentences.

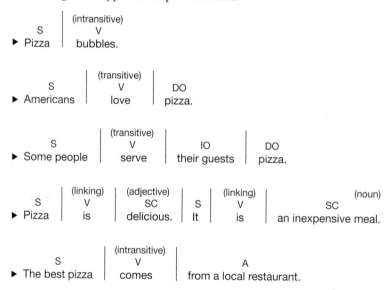

```
           (transitive)
    S          V          DO          OC
▶ Vegetarians | consider | pepperoni pizza | appalling.
```

```
           (transitive)
    S          V          DO          A
▶ They  |   prefer   |  cheese pizza  |  any day.
```

R1-d Combinations and Transformations

The simple sentence patterns shown in R1-c can be combined and transformed to produce all of the sentences writers of English need.

Two or more clauses may be combined with a coordinating conjunction (such as *and* or *but*) or a pair of correlative conjunctions (such as *either . . . or*) to create a **compound sentence**:

COMPOUND   Pizza is delicious, and it is an inexpensive meal.

Either Americans love pizza, or they consider it junk food.

Writers create **complex sentences** by combining independent clauses with a subordinating conjunction (such as *although* or *because*) or by linking two clauses with a relative pronoun (such as *which* or *who*):

COMPLEX   Vegetarians consider pepperoni pizza appalling

```
       ─── dependent clause ───
because pepperoni is red meat.
```

Clauses that contain subordinating conjunctions or relative pronouns are *dependent clauses* and cannot stand on their own as simple sentences.

Clauses can also be combined to produce **compound-complex sentences**, compound sentences that contain dependent clauses:

```
                 ─── dependent clause ───
COMPOUND-   Even though pepperoni pizza is unhealthy, it is a delicious meal,
COMPLEX
            and Americans love it.
```

(Conjunctions and dependent clauses are discussed in more detail in R2.) Simple sentences can take the form of *declarations, questions, commands,* and *exclamations*:

QUESTION   Why is pizza popular?

COMMAND   Bake the pizza in a brick oven.

EXCLAMATION   This pizza is delicious!

(In addition, sentences that are in the *active voice* can generally be transformed into the *passive voice* if they have transitive verbs and objects.)

PASSIVE   Pepperoni pizza is considered unhealthy.

R2   Basic Sentence Elements

This section reviews the parts of speech and the types of clauses and phrases.

R2-a   Parts of Speech

There are ten parts of speech: nouns, pronouns, adjectives, adverbs, verbs, prepositions, conjunctions, articles, demonstratives, and interjections.

subject The part of a clause that identifies who or what is being discussed.

object The part of a clause that receives the action of the verb or the part of a phrase that follows a preposition.

subject complement A word or word group that follows a linking verb and describes or restates the subject.

appositive A word or word group that identifies or gives more information about a noun or pronoun that precedes it.

Nouns   Nouns function in sentences or clauses as **subjects**, **objects**, and **subject complements**. They also serve as objects of various kinds of phrases and as **appositives**. They can be proper (*Burger King, Bartlett pear, Rachael Ray, Trader Joe's*) or common (*tomato, food, lunch, café, waffle, gluttony*). Common nouns can be abstract (*hunger, satiation, indulgence, appetite*) or concrete (*spareribs, soup, radish, champagne, gravy*). Nouns can be singular (*biscuit*) or plural (*biscuits*); they may also be collective (*food*). They can be marked to show possession (*gourmet's choice, lambs' kidneys*). Nouns take determiners (*that lobster, those clams*), quantifiers (*many hotcakes, several sausages*), and articles (*a milk shake, the eggnog*). They can be modified by adjectives (*fried chicken*), adjective phrases (*chicken in a basket*), and adjective clauses (*chicken that is finger-licking good*). (See also E3.)

Pronouns   Pronouns come in many forms and have a variety of functions in clauses and phrases.

Personal pronouns function as replacements for nouns and come in three case forms:

1. Subjective, for use as subjects or subject complements: *I, we, you, he, she, it, they.*
2. Objective, for use as objects of verbs and prepositions: *me, us, you, him, her, it, them.*
3. Possessive: *mine, ours, yours, his, hers, theirs.* Possessive pronouns also have a determiner form for use before nouns: *my, our, your, his, her, its, their.*

▶ Calvin Trillin says the best restaurants in the world are in Kansas City, but he was subjective born there.

▶ If *you* ever have the spareribs and french-fried potatoes at Arthur Bryant's, *you* will objective never forget them.

▶ Your memory of that lunch at Bryant's is clearer than *mine*. possessive   possessive

Personal pronouns also come in three persons (first person: *I, me, we, us;* second person: *you;* third person: *he, him, she, her, it, they, them*), three genders (masculine: *he, him;* feminine: *she, her;* neuter: *it*), and two numbers (singular: *I, me, you, he, him, she, her, it;* plural: *we, us, you, they, them*).

Reflexive pronouns, like personal pronouns, function as replacements for nouns, nearly always replacing nouns or personal pronouns in the same clause. Reflexive pronouns include *myself, ourselves, yourself, yourselves, himself, herself, oneself, itself, themselves*.

▶ Aunt Odessa prided *herself* on her chocolate sponge cake.

Reflexive pronouns may also be used for emphasis.

▶ Barry baked the fudge cake *himself*.

Indefinite pronouns do not refer to a specific person or object: *each, all, everyone, everybody, everything, everywhere, both, some, someone, somebody, something, somewhere, any, anyone, anybody, anything, anywhere, either, neither, none, nobody, many, few, much, most, several, enough*.

▶ Not *everybody* was enthusiastic about William Laird's 1698 improvement on apple cider—Jersey lightning applejack.

▶ In the Colonies, *most* preferred rum.

▶ Taverns usually served *both*.

Relative pronouns introduce **adjective (or relative) clauses**. They come in three forms: personal, to refer to people (*who, whom, whose, whoever, whomever*), non-personal (*which, whose, whichever, whatever*), and general (*that*).

▶ In 1846, Nancy Johnson invented a small hand-operated machine, *which* was the forerunner of today's portable ice-cream freezer.

▶ It was Jacob Fussell of Baltimore *who* established the first wholesale ice-cream business in 1851.

▶ The fact *that* we had to wait until 1896 for someone to invent the ice-cream cone is surprising.

Interrogative pronouns have the same forms as relative pronouns but have different functions. They serve to introduce questions.

▶ *Who* invented the ice-cream sundae?

▶ Of chocolate and vanilla ice cream, *which* do you prefer?

▶ The waiter asked, "*Whose* chocolate walnut sundae is this?"

Demonstrative pronouns are pronouns used to point out particular persons or things: *this, that, these, those*.

▶ *This* dish is what Mandy likes best for brunch: pecan waffles with blueberry syrup.

▶ Of everything on the menu, *these* must be the most fattening.

(See also G1–G4.)

adjective (or relative) clause A clause that modifies a noun or pronoun and is generally introduced by a relative pronoun (such as *that* or *which*).

Adjectives   Adjectives modify nouns and pronouns, and they usually appear immediately before or after nouns they modify. As subject complements (sometimes called predicate adjectives), they may be separated by the verb from nouns or pronouns they modify.

▶ *Creole* cooking can be found in *many* diners along the Gulf of Mexico.

▶ Gumbo is a *spicy* soup.

▶ Jambalaya tastes *delicious*, and it is *cheap*.
                              subject complements

Some adjectives change form in comparisons.

                      comparative
▶ Gumbo is *spicier* than crawfish pie.

                      superlative
▶ Gumbo is the *spiciest* Creole soup.

Some words can be used as both pronouns and adjectives; nouns are also sometimes used as adjectives.

       adj.   adj.   pron.
▶ *Many* people love *crawfish* pie, and *many* prefer gumbo.

(See also G7-b.)

Adverbs   Adverbs modify verbs (*eat well*), adjectives (*very big appetite*), and other adverbs (*extremely well done*). They often tell when, how, where, why, and how often:

▶ Walter started the charcoal fires *early*. [when]

▶ He basted the sizzling ribs *liberally* with marinade. [how]

▶ Pots of beans simmered *nearby*. [where]

Like adjectives, adverbs can change form for comparison.

▶ He ate the buttermilk biscuits *fast*. [*faster* than Bucky ate his biscuits, *fastest* of all the hungry diners]

A number of adverbs are formed by adding *-ly* to an adjective (*hearty* appetite, eat *heartily*). With adverbs that end in *-ly,* the words *more* and *most* are used when making comparisons.

▶ Junior drank the first cold lemonade *quickly*. [*more quickly* than Billy Joe, *most quickly* of all those at the table]

The *conjunctive adverb* is a special kind of adverb used to connect the ideas in two sentences or independent clauses. Familiar connectives include *consequently, however, therefore, similarly, besides,* and *nevertheless.*

▶ The inspiration for Tex-Mex food came from Mexico. *Nevertheless*, it is considered a native American cuisine.

Finally, adverbs may evaluate or qualify the information in a sentence.

▶ *Barbecue* comes from *barbacoa*, a word the Spaniards *probably* picked up from the Arawak Indians.

(See also G7-a.)

Verbs   Verbs tell what is happening in a sentence by expressing action (*cook, stir*) or a state of being (*be, stay*). Depending on the structure of the sentence, a verb can be **transitive** (*Jerry bakes cookies*) or **intransitive** (*Jerry bakes for a living*); an intransitive verb that is followed by a subject complement (*Jerry is a fine baker, and his cookies always taste heavenly*) is often called a **linking verb**.

Nearly all verbs have several forms (or principal parts), many of which may be irregular rather than follow a standard pattern. In addition, verbs have various forms to indicate *tense* (time of action or state of being), *voice* (performer of action), and *mood* (statement, command, or possibility). Studies have shown that because verbs can take so many forms, the most common errors in writing involve verbs. (See also G5.)

transitive verb A verb that needs an object — something that receives the action of the verb — to make its meaning complete.

intransitive verb A verb that does not need an object to make its meaning complete.

linking verb *be, seem, appear, become, taste,* or another verb that connects a subject with a subject complement that describes or modifies it: The chips *taste* salty.

Verb phrases.   Verbs divide into two primary groups: (1) *main (lexical) verbs* and (2) *auxiliary (helping) verbs* that combine with main verbs to create verb phrases. The three primary auxiliary verbs are *do, be,* and *have,* in all their forms.

> *do:* does, did, doing, done
> *be:* am, is, are, was, were, being, been
> *have:* has, had, having

These primary auxiliary verbs can also act as main verbs in sentences. Other common auxiliary verbs (*can, could, may, might, shall, should, will, would, must, ought to, used to*), however, cannot be the main verb in a sentence but are used in combination with main verbs in verb phrases. The auxiliary verb works with the main verb to indicate tense, mood, and voice.

▶ When the cheese curd forms, it *must be* separated from the whey.

▶ After cheddar cheese is shaped into a block, it *should be* aged for at least several months.

▶ By the year 2061, Americans *will have been* eating cheese for 450 years.

Principal parts of verbs.   All main verbs (as well as the primary auxiliary verbs *do, be,* and *have*) have five forms. The forms of a large number of verbs are regular, but many verbs have irregular forms.

Form	Regular	Irregular
Infinitive or base	sip	drink
Third-person singular present (*-s* form)	sips	drinks
Past	sipped	drank
Present participle (*-ing* form)	sipping	drinking
Past participle (*-ed* form)	sipped	drunk

The past and past participle for most verbs in English are formed by simply adding *-d* or *-ed* (*posed, walked, pretended, unveiled*). However, a number of verbs have irregular forms, most of which are different for the past and the past participle.

For regular verbs, the past and past participle forms are the same: *sipped*. All new verbs coming into English have regular forms: *format, formats, formatted, formatting*.

Irregular verbs have unpredictable forms. Their *-s* and *-ing* forms are generally predictable, just like those of regular verbs, but their past and past participle forms are not. In particular, be careful to use the correct past participle form of irregular verbs.

Listed here are the principal parts of fifty-three commonly troublesome irregular verbs. Check your dictionary for a more complete listing.

Base	Past Tense	Past Participle
be: am, is, are	was, were	been
beat	beat	beaten
begin	began	begun
bite	bit	bitten
blow	blew	blown
break	broke	broken
bring	brought	brought
burst	burst	burst
choose	chose	chosen
come	came	come
cut	cut	cut
deal	dealt	dealt
do	did	done
draw	drew	drawn
drink	drank	drunk
drive	drove	driven
eat	ate	eaten
fall	fell	fallen
fly	flew	flown
freeze	froze	frozen

Base	Past Tense	Past Participle
get	got	got (gotten)
give	gave	given
go	went	gone
grow	grew	grown
have	had	had
know	knew	known
lay	laid	laid
lead	led	led
lie	lay	lain
lose	lost	lost
ride	rode	ridden
ring	rang	rung
rise	rose	risen
run	ran	run
say	said	said
see	saw	seen
set	set	set
shake	shook	shaken
sink	sank	sunk
sit	sat	sat
speak	spoke	spoken
spring	sprang (sprung)	sprung
steal	stole	stolen
stink	stank	stunk
swear	swore	sworn
swim	swam	swum
take	took	taken
teach	taught	taught
tear	tore	torn
throw	threw	thrown
wear	wore	worn
win	won	won
write	wrote	written

Tense. As writers, even native speakers may find it difficult to put together sentences that express time clearly through verbs: Time has to be expressed consistently from sentence to sentence, and shifts in time perspective must be managed smoothly. In addition, certain conventions permit time to be expressed in unusual ways: History can be written in present time to dramatize events, or characters in novels may be presented as though their actions are in present time. The following examples of verb **tense** provide only a partial demonstration of the complex system indicating time in English.

tense The form of a verb that shows the time of the action or state of being.

Present. There are three basic types of present time: timeless, limited, and instantaneous. Timeless present-tense verbs express habitual action.

▶ Some Americans *grow* their own fruits and vegetables.

Limited present-tense verbs express an action in process and of limited duration.

▶ The neighbors *are preparing* watermelon rind preserves this week.

Instantaneous present-tense verbs express action being completed at the moment.

▶ Laura *is eating* the last ripe strawberry.

Present-tense verbs can also be emphatic.

▶ I certainly *do enjoy* homemade strawberry preserves in the middle of winter.

Past. There are several kinds of past time. Some actions must be identified as having taken place at a particular time in the past.

▶ While he *was waiting,* Jake *ordered* a ham sandwich on whole wheat bread.

In the *present perfect tense,* actions may be expressed as having taken place at no definite time in the past or as occurring in the past and continuing into the present.

▶ Jake *has eaten* more ham sandwiches than he can count.

▶ The Downtown Deli *has sold* delicious ham sandwiches on homemade bread for as long as he can remember.

Action can even be expressed as having been completed in the past prior to some other past action or event (the *past perfect tense*).

▶ Before he *had taken* a bite, Jake dropped his sandwich on the floor.

Future. The English verb system offers writers several different ways of expressing future time. Future action can be indicated with the modal auxiliary *will.*

▶ Fast-food restaurants *will grow* in popularity.

A completed future action can even be viewed from some time farther in the future (*future perfect tense*).

▶ Within a decade or two, Americans *will have given up* cooking their own meals.

Continuing future actions can be expressed with *will be* and the *-ing* form of the verb.

▶ Americans soon *will be eating* every second meal away from home.

The right combination of verbs with *about* can express an action in the near future.

▶ Jeremiah *is about to eat* his third hamburger.

Future arrangements, commands, or possibilities can be expressed.

▶ Junior and Mary Jo *are to be married* at McDonald's.

▶ You *have to be* there by noon to get a good table.

▶ If Fred *is to lose* weight, he must give up french fries.

Voice. A verb is in the *active* voice when it expresses an action taken by the subject. A verb is said to be in the *passive* voice when it expresses something that happens to the subject.

In sentences with active verbs, it is apparent who is performing the action expressed in the verb.

▶ The chef *disguised* the tasteless broccoli with a rich cheese sauce.

In sentences with passive verbs, it may not be clear who is performing the action.

▶ The tasteless broccoli *was disguised* with a rich cheese sauce.

The writer could reveal the performer by adding a phrase (*by the chef*), but the revision would also create a clumsy sentence. Graceful, clear writing relies on active, rather than passive, verbs. Passive forms do fulfill certain purposes, however, such as expressing the state of something.

▶ The broccoli *is disguised*.

▶ The restaurant *was closed*.

Passives can give prominence to certain information by shifting it to the end of the sentence.

▶ *Who* closed this restaurant? It was closed by *the Board of Health*.

Writers also use passives to make sentences more readable by shifting long **noun clauses** to the end.

> **noun clauses** Word groups that can function like nouns, acting as subjects, objects, or complements in independent clauses.

ACTIVE   *That the chef disguised the tasteless broccoli* with a cheese sauce disgusted Elvira.

PASSIVE   Elvira was disgusted *that the chef disguised the tasteless broccoli* with a cheese sauce.

Mood. Mood refers to the writer's attitude toward a statement. There are three moods: indicative, imperative, and subjunctive. Most statements or questions are in the *indicative mood*.

▶ The chuck wagon *fed* cowboys on the trail.

▶ *Did* cowboys ever *tire* of steak and beans?

Commands or directions are given in the *imperative mood*.

▶ *Eat* those beans!

The *subjunctive mood* is used mainly to indicate hypothetical, impossible, or unlikely conditions.

▶ If I *were* you, I'd compliment the cook.

▶ *Had* they *been* here yesterday, they would have had hot camp bread.

phrase A group of words that does *not* contain both a subject and a verb and is always part of an independent clause.

object The part of a clause that receives the action of the verb or the part of a phrase that follows a preposition.

Prepositions   Prepositions occur in **phrases**, followed by **objects**. (The uses of prepositional phrases are explained in R2-c.) Most prepositions are single words (*at, on, by, with, of, for, in, under, over, by*), but some consist of two or three words (*away from, on account of, in front of, because of, in comparison with, by means of*). They are used to indicate relations—usually of place, time, cause, purpose, or means—between their objects and some other word in the sentence.

▶ I'll meet you *at* El Ranchero *for* lunch.

▶ The enchiladas are stuffed *with* cheese.

▶ You can split an order *with* [Georgette and me].

objective case The form a pronoun takes when it is an object (receiving the action of the verb).

Objects of prepositions can be single or compound nouns or pronouns in the **objective case** (as in the preceding examples), or phrases or clauses acting as nouns.

▶ Herman began making nachos *by* [grating the cheese].

▶ His guests were happy *with* [what he served].

Conjunctions   Like prepositions, conjunctions show relations between sentence elements. There are coordinating, subordinating, and correlative conjunctions.

Coordinating conjunctions (*and, but, for, nor, or, so,* or *yet*) join logically comparable sentence elements.

▶ Guacamole is made with avocados, tomatoes, onions, *and* chiles.

▶ You may add a little lemon or lime juice, *but* be careful not to add too much.

Subordinating conjunctions (*although, because, since, though, as though, as soon as, rather than*) introduce **dependent clauses**.

dependent clause A word group that has a subject and a predicate but cannot stand by itself as a sentence; it must be connected to an independent clause.

▶ *As soon as* the waitress came, Susanna ordered an iced tea.

▶ She dived into the salsa and chips *because* she was too hungry to wait for her combination plate.

Correlative conjunctions come in pairs, with the first element anticipating the second (*both . . . and, either . . . or, neither . . . nor, not only . . . but also*).

▶ Charley wanted to order *both* the chiles rellenos *and* the enchiladas verdes.

Articles There are only three articles in English: *the, a,* and *an. The* is used for definite reference to something specific; *a* and *an* are used for indefinite reference to something less specific. *The Mexican restaurant in Westbury* is different from *a Mexican restaurant in Westbury.* (See T1.)

Demonstratives *This, that, these,* and *those* are demonstratives. Sometimes called demonstrative adjectives, they are used to point to something specific.

▶ Put one of *these* maraschino cherries at each end of the banana split.

▶ The accident left pineapple milk shake all over the front seat of *that* pickup truck.

Interjections Interjections indicate strong feeling or an attempt to command attention: *phew, shhh, damn, oh, yea, yikes, ouch, boo.*

R2-b Dependent Clauses

Like independent clauses, all dependent clauses have a **subject** and a **predicate**. Unlike independent clauses, however, dependent clauses cannot stand by themselves as complete sentences; they always occur with independent clauses as part of either the subject or the predicate.

subject The part of a clause that identifies who or what is being discussed.

predicate The part of a clause that includes a complete verb and describes the action or state of the subject.

INDEPENDENT   Ribbon-shaped pasta is popular in northern Italy.

DEPENDENT   . . . , while tubular-shaped pasta is popular in southern Italy.
. . . , which is generally made by hand, . . .

Although it originally comes from China, . . .

There are three types of dependent clauses: adjective, adverb, and noun.

Adjective clauses Also known as *relative clauses,* adjective clauses modify nouns and pronouns in independent clauses. They are introduced by relative pronouns (*who, whom, which, that, whose*) or adverbs (*where, when*), and most often they immediately follow the noun or pronoun they modify. Adjective clauses can be either *restrictive* (essential to defining the noun or pronoun they modify) or *nonrestrictive* (not essential to understanding the noun or pronoun); nonrestrictive clauses are set off by commas, and restrictive clauses are not (see P1-c and P2-b).

▶ Vincent bought a package of agnolotti, *which is a pasta used in soup*.

▶ We went back to the restaurant *where they serve that delicious veal*.

▶ Everyone *who likes Italian cooking* knows Romano cheese well.

Adverb clauses   Introduced by subordinating conjunctions (such as *although, because,* and *since*), adverb clauses nearly always modify verbs in independent clauses, although they may occasionally modify other elements (except nouns). Adverb clauses are used to indicate a great variety of logical relations with their independent clauses: time, place, condition, concession, reason, cause, circumstance, purpose, result, and so on. They are generally set off by commas.

> ▶ *Although the finest olive oil in Italy comes from Lucca*, good-quality olive oil is produced in other regions of the country. [concession]

> ▶ *When the tomato sauce comes to a boil*, reduce the heat and simmer. [time]

> ▶ *If you know mushrooms*, you probably prefer them fresh. [condition]

> ▶ Ken carefully watches the spaghetti *because he does not like it to be overcooked*. [reason]

independent clause
A word group with a subject and a predicate that can stand alone as a separate sentence.

Noun clauses   Like nouns, noun clauses can function as subjects, objects, or complements (or predicate nominatives) in independent clauses. They are thus essential to the structure of the **independent clause** in which they occur and so, like restrictive adjective clauses, are not set off by commas. A noun clause usually begins with a relative pronoun, but the introductory word may sometimes be omitted.

> ▶ *[—— subject ——]*
> *That we preferred the sausage* surprised us.

> ▶ Harold did not know for sure *[—— object ——] whether baloney came from Bologna*.

> ▶ *subject*
> He assumed *[complement] that it did*.

> ▶ Hillary claims *[—— direct object ——]* no one eats pizza in Italy. [relative pronoun *that* dropped]

> ▶ Gnocchi may be flavored *[prep.] with [—— object of preposition ——] whatever fresh herbs are available*.

R2-c   Phrases

dependent clause A word group that has a subject and a predicate but cannot stand by itself as a sentence; it must be connected to an independent clause.

Like **dependent clauses**, phrases can function as nouns, adjectives, or adverbs in sentences. However, unlike clauses, phrases do not contain both a subject and a verb. (A phrase, of course, cannot stand on its own but occurs as part of an **independent clause**.) The six most common types of grammatical phrases are *prepositional, appositive, participial, gerund, infinitive,* and *absolute*.

preposition A word (such as *between, in,* or *of*) that indicates the relation between a word in a sentence and its object.

Prepositional phrases   Prepositional phrases always begin with a **preposition** and function as either an adjective or an adverb.

> ▶ Food *in Hunan* is noticeably different from that *in Sichuan*.
>   adjective phrase   adjective phrase

▶ The perfect egg roll is crisp on the outside and crunchy on the inside.
    adjective phrase   adjective phrase

Appositive phrases   Appositive phrases identify or give more information about a noun or pronoun just preceding. They take several forms. A single noun may also serve as an appositive.

▶ The baguette, *the most popular bread in France,* is a loaf about two feet long.

▶ The king of the breakfast rolls, *the croissant,* is shaped like a crescent.

▶ The baker *Marguerite* makes superb croissants.

Participial phrases   Participles are verb forms used to indicate certain tenses (present: *sipping;* past: *sipped*). They can also be used as verbals—words derived from verbs—and function as adjectives.

▶ At breakfast, we were first served *steaming* coffee and a simple *buttered* roll.

A participial phrase is an adjective phrase made up of a participle and any complements or modifiers it might have. Like participles, participial phrases modify nouns and pronouns in sentences.

▶ Two-thirds of the breakfasts *consumed in the diner* included sausage and eggs.

▶ *Prepared in the chef's personal style,* the vegetable omelets are served with a cheese sauce *flavored with garlic and herbs.*

▶ *Mopping up the cheese sauce with the last of his roll,* Mickey thought to himself, I could get used to this.

Gerund phrases   Like a participle, a gerund is a verbal. Ending in *-ing,* it even looks like a present participle, but it functions as a noun, filling any noun slot in a clause. Gerund phrases include **complements** and any modifiers of the gerund.

    — subject —
▶ Roasting is the quickest way to cook a turkey.

    ——— subject ———
▶ Preparing a stuffed turkey takes several hours.

▶ You begin by mixing the dressing.
    object of preposition

complement A word or word group that describes or restates a subject or an object.

Infinitive phrases   Like participles and gerunds, infinitives are verbals. The infinitive is the base form of the verb, preceded by *to: to simmer, to broil, to fry.* Infinitives and infinitive phrases function as nouns, adjectives, or adverbs.

▶ Tamales can be complicated *to prepare.*
                            adverb

▶ *To assemble the tamales,* begin by cutting the kernels off the corncobs.

noun

▶ Remembering *to save the corn husks* is important.

object of gerund phrase

▶ Anyone's first tamale dinner is a meal *to remember for a long time.*

adjective

Absolute phrases   The absolute phrase does not modify or replace any particular part of a clause; it modifies the whole clause. An absolute phrase includes a noun or pronoun and often includes a past or present participle as well as modifiers. Nearly all modern prose writers rely on absolute phrases. Some style historians consider them a hallmark of modern prose.

▶ *Her eyes glistening,* Lucy checked out the cases of doughnuts at Krispy Kreme Doughnuts.

▶ She stood patiently in line, *her arms folded to control her hunger, her backpack hanging off one shoulder.*

GL Glossary of Frequently Misused Words

Sometimes writers choose a word that is incorrect, imprecise in meaning, pronounced the same as the correct word (a homophone), or used widely but unacceptable in formal writing situations. In addition, problems can arise with idiomatic phrases, common everyday expressions that may or may not fit, or words whose denotations or connotations do not precisely suit the context of a particular sentence. This list will help you avoid imprecise popular usages in formal writing.

accept/except *Accept* is a verb ("receive with favor"). *Except* may be a verb ("leave out") but is more commonly used as a preposition ("excluding"). Other forms: *acceptance, acceptable; exception.*

▶ None of the composition instructors will *accept* late papers *except* Mr. Siu.

▶ Her *acceptance* of the bribe *excepts* her from consideration for the position.

adapt/adopt *Adapt* means "adjust to make more suitable." *Adopt* means "take as one's own." Other forms: *adaptable, adaptation; adoption.*

▶ To *adopt* an older child, parents must be willing to *adapt* themselves to the child's needs.

advice/advise *Advice* is a noun; *advise* is a verb. Other forms: *advisable, adviser.*

▶ Everyone *advised* him to heed the expert's *advice.*

affect/effect *Affect* is commonly used as a verb, most often meaning "influence"; in psychology, the noun *affect* is a technical term for an emotional state. *Effect* is generally a noun ("result or consequences"); it is only occasionally used as a verb ("bring about"), although the adjective form (*effective*) is common.

▶ Researchers are studying the *effect* of stress.

▶ How does stress *affect* the human body?

all right *All right* is the preferred spelling, rather than *alright,* which many people regard as unacceptable.

a lot A common expression meaning "a large number," *a lot* is always written as two words. Because it is vague and informal, avoid it in college writing.

among/between Use *among* when you are referring to more than two objects; limit *between* to references to only two objects.

▶ It is hard to choose one winner *among* so many highly qualified candidates for the scholarship.

▶ *Between* the two extreme positions lies a vast middle ground.

amount/number *Amount* refers to the quantity of a unit ("amount of water," "amount of discussion"), whereas *number* refers to the quantity of individual items ("number of papers," "number of times"). In general, use *amount* only with a singular noun.

anxious/eager *Anxious* means "nervous" or "worried"; *eager* means "looking forward [impatiently]." Avoid using *anxious* to mean *eager.*

▶ The students were *eager* to learn their grades.

▶ They were *anxious* they wouldn't pass.

between/among See **among/between**.

capital/capitol *Capital* is the more common word and has a variety of meanings, among them the principal city in a state or country; *capitol* refers to the government building in which a legislature meets.

cite/site/sight *Cite* as a verb means "refer to as proof" or "summon to appear in court." *Site* is a noun meaning "place or location." *Sight* may be a verb or a noun and always refers to seeing or what is seen ("a sight for sore eyes").

▶ Can you *cite* your sources for these figures?

▶ When she *sighted* the speeding car, the officer *cited* the driver for recklessness.

▶ A new dormitory will be built at this *site*.

complement/compliment *Complement* refers to completion, the making of a satisfactory whole, whereas *compliment* indicates admiration or praise; both can be used as either nouns or verbs. *Complementary* means "serving to complete" or "contrasting in color"; *complimentary* means "given free."

▶ The dean *complimented* the school's recruiters on the full *complement* of students registered for the fall.

▶ The designer received many *compliments* on the way the elements of the room *complemented* one another.

▶ Buy a new refrigerator and receive a *complimentary* ice maker in a *complementary* color.

could of/should of/would of In standard speech, "could have," "should have," and "would have" sound very much like "could of," "should of," and "would of"; however, substituting *of* for *have* in this construction is too casual for written work. The same holds true for "might of," "must of," and "will of."

council/counsel *Council* is a noun ("an assembly of people who deliberate or govern"). *Counsel* is a verb meaning "advise" or a noun meaning "advice." Other forms: *councilor* ("member of a council"); *counselor* ("one who gives advice").

▶ The *council* on drug abuse has issued guidelines for *counseling* troubled students.

▶ Before voting on the important fiscal issue, City *Councilor* Lopez sought the *counsel* of her constituents.

desert/dessert As a noun or an adjective, *desert* (dez´ ert) means "a dry, uncultivated region"; as a verb, *desert* (di zurt´) means "abandon." A *dessert* is a sweet dish served at the end of a meal.

▶ The hunters were alone in the arid *desert*, *deserted* by their guides.

▶ After a heavy meal, sherbet is the perfect *dessert*.

eager/anxious See **anxious/eager**.

effect/affect See **affect/effect**.

emigrant/immigrant An *emigrant* moves out of a country; an *immigrant* moves into a country. Other forms: *emigrate, emigration, émigré; immigrate, immigration*.

▶ Congress passed a bill to deal with *immigrants* living in the United States illegally.

▶ Members of her family *emigrated* from Cuba to Miami and Madrid.

etc. An abbreviation of the Latin words *et cetera* ("and other things"), *etc.* should never be preceded by *and* in English. Also be careful to spell the abbreviation correctly (*not* "ect."). In general, use *etc.* sparingly, if at all, in college writing.

except See **accept/except**.

fewer/less Use *fewer* when referring to **count nouns** (nouns that name people or things that can be counted: one *teacher,* several *teachers*); reserve *less* for amounts you cannot count.

▶ The new cookies have *fewer* calories than the other brand because they contain *less* sugar.

fortuitous/fortunate Often used incorrectly, the adjective *fortuitous* means "by chance" or "unplanned" and should not be confused with *fortunate* ("lucky").

▶ Because the two candidates wished to avoid each other, their *fortuitous* meeting in the parking lot was not a *fortunate* event for either party.

hisself/theirselves In nonstandard speech, "hisself" is sometimes used for *himself* and "theirselves" for *themselves*, but such usage is not acceptable in written work.

hopefully In conversation, *hopefully* is often used as a convenient shorthand to suggest that some outcome is generally to be hoped for ("Hopefully, our nominee will win the election"); this usage, however, is not acceptable in most written work. Better substitutes include *I hope, let's hope, everyone hopes,* and *it is to be hoped,* depending on your meaning. The adverb *hopefully* ("full of hope") should always modify a specific verb or adverb.

▶ I *hope* my brother will win the election.

▶ We should all *hope* his brother will win the election.

▶ Her sister is *hopeful* that she will win the election.

▶ The candidate inquired *hopefully* about the results.

immigrant See **emigrant/immigrant**.

its/it's *Its* is a possessive pronoun; *it's* is the contraction of *it is*.

▶ This job has *its* advantages.

▶ When *it's* well grilled, there's nothing like a steak.

lay/lie The verb *lay,* meaning "put, place," is transitive (forms of *lay* are *lay, laid, laid*): It needs an object— something that receives the action of the verb—to make its meaning complete. The verb *lie,* meaning "recline," is intransitive (forms of *lie* are *lie, lay, lain*): It does not need an object to make its meaning complete. Writers may incorrectly use *laid* as the past tense of *lie,* or *lay* as the present tense of *lie.* Other forms: *laying, lying.*

▶ The lion *lies* in wait for the approach of its prey.

▶ Joseph *laid* down his shovel, took a shower, and *lay* down for a nap.

less/fewer See **fewer/less**.

literally *Literally* means "exactly as stated, actually" and is often used to suggest that a cliché has in fact come true. However, to say, "The movie made my hair literally stand on end" is to misuse the word (although a person who suffered a fatal heart attack brought on by a fearful shock might correctly be said to have *literally* died of fright).

lose/loose *Lose* is a verb ("mislay, fail to maintain"); *loose* is most often used as an adjective ("not fastened tightly").

▶ A *loose* board may make someone *lose* his or her balance.

number/amount See **amount/number**.

persecute/prosecute *Persecute* means "mistreat or oppress"; *prosecute* most often means "bring a legal suit or action against."

▶ A biased majority can easily *persecute* minority groups.

▶ The law may *prosecute* only those who are indicted.

prejudice/prejudiced *Prejudice* is a noun or a verb. When used adjectivally, it should take the form of the past tense of the verb: *prejudiced.*

▶ We should fight *prejudice* wherever we find it.

▶ He was *prejudiced* against the candidate because she spoke with an accent.

principal/principle *Principal* implies "first in rank, chief," whether it is used as an adjective ("the principal cities of the Midwest") or a noun ("the principal of a midwestern high school"). *Principle* is generally a noun meaning "a basic law or truth."

▶ In *principle*, you are correct.

▶ The *principle* of free speech will be the *principal* topic of discussion.

prosecute/persecute See **persecute/prosecute**.

sensual/sensuous Both *sensual* and *sensuous* suggest the enjoyment of physical pleasure through the senses. However, *sensual* generally implies self-indulgence, particularly in terms of sexual activity; *sensuous* has a more positive meaning and suggests the ability to appreciate intellectually what is received through the senses. Other forms: *sensuality; sensuousness.*

▶ When drunk, the emperor gave himself up to brutal *sensuality*.

▶ Anyone can enjoy a *sensuous* spring night.

set/sit The difference between the verbs *sit* and *set* is similar to that between *lie* and *lay: Sit* is generally intransitive ("rest on one's buttocks"), and *set* is transitive ("put [something] in a certain place"). *Set* also has a number of uses as a noun. The past tense and past **participle** forms of *sit* are both *sat;* these forms for *set* are both *set.* (Remember that a participle is a verb form showing present tense [*dancing, freezing*] or past tense [*danced, frozen*] that can also act as an adjective.)

▶ He would rather *sit* than stand and would rather lie than *sit*.

▶ He *set* his suitcase on the ground and then *sat* on it.

should of See **could of/should of/would of**.

sight/site See **cite/site/sight**.

stationary/stationery *Stationary* is an adjective meaning "fixed, remaining in one place" ("Concrete will make the pole stationary"). *Stationery* refers to writing paper. One way to keep the distinction in mind is to associate the *er* in *paper* with that in *stationery*.

that/which When used as a subordinating conjunction (a word or phrase [such as *although, because, since,* or *as soon as*] that introduces a dependent clause and relates it to an independent clause), *that* always introduces a restrictive word group (a group of words, not set off by commas, that provides information essential to defining or identifying the noun or pronoun it modifies). The word *which* is generally used for nonrestrictive word groups (groups of words, set off by commas, that provide extra or nonessential information). Although it is acceptable to use *which* before a restrictive word group, *that* is generally preferred to make it clear that the clause is restrictive. (See the discussion of restrictive and nonrestrictive word groups in P1-c and P2-b, and the review of sentence structure and sentence elements on pp. H-95–110.)

▶ Her first bid for the Senate was the only election *that* she ever lost.

▶ Her first bid for the Senate, *which* was unsuccessful, brought her to prominence.

▶ The Senate election *that* resulted in her defeat took place in 1968.

their/there/they're *Their* is a possessive pronoun, *there* specifies a place or functions as an expletive, and *they're* is a contraction of *they are*.

▶ The coauthors say *there* are no copies of *their* script in *their* office, but *they're* not telling the truth.

theirselves See **hisself/theirselves**.

to/too/two *To* is a preposition, *too* is an adverb, and *two* is generally an adjective. The most common error here is the substitution of *to* for *too*.

▶ It is *too* early *to* predict either of the *two* scores.

unique To be precise, *unique* means "one of a kind, like no other." Careful writers do not use it loosely to mean simply "unusual or rare." Nor can it correctly take a comparative form ("most unique"), although advertisers sometimes use it this way.

▶ Her generosity is not *unique*, although today it is increasingly rare.

▶ This example of Mayan sculpture is apparently *unique*; none other like it has so far been discovered.

used to In colloquial speech, *used to* often sounds like "use to." However, *used to* is the correct form for written work.

▶ My grandfather *used to* be a Dodgers fan, until the team moved to Los Angeles.

weather/whether *Weather* is a noun ("atmospheric conditions"); *whether* is a conjunction.

▶ The *weather* forecast indicates *whether* there will be sun or rain.

which See **that/which**.

who's/whose *Who's* is the contraction of *who is* or *who has; whose* is a possessive pronoun.

▶ *Who's* up next?

▶ She's the only student *who's* done her work correctly.

▶ *Whose* work is this?

▶ The man *whose* job I took has retired.

would of See **could of/should of/would of**.

Acknowledgments

Becker, Gary S. and Julio J. Elías. "Cash for Kidneys: The Case for a Market for Organs." *The Wall Street Journal*, January 18, 2014.

Bramson, Noam. "Child, Home, Neighborhood, Community, and Conscience." *The Huffington Post*, July 18, 2014. Reprinted by permission of the author.

Brownell, Kelly D. and Thomas R. Frieden. "Ounces of Prevention—The Public Policy Case for Taxes on Sugared Beverages." *The New England Journal of Medicine* 360: 1805-8, April 30, 2009. The New England Journal of Medicine by MASSACHUSETTS MEDICAL SOCIETY Reproduced with permission of MASSACHUSETTS MEDICAL SOCIETY, in the format reuse in a standard/custom book (basic rights) via Copyright Clearance Center.

Cain, Susan. "Shyness: Evolutionary Tactic?" *The New York Times*, June 26, 2011. Copyright © 2011 by The New York Times Company. All rights reserved. Used by permission and protected by the Copyright Laws of the United States. The printing, copying, redistribution, or retransmission of this Content without express written permission is prohibited.

Coyne, Amanda. "The Long Good-Bye: Mother's Day in Federal Prison." Copyright © 1997 Harper's Magazine. All rights reserved. Reproduced from the May issue by special permission.

Desmond-Harris, Jenée. "Tupac and My Non-Thug Life." *The Root*, Sept. 13, 2011. Copyright © 2011 by The Slate Group. All Rights Reserved. Used by permission and protected by the Copyright Laws of the United States. The printing, copying, redistribution, or retransmission of this Content without express written permission is prohibited.

Dillard, Annie. Excerpts from *An American Childhood*. Copyright © 1987 by Annie Dillard. Reprinted by permission of HarperCollins Publishers and Russell & Volkening as agents for the author. Copyright © 1987 Annie Dillard.

Etzioni, Amitai. "Working at McDonald's." Copyright © 1986 by Amitai Etzioni. Reproduced with the permission of the author.

Gibson, William. "The Art of Fiction No. 211." Interview by David Wallace-Wells, originally published in *The Paris Review*, Issue 197, Summer 2011. Copyright © 2011 by The Paris Review, used by permission of The Wylie Agency LLC.

Gladwell, Malcolm. "The Order of Things: What College Rankings Really Tell Us." First published in *The New Yorker*, Feb. 14, 2011. Reprinted by permission of the author.

Kincaid, Jamaica. "Girl." From *At the Bottom of the River*. Copyright © 1983 by Jamaica Kincaid. Used by permission of Farrar Straus & Giroux.

King, Stephen. "Why We Crave Horror Movies." Copyright © Stephen King. All rights reserved. Originally appeared in *Playboy* (1982). Reprinted with permission.

National Kidney Foundation. "Financial Incentives for Organ Donation." February 1, 2003. Reprinted by permission of National Kidney Foundation.

Nussbaum, Emily. "The Aristocrats." *The New Yorker*, May 7, 2012. © 2012 Conde Nast. Reprinted by permission.

Orner, Peter. "Writing About What Haunts Us." From *The New York Times* Opinion Page, January 12, 2013. Copyright © 2013 by the New York Times Company. All rights reserved. Used by permission and protected by the Copyright Laws of the United States. The printing, copying, redistribution, or retransmission of this Content without express written permission is prohibited.

Posner, Eric. "A Moral Market." *Slate*, October 17, 2014. Reprinted by permission.

Ronson, Jon. "The Hunger Games." From *Lost at Sea: The John Ronson Mysteries*. Copyright © 2012, 2013 by Jon Ronson, Ltd. Used by permission of Riverhead, an imprint of Penguin Publishing Group, a division of Penguin Random House LLC.

Rose, Naomi A. "A Win-Win Solution for Captive Orcas and Marine Theme Parks." Special to CNN.com, October 28, 2013.

Satel, Sally. "When Altruism Isn't Moral." *The American*, January 30, 2009. Reprinted by permission of the author.

Sedaris, David. Excerpt from *Me Talk Pretty One Day*. Copyright © 2008 by David Sedaris. Reprinted by permission of Little, Brown & Company. All rights reserved.

Solove, Daniel. "Why Privacy Matters Even If You Have 'Nothing to Hide.'" Excerpt as published in *The Chronicle of Higher Education*, May 15, 2011, adapted from *Nothing to Hide: The False Tradeoff between Privacy and Security*. Copyright © 2011 by Daniel J. Solove. Reprinted by permission of the publisher, Yale University Press.

Tan, Amy. Excerpt from "Mother Tongue." Copyright © 1989 by Amy Tan. First appeared in *The Threepenny Review*. Reprinted by permission of the author and the Sandra Dijkstra Literary Agency.

Thompson, Gabriel. "The Last Word: A Gringo In the Lettuce Fields." *The Week*, 2010, adapted from *Working in the Shadows: A Year of Doing the Jobs (Most) Americans Won't Do*. Copyright © 2010 by Gabriel Thompson. Reprinted by permission of Nation Books, a member of the Perseus Books Group.

Index

Index for Multilingual Writers